Jimmy Swaggart
Bible
Commentary

Jimmy Swaggart Bible Commentary

Mark

Volume Eight

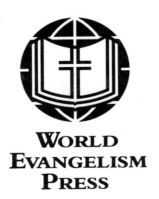

**WORLD
EVANGELISM
PRESS**

TABLE OF CONTENTS

■

INTRODUCTION

If the Bible Student derives half as much pleasure and enjoyment out of the study of the Book of Mark as I have in writing it, then my efforts will have been well worthwhile.

The Word of God being what it is provides not only instruction, guidance, and help in all things pertaining to life and Godliness, but, as well, provides a distinct pleasure that, in fact, can be derived from no other source. The Psalmist said it beautifully, *"How sweet are Thy Words unto my taste! Yea, sweeter than honey to my mouth!"* (Ps. 119:103).

DAILY ROUTINE

I generally start my day at the office at about 7 a.m., beginning work immediately on these Commentaries. Were you to see my desk, I'm afraid that it would not be one of tidiness and order. Books of every description are laying everywhere, including Concordances, Greek Texts, Bible Dictionaries, plus a cornucopia of other Bible helps.

I always begin the day with prayer, asking the Lord to give me guidance and to help me write that which should be written, and in a way that it is simple and easy to understand. I ask Him to give me light on the Scriptures, that I may be able to open its Contents in order that the Bible Student may be blessed and helped in his study. As well, at 10 o'clock, I break for prayer meeting. This meeting is conducted downstairs in our main Administration Building, with anywhere from 10 to 25 people present each morning.

I generally read a Passage of Scripture, commenting on it for a few minutes. Then we take prayer requests and go to the Lord in prayer. The entirety of the prayer meeting is not long, approximately 45 minutes to an hour. However, countless times the Lord has moved so mightily in these morning prayer meetings, giving strength and guidance which could not be derived in any other manner.

After prayer meetings is over, I pick up with the Commentary work. We break for lunch at 12 o'clock, and I start again at approximately 1 p.m.

I generally work to about 4 p.m., when I stop for the day and go home. I then come back to the office every evening at 6:30 p.m. for our evening prayer meeting. The crowd in this particular meeting is somewhat larger, anywhere from 20 to 100 people. The order of this meeting is identical to the one in the mornings.

I realize that this sounds like a bit much to most, two prayer meetings a day; however, I do not honestly know what I would have done, or would presently do, were it not for these times of seeking the Lord, and, above all, allowing Him to strengthen me, which I so desperately need.

Of course, along with this I have to write all the copy for our bi-monthly publication, The Evangelist, along with quite a bit of other correspondence work. Then, of course, there are the duties involved with Family Worship Center, the Television Ministry, overseas Crusades, and our recording schedule.

SOME REPETITION?

Of necessity, and as designed by the Holy Spirit, there is some repetition in the four Gospels. However, the repetition is never meaningless, but with purpose. I have noticed that the manner in which the Holy Spirit gave the various accounts, even though repeated in another Gospel, will, most, if not all of the time, give direction toward a particular Truth not found in other accounts of the same incident. If we probe, most of the time that Truth becomes evident.

In writing Commentary on particular experiences in the Ministry of Christ, which are given two to four times in the Gospels, I very seldom refer back to previous Commentary on the same incident. I have little interest in repeating what has already been said, desiring that the Holy Spirit would lead us into other pastures. He almost always does!

So, I think the repetition of the four Gospels only serves to enlarge the understanding of these Great

Truths presented by the Holy Spirit. At least, we have tried to be used in this manner. I trust we have.

THE GREEK

Beautifully enough, I have had access to Greek scholarship on the Book of Mark, that was not available on our Commentary regarding Matthew. Especially considering the manner in which the Holy Spirit designed the Book of Mark, and I speak of its beautiful simplicity, I believe this, the addition of the Greek, has helped us to bring out Truths which will greatly flavor the text. So, I guess I'm saying this:

If one feels that a knowledge of one of the Gospels is sufficient for all, then one is missing the entirety of the point designed by the Holy Spirit. As we have stated, the Holy Spirit designed these four Gospels as He did, and for purpose. Upon diligent study, that purpose will begin to surface. I pray that the Lord has helped us to show the difference intended in these Gospels. The Greek Text, I believe, has helped.

When one mentions *"Greek,"* many laymen automatically think in their minds that such is something they little understand, or even have any desire to understand. However, if presented correctly, which we have attempted to do, the addition of Greek instruction has the opposite effect, making it easier to understand.

ITS SIMPLICITY

I personally think, as stated, what makes Mark so beautiful is its simplicity. As the Holy Spirit nudged Mark to present Christ in the Form and Ministry of the Servant, of necessity, simplicity is the result. Consequently, and even though it is very difficult, if not impossible, to favor one Gospel ahead of the other, still, I suspect were I forced to make a choice, Mark would be my favorite. I think the beautiful, flowing, simplicity, at least has something to do with that. Mark wrote in such a way, and certainly designed by the Holy Spirit, that it seems as if the Bible Student is actually present when these great Miracles were performed by Christ, or even sitting at His feet, as He taught the multitudes. Mark has that wonderful capacity to make the reader a part of what is happening. I suppose that's what makes this Book so grand.

THE WONDER OF THE WORD OF GOD

I love the Bible more than I even have words or vocabulary to express. Until I began writing these Commentaries, I was reading the Bible completely through every six to ten weeks. I actually did this for years, with new Truths gleaned each and every time (Truths new to me, but not to the Word of God). Since beginning the Commentaries, my attention, and of necessity, is concentrated on the particular Book which I am addressing. And yet I never cease to be amazed at the wonder of the Word of God!

To illustrate what I am talking about, I have labored diligently at times respecting a particular Passage of Scripture, with the Lord giving me Truths which I had not seen heretofore. As well, I will peruse other Commentaries, and every help I can derive on that particular Passage, thinking surely I have gleaned most everything the Holy Spirit is saying, at least from that particular Passage.

On one such occasion I went over to our Bible College, hearing a first-year Bible Student preach his very first sermon from the Text which I had labored over diligently, and was amazed as he brought out a Truth completely new to me. Such is the Word of God! It is absolutely inexhaustible!

In my years of study of the greatest and most important subject on the face of the earth, the Bible, I have learned that one's life will be immeasurably blessed, and in every way, if one will make the Bible a life-long project. Consequently, my encouragement to you, the reader and student, regarding this all-important task, is done so from a lifetime of experience. I know what the study of the Word of God will bring about in one's heart and life. I have experienced it as millions of others! Consequently, I want every Believer to experience that of which I speak.

And yet I sadly realize that with many, if not most, the Bible is by and large an unread Book.

Why?

I suppose that Satan fights the Believer in this capacity as in no other. Satan knows what the Word of God can bring about in the life of the Believer. Consequently, he does everything he can to hinder that all-important spiritual progress.

This is at least one of the reasons I believe the Holy Spirit has moved upon me to write these Commentaries. In years of Ministry, I have had countless laymen tell me that they little read the Bible because they do not understand the Bible. Hopefully, at least for those who would take advantage of it, these Commentaries will help make the Word of God easier to understand.

Actually, the Bible is a story beginning with the Book of Genesis and concluding with the Book of Revelation. In Truth, it is a Revelation from beginning to end. That is the reason the Believer should study the Bible systematically, beginning at Genesis and going through to its conclusion. As the story was laid out in that fashion by the Holy Spirit, it should be studied in that fashion as well! So, if in this manner of study, I can get the Bible Student to read at least one chapter a day in these Commentaries, I believe he will have an understanding of that particular Chapter in the Word of God, which he has not had previously. I believe Truths will be brought to light that can literally change one's life, and in every capacity. The Word of God is designed to do that, and will accomplish that task if given the opportunity. If the student will make it a habit of studying one Chapter a day as suggested, I believe at the end of 12 months, there will be spiritual growth which will be obvious to all. If daily food is needed for the nourishment of our physical body, the Bible is likewise needed for our daily food respecting the spiritual man. Man does not live by bread alone, but by every Word which proceedeth from the Mouth of God.

If the Holy Spirit has moved upon me to write these Commentaries, then He has done so for purpose and reason. Consequently, when you begin their study, you are entering into His purpose and reason. As such, I believe you will be immeasurably blessed, instructed, helped, and strengthened in the Word of God. If, in fact, that is the case, then all Praise and Glory must go to the Lord for this help He has provided.

I WISH TO EXPRESS APPRECIATION

While knowing that the Lord is the Author of all good things, still, I would be remiss if I did not express my deepest appreciation to those who by their help have made it possible for me to devote the time required. I speak of Frances, who is my right arm. Actually, she attends to almost all of the daily duties of the operation of Jimmy Swaggart Ministries. That includes all personnel matters of the Ministry, as well as its daily operation. That, within itself, is a monumental task requiring her full attention. To be honest, she does it much better than I ever did. Her attention to detail is much more astute than mine. As well, I value her wisdom more than I have words to express, actually feeling that God has given her a special gift in this capacity.

Also, I must thank Donnie and Debbie for their full-time efforts at the Church and the Academy. Donnie attends to many, if not most, of the pastoral duties of the Church, as well as conducting Crusades all over the world. As I dictate these words, Frances and I have just returned from a series of meetings in South Africa, and Donnie left for Australia the day before we arrived home. Along with those duties, he as well attends to certain areas in the operation of the Ministry, which include Television, correspondence, etc. I depend on him greatly.

As well, I must mention my secretary, Linda Westbrook, who, in the midst of a mountain of work, tries to take the time to check these Volumes for grammar, punctuation, etc. Consequently, and regarding the Chapters which are not quite up to par in respect to this all-important aspect, etc., it should be understood that due to pressing duties, she was simply unable to peruse that particular part.

Also, I must not fail to extend gratitude to scholars, of which I am not one, who have gone before me, making my humble task immeasurably easier. What blessings there may possibly be in my efforts, they have helped to make possible. To their labor and faithfulness to the Word of God, I am grateful.

Actually, I am not a writer, and make no pretense in this direction. However, I suspect that if one would have the capacity to delve into the abilities of all the men who wrote the Bible, beginning with Moses, one would find that most of them, as well, were not writers. And yet, God used them to give the most important Message that mankind could ever receive — His Word.

Do not misunderstand, in no way do I place myself in their capacity, but, yet, I do claim the help of the same Holy Spirit Who helped them, as He, in Truth, helps all of us. Hopefully, He has helped us enough to make these efforts presentable. To Him, and for that, His wonderful help, we give all Praise and Glory.

As the Psalmist, I say, *"I entreated Thy favour with my whole heart: be merciful unto me according to Thy Word"* (Ps. 119:58).

THE
BOOK OF MARK

—■—

The author of this wonderful Book is John Mark (Acts 12:12; I Pet. 5:13). It was probably written about A.D. 60, some twenty-seven years after the Resurrection and Ascension of Christ. Some believe that Mark wrote his Gospel under the direction of Peter. Ancient writers, as Irenaeus, Tertullian, St. Jerome, and others, claim Peter as contributing to Mark's work. This much is obvious:

The manner in which the miracles and experiences of Christ are handled is definitely in the flavor of Simon Peter. However, even though what he heard orally from Peter concerning the life of our Lord, it seems also plain that he was not a mere copyist or story-teller. He was an independent witness as well! He often supplies a sentence, detailing some little incident which he could only have received from being an eye-witness.

Even though Mark's Gospel is the shortest of all the four Gospels, still, there is a unity and richness about it which quite excludes the notion that it is merely Mark relating what Peter had told him. Even though he avails himself of all the information he can procure, still, at the same time, he is an independent witness, giving, as all the sacred writers are permitted to do, the thoughts of his own mind which the Holy Spirit moved him to communicate.

Who, then, was Mark? He appears to have been of the Tribe of Levi. John was his original Jewish name; and Mark, his Roman prefix, which was added afterwards, and gradually began to supersede his Jewish name.

He was the son of a certain Mary who dwelt in Jerusalem. She appears to have been well known, with her house open to the friends and Disciples of our Lord. It is possible that her house may have been where our Lord *"kept the*

Passover" with His Disciples on the night of His betrayal; perhaps the house where the Disciples were gathered together on the evening of the Resurrection. It was certainly the house to which Peter came when he was delivered out of prison. Actually, this house may have been the first center of Christian worship in Jerusalem after our Lord's Ascension, which would have made it the site of the first Christian Church in that city.

It may come as a surprise to know that Mark was one who the Apostle Paul initially rejected.

He accompanied Paul and Barnabas as their attendant on their first missionary journey. However, when they reached Perga, in Pamphylia (Acts 13:13), Mark left them and returned to Jerusalem. The reason for his defection is not given; however, it placed an added burden on an already heavy-laden Paul and Barnabas.

Consequently, whenever the second missionary journey was begun, Barnabas desired to take Mark as at the first, but was rejected by Paul. Due to this, there was a temporary estrangement between Paul and Barnabas.

Even though very little information is given, it seems that Paul may have been wrong in his actions, with Mark acquitting himself favorably in further activity, and was accepted by Paul later on as well!

For instance, when Paul closed out the Epistle to the Colossians, which was written by him from Rome during his first imprisonment, he said at the close of that letter, *"There saluteth you ... Marcus, sister's son to Barnabas, (touching whom ye received commandments: if he come unto you, receive him;)"* (Col. 4:10).

Quite possibly the Christians at Colosse had heard of the temporary separation of Paul and Barnabas, and its cause. It is as if the Apostle

1

is saying, *"You have heard of the separation between Barnabas and myself on account of Mark. You will therefore now rejoice to know that Mark is with me, and a comfort to me, that he sends you Christian greetings by my hand. I have already given you directions concerning him: if he comes unto you, receive him."*

As well, in his Second Epistle to Timothy, written during his second imprisonment at Rome, which was the last he wrote before his death, he said, *"Take Mark, and bring him with thee; for he is profitable to me for the ministry"* (II Tim. 4:11). This is the last notice that we have of Mark in the New Testament, and it is beautiful as to how the Holy Spirit correlated these events that he would be mentioned by the great Apostle at the very last.

If one fails, as Mark, the Holy Spirit by these actions is telling us that the failure does not have to be permanent. As someone has said, *"It is not our actions, as important as they may be, but, rather, our reactions which really proclaim what we are."*

Mark overcame the failure in Pamphylia, and went on to write the Second Gospel in the New Testament. What an honor! What a privilege! And what a testimony of Faith to all!

It is said by some that Mark ultimately became the Pastor of the Church at Alexandria. It is further stated that he ultimately died a martyr's death in that city, although that cannot be proved.

Tradition says that his body was translated by certain merchants from Alexandria to Venice in A.D. 827. The Venetian Senate adopted the emblem of St. Mark — the lion — for their crest; and when they directed anything to be done, it is said that they affirmed that it was by the order of St. Mark.

This Second Gospel given by the Holy Spirit to Mark, portrays Jesus as the Servant of Jehovah (Zech. 3:8), as Matthew had portrayed Him as King.

As a result, parables and long discourses are almost entirely absent, for a servant does not teach. Though that purpose is to picture the Perfect Servant, yet through that service from time to time gleams the glory of the Godhead of Christ.

There is no genealogy given of Christ in Mark, for in a servant men seek a character and not a pedigree; hence there is no mention of the

NOTES

miraculous birth of Christ or reference to His childhood at Nazareth, as in Luke, or to His pre-existence and Deity, as in John; there is no Sermon on the Mount, for that became a King and not a Servant.

As well, there is no claim to authority, as, for example, in the Parable of the Tares, for the command to the reapers is omitted; here no sentence is passed upon Jerusalem, or woes denounced upon the Pharisees; no bridegroom as in Matthew 25; no Lord judging between faithful and unfaithful servants; and no king separating the nations to the right and left hand.

If parables and discourses are recorded, titles and actions are omitted. As in Gethsemane, nothing is said about Angels; on the Cross, no promise of the Kingdom is made to the dying thief. Prior to the Ascension of Christ, there is no statement as to His having all power in Heaven and in earth. He simply dismisses the Disciples to service and goes forth working with them as a Servant.

In Mark's account, the Apostles are regarded rather as companions than servants; they never call Him Lord in this Gospel; and in His miracles this title is suppressed.

And yet, if it would be possible to place one Gospel ahead of the other, at least in beautiful simplicity which makes it so easy to understand, the Gospel of Mark holds that distinction.

CHAPTER 1

(1) "THE BEGINNING OF THE GOSPEL OF JESUS CHRIST, THE SON OF GOD;"

This verse could read, *"The beginning of the Good News concerning Jesus, the Messiah, the Son of God."*

Consequently, the Holy Spirit begins this Book by testifying to the Kingship and Deity of Christ before setting out His perfection as a Servant.

The phrase, *"The beginning of the Gospel of Jesus Christ,"* refers to the Ministry of John the Baptist, which began that Gospel.

Matthew began with the ancestry and birth of the Messiah, Luke with the birth of the Baptist, and John with the pre-incarnate Word.

As stated, it was *"a Gospel of Good News."*

The Greek word for *"Gospel"* is *"Euaggelion,"* which means *"a Message of Good News,"* and was a word in common use in the first century for good news of any kind. Consequently, Mark appropriates the word, taking it out of the current secular usage, and links it to the Message of Salvation as Good News.

As a result, the word, *"Gospel,"* totally refers at present to the Message of Jesus Christ, and has no relationship to secular usage. Actually, this is forthright and truthful, because the *"Message of Jesus Christ"* is the only truly *"Good News"* in the world. The so-called good news claimed by the world is in reality, simply a momentary absence of bad news.

"Jesus Christ" actually means *"Jehovah saves, and is the Anointed One."* In Jesus, we have both His Deity and humanity, and in Christ, the Messiah of Israel.

This salutation means that this Good News is not preached, at least at this stage, by Jesus Christ, but is concerning Him. In other words, all of the Good News is wrapped up totally in Him.

The phrase, *"The Son of God,"* expresses His relationship to the Father, and that He is a separate and distinct Person from the Father. Jesus Christ is the Son of God by nature. Wuest says, *"He proceeds by eternal generation from God the Father in a birth which never took place because it always was. By virtue of all this, He possesses co-eternally the same essence as God the Father."*

Consequently, Mark begins His Gospel by telling us what it is all about, which is *"Good News,"* and, more particularly, Who it presents as the Author of this Good News, *"Jesus Christ, the Son of God."*

(2) "AS IT IS WRITTEN IN THE PROPHETS, BEHOLD, I SEND MY MESSENGER BEFORE THY FACE, WHICH SHALL PREPARE THY WAY BEFORE THEE."

The phrase, *"As it is written in the Prophets,"* proclaims the Old Testament as the Word of God, and that its records were carefully preserved and handed down from generation to generation. These records are, in the language of the Psalmist, *"For ever, O Lord, Thy Word is settled in Heaven"* (Ps. 119:89).

As someone has stated, almost everything said in the New Testament can be found somewhere in the Old Testament.

The word, *"Prophets,"* is used in the plural, because the quotation of verses 2 and 3 comes from both Malachi and Isaiah (Mal. 3:1; Isa. 40:3).

As well, it was common to combine, as here, quotations from various Prophets.

The phrase, *"Behold, I send My messenger before Thy face,"* refers to John the Baptist preparing the way for Christ. The Prophecy proclaimed that he was to immediately precede Christ, which he did!

The phrase, *"Which shall prepare Thy way before Thee,"* concerns preparation for the Ministry of the Lord by John the Baptist, of which the next two verses proclaim what type of preparation.

(3) "THE VOICE OF ONE CRYING IN THE WILDERNESS, PREPARE YE THE WAY OF THE LORD, MAKE HIS PATHS STRAIGHT."

The phrase, *"The voice of one crying in the wilderness,"* in the Greek actually says *"a voice,"* signifying that John was not the only *"voice"* sent to Israel, for many Prophets had preceded him and were sent by God.

The word, *"crying,"* signifies that John was a strong Preacher, whose preaching was full of emotion and feeling. It came from the heart, and was addressed to the heart.

Even though the voice used was John's, still, it was God Who was crying out. In other words, the Heart of God was in the Message, which meant that it was delivered by a powerful Anointing of the Holy Spirit, which greatly moved the people, as it was intended to do.

It was not psychology or mere emotionalism, as some modern skeptics claim, but the Holy Spirit greatly Anointing the Message and the Messenger, which meant what John said was the Word of God.

Regrettably, such Anointed preaching is frowned upon in modern ecclesiastical circles, and because such circles are almost entirely bereft of the Moving and Action of the Holy Spirit. Consequently, the words given by them are words of men and not of God, and are therefore of no consequence. Those words will bring no one to the Cross, cause no one to be saved, consequently, healing no broken hearts.

That which John gave did all of those things and more, as will all who follow in his train.

John ministered in the *"wilderness,"* which was probably close to Jericho, and was ordained thusly by the Holy Spirit for purpose and reason. There is very little, if any, evidence that he ministered in the cities.

Spiritually speaking, Israel was then a *"wilderness,"* and, therefore, the place and locality of John's Ministry was appropriate, and meant to serve as a symbol.

The phrase, *"Prepare ye the Way of the Lord,"* is actually given in the sense of a military command, and means that it is a command meant to be obeyed at once. In other words, *"Jesus Christ, the Son of God,"* is about to make His appearance, and everything must be ready. Therefore, Israel must do all the necessary things in the spiritual sense to prepare for the Advent of the Messiah. Tragically, Israel prepared not at all!

The *"Way of the Lord,"* is meant not only in the sense of preparation, but, as well, in the sense that Israel's ways must become God's Ways. In other words, get back to the Bible!

As I write these words, I sense the Presence of the Lord, in that the Holy Spirit is admonishing America, and the world for that matter, to do accordingly. The ways of man will destroy any and all, while the *"Ways of the Lord"* will bring life and prosperity.

I grieve, as do all True Believers, at the efforts of man to assuage his problems by his own abilities. As always, man seems to think that he either has the answer, or can find the answer in others. Never mind that all succeeding generations before him have failed, this generation thinks it can succeed.

However, without God there is no success! Solomon said, *"There is a way which seemeth right unto a man, but the end thereof are the ways of death"* (Prov. 14:12).

The phrase, *"Make His paths straight,"* simply means that the Ways of the Lord are *"straight,"* and that His people should be *"straight"* accordingly!

The word, *"straight,"* has to do with a *"plumbline."* Amos prophesied, *"Behold, I will set a plumbline in the midst of my people Israel"* (Amos 7:8). Christ is that *"Plumbline,"* with the definition of what is *"straight"* belonging to Him. As He was to Israel, He is to the Church, and to the entirety of the world for that matter!

Any time the *"Plumbline"* is tampered with, as it is oftentimes by men, and irrespective as to how much they claim it to be *"straight,"* as Israel of old, the fact remains, it is not *"straight,"* but crooked. That's what John was speaking of when he said, *"And the crooked shall be made*

straight" (Lk. 3:5). He was speaking primarily of the crooked way of the Religious Leaders of Israel.

(4) "JOHN DID BAPTIZE IN THE WILDERNESS, AND PREACH THE BAPTISM OF REPENTANCE FOR THE REMISSION OF SINS."

The phrase, *"John did baptize in the wilderness,"* was not exactly the type of Water Baptism practiced by Christians since Christ, but, in effect, very similar. It was connected with Israel and its acceptance of its Messiah.

The word, *"Baptism,"* or as given in the Greek, *"Baptizo,"* was not unknown to the Jews. It represented, or was symbolic of, the cleansing from sin which followed the Sin Offering, Trespass Offering, or Whole Burnt Offering. These ceremonial washings of Leviticus which followed the Sacrifices, were performed by the person himself, with one exception, and that was when Moses while installing Aaron and his sons, washed them himself (Lev. 8:6).

This is what Paul was speaking of when addressing the Law, *"Which stood only in meats and drinks, and divers washings"* (Heb. 9:10).

Even though these *"washings"* were practiced by the Jews, which meant they would have understood Baptism, still, the difference in the old washings which the person performed himself and John's Baptism, is that John personally baptized his converts.

One must, as well, be careful that he understands John's Baptism. Matthew 3:11 unfortunately translates, *"I indeed baptize you with water unto Repentance,"* which makes it seem like the Baptism is the cause of the Repentance. However, the original Greek makes it clear that John actually said, *"Repent, and be baptized because of the remission of sins."* The same holds true of Peter's words in Acts 2:38, where the same preposition is used.

Also, the word, *"for,"* is used in John's statement in verse 4, and should have been translated, *"because of."*

The error of *"Baptismal Regeneration"* is derived from these unfortunate translations, which in a simple way means that one is saved by Water Baptism. This is gross error, and has caused untold millions to die lost without God, hence our somewhat extended explanation.

The phrase, *"And preached the Baptism of Repentance,"* means that this all-important act is the foundation of moral intelligence.

Those who refuse to submit to it (Repentance) can neither understand Him nor the Book He wrote.

The Baptism that John preached was connected with the Repentance of the individual. It actually means, *"A change of mind,"* as it appears in a person who repents of a purpose he has formed or something he has done.

As well, the type of *"Repentance"* that John was preaching was far greater than a mere gloss or sorrow for one's wrongdoing, but was rather the Greek word, *"metanoia,"* which means, *"a change of mind which corresponds in a change of action consequent upon the realization that one has sinned and that sin is wrong."* In other words, the individual upon Repentance sees sin exactly as God sees it, not glossing over it in any fashion. As well, he sees himself, and says of himself, exactly what God says!

However, the type of Repentance John was speaking of, went even a step further. It not only addressed sin as God addressed the subject, but, as well, it renounced all the so-called good things that one was doing, which was thought to make one Righteous. So, a repentance was demanded that renounced not only the *"bad,"* but, as well, the *"good,"* which is extremely grievous to the prideful heart, and which such Repentance means to address.

That's the reason John said, *"Bring forth therefore Fruits worthy of Repentance, and begin not to say within yourselves, We have Abraham to our father"* (Lk. 3:8).

He was demanding that they repent not only of their sin, but, as well, of their dependence on who they were, the children of Abraham.

John was to *"preach"* this type of Repentance, which meant to do so with strength, power, and holy unction. The people were to have absolutely no doubt as to what he was talking about, nor a misunderstanding of what he meant.

One might quickly add, as the Message was desperately needed then, the Message is desperately needed now!

As the Message of Repentance had to be preached as a preparation for the First Advent of Christ, it, as well, must be preached as a preparation for the Second Advent, which definitely includes the Rapture (I Thess. 4:16-17).

Even though this particular Message is desperately needed at all times, still, its

proclamation at certain times, as here, is needed more than ever.

It is unfortunate that many claim the Message of Repentance is not needed presently, inasmuch as we are in the New Covenant. Those who proclaim such, little know their Bible. The Messages to the seven Churches of Asia by Christ, demanded that five of them repent. One could hardly deny that these were under the New Covenant (Rev. Chpts. 2 and 3).

The phrase, *"For the remission of sins,"* should have been translated as stated, *"Because of the remission of sins."*

In other words, the people were being baptized because they had already repented in their hearts, with their sins already remitted (forgiven), of which the Water Baptism was an outward act or sign.

The remission of sin is part of the Salvation which God gives the believing sinner when he places his Faith in the Lord Jesus. Therefore, remission of sins, as we have already stated, cannot be the result of Baptism, but rather its occasion. Baptism is the Believer's testimony to the fact that his sins are remitted.

The word, *"remission,"* in the Greek is *"aphesin,"* and refers to the act of putting something away. God did that at the Cross when He put away sin by incarnating Himself in humanity in the Person of His Son, stepping down from His Judgment Throne, assuming the guilt of man's sin, and paid the penalty, thus, satisfying His justice, and making possible an offer of Mercy on the basis of justice satisfied.

When a sinner avails himself of the merits of that atoning Sacrifice, he thus puts himself within the provision God made. His sins were put away at the Cross, and he comes into the benefit of that when he believes (Jn. 3:16). His submission to Water Baptism is his testimony to the latter fact, not only that all sin has been put away, but that he has taken advantage of that fact.

(The statement on remission of sins was derived from the teaching of Kenneth S. Wuest.)

(5) "AND THERE WENT OUT UNTO HIM ALL THE LAND OF JUDAEA, AND THEY OF JERUSALEM, AND WERE ALL BAPTIZED OF HIM IN THE RIVER OF JORDAN, CONFESSING THEIR SINS."

The phrase, *"And there went out unto him all the land of Judaea, and they of Jerusalem,"* specified they were coming and kept coming! It was a genuine Move of God, as would be obvious.

Naturally the news began to be spread all over Judaea and Jerusalem as well, concerning John the Baptist. His manner of attire, as the next verse proclaims, was somewhat different, and, above all, he spoke with the voice of a Prophet.

Inasmuch as Israel had not heard such a voice in about 400 years (since Malachi), the excitement caused by John's Ministry was excitement indeed!

Since Moses, and especially since Samuel, the voice of the God-called Prophet was that which whipped Israel into spiritual line, and actually served as a liaison between God and the people. Consequently, for that voice to be stilled for some 400 years was a tragedy of unparalleled proportions. However, every action by the Lord is for Divine purpose. There is some evidence that the Prophet Zechariah was murdered, with his Ministry taking place not so long before Malachi, who was the last. To be sure, Zechariah, if in fact he was murdered, was not the only one to suffer such a fate. However, the cup of iniquity for Israel, at least in this respect, was filling up; therefore, the Lord purposely silenced the prophetic voice.

However, John's Ministry was of far greater significance than any other Prophet, because his Ministry was the preparation of the coming of the Messiah, which was the greatest of all, and by far! So, this was a very special time for Israel, and the people responded accordingly, with the exception of most of the Religious Leaders.

With *"Jerusalem"* being specified, and it being the center of all religious activity, and especially considering that the Temple was located there, the Religious Leaders of Israel would have been dealt with especially by the Holy Spirit, but, sadly, with little favorable response. Hence, John would call them a *"generation of vipers"* (Lk. 3:7).

The phrase, *"And were all baptized of him in the river of Jordan,"* means they continually came and he continually baptized.

Even though, and as stated, Water Baptism was somewhat understood by the Jews, still, not in this fashion! As a result, some were being baptized who should not have been, causing John to say, *"Bring forth therefore fruits worthy of repentance"* (Lk. 3:8). In other words, he

was telling them in the account given by Luke that the water, or this act, could not save them.

The phrase, *"Confessing their sins,"* means that at times, as it certainly does, the act of Baptism and that of confessing sin went on at the same time. However, that means that the recipient of Baptism was not trusting in the water to save him, but rather his Repentance, of which the Water Baptism was an outward sign.

As well, the confession of sin is more than a mere acknowledgment of sin in the life. It is an agreeing with God as to all the implications that enter into the fact that one has sinned. It is looking at sin, as we have stated, from God's point of view, and acting accordingly. It means the putting away of that sin. It means the determination to be done with that sin.

(6) "AND JOHN WAS CLOTHED WITH CAMEL'S HAIR, AND WITH A GIRDLE OF A SKIN ABOUT HIS LOINS; AND HE DID EAT LOCUSTS AND WILD HONEY;"

The phrase, *"And John was clothed with camel's hair,"* proclaimed a possible imitation of Elijah by John, who wore a rough sackcloth woven from the hair of camels (II Ki. 1:8). As well, this garment was not made necessarily of the skin of a camel, but was a rough cloth woven of camels' hair.

In a spiritual sense, it was characteristic of the Doctrine which John taught, namely penitence and contempt of the world.

The phrase, *"And with a girdle of a skin about his loins,"* referred to a belt or sash of sorts used to pull the garment tight so as to give more freedom of movement.

The phrase, *"And he did eat locusts and wild honey,"* was a diet somewhat common in that day.

The *"wild honey"* was honey made by wild bees, whether in trees or the hollow of rocks.

As well, the *"locusts"* were dried to a crispness in the sun and eaten with the honey.

John's garb and diet were not without spiritual reference. Israel, in a sad state of spiritual declension, had succumbed to the things that money could buy, which included luxury, finery, and idleness. Consequently, the Holy Spirit drew John's attention to the simple and austere, which was 180 degrees opposite of what the majority in Israel was presently doing. Consequently, his food and clothing were meant to serve as a Message to Israel.

Looking at the modern Church, I wonder if

the similarity is not obvious! It, for the most part, has succumbed to the same evil as Israel of old. The Gospel has even been twisted and turned until presently money is the priority in many if not most Christian circles. The *"Prosperity Message"* has never had more followers and adherents. I wonder how similar everything else is?

As John introduced Jesus, the Son of God brought a moving of the Holy Spirit such as Israel had never seen before, but yet was rejected out of hand.

Likewise, I firmly believe that God is about to send a moving of the Holy Spirit on the Church and the world as it has never known before. I wonder if the modern Church will reject it even as the Hebrew Church rejected it?

I think the spirit of deception which is already laboring mightily in the modern Church gives us the answer to that question!

(7) "AND PREACHED, SAYING, THERE COMETH ONE MIGHTIER THAN I AFTER ME, THE LATCHET OF WHOSE SHOES I AM NOT WORTHY TO STOOP DOWN AND UNLOOSE."

The phrase, *"And preached,"* refers to strong, powerful proclamation of the Word of God, and, as stated, given with deep emotion. John's manner was an authoritative delivery which must be listened to and heeded.

The phrase, *"There cometh One mightier than I after me,"* means not merely *"one,"* but rather *"The One."* Actually, John was speaking of the Jehovah of the Old Testament. Consequently, the people of Israel, and especially the Religious Leaders, had absolutely no excuse for not knowing exactly Who Jesus was. John, with his powerful proclamation, introduced Him, telling exactly Who He was, and What He was! Not only was this *"The One,"* but, as well, *"The Almighty One!"*

The words, *"after me,"* proclaim that Jesus would immediately follow John. In other words, John was not speaking of someone who was coming in the distant future, but immediately!

The phrase, *"The latchet of Whose shoes I am not worthy to stoop down and unloose,"* has powerful meanings to it:

1. It meant that the majesty of the Word was shod with the sandal of our humanity — the Incarnation.

2. It meant that John and his Ministry would

decrease, while this *"One"* would continually increase. John was only the herald, while Jesus was the King Whom he announced.

3. This task of removing the shoes and washing the feet of a guest was the task performed by a slave in the household who held the lowest position in that status as a servant. So, John is telling us that one of the qualifications for being Baptized in the Holy Spirit, as the next verse proclaims, is humility.

(8) "I INDEED HAVE BAPTIZED YOU WITH WATER: BUT HE SHALL BAPTIZE YOU WITH THE HOLY GHOST."

The phrase, *"I indeed have baptized you with water,"* is not meant to introduce a Doctrine, but, rather, the fullness of Salvation which would be brought by Christ.

This 8th verse is meant to symbolize the difference in the Old Covenant and the New Covenant. There was as much difference there as between *"water"* and the *"Holy Spirit."* As is obvious, there is no comparison.

One pertained to ceremony, while the other pertained to newness of life.

The first was the promise, while the second was the performance.

The phrase, *"But He shall baptize you with the Holy Ghost,"* in effect, proclaims that the Lord will move His Spirit from the Temple in Jerusalem, where He had resided for about 1500 years (Temple and Tabernacle), and would now take up residence in the heart and life of the Believer, and because of what Jesus would do at Calvary and the Resurrection (I Cor. 3:16). Consequently, it has three meanings:

1. Water was the element with which John baptized. But the Holy Spirit is not the element with which Jesus baptizes. The Baptism connected with the Messiah is the act of the Holy Spirit Himself baptizing (placing) the believing sinner into Christ (Rom. 6:3-4), and thus the Body of Christ (I Cor. 12:13). John's Baptism was Water Baptism, while the Messiah's was Spirit Baptism. It is Jesus Who makes all of this possible, by what He did at Calvary and the Resurrection, and Who is the active Agent in carrying out this work.

2. This which Jesus would do, and which He has done in millions of lives, also respects that which happened on the Day of Pentecost, when Believers were baptized in the Holy Spirit, with the evidence of speaking with

other tongues as the Spirit of God gave the utterance (Acts 2:1-4), and continue to do so exactly in that manner.

There is a great difference in being *"born of the Spirit,"* of which this Passage also states, and as we have related, than being *"Baptized in the Spirit,"* which is strongly proclaimed.

Due to this Prophecy given by John concerning the great Work of Christ, if one stops at Salvation, as important as that is, and does not go on and be baptized in the Holy Spirit, one is greatly shortchanging himself in every respect (Acts 1:4).

3. The major purpose for Salvation is that one be a habitation of the Holy Spirit. Paul said, *"In Whom ye also are builded together for an habitation of God through the Spirit"* (Eph. 2:22).

The word, *"baptize"* referring to the Holy Spirit, means the same as *"baptize"* respecting water. It means for it to be in you and you to be in it!

(9) "AND IT CAME TO PASS IN THOSE DAYS, THAT JESUS CAME FROM NAZARETH OF GALILEE, AND WAS BAPTIZED OF JOHN IN JORDAN."

The phrase, *"And it came to pass in those days,"* respects the Ministry of John at its very close.

The phrase, *"That Jesus came from Nazareth of Galilee,"* respects the beginning of the Ministry of the Master.

As John in the wilderness, so Christ respecting His city of upbringing.

Nazareth was the home of Jesus for about thirty years until He was rejected (Lk. 2:39; 4:16, 28-31). He was therefore called *"Jesus of Nazareth."*

Nazareth lay close to several main trade-routes for easy contact with the outside world, and it is thought that a Roman garrison was stationed nearby. Consequently, the little town was held in contempt by strict Jews (Jn. 1:46).

However, and irrespective as to what Israel, and especially Jerusalem, thought of Nazareth, as the wilderness concerning John, the Holy Spirit would highlight Nazareth concerning Christ. It, as well, was to make a statement concerning humility, which characterized Christ.

The phrase, *"And was baptized of John in Jordan,"* concerned Jesus doing such to *"fulfill all Righteousness"* (Mat. 3:15).

John was commanded to baptize, and every

Godly Israelite was commanded to be baptized. Jesus was a Godly Israelite, and was such in order to save. Hence the obedience of Righteousness rested on them both in relation to this Baptism. But there was this difference — Righteousness brought Him there; sin brought His fellow-countrymen there.

The words, *"In Jordan,"* means that Jesus was baptized into the river and then came up out of the water. Jesus had no sins to confess, but nevertheless took His place with the Righteous of Israel, as we have stated, submitting to the baptism of John. Had He not done so, He would have been misunderstood as opposing John. As well, His Personal Baptism, although having nothing to do as an outward sign of inward repentance, as it did with all others, still, held tremendous meaning.

His going under the water signified His coming death and burial, with His coming out of the water signifying His coming Resurrection.

As well, that symbolism proclaimed the Salvation of the Believer, in that our Water Baptism symbolizes the same, with Christ serving as the example.

The old man dies and is buried, symbolized by the going down into the water, and is resurrected in newness of life, symbolized by the coming up out of the water.

So, this was a far greater moment with Christ than just an act performed in order that others may see it, consequently, sanctioning John's Ministry.

(10) "AND STRAIGHTWAY COMING UP OUT OF THE WATER, HE SAW THE HEAVENS OPENED, AND THE SPIRIT LIKE A DOVE DESCENDING UPON HIM:"

The phrase, *"And straightway coming up out of the water,"* concerning the Baptism of Christ, regards the beginning of His Ministry, which, as would be obvious, was the greatest Move of God the world had ever known. It would have an auspicious beginning, as this verse and the next proclaims!

The phrase, *"He saw the heavens opened,"* means He actually saw the heavens being rent asunder.

Six men have seen the heavens opened including Christ:

1. Ezekiel (1:1)
2. Jesus (vs. 10)
3. Nathanael (Jn. 1:51)

4. Stephen (Acts 7:56)

5. Peter (Acts 10:11)

6. John (Rev. 4:1; 11:19; 19:11)

However, the opening of the heavens on this occasion would signify the greatest of all! Even though all were extremely important, still, this pertained to the Redemption of humanity, and, therefore, was the fulfillment or the reason for this act of God. All of the Godhead would be here represented, Jesus upon Whom the Spirit descended, with the Voice of God speaking out of Heaven.

The phrase, *"And the Spirit like a Dove descending upon Him,"* actually should have been translated, *"Descending into Him."* This was the act of the Holy Spirit taking up His residence in the Messiah.

This precipitated and made possible the Words of Christ a little later at Nazareth, *"The Spirit of the Lord is upon Me* (within Me), *because He hath anointed Me..."* (Lk. 4:18).

Wuest said, *"This was the anointing with the Spirit for His three-fold Ministry of Prophet, Priest, and King, the dynamic power which would enable the Messiah to discharge the duties connected with these offices."*

As well, the act of the Holy Spirit coming into Christ was a preview of what would happen on the Day of Pentecost (Acts 2:1-4).

Even though Mark did not mention it, Luke said that Jesus was *"praying"* when *"the heavens were opened"* (Lk. 3:21). This plainly shows us that it was not through the Baptism of John which caused the heavens to open, but, rather, through the obedience and petition of the Son of God.

Exactly what is meant by the phrase, *"Like a dove,"* is not exactly known. Luke said, *"In a bodily shape like a dove,"* and concerning the Holy Spirit (Lk. 3:22). Quite possibly John saw this wonderful happening, as well as others who stood nearby! We dare not make more of this than we should, but, as well, must not make less!

It is my personal belief, although not shared by many others, that after the First Resurrection of Life, Believers in their Glorified State will be able to literally see the Holy Spirit. In effect, John the Beloved saw the Holy Spirit in his vision as outlined in Revelation 4:5. Admittedly, his description is beyond our pale of understanding, nevertheless, I think one could say without fear of contradiction that he did see Him.

NOTES

Consequently, I would assume from Mark's and Luke's description that those nearby literally saw something descend from Heaven in a *"bodily shape,"* and as Mark said it, *"Like a dove,"* which referred to similarity.

(11) "AND THERE CAME A VOICE FROM HEAVEN, SAYING, THOU ART MY BELOVED SON, IN WHOM I AM WELL PLEASED."

The phrase, *"And there came a Voice from Heaven,"* means that this Voice came from the rent or opened heavens. No form was seen, but a *"Voice"* was heard!

Incidentally, *"Heaven"* is a place, with this verse indicating that it has boundaries, etc. It is not merely a state of mind.

Revelation Chapters 21 and 22 tell us that Heaven has at least one city, with walls and gates, with the foundations of the wall *"garnished with all manner of precious stones"* (Rev. 21:19).

There is a river as well as streets and trees which bear fruits. Also, many people along with Angels are there (Rev. Chpts. 4 and 5).

One could probably say that Heaven is a planet somewhere in God's vast creation. At any rate, it is a real place, but far beyond our present knowledge. However, this we do know:

The Lord is going to change this earth into a replica of this place we call *"Heaven."* The Bible tells us so (Rev. 21:1-3)!

The phrase, *"Saying, Thou art My Beloved Son,"* means in contradistinction to all others.

Even though Believers are sons of God by adoption, still, we sustain a different relationship to the Father than the Son. As someone has stated, Jesus is the Son of God by a birth that never was, and, in fact, always has been. Therefore, He is the Son of God in a unique way that no mortal can ever hope to obtain.

The word, *"Beloved,"* means that Jesus is infinitely precious to God the Father. This love is pulled from the Heart of God because of the preciousness of the Son.

However, even though Believers are only adopted sons, still, in God's Eyes we are His Children, and, consequently, *"heirs of God, and joint-heirs with Christ"* (Rom. 8:17).

This means that everything Christ receives from the Father will also be given to the adopted sons.

Hallelujah!

The phrase, *"In Whom I am well pleased,"* means that the Father has always been pleased with the Son, is pleased with Him now, and will be pleased with Him forever! It is a delight that never had a beginning, because it always was, and will never have an end.

(12) "AND IMMEDIATELY THE SPIRIT DRIVETH HIM INTO THE WILDERNESS."

The words, *"And immediately,"* proclaim the first act of the indwelling Holy Spirit was to bring Jesus to the place of testing and temptation.

The phrase, *"The Spirit driveth Him into the wilderness,"* is not meant to imply reluctance of Jesus to go into this place. It does speak of the Holy Spirit moving upon Him so mightily and powerfully in respect to this thing, that it was almost as one would use force. It really pertained to an intense preoccupation of mind, which was set upon one thing only, and with fierce determination.

Some think that the *"wilderness"* here spoken of was nearby Jericho. Supposedly, John was baptizing in the Jordan near this city.

(13) "AND HE WAS THERE IN THE WILDERNESS FORTY DAYS, TEMPTED OF SATAN; AND WAS WITH THE WILD BEASTS; AND THE ANGELS MINISTERED UNTO HIM."

The phrase, *"And He was there in the wilderness forty days,"* proclaims the Second Adam being in the opposite setting of the First Adam, which was Paradise.

Even though Mark does not mention it, Jesus fasted the entirety of these *"forty days."*

Why forty days?

Even though the Bible does not say, is it possible that Adam and Eve lived forty days in innocence in the Garden before succumbing to Satan?

If so, Adam and Eve would have lived for forty days in bliss, then succumbing to Satan, while Jesus lived forty days in sheer torture and overcame Satan in every capacity, thereby doing what the First Adam did not do, and under the most difficult circumstances!

The phrase, *"Tempted of Satan,"* means to be tempted constantly during the forty days and nights.

The three temptations which Matthew speaks of at the end of the forty-day period, and which Mark does not allude to, merely indicate the additional intensity of the temptations as the period closed.

NOTES

The word, *"tempted,"* means to *"pierce or search into."* It means to discover what good or evil, power or weakness, is in a person. Since men so often break down under such a test, and, consequently, display the evil there is in them, the word, *"tempt,"* in its most simple form, means to solicit a person to do evil.

During this horrible time, the entirety of the universe was looking on, which included God the Father along with the Holy Angels, as well as the fallen angels and demons. In effect, this was the battle of the ages!

The very name or designation, *"Satan,"* means *"an adversary"* or *"slanderer."*

It means one who brings a false charge, and also those who spread the Truth concerning a person, but do so maliciously, insidiously, and with hostility.

A *"slanderer,"* although telling the truth, does so with the intention to destroy. Consequently, to spread something negative, although true, about a fellow Believer, can have but one intention, and that is to do the work of Satan. How many Believers have fallen into this trap, literally becoming emissaries of the Evil One!

Satan was once called Lucifer, seemingly the most powerful and beautiful Angel ever created by God. He served God for an undetermined period of time in Righteousness and Holiness. However, at some point he became lifted up within himself because of his great beauty, with pride entering his heart, which was the origination of sin, and, thereby, led a revolution against God, in which approximately one-third of the Angels joined with Him (Rev. 12:4).

How long this battle raged before Genesis 3:1-6 is not known. However, it has been the cause of all the heartache, pain, suffering, and bloodshed in this world (Isa. 14:12-15; Ezek. 28:11-19).

And yet the Bible predicts the total defeat of this evil one, which will at that time end this horrible period of suffering and bloodshed (Rev. 20:1-3, 7-10).

It is remarkable that God could speak the worlds into existence, but could not speak man's Redemption accordingly! To satisfy the Justice of God, the Lord had to become Man, thereby, coming down to this earth to accomplish as the Last Adam what the First Adam could not do. Due to the nature of the Fall of man, the victory of man, through the Substitute Man, the Lord

Jesus Christ, had to be in the same arena, but yet under worse circumstances.

The phrase, *"And was with the wild beasts,"* is said with intention. The *"beasts"* were not wild during the time of Adam and Eve, and therefore no harm was feared from them. However, and due to the Fall, some *"beasts"* became *"wild,"* but as we quickly add, were subject in totality to the Lord Jesus Christ. The only answer is that these wild beasts recognized and revered their Creator and their Lord. Paul said, and concerning the Fall, *"For we know that the whole creation* (which includes the animals) *groaneth and travaileth in pain together until now"* (Rom. 8:22).

However, Isaiah prophesied long before, of the time which is coming when Satan will be locked away, and Jesus will reign supreme. At that time, *"The wolf also shall dwell with the lamb, and the leopard shall lie down with the kid; and the calf and the young lion and the fatling together; and a little child shall lead them."*

He then said, *"And the cow and the bear shall feed; their young ones shall lie down together: and the lion shall eat straw like the ox"* (Isa. 11:6-7).

The phrase, *"And the Angels ministered unto Him,"* means they strengthened Him, but not with food. Even though we are not told exactly what they did, perhaps they ministered to His Soul, and, as well, only allowing Satan so much latitude.

The Great Plan of God for the Redemption of the human family was more vulnerable here than it ever had been or even would be. As God, Satan had no chance against Christ. However, as Jesus the Man, Satan was offered his greatest opportunity.

The efforts made against Jesus by Satan were basically, and irrespective of their direction, designed for one purpose. Satan attempted to get Jesus to step outside the perfect Will of God. Had he been able to do this, he would have won the conflict.

Others claimed that Jesus could not have failed. However, such thinking is unscriptural, and, therefore, specious. If Jesus could not fail, then at the same time by the very nature of such a position, He could not win.

As well, Satan would not have wasted his time for forty days and nights attempting to do something that was impossible.

No! For Jesus to be the Second and, therefore, Last Adam, it had to be possible for Him to fail. Actually, there is no record that Jesus had anymore help than any Child of God. He had the Holy Spirit as we have the Holy Spirit! (Acts 1:8). He had Angels to help Him, and we have Angels to help us, although unseen! (Heb. 1:14).

So, Jesus met Satan exactly as the First Adam had met him, although in much worse circumstances, such as the wilderness. As well, Satan's attack against Christ was much more powerful, many times so, than against Adam in the Garden of Eden.

The First Adam failed, but the Second Adam did not fail, and His defeat of Satan ensures our defeat of Satan.

(14) "NOW AFTER THAT JOHN WAS PUT IN PRISON, JESUS CAME INTO GALILEE, PREACHING THE GOSPEL OF THE KINGDOM OF GOD,"

The phrase, *"Now after that John was put in prison,"* concerns the ending of John's Ministry, and the beginning of Christ's. However, John wondrously and gloriously fulfilled that which he was called to do, the preparation for the Messiah.

As we have stated, John's prophetic voice was the first since Malachi, a time of approximately 400 years. Without a doubt, the people knew he was a Prophet of God, and knew that His Ministry was unique. Even though he plainly stated that One would follow him who would be much greater, still, it seems that only a few properly understood his Message — or else they understood, as the Religious Leaders, but would not believe it! Consequently, when he was put in prison these Religious Leaders who would later crucify Christ, would not lift a hand in His defense. Actually, they were probably very happy at the occasion of his arrest and imprisonment.

Such is religion!

The phrase, *"Jesus came into Galilee,"* specified this area as His Headquarters, which would be Capernaum by the Sea of Galilee.

This was in fulfillment of Bible Prophecy. Some 800 years before, Isaiah had prophesied..., *"Beyond Jordan, in Galilee of the nations. The people that walked in darkness have seen a great Light: they that dwell in the land of the shadow of death, upon them hath the Light shined"* (Isa. 9:1-2).

That Light was Jesus!

Consequently, this was the place chosen by God where His Eternal Son would carry out His earthly Ministry.

During the time of Christ, the Galilee area was bordered on the east by the Jordan River and the Sea of Galilee. On the west it did not quite extend to the Mediterranean. Its southern extension went down to the Kishon, which bordered Samaria. This was approximately ten to fifteen miles south of Nazareth.

There was actually an upper Galilee which extended to the northern most border of Israel, and a lower Galilee which incorporated the Sea of Galilee, Capernaum, and all of the cities which ringed that lake, as well as Nazareth, etc. It was in this area where most of the Ministry of Christ was carried out.

Judaea extended to the south as far as Beersheba, and included the cities of Hebron, Bethlehem, Jerusalem, the Capital of Israel. Between Judaea and Galilee, was Samaria. The Samaritans, who were somewhat half-breed Jews, were hated by the Jews proper, but were ministered to readily by Christ.

Galilee was a prosperous area, rich in olive oil and cereals, and especially fish from the Sea of Galilee.

Josephus, the Jewish Historian, said that cities ringed the eastern shore of the Lake, which teemed with fish, with the total population of Lower Galilee approximately 250,000 people.

It was well watered by streams flowing from the northern mountains, and possessed considerable stretches of fertile land in the limestone basins among its hills.

This, then, was the region in which Christ grew up — at Nazareth, in the limestone hills of Lower Galilee. Thanks to its position, it was traversed by several major route-ways of the Roman Empire, it was far from being a rural backwater region, even though its people were looked down upon by the intelligencia of Judaea.

Its agriculture, fisheries, and commerce, provided Jesus with His cultural background, and are reflected in His parables and teaching. Its people provided Him with His first Disciples, and its dense scattering of settlements formed their first mission field.

After the Baptism of Jesus in Jordan, the forty days and nights of wilderness temptation commenced. Then He came back to Galilee,

NOTES

with, it seems, Andrew and Peter, two of John's Disciples, who would become His Disciples. Shortly thereafter, He would turn the water into wine at the Marriage Feast in Cana, which would be His first Miracle (Jn. 1:43).

However, the Passover at this time was drawing near, therefore, He went back into Judaea that He might present Himself in the Temple, which occasioned its first purging (Jn. 2:14).

This is when Nicodemus visited Him by night, and when He began to openly preach and baptize (Jn. 3:26).

Almost immediately, the Scribes and Pharisees began to burn with envy toward Him. Shortly thereafter, He left Jerusalem, coming back into Galilee, which occasions this account by Mark.

The phrase, *"Preaching the Gospel of the Kingdom of God,"* says several things:

I. *"PREACHING"*: Matthew said, *"Preaching, teaching, and healing"* (Mat. 4:23; 9:35). As we have stated, preaching calls *"attention"* to Truth, while teaching *"explains"* the Truth.

As would be obvious, the *"preaching"* of Christ was powerful, in effect, the most powerful the world had ever known. Considering that He was Anointed by the Holy Spirit as no Prophet, Priest, or King had been Anointed before Him, one can well understand how it was said of Him, *"Never man spake like this Man"* (Jn. 7:46).

Respecting preaching, there are thirty things the Word of God tells us to preach:

1. Good tidings (Isa. 61:1; Lk. 4:18).
2. The Kingdom of Heaven (Mat. 4:17; 9:35; 10:7; 24:14; Mk. 1:14).
3. The Kingdom of God (Lk. 4:43; 9:2, 60; 16:16; Acts 8:12; 20:25; 28:31).
4. Repentance (Mat. 3:1-2; Lk. 24:47).
5. Water Baptism (Mk. 1:4; Lk. 3:3).
6. Spirit Baptism (Mk. 1:7-8; Lk. 3:16; Jn. 1:33; 7:37-39; Acts 1:4-8; 2:33, 38-39; 5:32; Gal. 3:13-14).
7. The Gospel (Mat. 11:5; Lk. 4:18; 20:1; Acts 8:25; 14:7, 21; 16:10; Rom. 1:15-16; 15:20; I Cor. 1:17; 15:1; II Cor. 10:16; Gal. 2:2; 3:8; 4:13; Heb. 4:2; I Pet. 1:12, 25; 4:6).
8. The Gospel of Peace (Rom. 10:15).
9. The Gospel of Christ (Rom. 15:19).
10. The Gospel of God (Rom. 1:1; II Cor. 11:7; I Thess. 2:9).
11. The Everlasting Gospel (Rev. 14:6).

12. The Word (Mk. 2:2; Acts 8:4, 25; 14:25; 15:36; 16:6; II Tim. 4:2; Heb. 4:2).

13. The Word of Faith (Rom. 10:8-17).

14. The Word of God (Acts 13:5; 17:13).

15. The Word of the Lord (Acts 15:35).

16. Jesus Christ (Acts 3:20; 5:42; 8:5, 35; 9:20; 10:42-43; 17:3, 18; II Cor. 1:19; 4:5; Gal. 1:16).

17. Christ crucified (I Cor. 1:23; 2:2).

18. The Cross (I Cor. 1:18, 21).

19. The Acceptable Year of the Lord (Isa. 61:1-2; Lk. 4:19).

20. The Unsearchable Riches of Christ (Eph. 3:8).

21. Deliverance (Lk. 4:18; Isa. 61:1).

22. Reconciliation (Acts 14:15; II Cor. 5:14-21).

23. The Bodily Resurrection of Jesus Christ (I Cor. 15:12).

24. Righteousness (Ps. 40:9; II Pet. 2:5).

25. Forgiveness of Sins (Acts 13:38).

26. Resurrection of the Dead (Acts 4:2).

27. Peace (Acts 10:36; Eph. 2:17).

28. All is vanity outside of God (Eccl. 12:8-14).

29. Mystery of Godliness (I Tim. 3:16).

30. Justification by Faith (Gal. 3:8).

II. *"THE GOSPEL"*: This is the *"Good News,"* but even more perfectly, *"The Good News that comes from God."*

In effect, the world has no Good News, and that which it calls *"Good News"* is only the absence of bad news. The only *"Good News"* is the Gospel of Jesus Christ.

Inasmuch as this is true, and certainly so, every Preacher must make certain that he preaches this *"Good News!"* If it is not heralded, preached, and proclaimed, there is nowhere else for the human heart to receive it. This is the reason that God calls Preachers. Consequently, and as stated, it becomes absolutely imperative, considering the consequences, that the Preacher preach the *"Gospel,"* only the *"Gospel,"* and nothing but the *"Gospel!"*

III. *"THE KINGDOM OF GOD"*: The word, *"Kingdom,"* as is here used, does not indicate a geographical area, but simply a realm in which a King, namely Christ, exercises His power to act and control. In this Kingdom, Jesus did not take up any earthly political power (Jn. 18:36); however, the miracles He performed showed His authority over every competing power. But Jesus the King was rejected and crucified, as His enemies struggled to force His Kingdom out of history.

NOTES

But Jesus' Death was not the end. During His days on earth, Jesus explained what life under His rule (i.e., in His Kingdom) would be like. It is best to take most Gospel descriptions of the Kingdom of Heaven and the Kingdom of God as explanations of life in Jesus' present Kingdom. (The Kingdom of Heaven and the Kingdom of God are basically the same, and have nearly the same meaning in some or all senses.)

According to His Gospel respecting the *"Kingdom of God,"* we are given powerful insights into how we can live today as Jesus' subjects and experience His Power. Because the New Birth brings us into union with Jesus and brings Jesus in a unique way into our experience here on earth, we live in a day in which the King is present, though still disguised. However, because Jesus is present, the unmatched Power of God can find supernatural expression in and through our lives.

It probably can be said that the Sermon on the Mount (Mat. Chpts. 5-7), is the foundation principle of the Kingdom of God lifestyle, with the Beatitudes serving as its core. These (the Beatitudes) describe the values of a person living a Kingdom lifestyle (Mat. 5:3-12). As King, Jesus acts to transform the character of His subjects. Jesus, in the present Kingdom, is working in our inner self to change our outward behavior. In the *"Sermon on the Mount,"* He goes on to show how we can experience this transforming power.

In this, we focus on our *"in secret"* relationship with the Lord, not on visible piety (Mat. 6:1-18).

We give priority to seeking God's Kingdom and Righteousness, and we trust our Heavenly Father to supply our material needs (Mat. 6:19-33).

We relate to other Kingdom citizens as brothers and sisters and reject every claim of a right to judge or control them (Mat. 7:1-14). As well, instead of relying on human leaders, we rely on the simple Words of Jesus and commit ourselves to obey them (Mat. 7:15-27).

To have entrance into this Kingdom of God, one must be *"born again"* (Jn. 3:3, 5). The New Birth gives entrance into the Kingdom — the realm in which Jesus' Sovereign Power is translated into action on behalf of His people.

And why this stress on being born again? Perhaps because of the fact that when a person is born again, Jesus enters his or her life, and there He takes up permanent residence through the Agency and Person of the Holy Spirit. Now and for all time Jesus is present in His people — in each Believer and in the corporate Body of Christ. In a mystical but real way, Jesus is present on earth in us. He is the key to release of the power needed to transform us and to shape the events that effect our lives according to His Will.

The Kingdom is here because Jesus is here. Because Jesus is here, the possibility of a new kind of life is laid open before us.

However, even though the Kingdom of Heaven, or the Kingdom of God is now real within our hearts, and, in Truth, we have entered that Kingdom, still, it is not evident on earth except in this capacity of the born-again experience.

However, the Old Testament along with the New proclaims a Kingdom which will not only reside in the spiritual, but the physical and material as well! In other words, there will be a Kingdom on earth, and Jesus will Personally rule over it. At that time, the entirety of the world will be transformed, with the *"Kingdom of God"* being realized in every facet of life, the spiritual, the academic, economic, agricultural, scientific, physical, and material. For the first time, the world and man will be seen as God originally created them.

Even though the Old Testament is full of these predictions, with Isaiah being the principle Millennial Prophet, still, Jesus Himself confirmed the Old Testament vision of this coming glad day (Mat. 8:11-12; 16:28; 20:21; 25:1, 34; 26:29; Mk. 11:10; 14:25; 15:43; Lk. 13:28-29; 14:15; 17:20; 19:11; 21:31; 23:43, 51; Acts 1:6-7).

(15) "AND SAYING, THE TIME IS FULFILLED, AND THE KINGDOM OF GOD IS AT HAND: REPENT YE, AND BELIEVE THE GOSPEL."

The phrase, *"And saying, the time is fulfilled,"* represented the most important *"time"* in history.

The older order of the Law was giving place to a new one, the Kingdom of Heaven, namely the Messianic earth-rule of the Messiah.

However, as is known, that was rejected by Israel, which subjected the entirety of the world to a time of suffering and heartache which has lasted now for nearly 2000 years. Christ was

rejected and Caesar was chosen (Jn. 19:15). Consequently, the world has seen approximately 2000 years of Caesar rule, which has resulted in heartache, starvation, war, death and destruction, causing untold suffering.

During this time, the Gospel of Grace and the age of Grace was brought in, with the Church, the Mystical Body of Christ, functioning in the interim between the rejection of Israel and its dispersion in A.D. 70, and its future regathering for the Millennial Kingdom. Then, the Kingdom of God will commence on earth, as was intended at the First Advent of Christ, but was rejected.

The word, *"fulfilled,"* means that God had allotted a specific period of *"time"* before Jesus would come. This was the period between the Garden of Eden with the first Prophecy of this coming event (Gen. 3:15), all the way to the beginning of the Ministry of Christ, which was about 4000 years. During this period, all the Prophets such as Abraham, Moses, David, Isaiah, etc., spoke of this coming time.

The phrase, *"And the Kingdom of God is at hand,"* meant that with the commencing of the Ministry of Christ, all that to which the Prophets had pointed, was about to be fulfilled, or at least given opportunity for fulfillment. All of it was wrapped up in Jesus.

The Kingdom of God can be further defined as God's rule over all moral intelligences willingly subject to His Will, including the Holy Angels and all Believers of all ages. This Kingdom was announced as at hand, but, as stated, was rejected.

However, and to be sure, the answer to our Lord's Prayer, *"Thy Kingdom come, Thy Will be done on earth as it is in Heaven,"* will ultimately be fulfilled (Mat. 6:10).

The phrase, *"Repent ye, and believe the Gospel,"* was the Message of Jesus Christ as well as John. It was also the Message of the Apostles (Mat. 10:7-10; Mk. 6:7-13); and of all True Gospel Preachers following them. It was not to be for Jews only or the early Church days only (Lk. 13:1-5; Acts 2:38-39; 3:19; 17:20; 19:8; 20:25; 28:23, 31; I Cor. 4:20).

The two words, *"repent and believe,"* may be regarded as a summary of the method of Salvation.

Repentance and Faith are the conditions of admission into the Christian Covenant.

Repentance has a special reference to God the Father, and Faith to Jesus Christ the Eternal Son.

It is in the Gospel that Christ is revealed to us as a Saviour; and therefore we find Jesus Christ as the object of our Faith, distinguished from the Father as the object of our Repentance.

Repentance of and by itself is not sufficient — it makes no satisfaction for the Law which we have broken; and hence, over and above Repentance there is required from us Faith in the Gospel, wherein Christ is revealed to us as a propitiation for sin, and as the only way of reconciliation with the Father.

Without Faith (believing) Repentance becomes despair, and without Repentance, Faith becomes only presumption. Join the two together, and the faithful soul instantly finds Redemption in Christ. Paul said, *"Testifying both to the Jews, and also to the Greeks, Repentance toward God, and Faith toward our Lord Jesus Christ"* (Acts 20:21).

(The remarks on Repentance and Faith were derived from Commentary of H. D. M. Spence.)

(16) "NOW AS HE WALKED BY THE SEA OF GALILEE, HE SAW SIMON AND ANDREW HIS BROTHER CASTING A NET INTO THE SEA: FOR THEY WERE FISHERS."

The phrase, *"Now as He walked by the Sea of Galilee,"* accounted this action as by design and purpose. This was probably near Capernaum. One can see Jesus slowly walking beside this body of water, maybe praying and meditating, which would occasion the call of Peter, Andrew, James, and John.

The Sea of Galilee is referred to by several names, *"Chinnereth"* (Num. 34:11), *"Chinneroth"* (Josh. 12:3), and in the New Testament as the *"Lake of Gennesaret"* (Lk. 5:1), and the *"Sea of Tiberias"* (Jn. 21:1).

The Lake is about seven miles wide and fourteen miles long. The River Jordan flows through it from north to south, and its waters are therefore constantly fresh.

As we have stated, the shores of this Lake were the site of towns, such as Capernaum, which Christ chose as His Headquarters, as well as Bethsaida, and others, along with Tiberias. Today, only Tiberias remains, with the others having faded into oblivion, and primarily because they little accepted the Ministry of Christ (Mat. 11:23).

The phrase, *"He saw Simon and Andrew his*

brother casting a net into the sea," signifies that such may have been done from the shore or from a ship close to the shore.

As stated, this was not Jesus' first acquaintance with Peter and Andrew, for He had met them on the trip to Judaea when He was baptized by John. They were Disciples of John the Baptist, along with John the Beloved (Jn. 1:35-42).

The phrase, *"For they were fishers,"* spoke of their occupation.

If one is to notice, the Holy Spirit did not at all select the religious elite of Israel to be the Disciples of Christ, but, instead, men of humble occupation.

This should portray to any and all the heart which God will use, which is seldom, if ever, the religious heart! That comes as a shock to most; however, religion and relationship with Christ are two different things altogether. Religion is man-devised, while relationship with Christ is God-devised.

(17) "AND JESUS SAID UNTO THEM, COME YE AFTER ME, AND I WILL MAKE YOU TO BECOME FISHERS OF MEN."

As an aside, the Holy Spirit, while guiding the minds of those whom He moved to write these records, did not use an overpowering influence, so as to interfere with their own natural modes of expression. Each sacred writer, while guarded against error, has reserved to him his own peculiarities of style and expression (Spence).

The phrase, *"And Jesus said unto them,"* would constitute the greatest words they would ever hear concerning their own personal lives.

The phrase, *"Come ye after Me,"* was a simple invitation, but yet containing the meaning of being His Disciple.

As stated, this was not their first encounter with Christ. As well, they no doubt had heard John's Messages when he spoke of One coming after him Who was mightier than he! Being dedicated to God, and even Disciples of John, they no doubt discussed long and hard among themselves that Jesus was the One of Whom John was speaking. Consequently, His appeal to them was something they probably had been eagerly awaiting for a period of weeks. And now it comes, with the thrill that must have penetrated their hearts which defies all description!

The phrase, *"And I will make you to become fishers of men,"* involves a long, slow process.

It is the same as when He spoke to the Church at Philadelphia, *"Him that overcometh will I make a Pillar in the Temple of My God"* (Rev. 3:12).

It was not a process that was easily arrived at, as the account of all four Gospels proclaim! And yet, it was arrived at, and greatly exacerbated by the outpouring of the Holy Spirit on the Day of Pentecost.

Someone has said:

"I can see far down the mountain, where
I've wandered many years,
"Often hindered on my journey, by the
ghost of doubts and fears.
"Broken vows and disappointments,
thickly strewn along the way,
"But the Spirit has led unerring, to the
land I hold today."

This first admonition of Christ proclaims to one and all that priority with God is the winning of souls. All who do not know of what Jesus did at Calvary and the Resurrection, as far as those people are concerned, Jesus died in vain!

So, even though many other things are greatly significant, still, priority must always be the proclamation of the Gospel of Jesus Christ, to bring men into the fold, i.e., *"fishers of men."*

(18) "AND STRAIGHTWAY THEY FORSOOK THEIR NETS, AND FOLLOWED HIM."

The words, *"And straightway,"* means this was done immediately! In other words, and as we have stated, this was something they had been waiting for.

The phrase, *"They forsook their nets,"* means they left the fishing business with no idea or thought of ever returning. It was not to be, nor intended to be, a brief excursion or sabbatical from the fishing business. They left with no intention of ever coming back. This is how powerful, how far reaching the invitation of Christ actually is. Of course, their understanding of Him and His Mission was limited at this time to say the least. Nevertheless, as early as this moment, they considered Him to be the Messiah, the Son of the Living God.

The phrase, *"And followed Him,"* in the Greek is *"akoloutheo,"* which means *"to walk the same road."* They were intent on following Him and irrespective as to where it would lead. (It actually means to walk alongside.)

Little did they know or realize that it would lead to ultimately judging the Twelve Tribes

of Israel forever, and, as well, to have their names inscribed on the Foundations of the coming New Jerusalem (Mat. 19:28; Rev. 21:14).

As the Apostles of old, the modern Believer little understands the tremendous spiritual benefit in living for Christ. The rewards are so absolutely far reaching that they beggar description! Consequently, our lives should be lived with this thought in mind, therefore, doing all that is possible to serve Him as diligently as we can.

(19) "AND WHEN HE HAD GONE A LITTLE FARTHER THENCE, HE SAW JAMES THE SON OF ZEBEDEE, AND JOHN HIS BROTHER, WHO ALSO WERE IN THE SHIP MENDING THEIR NETS."

The phrase, *"And when he had gone a little farther thence,"* respects the continued walk on the shore of the Sea of Galilee. There is a possibility even that Peter and Andrew were now walking with Christ, having left their *"nets."*

The phrase, *"He saw James the son of Zebedee, and John his brother,"* concerns two more fishermen who would be the Apostles of Christ.

At this time, Christ would merely request that these would *"follow Him."* It seems that quite a number ultimately were invited to do this. However, it was only after a night spent in prayer, that the actual Twelve were chosen (Lk. 6:12-16), which took place shortly thereafter.

The phrase, *"Who also were in the ship mending their nets,"* lends credence to the idea that even though they wanted and desired the call from Him, still, they were not expecting it at the moment. Their preparation, at least for now, was to continue in the fishing business.

(20) "AND STRAIGHTWAY HE CALLED THEM: AND THEY LEFT THEIR FATHER ZEBEDEE IN THE SHIP WITH THE HIRED SERVANTS, AND WENT AFTER HIM."

The phrase, *"And straightway He called them,"* constitutes the *"call"* of not only James and John, but, as well, every other person He has called into His service. Sadly, there are too many occupying pulpits who have never received that *"call!"* Conversely, there are many who have received the *"call,"* but have failed to heed and follow. And sadly, there are many who heard and answered the *"call,"* but have not lived up to its potential.

The Ministry of the Lord Jesus Christ is not

a vocation, avocation, career, or job. As here, it is a Call of God.

Regrettably, far too many are in the Ministry as a career, etc. They've actually never been called of the Lord.

Some time back, I heard a political figure say that the only way to get out of the grinding poverty into which he was born in West Texas, was either through politics or the Ministry. He went on to state how he had reasoned in his mind that Ministry would be the course he would take, when politics diverted his attention, with him choosing that direction instead.

Thank the Lord that was the direction he chose, because the Lord certainly had not chosen him for the direction of Ministry.

Some would ask the question as to how one can be sure that one is called?

The answer is not as difficult as one would think.

First of all, if it's possible to do anything else other than Ministry, then do it! To be sure, if one is truly called of the Lord, that *"call"* will rest so heavily upon him (or her) that they simply will not be able to do anything else.

Nevertheless, it should be well understood that a true *"call"* from the Lord will much of time ultimately result in a life of hardship, persecution, and sometimes even death! The world is not in sympathy with a true call from God, and, sadly enough, neither is the Church.

Those who are truly called of God will follow the Lord and nothing or no one else! Sadly, some who were truly called have ceased to follow Him, and as a result, experience no more Anointing by the Holy Spirit, neither His leading or guidance. One cannot follow man and God at the same time!

The reason the religious elite in Israel hated Christ so much, was because those who followed Him would not follow them. The situation has little changed even unto the present.

The God-called Preacher is going to have to make up his (or her) mind, that man, and especially religious man, will strongly seek to usurp authority over the Lord. Those who call themselves *"Religious Leaders"* too often demand total allegiance. This, also, too often characterizes Religious Denominations. So, the man of God will be faced with a choice. However, he must understand that he cannot serve both. *"No man can serve two masters: for*

either he will hate the one, and love the other; or else he will hold to the one, and despise the other" (Mat. 6:24).

The phrase, *"And they left their father Zebedee in the ship with the hired servants,"* is peculiar to Mark concerning the *"hired servants."* This shows that he was an independent witness of that which he wrote.

This narrative tells us that the fishing business of Zebedee was quite larger than that of Peter and Andrew, because no mention is made of servants (other employees) in their business. Actually, there is a good possibility that Peter and Andrew worked for Zebedee.

If this were the case, then the man was left with no one but the *"servants,"* with even his sons following Christ. However, every indication is that Zebedee gladly gave up his sons, and that he was rewarded greatly for his sacrifice. There is no indication whatsoever that he intended to stop them or even slow them, but actually encouraged them. He, as well, saw in Christ that which satisfies the hunger and thirst of the soul.

Zebedee was in the ship with them the day that they received the call of Jesus. Exactly what Jesus said is not registered, but more than likely it was the simple admonition as to Peter and Andrew, *"Follow Me!"*

The moment they looked up and saw Him, and His voice rang out to them of that clarion call, I believe the Presence of God instantly filled that ship as well as their hearts. This was a *"call"* that had been decided a long time before, and, consequently, it carried far more than just the weight of invitation. Zebedee no doubt sensed and felt the tremendous import of the invitation as much as his sons.

Mark does not say exactly what transpired at that moment, but Matthew did say that they *"left the ship and their father,"* meaning that they had his blessings (Mat. 4:22).

The phrase, *"And went after Him,"* means that they separated from their Father and the fishing business, never to go back. The call of God, as stated, transcends all affections, family ties, loyalties, and personal choices.

(21) "AND THEY WENT INTO CAPERNAUM; AND STRAIGHTWAY ON THE SABBATH DAY HE ENTERED INTO THE SYNAGOGUE, AND TAUGHT."

The phrase, *"And they went into Capernaum,"*

did not mean immediately, but rather some time later, possibly even several days. There is evidence that other things, such as the *"Sermon on the Mount,"* took place before the event of the deliverance of the man with an unclean spirit in the Synagogue on the *"Sabbath Day."*

The town of Capernaum was located on the northwest corner of the Sea of Galilee. It was inhabited continuously, it is said, from the first century B.C. to the seventh century A.D. It seems to have been the nearest village to the River Jordan as it made its entrance into the Lake.

On the western shore, Tiberias was the largest town closest to where the Jordan River made its exit from the Sea of Galilee, being about five miles distance from that site. About two miles north of Tiberias was Magdala, where Mary Magdalene lived. About two miles north of Magdala was a place called Heptapegon, and then about two miles further on Capernaum. On the northeast corner of the Lake was Bethsaida, about six miles from Capernaum. It was in Capernaum where Jesus made His Headquarters.

It is said that a lady by the name of Egeria visited this city in A.D. 383. She was shown a Church in the little town, and was told that it had been made from the house of the Apostle Peter, and the walls of this house were incorporated into it, still standing in their original form. Peter's house was probably the headquarters of Christ.

The phrase, *"And straightway on the Sabbath Day He entered into the Synagogue,"* constituted the Church of that day. The Jewish Synagogue was the place of worship other than the Temple at Jerusalem.

Synagogues were numerous among Jews from the Babylonian captivity on. They were erected in all cities and towns, and in the country on rivers, that there might be plenty of water for the many washings.

Ten Jews could start one, and it took this many to run and support such a place. There were many in all lands for each Jew was required to attend services in one or in the Temple every Sabbath. Jerusalem alone had 480 Synagogues. As stated, they were places of instruction and worship. They were also places for courts of justice (Lk. 12:11; Acts 9:2).

Officers and a council of three to thirteen men were chosen by the congregation that

NOTES

carried on the worship, to teach school and hold court concerning religious and civil cases (Mat. 10:17; 23:34; Jn. 9:22, 34; 12:42; 16:2; Acts 22:19; 26:11).

Priests were honored but had no official standing unless members of the council or serving as teachers. The leader or president could ask anyone to speak, read Scripture, or expound the Law. Christ often spoke in Synagogues (Mat. 4:23; 13:54; Mk. 6:2; Lk. 4:15-22; Jn. 18:20) as did the Apostles (Acts 13:5, 15; 14:1; 17:10-17; 18:19).

Services were held in them three times on the Sabbath. The Scribes and Lawyers in Israel in every community were the school teachers and interpreters of the Law and used such places for almost daily instruction.

They were built on the highest ground and were often without roofs, being situated so the worshiper entering could pray toward Jerusalem (Dan. 6:10).

In each Synagogue there was an Ark or Chest resembling the Ark of the Covenant, which contained the Law. It was from this Chest or Ark that the Scroll of Isaiah was handed to Christ when He taught on the Sabbath Day in Nazareth (Lk. 4:15-20).

There was a raised platform at one end of the Synagogue and a desk from which to read and expound the Law.

The men and the women were separated by a low partition, which ran down one side of the building.

As well, there were seats for officers in front of the platform facing the congregation, where the Pharisees enjoyed sitting (Mat. 23:6) (Dake).

The words, *"And taught,"* mean, according to the Greek scholars, that He brought an extended discourse to the people that day. What He taught is not stated; however, coming from His lips, as the next verse proves, meant that it was the greatest teaching on the things of God that the people had ever heard. What a privilege to have heard such explanation of the Gospel!

And yet, if a Preacher knows the Word and is Anointed by the Holy Spirit, it will be in the same realm as to what Jesus taught, because it is the same Holy Spirit Who Anoints now, Who Anointed then! This is the reason that two things are imperative respecting the Preacher of the Gospel:

1. He must know the Word of God, understanding that it alone holds the answer to all things pertaining to life and Godliness (II Pet. 1:3).

2. He must seek God incessantly in order that he (or she) be a proper channel through which the Spirit of God may flow. This speaks of a strong prayer life.

(22) "AND THEY WERE ASTONISHED AT HIS DOCTRINE: FOR HE TAUGHT THEM AS ONE THAT HAD AUTHORITY, AND NOT AS THE SCRIBES."

The phrase, *"And they were astonished,"* means they were literally *"bowled over"* at what He said and the way He said it! Whatever they were expecting to hear, as constantly brought to them by the Scribes, etc., they did not hear, and what they hardly expected to hear, a proclamation of the Word of God, which was actually greater than had ever been delivered in human history, they did not expect.

The phrase, *"At His Doctrine,"* once again respected <u>what</u> He taught, and the <u>way</u> He taught it.

What was His Doctrine?

His Doctrine was the Word of God, while the Scribes basically taught tradition.

Tradition was *"the commandments of men"* (Mat. 15:9; Mk. 7:6-7).

In other words, this tradition was human thought which did not measure up to the Word of God, and, in effect, was contrary to the Word of God.

Conversely, the teaching given by Christ not only agreed with the Word of God, but, in effect, was the Word of God. Thus in the Sermon on the Mount, Jesus quoted from the Law, but put beside it His Own Words, *"But I say unto you"* (Mat. 5:22, 28, 32, 34, 39, 44; 6:25).

His justification for so doing is found in His Person. As the Spirit-anointed Messiah, the Word made flesh, He Alone could make a valid and authoritative commentary on the Spirit-inspired Word of God. Likewise, the Epistles emphasize the Person of Christ in contrast to tradition. In Colossians 2:8, Paul warns against falling prey to *"philosophy and empty deceit . . . according to human tradition . . . and not according to Christ."*

And yet, the Early Church was commanded to hold to the traditions which came from Christ. Paul said, *"Therefore, Brethren, stand fast, and hold the traditions which ye have*

NOTES

been taught, whether by Word, or our Epistle" (II Thess. 2:15).

The difference was, this *"tradition"* encouraged by the Apostle Paul came from Christ, Who was and is God, and not man. Christ not only created the true tradition, but constitutes it.

Christian tradition, therefore, in the New Testament has three elements:

1. The facts of Christ (Lk. 1:2; I Cor. 11:23; 15:3).

2. The theological interpretation of those facts, which is the whole argument of I Corinthians 15.

3. The manner of life which flows from them (I Cor. 11:2; II Thess. 2:15; 3:6-7). In Jude 3, the *"Faith . . . once for all delivered,"* covers all three elements (Rom. 6:17).

Consequently, that written by the Apostles, which constitutes the Gospels and the Epistles, claimed that its tradition was to be received as authoritative (I Cor. 11:2; II Thess. 2:15; 3:6).

Christ told the Apostles to bear witness of Him, and for several reasons:

A. Because they had been with Him from the beginning, and, as such, they were to pass on what He taught them, as they did! This constitutes the four Gospels, Matthew, Mark, Luke, and John. It also includes Acts, for Luke, its writer, said, *"Forasmuch as many have taken in hand to set forth in order a declaration of those things which are most surely believed among us, even as they delivered them unto us, which from the beginning were eyewitnesses, and Ministers of the Word"* (Lk. 1:1-2).

It would also include the Books of James, Jude, I and II Peter, along with I, II, and III John, and the Book of Revelation.

As well, it includes all the writings of the Apostle Paul, which make up the entirety of the New Testament.

Even though Paul was not one of the Disciples of Christ during His earthly Ministry, still, he said, and concerning the visible appearance of Christ, *"And last of all He was seen of me also, as of one born out of due time"* (I Cor. 15:8).

Consequently, all the writers of the New Testament had either been with Christ, or had at least seen Him as Paul. (Paul is speaking of the time that Christ appeared to him on the road to Damascus, which resulted in his conversion, Acts 10.)

B. The Holy Spirit was promised to them, as

to us, Who would lead them into all Truth (Jn. 15:26-27; 16:13).

This combination of eyewitness testimony and Spirit-guided witness produced a *"tradition"* that was a true and valid compliment to the Old Testament. So, I Timothy 5:18 and II Peter 3:16 place apostolic tradition alongside Scripture and describe it as such.

In other words, and as stated, that passed down by the Apostles, and was called *"tradition,"* was not their own thoughts and ideas, as the *"tradition"* of the Scribes which Jesus rebuked, but rather, the Words and Actions of Christ, or direct revelation of the Holy Spirit.

That which transpired in Jesus' day, with the Scribes and Elders proclaiming their own thoughts and ideas which did not measure up to the Word, happens no less today! From behind most pulpits in America, the Word of God is either totally ignored, or twisted and perverted to mean something it did not originally proclaim. Paul called it *"another gospel"* (II Cor. 11:4).

As the True Word of God as proclaimed by Christ was very scarce during those days of long ago, likewise, it is very scarce presently! The greatest barometer of this is the condition of the nation as a whole.

The more of the True Word of God that is preached, proclaimed, and practiced, such will likewise show itself in the structure of government and the people in every sense. It does not necessarily mean that such proclamation will cause Righteousness to fill the land, but, instead, that it will serve as a bulwark against evil. As is obvious at the present, evil has never been more pronounced in America, whether academically, governmentally, economically, and, above all, socially! One will find the true cause of these afflictions as the lack of the proclamation of the True Gospel of Jesus Christ, i.e., the Word of God.

The phrase, *"For He taught them as One that had authority, and not as the Scribes,"* refers to the Scribes teaching their own thoughts and ideas, which were not the Word of God, and, consequently, not Anointed by the Holy Spirit, relative to what Christ taught, which definitely was Anointed by the Holy Spirit.

This is actually what we're speaking of, the Word of God Anointed by the Holy Spirit! Any God-called Preacher of the Gospel can have the same today, with but one exception, and that is the type of *"authority"* spoken of here.

The word, *"authority,"* as it is normally used, refers to power a person has that is delegated to him from someone else. In the case of the Preacher of the Gospel, or any Believer for that matter, it refers to the Lord giving that authority, which means *"delegated authority."*

However, the word *"authority"* as used here of Christ, is different in that His authority was in Himself, and not derived from others. (The Believer has authority within himself, only in the sense that the Holy Spirit resides in him. While it is true that the Holy Spirit abided in Christ, on Whom He depended constantly, still, Christ was the *"Living Word"* as no Believer can ever be, except to the degree that Christ abides in him.)

The *"Scribes"* were those learned in Mosaic Law and in the Sacred Writings, and, consequently, were supposed to be interpreters and teachers.

(23) "AND THERE WAS IN THEIR SYNAGOGUE A MAN WITH AN UNCLEAN SPIRIT; AND HE CRIED OUT,"

Several things are said in this Passage:

1. The man with the *"unclean spirit"* in the Synagogue, is indicative of a spirit (although different) which resides in, and, in fact, controls most modern Churches. Thankfully, it is not indicative of all, but, as stated, most!

It is somewhat startling to think of demon spirits controlling most Churches, especially considering that they are supposed to be the opposite, still, religion is the area where Satan works best, and, consequently, destroys the most!

As previously stated, each miracle performed by Christ was not only to benefit the individual involved, but, as well, to teach a greater lesson which applied to some or all in a spiritual sense.

2. The term, *"unclean spirit,"* is used some twenty-two times of demons, ten times in Mark alone. The word, *"unclean,"* runs the gamut of all the activity of Satan from immorality to deceptive, lying religious spirits (Rev. 16:13-16).

3. Demon possession speaks of spirits of darkness which enter into a person's body, taking up residence in it, and controlling the mind of the person in whose body he dwells. These spirits exercise control over the individual they possess at all times, but more so at some times

than others, as here illustrated. After Jesus finished His Message, the demon spirits screamed out, using the man's vocal chords. In other words, the man was the instrument, but the demon spirit was the actual control. (There is one Devil who is Satan, who controls a vast army of demon spirits, of which this was one.)

The torture of one afflicted by such, knows no bounds. Consequently, the torture of Mary Magdalene from whom Jesus cast out seven devils, must have been awful indeed! (Lk. 8:2).

4. From the fact that demons have no rest unless they are living in some physical body, it seems clear that at one time they did have physical bodies, and that they were deprived of them by a Judgment of God.

Some, including the writer, think that they are the disembodied beings of a pre-Adamite race who inhabited the first perfect earth (Gen. 1:1), and that they followed their leader Lucifer into sin, and were disembodied and deprived of residence upon the earth by the cataclysm of Genesis 1:2, which was coincident with the fall of Lucifer (Isa. 14:12-17). These are the principalities and powers of Ephesians 6:12, and comprise the kingdom of Satan in the atmosphere of this earth (Eph. 2:2) (Wuest).

The phrase, *"And he cried out,"* refers to a terrible cry of impending doom. It was a member of one race of beings, speaking through and by means of a member of the human race.

This spirit saw in Christ a Power far greater than his power of darkness, and, consequently, knew that it spelled his doom, at least regarding his habitation in this man.

Every human being in the world who does not know Christ as his personal Saviour, is more or less controlled in some way by demon spirits. It does not mean that all are possessed as this man, but it does mean they are controlled in one way or the other.

Even though a Believer cannot be *"possessed"* by demon spirits, as the man illustrated in this Text, still, Believers can definitely be controlled at times, and especially influenced. Such control or influence is denied by nearness to Christ. Christ having total control of one's life, will, of necessity, abrogate such activity by spirits of darkness.

(24) "SAYING, LET US ALONE; WHAT HAVE WE TO DO WITH THEE, THOU JESUS OF NAZARETH? ART THOU COME

NOTES

TO DESTROY US? I KNOW THEE WHO THOU ART, THE HOLY ONE OF GOD."

The phrase, *"Saying, Let us alone,"* represents the teaching and preaching of Jesus as having thrown the whole world of evil spirits into a state of alarm. Likewise, the True Proclamation of the Gospel will do the same presently.

In 1987, we were conducting a crusade in Monrovia, Liberia, in West Africa. The meeting was held in the Stadium which seated approximately 50,000 people. That Sunday afternoon, the newspapers reported that well over 100,000 were present, although possibly exaggerated. At any rate, the Stadium was completely filled, even with thousands standing in the infield.

As I began to minister, something took place which I had never encountered in all of my many years of ministry. Two or three individuals began to bark like dogs in this vast Stadium, with thousands of others immediately beginning to take it up. Soon a roar filled the Stadium of what seemed like thousands of dogs barking, but, in reality, were demon spirits.

Of course, it was impossible to continue to preach under such circumstances. Consequently, I stopped, and addressed these spirits by saying, *"In the Name of Jesus, I command you to cease this activity!"* The results were astounding!

The barking stopped in an instant. It was as if a faucet was running water, and then someone turned it off instantly. Whereas the noise of the barking had filled the Stadium, now there was nothing but silence.

To be sure, it was not necessarily to me that this vast number of demon spirits responded, but, instead, to the Name of Jesus proclaimed by me.

That afternoon, thousands responded to the invitation to come to Christ. No doubt, as Christ came into these many lives, evil spirits, as well, departed!

The question, *"What have we do with Thee, Thou Jesus of Nazareth?"*, means they resented the intrusion by Christ into their domain. As well, the question means that there was no association whatsoever between the world of Light, as represented by Jesus, and the world of darkness, as represented by these evil spirits. Incidentally, the pronoun *"us"* is used, denoting many demons in this man headed up by a head or chief demon.

As well, *"Jesus of Nazareth,"* is specified respecting this particular *"Jesus!"*

Actually, the demon would have said, *"Joshua of Nazareth,"* for Jesus is the Greek derivative of the Hebrew Joshua. As Joshua was a common name in Israel, Nazareth was specified, consequently, denoting a specific *"Joshua,"* i.e., Jesus.

The question, *"Art Thou come to destroy us?"*, has reference to the fact that they possibly thought they were at once to be judged. They knew He had Power to do whatever He desired.

The phrase, *"I know Thee Who Thou Art, the Holy One of God,"* proclaims these spirits knowing Who He was, but the Religious Leaders of Israel not knowing. Or if the Religious Leaders of Israel did recognize Him as the Messiah, the Son of God, with there being some evidence that they did, yet in their apostasy they rejected Him (Mat. 21:37-39).

(25) "AND JESUS REBUKED HIM, SAYING, HOLD THY PEACE, AND COME OUT OF HIM."

The phrase, *"And Jesus rebuked him,"* is interesting indeed!

First of all, Jesus desired no acknowledgment from the Devil whatsoever, and, therefore, told him to *"Shut up!"*

As well, the word, *"rebuked,"* in the Greek is, *"epitimao,"* which means a rebuke with no effort to bring the offender to the acknowledgment of his sin. In other words, Satan, the fallen angels, and demons are incorrigible. They refuse to be convicted of their sin, and they will not acknowledge it nor repent.

So, this one statement by Christ completely refutes the erroneous Doctrine of *"ultimate reconciliation,"* which means that ultimately everything will be reconciled unto God, even demon spirits and Satan himself. The Bible in no way teaches such gross, blatant error!

Inasmuch as the Bible is the story of the Fall of man, and his Redemption by Christ, only a little information is given concerning the Fall of Satan, along with his angels and spirits. Consequently, regarding their past opportunity to repent, we have no knowledge. And as here recorded, the die is cast, signifying that no reconciliation will ever be possible between God and Satan and the works of darkness.

The phrase, *"Saying, Hold thy peace,"* is glossed somewhat in the English translation.

NOTES

It should have been translated, *"Saying, Shut up!"* As we have stated, from this we can gather something of the attitude of God towards Satan, fallen angels, demons, and the enormity of their sin.

The phrase, *"And come out of him,"* would have been said, *"Shut up, and come out of him."*

Both commands, *"Shut up,"* and *"Come out of him,"* are military in their usage. It would be the same as a General giving orders to a Private, which would instantly be obeyed. However, it is much greater than that, although there is no idiom in any language to properly convey the authority here used by Christ, and heard by the demon.

This demon spirit knows that Christ has absolute Power, and can use it absolutely!

Consequently, the *"Name of Jesus,"* used according to the Word of God, and exclaimed by Mark, *"In My Name shall they cast out devils,"* expresses the same type of power (Mk. 16:17).

(26) "AND WHEN THE UNCLEAN SPIRIT HAD TORN HIM, AND CRIED WITH A LOUD VOICE, HE CAME OUT OF HIM."

The phrase, *"And when the unclean spirit had torn him,"* means that the exit of this spirit was of a violent nature. It can be looked at in two ways:

1. The spirit was angry at having to leave out of the man, and, consequently, showed his displeasure by his action against the man.

2. At the Command of Christ, this spirit was so overcome by fear that he hastened to remove himself from this man with such speed that it caused convulsions. Luke in his description, says, *"He came out of him, and hurt him not,"* emphasizing that the spirit was hastily trying to make his exit upon the Command of Christ (Lk. 4:35).

The phrase, *"And cried with a loud voice,"* represents a screech of fear — fear of Christ, and fear not to obey Christ immediately!

The phrase, *"He came out of him,"* is emphatic, meaning, *"forthwith!"* In other words, there was no delay.

Such is the Power of Christ, Who commands spirits and they instantly obey, and, as well, can change a person's life just that quickly.

(27) "AND THEY WERE ALL AMAZED, INSOMUCH THAT THEY QUESTIONED AMONG THEMSELVES, SAYING, WHAT THING IS THIS? WHAT NEW DOCTRINE IS

THIS? FOR WITH AUTHORITY COMMANDETH HE EVEN THE UNCLEAN SPIRITS, AND THEY DO OBEY HIM."

The phrase, *"And they were all amazed,"* means that the onlookers were frightened, even terrified. The short, simple Command of Christ to this demon spirit, which had caused his immediate exit, which was obvious to all, left the onlookers speechless at what they had seen, and even terrified at the power exhibited. Let us emphasize again that the change which instantly came about in this man's life is indicative of what Jesus can do for any and all who dare to believe Him. His Power is instant and can effect the New Birth, and, therefore, the instant change which man so desperately needs.

The phrase, *"Insomuch that they questioned among themselves,"* describes an animated, prolonged discussion.

The question, *"Saying, What thing is this?",* means that they had begun to reason that anyone who could bring about such instant miracles must be the Promised Messiah, the True God; for He Alone by His Power could rule evil spirits in such a fashion!

The question, *"What new doctrine is this?",* doesn't refer to *"new"* in respect to time, but, instead, in comparison to the day as dust droning of the Rabbis and Scribes. Someone has said compared to that, *"The teaching of Jesus was like the fragrance of a field of clover in the spring time. It was fresh with the dew of Heaven upon it."*

The phrase, *"For with authority commandeth He even the unclean spirits, and they do obey him,"* reflects the Lord as having the hosts of Satan under His absolute power at all times. Irrespective of their wickedness and evil, He can command them at will, and they instantly obey Him.

Notice that the military word, *"commandeth,"* is used, once again speaking of an *"authority"* that is all-powerful, as well as all-knowing.

The words, *"They do obey Him,"* means they do so forthwith, and without argument. While it is true that these spirits may at certain times seek a particular disposition, such as the account of them requesting that they be allowed to go into the swine, still, there was no doubt as to their obedience (Mk. 5:10-13).

With this one exhibition of power, and

especially the manner in which it was used, all present had absolutely no doubt as to Who Jesus was, the Messiah of Israel!

(28) "AND IMMEDIATELY HIS FAME SPREAD ABROAD THROUGHOUT ALL THE REGION ROUND ABOUT GALILEE."

The phrase, *"And immediately His fame spread abroad,"* refers to word of mouth, but with great haste. In other words, everybody was talking about what Jesus had done and was doing!

In these conversations, no doubt, the question of His Messiahship was discussed constantly.

The phrase, *"Throughout all the region round about Galilee,"* mostly spoke, at least at this time, of Lower Galilee. This would have included the Western Shore of the Sea of Galilee, and to Nazareth and Cana in the East, down to Nain in the South.

This was the beginning of His Ministry, with His fame spreading to the entirety of Israel a short time later, which would infuriate the Religious Leaders of Israel.

(29) "AND FORTHWITH, WHEN THEY WERE COME OUT OF THE SYNAGOGUE, THEY ENTERED INTO THE HOUSE OF SIMON AND ANDREW, WITH JAMES AND JOHN."

The phrase, *"And forthwith, when they were come out of the Synagogue,"* means only after the Work of God had been accomplished. Whatever had been in the past, those in the Synagogue had seen a moving of the Spirit, and by none other than Christ such as they had never seen before. In other words, they had *"Church"* that day!

The phrase, *"They entered into the house of Simon and Andrew,"* refers to Peter who was married, and Andrew, his brother, and Peter's mother-in-law living with him. It seems that Jesus made His home with Peter when He was in Capernaum, and, as well, made Peter's house His Headquarters. What an honor for Peter to have been so blessed to have Jesus reside with him, as we soon shall see!

Actually, that honor can be had by any and all! All one has to do is simply invite Jesus in.

The phrase, *"With James and John,"* also intimates that these four were the only Disciples He had at the time, or else were the only ones involved in this particular incident concerning Peter's wife's mother.

(30) "BUT SIMON'S WIFE'S MOTHER

LAY SICK OF A FEVER, AND ANON THEY TELL HIM OF HER."

The phrase, *"But Simon's wife's mother lay sick of a fever,"* means that she had been sick for some time, was actually burning up with a fever, and had taken to her bed unable to rise.

The phrase, *"And anon they tell Him of her,"* means they immediately made Jesus aware of her serious condition. Luke speaks of Jesus standing over her like a doctor, exactly as He was, the Great Physician.

There is no mention of the wife of Peter by name in the New Testament. Along with this, Paul also intimates that Peter was a married man, and that his wife accompanied him on his missionary tours (I Cor. 9:5).

According to the testimony of Clement of Alexandria, and of Eusebius, she suffered martyrdom, and was led away to death in the sight of her husband, whose last words to her were, *"Remember thou the Lord."*

(31) "AND HE CAME AND TOOK HER BY THE HAND, AND LIFTED HER UP; AND IMMEDIATELY THE FEVER LEFT HER, AND SHE MINISTERED UNTO THEM."

The phrase, *"And He came and took her by the hand,"* meaning that He stood over her, and as Luke also said, *"And rebuked the fever"* (Lk. 4:39). The same word, *"rebuked,"* is here used, as is used in verse 25, when Jesus rebuked the unclean spirit.

Consequently, this *"fever"* could well have been, and no doubt was, caused by a demon spirit. However, this in no way means that Peter's mother-in-law was demon possessed as the man, for she was not!

Even though all sickness is not caused directly by demon spirits, still, all sickness has as its origin, demon spirits.

This means that many sicknesses can be treated successfully by proper medicines (Ezek. 47:12; Rev. 22:2), but some will not respond to such treatment, as here, and must be *"rebuked,"* as Jesus here did. He rebuked the spirit causing the *"fever."*

This spirit was no doubt trying to kill her with this *"fever,"* as evil spirits seek to kill many Believers, and at times may even succeed, especially considering that many Believers, even Preachers, do not properly understand the spirit world as they should.

A Preacher friend of mine, who has been

used greatly by the Lord respecting healing and such type deliverance, gave this testimony.

He was in a particular city years ago in a meeting when a lady was brought in for healing. She actually came to three different services.

Even though he laid hands on her and prayed for her each time, still, there were no visible results.

There was some discussion as to whether the meeting should continue another week, with the decision finally being made to continue on. The next Friday night, and despite not having received her healing the previous three times, the woman was brought again, even though bed-ridden. Her disease had been diagnosed as cancer and she was in the final stages. Too sick to walk, she was carried to the front on a cot.

Once again, for the fourth time in several weeks, he laid hands on her asking for healing. All of a sudden the scene seemed to change, with the Lord showing him exactly what was wrong.

In the vision, he saw a demon spirit which looked to be the size of a small dog, sitting somewhat on her shoulder, and clutching her flesh with his claws. Even though many were standing nearby, no one else saw this appearance but the Evangelist in question!

Instantly, in the Name of Jesus he began to demand this spirit to leave.

It argued with him for a moment, stating that it would not leave, as it was going to kill her.

Again, and in the Name of Jesus the command was given, with the spirit loosing its grip on the woman, and then vanishing. Immediately when this happened, the Power of God swept the building, with everyone sensing it, and especially the woman who had been so ill.

Previously unable to rise to her feet, she now jumped up, gathering strength by the moment, and shouted all over the Church. They did not take her home that night on her bed, but, instead, she walked out Praising God!

As I heard my friend relate this experience from his Ministry, he went on to give the time that the healing and deliverance took place, which had then been some fifteen years ago, with the woman still alive and in good health.

As to why the Lord did not show my friend the cause of this woman's sickness the previous three times he prayed, I have no answer, and neither did he! Perhaps the Lord wanted an exhibition of Faith from this woman, which she exhibited by her continuing to seek for healing, even though she had not succeeded the previous three times.

At any rate, simply praying for her to be healed seemed to be unsuccessful. Until the true cause of this disease was shown, which was a demon spirit, and properly rebuked in the Name of Jesus, this woman did not receive her healing. Immediately this was done, her healing was instant and complete.

Even as I dictate these words, I sense the Presence of God. I feel like we miss so much and, in fact, could see so much more accomplished for the Cause of Christ if we only followed much more after the Spirit of God, instead of our own human inclinations (Rom. 8:1).

The phrase, *"And lifted her up,"* is what Jesus does. He never knocks anyone down, at least in a spiritual sense.

The phrase, *"And immediately the fever left her,"* means that as quickly as the demon spirit left the man of verse 26, likewise, the evil spirit causing this *"fever"* left Peter's mother-in-law, and instantly!

(The above illustration given concerning cancer, does not mean that all cancer, as all fever, is caused by a demon spirit, but definitely does mean that in some cases they are.)

The phrase, *"And she ministered unto them,"* means most probably that she began to prepare a meal for them, which means, as well, that she was healed immediately. She did not improve by degrees, but, instead, was well instantly!

What a joy must have filled that dear lady, as well as the entirety of the house!

(32) "AND AT EVEN, WHEN THE SUN DID SET, THEY BROUGHT UNTO HIM ALL THAT WERE DISEASED, AND THEM THAT WERE POSSESSED WITH DEVILS."

The phrase, *"And at even, when the sun did set,"* has reference that it was Saturday and therefore the Sabbath, which ended on sunset. As we have previously stated, the Jewish reckoning of the twenty-four-hour day was somewhat different than ours presently.

The new day begins for us at 12 o'clock midnight, whereas the new day then began at sunset.

So, in their reckoning, their Sunday began at approximately 6 p.m. on what we refer to as Saturday evening.

The phrase, *"They brought unto Him all that were diseased,"* means that the people could

NOTES

now go about and bring the sick and diseased to Jesus, inasmuch as the Sabbath was now past. (The people were very limited as to what they could do on the Sabbath, due to the many rules made up by the Scribes and Pharisees, with which Jesus was constantly coming into conflict because of His healing on this day.)

The *"diseased"* consisted of any and all types of sicknesses, ailments, afflictions, and diseases.

The words, *"They brought,"* means that the people were carrying the sick in a steady stream to Jesus. Quite possibly they heard of Jesus healing Peter's mother-in-law, or even other healings He no doubt performed at this time.

As well, it is said that Tiberias, which was about ten miles south of Capernaum, contained hot mineral baths, which were claimed to have certain curative properties. Consequently, the sick came from all over Israel to this place. Therefore, quite a few of these people, no doubt, made their way to Jesus, with every need being met.

How much good the health spa did is anyone's guess; however, for those who came to Jesus, which no doubt were many, they were not merely *"helped,"* but totally healed.

The phrase, *"And them that were possessed with devils,"* was probably a result of the man who had been delivered hours earlier in the Synagogue.

All through the Gospels, attention is given repeatedly to the extremely high number of individuals who were demon possessed, and consequently delivered by Christ.

The Book of Acts, along with the Epistles, although recording such activity, does not do so with nearly the frequency as the Gospels. Why?

There are possibly several reasons for this:

1. Some have suggested that due to the Advent of Christ, that demon spirits congregated in Israel to oppose Him.

While this is possible, it is doubtful that they would have done such a thing, due to His Mighty Power, over which they would have had no defense.

2. Israel had opened herself up to a tremendous influx of demon spirits, due to her heavy religious activity, which was a departure from the Word of God.

Religion is man-made and man-devised, and, consequently, not of God. As such, it is fostered and nurtured by demon spirits. Consequently, wherever false religions are predominant, as Judaism had become, there is heavy activity of demon spirits. Such is the case in Central and South America with its heavy domination of Catholicism. The same could be said for Mexico, or anywhere in the world for that matter, where Catholicism is predominant.

The same can be said for the areas where Islam, Hinduism, Shintoism, or Buddhism dominate. These areas are rife with demon activity.

The same can be said for Africa, as well as Haiti and other such like countries, where demon spirits are worshiped openly.

In America and Canada, along with other countries where True Bible Christianity has at least some influence, the activity is less, although increasing because the Word of God is being preached less and less!

(33) "AND ALL THE CITY WAS GATHERED TOGETHER AT THE DOOR."

The word, *"all,"* doesn't mean literally everybody, but does refer to *"all"* who needed the touch of Christ.

Them being *"gathered together at the door,"* means that they came to the door of Peter's home, with the determination to remain there until Jesus healed and delivered them. It must have been quite a sight!

Please forgive my repetition, but even as I dictate these words I sense His Presence. One day soon, the entirety of the world is going to be at the door of Christ. This will be during the coming Kingdom Age, and, to be sure, as He did not fail them then, He will not fail them now. He Alone holds the answer to the ills of mankind, be they spiritual, economical, physical, or domestical.

I grieve as any True Believer does, realizing that most of mankind simply will not come to Him that they might have life. Just this morning, I overheard a speaker for the United Nations stating that if they were given more money they could solve the problems of the world.

How foolish!

All of humanity keeps attempting man-devised solutions, which, in reality, are no solutions at all, and upon implimentation automatically show their inherent uselessness. Regrettably, the modern Church holds up humanistic psychology as a solution for the behavior problems of man. This, as well, is no solution at all. It is tragic when most of the Church will

not recognize Jesus as the Answer to the problems of man. However, the so-called Church in Jesus' day did the same thing, rejecting Him, and holding up their religion as the answer for man's dilemma! Consequently, the more things change, the less they change!

(34) "AND HE HEALED MANY THAT WERE SICK OF DIVERS DISEASES, AND CAST OUT MANY DEVILS; AND SUFFERED NOT THE DEVILS TO SPEAK, BECAUSE THEY KNEW HIM."

The phrase, *"And He healed many that were sick of divers diseases,"* does not mean what it seems to mean on the surface respecting numbers. He actually healed all, which were *"many!"*

"Divers diseases" spoke of many and varied types of diseases, and of every kind.

In other words, it didn't matter what type of disease it was, or how serious, all were healed!

The phrase, *"And cast out many devils,"* is the same as above, casting out all, which were *"many!"*

Not one person who came sick, went away sick. Likewise, not one person who came demon possessed, went away in that condition. All were healed and delivered!

The phrase, *"And suffered not the devils to speak,"* means the demons clamored to be heard.

To be sure, as the evil spirit of verse 24 said positive things, no doubt these would have as well! However, the Lord, as is here obvious, had no interest in whatever they said, irrespective as to what it was.

The phrase, *"Because they knew Him,"* means they knew Him to be the Messiah. Nevertheless, to have them screaming such information, and irrespective of its Truth, was not something desired.

Truth in the mouth of a liar, at least in some form, becomes a lie!

(35) "AND IN THE MORNING, RISING UP A GREAT WHILE BEFORE DAY, HE WENT OUT, AND DEPARTED INTO A SOLITARY PLACE, AND THERE PRAYED."

The phrase, *"And in the morning, rising up a great while before day,"* concerns the last watch of the night, which was between 3 a.m. and 6 a.m. So, this was probably about 4 a.m. in the morning.

This was done after a very heavy evening of healing the sick and casting out devils, which could have well lasted to near midnight, or even after.

The phrase, *"He went out, and departed into a solitary place, and there prayed,"* portrays an example for all and in many ways.

1. The example of a strong prayer life, which was a habit with Him (Mat. 14:23; Mk. 1:35; 6:46; Lk. 6:12; 9:28; 11:1).

It is absolutely impossible for any Believer, and especially Preachers, to know the Mind of God, without having a strong prayer life. This is, to say the least, imperative!

Unfortunately, in the last few years the *"Confession Message"* has pretty much eliminated intercessory prayer. People have been led to believe they can confess their loved ones to Christ or consecration into being, etc.

However, we should stop to think that if Jesus or the Apostles did not employ such theology, then quite possibly it just might not be Scriptural, at least in this manner.

In fact, even though a proper confession is important, and should be astutely practiced, still, absolutely nothing can take the place of intercessory prayer. If Jesus practiced such, and, in fact, had to do so, as is here obvious, where does that leave those of us who are supposed to *"follow Him"*?

2. He set the example of looking entirely to His Heavenly Father, giving little thought to the accolades of the crowd. In no way did man make His decisions, or even influence them. He was led strictly by His Heavenly Father.

3. He set the example of finding the Will of God and following it, which, in this instance, pertained to His first preaching mission respecting an evangelistic tour, as the next verses proclaim.

(36) "AND SIMON AND THEY THAT WERE WITH HIM FOLLOWED AFTER HIM,"

At some point after Jesus had left Peter's house, having gone out that early morning hour to pray, He was missed.

Their *"following after Him,"* meant that they sought Him out. Exactly how they were able to find Him, is anyone's guess.

Maybe they had an idea where He had gone, possibly having overheard Him speak of this *"solitary place."* It was probably on the outskirts of this small town, perhaps even close to the Lake.

The group seeking Him would have been Peter, along with his brother Andrew, as well as James and John, and possibly even others.

(37) AND WHEN THEY HAD FOUND HIM, THEY SAID UNTO HIM, ALL MEN SEEK FOR THEE."

The phrase, *"And when they had found Him,"* infers that they had to look for a while.

The phrase, *"They said unto Him, All men seek for Thee,"* means that individuals were seeking for Him at that very moment. Even at that early morning hour close to daylight, the sick were at Peter's door to be healed.

Inasmuch as scores had been healed a few hours earlier, they had, no doubt, told many others about their joyful experience. This would have precipitated many who were sick in going, or being taken to the home of Peter even at daylight. It was not a question that maybe they would be healed or delivered, but of a certainty, at least if they could be in His Presence.

However, it seems that Jesus, as important as this was, knew that it was more important for Him to be Alone with the Father for a period of time in prayer. Consequently, He would leave Peter's home at a very early hour, for this all-important task.

The pronoun, *"Thee,"* is emphatic, meaning that those who sought Jesus would not be satisfied with seeing His Disciples. They must see Him Personally.

Even though the Disciples a little later would be given miracle-working power, still, at this time they did not have such power, with Jesus Alone being able to perform these miracles.

(38) "AND HE SAID UNTO THEM, LET US GO INTO THE NEXT TOWNS, THAT I MAY PREACH THERE ALSO: FOR THEREFORE CAME I FORTH."

The phrase, *"And He said unto them, Let us go into the next towns,"* infers that He had heard from Heaven, and had been given direction respecting what to do and where to go.

This is beautiful, and as we have stated, sets an example for all who follow Christ, to be minutely directed by the Lord, which can come about only by intercessory prayer.

According to Josephus, Galilee was a densely-populated district, with upwards of 200 villages and towns, each containing from several hundred to several thousand inhabitants.

The phrase, *"That I may preach there also,"* proclaims healing and deliverance as being very important, but secondary to the *"preaching"* of the Word.

The phrase, *"For therefore came I forth,"* has two meanings:

1. It refers to coming out of Capernaum and seeking the Face of His Father in respect to this mission.

2. More importantly, it refers to Him coming from Heaven, carrying out the Plan of God to redeem fallen humanity.

(39) "AND HE PREACHED IN THEIR SYNAGOGUES THROUGHOUT ALL GALILEE, AND CAST OUT DEVILS."

The phrase, *"And He preached in their Synagogues throughout all Galilee,"* does not mean that He preached in every Synagogue, but in a different Synagogue every Sabbath.

How so much these towns and villages must have buzzed with excitement, as Jesus began to heal the sick and cast out devils, as well as proclaiming the Gospel in a manner they have never heard it before.

The phrase, *"And cast out devils,"* does not mean that's all He did, but that along with *"preaching"* and *"healing,"* He continued to perform this work. Mark is letting us know that the *"casting out of devils"* was a constant part of the Ministry of Christ.

Once again, this signals the fact that Israel was in a terrible spiritual condition at this time, which, as well, affected them in every other way!

What joy must have filled the hearts of those delivered! The torment they had experienced was now gone! And all because of Jesus.

(40) "AND THERE CAME A LEPER TO HIM, BESEECHING HIM, AND KNEELING DOWN TO HIM, AND SAYING UNTO HIM, IF THOU WILT, THOU CANST MAKE ME CLEAN."

The phrase, *"And there came a leper to Him,"* proclaims an extremely important episode in the Ministry of Christ. As we have stated, this healing would deal with the particular man; however, even more importantly, it would serve as a symbol of Christ dealing with the even more horrible effect of sin, of which leprosy was a type.

This *"leper,"* as Luke describes him, was *"full of leprosy"* (Lk. 5:12), which meant it had spread over his entire body. He was leprous from head to foot.

This meant that he was in the last stages, and even near death. Quite possibly, and even likely, body parts, such as fingers, toes, or even his nose or lips, had been eaten away. This

happened often regarding lepers in the last stage of this disease.

It is said that most of these were filled with an odor that was unbearable!

As stated, this awful thing for which there was no human cure, was meant as a type of sin as proclaimed in the Old Testament. The revolting appearance of this disease was meant to serve as a symbol of what it represented, the terrible spiritual death of sin.

It was cured, as sin is cured, only by the Mercy and Favor of God. No wonder, then, that our Lord especially displayed His Power over this terrible malady, that He might thus prove His Power over the still worse malady of sin.

The phrase, *"Beseeching Him,"* means to plead. The Mosaic Law stated that he must remain about a hundred feet away from any and all contact with fellow human beings. If a leper approached any closer, he could be stoned! Therefore, his approaching Christ proclaimed his absolute desperation.

No doubt it had come to his ears concerning the miracle-working Power of Jesus. Consequently, he was determined to approach Christ, even if it meant his life. He felt he had nothing to lose!

There is no way that one could comprehend the pain and suffering this poor wretch had endured. He was dying and he knew it; however, his death would not be pleasant or easy. In fact, it would be one of the most horrible deaths that one could ever die. He was actually dying by degrees and by the hour.

This incident is so important that it is recorded by Matthew, Mark, and Luke.

The phrase, *"And kneeling down to Him,"* is proclaimed by Matthew as saying, *"He worshipped Him"* (Mat. 8:2).

Luke said, *"He fell on his face"* before Jesus (Lk. 5:12), which probably was after he had knelt, as recorded by Mark.

His prostration of himself before Christ was not merely a rendering of honor to an earthly being; it was a rendering of reverence to a Divine Being (Bickersteth).

The phrase, *"And saying unto Him,"* indicates that it was a statement he had carefully planned.

The phrase, *"If Thou wilt, Thou canst make me clean,"* refers to the fact that he <u>knew</u> Jesus was able to do this thing.

He had probably heard of others who had had

terrible diseases, but had been instantly healed by Christ. How this information came to his ears, considering he was a leper and not allowed to mix with people, is not known. At any rate, the indication is that he knew Who Jesus was, and what Jesus could do! So, he does not question His Power, only His Will!

This was done for the following reason:

His disease was so awful, and especially with him in the final stages, even near death! As well, and which he well knew, leprosy was looked at as a curse of God, and, as such, most of Israel did not believe a leper could be saved. Consequently, there was nothing more horrible than for a person to be told by a Priest, *"You have leprosy."* It meant his death warrant, and a horrible death at that, as well as being spiritually cursed.

To all men the leper was a living lesson portraying sin, of which death was the penalty. He carried about perpetual signs of mourning for the dead, himself being an example of living death.

He was a symbol of sin, teaching that he was not only lost and ruined because of what he had done, but on account of what he was. The sinner must not only confess that he is a sinner, but also admit that there is no Righteousness in him (Ps. 51:5; II Cor. 5:21; Eph. 2:1-8; I Jn. 1:9).

The following is what the leper had to do:

1. *"His clothes shall be rent"*: This meant that his garment or robe had to be split up the back to the hem at the neck, in order to portray him being undone before God. The torn garment signified his utter lack of Righteousness.

2. *"His head bare"*: This signified that the Judgment of God was upon him as a result of the Covenant being broken. The men of Israel were to wear a little cap, signifying that the Lord was their protection. He could wear nothing on his head, signifying he had no protection.

3. *"He shall put a covering upon his upper lip, and shall cry, Unclean, unclean"*: Anytime anyone came within approximately a hundred feet of him, he must shout these words.

Whenever anyone attributes his supposed Salvation to anything other than Christ, whether they realize it or not, they are, in effect, crying, *"Unclean, unclean!"*

4. *"He shall dwell alone"*: Even though he could be with other lepers, he could not be with anyone else. Such signified the terrible loneliness of sin, and of being cut off from God (Lev. 13:45-46).

NOTES

As the Law was for leprosy, likewise, the Law was for cleansing (Lev. 14). It is as follows:

1. *"He shall be brought unto the Priest"*: Being brought to the Priest showed that the problem was spiritual rather than physical, but had manifested itself in a physical way, as well as every other manner. Here the Priest is a type of Christ. Consequently, the leper (sinner) is to be brought to Jesus, as He is the only Hope.

2. *"And the Priest shall look"*: This spoke of minute inspection, which determined if the disease was gone.

Even though men constantly pronounce that the sinner is clean as a result of joining certain Churches or participating in certain religious ceremonies, still, such holds no validity with the Lord whatsoever. Only He can pronounce one as *"clean!"*

3. *"Two birds alive"*: This ceremony of old was meant to portray, when the act was completed, the dead and risen Christ.

4. *"And clean"*: This spoke of two pigeons or turtledoves, which were often mentioned as Sacrifices. They typified Jesus as being absolutely perfect in His Body and Life.

5. *"And cedar wood"*: This spoke of the Cross on which Jesus would die.

6. *"And scarlet"*: This spoke of the shedding of His Blood.

7. *"And hyssop"*: This was a type of branch which was used to dip into the blood. It referred to the vinegar which was offered to Christ while He was on the Cross, which was on a sop made from the leaves of hyssop.

8. *"One of the birds be killed"*: This typified the coming death of Christ.

9. *"In an earthen vessel"*: This spoke of Christ's human Body.

10. *"Over running water"*: This spoke of the Word of God which dictated the actions of Christ at Calvary, energized by the Holy Spirit.

11. *"The living bird"*: This symbolized the Resurrected Christ.

12. *"He shall take it (the living bird), and the cedar wood, and the scarlet, and the hyssop, and shall dip them and the living bird in the blood of the bird that was killed over the running water"*: This spoke of the Resurrected Christ Who had purchased our Redemption by His Death at Calvary.

13. *"And He shall sprinkle upon him that is to be cleansed from the leprosy seven times"*:

Seven is God's number, symbolizing perfection, and, consequently, the completeness and perfection of the remedy, and foreshadowing the removal of all sin, sickness, pain, and suffering through Jesus Christ (Isa. 53; Mat. 8:17; 11:1-6; 13:15; Jn. 10:10; Acts 10:38; I Pet. 2:24).

14. *"And shall pronounce him clean"*: This refers to God's Word proclaiming Salvation to the believing sinner.

15. *"And shall let the living bird loose into the open field"*: As this living bird represented the Resurrected Christ, likewise, it represents the believing sinner who has been cleansed, washed, and set free by the Power of God.

There were many other things that the cleansed leper was to do; however, that which we have given in brief proclaims the Law of cleansing. The Believer, however, would be blessed greatly by doing an entire study on Leviticus 14 in order to investigate the entirety of this ceremony, and, more importantly, what it represented and symbolized respecting one's Salvation in Christ.

So, even though the Law of Moses did not say that a leper could not be cleansed and thereby saved, still, the paucity of such cleansing spoke of its improbability. Actually, there is record of only three being cleansed from this terrible malady. One was Naaman, the Syrian General (II Ki. 5:10, 14); Miriam, the sister of Moses who became leprous as a result of criticizing her brother Moses, but was healed as a result of Moses' intercession (Num. 12:13-15); and Moses himself, who the Lord used as an example by causing his hand to become leprous, and then healing him (Ex. 4:6-7).

Considering this dismal record, one can well understand the absolute hopelessness, at least until Jesus came!

So, in light of all of this, the leper felt that his disease was so loathsome that maybe Jesus simply would not heal him, even though He had the power! Consequently, when he uttered these words, *"If Thou wilt,"* he was either uttering his death warrant or his resurrection!

One can well imagine his thoughts as he awaited the answer of Jesus. He would know in just a moment, and so would the whole world.

(41) "AND JESUS, MOVED WITH COMPASSION, PUT FORTH HIS HAND, AND TOUCHED HIM, AND SAITH UNTO HIM, I WILL; BE THOU CLEAN."

NOTES

The phrase, *"And Jesus, moved with compassion,"* is a portrayal of the Heart of God. Salvation in Christ is not a cold, calculating formula, neither is it a philosophic superiority. It is a warm, moving, touching, heart-feeling sympathy and compassion for the plight of humanity. Such is instigated by love, and, in fact, such can only be instigated by love.

The religions of the world have no concern or compassion for the hurts of people. Whatever they do is from a motivation of selfishness. In other words, if there is nothing in it for me, I have no concern or regard. Consequently, life is cheap in such a spiritual climate.

The idea of hospitals, nursing homes, orphan homes, a government which cares, has its roots in Christianity. Regarding a caring government, it may very well be true that political motivation is the guiding force; however, it was the rudiments of Christianity which charted the course in the first place.

Consequently, when the Church begins to leave the True Principles of Bible Christianity, rather instituting its own, compassion and love is the first casualty. Then the Church becomes hard, cold, unfeeling, and unmoved at the plight of others. It becomes more concerned about self-preservation and, consequently, its rules and regulations.

The compassion shown by Christ in this example was not directed toward a multi-millionaire who could swell the coffers of this evangelistic party, but, rather, a pitiful leper who at best could only say *"thank you"* for the great miracle he was about to receive.

There are basically three types of love in the world. They are as follows:

1. Agape: This is the God-kind of love shown here by Christ, which is imparted to all True Believers. It is a type of love that the world does not have, and, in fact, cannot have without making Christ the Lord of one's life. It is the type of love that is here evidenced toward the leper (I Jn. 4:7).

2. Phileo: This is the Greek word expressed in the Bible, as agape, which expresses another type of love. It could be better described as fondness or affection.

For example, when Jesus asked of Peter, *"Lovest thou Me more than these?"*, He was speaking of *"agape"* love. However, when Peter answered Him, saying, *"I love Thee,"* the word, *"love,"* used by the Apostle was *"phileo,"* which means, as stated, fondness or affection (Jn. 21:15).

(Peter is not to be chided for this, because his answer was not predicated on what he really felt toward the Lord, which was a deep, abiding agape love, but, rather, on his recent denial. He was now fearful of claiming too much as he had once done, and was greatly humbled.)

The *"phileo"* type of love is the highest form of love the world can have. Consequently, it can turn or change almost overnight, hence the great *"love affairs"* promoted by Hollywood and country/western songs suddenly turning sour.

3. Eros: This type of love so prominent in the world and even the Church, is not even once mentioned in the Bible. Consequently, from that omission we learn exactly what the Lord thinks of such.

Eros is a Greek word which actually means *"the sum of all instincts for self-preservation."* In other words, I love you, if you, in turn can help me in some way. It is the epitome of selfishness, hence self-preservation.

This type of love is understandable in the world, but should have no place in the Church. However, and sadly, the Church is full of it!

Consequently, scores of Churches either subtly or not so subtly, suggest or blatantly state that they desire only a certain type of clientele. In other words, they want people that make their Church look good. This would speak of people with money, education, talent, or some type of ability that is useful. Anyone who does not fit that mold in some way is made to feel somewhat less than welcome.

This is the type of love that uses up someone, and then when they have nothing left to give, are discarded. Sadly and tragically, this type of love permeates and fills society. As stated, it is, as well, all too prominent in the modern Church!

As is obvious, this was not the type of love evidenced by Christ toward the leper. Everything Jesus did, not only with this man, but with everyone, was done with no idea or thought of any type of financial, physical, material, or even spiritual return. It was done simply because He loved the person, and not because the person necessarily loved Him. In fact, most didn't!

The phrase, *"Put forth His Hand,"* as it is stretched out toward the leper, is symbolic of what Christ had to do to save lost humanity.

God was able to speak the worlds into existence; however, due to the fundamentals of sin and the subtle way that Satan had woven his web of destruction, God could not speak Salvation into existence. He had to come down here and die, actually taking upon Himself the penalty for the sin of man, in essence, *"putting forth His Hand!"*

The phrase, *"And touched him,"* was symbolic of what Jesus had to do in order to save lost souls. *"For He hath made Him to be sin for us, Who knew no sin; that we might be made the Righteousness of God in Him"* (II Cor. 5:21).

However, Jesus touching the leper, was not done, in effect to heal him, because he was actually already healed.

The Levitical Law forbade a Jew to touch a leper. Our Lord lived under the Law and obeyed it, because He, in effect, was the One Who gave it originally. So, what actually happened here?

The first kind touch of a human hand this leper ever experienced was the gentle touch of the Son of God.

The phrase, *"And saith unto him, I will; be thou clean,"* tells us exactly what happened!

The rule of Greek grammar, we are told, that governs this sentence construction is that the action of the proclamation, *"I will,"* is going on at the same time, or immediately preceding the action of the touch. That is, Jesus was saying, *"I will,"* at the time He was touching the leper. However, the thought in His Mind, *"I will,"* actually preceded the act of touching him. In other words, when Jesus touched the leper, he had consequently already been healed.

All of which means that our Lord did not touch the leper in order to cleanse him, but to show him and the people around that he was already cleansed of his leprosy.

So, as this symbol bears out, when the Lord touches the forgiven sinner, which speaks of fellowship, it is not in order to save him, for that has already been accomplished by God's favorable response to Faith.

When the believing sinner cries to the Lord, as the leper, love is already big in the Heart of God for the sinner, and the answer is an immediate *"I will,"* which is followed by the touch. Jesus does not touch the sin, but the forgiven sinner.

When He died on Calvary for humanity, He in no way sinned, or even touched our sin. What He actually did was according to the following:

First of all, He provided the Perfect Sacrifice in the giving of His perfect human Body, which had never been tainted by the terrible ruin of sin. Consequently, it was a Sacrifice that God could and would accept.

When Paul wrote, *"He hath made Him to be sin for us,"* he actually said, *"He hath made Him to be a Sin-Offering for us,"* for this is what the Hebrew word *"sin"* means (II Cor. 5:21), at least in this instance. So, Jesus became the Sin-Offering, thereby suffering the penalty and judgment for sin in our place.

He did not become adultery, theft, lying, stealing, rape, murder, hate, etc., in order words, *"sin,"* but, instead, a *"Sin-Offering,"* which means He paid the penalty, thereby suffering the judgment.

So, this beautiful example of Christ cleansing the leper, typifies in brief that which He does for the believing sinner.

No doubt, the Priests would have gladly censored Christ for touching this leper, if there had been any evidence. However, he was no longer a leper, which was obvious to all, and, therefore, no evidence with which to charge Christ.

As well, Satan would charge Christ with touching unclean sinners, if there were any evidence. However, the evidence, i.e., sin, is gone, with the person in Christ becoming *"a new creature: old things are passed away; behold, all things are become new"* (II Cor. 5:17).

In John 1:12, Justification precedes Regeneration in the Divine economy. Mercy is only given on the basis of justice satisfied. So, as the sinner recognizes the Lord Jesus as the One, Who, through His out-poured Blood on the Cross, procured for sinful man a legal right to the Mercy of God, he becomes the recipient of Regeneration and of all the other blessings of Salvation.

The words, *"Be thou clean,"* means that the leper was cleansed at once. It was an immediate cure. Likewise, all who come to Christ are instantly saved upon Faith.

(42) "AND AS SOON AS HE HAD SPOKEN, IMMEDIATELY THE LEPROSY DEPARTED FROM HIM, AND HE WAS CLEANSED."

The phrase, *"And as soon as He had spoken,"* proclaims, and as we have stated, that it was not the touch that cleansed him, but, rather, the Will of God evidenced in the spoken word. Hallelujah! If God says it, I believe it!

NOTES

The phrase, *"Immediately the leprosy departed from him,"* must have been a sight to behold!

Leprosy leaves terrible marks on the human body. As stated, fingers and toes, plus other body members, at times, literally are eaten away and fall off. So, the meaning is that immediately every sore was healed on this man's body. As well, and as miraculous as it is, if, in fact, body members had been eaten away, they were instantly replaced. It was a miracle of transformation which took place immediately in front of the eyes of all who were standing there.

As well, as quickly as this leprosy departed at the Word of Christ, likewise, sin departs upon Faith in the Glorious Name of Jesus.

The phrase, *"And he was cleansed,"* means that he would never again have to cry, *"Unclean, unclean!"* The evidence was so obvious that no one could deny what had happened to him.

Now he could say, *"Clean, clean!"*

As well, the new person in Christ Jesus can say:

"Saved by His Pow'r Divine,
"Saved to new life sub-lime!
"Life now is sweet and my joy is complete,
"For I'm Saved, Saved, Saved!"

(43) "AND HE STRAIGHTLY CHARGED HIM, AND FORTHWITH SENT HIM AWAY;"

The phrase, *"And He straightly charged him,"* refers to what was said in verse 44.

The word, *"straightly,"* means to forcibly charge. In other words, Christ was stern in His admonition. The reason was this:

One can well imagine the joy that filled the leper's heart upon his instant cleansing. As a result, he was desiring to show everyone exactly what had happened to him. Consequently, the idea of going to the Priests as the Law demanded, was the furthest thing from his mind, as would be obvious!

By not obeying this injunction, consequently going out among the people, the Religious Leaders would have occasion to accuse Christ of disobeying the Law of Moses, or they may have even denied that the man had been a leper.

At any rate, Jesus, knowing the man's intense joy and desire to proclaim his great miracle to others, sternly charges him to first go to the Priest, as the Law demanded (Lev. 14:2).

The phrase, *"And forthwith sent him away,"* refers to sending him away for this purpose, and this purpose alone!

(44) "AND SAITH UNTO HIM, SEE THOU SAY NOTHING TO ANY MAN: BUT GO THY WAY, SHEW THYSELF TO THE PRIEST, AND OFFER FOR THY CLEANSING THOSE THINGS WHICH MOSES COMMANDED, FOR A TESTIMONY UNTO THEM."

The phrase, *"And saith unto him, See thou say nothing to any man,"* portrayed the utter excitement of this man who desired to tell any and all as to what Christ had done for him.

This, within itself, was not wrong, except that Christ said not to do it, and for a reason. Regrettably, as the next verse shows, the man was not obedient, and even after receiving one of the greatest miracles ever!

The phrase, *"But go thy way, shew thyself to the Priest,"* was meant to fulfill Leviticus 14:1-32, respecting the Law of the cleansed leper, and as we have alluded to.

The phrase, *"And offer for thy cleansing those things which Moses commanded,"* pertained to all the things listed regarding Leviticus 14.

The Law of the cleansing of the leper was complicated indeed! All the ceremony as outlined, was meant to portray the Sacrifice of Christ in His expiatory work. However, there is little if any record that it was ever done, because no lepers were cleansed other than Naaman, who was a Gentile, and would not have been subject to the Law of Moses.

As well, Moses and Miriam were healed of their leprosy before the Law was given.

So, if this man had obeyed Christ, which he did not, and the Priests would have faithfully followed the Law, this would have been the first time for such action, at least that is recorded. As such, it would have beautifully fulfilled the type.

The phrase, *"For a testimony unto them,"* refers to the testimony of the Priests to the people, to the effect that the leper was officially pronounced clean.

(45) "BUT HE WENT OUT, AND BEGAN TO PUBLISH IT MUCH, AND TO BLAZE ABROAD THE MATTER, INSOMUCH THAT JESUS COULD NO MORE OPENLY ENTER INTO THE CITY, BUT WAS WITHOUT IN DESERT PLACES: AND THEY CAME TO HIM FROM EVERY QUARTER."

NOTES

The phrase, *"But he went out, and began to publish it much, and to blaze abroad the matter,"* spoke of him disobeying the Lord.

It is hard to understand how that he could be so sternly charged by Christ, and then not obey, especially considering what Jesus had done for him! However, his example, I'm afraid, is too often our example.

How often does He do great things for us, of which makes us so gloriously joyful, and yet we turn around and disobey Him! Such is Christ and such is man!

The phrase, *"Insomuch that Jesus could no more openly enter into the city,"* means that He could not minister anymore in Capernaum, at least at this time.

The entirety of the city, upon seeing the healings which Christ had previously performed, was no doubt greatly overjoyed. However, upon hearing the testimony of the leper, and, no doubt, knowing him, and realizing this was the first leper cleansed since Naaman, the Syrian, their joy knew no bounds. Everyone was wanting to see Jesus, and irrespective of the need! So, if He attempted to enter the city, He would be mobbed!

The word, *"openly,"* means that He did go into Capernaum at times, probably very late at night, or disguised in some way.

The phrase, *"But was without in desert places,"* not only meant that Jesus could not openly enter Capernaum, but, could not openly enter any city. If so, He had to be as discreet as possible! Even then He would be mobbed! Consequently, at least at this time, much of His Ministry was carried out in the countryside.

The phrase, *"And they came to Him from every quarter,"* means they kept coming to Him for healing and deliverance, and irrespective as to where He was!

The first Chapter of Mark is thought to encompass the first twelve months, approximately so, of the Ministry of Jesus. At this time, the animosity and hatred of the Pharisees and Scribes, had not yet risen to the fore, which actually this adulation helped arouse.

Due to this hatred and opposition by the Religious Leaders of Israel, and their threat to excommunicate anyone who showed love for Christ or followed Him, the coming last year of His public Ministry showed the crowds thinning out considerably (Jn. 9:22).

CHAPTER 2

(1) "AND AGAIN HE ENTERED INTO CAPERNAUM AFTER SOME DAYS; AND IT WAS NOISED THAT HE WAS IN THE HOUSE."

The phrase, *"And again He entered into Capernaum after some days,"* probably referred to several weeks, or maybe even months. He had been on a preaching tour to other parts of Galilee, which would have taken some time.

At any rate, He probably slipped into the city during the night, or was spirited into Peter's home by the back streets, etc.

The phrase, *"And it was noised that He was in the house,"* referred to Peter's house where He had made His Headquarters.

Somehow the news got out that Jesus was there. And I don't wonder!

He Alone was and is the Answer to every problem that faces mankind. Consequently, they would mob the house, because only He could heal, could deliver, could save!

Even as I dictate these words, I greatly sense the Presence of God. And yet, too oftentimes men desire Him, not because of Who He is, but, instead, for what He can do.

(2) "AND STRAIGHTWAY MANY WERE GATHERED TOGETHER, INSOMUCH THAT THERE WAS NO ROOM TO RECEIVE THEM, NO, NOT SO MUCH AS ABOUT THE DOOR: AND HE PREACHED THE WORD UNTO THEM."

The phrase, *"And straightway many were gathered together,"* concerned those who were sick, demon possessed, or were there as onlookers.

The phrase, *"Insomuch that there was no room to receive them, no, not so much as about the door,"* means that the house was filled, along with the courtyard, and even all around the outside of the house.

I have been to the ruins of Capernaum, as have many, and have observed where it is said that Peter's house sat. Actually, it is only a few yards from the Sea of Galilee. Consequently, and irrespective as to what type of house it was, its location, I imagine, would have been beautiful.

On this day, people were no doubt all around the house, even on the shore of the

Lake, attempting to catch a glimpse of Jesus. I hope the reader can understand the majesty of this moment. The terrible opposition of the Scribes and Pharisees had not yet begun, and, consequently, the people did not fear their wrath, and felt free to seek the help of Christ. Some were hungry; some were hurting; some were curious; however, all were in need of what He had to give.

The phrase, *"And He preached the Word unto them,"* proclaims to all that this was the object of His Ministry. The exercise of miraculous power was subordinated to this; the miracles being simply designed to meet the need of the person in question, and to fix the attention upon the Teacher as One sent from God.

The manner in which the word, *"preached,"* is used, is not the normal word for preaching. This word, *"preached,"* means to speak to the people, in this instance, and because He was in a house, in a conversational tone, but yet loud enough for all to hear.

The emphasis concerns not only what He said, but, as well, His Person. His kindness exhibited in the beauty of His Voice, and especially considering what He said, must have been like rain on dry ground. It must have been like a fragrance that came from a newly-opened flower.

As well, and what made His Message so powerful, was because He preached *"the Word."* This consisted of Genesis through Malachi at that time. To be sure, the people had heard it expounded many times before, but never in this fashion.

So, the meaning is that He *"preached the Word,"* but His Person made the Word come alive.

Even though my statement will be rejected by some, still, this very Passage bears out that the mere preaching of the Letter is not enough, as truthful as it may be, but that it must be, as well, Anointed by the Holy Spirit for it to accomplish its intended purpose. Paul said, *"For our Gospel came not unto you in word only, but also in power, and in the Holy Ghost"* (I Thess. 1:5).

(3) "AND THEY COME UNTO HIM, BRINGING ONE SICK OF THE PALSY, WHICH WAS BORNE OF FOUR."

The phrase, *"And they come unto Him,"* is said by Mark in such a way that it places the reader in the very presence of the desperate ones.

They were coming to *"Him,"* not someone else, for only Jesus would do. Tragically, most of the world, at least as it relates to Christianity, comes to Churches, Religious Denominations, men, or even particular Doctrines. Few actually come to Christ; but those who do, receive the help this man received so long ago.

The phrase, *"Bringing one sick of the palsy,"* actually refers to paralysis, and not *"palsy"* as we presently know it. Being paralyzed, the man could not walk, and was consequently placed on some type of cot, being borne on the shoulders of four men.

The phrase, *"Which was borne of four,"* means that these men were not just doing a duty as servants, but, instead, that they were expressly bringing him to Jesus. As well, and as the following verses show, their Faith was joined with that of the sick man, which helped bring about his healing.

This is a perfect example of Believers showing care and concern in bringing one to Christ.

The paralyzed man represents the unsaved who on their own cannot come to Christ. They must have help, which is described by these *"four."*

These *"four"* represent not only those who personally bring someone to Christ, but, as well, those who earnestly seek the Lord for the Salvation of others, or even revival in particular places. It, as well, refers to those who give of their financial resources in order that others may have opportunity to hear the Gospel and be saved. All of us were once in the place of the *"paralytic,"* and all of us now, after we have come to Christ, should be in the place of the *"four!"*

These *"four"* did not beg off, claiming they did not have the time. Neither did they complain about the difficulty of their task. They were determined to get to Jesus, and irrespective of the cost, and this they would do. They would not be disappointed!

(4) "AND WHEN THEY COULD NOT COME NIGH UNTO HIM FOR THE PRESS, THEY UNCOVERED THE ROOF WHERE HE WAS: AND WHEN THEY HAD BROKEN IT UP, THEY LET DOWN THE BED WHEREIN THE SICK OF THE PALSY LAY."

The phrase, *"And when they could not come nigh unto Him for the press,"* concerns them coming to the front of the house, but with the crowd surrounding the place, there was no way they could gain entrance.

Faith in Christ has never presented an easy path, but Faith in Christ, being Faith, always finds a way.

For those who have no Faith, the *"press"* will always serve as a sufficient obstacle. As the *"press"* hindered then, the *"press,"* i.e., media, seeks to hinder now!

The phrase, *"They uncovered the roof where He was,"* concerned drastic measures, to say the least!

The *"roof"* on houses in those days, as in many parts of that country presently, were flat. Steps on the outside led to the roof, which was no doubt used by these *"four."*

On the roof was a trap door which led down into the house, where people could come and go, for many used the roof for many and varied things. Some even slept there during the Summer, obtaining the benefit of night breezes.

The phrase, *"And when they had broken it up,"* probably refers to them enlarging the opening where the trap door was located, it being too small to accommodate the prostrate man on the cot.

I wonder what the thoughts of Peter were, at seeing his roof being torn up in this manner? At the same time, and considering the miracle performed on this man, I am certain that the matter was favorably resolved.

The phrase, *"They let down the bed wherein the sick of the palsy lay,"* means they sufficiently made an opening large enough for the entrance of the man on the cot. There is every evidence that he was paralyzed, and unable to help in any way, or even move. Therefore, he would have been dead weight.

Either they had ropes, or else the people in the room, upon seeing what was being done, may have joined in to help from inside the room, as the man was being lowered down by the *"four."*

At any rate, it must have been quite a sight, and, no doubt, it interrupted the Message Christ was preaching. However, it must always be remembered, that the Message is for people, and not people for the Message! So, the interruption representing the need, in effect, would be no interruption at all, because this is what Jesus came for.

(5) "WHEN JESUS SAW THEIR FAITH, HE SAID UNTO THE SICK OF THE PALSY, SON, THY SINS BE FORGIVEN THEE."

The phrase, *"When Jesus saw their Faith,"* presents a startling revelation concerning this great subject. Several things are here said:

1. Faith can be seen: This means the action of Faith, which is never passive. This is what James was speaking of when He said, *"What doth it profit, my brethren, though a man say he hath Faith, and have not works?"*

He then said, *"Even so Faith, if it hath not works, is dead, being alone"* (James 2:14, 17).

He is saying that Faith will always show itself in works, as here by the *"four."*

2. Faith in God never says anything is impossible, because with God all things are possible. Consequently, these men did not allow the hindrances to stop them.

3. The very ingredient of Faith demands, and irrespective of the obstacles, that it be pushed through to its intended purpose and successful conclusion. In other words, it will not stop until the goal is reached.

4. The very ingredient of Faith demands that it be tested. Consequently, great Faith is tested greatly! However, the test is not meant to stop Faith, because True Faith cannot be stopped, but only to guarantee that it is Faith.

So Jesus *"saw their Faith,"* and inasmuch as it is here recorded, it means that it gladdened His Heart.

How much the Lord must constantly observe His Children, and in respect to this very subject. Are we evidencing Faith or doubt?

Are we taking the paralytic back home, mumbling that the situation is impossible, or busy tearing up the roof in order to get to Jesus? It is easy to imagine which one will be rewarded!

The phrase, *"He said unto the sick of the palsy, Son, thy sins be forgiven thee,"* tells us several things:

1. The wretched physical condition of the sick man was due to his sinful life, and, therefore, Jesus first of all, addressed the real cause.

2. He uses the word, *"Son,"* intimating kindness, and irrespective of his wretched spiritual and physical condition. There is not even a hint of condemnation. What a lesson we should learn from this encounter.

3. The Greek word for *"forgiveness,"* is *"aphiema,"* and means *"to send away,"* or *"to remit, forgive."* It is altogether different than the word, *"forgive,"* used by men in relationship to each other.

NOTES

When we forgive someone who has wronged us, it means we no longer hold any animosity against them, and the situation has changed to one of renewed friendliness and affection, providing, that is, the other party acts accordingly!

However, even though such an act of *"forgiveness"* does not hold the wrong against the person anymore, still, as far as the act itself is concerned, it is still there, and there is nothing anyone can do about it.

However, the word used by Christ has a double meaning.

A. The sin is put away on a judicial basis by the poured-out Blood of Christ. He paid the penalty the broken Law required, and thus satisfied Divine Justice.

B. The Lord not only forgives the sin, but removes the guilt of that sin in such a way that the believing sinner is looked at by God as if the sin was never committed. It is called *"Justification by Faith,"* and is what is meant by Bible forgiveness in the case of God and a believing sinner.

This can be legally done because Jesus Christ not only paid the price for our forgiveness of sin by the shedding of His Blood, but, as well, took upon Himself the Judgment of God, which we should have taken, by giving His Life. Consequently, not only are we forgiven, but we are justified as well, meaning that the act is not only forgiven, but its very existence is removed from the Books.

That's the reason *"There is therefore now no condemnation to them which are in Christ Jesus, who walk not after the flesh, but after the Spirit"* (Rom. 8:1).

Hallelujah! When Jesus said, *"Son, thy sins be forgiven thee,"* He also said it to multiple millions of others.

(6) "BUT THERE WERE CERTAIN OF THE SCRIBES SITTING THERE, AND REASONING IN THEIR HEARTS,"

The phrase, *"But there were certain of the Scribes sitting there,"* pertains to individuals who were opposed to Christ, and had come early, or else had pushed their way to the front so they could stand near Him, but with the purpose in mind of finding fault. These were some of the Religious Leaders of Israel!

The phrase, *"And reasoning in their hearts,"* represents a hostile spirit on their part, which could be felt by Christ.

It did not stop anything He did, but it did sully the atmosphere.

Bringing the subject to modern times, how many services have been greatly hindered because of the same type of hostile attitude and spirit!

There was no record in the Ministry of Christ of any such attitude or spirit on the part of the common people. All the opposition came from the Religious Leaders of Israel. Sadly, it is no different today!

What were they reasoning?

They were jealous of His popularity, and even more so of His Power with God. As a result of their evil hearts, they did not for a moment believe that He was the Messiah, and, as such, qualified to forgive sins. So we are looking here at a denial of His Messianic claims.

(7) "WHY DOTH THIS MAN THUS SPEAK BLASPHEMIES? WHO CAN FORGIVE SINS BUT GOD ONLY?

The question, *"Why doth this man thus speak blasphemies?"*, would have been correct had Christ been only a man. In that case, their logic would have been correct. However, inasmuch as He was God manifest in the flesh, they were totally incorrect. Consequently, they now come face to face with the Deity of Christ, and reject it.

Not only was their unbelief registered in their question, but, as well, it was registered in the way the question was framed.

The word, *"man,"* was inserted by the translators, but was not in the original Text. Consequently, they referred to Jesus as merely *"This,"* thereby, showing their contempt!

The question, *"Who can forgive sins but God only?"*, proclaims a Truth, but yet, Jesus was God!

Even though this question was posed in unbelief by the Scribes, still, the question is valid and demands only one answer, *"God!"* Consequently, the Catholic Confessional, where the Priests forgive sins, is not only unscriptural, but, and as the Scribes said, *"blasphemous."*

(8) "AND IMMEDIATELY WHEN JESUS PERCEIVED IN HIS SPIRIT THAT THEY SO REASONED WITHIN THEMSELVES, HE SAID UNTO THEM, WHY REASON YE THESE THINGS IN YOUR HEARTS?"

The phrase, *"And immediately when Jesus perceived in His spirit that they so reasoned within themselves,"* means that He knew fully

NOTES

what they were thinking. It was not guess-work on His part.

The manner in which this was done, was through the agency of the Holy Spirit Who spoke to His spirit, revealing this knowledge unto Him. This was not by any Divine attributes on His part. Even though He was God and never ceased to be God, and, as such, could forgive sins as here illustrated, still, every miracle He performed was by the Power of the Holy Spirit and not His Own. The same could be said for all Revelation Knowledge as well!

It was the same as, and, in fact was, the twin gifts in operation of: A. *"The Word of knowledge"*; and, B. *"Discerning of spirits"* (I Cor. 12:8-10).

The question, *"He said unto them, Why reason ye these things in your hearts?"*, must have been somewhat startling to them.

What were their thoughts when He posed this question to them? Did not this within itself lend even more credence to His Deity?

Faith *"sees"* when there is nothing visible to see, but unbelief will not *"see"* even though the proof, as here, is obvious!

(9) "WHETHER IS IT EASIER TO SAY TO THE SICK OF THE PALSY, THY SINS BE FORGIVEN THEE; OR TO SAY, ARISE, AND TAKE UP THY BED, AND WALK?"

The question that Christ here poses will answer the *"reasonings"* of unbelief in their hearts. His proof will be irrefutable. However, proof is not what they were looking for.

(The following is derived from an exposition of Spence and Trench, and proclaims, in essence, what Jesus may have said.)

"You accuse Me of blasphemy. You say that I am usurping the attributes of God when I claim the power of forgiving sin. You ask for the evidence that I really possess this power; and you say it is an easy thing to lay claim to a power which penetrates the spiritual world, and which is therefore beyond the reach of material proof. Be it so.

"I will now furnish that evidence. I will prove, by what I am now about to work upon the body of this man, that what I have just said is effectual upon the spirit. I have just said to this paralytic 'Thy sins are forgiven.' You challenge this power; you question My authority. I will now give you outward and sensible evidence that this is no fictitious or imaginary claim.

"You see this poor helpless, palsied man. I will say to him in the presence of you all, 'Arise, take up thy bed, and go unto thy house.' And if simply at My bidding his nerves are braced, and his limbs gather strength, and he rises and walks, which you know within himself, he is unable to do, then judge ye whether I have a right to say to him, 'Thy sins are forgiven.'

"Thus, by doing that which is capable of proof, I will vindicate My power to do that which is beyond the reach of sensible evidence; and I will make manifest to you, by these visible tides of My Grace, in what direction the deep undercurrent of My Love is moving."

(10) "BUT THAT YE MAY KNOW THAT THE SON OF MAN HATH POWER ON EARTH TO FORGIVE SINS, (HE SAITH TO THE SICK OF THE PALSY,)"

The phrase, *"But that ye may know that the Son of Man hath power on earth to forgive sins,"* proclaims the irrefutable proof, which will be evidenced by his healing. However, even though they would *"know"* by the actions of Christ, still, they would not admit it. For to have done so, would have been admitting that He is the Messiah, the Eternal One, the Lord of Glory, the Son of God.

Their pride and religious jealousy would not allow them to do that, so in the face of irrefutable proof, they will continue in unbelief.

Actually, the entirety of the world travels the same course. The proof that there is a God, and, furthermore, Who He is, and that He sent His Son Jesus Christ to die for lost humanity, and that He rose from the dead, is irrefutable, as well! And yet, most, by far, will not believe.

Why?

Men love their sins, and in their sins is deception. In this deception, right seems to be wrong, and wrong seems to be right! (Mat. 13:13-15).

The phrase, *"He saith to the sick of the palsy,"* proclaims Him doing this in full view of everyone, even the skeptics, and especially the skeptics!

(11) "I SAY UNTO THEE, ARISE, AND TAKE UP THY BED, AND GO THY WAY INTO THINE HOUSE."

The phrase, *"I say unto thee, Arise,"* is an order not only to the man, but to the spirit world as well!

It must be kept in mind that the same One

Who said this, also said, *"Let there be light, and there was light"* (Gen. 1:3).

Upon His Word, a burned-out planet which we call the *"sun"* suddenly ignited, and began to flame.

Likewise, at the moment of His Word, strength began to flood this man's physical body, and instantly he does something that he had not heretofore been able to do. He instantly arises, and in perfect health!

The phrase, *"And take up thy bed,"* was the proof of his immediate healing. Now that which had been his support, becomes supported by him.

The phrase, *"And go thy way into thine house,"* means that he can now go back under his own power, and any way he chooses, and not be dependent on the *"four"* who brought him.

Such not only proclaims healing, but, as well, epitomizes the Salvation experience.

All unsaved are spiritual cripples, consequently, being unable to walk, at least in a spiritual sense. However, at the Word of Jesus, this situation is instantly changed, with spiritual strength given and the individual now able to spiritually walk upright.

The *"bed"* spiritually symbolizes dependence on things of the world. The taking up of the *"bed"* symbolizes that dependence broken, with whatever it was becoming the servant instead of the master.

Before, the bed mastered him, now he masters the bed!

(12) "AND IMMEDIATELY HE AROSE, TOOK UP THE BED, AND WENT FORTH BEFORE THEM ALL; INSOMUCH THAT THEY WERE ALL AMAZED, AND GLORIFIED GOD, SAYING, WE NEVER SAW IT ON THIS FASHION."

The phrase, *"And immediately he arose,"* portrays no hesitancy whatsoever in his actions. He can do so because he is healed!

The phrase, *"Took up the bed,"* portrays him bending down and picking up this which had once carried him, but him now carrying it.

The phrase, *"Insomuch that they were all amazed,"* refers to the fact that they evidently all knew him, and that he had not been able to walk, which had been obvious to all! Consequently, there was no doubt or argument concerning the miracle which had been performed upon his physical body.

The phrase, *"And glorified God,"* means they

glorified the Lord for the healing and not for the sickness.

The Lord may get glory out of lives despite sickness, but not because of it.

Sickness should never be used as an excuse in glorifying God. This one healing should serve an excellent lesson refuting that particular fallacy.

If sickness is of Satan, and, consequently, a direct result of the Fall, which it is, as is clear in Matthew 8:17; Luke 13:16; John 10:10; Acts 10:38; etc., then it is not of God.

If such be of God, then He sent Jesus to destroy His Own Works, which is absurd!

If sickness is of Satan, which it is, then healing must be of God, if done in the Name of Jesus Christ. As in this case and all others, if God became glorified by healing, which the Word of God here declares, then He is not glorified by the sickness.

As long as the man was sick, God did not get glory. Satan's work continued to be manifest, with him (Satan) continuing to be glorified up to the point of healing.

When Believers begin to recognize Satan as the true cause of their problems, and then turn to God, thereby discontinuing their unbelief and cooperation with Satan, they will then begin to receive the great benefits promised in the Word of God (Dake).

There is no record in the four Gospels, which records the Life and Ministry of Christ, that Jesus ever refused to heal anyone, claiming it was the Will of God for them to be sick. If such were the case, even remotely so, surely, considering the thousands He healed, one or two such examples would have surely shown up. Nothing of this nature surfaced, because it is absurd to think that it is the Will of God for Believers to be sick.

No! Jesus healed all who came to Him, and irrespective as to whom they were, or their physical problem.

Some would argue that if it's the Will of God for Believers to never be sick, then they would never be sick. However, all would have to agree that it is always the Will of God for Believers to be overcomers. But, as we all know, all Believers are not overcomers, and, in Truth, no Believer has ever been an overcomer all the time.

It is the Will of God that no Believer ever fail, but, tragically, we all have failed at one time or the other.

NOTES

Unbelief has many arguments, but only Faith in Christ has positive results.

The phrase, *"Saying, We never saw it on this fashion,"* referred to several things:

1. They had never seen anyone whose sins had been instantly forgiven, along with his physical body being instantly healed.

2. As only Jesus could do this, truly they had never seen it *"on this fashion."*

3. They had never in their lives seen a healing so total and quick, especially considering the former helplessness of the man.

4. They had never seen such power demonstrated.

5. They had never seen such proof given in the answering of an argument, and so irrefutably!

They were seeing the Lord in action doing what only He could do. This is the difference in man and Christ.

Man can only register unbelief, as these Scribes, or marvel. He cannot carry forth the work, and it is foolish to think he can do so.

Consequently, modern psychologists could have counseled this man until the sun rose in the West, and no forgiveness of sins or healing of the body would have taken place. Only Jesus could do such a thing.

Therefore, one grieves when one looks at the modern Church, knowing that she has traded the Miracle-Working Power of God for the prattle of poor helpless man!

What a sorry trade!

We are not informed of the effect of this miracle upon the Scribes and Pharisees, but it is all too evident that, though they could not deny the fact, they would not acknowledge the power.

The multitude gave Praise and Glory to God, as they should have, while unbelief was working its deadly result of envy and malice among those who ought to have been their guides and instructors.

(13) "AND HE WENT FORTH AGAIN BY THE SEA SIDE; AND ALL THE MULTITUDE RESORTED UNTO HIM, AND HE TAUGHT THEM."

The phrase, *"And He went forth again by the sea side,"* has reference to the fact that Christ did not walk this way of necessity, but by choice. It suggests the idea that He loved to walk along the shore in order to be alone with His Heavenly Father, as well as to enjoy the beauty of His creation.

This area, which the Holy Spirit chose from eternity to be the site of the Ministry and Miracles of Christ, is beautiful to say the least! However, even though the topography has not changed from that day until now, still, its appearance probably has changed. Then it would have had a quite heavy growth of trees on the hills, which are now, at least for the most part, denuded, except those planted by modern Israel.

Then Lower Galilee was very thickly populated, with hundreds of fishing boats plying the waters of the Lake.

As a result, there probably wasn't much solitude along the Western Shore of the Sea of Galilee, but yet which Christ would have enjoyed immensely irrespective of the activity.

Not attempting to read more into the Passage than one should, still, I think the implication is that Jesus attempted to resort to this activity often, but as we soon shall see, without much success.

The phrase, *"And all the multitude resorted unto Him,"* proclaims Him being eagerly sought out, and no wonder!

The phrase, *"And He taught them,"* means that as the crowd kept on coming to Him, which they did, He kept on teaching them.

What a wonder and joy it must have been to have sat at the Feet of Jesus.

(14) "AND AS HE PASSED BY, HE SAW LEVI THE SON OF ALPHAEUS SITTING AT THE RECEIPT OF CUSTOM, AND SAID UNTO HIM, FOLLOW ME. AND HE AROSE AND FOLLOWED HIM."

The phrase, *"And as He passed by,"* refers to Jesus continuing His Walk. However, He could have well spent several hours teaching or even healing among the people.

At any rate, at some point He continues His Walk, with maybe Peter, Andrew, James, and John with Him, although not specified.

(It is hard to imagine that at this stage of His Ministry, and considering His fame, that He could have gone anywhere alone. Consequently, it stands to reason that some, if not all of His Disciples, at least as many as He presently has, are with Him.)

The phrase, *"He saw Levi the son of Alphaeus,"* speaks of Matthew.

This was not the first time the Lord had seen Levi. His choice of this man as one of the Twelve was based on long observation of him

as he sat at his tax-collector's desk. As well, this is not the first time that Levi had seen the Lord. The whole city of Capernaum, of which Matthew was a citizen, was flooded with the fame and reputation of the Lord. Consequently, this was no chance, or sudden meeting, or calling. It was designed by the Holy Spirit.

The phrase, *"Sitting at the receipt of custom,"* is a revealing portrait of this man.

Most Jews who were tax collectors, and, consequently, considered as traitors by their fellow countrymen, usually hired others to collect the actual taxes. However, Matthew seems to show his defiance by his actions of performing this chore himself, seemingly not caring what others thought.

His toll-gate would have been on the Great West Road from Damascus to the Mediterranean. It was the Customs Office as well of Capernaum, and the landing place for the many ships that sailed the Lake or coasted from town to town. He was a tax collector who collected toll for Herod Antipas.

In a sense, he was in the employ of the Roman Government, which meant he was hated and despised by the Jews, and classed with sinners, and thought by them to be a *"lost soul,"* in other words, one who could not be saved.

At his toll-gate, there would have been an elevated platform or bench on which he sat, and which would have been obvious to all. Here he collected the taxes, and had power to stop anyone, as well as rummage through their belongings at his pleasure. He could assign and collect taxes on the spot, or confiscate goods, and was backed by the mighty Roman Government. The manner in which one became a tax-collector varied from district to district.

One of the principle ways employed by Rome, was to auction off particular districts to the highest bidder. In this manner, Rome would collect a lump sum, with the tax-collector free to collect as much as the traffic would bear.

If, indeed, he had bid high, it was up to him to levy enough taxes to get back his investment, plus a good return. To be sure, inasmuch as he was free to tax within reason, most tax-collectors became very wealthy, and, in turn, were hated and despised by their countrymen.

First of all, the idea of an Israelite having to pay taxes to a Gentile power was unthinkable! And then to have to pay those taxes to a renegade Jew was adding insult to injury. Consequently, such a person was thought not only to be a traitor, but a sinner of the worst kind.

The phrase, *"And said unto him, Follow Me,"* is the same command given to Peter, Andrew, James, and John. As well, it had the same meaning respecting Matthew, as it did the others.

However, this was more than an invitation, it was a command!

It is not as Wuest, the Greek Scholar, says, *"Would you like to follow Me? I extend this invitation to you."* Here was a King, sovereign in His demands. Levi would have recognized the imperative tone of our Lord's Voice. This was an effectual call, like the call to Salvation.

In other words, this call of Christ was Anointed heavily by the Holy Spirit, and would have had its intended effect upon Matthew, just as the Holy Spirit convicts sinners to come to Christ. It is a power that one, if he so wills, can resist, but, at the same time, is strong enough to overcome all obstacles and hindrances.

The phrase, *"And he arose and followed Him,"* proclaims Levi leaving his toll-booth, instantly responding to the Master's Command.

The statement actually meant, *"Start following Me, and continue as a habit of life to follow Me."* This meant that Levi was henceforth to walk the same road that Jesus walked, a road of self-sacrifice, a road of separation, a road of suffering, if you please!

However, it was more than just *"Follow Me,"* but, instead, *"Follow with Me."*

As such, it did not mean one following after another, but rather walking side by side down the same road. And, as well, as Wuest brings out, *"This blessed fellowship is for every Believer in the Lord Jesus."*

What an honor!

What a joy!

As far as the world was concerned, to do this thing meant poverty for Levi, instead of the affluence and luxury to which he had been accustomed.

Sadly, the modern Church, at least a large segment of it, has attempted to materialize this call. Matthew is urged to continue in his tax-collecting business, while he follows Jesus on the side.

Or he is promised that his material riches will not only not be left behind, but, in fact, will be increased.

It is a heady doctrine for modern Matthews, but totally unscriptural, and, thereby heresy!

While it is certainly true that the Lord does bless His Children financially, still, to lower the *"Blessing of Abraham,"* to the level of money, as I heard one Preacher do, is woefully perverting the Gospel of Christ, which is a gross understatement.

Salvation has Christ as its object, and not money. Jesus did not say, *"Follow Me for the things I will give you,"* but, instead, *"Follow Me,"* which is something else entirely!

The Believer must never misunderstand this call, in that it is reduced to *"things."* Christ is always the object, and must never cease to be the object.

The idea is, and as stated, that Matthew left his toll-house immediately. Whether others were there or not, is not known, although there probably were.

The moment that this tax-collector said, *"Yes,"* was the greatest moment of his life. Thank God he did not hesitate!

(15) "AND IT CAME TO PASS, THAT, AS JESUS SAT AT MEAT IN HIS HOUSE, MANY PUBLICANS AND SINNERS SAT ALSO TOGETHER WITH JESUS AND HIS DISCIPLES: FOR THERE WERE MANY, AND THEY FOLLOWED HIM."

The phrase, *"And it came to pass, that, as Jesus sat at meat in his house,"* refers to Matthew's house. Luke 5:29 makes it clear that it was the home of this Disciple.

The phrase, *"Many Publicans and sinners sat also together with Jesus and His Disciples,"* expresses a gathering called by Matthew, evidently to celebrate his being called by Christ. In other words, he was giving up his tax-collecting business, which, this gathering, in effect, had nothing to do with business, but rather the call of God. No doubt, and quickly, the news had spread all over Capernaum at Matthew's decision. As well, there is some evidence that he was held in high regard by fellow tax-collectors and quite possibly could have been a man of some wealth.

The phrase, *"For there were many, and they followed Him,"* does not necessarily mean that they wholeheartedly gave their hearts to Christ, but rather that they were very interested in what was being done, and especially that the influence of Christ had been so powerful on one of their fellow Publicans.

As well, it seems that some had not received a formal invitation to this gathering, but upon hearing the news came anyway!

It is evident that these *"Publicans"* (tax-collectors) felt totally cut off from the mainstream of Jewish life, and the evidence seems clear that they were excluded from the Synagogue. In other words, they were not wanted there, and would have been told to leave had they attended. But yet, they felt comfortable with Jesus, as this Text graphically proclaims.

Why?

Religious Leaders had long since left the precepts of the Word of God, introducing their own concepts, which obviously were man-instituted, and therefore not of God. As such, it had become a Religion of the Jews.

To become a part of this Religion, one had to subscribe to a plethora of rules and regulations to which the Word of God had been twisted from its original context. It little offered God anymore to the people, but, rather, man-made philosophies and traditions. Consequently, these Publicans and no doubt others, seeing a way to make a great amount of money as a tax-collector for the Romans, opted for the money. They knew they would become cast-offs from Jewish tradition, but felt they were losing nothing in the process! Some, as stated, like Matthew, brazenly flaunted their defiance by openly collecting the taxes themselves, instead of hiring others to do it.

When Jesus came teaching, preaching, healing, and performing miracles, He seemed to be totally different than this mish-mash of Religion. His Words were not endless arguments generating continued debates over trifles, but rather, exploded with Life. As well, His demeanor was one of friendliness and kindness, which was totally unlike the Pharisees and Scribes with their long religious faces. As well, it was obvious that the Power of God was with Him, considering the tremendous miracles being wrought on a daily basis.

And then, miracle of miracles, He made no harsh statements about their tax-collecting business, and now had even called one of their own to be His close Disciple. As a result, they wanted to know more about Him.

Why did not He condemn the tax-collecting business? The next two verses will tell us!

(16) "AND WHEN THE SCRIBES AND

PHARISEES SAW HIM EAT WITH PUBLICANS AND SINNERS, THEY SAID UNTO HIS DISCIPLES, HOW IS IT THAT HE EATETH AND DRINKETH WITH PUBLICANS AND SINNERS?"

The phrase, *"And when the Scribes and Pharisees saw Him eat with Publicans and sinners,"* means that some of these had heard of the call of Matthew, and this resultant gathering, and had come, although uninvited, to see what was taking place.

As we have explained many times, the Scribes were supposed to be those who were scholars in the Law of Moses, and, consequently, instructors of the people in these fundamentals.

The Pharisees were a sect in Israel, numbering approximately 7,000 at this time, who would have been called the fundamentalists of our day. In other words, those who claimed to believe all of the Bible. They by and large controlled the religious life of Israel. Some few accepted Christ, but the majority of them hated Him with a passion, which meant that they really did not know God, despite their profession. Jesus denounced them with scathing rebukes (Mat. 23).

What we are seeing here is the beginning of the terrible animosity that would result in them crucifying Christ. They hated Him with a passion, and because of many and varied reasons. In effect, they were the apostate Church, while He was the True Church.

This hall in Levi's home where this gathering was held, and according to students of the customs of that day, was probably about 50 feet long, and about 20 feet wide. Most of these type banquet halls in well-to-do houses, which Matthew seemed to have had, were about 20 feet in height.

The walls were covered with a type of stucco, either washed brown or white. The roof was of timber, and flat; the floor, it is said, was strewn with fine, clean sand, and garnished with strips of carpet upon which cushions had been placed.

The phrase, *"They said unto His Disciples,"* refers to the Scribes and Pharisees questioning Peter, Andrew, James, and John, etc., concerning this gathering, which, in their minds, was unthinkable!

The question, *"How is it that He eateth and drinketh with Publicans and sinners?",* posed the idea that they thought He was committing a great sin by associating with these people.

In their minds, they were too holy and righteous to associate with such. To have done so would have greatly degraded their lofty claims of great piousness.

To be sure, it was this attitude that the Publicans hated, and which Christ hated as well!

The Scribes and Pharisees detesting the tax-collectors, went much further in their hatred than the mere practice of collecting taxes. Israel was now subject to Rome, and greatly chaffed at this, thinking themselves to be greatly superior. They maintained that they were Abraham's seed, and protested that as a people dedicated to God, they ought not to be subject to the Romans, who were Gentiles and idolaters. They considered that it was contrary to the liberty and dignity of the Children of God that they should pay tribute to them, a view which increased their prejudice against these tax-gatherers.

They felt that Israel's destiny was to be the premier nation in the world, which, in fact, they had been under David and Solomon.

In Truth, this was the Plan of God for these people. However, they had by their own sin, wickedness, and rebellion, abrogated this position. The Lord had repeatedly sent the Prophets such as Jeremiah, who made every effort to turn them away from their sin and rebellion, but without success. Consequently, Israel fell to the Babylonians, and had remained under the Gentile yoke for these many years, and that despite the fact that they had fought continuously to regain their place of superiority.

Even at this time, there were constant insurrections against Rome attempting to throw off this yoke, which would ultimately result in their destruction by Titus and Vespasian in 70 A.D.

What they little knew or realized in their self-righteousness was that Jesus actually was the Son of God, and, in reality, the Messiah. Had they accepted Him, doing so sincerely from a broken and contrite spirit, their nation could have been vaulted once again to prominence. But this they did not do, and, in fact, would not do!

So, they hated these *"Publicans,"* which were symbolic of their domination by the Romans.

The word, *"sinners,"* is here interesting! In the 15th verse and following, they are separated from the Publicans. However, inasmuch as the word, *"Publicans,"* is listed first, their sin would have been looked at by the Jews as greater even

than these *"sinners,"* whomever they may have been, and whatever they had done! And yet, Jesus was *"eating and drinking"* with them, and seemingly without censure.

To the Scribes and Pharisees this entire scene would have been, as stated, unthinkable! First of all, for Jesus to mix with these people was bad enough, but to do so with the enjoyment that seemed to permeate the gathering was not only unthinkable, but in their minds, blasphemous!

(17) "WHEN JESUS HEARD IT, HE SAITH UNTO THEM, THEY THAT ARE WHOLE HAVE NO NEED OF THE PHYSICIAN, BUT THEY THAT ARE SICK: I CAME NOT TO CALL THE RIGHTEOUS, BUT SINNERS TO REPENTANCE."

The phrase, *"When Jesus heard it,"* means that He overheard their murmuring and complaining respecting His Presence in this place.

The phrase, *"They that are whole have no need of the physician, but they that are sick,"* explains fully as to the <u>why</u> of His Presence.

As someone has said, as the physician is not infected by the disease of the patient, but rather overcomes it and drives it from him, so it is no disgrace but rather an honor to the physician to associate himself with the sick, and so much more, the greater the sickness.

Jesus was in this place, not because He especially enjoyed this type of company, for He did not. There was sin all about Him, and because there were sinners, and His Righteous, sensitive soul shrank back from it. But He was there to reach their souls for Salvation.

Bickersteth, a Greek expositor of the last century, said that the following may have been the thoughts of Christ regarding the question of the Scribes and Pharisees:

"I Who am sent from Heaven by the Father, that I might be the Physician of the souls of sinners, and not defiled by their sins and spiritual diseases when I converse with them; but rather I cure and heal them, which is alike for My Glory and for their good, and so much the more, the greater their sins.

"For I am the Physician of sinners, not their companion. But you, O Scribes and Pharisees, are not the physicians but the companions of sinners, and so you are contaminated.

"Nevertheless, you desire to be thought righteous and holy; and therefore I do not associate

with you, *(1) because you think you are righteous, when in Truth you are not, actually not even as good as these Publicans and sinners; and (2) because your insincerity and hypocrisy are an offense to Me."*

Many in the modern Church mistake and misunderstand the actions of Christ, thinking by His association with sinners, that He condoned their activity. Consequently, to many in the modern Church, very little is wrong or sinful. As a result, any and all are embraced as fellow Believers, and irrespective of their erroneous Doctrine, such as Catholicism, etc.

The world is thus brought into the Church under the guise of winning them to Christ. Regrettably, such does not win the world, but rather destroys the Church.

Christ was no companion of the sinful activities of these *"sinners,"* whatever they may have been. But He was a companion in the sense of loving these people, and irrespective of what they had done. He was not there to criticize or to condemn them, but rather to show them a better way.

In effect, they were on His territory, instead of Him being on their's. Not for a moment did He condone their sinful activities, nor did He show any inclination to such by His attitude toward them. To love them did not mean to accept them, and neither did it mean to condemn them. He was there to bring them out of their sin, instead of accepting them in their sin. A holier-than-thou attitude would in no way have accomplished this purpose. He was in their company, but not of their company! As such, we, as well, are to be in the world, but not of it! This we must never forget, conducting ourselves as Christ conducted Himself.

One does not win the drunk or the thief, etc., to Christ by condemning him. But by loving him.

However, at the same time, condemning the act is not condemning the person. Jesus, by His lifestyle, Messages, conduct, and actions, constantly condemned the acts of sin. However, he never condemned sinners. There is a vast difference!

As I dictate these words, America has just come through a wrenching trial which lasted nearly a year. Many accusations came out of this trial, not the least being the labeling of some certain individual or individuals as *"racists."* While this may have been true, still, many

NOTES

of those screaming the loudest were just as racist as the individual they were condemning.

While racism is wrong, racists can seldom be won to the Lord, and brought out of their sin by condemning them personally.

So, Jesus did not use this occasion to condemn the sinners who were present, but rather to show them a better way by His Love for them.

In effect, sinners, and especially these kind, know they are sinners. They don't really have to be reminded of it. They actually live under constant condemnation, and more condemnation heaped upon them personally does not tend to pull them out of their sin, but actually drives them further into it.

That is the reason a parent seldom does any good by constantly haranguing a son or daughter over their waywardness. Certainly the waywardness cannot be condoned, but, at the same time, it is only love which will bring them back. Taking the example of Christ, this is the only method which will work. No, it doesn't work with all, but it worked with Matthew, and it has worked with a host of others!

The phrase, *"I came not to call the Righteous, but sinners to repentance,"* tells us the very reason why He came. Thank God He did, because His Call reached me, and prayerfully you.

Some time back, we began placing our Telecast on *"Public Access"* Channels in various cities in America. These are Cable Channels set aside by Congress, with one supposedly in each city, to be used for whatever the public desires to air over it, within bounds of certain decency, which, at times, seems not to exist at all. In other words, about anything, as inane as it may be, can be aired over these Channels.

While nothing is charged for the air time, still, no appeal for financial help can be made to offset production cost, etc. At any rate, at this particular time (10-95) we are airing the Telecast on approximately 200 Channels in as many cities in America.

It has been inferred by some that it might not be proper to air a Gospel Program on such a Channel, especially considering the type of programming which surrounds it, and that only hard-core *"sinners"* watch it!

Of course the answer is simple, that is the very reason for airing it on these Channels. If you want to catch fish, you go where the fish are, exactly as Jesus did at this gathering. To think any other way, is to place oneself in the same position as the Scribes and Pharisees!

Beautifully enough, some of the greatest testimonies we have ever received are coming from these *"Public Access"* Channels. These are testimonies of deliverance and victory that beg description. And beautifully enough, most of them are from young people who are caught so terribly in such a bondage of sin and iniquity that it defies description. And yet, by the Power of God, they are being set free. I will give one brief example:

A seventeen-year-old girl wrote (9-95) and told of what Jesus had done for her. She related how she had been an alcoholic at thirteen years old, which is unthinkable to a rational mind. Yet she found herself in this terrible bondage.

She related as to how her step-father had sexually abused her over and over again, but her Mother would not do anything about the situation, causing her to be driven further into this prison of darkness.

As a result of the abuse and alcoholism, and seeking companionship and acceptance from almost anyone, she became pregnant at sixteen years old. As a result, she was driven out of the house and forced to live on her own.

She related how she sought employment at a service station, and rented a small mobile home for $60 a week in order to have a place to live. There was nothing in this small mobile home but a couch, a table and a bed, with a small black and white TV.

Not knowing what to do about her situation of pregnancy, she had scheduled an abortion. The day before she was to have the abortion, and having gotten two or three days off from her employment for this task, she came home that afternoon. Her shift had ended and it was 4 p.m.

She related as to how she laid down on the couch, after turning on the small television set. It was on the Public Access Channel.

Having no idea what was coming on, all of a sudden she was surprised to see our program beginning to air. She really did not know who we were, and really had little interest. However, she enjoyed the music and remained to listen to the Message.

During the course of the Message, I mentioned something about abortion. I stated, *"The answer to abortion is not killing doctors*

NOTES

or bombing abortion clinics, but, instead, bringing the precious soul to Jesus Christ."

As she heard those words, she came under great conviction by the Holy Spirit.

She went on to say that when the Message ended, and I began to pray, she slipped on her knees beside the couch and began to pray with me.

"Brother Swaggart," she said, *"even though I knew nothing about the Lord, not having been raised in a Christian family, when I began to pray with you, something happened to me such as I had never experienced before. For the first time I knew that someone loved me, and I knew it was Jesus."*

She related how she did not really know too much about what had happened to her; but she did know something had changed within her. In the first place, she almost instantly went to sleep, and without drinking the two or three glasses of vodka which she normally consumed before going to bed. She related how she slept all night, waking the next morning with no desire for alcohol.

In her mind, she had already canceled the abortion, but yet she did not know what she was going to do. She stated that she only had $3 to her name. With that, she walked over to a nearby Denny's Restaurant, and ordered some breakfast, which she seldom ever did.

She had just turned in her order, when a lady walked up to her table holding a Bible under her arm. The lady, without introducing herself, looked down at her and said:

"I come into this Restaurant every morning, and the Lord generally gives me someone to witness to. However, yesterday something happened to me that was special."

She went on to say, *"I was watching Brother Swaggart on the Public Access Channel, when he mentioned something about abortion. The Lord spoke to my heart and told me that I was, without fail, to be in this Restaurant this morning, and there would be a young lady present who was pregnant and needed help!"*

The lady then looked straight at the girl and said, *"You are that person, aren't you?"*

Startled, the girl began to weep, actually sobbing! The lady sat down across from her and began to console her and pray with her.

As the lady continued to speak with her, she again mentioned my name and the Message I had brought the day before, and then said, *"But you probably don't know who or what I'm talking about."*

The young lady began to weep again, saying, *"Oh yes I do, yesterday afternoon I saw that same program, and gave my heart to Jesus Christ."*

The girl wrote as to how this Christian lady immediately took her into her home, buying her some clothes, and helping her to find a better job.

She went on to state that a few weeks later, watching the Telecast, she was Baptized in the Holy Spirit with the evidence of speaking with other tongues. She then said, *"Brother Swaggart, my little son was born just a few days ago. He was two or three weeks early, but in perfect health."*

This testimony that I have related to you in part, could be construed as none other than a miracle. Not only was this girl's soul and life saved, but, as well, her baby was saved also! To be sure, this is why Jesus came. This is His very purpose!

In the word, *"Repentance,"* is the seed of Salvation. Men have sinned against God, and they must repent to Him, admitting they are a sinner and in desperate need of His help. The words may vary, and, in fact, the sinner may not even know what Repentance is. Nevertheless, their heart action toward God must be in that spirit.

As well, they must have Faith in Jesus Christ, even though they may know very little about Him, or what He has done respecting His Death at Calvary, which was for lost sinners.

Repentance toward God and Faith in Christ, guarantees Redemption for any and all! (Acts 20:21).

(18) "AND THE DISCIPLES OF JOHN AND OF THE PHARISEES USED TO FAST: AND THEY COME AND SAY UNTO HIM, WHY DO THE DISCIPLES OF JOHN AND OF THE PHARISEES FAST, BUT THY DISCIPLES FAST NOT?"

These following Passages will prove to be a tremendous insight into the world of religion versus the following of Christ, i.e., a relationship with Christ.

The phrase, *"And the Disciples of John and of the Pharisees used to fast,"* concerns the Disciples of John the Baptist, who was now in prison, and their joining with the Pharisees.

Why would they have done this, especially considering that John had called the Pharisees

a brood of vipers? Here they join with these vipers in criticizing Jesus.

Quite possibly, they were hurt and jealous respecting the incarceration of their leader, and the gaining influence of Christ. They may have reasoned within their hearts that if Jesus were actually the Messiah, He would effect the release of John.

If, in fact, these thoughts were in their mind, it shows they did not properly understand the mission of John, which was to introduce Christ, which he capably did.

In fact, Christ could have delivered John from prison, but that was not the Will of God. He had finished his mission, and had done it well. Even though he would die an early and violent death, still, he would do so knowing that he had carried out in totality that which he was called to do. There is no greater accomplishment than that.

As well, each of these Disciples that Jesus called, with the exception of John the Beloved, the brother of James, would ultimately die a martyr's death, and would not be delivered by the Lord. But at this time, their work would be finished as well!

It seems that John's Disciples allowed personal ambition to crowd out the Will of God, with them joining, in effect, the enemies of God.

The modern Believer must be very careful in respect to this temptation. Self interest must be laid aside in favor of the Will of God. To side with the enemies of God is a position that cannot be blessed, and irrespective of its seeming present prosperity.

"Fasting" was a ritual practiced two days a week by the Pharisees, and possibly the Disciples of John. More than likely, the day on which this Feast was held in the home of Matthew, was on one of these fast days.

This was not one of the fasts prescribed by the Law; had it been so, it would have been observed by our Lord. Actually, in the Law of Moses, only one day a year was to be set aside for fasting, and that was on the *"Great Day of Atonement"* (deny yourselves — Lev. 16:29, 31; 26-32). However, fasting was undertaken in times of deep trouble and underlined the seriousness of personal and national appeals to God (II Sam. 12:16-22; II Chron. 20:1-29; Neh. 1:4; Jer. 36:1-10; Dan. 9:3-19).

As well, fasting at times was carried out as a

sign of honest Repentance (I Ki. 21:27; Joel 2:12-15; Jonah 3:5-10).

However, the Pharisees, evidently thinking that more is better, now fasted 104 days a year. This was a part of their self-righteousness, which they, as here, loudly trumpeted.

To be sure, this type of fasting may have been of some benefit to them physically, but it held absolutely no spiritual significance.

Seeing Jesus along with His Disciples, as well as all these *"Publicans and sinners,"* feasting along with laughing and talking, was an offense to the Pharisees and the Disciples of John. Therefore they asked the following:

"Why do the Disciples of John and of the Pharisees fast, but Thy Disciples fast not?"

Actually, there is no record that Jesus or His Disciples fasted at all, even on the *"Great Day of Atonement."*

(In effect, the Great Day of Atonement could not now be carried out, because there was no Ark of the Covenant in the Holy of Holies in the Temple.

On this special day, which came once a year, the High Priest, who was a type of Christ, was to kill a goat, and offer its blood on the Mercy Seat of the Ark of the Covenant. This was to atone nationally for the sins of the people. Due to the Ark of the Covenant being missing since the Babylonian invasion of some 600 years earlier, this ritual could not be carried out.)

(19) "AND JESUS SAID UNTO THEM, CAN THE CHILDREN OF THE BRIDECHAMBER FAST, WHILE THE BRIDEGROOM IS WITH THEM? AS LONG AS THEY HAVE THE BRIDEGROOM WITH THEM, THEY CANNOT FAST."

The phrase, *"And Jesus said unto them,"* concerns an answer that will explain many things, as well as answer their question.

The question, *"Can the children of the bridechamber fast, while the bridegroom is with them?"*, tells us several things:

1. Jesus was alluding to Himself as the Bridegroom. John the Baptist had even called himself the friend of the Bridegroom, that is, of Christ.

2. People do not fast, as would be obvious, in the midst of a wedding feast.

3. By using this type of illustration, Jesus is actually referring to Himself as the Messiah, the One for Whom Israel had been waiting!

The phrase, *"As long as they have the bridegroom with them, they cannot fast,"* gives us some idea as to what fasting is all about.

Even though, and as we have stated, fasting should be done for many reasons, still, the primary reason for fasting is that Jesus is not here visibly present, resulting in the Will of God being done on earth as it is in Heaven. Consequently, people fasted before Jesus came, and we fast now because He has been rejected. However, when He comes back, as He shall, thereby beginning the Kingdom Age, there is no record in the Bible of people fasting at that time.

Fasting speaks of the Believer being in a hostile environment, which this world is, with the flesh subject to the pull of the world. This is because Jesus is not reigning Personally in this world, even though reigning in our lives. Consequently, we fast to subdue the *"pride of life,"* the *"lust of the eyes,"* and the *"lust of the flesh."* When Jesus comes back, and considering the great change which will take place, fasting will not then be necessary.

(20) "BUT THE DAYS WILL COME, WHEN THE BRIDEGROOM SHALL BE TAKEN AWAY FROM THEM, AND THEN SHALL THEY FAST IN THOSE DAYS."

The phrase, *"But the days will come, when the bridegroom shall be taken away from them"* is a statement, whether understood at that time or not, that Jesus would be rejected as the Messiah of Israel, and would be *"taken away"* which He was at the Ascension.

The phrase, *"And then shall they fast in those days,"* refers to the time after His Ascension on through to the present, and unto His Coming.

After the Lord's Ascension, His Disciples frequently fasted as of necessity, and because they went through much privation and trial.

As stated, such continues unto this moment, and will be the part and parcel of all who live Godly in Christ Jesus, until He returns to take to Himself His Kingdom, when there will then be a constant camp meeting and everlasting festival filled with joy, which will require no fasting.

(21) "NO MAN ALSO SEWETH A PIECE OF NEW CLOTH ON AN OLD GARMENT, ELSE THE NEW PIECE THAT FILLED IT UP TAKETH AWAY FROM THE OLD, AND THE RENT IS MADE WORSE."

The phrase, *"No man also seweth a piece of*

new cloth on an old garment," once again portrays Christ using something familiar to all to explain a great Truth. The idea is this:

The *"new cloth"* here spoken of, referred to cloth which had not been made usable by the process of cleansing, shrinking, and thickening, through the use of moisture, heat, and pressure. If such cloth was used as a patch on an *"old garment,"* the *"new cloth"* would tend to shrink, thereby tearing away from the *"old garment."*

The phrase, *"Else the new piece that filled it up taketh away from the old, and the rent is made worse,"* was easily understood by all, by which they should as well have understood the spiritual implication.

The patch refers to the Messiah's new type of Ministry which was Grace, as compared to the Mosaic Law, the old worn-out garment which was ready to be set aside.

It speaks of those today who attempt to retain the Mosaic Law which God set aside at the Cross, and put upon it the patch of Grace. It happens as our Lord said, *"The new piece that filled it up taketh away from the old, and the rent is made worse."* When the attempt is made to mix Law and Grace, both lose their true identity, and one is left with the doctrine of the Judaizers, as in the Galatian heresy.

(22) "AND NO MAN PUTTETH NEW WINE INTO OLD BOTTLES: ELSE THE NEW WINE DOTH BURST THE BOTTLES, AND THE WINE IS SPILLED, AND THE BOTTLES WILL BE MARRED: BUT NEW WINE MUST BE PUT INTO NEW BOTTLES."

The phrase, *"And no man putteth new wine into old bottles,"* has nothing to do with glass bottles as thought of presently. The Greek word is *"wineskins."*

The Gospel of Jesus Christ is here referred to as *"new wine,"* with the *"old bottles,"* or *"wineskins"* referring to the Law.

The phrase, *"Else the new wine doth burst the bottles, and the wine is spilled, and the bottles will be marred,"* refers to unfermented wine placed in *"old bottles,"* which upon beginning to ferment, would expand, and, consequently, *"burst the bottles,"* i.e., *"wineskins."*

The phrase, *"But new wine must be put into new bottles,"* was something that everyone understood.

Once again, Jesus uses an illustration of material things familiar to all. He is actually

saying the same thing that He said in the previous verse, except in a different way.

To attempt to attach the Gospel of Grace to the Law of Moses, would only destroy both! Consequently, the *"new wine"* of the Gospel must likewise have *"new bottles,"* i.e., a new presentation, which would actually be a *"New Covenant."*

Jesus is actually referring back to the statement in the 20th verse, *"The Bridegroom shall be taken away from them,"* speaking of Himself.

The Church would then be ushered in, founded not on the old Mosaic Law, but, instead, on the foundation of Grace, which was an entirely new presentation. In this new presentation, i.e., *"new bottles,"* both Gentiles and Jews would come the same way. All would be by Faith, with the Sacrifices coming to an end, because Jesus as the Perfect Sacrifice would fulfill that type.

The Disciples probably little understood what He was speaking of at that time, but which they would graphically understand after the Day of Pentecost.

(23) "AND IT CAME TO PASS, THAT HE WENT THROUGH THE CORN FIELDS ON THE SABBATH DAY; AND HIS DISCIPLES BEGAN, AS THEY WENT, TO PLUCK THE EARS OF CORN."

The phrase, *"And it came to pass,"* does not necessarily mean that the incident concerning the *"corn"* happened immediately after the teaching concerning the *"new cloth"* and *"new bottles,"* etc.

The phrase, *"That He went through the corn fields on the Sabbath day,"* does not refer to the type of corn which we have in America. The word was a generic name for all cereals and vegetables. On this occasion, it probably referred to barley, or more likely wheat.

The phrase, *"And His Disciples began, as they went, to pluck the ears of corn,"* spoke of their doing this in order to eat the grain.

This was a common practice, with the individual taking the ripened grain, rubbing it briskly in his hands to remove the chaff, and then eating it raw. It was, incidently, very nutritional.

Bede, one of the expositors of the past, in remarking on the fact of the Disciples plucking the ears of corn, and rubbing them until they get rid of the husks, and obtain the food itself, says; *"They do this who meditate upon the Holy Scriptures, and digest them, until they find in them the kernel, the quintessence of delight."*

St. Augustine, in essence, said, *"Those who merely please themselves with the flowers of Holy Scripture, not rubbing out the grain by meditation, greatly shortchange themselves in the spiritual sense."*

(24) "AND THE PHARISEES SAID UNTO HIM, BEHOLD, WHY DO THEY ON THE SAB-BATH DAY THAT WHICH IS NOT LAWFUL?"

The phrase, *"And the Pharisees said unto Him,"* actually means in the Greek that they kept on speaking to Him about this matter. In other words, they badgered Him!

The question, *"Behold, why do they on the Sabbath day that which is not lawful?",* pro-claims them taking issue with Him on the le-gality of gathering the grain on the Sabbath, which was to them, reaping on a small scale.

They did the same with the dragging of a chair across the floor on the Sabbath, or even a woman combing her hair. They claimed this should not be done because a speck of dust may be moved and could be construed as *"plowing,"* which was forbidden on the Sabbath.

The Law of Moses actually stated that any-one walking through a vineyard or field of grain, could feel free to pluck some grapes or grain to eat, although they must not pluck enough to put into a vessel (Deut. 23:24-25). Consequently, Jesus and His Disciples were not doing any-thing wrong by the taking of this small amount of grain from someone else's field, because, as stated, it was a common practice.

As well, the idea in Deuteronomy is that it was to be eaten immediately, and not taken home, etc. As well, no stipulation in the Law prevented such being done on the Sabbath. This was strictly an addition by the Pharisees.

Actually, most criticism by the Pharisees con-cerned outward religion, the things they held as proof of religion, which anyone could do, even the ungodly. This was the cause of the constant conflict between these hypocrites and Christ.

(25) "AND HE SAID UNTO THEM, HAVE YE NEVER READ WHAT DAVID DID, WHEN HE HAD NEED, AND WAS AN HUNGRED, HE, AND THEY THAT WERE WITH HIM?"

The phrase, *"And He said unto them,"* por-trays Him taking them to I Samuel 21, which, of course, they knew very well. He could have argued the point that there was nothing in the

NOTES

Law that forbade them eating this grain on the Sabbath day, but, instead, He would take them at their own game. In all of this we will learn several lessons:

1. The futility of outward religion and cer-emony, when there is no change in the heart.

2. That one can study the Word of God in-cessantly, as these Pharisees, but yet not know its true intent.

3. Rules and regulations, which translate into Law, never saved anyone, which consti-tutes religion.

The question, as asked by Christ, *"Have ye never read what David did, when he had need, and was an hungred, he, and they that were with him?",* took them back to an incident which would embrace His position in total.

(26) "HOW HE WENT INTO THE HOUSE OF GOD IN THE DAYS OF ABIATHAR THE HIGH PRIEST, AND DID EAT THE SHEW-BREAD, WHICH IS NOT LAWFUL TO EAT BUT FOR THE PRIESTS, AND GAVE ALSO TO THEM WHICH WERE WITH HIM?"

The beginning of the question, *"How He went into the House of God in the days of Abiathar the High Priest . . . ,"* seems to be a discrepancy for Ahimelech was High Priest at that time (I Sam. 21:1; 22:9). Consequently, it can be explained in one of two ways:

1. It seems that Ahimelech was Abiathar's father. However, both the father and the son could have had both names, which was some-times the case.

2. It is said that both, Ahimelech the father and Abiathar the son were present when David came in his distress and obtained the shew-bread. However, shortly after, Ahimelech was killed by Saul, with Abiathar fleeing to David, and became his companion in exile. A short time later, he succeeded to the High Priesthood, taking the place of his father, and did far more good than his father had done. In view of this, the possibility is that he was given this special commendation at this time, as though he was actually the High Priest, even though his father was then living.

Consequently, the words may be properly translated, *"In the days when Abiathar was liv-ing who became High Priest."*

The conclusion of the question, *"And did eat the shewbread, which is not lawful to eat but for the Priests, and gave also to them which were with him?",* concerned the bread which was called the *"bread of the face,"* that is, *"of the Divine Presence,"* symbolizing the Divine Being Who is the Bread of Life.

It was directed by the Law that within the Sanctuary there should be a table of shittim (acacia) wood; and every Sabbath twelve newly-baked loaves were placed upon it in two rows. These loaves were sprinkled with incense, and then remained there until the following Sabbath.

They were then replaced by twelve newly-baked loaves, the old loaves being eaten by the Priests in the Holy Place, from which it was unlawful to remove them. These twelve loaves corresponded to the Twelve Tribes.

When David came, even though he was not a Priest, still, he ate the loaves, which under ordinary circumstances were not lawful for lay people to eat. However, he wisely judged that a positive Law forbidding the laity to eat this bread, ought to yield to a Law of necessity and of nature, which it did!

As well, David divided them out with those who were with him, it seems, at a later time.

(27) "AND HE SAID UNTO THEM, THE SABBATH WAS MADE FOR MAN, AND NOT MAN FOR THE SABBATH:"

Jesus, as Lord of the Sabbath, could not submit to the authority of men, who, in their spiritual ignorance, opposed the true meaning of the Sabbath. The Scribes, being unspiritual men, did not understand the Sabbath or its purpose. They limited God's goodness and refused the New Wine of the Kingdom.

The phrase, *"And He said unto them,"* has in its original construction the idea that He said these things, and kept on saying them. It took some talking to get the idea across to minds warped with warped theology.

One can hear Christ making the statements of verses 27 and 28 over and over again, until they finally heard what He was saying. And yet, after they finally heard it, knowing what He was saying, and that it was correct, still, there is no evidence that they believed.

Why? To have done so would have meant unraveling all of their man-made rules and regulations. Doing such would be an admittance that they were wrong in their theology. Self-righteousness, even when coming face to face with its error, as here, is loathe to do that which is demanded of the humble penitent heart.

The phrase, *"The Sabbath was made for man, and not man for the Sabbath,"* in a few words proclaimed what the Sabbath was all about!

The principle is that the Sabbath is only a means to an end, the good of man. The Rabbis, with all their petty rules, seemed to think that man was made for it.

The force of the argument is this: The Sabbath was made on account of man, not man on account of the Sabbath.

In this Truth, Christ is showing these Religious Leaders that as great as the Sabbath is, it must be subordinate to man. If something is needed to be done on the Sabbath that will benefit man, such as His Disciples gathering a little grain to eat, then the Sabbath must be subordinate to that.

The Sabbath, as all Bible Students understand, was a part of the Law of Moses. This Law which was instituted in totality by God, was meant to serve as a way of life for Israel, God's people. It covered every aspect of the human endeavor from the minute to the mighty. It was meant to show man how to live, what to do, and how to conduct himself toward his fellow man and God. To be sure, there were other laws in the world, which had been devised by man, but as should be obvious, God's Law as given to Moses was so superior that there was no comparison. The Sabbath was supposed to be a day of rest for man; however, in doing that, it was not to be a sword over people's heads. While there were rules involved in the Sabbath regarding what man could and could not do, still, those rules were always subordinate to the actual needs of man. However, the Scribes and Pharisees had made man subordinate to the Sabbath, and, consequently, had added a myriad of rules of their own making, and then judged men's consecration to God by the keeping of their petty rules. In doing so, they completely missed the design and purpose of God in instituting the Sabbath in the first place!

(28) "THEREFORE THE SON OF MAN IS LORD ALSO OF THE SABBATH."

This Scripture, although short, encompassing only one sentence, is, nevertheless, freighted with meaning.

The phrase, *"Therefore the Son of Man,"* and referring to Himself, in effect, proclaims God the Son manifest in human flesh, identifying Himself in Incarnation with mankind. He was saying, *"I am the Messiah,"* and these Religious Leaders knew what He was saying!

The phrase, *"Is Lord also of the Sabbath,"* means that He is the Owner of the Sabbath, and because He is the Creator of it, as well as all things! The Creator is Lord of creation, and thusly, the Lord of the Sabbath, which He brought into being for the sake of mankind.

The title, *"Lord,"* is the august title of God, which we know as Jehovah, and thus proclaims Deity.

To be sure, Jesus, even as Lord of the Sabbath, was no Sabbath breaker; however, He set Himself against an attitude towards the Sabbath that would not permit the doing of good to a fellow-human because it involved what the Pharisees called *"work,"* such as His healing of the sick on the Sabbath (Wuest).

Robertson says that Jesus completely upset the ritualistic and ceremonial, which was a total shock to the Religious Leaders, insisting rather that emphasis be placed on the spiritual. In the other words, the true meaning of the Word of God!

Men love to make rules, and they rather enjoy forcing other men to obey them, and especially religious rules and religious men.

Consequently, not only is the Letter of the Word important, but the spiritual emphasis and intent must be taken into account as well, exactly as Christ did in these circumstances, thereby setting an example for us in our interpretation of the Word.

CHAPTER 3

(1) "AND HE ENTERED AGAIN INTO THE SYNAGOGUE; AND THERE WAS A MAN THERE WHICH HAD A WITHERED HAND."

The phrase, *"And He entered again into the Synagogue,"* spoke of the Sabbath, because this is when Synagogue services were conducted. Which Synagogue it was, is not stated, but most likely it was in Capernaum.

The phrase, *"And there was a man there which had a withered hand,"* sets the stage for the next confrontation with the Pharisees, although this was not the intention in the healing of this man.

The implication in the language is that the

man's hand had not always been this way, but had withered due to an accident or disease. Luke tells us it was his right hand. Several things will happen in this scenario:

1. This man's *"withered hand"* is a symbol of withered, undone humanity, as a result of the Fall. As the hand could little function in its present capacity, consequently, man little functions properly.

2. Only Jesus could straighten this hand, as only Jesus can straighten the crooked walk of mankind. This means that He is the only Remedy, and not the Synagogue itself.

Many mistake the Church for the Saviour. Emphatically, it is not! It took Jesus' presence in the Church (Synagogue) to bring about this miraculous result. Consequently, Church without Jesus, is no more than any other gathering. But with Jesus, it becomes a powerful conduit to bring about change for the better.

The Religious Leaders had absolutely no concern about this man being healed, they were only concerned that their petty rules be obeyed. The man meant nothing to them, as humanity means nothing to any religion. They did not care that his hand was withered, and, consequently, had no regard or concern that he be healed. In effect, he was nothing to them, and probably they wished he had not come to the Synagogue, because the *"withered hand"* was unsightly, and, therefore, made their gathering a little less than they desired.

So, in this scenario, the entire aspect of the God-man relationship becomes obvious, as well as the great hindering force of religion, which is inspired by Satan.

(2) "AND THEY WATCHED HIM, WHETHER HE WOULD HEAL HIM ON THE SABBATH DAY; THAT THEY MIGHT ACCUSE HIM."

The phrase, *"And they watched Him,"* spoke of the Pharisees, and, means that they dogged His footsteps, which spoke not only of this occasion, but, in fact, continuously.

In the situation regarding His Disciples plucking the grain on the Sabbath, they had not been able to lay much to His charge, due to the fact that He did not do it Himself. However, knowing His propensity to heal, they suspected that an occasion would arise on this Sabbath which would call for His healing Power, which it did!

The evil of these Pharisees knew no bounds! They who talked of God constantly, in fact, did not know God. This is the reason that Church without Christ is so damning. It is the reason that any form of religious activity without Christ, is anathema to the human soul.

As well, even though Christ be lauded, if denominational structure, doctrine, or religious activity, take precedent over Christ in any way, therefore, ceasing to be subordinate to Him, then it becomes Christ plus, whether it is realized or not, and, consequently, of no effect!

These Religious Leaders knew full well that Jesus claimed to be the Messiah, even though at this time He had not said it outright. Nevertheless, they understood His implications. They did not at all believe, even though His proof was irrefutable.

Why?

To have done so, would have meant subordination to Him, and, this, religion refuses to do. The entirety of religion is wrapped up in its man-devised ways, which placed these Religious Leaders in a position of authority, consequently, lording it over others, which religious man loves to do. In a nut shell it comes down to Christ being Lord, or man being lord!

In fact, the far greater majority of that which calls itself *"Christianity"* is ruled and guided by man, and, therefore, not by God. In other words, even though Jesus may be spoken of, He is not Lord, because man and Lord cannot reign at the same time.

This would include almost all organized religion, and of every stripe. It would as well include most of that which calls itself *"independent!"* Too often, even in these circles, man is still lord.

Tragically, now, as then, Jesus is Lord in only a few lives. Consequently, all Believers should resolutely investigate that which they are associated with regarding Church, and that which they are supporting. If it is ruled, regulated, and devised by man, it cannot be ruled by the Lord, and, consequently, their association would be the same as those who sided with the Religious Leaders of Jesus' day.

(Incidentally, our term *"Religious Leaders"* is not used in a positive fashion. In effect, there is no such thing as *"Religious Leaders"* in the Work of God. If they are called such, they are improperly designated. It is unscriptural.

There is only one *"Spiritual Leader,"* and that is Christ — Mat. 23:8-12.)

The phrase, *"Whether He would heal him on the Sabbath day,"* brings us to the crux of the situation.

St. Jerome informs us that the man whose hand was withered is described as a Mason, and is said to have asked for help in the following terms: *"I was a Mason, seeking my living by manual labor. I beseech Thee, Jesus, to restore to me the use of my hand that I may not be compelled to beg bread."*

The phrase, *"That they might accuse Him,"* refers to the Pharisees, and they, as the watchdogs of Israel's religion, attempting to discredit the claims of Christ as Messiah, by finding Him violating its regulations.

These Religious Leaders would have nothing to do with the Lord, and kept themselves away from any fellowship with Him, lest they be understood to be in sympathy with Him. They maintained an attitude of aloofness. They had only one thing in mind:

There was no desire to see if He really was the Messiah. Their minds were closed on the subject. Consequently, the entire framework of their thoughts and action was one thing only, and that was to see how they could take anything He did, twisting it to their own satisfaction in order that they might *"accuse Him!"*

In effect, and as stated, they were watchdogs and spies.

This somewhat hits home, as individuals designated by a particular Religious Denomination have stood in front of auditoriums where we were conducting meetings, in order that they may note anyone going into our meetings who they thought may be a member of the Denomination in question.

Why did they object to their people coming to our meetings?

I suppose my question answers itself.

They would like to have objected to what we preached, but this they could not do, at least Scripturally, because its Truth was undeniable.

Did they object to souls being saved or people being Baptized in the Holy Spirit, of which there were many?

Actually, their actions proved that they had little regard or concern about people being saved. As the Pharisees of old, the people meant little to them, except as to how they could be used. Precious lives being totally changed by the Power of God were of no consequence! Alcoholics being made sober, with drug addicts being delivered, meant little to them! Broken homes put back together by the Power of God, were not worthy of mention. Actually, all the things that pertained to the True Gospel of Jesus Christ were of no consequence whatsoever. There was only one thing in which they were interested.

Control!

As the Religious Leaders of Israel, the Denomination was supreme, therefore, its rules and regulations, and no matter how unscriptural, were sacrosanct.

To be frank, there is little difference in the two. Both, the Pharisees and those of whom I speak, talked much about God, but little knew Him. As the Pharisees, had they known Him, they would not have fought Him, or those who were His. It is impossible to be of God, and to oppose God at the same time! One cannot love God and fight God. So, to oppose His (that which belongs to Him) is to oppose Him.

(3) "AND HE SAITH UNTO THE MAN WHICH HAD THE WITHERED HAND, STAND FORTH."

The phrase, *"And He saith unto the man,"* is meant to bring the entirety of this situation out into the open. Whatever Christ would do, would be in full view of everyone, leaving no doubt regarding His action or purpose. In other words, He threw this challenge to the Pharisees and into their teeth.

I suppose if He had conducted Himself as many today, He would have told the man to wait until after the service, where He would have subtly taken him out back, and there performed the healing, telling him He was doing it in this manner so as not to arouse animosity. However, in this scenario, we see the very opposite!

To give one inch to ungodliness, is, in effect, to be ungodly! To compromise the standards of the Word of God even in the slightest, is to compromise all! There is only one way to do a thing, and that is the right way. One cannot be in union with both the Pharisees and Christ, one or the other must go. It is identical today. One either follows the Lord, or one follows man. One cannot follow both!

The phrase, *"Which had the withered hand,"* proclaims this man as the object.

NOTES

The religion of that time did not want him healed, and, in fact, had no regard for him. By contrast, Jesus wanted him healed, because that's the very reason why Christ came.

The Lord did not come to this earth to perpetuate Religious Denominations. He did not come to build the *"Baptists,"* or the *"Assemblies of God,"* or the *"Catholics,"* etc., but rather to liberate fallen humanity. What I'm about to say is strong, but I feel it needs to be said.

Those which I have mentioned, plus many not mentioned, are probably the greatest hindrance, as the Pharisees of old, to this all-important work being carried out.

As should be glaringly obvious, the greatest opposition to Christ during His Ministry, was not the Roman Government, or even the known vices of that day, such as alcohol, immorality, gambling, etc., as bad as they may have been, but rather, the *"Church!"*

It is the same now!

The Work of God on earth is not the perpetuation of Religious Denominations, or even particular Religious Doctrines, but, rather, the healing of the *"man with the withered hand,"* i.e., Salvation of withered souls.

The phrase, *"Stand forth,"* in the literal Greek is, *"Be arising into the midst."* That is, according to Wuest, *"Step into the midst of all the people so that all can see you."* Consequently, Jesus answered the attitude of these Pharisees by this daring act. He brought things out into the open at once, so that all may know exactly why and what He was doing. He demands no less of His followers presently!

Any yielding, and to any degree, to that which is wrong, is to yield totally to the wrong.

There are many reasons to do wrong, while there is only one reason to do right.

"If I do this, which I know in my heart to be right, I will lose my Church," is the answer of many Preachers.

Consequently, the question must be asked as to whose Church it is? Or who gave it to you in the first place? Which brings up the greatest question of all!

Who are you following, God or man?

The declaration of man is, *"If I do what I know to be right, they will crucify me!"*

Yes they will, exactly as they did Christ!

Consequently, many opt to follow man instead of the Lord.

(4) "AND HE SAITH UNTO THEM, IS IT LAWFUL TO DO GOOD ON THE SABBATH DAYS, OR TO DO EVIL? TO SAVE LIFE, OR TO KILL? BUT THEY HELD THEIR PEACE."

The phrase, *"And He saith unto them,"* points His statement directly to these Pharisees. He didn't want anyone to misunderstand as to whom He was speaking, and, consequently, pointed them out for all to see and hear.

The question, *"Is it lawful to do good on the Sabbath days, or to do evil? to save life, or to kill?"*, is what it is all about.

It was not a question of keeping rules and regulations, but a question of *"doing good or evil!"* It was not really a question of the Sabbath, but whether to *"save life, or to kill!"*

To have the power to set this man free and not do so, was *"evil."* Likewise, to have the power to save his life, and not do so, in effect, was to *"kill"* him.

Consequently, the Pharisees opted for "evil," and desired to *"kill,"* which was actually the intent of their murderous hearts. Please allow me to state it in this way, and once again, to be personal.

God has called me for World Evangelism. Consequently, I live, eat, and breathe this all-important task. The taking of the Gospel of Jesus Christ to lost and hurting humanity, is ever paramount in my heart. And as Paul said, *"I must not be disobedient to the heavenly vision."*

Almost all the world at the present sits in a lonely stygian darkness, with a sordid past, hurting present, and an unknown future. Jesus Christ, and Jesus Christ Alone, is their only answer.

Consequently, I must use everything at my disposal to get the Message of Redemption to them.

To do this, the Lord has instructed me to use Television and Crusades. In this manner, more people can be reached, with the Lord helping us to see many people saved.

I will pose this question!

Preachers who attempt to get our Telecast off the air, even going to the station demanding it be taken off, would they not be doing the same as these Pharisees of old?

One cannot claim to be doing *"good,"* while at the same time opposing *"good."* By their actions, as these Pharisees, they opted for *"evil."*

Likewise, one cannot claim to be giving

NOTES

"life," while, at the same time, opposing the giving of *"life"* to others. So, by their actions, they have said, *"We will kill them!"*

Consequently, Christ placed the Pharisees in a juxtaposition with Himself. The two Doctrines, that of the Pharisees and that of Christ, were placed side by side. One was shown to be good, while the other was shown to be evil, and by its actions. One was shown to give life, while the other was shown to give death, and by its actions.

Therein essentially lay the difference between Him and the Pharisees, in whose theory and practice, duty and benevolence, the Divine and the human, were divorced. To do good or to do evil, these were the only alternatives, not some petty rule about the Sabbath. To omit to do good in one's power is evil; not to save life when one can, is to destroy it.

So, what are we going to do, save souls or keep our silly man-made rules?

The phrase, *"But they held their peace,"* means they had no answer to the question posed by Christ. Not only were they quiet, but they kept on being quiet. Wuest says, *"Theirs was a painful, embarrassing silence."*

Someone else said, *"What could they have replied to a question which looked at the subject from a wholly different point of view, the ethical, from the legal one they were accustomed to?"* There was nothing common between them and Jesus, and that was the crux of the whole matter.

They were obstinate in their infidelity, who, when they can say nothing against the Truth, refused to say anything for it.

(5) "AND WHEN HE HAD LOOKED ROUND ABOUT ON THEM WITH ANGER, BEING GRIEVED FOR THE HARDNESS OF THEIR HEARTS, HE SAITH UNTO THE MAN, STRETCH FORTH THINE HAND. AND HE STRETCHED IT OUT: AND HIS HAND WAS RESTORED WHOLE AS THE OTHER."

The phrase, *"And when He had looked round about on them with anger,"* proves that *"anger"* is not necessarily a manifestation of sin and Satan. Both God and man have it and will always have it. Without *"anger,"* at least properly used, man would not be capable of waging warfare against sin and Satan. Consequently, the Believer should not pray to be de-humanized and uncreated, but pray to be able to control all faculties in the bounds of the Word of God (Gal. 5:22-23 - Dake).

With the man standing in the midst of all the onlookers, and the Pharisees standing or sitting nearby, Jesus, with a sweep of His eyes, stares at them for a few moments with anger registered on His countenance. In other words, the anger is obvious to all.

Here is the difference between the anger of fallen man and the anger of the sinless One. With fallen man, anger is the desire of retaliating, of punishing those by whom you consider yourself unjustly treated.

Hence, in men, unrighteous anger springs from self-love; in Christ, it sprang from the Love of God, which must always be opposed to sin, and especially this type of sin.

Jesus loved God above all things; hence He was distressed and irritated on account of the wrongs done to God by sins and sinners. Consequently, His anger was a righteous zeal for the honor of God; and hence it was mingled with grief, because, in their blindness and obstinacy, they would not acknowledge Him to be the Messiah, but misrepresented His kindnesses wrought on the sick on the Sabbath day, and found fault with them as evil (Bickersteth).

There are three Greek words speaking of anger in the New Testament:

1. *"Parorgismos"*: This speaks of anger in the sense of exasperation, and is forbidden in Scripture. Paul said, *"Let not the sun go down upon your wrath"* (Eph. 4:26). Actually, this type of anger is that most often exhibited.

2. *"Thumos"*: This speaks of a sudden outburst of anger that cools off quickly, and is the cause of much sin, including murder. By its very definition, it is prohibited in Scripture. Actually, the curtailing of this *"anger"* is one of the great changes brought about in the lives of those who are *"born again."* The explosive nature is changed to one of gentleness (Gal. 5:19-26).

A lady once said to the great Evangelist, Billy Sunday, *"I'll admit I have a temper, but it's over in just a minute!"*

Sunday answered her by saying, *"Yes Ma'am, and so is the blast of a shotgun, but it destroys everything it hits."*

3. *"Orge"*: This is an abiding and subtle habit of mind, not operative at all times, but

exhibiting itself in the same way when the occasion demands it. This is the word and type of anger used in relationship to Christ.

As would be obvious, under certain conditions the *"orge"* type of anger is a righteous passion to entertain. The Scripture has nothing in common with the Stoic's absolute condemnation of anger. So, as is here obvious, the Scripture permits, and not only permits, but on fit occasions demands it . . . there is a Wrath of God (Mat. 3:7). Who would not love good, unless He hated evil, the two being so inseparable, that either He must do both or neither (Wuest).

Gould says, *"Anger against wrong as wrong, is a sign of moral health."*

Consequently, Godly men and women must rise up in moral indignation at the sin and iniquity which destroy this generation. To not do so portrays an apathy or else ignorance of the true condition of mankind.

However, this righteous anger does <u>not</u> exhibit itself in the killing of doctors who perform abortions, as sinful and wicked as that may be. In other words, it does not become evil in order to oppose evil.

Such righteous anger is expressed in the utterances of the Prophets of the Old Testament and the Apostles of the New. Stephen said, and speaking to the Religious Leaders of his day, *"Ye stiffnecked and uncircumcised in heart and ears, ye do always resist the Holy Ghost: as your fathers did, so do ye."*

He then called them, *"betrayers and murderers"* (Acts 7:51-52).

If that is not righteous anger, I don't know what it is, and, as well, approved by the Holy Spirit! To be sure, His hearers did not take His Words kindly. The Scripture says, *"When they heard these things, they were cut to the heart, and they gnashed on Him with their teeth"* (Acts 7:54).

Most preaching presently little registers any anger, and because it mostly consists of motivation, and actually little of the True Word of God. Such is the sign that the Prophetic and Apostolic voice is silenced.

The phrase, *"Being grieved for the hardness of their hearts,"* means that His anger was tempered by grief. He knew to where it would lead, which was total destruction.

They were trying to defend their self-will, never dreaming that in about thirty-eight years, their nation would be so totally destroyed, that it would actually cease to exist.

What causes *"hardness of heart?"*

Almost without exception, hardness of heart is caused by rejection of the Gospel. This can refer to the unsaved who consistently say *"No"* to the appeal of Christ, or to Believers, so-called, who reject the True Gospel, turning more and more, as these Pharisees, to the false. Such creates a *"hardness of the heart,"* spiritually speaking, because of self-will and self-righteousness.

The *"hardness"* represents itself in their attitude toward the *"man with the withered hand,"* which is a perfect example. They had no regard for him or his needs. They were *"hard"* to true feeling and passion, as all are of this nature.

They would rather see the man's hand remain withered than to be healed by Christ.

Likewise, most who follow in their train, would prefer to see people die lost and go to an eternal hell, rather than be saved watching our Telecast. It is the result of a *"hardened heart."*

The phrase, *"He saith unto the man, Stretch forth thine hand,"* proclaims this being done in full view of all. Consequently, there would be absolutely no doubt as to the miracle which was about to take place.

I wonder what thoughts were in this man's mind, as he stretched forth that withered, shrunken hand and arm, in obedience to the Command of Christ? (The disease probably extended through the whole arm according to the wider meaning of the Greek word here used. It seems to have been a kind of atrophy, causing a gradual drying up of the limb.)

The phrase, *"And he stretched it out: and his hand was restored whole as the other,"* portrays a miracle instantly taking place without Christ even saying a word! The stretching out of the hand and arm was an act of Faith on the part of the man, with the Power of Christ instantly making it whole in front of the eyes of all onlookers. What must their thoughts have been?

One moment they are staring at a withered hand and arm, and the next moment, even in front of their very eyes, they watch it become whole as the other. This is so astounding, that it beggars description! Only God could do such a thing.

As well, this is a perfect picture of the immediate transformation of the believing sinner

upon Faith in Christ. That which is spiritually withered and shrunken, instantly is made *"whole."*

I can see the man as he looks from one hand to the other, hardly believing his own eyes, for this is what the Text means.

The willingness of Jesus to perform this gracious act, is equalled only by His ability to do so.

Now this man can lay brick, or stone, or do any other type of manual labor that is required. Jesus had made him whole! Dake says, *"This demonstrates the Power of God in creation. A creative act was necessary to make a withered hand normal in a moment of time. But this is nothing compared to creating bodies for all the dead in a moment of time, which the Lord will do at the Rapture"* (I Cor. 15:51-58).

"A God Who can do these things can be depended upon to answer the prayers of His people and meet His Own obligation to them according to the Promises" (II Cor. 1:20; II Pet. 1:4).

(6) "AND THE PHARISEES WENT FORTH, AND STRAIGHTWAY TOOK COUNSEL WITH THE HERODIANS AGAINST HIM, HOW THEY MIGHT DESTROY HIM."

The phrase, *"And the Pharisees went forth,"* means they made an immediate exodus, and full of wrath because the Sabbath, they said, was broken, and especially because it was broken by a miracle bringing fame to the alleged transgressor.

The phrase, *"And straightway took counsel with the Herodians against Him,"* means that they had now fully made their decision to oppose Him, and in every way!

This action indicates that they had come to the place that they must either accept His teaching, or they must take steps against Him.

However, what had He done?

The miracle had been wrought by no action on His part whatsoever. He had not even said anything, much less perform some type of labor, etc. Therefore, to get a judgment against Him, claiming He had broken the Sabbath, would be difficult to say the least! Consequently, they seek a meeting with the Herodians, who were their enemies. These individuals were the natural opponents of the Pharisees, and they of them! So what common ground would they have for such a meeting?

Jesus!

Herod the Tetrarch (Lk. 3:19), who also bore the distinctive name of Antipas, had inherited the Galilean and Peraean portions of his father's kingdom. He is the man who imprisoned and executed John the Baptist (Mk. 6:14-28) and was the Herod to whom Jesus was sent, by Pilate for judgment (Lk. 23:7). Jesus is recorded as having once described him as *"that fox"* (Lk. 13:32).

The Herods were not of proper Jewish descent, and were able to stay in power only because of the support of Rome. Consequently, they catered to their Roman patrons by doing everything they could to please them.

In this atmosphere sprang up the party known as the *"Herodians,"* and as is mentioned in this verse. They were a Jewish party who favored the Herodian dynasty. As such, they, as well, were willing to compromise any belief in order to appease Rome. They really had few religious leanings, and were more secular and political than anything else. Consequently, and as would be obvious, they had great influence at court.

The entirety of the lifestyle and belief system of the Herodians threw them into direct antagonism with the Pharisees. Consequently, they hated each other! But in the case of Jesus, they would unite in order to stop Him. The Pharisees no doubt felt that they would need the political assistance of this party to carry out their devious intent.

The phrase, *"How they might destroy Him,"* meant they were planning to kill Him.

It is difficult to imagine those who claim to be of God, and we speak of the Pharisees, and especially that they wore their religion so outwardly, who could be so evil as to plot the murder of a fellow human being, and especially the Christ of Glory. But they did!

Wickedness in any form or variety is awful. However, religious wickedness is the most wicked of all!

(7) "BUT JESUS WITHDREW HIMSELF WITH HIS DISCIPLES TO THE SEA: AND A GREAT MULTITUDE FROM GALILEE FOLLOWED HIM, AND FROM JUDAEA,"

The phrase, *"But Jesus withdrew Himself with His Disciples to the Sea,"* concerns itself somewhat with the hostility of the Pharisees and Herodians, but especially the Pharisees. To be sure, He did not retire because of fear, but that He may continue the Work of God without further confrontation. His purpose was not

NOTES

to confront the Pharisees, even though He was forced to do it repeatedly, but rather to preach, heal, and deliver!

Some have suggested that Jesus was not in Capernaum when the miracle of the withered hand occurred, but elsewhere, due to His now retiring to the Sea. However, while that may be true, still, Mark could well have spoken of Jesus and His Disciples leaving the Synagogue in Capernaum, and going out beside the Lake which He often did.

The phrase, *"And a great multitude from Galilee followed Him, and from Judaea,"* concerns the tremendous number of people who were now being attracted to Jesus because of what He preached, but mostly because of the healings and miracles. It said they *"followed Him,"* and no wonder!

(8) "AND FROM JERUSALEM, AND FROM IDUMAEA, AND FROM BEYOND JORDAN; AND THEY ABOUT TYRE AND SIDON, A GREAT MULTITUDE, WHEN THEY HAD HEARD WHAT GREAT THINGS HE DID, CAME UNTO HIM."

The phrase, *"And from Jerusalem,"* is interesting. The Religious Leadership of Israel resided in this city. That the Name of Jesus was no doubt the topic of every conversation, must have been galling to them.

The phrase, *"And from Idumaea,"* concerned the area south of the Dead Sea, and would have been over a hundred miles from the Sea of Galilee, the area of the Ministry of Christ. Inasmuch as most people had to walk in those days, the journey could have taken upwards of a week. Consequently, they were strongly desirous of seeing Jesus.

The phrase, *"And from beyond Jordan,"* spoke of east of the Jordan River, which would have included Paneas and Decapolis.

The phrase, *"And they about Tyre and Sidon,"* spoke of the twin cities on the Mediterranean, basically occupied by Gentiles.

The phrase, *"A great multitude,"* refers to an exceptionally large crowd. The idea is, that they did not gather in a short period of time, but over a period of several hours, or even two or three days. It took some time for this vast assemblage of thousands to gather.

The phrase, *"When they had heard what great things He did, came unto Him,"* concerned what the entirety of Israel was speaking of, His healings and miracles. John the Beloved said, *"And there are also many other things which Jesus did, the which, if they should be written every one, I suppose that even the world itself could not contain the books that should be written"* (Jn. 21:25).

Consequently, all the miracles He performed are not recorded in the four Gospels. As well, the things He did were so absolutely outstanding, they beggar description.

Not only was every type of loathsome disease healed, with even the dead being raised, but the indication from the Text is that missing limbs were replaced such as arms or fingers, etc. But of course, even that does not compare with one being raised from the dead!

This is what Israel could have had, and the entirety of the world for that matter, but they did not want Him.

Why?

Their deeds were evil, consequently, His Righteousness offended them, and greatly!

They would have rather had sickness and disease than healing and help! They would rather have had poverty than prosperity and plenty! They would rather have hate than love! They would rather have war than peace! They would rather have death than life!

We look back and marvel, and yet, is it any different now?

The peace that passeth all understanding, and which can only be given by Christ, is available to all, but with few takers.

More abundant life is free for the asking, but again, few takers!

The reason is the same now, as it was then.

However, the day is coming, and it's nearer than ever, that Jesus is coming back, then God's Will shall be done on earth, as it is in Heaven.

(9) "AND HE SPAKE TO HIS DISCIPLES, THAT A SMALL SHIP SHOULD WAIT ON HIM BECAUSE OF THE MULTITUDE, LEST THEY SHOULD THRONG HIM."

The phrase, *"And He spake to His Disciples,"* proclaims that which He continues to do unto this hour. As the song says:

"He speaks and the sound of His voice,
"Is so sweet, the birds hush their singing;
"And the melody that He gave to me,
"Within my heart is ringing.
"And He walks with me, and He talks with me,

"And He tells me I am His Own,
"And the joy we share as we tarry there,
"None other has ever known."

The idea is to live so close to Him, that His voice will always be heard. One should ever remember, that He is the only One Who knows the way through the wilderness.

The phrase, *"That a small ship should wait on him because of the multitude,"* speaks of a little rowboat.

There were, no doubt, thousands of people around Him at this time as He walked beside the Lake. In their haste to get to Him, at times He would employ a small boat, and that it should stand off the shore for a short distance, as He used it for a platform and pulpit.

In this instance, He was not actually in the boat, but walking slowly along the shoreline as He spoke to the people, and healed them. The small boat, no doubt manned by a couple of His Disciples, stayed off shore a few yards, slowly moving so as to keep up with Him, and be there if He needed it because of the press of the crowd.

The phrase, *"Lest they should throng Him,"* speaks of the crush of people attempting to get to Him, for healing, etc.

No doubt, His Disciples did the best they could to keep order in the crowd, but, at times, it would get out of hand, hence the small boat.

(10) "FOR HE HAD HEALED MANY; INSOMUCH THAT THEY PRESSED UPON HIM FOR TO TOUCH HIM, AS MANY AS HAD PLAGUES."

The phrase, *"For He had healed many,"* actually means that He healed all who came to Him, which were *"many."* There is no record of anyone leaving not healed, who came for healing!

The phrase, *"Insomuch that they pressed upon Him for to touch Him,"* now tells, at least somewhat, how the healings were brought about.

There was so much power that emanated from His Person, that at these times, anyone who touched Him, was instantly made whole, and irrespective of whatsoever type of disease or plague they had! What this cost Him, no one will really ever know. This much we do know:

When the woman with the *"issue of blood"* touched the hem of His garment, and was immediately healed, He said, *"Who touched Me?"*

Peter remonstrated that many were touching Him. But Jesus replied, *"Somebody hath touched Me: for I perceive that virtue is gone out of Me"* (Lk. 8:43-46).

Why Jesus spoke of this one woman as Luke records, even though many others were touching Him, is not fully known. No doubt, it had something to do with her Faith, as becomes quickly obvious! However, the point is, He felt power leave His Body and go into her.

As Mark records the incident of many touching Him, even throwing themselves against Him, the implication is that all were healed, which must have drained Him physically, which is the point we are attempting to make.

No doubt there were many sick ones in this huge crowd of thousands, with them quickly getting the idea that if they could only touch Him, they would be made whole. The Word, *"pressed upon Him,"* speaks of them literally throwing themselves against Him, to the extent that all decorum was thrown aside.

Sickness is a terrible thing, and a result of the Fall, with the advent of sin as the cause, and instituted by demon spirits. The Giver of Life was now in the midst of men, and, as such, the results of the Fall had to give way, at least for those who would believe. The scene must have been pathetic and glorious at the same time.

The Disciples were frantically attempting to keep some type of order in the crowd, with the sick becoming fearful that they may not have their turn, and then clamoring to get to Him.

On top of that, the joy of those healed would have known no bounds, expressing themselves with loud shouts of praises to God. Especially considering that blinded eyes were opened, deaf ears unstopped, paralyzed limbs instantly healed, as well as every other disease and scourge that one may think.

What a time that was for Israel! What a time it was for the world! And yet they rejected Him, and crucified Him! Such is the wickedness of man.

The phrase, *"As many as had plagues,"* actually means *"scourges"* which were destroying the people. The word, *"scourges,"* reminds us that these things were caused by their sins.

In other words, some of the people, even more than others, were physically ill because of their great sin. Satan had been allowed to scourge them greatly, and had taken advantage of the opportunity to do so. But yet, Jesus healed them

NOTES

all, and irrespective of their spiritual condition, and without a word of condemnation.

Consequently, the question begs to be asked, *"Is it always God's Will to heal the sick?"*

If so, *"Why aren't all Believers healed upon prayer?"*

Even though we have addressed ourselves to these questions elsewhere in these Volumes, due to their significance, perhaps we should briefly allude to them again!

If we take Jesus as the example, and as the only example, then most questions are cleared up immediately:

1. First of all, Jesus healed all who came to Him, without excluding anyone, irrespective of whatever spiritual condition they may have had. In this great crowd, I am positive that many of the people were not living as righteously as they should have, even as the Text brings out! But still, all were treated impartially. Not one time did Jesus say, *"I'm sorry, but your life does not measure up, consequently, I cannot heal you."*

Not only was nothing like that ever said, but actually the opposite was said, at least if we take His actions as any indication, which we certainly should!

2. As well, Jesus never said to a single soul, *"You need to remain sick, because you will live closer to Me if you do so,"* or, *"Your sickness brings Glory to God!"*

All of these excuses, and many more, are constantly used by Preachers, etc. However, there is nothing in the Word of God that lends credence to such a thing. Moreover, it would certainly seem that if such were Scripturally valid, Jesus would have alluded to such, at least a few times. However, He never did!

Consequently, we gather from these things, that it is always God's Will to heal the sick, and irrespective as to whom they may be.

3. Many Preachers claim that it's a lack of Faith on the part of the sick person, that keeps many from being healed.

At times, Jesus did allude to such, by making statements such as, *"If thou canst believe, all things are possible to him that believeth"* (Mk. 9:23). However, every indication is, if they did not have the Faith, He instantly gave it to them, with none being turned away. In other words, He never one time said, *"I'm sorry, you do not have Faith, consequently, I cannot heal you,"* or words to that effect!

So, even though there may be a lack of Faith on the part of the person who needs help, still, even that should not stop the healing.

4. It seems that the only requirement respecting healing, at least as far as Christ was concerned, was that they come to Him. As someone said concerning Salvation, *"All the person has to do to be saved, is to furnish the sinner, and Jesus will furnish the Saviour."* Likewise, it seems that the only requirement for healing was for the person simply to furnish the need, and it was instantly met!

As well, at times the person who was sick didn't even have to show up, with someone else coming in his place. The Bible records this happening several times (Mat. 8:5-10; Mk. 7:24-30).

5. If we use Jesus as an example, as I have already alluded to, the blame for people not being healed who come for healing must be laid at the feet of the one praying for them. We can use any excuse we like, as all of us are prone to do, still, the Biblical evidence is exactly that of which we have stated.

And yet, we must all admit, that no matter how close to God we may be, and no matter how much Faith we think we have, still, none of us even remotely compare to the Lord Jesus Christ. While it is true that we have the Holy Spirit, exactly as He, nevertheless, there was a difference, in that, *"Thy God, hath anointed Thee with the oil of gladness above Thy fellows"* (Ps. 45:7).

As well, John wrote, *"For God giveth not the Spirit by measure unto Him"* (Jn. 3:34).

This means that the Holy Spirit within us, is not in the same measure or degree that He was in Christ.

In view of this, I think it is impossible for the sheep to have the same degree of power as the Shepherd.

Realizing that Jesus said, *"He that believeth on Me, the works that I do shall he do also; and greater works than these shall he do; because I go unto My Father"* (Jn. 14:12), still, He also said, *"The servant is not greater than his Lord; neither he that is sent greater than He that sent him"* (Jn. 13:16).

Consequently, He was speaking of quantity and not quality! Due to modern technology, I can preach one Message over Television at the present, and reach more people with that one Message than Jesus reached in the entirety of His three and a half years of public Ministry.

Thus in quantity, His prediction is fulfilled. However, in quality, *"The servant is not above his Lord!"*

(11) "AND UNCLEAN SPIRITS, WHEN THEY SAW HIM, FELL DOWN BEFORE HIM, AND CRIED, SAYING, THOU ART THE SON OF GOD."

The phrase, *"And unclean spirits,"* says in the Greek, *"The spirits, the unclean ones."*

Some think that demons are the disembodied beings of a pre-Adamic race which inhabited the perfect earth of Genesis 1:1. At that time they were not demons, but created beings serving and worshiping God. However, when Lucifer fell, becoming Satan, the archenemy of God, it seems, along with one-third of the Angels, these beings threw in their lot with the Evil One. In some manner, they then became disembodied, consequently, seeking a person or animal to possess.

These *"unclean spirits,"* although unseen by the natural eye, are the contributors of much of the destruction in the world (Jn. 10:10). Actually, demon spirits, in the background, rule and control entire nations. Hence the starvation, witchcraft, religion, poverty, hatred, and war!

If one were to look into the spirit world, one would see evil spirits as causing every single war that's ever been fought, with either one or both sides heavily controlled by these spirits of destruction. The same can be said for most every other disorder in the world (Rev. 16:12-16).

The phrase, *"When they saw Him,"* means they instantly knew Who He was, the *"Son of God!"* Consequently, they were terrified, and acted accordingly.

However, there is no indication that they had any knowledge of what He would do respecting the Redemption of mankind, which would entail dying on the Cross, etc.

In their ignorance of the Plan of God, they would foment great hatred against Him, using the hearts of the Religious Leaders of Israel, not realizing that this action would ultimately spell their own doom! His Death at Calvary would defeat every power of darkness, as well as satisfying the claims of Heaven.

The phrase, *"Fell down before Him, and cried,"* means they kept on falling down before Him, and kept on constantly crying. They were using the bodies of those they possessed.

The phrase, *"Saying, Thou art the Son of*

God," proclaims their knowledge of Him, that the Father was His Own unique, private Father, in a sense in which He was not the Father of anyone else (Jn. 5:18). As well, this indicates a knowledge by the demons, of the Trinity.

(12) "AND HE STRAITLY CHARGED THEM THAT THEY SHOULD NOT MAKE HIM KNOWN."

The word, "charged," refers to a command such as would be given in the military. This indicates rank.

As a result, and in the ranks of spirit beings, these "unclean spirits" relative to Jesus, the "Son of God," were about the same as an Army private compared to the President of the United States. Actually, even though that is the greatest comparison that one could give in the natural, in the spiritual, which this relates to, it would be far beyond even that! So, whenever He "charged" them, they fell over themselves in order to obey, and instantly!

The phrase, "That they should not make Him known," did not imply that they were wrong in their statement about Him being the "Son of God," but that He wanted no advertisement from this sort. Actually, His attitude toward these spirits was one of total opposition and ultimate subjugation. He would spoil their goods and their house (Mk. 3:27).

The Lord wants all to "make Him known," but not these spirits of darkness, and under any circumstances! He had come to destroy these works of the Devil, and this He would do (I Jn. 3:8).

(13) "AND HE GOETH UP INTO A MOUNTAIN, AND CALLETH UNTO HIM WHOM HE WOULD: AND THEY CAME UNTO HIM."

The phrase, "And He goeth up into a mountain," has Luke saying that He went up into a mountain to pray (Lk. 6:12). Inasmuch as the mountain is not stipulated, it is useless to speculate. However, it must have been one not far from the Sea of Galilee, possibly the one on which the Transfiguration would later take place. He actually spent the entirety of the night in prayer. This is an especially interesting time, the lesson of which must not be lost upon the reader.

Due to the many healings and miracles, great fame had attached itself at this time to Christ. Consequently, there was no lack of followers. Even though it would change a little later, at this time many wanted to be His Disciples.

As He went to this mountain to seek God concerning the all-important selection of the Twelve, no doubt there was a number quite larger than that traveling and associating with Him at that time! Some months later He "appointed other seventy also, and sent them two and two before His face into every city and place, whether He Himself would come" (Lk. 10:1). However, at this time He would concern Himself only with the Twelve.

Considering that He spent the entirety of the night in prayer regarding this all-important selection, this should be, as well, and as stated, a lesson to all of us. Several things unfold before us:

1. Jesus sought the Heavenly Father incessantly concerning leading and direction, which would then be given to Him by the Holy Spirit. It is very obvious that He had a strong prayer life. As He was our Example, likewise, we should follow suit respecting prayer.

2. Inasmuch as He sought His Father all night long about this matter, this should, as well, tell us that some things require more intercession than others.

Regrettably, we are living in an age when intercessory prayer of this nature is almost unheard of. Actually, most, greatly influenced by the "confession message," do not even believe in such, much less practice it! This group, which is large, claim they can confess whatever they need into existence.

First of all, and irrespective of their boasts, they cannot do any such thing, and if they could, it would prove to be disastrous, because of not having the Will of God.

Many of the modern confession principle claim they automatically know the Will of God in any and all matters. One might quickly add that if this is true, then they must be far ahead of Christ, which is a preposterous idea to say the least!

No! There may be such a thing as a "Mc-burger," in the matter of fast food, but there's no such thing as a "Mc-Faith," or "Mc-Prayer!" Sometimes it takes more, much more, than a hurried petition.

3. The Twelve were not chosen respecting their personality, ability, talents, wealth, or eagerness. Each individual was selected by the Holy Spirit, with no man, even Christ, having a say in that selection. Consequently, this was at

least one of the reasons that a night of prayer was needed.

Much of the modern Church world is man-directed, man-guided, and man-instituted. Consequently, that which is man-ordered is not God-ordered, hence, most of that which calls itself *"Church,"* is little more than a meeting of the local Chamber of Commerce, at least as far as the Lord is concerned!

It is tragic that the modern Church knows almost nothing about prayer. Consequently, and as stated, the modern Church is little led by the Holy Spirit.

If the Believer could only realize the tremendous blessings from the Lord which are part of prayer, this all-important privilege would be far more heavily engaged.

In the act of prayer, far more is engaged than merely a request for help, as all-important as that is. The manner in which Jesus prayed, which is, as stated, our example, proclaims that He had total trust in the Heavenly Father, and sought Him accordingly. Consequently, if the modern Church little seeks the Lord, it shows that it little trusts the Lord.

On the way to whatever the Believer is seeking of the Lord, the Holy Spirit takes the occasion to greatly strengthen fellowship between the Heavenly Father and the seeker. In this is a joy unspeakable and full of glory that is almost beyond comprehension. It is a sense of security, well-being, and power, which can only come about through intercessory prayer.

I am constantly asked, or else it is intimated, as to what good is derived from the daily prayer meetings we have been conducting since the Fall of 1991?

The question is asked, because modern Believers, at least for the most part, have been so led astray by false teaching, that if they do not see some great spiritual eruption or outward manifestation of sorts, they feel that intercessory prayer is of little consequence. What they do not realize, evidently, is the tremendous communion and fellowship one has with the Lord in such activity. As well, I might quickly add, that the communion and fellowship of which I speak, can be derived no other way. It is impossible to confess such into existence, neither does it just happen on its own.

Just last night, as Frances and I, along with about twenty others, gathered for prayer

NOTES

(10-28-95), it would be very difficult to relate exactly how I felt. All day long, I had been wrestling with problems concerning the Ministry, respecting finances, as well as other particulars. At these times, spirits of oppression are extremely heavy. Consequently, when I drove to the Church for prayer meeting, my heart was heavy, with many problems seeming to have no solution whatsoever.

I had selected a Passage of Scripture, on which I would speak for about five or ten minutes, as was my usual custom, immediately before we went to prayer; however, just before arriving, the Holy Spirit moved upon my heart respecting another Scripture.

Upon arriving, and greeting our people, I read this particular Text, and began to comment on it. All of a sudden, the Spirit of God began to fall in the room. Hands began to be uplifted in prayer, and the Holy Spirit swept over the place in a way that it would be difficult to describe.

The joy that filled my heart, along with every other person there, could not be purchased with money, could not be given by anyone else, and actually could be obtained in no other way. One moment the troubles and problems pertaining to the Work of God were many, and the next moment there were no problems at all! Wave after wave of Holy Ghost Glory swept the place, as the Lord began to make real His Word to our hearts.

Admittedly, it does not happen this way constantly, but it does happen this way often! As such, not only is there tremendous leading given respecting the Will of God, but Communion and Fellowship with the Lord is enjoined, which draws the Believer ever closer to the bosom of the Heavenly Father. This Work of the Spirit in the life of the Believer is so very, very important, and, in fact, cannot be carried out any other way.

Even as I dictate these words, a lady was recently in our services, the wife of a Pastor from the Midwest. She introduced herself after the service, in which, incidently, the Holy Spirit had moved mightily.

She mentioned that she had been in the city for the past couple of weeks on business, and in the course of time had visited several Churches, of which ours was the last before she would return home the next day.

She said, *"Brother Swaggart, I sensed the Anointing of the Holy Spirit today in a mighty way."*

She said other things, of which I will not relate, but the idea that I wish to stress is, that the Anointing of the Holy Spirit she spoke of, and which had been so evident in the service that Sunday morning, was brought about as a result of intercessory prayer, which can be brought about no other way.

The phrase, *"And calleth unto Him whom He would,"* means those who were called did not have a say in the matter, being selected entirely by Christ, as He was given direction by the Heavenly Father. Once again, this emphasizes that man had absolutely nothing to do with this calling, all being strictly a Work of the Holy Spirit.

The phrase, *"And they came unto Him,"* means that He called out to them, and they stepped out from the larger group.

It is doubtful, at least at this moment, that they understood exactly what He was doing, or why they were being called out. Likewise, most who are called by God, have little understanding at the beginning as to the Plan of God.

The idea that they would judge the Twelve Tribes of Israel forever, and have their names inscribed on the foundations of the New Jerusalem, was something, at least at that time, that they could not have even remotely comprehended (Mat. 19:28; Rev. 21:14). Above that, they would be privileged to stand side by side with Christ for the entirety of His earthly Ministry, which would culminate at Calvary and the Resurrection, where He would redeem mankind.

(14-15) "AND HE ORDAINED TWELVE, THAT THEY SHOULD BE WITH HIM, AND THAT HE MIGHT SEND THEM FORTH TO PREACH,

"AND TO HAVE POWER TO HEAL SICKNESSES, AND TO CAST OUT DEVILS:"

The phrase, *"And He ordained Twelve,"* was for a purpose. *"Twelve"* symbolizes Government, and, more perfectly, the Government of God. It is God's Government versus man's Government, which is symbolized by the choice of the Twelve Tribes of Israel, along with the *"twelve gates"* in the wall of the New Jerusalem, with *"twelve Angels"* at those gates, and with the names of the *"Twelve Tribes of the Children of Israel,"* written on the gates.

NOTES

As well, the wall of the city had *"twelve foundations,"* and in them the *"names of the Twelve Apostles of the Lamb."*

The city is *"twelve thousand furlongs"* in measurement, which is about fifteen hundred miles square, with the foundations garnished by *"twelve types of precious stones."* As well, the *"twelve gates"* were made of *"twelve pearls"* (Rev. 21:12-21).

All of this is meant, and as stated, to express God's Government. Unlike man's Government, it is a Perfect Government.

From this, we should learn that the Government of the world must never be allowed to enter into the Government of the Church. And yet, most Church Government is plagued by man's Government, consequently, with little or none of the Government of the Lord. The Holy Ghost-filled Church does not take its cue from the world; does not get its advice from the world; does not conduct itself according to the world. Consequently, if the world accepts the Church, then it becomes very obvious that the Government of God is not ruling in that particular Church.

The word, *"ordained,"* means to *"appoint,"* or to *"choose."* It is a calling to a specific work, and is done by the Lord and not man.

Whenever God calls a man or woman to preach the Gospel, and for a specific work as here designated, that is actually the only ordination that counts. Man cannot give this *"ordination,"* and man cannot take it away. All man can do is recognize that which God has already done, which sadly is not too often the case! Man generally only recognizes what he has *"ordained,"* which, in turn, will not be recognized by God.

This system of man-control was already rearing its ugly head in the Early Church. Some were demanding of the Apostle Paul that he produce his letter of *"commendation"* or *"ordination."* His answer to them was revealing:

"Do we begin again to commend ourselves? or need we, as some others, Epistles of commendation to you, or letters of commendation from you?

"Ye are our Epistle written in our hearts, known and read of all men:"

He then went on to say, *"Forasmuch as ye are manifestly declared to be the Epistle of Christ ministered by us, written not with ink, but with the Spirit of the Living God; not in tables of stone, but in fleshly tables of the heart."*

He then said, *"But our sufficiency* (ordination) *is of God"* (II Cor. 3:1-5).

In other words, Paul was saying that the proof of his credentials or *"ordination,"* was not in a piece of paper that some man had given him, but rather the fruit of his calling, which translated into souls.

Sadly and regrettably, most of the modern Ministry, to prove their ordination, can only produce a card from a particular Religions Denomination. The true proof, and, in fact, the only proof that God will accept, is the fruit of souls won to Christ, which will always accompany a True Ordination.

The phrase, *"That they should be with Him,"* was the secret of all that the Disciples would ever do for the Kingdom of God. It is the secret no less today.

Actually, the Disciples were not only to be with Christ, they were to be with Him constantly!

If the following is to be proclaimed in the life and Ministry of the Preacher, being with Christ Alone will bring it about.

Most Preachers are with Religious Denominations, family, or personal interests, but few are with Christ.

As a result of being called by Him, and being *"with Him,"* the following is what Christ would do:

1. *"And that He might send them forth to preach":* Preaching was their actual mission, even though the power to heal the sick and cast out devils would be given. However, the healing and delivering must not overpower the preaching, because it is from the *"preaching"* that the other is derived.

Please notice that He was to send them, and not some Religious Denomination, etc. In fact, if the Church of that day, which obviously was comprised of the Religious Leaders of Israel, had had their way, they would have stopped them immediately. Consequently, the God-called Preacher will fight the battle most of his life, of whether he is to be controlled by God or man. That struggle is pretty much an unending struggle.

I am <u>not</u> saying that one associated with a Religious Denomination, cannot, at the same time, be led of the Lord. In fact, some are led exclusively by the Lord in these situations.

However, almost invariably, Religious Denominations seek to control men. Quite possibly, many of them do not begin that way, but almost, if not all, conclude in that manner.

So, the Preacher affiliated with a Religious Denomination, must ever be cognizant of the fact that the Word of God must be obeyed at all times, and irrespective of how small the matter may seem to be. God must ever take precedent over man.

This does not mean that one should not solicit the advice and counsel of others of like Faith, but it does mean that the Holy Spirit, and irrespective of the advice and counsel of others, has the final say.

Any time a controlling spirit comes into men (a desire to control others), one can be sure that it's not of God, and, consequently, should be resisted strongly. And yet, at the same time, every action must be judged by all respecting its Scriptural validity. It is the responsibility of every Minister of the Gospel, as well as every Believer, to apply Scripture to any and all situations. If it is not Scriptural, it is not of God (I Cor. 14:24, 32-33).

Again we emphasize that Jesus sent these individuals, and not man. The indication is that wherever they went, He designated the place or places they were to go.

The idea is that the Preacher of the Gospel is to seek the Face of the Lord incessantly concerning direction. He is not to be sent anywhere by any man unless he first has the direction of the Holy Spirit that this is the place the Lord desires that he go. Regrettably, most Preachers are occupying pulpits, because they were sent there by man. However, unless the Lord sends one, the Lord will not bless one!

This is where Religious Denominations too often, little by little, take on an authority that is not theirs. In the desire to control, they want to tell the Preacher <u>where</u> he can preach. As well, they want to tell him <u>who</u> can preach for him. Little by little, they also desire to tell Preachers <u>what</u> to preach. Therefore, such action must be resisted at all times, which means that if a Preacher of the Gospel is truly called of God, he will find it very difficult, if not impossible, to remain in some Religious Denominations or Churches. As stated, the battle for control goes on constantly. Either the Lord controls the man, or man controls the man.

Both cannot! If man controls, God will not, and if God controls, man cannot!

However, control exercised by the Holy Spirit will always be that which is freely given to Him by the Believer. He will never coerce, threaten, or force His Way into the life of anyone. The Believer is exhorted, *"Be filled with the Spirit"* (Eph. 5:18), and could well be translated, *"Be controlled by the Spirit."*

However, the Believer is not automatically controlled by the Spirit just because the Spirit indwells him. The control which the Spirit exerts over the Believer is dependent upon the Believer's active and corrective adjustment to the Spirit.

The Lord Jesus did not save us until we recognized Him as the Saviour and put our trust in Him for Salvation. Consequently, the Holy Spirit does not control us in the sense of permeating our will, reason, and emotions, until we recognize Him as the One Who has been sent by the Father to sanctify our lives, and trust Him to perform His Ministry in and through us.

There must be an ever-present conscious dependence upon and definite subjection to the Holy Spirit, a constant yielding to His Ministry and leaning upon Him for guidance and power, if He is to control the Believer in the most efficient manner and with the largest and best results.

Even though the Lord is the One Who sends, nevertheless, it is through the Agency and Person of the Holy Spirit which He does this. So, the more fullness of the Spirit in a person's life, the greater control and the greater leading.

In St. John 7:37-38, Jesus lays down two simple requirements for the fullness of the Spirit: A. Thirst for His control; and, B. Trust in the Lord Jesus for the Spirit's control.

"If any man thirst," refers to a desire on the part of the Believer that the Holy Spirit be the One to control his every thought, word, and deed. We do not take a drink of water unless we are thirsty. We do not appropriate the control of the Spirit unless we desire Him to control us. A desire for His control will include, among other things, a desire that He calls us to judge sin in our lives, a desire that He put sin out of our lives and keep it out, a desire that He separate us from all the ties we might have with that system of evil called the world, a desire that He dethrone our self-life and enthrone the Lord

Jesus as absolute Lord and Master, a desire that He produce in us His Own fruit, a desire that He make us Christlike, a desire that He lead us and teach us.

Such a desire is a serious thing. It involves crucifixion of self, and self dies hard. The Spirit-controlled life is a crucified life. The other requirement is trust.

Our Lord said, *"He that believeth on Me, out from His inmost being shall flow rivers of living water."* The trust here in this context is not only trust in Him as Saviour, but trust in Him as the One Who fills with the Spirit. The Spirit-controlled life is, therefore, a matter of Trust. Salvation is by Faith. We received our Justification by Faith. We are to receive our Sanctification by Faith. It is this constant desire for the Spirit's control and a trust in the Lord Jesus for the Spirit's control that results in the Spirit-controlled life. When one faces a new day, it is well to include in our prayers thanksgiving for the Presence of the Holy Spirit in our hearts, the expression of our desire for His control, and a definite assertion of our trust in the Lord Jesus for the Spirit's control during that day.

It is well at intervals during the day when we are faced with temptation or when we have a definite work of Christian service to perform, or are in need of instruction from the Word, or of strength for some duty, to recognize quietly the Ministry of the Spirit and depend upon Him for all needed guidance, wisdom, and strength. He is waiting for us to recognize Him and trust Him for His aid. He is there, the indwelling Spirit, always at the service of the Believer. But the point is that He comes to our aid when we avail ourselves of His help. He is a perfect Gentleman at all times, and will never exert control, take control, or force Himself. Consequently, and as stated, there are just two things therefore which the Believer must do in order to be controlled by the Spirit, desire that control and trust the Lord Jesus for that control.

As well, this is not for Preachers only, but for every single Believer, and irrespective as to who that Believer may be. The idea that the Holy Spirit is needed only by one who is engaged in some type of Christian service, is erroneous to say the least. That idea may possibly come from the Old Testament Ministry of the Holy Spirit. Before Pentecost, the Holy Spirit came upon Believers in order to equip them for a certain work they were to do for God, and left them when that service was over. However, every Believer can now be filled with the Spirit and, actually, is admonished to be so. That is God's Plan for every Christian life, in that it should be a life constantly, consciously, and definitely subjected to the Spirit, a life that has a consuming desire for His control over every thought, word, and deed, thus a life unceasingly controlled by the Holy Spirit.

In this context, one could probably say that it is a sin not to be filled constantly with the Spirit. Actually, the words, *"Be filled with the Spirit"* (Eph. 5:18), are a command and not a request. Failure to obey any Command of Scripture is sin.

(The thoughts concerning the leading and operation of the Holy Spirit in one's life were derived from the teaching of Greek Scholar Kenneth Wuest.)

2. *"And to have power to heal sicknesses"*: This is a powerful statement, but needs some understanding.

The word, *"power,"* as here translated, is the Greek word *"exousia,"* which means *"delegated authority."* Consequently, it does not mean that God puts His supernatural power into the hands of the Twelve to be exercised by them. What He did do, was delegate to them the authority to cast out demons in the sense that they would speak the word declaring the casting out, and God's Power would effect the work. Regrettably, this is where some Pentecostals and Charismatics miss it. We tend to have it in our minds that the *"power"* is ours, and in a sense to do with as we like. Nothing could be further from the truth!

Too oftentimes such thinking results in such Preachers, who once may have had this power, but no longer do, continuing to exercise it within their own abilities. The power of suggestion, psychological gimmicks, with even the edge of witchcraft being skirted, now become the *"gimmick."* To run the charade out to its conclusion, Believers are oftentimes told they are healed of diseases they never even knew they had, or told to confess their healing to all and sundry, even though there is no evidence of it. Thank God all who pray for the sick do not function in that capacity, but many do! And, I might quickly add, far too many Believers have such little Biblical foundation, that they little know

the false from the real. Nevertheless, Jesus Christ continues to heal the sick for those who will dare to believe Him.

The *"power"* granted, is strictly a work of Grace on the part of the Lord, delegating such to the humble heart and life. The continued understanding of this Truth is absolutely imperative, if He is to continue to use us.

3. *"And to cast out devils"*: The word, *"devils,"* should have been translated *"demons,"* because there is actually only one Devil, but many demons. As well, Satan and demons are actually two different categories of beings. Satan is a fallen angel, whereas demon spirits are not in the angelic category. As previously stated, many believe, as this writer, that these spirits of darkness come from a pre-Adamic creation which fell with Lucifer in his revolution against God (Isa. 14:12-15; Ezek. 28:11-19).

Even though we have already alluded to the following, please allow us the latitude of addressing it once again, especially in lieu of its significance.

As is obvious, it is mentioned over and over again in the four Gospels of the tremendous demon activity in Israel during the time of Christ. Constantly, it mentions that Jesus *"cast out demons."*

In the Epistles, there was definitely demon activity, which was addressed by the Apostles, but not nearly to the degree as in the four Gospels.

Why?

Most of the Ministry conducted by the Apostles, which included Paul, was conducted outside of Israel. These areas were definitely controlled by demon spirits, still, they were different types of spirits, such as immorality, idol worship, etc.

As for Israel, the nation was infested with, and controlled by religious spirits, who hated Christ with a passion, and for the obvious reasons. Even though these other spirits mentioned hated the Work of God, and definitely caused problems, nevertheless, it was not near the hatred or the resultant activity, as religious spirits. Consequently, Jesus faced them constantly, as did the Apostles when ministering in Israel.

Consequently, it is very difficult for people who are steeped in religion, which includes the far greater majority of *"Christianity,"* to be brought to a saving knowledge of Jesus Christ.

They are made to believe by these religious spirits, who they don't even know exist, that they are already saved, and, in fact, have the true way of Salvation. They are blind and deceived, and, as a result, cannot see their true spiritual condition, which is one of spiritual darkness.

This is the basic reason that the greatest opposition to the True Church of Jesus Christ is the apostate Church. This is the reason the Religious Leaders of Israel crucified Christ. Consequently, these individuals, whomever they may be, instigated and prompted by religious spirits, will, as well, attempt to crucify all who truly follow Christ.

As well, it is the task and responsibility of all True Believers to function in the Ministry of deliverance.

To be sure, the Lord is the One Who does the *"calling,"* the *"sending,"* and the *"giving"* of power to carry forth His Work. However, He will use every single Believer, at least in some capacity, who will dare to step out in Faith claiming His Promises.

Years ago, while in a Midwestern city in a Crusade, a lady approached me one night after service, and related as to how the Lord had saved her and Baptized her in the Holy Spirit. If I remember correctly, she stated that she had been Presbyterian all her life, when one day she came to the realization, and by the convicting power of the Holy Spirit, that she really had not previously had Salvation, but only religion. As a result, she gave her heart to Christ, and was shortly Baptized with the Holy Spirit, with the evidence of speaking with other tongues (Acts 2:4).

She went on to relate how that almost immediately the Lord began to use her in the very Ministry of which we are speaking, the *"casting out of demons."* However, it had come about in a rather odd way.

Being a lay person and not a Minister of the Gospel, and a woman as well, she was quite unprepared for that which the Lord was about to do.

However, feeling this burden for those who were bound by spirits of darkness, and especially in the realm of witchcraft, drugs, alcohol, immorality, etc., she began to invite them to prayer meetings, etc. Amazingly enough, they began to come!

At the outset, she did not pray for them herself, and because she felt that she really was not

NOTES

capable or qualified to do so. Consequently, she found three or four pastors in the city who believed that Jesus answered prayer, and that He was still in the business of deliverance. (It's sad, when in any given city, only a few Preachers actually believe the Bible.)

She would call one or more of these Preachers at these particular times, and they would come and lay hands on these people, and the Lord effected some great deliverances.

However, on one particular night, and with a desperate situation at hand concerning a young man, she called all four of the Pastors, but found none of them available. Looking at the young man who was obviously demon possessed, and with the others who were praying with her, she did not really know what to do.

Very quietly she whispered a prayer to the Lord asking for guidance, when He gently suggested to her, that even though the particular Preachers were not available, He was!

She went on to say how His gentle rebuke jarred her to her senses. And then the Lord quietly spoke to her again, telling her that this power was not given only to Preachers, but to any Believer (Mk. 16:17).

With that great Truth dawning on her, she instantly stepped forward and laid her hand on the young man.

She went on to say how she shouted out the Name of Jesus, and instantly this boy was delivered from the powers of darkness. With a smile, she said, *"Brother Swaggart, I don't have to call anyone now, and the Lord is doing great things, using this handmaiden!"*

Yes, He was using her, and, yes, He will use anyone who will dare to believe Him!

(16-19) "AND SIMON HE SURNAMED PETER;

"AND JAMES THE SON OF ZEBEDEE, AND JOHN THE BROTHER OF JAMES; AND HE SURNAMED THEM BOANERGES, WHICH IS, THE SONS OF THUNDER:

"AND ANDREW, AND PHILIP, AND BARTHOLOMEW, AND MATTHEW, AND THOMAS, AND JAMES THE SON OF ALPHAEUS, AND THADDAEUS, AND SIMON, THE CANAANITE,

"AND JUDAS ISCARIOT, WHICH ALSO BETRAYED HIM: AND THEY WENT INTO AN HOUSE."

Some of these, as we shall see, were given

added names by the Lord, with the others not mentioned accordingly.

1. To *"Simon,"* Jesus added the name of *"Peter."* It means *"a stone,"* which presently had reference to that which, as is obvious, Peter was not, but which the Lord would make of him. What a blessing it is to read this, knowing that the Lord can change one in such a manner that it is the total opposite of what one once was.

This is what Jesus was speaking of when He said in Matthew 16:18, *"As for you, you are Petros (a fragment of rock), and upon this Petra (Jesus, a massive living rock), I will build My Church."*

So, Jesus, by giving Simon the name of *"Peter,"* was actually saying to him, *"I will make of you a rock-like man, dependable, immovable, and equal to the emergencies and crises that confront you."*

2. James and John, as Peter, were surnamed *"Boanerges,"* which means, *"Sons of thunder."* It was intended, as Peter, to be a title of honor, although it was not perpetuated like the surname Peter.

The name suggested their impetuosity and zeal which characterized both the brothers (Wuest).

Christ would take the natural dispositions of these men, elevate them by His Grace, which would channel this fiery zeal into the proclamation of the Gospel.

Actually, John the Beloved was called *"the thunder-voiced."* This may have been after his death, and due to the visions he saw, which included the *"thunders,"* and resulted in the Book of Revelation.

However, it could also have had an earlier meaning referring to his manner of preaching, which well could have been with power and authority.

It is interesting that Jesus selected the three, Peter, James, and John, as recipients of these surnames, who alone would share great intimate experiences with Christ, even apart from the remainder of the Twelve.

3. *"Andrew"*: This name means *"manly."*

4. *"Philip"*: This name means *"fond of horses,"* and in Ecclesiastical legend he is said to have been a *"chariot-driver."*

5. *"Bartholomew"*: This is Nathanael, of whom we first read in John 1:46, as having been found by Philip and brought to Christ.

6. *"Matthew"*: This name means *"a gift of*

God," with the meaning of His name truly being brought to pass in that he was selected to this all-important Twelve.

7. *"Thomas"*: This name means *"twin."*

8. *"James, the son of Alphaeus"*: He is not the same as the other *"James"* listed above, which should be obvious, and neither is he the half-brother of Jesus. His name, as the other James, in the Hebrew, means *"Jacob."* He is thought to have been a brother to Judas (not Iscariot), Matthew, and Simon Zelotes. If, in fact, that is correct, he would have been a member of four brothers selected by Christ as His chosen Disciples, as well as the two brothers, James and John, and the two brothers, Peter and Andrew.

9. *"Thaddaeus"*: He is the same as Judas of John 14:22 (not Iscariot). Martin Luther called him the *"good Judas."*

10. *"Simon the Canaanite"*: His name is properly called, *"Simon, the Canaanaean."* As well, he was called *"Simon the Zealot,"* which meant that he had formerly been connected with one of the fierce war-parties of that day, dedicated to the overthrow of Rome respecting the occupation of Israel. As well, his life would be gloriously changed.

11. *"Judas Iscariot"*: This man was born in Kerioth, which is a small town mentioned in Joshua 15:25, and was one of the uttermost cities of Judah toward the coast of Edom southward. In this town was born the betrayer of the Saviour, and, as well, was the only one of the group who was of the Tribe of Judah, as Christ.

The phrase, *"And they went into an house,"* probably referred to Peter's house in Capernaum. Once again, as the following verses proclaim, they would be besieged by those needing healing and deliverance.

(20) "AND THE MULTITUDE COMETH TOGETHER AGAIN, SO THAT THEY COULD NOT SO MUCH AS EAT BREAD."

The phrase, *"And the multitude cometh together again,"* refers to the people in Capernaum hearing that Jesus was here once again, which would result in scores coming for healing, or for whatever purpose.

The phrase, *"So that they could not so much as eat bread,"* proclaims the impossibility of even carrying on the necessary affairs of life. They could not even eat!

There were many reasons for the gathering

of these tremendous crowds, but probably the greatest reason was that every single person that came to Christ for healing or deliverance, received exactly what they came for. Some twenty-three times it is stated that He healed them all.

So mighty were His works that Christ drew vast multitudes even out in the desert places where men would go willingly for days without food to hear Him and to be healed by Him (Mat. 14:13-21; 15:29-39).

Twice on such occasions He fed the hungry multitudes with food miraculously multiplied as He *"blessed, and brake, and gave"* (Mat. 14:15-21; 15:32-38 - Dake).

(21) "AND WHEN HIS FRIENDS HEARD OF IT, THEY WENT OUT TO LAY HOLD ON HIM: FOR THEY SAID, HE IS BESIDE HIMSELF."

The phrase, *"And when His friends heard of it,"* spoke of His immediate relatives, such as His mother and brothers, as verse 31 proclaims.

Of course, His family had heard of the massive crowds, the healings and miracles, and great deliverances. This was the talk of all of Israel. However, what prompted them to make this journey from Nazareth to Capernaum, a distance of approximately thirty miles, and by foot at that, was, no doubt, the tremendous animosity being stirred up against Christ by the Religious Leaders of Israel. As the next verse proclaims, they were accusing Him of performing these mighty miracles and casting out demon spirits by the power of Satan. Fearful of what this animosity would lead to, they came apparently to talk Him into returning to Nazareth with them, and ceasing His Ministry.

The phrase, *"They went out to lay hold on Him,"* means they intended to stop Him, even by using force and against His Will, if necessary!

The phrase, *"For they said, He is beside Himself,"* means they actually felt He was insane.

Their concern for His welfare is not doubted; however, other factors were involved as well!

First of all, John said, *"Even His brethren did not believe on Him"* (Jn. 7:5). In other words, they did not believe, at least at this stage, that He was the Messiah, and really could give little explanation as to the source of His great power. It was all an enigma to them, not being able to put it together, in that the older Brother they knew, they could not equate with what was now happening!

NOTES

Such is not meant to impugn His life before His Ministry, in that it was perfect before man and God. Still, He exhibited no miraculous powers during this time of some thirty years, and how was it that He was now able to do all of these miraculous things?

There is no hint that Mary, His Mother, joined in with the unbelief registered by His brothers. She was here on this day because she was truly concerned about His welfare.

And yet, it is doubtful that she fully understood all the things which were happening. Of course, His miraculous conception was, no doubt, constantly in her mind. As well, what the great Angel Gabriel had said to her was ever before her; *"He shall be great, and shall be called the Son of the Highest: and the Lord God shall give unto Him the Throne of His father David:*

"And He shall reign over the house of Jacob for ever; and of His Kingdom there shall be no end" (Lk. 1:32-33).

She had written down these words, and had, beyond doubt, memorized them, quoting them to herself over and over again.

Also, she no doubt remembered very well the words given to her by the Holy Spirit when she came to Elizabeth, the soon-to-be mother of John the Baptist. These Words extolled what God had done, and would do, which all pertained to this miracle child which she carried in her womb (Lk. 1:46-55).

I think without a doubt, she knew Who He was, and that He was the Messiah. And yet, as a Mother, and especially His Mother, she grieved in her heart at the anger and animosity that were fastly building in Israel against Him, remembering the words that were uttered in the Temple by Simeon concerning the Child, and, as well, of her, *"Yea, a sword shall pierce through thy own soul also!"* (Lk. 2:35).

Fearful of what might come, and, in fact, which did come, she was here this day, because she hoped that somehow something could be done that would cool the burning hatred toward her Son, and, above all, God's Son!

As stated, there is almost no evidence that she thought He was *"beside Himself,"* as was thought by His half-brothers!

(22) "AND THE SCRIBES WHICH CAME DOWN FROM JERUSALEM SAID, HE HATH BEELZEBUB, AND BY THE PRINCE OF THE DEVILS CASTETH HE OUT DEVILS."

The phrase, *"And the Scribes which came down from Jerusalem,"* proclaims these individuals as evidently being sent by the Sanhedrin in order to watch Him, and, thereby, to find something in which they could undermine His influence.

The evidence as to Who He is, presents an overwhelming case, not only to the Religious Leaders of Israel, but to the entirety of the world for that matter!

As to the fact that such a person as Jesus of Nazareth flourished in the first century A. D., there is hardly any dispute today. Actually, there is far more proof that Jesus lived, even than Julius Caesar.

And yet, concerning the writings of the first century, there isn't much said about Him by the secular historians. There is a reason for that:

He was born in an obscure part of the Roman Empire. Israel was far removed from Rome, with few secular historians noting anything of this region.

As well, He was not a person of high birth, at least as far as the world was concerned, although His lineage was in the royal line of David. However, that dynasty was not in power then, nor had it been in power for about 600 years. So, that historians did not take note of a peasant (for that's what Jesus was) of a province far removed from Rome, is not without understanding.

Even though we think today of His Crucifixion marking Him as the subject of an outstanding event, still, from the standpoint of the first century it was a common event. The Roman roads were literally lined with crosses upon which victims writhed in agony until death put an end to their struggles.

As well, His claiming Deity for Himself, which He did, was anything but uncommon. The Roman Emperors claimed to be divine, and required their subjects to worship them. Other officials (Herod, for example) deified themselves. Thus, the secular historians of the first century took little notice of Jesus of Nazareth, and for the obvious reasons. However, He was not totally ignored, as we shall see.

Josephus, the Jewish historian, was born in 37 A. D. His works were accepted by the Imperial Library of Rome, and he had this to say about Jesus:

"Now there was about this time, Jesus, a wise

man, if it be lawful to call Him a man, for He was a doer of wonderful works, a teacher of such men as received the truth with pleasure. He drew over to Him both many of the Jews and many of the Gentiles. He was (the) *Christ; and when Pilate, at the suggestion of the principle men among us, had condemned Him to the Cross, those who loved Him at the first did not forsake Him, for He appeared to them alive again the third day, as the Divine Prophets had foretold these and ten thousand other wonderful things concerning Him; and the tribe of Christians so named after Him is not extinct at this day"* (Antiquities of the Jews, by Josephus, Book 18, Chapter 3, Paragraph 3).

Tacitus, a Roman historian, lived during the first century. His high character as an historian is generally conceded. He wrote about Jesus of Nazareth in the following words, which are most informative, especially considering the attitude of the Roman Empire towards Jesus and Christianity. He spoke of Nero who burned Rome, and then attempted to place the blame on the Christians. He said, *"Nero caused others to be accused, on whom he inflicted exquisite torments, who were already hated by the people for their crimes, and were commonly called Christians. This name they derived from Christ their leader, Who in the reign of Tiberius was put to death as a criminal, while Pontius Pilate was procurator."*

Suetonius, another Roman historian who lived in the first century, said, *"He* (Claudius) *banished the Jews from Rome who were continually raising disturbances, Christ* (Chrestus) *being their leader."*

Even though the statements given by these Roman Historians, which others we could name, were not positive, still, they admitted to His existence.

Among all the other proofs of His Deity, it must be understood that Jesus of Nazareth was much more than just a man, for His followers must have been convinced of that fact, for many willingly suffered a horrible martyrdom for their testimony to His Deity. Thousands upon thousands of people do not go to a violent death for something they know or suspect is a fraud.

One cannot explain the willing acceptance of Jesus of Nazareth as Saviour by a sin-loving pagan who accepted with Him that which he formerly hated, namely, Righteousness, and by that forsook his sin which he loved, knowing that by so doing he would be liable to capital punishment for his act, except upon the basis of a supernatural working in his heart, providing for the willing acceptance of that which he formerly hated, Righteousness.

Jesus of Nazareth therefore stands as history's outstanding enigma, unless He is accorded the place which the Bible gives Him, Very God of Very God.

One cannot explain Him without this fact of His Deity. One can dismiss Him with an *"I do not believe that,"* but that does not solve the problem nor blot Him from the pages of history. He stands there, astride the world of mankind, a unique individual, God and Man in One Person.

As well, it must be considered that of all the founders of religions of this world, including Islam, Buddhism, Confucianism, etc., Jesus of Nazareth stands Alone in asserting that He was God, and in accepting the worship of individuals.

The phrase, *"Said, He hath Beelzebub,"* actually meant that Beelzebub had Him, and was using Him as his agent. Wuest says, *"The expression points to something more than an alliance, as in Matthew, to possession, and that on a grand scale: a divine possession by a base deity doubtless, god of flies* (Beelzebub) *or god of dung* (Beelzebul), *still a god, a sort of Satanic incarnation."*

Consequently, the accusation of these Religious Leaders was serious indeed, so serious in fact that they blasphemed the Holy Spirit, thus dooming themselves for time and eternity.

The phrase, *"And by the prince of the devils casteth He out devils,"* presented these Religious Leaders accusing Jesus of casting out demons by the help of Satan, i.e., *"Prince of Devils."* They were trying to break the force of the attesting power of the miracles performed by Jesus, and done in the energy of the Holy Spirit. If, of course, this could be done, it would disprove His claims to Messiahship. Consequently, they attributed the Works of God to the Devil, which Jesus labeled as *"blasphemy against the Holy Ghost"* (vs. 29).

Why did they do this?

They rejected Him and His claims because of sin in their lives, sin, incidentally, of which they would not repent, and by reason of their entrenched ecclesiasticism which would allow

NOTES

no interference with its position. It would be well to remember that here the testimony to the effect that Jesus claimed Deity in these exchanges (Jn. 10:20-30), did not come from His followers, but from the ranks of the opposition.

His family pronounced Him a lunatic (vs. 21), and the Scribes declared Him a demoniac. Thus the natural heart judged the Lord of Glory!

(23) "AND HE CALLED THEM UNTO HIM, AND SAID UNTO THEM IN PARABLES, HOW CAN SATAN CAST OUT SATAN?"

The phrase, *"And He called them unto Him,"* means that He called these *"Scribes"* close to Him, in order that He might answer their accusation.

The manner in which the language is constructed, tells us that He was not in the least bit awed by their alleged scholarly claims. In fact, there is a slight note of contempt in that which He did!

The phrase, *"And said unto them in parables,"* refers to Him using illustrations which would not only be easily understood by them, but also by all who stood nearby. This was done for a purpose.

The Scribes generally taught with an air of superiority, talking down to the people, and in terminology that was little understood. Jesus did the very opposite!

The question, *"How can Satan cast out Satan?"*, declares the impossibility of such ludicrousness. Wuest said, *"Our Lord's argument is briefly; — granted for the moment that spirits may be cast out by the aid of other spirits, which they cannot! More is needed in the latter than superior strength. There must be a motive, and Satan would have no desire to operate against himself."*

(24) "AND IF A KINGDOM BE DIVIDED AGAINST ITSELF, THAT KINGDOM CANNOT STAND."

This is the first of three illustrations which will be given by Christ respecting the absurdity proposed by the Scribes.

In essence, Jesus is saying that it should be obvious to all, that a kingdom warring within itself will ultimately destroy itself. Consequently, if Satan is busily engaged in placing spirits of darkness into people, then for him at the same time, to cast those spirits out, would be absurd! He would destroy himself, and, to be sure, he will not do that!

(25) AND IF A HOUSE BE DIVIDED AGAINST ITSELF, THAT HOUSE CANNOT STAND."

Internal fighting respecting a family, will ultimately lead to the destruction of that family, as was obvious to all who stood nearby, including the Scribes. So, the family of Satan is not warring against itself, as the Scribes should know!

(26) "AND IF SATAN RISE UP AGAINST HIMSELF, AND BE DIVIDED, HE CANNOT STAND, BUT HATH AN END."

So, and as Jesus continues, the third illustration proposes that if the *"kingdom"* and *"house"* were to war internally against themselves, as they would be obviously destroyed, likewise, Satan would come to the same *"end."*

So, their accusation and claim are preposterous!

(27) "NO MAN CAN ENTER INTO A STRONG MAN'S HOUSE, AND SPOIL HIS GOODS, EXCEPT HE WILL FIRST BIND THE STRONG MAN; AND THEN HE WILL SPOIL HIS HOUSE."

The phrase, *"No man can enter into a strong man's house,"* refers to Satan as a *"strong man."*

However, even though he is *"strong,"* nevertheless, Jesus is much *"stronger,"* because He is able to enter into this house of evil, and there is nothing that can be done about it. This is proved by Jesus casting out the demons. If Satan could have stopped Him, he would have done so. However, by his not doing so, proves that he simply does not have the power.

The phrase, *"And spoil his goods,"* means that not only will He enter Satan's domain of darkness, but, as well, He will destroy his kingdom, *"spoil his goods."*

Satan's *"goods"* are sin, bondage, poverty, sickness, ignorance, superstition, error, and the lie. Jesus has spoiled all of this, as the Scripture says, *"For this purpose the Son of God was manifested, that He might destroy the works of the Devil"* (I Jn. 3:8).

The phrase, *"Except He will first bind the strong man,"* means that Satan is rendered defenseless in the face of Christ, and is unable to protect his kingdom of darkness. Jesus did this by His Power, and especially at the Cross of Calvary.

As a result, when Jesus cried on the Cross, *"It is finished,"* He, in effect, was saying, *"Sin*

NOTES

is finished!" "Bondage is finished!" "Poverty is finished!" "Ignorance is finished!" "Satan is finished!"

The phrase, *"And then He will spoil his house,"* has reference to two things:

1. It speaks of the Gospel of Jesus Christ proclaimed by God-called Preachers, and, in effect, by every Believer, which spoils Satan's house. Lives are changed! Sick bodies are healed! Bondages are broken! And Believers are Baptized in the Holy Spirit!

2. Even though Satan, along with his minions of darkness, is a defeated foe, still, he is allowed to continue by the Lord on a limited basis, which has now lasted for about 2,000 years. However, very soon Jesus Christ will come back, and at that time Satan will be locked away in a bottomless pit, along with all his forces of darkness (Rev. 20:1-3). Then Satan's house will be effectively spoiled!

(28-29) "VERILY I SAY UNTO YOU, ALL SINS SHALL BE FORGIVEN UNTO THE SONS OF MEN, AND BLASPHEMIES WHEREWITH SOEVER THEY SHALL BLASPHEME:

"BUT HE THAT SHALL BLASPHEME AGAINST THE HOLY GHOST HATH NEVER FORGIVENESS, BUT IS IN DANGER OF ETERNAL DAMNATION:"

The phrase, *"Verily I say unto you,"* presents a change of tone in Jesus' response. Heretofore, He had reasoned with the Scribes, but now takes a more commanding tone. What He will speak of will be the most serious thing in which a person can engage themselves.

The phrase, *"All sins shall be forgiven unto the sons of men, and blasphemies wherewith soever they shall blaspheme,"* presents a glorious and wonderful promise. These *"sins and blasphemies"* include every vile thing that can be thought of, such as murder, rape, treason, incest, homosexuality, adultery, hate, pride, etc. However, an addendum will be added to this statement that must be seriously heeded.

The phrase, *"But he that shall blaspheme against the Holy Ghost hath never forgiveness,"* constitutes a chilling thought to say the least! It means that the sin is an eternal sin, which cannot be forgiven, which means the sinner is bound by a chain of sin from which he can never be loosed. Consequently, Jesus said to some of the Pharisees, *"Therefore your sin remaineth,"* i.e., meaning these Pharisees could not be forgiven, because they would not be forgiven (Jn. 9:41).

The word, *"blaspheme,"* is here used concerning the Holy Spirit, but does not speak of all sin. Actually, any and all sin, and irrespective of its nature, is, in effect, a sin against God the Holy Spirit, as it is against God the Son, or God the Father. However, the word, *"blaspheme,"* as it applies to the Holy Spirit, means to *"speak reproachfully, to rail at, revile, calumniate."* It means in its simple sense, *"malicious misrepresentation."*

Wuest says, *"It is used specifically of those who by contemptuous speech <u>intentionally</u> comes short of the reverence due to God or to sacred things. Here the words speak of the action of the Scribes, who, knowing that our Lord was performing miracles in the power of the Holy Spirit, deliberately and knowingly attribute them to Satan, and do this in an attempt to break the attesting power of the miracles our Lord was performing. This is the unpardonable sin."*

It is possible to blaspheme the Son or the Father, without committing the unpardonable sin. Jesus said, *"Whosoever speaketh a word against the Son of man, it shall be forgiven him"* (Mat. 12:32).

However, if one speaks against the Holy Spirit in such a malicious tone as these Scribes, it is a sin which cannot be forgiven, and, in fact, will not be forgiven!

The phrase, *"But is in danger of eternal damnation,"* according to Greek scholars, should have been translated, *"But is in danger of eternal sin."* The idea is this:

As the Text presently reads, it seems that Jesus is saying that upon the committing of such a sin, the person is merely in *"danger"* of damnation, instead of such being guaranteed, which is not the case.

As we have stated, and as the original Greek of this Text proves, this sin committed is an eternal sin, and, as a result, carries with it an eternal damnation.

Jesus is impressing upon all, that when one begins to speak in any manner disparaging of the Holy Spirit, the *"danger"* of committing this unpardonable sin becomes acute! Consequently, and in view of that, nothing must be said that could even be remotely construed as opposition to the Holy Spirit.

NOTES

(30) "BECAUSE THEY SAID, HE HATH AN UNCLEAN SPIRIT."

The phrase, *"Because they said,"* means that these Scribes knew full well that Jesus was casting out these demons by the Spirit of God. There was no doubt about that, by its disposition, or in their minds.

The phrase, *"He hath an unclean spirit,"* proclaims them hatching up this idea that Jesus cast out demons by the power of the Devil. In effect, they were saying that Jesus was an *"incarnate Devil,"* i.e., a Devil in human form!

They knew beyond the shadow of a doubt that it was not true, but hatched up this scheme among themselves in order to attempt to discredit Him in the eyes of the people. Thus their sin was willful, malicious, knowing, arbitrary, and deliberate.

The lie they were projecting was bad enough! But to attribute the Works of God, which were blatantly obvious, to the Devil, was blaspheming the Holy Spirit. Thus, at that moment, they were condemned to an eternal hell, from which there was no escape, which meant they were eternally doomed.

Inasmuch as we have given extended coverage to this important subject in Volume VII in our Commentary on Matthew 12, consequently, we will address it here in a more abbreviated form, but yet, we trust, answering questions held by some:

1. Who can commit the sin of blaspheming the Holy Spirit?

The only record in the Word of God of anyone blaspheming the Holy Spirit, is found among these professors of religion called *"Scribes and Pharisees."* There is no record of unsaved people committing this sin, only professors of religion, and we might quickly add, only those who claim to be involved in that which we presently call *"Christianity."*

2. Are there people who attempt to give their heart to God, and cannot, because they have committed this sin?

No! Any person who wants to be saved, can be saved (Rev. 22:17).

Some Preachers have claimed such, stating that some people have refused the Lord so many times, that when they finally desire to be saved, the Lord refuses to save them, and because they have committed this sin.

That is totally incorrect! There is no record

in the Word of God, which must be our criteria, that anyone who came to Christ was turned away. They were not then, and they are not now! As stated, anyone who desires in their heart to be saved, and who turns to the Lord, will <u>always</u> find Him a willing recipient of their lost person. Actually, Jesus is actively seeking those who are lost (Mk. 2:17).

Actually, one of the greatest signs that one has not blasphemed the Holy Spirit, is their desire for God and His Ways.

3. What is blaspheming the Holy Spirit?

It is, as stated, the willful ascribing of the Works of God to Satan. It is done so when all the evidence is contrary to the accusation.

Since the Day of Pentecost (Acts 2:1-4), the Holy Spirit has been poured out on all who would believe. As a result, multiple millions have been Baptized in the Spirit, with the evidence of speaking with other tongues.

This Gift of God has been multiplied since the turn of the century, with more receiving the Holy Spirit than probably all the previous centuries put together. This is in direct fulfillment of Bible Prophecy where Peter said, *"And it shall come to pass in the last days, saith God, I will pour out of My Spirit upon all flesh"* (Acts 2:17).

Even though the *"last days"* actually began on the *"Day of Pentecost,"* still, verses 19 and 20 of Acts 2 tell us that this *"pouring out of the Spirit"* will exacerbate in the last of the last days.

And yet, even though many have received, many have, as well, opposed this of which the Lord is doing. The opposition has almost entirely come from the religious sector, exactly as it did in the days of Christ.

In this opposition, I am concerned that some have blasphemed the Holy Spirit. Most of the opposition has centered up on *"speaking with tongues."*

For one to say, *"I do not believe in it,"* or *"I do not see this Doctrine in this manner,"* or some other such term, is one thing! However, to say that speaking in tongues is *"of the Devil,"* or *"inspired by demon spirits,"* puts one in the very position that Jesus spoke of when He said, *"is in danger of eternal damnation."*

Only the Lord can make the final determination that one has blasphemed the Holy Spirit, but, if, in Truth, *"speaking with other tongues as the Spirit gives utterance,"* is of God, as should be obvious by its Biblical terminology

(Acts 2:4), then attributing such to Satan is dangerous indeed! And yet some, if not many, have done this!

Were these, who have committed such acts, unsaved people rather than professors of religion, that would be one thing altogether. In other words, as the Scribes and Pharisees of old, the proof is irrefutable, and Scriptural. So, there is no excuse for them to make such statements. Consequently, such is done willfully, deliberately, and intentionally.

4. Will one know he has blasphemed the Holy Spirit?

No, they will not know such a thing, and neither will they have any desire to follow God's Way, in fact, continuing on with their own religious way, as the Scribes and Pharisees of old!

These individuals did not even remotely agree with Christ as to what they had done, neither did they turn their way at all toward God. They continued to think they were right with God, and that all was well. In other words, there was no desire for repentance, because such desire can only be generated by the Holy Spirit, Whom they had denied.

So, a person who has blasphemed the Holy Spirit, will not know they have done so, will not think they have done so, and will have no desire to change their way.

In fact, if there is a fear which arises in the heart of a person over something they may have said in this respect, such is a sign that they have <u>not</u> blasphemed the Holy Spirit.

Any attitude toward God in the hearts of people must be generated by the Holy Spirit. He works or acts upon the Word of God being presented to individuals. Without that, the drawing of the Holy Spirit, it is impossible for the individual to come to God (I Jn. 5:6; Rev. 22:17).

If the Spirit of God is not present to draw the person, or to perform His office work in any way, and because He has been rejected by attributing to Him works of Satan, there is no way for that person to be drawn to the Truth. Consequently, they are lost, and hopelessly so!

I am persuaded, and sadly so, that some, if not many Preachers, who occupy modern pulpits, have committed this grave sin. As such, and as would be obvious, there is absolutely no moving or operation of the Holy Spirit whatsoever in their Ministries or Churches. If it was so in Jesus' day, and it definitely was, it is so at present!

(31) "THERE CAME THEN HIS BRETHREN AND HIS MOTHER, AND, STANDING WITHOUT, SENT UNTO HIM, CALLING HIM."

The phrase, *"There came then His brethren and His mother,"* proclaims Mark resuming this account which had been interrupted by the encounter with the Scribes.

The phrase, *"And standing without,"* refers to them standing outside the house at the edge of the crowd. To be sure, this is sad!

Did He know they were out there, and yet failed to invite them in?

There is evidence according to His answer, that He did. So why did not He invite them in, if, in fact, He knew they were there, paying them proper respect as His close relatives?

Sadly and regrettably, He knew their intentions were not right or Scriptural. They had not come to rejoice with Him at the great work for God that was being carried out, but, rather, to attempt to stop that work. Whether their motives were right or wrong, is not really called into question. However, their actions are perfectly clear, in that they thought He was *"beside Himself,"* i.e., *"out of His mind"* (vs. 21).

As much as He loved His Mother and His brethren, He must not, and, in fact, could not allow them to hinder His Work. God must come first in all things.

Inasmuch as their attitude was antagonistic, there was really very little He could do, with them leaving without ever really having seen Him. (As we have stated, His Mother probably did not have the same attitude and thoughts as her other sons, the half-brothers of Christ. Nevertheless, the very fact that she was with them, would, of necessity, place her, at least in some respect, in a matter of denial.)

Consequently, all who do not line up exactly with the Ways of the Lord, in effect, promoting their own ways, will be, as these, *"standing without."*

The phrase, *"Sent unto Him, calling Him,"* means that they sent Him word by way of the crowd that they desired to see Him.

According to verse 21, the possibility definitely exists that they made it known to the crowd that they thought He was *"beside Himself."* If so, how much this must have hurt the Son of God, Who loved them more than they would ever know!

(32) "AND THE MULTITUDE SAT ABOUT

HIM, AND THEY SAID UNTO HIM, BEHOLD, THY MOTHER AND THY BRETHREN WITHOUT SEEK FOR THEE."

The phrase, *"And the multitude sat about Him,"* referred to as many as possible coming as close as they could to Him. Evidently, He was seated while He taught and healed, and they were seated around Him, whether on the floor or wherever.

The phrase, *"And they said unto Him, Behold,"* refers to the information that filtered to them from the outside respecting the desire of His relatives to see Him.

The phrase, *"Thy Mother and Thy brethren without seek for Thee,"* will serve as the occasion for a tremendous Truth to be presented.

(33) "AND HE ANSWERED THEM, SAYING, WHO IS MY MOTHER, OR MY BRETHREN?"

The phrase, *"And He answered them,"* concerns what He will say, but, also probably means that His teaching and healing were interrupted.

The question, *"Saying, Who is My mother, or My brethren?"*, seems, on the surface, to be harsh! However, He knew the reason for which they had come.

In this question, and its answer, He in no way meant to disavow or even to demean human relationship. However, He did mean to place this relationship in its proper setting.

(34) "AND HE LOOKED ROUND ABOUT ON THEM WHICH SAT ABOUT HIM, AND SAID, BEHOLD MY MOTHER AND MY BRETHREN!"

The phrase, *"And He looked round about on them which sat about Him,"* presents a look that is serious, but yet not critical.

When He asked the question, it is positive that it occasioned a deep contemplation in the hearts of those who heard it. In the silence that followed, He looked at them closely, which, as well, they probably observed.

Those who were closest to Him would have been the Twelve. And yet, some of the Twelve may have been with the crowd, helping them respecting their coming to Jesus. At any rate, those who hungered greatly for Him, not only for His healings, but for His teaching, would have lingered close. They were there because they wanted and desired Him. They saw in Him the answer to their heart's cry. As a result, they lingered close!

The phrase, *"And said, Behold My Mother*

and My brethren," may have been spoken as His outstretched Hand swept those assembled.

He answers His Own question by pointing out those who He considered as His *"Mother and brethren!"*

At the same time, He was not demeaning His Personal relationship with Mary, or His half-brothers. He was rather showing that spiritual relationship with Christ is on a higher level even than earthly family relationships. Consequently, the spiritual relationship with Christ always takes precedent over any other relationship, as dear as they may be. This relationship refers to the great family of God.

If one is to notice, Jesus never mentioned *"father"* in His statement.

Why?

He had no earthly father, as Joseph was only His foster father. God was His Father, and in a unique way, in which He is *"Father"* to no other.

At the same time, Jesus is addressing Himself to the cult of Mary worship, which would later come, and which now characterizes the Catholic Church.

While the Catholics claim they do not worship Mary, their actions prove differently.

Just last evening, over a Catholic program, while the Pope was being taken through a large crowd in his *"Popemobile,"* a song was playing in the background, *"You are the light of my life,"* or words to that effect, with further lines stating such to be *"Mary!"*

Anytime anyone proclaims that something or someone is the *"light of their life,"* that is worship, pure and simple!

In their elevating of Mary, she is called *"the Mother of God."*

Is this true?

No, Mary is not the Mother of God. Mary was the Mother of the human being, Jesus. Mary served a biological function that was necessary to bring about a unique situation. The preexistent Son of God was to take on human form. As He walked the earth (in human form), He was Very God and Very Man. As God, He had always been. As Man, He came into being in His Mother's womb. While Mary had something to do with the Incarnation, in that she provided a harbor (her womb) for His developing human form (for nine months), she had absolutely nothing whatsoever to do with His Godhead! Mary was, therefore, the Mother of

Jesus, the Man. She was not, by any stretch of the imagination, the Mother of God.

God has no Mother. If one understands the Incarnation, one understands that God, while never ceasing to be God, became completely Man.

"Wherefore when He cometh into the world, He saith, Sacrifice and offering Thou wouldest not, but a body hast Thou prepared Me" (Heb. 10:5).

It was this Body that God prepared for His Son — Jesus Christ — Who would become Man. Of necessity, He would be born into the world as are all other human beings, but with one tremendous difference:

"Therefore the Lord Himself shall give you a sign; Behold, a Virgin shall conceive, and bear a Son, and shall call His Name Immanuel" (Isa. 7:14).

This Virgin was the little maiden Mary, who was probably in her late teens, who was to bring the Son of God into the world. But it was not God Who would be born, it was *"The Man Christ Jesus"* (I Tim. 2:5).

Even though we have dealt with *"Mary worship"* in Volume VII in our commentary on Matthew (Ch. 12), still, due to the significance of the subject, please allow us to make a couple of other statements.

The Catholic Doctrine of *"The Immaculate Conception,"* is another case in point. This erroneous (and confusing) term does not refer to the conception of Jesus Christ (as most non-Catholics and many Catholics believe). It refers to the conception of Mary in her mother's womb.

The Catholic Catechism says:

"The Blessed Virgin Mary alone, from the first instant of her conception, through the foreseen merits of Jesus Christ, by a unique privilege granted her by God, was kept free from the stain of original sin.... From the first moment of her conception (she) possessed justice and holiness, even the fullness of Grace, with the infused virtues and the gifts of the Holy Ghost."

This Doctrine, a total fiction with no Scriptural support, was *"infallibly"* defined by Pope Pius IX as part of the *"revealed deposit of Catholic faith"* in 1854. There was great opposition to this pronouncement, at the time, within the Catholic Church.

The Doctrine of the Immaculate Conception implies that for Mary to be born without original sin, her mother also had to be a sinless virgin. The only other alternative is that God granted her a unique immunity to the all-pervasive original sin that is an inescapable element of the human condition.

To be frank, Roman Catholic theologians lamely defend their assertion of the Immaculate Conception by saying that *"God could have done it"* or *"It was fitting that He should do so — and therefore He did it."*

However, if God had decided on such a course, it would have meant that He was replacing the Plan of Salvation described in the Bible with a totally new concept. If this had happened, it is conceivable that we would have a *"quadrinity"* instead of the Trinity. God's Word then would have stated that the Godhead consists of God the Father, God the Son, God the Holy Spirit, and Mary, the Mother of God. Or, as Catholics now put it, Mary would have come first!

The Bible does not so state, so we can then conclude that this aberrant Doctrine is not of God.

Mary is looked at by the Catholic Church as an intercessor and a mediatrix. Is this Biblical?

No, it is not Biblical! Jesus Christ is our only Intercessor. The Scripture says:

"Wherefore He is able also to save them to the uttermost that come unto God by Him, seeing He ever liveth to make intercession for them" (Heb. 7:25).

There is no hint or suggestion in the Word of God that Mary should or would occupy such a role. Whenever Mary is inserted into the role of intercessor (as she is by the Catholic Church, to intercede with her Son, Jesus Christ, on behalf of individuals on earth), this, in effect, robs Christ of the rightful position He earned through His tremendous Sacrifice on Calvary. He paid the full price on the Cross with the shedding of His Precious Blood.

Christ Alone is worthy to make intercession for us. Christ Alone paid the price. Mary did not suffer and die on the Cross. She did not shed her blood. And neither does Christ need an assistant to motivate Him to intercede for the Saints. He is perfectly capable of performing this duty Himself, as He ever sits at the right hand of God making intercession for us.

"It is Christ that died, yea rather, that is risen again, Who is even at the right hand of God, Who also maketh intercession for us" (Rom. 8:34).

We blaspheme when we imply that Jesus Christ would not satisfactorily accomplish His eternal work of intercession without persuasion from His earthly Mother.

We blaspheme when we add to the Word of God:

"For there is one God, and one Mediator between God and men, The Man Christ Jesus; Who gave Himself a ransom for all" (I Tim. 2:5-6).

Please note, there are not two mediators, not three or four, just One! And then, if there is any confusion, the identity of that One Mediator is revealed:

Jesus Christ (I Tim. 2:5).

The Roman Catholic position is that God the Father and His Son, Jesus Christ, are, through normal human efforts, unreachable. By extension, they then propose that since Christ's Mother is available, that petitions delivered by her will not be ignored. Who would turn away his own mother, they reasoned, if she came seeking a minor favor?

Thus, in Catholic tradition, when a person goes through the Mother, he gets through more quickly and more surely. No doubt Jesus will look with more favor on her requests than on any delivered directly. Hence, the bumper stickers: *"Can't find Jesus? Look for His Mother."*

Such statements totally misinterpret the Person of God and the Incarnation, Redemption, and Plan of God for the human family.

Paul said it well:

"Now the Spirit speaketh expressly, that in the later times some shall depart from the Faith, giving heed to seducing spirits, and doctrines of devils;

"Speaking lies in hypocrisy; having their conscience seared with a hot iron;

"Forbidding to marry, and commanding to abstain from meats, which God hath created to be received with thanksgiving of them which believe and know the Truth" (I Tim. 4:1-3).

Obviously, Catholics do not know the Truth!

In all of Early Church history, no statement is reported of an Apostle referring to Mary as the *"Mother of God."* There is no hint of prayers being offered to her, nor admonitions given to the Saints to honor her beyond what the Bible suggests as normal deference.

Surely, if this great fabrication were valid, we would have at least a word from the Early Church concerning Mary.

The silence is deafening!

(35) "FOR WHOSOEVER SHALL DO THE WILL OF GOD, THE SAME IS MY BROTHER, AND MY SISTER, AND MOTHER."

The phrase, *"For whosoever shall do the Will of God,"* proclaims the qualifications for the high and lofty position of being His *"brother, sister, and mother."*

What is the *"Will of God?"*

The *"Will of God"* is the *"Word of God."* It alone is the criteria, and not the statements of a Pope, be he Catholic or otherwise! Neither is it a Church or Religious Denomination. As well, it is not Harvard, Yale, Oxford, or any other institution of higher learning. Neither is it Congress, the Supreme Court, Government, or the Law of the Land.

These things may all have their place, but the criteria for life, conduct, and, above all, the Plan of Salvation is the Bible.

As well, it is not enough to just believe the *"Word of God,"* i.e., *"Will of God,"* but, rather, to *"Do"* the Will of God.

This means for one to, *"Love the Lord thy God with all thy heart, and with all thy soul, and with all thy mind . . . And . . . , Thou shalt love thy neighbour as thyself"* (Mat. 22:37-39).

The phrase, *"The same is My brother, and My sister, and mother,"* places all born-again Believers in a status even greater than flesh-and-blood relationships, while never for a moment demeaning those relationships.

CHAPTER 4

(1) "AND HE BEGAN AGAIN TO TEACH BY THE SEA SIDE: AND THERE WAS GATHERED UNTO HIM A GREAT MULTITUDE, SO THAT HE ENTERED INTO A SHIP, AND SAT IN THE SEA; AND THE WHOLE MULTITUDE WAS BY THE SEA ON THE LAND."

The phrase, *"And He began again to teach by the sea side,"* reflects that teaching and preaching is more important than healing, as important as that may be!

Had He stayed on the shore, the diseased could have touched Him and been healed. But His business as a Servant was to deal with sin rather than its effects.

The words, *"To teach,"* do not address themselves in the Greek to the fact of teaching, but

to the process. Consequently, the teaching was simplicity itself, and may be repeated over and over, at least in a sense, in order that the people may understand.

At this stage, He was standing next to the water, while the people stood in a group around Him.

The phrase, *"And there was gathered unto Him a great multitude,"* probably refers to several thousand people. It had been a *"multitude,"* and now it is a *"great multitude!"*

The action of the words proclaims the fact that not only were they there for the healings and miracles, but, as well, to hear what He had to say. His subject was always the Word of God, but two things were in focus:

1. He had a knowledge of the Word, which no one else had. As well, this knowledge did not come automatically, but was acquired. It is said of Him, *"O how I love Thy Law! it is My meditation all the day"* (Ps. 119:97). Actually, the entirety of Psalm 119 speaks of Christ, but with verses 97-105 speaking more particularly of Him relative to the Bible.

Our last trip to Nazareth, the little town in which He was raised and lived even until His thirtieth year, was extremely interesting.

I asked to be taken, along with all our Television people, to the brow of the hill from which the good city fathers were determined to cast Him down (Lk. 4:29).

As it was a place of solitude now, more than likely it was the same then. Probably He had stood on this very hill countless times as He meditated on the Word of God. As well, there is every evidence that He began this prayerful study and meditation of the Word at a very young age. Even at twelve years old, He would ask the question, *"Wist ye not that I must be about My Father's business?"* (Lk. 2:49). So, His life was spent in the Word of God.

2. He was Anointed to teach and preach the Word as no man had ever been (Lk. 4:18-19). As a result, this combination produced not only an understanding of the Word as none other, but, as well, a presentation as no other!

What a privilege for those people to hear Him teach and preach.

Likewise, what a privilege we have today to study and learn His Word!

The phrase, *"So that He entered into a ship, and sat in the sea,"* refers to a vessel that was somewhat larger than the small rowboat of 3:9.

This larger vessel was brought as close to the shore as possible, with only a narrow strip of water between Jesus and the crowd. There He sat on the deck of the boat encircled by the water, and taught the people.

This was done, as would be obvious, because of the press of the crowd.

The phrase, *"And the whole multitude was by the sea on the land,"* referred to their listening to Him attentively as He taught!

(2) "AND HE TAUGHT THEM MANY THINGS BY PARABLES, AND SAID UNTO THEM IN HIS DOCTRINE,"

The phrase, *"And He taught them many things,"* means that He kept on teaching them, and, in fact, was constantly teaching them. His form of address was of two kinds:

1. He preached: This means *"To make a proclamation,"* to *"Call attention to Truth."*

2. He taught: This refers to imparting information, or rather to explain Truth.

The phrase, *"By Parables,"* proclaims a new system of teaching. Previously, He had spoken directly concerning particular Truths. However, inasmuch as this was met too often by ridicule and scorn, he now resorted to *"Parables."*

This method used illustrations taken from everyday life which was thrown alongside a Truth in order to explain it. It could be used to make the subject easier to understand, or, if so desired, to shade its meaning, which He sometimes did.

It would seem somewhat inconceivable that He would purposely attempt to conceal what He was giving to the people, but yet, this is exactly what happened. He possibly did it for several reasons; however, the major reason was to draw closer those who were sincere, while, at the same time, repelling those who were merely there out of idle curiosity. Verses 10 through 13 proclaim this.

The phrase, *"And said unto them in His Doctrine,"* refers to what He taught and the manner in which it was taught.

(3) "HEARKEN; BEHOLD, THERE WENT OUT A SOWER TO SOW:

This Parable is given in Matthew 13, and repeated in Luke 8, but worded somewhat different.

The word, *"Hearken,"* begins this Parable, and does so intentionally. It means *"Be listening."*

The crowd, as usual, even though interested

in what He had to say, still, was more interested in the healings and the miracles. Consequently, He would proclaim to them that the Salvation of their souls was far more important than the healing of their sick bodies, as important as that was!

To proclaim the significance of what is about to be said, in addition to the word, *"Hearken,"* Jesus follows with the word, *"Behold,"* which gives added strength to the first word, and means, *"Give attention to this!"*

The phrase, *"There went out a sower to sow,"* presents the first Parable and the key to understanding all other Parables.

The illustration of the *"sowing of seed,"* was something understood by all. And yet, even though the Parable was given, what it represented and meant regarding its explanation was not given to the people, but only to the Disciples. Why?

Knowing that Israel would not accept the Gospel, Jesus shaded its presentation and meaning to a certain extent, in order that the merely curious would not know, but the truly hungry would press in for the true meaning. As we previously stated, it was somewhat as the Disciples who plucked the grain, and then rubbed it briskly in their hands in order to rub away the chaff to obtain the kernel. It is the same with the Gospel even now, of which this Parable sets the stage.

The merely inquisitive and curious will find little solace, but those who truly *"Hunger and thirst after Righteousness shall be filled"* (Mat. 5:6). Jesus outlined this in verses 11-13.

The method in those days for sowing, and still is the method in some places, was for plows to be run over the ground, which actually only scratched the surface a few inches deep. In the doing of this, stones were upturned which were meant to be cleared, as well as all other obstacles. For the ground to produce a good harvest, the proper preparation had to be made, which is emphasized in this Parable.

The time of plowing for some crops began with the early rains in September and October, and continued until March.

After the ground was properly prepared, the farmer would walk over it scattering the seed around him which he took from a bag or bushel measure. After the grain was sowed, sometimes a harrow was dragged across it, or a flock of sheep or goats driven over it to tread the seed into the soil and give it enough depth of earth to grow and produce properly. All of this, as we shall see, is an illustration of the presentation of the Gospel, and its resultant fruit. We will see what happens when the ground is improperly prepared, somewhat prepared, and well prepared.

(4) "AND IT CAME TO PASS, AS HE SOWED, SOME FELL BY THE WAY SIDE, AND THE FOWLS OF THE AIR CAME AND DEVOURED IT UP."

Inasmuch as the explanation of the Parable is given in verses 14-20, we will not attempt to cover that ground with the presentation of the Parable, but only to provide foundation.

The farmer sowing seed, and birds of the air swooping down to retrieve it off the ground before it had any opportunity to germinate, was a familiar sight to all who were listening to Christ.

(5) "AND SOME FELL ON STONY GROUND, WHERE IT HAD NOT MUCH EARTH; AND IMMEDIATELY IT SPRANG UP, BECAUSE IT HAD NO DEPTH OF EARTH:"

This was ground which had not been properly broken up by the plow, with a layer of topsoil immediately above the stone which was too thin to nurture the plants, even though it would germinate and flower.

The farmer knew there was little hope of any grain being produced in this type of soil, but would sow the seed anyway in hope that there would be at least some harvest.

(6) "BUT WHEN THE SUN WAS UP, IT WAS SCORCHED; AND BECAUSE IT HAD NO ROOT, IT WITHERED AWAY."

Actually, all the seed was identical, as is here illustrated, so the fault was not in the seed, but rather the type of ground on which it fell, which determined the amount and kind of fruit that would result. On this particular ground, because the sun was hot and there were no roots to speak of, the plant soon withered away.

All of this is meant to describe the hearts of men in receiving the Gospel, whether receptive or unreceptive, and the reasons why!

(7) "AND SOME FELL AMONG THORNS, AND THE THORNS GREW UP, AND CHOKED IT, AND IT YIELDED NO FRUIT."

This particular ground seemed to be sufficient, with the plant developing a suitable root system, but the seed was sown in the midst of *"thorns,"* consequently, the bramble-bush or briers wrapped themselves around the plant and chocked it to death.

As well, those who stood before Christ fully understood what the Parable said, even though they would have had little knowledge as to what it represented. However, and to be sure, it was something they would easily remember, and no doubt mull over in their minds long after it had been uttered. Without a doubt, some few later asked the Disciples as to the meaning, and it was readily given unto them, with their *"spiritual hunger and thirst"* then satisfied.

(8) "AND OTHER FELL ON GOOD GROUND, AND DID YIELD FRUIT THAT SPRANG UP AND INCREASED; AND BROUGHT FORTH, SOME THIRTY, AND SOME SIXTY, AND SOME AN HUNDRED."

The *"good ground"* producing different amounts in different places, was, as well, very familiar to those who heard Jesus speak. Consequently, the entirety of the Parable presented four different stages.

1. In the first case the seed produced nothing.

2. In the second it produced only the blade, then it quickly withered.

3. The third case was near the point of producing fruit, and even looked like it would, but was choked by briers and brambles, therefore producing nothing.

4. This ground produces fruit, but in different measures.

All, as stated, represent the hearts of men in the reception of the Gospel.

(9) "AND HE SAID UNTO THEM, HE THAT HATH EARS TO HEAR, LET HIM HEAR."

The phrase, *"And He said,"* is proclaimed in Luke 8:8 as *"He cried,"* signifying the significance of what He has said, and of what He is now saying.

The phrase, *"He that hath ears to hear, let him hear,"* gives us the explanation as to the reason Jesus proclaimed the Parable, and did not explain it, at least to the people.

These *"ears"* which would properly *"hear,"* would attend to these Words of Christ, pondering them, until somehow the Truth was eventually revealed. As stated, it was designed this way by the Holy Spirit in order that the preciousness of the Gospel not be lost on mere curiosity seekers. It is a principle that holds even unto this moment. Several people can hear the Gospel, and even though it is the same in all cases, it will be received differently by most. Some have ears for it, and some don't.

From this, some have arrived at an improper explanation of predestination or election. They erroneously conclude that all are born predestined to be either saved or lost, of which the individual has no say! However, the very tenor of these Passages proclaims the very opposite. While it is true that God in His Omniscience, which means that He knows all things, past, present, and future, can very well know the eternal destiny of all, still, the choice is always left up to the individual, with *"Whosoever will"* eternally stamped upon the Gospel (Rev. 22:17). While predestination is a viable Bible Doctrine, still, it must be properly understood, therefore, *"Rightly dividing the Word of Truth"* (II Tim. 2:15).

Predestination in its most simple form, means that the Plan of God is predestined, and, consequently, cannot be changed. In this Plan, it is predestined that God will have a people who will serve Him, thereby bringing Him glory. However, as to who those individual people will be is not predetermined. That is decided by the individual in their reception or rejection of the Gospel, in respect, and as stated, *"Whosoever will!"*

While it is true that the Lord through foreknowledge will proclaim something in detail which will happen hundreds of years in the future, such as Judas betraying Christ, still, it was not predestined that Judas would do this, but that the Lord would simply look into the future and see what Judas would do of his own free will (Ps. 41:9; 55:12-14; 109:6-20).

Actually, every human being begins life on a level playing field respecting their personal heart toward God. In other words, none are born with a predisposition more or less toward the Lord. The Scripture says, *"He fashioneth their hearts alike"* (Ps. 33:15).

This means that the Lord designs or molds every heart identical respecting the all-important aspect of predisposition toward God.

(As I'm sure it is understood, the *"heart"* as here proclaimed, has nothing to do with the physical organ in one's body, but rather speaks of one's passions, will, emotions, and disposition. As it is used by the Lord, it is used by the world in the same manner. Men are accustomed to saying, *"He lost heart,"* or some such term, which,

NOTES

as is obvious, does not mean that the individual's heart falls out of his body, but simply that he lost his courage, will, or strength to continue.)

So, if all begin alike, as they do, why do some accept the Gospel and some reject?

The answer is found in the *"will"* of the individual. They either want the Lord or they don't, or they want Him, but are not willing to forsake all and follow Him. At any rate, whatever the person does, be it toward the Lord or in opposition to the Lord, the disposition is found strictly in the person, even though both the Lord and Satan deal with the individual attempting to pull them accordingly. However, even though dealt with by both, the final decision is strictly up to the individual. Satan cannot force a person against his will, although greatly persuading him, while the Lord will not force a person against his will, while, at the same time, persuading him.

So, the *"ears to hear,"* is strictly up to the individual!

Sadly, many have no opportunity to *"hear!"* Paul said, *"And how shall they hear without a Preacher?*

"And how shall they preach, except they be sent?" (Rom. 10:14-15).

If one properly understands the Word of God, he will understand that the entire complexion of all that it teaches is that all of mankind, and irrespective as to whom they are or where they may be, must have the opportunity to *"hear"* the Gospel. For those who do not have that opportunity, Jesus, as far as they are concerned, died in vain! If we properly understand that, then we properly understand how serious this situation is.

For God to do what He did in the sending of His Son, and considering the price paid by the Lord of Glory in dying on Calvary's Cross, and then for a high percentage of the world's population to know little or nothing about it, constitutes a crime of the highest order. No wonder the Lord told Ezekiel that if he did not warn the wicked, *"His blood will I require at thine hand"* (Ezek. 3:18). It is a sobering thought that the entirety of the Church must consider constantly.

I do not have to answer, and neither can I answer, for the generation of human beings which preceded me, and had no opportunity to hear and know. However, I am responsible, as you, for this generation.

That is the reason that we at Jimmy Swaggart Ministries struggle daily, even against impossible odds, to place the Telecast in any and every country of the world where possible, even translating into the language of the people, in order for them to better understand. This is what God has called me to do, and I must be able to say as Paul said, *"I was not disobedient unto the heavenly vision"* (Acts 26:19).

And yet, I cannot carry out this task without your help, for as Paul also intimated, the one who does the sending is just as important as the one who is sent (Rom. 10:14-15).

(10) "AND WHEN HE WAS ALONE, THEY THAT WERE ABOUT HIM WITH THE TWELVE ASKED OF HIM THE PARABLE."

The phrase, *"And when He was alone,"* proves according to the following that Jesus did not explain this Parable to the multitude, and for the reasons that will be given.

The phrase, *"They that were about Him with the Twelve,"* refers not only to the chosen Disciples, but, as well, another group from which the Twelve were chosen, which could have numbered as many as a hundred or more. We know the Lord a little later, *"Appointed other seventy also, and sent them two and two before His Face into every city and place, whither He Himself would come"* (Lk. 10:1).

The phrase, *"Asked of Him the Parable,"* presents all of them wanting to know the meaning to the simple illustration He had just given to the people. Thank the Lord, they had *"ears to hear,"* and, no doubt, others did as well!

(11) "AND HE SAID UNTO THEM, UNTO YOU IT IS GIVEN TO KNOW THE MYSTERY OF THE KINGDOM OF GOD: BUT UNTO THEM THAT ARE WITHOUT, ALL THESE THINGS ARE DONE IN PARABLES:

The phrase, *"And He said unto them,"* will proclaim the patient explanation which He will give to any and all who earnestly seek Him. He is no respecter of persons.

The phrase, *"Unto you it is given to know,"* refers to all honest, earnest, sincere hearts who seek after God, humbly inquiring into the full meaning of the Gospel, in order that they may *"know."*

The word, *"given,"* shows that this efficiency cannot be obtained by our own strength or ability, but must be humbly sought from God. It is His Own gift which He bestows on all who

earnestly seek His Face, while denying it to those who are not sincere. Hence Paul would say, *"And be not conformed to this world: but be ye transformed by the renewing of your mind, that ye may prove what is that good, and acceptable, and perfect, Will of God"* (Rom. 12:2).

The phrase, *"The mystery of the Kingdom of God,"* refers to the secret councils of God which are hidden from the ungodly, but when revealed to the Godly, are understood by them.

The Mystery is not in the fact that they are difficult of interpretation, but that they are actually impossible of interpretation until their meaning is revealed by the Holy Spirit, when they become plain.

There is another type of *"Mystery"* such as the *"Mystery of iniquity,"* which the Lord is not addressing here.

The first mystery is what Paul was speaking of when he said, *"But the natural man receiveth not the things of the Spirit of God: for they are foolishness unto him: neither can he know them, because they are spiritually discerned"* (I Cor. 2:14).

Regarding the overall picture, the meaning of the *"Mystery of the Kingdom of God"* as Jesus here uses it, refers to the New Covenant, which was shaded in the Old Covenant, but now revealed, at least to earnest, seeking hearts.

The phrase, *"But unto them that are without,"* means those outside this circle, referring to the Pharisees with their hostile minds, and all who follow in their train.

The phrase, *"All these things are done in Parables,"* records the reason for this type of teaching, which will be given in the next verse.

(12) "THAT SEEING THEY MAY SEE, AND NOT PERCEIVE; AND HEARING THEY MAY HEAR, AND NOT UNDERSTAND; LEST AT ANY TIME THEY SHOULD BE CONVERTED, AND THEIR SINS SHOULD BE FORGIVEN THEM."

The intent of this verse is that Judicial blindness and deafness justly befall those who do not wish to see and hear. It doesn't mean they cannot, but that they will not!

The phrase, *"That seeing they may see, and not perceive; and hearing they may hear, and not understand,"* has to do with what is presented and the manner in which it is received.

As stated, these Parables, and thus this manner of teaching, which actually constitute much of the Word of God, are designed to blind further or to give light, according to the disposition of the heart of the listener. The Word or Parable is the same to all. It is similar to the Sun, which either hardens clay or softens wax. The change brought about is not in the Sun, but, rather, in the material which is exposed to the Sun.

Upon reading this verse, many may erroneously think, and according to the English translation, that the Parable was purposely designed to blind and deafen. However, that is totally untrue! The same Parable which definitely does blind and deafen some, at the same time enlightens others. The Parables are thus a condemnation on the wilfully blind and hostile, while a guide and blessing to the earnest seeker.

This is what Jesus was speaking of when He said, *"For whosoever hath, to him shall be given, and he shall have more abundance: but whosoever hath not, from him shall be taken away even that he hath"* (Mat. 13:12).

From the Scribes and Pharisees who would not believe Jesus, God took away even that small knowledge which they had of Him and His Kingdom, as well as all who had the same spirit.

This is on the same principle that God hardened Pharaoh's heart by forcing him to an issue which he did not want to meet (Rom. 9:14-18). Light resisted, blinds. The Pharisees attempted to show that the Lord was in league with Satan. They did not want the Truth. Thus, rejecting the Truth, they, in a sense, blinded themselves. As we have repeatedly stated, the Parables are so adjusted that they blind the one who wickedly rejects the Truth, and enlighten the one who desires it.

The phrase, *"Lest at any time they should be converted, and their sins should be forgiven them,"* means they have wilfully rejected the Truth, and, consequently, cannot have their sins forgiven, and, therefore, *"converted."*

(13) "AND HE SAID UNTO THEM, KNOW YE NOT THIS PARABLE? AND HOW THEN WILL YE KNOW ALL PARABLES?"

The question, *"And He said unto them, Know ye not this Parable?",* actually contains a gentle reproach. They wanted to know, but they did not know! Actually, the question indicates that they should have known!

Could not the same be said to us?

Too often the Believer is so taken up with the

things of the world, even though innocent within itself, that little time or attention is given to the things of God. Consequently, there is a dullness of *"hearing"* and a blindness of *"seeing."*

The question, *"And how then will ye know all Parables?",* signifies two things:

1. The Parable of the Sower lays down the principle of all Parables, and the understanding thereof.

2. Consequently, the Disciples, as well as every Believer, must learn the full meaning of this particular Parable.

(14) "THE SOWER SOWETH THE WORD."

The phrase, *"The sower,"* refers to the Lord Jesus Christ, and all He calls to minister His Word (Mk. 16:15-20; I Cor. 1:18-21). However, it should be clearly understood that all Believers are called in some respect to minister the Word. It may not necessarily be one of the fivefold callings (Eph. 4:11), but it definitely is a calling, which includes all!

The phrase, *"Soweth the Word,"* means that the seed is the Word of God, exactly as the sower sowed natural seed (Mat. 13:19; Lk. 8:11; Rom. 1:16).

So, by its very application, this Parable, which is the key to all Parables, begins with the admonition that the *"sowing"* of the Gospel is the foundation of the *"Kingdom of God."* If this is priority with God, and it is, then it should be priority with the Church.

Regrettably, it is of little priority with much of the Church, with other things taking its place. Priority in too many Church circles is beautiful buildings, education, manifestations of what purports to be the Spirit, getting rich, etc. Regrettably, very few are properly sowing the seed.

As well, and as Mark relates at the conclusion of his Book, this *"seed"* must be sowed to the entirety of the world (Mk. 16:15).

The Early Church understood this perfectly, inasmuch as they evangelized in the first century almost all of the civilized world of that day. Remarkably, they did it without the aid of modern transportation, communication, or assimilation, which made their task more difficult! However, they did have the one thing that truly mattered, and that was the Holy Spirit in all His Power and Glory, Who aided and abetted them in all they did, which made the impossible possible. If there is any one thing the modern Church truly lacks, it is the Holy Spirit. To have all the other and not have Him, is to have nothing.

(15) "AND THESE ARE THEY BY THE WAY SIDE, WHERE THE WORD IS SOWN; BUT WHEN THEY HAVE HEARD, SATAN COMETH IMMEDIATELY, AND TAKETH AWAY THE WORD THAT WAS SOWN IN THEIR HEARTS."

The phrase, *"And these are they by the way side, where the Word is sown,"* refers to the first group who hears the Word, even with it properly given unto them, but really goes no further, with the next phrase explaining why!

The phrase, *"But when they have heard, Satan cometh immediately, and taketh away the Word that was sown in their hearts,"* proclaims the adversarial position of the Evil One against the Word of God, and especially it being received by the unbeliever. Several things are said here:

1. *"But when they have heard"*: Such refers to the grand time the Gospel is given to this particular individual. It is the single most important day of his or her life. Once again we state, the Holy Spirit is insistent that they have the opportunity, whether they accept or reject.

2. *"Satan"*: The Greek says, *"The Satan,"* meaning a concentrated plan engineered and devised by Satan himself, in his attempt to keep men from accepting the Gospel.

In other words, this is not a haphazard, last minute effort, but, instead, a carefully designed plan. It includes all of the minions of darkness, such as demon spirits and fallen angels, which carry out the directives issued by the Prince of Darkness, himself, Satan.

3. *"Cometh immediately"*: The plan is designed, that the moment the Gospel is presented, it is, as well, attacked within the heart of the recipient.

I would pray that God's people would be as diligent in getting the Gospel to others as Satan is diligent in attempting to stop it.

4. *"And taketh away the Word that was sown in their hearts"*: This refers to the plan being carried out to its intended conclusion, but with the permission of the one who has heard the Gospel.

This is what Jesus meant by the fowls of the air devouring the seed (vs. 4). However, there is a difference!

The ground on which the seed fell in the

illustration had no will of its own, and, consequently, could do nothing to stop the devouring. However, the human heart does have the power of choice, and can, therefore, say *"yes"* or *"no"* to Satan.

This group, as outlined by Christ, portrays the Seed of the Gospel coming to their hearts, and with them entertaining it for some time, but then of their own volition allowing Satan to pull the Seed out.

(16-17) "AND THESE ARE THEY LIKEWISE WHICH ARE SOWN ON STONY GROUND; WHO, WHEN THEY HAVE HEARD THE WORD, IMMEDIATELY RECEIVE IT WITH GLADNESS;

"AND HAVE NO ROOT IN THEMSELVES, AND SO ENDURE BUT FOR A TIME: AFTERWARD, WHEN AFFLICTION OR PERSECUTION ARISETH FOR THE WORD'S SAKE, IMMEDIATELY THEY ARE OFFENDED."

This is the second group to which Jesus refers. It falls out as follows:

1. *"And these are they likewise which are sown on stony ground"*: This pertains to the Word of God presented and received, and actually with a better reception than the previous. In other words, the heart is more receptive, and Satan is not able to snatch it away, as before.

2. *"Who, when they have heard the Word, immediately receive it with gladness"*: These actually make a start, and with great joy, giving every appearance of a true *"born-again"* experience, which it actually is! Such characterizes so many. They show such promise, but after a while they fall by the wayside. The next phrase tells us why.

3. *"And have no root in themselves, and so endure but for a time"*: These are like the seed sown on the ground which looked fine on the surface, but almost immediately beneath was rock. Consequently, as the *"root"* could not extend down because of the rocks, likewise, the Seed of the Gospel is hindered. Until the root hits the rock, everything looks and seems well. However, Satan, being unsuccessful in snatching the Seed away, will now try another tactic.

4. *"Afterward, when affliction or persecution ariseth for the Word's sake, immediately they are offended"*: Satan's next step is to bring *"affliction"* and *"persecution."* Likewise, it is clear from the Text that this *"affliction and persecution"* come strictly because of the *"Word of God"* being received into the heart.

I remember years ago working with a particular individual, who made the remark several times that when he was unsaved, it seemed as if he had few if any problems. Now that he had come to the Lord, he remonstrated, it seemed there were problems galore. He was right!

Satan was attempting to discourage him, as he attempts to do so with all, hoping the individual will give up and quit. Regrettably, many do!

Many in the modern Church have erroneously attempted to do away with all *"affliction and persecution,"* claiming that proper confession, based on great Faith, will eliminate these things. If that is true, then Jesus did not know what He was talking about!

Realizing that He did know very much as to what He was talking about, we must conclude that this modern Gospel is, in effect, *"another Gospel,"* and, therefore, has no Scriptural validity (II Cor. 11:4).

This group is *"offended,"* when the affliction or persecution comes, as come it shall, and even though making an excellent start, falls by the wayside.

(18-19) "AND THESE ARE THEY WHICH ARE SOWN AMONG THORNS; SUCH AS HEAR THE WORD,

"AND THE CARES OF THIS WORLD, AND THE DECEITFULNESS OF RICHES, AND THE LUSTS OF OTHER THINGS ENTERING IN, CHOKE THE WORD, AND IT BECOMETH UNFRUITFUL."

Jesus now explains the third group, who, likewise, heard the Word, making an excellent start, even with some progress, but ultimately lost their way as well!

1. *"And these are they which are sown among thorns; such as hear the Word"*: This ground was far better prepared than the other two. Satan was not allowed to come and snatch away the Word when it was presented, likewise, the soil had proper depth, and was not hindered by the hardness of the rocks. Consequently, the roots could reach down as they desired. So, this shows and portrays spiritual depth, with every indication that the Word will have its desired effect, and the individual will bring forth *"much fruit."* However, as we will see, the one who sows the Word is to be disappointed.

2. *"And the cares of this world"*: This really speaks of the *"worries"* of this world. In other

NOTES

words, this person allows, at least after a period of time, the disturbances of the world to effect him adversely. He is not properly tuned to Christ, with one hand actually holding to the world, and the other to the Lord. After a while, one or the other must go, because no man can serve two masters. Consequently, at least in this case, the world is embraced, with Christ ultimately being spurned. It is not so much the things of the world serving as an enticement, as it is the individual allowing the adverse things of the world to distract. Luke called it the *"cares of this life"* (Lk. 21:34).

In mundane terms, it refers to someone else getting the promotion, or the job being lost, with the house note unpaid, etc.

3. *"The deceitfulness of riches"*: Two things are here said: A. The Believer is not to seek riches. While such may come to some, and in fact have, it is not wrong if the Lord and His Work have priority. Many times, however, the priority is the seeking of riches, with right and wrong becoming blurred, and the person being consumed with this quest. This is what the Lord condemns.

B. Riches are *"deceitful"* in the sense that oftentimes the rich feel superior. Others feel their riches constitute the Blessings of God, with others not so materially blessed, evidently and obviously not having as much Faith. Consequently, the individual is deceived.

Sometime riches are the Blessings of God, and sometime they are the curse of Satan.

As well, others who have little of this world's goods whatsoever, at times, have great Faith. So, the acquiring of great wealth does not necessarily mean that one has Faith at all, at least in God.

If money is used for the Glory of God, it can be a tremendous blessing. However, it is seldom used accordingly. Too often, those who claim the Lord as their Saviour, and have acquired great wealth, much of the time give little of it for the furtherance of the Gospel. Thankfully, there are some exceptions, but precious few!

What a blessing it is to see someone, who the Lord has greatly blessed in material things, who will keep enough for himself and his family, but give the rest to the taking of the Gospel around the world. These are few and far between, but have made a tremendous impact for the Cause of Christ.

4. *"The lusts of other things"*: The word, *"lusts,"* as it is here used, does not necessarily mean things which are wrong or bad, but could, in effect, be something good, but yet not *"things"* which pertain to the Work of the Lord.

The sense of this statement is, that the Believer, and irrespective as to whom he may be, must not become engrossed in anything, no matter how innocent, unless it pertains to the Lord and His Work. This would mean that some Christians are far too involved in sports, business, hobbies, etc.

While it is certainly not wrong to be involved in business, still, the overlording passion, drive, concern, and interest, must be the Work of the Lord. He has promised, if we will seek first the Kingdom of God, and His Righteousness, that He will add all of these other things to us (Mat. 6:33).

Probably this one thing, the *"lusts of other things,"* is the greatest hindrance to the Child of God, and because it covers both the legitimate and the illegitimate.

The phrase, *"Choke the Word, and it becometh unfruitful,"* proclaims that which Satan attempts to do.

We are told here that it is the resident Word of God in the life of the individual, which, when properly acted upon, brings forth Fruit. Consequently, if there is no Word, there is no Fruit. Tragically, this would be the case in most who call themselves *"Christians,"* simply because they attend a Church where the Word of God is not preached, or else it is preached, but it finds no favorable lodging in their hearts.

The Bible, sadly enough, is an unread Book in many if not most Christian circles. Probably one could say without any fear of contradiction, that most Christians have never even read the Bible completely through one time, much less made it an habitual part of their daily spiritual exercise.

Actually, Jesus placed the daily necessity of the Word of God alongside the daily necessity of food (Mat. 4:4). We would greatly benefit ourselves if we heeded His Words.

Inasmuch a the Bible is the Word of God, it is, in effect, a Living Organism. The more it is studied, the more one wants to study it, and the more one derives from it. It is inexhaustible!

Consequently, Satan will do everything within his power to steer the Believer away from

the Word. Tragically, he has been very successful respecting many Preachers in modern Churches. All one has to do is to look at that which is offered in most Christian bookstores. He will find that much, if not most, is based on psychology instead of the Word of God. In fact, one of Satan's greatest ploys is to co-mingle his false teaching in with the Word of God. To be sure, the *"little leaven"* is not purified by the pure, but rather the opposite takes place, with the pure being totally leavened (I Cor. 5:6).

What type of *"Fruit"* is Jesus speaking of?

It is in the Gospel of John and the Epistles of Paul that the concept of Fruitfulness shifts from that of the product of character to the product of God's Work within us.

THE IMAGE OF THE VINE

In John 15:1-16, Jesus takes the image of the vine, with God as Gardener, from Isaiah. We Believers are carefully tended by the Father, pruned and cared for, that we may *"bear much Fruit."* Fruitfulness is possible, He said, if we remain in Him, and His Words remain in us. The point Jesus makes is that Fruitfulness is rooted in our personal relationship with Him, and our personal relationship with Him is maintained by living His Words: *"If you obey My Commands you will remain in My Love"* (Jn. 15:10).

God has chosen us. It is His intention that we be Fruitful. It is for this reason that He has given us the most intimate of relationships and Jesus's Own Words to guide us, and it is our responsibility to walk in close fellowship with our Lord.

Consequently, we learn from these Passages in John, that relationship with Christ is the key to successful Fruit-bearing.

THE LESSON GIVEN BY THE APOSTLE PAUL

In Romans 7:4-6, it is explained that human actions are energized from one of two sources. We can, on the one hand, be energized by our sinful nature; but when we are, we produce *"fruit for death."* Or we can be energized by the Holy Spirit. When we are controlled by the Spirit, we bear *"Fruit to God."*

In Galatians 5:16-26, Paul defines the fruit of sinful human nature and the Fruit that the Spirit-energized nature produces. It is striking that the Fruit God seeks, as defined here, is exactly as the Fruit sought in His Old Testament people! Bad fruit, the acts of the sinful nature, are *"sexual immorality, impurity and debauchery; idolatry and witchcraft; hatred, discord, jealousy, fits of rage, selfish ambition, dissensions, factions and envy; drunkenness, orgies, and the like."*

The Fruit of the Spirit, which is the opposite of the fruit of the flesh, is both inner (in the quality of our personal experience) and external (in the quality of our relationship with Christ); because *"The Fruit of the Spirit is love, joy, peace, patience, kindness, goodness, faithfulness, gentleness, and self-control"* (Gal. 5:22-23).

IN CONCLUSION

Fruitfulness is a consistent concept in the Old Testament and the New Testament. The Fruit God seeks in human beings is expressed in righteous and loving acts that bring peace and harmony to the individual and to society. But that Fruit is foreign to sinful human nature. Energized by sinful passions, fallen humanity acts in ways that harm and bring dissention.

God's solution is found in a personal relationship with Jesus and in the supernatural working of God's Spirit within the Believer. As we live in intimate, obedient relationship with Jesus, God's Spirit energizes us as we produce the peaceable Fruits of a Righteousness that can come only from the Lord.

(The summary on Fruitfulness was derived from the teaching of Lawrence Richards.)

(20) "AND THESE ARE THEY WHICH ARE SOWN ON GOOD GROUND; SUCH AS HEAR THE WORD, AND RECEIVE IT, AND BRING FORTH FRUIT, SOME THIRTYFOLD, SOME SIXTY, AND SOME AN HUNDRED."

The phrase, *"And these are they which are sown on good ground; such as hear the Word, and receive it, and bring forth fruit,"* presents that which the Holy Spirit strives for in the life of the Believer. The *"good ground"* refers to the heart of the individual which is prepared and cultivated in order that the Seed of the Word will have a proper lodging place. They *"hear the Word,"* and then they *"receive the Word,"* which means they *"act upon the Word,"* allowing it to *"bring forth Fruit."*

If one properly understands this Parable (The Parable of the Sower), one will properly understand the Ways of God in this world.

NOTES

For instance, the *"Fruit"* here spoken of by Christ, and outlined by the Apostle Paul in Galatians 5:22-23, can only be brought about by a proper relationship with Christ, which is the only way the Holy Spirit can work. The world thinks they can bring it about by education, or proper psychological counselling. However, such is impossible! Had it been possible, Jesus would not have had to go to Calvary in order to redeem man.

It is sadder still, when one realizes that the Church for all practical purposes has departed from Christ and His Word, gravitating toward worldly wisdom.

Just the other day, I happened to hear an exchange on an interview talk program over radio. It concerned racism.

After much discussion, the moderator made mention that legislation had failed to cure this evil, so what is the answer? Some ventured that the answer was now education. Regrettably, that won't work either!

The only cure for racism, or any other sin for that matter, is the heart of the individual changed by the Power of Christ, in order that the Fruit of the Spirit be brought about.

If one understands this, then one understands this Parable, and, in effect, the entirety of the Word of God, at least what the Plan of God for humanity is all about.

The phrase, *"Some thirtyfold, some sixty, and some an hundred,"* presents, as is obvious, various stages. However, the goal of the Holy Spirit in the life of the Believer, is always *"an hundredfold."* This is what Jesus meant when He said, *"He purgeth it, that it may bring forth more fruit"* (Jn. 15:2).

He then said, *"He that abideth in Me, and I in him, the same bringeth forth much Fruit"* (Jn. 15:5).

He further said, *"For without Me you can do nothing,"* which should settle once and for all, that all the efforts of man are fruitless, regarding changing men by any other means.

The Believer is to never be satisfied with merely bearing *"thirtyfold,"* or even *"sixtyfold."* The goal must always be *"an hundredfold."* This, the Spirit of God will do, if allowed to have His Way.

Even though Jesus does not mention it here, but does elaborate on it more fully in John 15, this process of *"an hundredfold,"* is not easily arrived at. It takes *"purging,"* and the purging process is not pleasant, easy, or of short duration.

Concerning my own personal situation, a dear lady in our Church (Family Worship Center) made this statement to me.

She said, *"Brother Swaggart, it is never pleasant to die, nor is it pleasant to watch someone else die."*

When she said it to me, I had to think for a moment before the full impact of her statement settled in on me.

She is right!

The adage would apply to both the physical and the spiritual realm. In the natural, to see someone die is a very distasteful thing. Regrettably, in the Spirit it is the same.

But yet in the Spirit, it has an entirely different result, with Jesus saying, *"Verily, verily, I say unto you, Except a corn of wheat fall into the ground and die, it abideth alone: but if it die, it bringeth forth much fruit"* (Jn. 12:24).

(21) "AND HE SAID UNTO THEM, IS A CANDLE BROUGHT TO BE PUT UNDER A BUSHEL, OR UNDER A BED? AND NOT TO BE SET ON A CANDLESTICK?"

This verse tells us that the secrets of Divine teaching are not to be privately enjoyed but to be imparted as a lamp imparts its light. Christians are responsible to proclaim the Gospel.

It may seem as if Jesus is changing the subject, however, He is merely proclaiming the result of those who *"bring forth Fruit."*

The phrase, *"And he said unto them,"* is meant to explain what the Work of God is all about as it is carried forth in the life of the Believer.

The question, *"Is a candle brought to put under a bushel, or under a bed?",* is meant to proclaim the lamp or *"candle"* as Divine Truth, shining in the Person of Christ and evidenced in the life of the Believer.

In other words, all of this work carried out by Christ in the life of the Believer, is meant to do two things:

1. To change the Believer from the fruit of the flesh, which is listed in Galatians 5:19-21, to the *"Fruit of the Spirit"* listed in Galatians 5:22-23.

2. The changed life of the Believer made possible by Christ, is to be a *"Light"* to the world.

The world is covered by spiritual darkness, which can only be penetrated by the Light of

NOTES

Christ, as it is presented in the Gospel. Consequently, it is imperative that this *"Light"* not be hid, as should be obvious!

Not too long after the turn of the century, efforts were made by a group of Christians to establish a Christian community in America, and incorporate a town, if you please! The result was Zion, Illinois. This was to be the perfect community, with the perfect environment, etc. To live in this town, one must be born again, plus subscribe to a host of rules and regulations, etc.

In short, it did not work, even though the town was established, and thrives even unto today, but in a different manner.

It is not God's Will, as is evidenced in these very Passages, for Believers to be bunched up in this manner. The Lord desires that we be in the world, though never of it, and that we let our light shine. Actually, this is the only Saving Grace in the world today, this Light brought out in the life of the Believer, as given by Jesus Christ.

The question, *"And not to be set on a candlestick?",* means that its purpose is illumination, which is an apt description!

To extend this to its proper conclusion, one must understand that this question as tendered by Christ, is definitely meant to include the presentation of the Gospel to the entirety of the world. Every single Believer is called for this task, in that the Light given to him by the Lord can be shed abroad to others. It is not meant to *"be put under a bushel, or under a bed."*

As I dictate these words (11-15-95), Frances and I have just returned from Brazil, where we were privileged to conduct a series of Evangelistic Crusades.

Our first service was in the Maracana Stadium, which seats 150,000 people, consequently, the largest in the world. Over 100,000 were in the Stadium that night. Dr. Manoel Ferriera, the President of the Assemblies of God in Brazil, the largest Pentecostal Organization in the world, with some 12,000,000 adherents, hosted this event, as well as all the other meetings in that great country. Actually, there were overflow crowds in each meeting, with thousands participating in the service outside the various auditoriums, watching the service on giant screens.

However, it was even a greater thrill to see scores of people who had been saved through the Telecast, and are now living productive Christian lives.

As I have stated many times in these Volumes, the Lord has called me for World Evangelism, with our primary objectives being Crusades and Television. That is the reason we see so many people saved in the Crusades and through the Telecast. The Lord has given us a special calling, which constitutes a special Message, and even a special Anointing. To be sure, it is all of the Lord and none of us. However, even though my burden may be somewhat heavier due to my calling, still, every Believer must have this burden at least in some degree. To do otherwise, is to hide the *"light."*

Any Church which is wrapped up only in its own locality, consequently ignoring the rest of the world, is, in effect, *"hiding its Light."* To do such, is to spiritually die. Because Light hidden is no Light at all! Jesus said, *"Remember therefore from whence thou art fallen, and repent, and do the first works; or else I will come unto thee quickly, and will remove thy candlestick out of his place, except thou repent"* (Rev. 2:5).

(22) "FOR THERE IS NOTHING HID, WHICH SHALL NOT BE MANIFESTED; NEITHER WAS ANY THING KEPT SECRET, BUT THAT IT SHOULD COME ABROAD."

The phrase, *"For there is nothing hid, which shall not be manifested,"* could be better translated, *"There is nothing hid save that it should be manifested."*

In other words, He is saying that the New Covenant of Grace, which was hidden in the Old, is to now be manifested, and to the entirety of the world. These great Truths will no longer be *"hidden,"* but will be manifested to all! A tremendous Truth is given here:

Inasmuch as the Light is given to any and all who will believe, with Fruit being realized in their lives, accordingly it must be given to others. To not *"manifest"* this Light, is to deny Christ.

The phrase, *"Neither was any thing kept secret, but that it should come abroad,"* means that even though this great Gospel of Grace was kept secret for a period of time, and for a reason, now this *"secret"* is to be manifested to all. And what is that secret?

"And the Spirit and the Bride say, Come. And let him that heareth say, Come. And let him that

is a thirst come. And whosoever will, let him take the Water of Life freely" (Rev. 22:17).

(23) "IF ANY MAN HAVE EARS TO HEAR, LET HIM HEAR."

In the Greek, the *"If"* does not mean that some did have ears to hear, and some did not, but, in fact, that all had ears to hear, and, therefore, they ought to use them.

In effect, Jesus is saying, *"Since a person has ears to hear, let him be hearing."* Two things are said:

1. We are meant to *"hear"* what He is saying about bearing Fruit, and taking the Gospel to the world, i.e., letting our Light shine.

2. The world, must have the opportunity to *"hear,"* whether they accept Christ or not! Paul said, *"How shall they hear without a Preacher?"* (Rom. 10:14). All Believers are held responsible to hear what Christ is saying regarding this all-important subject, even as all unbelievers will be held responsible for their actions upon hearing the Gospel.

(24) "AND HE SAID UNTO THEM, TAKE HEED WHAT YE HEAR: WITH WHAT MEASURE YE METE, IT SHALL BE MEASURED TO YOU: AND UNTO YOU THAT HEAR SHALL MORE BE GIVEN."

The phrase, *"And He said unto them, Take heed what ye hear,"* is a solemn statement indeed!

First of all, He means for us to hear what He is saying correctly, and that there is no excuse for us not to hear correctly.

Second, the implication given here is that tares (false doctrine) will be sown among the wheat (the True Gospel), and we must know and understand the Word well enough, to be able to recognize what is false.

The phrase, *"With what measure ye mete, it shall be measured to you,"* explains the increase from *"thirtyfold"* to *"an hundredfold,"* or, conversely, the opposite!

The phrase, *"And unto you that hear shall more be given,"* means not only to *"hear,"* but to act upon that which is heard, i.e., take the light to the world. If this is done, the fruit-bearing increases accordingly!

(25) "FOR HE THAT HATH, TO HIM SHALL BE GIVEN: AND HE THAT HATH NOT, FROM HIM SHALL BE TAKEN EVEN THAT WHICH HE HATH."

In proportion to the diligence given to this of which Christ speaks, so will spiritual intelligence be measured to the student. Spiritual gifts, if exercised, will be developed; if not, they will be lost.

The action of this True Servant, and of the under servants and the fortunes of the Gospel Kingdom between the First and Second Advents are set out in this Chapter. The history of that service, the responsibility of its agents, their quietness and Faith in danger, and the storms (vss. 35-41) which must exercise that Faith are here foreshadowed.

The phrase, *"For he that hath, to him shall be given,"* means that he is properly using that which is given him, therefore, more can be entrusted.

The phrase, *"And he that hath not, from him shall be taken even that which he hath,"* is the very opposite, and presents a startling concept. In other words, and according to Christ, we bear Fruit, or else we die (Jn. 15:6).

This one verse epitomizes the Parable of the *"Talents"* as given by Christ (Mat. 25:14-30). The ones who used their talents and gained others, were rewarded accordingly, while the one who did not use his talent, but rather hid it, was *"taken away even that which he hath"* (Mat. 25:29).

If the Believer does not walk in the Light as it is given to him, he will, of necessity, regress into darkness.

That is one of the reasons that the particular Religions Denominations which were given the Light of the Baptism in the Holy Spirit, and rejected it, are now void of any spiritual move whatsoever. In other words, all their activity (at least those who fall into this category) is man-inspired, and, consequently, man-led, and, of necessity, of no spiritual consequence.

As well, those Religious Denominations, which fall under the heading of Pentecostal, etc., which no longer depend on the Holy Spirit, but, instead, their own human endeavors, are losing all spiritual effectiveness. Not only are they gaining nothing, but, even that which they have had, is being *"taken away."* As someone has said, *"Use it, or lose it."*

(26) "AND HE SAID, SO IS THE KINGDOM OF GOD, AS IF A MAN SHOULD CAST SEED INTO THE GROUND;"

This has been called the *"Parable of the Wheat."* It speaks to the consciousness of Jesus as to the success and non-success of His preaching as it appears in the Parable of the

Sower; but only success is predicted in this beauteous Parable of the Man and the Seed. Christ sows, He reaps, and between these actions He waits. This is His present attitude. He is absent; He does not outwardly interpose. The Seed (Gospel) is left to itself to accomplish its purpose, which it definitely shall! During His absence, the laborers are responsible to work in the field (Williams).

The phrase, *"And He said, So is the Kingdom of God,"* is meant to express the manner in which the Gospel will take its course.

The phrase, *"As if a man should cast seed into the ground,"* is meant to explain how this will be done.

(27) "AND SHOULD SLEEP, AND RISE NIGHT AND DAY, AND THE SEED SHOULD SPRING AND GROW UP, HE KNOWETH NOT HOW."

The phrase, *"And should sleep, and rise night and day,"* means that after planting the Seed (Gospel), there is nothing more he can do.

The phrase, *"And the Seed should spring and grow up,"* refers to the germination of the Seed, which is brought about if the Seed is properly planted.

The phrase, *"He knoweth not how,"* means that he has no understanding how the Seed germinates after it is properly planted in the soil.

This verse is meant to proclaim the Power of the Gospel. It is up to the laborers (Christian Workers) to sow the Seed, but how it is received is according to the hearts of the individuals.

As well, after sowing the Seed, there is nothing more he can do, but must depend on the Power of God for the Seed to bring forth Fruit in the life of the hearer. Being finite, he does not know nor understand how this is carried out, and is not responsible for that part of the process. It is our responsibility to plant the Seed (Gospel) and God's responsibility to make it germinate, at least in the hearts of those who will believe.

However, the Seed cannot *"spring and grow up"* unless it is first *"cast into the ground,"* i.e., presented to the world.

(28) "FOR THE EARTH BRINGETH FORTH FRUIT OF HERSELF; FIRST THE BLADE, THEN THE EAR, AFTER THAT THE FULL CORN IN THE EAR."

The phrase, *"For the earth bringeth forth Fruit of herself,"* is meant to explain that sowing

Seed and the Gospel are very similar. If the Seed is planted, it will ultimately *"bring forth Fruit of herself."* While the sowing of the Seed is the responsibility of the laborer (Christian Worker), the bringing forth of the *"Fruit"* is the responsibility of the Holy Spirit.

The phrase, *"First the blade, then the ear, after that the full corn in the ear,"* is meant to express a Law, not only of seed in the earth, which is obvious to all, but, as well, the Law of the Gospel in *"sowing and reaping."* The Work of the Holy Spirit is developed in three stages:

1. *"First the blade"*: After the Seed is planted, the first little shoot comes above the soil, which represents the germination of the Seed. This is the acceptance of the Gospel by the hearer after it is presented.

2. *"Then the ear"*: This speaks of what surrounds that which will ultimately be brought forth. In other words, it is a sort of protective shield, for the *"full corn"* which will ultimately spring forth. Were this not done, Satan would be able to destroy it!

3. *"After that the full corn in the ear"*: This presents the finished product, and is the result of the labor of sowing the Seed.

Consequently, the Lord is telling us that our part of the task is simple to say the least. We are to just present the Gospel, with the Holy Spirit doing all the work in the hearts and lives of those who believe. As we have repeatedly stated, the Worker is not responsible for the developed Fruit, but is definitely responsible for the sowing of the Seed, without which no Fruit is possible.

(29) "BUT WHEN THE FRUIT IS BROUGHT FORTH, IMMEDIATELY HE PUTTETH IN THE SICKLE, BECAUSE THE HARVEST IS COME."

The phrase, *"But when the Fruit is brought forth,"* actually has reference to the end of this age, when the Church will be called to account.

The phrase, *"Immediately He putteth in the sickle, because the harvest is come,"* has two meanings:

1. It means that there definitely will be a *"harvest."* Thankfully, millions of souls have heard the Gospel, and many have accepted.

2. What Jesus did at Calvary and the Resurrection, will bring forth that which He intended, and, in effect, has brought forth that which He intended!

As well, there is a double meaning to the entirety of this Parable. It is as follows:

1. It pertains to each individual who sows the Seed of the Gospel, as well as those who hear it. It promises that some will receive, and will bring forth Fruit. God's Word will not return void.

2. The meaning of the Parable concerns the entirety of the Plan of God regarding the Church. It speaks of all the efforts which have been made for all time, and for the time that remains. Soon it will be over, and the *"harvest is come."* As stated, this will be at the end of the age, actually at the Second Coming.

(30) "AND HE SAID, WHEREUNTO SHALL WE LIKEN THE KINGDOM OF GOD? OR WITH WHAT COMPARISON SHALL WE COMPARE IT?"

The question, *"And He said, Whereunto shall we liken the Kingdom of God?"*, is meant, by the Master, to forearm all those who follow Him against disappointment and confusion. While the inner Kingdom of God (vss. 26-29) would be, and continue, pure, the outward professing Kingdom (vss. 30-32) would become a great earthly institution having great branches, and would become the home of Satan and his angels; and so it has come to pass (Williams).

The question, *"Or with what comparison shall we compare it?"*, is meant to proclaim the manner in which Satan will endeavor to corrupt the Work of God.

(31) "IT IS LIKE A GRAIN OF MUSTARD SEED, WHICH, WHEN IT IS SOWN IN THE EARTH, IS LESS THAN ALL THE SEEDS THAT BE IN THE EARTH:"

The phrase, *"It is like a grain of mustard seed,"* is the illustration that Jesus will use as a comparison to the Kingdom of God.

The phrase, *"Which, when it is sown in the earth, is less than all the seeds that be in the earth,"* has reference to the size of the plant that can come from this particular type of seed. It does not mean that it is actually the smallest seed, for there are actually other seeds which are smaller, but, rather, the smallest seed which produces such a large plant.

The Lord is here referencing the beginning of the Church as being small and insignificant, but rapidly expanding until it covers the entirety of the earth.

(32) "BUT WHEN IT IS SOWN, IT GROWETH UP, AND BECOMETH GREATER

THAN ALL HERBS, AND SHOOTETH OUT GREAT BRANCHES; SO THAT THE FOWLS OF THE AIR MAY LODGE UNDER THE SHADOW OF IT."

The phrase, *"But when it is sown, it groweth up, and becometh greater than all herbs,"* refers to Christianity being larger than all other efforts of religion in the world.

One could probably say, that if Catholicism (which claims to be Christian, but actually is not), and Christianity were joined together, it would be larger than all the other religions of the world combined. (Catholicism and Christianity combined boast approximately 2 billion adherents.)

The phrase, *"And shooteth out great branches,"* refers to all the various divisions of Christianity, as Catholicism, etc. (Actually, Mormonism also claims to be Christian, etc.)

The phrase, *"So that the fowls of the air may lodge under the shadow of it,"* refers to Satanic powers as explained in Matthew 13:19 and Luke 8:12.

This is another way of Jesus saying what He said in the Parable of the Leaven, *"The Kingdom of Heaven is like unto leaven, which a woman took, and hid in three measures of meal, till the whole was leavened"* (Mat. 13:33).

This is what I have repeatedly warned the reader about in all of these Commentaries respecting the True Church and the Apostate Church. In all called *"Christianity"* the True Church, although present, is far smaller than the Apostate Church. The apostasy is so great and widespread, that it looks as if the *"whole is leavened,"* but, in fact, the True Church is present, but not so easily discerned or observed.

It is somewhat as ancient Israel when Elijah complained, *"And I, even I only, am left; and they seek my life, to take it away"* (I Ki. 19:10).

However, the Lord told him, *"Yet I have left me seven thousand in Israel, all the knees which have not bowed unto Baal, and every mouth which hath not kissed him"* (I Ki. 19:18).

Satan has sought to infiltrate the Church, and he has succeeded admirably so! Consequently, every Believer must be diligent that he follows the Word of God only, and not man.

In our series of meetings in Brazil, which we have just mentioned, one can get an idea of what I speak.

There are two branches in this particular country of a particular Pentecostal Denomination.

NOTES

One has about 12,000,000 adherents, with the other approximately 3,000,000. As far as I can tell, at least in this case, the larger (which is unusual) follows the Lord, while the smaller, at least its leadership, follows man.

As an example, a particular Evangelist recently joined this Pentecostal Denomination, which has its Headquarters in the U.S.A. Before he joined it, he was black-balled, black-listed, and roundly rejected by the smaller Pentecostal Organization. However, the moment he joined this Denomination, their statements concerning him changed 180 degrees. Now he is a Godly Evangelist, according to them!

Why did they change so quickly?

They changed because they were parroting the party line. Whatever the Denominational Leaders said, they said the same.

Before this Brother became a part of that Denomination, and because he was not a part of that Denomination, he was spoken of very negatively by its Leadership. But when he joined the Denomination, all of a sudden he became pure and holy. All of this tells us several things:

1. They had equated belonging to their Denomination as belonging to the Kingdom of God. They may deny that, but their actions prove otherwise.

2. It is obvious that this group in Brazil was following man instead of the Lord. It did not really matter what the true spiritual condition was, but only what the Religious Leadership said about him. The day before he joined, he was not a *"True Apostle,"* but the day after he joined, he was a *"True Apostle!"* Such is man-directed, and not God-directed!

3. Anyone who is not led by the Holy Spirit is Apostate.

This does not mean that everyone associated with that Denomination is Apostate, but definitely does mean that a part or all of its Leadership is Apostate.

If one is led by the Holy Spirit, one is led by the Word of God. If one is not led by the Holy Spirit, one is led by the word of man.

Actually, whatever the man was before he joined this Denomination, he was the same after he joined it. His spiritual status did not change, but yet in the eyes of these individuals, whoever they may have been, his status did change, and because he had associated himself with this earthly organization.

In Truth, many Religious Denominations feel and do the same about their own particular group. Actually, this even occurs in local Churches. In other words, if you're not a member of our group, you are not accepted by the Lord, etc.

Even though this is only a small part of the apostasy which Christ speaks of, still, it is an important part.

Considering that these *"fowls of the air,"* i.e., religious demon spirits, are *"lodged under the shadow of the Church,"* millions think that they are legitimate, and, consequently, accept their teaching which leads to destruction. Paul called them, *"False apostles, deceitful workers, transforming themselves into the Apostles of Christ."*

He then said, *"And no marvel; for Satan himself is transformed into an angel of light."*

And lastly, *"Therefore it is no great thing if his ministers also be transformed as the ministers of righteousness; whose end shall be according to their works"* (II Cor. 11:13-15).

He likened it all to *"another Jesus,"* *"another Spirit,"* and *"another Gospel"* (II Cor. 11:4).

For instance, in the 1980's, hundreds of millions of dollars were poured into a religious amusement park, which went under the guise of the Gospel. Regrettably and sadly, in the 1990's, the same thing is happening all over again. Hundreds of millions of dollars are being squandered in the same capacity in respect to some religious television networks. *"Another Jesus, another Gospel, and by another Spirit,"* is being presented, and most Christians do not even have enough spiritual discernment to know the true from the false. This is the sad part!

Why can't they tell?

They cannot tell because they do not know the Word of God. The Psalmist said, *"Thy Word is a Lamp unto my feet, and a Light unto my path"* (Ps. 119:105). They have no *"Lamp"* or *"Light"* because they do not know the *"Word."*

(33) "AND WITH MANY SUCH PARABLES SPAKE HE THE WORD UNTO THEM, AS THEY WERE ABLE TO HEAR IT."

The phrase, *"And with many such Parables spake He the Word unto them,"* means it was done in order for them to understand what He was speaking of.

At times, He used Parables to shade what He was saying, while at other times, as here, to make clear and plain.

NOTES

The phrase, *"As they were able to hear it,"* refers not only to the act of hearing, as is its usual meaning, but also to the act of understanding. It is thereby clear that these Parables were used to make Truth clear and plain.

(34) "BUT WITHOUT A PARABLE SPAKE HE NOT UNTO THEM: AND WHEN THEY WERE ALONE, HE EXPOUNDED ALL THINGS TO HIS DISCIPLES."

The phrase, *"But without a Parable spake He not unto them,"* means that this was the method He used to impart teaching unto the hearers.

The Greek word for *"Parable"* means something *"set alongside."* Sometimes Scripture records people illustrating what they are saying by setting a concrete situation alongside an abstract concept (Jud. 9:8-15; II Sam. 12:1-7; Isa. 5:1-7).

However, and as is obvious, the most well-known Parables in the Bible are those of Jesus. Many of these have an illustrative thrust, and a true to life experience, such as those of the Good Samaritan (Lk. 10:27-37), the Prodigal Son (Lk. 15:11-32), and the Talents (Lk. 19:11-27).

However, some Parables, related to a yet hidden form of the Kingdom, were told in such a way (as we have stated), that they concealed rather than illustrated Jesus' meaning (Richards).

The phrase, *"And when they were alone, He expounded all things to His Disciples,"* means that He explained it plainer and clearer.

The idea is, that He took the time to explain fully what He was speaking of, which actually amounted to fresh revelations concerning the mysteries of the Kingdom of God.

The word, *"Disciples,"* refers to the *"Twelve,"* even though Jesus had other Disciples as well!

How wonderful it must have been to be able to sit at the feet of Jesus, and to hear Him expound more fully the Word of God. Considering that He was the Living Word, if you please, the Incarnate Word, how wonderful these times must have been to the Disciples!

And yet, He does the same identical thing with us, if we will only wait on Him.

In the prayer meetings of which I have mentioned, time and time again the Lord through the Agency and Person of the Holy Spirit, would open up His Word to me in such a fashion, that my soul would be greatly blessed.

Even last night (11-14-95), the Lord made something so very, very special to me. It concerned something which I felt was extremely important, and yet, for which I had no answer.

On the last day of our meetings in Brazil, which was a Monday, I preached three times that particular day, beside driving about 200 miles. The first message was to approximately 500 Preachers, with the second message to approximately 700 Preachers. And then that night we were in one of the Churches, with it packed to capacity. Immediately after the service ended, we caught a plane out of Sao Paula, for the States. Frances and I flew all night, actually getting very little rest. Consequently, when we finally arrived in Baton Rouge the next day, to say I was exhausted would have been an understatement.

If I had left it up to my feelings, I would not have gone to Prayer Meeting that night. However, how so glad I am that I went.

As I laid this petition before the Lord, His Spirit came upon me, and in His Word He outlined to me exactly what He would do and could do, which was whatever is needed. Along with that revelation was a powerful moving of His Spirit, that rejuvenated me, insomuch that I felt so much better when I left than when I came.

So, what He did then, He does now, at least for those who will bother to take the time to seek His Face.

(35) "AND THE SAME DAY, WHEN THE EVEN WAS COME, HE SAITH UNTO THEM, LET US PASS OVER UNTO THE OTHER SIDE."

The phrase, *"And the same day, when the even was come,"* refers to the same day that He had been teaching the people through Parables.

The phrase, *"He saith unto them, Let us pass over unto the other side,"* is freighted with meaning.

First of all, the *"other side"* represents that to which Christ came. He left the portals of Glory, in order to come down to a world infested by demon spirits, and, for the purpose of redeeming mankind, represented by the maniac of Gadara.

The storm He calmed on the Sea of Galilee, was representative of the storm in this man's soul, as the next Chapter reveals.

Last of all, He would be opposed greatly by the powers of darkness in the realm of the

NOTES

storm, but as long as Jesus is in the boat, it cannot sink.

(36) "AND WHEN THEY HAD SENT AWAY THE MULTITUDE, THEY TOOK HIM EVEN AS HE WAS IN THE SHIP. AND THERE WERE ALSO WITH HIM OTHER LITTLE SHIPS."

The phrase, *"And when they had sent away the multitude,"* means such was done only after they had been amply fed by the Word of God, with, as well, many, no doubt, being healed.

The phrase, *"They took Him even as He was in the ship,"* refers more than likely to one of the vessels owned by Zebedee, which Jesus often used as a platform from which to preach and teach.

The idea of the phrase is that Jesus was so exhausted from the full day of teaching and preaching, and, no doubt, healing, that they almost had to carry Him to the ship. In His Incarnation, He grew tired exactly as any other man.

The phrase, *"And there were also with Him other little ships,"* referred, no doubt, to those who wanted to be near Him wherever He went. Consequently, they, as well, would experience the stilling of the storm.

(37) "AND THERE AROSE A GREAT STORM OF WIND, AND THE WAVES BEAT INTO THE SHIP, SO THAT IT WAS NOW FULL."

The phrase, *"And there arose a great storm of wind,"* refers to a furious storm or hurricane. Wuest says, *"A storm breaking forth from black thunder-clouds in furious gusts, with floods of rain, and throwing everything topsy-turvy."*

The phrase, *"And the waves beat into the ship, so that it was now full,"* meant that it was full of water. The phrase has reference to the waves beating into the ship, and repeatedly doing so.

As well, the inference is that the storm came up suddenly, and, consequently, without warning. This account is given that the lesson not be lost upon the reader.

1. In this Christian life, there will be opposition, as is evidenced by this storm. Some foolishly and erroneously claim that they can confess such away, claiming an idealistic life free from such disturbances. However, such is not Scriptural. It is not a question of if the storm may come, but, rather, when it comes!

2. Some claim they can have Faith enough,

that they can ward off all such things. However, are they accusing Christ of not having enough Faith?

I seriously doubt anyone would want to be guilty of such an accusation.

No! The storm did not come up because of a lack of Faith, but rather that their Faith (the Disciples) might be tested. Great Faith must be tested greatly!

3. Even though Satan sent the storm, he had to have permission from God to do such. Satan cannot do anything to a Believer unless the Lord permits or allows it. Consequently, the Lord allowed this storm to come up, and for a reason (Rom. 8:28).

(38) "AND HE WAS IN THE HINDER PART OF THE SHIP, ASLEEP ON A PILLOW: AND THEY AWAKE HIM, AND SAY UNTO HIM, MASTER, CAREST THOU NOT THAT WE PERISH?"

The phrase, *"And He was in the hinder part of the ship, asleep on a pillow,"* referred to His exhaustion from the long day of teaching, preaching, and healing. As well, the *"pillow"* here in question was not a soft pillow, but rather the leather cushion of the steersman, or the low bench on which the steersman sometimes sits.

The phrase, *"And they awake Him, and say unto Him,"* concerns their desperation!

Inasmuch as the boat was filling up with water, and even was now *"full,"* and due to the ferocity of the storm, their efforts to keep the ship afloat were in vain. Consequently, they resort to Christ, but only after all their efforts had failed.

No doubt, knowing of His physical exhaustion, they did not want to disturb Him. Nevertheless, they soon arrive at a place to where they have no choice.

It is amazing that He was able to continue sleeping, especially considering that the ship was violently rocking from side to side, being beaten violently by the waves. As well, the water had to be pouring over Him, even as it did the Disciples. And yet, there is a possibility that the ship was large enough that the waves did not reach Him, which is probably the case.

The question, *"Master, carest Thou not that we perish?"*, is claimed by some to have been impertinence on the part of the speaker. Some have attributed the question to Peter.

However, those who would accuse the Disciples of impertinence, obviously have not been

where the Disciples were. Oftentimes the Lord allows things to come very close to destruction before He steps in and takes a hand. Personally, I know what it is to cry, *"Master, carest not that I perish?"*

The powers of darkness can be so strong, as evidenced by this storm, that it looks like there's no way out. But yet, we hear the Words of Christ, *"Let us pass over unto the other side."* He did not say, *"Let us go out into the sea and perish!"*

So, He does care, enough I might quickly add, to go with us through the storm, and then to calm it when it looks like we will surely perish.

I might quickly add, that even though the storms have beaten furiously upon this old ship of the Church, still, not a single ship or passenger has ever been lost, at least for those who trust Him.

(39) "AND HE AROSE, AND REBUKED THE WIND, AND SAID UNTO THE SEA, PEACE BE STILL. AND THE WIND CEASED, AND THERE WAS A GREAT CALM."

The phrase, *"And He arose,"* literally means, *"He awakened!"*

The phrase, *"And rebuked the wind, and said unto the sea,"* implies in the original Greek that before the Word was uttered, the thing was done by the simple power of His Will, which preceded His Word.

The phrase, *"Peace, be still,"* is a beautiful Word. Wuest says it probably meant, *"Silence! Hush!"*

The phrase, *"And the wind ceased, and there was a great calm,"* means that the wind instantly ceased, and the sea instantly calmed.

This miracle invaded the laws of nature, interposing a greater Law, which was the Word of God. Consequently, Jesus proved Himself as the Creator of all things, and, therefore, God, although manifest in the flesh. In other words, only God could do such a thing!

To emphasize the point, there was no gradual subsiding of the storm, as in the ordinary operations of nature, but almost before the Word had escaped His lips there was a perfect calm (E. Bickersteth).

(40) "AND HE SAID UNTO THEM, WHY ARE YE SO FEARFUL? HOW IS IT THAT YE HAVE NO FAITH?"

The phrase, *"And He said unto them,"* refers to Him speaking to men who were transfixed with amazement at that which had happened before their very eyes, the instant stilling of the storm. Even though He would give them the lesson intended by the Holy Spirit, nevertheless, at least at this moment, their minds were totally on Him and what He had done, rather than learning the lesson He taught. However, as is here recorded, the lesson would ultimately become unmistakably clear to them.

The question as asked by Christ, *"Why are ye so fearful?"*, refers to an imperfect love on the part of the Disciples for the Lord (I Jn. 4:18).

This question as it was asked of them so long ago, is also asked of each and every Believer. As the Disciples, there has not been a single Believer, at one time or the other, who has not *"feared."* Nevertheless, the *"fear"* shows an imperfect love and an imperfect Faith.

Perfect Love trusts, while Perfect Faith believes!

The storms are allowed to teach us Trust, and, as well, that we may learn how to use our Faith. No! No one enjoys such, and admittedly many storms come upon us because of our own foolishness, etc. However, some are allowed, as here, and as stated, for a purpose. Great Faith must be tested greatly!

The question, *"How is it that ye have no Faith?"*, is actually saying, *"Do you think any harm could come to you, while I am in the ship?"*

The question is not meant to infer that the Disciples had no Faith at all, but that they did not have Faith for this particular situation. According to what the Lord asks of us, accordingly is the Faith we must have. Oftentimes, such Faith is not readily available. Nevertheless, whatever the Lord asks us to do, will always be accompanied by the necessary Faith, that is, if we will dare to believe Him.

By these questions, was He meaning that they should have calmed the storm themselves without awakening Him?

No! That is not the idea at all. These questions cover the entirety of the scenario, meaning they were afraid they were going to die. So, He is asking them how such could happen with Him in the ship?

In Truth, it could not happen! The Creator and Sustainer of the Universe was with them in the boat. Wuest said that the Disciples had accepted His Messiahship, but had a most inadequate view of what that office carried with it.

(41) "AND THEY FEARED EXCEEDINGLY, AND SAID ONE TO ANOTHER, WHAT MANNER OF MAN IS THIS, THAT EVEN THE WIND AND THE SEA OBEY HIM?"

The phrase, *"And they feared exceedingly,"* means their fear of Him was greater even than their fear had been of the storm. To see the storm raging one moment, and then to see utter calm the next, was beyond their power of comprehension.

The question, *"And said one to another, What manner of Man is this, that even the wind and the sea obey Him?"*, actually said, *"What manner of is this?"*, with the word, *"Man,"* not found in the Greek. According to Wuest, Mark has it, *"Who then is this Person?"*

We know that Satan was the cause of this storm, even though permitted by God. So, how could Satan think that he could do damage to someone as powerful as Christ?

I am certain he knew that he could not do anything to Christ, but, perhaps, with Christ being asleep, he thought he might be able to swamp the boat and possibly even kill one or more of the Disciples. But, of course, that was futile as well, inasmuch as Christ had said at the beginning of the journey, *"Let us pass over unto the other side."*

But still, the Evil One would try to wreak havoc, even though he had little or no chance of succeeding!

The Disciples were right! The *"wind and sea do obey Him,"* as well as everything else, other than most people.

CHAPTER 5

(1) "AND THEY CAME OVER UNTO THE OTHER SIDE OF THE SEA, INTO THE COUNTRY OF THE GADARENES."

The phrase, *"And they came over unto the other side of the Sea,"* refers to the eastern shore of the Sea of Galilee.

The phrase, *"Into the country of the Gadarenes,"* is the only reference to this area in the Bible, and concerns the deliverance of the man called *"Legion."*

Gadara was a city south of the Sea of Galilee and east of Jordan in the Decapolis area. This *"country"* simply referred to the parts outside the city which reached down to the Sea. The city of Gadara was probably about three miles from the Sea of Galilee proper.

(2) "AND WHEN HE WAS COME OUT OF THE SHIP, IMMEDIATELY THERE MET HIM OUT OF THE TOMBS A MAN WITH AN UNCLEAN SPIRIT,"

The phrase, *"And when He was come out of the ship,"* concerns the very reason for which He came, which was to deliver the Maniac of Gadara. As we have stated, this in a way symbolizes the great mission for which Christ came to the world.

Many may object, claiming that man is not nearly in the condition of the Maniac of Gadara, and, hence, such would not provide a suitable example.

To be sure, only those who hide their heads in the sand would think such a thing. Even at the present time, and despite the thousands of years of intellectual pursuit and education, the fallen nature of man has never been more obvious. As I dictate these words, just days ago a mass grave was found in former Yugoslavia, containing the bodies of approximately 5,000 people. They had recently been shot, in what was referred to as *"ethnic cleansing."*

And lest the reader thinks that such is indigenous only to the guilty ones, if the ones shot had had the opportunity, they would more than likely have visited the same on their assailants.

Some time ago, Frances and I, along with friends, were in Munich, Germany. A few miles from this beautiful city is the concentration camp called *"Dachou,"* actually, the first such camp built by Hitler. I personally looked at the ovens, where thousands of Jews were gassed to death, and then burned. It is said that when the wind was blowing toward Munich, the smell of burning bodies filled the air.

How could educated, civilized, so-called human beings engage themselves in such horror?

Man should learn from that horrid debacle of World War II, that education, as helpful as it is in many respects, is not the answer to the evil hearts of men. The men who murdered 6,000,000 Jews, plus millions of others, were educated men. However, an evil heart which undergoes education, is only an educated evil heart when it's all over!

No! The example of the Maniac of Gadara is not an overemphasis of the state of man.

Actually, it perfectly symbolizes the unregenerate heart.

The phrase, *"Immediately there met Him out of the tombs a man with an unclean spirit,"* instantly proclaims the one Jesus had come to deliver.

Matthew says there were two, while Mark as Luke only mentions one. Actually, there were two, but the one mentioned by Mark and Luke was no doubt the more prominent and fierce of the two.

More than likely, there were others in the general area as well! However, only two were delivered, and because the others, if in fact there were others, would not come to Christ.

The Jews did not have their burial-places in their cities, lest they should be defiled. Consequently, they buried their dead without the gates in the fields or mountains, etc. Their sepulchers were frequently hewn out of the rock in the sides of limestone hills, etc.

The demon spirits that possessed this man guarded their territory with diligence. Consequently, when the ship carrying Jesus and His Disciples came close to the shore, with them disembarking, their response was immediate!

Matthew, speaking of the two, says they were *"exceeding fierce, so that no man might pass by that way"* (Mat. 8:28). However, they did not know Who this *"Man"* was!

The phrase, *"Unclean spirit,"* seems to be a designation applied to any and all spirits, irrespective of their activity. However, some were given other designations such as a *"dumb and deaf spirit"* (Mk. 9:25), *"a spirit of infirmity"* (Lk. 13:11), and *"a spirit of divination"* (Acts 16:16). However, and as stated, the catch-all phrase seems to be *"unclean spirit."*

The Scripture is silent respecting the origin of demons. However, some scholars (and I share this view), believe that these disembodied spirits are the product of a pre-Adamic creation which fell with Lucifer. Consequently, having been deprived of their original body, they seek a body to inhabit, whether human or animal.

Some have thought these to be the fallen angels; however, there is no record of an Angel, fallen or otherwise, possessing anyone. Since angels are not disembodied, it would be impossible for them to do such a thing. Therefore, demon spirits are not fallen Angels.

To be demon possessed is an awful thing, and from what description we have, it seems to always include at least some form of insanity. To be sure, everyone, even consecrated Believers, are oppressed by demon spirits at times, or even influenced. However, oppression or influence is not possession.

Despite the teaching of some, a Believer cannot be demon possessed. Influenced and oppressed, yes!

Why was this man demon possessed? In fact, why is any person demon possessed?

The answer to that would not be simple, but would probably come under the category of one of several things.

Environment may well be one of the principle causes of demon possession. Individuals who live in areas where demons are actually worshiped, as some places in Africa and elsewhere, possession, as should be obvious, is rife.

Association is another cause. This is the cause, I believe, of homosexuality and such perversions. A child is molested, and then at times (but not always) takes upon himself (or herself) the spirit of the molester.

As well, association with any perverted activity will, sooner or later, wreak its terrible toll, and can result in demon possession.

Lastly, territorial possession may be more extended than one realizes. I speak of families. I feel it is improper to take this too far; however, I think there is some evidence that demon possession can literally be handed down from father to son, etc. Of course, the terrible chain is broken upon any member of the family coming to Christ.

At the same time, I do feel that some have made more of this than they should, but to disavow the possibility, I think is unwise.

If, in fact, this is correct (and I believe it is), the Salvation of any member of a family, and especially an entire family coming to Christ, is of far greater consequence than even the immediate Salvation of the principles involved, as wonderful as that may be. This horrible chain of demon influence, oppression, and even possession is now broken. It does not mean that demon powers cannot have some access, even to Believers, but it does mean that their authority to steal, kill, and destroy, is broken.

When my family came to Christ in 1941, as far as I know, this was the first time that anyone

NOTES

with the name of Swaggart had ever come to know Christ. Beautifully enough, my entire family was saved, with me coming to Christ in 1943 at eight years of age.

Now, the son given to Frances and me, along with his wife wonderfully serve the Lord. As well, their three children, our grandchildren, also serve Jesus. In fact, all three are Baptized in the Holy Spirit. I believe when they are old enough to be married, that their children will as well serve the Lord, at least when they are old enough to accept Christ as their Saviour.

As a result of my Mother and Dad accepting Christ so long ago, the entire direction of our family changed, as would be obvious. Whatever hold Satan had was broken. I am not aware of any demon possession in our family, but I do know there was tremendous demon influence and oppression. To be sure, without Christ, the future would have been foreboding. But with Christ, everything changed, and for the better.

That is one of the reasons that we must allow this Light to shine, in order that others may hear and know, as Jesus outlined in 4:21.

(3) "WHO HAD HIS DWELLING AMONG THE TOMBS; AND NO MAN COULD BIND HIM, NO, NOT WITH CHAINS:"

The phrase, *"Who had his dwelling among the tombs,"* is meant to insinuate more than a place of abode. There was a spiritual attraction to the death represented by the *"tombs."* The man was possessed by an *"unclean spirit,"* which was the epitome of death, even while he lived. The further away from God, Who is Life, the closer to death. If one does not have Light, he has darkness! There is no in-between.

A perfect example is the rock 'n roll craze, which has gone to the depths of iniquity, and personifies death. The songs of these people glorify death, whether it be by suicide or murder. *"He that hath the Son hath life."* It might also be said, *"He that hath not the Son hath death"* (I Jn. 5:12).

So, this man dwelt among the tombs, because every fiber of his being spoke of death! Death is the ultimate conclusion of sin!

The phrase, *"And no man could bind him, no, not with chains,"* spoke of the superhuman strength he possessed due to the *"unclean spirit."* In effect, there was no earthly remedy for his terrible condition, and yet Jesus would come to this forsaken place to deliver this poor soul.

(4) "BECAUSE THAT HE HAD BEEN OF-TEN BOUND WITH FETTERS AND CHAINS, AND THE CHAINS HAD BEEN PLUCKED ASUNDER BY HIM, AND THE FETTERS BROKEN IN PIECES: NEITHER COULD ANY MAN TAME HIM."

The phrase, *"Because that he had been of-ten bound with fetters and chains,"* proclaims the efforts of men to restrain him. These bind-ings were probably made of ropes, etc.

The word, *"often,"* proclaims that they had done this many times, but, as well, had in-creased the strength of the bindings each time, but with no success.

The phrase, *"And the chains had been plucked asunder by him, and the fetters broken in pieces,"* represents his superhuman strength.

Such is not uncommon, even at the present time. In certain parts of Africa, and elsewhere, where Satan is openly worshiped through the fetish of the witch doctors, human bodies, at times, are made to levitate in mid-air.

Many years ago, *"Readers Digest"* carried an article respecting the country of Tibet. At that time, very few westerners penetrated the con-fines of that country steeped in heathenistic darkness. Some few who did, told of stones be-ing thrown through the air, with no visible hand providing the motion.

The writer of the article had no explanation for it, but, of course, we know that it was de-mon spirits, which, by and large, controlled this land, as demon spirits control, more or less, many, if not most countries of the world.

The phrase, *"Neither could any man tame him,"* was the conclusion then, and is the con-clusion now. In other words, this is beyond the pale of human endeavor, and irrespective of its intellectual knowledge.

Despite this plain statement as written by Mark, and inspired by the Holy Spirit, man now feels he is able to do what his ancient counter-parts could not do. I speak of the field of hu-manistic psychology.

Of course, the advocates of this philosophy would disavow their abilities in such desperate situations; however, my question would be, *"To what degree can psychology be of service?"*

If, in his demon possession, he can break ropes an eighth inch in diameter, could psychol-ogy help him then, but not if he can break ropes up to a quarter of an inch in diameter?

NOTES

I do not mean to be sarcastic, but the truth is, psychology holds no answer whatsoever, and despite the fact that the modern Church has bought this humanistic line, proverbially speak-ing, hook, line, and sinker.

Even though the following has been given elsewhere in these Volumes, I personally feel that the significance of this subject demands that we repeat the information.

THE REPLACEMENT OF BIBLICAL COUNSELING

I am absolutely convinced that psycho-therapy (psychological counseling) is rapidly replacing Biblical counseling, and that the whole Christian structure is being, to a great extent, subverted by this *"false religion,"* and a *"false religion"* it is!

Perhaps some of the statements which will be made might shock or annoy, or even make some angry, but I am convinced they must be said.

PSYCHOTHERAPY AND BIBLICAL COUNSELING

In a recent book review in a major Pentecos-tal publication, a book entitled *"The Holy Spirit In Counseling"* was lauded. Here is what was said:

The authors, who I will leave nameless, and Ministers in this particular Pentecostal De-nomination, examined (according to the book report) the Biblical foundations of the Holy Spirit's dynamics as Comforter in the counsel-ing process.

Both authors during the time of writing, were professors in one of the schools in this Pentecostal Denomination. The following is a statement they made in their book:

"It is impossible to separate psychology and theology — as they relate to the counseling pro-cess. The object of counseling is a human being created in God's Image. Wholeness is achieved only when life is lived in the manner in which He intended. Therefore, it is not a question of whether therapists rely upon the Holy Spirit or upon their counseling skills. We must equip ourselves with the best tools available, while being certain that the Presence and Power of the Holy Spirit permeates our personalities."

If one is to notice, even though cleverly stated, they are saying that it doesn't really mat-ter what one uses, the Holy Spirit or their coun-seling skills (psychology).

They went on to say, *"We must equip our-selves with the best tools available,"* which actually says that at times psychology is a better tool than the Holy Spirit.

They then tried to gloss it over by saying that while they're using the psychological tools, they must make certain *"that the Presence and Power of the Holy Spirit permeates our personalities."*

First of all, to conclude that poor, failing, perverted man, has developed greater means for dealing with the human problem than the Holy Spirit, is ignorance at its best, and blasphemy at its worst.

As well, how can the Holy Spirit permeate personalities, who are using false methods of humanistic philosophy devised mostly by agnostics and atheists?

WHAT IS PSYCHOLOGY?

The primary Greek word, *"psycho,"* is the root from which we derive the English terms *"psychology"* or *"psychologist."* Interestingly, the word, *"psycho,"* is utilized in the New Testament for *"soul."* Hence, a psychologist is a *"worker with souls,"* that is, if the true meaning of the word is maintained. However, the foundation of psychological teaching does not even believe that man has a soul.

Consequently, a specific distinction should be made. The secular psychotherapist considers himself a worker with *"minds,"* while the (so-called) *"Christian"* psychologist considers himself a worker with *"souls."*

Most Bible Colleges and Seminaries today offer at least some basic introduction to psychology for their would-be Preachers of the Gospel. Thus a foundation is laid for a subtle deflection away from the Bible and towards psychotherapy.

Actually, I suspect that the psychology offerings in most Bible Colleges and Seminaries do far more than offer a basic introduction to psychology. A short time ago, I happened to pick up a catalog advertising the course offerings of a long list of Bible Colleges and Seminaries.

Almost all of the subjects were in the field of psychology, or at least leaned in that direction. So I feel that the subtle deflection away from the Bible and towards psychotherapy has turned into something that is not so subtle after all. Actually, it could better be described as a wholesale rout.

NOTES

Consequently, the Preachers graduating from these schools, come away with little knowledge of the Bible, if any, but steeped in the new *"psychological way,"* and, therefore, those who sit under their charge have the terrible misfortune of being led astray.

It is even suggested today that if a person has only Bible knowledge, he is ill-equipped to handle the pressing problems of humanity. He must (they say) be grounded also in psychology to meet *"human"* needs. This is implanted early, with the unspoken implication that the Bible in itself is insufficient to solve human problems.

As well, it is constantly being suggested that Ministers are ill-prepared and ill-equipped to meet the needs of modern man. If the Preacher is to be truly effective and proficient in his role, he should be referring a large percentage of those who seek his help to *"professionals."*

"Professionals" or *"therapy"* used within this context means, of course, psychologists or psychotherapy.

Some time back, I received a letter from a *"Christian Psychologist,"* telling about his wife who once had serious problems. He said, *"We needed competent Christian mental health care. We couldn't find it in the Church; people didn't understand her emotional problems. We couldn't find it in the world; mental health professionals didn't understand our Faith."*

He went on to say that psychotherapy combined with the Holy Spirit, gave her the victory.

Now I don't know exactly what he meant when he said, *"We couldn't find it in the Church."* Perhaps he was speaking of a specific Church they attended or a particular Pastor — which is certainly understandable. But if he was speaking of *"The Church,"* meaning the Body of Christ and the Work of the Holy Spirit within this Church, he was in effect saying that the Bible does not hold the answer to human problems, and that we must look outside the Word of God for help.

At the very least, it would seem that his statement (as the two authors' statements), suggests that we must combine the Work of the Holy Spirit with secular psychotherapy. The end-product of this growing dependence on *"scientific"* compromise is that:

• Psychotherapy has been widely accepted as *"scientific,"* and, therefore, must be a useful tool. As a consequence, it has become accepted within Pentecostal and Charismatic fellowships. (It has been long accepted within the Denominational world of the Baptists, Methodists, etc.)

• Most Pentecostal Bible Colleges and Seminaries now promote psychotherapy as a legitimate tool for meeting *"the human need."*

• As a result, most of our younger Preachers are now convinced that psychotherapy is *"spiritually neutral."* It is, therefore, a legitimate tool to be employed with a clear conscience when trying to help humanity.

• The old-fashioned, tried-and-true Word of Almighty God is given lesser place when considering methods for solving man's problems, if any place at all!

COUNSELING — THE EXPRESSWAY FOR HELP

The other day I spoke with a professor who has many years of experience teaching in Pentecostal Bible Colleges. I asked him why homiletics (the preparation of sermons) is seldom taught anymore in Bible Colleges.

His answer shocked me. He said, *"Most are no longer looking to preaching as a means of meeting humanity's needs. Counseling has now become the expressway for help in this area."*

Hence, there is no longer a need for sermon preparation. The Colleges are gradually shifting over to a definite bias towards psychotherapy.

IS PSYCHOTHERAPY (COUNSELING PSYCHOLOGY) TRULY SCIENTIFIC AND THEREFORE NEUTRAL?

Proponents of psychotherapy call it scientific and camouflage its discrepancies with scientific jargon and medical terminology. However, the questions must be asked: Is psychotherapy a science or a superstition? Is it fact or fabrication?

These questions must be asked, because we have come to venerate almost anything labeled as *"science."* If, indeed, psychology and psychotherapy are scientific, they should command our respect and be used within every community. However, if they are not, we have valid grounds for questioning the propriety of intruding them into the Preachers' methodology.

In Martin and Deidre Bobgan's book, *"The Psychological Way / The Spiritual Way,"* they state on page 44:

NOTES

"In attempting to evaluate the status of psychology, the American Psychological Association appointed Sigmund Koch to plan and direct a study which was subsidized by the National Science Foundation. This study involved 80 eminent scholars in assessing the facts, theories, and methods of psychology. The results of this extensive endeavor were then published in a seven-volume series entitled 'Psychology: A Study Of A Science.'"

After examining the results, Koch concluded, *"I think it is by this time utterly and finally clear that psychology cannot be a coherent science."* He further declares that *"such activities as perception, motivation, social psychology, psychopathology, and creativity cannot be properly labeled science."*

E. Fuller Torrey says, *"The medical model of human behavior, when carried to its logical conclusion, is both nonsensical and non-functional. It doesn't answer the questions asked. It doesn't provide good service, and it leads to a stream of absurdities worthy of a Roman Circus."*

The Lord through Jeremiah said, *"For My people have committed two evils; they have forsaken Me the Fountain of Living Waters, and hewed them out cisterns, broken cisterns, that can hold no water"* (Jer. 2:13).

William Kirk Kilpatrick says, *"True Christianity does not mix well with psychology. When you try to mix them, you end up with a watered-down Christianity instead of a Christianized psychology.*

"But the process is subtle and is rarely noticed. It is not a frontal attack on Christianity. It is not even a case of the wolf at the door. Actually, the wolf is already in the fold, dressed in sheep's clothing. From the way it was petted and fed by some of the shepherds, one would think it was a prized sheep."

Jacob Needleman says, *"Modern psychiatry arose out of the vision that man must change himself and not depend for help on an imaginary God. Over half a century ago* (mainly through the insights of Freud and through the energies of those he influenced), *the human psyche was wrested from the faltering hands of organized religion and was situated in the world of nature as a subject for scientific study."*

Incidentally, Freud opened his office in Vienna, the first devoted to psychotherapy, a little over a hundred years ago.

Martin Gross, in his book, *"The Psychological Society,"* says: *"When educated man lost faith in formal religion, he required a substitute belief that would be as reputable in the last half of the twentieth century as Christianity was in the first. Psychology and psychiatry have now assumed that special role."*

WHAT IS THE ORIGINATION OF PSYCHOLOGY?

Modern-day psychotherapy has its roots in Atheism, Evolution, and Humanism. Psychology pretends to have a cure for troubled souls. It is taught in atheistic universities, oftentimes by atheistic professors. And this same subject, with the same foundations and influences, is accepted today as an integral part of the Christian curriculum in most Bible Colleges and Seminaries. There aren't two kinds of psychotherapy, there is only one. And, as Paul Vitz says, *"It is deeply anti-Christian."*

Someone else said, *"America's problem is not ignorance; America's problem is that she accepts a lie."*

One might say that the Church has done the same!

The problems with our Preachers may once have been ignorance, but this is no longer the case. I am concerned at present that what they now accept (psychotherapy) is not truth — it is a lie.

I maintain that psychotherapy is not scientific, that it is not even an *"art"* as claimed. It is a lie, pure and simple, and has no basis in scientific or Biblical fact. When Bible Colleges offer it, they are offering a bald fabrication. When Seminaries teach it, they are teaching a lie. When would-be Preachers immerse themselves in it, they immerse themselves in falsehood. When individuals accept a doctorate in this nefarious shamanism, they are receiving a certificate without scientific validity.

I say that Preachers of the Gospel attempting to meld psychotherapy with the Word of God, will help no one. They will deliver only confusion. People will be led away from the true aid available through the Word of God.

The two are as different and antagonistic as oil and water.

What is the Biblical system for counseling and helping the *"human condition"*?

Jesus Christ said:

NOTES

"Come unto Me, all ye that labour and are heavy laden, and I will give you rest.

"Take My yoke upon you, and learn of Me; for I am meek and lowly in heart: and you shall find rest unto your souls.

"For My yoke is easy, and My burden is light" (Mat. 11:28-30).

When it was suggested that modern-day psychology is not found in the Bible, one Preacher stated that neither is the automobile, the airplane, or the computer. *"We do not,"* he reasoned, *"resist utilization of these tools in our lives, so why should we resist the tool of psychology* (or any other self-help method or technique)*?"*

My answer is this:

Admittedly, the Bible has nothing to say about the automobile, computer, airplane, or a host of other crafts developed since it was written. The Bible does not claim to be a handbook on engineering, science, or whatever because these extraneous subjects are not man's problems. Man can be an expert scientist, a qualified engineer, or a host of other things — and still be a moral and spiritual wreck.

However, the Bible does claim to be a handbook on *"the human condition"* — and does come right out and claim to hold all the answers to this particular human area.

This is what the Holy Spirit said through Peter:

"According as His Divine Power hath given unto us all things that pertain unto life and godliness, through the knowledge of Him that hath called us to glory and virtue:

"Whereby are given unto us exceeding great and precious promises: that by these ye might be partakers of the Divine nature, having escaped the corruption that is in the world through lust" (II Pet. 1:3-4).

Now either the Bible did give us all things that pertain unto life or it didn't. If it didn't, it lied, and we then need to turn to the book, *"The Holy Spirit in Counseling,"* by the particular authors referred to. We can then, forever after, rely upon therapists who will combine their modern-day *"science"* with the Word of God.

(Incidentally, even though the Bible is not a handbook on engineering, etc.; however, whatever it does say on these subjects, is absolute in its correctness.)

IS THERE SUCH A THING AS A CHRISTIAN PSYCHOLOGIST?

No! The term is misleading. It insinuates that the type of psychology offered by these who call themselves *"Christian Psychologists"* is different than that offered by their worldly counterparts. However, there is only one type of psychology, which is taught by all, Christian or non-Christian. There may be Christians who are psychologists, but in the true sense of the word, there is no such thing as a *"Christian Psychologist."*

If we have Christian Psychology, why not have Christian Medicine, Christian Physics, or Christian Biochemistry?

Of course, the reason we don't have all these things is that such things don't exist in real-life terms. Medicine is the same for the Christian or the non-Christian. Chemistry is the same for the Christian or the non-Christian, etc.

However, some educators who are Christians have attempted to take an ungodly, atheistic, anti-Christian, immoral, unbiblical, worldly system called psychology, and integrate it into Biblical Counseling.

It cannot be done!

CAN A TRAINED COUNSELOR HELP PEOPLE IF HE LOVES GOD AND HAS A TRUE DESIRE TO BE OF SERVICE?

If one is speaking of a counselor trained in psychology, no! Even though we do not question his motives or desire to help people, still, we maintain that he cannot be effective until he totally and completely renounces all psychological training and turns to the Word of God as his sole source and guide. It is like mixing light with darkness. Scripture asks us this question:

"And what concord hath Christ with Belial? or what part hath he that believeth with an infidel?" (II Cor. 6:15).

IS THE PREACHER OF THE GOSPEL QUALIFIED TO DEAL WITH THE PROBLEMS OF MANKIND?

If the Preacher of the Gospel is thoroughly grounded in the Word of God, he is actually the only one who is capable of meeting these particular needs.

I realize it is being suggested today that the Preacher of the Gospel is not qualified to

address the *"human condition."* He has not been specifically educated and trained in these areas. But the fact is, the so-called professional in the field of *"the cure of the soul"* is actually the one who is unqualified to help the individual in need.

Now this might seem ludicrous to some. Don't they have Masters or Doctorates in counseling or psychotherapy? Still, I am stating that they are not qualified to help the individual. They hold certificates in a system that is grounded in Atheism and Humanism. As such, the whole system has no basis in truth and has no inherent qualification for addressing itself to *"the cure of the soul."*

I want to say it again:

The Bible is the only casebook for the cure of souls. Only it holds the answers.

As a consequence, the Preacher of the Gospel (or, for that matter, anyone who is well-versed in the Word of God and committed to Christ) is eminently well-qualified to deal with human needs.

DOESN'T THE BIBLE SUGGEST COUNSELING AS A PROPER HELP?

Yes, it does! But it is merely speaking of advice. It is not, by any trick of modern-day interpretation, recommending psychology or psychotherapy.

The Bible is full of advice specific to the human condition and doesn't need any help. To be completely frank, there is no help other than the Word of God.

If a person will apply the Bible to his problems, he will find the solution. If he goes to man for his advice, he will only receive man's solution — which will prove of little value.

Yes, I believe in Biblical counseling. But I believe it should be of short duration, and with individuals directed to specific areas of the Bible — and to their knees. At this point, the Holy Spirit should be invited to perform His Work of reconciliation. In this situation, the counselor is no longer a counselor in any sense, he is a Minister.

However, something more should be added:

Counselors can develop an unwarranted sense of self-importance. People come to them for advice and counsel. All too often, their troubled wards become emotional addicts, totally dependent upon a succession of counseling *"fixes"* to carry them through the short periods between visits.

Of course, this can become heady stuff for the therapist. With the steady parade of fawning clients at his or her feet, it is easy for the therapist to lose perspective and end up more confused than the patients.

Consequently, the individual must ever be pointed to Christ as the only solution, and away from the Preacher or counselor in question.

In Truth, psychology and Christianity cannot be reconciled. Truth and lies cannot live together.

It might be said of psychology, as it was said of a particular sinister prison:

"Abandon hope, all ye who enter here."

Paul said, *"Beware lest any man spoil you through philosophy and vain deceit, after the traditions of men, after the rudiments of the world, and not after Christ.*

"For in Him dwelleth all the fulness of the Godhead bodily.

"And ye are complete in Him, which is the Head of all principality and power" (Col. 2:8-10).

The following is a letter we received, and we felt would be helpful as it relates to the subject at hand.

The man signed his letter as a *"Born-again"* Psychologist.

He said:

"Dear Brother Swaggart:

"There are two issues which I feel the need to discuss briefly.

"First of all, I want to express the sincere gratitude of our family for the Ministry of Family Worship Center. Worship and service at Family Worship Center have been a rich spiritual blessing to each of us and we are so glad to be a part of the family of Family Worship Center.

"Next, I want to comment on the stand you have taken regarding the issue of secular psychology and, in particular, psychotherapy. As you know, I attended a Theological Seminary and earned a Doctorate of Education Degree there. What you may not know is that my major field of study was in the area of psychology and counseling. While there was some emphasis on Biblical counseling in my studies, the primary emphasis was on secular psychological theories and the adaptation of those theories to pastoral counseling. I left the Seminary ill-equipped to do Bible-based pastoral counseling. My studies

left me with a strong background in the area of relationship with self and others but with a weak background in the area of man's relationship with God. My years of Seminary training prepared me for a passive Ministry.

"My vocational background has been varied. Aside from my administrative and consulting experience in corrections, I have served as a Prison Chaplain, an Associate Pastor of a large urban Church, and as the Director of a Community Mental Health Center. I know what I'm talking about, then, when I tell you that you are absolutely correct in your position regarding psychotherapy.

"Psychotherapy is one of the most hellish and devastating practices that mankind has contrived. Psychotherapy manipulates, abuses, and destroys those persons who seek help for their problems through it. Psychotherapy makes the 'patient' dependent upon the psychotherapists, and I have found psychotherapists to be, for the most part, unspiritual, anti-God, egotistical, and wrong. Many psychotherapists suffer from the same, or worse, life and personality problems as the persons they pretend to help.

"In my 16-year career, I have interacted and worked with many clinical psychologists. I have watched as they dealt with alcoholism, marital problems, family problems, etc., treating them either as diseases or dysfunctions. Never have I known a clinical psychologist to deal with such problems as the product of sin. Sin is never mentioned; rather, an attempt is made to justify sin through the use of sterile and non-offensive terms as dysfunction and disorder.

"While many psychologists perform valuable services in the diagnosis and treatment of educational problems, mental retardation, etc., those who practice psychotherapy are inflicting suffering, damage, and doom upon those whom they claim to help. Psychotherapy is not therapeutic.

"Man's essential problem is his alienation from God, which results from sin. Man's sinful nature and his sinful behavior have separated him from God and worked havoc. Ultimately, sin is at the bottom of all of man's physical and mental distress. The psychotherapist denies this and is ill-equipped to help anyone.

"I thank God for your boldness in speaking the truth about such things. I stand with you."

Consequently, the words given by the Holy Spirit to Mark, *"Neither could any man tame him,"* still holds true today. However, Jesus Christ, as here exampled, can tame this individual, as well as all brought to Him.

(5) "AND ALWAYS, NIGHT AND DAY, HE WAS IN THE MOUNTAINS, AND IN THE TOMBS, CRYING, AND CUTTING HIMSELF WITH STONES."

The phrase, *"And always, night and day,"* proclaimed the constant misery which never ended, as a result of the demon possession.

The phrase, *"He was in the mountains, and in the tombs, crying, and cutting himself with stones,"* referred to the shrieks that must have pierced the air, especially at night.

As well, he gashed his body with sharp stones, until, no doubt, it was covered with cuts and scars.

The horror of this knows no bounds! And yet, to one degree or the other, much of the human family falls into this category. In America alone, some 20,000,000 people a day drink themselves into a stupor, trying to ease emotional and spiritual pain. Untold millions of others ingest themselves with drugs for the same purpose. Their dilemma may not be as bad as what is described here, but yet, it is pain and heartache for which the world has no cure.

(6) "BUT WHEN HE SAW JESUS AFAR OFF, HE RAN AND WORSHIPPED HIM,"

The phrase, *"But when he saw Jesus afar off,"* is not meant to insinuate that he recognized Him at that distance, but that the demons within the man thought he was another intruder. Therefore, they would take action!

The phrase, *"He ran,"* at the moment has nothing to do with the *"worship."* He probably runs toward Jesus with hostile intentions, not knowing who He was.

The phrase, *"And worshipped Him,"* refers to him drawing closer, with the spiritual power and grace that always pervaded the personality of the Son of God, quieting his spirit and causing him to fall on his knees in reverence.

The word, *"worship,"* is here used of homage shown to men of superior rank, or of homage shown to God. Here it speaks of homage to God, the act of worship, for the demon recognizes our Lord as the Son of God. Here, we have a being, incorrigible in his nature, destined to be damned for all eternity, one of the cohorts of Satan, bending the knee to God the Son.

This is what Paul was speaking of when he referred to the universal adoration of the Lord Jesus, even by beings *"under the earth"* (Phil. 2:10). They are even now bending the knee to the Son of God.

Actually, it was not just the man who was prostrating himself before the Lord Jesus. He was under the control of the demon, and the latter was the source of the homage paid to the Son of God (Wuest).

It should be quickly added, that even though demon spirits worship the Lord, most of the human family does not have sense enough to do so. Even most of the Church little worships Him!

However, as we have stated, the type of worship here enjoined was not in *"Spirit and Truth,"* but, rather, a worship of deference or homage, as one would pay to a superior being.

(7) "AND CRIED WITH A LOUD VOICE, AND SAID, WHAT HAVE I TO DO WITH THEE, JESUS, THOU SON OF THE MOST HIGH GOD? I ADJURE THEE BY GOD, THAT THOU TORMENT ME NOT."

The phrase, *"And cried with a loud voice,"* refers to the demon spirit using the vocal chords of the man, thus speaking to Christ.

The question, *"And said, What have I to do with Thee, Jesus, Thou Son of the Most High God?",* refers to this evil spirit knowing exactly as to Who Jesus was!

Some have suggested that Satan in the wilderness using the exclamation, *"If Thou be the Son of God . . . ,"* means that he was not quite sure respecting the status of Christ.

Possibly that may be true. However, after an approximate year of Ministry which saw great miracles, and more especially the Power of Christ over evil spirits, there was now no doubt among the hosts of darkness, that Jesus was indeed the Son of God, the Messiah.

The phrase, *"I adjure thee by God, that Thou torment me not,"* was actually an effort by this demon spirit to put Jesus under oath.

Matthew used the phrase, *"To torment us before the time,"* meaning that a certain time has been appointed by God to which these spirits will be confined to the pit, which is without doubt described in Revelation 20:1-3 (Mat. 8:29).

As severe as the misery may be at present for these spirits of darkness, still, it is nothing compared to what they will yet suffer.

It seems they are now allowed to wander about and find their depraved pleasure in tempting men; so that, if possible, they may at last drag them down with them into the abyss. For they are full of hatred of God and envy of man; and they find a miserable satisfaction in endeavoring to keep men out of those heavenly mansions from which, through pride, they are themselves forever excluded (Bickersteth).

(8) "FOR HE SAID UNTO HIM, COME OUT OF THE MAN, THOU UNCLEAN SPIRIT."

The phrase, *"For He said unto him,"* could have been translated, *"For He had been saying . . . ."*

The phrase, *"Come out of the man, thou unclean spirit,"* constituted a direct order in which the spirit knew he must obey!

(9) "AND HE ASKED HIM, WHAT IS THY NAME? AND HE ANSWERED, SAYING, MY NAME IS LEGION: FOR WE ARE MANY."

The question, *"And He asked him, What is thy name?"*, actually meant *"He kept on asking him."* It seems at first the demon would not respond, but finally did after repeated questioning.

The phrase, *"And he answered, saying, My name is Legion: for we are many,"* finally proclaims the answer as elicited by Christ.

A *"Legion"* was a designation for a company of Roman soldiers numbering 6,826 men, although at times it could refer to an undetermined number. Quite possibly this latter is the meaning respecting the *"many"* which possessed this unfortunate man.

Why did Jesus ask this question concerning the name of the demon?

No doubt Jesus knew there were other demons there, and wanted this head demon to admit it. Possibly the demons were conspiring among themselves, that one or more would depart, with the others remaining. The question asked by Christ, would forestall these darkened plans.

Even though these spirits were liars, still, they knew it was pointless to lie to Christ, therefore, the head demon related the truth as to their infestation.

(10) "AND HE BESOUGHT HIM MUCH THAT HE WOULD NOT SEND THEM AWAY OUT OF THE COUNTRY."

The phrase, *"And he besought Him much,"* means that the demon kept on pleading with

Christ. This one who called himself *"Legion,"* was asking on behalf of all the other demons as well.

The phrase, *"That He would not send them away out of the country,"* seems to insinuate that they enjoyed this particular area better than others.

It is said that Decapolis, of which Gadara was a part, was full of hellenistic, apostate Jews, and was loved by the demons.

From this statement, we learn that demon spirits enjoy places that have little or no mention of Christ. Consequently, in countries of the world, such as those ruled by Islam or Buddhism or Hinduism, etc., demon activity is rampant. The same can be said for those ruled by Catholicism. All of these are false religions, actually instigated and energized by Satan. Therefore, demon activity is plentiful and abundant.

Only True Bible Christianity is a ward against these spirits of darkness. They fear only the Name of Jesus, and that wielded by Faith-filled hearts and lives.

In this one verse we find the answer to poverty, sickness, suffering, murder, slavery, bondage, filth, disease, man's inhumanity to man, and every other vice imaginable! Sadly and regrettably, most countries of the world fall into this category, and because there is little or no light of the Gospel which penetrates this darkness. Consequently, demon spirits are rampant in their stealing, killing, and destroying (Jn. 10:10).

Actually, the terrible increase of crime in America, is a direct result of improper Bible preaching of the Gospel. As the spiritual temperature of this nation, or any nation, rises, conversely, the crime rate, etc., falls. As the spiritual temperature falls, as it is now doing, the crime rate rises, plus every other type of problem imaginable.

When Jesus comes back, as He certainly shall, the world will be ridded of these spirits of darkness, which are now the cause of so much suffering and pain. Then the earth will be *"filled with the Glory of the Lord, as the waters cover the Sea"* (Hab. 2:14).

Then the sorrow and heartache will end!

(11) "NOW THERE WAS THERE NIGH UNTO THE MOUNTAINS A GREAT HERD OF SWINE FEEDING."

This *"herd of swine,"* which Mark said numbered *"about two thousand,"* was no doubt owned by the Jews. Even though Jews were forbidden by the Law to eat pork, yet, they were not forbidden to breed swine for other uses, such as provisions for the Roman Army.

Jesus was on the seashore when this confrontation took place with the Maniac of Gadara, while the hogs were at some distance, feeding on the slopes of the mountain.

As stated, this was the Decapolis area, which actually referred to ten cities, mostly occupied by the Romans, with some Jews.

(12) "AND ALL THE DEVILS BESOUGHT HIM, SAYING, SEND US INTO THE SWINE, THAT WE MAY ENTER INTO THEM."

The phrase, *"And all the devils besought him,"* proclaims these spirits as frantic, with many of them using the man's vocal chords to express their desire of the entrance into the swine.

As well, we learn from this request made by the demons, that they could not even enter into the hogs without the express permission of Christ, so how much less could they enter into *"the sheep of His pasture!"*

The phrase, *"Saying, Send us into the swine, that we may enter into them,"* shows that demons at one time had physical bodies, for they have no rest unless they inhabit a physical body, either that of a human being or an animal.

(13) "AND FORTHWITH JESUS GAVE THEM LEAVE. AND THE UNCLEAN SPIRITS WENT OUT, AND ENTERED INTO THE SWINE: AND THE HERD RAN VIOLENTLY DOWN A STEEP PLACE INTO THE SEA, (THEY WERE ABOUT TWO THOUSAND;) AND WERE CHOKED IN THE SEA."

The phrase, *"And forthwith Jesus gave them leave,"* means that He did not command them to do this, but, instead, gave them permission.

The phrase, *"And the unclean spirits went out, and entered into the swine,"* reflects, as is obvious, the demons doing what Jesus had given them permission to do. The functional abilities of these spirits seem to be very limited unless they can inhabit a physical body, be it human or animal. However, the reaction of the animals, as the next phrase portrays, would result in their deaths. Consequently, these spirits would not help themselves that much!

The phrase, *"And the herd ran violently down a steep place into the sea, (they were about two thousand); and were choked in the sea,"* represents a loss of approximately $250,000 in 1995 dollars.

NOTES

The question has been asked repeatedly as to the right or wrong of Jesus allowing these spirits to go into these swine, resulting in this tremendous loss for the owners?

First of all, we know that Jesus did not do wrong, because everything He did was in the Will of the Heavenly Father (Jn. 8:28).

Everything done by the Lord, whether constructive or destructive, is meant but for one purpose, to draw the individual(s) to Christ. Even if it is extended judgment on a person or nation such as Egypt of old, and after much pleading and mercy, still, the act itself is meant to serve as an example to hopefully draw others to Christ. Consequently, this act of allowing the spirits to enter the swine, with their resultant loss, was an act of mercy on the part or God. It was designed to bring their owners to Christ, which it did! However, as we shall see, they did not allow the transformation enacted on the former Maniac to extend to them.

Oftentimes the Lord allows inclement weather, such as hurricanes, earthquakes, etc., to wreak a deadly toll, destroying property and even lives. Even though some may question His right to do this, that is if they confess His existence at all, still, as Creator, and, therefore, having all knowledge and all power, and always doing what is best for man, the wise individual will say as Job of old, *"The Lord giveth, and the Lord taketh away; Blessed be the Name of the Lord"* (Job 1:21).

Many erroneously claim that it was not the Lord Who took away Job's possessions, but Satan. They also attribute all natural disasters to Satan! However, the Holy Spirit said, concerning Job, *"In all this Job sinned not, nor charged God foolishly"* (Job 1:22).

While it certainly may be true that Satan is, at times, the instrument, nevertheless, he can only do what God allows him to do. To think he has unlimited latitude in given areas, is to limit God's Power, which no right thinking person desires to do.

God controls all, even Satan and his minions of darkness, and to attribute less to Him, denies Who He is!

(14) "AND THEY THAT FED THE SWINE FLED, AND TOLD IT IN THE CITY, AND IN THE COUNTRY. AND THEY WENT OUT TO SEE WHAT IT WAS THAT WAS DONE."

The phrase, *"And they that fed the swine fled, and told it in the city, and in the country,"* represents a scenario that must have been played out in this fashion.

Evidently, those who tended the hogs were nearby, or even observing, when Jesus cast the spirits out of the Maniac. They may have even heard the unclean spirits asking permission for all the demons to go into the swine, or else the Disciples told them what had happened. At any rate, they knew what had taken place, and made certain that the owners of the swine knew they were not responsible for this large loss.

As well, the implication is that they related the story of Jesus delivering the Maniac, who was probably well known in the area.

The phrase, *"And they went out to see what it was that was done,"* concerned a large group of people, who, upon hearing the story of the swine-herders, immediately come to see for themselves.

(15) "AND THEY COME TO JESUS, AND SEE HIM THAT WAS POSSESSED WITH THE DEVIL, AND HAD THE LEGION, SITTING, AND CLOTHED, AND IN HIS RIGHT MIND: AND THEY WERE AFRAID."

The phrase, *"And they come to Jesus,"* actually gives us the reason, and as we have stated, that the Lord allowed the loss of the large herd of swine. It was done, at least in part, by the Holy Spirit in order to bring this crowd to Jesus, which, if they had taken advantage of it, would have been the greatest day of their lives. The loss of the animals would have been nothing in comparison to what they would have received upon their acceptance of Christ, i.e., eternal life.

The phrase, *"And see him that was possessed with the devil,"* means that they minutely inspected him, because, evidently, they had known him in his previous state. They were flabbergasted at what they saw!

The phrase, *"And had the Legion, sitting, and clothed, and in his right mind,"* gives a compendium of what spiritually happens in the Salvation of a soul.

1. *"Sitting"*: This speaks of the *"rest"* that is given to those who put their trust in Christ (Heb. 4:9).

There is a terrible tumult in the hearts and lives of all unbelievers, which expresses itself in many and varied ways. As well, it is impossible for the unbeliever to know or understand

the opposite of that, because he has never experienced it. However, upon coming to Christ, the unrest is quieted and settled, with a beautiful *"peace"* given to the recipient. It is, no doubt, the greatest attribute of Salvation, hence, given first.

2. *"And clothed"*: This speaks of being clothed in Righteousness, which can only be given by Christ. Isaiah called it, *"The garment of praise for the spirit of heaviness"* (Isa. 61:3).

There is a chorus which says:
"The windows of Heaven are open,
"The Blessings are falling tonight.
"There is joy, joy, joy in my heart,
"Since Jesus made everything right.
"I gave Him my old tattered garments,
"He gave me a robe of pure white.
"I'm feasting on manna from Heaven,
"That's why I'm singing tonight."

3. *"And in his right mind"*: Irrespective of one's education, intellect, or genius, if one does not know Christ as one's personal Saviour, to one degree or the other, one is not in his right mind.

Of course, the case illustrated in this Chapter would be in the extreme. However, the principle holds for all, and irrespective of their state, position, status, race, or educational accomplishments.

In other words, a correct view of the world and mankind, cannot be obtained outside of Christ. The illustrations are obvious!

One need only recall the horrors of Nazi Germany, to observe education and intellect without God. Unfortunately, that scene has been repeated, albeit to a lesser degree, tens of thousands of times, before and since.

As well, the world has many, and always has had, of those who are rich respecting money, but with no solutions for the ills of humanity. In other words, they hurt, sicken, and die, just like the most poverty-stricken.

The only *"Light"* in the world is Jesus. To be sure, He does not merely contain light, but, in effect, is Light (Jn. 8:12).

The only *"right mind"* is that which knows Christ, and it is *"right"* only as it remains in Christ, and is led by Christ. Unfortunately, Christians, at times, do foolish things, but never because of Christ, but because of departing from Christ.

The phrase, *"And they were afraid,"* means they were afraid of the Power of Christ.

They had no doubt known the man in his previous condition, with some of them possibly even having attempted to restrain him with ropes, etc. As well, his insanity had been such that he had been a raving maniac. And now they observe him sitting and clothed, with them possibly even questioning him. His answers, if, in fact, that did happen, were lucid, intelligent, as he related what Jesus had done for him.

In their minds, it was very little different than someone being raised from the dead. And then on top of that, these spirits of darkness, which had been the cause of this man's terrible condition, were allowed to go into the swine, with the hogs, consequently, destroying themselves. They realized they were in the presence of a power far greater than anything they had ever known, experienced, or witnessed. And yet, this fear, which was proper, did not bring them to Christ, but rather the very opposite.

(16) "AND THEY THAT SAW IT TOLD THEM HOW IT BEFELL TO HIM THAT WAS POSSESSED WITH THE DEVIL, AND ALSO CONCERNING THE SWINE."

The phrase, "And they that saw it," lends credence to the thought that the swine-herders had witnessed the entire episode, concerning the action of Christ in delivering the Maniac.

The phrase, "Told them how it befell to him that was possessed with the devil," relates the swine-herders giving a blow-by-blow account of what Jesus had done, with the owners and others now observing with their own eyes what they had been told.

The phrase, "And also concerning the swine," means they made certain that the owners knew that dereliction of duty had not been a part of this episode, but, rather, the demon spirits.

At the outset, every evidence is that the story was completely preposterous! The idea that this Maniac was completely delivered was, no doubt, unbelievable whenever it was first told. And then, for the owners of this herd of swine to be told that all two thousand of the hogs had run into the Sea and drowned, and because of demon spirits, was even more preposterous. But to their amazement, they find it exactly as they had been told.

(17) "AND THEY BEGAN TO PRAY HIM TO DEPART OUT OF THEIR COASTS,"

This verse has to be one of the saddest in the entirety of the Bible. Instead of accepting

Him as their Lord and Saviour, they wanted Him to "depart."

The evidence was irrefutable! What He had done for this Maniac, He could do for them. Every need in their lives, whether physical, spiritual, mental, or domestical, could be easily handled by Christ. The opportunity of the ages was before their eyes, and with irrefutable proof, but yet, they did not want it.

Why?

Sadly and regrettably, the decision of these people was not unique or isolated. Almost all the world follows in their train. The proof is irrefutable, as to Who Christ is, and what He can do! And yet, even despite the dire need, most of the world conducts themselves exactly as these citizens of Decapolis.

The "Why?", is answered in the fact that they loved their sin more than they desired a change. In other words, they did not want to change!

A newsman mentioned to me once, that most of the people who accept the Lord do so in dire circumstances. He was correct.

As someone has said, "Man's extremity, is God's opportunity." The Maniac was thrilled to turn to Christ, when given the opportunity, but his neighbors, not nearly in the condition he was in, did not see their need. Therefore, most of the world follows suit!

And yet, no doubt some of these very people who urged Jesus to leave their locality, would later come to dire straits in life. But now they do not see themselves in that position.

Some have ventured that they were more concerned about the loss of the swine than the deliverance of the Maniac. While that is certainly true, still, that, I think, was not their real reason for refusing Christ.

They refused Him, because they simply did not see their need of Him.

I have had the occasion on various news programs in Washington, New York, or elsewhere, to enter into discussion with various intellectuals. Most all, if not exclusively, their attitude was and is, that accepting Christ may be proper for some people, but not for them. In other words, they think they are above that need. "Those who are less educated, less knowledgeable in the ways of the world, may need such," but not them!

There are a few exceptions, but not many. That is one of the reasons Jesus said, "How *hardly shall they that have riches enter into the Kingdom of God"* (Mk. 10:23).

I happened to be in the presence once of the Vice-President of the United States, who shortly became President, when he was asked the question, *"Mr. Vice-President, are you born again?"*

He was honest and forthright in his answer. He claimed that he did not understand the born-again experience. He related as to how he and his wife had attempted to live a *"good, clean life,"* but, still, some things had happened which they did not understand. Consequently, they had rejected the Lord.

Let it ever be understood that men never reject the Lord for good and noble purposes. Those reasons are always sinister, dark, foreboding, and ultimately destructive!

The implication in the Greek is that the moment they began to urge Christ to depart, He withdrew on the first hint of their wish. However, when He walked away, eternal life walked away with Him as well! For such is in no other.

(18) "AND WHEN HE WAS COME INTO THE SHIP, HE THAT HAD BEEN POSSESSED WITH THE DEVIL PRAYED HIM THAT HE MIGHT BE WITH HIM."

The phrase, *"And when He was come into the ship,"* refers to the departure of Christ.

The phrase, *"He that had been possessed with the Devil,"* is spoken of in the past tense, meaning that he was no longer possessed, and would never be possessed again. One can only shout *"Hallelujah!"*

As I dictate these words, I think of the multiple millions of letters we have received over the years, with many of them containing some of the most wonderful stories of Redemption that could ever be related. Actually, they are little different than the story of the former Maniac of Gadara. Lives which were totally ruined and wasted, were suddenly changed by the glorious Power of Jesus Christ. As He did it then, the evidence is glaringly obvious that He does it today.

The phrase, *"Prayed Him that he might be with Him,"* is certainly understandable in all its implications. What this man had been was horrible, and what he now is, is wonderful to say the least, and all because of Jesus. Consequently, he wants to be with Jesus, even as His Disciple.

(19) "HOWBEIT JESUS SUFFERED HIM NOT, BUT SAITH UNTO HIM, GO HOME TO

THY FRIENDS, AND TELL THEM HOW GREAT THINGS THE LORD HATH DONE FOR THEE, AND HATH HAD COMPASSION ON THEE."

The phrase, *"Howbeit Jesus suffered him not,"* speaks of a gentle persuasion. The Lord spoke kindly to him, even giving him explicit directions, which the evidence is that he carried out totally.

The phrase, *"But saith unto him, Go home to thy friends,"* actually in the Greek says, *"Go into your home to your own."* He was directed by the Lord to first of all testify to his own flesh and blood, his own family.

I think one should not make more of this episode than one should, but yet the following may well have happened.

If the man had been married and with children, the terrible horror of his past life had, no doubt, been woefully destructive on those he loved the most, and who loved him in return.

No doubt, they had painfully observed his deterioration until finally he could no longer remain at home, but was forced in his demon-possessed agony to leave. What brought it on, the Bible does not say. But yet, we know that Satan is the one who *"steals, kills and destroys"* (Jn. 10:10). Maybe the man was profligate in his lifestyle! Maybe he courted evil! And then again, maybe none of those things happened, but yet through a series of events not exactly of his choosing, he finds himself in this awful condition.

The grief that must have followed his departure and being driven to the tombs, must have been awful to say the least! The children along with their Mother, would have grieved terribly. And yet, they were helpless! There was nothing they could do.

Maybe at night they could hear his screams, and then most assuredly, it was related to them how men had attempted to restrain him, but with no success.

Whether the news of his deliverance came to his wife (or Mother, etc.), before he personally related such, is anyone's guess.

No doubt, upon hearing the swine-herder's story, the news quickly spread abroad of this man's deliverance. And yet, there were others in this area in the same condition, so, whatever his loved ones heard, if anything, the information would have been scant. And then it happened!

One can see him swiftly walking down the road, with others no doubt close to him, desiring to hear his story. As he gets closer to his house, he can hardly believe what has happened to him. There is no explanation for it, at least that one could ever begin to understand. A Man called Jesus . . . .

As he draws closer to his house, almost running, no doubt others have gone ahead to inform his wife (or loved ones) as to his coming.

Immediately upon receiving the news, the wife would have run out of the house with the children closely following, and would have run to meet him. The crowd, no doubt, stands with happy smiles on their faces, as they observe this meeting. It should have been private, but there is no way that such could have been. Despite the owners of the swine telling Jesus to depart, undoubtedly, there were many who were thrilled at what had happened with this former Maniac of Gadara.

After holding him close for a period of time, his wife (or Mother, etc.), must have asked the all-important question! What happened?

One can almost feel the words tumbling out of his mouth. He relates how Jesus came with His Disciples. To the best of his ability, he describes how he was set free by the Power of Jesus Christ.

Undoubtedly, he proceeded to tell her about the Person of Christ. What He was like! How He sounded! How His eyes seemed to look into the very depths of one's soul!

He would have said, *"I have never seen anyone like Him! His very Presence seemed to permeate everything in the immediate vicinity. And it was a Presence that spoke of goodness, kindness, and love as I have never known before."*

Maybe this is not exactly the way it happened, but from the description given by Mark, it may have been similar.

The phrase, *"And tell them how great things the Lord hath done for thee,"* had reference to three things:

1. He was to testify to any and all what was done.

2. He was to tell that it was Jesus Who had done it.

3. He was to understand that the cure was permanent. The demons would never return!

The phrase, *"And hath had compassion on thee,"* is a statement of depth!

NOTES

The culpability of humanity, such as this man, is not denied. But yet, in the word *"compassion"* Christ proclaims the scheme of evil perpetrated by Satan, which wreaks havoc in the human family.

Even though man is responsible, still, the scope of this evil is so wide and deep as to be beyond the pale of comprehension. In other words, it is a dilemma from which the human family cannot even hope to extricate itself, at least according to its own ability and ingenuity. This is the reason for the *"compassion,"* and it is the reason for the Coming of Christ. He Alone can lift man out of this terrible and horrible dilemma, even as He lifted the Maniac from this demon possession.

As valuable as education is, man cannot be educated out of this pit of darkness. As necessary as right legislation is, laws can never set the captive free.

Men use the word, *"rehabilitation,"* but it is a word which results cannot be realized in the domain of human ability. In effect, the Lord does not rehabilitate anyone! He, instead, makes of them a new creature in Christ Jesus (II Cor. 5:17).

(20) "AND HE DEPARTED, AND BEGAN TO PUBLISH IN DECAPOLIS HOW GREAT THINGS JESUS HAD DONE FOR HIM: AND ALL MEN DID MARVEL."

The phrase, *"And he departed,"* means that he determined to do that which Christ had instructed him.

The phrase, *"And began to publish in Decapolis,"* means *"to make a public proclamation."* In other words, he probably stood on the corner of busy intersections, and in all the ten cities of the region, giving his testimony as to what Christ had done for him. He became an Evangelist.

The phrase, *"How great things Jesus had done for him,"* proclaims for a certainty that it was *"great!"*

The giving of one's testimony as to what Christ has brought about in one's life, is the greatest, most compelling witness that can ever be given. The Apostle Paul, as the Book of Acts records, gave his testimony over and over (Acts Chpts. 9, 22, 26).

So, every Believer should follow this example in telling others what *"Jesus has done for him."*

The phrase, *"And all men did marvel,"* proclaims the fact that many, no doubt, had known him previously, and now saw the astounding change. Consequently, they *"marvelled!"*

To be sure, what Christ does in the human heart, is a *"marvel!"*

What a story of the miracle-working Power of Christ! What a story of Redemption!

(21) "AND WHEN JESUS WAS PASSED OVER AGAIN BY SHIP UNTO THE OTHER SIDE, MUCH PEOPLE GATHERED UNTO HIM: AND HE WAS NIGH UNTO THE SEA."

The phrase, *"And when Jesus was passed over again by ship unto the other side,"* refers to Him going back to Capernaum on the west side of the Sea of Galilee.

The phrase, *"Much people gathered unto Him,"* speaks of a great crowd, with Luke saying, *"For they were all waiting for Him"* (Lk. 8:40). No doubt, there were many who needed healing, and who had come perhaps from afar.

The phrase, *"And He was nigh unto the Sea,"* means that He had departed out of the ship, and was on the shore.

(22) "AND, BEHOLD, THERE COMETH ONE OF THE RULERS OF THE SYNAGOGUE, JAIRUS BY NAME; AND WHEN HE SAW HIM, HE FELL AT HIS FEET,"

The phrase, *"And, behold, there cometh one of the rulers of the Synagogue,"* refers to a sudden appearance by this man. As well, the words, *"And, behold,"* exclaim a happening of great significance which is about to take place.

There were several rulers in each Synagogue, of which Jairus was one, with their duties being to select the readers or teachers on the Sabbath, and to examine their discourses, seeing that all things were done with decency and in accordance with ancestral usage.

The phrase, *"Jairus by name,"* was this man whose name meant *"Whom Jehovah enlightens."* To be sure, he was to be enlightened more so than he could ever begin to realize.

The phrase, *"And when he saw Him, he fell at His feet,"* means that he had heard that Jesus had arrived, and he rushes to seek His help. His request is preceded by his *"Falling at Jesus' feet,"* in a posture of worship, and because the need is so great, the saving of his daughter from death.

(23) "AND BESOUGHT HIM GREATLY, SAYING, MY LITTLE DAUGHTER LIETH AT THE POINT OF DEATH: I PRAY THEE, COME AND LAY THY HANDS ON HER,

THAT SHE MAY BE HEALED; AND SHE SHALL LIVE."

The phrase, *"And besought Him greatly,"* proclaims an impassioned plea.

The phrase, *"Saying, My little daughter lieth at the point of death,"* means, as is obvious, that the child is about to die. Actually, in a few minutes, someone would come from the home of Jairus, telling him that his daughter, in fact, was dead. In other words, she probably died about the time that her father was imploring Christ to heal her.

The phrase, *"I pray Thee, come and lay Thy hands on her, that she may be healed; and she shall live,"* in the Greek actually says, *"To save her from death."*

A point should be brought out, that the Gentile Centurion had said to Jesus, *"Speak the word only,"* referring to his servant, but the Faith of Jairus does not seem to have risen to such degree (Mat. 8:5-13).

(24) "AND JESUS WENT WITH HIM; AND MUCH PEOPLE FOLLOWED HIM, AND THRONGED HIM."

The phrase, *"And Jesus went with him,"* proclaims a like response to the man's Faith. If Jairus had requested for Christ to *"Speak the word,"* as the Centurion, Jesus would have, undoubtedly, done so, and the child would have been healed or even raised from the dead at that moment. Nevertheless, Jesus meets him on his own level, and proceeds to go to his house.

This tremendous lesson of Faith, relative to comparing the Centurion with Jairus, must not be lost upon the reader. God responds to Faith, and at whatever level. The evidence is, that He seldom seeks to increase the Faith at the moment, but rather responds to its present level, whatever that may be! The level of Faith receives the same level of response. Actually, Jesus, at times, would say, *"According to your Faith be it unto you"* (Mat. 9:29).

He also used terms such as, *"O thou of little Faith, wherefore didst thou doubt?"* (Mat. 14:31).

He as well said, *"O woman, great is thy Faith"* (Mat. 15:28).

So, we are made to see in these responses by Christ, that there are levels of Faith which receive the same level of response.

Jairus seemed to need Jesus to come Personally to his house, and even to physically *"Lay*

His hands on his daughter." Consequently, that is what Jesus would do!

The phrase, *"And much people followed Him, and thronged Him,"* sets the stage for the next great miracle, and another lesson in Faith, which is astounding to say the least!

The crowd was so intense around Christ, so as to almost suffocate Him. There were many people with many needs, and they knew that He Alone had the answer.

(25) "AND A CERTAIN WOMAN, WHICH HAD AN ISSUE OF BLOOD TWELVE YEARS,"

The phrase, *"And a certain woman,"* is said by tradition to have been named *"Veronica,"* and a native of Caesarea Philippi.

The phrase, *"Which had an issue of blood twelve years,"* spoke of a constant hemorrhage, and which she had suffered for twelve years.

(26) "AND HAD SUFFERED MANY THINGS OF MANY PHYSICIANS, AND HAD SPENT ALL THAT SHE HAD, AND WAS NOTHING BETTERED, BUT RATHER GREW WORSE,"

The phrase, *"And had suffered many things of many physicians,"* means that she had suffered extreme pain at the hands of these doctors, but to no avail.

Luke, himself a physician, added, *"Which had spent all her living upon physicians, neither could be healed of any"* (Lk. 8:43).

Their manner of treatment in those days for sicknesses such as this, was primitive to say the least. In effect, there was really nothing they could do, with whatever they did, as is here obvious, mostly exacerbating the problem instead of relieving it.

The phrase, *"And had spent all that she had,"* infers that many of these doctors had attempted to treat her, merely for the money they would receive out of it, knowing they could not help her. The implication is, that she had once been quite wealthy, and had spent basically all her worth on this effort to obtain relief.

The phrase, *"And was nothing bettered, but rather grew worse,"* meaning that the physicians had not helped her at all, but, if anything, had made the situation worse.

(27) "WHEN SHE HAD HEARD OF JESUS, CAME IN THE PRESS BEHIND, AND TOUCHED HIS GARMENT."

The phrase, *"When she had heard of Jesus,"* is interesting indeed!

First of all, the idea is that she had not known of Jesus before her trip at this present time to Capernaum. Upon arriving in the city, she no doubt heard of the One Who was the topic of every conversation, and, upon inquiring, learned of His great healing Power. She had tried all the doctors, and for twelve long years, now she must try Him. However, this experience with the Great Physician will not be as with the other physicians.

As well, the Greek actually says, *"When she had heard of The Jesus,"* meaning that He had become so popular, that even though this Name was commonly used, still, He was distinguished from all others, hence, *"The Jesus."*

(Jesus in the Hebrew means Joshua, which He was actually called.)

The phrase, *"Came in the press behind,"* means that she made her way through the crowd which was at the back of our Lord.

The phrase, *"And touched His garment,"* probably referred to touching the hem of the shawl thrown over His shoulder, which contained a blue fringe which the Jews were required to wear, to remind them they were God's people.

Even though there are indications she may have been a Gentile, even with tradition saying so, this particular phrase seems to indicate she may have been Jewish, although living in a Gentile area. Otherwise, it seems she would have had little knowledge or understanding respecting the touching of this part of His garment (Num. 15:38-41; Deut. 22:12). At any rate, this is the part of His garment she touched, and with reason!

(28) "FOR SHE SAID, IF I MAY TOUCH BUT HIS CLOTHES, I SHALL BE WHOLE."

The phrase, *"For she said,"* means she kept saying it to herself over and over, or even possibly to others nearby.

The phrase proclaims the fact that something had transpired within her heart respecting a way to be healed. No doubt, she would have loved to have approached Him, with the opportunity to tell Him of her difficulties and problems. But such, as is now obvious, was not possible. The crowd is too great, with too many clamoring to get to Him. So, the Holy Spirit dropped a word within her heart, which generated Faith, and found a way. She would touch the hem of His garment (Lk. 8:44).

The phrase, *"If I may touch but His clothes, I shall be whole,"* concerns her level of Faith.

Jairus wanted Jesus to touch his daughter, while this *"certain woman"* knows this is not possible, therefore, she will touch Him.

The entire scenario tells us that Faith will find a way. It will not take *"no"* for an answer, neither will it be hindered by seemingly impossible circumstances.

So, if Jesus has not touched you, that doesn't mean that all hope is gone. You can touch Him! And if you touch Him by Faith, and with Faith, you will receive just as much as if He had touched you.

This opens up the possibility for the receiving of whatever is needed to any and all. No one is excluded, except those who will not believe.

Sometimes the Power of God is so real, that the Lord touches all in the place, or at least some. But sometimes there is no touch. But yet, and according to this woman, which is at least a part of the lesson the Holy Spirit desires that we learn, whatever is needed can still be obtained. Even though He may not touch you, you can touch Him!

What does it mean to touch the Lord?

Well, of course, regarding this *"certain woman,"* realizing she would not be able to get Him to touch her, she reasoned in her mind and spirit, and no doubt inspired by the Holy Spirit, that she could touch Him, and the effect would be the same. It was! It was just that simple.

However, the situation presently, and because Jesus is not here physically as then, is a tiny bit different. The difference is that it only requires a slightly higher level of Faith. In effect, He <u>is</u> here, but not physically.

When individuals are in a Church service, or wherever, and the Spirit and Power of God are moving greatly, with many being touched and healed, it doesn't really take near the Faith as of this of which we speak. However, some, if not many, at these times, do not receive a touch from the Lord, and are led to believe by the lack of obvious evidence, that they are not able to receive what others have received. This tells us different.

1. First of all, understand that no formula is given in the Word of God concerning receiving from the Lord. The reason is obvious. Each individual, plus their situation, is different. Faith always requires different things of different people. Consequently, the formulas given by most Preachers, simply do not work. Therefore,

one must understand that no formula is available, and the few steps I will give, as well, must not be construed as a formula.

2. The individual, exactly as this woman, must settle it in his or her mind, that it is the Will of God for them to receive from the Lord. If they vacillate on this point, it shows a lack of Faith. We must believe that *"God is, and that He is a rewarder of them that diligently seek Him"* (Heb. 11:6).

James told us that Faith cannot work in a double minded atmosphere. He said, *"A double minded man is unstable in all his ways"* (James 1:8).

He also said, *"But let him ask in Faith, nothing wavering"* (James 1:6).

3. Touching the Lord, as this woman, must be anchored in God's Word, in other words, *"Claiming His Promises."* In effect, this is exactly what she did. She must have had an inkling of knowledge as to what this blue tassel meant on Jesus' garment. Therefore, she touched it, and in Faith. So, claim the Word for your particular case, and believe it.

4. Persevere until the answer comes. This is where many Believers break down. They do the things mentioned, and no answer is forthcoming, at least at that particular time, and they soon weary and quit. The Holy Spirit desires that we keep believing, even though circumstances may say the opposite, as they often do.

The answer will come, even though at times it may be delayed.

As stated, and as by now should be obvious, it is not nearly as simple to touch the Lord, as Him touching us, and for the obvious reasons. However, it can be done as evidenced by this dear lady, and given for this very purpose by the Holy Spirit.

(29) AND STRAIGHTWAY THE FOUNTAIN OF HER BLOOD WAS DRIED UP; AND SHE FELT IN HER BODY THAT SHE WAS HEALED OF THAT PLAGUE."

The phrase, *"And straightway the fountain of her blood was dried up,"* contains a powerful meaning.

It not only means that the bleeding stopped, and instantly, but that what was causing the bleeding, the fountain if you please, was instantly dried up. In other words, she was totally and completely healed.

The phrase, *"And she felt in her body that she was healed of that plague,"* means that she had felt oftentimes the efforts of the doctors attempting to help her, but only hurting her. As she felt that, she feels this, but with a great difference.

Then she felt pain, now she feels healing! She knows, and beyond the shadow of a doubt, and because of what she feels in her body, that *"She was healed of that plague."*

And so she was! The cure was instantaneous.

(30) "AND JESUS, IMMEDIATELY KNOWING IN HIMSELF THAT VIRTUE HAD GONE OUT OF HIM, TURNED HIM ABOUT IN THE PRESS, AND SAID, WHO TOUCHED MY CLOTHES?"

The phrase, *"And Jesus, immediately knowing in Himself that virtue had gone out of Him,"* tells us several things:

1. That which was done by Christ for others, had a price tag attached to it, as is obvious in this verse. *"Virtue* (power) *went out of Him."* This would have had at least some effect on Him physically, emotionally, and spiritually.

2. We learn from this the tremendous power of Faith in God.

In mid 1995, Frances and I were in a series of Evangelistic meetings in Mexico, with a couple of services on the U. S. side of the border. This particular Monday night, we were to be in Harlingen, Texas.

I was almost ready to leave for the service that night, when I greatly sensed the Presence of the Lord. My mind was on the Message I would preach that evening, which was this very Text.

The Lord spoke to my heart, saying, *"I'm going to show you something about this illustration of the woman touching the hem of My garment, that you have not seen previously."*

Actually, as my memory comes back even as I dictate these notes, some of it began to unfold even then. However, it was only during the Message that the Spirit of God greatly outlined that of which He had spoken.

The auditorium was jammed to capacity that night, and, correspondingly, there was a mighty moving of the Holy Spirit in the entirety of the service.

As I began to preach, greatly sensing the Presence of the Lord, with the congregation sensing it as well, when I came to the part of the woman touching the hem of Jesus' garment,

the Holy Spirit fully brought out that which He had only given me in part before the service. It was as follows.

Jesus did not know this woman was in the crowd, did not know of her illness, did not know of her determination to receive her healing, and actually didn't even know she existed. And yet, her experience portrays to any and all that Faith in God is such a powerful force, even such a powerful commodity if you please, that it would pull healing from Jesus, even though He did not even know this woman existed.

As I began to expound this to the congregation, you could sense Faith building greatly in the audience. As well, it was so powerful on me all night long, that I actually slept very little that night.

On the way to the airport the next morning, if anything, it increased respecting that which the Lord had given me.

God loves Faith! Actually, one cannot even please God without Faith (Heb. 11:6). He wants His Children to believe Him! If something is so powerful, as this obviously is, that it would bring healing from Christ, even though He did not even know the woman existed, then we're talking about something that is powerful beyond our comprehension. Consequently, every Believer should diligently seek to increase his Faith in the Lord.

Such is done by the diligent study of the Word of God, for *"Faith cometh by hearing, and hearing by the Word of God"* (Rom. 10:17).

The question, *"Turned Him about in the press, and said, Who touched My clothes?"*, actually says in the Greek, *"Who touched Me on My clothes?"*

Considering the great press of people around Him, and that many were attempting to touch Him, as the next verse proclaims, but without any recorded results, the difference was, this woman had Faith. Consequently, He felt it.

(31) AND HIS DISCIPLES SAID UNTO HIM, THOU SEEST THE MULTITUDE THRONGING THEE, AND SAYEST THOU, WHO TOUCHED ME?"

The phrase, *"And His Disciples said unto Him,"* proclaims their exclamation! They did not understand His question, especially considering that scores of people were pressing Him, even thronging Him, and, consequently, touching Him. What did He mean, *"Who touched My clothes?"*

Consequently, we see from this act of Faith performed by this dear woman, that the only thing she actually needed was Faith in God. She didn't have to go through the Disciples, and, in fact, did not do so! So that shoots down the Roman Catholic appeal to dead Saints, or live ones for that matter! She went personally to Jesus, without Him even knowing she was there, and by her Faith was able to receive exactly what she wanted.

Peter asking the question, *"Thou seest the multitude thronging Thee, and sayest Thou, Who touched me?"*, portrays that this was completely beyond his understanding or any of the other Disciples (Lk. 8:45).

Why would one touching Him, mean more, or be different, than others touching Him?

The difference was Faith!

Why did this woman have Faith and the others did not?

There is no answer to that. Actually, they should have had more Faith than her. They had already witnessed many of the miracles of Christ, while she had only recently heard what Jesus could do. But yet she had great Faith in Christ.

When I was eight years old, I asked the Lord to give me the talent to play the piano. It happened in a particular Church service, with a visiting Evangelist. He played the piano fairly well, and as a child, I became more and more enamored each night as the meetings progressed.

On the night in question, I began to ask the Lord to give me this particular talent. I had never tried to play a piano before, and at eight years of age, had absolutely no musical expertise.

Immediately after the Evangelist concluded with his musical rendition and singing, very quietly under my breath I began to implore the Lord to give me this talent. I promised Him if He would do so, that I would forever use it for His Glory.

Being only eight years old, I did not know much about sin or the world, but I promised the Lord, if He would give me this talent, I would never use it in the world, and would never play in a nightclub. Actually, I had never seen a nightclub, but somehow I knew this was a place where the Lord was not glorified.

At any rate, when the service ended, I could hardly wait to go to the platform and see if I could play the piano. I was that serious with my request, and that expectant!

I remember the service finally concluding with the final *"Amen,"* and very slowly and hesitantly I made my way to the small platform, walking up to the piano. I did not really even sit down on the piano stool, but just stood in front of the black and white keys and placed my hands on them. Instantly, I began to make chords.

At that time, I actually did not know they were chords, but I did know they sounded right.

Some may argue that musical talent was in my family, which is true, and that accounts for this ability, with my petition to the Lord having nothing to do with it.

I don't believe that! I believe the Lord heard my prayer, and answered me by giving me what I had asked for.

Upon arriving home after service, My Dad asked me, where I had learned the chords he had heard me make after the service? He wanted to know if I had been practicing at the Church, or elsewhere?

I remonstrated to him, that I had not touched a piano before, but that I had asked the Lord that night to give me the talent, and *"I suppose He has already started,"* I exclaimed!

Yes, it took many months, even years, of practice, and practice, and more practice, but eventually it came. By God's Grace, I have kept that promise made to Him, and He certainly has blessed abundantly.

I know beyond the shadow of a doubt, that the Lord heard and answered that prayer, and because of my Faith in Him. With this talent, He has helped us to bless untold millions, for which I will ever be thankful.

However, I related that in order to emphasize the childlike Faith I had, which brought about the request in the first place, and the belief that He heard me, and would answer, which He did!

From the time the Lord spoke to my heart in Harlingen, Texas respecting this small Truth that I have attempted to relate to you, I have sensed an urgency of the Holy Spirit respecting the increase of my Faith. It is as if He is telling me, *"Do not look at circumstances, or situations, but look to Me, and believe Me."* I have sensed and felt that as never before! As well, I believe it is Faith which will be used to touch untold millions for the Cause of Christ. For God never does anything of this nature, but that it is for an intended purpose.

(32) "AND HE LOOKED ROUND ABOUT TO SEE HER THAT HAD DONE THIS THING."

Irrespective of the question Peter had asked, Jesus begins a scrutinizing gaze in search for the woman.

It is amazing as to how the Holy Spirit works. Jesus knew someone had touched Him with great Faith, and that it was a woman, but that is as much as the Spirit gave to Him. He did not tell Him where the woman was in the crowd. All of this was for purpose. There is a possibility she was very shy, and, again, she had actually broken the Law of Moses by touching Him because of her disease. In other words, she was unclean! Consequently, the Holy Spirit would give her time to compose herself, before she would give her testimony.

As well, she had only *"touched"* the garment, and had not by any means grabbed it. Therefore, His knowing of this touch, was not because of its action, but because of what it represented, her Faith.

(33) "BUT THE WOMAN FEARING AND TREMBLING, KNOWING WHAT WAS DONE IN HER, CAME AND FELL DOWN BEFORE HIM, AND TOLD HIM ALL THE TRUTH."

The phrase, *"But the woman fearing and trembling,"* pictures something going on in her soul. Luke prefaced this statement by saying, *"And when the woman saw that she was not hid"* (Lk. 8:47).

Perhaps the knowledge that she had broken a ceremonial law by touching Him inasmuch as she was unclean, caused the consternation! She had not asked His permission, carrying out her act of Faith, so to speak, behind the scenes. And now He had stopped the entire procession, looking earnestly through the crowd, proclaiming that *"Virtue had gone out of Him!"* She was found out; however, the results would not be at all what she feared. This, she did know, the disease was gone!

The phrase, *"Knowing what was done in her,"* has a double meaning:

1. First of all, and as stated, she knew the disease was gone. Especially considering that she had spent all her living on doctors, and for some twelve years, and had grown no better at all, but rather worse, there was no doubt in her mind or body that she was whole of that plague. Actually, she could feel it deep within her that the problem was gone, and, furthermore, she

NOTES

would never be troubled with it again. It was a complete and permanent cure.

2. And yet she was fearful that she had done something wrong! She no doubt knew of the strict censure of the Pharisees, and not knowing Jesus before now, due to living a goodly distance away (according to tradition), she wondered if He might be angry?

The phrase, *"Came and fell down before Him,"* proclaims her seeking Mercy as she had previously sought healing. This much she did know, anyone who had the type of power manifested in Him as Jesus, was more than ordinary, and deserved worship, which she freely gave! She did not know what He might do, but she did know what had already been done. She had been gloriously and wondrously healed, and of that there was no doubt!

The phrase, *"And told Him all the truth,"* proclaims her giving exactly the thoughts of her heart concerning the touching of the hem of His garment. Luke, being a doctor, added the words, *"How she was healed immediately"* (Lk. 8:47).

The song says:
"Tell it to Jesus, tell it to Jesus,
"He is a friend that's well known;
"You've no other such a friend or brother,
"Tell it to Jesus alone."

She told everything and exactly as to how it happened, because in her heart she knew that anyone who had such power, would, as well, know it if she told otherwise.

(34) "AND HE SAID UNTO HER, DAUGHTER, THY FAITH HATH MADE THEE WHOLE; GO IN PEACE, AND BE WHOLE OF THY PLAGUE."

The phrase, *"And He said unto her, Daughter,"* proclaims far more than meets the eye and ear.

First of all, the word, *"Daughter,"* was a word of endearment. In effect, He was claiming her.

In the 25th verse, she was addressed merely as *"a certain woman,"* now she is called *"Daughter,"* which refers to ownership. In other words, not only was she healed, but she was saved as well! She was now a member of the Family of God, the same family to which the Disciples belonged, as well as all who have prostrated themselves, as her, before the lowly Galilean.

Even though she was near His age, or possibly even older, His using the word, *"Daughter,"* proclaimed Him as the Messiah, therefore, He spoke as a Father to a Daughter.

Second, this entire episode has a far greater meaning than just the healing of an individual, as wonderful and gracious as that was.

It is here obvious to remark that this malady represents to us the ever-flowing bitter fountain of sin, for which no treatment can be found in human philosophy. The remedy is only to be found in Christ.

To touch Christ's garment is to believe in His Incarnation, whereby He has touched us, and so has enabled us by Faith to touch Him, and to receive His Salvation of Grace (Bickersteth).

As stated, there is no earthly remedy for sin, but there is a remedy! That remedy is Christ, and Christ Alone!

The phrase, *"Thy Faith hath made thee whole,"* carries a powerful statement. He said to her, *"Thy Faith,"* implying the ingredient that one must have in order to receive from God, be it physical, financial, domestical, or spiritual.

The word, *"Faith,"* is central to the Christian experience and Message. And yet at times, this word is corrupted by a misunderstanding of its true Biblical meaning.

Oftentimes, people use the word, *"Faith,"* to indicate what is possible but uncertain. This is what causes most people to not receive from God.

The Bible uses *"Faith"* in ways that link it with what is assuredly and certainly true, and, consequently, is the type of *"Faith"* this woman had, and that all are demanded to have, that is, if we are to receive from the Lord.

As well, the object of our Faith must not be ourselves, or others, but God Himself.

There is no limit to what Faith in God can do! It holds out a promise to all of mankind that can literally transform any situation, and because of a personal relationship with God in Jesus Christ.

THE OBJECT OF FAITH IN GOD MUST BE GOD!

The Old Testament speaks of false sources of security. It holds each of them up and examines them in contrast to the security that is ours in the Lord. Over and over again, it proclaims the foolishness of man in turning from reliance on God to seek the security of other men (Ps. 118:8; 146:3; Jer. 17:5).

NOTES

As well, we are warned not to have Faith in riches (Ps. 49:6; 52:7), in military power (Deut. 28:52; Ps. 44:6; Jer. 5:17), or in our own goodness (Ezek. 33:13; Hos. 10:13).

True Faith fastens on God as One, Who, by His nature, is the sole certain and sure reality. God is faithful and unchanging, established in eternity; and because He is Who He is, we can commit ourselves to Him.

Because of Faith in Him, God also commits Himself to us in Covenant relationship, and the placing of our confidence in Him brings us true well-being and safety.

THE OLD TESTAMENT VIEW OF FAITH

God demanded that those who followed Him in Old Testament times, which, as well, carries over into the present, that we do so because He is utterly faithful and trustworthy.

In the great Faith worthies, the New Testament points to Abraham as Faith's primary example.

Genesis 15 describes Abraham, then a very old man, in dialogue with God. Abraham complained that God had given him no children of his own, despite an earlier promise (Gen. 12:2). God responded by amplifying the Promise. Abraham looked to the sky, filled with its numberless stars, and heard God say, *"So shall your offspring be"* (Gen. 15:5).

The next verse tells us, *"Abram believed the Lord, and He credited it to him as Righteousness"* (Gen. 15:6). The Apostle Paul says of this incident: *"Against all hope, Abraham in hope believed...*

"He faced the fact that his body was as good as dead — since he was about a hundred years old — and that Sarah's womb was also dead.

"Yet he did not waver through unbelief regarding the Promise of God, but was strengthened in his Faith and gave Glory to God,

"Being fully persuaded that God had power to do what He promised" (Rom. 4:18-21). Abraham examined the circumstances, and, despite everything, decided that God was to be trusted. Abraham consciously chose to put his trust in God, and this act of Saving Faith was accepted by the Lord in place of a Righteousness that Abraham, within himself, did not possess.

Abraham was not perfect, as the Scriptures bear out, by any standard. But his life, as reported in the Old Testament, shows again and again that he trusted God and acted on God's Promises, certain the Lord could be counted on (Heb. 11:8-12).

THE EXAMPLE

The example of Abraham stands as the Biblical illustration of Faith as believing response to God. God spoke in Promise and Command. Abraham trusted himself to God. And Abraham's Faith was demonstrated as he subsequently acted on what God had said (Gen. Chpts. 12-22).

AN EXAMPLE OF UNBELIEF, OR LACK OF FAITH

A study of Abraham's life helps us to understand the nature of belief or Faith. By contrast, the history of the generation of Israelites that was redeemed from Egypt helps us to understand the nature of unbelief.

Exodus 4:1-8 is a foundation. Numbers 14 the culmination of a theme. Exodus 4 reports a dialogue between the Lord and a hesitant Moses.

Moses had been told to return to Egypt. He would become the instrument of Israel's deliverance. But Moses objected: *"What if they do not believe me or listen to me?"* (Ex. 4:1). God gave Moses the power to perform three minor miracles and explained that, *"If they do not believe you or pay attention to the first miraculous sign, they may believe the second"* (Ex. 4:8).

Moses returned to Egypt, and through many striking wonders, delivered the people of Israel. That generation experienced many miraculous events, all providing unmistakable evidence of God's reality and His Power. Yet these miracles failed to produce anything beyond moments of belief (Ex. 14:31).

Instead, when led to the edge of the Promised Land, these people who had experienced many miracles, refused to respond to God's Command to go up and take the land. Angrily, God exclaimed, *"How long will these people treat Me with contempt? How long will they refuse to believe in Me, in spite of all the miraculous signs I have performed among them?"* (Num. 14:11).

The Old Testament and New Testament return to this incident often, just as they return again and again to Moses. In a review of history for the next generation, Moses reminded

NOTES

them, *"You did not trust Him or obey Him"* (Deut. 9:23). Psalm 78 speaks of God being angry because the Exodus generation would *"not believe in God or trust in His deliverance"* (Ps. 78:22) *"in spite of His wonders"* (Ps. 78:32).

The writer to the Hebrews warns New Testament Believers not to permit a hardened heart to drag them into error so that they would become like the evil generation that heard God's Word, but whose *"unbelieving heart"* was shown by their refusal to obey (Heb. 3:12).

The stories of Abraham and of the Exodus generation show the meaning of Faith in positive and negative frames. Through them we see several basic aspects of Faith.

THE BASICS OF FAITH

First, Faith is not some response to evidence, even when that evidence is clearly miraculous. Abraham believed God. His Faith was a response to God Himself, Who met Abraham directly in a word of promise. That Word from God is far more compelling for Faith than any miracles performed in the material universe.

Second, Faith in God engages the total person. It is expressed in perception and action. Abraham was well aware of his and Sarah's advanced age. But Abraham also considered God's Power and Faithfulness. The fact of God so transformed Abraham's perspective that he easily accepted God's Promise, although fathering a son was humanly impossible for him.

But Israel, poised on the borders of Canaan, could see only the military strength of that land's inhabitants. They treated God *"with contempt"* (Num. 14:11; 16:30) by refusing to consider His Power and reality.

Faith is also expressed in actions. When Abraham was told to go to Canaan, he packed up and went (Gen. 12). When the Exodus generation was told to conquer the land, they refused even to try. They were betrayed by their *"unbelieving heart."*

Third, the outcome of Faith is demonstrated. When a person responds to God's self-disclosure, Faith-generated obedience leads to blessing. Abraham believed God and knew God's protection during his lifetime. Conversely, the unbelieving generation of Israelites wandered back into the wilderness to die in its desolate wastes.

FAITH AS EXPRESSED IN THE NEW TESTAMENT

The object of Faith in the New Testament continues to be God as in the Old, but now, through Jesus, Who is a reality, whereas in the Old Testament, He was only a shadow. Consequently, Faith as expressed in the New Testament, and in Christ, is far more developed than in the Old. The reason is clearly expressed by Jesus Himself: *"I am the Way and the Truth and the Life. No one comes to the Father except through Me"* (Jn. 14:6). God the Father has revealed Himself in the Son. The Father has set Jesus before us as the One to Whom we must entrust ourselves for Salvation. It is Jesus Who is the focus of Christian Faith.

In the context of our Faith and in our relationship with Jesus, which is inseparable, *"Believing"* has come to mean: A. The happy trust that a person places in the Person of Jesus; and, B. The allegiance to Him that grows out of that very personal commitment.

FAITH AS EXPRESSED IN THE GOSPELS

The Gospels report many signs (miracles) that Jesus performed as He travelled and taught. Often, but not always, Jesus' healings were intimately associated with the Faith of the sick person, exactly as is expressed in this woman who touched the hem of His garment (Mat. 9:2, 22, 29; Mk. 2:5; 5:34; Lk. 17:19; 18:42).

However, a survey of the Gospels shows that for most of the people, Jesus' miracles failed to produce True Faith. Even as Jesus hung on the Cross, the mocking promise of his watching enemies was a lie. *"Come down now from the Cross,"* they pledged, *"and we will believe"* (Mat. 27:42; Mk. 15:32). And when Jesus was raised from the dead, what happened? These men were the first to attempt to hide the evidence (Mat. 28:11-15).

In this, we see the phenomenon we noted in the Old Testament report of ancient Israel's unbelief. The Exodus miracles provided incontrovertible proof of God's Power and His Presence. Yet the Exodus generation would not commit themselves to Him. The nation in Jesus' day saw His healings, watched Him cast out demons, and even saw Him raise Lazarus from the dead; yet they refused to believe.

But belief in the full flow of God's Power was difficult, even for the Disciples. They had

trusted themselves to Jesus as the Son of God. But when the Lord was crucified, their hope and confidence drained away. They could not, on the day of the Resurrection, bring themselves to believe that the One they trusted had come to life again (Mat. 28; Mk. 16; Lk. 24).

But in the Gospels, one vital fact is made clear in Jesus' Words about Faith: A lack of trust in the God in Whom we have Faith closes off lives' possibilities. When we fail to believe, we do not experience the full range of God's activity (Mat. 21:22). But when we trust, we open up our future to a full experience of God's Power in and through us (Mat. 17:20; 21:21; Lk. 7:9-10). All things are possible to the one who believes.

For you and me, Faith in Jesus does not come through an observation of miracles, as wonderful as they may be. Faith is born as we learn about Jesus, find out what He said, and put our trust in Him. We then go on to deeper Faith, an active reliance on the Power and Presence of God. And as we trust, our life opens up to all sorts of possibilities. Miracles follow Faith. Believing, we experience God at work in our lives.

FAITH AND JOHN THE BELOVED

John looks at the relationship between believing and evidence. He examines superficial belief. And he connects True Faith with life and death. In addition, several Passages of John's Gospel call for careful study.

BELIEVING AND EVIDENCE

In Christian Faith, knowing and believing are linked. We respond to testimony about Jesus with our intellect as well as with our heart. John's Gospel looks at two kinds of testimony. There is the testimony of Jesus' Miracles and the testimony of Jesus' Words.

At times these two lines of testimony enhance each other. Thus the Twelve, who were already committed to Jesus, saw the miracle at Cana (Jn. 2:11) and found their belief in Jesus strengthened. It is not unusual to find that many of the observers of Jesus' Works were moved to some kind of belief. The testimony of His Miracles was compelling (Jn. 7:31; 11:45; 12:11). Yet others who saw the same signs chose not to believe, rejecting Jesus against the evidence of the Lord's Works (Jn. 10:38; 14:11).

In John, we see that the testimony provided by miracles and signs forced observers to take

Jesus seriously. But signs and miracles alone did not bring about Saving Faith.

SUPERFICIAL BELIEF

John distinguishes between two types of *"believing."* His Gospel was written, he told his readers, *"That you may believe that Jesus is the Christ, the Son of God, and that by believing you may have life in His Name"* (Jn. 20:31). Yet when John describes the response of the crowds to the testimony of Jesus' Miracles, it is clear that those who *"believed"* did so in a way that fell short of life-giving belief in Jesus as the Son of God.

John 2:22-23 tells us of many who saw His signs and *"believed in Him."* But later, after that same crowd of shallow Disciples heard Jesus speak about Himself as the Bread of Life (Jn. 6), they complained: *"This is a hard teaching. Who can accept it?"* (Jn. 6:60). John observes that *"From this time many of His Disciples turned back and no longer followed Him"* (Jn. 6:66).

Superficial Faith came in response to the miraculous, and it died when Jesus communicated the Divine content of His Message.

Nicodemus, a Religious Leader, confessed, *"We know You are a Teacher Who has come from God. For no one could perform the miraculous signs You are doing if God were not with Him"* (Jn. 3:2). Yet when other Religious Leaders heard the Message that Jesus spoke (Jn. 7:16-17), they refused to go on to the belief that involves commitment to Jesus as Lord (Jn. 7:45-47).

Wonder at Jesus' Powers and even agreement that God must have sent Him, falls far short of Saving Faith.

Only when one recognizes Jesus as the Son of God and commits himself completely to Him, does a person believe in the fullest, saving sense. This commitment involves accepting His Words and making them the framework of one's life.

FAITH AND LIFE

Over and over in his writings, John links Faith with life, and unbelief with death. The one who believes in Jesus has eternal life. The one who does not believe is already condemned to eternal death.

The intimate connection between life and believing is as marked in John's Gospel and Epistles as is the connection between Faith and Righteousness in the writings of Paul.

NOTES

In John 8, this Chapter explores the link between the testimony of the miraculous and the testimony of the Message. Jesus teaches clearly that He and the Father are inseparably One. Thus, belief in Jesus is the critical issue for every hearer: *"If you do not believe that I am the One I claim to be, you will indeed die in your sins"* (Jn. 8:24).

The Miracles of Jesus likewise, cannot be argued away. But when Jesus spoke the Truth, the Religious Leaders attacked Him. Unlike Abraham, who heard God speak and responded with belief in the Lord, this generation did not respond to the Word of Truth.

When the physical descendants of Abraham rejected the fresh Word of God that came through Jesus, they proved themselves to be of a different spiritual family, for Abraham believed God, and these men refused to believe God's Son.

John 11, tells the story of the raising of Lazarus. While many accepted the testimony of this miracle and accepted Jesus' Word about Himself, the story itself looks at believing from a slightly different perspective. Mary and Martha, the sisters of Lazarus, did believe in Jesus. They believed that Jesus as the source of life would raise Lazarus *"at the last day"* (Jn. 11:24), for Jesus was the Christ and the Son of God (Jn. 11:27). But although Saving Faith was present, the women still failed to understand the life-giving Power of Jesus, Power that enabled Him to raise their brother then and there, recalling him to life even though he had been dead for four days.

This proclaims to us that one may have Saving Faith in Jesus, as the sisters of Lazarus, and yet limit His Power. When we put our trust in Jesus, the Son of God, we enter a relationship with One Who is Lord and Whose ability to act in our world is without limitations.

Actually, this characterizes the greater majority of the modern Church. Saving Faith in Christ is believed and maintained. Yet, many limit Him thereafter!

PAUL AND FAITH

It fell to Paul the task of not only presenting the Gospel, but, as well, of giving testimony and explanation. Consequently, he deals with Faith and Salvation, Faith and Righteousness, and Faith and Fellowship with God.

In the first three Chapters of Romans, Paul demonstrated the fact that all humanity is lost, without a shred of Righteousness that would permit God to accept any individual, at least on their own merit. He said, *"Therefore no one will be declared Righteous in God's sight by observing the Law"* (Rom. 3:20). Yet, God has determined to bring mankind a Salvation that necessarily involves sinners becoming Righteous in His sight. This, Paul explains, is accomplished in the Death of Christ, which was a Sacrifice of Atonement. Through *"Faith in His Blood,"* the individual who believes is declared Righteous. Thus Salvation and Righteousness come through Faith in Jesus; and through Faith Salvation and Righteousness are available to all.

THE NATURE OF FAITH

In Romans 4, Paul argues that Faith is the same today as it was when it was exercised by Old Testament Saints such as Abraham and David. And Faith has the same result. Abraham and David won forgiveness by Faith (Rom. 4:1-8); and for us today, forgiveness is also found by Faith. In Romans 4, we see that to believe means simply to count on God's Promise. We accept the Word of God Who spoke, and in doing so, we accept God Himself.

Paul shows that the God Who spoke with promise to Abraham, is the same God Who, in Jesus, speaks with promise to us: The God *"in Whom he* (Abraham) *believed — the God Who gives life to the dead and calls things that are not as though they were"* (Rom. 4:17).

In Romans 4:18-25, Paul further defines Faith. Here he analyzes Abraham's Faith. Abraham faced the fact of his and Sarah's advanced age. He knew this meant that conceiving a child was impossible. But Abraham *"Did not waver through unbelief regarding the Promise of God."* Instead, he was *"Fully persuaded that God had power to do what He had promised."* And so Paul concludes, *"This is why it was credited to him as Righteousness."*

Abraham heard the Promise. He looked beyond the impossibility of its fulfillment and considered God. Abraham, confident that God would keep His Promise, accepted what God announced would come to pass.

The Promise Abraham believed was the Promise that he would father a child. The Promise held out today in the Gospel and which

NOTES

we are to believe, is the Promise that God, Who has delivered Jesus up for our sins and raised Him to life again for our justification, will save us because of Jesus. We look beyond the impossibility that the natural person sees. We consider God. And we too are convinced that what God has announced will come to pass.

Believing, we receive the Gifts of Salvation and Righteousness.

MAINTAINING OUR SALVATION

In Galatians 3, Paul not only proclaims the necessity of Faith in Christ for one's Salvation, but, as well, he argues that our relationship with the Lord is also maintained by Faith. We are not to attempt to live in fellowship with God by trying to keep the Law. Paul reminds us, *"The Righteous will live by Faith"* (Gal. 3:11).

Law is based on a contrary principle: Reliance on human activity and performance. It is not based on Promise. Since we must relate to God through His Promise, rather than through His Works, we must continue on in our relationship with the Lord by Faith. We must hear the Words of Scripture as promised, and we must rely on them as promised.

In his personal testimony, Paul says, *"I have been crucified with Christ and I no longer live, but Christ lives in me. The life I live in the body, I live by Faith in the Son of God, Who loved me and gave Himself for me"* (Gal. 2:20). The life of Faith is ours as we continue to count on God's Words to us. We hear them as Promise and believe that God will do in us all that He has spoken.

As we live by Faith, the Righteousness of which the Bible speaks as being ours in God's sight, gradually infuses our life and character, and we become Righteous persons in fact and in deed. It is all by Faith in Christ.

LOOKING BACK AT FAITH

The object of Faith, we find as we study the Word of God, has differed somewhat from age to age. For in different ages, God has spoken different Words of Promise.

At the very dawn of time, and at the Fall of man, God promised that a Redeemer would come (Gen. 3:15).

To Abraham, and in keeping with that Promise, He promised a Son and multiplied descendants.

To those under the Law, there was the Promise of Blessing to accompany obedience.

To us, there is the Promise of cleansing and acceptance through Jesus, Who all the other promises pointed to.

In each age, Faith is man's response to the Promise. In each age, Faith is trusting oneself to the God Who has spoken. In each age, Faith is accepted by God in place of a Righteousness that no human being had, or, in fact, could have, at least on his own.

In the New Testament, to which the entirety of the Old pointed, we see with unmistakable clarity that it is through Faith that God gives Salvation and Righteousness. It is in the New Testament that we see with unmistakable clarity that Faith is a personal response to God and a complete commitment of ourselves to Him. There, also, we see that Faith calls for a continuing relationship of response to Jesus' Word. It is in the New Testament that we see with unmistakable clarity that Faith transforms human beings, bringing us a life that is eternal, and, as well, can be experienced now. Through Faith, we come into a relationship with God, in which He commits Himself not simply to declare us Righteous, but also to make us truly good persons after the example of Christ.

Trusting God is the heart and soul of the Faith that centers in our Lord Jesus Christ.

ONCE AGAIN, FAITH OR CHRIST AS THE OBJECT

The Believer must be careful not to fall into the trap to which Abraham almost succumbed.

Distraught and discouraged because the promised Son had not yet appeared, and, as well, inasmuch as it seemed the obstacles were abundant, he began to gradually take his eyes off the Giver onto the gift. This is a danger for many Believers.

In response to this, *"The Word of the Lord came unto Abram in a vision, saying, Fear not, Abram: I am thy shield, and thy exceeding great reward"* (Gen. 15:1).

In this Passage, the Lord brings Abraham back to the correct position of Faith. The Believer must never allow himself, and for whatever reason, to be pulled away from the Giver to the gift. While it was certainly important, and exceedingly so, that the gift, the Promised Son,

be brought into the world, still, the Lord would tell the Patriarch, it is not the gift, but rather My Person Who is *"Thy exceeding great reward."*

The modern Faith Movement, while bringing some needed Truths to the Body of Christ, has, at the same time, at least in a measure, fallen to the error in which Abraham found himself. Faith has become the object with many, instead of the Giver of Faith. In so doing, the danger is always prevalent that God's Word will in turn be used against Himself. In other words, with Faith as the object, instead of Christ, the Believer automatically concludes that he knows the Will of God in any and all situations, and thereby sets about to use his Faith to bring about that which he desires, instead of what God desires.

Actually, this is what Satan attempted to get Christ to do respecting the temptations in the wilderness. Christ was hungry, so why not introduce His Power to His need? It was a logical conclusion, at least the manner in which Satan proposed it. There was nothing sinful in bread, and, as well, there was nothing sinful in the Lord using His Power accordingly. And so reason millions!

However, if Jesus had done so, He would have been stepping outside the Will of God, which was the primary focus. Consequently, He will say to Satan, *"It is written, Man shall not live by bread alone, but by every word that proceedeth out of the Mouth of God"* (Mat. 4:4).

So, to use Faith as an object, which means to acquire things at random pleasure, is not the Will of God at all! The object of Faith must ever be the Giver of Faith, Who is the Lord Jesus Christ. While the gift is always important, such as the promised Son to Abraham, still, the Giver of that gift, and as stated, was the *"exceeding great reward,"* and not the gift itself.

(Most of the thoughts on Faith were taken from the teaching of Lawrence O. Richards.)

The phrase, *"Go in peace, and be whole of thy plague,"* adds a new dimension to the entirety of this episode. This woman not only gained healing, but Salvation as well! The word, *"peace,"* assures this. It spoke of the health of both body and soul.

As such, the proclamation of Salvation, and in few words, is beautifully given.

The *"peace"* spoken of, refers to *"peace"* with God.

As a result of the Fall, man lost his peace with God. As a result of sin which entered, there was an enmity which entered between God and man. Man was estranged from God, and because of his disobedience, which brought about this enmity (Rom. 8:7; Eph. 2:15-16).

This lack of *"peace"* presents a troubled soul to the individual, which expresses itself in many ways, all adverse, whether physical, mental, domestical, and, above all, spiritual. Such flows from a twisted human nature. It can only be assuaged by Christ, as Faith is evidenced in Him, as exampled by the woman who touched the hem of His garment.

THE OLD TESTAMENT CONCEPT OF PEACE

The Hebrew word for *"Peace"* is *"Shalom."* It is derived from a root that conveys the image of wholeness, unity, and harmony — something that is complete and sound. It also conveys the idea of prosperity, health, and fulfillment.

In the Old Testament, Peace takes on its deepest significance when we move into the Psalms and the Prophets. Although the word is expressed in other ways, still, its greatest fulfillment comes to human beings when they experience God's Presence.

As an example, the Lord said that He would bless *"His people with Peace"* (Ps. 29:11). But more than national blessing is involved in the Peace that God gives. David, fleeing from Absalom during that son's rebellion, felt intense strife and pressure (Ps. 4:1-2). But David fixed his thoughts on God and remembered the joy that came with trust in Him.

Comforted and at rest despite overwhelming danger, David concluded, *"I will lie down and sleep in peace, for You Alone, O Lord, make me dwell in safety"* (Ps. 4:8). For us, as for David, Peace in difficult circumstances is a result of our relationship with the Lord. *"Great peace,"* David says, *"have they who love Your Law"* (Ps. 119:165). The one whose life is in harmony with God's revealed Will experiences inner harmony as well. It is not surprising, then, to find Psalm 37 contrast the wicked and ruthless with *"the man of peace"* (Ps. 37:35-37). The man of peace lives in a right relationship with God, for God Alone is the Source of human rest and fulfillment.

For those who have missed the way of Faith and are struggling to find fulfillment apart

from God, there is no such blessing. As Isaiah warns, *"The wicked are like the tossing sea, which cannot rest, whose waves cast up mire and mud. There is no peace, says my God, for the wicked"* (Isa. 57:20-21).

Consequently, peace in the Old Testament speaks of the blessing of inner and outer harmony that comes to a person or people who live in a close relationship with God. Believers can, like David, experience peace despite dangerous circumstances by being conscious of God's Presence, or at least of His sure Promises. Ultimately the world will know international and interpersonal peace as well, as the very Presence of God in the Person of Jesus halts strife and war. One day it will come!

THE PEACE OFFERING IN THE OLD TESTAMENT

One of the Old Testament offerings was called *"The Peace Offering."* It is mentioned over eighty times. This Offering, which came after the Sacrifices for sin, was partially burned and partially eaten by the worshipers. Thus it symbolized the *"Shalom,"* the overflowing joy and fulfillment, that forgiveness brings us, causing us to be at peace with the Lord. This was fulfilled by Christ at Calvary, thereby becoming our Peace (Col. 1:20).

THE PEACE THAT JESUS BRINGS

There are multiplied greetings and farewells in the Epistles proclaiming that believing readers will receive Grace, Mercy, and Peace. This Peace is *"From God our Father and from the Lord Jesus Christ"* (Rom. 1:7; I Cor. 1:3; II Cor. 1:2; Gal. 1:3; Eph. 1:2, etc.).

First and foremost, the peace human beings need is peace with God. This is ours in Jesus, and Jesus Alone, *"Since we have been justified through Faith, we have peace with God through our Lord Jesus Christ"* (Rom. 5:1). Ephesians 2:14 adds that Jesus *"Himself is our peace."*

Among God's people, peace means that hostility has been replaced by unity (Eph. 2:14-17; 4:3).

PEACE IN THE EPISTLES

Peace, in the Epistles, is most often that restored wholeness that Jesus brings to our relationship with God and others, although this cannot be separated from the inner sense of well-being that accompanies them. However, this does not necessarily mean the absence of all outward strife.

Jesus warned His Disciples not to imagine that serving Him meant that they would be freed from all external pressures and strife *"on earth"* (Mat. 10:34; Lk. 12:51). Instead, Jesus focuses on peace despite external pressures, and even suffering.

John most clearly developed that theme. He reports Jesus' Words of peace: *"Peace I leave with you; My peace I give you. I do not give to you as the world gives. Do not let your hearts be troubled and do not be afraid"* (Jn. 14:27).

"I have told you these things, so that in Me you may have peace. In this world you will have trouble. But take heart! I have overcome the world" (Jn. 16:33).

Jesus provides an inner peace that lets the Believer face danger and suffering without fear or a trembling heart. Through Jesus, an inner peace is possible, no matter how turbulent the external situation may be.

As well, from the phrase, *"Go in peace, and be whole of thy plague,"* one can make an excellent Scriptural case that healing for the body, as well as Salvation of the soul, is a part of the Atonement, i.e., the price that Jesus paid at Calvary. Man cannot be *"whole"* unless he is whole in every capacity. To argue that the *"Atonement"* only included Salvation from sin, is a failure to understand the total Fall of man, and, consequently, the total Redemption of man by Christ at Calvary and the Resurrection. He is either totally redeemed, and made whole in every respect, or not redeemed at all! Of course, we know that Jesus redeemed the *"whole"* man.

To argue that healing was not included in the Atonement, and because Christians still get sick, is to argue that Salvation from sin is not in the Atonement, because Christians, at times, still sin. In Truth, the total Redemption of man in the Atonement, including both spiritual and physical, is not affected by the fact of both continued sin and sickness.

The idea is, that the entirety of the Salvation process, as provided at Calvary and the Resurrection is not yet completed as far as results are concerned, even though it is completed as far as the fact is concerned. Consequently, the Believer has been saved, is being saved, and shall be saved! (Jn. 3:16).

NOTES

The Believer has presently been Sanctified and Justified *"In the Name of the Lord Jesus, and by the Spirit of our God"* (I Cor. 6:11).

However, the Believer has not yet been *"Glorified"* which will take place at the Resurrection of Life, which will then, and for all time, complete the Salvation process. Then sin or sickness will no longer be possible (Rom. 8:17-25; I Cor. 15:51-54).

(35) "WHILE HE YET SPAKE, THERE CAME FROM THE RULER OF THE SYNAGOGUE'S HOUSE CERTAIN WHICH SAID, THY DAUGHTER IS DEAD: WHY TROUBLEST THOU THE MASTER ANY FURTHER?"

The phrase, *"While He yet spake,"* refers to someone coming from the home of Jairus, and bringing a message, even while the Lord was speaking to the woman who had just been healed. The message would not be good!

The phrase, *"There came from the ruler of the Synagogue's house certain which said, Thy daughter is dead,"* constituted a terrible blow to Jairus. He no doubt was very pleased at the healing of this dear woman, but, at the same time, his heart was breaking for his little daughter. Consequently, he must have been extremely concerned regarding the delay brought about by the healing of the woman. Jesus, searching for her after the healing, and the time it took for her to give her testimony, must have caused terrible anxiety in the heart of this man. And now he receives the worst message of all, confirming what were no doubt his fears, *"Thy daughter is dead!"*

The question, *"Why troublest thou the Master any further?"*, proclaims the end of their Faith, at least those who had brought the disconcerting message. I think the next verse proclaims, that Jairus, as well, felt that it was now too late!

(36) "AS SOON AS JESUS HEARD THE WORD THAT WAS SPOKEN, HE SAITH UNTO THE RULER OF THE SYNAGOGUE, BE NOT AFRAID, ONLY BELIEVE."

The phrase, *"As soon as Jesus heard the word that was spoken,"* means that Jesus overheard what was being said.

The phrase, *"He saith unto the ruler of the Synagogue,"* proclaims the fact, and according to the statement given by Christ, that Jairus had ceased to believe on the news of the death of his daughter.

The phrase, *"Be not afraid, only believe,"* constituted at least some of the greatest words that Jairus would ever hear, but yet completely beyond his comprehension. In effect, Jesus said, *"Stop fearing,"* and *"Be believing,"* which means to continue believing, even in the presence of death. What a valuable lesson this should be to all!

To believe is one thing, but to continue to believe, even in the face of extremely adverse circumstances, as here proclaimed, is the key to receiving what we want from the Lord. At what level does our Faith weaken and die?

The Lord is ever seeking to strengthen our Faith, which is always done through the Word of God (Rom. 10:17). This simply means we are to believe the Word of God, and to believe it despite the circumstances.

I am convinced, that the more mature one is in Christ, that the Lord allows circumstances to build, which, at times, make the situation even more impossible, in order that our Faith may be increased, by trusting solely in God's Word.

The idea is, that we walk by Faith and not by sight (II Cor. 5:7).

Consequently, the Lord will allow the *"sight"* to be increased by adverse circumstances, difficulties, and even impossibilities! It becomes very easy to look at these things, and because of their loud clamor and obvious disabilities. The secret is to keep one's eye and heart on the Word, and despite the circumstances or difficulties.

I think the difficulties could not be any worse than here recorded, with the child actually dying. And yet Jesus says to him, *"Don't fear, keep believing!"*

He says the same to us, as well!

(37) "AND HE SUFFERED NO MAN TO FOLLOW HIM, SAVE PETER, AND JAMES, AND JOHN THE BROTHER OF JAMES."

Why these three, *"Peter, James, and John?"*

This is the first of three occasions when Jesus will single them out from the other Disciples.

1. On this occasion, the raising of the girl from the dead, Jesus would portray to these three His *"Power."*

2. At the Transfiguration, only these three were allowed to witness this event (Mk. 9:1-2). Here, He showed them His *"Glory!"*

3. During His passion in the Garden of Gethsemane, likewise, only the three were

NOTES

allowed (Mk. 14:32-35). Here, He showed them His *"Sufferings!"*

The only answer as to why these three were included, with the others excluded from these momentous occasions, is that the three showed by their actions that they desired a closer walk with Him. There is no other explanation that I'm aware of. Those who *"Hunger and thirst after Righteousness are filled."* Consequently, it stands to reason that they who *"Hunger and thirst"* the more, are filled the more (Mat 5:6).

(38) "AND HE COMETH TO THE HOUSE OF THE RULER OF THE SYNAGOGUE, AND SEETH THE TUMULT, AND THEM THAT WEPT AND WAILED GREATLY."

The phrase, *"And He cometh to the house of the ruler of the Synagogue,"* spoke of the home of Jairus. I wonder what was in the mind of Jairus all the time they were on the way to his house? Did he really realize what Jesus was about to do?

It seems from Luke 7:11, that this was not the first occasion of Jesus raising one from the dead, although that chronology is not confirmed.

The phrase, *"And seeth the tumult,"* referred to the activity of the paid mourners, and Jesus examining their actions with a critical and careful eye.

The phrase, *"And them that wept and wailed greatly,"* had to do with the practice and custom of that time of hiring mourners to do this thing. Their mourning was not real, only fake, due to most of them probably not even knowing the child.

The actions of Christ, as the next verse portrays, proclaim the fact that He was not in sympathy with such activity.

(39) "AND WHEN HE WAS COME IN, HE SAITH UNTO THEM, WHY MAKE YE THIS ADO, AND WEEP? THE DAMSEL IS NOT DEAD, BUT SLEEPETH."

The phrase, *"And when He was come in,"* refers to Him entering into the midst of the paid mourners. No doubt, Jairus, along with Peter, James, and John, were with Him.

The question, *"He saith unto them, Why make ye this ado, and weep?"*, refers to all the uproar, and constant wailing. As stated, Jesus was not in sympathy with this custom and practice.

The phrase, *"The damsel is not dead, but sleepeth,"* did not mean that she was not actually dead, but that the child was not dead to stay dead.

As well, the word, *"sleepeth,"* brings us to the fact of the Resurrection. In the Scriptures, the dead are constantly referred to as *"sleeping,"* in order that the terror of death be assuaged.

Again, it is only the body that *"sleeps,"* with the soul and spirit of the individual fully alive and active in the Presence of Christ. Hence Paul would say, *"Having a desire to depart, and to be with Christ"* (Phil. 1:23).

Jesus, consequently, would say of Lazarus, *"Our friend Lazarus sleepeth; but I go that I may awake him out of sleep"* (Jn. 11:11).

Some false cults teach soul-sleep, meaning that at death the soul sleeps until the Resurrection, etc. Such is not taught in Scripture.

All the Scriptures used by these cults clearly refer to the body which does sleep in the dust of the earth until the Resurrection of the body (Dan. 12:2; Jn. 5:28-29).

The body is the only part of man that dies at physical death (James 2:26). The reason it dies is because the inner man, the soul and spirit, the life of the body, leaves the body. It then goes back to dust and is spoken of as being asleep (Gen. 3:19; Eccl. 3:19-21; Mat. 9:24; Jn. 11:11; I Cor. 11:30; 15:6, 18-20, 51; I Thess. 4:13-17).

(40) "AND THEY LAUGHED HIM TO SCORN. BUT WHEN HE HAD PUT THEM ALL OUT, HE TAKETH THE FATHER AND THE MOTHER OF THE DAMSEL, AND THEM THAT WERE WITH HIM, AND ENTERETH IN WHERE THE DAMSEL WAS LYING."

The phrase, *"And they laughed him to scorn,"* refers to their weeping suddenly turned to laughing. I think it now becomes obvious as to why Jesus was opposed to this custom.

As well, their deriding and jeering were at Him! They were not content to merely disagree with Him, concerning the child being dead, but, felt they must loudly proclaim their disagreement by jeering Him.

The phrase, *"But when He had put them all out,"* is a strong statement, meaning that He had to use pressure to make these individuals leave. It was somewhat akin to the forceful ejection when He cleansed the Temple. There is no evidence that it went quite that far, but very close to it!

The phrase, *"He taketh the father and the mother of the damsel, and them that were with Him,"* referred to Jairus, his wife, along with Peter, James, and John.

NOTES

The phrase, *"And entereth in where the damsel was lying,"* is an interesting statement. The word, *"entereth,"* actually refers to a person going on a journey.

Wuest says that the word was chosen because it conveyed the idea of distance. Even though it was only a few feet from this room to where the child was lying dead, still, what would transpire, the raising of the child from the dead, would portray a journey of incomprehensible proportions. All would be taken to a dimension of Faith and Power, that are impossible in the natural sense.

(41) "AND HE TOOK THE DAMSEL BY THE HAND, AND SAID UNTO HER, TALI-THA CUMI; WHICH IS, BEING INTERPRETED, DAMSEL, I SAY UNTO THEE, ARISE."

The phrase, *"And He took the damsel by the hand,"* refers to a strong grip.

I wonder what the thoughts of Jairus and the girls' mother were when Jesus reached down and took her hand?

The phrase, *"And said unto her, Tali-tha cumi,"* is Aramaic, and means, *"Little girl, I say unto thee, arise."* Consequently, it means that Mark gave us the original language in which Jesus spoke this Word.

As well, the other time that the mother tongue of Aramaic was given, concerned our Lord's Words on the Cross, *"My God, My God, Why hast Thou forsaken Me?"* As this occasion at the home of Jairus, it was as well interpreted for Gentile readers (Mat. 27:46).

Inasmuch as the original language was reported in these two cases, quite possibly they relate to each other. As Jesus defeated death at the home of Jairus, likewise, and for the whole world, He defeated death at Calvary. Perhaps, the Holy Spirit desired to interrelate the two. That which He did this day, He would do, and on a worldwide scale.

The phrase, *"Which is, being interpreted, Damsel, I say unto thee, arise,"* presents His exact words in Greek, in which this Text was originally written.

Some claim that Jesus may possibly have been bilingual, sometimes using Greek, sometimes Syrian (Aramaic).

(42) "AND STRAIGHTWAY THE DAMSEL AROSE, AND WALKED; FOR SHE WAS OF THE AGE OF TWELVE YEARS. AND THEY WERE ASTONISHED WITH A GREAT ASTONISHMENT."

The phrase, *"And straightway the damsel arose, and walked,"* means that she immediately arose upon the Command of Christ, and began to walk about the room, possibly to her Mother and Father, and then maybe even to Christ.

The phrase, *"For she was of the age of twelve years,"* simply relates her age. What her sickness had been which had caused her death, we are not told. However, whatever it was, she no longer has it.

The phrase, *"And they were astonished with a great astonishment,"* means they were simply amazed beyond words. Peter, James, and John, along with the Mother and Father, simply stood there as if in a trance, knowing that what they had seen was true, yet, hardly able to believe it.

As someone has said, He raised the dead then to show that He will be able to raise the dead on that Resurrection Morn!

(43) "AND HE CHARGED THEM STRAITLY THAT NO MAN SHOULD KNOW IT; AND COMMANDED THAT SOMETHING SHOULD BE GIVEN HER TO EAT."

The phrase, *"And He charged them straitly that no man should know it,"* was done, in order that the Religious Leaders may not be further aroused.

However, His Command was probably futile, inasmuch as the paid mourners knew what He had proposed to do, and certainly the very appearance of the child would prove beyond the shadow of a doubt that He had done it — raised her from the dead. So, even though they were *"charged straitly,"* i.e., with insistence, still, it is doubtful that the secret was kept for very long.

The phrase, *"And commanded that something should be given her to eat,"* probably was in reference to her past illness.

Maybe whatever she had, had caused food to exacerbate the problem. Nevertheless, if that was the problem, it no longer is, and now she can eat anything she desires.

Consequently, this Chapter begins by the former Maniac of Gadara being commanded to go into the Gospel field (vs. 19); the woman, to go into peace (vs. 34); and the child to go into dinner (vs. 43).

These three Commands in reverse order apply to all who have experienced the Saving Grace and Power of Christ. The Bible must be their

food; assurance of Salvation their experience; and preaching the Gospel their employment.

Consequently, all Christians, honorably earning their bread, should regard preaching the Gospel as their main business (Williams).

CHAPTER 6

(1) "AND HE WENT OUT FROM THENCE, AND CAME INTO HIS OWN COUNTRY; AND HIS DISCIPLES FOLLOW HIM."

The phrase, *"And He went out from thence,"* refers to Him leaving Capernaum. Quite possibly, He left before the news got out concerning the raising of the daughter of Jairus from the dead.

The phrase, *"And came into His Own country,"* refers to Nazareth. Even though He was born in Bethlehem, still, Nazareth had been His home from the time that Joseph, His foster father, had been warned of the Lord in a dream, concerning where He should live. Consequently, the Scripture says, *"And He came and dwelt in a city called Nazareth"* (Mat. 2:23). Nazareth was about a day's journey from Capernaum.

There is debate over whether this is the same journey recorded in Luke 4, or another. Most think that Luke 4 was His first, with this being His second. And yet, the terminology is such that the possibility definitely exists that Luke 4 and Mark 6 are one and the same. Luke 4 could well be given out of chronological order, as some of the experiences often are.

The phrase, *"And His Disciples follow Him,"* speaks of the entirety of the Twelve.

(2) "AND WHEN THE SABBATH DAY WAS COME, HE BEGAN TO TEACH IN THE SYNAGOGUE: AND MANY HEARING HIM WERE ASTONISHED, SAYING, FROM WHENCE HATH THIS MAN THESE THINGS? AND WHAT WISDOM IS THIS WHICH IS GIVEN UNTO HIM, THAT EVEN SUCH MIGHTY WORKS ARE WROUGHT BY HIS HANDS?"

The phrase, *"And when the Sabbath Day was come,"* lends credence to the thought that He arrived in Nazareth several days before the Sabbath.

The phrase, *"He began to teach in the Synagogue,"* records the practice of most Synagogues.

If a speaker of note came by, the rulers of the Synagogue could, if he so desired, request that he speak. Having heard many wonderful things about Jesus, and especially considering that He was a home boy, they, no doubt, eagerly requested that He teach them. The method varied in different Synagogues. Sometimes a Text was appointed, and sometimes the speaker was allowed to choose that which he desired.

The phrase, *"And many hearing Him were astonished,"* actually proclaims two reasons why!

1. The tremendous insight He had in the Scriptures, far eclipsed any and all they had ever heard. Little did they realize it, but while growing up among them, the Psalms declared His attention to the Word. It said, *"O how love I Thy Law! It is My meditation all the day.*

"Thou through Thy Commandments, hast made Me wiser than Mine enemies: for they are ever with Me" (Ps. 119:97-98).

Consequently, on these very hills around Nazareth, in places of solitude and privacy, He had sought the Lord earnestly, and for all of his life. His knowledge of the Word was far greater than any had ever been. For it further said, *"I have more understanding than all My teachers: for Thy Testimonies are My meditation.*

"I understand more than the ancients, because I keep Thy Precepts" (Ps. 119:99-100).

2. He was but a peasant's Son, and, consequently, a peasant Himself. Therefore, how was it possible, at least in their thinking, that He would have such understanding?

The question, *"Saying, From whence hath this Man these things?",* is asked in contempt. The word, *"man,"* was inserted by the translators; however, it was not in the original, with them actually asking, *"From whence hath this these things?"* They were overly contemptuous in their question.

The question, *"And what wisdom is this which is given unto Him, that even such mighty works are wrought by His Hands?",* proclaims them questioning both that which He taught, and the *"mighty works"* which He performed. They did not deny the *"wisdom,"* or the *"mighty works,"* nor that they were *"wrought by His Hands,"* but actually that He had no right to do such things. This has ever been the criticism of those who do not desire God's choice. They could not attack what He said or did, consequently, they will attack Him.

He wasn't worthy! He wasn't qualified! He did not pass their test, whatever that test was! It has little changed unto the present.

Those who pass God's test, will not pass man's. Those who pass man's, will not pass God's.

(3) "IS NOT THIS THE CARPENTER, THE SON OF MARY, THE BROTHER OF JAMES, AND JOSES, AND OF JUDA, AND SIMON? AND ARE NOT HIS SISTERS HERE WITH US? AND THEY WERE OFFENDED AT HIM."

The beginning of the question, *"Is not this the carpenter,"* no doubt, actually meant that He worked at the trade of a carpenter, and continued to do so until He entered public Ministry. Chrysostom said that He made ploughs and yokes for oxen. He could well have made other things such as tables, chairs, etc.

So, their complaint was that He was a carpenter, and, consequently, ill-prepared to be a great Teacher, etc. The contrast between a peasant of Galilee Who had earned His daily bread by the sweat of His brow for the first thirty years of His life, with the Person Who delivered those wonderful discourses and performed those miracles, was too much for His townspeople. They could not see past His role and position as a carpenter. In their estimation, this was lowly, and certainly offered no preparation for a position as one of the great Teachers of Israel. So, they were offended!

The continuing of the question, *"The Son of Mary, the Brother of James, and Joses, and of Juda, and Simon?",* concerns the firstborn of Mary, along with His brothers.

Some have contended that the word, *"brother,"* could refer to *"cousins,"* which they claim these were, with Mary remaining a perpetual virgin. However, that is incorrect. Had they been *"cousins,"* the term would have been *"sungenes,"* which is used of *"kin,"* *"kinsman,"* or *"kinsfolk."*

The question, *"And are not His sisters here with us?",* probably means that He had more than two sisters, for if there had been only two, the word *"both"* would probably have been used.

The phrase, *"And they were offended at Him,"* means that He did not meet their approval, and, consequently, they were scandalized that He was able to do these great things. In some weird way, they felt it brought reproach on their town of Nazareth. They were fearful they would become a laughing-stock over Israel.

The very idea that this peasant, or this *"oaf,"* as they would have put it, would aspire to be one of the great Teachers of Israel, is what was beyond their comprehension. Never mind, that His Words were given with more wisdom than any they had ever heard before, and that *"mighty works"* were performed constantly by His Hands, still, they could not, or, in Truth, would not, accept Him irrespective of the great things He did! As stated, they could not explain Him, so they rejected Him.

The saddest part of all was that His Own half-brothers and half-sisters, sons and daughters of Mary and Joseph, disbelieved His Messianic claims. They had lived in the same home with Jesus for many years, and had been the recipients of the financial support He brought in to the family by His carpentry work. As well, His singularly beautiful life had made no effective impression upon their dull, cold hearts (Wuest).

(4) "BUT JESUS SAID UNTO THEM, A PROPHET IS NOT WITHOUT HONOUR, BUT IN HIS OWN COUNTRY, AND AMONG HIS OWN KIN, AND IN HIS OWN HOUSE."

The phrase, *"But Jesus said unto them,"* represents His answer to their unbelief.

The phrase, *"A Prophet is not without honour,"* is actually a catch-all phrase referring to any and all who hold this office. A *"Prophet"* is a *"forth-teller,"* which means, *"one who speaks out God's Message."* It also includes the predicting of future events, but such is only incidental to the chief work of proclaiming the Message.

Even though the phrase was a catch-all, still, in the phrase, Jesus makes a definite claim to being a Prophet. He had already claimed to be the Jewish Messiah (Lk. 4:21; Jn. 4:26), the Son of Man, with power of God (Mat. 9:6; Mk. 1:10; Lk. 5:24), the Son of God (Jn 5:22).

The word, *"honour,"* means to show respect, deference, and reverence (Wuest).

The phrase, *"But in His Own country, and among His Own kin, and in His Own house,"* not only speaks of all *"Prophets,"* but, as well and more specifically, of Christ Himself.

There was no way that these people would even remotely consider that He was born of a Virgin and had God Alone for His Father.

As stated, the phrase also proclaims the disbelief of His *"kin"* and *"house."*

And yet, I cannot believe that Mary shared the unbelief of her other sons and daughters.

NOTES

From what little description is given, it seems that she was not a forceful woman, and, consequently, said very little during these times, although hurting very deeply in her heart. She knew what the Angel Gabriel had said unto her, and, as well, she remembered the spirit of Prophecy that came on her at this occasion (Lk. 1:26-38, 46-56).

So, I think we must confine the unbelief to the half-brothers and half-sisters! (By this time, Joseph seems to have passed on.)

The rejection suffered here by Christ, had to be the *"unkindest"* cut of all. These people knew Him, and especially His Own loved ones. They knew of His impeccable life and perfect character. They knew He was the personification of kindness. Consequently, there was no reason for their actions. It could only be summed up as the result of a cold, calculating, hardened heart, which was so removed from God, that even though they constantly spoke of Him, they did not, in reality, know Him at all! Consequently, if they did not know Him, they did not know His!

(5) "AND HE COULD THERE DO NO MIGHTY WORK, SAVE THAT HE LAID HIS HANDS UPON A FEW SICK FOLK, AND HEALED THEM."

The phrase, *"And He could there do no mighty work,"* actually means, *"Not even one."*

The phrase does not mean that He attempted to bring deliverance to the worst cases and failed, but, instead, that no one would bring their sick and afflicted to Him. These people of Nazareth were so consistently unbelieving that they would rather see their loved ones remain sick than to be healed by Christ.

Such is the world today!

The phrase, *"Save that He laid His Hands upon a few sick folk, and healed them,"* actually meant that a few sickly ones came to Him, and did receive their healing. From the terminology, it seems that they would have been belittled greatly for their coming to Christ.

Unbelief shuts Heaven out of men and men out of Heaven; but where need was, His pity, never chilled or tired, continued to work. The few sick folk profited by a love that overleaps every obstacle because it never seeks *"self"* (Williams).

(6) AND HE MARVELLED BECAUSE OF THEIR UNBELIEF. AND HE WENT ROUND ABOUT THE VILLAGES, TEACHING."

The phrase, *"And He marvelled because of their unbelief,"* expresses the view of His humanity. As Deity, He, of course, would not have marvelled at anything.

The idea is, that He did not expect the negative reception that He received in Nazareth. Inasmuch as there was no cause or reason for their attitude and action, it surprised Him at their wholesale rejection. A sincere, honest, pure heart, as the Heart of Christ, which has nothing but good for anyone, does not expect the hatred and opposition as here evidenced. There was no reason for them to do this, inasmuch as He had lived among them for about thirty years, and during all of that time had conducted Himself in a manner that was perfect. In Truth, their hatred of Him did not spring from anything He had done, but for Who He was! Their unrighteousness rebelled at His Righteousness.

The Holy Spirit only brings it out twice in the entirety of the four Gospels that He marvelled, once at the Faith of a Gentile (Mat. 8:10), and at the unbelief of His Own!

The phrase, *"And He went round about the villages, teaching,"* means that He visited all the villages around Nazareth, teaching, more than likely, in their Synagogues. What a privilege it was to have Him in their midst, and, yet, the far greater majority did not know Him, and, actually, never would know Him!

(7) "AND HE CALLED UNTO HIM THE TWELVE, AND BEGAN TO SEND THEM FORTH BY TWO AND TWO; AND GAVE THEM POWER OVER UNCLEAN SPIRITS;"

The phrase, *"And He called unto Him the Twelve,"* spoke of their first mission where they were sent out without Him, in order to carry forth the Work of the Lord.

The phrase, *"And began to send them forth by two and two,"* records the manner in which they were sent.

Dake gives six reasons why two are better than one:

1. To help each other in tests, loneliness, and discouragements (Eccl. 4:9-12; Rom. 15:14).

2. To lift up when one falls and to be a balance in success (Eccl. 4:9-10; 12:9-10; Gal. 6:1).

3. To strengthen in weakness when burdened (Rom. 15:1-5; Gal. 6:2).

4. For unity in prayer (Mat. 18:19).

5. For protection in attack (Deut. 32:30; Eccl. 4:12).

NOTES

6. For confirmation of preaching (Deut. 17:6; 19:15; Mat. 18:16).

The phrase, *"And gave them power over unclean spirits,"* presents a great Truth.

Bickersteth said that Mark here fixes the attention upon the great central object of Christ's mission — to contend against evil in every form, and especially to grapple with Satan in his stronghold in the hearts of men.

If one is to notice, it is not mentioned here about praying for the sick, even though they did this, and the 13th verse says that many were healed. Neither were other problems mentioned, only the *"unclean spirits."*

As we have stated, *"unclean spirits"* as a designation, covers all spirits of darkness. As well, the Holy Spirit mentioned this alone, because, either directly or indirectly, evil spirits are the cause of all problems that beset humanity, be it physical, domestical, material, or spiritual.

This does not mean that demons are the direct cause of any and all problems, but it does mean that if not directly, then indirectly!

For instance, demon spirits are the instigators of all false doctrine (I Tim. 4:1). As well, they are the originators of all sicknesses and diseases, at least in their original form. That does not mean that the cause of every headache, etc., is a demon spirit, for it isn't. But it does mean that evil spirits are the cause of original sickness in man as a result of the Fall (Mk. 6:13).

Also, evil spirits are the cause of anarchy and war (Rev. 16:13-16).

Verse 7 proclaims to the Church the area of its warfare. Tragically, the greater majority of the Church has absolutely no idea of what it is or what it means to oppose demon spirits in the Name of Jesus. About half of the so-called Church, doesn't even believe in the Holy Spirit, at least as He is proclaimed in the Word of God, consequently, they do not believe in the Work of the Holy Spirit, which is healing the sick and casting out devils, or in any capacity. Therefore, it is by and large a man-led Church, which in no way engages Satan in spiritual warfare. It is pretty much a social club and little else!

Regrettably, great segments of the Pentecostal and Charismatic community, who claim to believe in the Power of God, still, for the most part, are promoting the *"political message"* and the *"prosperity message,"* both false doctrines. While the Lord does bless people financially, and while Believers should take a hand in the political process, still, the culture is not going to be Christianized, nor is society going to be changed. There is nowhere in the Bible that men are called to change society, but, rather, to save men out of society.

Consequently, only a handful of Believers throughout the world are truly filled with the Holy Spirit, and are truly carrying out the Work of God in combating the forces of darkness by using the Biblical principles laid down by Christ.

Jesus *"gave them power"* at that time, but now power automatically comes with the infilling of the Holy Spirit (Acts 1:8). Regrettably, it is little used by most Believers!

The *"power"* here given by Christ, is little sought by most Preachers, or anyone for that matter. Most are seeking Doctorates or recognition by the world, etc. The desperate need, however, is *"Power from on High."*

(8) AND COMMANDED THEM THAT THEY SHOULD TAKE NOTHING FOR THEIR JOURNEY, SAVE A STAFF ONLY; NO SCRIP, NO BREAD, NO MONEY IN THEIR PURSE:"

The phrase, *"And commanded them that they should take nothing for their journey,"* does not present a suggestion, but, as stated, a *"command."*

The phrase, *"Save a staff only,"* referred to a wooden staff for walking.

The phrase, *"No scrip, no bread, no money in their purse,"* referred to the obvious! There are actually two meanings in this phrase:

1. The idea is that they were not to make any special provisions for their journey, but to go forth just as they were, depending upon God.

Some have been called by God, and then thought they would earn a goodly sum of money before answering the call, in order that their needs may be met, etc. Such shows a lack of trust in God, and is forbidden by the Lord.

2. The idea of *"no money in their purse,"* is that the emphasis be placed on the rightful priority, which was doing the Work of God, and not specializing in money. It did not mean they were to never take money, or bread, etc., but that they were to trust God to meet their needs on these Evangelistic tours. As well, and as stated, money was never to be an overriding object.

Tragically and sadly, many Preachers have sold out for money, and, consequently, have lost their way, and cease to be effective for the Lord.

NOTES

(9) "BUT BE SHOD WITH SANDALS; AND NOT PUT ON TWO COATS."

Matthew said that shoes were forbidden, while Mark says, *"Be shod with sandals."* There is no contradiction.

In that climate and culture, the *"sandals"* spoke of association with the common people, etc., where *"shoes,"* which covered the entirety of the foot, spoke of the aristocracy, etc.

Bickersteth says that it is worthy of notice that after the Lord's ascension, we find Peter using sandals when the Angel, who delivered him out of prison, said to him, *"Gird thyself, and bind on thy sandals"* (Acts 12:8).

These commands applied only to those missions on which the Disciples were then sent. Later this was changed (Lk. 22:35-36). However, the fundamental principle of what was here taught, and which was actually intended, was not changed.

(10) "AND HE SAID UNTO THEM, IN WHAT PLACE SOEVER YE ENTER INTO AN HOUSE, THERE ABIDE TILL YE DEPART FROM THAT PLACE."

Several things are said here:

1. They were not to stay too long anywhere, lest they should be burdensome to any.

2. They were not to go from house to house, seeking better quarters. Wherever they were first invited, there they were to remain, and irrespective of the circumstances, at least if hospitality was afforded them.

3. They were always to conduct themselves in a manner that was befitting of their mission, as Ambassadors for Christ. Consequently, they were not to be a burden, but kind and hospitable at all times.

4. If truly sent by the Lord, they would be a blessing to the house, which is here intended!

(11) "AND WHOSOEVER SHALL NOT RECEIVE YOU, NOR HEAR YOU, WHEN YE DEPART THENCE, SHAKE OFF THE DUST UNDER YOUR FEET FOR A TESTIMONY AGAINST THEM. VERILY I SAY UNTO YOU, IT SHALL BE MORE TOLERABLE FOR SODOM AND GOMORRHA IN THE DAY OF JUDGMENT, THAN FOR THAT CITY."

The phrase, *"And whosoever shall not receive you, nor hear you,"* basically refers to the area, even the city, and not the house in which they were invited.

The phrase, *"When ye depart thence,"* is meant to express the significance of the visit. The Lord had sent His emissary to this particular city, and, accordingly, this visit would be held against this place in the Judgment.

Maybe most in the city were not even aware of the visit, and even if they had been aware, would have greeted it with skepticism and rejection. Still, in the eyes of God, the city had been visited with Mercy and Grace, irrespective of its rejection or lack of interest.

Inasmuch as the Lord has called me for Televangelism, as well as Crusades, everywhere we conduct a meeting, or where we are privileged to go on Television in any given area, such is looked at by the Lord as a visitation to that area, with every person there being held responsible for either their acceptance or rejection. The same can be said for any God-called Preacher of the Gospel.

The phrase, *"Shake off the dust under your feet for a testimony against them,"* is not necessarily to be taken literally, but is actually a symbolic act. If the Message is rejected, there is no point in the effort continuing to be made. However, the following should ever be noted:

Acceptance of the Gospel is the greatest thing that could ever happen to a person or community. The entire nature is changed for the better, and visibly so!

However, if rejected, the person or area is not left as it was found, but measurably worse!

I have had a number of discussions with Moslems about this very thing. They label the sin and debauchery in America as the failure of Christianity. What they fail to understand is, that it's not the failure of Christianity, but the failure to accept what Christianity offers, namely Christ. This failure has left America the worse!

However, what little Gospel America has accepted, has made it, without a doubt, the greatest nation of freedom in the world, the nation of which most people in the world would like to be a part.

With Islam, or any other religion for that matter, a person or nation is made worse only by accepting it, and greatly bettered by rejecting it. All one has to do is look at the nations where these various religions are predominate. The proof speaks for itself!

The phrase, *"Verily I say unto you, It shall be more tolerable for Sodom and Gomorrha in the*

Day of Judgment, than for that city," has reference to the fact that Sodom and Gomorrha had no Gospel Witness, while these places did.

The same holds true presently! Every city in the world that has had the privilege of hearing the Gospel of Jesus Christ, will be judged more severely even than the twin cities mentioned here, which were burned for their sin and iniquity (Gen. 19:24-25).

As well, and despite the denial of many Preachers and the majority of the world, *"The Day of Judgment"* is coming, where all will have to answer!

Man, today, rejects out of hand the idea that he must one day render account for his life and its decisions. His loss of conviction concerning an after-life, combined with the erosion of the notion of moral responsibility on the basis of popular understanding of psychological and psycho-analytical theories, has contributed to the moral indifference and pragmatism of our times.

According to the basis of psychology, moral issues, insofar as they matter at all, relate only to the present moment, and to considerations of personal happiness. The thought that they might relate to some Divine dimension, or that all men will one day be inescapably summoned to accept responsibility for these very moral decisions in the all-seeing presence of their Creator, is foreign to such thinking.

Unfortunately, for modern man it happens to be true. Judgment is inevitable and awaits us all. In face of this modern tendency to dismiss future Judgment, there is the greater and more urgent responsibility placed upon the Church tenaciously to maintain the Biblical perspective.

PRESENT ATTITUDES

There are few points at which the teaching of the Bible is more sharply in conflict with the assumptions of our age than in its teaching concerning God's future Judgment of all men. It is correspondingly one of the most serious contemporary expressions of Christian intellectual and spiritual capitulation that this particular Truth should be so little reflected in modern preaching and writing. Regrettably, the world has been permitted at this point, only too clearly, to squeeze the Church into its own mold (Rom. 12:1-2). Thus a theological commentator can complain with full justice that today the notion of final Judgment *"figures so little in the theology and preaching of the modern Church."*

This is even more inexcusable in that this century has witnessed an unprecedented recovery of the Biblical prophetic perspective. However, a future Divine Judgment has been largely set aside in favor of the more popular doctrines of the now and present.

THE OLD TESTAMENT TEACHING OF JUDGMENT

God appears in the Old Testament very commonly in the role of *"Judge of all the earth"* (Gen. 18:25), or more generally as a *"God of justice"* (Deut. 1:17; 32:4; Ps. 9:8; 94:2; 97:2; Isa. 30:18; 41:1; 61:8; Mal. 2:17). Judgment does not simply imply an impartial and detached weighing up of good and evil, but rather the thought of vigorous action against evil. It is on this understanding that the people of God are summoned to exercise Judgment in turn (Isa. 1:17; Micah 6:8; Zech. 8:16).

The Judgment of God is not impersonal, the operation of some undeviating principle, it is a strongly personal notion. It is closely linked to the thought of God's character of Mercy, Lovingkindness, Righteousness, and Truth (Ps. 36:5; Ezek. 39:21; Hos. 2:19).

It is the working out of the Mercy and Wrath of God in history and in human life and experience. Thus the Judgment of God can bring deliverance for the Righteous (Deut. 10:18; Ps. 25:9-10), as well as doom for the wicked (Ex. 6:6; Num. 33:4; Deut. 32:41; Isa. 4:4; Jer. 1:10; 4:12; Ezek. 5:10).

As the Old Testament draws toward its close, the thought of God's Judgment becomes increasingly bound up with the eschatological expectation of this coming Day of the Lord (Joel 2:1; Amos 5:18; 8:9; Obad. 15; Zeph. 1:7, 14; Mal. 4:1).

JUDGMENT IN THE NEW TESTAMENT

The New Testament, as we should expect, continues the Old Testament stress upon Judgment as belonging to the nature of God, and as part of His essential activity (Rom. 1:18; Heb. 12:23; I Pet. 1:17; 2:23; Rev. 16:5).

As in the Old Testament, God's Judgments are not confined to the future, but are already at work in man's life in the present age (Jn. 8:50; Rom. 1:18-22, 24, 26, 28; Rev. 18:8). Judgment

is associated even now with Christ Who exercises the Father's Judgments (Mat. 3:11-12; 10:34; Jn. 3:19; 5:30; 8:12, 16; 9:39).

The Light of God's Word is already shining into the world through His self-revelation in man's moral experience, and supremely in the Incarnate Word, Jesus Christ. The Judgment of men is therefore already in operation, for they show by their evil deeds that they *"love darkness rather than light"* (Jn. 3:19).

The spotlight in the New Testament, however, falls upon the *"Judgment to come,"* a future and final Judgment which will accompany the Return of Christ (Mat. 25:31-46; Jn. 5:22, 27; Rom. 3:5; I Cor. 4:3-5; Heb. 6:1).

This great culminating Judgment will be that which is referred to as *"The Great White Throne Judgment"* (Rev. 20:11-15).

Even though there have been, and are, many Judgments, still, the culminating Judgment of all will be this particular time. It will take place at the conclusion of the thousand-year Millennial Reign. Satan will then be locked away in the Lake of Fire, along with all his minions of darkness, which will include all demon spirits and fallen angels (Rev. 20:10). At that time, all men, and from the beginning of time, who have rejected Christ, will then stand before Him. Today, He is the Saviour; then, He will be the Judge!

No Believer will be at this *"Great White Throne Judgment,"* for their sins have already been judged at Calvary. This Judgment will be strictly for unbelievers, and *"according to their works"* (Rev. 20:12).

The eternal destiny of all who will appear at that Judgment, will be *"The Lake of Fire"* (Rev. 20:15).

Once again, we emphasize that it doesn't really matter what the world thinks concerning this Coming Judgment, nor does it matter that the Church is lax in its presentation and proclamation of this coming Day, still, it will come about, and exactly as given in the Word of God. Consequently, it behooves the God-called Preacher to proclaim that which is so prominent in Scripture, and so certain of fulfillment.

(12) "AND THEY WENT OUT, AND PREACHED THAT MEN SHOULD REPENT."

If the Message of *"Repentance"* was then their Message, it should be our Message presently!

Are men any different today than they were then?

Is the spiritual need any different now than then?

The word, *"preached,"* means that they made a public proclamation with gravity, formality, and authority which demanded it be heeded.

In essence, it was *"Good News,"* even though it proclaimed Judgment to those who would not accept, still, it proclaimed eternal life to those who would heed its clarion call. Consequently, it was Good News to the sinner, in that this Message of Repentance, which demanded a turnabout, was, as well, accompanied with the announcement of Salvation from sin as provided by the Lord.

If one is to notice, the preaching of the Gospel was their great work, to which the miracles were subordinate. If the order is reversed, it ceases to be the Gospel!

As we have stated before, Salvation demands *"Repentance toward God, and Faith toward our Lord Jesus Christ"* (Acts 20:21).

Why is it in this order?

Repentance comes first because God has been offended by the sin in the lives of unbelievers. Consequently, the sinner must repent of that sin. It is not so much the words said, but, rather, the attitude of the heart.

Along with Repentance, there must be Faith evidenced in Jesus Christ relative to what He did at Calvary and the Resurrection, in paying the price for man's sins. To be sure, the sinner may understand very little of what Jesus actually did, but there must be Faith extended in some manner, even though little understood, as to what Christ did at Calvary.

It is somewhat the Doctrine of Substitution and Identification. Jesus became our Substitute in all things, and we identify with Him.

For instance, He took our place at Calvary, and we identify with that. He took the Judgment of God in our place, thereby becoming our Substitute, and we identify with Him.

Actually, this principle holds true, not only in accepting Christ as one's Saviour, but, as well, in maintaining a victorious life in Christ (Gal. 2:20).

(13) "AND THEY CAST OUT MANY DEVILS, AND ANOINTED WITH OIL MANY THAT WERE SICK, AND HEALED THEM."

The phrase, *"And they cast out many devils,"* goes back to verse 7. They first attacked the cause of the problem which was demon spirits, and then the result of the problem which was sickness.

The phrase, *"And anointed with oil many that were sick, and healed them,"* proclaims them doing what Christ, no doubt, commanded!

The *"oil"* used then, continues to be used today (James 5:14).

Contrary to some thinking, *"oil"* has nothing to do with medicine, but rather is symbolic of the Holy Spirit (Ex. 27:20; 30:25; Num. 6:15; I Sam. 16:1, 13; Ps. 45:7).

The Disciples were able to do these things only because Jesus *"gave them power"* (vs. 7).

As Jesus sent out the Disciples *"two and two,"* likewise, He is still sending out Believers whom He has called to do His Work.

(14) "AND KING HEROD HEARD OF HIM; (FOR HIS NAME WAS SPREAD ABROAD:) AND HE SAID, THAT JOHN THE BAPTIST WAS RISEN FROM THE DEAD, AND THEREFORE MIGHTY WORKS DO SHEW FORTH THEMSELVES IN HIM."

The phrase, *"And King Herod heard of Him,"* refers to Herod Antipas, son of Herod the Great, who had appointed him *"Tetrarch"* of Galilee and Peraea. (The title, *"Tetrarch,"* means *"a rule by four,"* and, consequently, meant that King Herod was one of four men at that time ruling Israel. As well, Mark was correct in calling him a King, for this title was applied freely in the Roman world to all Eastern Rulers.)

To only hear of Jesus now is, as one man said, *"A palace is late in hearing spiritual news."*

The phrase, *"For His Name was spread abroad,"* actually referred to the miracles performed by Christ, and the fame that such had gained.

The phrase, *"And he said, That John the Baptist was risen from the dead,"* proclaims a troubled and guilty conscience more than anything else, for Herod had put to death an innocent and holy man. As well, it is a high testimony to John the Baptist, that Herod should have such a testimony of him.

The phrase, *"And therefore mighty works do shew forth themselves in him,"* actually has reference to the idea that vengeance may be taken on Herod. A sinful conscience imagines all sorts of things, and, consequently, never knows peace. Chrysostom said, *"What a great thing is virtue, for Herod fears him, even though dead."*

(This is the same Herod who mocked Jesus, when Pilate sent Jesus to him in the hope of

NOTES

NOTES

relieving himself of the terrible responsibility of condemning One Whom he knew to be innocent.)

(15) "OTHERS SAID, THAT IT IS ELIAS. AND OTHERS SAID, THAT IT IS A PROPHET, OR AS ONE OF THE PROPHETS."

The phrase, *"Others said,"* referred to the Court, as well as many in Israel.

The idea was that Israel would admit to anything, except the Truth, which was that He was the Messiah, the Son of God.

And then, again, these were other comments, with most of the Religious Leaders of Israel calling Him a *"deceiver"* (Mat. 27:63; Jn. 7:12).

(16) "BUT WHEN HEROD HEARD THEREOF, HE SAID, IT IS JOHN, WHOM I BEHEADED: HE IS RISEN FROM THE DEAD."

The phrase, *"But when Herod heard thereof,"* proclaims his prediction, and because of his troubled conscience.

The phrase, *"He said, It is John, whom I beheaded,"* means he kept saying it over and over, in response to the predictions of others as to Who Christ was!

It was not just the Prophet John he remembered, but that he beheaded him. The sight of that head dripping blood would not leave his conscience, tormenting him day and night! So, the expostulation of others concerning the identity of Christ, was always met by Herod with his pronouncement that it was John.

The phrase, *"He is risen from the dead,"* is said with the thought in mind that this is done for one purpose, and he, Herod, is the target.

(17) "FOR HEROD HIMSELF HAD SENT FORTH AND LAID HOLD UPON JOHN, AND BOUND HIM IN PRISON FOR HERODIAS' SAKE, HIS BROTHER PHILIP'S WIFE: FOR HE HAD MARRIED HER."

The phrase, *"For Herod himself had sent forth and laid hold upon John, and bound him in prison,"* is looking back in the past tense to what Herod had done. As well, it is as if the Holy Spirit is wanting to make certain that no one misunderstands that it was *"Herod"* who had done this dastardly thing. John had been imprisoned in the fortress of Machaerus, situated on the barren heights of Moab above the Dead Sea.

The phrase, *"For Herodias' sake, his brother Philip's wife,"* means that John had been imprisoned because Herod's wife, Herodias, had demanded it.

The phrase, *"For he had married her,"* constituted the reason for John's pointed Message to the *"Tetrarch."*

Herod had originally married the daughter of the Nabataean King Aretas IV, but divorced her in order to marry Herodias, the wife of his half-brother Herod Philip. John denounced this second marriage as unlawful, consequently incurring the wrath of Herod. Josephus says that along with the carping of Herodias, Herod was afraid that John's great public following might develop into a revolt. Consequently, he imprisoned him in order to silence him.

Aretas, at this time, resented the insult offered to his daughter, and seized the opportunity a few years later to wage war against Herod. At this time, A.D. 36, the forces of Herod were heavily defeated, and Josephus says that many people regarded the defeat as Divine retribution for Herod killing John the Baptist.

In A.D. 39, Herod was denounced to the Emperor Gaius by his nephew Agrippa as a plotter; he was deposed from his tetrarchy and ended his days in exile.

(18) "FOR JOHN HAD SAID UNTO HEROD, IT IS NOT LAWFUL FOR THEE TO HAVE THY BROTHER'S WIFE."

The phrase, *"For John had said unto Herod,"* means that he said it not only once, but many times, and pointedly so!

The phrase, *"It is not lawful for thee to have thy brother's wife,"* pulls no punches and minces no words. Herod knew exactly what John was saying, and so did the people. No one could accuse this Preacher of compromise! And yet Jesus had very little to say about Herod, with the exception of once describing him as *"that fox"* (Lk. 13:32).

(19) "THEREFORE HERODIAS HAD A QUARREL AGAINST HIM, AND WOULD HAVE KILLED HIM; BUT SHE COULD NOT:"

The phrase, *"Therefore Herodias had a quarrel against him,"* means that she *"had it in for him."* Wuest said that she never let up on this fury of her's toward the Baptist for daring to denounce her private relations with Herod, and waited her time for revenge.

The phrase, *"And would have killed him; but she could not,"* means that she did not lack the will, only the way!

Matthew had stated that Herod, as well, desired to kill John, but feared the people (Mat. 14:5).

However, there is no contradiction in the account given by Matthew and Mark, because it seems that Herod at the first desired to put John to death, but, little by little, as Herod observed the Prophet, the force of his character and holy life made an impression upon him, as the next verse portrays.

(20) "FOR HEROD FEARED JOHN, KNOWING THAT HE WAS A JUST MAN AND AN HOLY, AND OBSERVED HIM; AND WHEN HE HEARD HIM, HE DID MANY THINGS, AND HEARD HIM GLADLY."

The phrase, *"For Herod feared John,"* means in the Greek, that he was in a continual state of fear respecting the Prophet. There was a reason for the fear.

He knew that John was right respecting his sin, and he knew that John was a Prophet sent from God. Considering that he had arrested him, he fears the Wrath of God.

The phrase, *"Knowing that he was a just man and an holy,"* proclaims John's character, and that compliment from the man who had been his bitter enemy.

The phrase, *"And observed him,"* means that he watched over John to keep him safe from the evil plots of Herodias, who was seeking to kill him. He kept a constant watch over the Prophet. The phrase, *"And when he heard him, he did many things, and heard him gladly,"* means that John's Messages to him caused him consternation of soul, but yet he kept going back to this dank prison cell over and over again to speak with the Prophet. In other words, he was under great conviction, as the Holy Spirit made a plea for his soul.

There is a possibility that the King sent for John and brought him to his chambers. However, it is more probable that he visited John in prison.

What a sight this must have been, the King coming down into this dungeon, dressed in his royal robes, and then going in to talk with the Prophet sometimes hours on end. He came so close, but yet not quite close enough.

Herod fought the battle that most all have to fight. If he accepted the teaching of John the Baptist, and, therefore, the Lord as his Saviour, the entirety of his lifestyle would change. He would probably have to give up everything, and he was not sure that he was willing to do that.

The tragedy is, as always, he lost his soul and his kingdom.

That for which we sell the soul, is lost as well!

(21) "AND WHEN A CONVENIENT DAY WAS COME, THAT HEROD ON HIS BIRTHDAY MADE A SUPPER TO HIS LORDS, HIGH CAPTAINS, AND CHIEF ESTATES OF GALILEE;"

The phrase, *"And when a convenient day was come,"* refers to a convenient time for Herodias to kill John the Baptist. She would now spring her trap!

Bede said, *"She feared lest Herod should at length repent, and yield to the exhortations of John, and dissolve this unreal marriage, and restore Herodias to her lawful husband."*

The phrase, *"That Herod on his birthday made a supper to his lords, high captains, and chief estates of Galilee,"* referred to a notable gathering, composed of men from governmental, military, and civil life. So, not only were there Romans present, but, as well, the chief Jews of Galilee. Regrettably, these Jews would raise no protest against the death of the Baptist.

(22) "AND WHEN THE DAUGHTER OF THE SAID HERODIAS CAME IN, AND DANCED, AND PLEASED HEROD AND THEM THAT SAT WITH HIM, THE KING SAID UNTO THE DAMSEL, ASK OF ME WHATSOEVER THOU WILT, AND I WILL GIVE IT THEE."

The phrase, *"And when the daughter of the said Herodias came in, and danced,"* refers to Herodias' own daughter who degraded herself in a licentious dance in which only professional actors of loose morals normally would engage.

The phrase, *"And pleased Herod and them that sat with him,"* presents a scene of debauchery. No doubt all were drunk, or nearly so!

The phrase, *"The king said unto the damsel, Ask of me whatsoever thou wilt, and I will give it thee,"* presents the trap set by Herodias, and ready to be sprung.

No doubt Herod was accustomed in his drunkenness and debauchery to offering such sweeping gifts. It made him look big in the eyes of all who were present!

Herodias, no doubt having observed this many times, sets the trap by having her daughter dance before the king and his gathering, even in a licentious manner, which elicited exactly what she thought it would.

(23) "AND HE SWARE UNTO HER, WHATSOEVER THOU SHALT ASK OF ME, I WILL

GIVE IT THEE, UNTO THE HALF OF MY KINGDOM."

The phrase, *"And he sware unto her,"* refers to the daughter of Herodias.

Did he really mean what he said, concerning giving her whatever she wanted?

Consequently, he assures her he does, by putting himself under an oath.

The phrase, *"Whatsoever thou shalt ask of me, I will give it thee, unto the half of my kingdom,"* was not really to be taken literally, but was meant to add tremendous force to the answering of any reasonable request.

Now he is on the hook!

(24) "AND SHE WENT FORTH, AND SAID UNTO HER MOTHER, WHAT SHALL I ASK? AND SHE SAID, THE HEAD OF JOHN THE BAPTIST."

The phrase, *"And she went forth, and said unto her mother,"* implies her knowledge of at least a part of the plan. Whether her mother had related her full intentions to the girl is not known!

At any rate, she knew to go to her mother when the trap was sprung.

The question, *"What shall I ask?",* seems that she knew of a plan, but not exactly as to its direction.

She had done her part. She had enflamed the passions of the king and all with him, causing him to make this wild gesture! Everything had played into this wicked woman's hands.

The phrase, *"And she said, The head of John the Baptist,"* meant that she wanted him to die, and by being beheaded!

(25) "AND SHE CAME IN STRAIGHTWAY WITH HASTE UNTO THE KING, AND ASKED, SAYING, I WILL THAT THOU GIVE ME BY AND BY IN A CHARGER THE HEAD OF JOHN THE BAPTIST."

The phrase, *"And she came in straightway with haste unto the king,"* presents her immediately making her demand, so the king will have no opportunity to renege on his promise. Little did Herod realize as to what she was about to ask.

The phrase, *"And asked, saying,"* presents the evil of this moment about to unfold in all its horror.

No doubt, the crowd is mostly drunk, including Herod! As well, prominent Jews were at this so-called celebration, but none would lift a hand or voice in defense of the Prophet. So much for the world and so much for the Church!

The phrase, *"I will that thou give me by and by in a charger the head of John the Baptist,"* actually meant immediately, with the words, *"by and by,"* having a different meaning then, than now. The evil of this woman in asking this, knew no bounds! She would not rest until she had silenced the voice of the greatest Prophet who ever lived. However, and even though she would carry out this bloody scheme, still, John had finished the work that God had called him and sent him to do.

(26) "AND THE KING WAS EXCEEDING SORRY; YET FOR HIS OATH'S SAKE, AND FOR THEIR SAKES WHICH SAT WITH HIM, HE WOULD NOT REJECT HER."

The phrase, *"And the king was exceeding sorry,"* means that Herod now realizes what he has done. He is now to become the murderer of the Prophet whom he feared and respected.

The phrase, *"Yet for his oath's sake,"* means that when he extended this offer, it really was not taken seriously to begin with, but then he restated it with force, which made it harder to back down.

The phrase, *"And for their sakes which sat with him,"* referred to him saving face. All had heard him make the oath, verify it, and now eagerly awaited as to what she would request.

The phrase, *"He would not reject her,"* means that the life of John the Baptist, at least to these men, had boiled down to the worth of a lewd dance.

(27) "AND IMMEDIATELY THE KING SENT AN EXECUTIONER, AND COMMANDED HIS HEAD TO BE BROUGHT: AND HE WENT AND BEHEADED HIM IN THE PRISON,"

The phrase, *"And immediately the king sent an executioner,"* is the beginning of the horrible deed which will haunt him for the rest of his life.

The phrase, *"And commanded his head to be brought,"* proclaims the manner in which he was executed.

As stated, John was incarcerated in the fort of Machaerus. As well, Herod's father had built a magnificent palace within that fort. Consequently, this, no doubt, is where this birthday celebration was conducted. It was only a short distance to the dungeon where John was being held.

The phrase, *"And he went and beheaded him in the prison,"* concerns the dastardly deed being carried out!

(28) "AND BROUGHT HIS HEAD IN A CHARGER, AND GAVE IT TO THE DAMSEL: AND THE DAMSEL GAVE IT TO HER MOTHER."

The phrase, *"And brought his head in a charger,"* must have been a gruesome sight, with it dripping blood as it was brought into the banquet hall.

The phrase, *"And gave it to the damsel,"* referred to the girl who had danced, the daughter of Herodias.

The phrase, *"And the damsel gave it to her mother,"* proclaims Herodias, according to Jerome, thrusting the tongue through with a long pin.

Someone said, *"Because they could not bear to hear the truth, therefore they bored through with a needle the tongue that had spoken the truth."*

However, *"Vengeance is Mine; I will repay, saith the Lord"* (Rom. 12:19).

Herodias and Herod, a short time later, were banished by a decree of the Roman Senate to Lyons, where they both perished miserably.

Nicephorus relates that Salome, the daughter who danced, died by a remarkable incident. She fell through some treacherous ice over which she was passing and fell through it in such a manner that her head was caught while the rest of her body sank into the water, and thus it came to pass that in her efforts to save herself her head was nearly severed by the sharp edges of the broken ice.

(29) "AND WHEN HIS DISCIPLES HEARD OF IT, THEY CAME AND TOOK UP HIS CORPSE, AND LAID IT IN A TOMB."

The phrase, *"And when His Disciples heard of it,"* proclaims that the corpse lay uncared for and unburied until the Disciples showed their respect for it. Josephus says that after the beheading, the mutilated remains were cast out of the prison and left neglected.

The phrase, *"They came and took up his corpse, and laid it in a tomb,"* concludes the life and Ministry of the greatest Prophet who ever lived.

(30) "AND THE APOSTLES GATHERED THEMSELVES TOGETHER UNTO JESUS, AND TOLD HIM ALL THINGS, BOTH WHAT

NOTES

THEY HAD DONE, AND WHAT THEY HAD TAUGHT."

The phrase, *"And the Apostles gathered themselves together unto Jesus,"* relates back to verse seven where the Twelve had been sent forth *"two and two."* They now come back to report to Christ.

The phrase, *"And told Him all things, both what they had done, and what they had taught,"* represents a victorious mission. They had seen many healings and miracles, and had taught the Word with Power.

The word, *"Apostle,"* simply means *"One sent forth on a particular mission, and representing a particular person, in this case Christ!"*

Consequently, not all who are called of the Lord have the designation of *"Apostle!"* Actually, the Scripture says, *"And He gave some, Apostles; and some, Prophets; and some, Evangelists; and some, Pastors and Teachers"* (Eph. 4:11).

Concerning the calling of the *"Apostle,"* I think the following information will be helpful:

1. The original Twelve are not the only Apostles named in the New Testament, with twenty-four being recorded, if one is to include Christ (Heb. 3:1). However, no one can be an Apostle as the original Twelve (with Matthias taking the place of Judas — Acts 1:26), and because they had personally been with Jesus for some three and a half years.

2. Apostles, exactly as Pastors, etc., are still being called by the Lord presently.

3. An Apostle is anyone who is truly called by the Lord, and for a particular purpose and mission.

For instance, a Pastor being called by the Lord to take a particular Church in a particular city, would not constitute a direct Mission, as important as this particular work may be. However, if one was sent by the Lord to open up Churches, as Paul, in a number of cities, etc., that would definitely be a Mission, and would constitute one directly sent, and, therefore, an Apostle. As well, if a Preacher was called by the Lord to a foreign field where there was little Gospel or none at all, this would be the office of an Apostle. However, if one went later as a Missionary to the same area, and to serve in an administrative capacity, even though called by the Lord, still would not be constituted an Apostle.

There must be a direct Mission involved, as the result of a direct calling by the Lord, and must be more than the work of a Pastor or an Evangelist, as important as those offices may be.

4. The Scriptural evidence is, that an Apostle, as well as having a special, direct calling regarding a particular Mission, can, as well, carry out the work of the *"Prophet, Evangelist, Pastor, and Teacher."* In other words, he can, and often is, called upon by the Holy Spirit to function in any of these capacities. The Ministry of the Apostle Paul and others graphically portrays this Truth.

(31) "AND HE SAID UNTO THEM, COME YE YOURSELVES APART INTO A DESERT PLACE, AND REST A WHILE: FOR THERE WERE MANY COMING AND GOING, AND THEY HAD NO LEISURE SO MUCH AS TO EAT."

The phrase, *"And He said unto them, Come ye yourselves apart into a desert place, and rest a while,"* concerns the tremendous activity which engaged Jesus and His Disciples regarding the preaching of the Word, healing the sick, and casting out devils.

The needs among the people, as would be obvious, were abundant. As well, Jesus was the only One Who could meet these needs, as He is the only One today. Unceasing activity in dealing with the crowds, would have taken its toll both physically and spiritually. Consequently, and despite the needs, they must *"rest a while."*

The phrase, *"For there were many coming and going, and they had no leisure so much as to eat,"* gives one an idea as to the press of the crowds, the needs of the people, and the attention given to these needs.

It should be quickly added, that some few Ministers of the Gospel work themselves into exhaustion respecting the same type of activity as Jesus and His Disciples; however, the far greater majority of physical and emotional breakdowns are caused among Ministers, not necessarily from overwork, but, rather, from an improper relationship with Christ. It could fall into one of two categories:

1. An improper relationship could speak of a weak prayer life and attention to the Word. If such is weak or missing, the inner peace that such gives will be missing as well, giving fertile field for Satan, and, consequently, emotional breakdowns, etc.

2. Any effort made in the flesh, which regrettably constitutes much if not most of that done in the Name of the Lord, will exact a heavy toll and, in fact, accomplish nothing for the Lord.

A perfect example is the *"bush which burned with fire,"* in front of Moses, and yet, *"the bush was not consumed"* (Ex. 3:2).

If the bush burns in the Spirit, it will not be consumed. But if it is a man-directed effort, and, consequently, the flesh, the bush will be consumed, i.e., emotional breakdowns, etc.

Of course, and as is obvious, neither Jesus nor His Disciples would have fallen into either of these categories, but simply became exhausted because of overwork.

As someone has humorously said, *"If after much effort we do not come apart and 'rest a while,' we will simply, 'come apart!'"*

(32) "AND THEY DEPARTED INTO A DESERT PLACE BY SHIP PRIVATELY."

The *"ship"* they used was probably one of the vessels belonging to Zebedee. From the frequent mention of the usage of such vessels, it seems that Zebedee may have kept one of these ships ready at all times for the Master's use. Quite possibly he donated the use of it.

The *"desert place"* referred to, we learn from Luke, was near to *"a city called Bethsaida,"* the one to the northeast of the Sea of Galilee.

The word, *"privately,"* means that other ships, at least at this time, did not go with them. And yet, as the following verses proclaim, it seems as if their efforts to get a little rest, would be in vain.

(33) "AND THE PEOPLE SAW THEM DEPARTING, AND MANY KNEW HIM, AND RAN AFOOT THITHER OUT OF ALL CITIES, AND OUTWENT THEM, AND CAME TOGETHER UNTO HIM."

The phrase, *"And the people saw them departing, and many knew Him,"* refers to the action which will follow.

The phrase, *"And ran afoot thither out of all cities,"* means that some ran from village to village, telling them that Jesus was coming their way. Quite possibly they did not know exactly where He was going, but yet, being able to visibly follow the ship, it quickly became obvious as to His destination. When the boat would land, Jesus would be met by about 5,000 men, beside the women and children.

The needs were obvious, with many no doubt very ill, and others desperately needing miracles, with scores needing deliverance from demon spirits, etc.

When the day would end, it would result in many miracles being performed, not the least of which was the feeding of this tremendous crowd with five loaves of bread and two fish. However, according to St. John 6, this would prove to be the height of His popularity. After this, the crowds, at least for the most part, would begin to thin out, and for varied reasons. What He taught seemed to be more than many could bear, and then, the Pharisees were beginning to threaten excommunication to anyone who followed the Lord (Jn. 6:66).

The phrase, *"And outwent them, and came together unto Him,"* presents them waiting for Him whenever the boat docks in this desert place.

(34) "AND JESUS, WHEN HE CAME OUT, SAW MUCH PEOPLE, AND WAS MOVED WITH COMPASSION TOWARD THEM, BECAUSE THEY WERE AS SHEEP NOT HAVING A SHEPHERD: AND HE BEGAN TO TEACH THEM MANY THINGS."

The phrase, *"And Jesus,"* presents the Master as being the principle One, Who was concerned about the people. His great heart went out to them, as would be obvious!

The phrase, *"When He came out, saw much people, and was moved with compassion toward them,"* presents the heart of God for the human family.

WHAT IS COMPASSION?

The word means *"to love deeply,"* and thus *"to be compassionate,"* or *"to have mercy."* The word or one of its derivatives is found 133 times in the Old Testament, and nearly that many times in the New, as it is coupled with the word, *"Mercy."*

In the Old Testament, God is looked at somewhat more in the sense of judgment than in the New. However, even then His compassion is presented as a strong earmark of His nature and character. Even when His people are being disciplined, Malachi records promise and restoration, which of necessity must be linked with compassion. *"They will be Mine, says the Lord Almighty, in the day when I make up My treasured possession. I will spare them, just as in*

NOTES

compassion a man spares his son who serves him" (Mal. 3:17).

GOD TRULY CARES

The entire theme of the Bible is that God compassionately and truly cares about what happens to us (Rom. 12:1; II Cor. 1:3). Consequently, we are to imitate our Heavenly Father (Lk. 6:36) and let His kind of caring bind Believers to each other in unity (Phil. 2:1; Col. 3:12).

When the Scripture mentions Jesus being moved by compassion, it is usually the occasion of a turning point in someone's life. A leper came to Jesus and begged for healing. Jesus, *"filled with compassion,"* reached out to touch and heal (Mk. 1:40-42). Travelling in the towns and villages of Judea, and Galilee, Jesus saw the confused crowds and *"had compassion on them"* as we are studying here.

From these incidents, we learn that it is compassion which moves Jesus to take action that affects the lives of those whose needs moved Him.

THE ROOT OF COMPASSION

We see the same active aspect of compassion in two Parables Jesus told. In Matthew 18, there is the story of a servant who owed an unpayable debt. He begged the King to whom he owed the money to give him time to pay it. But the King was so *"moved by compassion"* that he canceled the debt.

As well, Luke 15 tells the story of the prodigal son. The wayward youth returned home to confess his sins and beg for a job as a hired man. But the father was *"filled with compassion for him,"* and welcomed him back as a son.

The loving compassion of one person literally changed the life of another, for the person who cared was moved to act and so set the needy person on a new course in life.

God called you and me to have compassion on others. That call is more than an appeal for us to feel with and for the needy. It is a call to care enough to become involved and to help by taking some action that will set others' lives on a fresh, new course.

COMPASSION AS A WORD

As a word, compassion indicates the inner parts of the body and came to suggest the seat of the emotions — particularly emotions of pity, compassion, and love. This is the word used in the Gospels to speak of Jesus having compassion on someone in need.

The word originated, it is believed, from the Greek language, and more specifically from the offering up of heathen sacrifices.

When the animal slated for the sacrifice was killed, it was dissected with its intestines removed. This entire mass was held up toward the heavens in the hands of the Priests, and called *"the compassion."* As is obvious, it pertained to the very inward parts of the animal, hence, an apt description of one's emotions, etc.

So, when it said that Jesus was *"moved with compassion,"* it meant that every fiber of His Being was involved.

WHO CAN HAVE COMPASSION?

While the word may be used regarding any and all, still, true *"compassion"* can only be had by those who truly follow Christ. It has to do with Agape Love, which is the God kind of Love, and is the kind that caused God to send Jesus to this world to die for lost humanity.

The word really comes into play, and has its deepest root, and, in fact, its only root, in doing for those who cannot return such kindness. It is perhaps explained in its totality by Jesus dying for those who did not love Him. *"But God commendeth His love toward us, in that, while we were yet sinners, Christ died for us"* (Rom. 5:8).

Consequently, the only true *"compassion"* shown in the world, is that evidenced by Christ through His people. Islam, Buddhism, Hinduism, etc., have no compassion, and because they do not have the God kind of Love. Regrettably, many alleged Christians have little compassion as well! However, the closer to Christ, the more compassion.

Actually, *"compassion"* is the greatest cause of the spread of the Gospel. The closer to the Lord men are, the more they desire to get the Gospel to others, and because they feel exactly as Christ, *"moved with compassion toward them."*

If there is little nearness to Christ, there is, as well, little compassion.

The phrase, *"Because they were as sheep not having a shepherd,"* presents Israel at that particular time.

The nation was perhaps more religious then than ever before, but with few true shepherds. Chrysostom observes that the Scribes, who were supposed to serve as the Pastors of the people,

were not so much Pastors as wolves, because, by teaching errors both by word and by example, they perverted the minds of the simple.

As well, the description of *"sheep"* is appropriate, in that no animal is more helpless, more in need of a shepherd, than sheep. This is the reason that the Lord has given, *"Some, Apostles; and some, Prophets; and some, Evangelists; and some, Pastors and Teachers."*

He then said, *"For the perfecting of the Saints, for the work of the Ministry, for the edifying of the Body of Christ"* (Eph. 4:11-12).

But sadly, there are many *"false apostles"* now, as then, and if the sheep follow these *"false prophets, which come to you in sheep's clothing, but inwardly they are ravening wolves,"* the results are obvious (Mat. 7:15).

This is perhaps Satan's greatest and most effective weapon, *"wolves in sheep's clothing."* If we are to take an example from the time of Christ, such example is shocking.

There were almost no true Shepherds in Christ's day. Hopefully there are a few more at present, but the true number would probably be shockingly small. In fact, the most dangerous place in town for the Christian, or anyone for that matter, is, most of the time, *"the Church."* There, too often, people are led astray by *"wolves in sheep's clothing."* They are taught false doctrine, used and abused, with no true Salvation of Christ offered.

Tragically, many who claim to be Believers, but really aren't, desire this religious facade.

Religion is the biggest business in the world, far eclipsing any and all giant corporations. However, all religion is of man, and, ultimately, of Satan. It is a way devised, instigated, instituted, and developed by man, and, therefore, not of God. True Salvation is all of God and none of man. That is the reason Bible Christianity is not a religion, but, rather, a relationship — a relationship with Christ (Mat. 11:28-30).

The phrase, *"And He began to teach them many things,"* presents the only True Gospel that many of them had ever heard.

Wuest said, *"The crowd tired of the powerless teaching of the Rabbis, sensed a new type of teaching and was eager to hear the new Teacher. What they were hearing was 'Truth!'"*

If those who follow in the train of Christ, do not teach exactly as He taught, which is the Word of God, and the Word of God exclusively, the people will not be helped. Only the Word of God is the Truth. It must not be added to or taken from.

(35) "AND WHEN THE DAY WAS NOW FAR SPENT, HIS DISCIPLES CAME UNTO HIM, AND SAID, THIS IS A DESERT PLACE, AND NOW THE TIME IS FAR PASSED:"

The phrase, *"And when the day was now far spent,"* referred to the sun near setting.

The phrase, *"His Disciples came unto Him, and said,"* represents human thinking, which did not bring Jesus into the equation.

The phrase, *"This is a desert place, and now the time is far passed,"* means that no accommodations were nearby, with the time fastly slipping away in order that they may find such accommodations in nearby villages, etc.

(36) "SEND THEM AWAY, THAT THEY MAY GO INTO THE COUNTRY ROUND ABOUT, AND INTO THE VILLAGES, AND BUY THEMSELVES BREAD: FOR THEY HAVE NOTHING TO EAT."

The phrase, *"Send them away,"* is about all that one person can do for another, that is, if they are not depending on Christ.

It is tragic, that the world claims to be able to help mankind with all of the attendant problems, but despite the great claims and the large sums of money charged, the end result is to *"send them away,"* and without any help whatsoever. It is sad and tragic, but the Church has bought into this ungodly, humanistic concept of psychology as well. There is no answer other than Christ, and the Church, of all people and places, should be the first one to say so!

As an example, the modern Church has, by and large, embraced humanistic psychology as the answer to the emotional and even spiritual needs of man. It has done so, even though the roots of psychology are in humanism, atheism, and evolution. The Church has taken this direction because it no longer believes the Bible. As well, there is no way the two can be mixed. The little leaven ultimately leavens the entirety of the lump. Consequently, at present, precious few Preachers claim Christ as the answer to the problems of man, with almost all recommending humanistic psychology.

And yet, there is a refreshing glimmer of hope here and there.

From an August 14, 1995 article in *"Christianity Today,"* entitled *"Putting an End to Christian Psychology,"* one, thankfully, sees

NOTES

some sanity in this previously untouchable area. The article concerns an interview with Larry Crabb, who is founder and director of the Institute of Biblical Counseling in Morrison, Colorado, and a professor at Colorado Christian University. Books such as *"Inside Out"* and *"Finding God,"* have made him a popular author and speaker in the Christian community.

THE ARTICLE BEGINS

"'You're committing professional suicide,' a colleague recently told Psychologist Larry Crabb. In recent speeches, Crabb has been raising eyebrows by joining in the chorus of those questioning the utility of psychotherapy for Christians. According to Crabb, who is a psychologist, the Church must reclaim its job of healing people who are struggling emotionally — including those with problems that are generally referred to psychologists and therapists.

"Lately, with his idea of dismantling the Christian counseling industry, Crabb seems on the verge of bewildering more than a few of his followers. Here he talks about his vision for the Church becoming a healing sanctuary, and is questioned accordingly.

WHAT HAS BEEN THE EFFECT OF PROFESSIONAL COUNSELING IN THE CHURCH?

"The Church has bought into the idea that its spiritual role is a very limited one. If a woman struggles with depression or lacks sexual desire for her husband because of past sexual abuse, the immediate response is to send the woman to a professional counselor. The underlying assumption is that spiritual resources aren't sufficient to deal with what's going on — that only people with massive levels of professional training can help.

"Ultimately, we are saying the Scriptures and Christianity don't meaningfully address the core concerns of our lives.

YOU DON'T HOLD TO THE THREE-SIDED MODEL THAT THERAPISTS ARE QUALIFIED TO TREAT PSYCHOLOGICAL PROBLEMS, PASTORS SPIRITUAL PROBLEMS, AND DOCTORS PHYSICAL ONES?

"I say 'no' for two reasons. First, as a professional, I don't know what we don't know. We can't diagnose what's really happening in

people's souls — not the way my dentist can when he looks at x-rays and tells me what's wrong with my tooth. He's not pretending; he knows, and because of the x-ray.

"But as a psychologist, I don't know, and it's not because I'm stupid or poorly trained; it's because there's no such thing as a scientifically-trained expert on the soul.

"Second, theologically I am more comfortable with a dichotomous position — that human beings consist of spirit and body — than a trichotomous one. This leads me to suggest that what we call emotional/psychological problems are really spiritual/theological ones; that nonorganic problems really stem from a troubled soul, not some damaged self, which psychotherapists claim to fix.

BUT HASN'T PSYCHOTHERAPY WORKED FOR MANY PEOPLE?

"Yes; but ask most people who have had two or three years with a good therapist what it was that helped them. Nine times in ten they say, 'This guy really cared about me. He looked at me and said, "I really want to see you feel better."' The therapist's caring was much more important than his or her professional interpretations. Those therapists who are doing really good work are, in fact, doing what I'm calling 'eldering.' And if eldering is being done within a professional setting, why can't it be done in the nonprofessional setting of the Church? I think it can be, and I think that's where it really belongs.

WHY SPECIFICALLY THE CHURCH?

"When a patient goes to see a therapist, he's really asking the therapist to do the sanctifying work that the Spirit of God does through His Word. In the end, all counseling — intentionally or not — deals with issues of Sanctification. The primary context for healing, then, should be the Christian community, not the antiseptic world of a private-practice therapist.

BUT DON'T SOME PROBLEMS LIKE EATING DISORDERS OR MANIC DEPRESSION HAVE A PHYSICAL DIMENSION THAT UNTRAINED INDIVIDUALS ARE NOT EQUIPPED TO DEAL WITH?

"Yes, some personal problems have an organic root. Antidepressants, for example, can

sometimes effectively treat depressive moods, but only because there really is an organic background to the depression. But if you eliminate those kinds of problems — which is anybody's guess how to do this — then I think we're talking about the problems of the soul and not psychopathology, nor damage to an entity that spiritual categories don't include. If, in fact, all nonorganic psychological problems are spiritual problems, they belong more to the role of an Elder than to the expert.

WHAT DO YOU MEAN BY ELDER?

"I am not referring to the official Church position as such, but to Godly people. To whatever degree you or I have pursued the Lord with our heart and soul and mind and strength, we have something to offer those around us, either in a discipleship or friendship capacity. The Church needs to take the role of spiritual, Godly men and women far more seriously. They have a lot more power to deeply affect souls of other people than they generally are given credit for.

"A key Passage is Ephesians 4:16, which says the whole Body grows when each part does its work. We are 'joined and held together' by God — there is an inner connection. So when I meaningfully relate to another person, deep things happen inside him or her. That is what we have taken out of the Christian community and put into a therapist's office.

IS THERE STILL A PLACE FOR THE SKILLED PROFESSIONAL IN THE IDEAL FUNCTIONING CHURCH?

"In the ideal functioning Church, no. But since we are never going to get there, there will always be a place. There is obviously a need for professional counselors for hurting folks who cannot find the kind of help that should be available elsewhere.

ASSUMING PSYCHOLOGICAL PROBLEMS ARE REALLY SPIRITUAL PROBLEMS THAT ARE BETTER TREATED IN THE CHURCH, HOW WOULD A CHURCH MEMBER BE ABLE TO SAFELY HELP SOMEONE SUFFERING FROM, SAY, BULIMIA?

"I envision a woman in the Church suffering from bulimia meeting with an older woman who would get to know her in a profound way so she could nourish her spiritually. The older woman would also recommend she see a physician for medical assessment and treatment. There may also be another Elder in the Church they call on for the special help that that person could offer on the internal spiritual struggles under-lying bulimia.

IN ORDER TO STAY OBJECTIVE, THERAPISTS MAINTAIN A "PROFESSIONAL DISTANCE" FROM THOSE THEY COUNSEL. HOW WOULD THAT WORK IN THE ELDERING MODEL?

"In Acts 20, Paul talks to the Elders of Ephe-sus, saying that he gave himself to them 'day and night with tears.' This implies that there is no 'distance' in eldering. The meaningful connection of shepherding will require an enor-mous emotional price and Elders must be pre-pared to pay that. Certainly, though, the wis-dom and support of fellow Elders will be re-quired to avoid emotional burn-out.

WHAT ABOUT LEGAL LIABILITY ISSUES?

"That is a crucial question. Government regulations often do regulate the offering of psychological services. In the eldering model, the Elders would need to state clearly and pub-licly, that what they are offering is not what modern culture calls 'professional treatment.' And no one should be pressured into accepting the eldering model. Those who believe in the traditional expert model should be encouraged to find a professional counselor.

HOW IS YOUR VISION DIFFERENT THAN THAT OF THE LAY COUNSELING MOVEMENT?

"The Lay Counseling Movement has not challenged the basic thing I'm challenging, which is the expert-elder distinction. I think they still operate under the assumption that people need a specialist — an expert with cer-tified training who has more than Biblical wis-dom, personal Godliness, and deep compassion. Lay counseling programs have organized lists of recognized lay counselors, and the whole approach is to train nurses, so to speak, to care for those folks who aren't so bad off that they need a doctor. I am saying the Elders are the doctors. Half the training of lay counselors is

NOTES

knowing your limits. In contrast, I am saying, know your possibilities.

WHAT ABOUT THE CELL AND SMALL GROUP MOVEMENTS THAT ARE CURRENTLY TAKING ROOT WITHIN THE CHURCH?

"I see a lot of potential in these groups for building the kind of relationships in which people connect deeply and where the kind of eldering I'm talking about could at least begin.

"If these groups can avoid being gatherings of either emotional gushers or rigid Bible stu-dents, they are a wonderful direction to go.

WHAT WILL YOU SAY TO CRITICS WHO THINK YOU ARE BEING TOO SIMPLISTIC?

"I think I am being very simple-minded, but I hope not simplistic. One of my favorite sayings is: 'Simplicity on this side of complexity is not worth anything, but simplicity on the other side of complexity is worth everything.' I believe I have been complicated for twenty-five years and am now finding a little bit of simplicity.

"At the same time, when people try to pin me down on how exactly all of this is going to work, I feel like a ten-year old describing his wife. He has not met her yet; he is not quite sure what she is going to look like. She will be female, and he hopes, pretty; but beyond that, he hasn't got a clue. At one level, I haven't got a clue what I am doing. But I have a couple of central convictions, and I don't think I have ever felt more directly led by the Lord. It leaves me feeling more scared than I have ever felt in my life, but also more excited."

First of all, I want to briefly comment on this article, making a few statements which I feel will possibly be of some help.

Our brother is right, that the Church has bought into the idea that its spiritual role is a very limited one. By that, they are saying, and blasphemously so, that the Scriptures and Christianity do not meaningfully address the core concerns of our lives.

The question is, "Why?"

The answer is relatively simple. Most Preachers, as stated, simply do not believe the Bible anymore because they actually aren't "born again." And then again, there are many who are *"born again,"* but are not at all following the Spirit, but, rather, the flesh. Paul addresses this carefully in Romans 8.

If they followed the Holy Spirit, they would know, and beyond the shadow of a doubt, that the Lord *"Hath given unto us all things that pertain unto life and Godliness, through the knowledge of Him that hath called us to glory and virtue"* (II Pet. 1:3).

The trouble is, most Preachers simply do not have any *"knowledge of Him,"* i.e., Christ.

If the Preachers do not know Him, then the people have no Shepherd, and they, consequently, follow whatever is offered, as erroneous as it may be, as is presently happening.

As well, the Brother is right, when he spoke of the *"dichotomous position"* which addresses the spirit, soul, and body. (He only mentioned spirit and body, but the soul should have been included, with the soul and spirit addressed as one entity, at least in this case.)

He has hit at the very core of the problem of man and the error of psychology. Man is a *"troubled soul,"* and not a *"damaged self."* Psychology addresses the *"self"* or *"mind,"* while the Word of God addresses the *"soul,"* which is the proper terminology, and because of the way man is created.

The problem is, the roots of psychology, and despite the smearing of Christianity, does not even believe that man has a soul and spirit. Or if it does, its explanation steers it away from its Creator, which, in reality, actually denies its existence.

Most of the world, and including the Church, is preoccupied with *"self."* However, while man is certainly a person or *"self,"* still, such is only the result of the soul and spirit. Consequently, to treat *"self"* is to treat only the symptoms instead of the cause. The Word of God goes to the cause.

Consequently, his answer to the question, *"But hasn't psychotherapy worked for many people?"*, with him answering, *"Yes,"* is error. He went on to explain that it was not really any professional skills that helped the individual, but only the care and concern of the professional therapist.

However, this means that psychotherapy did not really help anyone at all, but only care and concern, which can be offered by anyone, which our Brother is quick to bring out.

The *"Elder"* or *"eldering,"* as he refers to it, is excellent and Scriptural. This is the Bible way. As such, it gets Bible results.

However, one key element is missing in this entire scenario. While *"eldering"* is important and Scriptural, and, consequently, the Bible Way, still, the Lord's answer to the problems of mankind is strong preaching of the Gospel, which our Brother little mentions, if at all, with the hurting one brought to a place of prayer and consecration before the Lord, where the Holy Spirit can have an opportunity to deal with the individual.

There is too much of counselors, as dedicated as they may be, telling someone else what to do, other than the preaching of the Gospel. While some small amount is certainly proper and even needed, still, the idea is to get the individual on his knees before God, pouring out his heart to Him, consequently, allowing the Holy Spirit to perform His Work of Healing and Redemption in the soul.

Sound advice is good. However, if it does not lead to the *"Altar,"* it will not really perform its intended task. Sadly, most Churches do not practice that of which I speak anymore, even though some once did.

People who attended Baptist, Methodist, and Holiness Churches, once sought God eagerly in the Altars. The same could be said for Pentecostals. However, this is seldom, and sadly, the case anymore! Regrettably, most Charismatic Churches do not even see any need to seek God, inasmuch as seeking the Lord, at least in their thinking, admits that something is wrong, and according to their doctrines, nothing can be wrong in the new creation man.

So, the upshot is, that there are almost no Biblical methods practiced, and because of what we've stated, Preachers who are not true Shepherds of Jesus Christ.

Sadly, the Church has been busy *"sending them away,"* when all the time, Jesus, and Jesus Alone, has the answer.

The phrase, *"That they may go into the country round about, and into the villages, and buy themselves bread,"* is certainly understandable in the literal sense. However, the *"bread"* which Jesus Alone gives, cannot be obtained in the places of the world. *"Bread"* of the world will not satisfy. Only He is the True Bread of Life. Actually, this is what Jesus was teaching His Disciples.

The phrase, *"For they have nothing to eat,"* was true in the literal sense, and is also true in the spiritual sense.

This is the great error of the modern Church. It tries to exist on *"bread alone,"* or else it substitutes another type of spiritual bread for Jesus Christ, which, in reality, is no bread at all, hence *"nothing to eat."*

One must always remember, that the Church is not the *"bread,"* it only is supposed to show people where the Bread, i.e., Jesus Christ, actually is, i.e., the Bible.

(37) "HE ANSWERED AND SAID UNTO THEM, GIVE YE THEM TO EAT. AND THEY SAY UNTO HIM, SHALL WE GO AND BUY TWO HUNDRED PENNYWORTH OF BREAD, AND GIVE THEM TO EAT?"

The phrase, *"He answered and said unto them, Give ye them to eat,"* is meant to address the subject on a spiritual level, which they at that time could not begin to grasp. Even though Jesus definitely was speaking of the physical, even more so, He was speaking of the spiritual.

This, which they would understand later, referred to the Word of God. This corresponds with what Jesus answered Satan, *"Man shall not live by bread alone, but by every Word that proceedeth out of the Mouth of God"* (Mat. 4:4).

The tragedy is, and as stated, that the majority of Preachers are not giving the Word for their listeners to eat, but, rather, something else!

The question, *"And they say unto Him, Shall we go and buy two hundred pennyworth of bread, and give them to eat?"*, pertains to the problem at hand, and the Disciples trying to solve it.

The people had been without physical food for some time, although having received the greatest spiritual food they would ever have. But still, their physical bodies demanded nourishment. The Disciples had one of two solutions. They would either send the people away for them to obtain food on their own, or else they would buy enough food to feed this massive crowd, which was actually impossible, at least in this *"desert place."*

Even though numbers are readily given in some Commentaries, still, the consensus is that there is actually no way to presently know, at least according to inflated dollars, exactly how much bread *"two hundred pennyworth"* would buy. The consensus is, that it was a sizeable

amount of money, probably equivalent to $7,000 or $8,000 presently.

(38) "HE SAITH UNTO THEM, HOW MANY LOAVES HAVE YE? GO AND SEE. AND WHEN THEY KNEW, THEY SAY, FIVE, AND TWO FISHES."

Jesus does not at all comment on their question. He ignores it, as if it is of no consequence, which it wasn't. The phrase, *"He saith unto them,"* shows them what He will now do.

It is very easy to criticize the Disciples, but most of us, as they, do not think in spiritual terms nearly as much as we should. Too often, we try to figure the thing out from a natural basis, when those things certainly should be considered, but, at the same time, realizing that God is able to do all things. Actually, Jesus will take the Disciples to a dimension they had never dreamed possible. He would take them from the natural to the supernatural! He would take them from the impossible to the possible! He would take them to the miraculous! Among all the lessons He is now teaching, this is perhaps the greatest lesson of all.

The Believer must look at every situation, whether little or large, in the context of what God is able to do, instead of what man is able to do. If Jesus would go to this length to teach this lesson, surely it must be learned. This is the reason He made such statements as, *"If ye abide in Me, and My Words abide in you, ye shall ask what ye will, and it shall be done unto you"* (Jn. 15:7).

Or, *"If ye shall ask any thing in My Name, I will do it"* (Jn. 14:14).

Actually, the four Gospels are replete with such glorious and miraculous Promises. To be sure, He meant what He said, and said what He meant!

The question, *"How many loaves have ye?"*, pertains to literal loaves of bread. In fact, most everything the Lord does, addresses itself to literal things. However, He turns it into a miracle.

They were thinking of thousands of loaves to feed this massive crowd, while He addressed Himself to whatever they had, as little as it might have been. He is asking the same question to every Believer, *"How many loaves have ye?"*

It is meant to tell each and all, that whatever we do have, as little as it may be, can be miraculously touched by Him, and made to serve in great capacities. In fact, the *"five loaves and two fishes"* supplied, were about as nothing as could ever be, at least respecting the size of this great crowd. So, the Lord is trying to pull us away from what little we have, to how big He is, and what He can do!

The phrase, *"Go and see,"* as directed to them, is directed to us as well!

We may think we have nothing, especially considering the tremendous task ahead, but all of us have at least something. The problem is, we have considered it without Him, instead of with Him. We keep looking at the smallness of our assets instead of the bigness of His abilities.

Many people refuse to give to God for this very reason. They reason within themselves, that it is so little that it is of no consequence.

The lesson here taught, and as stated, is not the smallness of our gift, but the miracle manner in which He is able to enlarge it.

What a lesson, that is if we can only learn it!

The phrase, *"And when they knew, they say, Five, and two fishes,"* means that at first they did not even really know if they had that. Actually, and according to Andrew, this small collection belonged to a boy (Jn. 6:8-9). He had sent them to find whatever bread they could find, and this is what they came back with, *"Five loaves, and two fishes."*

(39) "AND HE COMMANDED THEM TO MAKE ALL SIT DOWN BY COMPANIES UPON THE GREEN GRASS."

The phrase, *"And He commanded them,"* proclaims Him taking charge, as He will do, if we will only allow Him. When He is given that latitude, He will begin to give instructions, and things will begin to fall in place. We do not really know how He does it, but we just know things start to happen!

The phrase, *"To make all sit down by companies upon the green grass,"* tells us that it was Passover time, and therefore in the month of April (Jn. 6:4).

The *"companies"* spoke of order, which always characterizes that which the Lord does. He is not a God of confusion!

(40) "AND THEY SAT DOWN IN RANKS, BY HUNDREDS, AND BY FIFTIES."

The word, *"ranks,"* probably best describes this which was done. In other words, the entirety of the gathering of at least ten thousand people, and possibly more, was organized that all may be properly cared for.

There is even some slight evidence, that the men were separated from the women and children (Mat. 14:21).

Other than *"order,"* which is always characteristic of the Work of the Lord, perhaps this suggests to us all the nations of the world which must be equally fed. The organization was such, that those in the very back ranks were given just as much as those in the forward ranks. This is the intention of the Lord respecting the dissemination of the Gospel. Unfortunately, it has not worked quite that way, at least at the present time. Some nations seem to be given far more than others.

(41) "AND WHEN HE HAD TAKEN THE FIVE LOAVES AND THE TWO FISHES, HE LOOKED UP TO HEAVEN, AND BLESSED, AND BRAKE THE LOAVES, AND GAVE THEM TO HIS DISCIPLES TO SET BEFORE THEM; AND THE TWO FISHES DIVIDED HE AMONG THEM ALL."

The phrase, *"And when He had taken the five loaves and the two fishes,"* signifies the beginning of the miracle, and because it was in His Hands. That is the secret! In our hands it is nothing; in His Hands it is everything! Sadly, mankind is reluctant to place it in His Hands, even though it is insignificant to begin with.

The phrase, *"He looked up to Heaven,"* proclaims that it is from God from whence the blessings come. Man keeps thinking it is his ability, when the opposite is true. Even regarding those who do not live for God, or even recognize Him, it is the Lord Who gives the breath that man breathes, and the strength to do what is done both mentally and physically. However, precious few give Him the praise and the glory.

GOD AS THE SOURCE

The phrase, *"And blessed,"* signifies thanksgiving, and God as the Source of all Blessing.

"Lord, you bless the Righteous," says the Psalmist (Ps. 5:12). God not only gives life, but also enriches life. Even the power to get wealth (Deut. 8:18) comes from the Lord. We are totally dependent on Him. Jesus' action consequently portrays this.

COVENANT BLESSINGS

Basically, the beginning of Blessings, at least as far as Covenant was concerned, began with Abraham and followed through to his descendants. The Lord committed Himself to bless them (Gen. Chpts. 12; 17). But the Covenant had to be accepted by Faith by each succeeding generation, and Blessing was found in obedience to a way of life that God later laid down. *"I am setting before you today a Blessing and a curse,"* Moses said in restating God's Law to one generation, *"The Blessing if you obey the Commands of the Lord your God that I am giving you today; the curse if you disobey … and turn from the way … by following other gods"* (Deut. 11:26-28).

Actually, this Truth, restated often in Deuteronomy (Deut. Chpts. 12; 15; 28), is basic to the Old Testament concept of Blessing. The abundant life, enriched by God, is to be found in the Lord and experienced as we live His Way.

The Old Testament rightly assumed from God's Covenant Promises that the enriched life included material blessings. These follow consecration as the individual lives by Faith and in obedience to God. However, Jesus moved beyond the Old Testament Covenant regarding Blessing.

JESUS AND BLESSINGS

He makes the startling statement that God's Kingdom is a present Kingdom and that His blessed ones already know (are happy with) a unique joy, which comes from living in that Kingdom.

The Old Testament describes the path that leads to God's Blessing. Jesus describes that Blessing itself. God's Blessing comes to us in all our circumstances and makes us fortunate no matter how others may view our lives.

The New Covenant takes us even further into God's Blessings, as Paul announced it in Ephesians 1:3, *"Blessed us with all spiritual Blessings."* All of this is in Christ. Because our Blessing is found in personal relationship with Jesus and because that relationship is so intimate and real, we have in Jesus Himself the abundant life for which we yearn and which God has ever yearned to give straying mankind.

However, and as stated, the main thrust of the action of Christ in blessing the food, is the reminder that God is the Source of all Blessings.

The phrase, *"And brake the loaves,"* signifies the act of the Miracle. In other words, the Greek structure of the language tells us that the Miracle of the multiplication took place

between the breaking and the giving. There is a tremendous lesson in this, of which we will mention in greater detail momentarily!

The phrase, *"And gave them to His Disciples to set before them,"* means that the provision was not to be kept by the Disciples, but, instead, to be given to the hungry.

The phrase, *"And the two fishes divided He among them all,"* proclaims as well that they were multiplied as the bread.

There is a tremendous pattern outlined in the action of Christ, which addresses itself to every Believer, and, as well, proclaims the manner in which God carries out His Work in our lives.

1. *"When He had taken"*: Of course, this is speaking of the bread and fish, still, it pertains as well to our lives. Whenever we, as individuals, come to Christ, the Lord is kind and generous to take us, even though we really have nothing to offer Him.

2. *"And blessed"*: Almost immediately after Salvation, the Lord blesses the individual greatly. These Blessings come in all shapes and sizes, and from every direction. It is somewhat like an initiation into Christianity, which is the opposite of most initiations of the world.

3. *"And brake"*: Then comes the *"breaking,"* which is a very painful experience for any and all Believers. However, if we are to be used by the Lord, this process must be engaged. It is the struggle between the flesh and the Spirit.

For a while it seems as if all Blessings stop, with everything we hold dear being stripped away. Actually, and in some manner, this *"breaking"* never ends. This is done that the flesh may be subdued, and Christ may be all in all. As stated, it is a debilitating process, and is meant to be so. Unfortunately, many of our Faith friends have endeavored to confess this part of the Christian experience away, entertaining only the Blessing. However, such cannot be done, and, in fact, is not meant to be done.

David is a perfect example! He was Anointed by the Lord, which constituted tremendous blessing. Very shortly thereafter he killed the giant, with all the attendant blessings that followed. However, the time soon came that it seemed like all blessings left, with David persecuted by Saul, even to the place he thought he would lose his life. It was the *"breaking"* process, and was necessary before he could take the Throne.

4. *"And gave"*: The breaking, as stated, constitutes Miracles, and because it is totally of Christ. Without the *"breaking,"* the flesh is given to the world, which constitutes man-devised efforts, which will bless or help no one.

After the *"breaking,"* the flesh is subdued, with Christ being supreme, and given to lost humanity. Consequently, miracles result in changed lives, and because Christ is properly presented.

If one is to notice, and as we have alluded to, the Disciples did not hoard the food for themselves, but, instead, gave it to the multitude as intended! Regrettably, the modern Church, and especially most in the Pentecostal and Charismatic community, have attempted to do the opposite of what is proclaimed here. Most of the so-called faith is used to confess personal riches, etc. Very little of the Gospel is given to a hurting world, at least from this part of the Church.

Regrettably, and even though my statement may offend some, I must say it because it is true, *"The modern faith message is a selfish message, which is the opposite of the True Bible Message."* Even though it talks about *"giving,"* still, its action is the very opposite. Even if it does give, it is not without great strings attached, demanding much more in return than was given. Such is not giving, but rather covetousness.

If *"self"* is properly hidden in Christ, as it must be, it will do exactly as Christ said, *"Take no thought for your life, what ye shall eat, or what ye shall drink; nor yet for your body, what ye shall put on"* (Mat. 6:25).

While the Lord certainly does bless materially, and as we have already stated, still, that is a by-product of His great Salvation, and certainly not the main thrust, which is Salvation from sin.

(42) "AND THEY DID ALL EAT, AND WERE FILLED."

Such is always the case with Christ.

When men eat that which is offered by the world, at least in the spiritual sense, it never satisfies, and, consequently, they are never *"filled."* However, that which Christ gives is filling, i.e., satisfying.

As well, that which was given satisfied *"all,"* and not just a few. In other words, what Christ has to offer is meant for all, with the need in all for what Christ has to offer.

I have had the opportunity to appear on nationally televised news and interview programs with some of America's most noted political

NOTES

pundits. Of course, many of these individuals consider themselves to be the cream of the intelligentsia of the nation.

Almost entirely, they place themselves beyond the need for Christ and what He offers. Their attitude is, that the ignorant and unlearned may need this *"crutch,"* but not them. They have it altogether, at least in their thinking.

The Truth is, the only difference in these individuals and the ignorant and unlearned, as they put it, is a little education, which, for the most part, is no education at all, simply because it is error. The truly ignorant are these pseudo intellectuals. To be uneducated, is simply not to know. To be ignorant, is to not know that you don't know! Such describes those who think they know so much, but, in reality, know so little! Solomon said, *"The fear of the Lord, is the beginning of wisdom"* (Prov. 9:10).

The Truth is, all, rich, poor, great, small, educated, uneducated, young and old, need the Lord Jesus Christ. As well, and as stated, He Alone can provide what the soul of man desperately needs.

(43) "AND THEY TOOK UP TWELVE BASKETS FULL OF THE FRAGMENTS, AND OF THE FISHES."

The number *"Twelve,"* speaks of Government, and God's Government at that! The idea is, that if God's Government was paramount in the world, the entirety of the world would be fed and prosperous. One day it will be!

They begin with *"five loaves and two fishes,"* fed ten thousand or more people, and ended up with *"twelve baskets full of the fragments, and of the fishes."*

What a Miracle!

As is obvious, Christ does not carry out His Work according to the particular laws of this earth, laws, He, in fact, originally created, but no doubt twisted by the Fall of man. Christ brings Heaven down to earth, which introduces a completely new way of doing things. That is the reason He prayed, *"Thy Kingdom come, Thy Will be done in earth, as it is in Heaven."*

He then said, *"Give us this day our daily bread"* (Mat. 6:10-11).

To be sure, and as is obvious, He can give bread in a manner in which the world cannot, and, in fact, does not even understand.

There is a law called *"Hamilton's Law."* It basically states, that for everything built, something must be destroyed. In other words, if a house is built, trees must be cut down, thereby providing the lumber, with rock and sand, etc., depleted from the earth, thereby making the bricks, etc.

However, with Christ no such law exists. Even though the original five loaves and two fishes caused depletion, at least to a small degree, still, the multiplication caused no depletion whatsoever.

Where did the extra bread and fish come from?

Of course, what the Lord carried out was a Miracle. Such sets aside natural law, and can only be done by the supernatural Power of God. Actually, the Power was in Jesus, not in a formula or some type of magical control of the supernatural.

The Message of Miracles is that God has shown us His Power and has proved that His Power will be used for our benefit. We can trust Jesus fully. He is able, and He wills only our good.

To be sure, if it can be explained as to how the Lord performed Miracles, then, in actuality, it really was not a miracle. A miracle simply cannot be explained by natural means or according to phenomenon.

Some time back, I had the occasion to see a program over Television which addressed itself to this very subject — the subject of miracles. One group did not believe at all, with the other group claiming to believe, but, in reality, was faithless as well!

The ones who claimed to believe, attempted to explain the Miracles of the opening of the Red Sea, and the Hebrew Children in the fiery furnace, as a result of natural means. In other words, they said the opening of the Red Sea was caused by an earthquake.

While it certainly may have been possible that the Lord used an earthquake to carry out this grand Miracle, still, for it to happen at the exact time the Children of Israel were standing on the banks of the Red Sea, and then for it to conclude at the very time the last Israelite gained the opposite shore, is more, much more, than just a mere earthquake. It cannot be explained according to natural phenomenon, earthquake or no earthquake.

As well, they attempted to explain the Hebrew Children in the fiery furnace, as finding a *"cool spot"* in the midst of the furnace. They claimed that *"cool spots"* are found in all furnaces, etc.

In all honesty, the unbelief of the Believers is worse even than that of the unbelievers.

If they were saved by this *"cool spot,"* how did they get to the cool spot in the first place? The fire was already raging when they were thrown in, so much in fact that it killed those who threw them in the furnace (Dan. 3:22).

No! The Truth is, the Lord performed a Miracle by suspending the heat and its effect on the Hebrew Children. In Truth, it cannot be explained by any natural law or phenomenon, only by the Power of God.

So, how the Lord performed the Miracle of multiplying the loaves and the fishes, is not known. But that He did it, is obvious! He is a God of Miracles, and is the same today as He was yesterday (Heb. 13:8).

(44) "AND THEY THAT DID EAT OF THE LOAVES WERE ABOVE FIVE THOUSAND MEN."

Wuest says that the word for *"men"* here is not *"anthropos,"* the generic term which could include men and women, but *"aner,"* the word for a male individual. Matthew added that there were women and children. Consequently, there must have been at least ten thousand or more who were fed that day.

I have to believe that the *"bread and fish"* multiplied by Jesus, and given to the multitude, were the finest *"bread"* and *"fish"* that these people had ever eaten. I can imagine that thousands exclaimed as to how delicious the food was.

While we must not be carried away, still, everything the Lord does is perfect. Consequently, this must have been a perfect meal as well! Likewise, the Salvation afforded by Christ is a perfect Salvation!

(45) "AND STRAIGHTWAY HE CONSTRAINED HIS DISCIPLES TO GET INTO THE SHIP, AND TO GO TO THE OTHER SIDE BEFORE UNTO BETHSAIDA, WHILE HE SENT AWAY THE PEOPLE."

The phrase, *"And straightway He constrained His Disciples to get into the ship,"* proclaims their reluctance to do so, with Jesus having to sternly command them to obey. They had witnessed a tremendous Miracle, and did not desire to leave Him, and, as well, were perplexed at His action.

Why would He want to stay there alone?

He offered no explanation, but, rather, demanded their obedience.

The phrase, *"And to go to the other side before unto Bethsaida,"* probably referred to the Bethsaida near Capernaum. Actually, there were two Bethsaidas.

One was at the northeast end of the lake, where they probably were near at the moment, with the other, as stated, across the lake near Capernaum. (The one in the northeast was called *"Bethsaida Julias."*)

The phrase, *"While He sent away the people,"* proclaims Him doing so only after they were fed and filled.

Also, it seems as if the people, as the Disciples, did not desire to leave Him, with Him having to ask them to go their respective ways. Nevertheless, the admonition to the Disciples was far stronger than to the crowd.

(46) "AND WHEN HE HAD SENT THEM AWAY, HE DEPARTED INTO A MOUNTAIN TO PRAY."

The phrase, *"And when He had sent them away,"* proclaims the reason for His action.

The phrase, *"He departed into a mountain to pray,"* gives the reason for His desiring to be alone.

PRAYER

The word, *"pray,"* as used in this sentence, speaks of the consciousness on the part of the one who prays, of the fact of God's Presence and His listening ear (Wuest).

Prayer is not understood too well by most Christians. Actually, it remains one of the mysteries of our Faith.

The questions are asked, *"How can prayer change the mind of God or modify events?"* or *"How does prayer relate to Divine Sovereignty?"*

Actually, prayer does not change the mind of God, though it does modify events.

Respecting Divine Sovereignty, the Lord has so designed His Work and Word, that He allows the Believer to enter into the carrying out of God's Will by using our Faith, and seeking His Face.

Believers are commanded to pray about everything, confident that God hears prayer, cares, and is able to act (I Thess. 5:17).

PRAYER IN THE OLD TESTAMENT

The Old Testament is filled with references to prayer. God's people pray to Him, call on Him, and cry out to Him.

Using David as an example, the Passages of Scripture which deal with David's life, portray

NOTES

the Shepherd King consistently inquiring of the Lord (Ps. 4:1; 69:16-17).

Prayer indicates an humbling of oneself before the Lord, and, consequently, a submission to God.

THE FOUNDATIONS OF OLD TESTAMENT PRAYER

Prayer in the Old Testament is an expression of personal relationship. This relationship is initiated by God, Who is recognized as Creator and Redeemer.

As Creator, God is recognized as the Source of each life, as well as of the Universe. His limitless Power is expressed in the material world and in history itself, which unfolds according to His purposes.

As Redeemer, God acted in history to deliver His people in their need. While the Exodus is the prime example of Redemption, God continued to act on Israel's behalf. He is a God Who saves, and His people can depend on His intervention.

God's basic commitment to the descendants of Abraham was given formal expression in the Covenant. God had chosen this race and blessed them. When Israel turned to God, they turned to the One Who had made Himself their God.

All this — knowing God as Creator, Redeemer, and Covenant-Giver — was the basis of the relationship within which God's Old Testament people approached Him in prayer. Knowing God, also taught the Israelites their own place. Compared to God, the most exalted individual is but a humble supplicant. Matched against God's unlimited power, the greatest human force is wholly insignificant. It is appropriate, then, for God's people to depend completely on Him. In the final analysis, His favor is all that matters. Every issue of life hinges on His Grace alone. The Old Testament Believer was dependent on God in everything, just as a little child is completely dependent on his or her parents.

Prayer, then, is the appeal of a child who recognizes his dependence. It is made to an all-powerful Person Who cares. It is not surprising that Old Testament prayers are personal, often motivated by need, and beautiful in their child-like simplicity.

Moreover, prayer in the Old Testament is a spontaneous expression. God can be approached at any time in any place. It is significant, consequently, that the Old Testament presents no prayer liturgy. Prayer is not a matter of ritual religion. Prayer is a living, vital expression of relationship. Thus, true prayer is always a matter of the heart (Jer. 29:12-14), while false or meaningless prayer is only a matter of the lips (Isa. 29:13; Amos 5:23-24).

PRAYER IN THE NEW TESTAMENT

It is made obvious in the New Testament that the view of prayer established in the Old Testament also permeates the New as does approach to God in prayer. As in the Old Testament, prayer is an expression of relationship and must always be understood as an expression of fellowship between God and human beings, made possible by Jesus.

In the New Testament, prayer is related to the intimate relationship that the Believer sustains with the Father, the Son, and the Holy Spirit.

Jesus condemns a ritualistic, hypocritical approach to prayer and presents true prayer as an intimate expression of relationship with a God Who is one's Father (Mat. 6:5-8). Jesus' model prayer, known to us as the *"Lord's Prayer,"* sums up the beautiful relationship we have with God.

We approach Him as we would a Father. We acknowledge and praise Him as the hallowed One in Heaven. We express our joyful submission to His Will. We acknowledge our dependence on the Lord for material and spiritual sustenance, and we ask for forgiveness as well! We acknowledge His right to direct our lives (Mat. 6:9-13).

Actually, Jesus taught His Disciples, assuring them by explaining the freedom from worry that Believers have: *"Your Heavenly Father knows what you need"* (Mat. 6:32). Coming in prayer to a God Who is Father and resting in all that this means, we are free to *"Seek first His Kingdom and His Righteousness"* (Mat. 6:33).

JESUS

In the New Testament, Jesus is seen as the key to that personal relationship with God that is central to prayer. Through Jesus, and Jesus Alone, can we *"Approach the Throne of Grace with confidence,"* sure that we will *"Receive Mercy and find Grace to help us in our time of need"* (Heb. 4:16).

NOTES

However, a continuing intimate walk with Jesus is vital to prayer. Jesus, using the image of the Vine and Branches (Jn. 15), told the Apostles, *"If you remain in Me and My Words remain in you, ask whatever you wish, and it will be given you"* (Jn. 15:7). That intimate relationship with Jesus, enhanced by His Words, reshape our personalities to fit with His values and character, brings us into so rich a harmony with the Lord that what we wish is what God desires us to ask.

PRAYER AND THE HOLY SPIRIT

The Holy Spirit lives within Believers. He has a unique role in this intimate exchange known as prayer. *"The Spirit Himself intercedes for us with groans that words cannot express"* (Rom. 8:26), and *"The Spirit intercedes for the Saints in accordance with God's Will"* (Rom. 8:27).

While the Spirit may assist us in prayer without our conscious awareness, our understanding clearly must be involved (I Cor. 14:13-15). Jesus told the Apostles that the Spirit would take from what belonged to Jesus and make it known (Jn. 16:15).

Prayer is a continuous expression of relationship. The New Testament speaks of prayer as a continuous, constant experience for Christians (Acts 1:14; I Cor. 7:5; I Thess. 5:17; II Thess. 1:11; I Tim. 5:5). Just as we talk with members of our family naturally and spontaneously, so we converse with God Who also shares our lives.

INTERCESSORY PRAYER

One of the most striking features of New Testament prayer as it is portrayed in the Epistles is its intercessory nature. We read again and again of prayer being offered by Believers for one another. In this, we learn that prayer is an expression of relationship within the Body of Christ, as well as an expression of relationship with God. Out of the intimacy of shared lives grows a deep concern for others and their needs, and this provides the primary content for prayer in the Epistles.

CONDITIONS FOR ANSWERED PRAYER

Too often prayer is placed in the position of an obstacle course. Erroneous conditions for answered prayer are laid down. Often the treatment suggests that only if certain obstacles are overcome, will prayer be answered. In other words, if we do not successfully negotiate the obstacle course, these false teachers tell us, God will not hear us. Too often the reader is given the impression that God stands watching like a tennis judge, ready to disqualify us if we are even slightly out of bounds. Consequently, the relational nature of prayer is missed, and prayer is recast as a spiritual exercise, with answers depending on our efforts rather than on God's Grace and good will.

Everyone knows that if a child asks something of his parent, that even though the grammar may be wrong, or even the request somewhat out of order, still, the parent will do all he can to grant the request for the child, and because he loves him. Jesus said, *"If ye then, being evil, know how to give good gifts unto your children: how much more shall your Heavenly Father give the Holy Spirit to them that ask Him?"* (Lk. 11:13).

DISOBEDIENCE

In Truth, disobedience is about the only thing which will prevent God from hearing and answering prayer (Deut. 1:43-45).

It should be obvious that disobedience means that people are not living in fellowship with God, for the people who are close to Him are obedient and loving, and seek to do justice. It is in the context of a growing relationship with the Lord that prayer finds its place. Outside of such a relationship, prayer is a meaningless exercise.

The New Testament offers us encouragement that our request will surely be answered. This encouragement comes as a listing of indicators that reassure us that our relationship with God is vital and real. Those who seek, knock, and ask, receive what they request (Mat. 7:7-11).

Jesus told the Apostles that when two agreed regarding a matter, it would be done by the Lord (Mat. 18:19). To pray *"In Jesus' Name"* means to identify with His character and purposes (Jn. 14:13-14; 15:16; 16:23). The trust that we have in God, which calms our doubts and uncertainties, also testifies to us that God's answer will come. Only those who show contempt for God by questioning His ability or willingness to act in human affairs, and thus violate the relationship, will not be answered when they call (James 1:5-8).

As we obey the Lord, we are assured that we live in a relationship with Him in which our prayers are heard and answered (I Jn. 3:22). As the Scripture and the Holy Spirit testify to us that what we ask is in the framework of God's Will, we can have confidence that what we ask for will be granted (I Jn. 5:14-15).

Actually, disobedience, and in whatever form, is the reason that many, if not most, Christians do not pray. Automatically, the Holy Spirit makes us very much aware of such disobedience, and unless it is properly handled, continued prayer is a fruitless exercise. So, disobedient Christians seldom pray.

Other than being obedient, there are really no conditions that a person must meet before God will hear prayer. The Bible provides indicators that force our attention back to the quality of our personal relationship with the Lord. In fact, those whose lives demonstrate that they have no significant relationship with God, as well, have no basis on which to expect prayer to be heard.

But those who experience a growing relationship with the Lord, marked by trust, obedience, love, harmony with other Believers, and a growing commitment to the revealed Will of God, can rest assured that the Lord will hear and answer prayer in His time.

(Most of the thoughts on prayer were supplied by Lawrence O. Richards.)

Verse 46 indicates that Jesus prayed. And as someone has said, if He had to pray, what about us?

The Truth is that most Christians do not pray, simply because they have little or no relationship with Christ. As a result, they little believe Him, and, consequently, little resort to Him. In other words, they simply do not know Him.

(47) "AND WHEN EVEN WAS COME, THE SHIP WAS IN THE MIDST OF THE SEA, AND HE ALONE ON THE LAND."

The phrase, *"And when even was come,"* represents the early evening after nightfall.

The phrase, *"The ship was in the midst of the sea,"* refers to the problem the ship was now encountering.

The phrase, *"And He Alone on the land,"* represents Him coming down to the beach from the mountain where He had been praying. He did so on their behalf.

(48) "AND HE SAW THEM TOILING IN ROWING; FOR THE WIND WAS CONTRARY UNTO THEM: AND ABOUT THE FOURTH WATCH OF THE NIGHT HE COMETH UNTO THEM, WALKING UPON THE SEA, AND WOULD HAVE PASSED BY THEM."

The phrase, *"And He saw them toiling in rowing,"* uses the Greek word, *"eidon,"* and means the actual perception of the object, and not the mere seeing with the eyes.

The Sea of Galilee is about seven miles wide, and especially considering that it was night, He could not have seen them physically. Consequently, He saw what was happening to them in His spirit, which was revealed to Him by the Holy Spirit.

The word, *"toiling,"* means they were making no headway against the contrary wind.

The phrase, *"For the wind was contrary unto them,"* concerns considerably more than an adverse wind, and somewhat less than an outright storm. John called it, *"a great wind that blew"* (Jn. 6:18).

The phrase, *"And about the fourth watch of the night He cometh unto them, walking upon the Sea,"* referred to somewhere between three and six in the morning.

The inference is that the sandals of our Lord actually had contact with the water. Wuest said that He walked on the surface of the Sea as we walk on a hard pavement.

The phrase, *"And would have passed by them,"* is an unfortunate translation.

The Greek word, *"parerchomai,"* has the meaning of *"passing by,"* but it also means *"to come near."* Consequently, the entirety of the Text tells us that Jesus had come near to help them rather than to pass them by.

(49) "BUT WHEN THEY SAW HIM WALKING UPON THE SEA, THEY SUPPOSED IT HAD BEEN A SPIRIT, AND CRIED OUT:"

The phrase, *"But when they saw Him walking upon the Sea,"* refers to something they in no way understood, and, consequently, did not believe — His appearance! In other words, they could not believe their eyes.

The phrase, *"They supposed it had been a spirit, and cried out,"* means they did not believe it was really Jesus, but rather a phantom or apparition. Under the circumstances, it is not difficult at all to understand their dilemma and response.

NOTES

Inasmuch as they had left late in the afternoon, they had probably been rowing for eight or nine hours, and had only covered about three miles. The Scripture says they were *"in the midst of the Sea,"* and with the lake about seven miles wide, they were making very little headway.

They knew that Jesus had pointedly told them to go to the other side, but, still, they seemingly were unable to carry out His Command. The wind was contrary, and despite their efforts, little headway was being made. Consequently, they were confused, as well as physically exhausted. And now they see Jesus, or at least something that looks like Jesus, walking these choppy waves, and coming toward them.

Someone has suggested that the first watch of the night represented the age of the Law, the second of the Prophets, the third of the Gospel, with the fourth representing His Glorious Advent, when He will find Israel buffeted by the spirit of the Antichrist and by the storms of the world.

His reception into the ship and the consequent calm prefigures the eternal peace of the Church and the world after His Second Coming.

(50) "FOR THEY ALL SAW HIM, AND WERE TROUBLED. AND IMMEDIATELY HE TALKED WITH THEM, AND SAITH UNTO THEM, BE OF GOOD CHEER: IT IS I; BE NOT AFRAID."

The phrase, *"For they all saw Him,"* means that this was not merely the hallucination of one member of the group, but, instead, that all Twelve *"saw Him."* Consequently, there was no doubt about what they were seeing, even though they did not understand it, at least at the time.

The phrase, *"And were troubled,"* pertains to all the difficulties which had accrued that night.

The phrase, *"And immediately He talked with them,"* presents Him calming their fears. When they heard Him speak, and to them directly, they knew they were not dealing with *"a spirit"* or ghost.

The phrase, *"And saith unto them, Be of good cheer: it is I; be not afraid,"* presents His Message. It is one of comfort, strength, and encouragement. It has not changed at all today!

Several things are said here:

1. *"Be of good cheer"*: It means *"to be of good courage,"* and, consequently, not to be discouraged.

It is so easy for one to get one's eyes on circumstances, such as the contrary wind, and the difficulties of the night. Despite His Command for them to go to the other side, their journey had been fraught with peril. As well, they were physically and mentally exhausted.

To be sure, in one's labor for the Lord, and even in the midst of His Will, doing exactly as He has said, difficulties, as here, will arise. Irrespective, at least part of the lesson of this episode is that we are not to be discouraged by adverse events. What Jesus said to them then, He says to us now!

As well, He is telling us that these times will come, and, to be sure, cannot be confessed away. Unfortunately, a large segment of the modern Church thinks that such things happen only because of a lack of Faith on the part of the Believer. While that certainly could be true in some cases, still, in most it is not true at all.

Why does the Lord allow such?

When Jesus sent the Disciples away, He knew He was sending them into difficult circumstances. He did it purposely! The only way some lessons can be learned, is for the actual difficulty to be experienced. He could tell them all day long, and, in fact, did tell them, but until they were in such circumstances, they really did not fully understand His meaning.

Some people erroneously think that if one is in the Will of God, there will not be any difficulties. To be sure, and I think one could say without fear of contradiction, that the opposite is generally the case. The Will of God, as here, will be contested mightily, and for the obvious reasons. Satan hates the Will of God, and will do all within his power to get the Child of God in an opposite direction, either by disobedience or by discouragement. In this case, it was discouragement.

So, Jesus says, and right in the midst of their difficulties, *"Be of good cheer,"* which shows Faith, Trust, and dependence on the Lord.

2. *"It is I"*: Wuest said that the pronoun, *"I,"* is used here for emphasis. Literally, *"It is I and nobody else."*

It is said in this manner in order that the Child of God will know and understand that whatever the Lord requires that we do, He will see to it that we are able to carry it out, even if He has to perform a Miracle, as here, to bring it about. If He tells us to do something, He, to be

NOTES

sure, will help us do it, and irrespective of what it takes. The emphatic *"I"* guarantees His Presence, and, therefore, our success.

Hallelujah!

3. *"Be not afraid"*: In other words, *"stop being afraid."*

Fear is that which is brought on by circumstances, our reaction to them, and a failure to trust God. *"There is no reason for any Believer to ever be afraid,"* is actually what the Lord is telling us. In fact, if our love for the Lord is as it should be, there will be no reason to fear, because *"Perfect love casteth out fear"* (I Jn. 4:18). He then went on to say, *"He that feareth is not made perfect in love."*

(51) "AND HE WENT UP UNTO THEM INTO THE SHIP; AND THE WIND CEASED: AND THEY WERE SORE AMAZED IN THEMSELVES BEYOND MEASURE, AND WONDERED."

Mark does not mention Peter walking on the water to go to Jesus, as recorded by Matthew (Mat. 14:28).

Why?

Inasmuch as the Holy Spirit superintended and guided all that was said and done respecting the recording of these events, the account of Peter in this incident was left out by design. Among other reasons, the Holy Spirit desired that the reader's attention not be diverted to Peter, as important as that incident was. Matthew's account concerning Peter was enough, with this account focused more directly on the entirety of the Disciples, and, consequently, all Believers.

As well, Peter probably divulged this account to Mark, as he did most of the accounts in Mark's writings, and purposely left out his own experience. Many scholars feel that Mark wrote his Book in collaboration with Simon Peter. There are homey and personal touches in it, which lend themselves to Peter's involvement. Even as I dictate these words, I sense the Presence of the Lord! That the Lord would choose humble fishermen, as Peter, and others such as Mark, giving them the privilege of associating with Him, and then allow them to give an account of the greatest events in the history of mankind, leaves one utterly astonished! But such is the Grace of God!

During the earthly Ministry of Christ, Peter was a boastful man. And then came his terrible difficulty with him denying Christ. Ever after, this boastful nature was completely gone, replaced by a quiet humility, which always sought to demote self and, as here, promote Christ.

The phrase, *"And He went up unto them into the ship,"* proves beyond the shadow of a doubt that it was really Jesus, and not an apparition.

The phrase, *"And the wind ceased,"* emphasizes the fact that such was done solely because He was now in the ship. To be sure, He will come, although at times it seems like He waits forever. However, as the spiritual says, *"He's an on-time God."*

He may not be early, but He's never late.

The phrase, *"And they were sore amazed in themselves beyond measure, and wondered,"* registers their response to His action. He never ceased to amaze them, and *"beyond measure,"* which means that they had witnessed something beyond their power of comprehension.

(52) "FOR THEY CONSIDERED NOT THE MIRACLE OF THE LOAVES: FOR THEIR HEART WAS HARDENED."

Williams says that the spiritual blindness occasioned in this verse was most probably caused by their political unity with the world in its carnal enthusiasm and purpose (Jn. 6:15). Nothing dulls spirituality like the religious enthusiasm of the carnal nature acting in fellowship with the religious world.

The desire to make Jesus King, as John mentioned, was paramount, as well, in the minds of the Disciples. Consequently, the True Mission of Christ was lost on them, at least at this time. Any deviation from the True Will of God always *"hardens the heart."*

The phrase, *"For they considered not the Miracle of the loaves,"* has the implication that they did not understand the true meaning of this Miracle. Jesus said, *"Ye seek Me, not because ye saw the miracles, but because ye did eat of the loaves, and were filled"* (Jn. 6:26). The people saw Him using His Miracle-working Power to bring about an earthly government of prosperity, which would make Israel once again the leading nation in the world. As stated, the Disciples were tainted with this thought as well. The True Bread of Life, which He was, and which the Miracle of the loaves and the fishes was meant to symbolize, was lost upon them. Consequently, *"Their heart was hardened"* to the True Purpose of God.

As then, so now!

I have personally watched individuals get out of the Will of God, and, consequently, become totally blind to what the Lord was actually doing. They were *"hardened,"* and because their agenda was not God's agenda.

In a sense this has happened to almost the entirety of the Church. Most have long since deserted the Bible, i.e., the Will of God, and, consequently, have become *"hardened."* The Faith community is an excellent example!

Even though this holds true in every aspect, still, the manner in which the Word of God is used by much of the Faith community is almost identical to Israel and the Disciples of old. They saw everything that Christ did in a secular, carnal way, which would bring glory to Israel. As stated, they did not see or know His True Mission.

Likewise, the Faith community too often turns the great Promises of God into a selfish spectacle, claiming riches for themselves, etc. They forget that Jesus came to save sinners, and not to make men rich.

One particular Preacher of my acquaintance proclaimed that he was confessing a Mercedes Benz for Christmas, and for his wife, some other such type thing. It is all said under a heavy canopy of religion, claiming this is the Blessings of God, etc.

In Truth, it is selfishness of the highest order, and a gross perversion of the Word of God. Consequently, the True Mission of Christ, and the true purpose of the Word of God is completely lost upon them. Their hearts are hardened.

Regrettably, there is no lack of takers respecting this heady doctrine, and because, I am afraid, that at least a seed of covetousness lurks in the heart of most, if not all, of us.

(53) "AND WHEN THEY HAD PASSED OVER, THEY CAME INTO THE LAND OF GENNESARET, AND DREW TO THE SHORE."

The phrase, *"And when they had passed over,"* refers to them coming, as is obvious, to the other side. The ship had begun without Jesus, but concludes with Him. What a Miracle!

The phrase, *"They came into the land of Gennesaret, and drew to the shore,"* was a fertile plain on the north shore of Galilee and west of Jordan about four miles long and two miles wide. It is said that it produced both temperate and tropical fruits (Dake).

(54) "AND WHEN THEY WERE COME OUT OF THE SHIP, STRAIGHTWAY THEY KNEW HIM,"

The phrase, *"And when they were come out of the ship,"* insinuates a ship of some size. It was probably one of the larger fishing vessels of Zebedee.

The phrase, *"Straightway they knew Him,"* proclaims no surprise at all, in view of the fact of His fame, due to the Healings and Miracles.

(55) "AND RAN THROUGH THAT WHOLE REGION ROUND ABOUT, AND BEGAN TO CARRY ABOUT IN BEDS THOSE THAT WERE SICK, WHERE THEY HEARD HE WAS."

The phrase, *"And ran through that whole region round about,"* proclaims runners going from village to village, announcing that Jesus was in the vicinity.

The phrase, *"And began to carry about in beds those that were sick, where they heard He was,"* proclaims the sick being carried any place they thought Jesus might be. It was a pathetic, yet understandable sight! This was the very height of His popularity, with the entirety of the countryside clamoring after Him. To be sure, this fame would arouse the ire of the Pharisees until they literally hated Him. Hence, at the time of the Crucifixion, it is said of Pilate, *"For he knew that for envy they had delivered Him"* (Mat. 27:18).

(56) "AND WHITHERSOEVER HE ENTERED, INTO VILLAGES, OR CITIES, OR COUNTRY, THEY LAID THE SICK IN THE STREETS, AND BESOUGHT HIM THAT THEY MIGHT TOUCH IF IT WERE BUT THE BORDER OF HIS GARMENT: AND AS MANY AS TOUCHED HIM WERE MADE WHOLE."

The phrase, *"And whithersoever He entered, into villages, or cities, or country,"* refers to the entirety of the countryside, which was looking to Him for healing and deliverance. The situation was the same whether it was a *"village,"* *"city,"* or *"countryside."* The idea is that the need was the same in all places, as the need is the same presently! If it is truly the Lord, it will be the same, and irrespective of the place or people.

The news media once questioned me as to the size of our largest audience respecting Television? At that time it happened to be New York City. Upon relating that to them, it was met with derision. In their thinking, how in the world could someone from the South garner

NOTES

that type of audience in New York City? This was the *"Big Apple,"* and they did not fall for such foolishness, etc.

However, my information was correct, which they found out when they checked the various ratings systems.

While it may have been a mystery to them, it was no mystery to me, simply because the need is the same, and the True Gospel of Jesus Christ meets that need.

The phrase, *"They laid the sick in the streets,"* referred to the tremendous number, and, as well, the logical place to meet Him, that is, if He came down that particular street. This would have been a situation astounding to behold!

No doubt, there were thousands of people who had come in from villages, cities, and the countryside, who desperately needed His Healing Power. They were not to be disappointed!

The Power of God must have been so strong at these particular times, that it could be sensed and felt by all. It was the greatest visitation by the Holy Spirit the world had ever known, and because it was through the Incarnate Son of God.

The phrase, *"And besought Him that they might touch if it were but the border of His garment,"* may well have been derived from the woman who touched the hem of His garment and was healed (Lk. 8:44). She had no doubt told many of her healing, and the manner in which it was derived, which will now be copied by many, possibly thousands.

The *"Border of His garment,"* consisted of a *"hem"* or *"tassel,"* which was attached to the garment, and was normally blue, and was meant to be a constant reminder of the Law of Moses, and that Israel's help came from the Lord.

The phrase, *"And as many as touched Him were made whole,"* must have spoke of thousands.

One can well see the thousands which gathered wherever Jesus was, and with these thousands attempting to touch Him. What a sight that must have been!

The moment they *"touched,"* they were made perfectly *"whole,"* and because of the Power of the Holy Spirit which emanated from Jesus.

As well, the moment they were healed, which was instantly, tremendous joy must have flooded the hearts and lives of those who experienced this Move of God, with shouts and acclamations of Praises to God literally filling the air. In effect, this could have happened to the entirety of Israel, and even the entirety of the world, had Israel accepted Christ, instead of rejecting Him.

In Truth, it was the Religious Hierarchy which rejected Him, with the ordinary people having very little to say in the matter. Actually, the Scripture says, *"The common people heard Him gladly"* (Mk. 12:37).

The world had never seen such before, and it will not see such again until Jesus comes back.

*"Hear the Blessed Saviour calling
   the oppressed,
"Oh ye heavy laden, come to Me and rest;
"Come, no longer tarry, I your load
   will bear,
"Bring Me every burden, bring Me
   every care."*

*"Have you by temptation often
   conquered been,
"Has a sense of weakness brought
   distress within?
"Christ will sanctify you, if you'll claim
   His best,
"In the Holy Spirit, He will give you rest."*

CHORUS:

*"Come unto Me; I will give you rest;
"Take My yoke upon you, hear Me and
   be blest;
"I am meek and lowly, come and trust
   My might;
"Come, My yoke is easy, and My
   burden's light."*

CHAPTER 7

(1) "THEN CAME TOGETHER UNTO HIM THE PHARISEES, AND CERTAIN OF THE SCRIBES, WHICH CAME FROM JERUSALEM."

The phrase, *"Then came together unto Him the Pharisees, and certain of the Scribes,"* should have been translated, *"And then . . . ."* Mark used the Greek word, *"kai,"* which means *"and."* This means that what is now given follows very closely that which went before.

In other words, the Religious Leaders were becoming alarmed at the tremendous popularity of Jesus.

The phrase, *"Which came from Jerusalem,"* concerns the Religious Hierarchy, or at least those sent by such.

The greatest hindrance to the Work of God has always been that which calls itself *"The Church."* It is Satan's master stroke. As such, it has taken more people to eternal hell than all the vice in the world.

If Satan can make people think they are saved, when, in reality, they aren't, he, in effect, does two things:

First, the deceived soul will be eternally lost. Second, the deceived soul will deceive others. That is why it was said of Jesus, *"And was moved with compassion toward them, because they were as sheep not having a shepherd"* (Mk. 6:34).

Jerusalem was supposed to be the city of the King, i.e., Jesus Christ, but it was the city that rejected and murdered its King. Hence Jesus would say, *"O Jerusalem, Jerusalem . . ."* (Mat 23:37).

(2) "AND WHEN THEY SAW SOME OF HIS DISCIPLES EAT BREAD WITH DEFILED, THAT IS TO SAY, WITH UNWASHEN, HANDS, THEY FOUND FAULT."

The phrase, *"And when they saw,"* means they were earnestly seeking some fault, for which they might accuse Him. How sad! They did not see the Healings, the Miracles, or the people delivered from demon spirits. Neither did they hear the gracious words which proceeded out of His Mouth. As well, they did not see that He fulfilled all the Prophecies concerning Himself as the Messiah.

Why could not they see the obvious?

As the Disciples were momentarily afflicted with the *"hardened heart,"* they were permanently afflicted.

What they would *"see"* would be nothing, but, yet, they would attempt to make a case of it.

It is sad that they were so close, and yet so far away! Tragically and sadly, millions fall into the same category. They are in the Church, but not in Christ. They talk about the Lord, but they do not know the Lord!

The phrase, *"Some of His Disciples eat bread with defiled, that is to say, with unwashen, hands,"* concerned a ceremonial law. It had nothing to do with sanitary cleanliness.

The Pharisees taught that demons (unseen) could sit on the hands of anyone, and, consequently, if the hands were not washed, the demons could be ingested. In effect, they were saying that the Disciples, by eating with unwashed hands, could now be looked at as *"demon possessed."*

NOTES

To be sure, there was absolutely no Scriptural foundation for this foolishness. However, as most who follow in that train, a little thing such as lacking Scriptural foundation, has never stopped them. In fact, the modern Church, and especially the Pentecostal and Charismatic variety, is rife with foolishness which has no Scriptural foundation. I speak of people barking like dogs, roaring like lions, and Preachers manipulating congregations, in order that they giggle and laugh, etc., all being referred to as a Work of the Holy Spirit. Most are not of the Holy Spirit, and because it has no Scriptural basis.

If any type of phenomenon cannot be adequately proved by Scripture, it is best to leave it alone. While the Lord certainly can give great joy to particular people, in fact, causing tremendous laughter, still, the idea that this is some type of *"gift"* to receive, is foolish. Unfortunately, many take something which is legitimately of the Lord, and make heresy of it.

The phrase, *"They found fault,"* means that this is exactly what they came to do.

(3) "FOR THE PHARISEES, AND ALL THE JEWS, EXCEPT THEY WASH THEIR HANDS OFT, EAT NOT, HOLDING THE TRADITION OF THE ELDERS."

The phrase, *"For the Pharisees, and all the Jews, except they wash their hands oft, eat not,"* presents the schism between Christ and the Religious Leaders of Israel. They constantly carried out this type of ceremonial religion. The placing of the *"Pharisees"* ahead of *"all the Jews,"* insinuates that the Pharisees were the promoters of these things, demanding that all of Israel follow.

Not only did they wash their hands, but they had to do it in a certain prescribed way. The washing was done with the clenched fist, the individual rubbing one hand and the arm up to the elbow with the other hand clenched. He then rubbed the palm of one hand with the other closed, so as to make sure that the part that touched the food would be clean. As stated, this was done because it was thought that an evil spirit by the name of Shibta sat upon the hands at night. Consequently, he must be washed off or he might be eaten, etc.

As well, the Pharisees had linked Salvation with the keeping of these ceremonial rulings.

The phrase, *"Holding the tradition of the Elders,"* presented the Pharisees claiming that

God had orally delivered this tradition to Moses on Mount Sinai, with it then being transmitted orally down to their time.

Of course it was totally untrue, and Jesus was quick to say so! The problem of men adding to the Word of God, or taking from it, has always been one of Satan's chief ploys.

The *"Elders"* were a group of men who held rank and position in Israel as members of the Great Council or Sanhedrin. Consequently, the entire weight of these Religious Leaders was ensconced behind these ceremonies which Jesus bitterly opposed, and which, therefore, placed Him in direct confrontation.

It is basically the same, as a Preacher of the Gospel today publicly stating that the ceremonies of Roman Catholicism or the denominationalism of many, if not most, Church organizations are unscriptural. As the position of Christ was not met with Grace and Kindness, likewise, it is not met with much Grace and Kindness presently!

However, if Jesus stood firmly for the True Gospel, which He certainly did, should not His Ministers follow suit? While it should be done with wisdom, still, it should be, and, in fact, must be done! Jude said, *"That ye should earnestly contend for the Faith which was once delivered unto the Saints"* (Jude 3). Regrettably, there aren't many true *"watchmen"* gracing modern pulpits.

(4) "AND WHEN THEY COME FROM THE MARKET, EXCEPT THEY WASH, THEY EAT NOT. AND MANY OTHER THINGS THERE BE, WHICH THEY HAVE RECEIVED TO HOLD, AS THE WASHING OF CUPS, AND POTS, BRASEN VESSELS, AND OF TABLES."

The phrase, *"And when they come from the market, except they wash, they eat not,"* presented these Religious Leaders and their followers spending an inordinate amount of time engaging in this foolishness — and foolishness it was!

The phrase, *"And many other things there be,"* presented the fact that there were many other ceremonies of similar nature as well. Actually, they were to even wash their *"cups"* and *"pots,"* etc., in a certain way. In fact, the entirety of the Law of Moses had been reduced by these individuals to mere ceremony.

These people were meticulous in holding to these outward ceremonies, and roundly condemning all who did not follow suit, but registered hate toward their fellowman, as well as all other types of heart impurities.

Regrettably, many foolish things, such as these *"washings"* of old, have made their way into modern Churches, making some Christian groups as ridiculous as the Pharisees (Mat. 15:1-3; 16:12; 23:1-33).

The true manner of the Believer should be that if something is condemned in the Scripture, then it should be left alone. However, if it is not definitely condemned, then each person should answer to the Lord according to his own conscience as to what He allows (Rom. 14:1-23; 15:1-3; I Cor. 8). Actually, sins that will cause the soul to be lost are listed in Mark 7:19-23; Romans 1:29-32; I Corinthians 6:9-11; Galatians 5:19-21; and Colossians 3:5-10.

Believers need to be careful that their Salvation does not consist merely of rules and regulations. And yet, there are things a Christian should do or not do!

Christians live on this earth, scattered in every society. As such, the Believer must be careful that the culture of the society in which he lives does not impact him in a negative way. Actually, upon accepting Christ, the Bible becomes the yardstick for life and conduct, thereby presenting its own culture.

The Bible teaches that every human culture is warped and twisted by the impact of sin. The perceptions of each generation, the basic desires that move human beings, the injustices institutionalized in every society, testify to sin's warping power.

Believers, constituting the Church, are gatherings called to display on earth a completely different set of values, not based on the cravings, lusts, or the boasting of sinful humanity. Rather than being squeezed into the world's mold, we are to be *"transformed by the renewing of our minds"* (Rom. 12:2).

Bluntly put, the Believer is one who *"does not live his earthly life for evil human desires, but rather for the Will of God"* (I Pet. 4:2).

If we remember that the world represents the systematic expression of human sin in human cultures, we understand why the Believer is not to be of the world, though he is in it (Jn. 17:14-18).

We are members of our society, yet the values we display and the structures we create in Church, home, and occupation are to be distinctively Christian, consequently of the Bible.

NOTES

This understanding helps us sense the deadliness of worldliness. Worldliness is not a matter of engaging in those practices that some question. It is unthinkingly adopting the perspectives, values, and attitudes of our culture, without bringing them under the Judgment of God's Word. It is carrying on of our lives as if we did not know Jesus (Mat. 16:26; Mk. 8:36; Lk. 9:25; I Cor. 5:10; 7:31, 33-34; II Cor. 7:10; I Jn. 2:15-16; 4:17 — Richards).

(5) "THEN THE PHARISEES AND SCRIBES ASKED HIM, WHY WALK NOT THY DISCIPLES ACCORDING TO THE TRADITION OF THE ELDERS, BUT EAT BREAD WITH UNWASHEN HANDS?"

The phrase, *"Then the Pharisees and Scribes asked Him,"* means in the Greek, that they kept on asking Him, therefore demanding an answer.

The question, *"Why walk not Thy Disciples according to the tradition of the Elders, but eat bread with unwashen hands?"*, hits at the very heart of what was then taking place in Israel, which was outward show only, and, therefore, brought Christ into direct conflict with these Religious Leaders.

At this time, Israel was eaten up with all of these ceremonies, which made the people very religious, consequently thinking they were very saved, but, in reality, were very lost!

When the *"six waterpots of stone"* were mentioned at the Marriage Feast in Cana (Jn. 2:6), these contained water, and were there for these ceremonial cleansings, in which the Jews constantly engaged.

Even though there was some water in these pots, Jesus gave instructions for them to be filled to the brim, and then proceeded to change it to wine. Consequently, His Miracle was a proclamation that He was going to bring men out of ceremonial religion, which, in effect, afforded no Salvation at all, into the Glory and Grace of God, which gave all Salvation. However, it is doubtful that anyone understood what He was doing, at least at that particular time.

Sadly, many if not most still cling to religious ceremonies, and, in Truth, do not really know the Saviour. As then, so now!

(6) "HE ANSWERED AND SAID UNTO THEM, WELL HATH ESAIAS PROPHESIED OF YOU HYPOCRITES, AS IT IS WRITTEN, THIS PEOPLE HONOURETH ME WITH

THEIR LIPS, BUT THEIR HEART IS FAR FROM ME."

The phrase, *"He answered and said unto them,"* runs through verse 13, and constitutes the startling answer given by Christ, which pulled no punches and minced no words. In other words, they knew exactly what and who He was talking about.

The phrase, *"Well hath Esaias (Isaiah) prophesied of you hypocrites,"* did not mean exactly that the Prophet had these people in mind when he prophesied these words, but that they (Pharisees) definitely fit what Isaiah said. As well, these Prophecies fit many others.

Actually, all should seriously ponder the answer given by Christ, consequently, checking our own hearts.

The word, *"well,"* adequately describes the spiritual condition of Israel at this time, proclaiming, and definitely so, that they fulfilled this Prophecy of Isaiah completely, with Jesus using the word again in verse 9.

The words, *"You hypocrites,"* actually say in the Greek, *"You, the hypocrites,"* which meant the outstanding ones.

The word, *"hypocrites,"* means that these people pretended to be something on the outside, which they were not on the inside.

The phrase, *"As it is written, This people honoureth Me with their lips, but their heart is far from Me,"* hits at the very heart of what True Salvation is and isn't (Isa. 29:13).

The Jews talked about God continuously, but, in reality, most did not know Him.

What did Jesus mean by the statement, *"But their heart is far from Me"*?

Wuest said that the picture is of one holding himself a great distance from someone else. He went on to say that the person is far off because he wants to be. In other words, they wanted their sin, while all the time professing their great closeness to God.

As Jesus called the Religious Leadership of Israel *"hypocrites,"* I wonder what His statement would be today concerning Religious Leaders?

If one is to look at the condition of the Church, especially in America and Canada, one would have to come to the conclusion that the assessment as given by Christ would be, and, in fact, is little different, concerning the modern Church, than Israel of old!

NOTES

Most of the old-line Churches, such as Baptists, Methodists, etc., *"have a form of Godliness, but deny the power thereof."* Paul then went on to say, *"From such turn away"* (II Tim. 3:5).

Respecting the Pentecostal and Charismatic varieties, every fad and phenomenon are being chased with vigor. We are laughing when we ought to be mourning, praising (by rote) when we ought to be praying, proclaiming fakery as Revival, when we ought to be repenting. The Pentecostal and Charismatic communities have come to the place that most little know anymore what is God or not God! The spirit of discernment is gone because the *"Spirit"* is gone!

(7) "HOWBEIT IN VAIN DO THEY WORSHIP ME, TEACHING FOR DOCTRINES THE COMMANDMENTS OF MEN."

The phrase, *"Howbeit in vain do they worship Me,"* presents a powerful statement indeed!

The word, *"vain,"* means *"without profit,"* or *"empty nothings."* In other words, it was *"worship"* that the Lord would not accept. Jesus had recently said to the woman at the well, *"The True worshiper shall worship the Father in Spirit and in Truth"* (Jn. 4:23).

A Prophecy was given a little after the turn of the century in the great Azusa outpourings, which said, *"In the last days My people will worship Me, to Whom they no longer pray!"*

I think it can properly be said that there has never been more worship than that presently offered in Pentecostal and Charismatic Churches. Worship has been carefully honed into a fine art. But yet, is it worship that God will accept?

Worship which He accepts, first of all, must be *"Truth,"* thereby accounting to the Word of God, and will always be inspired and attended by the Holy Spirit. As someone has said, *"The Lord is not looking for holy worship, but, instead, for 'holy worshipers.'"*

One should carefully analyze that statement, because it hits at the very heart of what Jesus was speaking of, and what the Spirit continues to speak of presently. In fact, there can be no holy worship without there first being *"holy worshipers!"*

Paul said this, *"Though I speak with the tongues of men and of angels, and have not charity (love), I am become as sounding brass, or a tinkling cymbal"* (I Cor. 13:1).

In other words, the Holy Spirit is saying through the Apostle, that the worship will sound in God's ears *"as sounding brass, or a tinkling cymbal."*

I am afraid that in many circles, the applauding of the flesh has been mistaken for *"worship."* The singer sings, and we applaud! The Preacher says something that we like, and we applaud! Has show business crept into our Churches?

While applauding or clapping with the hands is not condemned, and can be of the Lord if properly understood, still, applauding talent, presentation, or ability, can never be sanctioned by the Lord. The Lord will never honor the flesh, therefore, the Holy Spirit through Paul said, *"So then they that are in the flesh cannot please God"* (Rom. 8:8).

Is it possible that much of our so-called worship, is actually little more than the flesh, and, therefore, displeasing to God?

The phrase, *"Teaching for doctrines the commandments of men,"* presented the problem then, and presents the problem now!

What are *"commandments of men"* ?

Anything that is not Bible, or with the Word rightly divided, is, consequently, *"commandments of men,"* and must be rejected out of hand (II Tim. 2:15).

This would have included much, if not most, of the religious doctrine of Israel of that day.

Presently, it would include most, if not all, of Catholicism, as well as much of that taught in Protestant Churches.

For instance, the *"Kingdom Now"* or *"Political Message,"* is a *"commandment of men."* This teaching, by and large, denies the Rapture of the Church, claiming that the Book of Revelation and Daniel have mostly been fulfilled. It is a man centrist teaching, thereby placing man at the forefront, and, consequently, denying the rightful place of Christ. It teaches that by political means, the Millennium will ultimately be ushered in, with the Church at some point then notifying Christ that He can come back. It furthermore claims that the world is getting better, with the culture being Christianized and society being sanctified. As stated, all of this is to be done by Christians being voted into political office, etc.

Many Churches have bought into this *"Christian Coalition,"* declaring unity in favor of the political process.

The Bible declares the opposite, claiming that the world at the end time will face *"perilous*

times," ultimately being judged by God (II Tim. 3:1-5; Rev. Chpts. 6-19).

As well, the Faith Message or *"Prosperity Message,"* is another *"commandment of men."*

This, as well, shifts the emphasis from Christ to men. The end result is money, and irrespective of the heavy religious canopy.

This teaching openly concludes the *"Blessing of Abraham"* as material prosperity, which is not only error, but, actually, borders on blasphemy.

Inasmuch as greed permeates the hearts of most, if not all of us, at least in some fashion, this Doctrine is heady, and demands a wide following. Most want to be rich, and if they can do so under the guise of the *"Blessings of God,"* then it is legitimized, and despite the plain Command of the Word otherwise. Paul said, *"Perverse disputings of men of corrupt minds, and destitute of the truth, supposing that gain is Godliness: from such withdraw thyself"* (I Tim. 6:5-11).

In effect, this Doctrine, and whether it admits to it or not, claims that poverty is man's problem instead of sin, and, therefore, money is the solution instead of Salvation. As stated, they will deny this, but the *"fruit"* of their teaching borders down to prosperity instead of Salvation.

The *"Blessing of Abraham"* is *"Justification by Faith"* (Gen. 15:6). Paul said, *"That the Blessing of Abraham might come on the Gentiles through Jesus Christ; that we might receive the Promise of the Spirit through Faith"* (Gal. 3:14).

Even though there are many other *"commandments of men"* at this present time, still, these two mentioned are the most prominent at the moment, cutting across all denominational lines, thereby affecting the entirety of the Church, at least in one way or the other!

"Baptismal Regeneration" is another *"commandment of men,"* as is *"Sacrament Salvation"* (The Lord's Supper). *"Unconditional Eternal Security,"* *"Ultimate Reconciliation"* (the teaching that all will ultimately accept Christ, even the Devil, etc.), *"Denominationalism"* (the Church saves), *"Law-keeping"* (Seventh Day Adventism, as do many other Churches), are but to name a few!

Millions have lost their souls, simply because they did not know the Bible, and accepted for Gospel, Doctrines which were, in effect, *"commandments of men,"* and, thereby, not of God.

That is the reason it is incumbent upon every single Believer to know and understand the Word of God, and not to depend on others to interpret it for them.

(8) "FOR LAYING ASIDE THE COMMANDMENT OF GOD, YE HOLD THE TRADITION OF MEN, AS THE WASHING OF POTS AND CUPS: AND MANY OTHER SUCH LIKE THINGS YE DO."

The phrase, *"For laying aside the Commandment of God,"* refers to the Word of God laid side by side with traditions. The Religious Leaders, purposely and with forethought, made the decision to accept the *"tradition"* instead of the *"Word."*

(The Bible in that day consisted of the entirety of the Old Testament.)

It was not that the Religious Leaders did not have the Word of God, for, in fact, they did! It was that they did not want or desire the Word of God.

The phrase, *"Ye hold the tradition of men, as the washing of pots and cups,"* is said with some sarcasm. In other words, Jesus is saying that they had purposely selected these *"traditions"* which were not *"Commandments of God,"* and had purposely accepted these silly ceremonies relating to *"pots and cups."*

Tragically, the *"pots and cups"* would describe many Churches. In other words, they have a *"pot and cup"* religion!

As stated, these *"pots and cups"* were washed in particular ways, holding them in a certain manner, allowing the water to run in and on them in a certain fashion, with even the drying done a certain way. Great care was taken that all of this was done properly.

Jesus bitterly opposed this foolishness, while stating that True Salvation pertained to one's love of God, and fellow man, which had nothing to do with *"pots and cups."* Consequently, the contrast was succinctly drawn, and made glaringly obvious to all, as it was intended to do!

The phrase, *"And many other such like things ye do,"* which spoke of reams of other ceremonial laws which the Religious Leaders demanded that the people keep.

(9) "AND HE SAID UNTO THEM, FULL WELL YE REJECT THE COMMANDMENT OF GOD, THAT YE MAY KEEP YOUR OWN TRADITION."

NOTES

The phrase, *"And He said unto them, Full well ye reject the Commandment of God,"* speaks of biting sarcasm, as it was delivered by Christ. The word, *"reject,"* means they studied it minutely, and then purposely made the decision that it was not sufficient, and needed additional laws and commandments, etc. It was a studied and deliberate rejection.

Actually, this describes most all of mankind. The Holy Spirit so deliberately convicts men of sin, that there is no doubt as to Who and What He is, even though further knowledge may be limited. Consequently, any and all rejection is deliberate and studied.

The phrase, *"That ye may keep your own tradition,"* means these Religious Leaders purposely chose their own *"tradition"* over the Word of God.

This is not surprising at all, considering that man has by and large ever followed this course. Consequently, this is the choice that men must make the world over. It is either the Word of God or Islam, or Buddhism, or Shintoism, or Hinduism, or Catholicism, or Mormonism, or corrupt forms of Christianity.

The world now, as then, has two choices. It can accept God's Word, or man's word which includes all of these things we have named plus others.

Despite what the Mormons say, the Book of Mormon is not another *"Word of God,"* and neither is the *"Koran."*

As well, Churches, in their Constitution and Bylaws, must be very careful that the Word of God is strictly adhered to, and not their own fabrications.

As a minor example, one large Pentecostal Denomination had a ruling in its Bylaws opposing the wearing of any type of jewelry by women. However, in one of their bi-annual conclaves, this particular ruling was voted down, and, thereby, stricken from their Bylaws.

On the way to their meeting, some stopped by our Church for service. Of course, inasmuch as they were on their way to this meeting, the ladies had on no jewelry at all.

About a week later after their meeting had concluded, some, stopped again at our Church on the way back. This time many of their ladies had on much jewelry.

Even though this is a simple matter, and hardly worthy of mention, still, it does show the attitude of the heart.

The sudden appearance of jewelry on the advent of the abrogation of their ruling, means that in their heart they wanted to wear it all along. Such is obvious, because law cannot change a person's heart.

As well, if it was wrong all of those years, and before they went to this particular convention, how was it suddenly right after this convention? The Word of God does not change. It is the same one generation as the next.

The Truth is, this ruling of no jewelry was a *"tradition of men,"* and not of God. God's Word cannot be changed, while man's word can be changed, and is, in fact, changed constantly.

So, the Believer should set himself to keep only the Word of God, and not the commandments or traditions of men. If one keeps these silly traditions, even though he does not believe them in his heart, he is, whether he realizes it or not, abrogating the Word of God.

In fact, millions keep silly rules of Religious Denominations, even though they do not believe them, but do so in order to curry favor, or else to get along. Such is wrong!

If it is not the Word of God, and plainly so, it should be rejected out of hand, and refused to be kept. This is the position that Jesus took, as well as the Apostle Paul, and, consequently, should be taken by all.

How many times have Preachers said, *"I don't believe it that way, and I know it's not Bible, but it's what my Religious Denomination wants, and I suppose I have to do it"*?

No, they don't have to do it! They can get out of that Religious Denomination, and, in fact, should do so! Because, *"Whatsoever is not of Faith is sin"* (Rom. 14:23).

The phrase, *"That ye may keep your own tradition,"* means that to keep this *"tradition,"* is to reject the Word of God.

(In fact, some tradition may be right and Biblical, and should be kept, but not if it violates the Word of God — II Thess. 2:15.)

The State (Herod) put to death the Preacher of Righteousness, John the Baptist (Mat. 14:10), and the Church (the Scribes) corrupted the Word of Righteousness.

The Scribes and Pharisees washed cups and pots, but not their hearts. The ceremonial washing of their hands could not remove the guilt that stained them (Williams).

(10) "FOR MOSES SAID, HONOUR THY

FATHER AND THY MOTHER; AND, WHOSO CURSETH FATHER OR MOTHER, LET HIM DIE THE DEATH:"

The phrase, *"For Moses said,"* is meant to draw the people back to the Bible in relationship to their own tradition which is given in verse 11. In verses 6-10 and 13, the Lord declares the Bible, as written by Moses and Isaiah, to be *"The Word of God."* This is why it *"cannot be broken,"* because it is the Word of God; man's word can be broken, whether written or spoken, and often is, but not God's Word (Jn. 10:35).

The phrase, *"Honour thy father and thy mother,"* concerns honor that is due and not honor that is given out of the kindness of one's heart. It is in view of who and what they are, and their worth, which is their due. It is linked to reverence for the Heavenly Father.

The idea is, if there is no reverence for earthly parents, and irrespective as to what they may be, there will be little reverence for our Heavenly Parent.

Ideally, parents are to be as God, until the child reaches the age of accountability. During this formative time, and even thereafter, if the *"child is trained in the way he should go, when he is old, he will not depart from it"* (Prov. 22:6).

Regrettably, most parents do not do this, and suffer the bitter results. However, the attitude of sons and daughters must always be of reverence and respect toward their parents, and because of the symbolism of earthly parents in relationship to the Heavenly Parent.

The phrase, *"And whoso curseth father or mother, let him die the death,"* means *"to speak ill of,"* to *"revile,"* or *"abuse."*

According to Wuest, it does not mean *"to curse"* in the sense of Galatians 1:9, where *"accursed,"* in that instance is a Divine curse, and speaks of one eternally losing his soul.

The type of *"curse"* spoken of by Jesus is of far less severity, but yet carries with it a dire sentence. The idea is this:

If he, who, by words, only speaks evil of his Father or his Mother is, by law, deserving of death, how much more is he deserving of death who wrongs them by deed, and deprives them of that support which he owes them by the law of nature; and not only so, but teaches others so from Moses' seat, as you Scribes and Pharisees do when you say, *"It is Corban,"* i.e., *"Given to God"* (Bickersteth.)

The sin of ill treatment of parents, as spoken here by Christ, is one of the crowning sins presently of America. Consequently, this is, at least one of, the reasons for the terrible mayhem now prevalent among the youth. Death, and even violent death, ultimately follows in the train of those who disregard this Commandment.

The honoring of the Father and Mother is the Fifth Commandment, and concludes with a Promise, *"That thy days may be long upon the land which the Lord thy God giveth thee"* (Ex. 20:12). Consequently, the young in America, and even down to sub-teens, are dying violent deaths by the tens of thousands, and if the root cause could be traced, it would be the disregarding of the Fifth Commandment. Honor of parents brings long life, while dishonor brings the opposite!

(11) "BUT YE SAY, IF A MAN SHALL SAY TO HIS FATHER OR MOTHER, IT IS CORBAN, THAT IS TO SAY, A GIFT, BY WHATSOEVER THOU MIGHTEST BE PROFITED BY ME; HE SHALL BE FREE."

The phrase, *"But ye say,"* presents a stark contrast to the Word of God. In essence, the entirety of the Church falls into this choice. It is either *"The Word says,"* or *"You say!"* Regrettably, *"You say,"* has replaced, *"The Word says,"* in too many religious circles.

The phrase, *"If a man shall say to his Father or Mother, It is Corban, that is to say, a gift,"* gives the explanation of the word, *"Corban."* In other words, the erring son could absolve himself of responsibility to his parents respecting their support and upkeep during their old age, by simply declaring that his material possessions were dedicated to God, and, consequently, he could not help his parents.

The phrase, *"By whatsoever thou mightest be profited by Me; he shall be free,"* presents a serious spectacle indeed!

The idea is this: The Pharisees were teaching these people to twist the Word of God for their own pecuniary gain. By claiming their material possessions had been given to God, and, therefore, could not be used for support of their parents, made God a part of their lie. Consequently, their sin was compounded. They were making *"profit"* by the elicitation of God's Word, hence the phrase, *"profited by Me."*

All sin is evil, but this sin is even worse, because it makes God a part of these nefarious

activities. Actually, the *"Prosperity Message"* is very similar, at least as far as making God a part of the sin.

As an example, a Preacher addressing his Television audience, suddenly acted as if the Spirit of the Lord was upon him, then told his audience if they would call in the next five minutes, whatever they gave to the Work of God, would be given back to them a hundredfold, or some such number.

In Truth, the Lord had not told him any such thing, and because the very nature of his statement spawned covetousness in the heart instead of love for God. Consequently, by claiming the Lord had told him this, he made the Lord a part of his sin. To be frank, it was a far worse sin than someone pulling a gun on a bank teller and demanding money. At least the bank robber did not include God in his activity. To be sure, the *"Prosperity Message"* is made up mostly of these types of sins.

While it is certainly true that God does bless those who give to Him, still, if that is the motivation, then the entirety of what the Holy Spirit is teaching is lost. The Believer is to give to God to *"prove the sincerity of his love,"* and not because God is some type of Las Vegas slot machine (II Cor. 8:8).

As well, any time a person says, *"The Lord told me,"* when, in reality, the Lord has said nothing, the lie of this person is compounded by the effort to make God a part of it. Among other things, this is *"taking the Name of the Lord in vain,"* with the penalty stated, *"For the Lord will not hold him guiltless that taketh His Name in vain"* (Ex. 20:7).

Even though no set penalty is stated in the Third Commandment, death is specified in Leviticus 24:10-16, 23, and Numbers 15:30-31.

While we are no longer living under Law, but under Grace, the penalty of these Commandments is still in force. And while it is true that people are not presently stoned to death for breaking these Laws, God still continues to exact the toll.

Even though the Pharisees told their followers, *"You shall be free,"* by following their nefarious counsel, thereby not having to care for their aged parents, still, Jesus, in effect, is saying, *"You will not go free,"* God will collect!

(12) "AND YE SUFFER HIM NO MORE TO DO AUGHT FOR HIS FATHER OR HIS MOTHER;"

The word, *"Corban,"* came from the area in the Temple where offerings were deposited and were called the *"Corbanas,"* or *"Sacred treasury."* Hence to say of anything, *"It is Corban,"* was to say that it had a prior and more sacred destination. Consequently, when the son or daughter said to the parent, *"It is Corban,"* it meant it was already appropriated for another purpose, and could not be given to them. Thus the parents would be silenced and alarmed, choosing rather to perish of hunger than to rob God.

To such extremities did these covetous Scribes and Pharisees drive their victims, who were the aged parents, with no way to care for themselves.

In actuality, what was happening was grievous indeed! The Scribe would make a deal with an individual who did not want to care for his parents. For a percentage, the son could claim that his material possessions were dedicated to God, with the Scribe verifying his action. Consequently, the Scribe was enriched, with the son side-stepping his responsibilities, but with the helpless parent suffering greatly.

There was no separation of Church and State in those days, with the Church, in effect, being the State. Consequently, the actions of the individual were legalized, and because of the crookedness of both, the Scribe and the son (or the daughter).

(13) "MAKING THE WORD OF GOD OF NONE EFFECT THROUGH YOUR TRADITION, WHICH YE HAVE DELIVERED: AND MANY SUCH LIKE THINGS DO YE."

The phrase, *"Making the Word of God of none effect through your tradition,"* constitutes a serious sin indeed, and is the crowning sin of the present as well! It means, *"To render void, deprive of force and authority, to invalidate."*

In other words, they figured out a way to get around the Word of God, thereby, absolving themselves of responsibilities, and, at the same time, making themselves believe they were righteously keeping the Laws of God.

This is one of the greatest ploys of Satan, attempting to get people to twist the Word, making it seem to justify their sinful actions.

Primarily, that is what Paul was speaking of when he asked the question, *"Shall we continue in sin, that Grace may abound?"* (Rom. 6:1).

He answered, *"God forbid."* Individuals were taking the great Doctrine of Grace to mean that

it really didn't matter what type of sin they committed, Grace would cover it. In other words, they were using Grace as a license to sin. In doing so, they were subtly twisting the Word of God, in order to make it justify their sinful actions. As stated, this sin abounds even now, and maybe more than ever!

The phrase, *"Which ye have delivered,"* referred to the oral laws of the Pharisees, which were handed down from generation to generation. The Pharisees, to whom our Lord was speaking, were adding weight to these laws by themselves transmitting them to their posterity (Wuest).

The phrase, *"And many such like things do ye,"* means that this of which Christ has spoken was only a sample of the many ways in which the Commandments of God were twisted, distorted, and annulled by these rabbinical traditions of men.

No doubt, there were many cases of parents who lived profligate lives, squandering their income, thereby making no provisions for their old age, thereby, putting a hardship on their sons and daughters. In these cases, which no doubt were many, some offspring, at times in dire straits themselves, balked at caring for such parents. However, the Commandment of the Lord to honor parents, was not predicated on their conduct, but, instead, on the symbolism of the Heavenly Father. In other words, irrespective as to the conduct of the parents, the obligation of the offspring did not change. Showing *"honor"* and despite conduct, showed a respect and understanding of the Word of God. As stated, and in a sense, the parents were a symbol of the Heavenly Father, and should be treated accordingly, at least as far as possible, and irrespective of their actions.

(14) "AND WHEN HE HAD CALLED ALL THE PEOPLE UNTO HIM, HE SAID UNTO THEM, HEARKEN UNTO ME EVERY ONE OF YOU, AND UNDERSTAND:"

The phrase, *"And when He had called all the people unto Him, He said unto them,"* constitutes a serious clash between Christ and the *"Pharisees and certain of the Scribes, which came from Jerusalem"* (vs. 1).

Inasmuch as these dignitaries, fault-finders we might quickly add, had come on the scene, quite possibly the crowd of people had retired into the background. Now Jesus calls them forth, because what He has to say primarily is to them.

The phrase, *"Hearken unto Me every one of you, and understand,"* will contain the most serious and important words they had ever heard. The people have a choice, they can hear Him, or the Pharisees. They cannot hear both, because the teaching of each is diametrically opposed to the other. Several things of immeasurable significance are done here. They are:

1. Jesus, would not go over too well with present-day modern unity Preachers. As a result of His bold statements, He would not be, presently, as then, appreciated at all!

2. Inasmuch as what He was saying concerned the very Salvation of the souls of these people, and all others for that matter, He would be bold in His assertions, leaving absolutely no room for doubt respecting what He was talking about.

3. In His delivery, and publicly, He did not mince words, plainly pointing out the error of the Pharisees and Scribes, and doing it in no uncertain terms. As stated, His manner of approach would not have been too very much appreciated at the present.

4. Any modern Preacher of the Gospel should desire to follow Christ in this respect. While we should not go out of our way to antagonize, and we certainly must use wisdom, still, the Truth must be presented, and in a way that leaves no room for misunderstanding. To do this, error must be pointed out, as well as Truth. If Jesus set the example, and He did, then we must follow!

(15) "THERE IS NOTHING FROM WITH-OUT A MAN, THAT ENTERING INTO HIM CAN DEFILE HIM: BUT THE THINGS WHICH COME OUT OF HIM, THOSE ARE THEY THAT DEFILE THE MAN."

The phrase, *"There is nothing from without a man, that entering into him can defile him,"* is referring to food, and not intoxicating drinks, narcotics, poisons, tobacco, and numerous other things. Actually, Paul dealt with this extensively, and quite possibly from these very Words of Christ (I Cor. 8:7-8; II Cor. 7:1).

The Pharisees and Scribes dealt exclusively with that which is outward, even to the washing of cups and pots in a certain way, but not their hearts. The ceremonial washing of their

hands could not remove the guilt that stained them, as Jesus mentions here.

Too much of the modern Church world is made up, as well, of rules and regulations that have little to do with one's spirituality. It is all of religion and not of God. However, religious men love to make rules, which only gender more strife. Somehow it makes them feel religious, and, therefore, acceptable to God. In Truth, these things pull people away from the Lord, instead of closer to Him.

The phrase, *"But the things which come out of him, those are they that defile the man,"* presents the very heart of the problem of humanity.

Concerning this statement, Bickersteth translated the Words of Christ in this fashion: *"The Scribes teach you that it is not lawful to eat with unwashed hands, because unwashed hands make the food unclean, and unclean food defiles the soul. But in this they err; because it is not that which enters from without into the mouth, but that which proceeds from within through the mouth, and so from the heart, if it be impure — this defiles the man."*

(16) "IF ANY MAN HAVE EARS TO HEAR, LET HIM HEAR."

This statement is used some fifteen times by Christ, seven times in the Gospels, and eight times in the Book of Revelation (Mat. 11:15; 13:9, 43; Mk. 4:9; 7:16; Lk. 8:8; 14:35; Rev. 2:7, 11, 17, 29; 3:6, 13, 22; 13:9).

In effect, the Lord is telling the people that they have a choice. They can hear Him or the Pharisees, but, as stated, not both! They now know the Truth, and will have to make a decision. Of course, it will cost something to side with Christ, as it always does. This is what Jesus was speaking of in the Beatitudes, when He said, *"Blessed are they which are persecuted for Righteousness' sake"* (Mat. 5:10).

Of course, it should be obvious to all as to how important it is for the True Gospel of Jesus Christ to be preached. Tragically, most people only hear error, or a mixture of Truth and error. As a result, it reaps its deadly harvest.

It should be obvious that very little True Gospel was preached and taught in the Israel of Jesus' day. It is the same presently, and, in fact, always has been.

Sadly, few Believers are truly led by the Spirit, resulting in most not even really knowing what is right and wrong. They are rather led by the flesh (self), which leads to corruption.

John said, *"But the anointing which ye have received of Him abideth in you, and ye need not that any man teach you: but as the same anointing teacheth you of all things, and is Truth, and is no lie, and even as it has taught you, ye shall abide in Him"* (I Jn. 2:27).

John wasn't meaning by this statement that Spirit-led Teachers are not needed. Instead, he is saying that if one is truly filled with the Spirit and, correspondingly, led by the Spirit, a part of the Spirit's office work will be to anoint the Believer to discern between right and wrong teaching.

I heard a dear friend years ago, who is now with Jesus, make a statement which impressed me greatly. He mentioned how he was baptized in the Holy Spirit when he was fourteen years old. He went on to tell how his entire life was changed, with the Holy Spirit drawing him to Christ in a manner he had never known before.

He told how he was so hungry for God that he looked for Revival meetings to attend each and every night.

He attended a particular meeting, not really knowing the Doctrine espoused by these people. He went on to say how certain parts of the service were very helpful and blessed, but yet certain things were said and done that did not quite witness with his spirit. As stated, he was only fourteen years old, knew very little about the Word, and had only been filled with the Spirit a short time. And yet, the Spirit of God, in keeping with this very Passage in I John 2:27, told him that something was wrong.

He then found out they were teaching the *"Oneness Doctrine,"* which is unscriptural. As stated, being only fourteen years old, he had no knowledge at all of this Teaching, except that the Holy Spirit informed him that something was not quite right. Upon looking into it, he would find the error of which the Holy Spirit had already informed him.

Why is it that all Believers, even Spirit-filled Believers, are not led accordingly?

To be saved or even Spirit-filled, does not necessarily mean that one is Spirit-led. To be Spirit-led, one has to walk close to God, which necessitates a strong prayer life and deep consecration. As well, the Holy Spirit will always draw one close to the Word, that he may *"hear*

and understand." In Truth, this fourteen-year-old boy just mentioned, probably had a greater knowledge of the Word of God even at that tender age, than most many years his senior. Therefore, the Spirit of God had a foundation on which to lead and guide. With the scant attention most Believers give to the Word of God, it is no wonder that they are not Spirit-led! To be Spirit-filled, as stated, is not necessarily to be Spirit-led. That takes a consecration to the Lord that most, regrettably, do not have.

To be led other than by the Spirit, is to be led by the flesh, and, therefore, to fall into the trap of Romans 7:15, *"For that which I do I allow not: for what I would, that do I not; but what I hate, that do I."*

To be led by the Spirit, is to *"walk not after the flesh, but after the Spirit"* (Rom. 8:1).

(17) AND WHEN HE WAS ENTERED INTO THE HOUSE FROM THE PEOPLE, HIS DISCIPLES ASKED HIM CONCERNING THE PARABLE."

The phrase, *"And when He was entered into the house from the people,"* probably referred to Peter's house.

It seems that He made the statement as outlined in 14-16, and then went into the house, which may have been immediate or some hours later.

The phrase, *"His Disciples asked Him concerning the Parable,"* proclaims their curiosity as to what He was talking about. Matthew said that Peter is the one who posed the question, with the others joining in (Mat. 15:15).

(18) "AND HE SAITH UNTO THEM, ARE YE SO WITHOUT UNDERSTANDING ALSO? DO YE NOT PERCEIVE, THAT WHATSOEVER THING FROM WITHOUT ENTERETH INTO THE MAN, IT CANNOT DEFILE HIM;"

The question, *"And He saith unto them, Are ye so without understanding also?"*, shows some disappointment on the part of Christ respecting His Disciples.

The teaching of the Pharisees and Scribes was so ingrained in them, as well as all of Israel, that most all had bought into this theology. Their Salvation had become a series of *"dos"* and *"don'ts."* As well, it was almost, if not altogether, pertaining to the externals. The Law of Moses had been so twisted and perverted, that its true meaning had long since been lost on the people.

In this, we find the terrible sin of man in trying to make a religion out of anything, even the very Word of God. Man is not content to accept the Word at face value, but must put his own gloss onto it, thereby, perverting its true meaning, which is Satan's intention! That is the reason Paul said, *"Study to shew thyself approved unto God, a workman that needeth not to be ashamed, rightly dividing the Word of Truth"* (II Tim. 2:15).

Regrettably, most Preachers do not *"rightly divide the Word of Truth!"* So, the Words of Jesus, as straight to the point as they were, came as a shock to His listeners, with even His Disciples little understanding what He said.

The question, *"Do ye not perceive, that whatsoever thing from without entereth into the man, it cannot defile him,"* was the exact opposite of what the Pharisees and Scribes taught. As stated, almost, if not entirely all, which they taught and believed pertained to the externals.

By this statement, Jesus shoots down the moralists, as well as every other religion in the world, for all religions work from the same principle, the externals.

As well, He shows, and in no uncertain terms, that man's problem cannot be solved by whatever is addressed externally, but only by a change of the heart, which is the cause of man's difficulties.

Consequently, this means that all psychology, at least as it attempts to adjust man's behavior patterns, is doomed to failure. This would go, as well, for all self-help programs. All are a waste of time, which should be obvious, considering the one-hundred percent failure rate.

This means that all the rehab centers in America and around the world are of no use whatsoever to the poor individual who desperately needs help.

This means that Alcoholics Anonymous is of no avail, even though in some few cases it may help the person to quit drinking. While that is certainly commendable, still, the individual, at least as far as his heart is concerned, is unchanged. Consequently, he (or she) continues to be what he says he is, *"a recovering alcoholic!"*

However, when Jesus changes the heart, He, as well, changes the life. He does not try to patch up the old man, but, in reality, makes of the person *"a new creature,"* and does so *"in Himself, Christ Jesus"* (II Cor. 5:17).

When man fell in the Garden of Eden, he fell from a position of God-consciousness to a position of self-consciousness, hence, the constant preoccupation with *"self."* As well, he changed lords, in that Satan is now man's lord. Consequently, *"The lust of man's father* (the Devil) *man will do"* (Jn. 8:44). This is the reason for all the hate, evil, murder, violence, and mayhem in the world today! Regrettably, the so-called intelligentsia of America and the world, continues to look for the cause of evil elsewhere! However, it is found in man's own heart (Jer. 17:9).

So, man's defilement is not his surroundings, and neither are the surroundings his cure.

The Federal Government has spent, and continues to spend, hundreds of billions of dollars on housing, environment, and education, thinking that such will stem the crime rate among certain segments of society, but to no avail! Almost everyday a new program is announced, which the social planners believe will solve the problem. However, with the passing of time and the spending of more billions of dollars, the situation is no better, but, instead, worse. It is, as someone has said, *"about like putting lipstick on a hog!"*

To these ills of humanity, which cause all the heartache in the world, Jesus is the only Answer. To be sure, He is not a part of the answer, but, in Truth, the only Answer!

(19) "BECAUSE IT ENTERETH NOT INTO HIS HEART, BUT INTO THE BELLY, AND GOETH OUT INTO THE DRAUGHT, PURGING ALL MEATS?"

The phrase, *"Because it entereth not into his heart,"* proclaims every effort by man to change human behavior, and, as stated, to be futile. How can it change man, when it does not go to the source of the problem, i.e., the heart, the seed of all intellect and will?

The phrase, *"But into the belly, and goeth out into the draught, purging all meats,"* refers to the digestive and elimination system of the human body. As an aside, this, as well, destroys the Seventh Day Adventist teaching that it is sinful to eat pork.

The teaching of Jesus is so simple, simple enough in fact that no one need have any problem understanding, and, yet, most of the world does not understand it. It keeps trying to change man by dealing with the externals.

(20) "AND HE SAID, THAT WHICH COMETH OUT OF THE MAN, THAT DEFILETH THE MAN."

The phrase, *"And He said,"* refers to the Words of Jesus, and that which is Law and Gospel. As such, it is said in contradistinction to the Pharisees and Scribes. In other words, He totally contradicted them.

The phrase, *"That which cometh out of the man, that defileth the man,"* gives the cause of all of man's inhumanity to man, and is listed in the following verses.

It means, and as we have said, that man's problem comes from within him, and not from without. Consequently, a change of environment will not solve the problem; education will not solve the problem; psychology will not solve the problem. Actually, other than Christ, the problem, and whatever it is, is unsolvable.

(21-22) "FOR FROM WITHIN, OUT OF THE HEART OF MEN, PROCEED EVIL THOUGHTS, ADULTERIES, FORNICATIONS, MURDERS,

"THEFTS, COVETOUSNESS, WICKEDNESS, DECEIT, LASCIVIOUSNESS, AN EVIL EYE, BLASPHEMY, PRIDE, FOOLISHNESS:"

The phrase, *"For from within,"* now, and in no uncertain terms, gives the cause of man's inhumanity to man, the heart, and what proceeds from it.

The phrase, *"Out of the heart of men,"* proclaims the evil things that come from within and defile the man. This statement by Him, Who is the Truth, destroys the belief that the natural heart is good, and makes foolish modern efforts to improve human nature.

The assumption that only what goes into the heart defiles it, is here denied; and the necessity of the creation of a new heart declared. It is evident that what comes out of the heart must exist in the heart (Williams).

As well, the word, *"proceed,"* means that it is a fountain constantly producing that which is evil. Consequently, it is a sobering thought. The action which proceeds from the evil heart is as follows:

1. *"Evil thoughts"*: Wuest says that the word, *"thoughts,"* carries the idea of discussion or debate, with an under-thought of suspicion or doubt, either in one's own mind, or with another. The idea is that in the unconverted heart and mind, all the thoughts which proceed, are *"evil,"*

NOTES

and irrespective as to how they may appear the other way. The unregenerate man is not capable of any other type of *"thoughts."* Whether those thoughts are *"good"* or *"evil,"* they all come from the same *"Tree of the knowledge of good and evil,"* and are, consequently, wrong (Gen. 2:17).

The *"good"* side of this tree greatly deceives men, because they think it is the opposite of the *"evil,"* not realizing that it all comes from the same tree.

2. *"Adulteries"*: Adultery is unlawful sexual relationship between men and women, single or married. It is not as some think, sexual relationship between married people, with fornication pertaining to those not married.

Dake says this term is not used in the broader sense of all forms of unchastity as is fornication. All adultery is fornication, but all fornication is not adultery.

3. *"Fornications"*: This speaks of an individual going from one sexual partner to the next. In other words, no sooner is one conquest made than another is sought. For instance, Esau was a fornicator (Heb. 12:16).

As well, the sin of fornication refers to *"incest"* (I Cor. 5:1; 10:8); idolatry and adultery in honor of idol gods (II Chron. 21:11; Isa. 23:17; Ezek. 16:15; Acts 15:20, 29; Rev. 2:14-21; 14:8); natural harlotry (Jn. 8:41; I Cor. 6:13-18); spiritual harlotry (Ezek. 16:15, 26, 29; Rev. 17:2-4; 18:3-9; 19:2); sodomy and male prostitution (Rom. 1:24-29; I Cor. 6:9-11; II Cor. 12:21; Gal. 5:19; Eph. 5:3; Col. 3:5; Heb. 12:16; Jude 6-7).

I think it is obvious that these Scriptures do not apply to single people only. If not, then fornication does not apply only to single people as some teach.

4. *"Murders"*: The Greek word is *"phonoi,"* and means *"to kill,"* or to *"spoil or mar the happiness of another."* It also refers to "hatred" (I Jn. 3:15).

Consequently, this sin of *"murder"* refers to a lot more than the malicious taking of another human life.

5. *"Thefts"*: This sin is the secret or open removal of the property of another, any injury done to it, and carelessness about that which belongs to a neighbor. However, it refers to more than just the act of taking real property, but also refers to the destruction of one's name by slander or whispering, etc.

6. *"Covetousness"*: This is a greedy desire to have more. As one American Industrialist said, upon being asked as to how much more property he wanted, his answer was revealing, *"Only that which borders mine!"*

However, the word, *"covetousness,"* speaks of far more than just the desire, but speaks of the action of the individual in eagerly attempting to obtain it, if at all possible.

This is what Paul was speaking of when he spoke of his efforts to keep the Law. He found that not committing the act was not enough. As well, he must not desire to do it, which came under the last Commandment, *"Thou shalt not covet."* In other words, when he was about to congratulate himself, *"The Commandment came, sin revived, and he died,"* i.e., failed spiritually, because the desire was still there (Rom. 7:7, 9).

All religion is made up more or less of rules and regulations, which automatically throw the adherent into *"covetousness."* In other words, he may not do what his rule says he cannot do, but that rule cannot keep him from desiring to do it. Consequently, the evil heart is shown to be what it is, and, therefore, produces.

7. *"Wickedness"*: This speaks of depravity, and not merely in the abstract, but, in effect, active wickedness. It has the idea of being *"dangerous and destructive."* In other words, this type of wickedness is in active opposition to the good.

Some types of the wicked are content to perish in their own corruption. That is bad enough! However, the type of wickedness here spoken of by Jesus, speaks of the individual who is not content unless he pulls everything else down with him in his own destruction.

An excellent example is Adolph Hitler, who gave instructions that everything was to be destroyed in Germany, when it became obvious that the war was lost.

Even though that is an extreme example, millions follow in his train, and because they have the same evil heart.

8. *"Deceit"*: Deceit is more than a *"lie."* In its most simplistic definition, it is a complex web of ideas, which lead one astray. The word suggests undependable behavior in a given relationship. The person who thus deals falsely, ultimately causes harm to others.

The word violates the basic relationship of trust and honesty that ought to exist between

human beings, and is intended to mislead and so to harm another person.

The word, *"deceit,"* has to do with error urged by external evil powers and by things locked into the world's way of thinking.

Satan is the epitome of deception, having used this method to ensnare Adam and Eve. Consequently, man is very easily deceived, because his entire premise operates on a foundation of deception, as a result of the Fall. *"Deceit"* is still Satan's greatest weapon.

The world is fond of what it refers to as *"subjective truth,"* which means it may not be true for all, but it is *"true for you."*

In contrast, the Lord and His Word operate on absolute (objective) Truth. The Bible clearly affirms objective Truth, and it grounds that belief in the Biblical concept of God. God is Truth. All that He says is in strict accord with reality. His Words are therefore firm and trustworthy.

By contrast, we human beings are trapped in illusion. We struggle to understand the meaning of the world around us and of our experiences. Unaided, we cannot distinguish between the real and the counterfeit, the Truth and the lie. Consequently, all who do not know Christ, and all who know Him, but do not rely solely on Him, are perfect targets for Satan.

Only reliance on God's Word, which is true, enables us to build our lives on a firm foundation.

That is the reason, if something is not grounded firmly in the Word of God, it must be firmly denied.

9. *"Lasciviousness"*: This is unrestrained sexual instinct. Regrettably, it is the sin of the age!

10. *"An evil eye"*: This speaks of those who look at other people, and things, with the idea of positive, injurious activity in order to secure what is desired.

As well, it speaks of one who sees *"evil"* wherever he looks, and because his eye is *"evil."* To this *"eye,"* Godliness is looked at as a scheme, etc.

This is at least one of the reasons the news media cannot write anything good about the Work of the Lord. They see it through *"an evil eye,"* consequently, attributing to it every devious practice.

Years ago, when our Television audience became quite large, we attracted media attention. I had the erroneous idea that if I was totally open with reporters, they would not write or say that which was error. However, I was soon to find out differently.

I found they had no interest in the Truth. They had already made up their minds before the investigation started, consequently, the situation was whatever they wanted it to be, and because their eye was *"evil."* They saw falsehood, chicanery, dishonesty, and deception in every act.

One noted investigative reporter went with us to a particular Crusade, and upon coming back, he hit me with this bombshell.

"I believe you're stealing money!", he said.

I looked at him a moment, taken aback somewhat by his accusation, and then patiently attempted to explain to him how difficult such would be even if I wanted to.

After the explanation, I asked him why I would want to do such a thing, especially considering that I sold more Gospel records (at that time) than anyone. *"All I have to do,"* I said to him, *"is to take a royalty on all these records, which is legal and moral; however, I don't even do that!"* I explained to him.

Completely discounting all I had said, he remonstrated, *"I still believe you're stealing money!"*

I then looked at him and said, *"I know why you think that!"*

"Why?", he exclaimed!

"If you were in my shoes, you would steal money!"

I will never forget his answer. He turned to me and stared at me for a while without saying anything, and then said, *"Yes, if I could do it and get by with it, I would steal every dollar I could lay my hands on."*

Consequently, he was judging me according to his own evil heart. He had *"an evil eye!"*

I learned the hard way that Truth meant nothing to these people, and because of this very Word spoken here by Christ.

11. *"Blasphemy":* Wuest said that this word does not necessarily speak of blasphemy against God, but can be used of malicious misrepresentation of another person or thing.

12. *"Pride":* This is the sin of an uplifted heart against God and man, and is the foundation sin of all sin.

13. *"Foolishness":* This proclaims the fact that all evil terminates in the loss of all moral

and intellectual illumination. Consequently, it becomes easier to understand the foolish ideas presented by those who call themselves *"intellectuals"* respecting the solving of the human problem.

It also speaks of the Church, and, above all, the Church, which has left the tried and true Ways of the Lord, and resorted rather to the *"foolishness"* of the ways of the world.

(23) "ALL THESE EVIL THINGS COME FROM WITHIN, AND DEFILE THE MAN."

Men, that is to say, are the efficient causes of their own choices. But yet, that is only half right. Because without God in the soul, man's choices are heavily influenced and weighted by Satanic influence.

Jesus ended this statement in Matthew 15:20, by saying, *"But to eat with unwashen hands defileth not the man."*

Once again, He is not speaking of proper sanitary necessity, but, instead, the religious practice of washing demons off before eating, etc.

With His short statements, He succinctly addresses the real cause of man's problems, and the real cure. Men are ever treating symptoms, while ignoring the cause. Jesus addresses the cause, but instead of responding to it with treatment, He responds with deliverance (Lk. 4:18).

That, in a nutshell, is the basic difference between the gospel of psychology and the Gospel of Jesus Christ. The first treats the problem, which, in reality, only treats the symptom, while Jesus delivers man from the problem.

(24) "AND FROM THENCE HE AROSE, AND WENT INTO THE BORDERS OF TYRE AND SIDON, AND ENTERED INTO AN HOUSE, AND WOULD HAVE NO MAN KNOW IT: BUT HE COULD NOT BE HID."

The phrase, *"And from thence He arose,"* speaks of the clash between Himself and the Pharisees and Scribes. He takes leave of this area.

The phrase, *"And went into the borders of Tyre and Sidon,"* has the idea from the Greek Text, as meaning that our Lord did not merely cross over the border into Phoenician territory, but, instead, went deep into the heart of that country.

The phrase, *"And entered into an house, and would have no man know it,"* seemingly refers to a desire to seek rest, as had been admonished in 6:31.

The phrase, *"But He could not be hid,"* referred to His fame which had preceded Him.

Consequently, the stage is set for the deliverance of a Gentile girl.

To whom the house belonged is not stated; however, what a privilege it was to have Jesus enter under its roof. As well, He stands ready to come into any house, which alone can make it a home.

When I was a child, my parents did not have much as far as worldly goods were concerned. However, the day my Mother and Dad said *"Yes"* to Christ, was the greatest day of my life. Everything changed, and for the better!

Before, we had only a *"house,"* and now, we had a *"home!"* To be sure, nothing had really changed as far as the furnishings or the house itself were concerned. However, the hearts of my parents had changed, with love replacing hate. Now this *"home"* became the most wonderful place on earth!

As well, had my parents come into millions of dollars, and, consequently, been able to construct a mansion, at least as far as externals are concerned, it would still have been a place of misery, if they had not found Jesus.

Millions think that by building a new house, they have found the secret to life. They soon find that life really has not changed. In fact, and in Truth, it can only change when Jesus comes into the heart.

So a *"home"* does not consist of finery, but, rather, who lives in it. And who lives in it determines what it will be, according to who lives in them, whether Christ or Satan.

(25) "FOR A CERTAIN WOMAN, WHOSE YOUNG DAUGHTER HAD AN UNCLEAN SPIRIT, HEARD OF HIM, AND CAME AND FELL AT HIS FEET:"

The phrase, *"For a certain woman,"* refers to a Gentile, and as Mark will say, *"a Syrophenician."*

The phrase, *"Whose young daughter had an unclean spirit,"* is verified by the Holy Spirit in the giving of this account, that the woman's summation of her daughter's condition was correct.

It is ironical that this heathen woman some 2,000 years ago knew the problem of her daughter, but modern intellectuals, with all their vaunted knowledge, do not know!

As we have previously stated, the designation, *"unclean spirit,"* covers all evil spirits, and of whatever kind. That an evil spirit could possess a young girl, would come as a shock to most.

How could such happen?

First of all, this woman being a Gentile, was an idol-worshiper, or at least was the citizen of a nation of idol-worshipers. At any rate, demon spirits ruled this country of Tyre and Sidon, as evil spirits rule most countries today. As such, many were demon possessed, with many more demon oppressed.

Any parents who do not know Jesus, are open to demon possession and oppression, whether in themselves or their children. That holds true now, as then!

The only protection against the powers of darkness is the Lord Jesus Christ. Education, money, or environment, are no protection whatsoever!

Consequently, when unsaved parents bring a child into the world, due to its exposure to the powers of darkness, not many months after birth, it is possible for it to become demon possessed.

If one could pull back the cover and find the cause of all gang violence, teen murders, immorality among teenagers and even sub-teens, etc., one would find demon possession, or, at the least, extreme demon influence, as the cause.

Even if only one parent is a Believer, *"The unbelieving husband is sanctified by the wife, and the unbelieving wife is sanctified by the husband: else were your children unclean: but now are they holy"* (I Cor. 7:14). (Meaning that one believing parent can sanctify the family.)

As well, if the parents, or at least one parent, come to Christ after the birth of their child or children, Satan's power is broken in that family. It does not necessarily mean that he will discontinue all efforts of corruption and destruction, but it does mean that the believing parent(s) has powerful weapons at his or her disposal, which will, and without fail, subdue the powers of darkness, upon proper Faith (Jn. 15:7).

The phrase, *"Heard of Him,"* means that His Presence was related to her, probably after He had already arrived at the house.

The phrase, *"And came and fell at His feet,"* concerns her desperation. Whatever she knew about Him, the results will show that she believed He was the answer to her dilemma.

It was at this moment, more than likely, as Matthew records, that she addressed Jesus as *"Lord, Thou Son of David"* (Mat. 15:22). Mark omits this, and for purpose and reason.

Matthew proclaims Christ as King, and of the entire world, consequently, the woman's acclamation in his account would be included.

Mark proclaims Jesus as a servant, but, such titles would not be given by Gentiles, although recorded if spoken by a Jew (Mk. 10:48).

(26) "THE WOMAN WAS A GREEK, A SYROPHENICIAN BY NATION; AND SHE BESOUGHT HIM THAT HE WOULD CAST FORTH THE DEVIL OUT OF HER DAUGHTER."

The phrase, *"The woman was a Greek, a Syrophenician by nation,"* means she was Greek by religion, spoke the Syrian language, and was Phoenician by race. Wuest says she was a Phoenician of Syria as distinguished from a Phoenician of North Africa.

Matthew was a little more specific, calling her *"a woman of Canaan,"* meaning that she was a descendant from those seven nations of Canaan which had been driven out on God's Command by Joshua.

In the context of this explanation as to who the woman was, one finds all the attendant horror of a life without God. She was an *"alien from the Commonwealth of Israel, a stranger from the Covenants of Promise, having no hope, and without God in the world"* (Eph. 2:12).

In these very words as given by Paul, one can literally feel the lost condition of such a person! Everything that truly makes life worth living is denied such an individual. And yet, sadder still, most of this present world is in that condition. They do not know the Lord.

I will ever thank God for that day so long ago when the Gospel of Jesus Christ was brought to my community. As the songwriter said:

"Oh happy day, Oh happy day,

"When Jesus washed, my sins away."

That is at least one of the reasons I have a burning burden to take this Glorious Message of Redemption to a lost and dying world. In Truth, every Believer feels the same way, at least if they truly understand what Jesus has actually done for them! That is the reason Paul said, *"I am debtor"* (Rom. 1:14).

He meant that he was under an obligation and bound by duty to take the Gospel to others, because the Lord had been gracious and kind to bring the Gospel to him.

The phrase, *"And she besought Him that He would cast forth the devil out of her daughter,"* actually means that she kept asking the Lord

NOTES

over and over to do this thing, which was the cry of her heart.

Someone has said that parents love their children more than their children love them, and because love descends.

Quite possibly that is correct, inasmuch as God loves us more than we love Him.

At any rate, this woman has come to Christ, and the results will proclaim that she means to receive what she came for, deliverance for her daughter.

The suffering and pain her daughter's condition had caused, must have been extremely debilitating. As it is, she sees no future for the girl. Actually, there is no future for anyone outside of Christ.

As well, there was absolutely no way this girl could be delivered except by Christ. Even though the long span of years has crossed the bridge of time, still, and irrespective of vaunted science and the increase of medical knowledge, there is no deliverer except Christ. He Alone can set the captive free.

As we have repeatedly stated, this is the reason that the Gospel is so very important. It is not one of several solutions, but, in fact, is the only solution.

(27) "BUT JESUS SAID UNTO HER, LET THE CHILDREN FIRST BE FILLED: FOR IT IS NOT MEET TO TAKE THE CHILDREN'S BREAD, AND TO CAST IT UNTO THE DOGS."

The phrase, *"But Jesus said unto her,"* begins the odyssey which will proclaim one of the greatest displays of Faith ever!

The phrase, *"Let the children first be filled,"* had reference to Israel.

This order of procedure was not favoritism, but only the method of reaching the larger number through a selected smaller group, in this case Israel. The Jew was the chosen channel through which God had elected to reach the Gentiles. Consequently, it was proper that the *"children"* (Israel) receive first, in order that they may be able to give it to others. As stated, this was God's Plan, but sorrow of sorrows, Israel would not receive it! Nevertheless, Jesus would offer it to them first, as it should be.

The phrase, *"For it is not meet to take the children's bread, and to cast it unto the dogs,"* is not nearly as harsh as it seems on the surface.

In fact, Jews looked on all Gentiles as dogs. It was a term of reproach. Paul even called the

Judaizers *"dogs"* when he said, *"Beware of dogs"* (Phil. 3:2).

However, the word used by Christ was not the word for *"dog,"* as it is commonly used, but the word for *"a little dog,"* actually referring to *"pets."*

Wuest suggests that Jesus may have spoken Greek to this woman, for she possibly would not have known the Aramaic of the Jews. As well, Greek was the international language of the day.

Why did the Lord address this woman in this manner?

1. As we have repeatedly stated, everything He did had a far larger scope than the immediate need, although it certainly included that. His miracles basically pertained to three directions:

A. To meet the present need, as stated!

B. To serve as a lesson for the entirety of the Church, and for all time!

C. To serve as a lesson for each individual, and for all time!

2. He was testing her Faith. As Satan's every effort is meant to weaken or even destroy our Faith, likewise, everything done by the Lord is meant to increase our Faith. Faith is the currency, and, in fact, the only currency which spends in Heaven.

Some may question as to how this woman could have Faith, inasmuch as she was a heathen, and, consequently, a stranger to the Promises of God?

Actually, her condition was no different than anyone else. The moment an individual comes in contact with God and His Word, a *"measure of Faith is dealt to them"* (Rom. 12:3).

She had come to Christ, therefore, her Faith is automatically increased, and strictly by association with Him. As stated, His very Words were intended to increase her Faith, which they did!

3. He would show her how to have what she wanted, even though, at least at this time, she, as a Gentile, was not included in the Mission of Christ.

By Jesus using the word *"Dog,"* He was not insulting her, but rather showing her how she could receive what she wanted.

First she attempted to appeal to Christ by saying, *"Oh Lord, Thou Son of David."* However, she was not a Jew, and therefore had no right on that basis, and because she was not a part of the Covenant (Mat. 15:22). But as a *"Dog"* she could appeal on the merit of Mercy and Grace. As such

she could receive what she wanted. Actually she could receive far more, because Mercy and Grace always have a greater supply than Covenant.

This should be a tremendous lesson for us all, in that God will honor Faith wherever He finds it. Even as I dictate these words, I sense the Presence of God.

It does not matter what the circumstances are! If a person believes God, He will honor their Faith in Him, and without fail! This is at least a part of the lesson He is teaching us by the experience of this woman.

(28) "AND SHE ANSWERED AND SAID UNTO HIM, YES, LORD: YET THE DOGS UNDER THE TABLE EAT OF THE CHILDREN'S CRUMBS."

The phrase, *"And she answered and said unto Him,"* proclaims a level of Faith which should be a lesson to all Believers. What determination! Even what desperation! But yet, True Faith is always in this vein.

The phrase, *"Yes, Lord,"* is said by Wuest to be explained in this manner.

The word, *"Lord,"* in the Greek Text, as used by the woman, did not refer to Deity or of Jesus being the Jewish Messiah. She would have had scant knowledge of this. She, instead, used the word, *"Lord,"* in the sense of Jesus being an important Person, etc.

As well, she fully agrees with Him by using the word, *"Yes!"* Actually, she did exactly what He was desiring that she would do. She used His Own Words, which seemed to be in the negative, and turned them to the positive. I have to shout *"Hallelujah!"*

The phrase, *"Yet the dogs under the table eat of the children's crumbs,"* places her in the position, by Faith, to receive what she wanted.

In other words, she is saying that this table is so heavily laden, that surely a crumb will not be missed, which will meet her need.

Actually, this very illustration used by Christ, which seems harsh on the surface, rather appeals to this Gentile.

Jews did not look kindly on dogs at all, and would not have thought of having one in their house and around their person. However, most Gentiles had them as pets, even allowing them at times to come and go in the house, and, actually eating the crumbs which fell from the table. In the Gentile culture of that day, it was common for children to throw crumbs to the dogs at mealtime. Consequently, the statement as used by Christ would have been perfectly understandable to this Gentile.

Isn't our Lord wonderful!

(29) "AND HE SAID UNTO HER, FOR THIS SAYING GO THY WAY; THE DEVIL IS GONE OUT OF THY DAUGHTER."

The phrase, *"And He said unto her,"* constitutes a Divine answer to a terrible need, and, as well, to great Faith. Actually, Matthew proclaims Jesus saying, *"O woman, great is thy Faith"* (Mat. 15:28).

The phrase, *"For this saying go thy way,"* concerns her Faith, and great Faith at that! There is something else evident in this Text, which we must not overlook.

The humility registered here goes hand in hand with great Faith.

Humility, as a Grace is something not easily brought about. Humility is generally, if not always, brought about by the humbling process. This comes about, oftentimes, by the advent of great troubles and difficulties.

As stated, this woman was desperate! Her daughter was in serious condition, and possibly getting worse, with death shortly in the offing, if something was not done. Consequently, this dear woman was humbled in the face of this great need.

Much of that which is presently called *"Faith,"* is, in fact, precious little True Faith, if any at all, and because of the almost total lack of humility. The modern brand is self-aggrandizing and self-boasting, even though glossed with Scripture. In the modern variety, it is almost as if the louder one can boast, the more Faith he has.

In Truth, it is no Faith at all, but rather mere presumption!

I think one can say, and without fear of Scriptural contradiction, that True Faith will always be humble, or at least will be humbled in the process.

Naaman is a perfect example! What he was told to do by Elisha, regarding the cure of his leprosy, the Scripture says that he *"went away in a rage"* (II Ki. 5:12).

He was greatly offended because Elisha had not even bothered to come out himself, but had rather sent his servant to deliver the Message. He was Naaman, the great Captain of Syria, therefore, at least in his mind, he warranted more than this cavalier treatment.

However, he ultimately humbled himself, and did as the Prophet said, and was totally healed. However, had he not been humbled, there would have been no Faith (II Ki. 5:14).

The phrase, *"The devil is gone out of thy daughter,"* means that it is out, and will stay out. It is a permanent cure, with the Mother never again having to worry that this *"unclean spirit"* will have access to her daughter.

(30) "AND WHEN SHE WAS COME TO HER HOUSE, SHE FOUND THE DEVIL GONE OUT, AND HER DAUGHTER LAID UPON THE BED."

The phrase, *"And when she was come to her house,"* presents a beautiful picture indeed!

Previously, her house had been one of turmoil, suffering, and as one might say it, *"hell on earth."* Such is the condition of most *"houses."* However, her *"house"* has now changed, and, in fact, would be changed forever.

The phrase, *"She found the devil gone out,"* once again has in the Greek Text the idea that the cure is permanent. It is not a temporary thing, but, rather, an eternal deliverance. Hallelujah!

What joy must have filled this woman's heart! What Praises to God must have filled that house! To be sure, as it happened then, it can happen now, and, in fact, does happen countless times, but only when Jesus speaks the Word. To be sure, He stands ready, waiting, and willing to do for any and all who will believe Him exactly as He did for this woman of so long ago.

The phrase, *"And her daughter laid upon the bed,"* refers to a restful repose, which indicated that previously she had not been easily restrained.

There is every indication that the girl previously had been insane, or at least partially so! But now she is as perfectly whole and sound of mind as any human being could ever be. All of this, because of the *"Word of Christ."* And yet, most of the world turns Him away.

Just yesterday, a dear Brother gave me a testimony, which is beautiful to say the least. It took place in the mid 1980's.

He told me how his life was filled with sin, the situation was deteriorating almost by the hour, and he was on the very edge of losing his family and everything he held dear. At a particular time, the situation grew so bad that he contemplated suicide. Actually, he said he heard a voice telling him, *"Put a gun to your* head and pull the trigger, and your troubles will be over!"

This went on for several hours, but every time he would reach for the gun, another voice would speak to him, saying, *"That is not the way. I have a better Way."*

Almost absent-mindedly, he reached over and turned on the radio. The dial was on a Christian station, and at that moment my radio program was on the air. However, he did not know me, and, in effect, had never heard of Jimmy Swaggart.

The voice spoke to him again, saying, *"Listen to him, and go to his Church!"*

At the moment, he didn't even know what Church was being spoken of, and, as well, had never even heard of Family Worship Center.

He made inquiry, and found out that our Church was in Baton Rouge, not too far from where he lived. It was a Friday afternoon when all of this took place.

He got his wife and children in the car, and drove across town to our Church, in order that he may know where it was, so he would have no trouble finding it that Sunday morning. He told me this:

"Brother Swaggart, when I drove into the Ministry parking lot, and stopped my car, it was a Friday afternoon about 3 p.m." He went on to say, *"The moment we got out of the car to look at the Church, everything changed."* At that moment he gave his heart and life to Jesus Christ, and so did his wife.

They immediately began to come to Church, never missing a Sunday, and today, this dear Brother pastors a Church not far from Baton Rouge, and his son attends our Christian School.

In one moment his entire life changed. He was contemplating suicide, with the situation so bad that he seemingly could not endure it any longer.

A short time later, he was gloriously and wondrously saved by the Precious Blood of Jesus Christ. That is what Jesus can do, and Jesus Alone can do!

The situation I have just revealed, is actually little different than the deliverance afforded by Christ of this woman's daughter. Demon spirits were destroying that home, and demon spirits were destroying the home of which I have just mentioned. The same Christ who delivered the girl of so long ago, is the

NOTES

same Christ who delivered my Brother and set him free.

He has done it for millions of others as well!

(31) "AND AGAIN, DEPARTING FROM THE COASTS OF TYRE AND SIDON, HE CAME UNTO THE SEA OF GALILEE, THROUGH THE MIDST OF THE COASTS OF DECAPOLIS."

Leaving the Tyre and Sidon area, the Lord probably went east through Caesarea Philippi, then turning south, by the eastern side of Galilee, to the border of Decapolis. It could well have been a journey of some 60 or 70 miles, taking several days. Actually, this was not far from the area where He had delivered the maniac of Gadara.

Inasmuch as the Holy Spirit had Mark to carefully delineate the route of our Lord, Jesus came here by design. The opposition by the Pharisees and Scribes was not pleasant to say the least. Consequently, the trip to Phoenicia and back to Decapolis, would have been a respite from the venomous hatred of these Religious Leaders.

(32) "AND THEY BRING UNTO HIM ONE THAT WAS DEAF, AND HAD AN IMPEDIMENT IN HIS SPEECH; AND THEY BESEECH HIM TO PUT HIS HAND UPON HIM."

The phrase, *"And they bring unto Him one that was deaf, and had an impediment in his speech,"* proclaims the usual difficulties of the *"deaf."* Due to being unable to hear, speech impediments are normal, with total speech loss resulting many times. However, there was an added problem with the man's tongue, as we shall see!

The phrase, *"And they beseech Him to put His Hand upon him,"* refers to their belief that the man would be healed upon this action by Christ.

It seems that the fame of Jesus was just as prominent on the eastern side of the Sea of Galilee as on the other side. There will be a day, and soon, that His fame will be the same in the entirety of the earth.

Concerning the coming Kingdom Age, Isaiah prophesied, *"I will send those . . . afar off, that have not heard My fame, neither have seen My Glory; and they shall declare My Glory among the Gentiles"* (Isa. 66:19).

(33) "AND HE TOOK HIM ASIDE FROM THE MULTITUDE, AND PUT HIS FINGERS

INTO HIS EARS, AND HE SPIT, AND TOUCHED HIS TONGUE;"

The phrase, *"And He took him aside from the multitude,"* was done for purpose and reason. More than likely, the Disciples were very near, but the multitude would have been some yards away.

Why did He do this?

Many reasons have been given, but I suspect the strange manner in which He would bring about this healing, by using the spittle, He did not want the crowd to observe. Everything He did always had a reason to it. It may not be readily understood by the onlookers, but it was certainly understood by Him!

The phrase, *"And put His fingers into his ears,"* means that He put one finger (probably His index finger) of His right hand into one ear, and one finger of His left hand into the other.

The phrase, *"And He spit, and touched his tongue,"* is probably the most unusual means of healing recorded in the entirety of the Bible. The order of events seems to be the following:

First of all, He had the man to stick out his tongue. Inasmuch as he was deaf, quite possibly, Jesus, or one of the Disciples, protruded their own tongue in order that the man may know what Jesus was talking about. Upon understanding, and, thereby, extending his tongue, Jesus spat on His Own finger, and then touched the man's tongue with the saliva.

He then put a finger in each ear.

Why the spittle?

As stated, this was most unusual!

We know that whatever He did was never a matter of self-will, but, instead, the admonition of the Heavenly Father. So, He was directed to do as He did.

Everything about His Person was sacred, even the spittle! Being the Incarnate Son of God, He was the only Perfect Person Who ever lived. As such, there was no taint of corruption, disease, sickness, or that which was unsanitary about Him. So, the spittle that touched this man's tongue, was absolutely germ free. Not only that, it, as well, contained *"life."*

(Shortly before His Crucifixion, He spat on the ground, and made clay of the spittle, placing it on a blind man's eyes, John 9:6; however, this is the first time, at least recorded, that someone's tongue was touched with His spittle. A little later, Mark 8:23, spittle would be applied to a man's eyes.)

The incident in John was meant to serve as symbol of His Incarnation, while this incident is meant to serve in the same manner, but with a difference.

As the clay represented His Incarnation, the spittle represented His Life. As such, when His life touched the deformity of this man's tongue, the deformity was instantly healed.

(34) "AND LOOKING UP TO HEAVEN, HE SIGHED, AND SAITH UNTO HIM, EPHPHATHA, THAT IS, BE OPENED."

The phrase, *"And looking up to Heaven, He sighed,"* tells us two things:

1. Even though the power was resident totally within Him, still, He was from Heaven, signifying this is the place of God's Throne and the solution to man's problems. Regrettably, most Preachers presently are not looking up, but, rather, down toward themselves or others. To be sure, there is no help from that source, only from Heaven.

2. His *"sigh"* spoke of His response to hurting humanity. The *"sigh"* expressed the terrible dilemma in which man now found himself, and, as well, the fact of rebellion against God, incorporating most of mankind. It, as well, expressed the terrible price that would have to be paid in order to redeem mankind.

The phrase, *"And saith unto him, Ephphatha, that is, be opened,"* expresses the command.

(35) "AND STRAIGHTWAY HIS EARS WERE OPENED, AND THE STRING OF HIS TONGUE WAS LOOSED, AND HE SPAKE PLAIN."

The phrase, *"And straightway his ears were opened,"* means they were opened immediately. In other words, his hearing did not come back by degrees, but was instant. One second he could not hear, and the next second he could hear everything clearly and plainly. What a wonder this man immediately experienced!

The phrase, *"And the string of his tongue was loosed, and he spake plain,"* means that at the same time his ears were opened, the deformity of his tongue was healed as well!

Previously he had spoken with great difficulty, being very difficult to understand. But now he speaks clearly and plainly, which began instantly.

What a Miracle!

As well, the healing of the man's hearing and speech, symbolizes the Salvation of the soul. Undone without God, man cannot hear what God has to say. As well, when he speaks of the Lord, he has an *"impediment,"* which means that whatever he does say about the Lord is error, without understanding, and only breeds confusion.

Therefore, within himself, this situation cannot be rectified. As Jesus took the initiative with this man, likewise, there must be a revelation by the Spirit before man can be awakened to his need for God. Upon yielding to the petition of that revelation, the Miracle of the New Birth commences, with the individual then able to *"hear"* as the Lord speaks. As well, whatever he says about Christ now, is understandable and *"plain."*

(36) "AND HE CHARGED THEM THAT THEY SHOULD TELL NO MAN: BUT THE MORE HE CHARGED THEM, SO MUCH THE MORE A GREAT DEAL THEY PUBLISHED IT;"

The phrase, *"And He charged them that they should tell no man,"* was done, as well, for purpose and reason.

He gave the man, plus those who had witnessed this Miracle, clear and positive orders, that they were not to tell others what had happened.

Possibly, there were many reasons why He commanded this, and, as previously stated, it was done at the Father's instructions, still, it probably had to do with the fame of His Ministry.

The crowds were already gargantuan, with the sick and afflicted being brought from every quarter. Consequently, the major thrust of preaching and teaching the Gospel, was becoming lost in the constant prayer for the sick. Also, He desired that no more attention be directed toward Him than could be helped, simply because the situation could get out of hand. In fact, and at least once, they desired to make Him King then and there (Jn. 6:15). It was no doubt this attitude which prompted this Command.

The phrase, *"But the more He charged them, so much the more a great deal they published it,"* means that they did not heed Him the first time, with Him admonishing them again, but still to no avail!

Yes! They certainly should have obeyed Him. However, I suspect it was a Command which was very difficult to heed.

No doubt, many people knew this man who had formerly been deaf and partially dumb. Seeing him now perfectly whole, would have

occasioned much curiosity. It would have been very difficult for him to explain what had happened, without telling Who had done it.

So, despite His admonishment, *"So much the more a great deal they published it."*

I don't know why I sense the Presence of God so strongly as I dictate these words, but I do! Possibly, at least to a small degree, I can feel what this man and his friends must have felt, after experiencing this Miracle. He had been touched by the Son of the Living God, actually, the same One Who appeared to Moses on Mt. Sinai; in reality, the One Who made the world and all therein. Consequently, what he experienced was far more than just a healing, he experienced a deliverance. The prison of deafness in which he had been locked, had its doors thrown open wide, with him going free! As well, the touch of the saliva of Christ on his deformed tongue had given him the ability to express what he had experienced, and was now feeling. How could he help but speak!

I suspect it was a Command the Lord knew would little be obeyed. Perhaps the man's actions were wrong, but I believe his heart was right. The way the Holy Spirit instructs Mark to write this, seems to say, at least in some small way, that the Spirit took some delight, or at least was not offended, in the widespread proclamation of this man and his friends.

Perhaps I am wrong, but I suspect not!

(37) "AND WERE BEYOND MEASURE ASTONISHED, SAYING, HE HATH DONE ALL THINGS WELL: HE MAKETH BOTH THE DEAF TO HEAR, AND THE DUMB TO SPEAK."

The phrase, *"And were beyond measure astonished,"* means they were struck with astonishment, with the words, *"beyond measure,"* adding to their astonishment a double measure, which meant what Jesus had done was beyond comprehension.

The phrase, *"Saying, He hath done all things well,"* means they said this, and continued to say it over and over.

The phrase, *"He maketh both the deaf to hear, and the dumb to speak,"* spoke of the great Miracle which had been performed on this man, and which they knew was from God. Matthew proclaims that the Lord performed a vast number of Miracles in this area, which were not recorded by Mark (Mat. 15:29-31).

As someone has said, *"His whole life on earth was one connected, continued manifestation of lovingkindness."*

CHAPTER 8

(1) "IN THOSE DAYS THE MULTITUDE BEING VERY GREAT, AND HAVING NOTHING TO EAT, JESUS CALLED HIS DISCIPLES UNTO HIM, AND SAITH UNTO THEM,"

The phrase, *"In those days the multitude being very great,"* speaks of anywhere from 8,000 to 10,000 people, counting women and children. Exactly where Jesus was, Mark does not specify. Wuest says the words, *"In those days,"* indicate Mark's inability or purpose to assign to this incident a precise historical place. I think it is obvious that the rejection of Christ pertained basically to the Religious Leaders of Israel. In fact, Mark will later say, *"The common people heard Him gladly"* (Mk. 12:37).

While it is certainly true that many will not follow Christ, even though their shepherds are Godly, still, some will! However, with ungodly leaders, such as those in Israel, the people are left with no Shepherd, no one to point the True Way. Consequently, Israel would go to her doom, exactly as the apostate Church presently is going to its doom.

The phrase, *"And having nothing to eat,"* has a spiritual as well as physical meaning.

The later Text will show that many of these people had been following Christ for three days and nights, sleeping where they could and eating what little had been brought with them, which had, no doubt, long since run out.

As their physical provisions had run out, likewise, the spiritual. Outside of Christ, the world *"has nothing to eat."* He Alone is the True Bread of Life. This is what makes Bible Christianity so different than all else. Bible Christianity is a Person, and that Person is Christ. Christianity, even by the greatest stretch of the imagination, is not a system of *"dos"* and *"don'ts,"* which characterizes religions, but is Faith and confidence in a Person. Upon accepting Christ, men do not accept a creed, dogma, theory, doctrine, or system, but, instead, a Man, *"The Man Christ Jesus."*

The phrase, *"Jesus called His Disciples unto Him, and saith unto them,"* proclaims His care

NOTES

and concern for the people. To be sure, He is no less to each of those who seek unto Him.

(2) "I HAVE COMPASSION ON THE MULTITUDE, BECAUSE THEY HAVE NOW BEEN WITH ME THREE DAYS, AND HAVE NOTHING TO EAT:"

The phrase, *"I have compassion on the multitude,"* portrays the Love of God. It would be the same as saying, *"My heart goes out to them."*

If one is to notice, the word, *"compassion,"* is used of Christ constantly, and actually denotes His Character. His entire Life was spent for others. Consequently, the example He set, is that which the Church should follow.

The phrase, *"Because they have now been with Me three days, and have nothing to eat,"* shows their hunger for Him, and His concern for them.

"Nothing to eat," did not mean they had not had anything at all during the past three days and nights, but what little they had, if anything, had long since been exhausted.

(3) "AND IF I SEND THEM AWAY FASTING TO THEIR OWN HOUSES, THEY WILL FAINT BY THE WAY: FOR DIVERS OF THEM CAME FROM FAR."

The idea of this verse is that the Lord would not send them away without first meeting their need. As well, this is characteristic of Him. When coming to Christ, men receive what they come for.

All of these people who had been sick had been gloriously healed. As well, they had heard the Word of God as they had never heard it before. Now they will receive physical food as well!

In effect, the Gospel of Jesus Christ is the whole Gospel for the whole man! Jesus saves, Jesus heals, Jesus Baptizes in the Holy Spirit, and Jesus is coming again. It meets every need, spiritually, physically, financially, and domestically.

The phrase, *"Divers of them came from far,"* characterizes that which will happen in the coming Kingdom Age. In fact, they will come from all over the world at that time, and with every need met, and with prosperity for all!

(4) "AND HIS DISCIPLES ANSWERED HIM, FROM WHENCE CAN A MAN SATISFY THESE MEN WITH BREAD HERE IN THE WILDERNESS?"

The phrase, *"And His Disciples answered Him,"* will be an answer which speaks of unbelief.

The question, *"From whence can a man satisfy these men with bread here in the wilderness?"*, portrays the insensibility of the natural heart.

This is the second time that Jesus had fed a great multitude of people, and yet the Disciples seemed to have learned little or nothing from the previous Miracle. This blindness is recorded in 6:52 and 8:17.

They seemed to resort almost to the word to their previous position, attempting to address the problem in the natural sense.

In effect, the very tenor of their question actually answered it. Jesus furnished bread in the wilderness for the Children of Israel upon their deliverance from Egypt. This the Disciples knew, and yet, still walked in unbelief.

There was a reason for it, which verse 17 portrays.

(5) "AND HE ASKED THEM, HOW MANY LOAVES HAVE YE? AND THEY SAID, SEVEN."

Before they had *"five"* loaves, which is God's number of Grace, while now they have *"seven,"* which is God's perfect number of completion.

Whether the *"seven"* loaves were theirs or that which they had borrowed, as the *"five,"* is anyone's guess. At any rate, this is the amount they had, which is almost nothing considering the vast number of people to be fed. However, as in Chapter 6, so here, the lesson to be learned is that we should have Faith in God, not looking at the natural but the supernatural. Those loaves in the Disciples' hands were nothing, but in the Hands of Christ they will multiply into astounding proportions.

(6) "AND HE COMMANDED THE PEOPLE TO SIT DOWN ON THE GROUND, AND HE TOOK THE SEVEN LOAVES, AND GAVE THANKS, AND BRAKE, AND GAVE TO HIS DISCIPLES TO SET BEFORE THEM; AND THEY DID SET THEM BEFORE THE PEOPLE."

The phrase, *"And He commanded the people to sit down on the ground,"* once again concerns what He is about to do. As well, He now takes charge. In fact, He is always in charge; however, the result of His authority will now be brought out. They were to *"sit down"* in order to be served!

The phrase, *"And He took the seven loaves,"* represents them now in His Hands, and, consequently, will become a Miracle. In the Disciples' Hands they were nothing, in His Hands they are

everything! The action is not in the loaves, but rather in Him.

The phrase, *"And gave thanks,"* is with Him a habit! It should be our habit as well!

He *"gave thanks"* to His Heavenly Father, Who is the Source of all Blessings.

The phrase, *"And brake,"* was a custom among the Jews. Dake says that bread was baked in thin cakes about one-half to one inch think, which had to be broken to be divided. It was too hard to cut as we do our bread. As well, *"to brake bread"* means *"to eat food"* (Lk. 24:35; Acts 2:42, 46; 20:7; 27:35; I Cor. 10:16).

The phrase, *"And gave to His Disciples to set before them,"* seems to proclaim the actual time of the multiplication. The giving was a continual act, till all were filled.

The phrase, *"And they did sit them before the people,"* presents the Disciples acting as the agents of Christ in serving the people.

As then, so now, at least as it is supposed to be.

(7) "AND THEY HAD A FEW SMALL FISHES: AND HE BLESSED, AND COMMANDED TO SET THEM ALSO BEFORE THEM,"

The phrase, *"And they had a few small fishes,"* does not give the number, only a *"few,"* and small ones at that!

The phrase, *"And He blessed,"* refers to Him giving thanks for these, as He did the bread. In other words, there seems to have been two *"Blessings."* When we offer the blessing at the table before meals, we do what the Lord did at this time.

The phrase, *"And commanded to set them also before them,"* makes it seem as if the fish came a little after the bread, and was passed out accordingly to the people.

(8) "SO THEY DID EAT, AND WERE FILLED: AND THEY TOOK UP OF THE BROKEN MEAT THAT WAS LEFT SEVEN BASKETS."

The phrase, *"So they did eat, and were filled,"* of course speaks of this great Miracle performed, but, as well, speaks of the multiplicity of millions who have partaken of the Bread of Life and, to be sure, *"were filled."* In Truth, it is the only Bread that will satisfy. Everything else falls far short. As we have repeatedly stated, Jesus is that Bread.

The phrase, *"And they took up of the broken meat that was left seven baskets,"* is in contrast to the twelve of the last Miracle of this nature.

As we have stated, *"seven,"* speaks of perfection and completion, and rightly typifies all that which the Lord does. It proclaims that the whole world could partake of this Gospel, and to their fill, and there would still be more to receive if needed. Actually, it is impossible to exhaust the Gospel, or one's understanding of it.

The learning of every philosophy in this world can be exhausted in a short period of time. However, with the Gospel of Jesus Christ, and because it is the Living Word of God, if one studied it a lifetime, one still would not have even scratched the surface. Its depth, height, breath, and width are absolutely inexhaustible.

As I have stated elsewhere in these Volumes, at times I will think I have gleaned from a particular Passage of Scripture everything possible. I will then hear a first-year Bible Student in our Bible College preach on the same subject, and from a direction I never thought of. I never cease to be amazed at the Wonder and the Glory of the Word of God.

As well, the *"baskets"* spoken of in this Passage are different than the word for *"basket"* used in the record of the other Miracle (6:43).

Those baskets were small hand-baskets of wicker-work. The baskets here spoken of are much larger baskets, actually large enough to hold a man.

As well, this, along with a great deal of other evidence, records the fact that this Miracle of multiplication was different than the other, and took place on a different occasion.

(9) "AND THEY THAT HAD EATEN WERE ABOUT FOUR THOUSAND: AND HE SENT THEM AWAY."

We know from verses 19 and 20, that the *"four thousand"* here mentioned, spoke only of men. Consequently, the number of women and children added to this, would have raised the figure to approximately 8,000 to 10,000 people.

The phrase, *"And He sent them away,"* but only after they were filled, and in every capacity.

The Gospel containing the Words of Life had been spoken unto them, as well as their sick having been healed. Also, they were fed physically. Consequently, nothing was left undone.

I think the two incidents respecting the multiplication of the loaves and fishes, proclaims to all that Jesus is concerned about our material welfare as well!

NOTES

As I dictate these words, our ChildCare Program has been in force for about fifteen years. In the last ten years it has been confined basically to Africa, with our Headquarters in Harare, Zimbabwe.

For this ten years, we have had two giant tractor/trailer trucks constantly on the road taking food to the various refugee camps in that country. The individuals occupying these camps, by and large, came from Mozambique, and, I might quickly add, in a destitute condition.

At the present, most of these refugees have been taken back to their respective homes. However, our program continues, although on a smaller basis.

Some have contended that this has nothing to do with the Gospel. However, it has everything to do with the Gospel.

As stated, Jesus multiplying these loaves and fishes proclaimed to us His concern for the welfare of all, and in every category. So, this is important!

In these camps, we were able to build quite a number of Churches, with many people giving their hearts and lives to the Lord Jesus Christ. Many of these refugees were open to the Gospel, when it became obvious that we were concerned about them in every capacity. As stated, many accepted the Lord.

From the years of 1980 through 1987, we, as well, were able to construct nearly 100 schools in Haiti and Central America. These schools were elementary, providing education for an average of 500 students per school. As well, we furnished a hot meal each day for these students at that particular time, which was, in many cases, the only meal these children would receive each day.

Also, during those years we had approximately 15 Mobile Medical Units stationed in particular places in the world, treating people free of charge, etc.

Along with that, we helped fund, actually supplied almost all the funds, for Mark Buntain's Feeding Program in Calcutta, India, of about 25,000 people daily.

These were Ministries, which I believe were and are very important, with Jesus setting the example on these miraculous occasions.

John said, *"But whoso hath this world's good, and seeth his brother have need, and shutteth* up his bowels of compassion from him, how dwelleth the love of God in him?" (I Jn. 3:17).

However, it must ever be understood that even though these things are important, still, man's real need is the Gospel of Jesus Christ. Humanitarian efforts, as important as they may be and as pleasing as they are to the Lord, only proclaim the Love of God to these unfortunates, but really do not address the real issue, which is Salvation of the soul. That, far and away, is the most important!

Regrettably, many, if not most, Religious Denominations have ceased to preach the Gospel altogether, with most, if not all their efforts, pertaining to that which is humanitarian. As such, and due to the fact that their efforts are not combined with the Gospel, their efforts, in Truth, are of little consequence. The mission of the Church is to preach the Gospel of Jesus Christ. That is uppermost and foremost, and nothing must be allowed to circumvent this all-important effort. And yet, the other, the humanitarian side, must not be neglected either.

(10) "AND STRAIGHTWAY HE ENTERED INTO A SHIP WITH HIS DISCIPLES, AND CAME INTO THE PARTS OF DALMANUTHA."

The phrase, "And straightway He entered into a ship with His Disciples," probably refers to the same ship which brought Him. As stated, it probably belonged to Zebedee. It was probably quite large, having ample room for all the Disciples, etc.

The phrase, "And came into the parts of Dalmanutha," has Matthew calling it the "coast of Magdala" (Mat. 15:39).

This was on the western shore of the Sea of Galilee, and probably was about three or four miles south of Capernaum.

(11) "AND THE PHARISEES CAME FORTH, AND BEGAN TO QUESTION WITH HIM, SEEKING OF HIM A SIGN FROM HEAVEN, TEMPTING HIM."

The phrase, "And the Pharisees came forth," once again proclaims the opposition by the Religious Leaders of Israel. Matthew said the Sadducees were present as well (Mat. 16:1).

Why is it that Religious Leaders are almost always opposed to Christ?

In the first place, there is really no such thing as Religious Leaders or even Spiritual Leaders. While it is true that men love to refer to themselves as such, still, the only True Spiritual Leader is Jesus Christ as the Head of the Church (Col. 1:18). Whenever individuals attempt to abrogate the position of Christ, Paul addressed them as, "not holding the Head," in other words, taking the position of Christ as the Head of the Church (Col. 2:19).

So, even though the Lord has given for the benefit of the Church, "Apostles, Prophets, Evangelists, Pastors and Teachers," still, these offices pertain to particular Ministries, and not designations of authority, except in the spiritual realm (Eph. 4:11).

Consequently, this means that all the man-made offices in the Church, which many refer to as offices of spiritual leadership, are not recognized as such by God, and in many cases are in direct opposition to the Lord.

These man-devised offices are not necessarily wrong, as long as men understand that they carry no spiritual authority, and are administrative only. However, most do not leave it at that, but become "puffed up in their fleshly mind" (Col. 2:18).

Most of these individuals who occupy these particular offices, whether Catholic or Protestant, and which includes most of Christianity, claim their position as God-ordained, and, therefore, whatever they say must be obeyed. The idea is, if wrong is committed, it will not be the fault of the people, but the so-called, Spiritual Leader.

In effect, "control" is the key word in all Religious Leadership. These individuals desire to control what is said, what is done, and every aspect of the religious community. Consequently, the Headship of Christ is abrogated in almost all of Christianity.

The Truth is that multiple millions have died eternally lost, because they believed error as propagated by these individuals, be they Catholic or Protestant. It is the same as with the Pharisees and Scribes of old!

In Truth, the Lord demands responsibility of every single individual. This means that every person must learn the Word of God for themselves, and, consequently, be led by the Spirit accordingly. This is the same for the layman as the Preacher, with none being excluded.

While Preachers of the Gospel, and in various Ministries, are given by the Holy Spirit, "For the perfecting of the Saints, for the work of the Ministry, for the edifying of the Body of Christ"

NOTES

(Eph. 4:12), still, every person must know the Word of God well enough, that if error is presented, it will be immediately recognized and rejected.

However, it is sad that men not only desire to control other men, but many, if not most, desire to be controlled. It is somewhat like a select few saying, *"Leave the driving to us."* Many have the erroneous conclusion that if error is presented, it will not be their responsibility, but, rather, these Religious Leaders.

While these Religious Leaders, and whoever they may be, will certainly be held accountable, as well, those who look to them will be responsible also!

Men love to shift responsibility to others; however, the responsibility for one's soul cannot be shifted to others, with God demanding accountability from each and every one (Ezek. 18:4).

(In all my years of Ministry, I have witnessed only a few men who occupied these administrative offices who were truly Godly. The others fell into the category of the Pharisees of old.)

The phrase, *"And began to question with Him,"* concerned questions designed to get Him to say the wrong thing, which He never did.

It is ironical! These men were standing before the Creator of all things. Consequently, He knew the answer to anything that could be asked, and irrespective of its nature. And yet, they did not have enough spiritual sense to know Who He was. Consequently, they plied Him with arcane, inane questions.

The phrase, *"Seeking of Him a sign from Heaven, tempting Him,"* was not the first time such had been engaged. They had already asked from Him a sign from Heaven (Mat. 12:38).

In effect, they were questioning Him in respect to His Miracles, and wanting to know if He claimed to be the Messiah of Israel. Their questions were not sincere, inasmuch as they had already made up their minds that He was not the Messiah. Consequently, what He was doing had to be of Satan, at least in their thinking.

It is ironical that they would ask for a *"sign,"* when the signs were abundant!

His Miracles were in fulfillment of the Prophecies of old. As well, His genealogy was perfect. Actually, there was nothing they could put their finger on respecting wrongdoing on His part, with the exception of some of their silly rules which He ignored — rules which had no foundation in the Word of God.

NOTES

So, the words, *"tempting Him,"* mean that their inquiry was not honest, with their sole motive being to snare Him in some way.

Of course, they never were able to do so, because His intelligence was so far beyond their's, and as well, His knowledge of the Word of God far exceeded anyone who had ever lived (Ps. 119:99-100).

Why did they not recognize Him as the Messiah, the fulfillment of the Prophecies?

The reasons are varied and many. These men were not right with God, and, in fact, did not know God, despite speaking of Him constantly! As such, self-will ruled them, which caused them to twist the Word of God to their own selfish ends.

As well, their self-righteousness would not allow them to admit their need of anything, much less to heed this *"Peasant,"* as He was thought to be!

In effect, the same situation presents itself now.

Most in the modern Church little knows what is of the Lord, or not of the Lord. The reason is, they know the Word of God so little, and are so taken up with self-will, and lifted up in their own self-righteousness, and because of religious activity, that they little know the Spirit of God at all! Consequently, they follow that which is the most showy, ostentatious, entertaining, and boastful. Only those who are truly Spirit-led, which are few, truly follow the Lord, and recognize that which is of the Lord. Regrettably, that number is small, very small!

(12) "AND HE SIGHED DEEPLY IN HIS SPIRIT, AND SAITH, WHY DOTH THIS GENERATION SEEK AFTER A SIGN? VERILY I SAY UNTO YOU, THERE SHALL NO SIGN BE GIVEN UNTO THIS GENERATION."

The phrase, *"And He sighed deeply in His Spirit,"* actually means *"He groaned in His Spirit."* As well, the groan or *"sigh"* came from *"deep within Him."* This *"sigh"* pertained to several things.

1. He groaned because of the apostate rejection of His Ministry, knowing that it would bring doom to the rejecters. Jesus was not one of several solutions to the human dilemma, but, in fact, the Only solution. Consequently, to refuse Him, was to refuse Life.

2. As well, this rejection came from the Religious Leaders of Israel, who, entrenched in

their ecclesiasticism, later crucified the Lord of Glory, having recognized Him as such and having seen the attesting Miracles He had performed, even attempting to break the force of these attesting Miracles by attributing them to Satan (Mat. 12:22-24; 21:37-39), (Wuest).

3. His rejection not only spelled doom for the Religious Leaders and their followers, but, as well, for the entirety of the nation.

4. In this statement, we are given the Heart of God respecting the attitude of rejecters. In other words, it affects Him deeply!

The question, *"And saith, Why doth this generation seek after a sign?",* in effect speaks of their terrible unbelief.

In Truth, it is impossible for unbelief to see a *"sign,"* even though it be given! Actually, there were *"signs"* galore, therefore they were without excuse.

The great Miracles performed by Jesus were so astounding, that it was obvious a mere mortal, at least within himself, could not do such a thing! The blind were made to see, the lame made to walk, the deaf made to hear, lepers were cleansed, and even the dead raised. Israel or the world had never even remotely seen such an outstanding display of the Power of God. Consequently, the Religious Leaders of Israel had to admit that it was of God, or else come up with another reason. Consequently, they said He did these things by the power of Satan.

Of course, such an accusation and claim were preposterous to say the least! In all of history, Satan had never been known to do such a thing. Actually, such works of healing and life were in direct contrast to his works of sickness and death.

To be sure, men always reject God from a position of stupidity. Even though the statement is blunt, it cannot be explained any other way. Rationally, men cannot reject Christ. Therefore, they must do so from a position of absurdity.

So, in effect, Jesus says that *"this generation"* has had more signs than any other generation that has ever been, and why are those not sufficient, with them consequently seeking more?

The phrase, *"Verily I say unto you, There shall no sign be given unto this generation,"* in effect says, *"I will perform the sign of Miracles in healing the sick and casting out devils, etc., but I will not give a sign of performing Miracles*

NOTES

at the demand of apostates, who would not accept their attesting value, even if given!"

His denial of their demand is powerfully firm, and left absolutely no doubt as to His refusal.

In fact, they later refused to be convinced, even after He had arisen from the dead (Acts 3:15).

(13) "AND HE LEFT THEM, AND ENTERING INTO THE SHIP AGAIN DEPARTED TO THE OTHER SIDE."

The phrase, *"And He left them,"* is of far greater import than just geographical location. He, in Truth, left them to their doom, and because of their unbelief. Little did they realize, but it was to be the most significant departure they would ever know or witness. And yet, these Pharisees were so spiritually dull that they had no idea as to what was happening.

The phrase, *"And entering into the ship again departed to the other side,"* even though speaking of going to the other side of the lake, its portend speaks of a darkening gloom beginning to settle over Israel. The only hope for this country, as any country, is Christ! However, the Religious Leadership did not believe this, and, as a consequence, opposed Christ greatly!

However, Israel as the Covenant people, was of far greater significance than any other country. Actually, their rejection of Christ would postpone the material/physical advent of the Kingdom of God. As a result, the *"Times of the Gentiles"* has been lengthened for some 2,000 years. During this time the world has been bathed in blood as the result of countless wars. As well, starvation, disease, and plagues, have characterized the planet — all because of Israel's rejection of Christ.

Thank the Lord that this will soon be rectified, with Israel ultimately coming to Christ, but not without great Tribulation (Rev. Chpts. 6-19).

(14) "NOW THE DISCIPLES HAD FORGOTTEN TO TAKE BREAD, NEITHER HAD THEY IN THE SHIP WITH THEM MORE THAN ONE LOAF."

They were on their way from the western shore to the northeastern side of the Sea of Galilee. The short journey would take approximately six hours.

The statement about the *"one loaf"* is given only to set up the coming exchange between Jesus and the Disciples.

(15) "AND HE CHARGED THEM, SAYING, TAKE HEED, BEWARE OF THE LEAVEN OF

THE PHARISEES, AND OF THE LEAVEN OF HEROD."

The phrase, *"And He charged them,"* in the Greek Text, means that He kept on warning them, making certain they understood of what He was speaking. Through His Word, He charges us no less presently! Consequently, the reader must take this to heart just as much as the warning to the Disciples.

The phrase, *"Saying, Take heed, beware of the leaven of the Pharisees, and of the leaven of Herod,"* presented not only the dangers of that time, but of the present as well! Jesus is speaking of false doctrine, for that is what *"leaven"* represents.

The words, *"Take heed,"* and, *"Beware,"* speak of extreme caution, and that the teachings of these particular ones were to be put to the acid test. It speaks of the mind's eye, discerning mentally, understanding what is being said and done.

It means that every Believer is to look at Doctrine carefully, inspecting it minutely according to the Word of God, before it is accepted. How so much trouble would be avoided if this were heeded!

Regrettably, most Believers so little know the Word of God that they readily bite into any bait offered. With many, it is almost like a child being mesmerized by the glitter of a brightly-colored object.

Wuest says that *"leaven"* embodies the principle of fermentation which makes it the symbol of corruption, for fermentation is the result of the divine curse upon the material universe because of sin. Always in the Bible, it speaks of evil in some form, Matthew 13:33 being no exception, for the Kingdom of Heaven here refers to Christendom, in which is the true and the false, the evil and the good.

As well, *"Leaven,"* in I Corinthians 5:6-8, speaks of malice and wickedness as contrasted to sincerity and truth.

In Matthew 16:12, it speaks of evil doctrine in its threefold form of Pharisaism, which is externalism in religion, of Sadduceeism, which is skepticism as to the supernatural and as to the Scriptures, and of Herodianism, which is worldliness.

In effect, the Pharisees taught some things concerning the Law of Moses which were right. This was not to be disregarded, but only so far

as they corrupted the Law by their own vain traditions, which were contrary to the Law.

However, the mixture of Truth and error, which the Pharisees did, and which is common today, is probably the greatest danger of all. Leaven has this property, that however small it may be in quantity, it spreads its influence rapidly through the mass. And so if only a little spark of heretical doctrine be admitted into the soul, speedily a great flame arises, and envelopes the whole man (Bickersteth).

As an example, the unscriptural doctrine of Unconditional Eternal Security as leaven, which it is, has ultimately taken over the entirety of the Denomination(s) which teach and believe it. In other words, this unscriptural doctrine overshadows everything that is taught.

As well, those who teach that one has to speak in tongues to be saved, falls into the same category. Even though *"tongues"* is certainly Scriptural, even as Conditional Eternal Security is Scriptural, still, making it a part of Salvation is error, in fulfillment of the little leaven, which leaveneth the whole lump (I Cor. 5:6).

The same could be said for Seventh Day Adventism, respecting the keeping of Saturday, etc. This leaven of the Mosaic Law, which, in effect, was fulfilled in Christ, now overshadows the entirety of that particular Denomination.

At the same time, it does not mean that all who believe these particular erroneous doctrines are lost, for, in Truth, many of them are truly saved. If one truly trusts Christ for one's Salvation, one is saved irrespective of other types of error. Nevertheless, if allowed to remain, which proclaims a failure to heed the admonitions of the Holy Spirit as given in the Word of God, ultimately, the Christian life will be seriously hindered and weakened. The Holy Spirit always leads one toward Truth and Christ (Jn. 16:13-14).

The Holy Spirit can never bless or anoint error. To be sure, He, at times, will bless and anoint us, even though error is present, but such is done because of a sincere heart. Nevertheless, His help and anointing will gradually subside if we fail to heed His admonitions respecting our walk in proper Scriptural Light.

The greatest sign of Truth being properly lived and preached, is the fruit that it bears (Jn. 15:1-2). If the Word of God is properly practiced and taught, it will bring forth the Fruit of changed lives and Christian growth. If this is little present or not present at all, it is a sure sign that one of two things is taking place:

1. The Truth is not being preached, or else it is a mixture of Truth and error.

2. The Truth is being preached, but with no Anointing of the Holy Spirit (I Thess. 1:5).

As is obvious, the Ministry of Christ brought forth much Fruit, even though it also garnered much opposition. The same could be said for the Apostle Paul. To be sure, the same holds true for all who truthfully proclaim the Gospel of Christ. That which is corrupted with *"leaven"* will greatly oppose that which is True.

As well, the doctrine of the *"leaven"* as it is taught throughout the Bible, shoots down the theory propagated by the world and much of the Church, that man is getting better and better, with the world ultimately to be ushered into a utopian paradise.

Even though Bible Christianity has had a tremendous positive effect on the earth, still, most of humanity rejects the Gospel of Jesus Christ. Consequently, and despite thousands of years of education and technological advancement, especially in the last 100 years, man is not getting better, but rather worse. Despite intellectualism, the evil heart of man is not changed, and actually because of the *"leaven process"* is getting worse, and were it not for the Second Coming of Christ, man would ultimately destroy himself, and the world.

As well, the *"political message,"* as propagated by much of the modern Church, flies in the face of the leavening of the whole as taught in the Word of God. The various cultures of the world are not, and, in fact, will not be Christianized, with the world getting better and better, ultimately ushering in the Millennium. As stated, such teaching flies in the face of the Word of God. The sin problem cannot be educated out of people, and neither can proper politics curtail the terrible problem of evil. Only the Coming of Jesus Christ, which will be in great power, will solve this problem. As well, when He comes, it will not be to a world that has been Christianized, but, instead, to a world that is on the brink of total destruction. The account is given in Revelation 19.

As we have alluded to, the *"leaven of the Pharisees"* was the mixture of tradition with the True Word of God. As a consequence, there was

NOTES

not much of the True Word of God left, with the leaven, as is the custom of leaven, having taken over the whole.

The *"leaven of Herod,"* concerned the Herodians, and spoke of worldliness. This party followed Herod, and did all within its power to accommodate Rome, even at the expense of compromising the entirety of the Word of God.

Both, *"the leaven of the Pharisees,"* and *"the leaven of Herod,"* are prominent in the modern Church as well! So, the admonition of Christ to His Disciples so long ago was an admonition to us also!

(16) "AND THEY REASONED AMONG THEMSELVES, SAYING, IT IS BECAUSE WE HAVE NO BREAD."

The phrase, *"And they reasoned among themselves,"* concerned them discussing what He had said about the leaven back and forth among themselves. As the next phrase shows, they had not the slightest idea of what He was speaking.

The phrase, *"It is because we have no bread,"* concerns them having their mind on the *"one loaf,"* and thinking He was upset because they had not brought more.

His statement was spiritual, while their thinking and conversation were the opposite.

I am afraid we presently miss so much of what the Holy Spirit tells us, and because of the same problem. Our thinking is too much in the carnal realm, and not enough in the spiritual.

The erroneous statement that some *"are so spiritually minded, that they are of no earthly use,"* has taken root in many lives. In Truth, it is impossible to be too spiritually minded. Paul said, *"For to be carnally minded is death; but to be spiritually minded is life and peace"* (Rom. 8:6).

One of the greatest truths they would ever hear was being given to them, and they missed it altogether!

(17) "AND WHEN JESUS KNEW IT, HE SAITH UNTO THEM, WHY REASON YE, BECAUSE YE HAVE NO BREAD? PERCEIVE YE NOT YET, NEITHER UNDERSTAND? HAVE YE YOUR HEART YET HARDENED?"

The phrase, *"And when Jesus knew it,"* means, *"When Jesus perceived it!"* It was not so much a matter of Him overhearing the Disciples, but, instead, that the Spirit of God witnessed to His Spirit their confusion.

The question, *"He saith unto them, Why reason ye, because ye have no bread?"*, concerns the first of nine questions which will be asked. In fact, the Jews were very strict as to the kind of leaven that was to be used in bread, of which the Pharisees, no doubt, had much to say. This may have been on their mind, concerning the amount of leaven in the one loaf they had, as much as not bringing an ample supply.

Their thoughts concerning not having enough bread, and to which His question pointed, was of far greater import than meets the eye.

Not only were the Disciples forgetting His Miracle-working Power, but, as well, they wanted this multiplication of bread to springboard Jesus to the Throne of Israel as King, with Rome, consequently, being overcome. The entirety of their perception was wrong, as He will later say.

The question, *"Perceive ye not yet, neither understand?"*, concerns a wrong understanding of what the Miracles of the multiplication were all about. As a result of that misunderstanding, which was a total misconception of the Plan and Will of God, neither did they understand His statement concerning the *"leaven of the Pharisees,"* etc.

Once again, we see the leaven at work concerning their understanding, which, if not corrected, will ultimately corrupt the whole of their thinking. It is like a rotten apple in a barrel of good apples. The good apples do not make whole the bad one, but the bad one will definitely corrupt all the others, unless removed.

This is a lesson we should well learn. If erroneous doctrine is allowed to continue in our thinking, as we have repeatedly stated, our understanding concerning what Truth we do know, will ultimately be affected. Actually, it is impossible to have any leaven at all, no matter how small, without it ultimately corrupting the whole. All leaven must be removed!

The question, *"Have ye your heart yet hardened?"*, goes back to 6:52. Because this subject is so very important, and, consequently, affects so many people, allow us to repeat what was previously given in commentary on 6:52.

The Disciples misunderstood the reason for the multiplication of the loaves and fishes. They did not understand that Jesus, by doing this, was telling the world in essence that He was the Bread of Life, and Alone could satisfy

the spiritual hunger of the human family. They saw the multiplication of the loaves and fishes as a springboard to power. He would be made King, and Israel would once again rule the world. Consequently, their thinking, which was contrary to the Will of God, hardened their hearts. The product of self-will, which this was, is always the hardened heart.

This means that every single individual who does not follow the Word of God, but, instead, puts his own gloss on it, as the Pharisees of old, concludes with a hardened heart. Regrettably, almost all of the modern Church falls into this category.

As self-will intrudes, the heart, ceasing to be pliable in the Hands of the Lord, becomes hardened toward God. For one to be tender toward God, consequently able to hear His Voice, and to be led accordingly, one must be in the Will of God, which will always be according to the Word of God.

(18) "HAVING EYES, SEE YE NOT? AND HAVING EARS, HEAR YE NOT? AND DO YE NOT REMEMBER?"

The question, *"Having eyes, see ye not?"*, pertained to spiritual eyes they were not using. Once again, they were seeing things in the carnal, which was a result of self-will. They were not seeing things in the spiritual sense, and most today follow in their train.

The question, *"And having ears, hear ye not?"*, is the same as the *"eyes."* As they could not *"see"* correctly, neither could they *"hear"* correctly.

The question, *"And do ye not remember?"*, proclaims their understanding of what had happened regarding the multiplication of the loaves, as being faulty. So, they *"saw"* wrong; they *"heard"* wrong; they *"understood"* wrong!

When one considers that these men to whom Jesus was speaking were His chosen Disciples, and had the privilege of being under His tutelage constantly, one begins to understand how absolutely deadly this *"leaven"* actually is. Thank the Lord some personal problems, such as Peter's denial, along with the Day of Pentecost, would help cure these problems.

(19) "WHEN I BRAKE THE FIVE LOAVES AMONG FIVE THOUSAND, HOW MANY BASKETS FULL OF FRAGMENTS TOOK YE UP? THEY SAY UNTO HIM, TWELVE."

Jesus will now draw their attention back to the Miracle of the multiplication of the loaves, reminding them that they had *"twelve"* baskets of fragments left over, even after feeding multiple thousands of people. Consequently, the amount of bread they had in the boat should have been of no consequence to them.

(20) "AND WHEN THE SEVEN AMONG FOUR THOUSAND, HOW MANY BASKETS FULL OF FRAGMENTS TOOK YE UP? AND THEY SAID, SEVEN."

As He reminded them of the first Miracle of multiplication, He now reminds them of the second Miracle. In other words, if one was not enough to prove His Power, surely two were enough.

So, they had no reason to misunderstand His statements regarding the *"leaven of the Pharisees,"* etc., thinking He was speaking of their forgetting to bring more bread.

(21) "AND HE SAID UNTO THEM, HOW IS IT THAT YE DO NOT UNDERSTAND?"

Some have said that the question could have been better translated, *"Do ye not yet understand?"*

There is a hint in the Greek Text that, in fact, they finally did understand. Actually, Matthew tells us this was the case (Mat. 16:12).

They now know that He was not speaking of earthly leaven or earthly bread, but, rather, Spiritual Doctrine.

(22) "AND HE COMETH TO BETHSAIDA; AND THEY BRING A BLIND MAN UNTO HIM, AND BESOUGHT HIM TO TOUCH HIM."

The phrase, *"And He cometh to Bethsaida,"* probably refers to Bethsaida Julias, situated on the northeast shore of the Sea of Galilee.

The phrase, *"And they bring a blind man unto Him, and besought Him to touch him,"* seems to indicate that they imagined that healing could not come forth from Christ except by actual contact. Therefore, they will plead with Him to *"touch him."*

(23) "AND HE TOOK THE BLIND MAN BY THE HAND, AND LED HIM OUT OF THE TOWN; AND WHEN HE HAD SPIT ON HIS EYES, AND PUT HIS HANDS UPON HIM, HE ASKED HIM IF HE SAW OUGHT."

The phrase, *"And He took the blind man by the hand, and led him out of the town,"* was done for reason.

Jesus had already cursed this city because of their refusal to repent, and, consequently, would not perform another Miracle in its confines (Mat. 11:21). Light refused is light canceled.

NOTES

This means that America and Canada are possibly in the most dangerous period of their existence as a nation. One could possibly say, and without fear of contradiction, that more Gospel has been proclaimed in these two countries than any other country or countries in the world. As a result, America and Canada have been blessed in an unprecedented way.

And yet, both nations are fastly hardening themselves against God. No longer does it know or realize the Source of its blessings. It is as Israel of old!

Why?

Peter said, and which is the answer, *"For the time is come that Judgment must begin at the House of God: and if it first begin at us, what shall the end be of them that obey not the Gospel of God?"* (I Pet. 4:17).

For the nation to have Revival, the Church must first have Revival!

The phrase, *"And when He had spit on his eyes,"* pertains to the second time such was done (Mk. 7:33). The first concerned a malformed tongue of a man which caused an impediment in his speech, with this referring to blindness.

The cause for the *"spittle,"* is the same as in the previous incident. The saliva which came from a perfect body, which had not the taint of sin about it, therefore perfectly free of germs, was a symbol of His Life which was perpetual, and, therefore, eternal.

Exactly how the spittle was applied to his eyes, Mark does not say. He could have spat on His finger, as He probably did before, and then applied it to the man's eyes, or He could have spat fully on his eyes, which seems to be the case.

The phrase, *"And put His Hands upon him,"* now proclaims Him doing what the friends of the blind man had requested.

The phrase, *"He asked him if he saw ought,"* has in the Greek Text that He kept on asking him.

(24) "AND HE LOOKED UP, AND SAID, I SEE MEN AS TREES, WALKING."

The answer to the question as asked by the Lord, in the Greek Text is actually as follows: *"I see men; for I behold them as trees, walking."* The word, *"walking,"* refers to the men, and not to the trees, as is evident from the Greek.

There seemed to be a mist of sorts over his eyes, which disfigured everything, which meant he was still partially blind.

(25) "AFTER THAT HE PUT HIS HANDS AGAIN UPON HIS EYES, AND MADE HIM LOOK UP: AND HE WAS RESTORED, AND SAW EVERY MAN CLEARLY."

The phrase, *"After that He put His Hands again upon his eyes, and made him look up,"* records the only incident in the four Gospels of Jesus touching someone the second time in this fashion. Some have called this a gradual healing; however, it could hardly be labeled as that, inasmuch as the entire scenario probably took place in a minute or so!

The phrase, *"And he was restored, and saw every man clearly,"* records his complete healing.

Why did Jesus have to lay His Hands on him a second time?

The next verse possibly gives us a clue.

(26) "AND HE SENT HIM AWAY TO HIS HOUSE, SAYING, NEITHER GO INTO THE TOWN, NOR TELL IT TO ANY IN THE TOWN."

The phrase, *"And He sent him away to his house,"* implies that he was not a native of Bethsaida Julias.

The phrase, *"Saying, Neither go into the town, nor tell it to any in the town,"* refers, as we have mentioned, to the curse He had placed on this town for their refusal to repent. He had said this: *"Woe unto thee, Bethsaida! For if the mighty works which were done in you, had been in Tyre and Sidon, they would have repented long ago in sackcloth and ashes"* (Mat. 11:21).

Due to this, Christ seemed unwilling to give Bethsaida anymore evidence of the visitation of God.

This could well be the reason why Jesus had to lay His Hands on the man a second time. The curse had been pronounced and the die cast, consequently, it was as if the door was shut.

Many have claimed that the Lord led the man outside of town, in order to avoid the crowds, etc. However, it is very doubtful that was the case. It was more likely because of the pronounced Judgment.

The town had seen a display of the Power of God as only a few others had seen, namely, Capernaum and Chorazin, still, all refused to repent, with all, consequently, being cursed.

The man not being healed instantly when Christ first laid Hands on him, certainly was not because of a lack of power on the part of Christ, but, rather, that no more power would be displayed in this place. Consequently, the man had

NOTES

to be led out of town, and even then, hands laid on him twice.

As well, Jesus telling the man not to even relate the account of his healing to the people in Bethsaida, tells us two things:

1. No more Light was to be given to them, and because they had firmly rejected that already given.

2. If the man had said anything about it to the occupants, more than likely they would have ridiculed the Miracle. When men resist the Holy Spirit, He, by a just Judgment, abandons them to wrath.

Unbelief is the mother of many evils, and it has a mysterious power. Consequently, and as here stated, it is useless to give evidence to unbelief. Had Jesus given the most overwhelming proofs of His Messiahship, they would not have believed upon Him, and for the reason that Faith waits for repentance and the sense of sin against God, for the need of pardon, and for a desire to escape from its defilement. Inasmuch as Faith is the foundation of the Gospel, Jesus threw the responsibility upon the cities of Israel, calling upon them to repent and believe the Gospel. His whole mission rested upon this moral foundation; and the satisfactory evidence He gave of His Deity could only be perceived by those who had moral eyesight. The demonstration that the Scribes demanded had no value; it would not have affected the heart and produced repentance, even if done!

I wonder if there are cities in America and Canada, or elsewhere in the world for that matter, which have been cursed by God, and will, consequently, receive no further visitation?

As a spiritual lesson derived from this episode, Bede, the great scholar of long ago, said, *"Christ teaches us how great is the spiritual blindness of man, which only by degrees, and by successive stages, can come to the light of Divine knowledge."* Bickersteth said, *"The experiences of this blind man in gradually recovering his eyesight show as in a parable the stages of the spiritual change from absolute darkness to glimmering light, and thence to bright and clear vision."*

Back to the mysterious power of unbelief, such cannot be registered until Light is first given and rejected. Richards says, *"At heart, unbelief is staggering back from God's Revelation of Himself, refusing to respond as Abraham, with trust"* (Rom. 4:20). Thus, unbelief exhibits a sinful heart *"that turns away from the Living God"* (Heb. 3:12).

If Light is rejected, darkness can be the only result! However, it is a darkness that ever deepens. While it is possible for one to be pulled back from unbelief, it can only be done by the Power of the Risen Christ. Paul Rader experienced that Power.

It is said that he had a great experience with the Lord as a young Preacher, winning many souls and seeing great success. However, things happened which brought a bitterness to his soul, resulting in him turning his back on God.

He entertained great depths of sin, but with the greatest sin of all being that of unbelief, which disavowed even the fact of God's existence.

But, miracle of miracles, the Holy Spirit was able to reach through the gloom of that stygian night, and awakened the Light, though covered, that still resided in his soul. To be sure, it is not easy at all to turn out the Light that God has hung up in one's soul since infancy.

By the Power of God, he was brought back, and performed an even greater work for God. As well, he wrote the song:

> *"Only believe, only believe,*
> *"All things are possible, only believe.*
> *"Only believe, only believe,*
> *"All things are possible, only believe!"*

In the depths of his failure, he had had great difficulty in believing, because unbelief with its mysterious power destroys every vestige of Faith. However, even a shred of Faith is stronger than all unbelief. Consequently, Paul Rader was brought back to Jesus. Now the reason for this song becomes all the more obvious!

(27) "AND JESUS WENT OUT, AND HIS DISCIPLES, INTO THE TOWNS OF CAESAREA PHILIPPI: AND BY THE WAY HE ASKED HIS DISCIPLES, SAYING UNTO THEM, WHOM DO MEN SAY THAT I AM?"

The phrase, *"And Jesus went out, and His Disciples,"* represents Jesus leaving this place spiritually, even as He had left the *"parts of Dalmanutha"* (8:13). Even though the Text speaks of a geographical change, still, it has spiritual implications as well! They had rejected Him, so He *"went out!"*

The phrase, *"Into the towns of Caesarea Philippi,"* placed Him about 40 miles north of

the Sea of Galilee and about 40 miles south of Damascus. By the use of the word, *"towns,"* He probably did not go into Caesarea Philippi proper, but rather to the towns which were nearby.

Scholars have suggested that as the name *"Jesus"* is here expressly mentioned, it refers to something very important about to be narrated, which closely concerned His Disciples, because they are mentioned as well!

This is approximately six months before His Crucifixion. If one is to notice, Jesus spent more and more time away from Galilee and Judaea proper, and because of the tremendous opposition. By now, He was welcome in very few Synagogues. At least as far as Judaea was concerned, the people were threatened with excommunication from the Synagogue if they followed Him (Jn. 9:22).

Despite His Miracles, despite His Teaching and Preaching, which was the most enlightening that man had ever heard, and despite the fact that He was the Messiah, the Son of the Living God, He was no longer welcome in their Churches.

Were He on earth today and under the same circumstances, I suspect He would be no better received. In Truth, He is not welcome in most Churches at present.

While it is true that He is spoken of and talked about, still, if there is the slightest manifestation of His Power through the Holy Spirit, such is instantly stopped!

While most Preachers and Priests speak favorably of Him, still, if they truly loved Him, and, thereby, served Him, He would not be a stranger in their Churches.

The question, *"And by the way He asked His Disciples, saying unto them, Whom do men say that I am?",* constitutes Who He really was, and the drawing out of the Disciples as to Who they thought He was.

The Greek Text says, *"He kept on asking,"* meaning that the question so startled them, that at first they did not answer.

(28) "AND THEY ANSWERED, JOHN THE BAPTIST; BUT SOME SAY, ELIAS; AND OTHERS, ONE OF THE PROPHETS."

Their answers were strange, but yet reflected the thinking of much of Israel at that particular time.

Their answers portray the fact that most in Israel did not believe that He was the Messiah.

Bickersteth said, *"The great body of them were offended at His poverty and humility; for they thought that Messiah would appear amongst them with royal state as a temporal King."*

So, if He was not the Messiah, they reasoned, then He must be one of the great Prophets of old risen from the dead. Even though the Sadducees denied a Resurrection, the great body of the Jews believed in it.

Probably most of them thought He was Elijah, insomuch that Elijah had not died, but had been translated. As well, Malachi had prophesied that this Prophet would return. Some thought, therefore, that Elijah had returned, and that the Lord was Elijah the Prophet.

In effect, their unbelief stemmed from the fact that they would not believe the Word of God. The people were not altogether to blame for this situation, inasmuch as the Religious Leaders of Israel gave no credence at all to Biblical interpretation by the peasantry, with whatever they thought being passed off as inconsequential. The people were encouraged strongly to look to these so-called great scholars, who would interpret the Bible for them. Consequently, most did not know the Bible.

(29) "AND HE SAITH UNTO THEM, BUT WHOM SAY YE THAT I AM? AND PETER ANSWERETH AND SAITH UNTO HIM, THOU ART THE CHRIST."

The question, *"And He saith unto them, But Whom say ye that I am?"*, concerns the greatest question they would ever be asked, and the greatest question anyone could ever be asked! Actually, it is a question that all must ultimately answer.

Hundreds of millions say that He was a Prophet, but no more than a Prophet, consequently, denying His Deity. Others say He was a great Man, and a Miracle-worker, but somewhat deluded respecting Himself being the Son of God. Of course, it is difficult to understand how someone could be great, and at the same time a liar!

Actually, very few deny that He actually lived, and because the evidence of His Life and Ministry is overwhelming. Therefore, at least by most, He is passed off as merely a Great Man among other great men.

Years ago, I happened to read an article in Reader's Digest regarding the ten greatest men who ever lived. Jesus Christ was mentioned as One of the ten.

Possibly the editors of this magazine felt very kindly toward themselves for including Jesus in this august group. However, what they did was tantamount to blasphemy.

While it is certainly true that Jesus was a Man, still, and as Peter will proclaim, He is much more, actually, the Son of the Living God. He is Emmanuel, God manifest in the flesh. Even though He had a beginning as Man, as God He had no beginning, having always existed, and will always exist. He said, *"I am Alpha and Omega, the Beginning and the End, the First and the Last"* (Rev. 22:13).

The phrase, *"And Peter answereth and saith unto Him, Thou art the Christ,"* is the English spelling of the Greek word, *"Christos,"* which means *"The Anointed One."* Into the English it is translated *"Messiah."*

Some scholars feel that Peter actually said, *"Thou art the Messiah,"* with the word, *"Christos,"* translated accordingly.

In Psalm 2:2, the Kings of the earth are said to take counsel against the Lord and His Anointed, the word, *"Anointed,"* being here *"Messiah"* in the original. Wuest says, *"The word designates that King Whom God will provide for Israel, Who will occupy the Throne of David forever."*

As well, it should be noticed, that Mark omits the Great Blessing pronounced upon Peter for this confession by the Lord. However, Matthew did record it (Mat. 16:17-19).

This is probably because Peter is relating this account to Mark, and, consequently, not feeling comfortable in relating such Blessing, although he would relate the rebuke that Christ gave him in full (vs. 33).

Again, such proclaims the fact that the boastful Peter no longer exists, but only the Peter of humility!

(30) "AND HE CHARGED THEM THAT THEY SHOULD TELL NO MAN OF HIM."

The word, *"charged,"* is a strong word, meaning that He admonished or charged them sharply. It is almost a threatening tone.

The phrase, *"That they should tell no man of Him,"* relates the fact that it was now obvious that Israel had rejected Him, and, consequently, there was no further point in projecting the issue.

He was very concerned about His Disciples, and, therefore, made sure they knew Who He was. At all cost, they must not be pulled under by unbelief. Of course, the horror of the Crucifixion, which was only a few months away, would try their Faith to the fullest. However, the Resurrection, with the exclaimed, *"He's alive again,"* would instantly clear that up.

(31) "AND HE BEGAN TO TEACH THEM, THAT THE SON OF MAN MUST SUFFER MANY THINGS, AND BE REJECTED OF THE ELDERS, AND OF THE CHIEF PRIESTS, AND SCRIBES, AND BE KILLED, AND AFTER THREE DAYS RISE AGAIN."

The phrase, *"And He began to teach them,"* proclaims an explanation as to what was to happen, despite the fact that He was the Messiah.

Consequently, Peter's confession, although correct, was not given in the correct posture. Peter, as the others, thought surely that the Throne of David would be occupied now. This is proven by Peter's rebuke of Him in the following verse. Consequently, he begins to prepare them!

The phrase, *"That the Son of Man must suffer many things,"* proclaimed that they believed otherwise!

Jesus was speaking of suffering, while they were thinking of Glory.

The phrase, *"And be rejected of the Elders, and of the Chief Priests, and Scribes,"* concerned the entirety of the Religious Leadership of Israel. In other words, He was rejected totally, fully, and completely, by the Church.

The word, *"rejected,"* means that the Religious Leaders of Israel put Jesus to the test for the purpose of approving Him as the Messiah, for they were looking at this time for the Messiah. However, He did not meet their specifications. He was not the kind of a Messiah the Jews wanted. Wuest said, *"They wanted a military leader who would liberate them from the yoke of Rome, not a Saviour Who would free them from their bondage of sin."*

They rejected Jesus even though He fulfilled every Prophecy, and, in Truth, met every specification. However, these were Biblical specifications, and not of self-will.

Their vision of the Messiah was not what the Bible projected. Their tradition, however, would not allow them to believe the Bible, but rather twist its words to conform to their own unbelief.

In Truth, Jesus will one day take the Throne of Israel, consequently, putting down every enemy, and making Israel the greatest nation in

the world. However, it will be only after Israel has repented (Zech. 12:10-13:1), which did not take place at the First Advent.

The phrase, *"And be killed,"* was something the Disciples, and especially Peter, could not grasp or even believe. In their minds, how could such be?

They still did not realize how evil the Religious Leaders of Israel actually were, and neither did they realize the true mission of Christ. He did not come to catapult Israel to greatness and glory as they thought, but rather to lift man from the terrible bondage of sin which had enslaved him. At that time, they did not understand this!

The phrase, *"And after three days rise again,"* was completely lost upon them. It was as if they did not hear what He said.

Not only did they not believe it then, they had trouble believing it after the Resurrection.

In this statement by Christ, the two great principles of Faith are presented:

1. The Divinity and the Humanity of Christ.

2. His Cross and Passion, whereby He redeemed the world (Bickersteth).

At this time, they were not clear on these things, but would be after the Day of Pentecost.

(32) "AND HE SPAKE THAT SAYING OPENLY. AND PETER TOOK HIM, AND BEGAN TO REBUKE HIM."

The phrase, *"And He spake that saying openly,"* actually has two meanings:

1. In the Greek Text, the idea is that Jesus didn't say this one time, but actually several times. In other words, He kept saying it over and over, so they would not miss it.

2. It was said *"openly"* in that each Disciple heard Him, and unmistakably so, and, as well, it was not said as a Parable.

The idea is, that the Disciples know exactly what He was saying, what it meant, and would have no questions about the matter.

The phrase, *"And Peter took Him,"* means that the words hit the Disciples like a bombshell. Peter, as the leader, and inasmuch as he had just made the great confession, pulls the Lord aside in order to speak to Him privately. It is the same as someone taking another by the shoulders, which is probably what happened!

The phrase, *"And began to rebuke Him,"* means to speak with force, but, above that, to deny what Jesus has said.

Even though Mark does not relate what Peter said, Matthew did record his statement. He said, *"Be it far from Thee, Lord: this shall not be unto Thee"* (Mat. 16:22).

The terrible trials, and even His Death, expressed by Christ, flew in the face of what the Disciples were thinking. In their minds, He was going to be the King of Israel, making David's Throne the centerpiece of the world. Israel would once again regain her glory as under David and Solomon. Rome would be thrown off, and this hated subservience would end.

As well, they (the Disciples) would be His Chief Lieutenants in this new Kingdom, which was obvious, especially considering their association with Him.

Actually, this is what caused their *"hardness of heart!"* Their position was not one of Faith, but, rather, of presumption, and, therefore, of self-will. Anyone out of the Will of God, and irrespective as to whom the person may be, even the Disciples, takes unto himself the hardened heart.

They did not understand the Mission of Christ, neither did they properly understand the Scripture. While the Prophets had certainly spoken of a coming Kingdom, their assumption that it was coming now, was entirely wrong. Had they properly read Isaiah 53, Daniel 9, or Zechariah 11, they would have known better. But they, as so many others, read what they desired into the Word of God.

(33) "BUT WHEN HE HAD TURNED ABOUT AND LOOKED ON HIS DISCIPLES, HE REBUKED PETER, SAYING, GET THEE BEHIND ME, SATAN: FOR THOU SAVOUREST NOT THE THINGS THAT BE OF GOD, BUT THE THINGS THAT BE OF MEN."

The phrase, *"But when He had turned about,"* proclaims a sudden motion on the part of the Master, upon hearing Peter's rebuke. He did not at all take lightly what Peter had said, as will be obvious!

The phrase, *"And looked on His Disciples,"* means that what He will say, must be heard by them as well!

More than likely, the Disciples had heard Peter's rebuke, and now they must hear Jesus' answer. To be sure, it was not a pleasant time at all for Jesus. Even though they had been with Him constantly for about three years, still, they had little understanding as to what His True

Mission was all about. Instead of Salvation for the world, they saw power, position, riches, and glory. Regrettably, much of the Charismatic community sees the same thing, instead of the True Purpose of Christ.

The phrase, *"He rebuked Peter,"* did not, at least at that time, obtain its intended result. Mark uses the same word for *"rebuke"* concerning the answer of Jesus, as he did for Peter's answer to Christ.

Peter's rebuke did not cause Jesus to change His Mind, because it should not have. However, the *"rebuke"* given to Peter and the Disciples by Christ, should have brought Peter to repentance, but, sadly, it did not!

It was not that Peter was stubbornly rebelling against the Lord, but that he simply did not understand. However, ignorance, although not as bad as open rebellion, still, brings about the same results — the hardened heart (Mk. 8:17).

The phrase, *"Saying, Get thee behind Me, Satan,"* presents Jesus speaking directly to Satan, and not Peter. He spoke directly to the Tempter, including Peter in the rebuke. Consequently, the Lord, in His utterance, brands Peter's words as Satanic.

Jesus' rebuke has the same flavor as the temptation in the wilderness. Satan had said to Jesus at that time, and speaking of the great Roman Empire, *"All these things will I give Thee, if Thou wilt fall down and worship me"* (Mat. 4:9).

At this time, Satan does not ask Jesus to fall down and worship him, as he did previously, but, instead, he tempted the Lord to go around the Cross. To do this, he would use Jesus' most trusted Disciples.

The word, *"Behind Me,"* in essence, demands that Satan cease his temptations, in effect, *"Get out of My Face!"*

The phrase, *"For thou savourest not the things that be of God, but the things that be of men,"* is addressed to both Satan and Peter. Satan, as is obvious, did not want the things which were of God, and Peter was wanting the things that were *"of men."* Actually, there was no difference in the two desires.

This is perhaps one of Satan's greatest ploys. If he can get men to follow other men, even religious men, he will have succeeded in his purpose. The reasons are obvious. The Lord through Isaiah said, *"For as the heavens are higher than the earth, so are My Ways higher than your ways, and My Thoughts than your thoughts"* (Isa. 55:9).

In fact, *"There is a way which seemeth right unto a man, but the end thereof are the ways of death"* (Prov. 14:12).

At the moment of conversion, the Holy Spirit sets about to direct the ways of man toward God. This is done through the Word of God. Actually, there is not a single way which the Holy Spirit will lead a man, that is not found first in the Word.

At the same time, Satan sets about to lead men away from the Word. To be sure, his efforts are subtle, smart, religious, and to the carnal mind, plausible! To follow that way, will reap the applause of men, and especially religious men, but the frown of God.

To follow the Lord, and the Lord exclusively, will reap no applause from men, but rather their opposition, and especially from religious men. However, such will meet with the approval of God. This is what Jesus was speaking of when He said, *"Blessed are they which are persecuted for Righteousness' sake: for theirs is the Kingdom of Heaven"* (Mat. 5:10).

To follow the Lord as one should, one must follow very closely in order to hear His Voice. If he lags too far behind, the siren call of the world, and especially the religious world, will gradually drown out that Voice.

As well, it should be understood, that if Peter was so used by Satan, so can any Believer be thusly used.

(34) "AND WHEN HE HAD CALLED THE PEOPLE UNTO HIM WITH HIS DISCIPLES ALSO, HE SAID UNTO THEM, WHOSOEVER SHALL COME AFTER ME, LET HIM DENY HIMSELF, AND TAKE UP HIS CROSS, AND FOLLOW ME."

The phrase, *"And when He had called the people unto Him with His Disciples also,"* speaks of an interval of some period of time between His rebuke of Peter and this present statement. In the previous exchange, only the Disciples were included, with others now being addressed as well! What Jesus will say, will be the very heartbeat of what it means to be a Christian. Consequently, the Message is given not only to the Disciples, but to the people as well, and because it is a requirement of all!

The phrase, *"Whosoever will come after Me,"* refers to those who accept the call. It means to

be born again, thereby becoming His Disciple, following His Teachings, and, consequently, entering into His fellowship.

If one is to notice, Jesus didn't say, *"Come after the 'Church,'"* or Preacher, Priest, or Prophet, but, rather, Christ Himself.

Christianity without Christ, is no more than any other philosophy. Such produces the moralist, which number abounds, but does not produce a changed life. The moralists reduces Christianity to a mere religion, which makes it little different than the other religions of the world. Actually, Christianity cannot change anything or anyone. Only Christ can change hearts, and, thereby, lives! He actually makes a new creature of all who come to Him.

Regrettably, Christianity in most circles is Christless, inasmuch as Christ has been pushed to the periphery, if considered at all! When that happens, the Church becomes the Saviour, which, in effect, is no Saviour at all!

As a result, Jesus is the Center of controversy. The argument is not with God, because God, at least to most, is merely an abstract. He can be labeled anything, and usually is, and, consequently, does not offend anyone. However, Jesus is a Person Who actually lived, and actually claimed to be God, and, as well, the Way to the Father, and, to be sure, the Only Way! As such, He stands in contrast to Mohammed and a host of other false luminaries. So the argument is with Jesus.

The Bible teaches that no man can come to the Father but by Jesus, and, as well, it is through His Name Only that one can be saved (Jn. 14:6; Acts 4:12).

The phrase, *"Let him deny himself,"* hits at the very crux of man's problem, which is *"self."*

As we have previously stated, when man fell in the Garden of Eden, he lost God-consciousness, falling to the far lower level of self-consciousness. Before the Fall, his eyes were exclusively on God from Whom he drew sustenance, life, and strength. Now it is on *"self,"* which breeds acute selfishness, thereby, the cause of all the misery in the world.

THE GOSPEL OF SELF-ESTEEM

To correct this situation, man (not God) has come up with the false gospel of *"self-esteem."* This false way basically teaches that man's problem is that he does not readily know his self-worth, and, consequently, needs his self-esteem elevated. If this can be done, they teach, man's problems will be solved.

One of the foremost proponents of the self-esteem gospel, has called for a *"new reformation,"* stating that the 16th century movement (under Luther and Calvin) was a *"reactionary movement"* because it emphasized that men are sinners. He goes on to say, *"Once a person believes he is an 'unworthy sinner,' it is doubtful he can honestly accept the Saving Grace God offers in Jesus Christ."*

This man offers the following blueprint for bringing sinners to Salvation:

"If you want to know why — smiles on television, if you want to know why I make people laugh once in a while, I am giving them sounds and strokes, sounds and strokes (like you would a baby).

"It's a strategy. People who don't trust need to be stroked. People are born with a negative self-image. Because they do not trust, they cannot trust God."

Of course, if this man is right, accepted Evangelistic practices which have brought millions to Christ are wrong. We should then stop telling people they're sinners who need Jesus Christ as a Saviour. We must no longer convince them of their sin and rebellion against a Holy God. We must never speak of hell, nor warn of the terrible, eternal consequences of rejecting the wonderful offer of Salvation as an unmerited gift from God.

Instead, we should begin to stroke men and women into Faith, smile them into the Kingdom of God, and elevate their self-esteem. If one knows his Bible, he will agree that this is a major change in Christian perspective.

However, the proponent of this false gospel has an even broader concept in mind. He goes on to say:

"A theology of self-esteem also produces a theology of social ethics and a theology of economics — and these produce a theology of government. It all rises from one foundation: the dignity of a person who was created in the image of God."

Basically, this self-esteem theology states that we need a new reformation and a new theology. What it also suggests — but does not openly state — is that we need a new Bible.

The doctrine of self-esteem strikes at the very heart of the Gospel of Jesus Christ. The

True Gospel states that man is a lost sinner who cannot save himself, and who thus desperately needs a Redeemer.

WHERE DID THIS "OTHER GOSPEL" OF SELF-ESTEEM COME FROM?

In order to place this new teaching into proper perspective, we should realize that so-called *"Christian"* psychologists and psychiatrists transplanted it from outside the Church and, as well, from outside the Bible.

A leading evangelical psychologist who vigorously promotes self-worth teaching, explains in one of his books, *"You're someone special:"*

"Under the influence of humanistic psychologists like Carl Rogers and Abraham Maslow, many of us Christians have begun to see our need for self-love and self-esteem."

Satan's threefold humanistic plan for world domination is basically simple, and you might be surprised how well it correlates with this new theology.

1. Darwinism (Darwin) — The concept of evolution as it affects the social man, resulting in abortion, humanism, and *"the survival of the fittest."*

2. Marxism (Communism and Socialism) — Satan's economic foundation.

3. Freudianism (Psychology) — A profound influence on the morals of man.

And there you have it! Satan's three-pronged assault — social, economic, and moral. The self-esteem philosophy comes directly from Freudian principles, and it does demand an entirely different theology.

ALL TRUTH IS GOD'S TRUTH?

This is a standard statement offered by *"Christian"* psychologists to justify the *"self-help"* philosophies and *"new-speak"* theologies. It is an *"answer"* in sloganized format.

"It doesn't matter," we are told, *"if Adler and Maslow* (psychologists) *were humanists. If they stumbled upon truth, so be it. We must accept truth — no matter its source."*

One *"Christian"* psychologist told me that Jesus used psychology in his ministry. In other words, Jesus was *"a great psychologist."*

I wonder if he understands the blasphemy of such a statement?

"What kind of psychology did Jesus use?", we might ask. Was it Freudian? That is somewhat

difficult to imagine since Freud wasn't born until the 1800's. It should be noted also that Freud was a narcotics addict, a sexual pervert, and an unmitigated liar who falsified his medical results to make them conform to what he had already postulated as theory. These are well-known and accepted facts — admitted by even the most faithful of Freud's devotees.

Freud himself stated, in regard to his psychiatric method, *"I would trash the whole business, but I don't know what else to turn to."* How tragic that he never read John 14:6, which states:

"I am the Way, the Truth, and the Life."

Jesus is Truth. Without Him, there is no truth.

Jesus does not merely contain truth, He is Truth, which is a vast difference!

Consequently, Truth is not a philosophy, but actually a Person, The Man Christ Jesus!

All that purports to be truth without Him is a lie. Psychotherapy — the wellspring of the self-esteem philosophy — is a lie. And, basically, what is being touted as truth today (*"all truth is God's truth"*) is little more than disconnected facts taken out of context.

Pavlov's dogs were trained to respond by salivating at the ringing of a bell — and huge segments of the *"science"* of psychology are built on this minor point.

In keeping with this same policy of building great precepts on flimsy evidence, we are asked to accept this principle: *"Even though it's not in the Bible, it can still be truth. And anything that is truth is God's Truth, because all truth comes from God. We must, therefore, avail ourselves of any and all 'helps' that fall into our hands, whatever their sources."*

However, once again allow us to state this Truth! There is no Truth outside of Christ! Anything else which looks like Truth, but comes from another source, actually comes from the *"angel of light,"* Satan himself (II Cor. 11:13-15).

As well, we must quickly add, as Jesus is Truth, likewise, Satan is the lie. He does not merely lie, but, in fact, is the father of the lie (Jn. 8:44). Consequently, Truth related by a liar becomes a lie.

IS MAN'S TRUE PROBLEM ONE OF LOW SELF-ESTEEM?

To be completely objective, this much-touted philosophy is the precise opposite of reality.

When man fell in the Garden of Eden, he did so at the suggestion of Satan, and because he fell for the idea of wanting to be a god.

"And the serpent said unto the woman, Ye shall not surely die:

"For God doth know that in the day ye eat thereof, then your eyes shall be opened, and ye shall be as gods, knowing good and evil" (Gen. 3:4-5).

Yes, ye shall be as gods . . . .

And there's the problem. It is the ancient temptation Satan used to beguile Eve, and he is still using the same, tired ruse today. This is why there are so many dictators around the world. They see themselves as gods. It is the foundation for humanism. Man is the focal point, replacing God. The whole world is now fascinated and beguiled by the false god of man's importance.

Socialism and Communism follow hard on the heels of humanism. They are all man-centered concepts — and Satan is the author of all such worldly systems.

Regrettably, this is the basic source of manmade philosophies which are permeating Pentecostal and Charismatic circles today — philosophies such as *"Christian"* psychology, sociology, possibility thinking, positive thinking, the fourth dimension, dream your own dream, inner healing, self-esteem, etc. Man wants to play God.

In effect, the self-esteem teachers are saying that Jesus does not hold the answer to man's problems, and, therefore, new concepts are needed.

In some Pentecostal and Charismatic circles, such statements are being made as, *"We are little gods. As Adam was formerly god of this world and lost it, we have now regained it. And we are now little gods under the Lord Jesus Christ."*

This is a dangerous, man-centered philosophy, which has no foundation in the Bible whatsoever, and will undermine and grossly cheapen the magnificent Gospel of the Lord Jesus Christ.

"Because thou sayest, I am rich, and increased with goods, and have need of nothing; and knowest not that thou art wretched, and miserable, and poor, and blind, and naked:

"I counsel thee . . . (that)

"As many as I love, I rebuke and chasten: be zealous therefore, and repent" (Rev. 3:17-19).

In preaching to millions around the world of their need of a Saviour, I can state with assurance that at least one of the biggest problems the True Preacher of the Gospel finds in leading men to Christ, is the *"god syndrome."*

"What do you mean, I need a Saviour?" many say! *"I'm not a sinner, I'm doing just fine."*

Truly, the hardest thing in the world is to get a man to admit that he is a sinner. And one must admit to himself that he is lost before he can be saved.

One must admit that he needs a Saviour before he can be introduced to one. And the reason this matter of human pride is such a successful tool of Satan's, is that man's basic problem is not one of low self-esteem, it is one of inflated self-esteem. Ultimately, this single fact is causing millions to perish.

DOMINION TEACHING IS PART OF THE SELF-ESTEEM THEORY

Some time back, listening to a Charismatic Preacher over Television, I heard him espouse the Dominion Teaching Theory.

"We are going to take over the world . . . We are going to solve the problems of mankind." It was *"we this,"* and *"we that."* If Jesus Christ was mentioned, it was only in passing. I doubt very seriously that the proponents of this gospel even suspect what they are promoting. But at the core of it is the fact that Jesus Christ is relegated to an inferior position — with man occupying the Throne.

Dominion Teaching is doomed to failure, not only because it is unscriptural, but because it is man-centered. Whenever any philosophy ceases to be God-focused, it becomes unscriptural and heretical. It is easy to see the slimy trail of the serpent in this teaching as it parrots his original lie, *"Ye shall be as gods."*

A. W. Tozer said:

"If self occupies any part of the Throne, we cannot say that Jesus Christ is on the Throne of our heart. Self is man's greatest enemy. It embodies selfishness, greed, and all that opposes God. If Jesus Christ is centered on the Throne, self-will is eradicated. And until self-will is totally eradicated, there can be no Christ-centered Throne in our lives."

Self-esteem caters to man's basic nature. This first became apparent at the Fall in the Garden. It will lead no one to Christ. It will lead, instead, to the enshrinement of self. And the tragic fact is that thousands of Pentecostal and

Charismatic Preachers are falling all over each other to embrace this errant doctrine.

Sadly, the old-line Churches have long since embraced it, at least for the most part.

Jay E. Adams, in his book, *"The Biblical View of Self-Esteem,"* says:

"Any system that proposes to solve human problems, apart from the Bible and the power of the Holy Spirit (as all of these pagan systems, including the self-worth system do) *is automatically condemned by Scripture itself. Nor does this system in any way depend upon the Message of Salvation. Love, joy, and peace are discussed as if they were not the fruits of the Spirit, but merely the fruits of right views of oneself, which anyone can attain without the Bible and the Work of the Spirit in his heart.*

"For these reasons, the self-worth system with its claims of Biblical correspondences must be rejected. It does not come from the Bible. Any resemblance between Biblical teaching and the teaching of the self-worth originators is either contrived or coincidental."

Actually the only thing the Bible says about self-esteem can be found in Philippians 2:3:

"Let nothing be done through strife or vain glory; but in lowliness of mind let each esteem other better than themselves."

This teaches the precise opposite of puffed-up self-opinions. It clearly tells us to have a humble view of ourselves, being ever aware of our own secret faults and shortcomings. This does not state that man's crying need is enhanced self-esteem. It says that man needs less emphasis on ego and self-gratification.

J. I. Packer said:

"Modern Christians spread a thin layer of Bible teaching over their mixture of popular psychology and common sense. But their overall approach clearly reflects the narcissism — the 'selfism' or 'meism' as it is sometimes called — that is the way of the world in the modern west."

The Apostle Paul plainly tells us that the person who fails to love others is *"nothing":*

"Though I speak with the tongues of men and of angels, and have not charity (love) *. . . I am nothing"* (I Cor. 13:1-2).

One of the foremost proponents of self-esteem claims that to glorify God, we must first love ourselves. This is not Biblical! As we have stated, the Lord through Paul said that man is nothing — unless and until he loves others. It says nothing, incidentally, about loving one's self first.

In Psalm 8, the Psalmist expresses amazement that God visits man. *"What is man?"*, he asks. Then in Psalm 62, we have the answer to this question: Nothing! Man is nothing!

Obviously, God does not love man because of his moral traits, he loves him despite them. This is why the Psalmist expressed amazement. It is a testimonial to God's greatness — not man's.

Actually, in the statement of Christ in Mark 8:34, Jesus is saying, in effect, *"You must treat yourself — with your sinful ways, priorities, and desires — like a criminal. Your sins must be condemned and utterly done away with."*

This certainly says something about the self-image Christ expects us to have — and it is a far cry from the elevated self-esteem being promoted today.

THE WORK OF THE HOLY SPIRIT

John 16:8 tells us that the Work of the Holy Spirit is to *"reprove the world of sin, and of* (self) *Righteousness, and of Judgment."* This means, under the teaching of the Gospel (as in I Corinthians 1:21), that the Holy Spirit convicts men of sin — not of low self-esteem. It clearly states, furthermore, that man is a sinner.

When, according to the Gospel, an individual is convicted (reproved) of sin, he is brought to a place of repentance. He suddenly sees himself as he is — which is *"lost, undone, and without God."*

In Peter's sermon on the Day of Pentecost (Acts 2), some 3,000 were saved. Read this Passage and you will search in vain for any reference to elevating the listeners' self-esteem, as claimed by the proponent of such at the beginning of this article. Instead, he said:

"Therefore let all the house of Israel know assuredly, that God hath made that same Jesus, Whom ye have crucified, both Lord and Christ" (Acts 2:36).

Peter did not by any means appeal here to their vanities in an effort to raise their self-esteem.

And what happened?

"Now when they heard this, they were pricked in their heart, and said unto Peter and to the rest of the Apostles, Men and brethren, what shall we do?" Acts 2:37).

This is Holy Spirit conviction in fact.

In Peter's second great sermon, as quoted in Acts 3, he once more ignored the matter of the

NOTES

listeners' self-esteem. Instead, he refocused on the darker side of their natures.

"But ye denied the Holy One and the Just, and desired a murderer to be granted unto you;

"And killed the Prince of Life, Whom God hath raised from the dead; whereof we are witnesses" (Acts 3:14-15).

Again, what happened? This time, 5,000 were saved.

I think it is by now clearly obvious that this is the God-approved principle of confronting men with the fact that they are sinners and they are lost without God. It then becomes the responsibility of the Holy Spirit to convict them and bring them to Jesus Christ. And where does all this leave the gospel of self-esteem?

The two are certainly hard to reconcile. In Truth, even though Jesus is mentioned (and given lip service as Lord), the self-esteem gospel does not bring Biblical Salvation. It brings people to a man-centered philosophy instead.

As a result, individuals who respond to this siren song of deceit (and that's what it is) are not born again. They do not turn to the Lord Jesus Christ as their Saviour, but, to a vain philosophy. To be frank, it is impossible for them to be born again because the Gospel has not been preached to them; a vain philosophy has been tendered in its place. They are confronted with the impossible, the task of saving themselves.

"And if the blind lead the blind, both shall fall into the ditch" (Mat. 15:14).

THE FOOT-WASHING SPIRIT

The self-esteem spirit was the hardest spirit to purge out of the Disciples. It was a battle that raged in their lives and ministries up till the time of the Crucifixion of Christ.

"And there was also a strife among them, which of them should be accounted the greatest" (Lk. 22:24 — the account of the Last Supper).

The mother of James and John also evidenced this spirit, along with her sons, when she desired to have her sons seated at either side of Christ. The spirit of self-esteem is capable of invading any situation, no matter how holy in concept, and once there, can threaten the very future of that situation.

What it really amounts to is that man's standard of greatness lies in obtaining the position where he will be served, while God's standard involves serving.

Man's standard is to humble others, while God's is to humble oneself.

Failure to observe these Godly principles led to the downfall of both Adam and Lucifer. It was, and as stated, the *"Ye shall be gods"* principle in action, and this is again being promoted by way of the self-esteem gospel.

If this spirit of high self-esteem had not been purged from the Disciples, the entire Work of God would have been destroyed. And the only way this could be accomplished was for the Master to demonstrate the foot-washing spirit, which He did at the Last Supper.

"After that He poureth water into a basin, and began to wash the Disciples' feet, and to wipe them with the towel wherewith He was girded" (Jn. 13:5).

(And we should note that Judas' feet were washed, as well!) Jesus then asked them:

"Know ye what I have done to you?" (Jn. 13:12).

No, the Lord was not instituting some new form of Church ritual; He was instead demonstrating the principle of humility that He wanted them to adopt, and in fact that they must adopt in their Ministry.

THE ANSWER TO SELF

Christ is the answer to self, whether it is low-self, or high-self.

A man said to me some time ago, *"Well then you do believe that a person can have a low self-esteem?"* I answered him in the affirmative. However, the answer to that individual is not in elevating their self-esteem, but rather taking their problem to Christ. Jesus said:

"Come unto Me, all ye that labour and are heavy laden, and I will give you rest.

"Take My yoke upon you, and learn of Me; for I am meek and lowly in heart: and ye shall find rest unto your souls.

"For My yoke is easy, and My burden is light" (Mat. 11:28-30).

Attempting to get a person with low self-esteem into a mode of high self-esteem, only exacerbates the problem. They are exchanging one problem for another. In fact, all the self-help philosophies in the world are of no avail! Self, whether low or high, is evil, demented, perverted, wrong, in effect, of the flesh. Paul said, *"For to be carnally* (self) *minded is death; but to be spiritually* (Christ) *minded is life and peace"* (Rom. 8:6).

Paul also said, *"Because the carnal mind* (self mind) *is enmity* (hatred) *against God: for it is*

not subject to the Law of God, neither indeed can be."

He then went on to say, *"So then they that are in the flesh* (trying to change self by their own efforts) *cannot please God"* (Rom. 8:7-8).

So, all of this self-help effort in the realm of self-esteem, etc., is roundly condemned by the Holy Spirit.

If any individual, and irrespective of his problem, comes to Christ, learning of Him, consequently, following Him, He will give us *"rest"* from all of these self-help efforts, and, actually, make of us a *"new creature"* (II Cor. 5:17).

WHY DOES MAN INSIST ON THESE VAIN PHILOSOPHIES INSTEAD OF CHRIST?

Especially considering that no human being has been successful in these self-help efforts, why does he continue trying?

He does so because he is deceived. Deception is Satan's greatest weapon. He used this tactic in the Garden of Eden, which caused the Fall of man. Consequently, man comes quickly to the lie, but slowly to the Truth.

Self-esteem sounds good to the carnal mind. However, it does not sound good to the spiritual mind, and because it is doomed to failure. Consequently, the propagators of this false gospel, and a false gospel it is, will help no one, but rather lead them to destruction.

Allow us to say it again, the only answer is Christ, and not Christ plus some new philosophy dreamed up out of vapid minds.

The phrase, *"And take up his cross,"* is the central focus of the activity of Christianity.

First of all, the *"Cross"* spoke of death.

Death of what?

The death of *"self,"* or more perfectly, *"selfishness."* As we have attempted to bring out, the greatest enemy of man is self! Self-will is always opposed to God's Will. Consequently, self must be brought into Christ, for there alone can it realize its true worth.

To be sure, and as Jesus will say even in this short Message, man is extremely important. Actually, more important than all the things of the world. So important, in fact, that Jesus came from Heaven and died on a cruel Cross in order that man may be saved.

However, for man to properly know his true worth, can never be found in self, or its efforts at betterment, but only in Christ.

Many want to know as to exactly what it means to bear the Cross?

First of all, many Christians are confused about bearing the Cross, thinking that difficulties and problems fall into this category. However, any thing which can happen to the unsaved, cannot be looked at by the Christian as bearing the Cross. In other words, poverty is not a Cross, inasmuch as much of the world lies in poverty. Neither is sickness, for much of the world falls into that category.

The ill will of one's family is not bearing the Cross, as that happens to the worldling also!

Bearing the Cross is seeking and doing the Will of God, which will always place one at cross purposes with the world, and even with much of the Church.

As well, Luke added the word *"daily"* (Lk. 9:23), showing this is a decision we must make on a daily basis. In other words, the temptation will always present itself for the Cross to be aborted. Consequently, the Believer must resolve on a *"daily"* basis, to take up the Cross. It is something that continues through the whole life.

The phrase, *"And follow Me,"* does not actually refer to following behind another, but that of accompanying the other person, taking the same road that he takes, and fellowshipping with him along that road.

The words, *"Come after,"* and *"Take up,"* are to be a once-for-all act. They are to be looked at as a permanent attitude and practice of life.

Also, the word, *"follow,"* refers to a moment-by-moment continuance.

In this scenario, we have direction, which man desperately needs, as well as the actual living such direction brings. It incorporates a total and complete lifestyle.

There is a great difference between *"come after"* and *"follow."* Judas Iscariot went after Him, but did not follow Him. To follow demands affection and repentance, and loyalty of heart.

In this verse is the condition of Discipleship.

1. The attitude of the Disciple to himself — *"Let him deny himself."*

2. The attitude of the Disciple to the world — *"And take up his Cross."*

3. The attitude of the Disciple to Christ — *"And follow Me."*

(35) "FOR WHOSOEVER WILL SAVE HIS LIFE SHALL LOSE IT; BUT WHOSOEVER SHALL LOSE HIS LIFE FOR MY SAKE AND THE GOSPEL'S, THE SAME SHALL SAVE IT."

The phrase, *"For whosoever will save his life shall lose it,"* actually constitutes Jesus' philosophy of life. In this statement, Christ is not telling one how to be saved from sin, for that can only be brought about by Faith in the shed Blood of Jesus. Jesus is here giving, as stated, His philosophy of life, in effect, telling one how to live.

To be sure, it is the opposite of self-gratification, which characterizes the world.

Wuest says, *"God has so created man, that he does not find complete rest and satisfaction until his entire being is swallowed up in the sweet Will of God."*

The word, *"life,"* as Jesus uses it here, is not referring to one's physical existence and its needs. Instead, it is referring to one's purpose for living.

I read the other day of the passing of one of the Noblemen of England, who was a very wealthy man. The only thing they could say of him was his love for his butterfly collection.

Whenever a Hollywood actor or actress dies, their films and Broadway appearances are extolled.

Respecting the far greater majority, and even those who gain fame and notoriety, their lives are a waste. They simply lived and died without ever really knowing what true living actually is. Solomon is a perfect example of what I say.

In all of history, no one ever had the wisdom or riches to indulge his passions and appetites as Solomon. Nothing, at least as far as self-gratification was concerned, was out of his reach. Nothing was illegal and nothing was too expensive. And yet, when he did it all, his answer was, *"All is vanity and vexation of spirit"* (Eccl. 1:14).

Actually, the entirety of the Book of Ecclesiastes exposes the emptiness of earthly wisdom in hastening after impossible satisfaction, whether sensual, industrial, or philosophic.

In effect, in Ecclesiastes and the Song of Solomon, Christ and the world are contrasted. In the one Book the heart is too large for the portion; in the other, the portion is too large for the heart.

What does Christ mean by one losing his life?

The next phrase tells us: *"But whosoever shall lose his life for My sake and the Gospel's, the same shall save it."*

When Jesus spoke of *"losing one's life,"* He was not speaking of physical death. He was speaking of giving up one's selfish interests, desires, personal pursuits and pleasures, and doing it for His, i.e., *"My sake."* Actually He presents two conditions:

1. *"My sake"*: This means to seek the Will of God for one's life, which will be readily given if one properly yields to the Lord. Paul said, *"And be not conformed to this world: but be ye transformed by the renewing of your mind, that ye may prove what is that good, and acceptable, and perfect, Will of God"* (Rom. 12:2).

In other words, one's life is lived for Christ, instead of for *"self."*

2. *"And the Gospel's"*: To be sure, He is not speaking only of Preachers, but, actually, of every single Believer.

It is the responsibility of all who make Christ their Lord and Saviour, to tell others about Jesus. In other words, the businessman may deal in real estate or other things, but his primary objective is the propagation of the Gospel. Consequently, his money should be used primarily for that purpose.

Likewise, even the person who has little money to give, must concentrate his efforts of prayer toward the lost in order that the Gospel may reach them. (In Truth, all should pray to that end.)

When Jesus speaks of *"saving"* one's life, He is referring to the real purpose of living. To be sure, outside of Christ there is no purpose to life. This means that Islam, Mormonism, Hinduism, etc., hold no purpose or reason for living.

It also means that money, education, fame, popularity, position, state or status, present no purpose or reason for living. Only in Jesus can one find the true purpose for living. Only in Jesus can one truly find fulfillment.

That is the reason why the little grandmother who is trying to eke out a living on Social Security, but who knows Jesus, has a far more fulfilling and purposeful life, than the richest most powerful person in the country who does not know Christ.

(36) "FOR WHAT SHALL IT PROFIT A MAN, IF HE SHALL GAIN THE WHOLE WORLD, AND LOSE HIS OWN SOUL?"

The phrase, *"For what shall it profit a man,"* proclaims Christ bringing this all-important subject down to the level of the businessman. He now speaks of profit and loss!

NOTES

The great question of the world is, *"What's in it for me?"* Consequently, Jesus addresses the world on their own level.

The conclusion of the question, *"If he shall gain the whole world, and lose his own soul?"*, puts everything in stark contrast.

What is the soul of man?

First of all, the soul is one's personal existence. It is the life or self of an individual as marked by vital drives and desires. It is the seat of emotion and feelings.

The *"soul"* and *"spirit"* of man are indestructible. They were created by God to live forever, and actually make up the being of man. Man is tripartite, consisting of *"spirit and soul and body"* (I Thess. 5:23).

Of this trinity of being, the only part of man that dies physically is the body, and that because of the Fall in the Garden of Eden. (At the Resurrection, all Believers will be given new, Glorified Bodies, which cannot die — I Cor. 15:20-22, 51-57.)

At the moment of death, the soul and spirit of the unbeliever, which are inseparable, are consigned to hell to await the Second Resurrection of Death and Damnation which will take place at the conclusion of the Kingdom Age. It will be the time of the *"Great White Throne Judgment"* (Lk. 16:19-31; Rev. 20). At the Second Resurrection of Damnation, all unbelievers will be given an indestructible body as well, which will join their soul and spirit, and will be cast into the *"Lake of Fire"* forever. This is called *"the second death"* (Rev. 20:14).

At the moment of death, the soul and spirit of all Believers instantly go to be with Christ (Phil. 1:21-24). At the First Resurrection of Life, which will take place at the Rapture (I Thess. 4:13-18), the Believer will then be given a Glorified Body, which will then join the soul and the spirit, and be with Christ forever (I Cor. 15:51-57).

So, in this question posed by Christ, one learns that his soul is worth more than the entirety of the world, and because it is eternal.

(37) "OR WHAT SHALL A MAN GIVE IN EXCHANGE FOR HIS SOUL?

Considering that the soul is eternal, this question posed by Christ means that no material possessions, and irrespective as to how much they may be, are worth even one soul. And yet, hundreds of millions are selling their souls for a mere trifle.

As well, these questions as asked by Christ concerning the soul, completely refute the silly idea of evolution. Perhaps in history, the most preposterous foolishness ever conceived by foolish man is this absurdity. With not one shred of scientific evidence, this preposterous idea is taught to school children as fact.

WHAT IS THE THEORY OF EVOLUTION?

The theory of evolution is that all forms of life derived by gradual modification from earlier and simpler forms, or from one rudimentary form. It teaches a process in which something complex is developed by itself from a simple beginning. It accepts the existence of the cause or causes of the first substance and the force or forces working successive transformations from a lower to a higher form of matter and life.

THE THEORY OF COSMIC AND ORGANIC EVOLUTION

The theory of cosmic evolution claims that from lower units of matter (atoms and molecules) the vast material suns, moons, stars, planets, and universes, were formed by themselves.

That of organic evolution teaches that the vegetable and animal kingdoms evolved from lower forms of life to what they are today.

THE UTTER FOOLISHNESS OF EVOLUTION

Evolutionists do not deny the first cause. Their theory begins with matter or substance already in existence. They believe in primitive nebulosity and powers possessed by molecules. They do not try to account for how these came to exist, how molecules got their inherent powers, or how there came to be definite laws governing them so that they could produce, without failure, all things as we now have them.

Their theory does not show why there is such bitter hatred against the God of the Bible as being that first cause. It does not consider proved facts, but has absolute faith in a mere supposition which no fact has ever been produced to prove. Its teachers seemingly deny God, the Bible, and known facts and continue to rob multiplied thousands of boys and girls of their simple Faith in God and the Bible without a sting of conscience.

They manufacture multiplied drawings of human beings, different kinds, rising from a molecule through a monkey to the present man;

and add guess upon guess of how life was in each stage of evolution, but refuse to accept the Bible Truth of the origin of all things. They speak glibly of denying God and His Work in creation, and at the same time pose as having the only truth on the subject.

STATEMENTS OF EVOLUTIONISTS

Huxley said, *"It is clear that the doctrine of evolution is directly antagonistic to that of creation . . . Evolution, if consistently accepted, makes it impossible to believe in the Bible."*

Darwin taught that the more complex organs and instincts have been perfected by the accumulation of innumerable slight variations, each good for the individual possessor.

Spencer said that evolution was purely mechanical and anti-supernatural.

Earnest Haechel said, *"It entirely excludes the supernatural process, every prearranged and conscious act of a personal character. Nothing will make the full meaning of the theory of descent clearer than calling it the non-miraculous theory of creation."*

Thus the confessed evolution-theory leaders are clear that no true evolutionist can be a Christian or a Believer in the Bible. There is no place for God in evolution, hence no need of a belief in sin or a Saviour, Heaven or hell.

Those in the Church who try to harmonize evolution with the Bible rule God out despite themselves and are enemies of both God and the True Church of Jesus Christ.

No one branch of organic evolution has been proved, much less the main theory. It is a bankrupt, speculative philosophy — not a scientific fact.

TRUE SCIENCE REJECTS:

1. The theory that the hair is but elongated scales of prehistoric animals.

2. The legs of all animals developed from warts on aboriginal amphibians.

3. Eyes are but accidental development of freckles on blind amphibians that responded to the sun.

4. Ears came about by the airwaves calling to spots on early reptiles.

5. The theory of natural selection.

6. Man came from monkeys.

7. The vast universes came from a few molecules.

8. Nothing working on nothing by nothing, through nothing, for nothing, begat everything.

TWELVE FALLACIES OF EVOLUTION

1. It accepts heathen and pagan philosophers in preference to God, Christ, the Holy Spirit, the Bible, and Christians. Pagan, Hindu, and Greek philosophers invented such a theory. Aristotle taught an internal spontaneity, which is the same idea of modern evolutionists who call it resident forces or impersonal eternal energy.

2. It nullifies the idea of Bible creation by God. Blind force is substituted for the creative power of the Personal and Living God Who created all things (Gen. 1:1, 20-28; 2:7-22; 5:1-2; 9:6; Jn. 1:1-4; Eph. 3:9; Col. 1:15-18; Heb. 1:1-3).

3. It degrades man from creation by God in the Image of God to a monkey ancestry (Gen. 1:26-28; 2:7; 5:1-2).

4. It degrades God's image to a mere beast (Gen. 1:26-28; 9:6; James 3:9).

5. It makes Christ the second and last Adam, nothing more than a mere beast (Gen. 1:26-28; I Cor. 15:45).

6. Evolution does away with the Fall of man, for how can a mere beast who has evolved steadily from a molecule to an intelligent being go backward and have a fall (Gen. 3; Rom. 5:12-21).

7. Evolution does away with Bible miracles and the supernatural in all its forms. The only miracle or power of evolution is the inherent forces of molecules (Heb. 2:1-4).

8. Evolution does away with the Virgin Birth, makes it impossible and unnecessary, and makes Christ a product of evolution in the same sense that it does all other men (Isa. 7:14; 9:6-7; Mat. 1:18-25).

9. Evolution denies the bodily resurrection of Christ and declares that it is contrary to the process of evolution of resident forces making progress.

10. It denies the Atonement, for according to evolution there was no Fall of man and therefore no sin to make Atonement for. Regeneration by outside power is the direct opposite of resident powers, the only power accepted by evolution.

11. It denies the Second Coming of Christ and the final restoration and preservation of all things by the personal acts of God.

12. Evolution does away with the authority of the Bible as a real Revelation from a Personal and Living God, making it a lie, not only

NOTES

regarding creation but every other doctrine (II Tim. 3:16).

To argue that the Christian can accept evolution on the grounds that the Bible is not to be taken literally, is a surrender to the foes of God, Christ, the Holy Spirit, the Bible, and all Christian teachings. The theory, therefore, is anti-God, anti-Christ, anti-Bible, anti-Christian, and anti-intelligence.

CHRISTIANS MUST BELIEVE THE FOLLOWING:

1. The Bible is the Word of God, not that it merely contains the Word of God (II Tim. 3:16; Heb. 4:12; II Pet. 1:16-21).

2. God is a Person Who created (brought into existence all material and spiritual substance), and that out of the created material He Personally formed the worlds and each creature therein (Gen. 1:1; 2:7, 19; Ps. 8:1-9; 102:25; Jn. 1:3-4; Eph. 3:9; Col. 1:15-18; Heb. 1:1-3; Rev. 4:11).

3. God created man in His Own Image and Likeness in one day, fully mature and highly intelligent, not that he descended from molecules through the lower forms of life to monkey and man (Gen. 1:26-28; 2:7, 19; 9:6; Acts 17:26; I Cor. 11:7-9; James 3:9).

4. All Angels and spirit beings were created by God fully mature and intelligent (Ps. 104:4; Ezek. 28:15; Col. 1:15-18; Rev. 4:11).

5. God created man, animals, fish, fowls, and plants to reproduce themselves *"after their own kind"* (Gen. 1:20-31; 2:5-7, 19-25).

6. Jesus Christ is The Son of God in a sense no other man is — the Only Begotten of the Father, not that He is a Son of God in the sense all Believers are (Gen. 3:15; Isa. 7:14; 9:6-7; Mat. 1:18-25; Lk. 1:34-35; Jn. 1:18; 3:16; Phil. 2:5-11; I Tim. 3:16; Heb. 1:1-3, 8; Rev. 1:8-11).

7. The Holy Spirit is a Person separate and distinct from both the Father and the Son. All three Persons in the Godhead have their Own personal body, soul, and spirit, and make up the Divine Trinity (I Jn. 5:7).

8. The birth of Christ was supernatural, not natural, as in the case of all other men. He was *"Virgin-born,"* and *"of the Holy Spirit"* without a human father (Gen. 3:15; Isa. 7:14; 9:6-7; Mat. 1:18-25; Lk. 1:34-35; Jn. 1:1-14; 3:16-18; I Tim. 3:16; Heb. 1:1-3).

9. The death of Christ was *"expiatory,"* not exemplary. He died for all men. His Blood is

the only Atonement for sin and by His stripes we are healed (Isa. 53; Mat. 1:21; 8:17; 26:28; Jn. 3:16; Acts 4:12; Rom. 8:3; I Cor. 1:18-24; 5:7; Heb. 1:3; 2:9-18; 9:11-28; 10:5-29; I Pet. 2:24; I Jn. 2:1-2; Rev. 1:5; 5:8-10).

10. Jesus Christ rose *"bodily"* from the dead, not spiritually or as a spirit being. He is alive forevermore in His earthly, resurrected flesh-and-bone body, and represents men before God as their High Priest and Saviour (Zech. 13:6; Jn. 10:17-18; Lk. 24:39; Acts 1:3, 11; 2:22-34; 4:10-12; Rom. 1:4; 8:11; I Cor. 15; Phil. 3:20-21; I Thess. 4:13-16; Rev. 1:18).

11. Jesus Christ ascended into Glory bodily, and will come again in like manner to rule the world eternally, put down all rebellion, restore man's dominion, and God's Kingdom over all as before the Fall of Lucifer and Adam (Lk. 24:50-52; Acts 1:11; I Cor. 15:24-28; II Thess. 1:7-10; Jude 14; Rev. 19:11-21; Zech. 14).

12. Man is a sinner fallen from original Righteousness and a high, intelligent, and responsible place as head of the present creation. Apart from God's Redemption, man is lost. Man is not the unfortunate victim of environment, one who through self-help and self-culture, can remedy his fallen condition (Gen. 3; Jn. 3:16; Rom. 3:23-25; 5:12-21; Heb. 1:1-3; 7:25; 9:22; I Jn. 1:9; 2:1-2; Rev. 1:5; 5:8-10; 20:11-15).

13. Man is justified by Faith in the Atoning Blood of Jesus Christ, resulting in a supernatural regeneration from above (Mat. 1:21; 18:3; Jn. 3:1-8, 16; Rom. 5:1; II Cor. 5:17; Eph. 2:8-9; Col. 1:14, 20; Tit. 3:5; I Pet. 1:18-23). He is not justified by works or by natural development from within or self-effort.

14. Man, animals, and plant-life have degenerated and are under a curse. Man chooses to continue in sin, sickness, and sufferings of earth, and only through Redemption in Christ will the whole creation be restored to original perfection and goodness (Gen. 3; 6:5-22; Rom. 5:12-21; 8:17-24; I Cor. 15:24-28; Rev. 21:1-22:5). No single species has evolved from a lower to a higher plane of life.

15. All men who accept Christ and conform to God's Plan for man will be saved, will be resurrected from the dead to immortality, and will help God administer the affairs of the universe forever (Jn. 3:16; Jn. 5:28-29; Rom. 8:17-24; I Cor. 6:2; 15:1-54; II Tim. 2:12; Rev. 1:6; 2:26-27; 5:10; 11:15; 22:4-5).

NOTES

16. All men who reject Christ and do not conform to the Plan of God for man will pay the eternal death penalty for sin, will be resurrected to immortality, and will be punished eternally in the Lake of Fire forever (Mk. 16:15-16; Jn. 3:16-20; 5:28-29; Rev. 14:9-11; 20:11-15; 21:8; 22:15).

Any denial of God or His Plan for man in Scripture makes him a liar, and will damn the soul. If some through ignorance of the Bible think they can believe in evolution and the Bible at the same time, they are highly deceived by Satan, the deceiver of the world (II Cor. 4:3-4; 11:14-15; Rev. 12:9).

One cannot know the statements of both the Bible and evolutionists and believe both. Nor can he be neutral. He must take a stand either for God and the Bible or for evolution and mere guesswork.

FIFTEEN FACTS DISPROVING EVOLUTION

1. THE BIBLE

The Bible in its entirety condemns the theories of both cosmic and organic evolution. It declares in no uncertain terms that God created (brought into existence) all the material and moral creation; the animate and inanimate things, and that He is the first and last cause of all existing universes and the things therein.

The Bible declares: *"God created the heavens and the earth"* (Gen. 1:1; Ps. 8:1-9; 19:1-7; 102:25-27; Isa. 45:18); *"God created great whales and every living creature"* (Gen. 1:21); *"God created man in His Own Image, in the Image of God created He him; male and female created He them"* (Gen. 1:26-28; 2:7, 19-25; 5:1-2; 9:6); *"all things were made by Him; and without Him was not anything made that was made"* (Jn. 1:3); *"God, Who created all things by Jesus Christ"* (Eph. 3:9; Col. 1:15-18); *"and upholding all things by the Word of His Power"* (Heb. 1:3); *"Thou hast created all things, and for Thy pleasure they are and were created"* (Rev. 4:11).

2. IT IS A LAW OF NATURE THAT NOTHING REPRODUCES ANYTHING GREATER THAN ITSELF

If this is true of all species today, of which we have millions of examples, then it was true originally. The vast creations of matter and life had to come into existence by a superior power, not an inferior force. One thing is certain: All intelligence and matter could not have come from one or any number of molecules of un-intelligence.

The most that has ever been done or can possibly be done, is to demonstrate the law of improvement of a species through breeding and cultivation. No new species has been or can be produced by such law. If left alone, the plants and animals would degenerate, not improve themselves in any degree.

Therefore, we must conclude that no amount of unintelligent matter could produce intelligence or intelligent beings — anything higher than itself. The intelligent and innumerable self-producing species of creatures, each with its own eternal consistent traits, distinct flavors, and infinite combinations of chemicals, could never be the product of unintelligent matter. Each one of the millions of creature that reproduce their own kind by fixed and eternal laws must be the work of an all-powerful and all-wise Creator.

3. AFTER ITS OWN KIND

The Bible declares (ten times in Genesis 1) that everything created by God was given power to reproduce *"its own kind."* No one thing could break this law and produce any other (Gen. 1:20-28).

Some 1600 years later it had not been broken (Gen. 7:14). Now, after more than 6,000 years the law of reproduction is still unbroken. The sponge is still a sponge and has not become an oyster, octopus, a turtle, frog, fish, or crab. None of these have ever reproduced anything except *"their own kind."*

No lowly earthworm has ever turned into a spider, tarantula, scorpion, lizard, tortoise, snake, or crocodile. No bug, bird, or animal has ever changed from its own kind or reproduced another kind which was fertile and could produce a new kind.

The crossing of an ass and a mare, for instance, will produce a mule which cannot reproduce itself. No monkey has ever produced a man, and the missing-link is still missing, and, in fact, the whole chain is missing and always will be.

All this is quite remarkable in view of the fact that there are over 2,000,000 different species of plant and animal life. Each species proves the law of reproduction established by God — *"after His Own kind."*

It is claimed that there are more than 1,000,000 species of insects. Species of beetles

NOTES

number 250,000; butterflies and moths, 110,000; etc.

All species exist in great variety, and the so-called proofs of evolutionists are merely variations or minor changes within the same species. Out of billions of living organisms and fossils there is no evidence of the slightest tendency to evolve out of the original kind to which each belongs. There is only evidence of development and normal growth; but these are not evolution. Improvement of a species and new varieties within the species are not evolution.

The theory of evolution teaches transmutation, a change in nature, substance, form, and alteration of essence by a slow and gradual process of mutation from one species to another, and from the lower to the higher. This has never been done, nor can it be done. In nature we find endless variety in each species or kind, but no change from one species to another.

Without a change of species there could be no evolution. God has made life so that it interbreeds in closely related variation; and when interbreeding is attempted between different kinds of species, it is found that there is an impassable gulf which cannot be crossed.

Out of the billions of reproductions of nature, not one monkey's tail has been produced by anything except a monkey. There is no proof of man in various stages from a molecule to a monkey, or from a monkey to a man!

4. THERE CAN BE NO EVOLUTION WITHOUT THE POWER OF REPRODUCTION IN LIVING THINGS

Since reproduction is a prior condition to evolution, it cannot be a product of it. Hence, we face the logical necessity for the creation of life and its power of continued reproduction. The power of reproduction is not in the embryo, but only in the mature parent. An egg cannot produce an egg. It is also true that the egg is not improvable by itself. Improvement can come only in and through the mature form. Therefore, the parent-form of life must have been created in the beginning to have produced an egg from which offspring alone can come. So, the chicken came first!

5. SCIENCE HAS PROVED THAT DEAD MATTER CANNOT GENERATE LIFE

Life can come only from pre-existing life. When test tubes are filled with hay and other organic matter, and when all life-germs are completely destroyed, and when the tube is hermetically sealed to exclude outer air, and while it is absolutely free of living germs, not one vestige of life has ever appeared. The attempt to get the living out of the dead completely fails. The theory of spontaneous generation of evolutionists has had to be given up. It is now recognized that life can only come from life.

All life is dependent upon other life; the lower upon the higher; the simple upon the complex; the powerless upon the powerful; the impersonal upon the personal; the unintelligent upon the intelligent; the non-existing upon the existing; the natural upon the spiritual; the temporary upon the eternal. Nothing can come from nothing or be produced by nothing.

6. THE ARGUMENT OF EVOLUTION FROM EMBRYOLOGY

This theory argues that different forms of life are somewhat alike so they must have come from a common ancestor. This argument has totally failed, as have the theories of natural selection, and the survival of the fittest. The similarity of embryos and their fast development to full growth are contrary to the principles of the evolutionary hypothesis. The chief foundation of evolution is that of a slow and tedious process, it is claimed, over millions and millions of years. This, the evolution teachers have to argue due to the fact that no single example of evolution from one species to another can be cited.

Human and other embryos pass through various stages of growth very rapidly. In the case of some the progress of growth is so rapid that it is miraculous. Thus, evolutionists are forced to believe in miracles, which they deny in other fields, but sustain in their own, in the effort to prove their claims.

It is now known that there are radical differences between the embryos of vertebrates (backboned animals) and invertebrates (animals without backbones) which we would not have if all things had a common ancestor. Some similarity among embryos of all forms of life should be expected, since all start individually from a single life-germ or a combination of two.

If a botanist would be asked the difference between an oak, a palm tree, and a lichen, he would declare that they are separated from one another by the broadest lines of classification. But if the germs of these plants were placed

NOTES

before them, to choose one from the other, he could not do it.

Under the most powerful microscope they would yield no clue. If analyzed by the chemist, they would still keep their secret.

The same is true of the life-germ of various animals and man. No one can tell which is which. What makes the little speck grow in the millions of different kinds of creatures? What is there which the eye cannot see that determines which of the many creatures it shall be? Only a personal and an infinite intelligent being could make such unfailing laws of reproduction — *"after His kind."*

7. SIMILARITIES

It is further argued that man and monkey are so similar that they must have come from a common ancestor. This is neither sound logic nor sound science.

Resemblance proves nothing but resemblance. Similarity proves nothing but similarity. Resemblance and similarity run throughout all nature and things that have no connection with each other. Resemblance or similarity on some points is to be expected even though we accept creation by God.

Such only magnifies the fact of an intelligent Creator. This is true whether it is the Creator or a manufacturer as in every factory of man. The wheel, for example, is the same in the wagon, the car, locomotive, and airplane. But such similarity does not prove that the wagon evolved into an automobile, then into a locomotive, and finally into an airplane.

All animals and men have similar faculties to breath, eat food, and perform other bodily functions, but no such similarity proves close relationship. God made them thus so that all could exist alike in the same air and on similar foods.

The dissimilarities between man and lower animals, not only in body, but also in brain, spirit and soul faculties prove that they are <u>not</u> vitally related. The differences between man and monkey are so wide that any single bodily part is sufficient in itself to prove whether it is a part of man or monkey.

Evolutionists themselves confirm this fact by their promptness in deciding whether a bone is from a monkey or a man. There are hundreds of differences between the bodies of men and apes, and thousands of differences between these two in mental, moral, spiritual, and habitual matters which prove evolution of man from apes or lower life an impossibility.

8. DEGENERATION

The similarities between man and lower animals could be used to prove a process of degeneration from man more than a process of evolution to man. The Bible teaches that God made man <u>before</u> He made land animals — on day six. Therefore, man came first, and then the monkey (Gen. 2:7, 19-25).

Darwin's argument that plants and animals have within themselves tendencies to vary of their own accord in many and all directions to an unlimited degree, has been disputed many times.

Mendel's experiments prove conclusively that plants and animals either under man's selective skill in breeding, do not tend to vary in all directions and to an unlimited degree; but that the variations are within strict limits and work according to strict laws producing unvarying results. The theory of natural selection and inheritance of acquired characters has failed the test of proof.

The forms of vegetables, plants, and animals that man succeeds in improving by human selection and cultivation revert rapidly to type as soon as man's directing skill is removed. In all man's selection and cultivation, he can work only within the limits of the species. No change into new species has been produced either by natural or artificial selection.

The iron law of sterility stands guard at the far frontiers of the species and everything continues to reproduce *"after His kind."*

There is a certain potency of development implanted in all things, but such potential powers are let out into actual development or improvement, not through resident forces, as evolution teaches, but only through outside intervention and intelligent help.

Man can develop the wild rose into the American Beauty, or the wild pony into the Kentucky thoroughbred by selection, better environment, breeding, etc., but it is most significant that these improvements do not continue to increase, or even persist when things are left to themselves. The rose reverts to a wild rose if left alone, and the horse begins to go back to its degenerated type the very minute man's skill is omitted.

If one takes a flock of highly-developed pigeons, with all their shades of color and variety of markings, and turns them loose in the forest to see if they will improve or degenerate, he will find in a few years that they have all returned to one type. Compelled by an unfailing natural law, all will revert to common colors instead of being a variety with beautiful markings.

Improvements brought about by care and selection in breeding will be gone, proving the law of evolution a failure.

The same thing actually happens to man. If he neglects himself, he will revert to a worse and lower type of man — like those who have been discovered on desert islands or in jungles, etc.

As well, if the mind is neglected it will degenerate into imbecility and ignorance. Solitary confinement has the power to unmake men's minds and leave them less than what they were. If the conscience is neglected it will run off into lawlessness and sin. The soul that is neglected will go into ruin and depravity.

Only three possibilities are before the human family; *"balance," "improvement,"* only to a certain degree, or *"degeneration."* The Bible question is: *"How shall we escape if we neglect?"* (Heb. 2:1-4).

These three possibilities face every man. He has a desire to better himself, and yet he is constantly beset with a gravitation to sin and the law of death working in his very being. We say that nature is full of life, but, in reality, it is full of death. Plant life and animal life are kept alive by a temporary endowment which gives power over the elements that cause death.

Withdraw the elements of life and the true nature will be revealed. Life is merely the suspension of these destructive powers — the sum total of the functions that resist death. Spiritual life is the same — the sum total of the functions that resist sin. If we neglect the use of these powers, death will result.

The man who does not properly use the powers to live is as much dead as a man falling 500 feet is as good as dead as the first foot of the fall. Unless he is stopped, he is a dead man. One who continues to neglect life is dead. If we neglect, degeneration sets in. If we use the power of life to resist sin, we live.

To use the argument that the savages of heathen darkness are more like monkeys than men in the civilized world is no proof of evolution.

It is proof of degeneration. Man fell from original sinlessness and the highest degree of intelligence in the Garden of Eden, to the present status.

Adam had more intelligence the day he was created than all men together have now. He could name all things, and with their names explaining their function, and all men today who learn all their lives cannot yet do this (Gen. 2:19).

Degeneration explains the present uncivilized parts of the world, and the so-called cave men, etc. All problems between true science and the Bible can be solved by the facts of degeneration, or with the Bible Truth of a pre-Adamite world. Belief in the pre-Adamite system allows that the earth could be millions of years old.

Pre-historic animals could have been a part of that system, as well as any different type of creation similar to man, if such is ever excluded from Adam's race by established proof.

9. FOSSIL REMAINS

Fossil remains have been referred to as one of the strongest proofs of evolution. But evolutionists themselves acknowledge that this proof is extremely fragmentary, limited, and obscure, due to the fact of only a few fossil remains. Hence, they are forced to guess without proof.

The *"missing links"* between man and monkey have never been found. The manufactured bones of prehistoric men are fakes. The Piltdown man, for example, was no man at all.

In a gravel pit in Sussex, England, near Piltdown Common, two or three bits of a skull-bone, a piece of jawbone, and a tooth were found by different persons in different places in different years. From these few scraps so-called scientists destructed the Piltdown man and named it the *"Dawn-man"* of the dateless past.

From the same bones another later type was made by another team of scientists. Finally it was acknowledged that the jawbone and tooth did not belong to the skull, but were those of a chimpanzee.

The *"Java-man"* was built in Java from a skull-bone, leg-bone, two molars, and plaster-of-Paris; the *"Heidelberg-man"* was built in Germany from a jawbone which was unquestionably human; the *"Peiking-man"* of China was made from human skull fragments found in a cave in 1929, etc.

These, plus many we have not named, are the so-called proofs shown in school textbooks.

NOTES

Such are the hoaxes which are being passed upon innocent boys and girls by educators in the name of science!

10. THE GEOLOGICAL SCHEME

The old geological scheme to prove evolution has also been repudiated. Instead of the older rocks being found at the bottom and the younger rocks at the top, as would be the case if evolution were true, it is found that the opposite is often the case. This explodes the evolution-theory of natural building up of the strata.

11. THE TWO UNIVERSAL FLOODS

The fact of two universal floods instead of one (one in Lucifer's day and one in Noah's day) and a later division of the earth, can easily explain the fossil remains being where they are. In Lucifer's flood, God turned the earth upside down by earthquakes (Gen. 1:2). This accounts for fossil remains being found deep in the earth underneath many layers of solid rock. Such things never would have been there without the earthquakes and Judgment of God.

It is evident that many fossils came from a great catastrophe, being entombed in the strata instead of being slowly buried by sedimentation over millions of years. We read of whole schools of fish, covering large fields which have been found with every indication of a violent and sudden death.

They are not in a relaxed position but often with their heads twisted around to their tails, and every fin extended, which is the position in which a fish dies when overtaken by an enemy or some catastrophe.

Historians tell us that the earth has undergone one great and indescribable catastrophe. This happened at Lucifer's flood or when the earth was divided into continents (Gen. 1:2; 10:25).

That there was a dividing of the earth in the days of Peleg is clear from Genesis 10:25. Such a shaking up of the entire earth, as well as the flood-catastrophe of Lucifer's time, could have caused fossils to become deeply submerged.

The Arctic regions give clear evidence of a sudden calamity. In their extensive fields of fossilized and frozen mammoths, where multitudes of giant creatures have been found, some have been discovered with their stomachs filled with undigested food, and in some instances with their mouths full of the food they were eating. This shows that they were feeding quietly when the crisis came and that they were destroyed with suddenness.

That the Arctic regions had tropical climate when these beasts were destroyed seems true, for they had tropical food in their mouths. Evidently they were frozen immediately when God withheld the sun, moon, and stars from shining on the earth during Lucifer's flood (Gen. 1:2; Ps. 104:6-9; Isa. 14:12-14; Jer. 4:23-26; Ezek. 28:11-17; II Pet. 3:5-8).

12. NOAH'S FLOOD

Regarding Noah's flood, God commanded male and female of every species to be kept alive in the Ark to replenish the earth *"after His kind"* when the flood was over (Gen. 6:18-22; 7:2-16).

Had the evolutionists been right, this would have been unnecessary. Noah could have merely saved a couple of molecules, turned them loose after the flood and eventually, we could have the innumerable living things again in all their varieties in innumerable varieties.

13. WHY IS THE LAW OF EVOLUTION NOT WORKING TODAY?

If evolution is responsible for all the vast creations in space and the possible endless varieties of life on innumerable planets, then why is the law not working today? And why do we not have actual and unquestionable examples of the various stages of evolution from the lowest to the highest forms of life?

If evolution ever worked, it should be working today so that every form or stage of development could be seen as proof that the lower forms of life will eventually be the higher in the ages to come. Is it not strange that the process has been at a standstill for the period man has been on earth to observe the law of evolution at work. Is it not strange that man has not produced one example of change from one species to another, not even the losing of the monkey tail and hair?

In fact, if it was suspended during the time of man, which is absurd within itself, why then aren't there specimens left over from the time before the suspension? The further one goes, the more absurd the entire theory becomes.

14. THE WHOLE WORLD IS INSTEAD MOVING TOWARD JUDGMENT AND RE-CREATION

There is evidence now that the whole world and all in it are degenerating and moving toward some climax or judgment and re-creation,

NOTES

instead of evolving upward into higher and better forms. In chemistry, which is closest to the deeper facts and forces of inanimate matter and life, there is no evidence of a surge upward.

Not only are the laws of chemical affinity static and unchangeable as to their operations, but there is a disintegrating tendency downward instead of upward that seems to characterize all matter. The tendency of atoms of high atomic weight to break up into other atoms of lower weight, seems to be the universal tendency of all matter. Scientists declare that this is also true in the vegetable and animal kingdoms.

15. THE GUESSES OF EVOLUTION

The evolution theory is not only absurd — its so-called proofs are so contradictory that they cause increasing doubt regarding its guesses.

Tyndale says that the world began in a *"fire mist"* that contracted as it became cold; but Spencer says it was a *"cold-cloud"* that became heated and contracted.

As well, the age of man is estimated all the way from 550,000,000 years to as little as 6,000,000 years. The age of the earth is put by guessers as 10,000,000,000 to the lowest estimate of 10,000,000 years. This proves nothing but the unreliability of data which is used in the effort to prove diverse conclusions.

The truth is, God made the heavens and the earth, and all therein (Gen. 1:1). A creation demands a Creator. Blind chance, and according to all true laws of science, has never produced anything.

Evolution is an elaborate hoax by Satan, designed to insult God, and is believed by man because of his rebellion against God.
(The statement on evolution was derived from material compiled by Finis Jennings Dake.)

(38) "WHOSOEVER THEREFORE SHALL BE ASHAMED OF ME AND OF MY WORDS IN THIS ADULTEROUS AND SINFUL GENERATION; OF HIM ALSO SHALL THE SON OF MAN BE ASHAMED, WHEN HE COMETH IN THE GLORY OF HIS FATHER WITH THE HOLY ANGELS."

The phrase, *"Whosoever therefore shall be ashamed of Me and of My Words,"* actually proclaims a present tense, *"Whosoever is ashamed."* Robertson says that this is not a statement concerning the future conduct of a person, but, instead, the person's present attitude toward Jesus. The present conduct of the individual now determines Christ's future conduct with reference to that person. This speaks of *"shame"* respecting Christ and the Word of God.

Why would anyone be ashamed of Jesus?

Satan has made it his business to so insult the Person of Christ, and in every conceivable way, that this spirit permeates the entirety of the world and of mankind.

Unbelievers allude to His peasant upbringing, thereby declaring that He must have been deluded.

As well, the Jews, and from the time of their rejection of Him, have concocted the most evil lies about His Person, which could only have been spawned by Satan himself!

Islam, with its nearly 1,000,000,000 adherents, claims that He was a good man, but definitely not the Son of God.

Consequently, to accept Christ as one's Saviour, and, thereby, openly proclaim Him to any and all, as one must do, requires an attitude and spirit that flies in the face of world thinking.

One Nashville entertainer said the other day, *"I am a silent witness!"*

I don't know exactly what he meant by that statement; however, there is no such thing as a *"silent witness"* when it comes to Jesus Christ. One either confesses Him boldly, or not at all!

However, the cause of the greatest opposition to Christ pertains to the manner in which He died in order to redeem humanity from the grip of Satan and sin. The Cross of Christ appears to the great body of mankind to be shameful and contemptible. To the Jews it is a stumbling-block, and to the Greeks (Gentiles) foolishness. Hence vast numbers, whether through shame or fear, do not dare to confess it, and still less to preach it.

And therefore it is that Paul says (Rom. 1:16), *"I am not ashamed of the Gospel of Christ"* (Bickersteth).

The phrase, *"In this adulterous and sinful generation,"* pertains to the character of Israel at the time of Christ, and, as well, to every generation which has followed.

Mankind is ashamed of Him because it is *"adulterous and sinful."*

The word, *"adulterous,"* although pertaining to immorality, in this instance, pertains more to the worship of that which is not of God. That means that those who put the Church ahead of Christ, as do the whole of Catholicism, and many Protestants, are, according to Christ,

"adulterous." Paul said, *"Who changed the Truth of God into a lie, and worshipped and served the creature more than the Creator, who is blessed forever"* (Rom. 1:25).

The phrase, *"Of Him also shall the Son of Man be ashamed,"* means that such attitude will be reciprocated in like kind. In other words, no one can be saved and be ashamed of Christ at the same time!

The phrase, *"When He cometh in the Glory of His Father with the Holy Angels,"* speaks of the Second Coming, and not the Rapture (Rev. 19). The idea is this:

All the reasons for which man seems to be ashamed of Christ at present, will be proven baseless at the Second Coming. The Lord will come with such Splendor and Glory, that there will be absolutely no doubt as to Who and What He is!

His Coming will be with such Glory, that *"The sun shall be darkened, and the moon shall not give her light, and the stars shall fall from Heaven, and the powers of the heavens shall be shaken"* (Mat. 24:29).

No one will be *"ashamed"* of Him then. However, the die will have long since been cast regarding one's Salvation before this moment.

In fact, all who are born again, and, thereby, not ashamed of Christ, will actually come back with Him at this time of Glory and Splendor. Conversely, those who have been ashamed of Him, will not be with Him at the Second Coming.

CHAPTER 9

(1) "AND HE SAID UNTO THEM, VERILY I SAY UNTO YOU, THAT THERE BE SOME OF THEM THAT STAND HERE, WHICH SHALL NOT TASTE OF DEATH, TILL THEY HAVE SEEN THE KINGDOM OF GOD COME WITH POWER."

Some feel, and are probably correct, that the first verse of the 9th Chapter should have been the last verse (39) of the previous Chapter, and because it speaks of the coming Kingdom of God, which is alluded to in verse 38 of the last Chapter.

A. T. Robertson said that the first rule of Scripture interpretation is that one should ignore Chapter and Verse divisions as one studies the Word.

As one knows and realizes, the translation of Scripture, plus the Verse and Chapter divisions are not inspired by the Lord, as the original Text.

The phrase, *"And He said unto them, Verily I say unto you,"* proclaims by its manner a tremendously important statement about to be made.

The phrase, *"That there be some of them that stand here,"* referred, at least in this incident, to Peter, James, and John.

The phrase, *"Which shall not taste of death,"* did not mean they would not die, but, instead, that they would be given a very important experience concerning the coming *"Kingdom of God."* This would happen, as stated, some six days later.

The phrase, *"Till they have seen the Kingdom of God come with power,"* referred to, according to Wuest, an anticipatory picture of the coming Millennium.

Matthew used the phrase, *"Till they see the Son of Man coming in His Kingdom"* (Mat. 16:28). Luke said, *"Till they see the Kingdom of God"* (Lk. 9:27).

Actually, the terms, *"Kingdom of God,"* and, *"Kingdom of Heaven,"* are used interchangeably, and basically mean the same. This is also the *"Kingdom of Heaven"* of Matthew 3:2 and 4:17, announced by John the Baptist and the Messiah Himself, but rejected by Israel at that time. However, it will be accepted by Israel at the Second Advent (Second Coming).

The reason for these terms being used differently, but yet referring to the same thing, is probably because Matthew was writing for the Jews, and, therefore, used the phrase, *"Kingdom of Heaven."* Mark and Luke were writing for the Gentiles, and, therefore, used the term *"Kingdom of God."*

This *"Kingdom"* will come with *"Power,"* and because of necessity, thereby, refuting the *"Kingdom Now"* philosophy.

This teaching (Kingdom Now) proclaims that man is either now living in the Millennium, or society is getting better and better, and because of the influence of Christianity, which will shortly usher in the Millennium. The *"Prosperity Message"* and *"Political Message"* are, by and large, a part of this philosophy, and, consequently, eagerly embraced by many Christians.

In Truth, and as previously stated many times, the world is not getting better and better, but actually worse. In fact, Satan is going

to make his great bid for world dominion in the very near future by the advent of the Antichrist. The world at that time, and according to Revelation Chapters 6-19, is going to experience turmoil, suffering, war, and judgment, as it has never known before. Actually, the coming times of the near future are going to see *"tribulation"* as the world has never known in all of its history. These are the very Words of Christ (Mat. 24:21).

No! Jesus was not speaking of the conflict of 70 A.D., when Jerusalem was destroyed, as many teach.

The Disciples of Christ had asked Him the question as to the sign of His Coming and of the end of the world (age) (Mat. 24:3). Consequently, this is the question Jesus was answering.

As should be obvious, Jesus did not come in 70 A.D., and, as well, that certainly was not the end of the age.

Due to the advent of the Antichrist and his efforts to take over the world, the Coming of Christ with *"Power"* is a necessity. Daniel likened it to a *"Stone"* coming out of Heaven and smiting with great force, violence and power, the nations of the world (Dan. 2:45).

Consequently, this is a far cry from the world getting better and better, but actually proclaims it getting worse and worse (II Tim. 3:1-5).

(2) "AND AFTER SIX DAYS JESUS TAKETH WITH HIM PETER, AND JAMES, AND JOHN, AND LEADETH THEM UP INTO AN HIGH MOUNTAIN APART BY THEMSELVES: AND HE WAS TRANSFIGURED BEFORE THEM."

The phrase, *"And after six days,"* is spoken by Luke as *"eight days"* (Lk. 9:28). There is no discrepancy!

In Luke the Greek phrase is inclusive, meaning that two more days of time elements were counted which Matthew and Mark did not include.

The phrase in Mark is exclusive, which means all the days and time are not included.

Consequently, if the skeptics bothered to check the original language in which the Text was originally written, the truth would become obvious.

The phrase, *"Jesus taketh with Him Peter, and James, and John,"* speaks of the second experience in which they were included, but not the other Disciples.

1. These three were taken with Jesus at the raising of Jairus' daughter (Mk. 5:37). In this instance, they saw the *"Power"* of Christ.

2. This incident of the Transfiguration: Here they saw the *"Glory"* of Christ.

3. These three were taken even further with Christ in Gethsemane (Mat. 26:37). Here they saw His *"Suffering."*

Why Peter, James, and John, relative to the other Nine?

It was not an arbitrary decision on the part of Christ, therefore, there had to be a reason.

Inasmuch as the Bible does not say, we have to surmise that these three had a greater hunger for God, and, therefore, a greater love for Christ, and despite their faults and failings. Consequently, as they drew near to Him, He, consequently, drew near to them (James 4:8).

The phrase, *"And leadeth them up into an high mountain apart by themselves,"* does not tell us exactly where this mountain was. There is speculation that it was Mt. Hermon, with others claiming it was Mt. Tabor.

Even though it is only speculation, it is my thought that it was Mt. Tabor, which was only a few miles from Nazareth.

The phrase, *"And He was transfigured before them,"* simply refers to the act of giving outward expression of one's inner character, that outward expression coming from and being truly representative of that inner character.

The outward expression of the Lord was obvious to all. He was a travel-stained, itinerant Preacher, a peasant, if you will! As such, there was no evidence of His outward expression, Who He actually was.

Wuest says, *"But now, that outward expression was changed. Out from within the inmost being of the Son of God, there shown that dazzling glory of the essence of Deity which He possesses co-eternally with God the Father and God the Spirit."*

As such, it shown right through the clay walls of His humanity and through the clothing He wore. Wuest went on to say, *"It was that same dazzling radiance which the Angels saw in His pre-incarnate state* (Phil. 2:6), *but given through His physical Body, and not in the spiritual sense as in the case of the Angels."*

(3) "AND HIS RAIMENT BECAME SHINING, EXCEEDING WHITE AS SNOW; SO AS NO FULLER ON EARTH CAN WHITE THEM."

The phrase, *"And His raiment became shining,"* was a result of the Glory of God which did shine from Him, and, consequently, made His clothing translucent. Matthew as well said, *"His Face did shine."*

It should be quickly added, that the Glory that shown on His clothing and Face, was no borrowed radiance, as reflection of sunlight, but rather, the effulgence of Glory which came from within.

The word, *"shining,"* is *"stilbo"* in the Greek, and indicates that the shining was active, or, rather, *"a living light."*

As well, this is a picture of what He will be like in the coming Kingdom Age, i.e., Millennium.

The phrase, *"So as no fuller on earth can white them,"* means that whatever the color of His garment was, due to the powerful effect of the light which shown from within Him, it took on a radiating white.

(4) "AND THERE APPEARED UNTO THEM ELIAS WITH MOSES: AND THEY WERE TALKING WITH JESUS."

The phrase, *"And there appeared unto them Elias* (Elijah) *with Moses,"* proclaims a far greater portend than their mere appearance, as startling as that was. Their appearance had to do with the coming Kingdom Age, as did the Transfiguration of Christ.

Moses represents the Law, and, consequently, all those who died in the Faith, looking forward to the Coming Promise, Who was Christ.

Elijah represents Grace.

Moses points to the Saints from Adam's time to the First Advent of Christ. These who were under the Law, or before, will have as great a part in the Millennial Kingdom, as those under Grace.

Elijah speaks of the Saints dead or alive under Grace, who at the Rapture, will also be glorified and translated, and be a part of the Millennial Kingdom.

Actually, there will be no difference in the two groups.

Peter, James, and John represent Israel, cleansed and restored at the Second Advent.

The great multitude which was at the foot of the mountain, as spoken of in verse 14, speaks of the entirety of the world at the beginning of the coming Kingdom Age, in desperate need of the Ministry of the Messiah.

Consequently, the Transfiguration is a picture of the coming Millennial Kingdom, briefly given!

The phrase, *"And they were talking with Jesus,"* has the emphasis in the Greek Text that the conversation was a protracted one. Luke said they *"spake of His decease which He should accomplish at Jerusalem"* (Lk. 9:31).

I wonder what Peter thought when he saw and overheard this conversation concerning the coming death of Christ in Jerusalem, especially after he had rebuked the Lord concerning this very thing? (Mk. 8:31-32).

But yet, this tremendous experience of the Transfiguration would not give the Disciples, or even Peter, the Faith needed for that trying hour. Peter was still lifted up within his boastful self, and would not be deterred without bitter humiliation.

(5) "AND PETER ANSWERED AND SAID TO JESUS, MASTER, IT IS GOOD FOR US TO BE HERE: AND LET US MAKE THREE TABERNACLES; ONE FOR THEE, AND ONE FOR MOSES, AND ONE FOR ELIAS."

The phrase, *"And Peter answered and said to Jesus,"* refers to him answering something that he had not been asked.

However, it is easy to criticize Peter, when I suspect we do little better during the rare times of great visitations from the Lord.

The phrase, *"Master, it is good for us to be here,"* certainly is true; however, it completely begs the point.

If any response was warranted at all, which was doubtful, at the very most it would have been Praise to the Lord.

The phrase, *"And let us make three Tabernacles,"* is not as off the wall as it first seems.

There is a possibility that Peter had the Feast of Tabernacles in mind, which will be continued in the coming Kingdom Age (Zech. 14:16). As such, and if that is what he thought, he surmised that it was now beginning, hence the *"three Tabernacles,"* etc.

Having overheard the conversation concerning the coming Crucifixion in Jerusalem, perhaps he thought that the Kingdom Age would commence immediately after this time. This is evidenced by the question asked of Jesus immediately before the Ascension, *"Lord, Wilt Thou at this time restore again the Kingdom to Israel?*

"And He said unto them, It is not for you to know the times or the seasons, which the Father hath put in His Own Power" (Acts 1:6-7).

The phrase, *"One for Thee, and one for Moses, and one for Elias* (Elijah)*,"* even if Peter had the Feast of Tabernacles in mind, still, made little sense.

Peter's statement tells us several things:

1. First of all, he still was not properly evaluating the Mission of Christ, and because he had not properly evaluated the Word of God, i.e., of Christ. As such, his understanding of future events was skewed.

He was much like those of the modern *"Kingdom Now"* philosophy, attempting to pull the Millennium into the present, when the great suffering of Christ was just ahead.

Likewise, instead of Christ at this moment preparing for the Second Coming, He is rather preparing for the great suffering He will endure, and because of the suffering of His people, Israel, in the coming Great Tribulation.

2. As Peter, religious men are so prone to erect shrines where a great spiritual event has taken place. As such, and due to the penchant of man to worship, which actually is given by the Lord, in his carnality, he worships the gift instead of the Giver. Hence, millions worship the Church instead of the One Who builds the Church, i.e., Christ Jesus.

3. Whatever his error, Peter compounds it by placing Moses and Elijah in the same category as Jesus. This will be sharply rebuked by the Voice from Heaven, as outlined in verse 7.

As well, the modern Church, and especially Catholicism, has the tendency to place Mary on a par with Christ. Such is blasphemy!

(Incidentally, Elijah is spelled *"Elias"* here because the Greek language does not have a letter *"j."*)

(6) "FOR HE WIST NOT WHAT TO SAY; FOR THEY WERE SORE AFRAID."

The phrase, *"For He wist not what to say,"* is obvious by what he said, which would have been better not to have said anything.

The phrase, *"For they were sore afraid,"* actually speaks of being terrified. And no wonder!

All of a sudden, Jesus is shining with such a brightness that the Disciples are hard put to describe it.

And then, two men appear, one who has been dead for hundreds of years, with the other (Elijah) having never died . . . and then the Voice from Heaven!

(7) "AND THERE WAS A CLOUD THAT

OWED THEM: AND A VOICE
OF THE CLOUD, SAYING, THIS
ELOVED SON: HEAR HIM."

The phrase, *"And there was a cloud that overshadowed them,"* spoke of the Shekinah Glory Cloud which guided Israel out of Egypt, and which rested above the Mercy Seat beneath the Golden Cherubim in the Holy of Holies.

The word that Mark used for *"cloud"* is *"nephele,"* which speaks of a cloud which has definite form and is of a certain size.

Had he been speaking of a cloud which is a shapeless collection of vapor, which makes up the clouds in the heavens, he would have used the word *"nephos."*

The phrase, *"And a Voice came out of the cloud,"* proclaims the actual Voice of God. In Truth, God's audible Voice has been heard many times (Gen. 3:8; Deut. 5:22-25; Mat. 3:17; Jn. 12:28; Rev. 10:3). Nearly 3,000 times in the Bible, God is referred to as speaking to men, whether by impression upon their spirits, or audibly (Heb. 1:1-2) (Dake).

The phrase, *"Saying, This is My Beloved Son,"* says in the Greek Text, *"This is My Son, The Beloved One."* According to Wuest, this places emphasis equally upon two facts: A. That the Messiah is God's Son; and, B. That He is the Beloved One.

This is the second time God has declared by an audible Voice that Jesus of Nazareth is His Beloved Son (Mat. 3:17), the Only Begotten Son (Jn. 1:14, 18; 3:16-18; I Jn. 4:9).

Jesus is the only Person Who was brought into being in the sense of being conceived by the Holy Spirit and born of a woman (Isa. 7:14; 9:6-7; Mat. 1:18-25; Lk. 1:34-35; Gal. 4:4).

Men are *"born again,"* and, as such, are *"adopted sons"* (Rom. 8:14-16, 23; 9:4; Gal. 4:5; Eph. 1:5) (Dake).

The phrase, *"Hear Him,"* refers to Christ. In other words, Moses and Elijah are not to be placed on the same par with Christ, which should be obvious. Jesus is the One to *"hear"* and, consequently to *"listen."*

It actually means, *"Be constantly hearing Him."* As well, Wuest says that it does not merely refer to the act of hearing in the sense of listening, but also to the act of obeying what is heard.

In a sense, these Words of God signify the abolition of the Old Covenant, and the establishment of the New Covenant in Christ.

NOTES

Also, the entire portrayal of the Transfiguration is meant to portray, along with its symbolism of the coming Kingdom Age, the Deity of Christ. Consequently, He Alone was transfigured, and not Elijah and Moses. They did not have within them that which He had within Him.

(8) "AND SUDDENLY, WHEN THEY HAD LOOKED ROUND ABOUT, THEY SAW NO MAN ANY MORE, SAVE JESUS ONLY WITH THEMSELVES."

The words, *"And suddenly,"* proclaim, as is obvious, a change in this situation.

Matthew seemed to explain it a little more fully when he said, *"When the Disciples heard it* (the Voice of God out of Heaven), *they fell on their face, and were sore afraid"* (Mat. 17:6). As if the Transfiguration of Jesus wasn't enough, and with the sudden appearance of two of the great Prophets of the distant past, the Voice of God coming from the cloud which overshadowed them, placed them in a position little short of terror. Peter's foolish request concerning the Tabernacles are suddenly forgotten in the glory of the moment. They consequently hide their face on the ground with Matthew saying, *"And Jesus came and touched them, and said, Arise, and be not afraid"* (Mat. 17:7). The phrase, *"When they had looked round about,"* records their reaction to the touch of Jesus. In astonishment they slowly look around, surveying the situation.

The phrase, *"They saw no man any more, save Jesus only with themselves,"* proclaims the conclusion of this great happening.

Let it be known that this was not a dream or a vision, at least as a vision is commonly thought of, but rather an actual happening which was as literal as was possible for anything to be.

They had witnessed the Glory of God in a way that no human being had ever witnessed it before. While it is true that the Prophets of the past had seen great manifestations of the Glory of God, such as Isaiah (Isa. 6:1-7), and Ezekiel (Ezek. Chpt. 1), etc., still, none had seen Jesus as Peter, James and John. In Truth, all the manifestations of Glory in the Old Testament were not an end within themselves, but rather pointed to that which was to come, namely Jesus. And yet, that which was seen by these Disciples, as glorious and wonderful as it was, was only a preview of that which is even yet to come.

The fulfillment of the great Plan of God, will be the coming down out of Heaven, of the New Jerusalem, which will take up its abode on this earth. John the Beloved wrote, *"And the city had no need of the sun, neither of the moon, to shine in it: for the Glory of God did lighten it, and the Lamb is the light thereof"* (Rev. 21:23).

(9) "AND AS THEY CAME DOWN FROM THE MOUNTAIN, HE CHARGED THEM THAT THEY SHOULD TELL NO MAN WHAT THINGS THEY HAD SEEN, TILL THE SON OF MAN WERE RISEN FROM THE DEAD."

The phrase, *"And as they came down from the mountain,"* must have signaled a time of great reflection of heart, and burden of soul. They had witnessed what no human being had ever witnessed before, and in magnitude that left them speechless.

To be sure, occasionally the Lord takes us to the top of the mountain of Blessing and manifestation of the Holy Spirit, but then we have to come back down. However, we have the assurance that as He took us up, He, likewise, will come down with us.

The phrase, *"He charged them that they should tell no man what things they had seen,"* referred even to their fellow Disciples.

Why?

To have done so then may possibly have created jealousy in the hearts of the other Disciples, which after the Resurrection and Ascension would not occur.

As well, and especially at that time, even the three little understood what they had actually seen. Therefore, to explain it, they would have been hard put to have done so!

The phrase, *"Till the Son of Man were risen from the dead,"* means that things would begin to fall into place at that time!

They had seen much, and had understood little. The Resurrection, Ascension, and Day of Pentecost, when they would all be Baptized in the Holy Spirit, would then bring everything into focus.

(10) "AND THEY KEPT THAT SAYING WITH THEMSELVES, QUESTIONING ONE WITH ANOTHER WHAT THE RISING FROM THE DEAD SHOULD MEAN."

The phrase, *"And they kept that saying with themselves,"* means that they faithfully obeyed what the Lord had told them respecting what they had seen. They told no one!

The phrase, *"Questioning one with another what the rising from the dead should mean,"* means two things:

1. The manifestation of the Glory of God they had experienced was so startling, so unreal, so unexplainable, that the implication is that they discussed it very little among themselves. It was almost as if they were fearful of doing so, which they probably were.

2. However, they discussed intently the statement of Jesus about Him dying and rising from the dead. Despite His plain statements, they still did not understand what He was talking about.

The Power He manifested in healing the sick, cleansing the leapers, and even raising the dead, was, within itself, so absolutely astounding that they could not begin to see how anyone could take His Life. In their reasoning, *"How can you take the life of One Who can walk on water, or speak the Word and a mighty storm instantly subsides, and even raise the dead?"* In their minds they cannot put it all together. Jesus is the Messiah, and of that they are sure! While it was true that the opposition of the Pharisees and Sadducees was severe, still, there was really nothing they could do against such Power.

As we have repeatedly stated, they did not understand His True Mission was so much greater than once again bringing back the Glory of Israel. He had rather come to break the terrible grip that Satan had on humanity, a grip so severe in fact that man, within himself, could not break it. They looked at Him as a King, and not a Sacrifice. In Truth He was a King, and more than a King, but, in Truth, The King, but yet, The Sacrifice!

They had heard Elijah and Moses speak with Jesus concerning His coming death, and now they hear Jesus speak of His rising from the dead. It should have been an encouragement to them, which, in reality, Christ intended for it to be. However, they simply did not understand.

(11) "AND THEY ASKED HIM, SAYING, WHY SAY THE SCRIBES THAT ELIAS MUST FIRST COME?"

Their question concerning the coming of Elijah was based on His appearance before them on the Mt. of Transfiguration.

They were speaking of what the Scribes taught concerning the coming of Elijah as prophesied by Malachi some 400 years earlier,

"Behold, I will send you Elijah the Prophet before the coming of the great and dreadful day of the Lord" (Mal. 4:5).

However, the Scribes, even as the Disciples, had the time element somewhat confused. They did not distinguish the First Coming of Christ in the flesh from His Second Advent of Judgment, which is even yet to come.

The thinking of the Disciples seems to have been that immediately after the Resurrection of Christ, He would then set up the Kingdom. Consequently, they thought the appearance of Elijah on the Mt. of Transfiguration, pertained to that event. In their minds, Elijah should have remained, in view of the Kingdom soon to come. This is evidenced as well by their question to Christ immediately before the Ascension, *"Wilt Thou at this time restore again the Kingdom to Israel?"* (Acts 1:6). Even at that late moment, they continued to hold to Jesus ushering in the Kingdom, and, once again, making Israel great.

In Truth, the difference in the First and Second Advents of Christ was amply outlined in the Old Testament. Nevertheless, it seems that all of Israel confused them.

As we have stated, Isaiah 53 along with Daniel 9 adequately described His First Coming in the flesh, and His being *"cut off"* as Daniel put it. As well, basically all the Prophets spoke of His Second Advent, which would be in Glory and Power (Ezek. Chpts. 38-39; Zech. Chpt. 14). Isaiah 9:6-7 actually portrays both Comings. Irrespective, Israel viewed it all as one coming, with the Religious Leaders rejecting Jesus as the Promised One, and the Disciples accepting Him, but confusing His Coming, and, therefore, His Purpose.

(12) "AND HE ANSWERED AND TOLD THEM, ELIAS VERILY COMETH FIRST, AND RESTORETH ALL THINGS; AND HOW IT IS WRITTEN OF THE SON OF MAN, THAT HE MUST SUFFER MANY THINGS, AND BE SET AT NOUGHT."

The phrase, *"And He answered and told them,"* proclaims Him explaining the situation, but with them still lacking in understanding.

The phrase, *"Elias* (Elijah) *verily cometh first, and restoreth all things,"* refers to this Prophet coming as one of the two witnesses not long before the Second Advent (Mal. 4:5-6; Rev. 11:3-12).

Jesus is saying that the Scribes are correct in their statement about Elijah coming first, but that they are confusing the time.

Consequently, many of the Scribes, no doubt, disclaimed Christ because Elijah had not come. They completely misunderstood the mission of John the Baptist, who came in the spirit and power of Elijah (Mat. 17:13).

The phrase, *"And how it is written of the Son of Man, that He must suffer many things, and be set at nought,"* pertains to the First Coming (Birth of Christ, and His Ministry), which Elijah, at least in a personal sense, would have no part of.

The phrase, *"Restoreth all things,"* did not mean that Elijah would do this personally, but shortly after his appearance all things would be restored, which pertained to Israel, and the Kingdom Age which would affect the entirety of the world.

However, the phrase *"Restoreth all things,"* could also mean that Elijah, will, at that time (the coming Great Tribulation), preach the Truth to Israel, which they have not heard since John the Baptist and Christ, neither would they receive.

By the words, *"It is written,"* Jesus is plainly saying that His Present Coming is when He will *"suffer,"* exactly as He has been telling the Disciples, was adequately revealed in Isaiah 53, among other places. Consequently, and as we have stated, there was no reason for the Scribes or the Disciples, to confuse the issue.

Why didn't the Scribes understand these Prophecies as they should have?

The Pharisees, of which the Scribes were a part, had so added to the Word of God, that they no longer knew its true meaning. Self-will had degenerated into self-righteousness, and, consequently, clouded their understanding of the Word of God. In other words, they simply no longer understood the Bible. However, and as should be obvious, it was a willful rejection of the Word. Consequently, inasmuch as they did not want its true meaning, the Lord took from them what little understanding they did have (Mat. 13:12).

(13) "BUT I SAY UNTO YOU, THAT ELIAS IS INDEED COME, AND THEY HAVE DONE UNTO HIM WHATSOEVER THEY LISTED, AS IT IS WRITTEN OF HIM."

The phrase, *"But I say unto you, That Elias* (Elijah) *is indeed come,"* refers to John the Baptist who came in the spirit and power of Elijah (Lk. 1:17). He would do before the First Advent, as he did do, what Elijah in person will do before the Second Advent (Isa. 40:3; Mal. 3:1; Mat. 17:12-13).

Wuest said, *"We are not to understand that he was the actual Elijah of the Old Testament, nor that his appearance and ministry to Israel fulfilled the Prophecy of the future coming and ministry of Elijah, but that He came in the spirit and power of Elijah to prepare the hearts of Israel for the First Advent of the Messiah as Elijah will do for His Second Advent."*

The phrase, *"And they have done unto him whatsoever they listed, as it is written of him,"* refers to John's execution by Herod.

Elijah was persecuted by Jezebel, as John the Baptist was persecuted by Herodias. As well, Elijah will in the future be killed by the Antichrist (Rev. 11:8), as John the Baptist was killed by Herod.

Even though Mark did not mention it, Matthew said, *"Then the Disciples understood that He spake unto them of John the Baptist"* (Mat. 17:13).

(14) "AND WHEN HE CAME TO HIS DISCIPLES, HE SAW A GREAT MULTITUDE ABOUT THEM, AND THE SCRIBES QUESTIONING WITH THEM."

The phrase, *"And when He came to His Disciples,"* refers to the Nine, as Peter, James and John had been with Him.

The phrase, *"He saw a great multitude about them,"* spoke of the crowd which had assembled due to the argument that was now taking place between the Scribes and the Nine Disciples. It concerned the Disciples attempting to cast the demon out of a boy, but without success.

The phrase, *"And the Scribes questioning with them,"* meant they were taunting the Disciples with their failure, and suggesting that it was because the Power of Jesus was waning. No doubt the Disciples had used the Name of Jesus in attempting to cast the demon out of the boy.

What the Disciples were answering is not recorded, but it is possible they were saying very little, if anything!

Regrettably, the world of religion, at present, as then, has no regard for Christ. They may speak of Him, but most of the time it is in an unbelieving manner. As well, they have no regard or concern for those who are pitifully held captive by Satan, as this boy, and who can be set free only by Christ.

Religion is a cold, calculating business! Its task is the control of people and the taking in of money. Absolutely no one is helped by its efforts, but only hurt, and greatly so! God is not in it, so no one can be helped. Consequently, when one looks at these Scribes as they ridicule the Disciples, one is looking at the modern Church as well!

Also, and too often, the True Remnant is as the Disciples were, powerless. They use the Name of Jesus, but seemingly to little avail! Verses 28 and 29 tell us why.

(15) "AND STRAIGHTWAY ALL THE PEOPLE, WHEN THEY BEHELD HIM, WERE GREATLY AMAZED, AND RUNNING TO HIM SALUTED HIM."

The phrase, *"And straightway all the people, when they beheld Him,"* proclaims His sudden, unexpected arrival.

The word, *"beheld,"* denotes something more than mere recognition. As well, it is more than Him coming at this particular time, in the midst of the sarcasm of the Scribes. Quite possibly, traces of Glory which He had just experienced on the Mt. of Transfiguration, still lingered on Him.

The phrase, *"Were greatly amazed,"* means, *"Were utterly amazed."* The Greek expositors expressed something more than mere recognition. There was something about Him that stood out, and must have come as a shock to the Scribes as well! Their sarcasm must have stuck in their throats at this point.

The phrase, *"And running to Him saluted Him,"* pertained to His popularity among the people. This, as well, is what angered the Religious Leaders of Israel.

(16) "AND HE ASKED THE SCRIBES, WHAT QUESTION YE WITH THEM?"

The question was actually directed to the entirety of the multitude who came to Christ upon His arrival, but which eventually concluded with the Scribes. When the question was asked, more than likely the people turned and looked at the Scribes, in which they really did not answer. The next verse gives us the reason!

(17) "AND ONE OF THE MULTITUDE ANSWERED AND SAID, MASTER, I HAVE BROUGHT UNTO THEE MY SON, WHICH HATH A DUMB SPIRIT;"

The phrase, *"And one of the multitude answered and said,"* concerned the man who had brought his son to Jesus. The Scribes were probably very pleased that the man quickly answered, so they would not have to answer. They desired no confrontation with Christ.

The phrase, *"Master, I have brought unto Thee my son, which hath a dumb spirit,"* pertains to him hearing that Jesus was in the vicinity, and bringing his son for deliverance. However, he found nine of the Disciples, but Jesus was not present.

The *"dumb spirit"* was a correct analysis of the situation. The boy was demon-possessed, with the demon having bound his tongue and vocal organs.

It seems that knowledge of demon spirits was more pronounced at that time, even than presently. Inasmuch as the Holy Spirit did not contradict the findings of many of these people, if any, proclaims the truth of the situation.

While it is certainly true that modern Disciples can overemphasize the presence of evil spirits, still, I am persuaded that these spirits are just as active today as then, and the cause of far more problems than one realizes. If Satan cannot get one to become overly preoccupied with evil spirits, he will go in the other direction, tempting the Believer to ignore them altogether, thereby, not correctly analyzing the situation in a spiritual sense.

(18) "AND WHERESOEVER HE TAKETH HIM, HE TEARETH HIM: AND HE FOAMETH, AND GNASHETH WITH HIS TEETH, AND PINETH AWAY: AND I SPAKE TO THY DISCIPLES THAT THEY SHOULD CAST HIM OUT; AND THEY COULD NOT."

The phrase, *"And wheresoever he taketh him,"* means *"to seize upon,"* or *"take possession of."* The idea is that the power of the demon spirit is greater than the willpower or the strength of the individual. Consequently, the control by the one possessed, as this boy, is limited, if any at all.

While one certainly should not give too much credit to Satan, still, at the same time, one must not underestimate his power. To give the reader an example of how great God's power is, when He wanted light, He simply spoke it into existence (Gen. 1:3).

As well, the entirety of the restoration of a planet which *"was without form, and void; and darkness was upon the face of the deep,"* was brought about simply by the Word of God

(Gen. 1:2). Concerning this restoration, the phrase, *"And God said,"* was used five times in order to bring it about, and it was accomplished in four days (Gen. 1:3-19). However, when time came to redeem man from the terrible horror of the Fall which resulted in destruction, this power of Satan, as it gripped humanity, was so great that God could not speak Redemption into existence, as He did restoration. He had to come down to this hell-bound world, taking upon Himself the frame of man, and die on Calvary in order that the terrible bondage of sin could be broken. That is how powerful it was and is! To be sure, only Jesus Christ has overcome Satan, defeating the powers of darkness, and because He is stronger. As a result, He entered into Satan's house, spoiling his goods, and, in fact, the entirety of his house (Mk. 3:27). Consequently, to depend on anything other than Christ, is foolishness indeed!

Let's lay aside demon possession and even demon oppression for the moment, and deal with the struggle every Christian faces in his effort to live an overcoming life.

CAN SATAN OVERRIDE A BELIEVER'S WILL?

The question we have just asked, is powerful, and even somewhat frightful!

As we attempt to answer this question, let's look first at Simon Peter.

Jesus said to him, *"Simon, Simon, Behold, Satan hath desired to have you, that he may sift you as wheat:*

"But I have prayed for thee, that thy Faith fail not: and when thou art converted strengthen thy Brethren" (Lk. 22:31-32).

To that statement by Christ, Peter said, *"Lord, I am ready to go with Thee, both into prison, and to death"* (Lk. 22:33).

Was Peter serious concerning his acclamation? At that time, was he really serious about going to prison with Christ, should that arise, or even death?

I believe he was! I believe he meant every word he said. However, his acclamation or boast was in his own strength, and not True Faith as given by Christ.

If one is to notice, Jesus did not tell Peter He would pray for him that his strength fail not, but, instead, *"That thy Faith fail not."*

Did Peter want to do what he did? I believe

it is obvious he did not want to deny Christ. However, Satan overrode his will.

In Truth, Peter's strength failed, but his Faith did not fail. He lost a battle, but he did not lose the war.

Many years ago, I heard the great Pentecostal Preacher, A. N. Trotter, say, *"Every attack Satan directs against the Believer is in one way or the other designed to weaken and to ultimately destroy his Faith."*

If Satan can maneuver the Believer into a position where he has tried his hardest and still lost, Satan will then tell the Believer any lie he can get him to believe. He will tell him that Christianity does not work, or the Word of God does not work, etc.! That's when our Faith is at stake. At that time, it is not really a question of our strength; it is a question of our Faith.

Can our Faith fail?

It can fail, as it has failed in the hearts and lives of many. However, if one looks to Jesus, and despite the problem or the failure, we have the Promise that He is *"praying for us, that our Faith fail not"* (Lk. 22:32).

ROMANS CHAPTER 7

Many have argued that Romans 7 pertains to Paul's before conversion experience. That is probably correct through verse 13. However, beginning with verse 14, it is obvious that he was speaking of his experiences after Salvation. Here is what he said:

"For that which I do I allow not: for what I would, that do I not; but what I hate, that do I" (Rom. 7:15).

He then said this concerning the will:

"For I know that in me (that is, in my flesh,) *dwelleth no good thing: for to will is present with me* (to use his willpower to do right)*; but how to perform that which is good I find not"* (Rom. 7:18).

The Holy Spirit went on to emphasize this point again. For now Paul says this, which is basically the same as verse 15.

"For the good that I would I do not: but the evil which I would not, that I do" (Rom. 7:19).

First, we should notice that the language he is using here is not the language of an unconverted man. It is the language of a saved man.

No unsaved person hates sin (*"But what I hate, that do I"*). The unconverted may hate the results of sin, but he does not hate sin itself.

As well, no unconverted person even remotely has a will to try to live for God. Once again I emphasize: They may strongly detest the predicament their sin has put them in, but they don't hate the sin itself. It is impossible for a sinner to hate his sin. He actually loves his sin.

So, the statements we have quoted by Paul from Romans 7 are the statements of a saved man in deep struggle.

Most of us would never admit that we have fought this same battle. And, sadder still, many of us have not only fought it in the past, we are fighting it at present. We want to make the right choice in something, but we cannot do it. In other words, whether we understand it or not, Satan is overriding our will. The very thing we hate, at times, we conclude by doing. Romans Chapter 7, at least beginning with verse 14, is actually the story of the struggle of most of Christendom. Consequently, it should be obvious that Satan can override a Christian's will if he does not properly understand the Grace of God.

However, I emphasize that this does not mean that we are free of responsibility. Any wrongdoing committed by any Believer is the responsibility of that Believer, and he will be held accountable for it.

HOW CAN SATAN OVERRIDE A PERSON'S WILL AND FORCE HIM TO DO SOMETHING AGAINST HIS WILL?

Paul said: *"O wretched man that I am! Who shall deliver me from the body of this death?"* (Rom. 7:24).

How many Christians have uttered the same words, *"O wretched man that I am!"* How many are saying those words right now, *"O wretched man that I am?"* Once again, I want to emphasize that this is not the language of an unconverted person. This is the language of an individual who is struggling with all his strength to do right. He is trying to please God with every fiber of his being, but failing miserably. Let's look at Paul a little closer.

I think it is obvious that Paul was a tremendously strong (in self) individual. He was well educated; possibly the most educated person God used in the entire Old and New Testaments. As well, he was headstrong. I think if you study his life even slightly, you will have to agree.

Before his conversion, Paul prided himself on his strict adherence to Levitical Law. However, he only trumpeted the part of the Law he thought he was keeping, and said little or nothing about that which he couldn't keep. Read what he said:

"For I bear them record that they have a zeal of God, but not according to knowledge.

"For they being ignorant of God's Righteousness, and going about to establish their own righteousness, have not submitted themselves unto the Righteousness of God" (Rom. 10:2-3).

Paul said this of Israel, because that is exactly what he himself had been. Before his conversion on the Damascus Road, he went about trying to establish his own righteousness.

In Romans 7:9-11, Paul recounts some of his experiences before conversion.

"For I was alive without the Law once (as a child): *but when the Commandment came* (when he reached the age of understanding), *sin revived, and I died.*

"And the Commandment, which was ordained to life, I found to be unto death (in other words he couldn't keep the Commandment).

"For sin, taking occasion by the Commandment, deceived me, and by it slew me." (The Commandment said *"don't do it,"* but he was not able to obey because of the power of sin.)

After Paul came to Jesus, he thought, *"Surely, I can keep the Law now!"*

But then to his dismay, as is recorded in Romans 7:15, he found that even though he was now born again, he still couldn't keep the Law. (In other words, Satan would override his will and force him to do things he did not want to do.)

Little by little, it seems that Paul ultimately came to the conclusion that despite how hard he tried, he could not, at least within himself, keep the Law.

PAUL'S VICTORY

He gradually learned after he became a Believer, that even though the Law did not die, nevertheless, he became dead to the Law.

"For I through the Law am dead to the Law, that I might live unto God" (Gal. 2:19).

The struggle to keep the Law had ended. The Law, to be sure, was kept (the moral law), but it was really not kept by him; it was kept by Christ through him. This is what he learned. *"I am crucified with Christ: nevertheless I live;*

yet not I, but Christ liveth in me: and the life which I now live in the flesh I live by the Faith of the Son of God, Who loved me and gave Himself for me" (Gal. 2:20).

What did he mean by the statement, *"I am crucified with Christ"*?

He meant that when Jesus died on Calvary, in effect, every Believer died with Him. That means the old Paul died, just as with every Believer.

Thus, when Jesus rose from the dead, Paul rose with Him, along with every Believer, hence, *"Christ liveth in me."*

That means that Christ has already kept the Law perfectly, and if we allow His victory, and, in effect, Him Personally to live in us, we will perfectly keep the (moral) Law as well!

Even though we *"live in the flesh,"* still, our overcoming victory is not in the flesh, but rather in Christ.

As well, if we *"live by the Faith of the Son of God,"* we cannot fail, because His Faith cannot fail, and, consequently, our Faith cannot fail.

If you will notice, Paul did not say that he would live this life in the flesh, a life of victory, by his Faith, even though his Faith was very much present, but, instead, *"by the Faith of the Son of God."*

All of this means that the very moment we attempt to overcome Satan in our own strength, we lose — every time.

As well, Satan knows when the Believer is in his own strength instead of Christ's strength. And no matter how opposed to doing something the Believer may be, Satan will literally force the Christian's will and make him do what he doesn't want to do. Paul said it very succinctly:

"... For to will is present with me; but how to perform that which is good I find not" (Rom. 7:18). When we pit ourselves against Satan in any capacity, we have lost.

However, as Paul allowed Christ to live in him, consequently, the Holy Spirit became the Power within Paul, and *"The Law of the Spirit of Life in Christ Jesus hath made me free from the Law of sin and death"* (Rom. 8:2).

Then *"The Righteousness of the Law might be fulfilled in us, who walk not after the flesh, but after the Spirit"* (Rom. 8:4).

OUR VICTORY!

Now that Jesus lives within us, and that means an active performance within us on a daily basis, the Holy Spirit now has control, consequently, it is no longer possible for Satan to override one's will.

IS IT POSSIBLE WE CAN THINK WE ARE IN THE SPIRIT WHEN ACTUALLY WE ARE NOT?

This question has to be asked, because even after one begins to allow Christ to live within him, and, consequently, walking after the Spirit, the walk does not begin perfectly, and there are still failures at times simply because we are learning about this glorious Spirit walk. At times we have to pick up and start all over again, asking the Lord where we went wrong, and how we drifted back into the flesh!

However, Faith, and especially if we are leaning on His Faith, does not quit. It picks itself up, and as Paul said, *"Forgetting those things which are behind, and reaching forth unto those things which are before,*

"I press toward the mark for the prize of the high calling of God in Christ Jesus"(Phil.3:13-14).

To help us understand it a little better, the moment the Believer comes to Christ, he is freely given Sanctification (I Cor. 6:11). One could probably call it *"Positional Sanctification,"* meaning that this is our position in Christ, which does not change irrespective of our conduct, because its example is Christ, and not ourselves.

However, the Sanctification process in the Believer begins at conversion and actually never ends, and is really what the struggle is all about. One might call that *"Conditional Sanctification"*(I Thess. 5:23).

Now, even though our *"Position"* in Christ never changes, still, our *"Condition"* does change, and constantly. When the Holy Spirit is allowed control, as Romans 8 declares, it is the business of the Holy Spirit to bring the Believer's *"Condition"* up to his *"Position."* It is a task the Holy Spirit never stops working on, and, in fact, will not stop until He one day, *"Presents us faultless before the Presence of His Glory with exceeding joy"* (Jude 24).

Many years ago, I heard A. N. Trotter quote the following poem. It ministered greatly to me, and has done so through the years. I have quoted it countless times publicly and within my own heart. It perhaps says everything I'm trying to say, in its short verse.

NOTES

"I can see far down the mountain,
"Where I have wandered many years.
"Often hindered on my journey,
"By the ghosts of doubts and fears.
"Broken vows and disappointments,
"Thickly strewn along the way,
"But the Spirit has led unerring,
"To the hand I hold today."

The phrase, *"He teareth him,"* speaks of this spirit throwing the boy into convulsions.

The phrase, *"And he foameth,"* means he foamed at the mouth.

The phrase, *"And gnasheth with his teeth,"* spoke of intense pressure, which manifested itself in the grinding of the teeth. It was somewhat like a fierce anger.

The phrase, *"And pineth away,"* means after the contortions had ended, the boy would sink into a motionless stupor.

The pain and suffering this family underwent can only be imagined when one has experienced it!

The phrase, *"And I spake to Thy Disciples that they should cast him out; and they could not,"* presents the man bringing his son to Jesus, but, regrettably, Jesus was not there. Consequently, he asked the help of the nine Disciples.

They evidently attempted to cast the demon out of the boy, but to no avail! The idea is that they tried repeatedly, but without success; hence, the taunts of the Scribes.

We know that the Transfiguration of Christ on the mountaintop pointed toward the coming Kingdom Age. Consequently, and as we have stated, Jesus descending the mountain and delivering the boy, is symbolic of what He will do in that coming grand time, when Satan will be expelled by the Power of Christ from his present domain (Rev. 20:1-3).

Therefore, in a sense, the nine Disciples, who undoubtedly love Jesus, are a symbol of the True Church versus the apostate Church as evidenced by the Scribes.

I realize that some would object to that, especially considering they were unable to cast out the demon. However, at other times they were successful! Consequently, the True Church falls into the same category.

As powerful as the True Church in Christ may be, still, until Jesus comes (The Second Coming), Satan will not be totally cast out.

(19) "HE ANSWERETH HIM, AND SAITH,

O FAITHLESS GENERATION, HOW LONG SHALL I BE WITH YOU? HOW LONG SHALL I SUFFER YOU? BRING HIM UNTO ME."

The phrase, *"He answereth him, and saith, O faithless generation,"* means *"without Faith, unbelieving,"* and definitely included the Disciples in the rebuke.

The unbelief of the Pharisees which included the Scribes, had so ingrained itself in the entirety of Israel, that all were affected by it, even including the choice Disciples of Christ, as is obvious.

I wonder if this present generation doesn't fall into the same category? The closer to the end, the less True Faith there will be. Jesus said, *"Nevertheless when the Son of Man cometh, shall He find Faith on the earth?"* (Lk. 18:8).

The question, *"How long shall I be with you?"*, in effect asks if His time spent with them will be enough.

The question, *"How long shall I suffer you?"*, means *"to bear with, or endure."*

Once again, this includes the Disciples. Jesus is saying, and especially considering that they were constantly in His Presence, and, consequently, constantly under His Teaching, that they should not be so slow to learn.

The phrase, *"Bring him unto Me,"* implies that the boy was not immediately with the father, but was being held by others a short distance away.

(20) "AND THEY BROUGHT HIM UNTO HIM: AND WHEN HE SAW HIM, STRAIGHT-WAY THE SPIRIT TARE HIM; AND HE FELL ON THE GROUND, AND WALLOWED FOAMING."

The phrase, *"And they brought him unto Him,"* proclaims them obeying Christ, with the boy being brought into the Presence of the Lord.

The phrase, *"And when he saw Him,"* refers to the evil spirit within the boy seeing Christ.

In the phraseology, the idea presents itself of the spirit having seen the Disciples and was not affected accordingly. However, when he saw Christ, he knew his time was up.

The phrase, *"Straightway the spirit tare him,"* presents the demon's final effort, possibly even to kill the boy.

The phrase, *"And he fell on the ground, and wallowed foaming,"* means he kept rolling on the ground and foaming at the mouth. The sight had to be terrible to behold! However, this

NOTES

parent had undergone this suffering for quite some time.

(21) "AND HE ASKED HIS FATHER, HOW LONG IS IT AGO SINCE THIS CAME UNTO HIM? AND HE SAID, OF A CHILD."

The phrase, *"And He asked his father,"* presents the beginning of a question, and proclaims the humanity of Christ. As all men, He only knew what the Holy Spirit told Him, or by asking for information. However, and to be sure, the Holy Spirit was much more conversed with Him, than with any other man (Ps. 45:7).

The question, *"How long is it ago since this came unto him?"*, was for a purpose!

I feel the asking of the question had nothing to do with the casting out of the demon, but, rather, to ascertain how young the boy was when this thing happened.

It seems that Jesus sensed the answer given by the father, *"Of a child."*

How could a demon spirit enter into a child?

A child is innocent, and would not be able, at least within himself, to yield or resist. Therefore, the cause has to be other than himself.

Demons were rampant at this time in Israel. Some have suggested that they were there to oppose Christ. While that possibly may have played some part, still, it was not the main cause.

The True Word of God held no sway in Israel at that time. The *"leaven"* of the Pharisees ruled the land. Any country where religion rules, demon spirits abound.

Hinduism rules India, therefore, demon spirits are rampant. The same can be said for Moslem countries, etc. Catholicism is another example!

Judaism within itself was not a religion, and because it was originally given by God. However, the Pharisees had made the Word of God noneffective by their tradition. Consequently, religion ruled, i.e., demons ruled.

As well, any home that does not know Christ is open to the demon powers of darkness, even upon the children. Therefore, the possibility definitely exists, and probably was the case, that this family did not know the Lord. They no doubt knew this corrupt form of Judaism, but not the True Word of God. Consequently, their son was an open target for the powers of darkness.

If one could pull back the cover and find the true cause of the terrible problems that beset America, and the entirety of the world for that matter, one would no doubt be shocked at the operation of demon spirits as the original cause. Most homes in modern America do not know God, and, consequently, are as susceptible as this family of our Text.

Of course the question, *"What would be the spiritual condition of the child should he die in that condition?"*, begs to be asked.

As we previously stated, the child is not able to resist or accept, at least with understanding. Consequently, every child, and even one in the condition of our discussion, is protected by the Lord, at least regarding their soul, until they reach the age of accountability, whatever that may be. In other words, the Bible teaches that no child dies lost. Jesus verified this by saying, *"Verily I say unto you, Except ye be converted, and become as little children, ye shall not enter into the Kingdom of Heaven"* (Mat. 18:3).

So, the Salvation experience, among other things, makes one guileless *"as little children."*

(22) "AND OFTTIMES IT HATH CAST HIM INTO THE FIRE, AND INTO THE WATERS, TO DESTROY HIM: BUT IF THOU CANST DO ANY THING, HAVE COMPASSION ON US, AND HELP US."

The phrase, *"And ofttimes it hath cast him into the fire, and into the waters, to destroy him,"* reflects suicidal tendencies, as promoted by this spirit. Consequently, the parents had to watch him constantly, in view of these terrible impulses.

From this we know that this spirit had attempted to kill him again and again, but without success.

Even though it is impossible for us to go too deep into this scenario, could it be that Jehovah kept this child alive, and despite the efforts of Satan, until he could be brought to Jesus?

In fact, how much hand does the Lord take in matters of this nature, knowing that ultimately the Gospel will be brought to particular areas?

I was born into a home that did not know God. In fact, my Dad, until he was 25 years old had never seen a Bible, heard a Gospel Message, or darkened the doors of any type of Church. My Mother was pretty much the same, having only attended a funeral at a Church once or twice.

In fact, before my parents came to Christ, to my knowledge, not a single member of our family, whether immediate or otherwise, as far as I know, knew the Lord.

NOTES

When I was two years old, my Dad had an experience that can only be credited to the Lord, even some three years before they gave their hearts to Christ.

My Mother and Dad were in a particular place working at a certain job. Times were hard in those days (1937), as economic depression ravaged America and the world.

During the few days of this particular work, they were staying in a small room, which mostly contained only a bed and a chair or two. The accommodations were very spartan, with the lock on the door little more than a latch.

Some time after midnight, my Dad awakened, or rather was awakened. Even though he was fully awake, he felt somewhat strange.

He looked to his right, and he saw me sitting on the floor. As stated, I was only two years old. He wondered in his mind what I was doing out of the bed, and especially sitting on the floor?

About that time, he heard someone attempting to undo the latch on the door! He then shouted loudly to my Mother to get the gun, even though they owned no gun.

The action with the door stopped immediately. As well, strangely enough, I was no longer sitting on the floor, but was in the bed with my parents asleep. Actually, I had been there all the time. My Dad had seen a vision.

The next morning, it was discovered about two cabins down that two people had been murdered and robbed.

Even though one cannot say for sure, quite possibly, and most probably, the robbers who murdered the two people were attempting to come into our room, and, if so, would have killed my parents as well as me.

As stated, they were unsaved at this time. But yet, the Lord knew that in a short time the Gospel would be brought to them, with them wondrously and gloriously accepting Christ as their Saviour.

The year they were saved was 1941. I came to Christ at eight years old, in 1943.

Did the Lord purposely give my Dad a vision, even though he was unsaved, in order to keep him alive until the Gospel could be brought to him?

I believe He did!

And I believe He has worked accordingly in the lives of millions of others.

And yet, my heart breaks for the multiple millions of others who never have an opportunity to accept or reject.

In the mid 1980's, Frances and I, along with Donnie and others, were in Communist China, where we did a Television Special. Even though we visited several cities, one particular scene stands out in my mind. It was on the docks of Shanghai.

Being Westerners, we quickly drew a crowd. Many of the Chinese desired to practice their English on us. One young man of about 14 years old stands out. He was a very handsome young fellow, and very personable. He attempted to speak to us in his broken English.

At one point, Frances asked him, and very slowly so he would understand, *"Do you know Jesus?"*

For a few moments he stood there slowly repeating the Name, *"Jesus!"* And then he asked, *"Who is Jesus? I not know Jesus!"*

In fact, most Chinese do not know Jesus, with many never having even heard of Him.

However, something else happened at that moment which gave us hope.

Two young Chinese men were overhearing the conversation with the boy. With a raised eyebrow and then pointing to their hearts, they let us know they were Believers. They then pointed to the boy and shook their head in the affirmative, letting us know as well that they would witness to him after we left.

The phrase, *"But if Thou canst do any thing,"* portrays the man weak in Faith, and shaken by the failure of the Disciples. As well, the severity of the case was an obstacle!

The phrase, *"Have compassion on us, and help us,"* does not question the *"compassion"* of Christ. The structure of the sentence in the Greek Text proclaims that he saw compassion all over Christ, and especially in His Face. He wasn't questioning the *"compassion,"* only the ability of Jesus to do what the Disciples could not do.

Also, by using the pronoun *"us,"* he identifies himself with the misery of the son. As well, Wuest reminds us, the Syrophenician woman said, *"Have mercy on me,"* making her daughter's affliction her own.

To be sure, this scenario as it unfolds is so beautiful as to defy all description, even though it begins so ugly.

(23) "JESUS SAID UNTO HIM, IF THOU CANST BELIEVE, ALL THINGS ARE POSSIBLE TO HIM THAT BELIEVETH."

The phrase, *"Jesus said unto him,"* addresses itself to the unbelief of the man, and due to the recent events. In effect, Jesus will preach him a very short Message, which will build his Faith.

The phrase, *"If thou canst believe,"* addresses itself to all of the things which have happened.

The man has been faced with the powerless Disciples, and Jesus is telling him to rise above that.

As well, he has heard the taunts of the Scribes, and that weakened him further. Jesus is telling him to rise above that as well!

In Truth, this should be a valuable lesson to all of us. Faith is constantly battered by adverse circumstances. As we have just stated, every attack by Satan, and in whatever direction, is but for one purpose, to weaken or even destroy our Faith.

So, Jesus is telling him that he must believe despite these things. He is saying the same to us as well!

The phrase, *"All things are possible to him that believeth,"* is the second part of this short Message as preached by Christ. As always, the Lord could say so much in so little.

What did He mean, *"All things?"*

Dake said the following:

"Note the two 'ifs' of verses 22-23: one by the father of the child and one by Jesus. Deity can use 'If thou canst' just as much as man.

"In fact, God has the only lawful right to use such a term, for it is a settled fact that all things are possible with Him.

"So if man can quit his eternal questioning and satanic unbelief concerning God's Will and Power, 'all things' will be possible for the Believer (Mat. 17:20; 21:22; Mk. 11:22-24; Jn. 14:12-15; 15:7, 16; 16:23-26).

"It is not the question so much as to what God can do, but what man can do in believing God and His Word. Any question of God's Will concerning anything that He has already promised and provided for all men, is an excuse of unbelief and must be repented of" (Heb. 11:6; James 1:5-8).

All things are promised in the Gospel *"that pertain unto Life and Godliness"* (Ps. 84:11; II Cor. 1:20; II Pet. 1:3-4).

This Promise is an open invitation for Believers to have Faith in God. As a result, He has allowed Believers to enter into His Plan, helping to bring it to pass, and according to our Faith.

That He would allow us to do this is a privilege indeed! The Lord doesn't have to have us in order to get anything done. He is complete within Himself. And yet, He has allowed us this privilege!

A short time ago, the Lord graphically spoke to my heart (November 1995), saying this to me:

"You have believed I can, but you are not believing that I will."

And then He said, *"I want you to believe not only that I can, but, as well, that I will!"*

Even before then, the Holy Spirit had been dealing strongly with my heart about Faith in God. It has been as if the Holy Spirit has urged me constantly to *"believe!"* To be sure, whatever He does, is always for purpose and reason.

(24) "AND STRAIGHTWAY THE FATHER OF THE CHILD CRIED OUT, AND SAID WITH TEARS, LORD, I BELIEVE; HELP THOU MINE UNBELIEF."

The phrase, *"And straightway the father of the child cried out,"* speaks of a loud cry that comes from the very depths of the man's soul.

The phrase, *"And said with tears, Lord, I believe,"* proclaims belief, but yet imperfect belief! The *"tears"* proclaim the consternation of the battle that is raging in the man's soul.

The phrase, *"Help Thou mine unbelief,"* proclaims the deficiency of his Faith. In other words, he is asking the Lord to help him in this deficiency. It is a prayer the Lord will always answer.

Perhaps if the Truth be known, this man's statement, *"Lord, I believe; help Thou mine unbelief,"* is indicative of every Believer. Our Faith is not perfect. There are areas in which we fall down. And in those areas, we miss some of the things which would have been *"possible"* otherwise! So, this is a prayer that every Believer ought to pray.

As well, it should be noted that this man did not, and, in fact, could not confess this unbelief away. Neither was his *"unbelief"* caused by a bad confession. It was rather caused by adverse circumstances, which seemed to be impossible, and, therefore, insurmountable.

Even though one may habitually confess such away, still, the matter will not change unless

the Lord helps us in this, for which we are encouraged to pray.

As well, one will find that when the help comes, it will always be through the Word of God, for, *"Faith cometh by hearing, and hearing by the Word of God"* (Rom. 10:17).

(25) "WHEN JESUS SAW THAT THE PEOPLE CAME RUNNING TOGETHER, HE REBUKED THE FOUL SPIRIT, SAYING UNTO HIM, THOU DUMB AND DEAF SPIRIT, I CHARGE THEE, COME OUT OF HIM, AND ENTER NO MORE INTO HIM."

The phrase, *"When Jesus saw that the people came running together,"* concerns the crowd, no doubt, overhearing the loud cries of the boy's father.

It seems that Jesus and the man were somewhat away from the crowd, with the boy near them as well. How he managed this, is anyone's guess! Quite possibly the Disciples held the crowd back for a period of time, but now they will wait no longer.

The phrase, *"He rebuked the foul spirit,"* concerns, seemingly, Him desiring to deliver this boy before the multitude came upon them.

The word, *"rebuke,"* is not the type of rebuke offered to one desired to be brought to repentance, but, instead, one who cannot repent, and, therefore, commanded to cease and desist operations, for this demon could not repent, and, therefore, this *"rebuke"* was not meant in that fashion.

Wuest says that the word *"rebuke"* as here used in the Greek is *"epitimao."* He went on to say that normally the Greek word would have been *"elegcho,"* which is meant to lead one to repentance.

Consequently, one is able to observe in the use of this word, the meticulous accuracy with which the Holy Spirit leads the Bible writers in their choice of words or synonyms.

Truly this demon was *"foul,"* and may lend some credence to the idea that this evil spirit possessed more than ordinary power as well as malignity, and that this was the reason why the Disciples could not cast him out; so that this expulsion needed the mighty arm of One stronger than the strong (Bickersteth).

The phrase, *"Saying unto him, Thou dumb and deaf spirit,"* refers to what this spirit brought about in this boy as well as other things.

The phrase, *"I charge thee, come out of him,"* is a powerful term which means *"to order or* change." The order was powerful and firm, which left absolutely no room for disobedience. It is a military term.

The phrase, *"And enter no more into him,"* means that he was to leave out, and never again come back. Hallelujah!

As well, it seems from the Greek Text that this type of demon-possession was of the intermittent kind, which meant it came and went! Quite possibly when it went, the child was able to speak and hear, with the problem reoccurring upon the entrance of the spirit. Jesus is telling him to *"Go, and stay gone!"*

(26) "AND THE SPIRIT CRIED, AND RENT HIM SORE, AND CAME OUT OF HIM: AND HE WAS AS ONE DEAD; INSOMUCH THAT MANY SAID, HE IS DEAD."

The phrase, *"And the spirit cried, and rent him sore, and came out of him,"* concerns the last gasp of this spirit, and that he attempted to kill the boy as he came out.

Quite possibly, the thought that this spirit was of greater power than most, is correct, in the sense, that the description given here by the Holy Spirit through Mark, is of greater portend than hardly any other deliverance.

The phrase, *"And he was as one dead; insomuch that many said, He is dead,"* concerned the terrible ordeal he had just experienced, and the last gasp of this spirit. Wuest said that he *"lay motionless and pallid as a corpse."*

(27) "BUT JESUS TOOK HIM BY THE HAND, AND LIFTED HIM UP; AND HE AROSE."

The phrase, *"But Jesus took him by the hand,"* concerned more than just a helping hand. Healing power flooded the boy's body, giving strength to his weakness, and healing to that which the demon had damaged.

The phrase, *"And lifted him up,"* means that He gave him help in getting up.

How many millions has Jesus lifted up? How many millions has Satan almost destroyed, but Jesus changed them, instantly, totally, and completely!

The phrase, *"And he arose,"* spoke of strength flooding his body, even as he stood to his feet.

We do not know if his mother was alive or not, or if he had brothers or sisters! However, this we do know; whatever home he entered upon returning, was not the same home he left.

NOTES

The father took from that house a demon-possessed wretch, and brought back a young man, delivered, well, healed, and free. There would be joy in that house that night!

Just last night (12/12/95), a dear brother told me how Jesus came into his heart. Actually, each and every conversion story is a miracle within itself.

He was saved from alcoholism while watching the Telecast. He said, *"Brother Swaggart, I did not like you and wouldn't watch the program. However, my wife had turned it on, and I happened to walk into the room while it was on."*

He went on to say, *"I grabbed the remote in order to change the channel; however, I hit the wrong button, and turned the entire set off. Nevertheless, during the few seconds before I got it off, you pointed your finger at the camera, and therefore to me, and said, 'You are bound by alcohol, but Jesus can set you free!'"*

He then said, *"Brother Swaggart, that's all it took! Those words pierced my heart like a sword. All the anger and hatred for the Gospel, and even you, melted away in a moment's time. I cannot explain it, I do not even quite understand it to this day, but instantly I was free."*

He went on to say, *"I said nothing to my wife about it, at least for a few days; however, she noticed that when I got off from work, I now came home and didn't go to the bars. That's when she knew that Jesus had changed my life."*

He told me this story, as we were sitting in the bleachers at the gym at the Ministry, as our Academy Basketball Team was playing a home game. He pointed out his son on the team, and his daughter who was one of the cheerleaders.

They were two fine looking young people. I said to him, *"Had you not found Jesus, quite possibly your home would now be destroyed, and those children would not have a father, or else one estranged!"*

He looked at me and said, *"No doubt about it, our marriage was heading for disaster, and fast."*

But Jesus changed that marriage, because He changed that heart and life, and can change any heart and life!

(28) "AND WHEN HE WAS COME INTO THE HOUSE, HIS DISCIPLES ASKED HIM PRIVATELY, WHY COULD NOT WE CAST HIM OUT?"

The phrase, *"And when He was come into*

the house," spoke of lodging nearby, where they could escape the crowd.

The question, *"His Disciples asked Him privately, Why could not we cast him out?",* was a question they could not wait to ask. They had been successful in the past, so why did they fail in this instance? Perhaps all of us should ask the same question.

It is the business of the Church to be His Hand extended. We are to use His Name to *"cast out devils"* (Mk. 16:17).

But, sadly and regrettably, the far greater majority of the modern Church is too busy referring such to the psychologists and psychiatrists, which offer no help whatsoever. In fact, the Church has become one giant referral system.

Why?

The answer is that which Mark did not give but Matthew included, *"Because of your unbelief"* (Mat. 17:20).

Unbelief begins with, *"It may not be God's Will,"* or *"You may be under the chastening of God,"* or *"Power to heal was for the Apostles only,"* or *"Signs, gifts, and miracles ceased with the Apostles,"* or *"You may be exalted if God would hear your prayers,"* or *"Healing is not in the Atonement,"* or *"Healing is not for us today,"* etc.

Such unbelief leads to further unbelief!

Now the Lord is not addressed at all in most modern Churches, even in a negative sense, but completely ignored.

This is sad, considering the Church is the only real force against the Powers of Darkness. But, yet, the modern Church at present, exerts little force at all in this respect.

(29) "AND HE SAID UNTO THEM, THIS KIND CAN COME FORTH BY NOTHING, BUT BY PRAYER AND FASTING."

The phrase, *"And He said unto them,"* proclaims the answer. It is twofold:

1. *"Because of your unbelief"*: (Mat. 17:20). Two Greek words express unbelief, *"apistia"* and *"apeitheia."* Disobedience springs from *"apistia," "a want of Faith and Trust."*

"Apeitheia" connotes disobedience, rebellion, and contumacy.

"Apistia" is a state of mind, and *"apeitheia"* an expression of it.

Unbelief towards Himself was the prime sin of which Christ said that the Spirit would convict the world (Jn. 16:9). Unbelief in all its forms

NOTES

is a direct affront to the Divine veracity (I Jn. 5:10), which is why it is so heinous a sin.

The Children of Israel did not enter into God's rest (Grace) for two reasons. They lacked Faith (apistia, Heb. 3:19), and they disobeyed (apeitheia, Heb. 4:6). As stated, unbelief finds its practical issue in disobedience.

2. *"Prayer and Fasting"*: Prayer by man is communion with God, and God with man. If it is according to the Word, and which it definitely will be if in the Spirit, the results are staggering.

As well, when coupled with *"fasting"* its power is manifold. Actually, *"fasting"* concerns two aspects: A. Abstaining from food for a protracted period of time; and, B. Living a fasted life. This speaks of being immersed in God, and not the world. The Believer in this state is in the world, but not of it. He is not moved by the things of the world, neither does he plan his course of action according to the direction of the world. His total sustenance is God, drawing nothing from the world save natural food, etc.

However, this in no way means a withdrawal from fellow citizens, even the unsaved. Actually, True Christianity serves as *"salt"* and *"light."* Consequently, it is, as stated, to be a part of the world system, but not of it. This proclaims a vast difference!

Paul used the word, *"separate."* He said, *"Come out from among them, and be ye separate, saith the Lord"* (II Cor. 6:17). He also said of Jesus, *"Separate from sinners"* (Heb. 7:26).

However, it should be noted that the *"fasted life"* is not *"asceticism,"* which refers to a rigorous abstention from self-indulgence, which means that through the renunciation of the desires of the flesh and of pleasure in worldly things, and through self-mortification or self-denial one can subdue his appetites and discipline himself so as to reach a high spiritual state.

In fact, this is the opposite of the *"fasted life."* This is man devised, and, consequently, man controlled. It has its roots in Eastern mystic religions.

The *"fasted life"* is in Christ, and Christ Alone! It is led by the Spirit. As such, its power is not in *"dos"* and *"don'ts,"* but, rather, in the Holy Spirit. In fact, and as Paul said, it has nothing to do with *"Touch not; taste not; handle not;*

"Which all are to perish with the using; after the commandments and doctrines of men?"

He went on to say, *"Which things have indeed a shew of wisdom* (worldly wisdom) *in will worship* (worship which is not of God), *and humility* (which is not true humility), *and neglecting of the body* (asceticism): *not in any honour to the satisfying of the flesh* (powerless to deal with sin and the old man)*"* (Col. 2:21-23). They only feed self-righteousness and pride and do not change the heart.

So, Jesus told His Disciples, both then and now, that it was *"unbelief"* and a lack of *"prayer and fasting,"* which brought about their lack of power.

(Fasting at that time was not enjoined, because Jesus was still with them. When He left, they would then fast, Mat. 9:15.)

Jesus, by using the words, *"This kind,"* proclaims that some demons are stronger than others, requiring more power to cast them out.

(30) "AND THEY DEPARTED THENCE, AND PASSED THROUGH GALILEE; AND HE WOULD NOT THAT ANY MAN SHOULD KNOW IT."

The phrase, *"And they departed thence,"* concerns them leaving the area totally different than they had found it. God had moved mightily in this place, wherever it was. (Its location is unclear.)

Here, three of the Disciples had witnessed the Transfiguration of Jesus, plus the appearance of Elijah and Moses, and had heard the Voice of God. As well, a most powerful demon had been cast out of a boy, bringing joy, Salvation, and happiness to this family, and forevermore! So, they departed from it, leaving it much greater than when they found it. This should be, and, in fact, will be, the result of every God-called Preacher.

The phrase, *"And passed through Galilee; and He would not that any man should know it,"* was done for two reasons:

1. It is only months before He will die for the sins of the world, therefore, He desires to use as much time as possible in teaching His Disciples.

2. The opposition by now had become so fierce in Galilee, and especially in Judaea, that any activity spurred a confrontation. The Church is now His greatest enemy! I am afraid it is His greatest enemy presently! In fact, the most dangerous place in town (spiritually speaking) is often the Church!

(31) "FOR HE TAUGHT HIS DISCIPLES, AND SAID UNTO THEM, THE SON OF MAN

IS DELIVERED INTO THE HANDS OF MEN, AND THEY SHALL KILL HIM; AND AFTER THAT HE IS KILLED, HE SHALL RISE THE THIRD DAY."

The phrase, *"For He taught His Disciples,"* had as its main direction, the coming Crucifixion. This event would be so shattering that the possibility of them losing their Faith was ever present. It was very difficult for them to understand how the Messiah would die, and, in fact, could die!

It should be remembered that, notwithstanding these repeated warnings from their Lord, when these events actually took place, *"They all forsook Him and fled."*

They no doubt reasoned in their minds, that inasmuch as *"He that is hanged is accursed of God,"* consequently, He could not be the Messiah! (Deut. 21:23). They did not understand that Jesus, while truly cursed by God at that time, did not experience such because of His Own sin, but, rather, for the sin of the world. As we have stated, had they known Isaiah 53 and Daniel 9, they would have understood. However, they really did not know the Word of God as they should have!

The phrase, *"And said unto them, The Son of Man is delivered into the hands of men,"* means that His betrayal in the heart of Judas had already begun. It was imminent and in the process of accomplishment.

Actually, at that time, Judas possibly did not have such in his mind; however, this seed-bed of thoughts, which was the opposite of the Will of God, was already germinating.

There is an excellent possibility that the thoughts of all the Disciples, including Judas, were in the same vein. They felt the *"Kingdom"* was now coming, with Jesus at its Head, and with them as His Chief Lieutenants. The only difference in the thoughts of Judas and the others was that Judas, it seemed, pursued it more vigorously. However, with Jesus talking about being killed, such terminology confused and discouraged them.

In effect, this was at least one of the reasons that the Nine were powerless to cast the demon out of the boy. Thinking Jesus was going to establish the Kingdom at that time, and with them pushing hard for this purpose, they were actually out of the Will of God. Opposition to the Will of God always fosters unbelief.

Jesus had answered them, that they could not cast the demon out *"because of your unbelief"* (Mat. 17:20).

Consequently, we presently have a powerless Church which stems from unbelief, and which is caused by being out of the Will of God, i.e., man-led instead of God-led!

The phrase, *"And they shall kill Him,"* is bitter and to the point! It implies murder, which it actually was. And yet, they did not really take His Life, for He would say, *"No man taketh it from Me, but I lay it down of Myself"* (Jn. 10:18).

Because Jesus was born without original sin, He was not tainted by the Fall, and, therefore, had not suffered the curse of the Fall, which was death. Consequently, had He not laid down His Life freely, He would not, and, in fact, could not have died.

However, He was not going to the Cross by constraint, but as a willing Sacrifice, that He might do the Will of His Father, and so redeem mankind (Bickersteth).

The phrase, *"And after that He is killed, He shall rise the third day,"* pronounces a Miracle of such proportions, that it is beyond the comprehension of the Disciples.

That He would be *"killed,"* was not in their thinking at all, but to come from the tomb *"in three days"* was beyond the realm of plausibility to say the least!

(32) "BUT THEY UNDERSTOOD NOT THAT SAYING, AND WERE AFRAID TO ASK HIM."

In the natural it was difficult to understand. However, the Disciples, especially after being with Jesus for about three years, had seen Him time and time again do the impossible! Consequently, the *"rising on the third day,"* in that light, was something they should have known He was able to do.

Once again, *"They understood not,"* because of their unbelief. It was not unbelief in His Power, or that He was able to do it; instead, it was unbelief regarding direction.

They had heard Him as well as John the Baptist say, *"The Kingdom of Heaven is at hand,"* and, therefore, they could see nothing else (Mat. 3:2; 4:17).

They seemed to not realize that Israel had rejected the *"Kingdom,"* and, consequently, even though it would come in the Spiritual, at least to all who would believe, still, its material

and physical aspect would be delayed. Actually, it still has not come, awaiting the Second Coming!

The phrase, *"And were afraid to ask Him,"* stemmed back to Peter rebuking Him when He had previously made this announcement, and His response, which had been strong indeed! (Mk. 8:33).

(33) "AND HE CAME TO CAPERNAUM: AND BEING IN THE HOUSE HE ASKED THEM, WHAT WAS IT THAT YE DISPUTED AMONG YOURSELVES BY THE WAY?"

The phrase, *"And He came to Capernaum,"* referred, as is known, to His Headquarters.

The phrase, *"And being in the house He asked them,"* as well, probably referred to the house of Simon Peter. Evidently, all the Disciples were there with Him.

The question, *"What was it that ye disputed among yourselves by the way?",* would concern a very serious problem in their own lives.

Actually, He already knew what they were disputing, and because the Holy Spirit had told Him.

(34) "BUT THEY HELD THEIR PEACE: FOR BY THE WAY THEY HAD DISPUTED AMONG THEMSELVES, WHO SHOULD BE THE GREATEST."

The phrase, *"But they held their peace,"* means they were ashamed to relate to Him what they had been, in fact, discussing.

The phrase, *"For by the way they had disputed among themselves, who should be the greatest,"* constituted a problem in their lives, which if not eradicated, would completely destroy the Work of God. Unfortunately, this problem rears its ugly head no less today!

Bickersteth said, *"It is not unlikely that the preference given by our Lord to Peter, James, and John, may have given occasion for this contention."*

However, even though that may have played a part in the dispute, with the word *"dispute"* meaning they were arguing forcibly, still, the wrongheaded course they were taking, constituted the major offense. As we have repeatedly stated, the entirety of their thinking was wrong respecting what Christ was doing, and why He had actually come! They knew He was the *"Messiah,"* with Peter having confessed it (Mk. 8:29), and, therefore, at least in their thinking, the *"Messiah"* would take the Throne of

David. Their contention was right, but their date was wrong!

Irrespective, Jesus will address not their wrongheadedness referring to direction, but, instead, their own disposition of heart, which was the true cause.

(35) "AND HE SAT DOWN, AND CALLED THE TWELVE, AND SAITH UNTO THEM, IF ANY MAN DESIRE TO BE FIRST, THE SAME SHALL BE LAST OF ALL, AND SERVANT OF ALL."

The phrase, *"And He sat down, and called the Twelve, and saith unto them,"* reflects His posture, but, more so, that what He is about to say is extremely important!

The phrase, *"If any man desire to be first,"* is in response to their question as to *"Who should be the greatest?"* As well, He does not reprimand them for desiring to be *"first."* However, the direction to that position, as He will portray, is directly opposed to the direction of the world.

The phrase, *"The same shall be the last of all, and servant of all,"* is, as stated, the opposite of the way of the world, and, as well, the most revolutionary concept ever heard by man concerning *"greatness."* In other words, God's definition of *"greatness"* is totally opposite to that of the world.

To be *"last of all,"* means to think of oneself last, with all others first.

To be *"servant of all,"* means to minister to others.

By comparison, this short statement by Christ places Bible Christianity so far ahead of the religions of the world, that, in fact, there is no comparison. However, and sadly so, there are not many who practice this concept of greatness as looked at by the Lord. Too often the concept of the world, which is bloated egos and self-exaltation, is brought into the Church.

I have met thousands of people on this life's journey, and it's been my privilege to meet two or three who, in my opinion, so exemplified Christ that you left their presence, not entertained by, nor desiring to emulate, their abilities, but instead, to be like Christ. That is, perhaps, the greatest compliment that could be paid to anyone.

As well, those two or three men were taken up wholly with others, exemplifying this of which Jesus taught.

(36) "AND HE TOOK A CHILD, AND SET HIM IN THE MIDST OF THEM: AND WHEN

NOTES

HE HAD TAKEN HIM IN HIS ARMS, HE SAID UNTO THEM,"

The phrase, *"And He took a child, and set him in the midst of them,"* will be used as an example. Some say this child might have been Peter's. Another tradition not earlier than the ninth century says that this child was Ignatius. Irrespective, he will be the example!

Why a child?

First, a child is totally dependent on others. Such demonstrates the total dependency that the one of true greatness should have on the Lord.

Second, a child is trustful, the least self-conscious and self-sufficient.

Third, a child does not hold grudges, is quick to forgive, and retains anger only for a very short time.

The phrase, *"And when He had taken him in His arms, He said unto him,"* refers to Him holding the child in such a way, literally embracing it, which says that He will do the same for all who place their total trust in Him, even as this child is now doing.

(37) "WHOSOEVER SHALL RECEIVE ONE OF SUCH CHILDREN IN MY NAME, RECEIVETH ME: AND WHOSOEVER SHALL RECEIVE ME, RECEIVETH NOT ME, BUT HIM THAT SENT ME."

The phrase, *"Whosoever shall receive one of such children in My Name, receiveth Me,"* in effect, says that if the person is not of such posture (as a little child) he should not be received.

As well, one who is truly of this posture, is the same as Christ, and, in effect, witnesses in His stead. Consequently, to receive such a one, is to receive Christ.

The phrase, *"And whosoever shall receive Me, receiveth not Me, but Him that sent Me,"* proclaims the entirety of the foundation of Heaven and its Government being tied to this Philosophy or Doctrine.

To receive such a person is to receive Christ, and to receive Christ is to receive the Father, and to receive the Father, is to receive the Government of God. Consequently, Blessings on such are a given!

(38) "AND JOHN ANSWERED HIM, SAYING, MASTER, WE SAW ONE CASTING OUT DEVILS IN THY NAME, AND HE FOLLOWETH NOT US: AND WE FORBAD HIM, BECAUSE HE FOLLOWETH NOT US."

The phrase, *"And John answered Him,"* respects what Jesus has said, and occasions the only remark attributed by the synoptists (the Books of Matthew, Mark, and Luke) specifically to John.

The phrase, *"Saying, Master, we saw one casting out devils in Thy Name, and he followeth not us,"* registers conviction on John's part, especially considering what Christ has just said about receiving such a one.

The *"Followeth not us,"* portrays the sectarianism that is beginning to creep in.

The casting out of evil spirits was one of the foremost signs of apostleship. Consequently, John was somewhat nonplussed because one could do such a thing, even though he was not a member of the elite group. He admitted that the man was doing such in the Name of Jesus, but due to his lack of selective association, John felt he had no right to exercise this power or use this Name.

Justin Martyr said, *"While exorcism, as practiced by the Jews, often failed when it was attempted 'by the God of Abraham, Isaac, and Jacob,' was eminently successful when administered 'by the Name of the Son of God,' Who was born of a Virgin and crucified under Pontius Pilate."*

Consequently, it is given knowledge that this Name, the Name of Jesus, has power over evil spirits in such a way, which science has not yet been able to explain.

Of course, it cannot be explained scientifically because it is not scientific, but, instead, spiritual. It was Jesus Who defeated Satan and all his minions at Calvary's Cross, and, therefore, the Name that Satan fears the most.

The phrase, *"And we forbad him, because he followeth not us,"* seems to mean that such was done not out of envy or jealousy, but, rather, out of zeal for Christ, as though they were thus serving His Cause and upholding His Honor. However, this was *"a zeal, not according to knowledge."* It seems they did such without having first taken counsel with Jesus (Bickersteth).

(39) "BUT JESUS SAID, FORBID HIM NOT: FOR THERE IS NO MAN WHICH SHALL DO A MIRACLE IN MY NAME, THAT CAN LIGHTLY SPEAK EVIL OF ME."

The phrase, *"But Jesus said, Forbid him not,"* presents a striking Command that should be, and, in fact, must be the criteria of all Believers, that is, if one is to truly do the Work of the Lord.

However, if one is to note, Jesus did not say, *"Receive him,"* for the man's motive did not appear. However, He does say that the attitude toward such a one should at least be neutral. Swete says, *"Whatever his intention, the man is for the time practically committed to a course of action which at least cannot be unfriendly. Therefore, do not forbid him."*

The phrase, *"For there is no man which shall do a miracle in My Name, that can lightly speak evil of Me,"* proclaims many things!

First of all, if the miracle is performed by the use of the Name of Jesus, this automatically places the seal of legitimacy on the act and the man, for that matter!

Second, there is at least some relationship with Christ, or else such power would not be possible! So, in a sense, to forbid him is to forbid Christ, which no one desires to fall into, that is, if they are sane!

(40) "FOR HE THAT IS NOT AGAINST US IS ON OUR PART."

Regarding this statement, Morison says, *"Regarding applied morals and sitting in judgment on ourselves, we should in ordinary circumstances apply the law strongly and stringently, 'He who is not with Christ is against Him.' But when we are sitting in judgment on others, into whose hearts we cannot look directly, we should in ordinary circumstances apply the law with generosity and largeness of heart, 'He that is not against Christ is with Him.'"*

In other words, when forced to make a judgment, be hard on ourselves and lenient on others, especially concerning their Work for the Lord.

Dake has a lengthy thought which I think bears repeating:

"A lesson for divided Christendom today and a lesson Moses had learned many years before (Num. 11:26-29), is a lesson we should truly heed.

"True Christians will love every person of another Church and will appreciate him and his work just as much as if he belonged to their Church, that is if that Church is proclaiming the Truth, or anything close to it (Rom. 12:10; Phil. 2:1-3). No man doing miracles in Jesus' Name will speak lightly of Christ and no man for Christianity is against it, and on this basis men can detect True Christian workers.

"In general, anyone or any doctrine that denies a personal God and the Holy Spirit as a Person, or who denies the Incarnation of God

in human flesh, the literal Virgin Birth of Jesus, *His Sinless Life, His Divine Mission among men, His Claims and Doctrines, His miraculous Powers, His physical Death, Burial, and Bodily Resurrection to the Right Hand of the Father as the Head of the Church, is certainly not of God, but of Satan.*

"The marks of false teachers are numerous in Scripture, so that no mistake need be made in detecting them. To be sure, if such is supported, it is the same as supporting the work of Satan" (the last sentence is mine) Mat. 7:15-20; 23:1-33; Acts 8:9; 13:8; Rom. 1:18-32; 16:17; I Cor. 1:18-31; 6:9-11; II Cor. 11:13-15; Gal. 5:19-21; Phil. 3:17-19; Col. 2:8, 18; I Tim. 4:1-8; II Tim. 3:1-13; 4:3-4; II Pet. 2; III Jn. 9-10; Jude 4-19; Rev. 2:14, 20).

(41) "FOR WHOSOEVER SHALL GIVE YOU A CUP OF WATER TO DRINK IN MY NAME, BECAUSE YE BELONG TO CHRIST, VERILY I SAY UNTO YOU, HE SHALL NOT LOSE HIS REWARD."

The phrase, *"For whosoever shall give you a cup of water to drink in My Name,"* says three things:

1. Such knows Christ, because the act is being done in His Name.

2. The person has a spirit of giving, which is the Spirit of Christ.

3. No gift is to be looked at as unworthy or too small.

While it certainly may be true that the person could do more, still, the recipient is to be thankful for that given, even if only *"a cup of water."*

The phrase, *"Because ye belong to Christ,"* indicates that not only is it done in His Name, but, in effect, for Him. Consequently, it is to be received accordingly!

The phrase, *"Verily I say unto you, he shall not lose his reward,"* means that the spiritual significance of help offered to a brother for Christ's sake is independent of the material value of the gift. If sincerely given, it will be duly noted by the Lord, with the giver *"not losing his reward."*

As well, here the Believer is taught that small gifts, especially considering it is the best some can do, are looked at very highly by the Lord, and should be noted accordingly by other Believers.

(42) AND WHOSOEVER SHALL OFFEND ONE OF THESE LITTLE ONES THAT BELIEVE IN ME, IT IS BETTER FOR HIM THAT

NOTES

A MILLSTONE WERE HANGED ABOUT HIS NECK, AND HE WERE CAST INTO THE SEA."

The phrase, *"And whosoever shall offend one of these little ones that believe in Me,"* refers to Believers who, following the admonition of Christ, conduct themselves as *"little children,"* at least regarding the temperament of the child.

As a child is defenseless and absolutely dependent on someone else to protect it, likewise, the Believer who has the *"child spirit"* and, consequently, will not defend himself, is here boldly proclaimed to be defended by the Lord.

The phrase, *"It is better for him that a millstone were hanged about his neck, and he were cast into the sea,"* is a reference to Greek and Roman punishment. Consequently, one should well heed these words, for the punishment stated here is awful!

Contrasts are presented here; great reward for even the smallest kindness, and great punishment for even the slightest offense.

(43) "AND IF THY HAND OFFEND THEE, CUT IT OFF: IT IS BETTER FOR THEE TO ENTER INTO LIFE MAIMED, THAN HAVING TWO HANDS TO GO INTO HELL, INTO THE FIRE THAT NEVER SHALL BE QUENCHED:"

The phrase, *"And if thy hand offend thee, cut it off,"* presents a symbolic statement. It is not meant literally that the hands should be cut off, for sin does not originate with the hand, but, rather, the heart.

The *"hand,"* at least in this instance, figures power. It relates to the power of one to do things, and especially if that power is used against a True Child of God.

The phrase, *"It is better for thee to enter into life maimed, than having two hands to go into hell,"* means that rather than offending a Believer, one would be far better off to lose half his power, i.e., ability to do things. Jesus is proclaiming the need for extreme caution on the part of all when it comes to His Children. (This pertains to fellow Believers or unbelievers who attempt to hinder or hurt.)

These *"little ones"* (humble Believers) are doing the Work of God on earth, which is the only Work that really matters, and, therefore, nothing must be done to hinder them, with everything done, in fact, to help them. This is the lesson being taught by Christ.

The phrase, *"Into the fire that never shall be quenched,"* proclaims two things:

1. Hell is a literal place, with literal fire, which will literally burn forever, in which the person will literally be eternally imprisoned.

2. Considering the punishment, the loss of one's soul meted out to those who *"offend one of these little ones,"* one should understand just how seriously the Lord holds the value of the *"little ones"* and their work.

(44) "WHERE THEIR WORM DIETH NOT, AND THE FIRE IS NOT QUENCHED."

Dake says, *"This refers to the real consciousness and life of the individual who goes to hell. The word, 'worm,' is used of man several times (Job 25:6; Ps. 22:6; Isa. 41:14; 66:24). It has to do with the remorse of the conscience that each man will have over his failure to do what was necessary to escape hell.*

"It is the living, conscious, never-dying part of the human being that will feel eternal torments of fire in eternal hell. (Isa. 66:24; Mat. 8:12; 13:42-50; 22:13; 24:51; 25:30, 46; Rev. 14:9-11; 20:10-15; 21:8).

"It is that part that feels and knows, the inner man that dwells in the Resurrected Body. Both body and soul will be cast into hell at the Judgment" (Mat. 10:28; Rev. 20:11-15).

The metaphor used here is striking as well as terrible.

Ordinarily the *"worm"* feeds upon the disorganized body, and then dies. The fire consumes the fuel, and then itself expires.

But here the *"worm"* never dies; the fire never goes out.

The words of Cornelius Lapide, and regarding this Passage, are well worth repeating:

"I beseech you, O reader, by the mercies of our God, by your own Salvation, by that one little life entrusted to you and committed to your care, that you will ever keep before your eyes the living memory, as of eternity and of eternal torments, so also of the eternal joys on the other side offered to you by God, and concerning which you here cast the die, and that irrevocable.

"Let these two things never depart from your mind. In this world, 'Vanity of vanities, and all is vanity.' Oh, what a void there is in earthly things! Oh, how vain is all our life without Christ! In the world to come, Truth of truths, and all is Truth; stability of stabilities, and all is stability; eternity of eternities, and all is eternity.

"An eternity in Heaven most happy, in hell

NOTES

most miserable, 'Where the worm dies not, and the fire is not quenched.'"

(45) "AND IF THY FOOT OFFEND THEE, CUT IT OFF: IT IS BETTER FOR THEE TO ENTER HALT INTO LIFE, THAN HAVING TWO FEET TO BE CAST INTO HELL, INTO THE FIRE THAT NEVER SHALL BE QUENCHED."

The phrase, *"And if thy foot offend thee, cut it off,"* refers to self-will. It speaks of one's will, which is apart from God's Will, which always leads one astray. As such, it will offend, and easily so, *"One of these little ones that believe in Me."*

The phrase, *"It is better for thee to enter halt into life, than having two feet to be cast into hell,"* refers to the stupidity of self-will.

The idea is, that any measure which can be taken in order to miss hell, must be taken. It is not the idea that such will save one's soul, for that comes about only by Faith in Christ.

What it does refer to are things which keep us from accepting Christ. As well, if one refuses Christ, much of the time one will persecute those who follow Jesus. To do so only exacerbates the problem.

The phrase, *"Into the fire that never shall be quenched,"* is said now the second time, which gives added emphasis. Jesus desires that no mistake be made about it, referring to the certitude of the place called hell.

(46) "WHERE THEIR WORM DIETH NOT, AND THE FIRE IS NOT QUENCHED."

For the second time, this ominous statement is made by Christ.

A communications baron, we are told, made this statement; *"I want to go to hell when I die, because that's where all the fun is!"*

I don't know where he is getting his information regarding the *"fun"* in hell, because the Words of Jesus state otherwise! It is a place too dreadful for human language to describe or human thought to conceive. No! There is no *"fun"* there!

(47) "AND IF THINE EYE OFFEND THEE, PLUCK IT OUT: IT IS BETTER FOR THEE TO ENTER INTO THE KINGDOM OF GOD WITH ONE EYE, THAN HAVING TWO EYES TO BE CAST INTO HELL FIRE:"

The phrase, *"And if thine eye offend thee, pluck it out,"* figures covetousness, or the wealth gained by covetousness, *"Lust of the eyes."* In fact, the hands could well speak of the *"Lust of the flesh,"* and the feet *"The pride of life,"* (I Jn. 2:16).

As we have previously stated, Jesus is not meaning that one should literally pluck out one's eye. He is speaking of the severity of the situation, and even if drastic measures must be taken, and in whatever capacity, such should be done without hesitation in order to gain victory over the powers of darkness.

The phrase, *"It is better for thee to enter into the Kingdom of God with one eye, than having two eyes to be cast into hell fire,"* lets us know the reason that Jesus is saying this, i.e., *"hell fire."* I think the analogy could be drawn in this manner:

If a man and his family live in a certain area, and that area has some serious spiritual drawbacks of whatever capacity, which is dragging down this family, even though their economic welfare may be excellent in this particular place, still, if the situation can be bettered spiritually by moving elsewhere, even counting great loss economically, by all means it should be done, and instantly. First of all, a good, spiritual Church is absolutely necessary, at least where possible to find and attend. Regrettably, many Christians put money first and Church last. If the income is improved in a particular area, and irrespective as to the spiritual condition of the Churches in that area, many opt for the money. Jesus is plainly saying in these Passages that such a move is foolish. In effect, his admonition is far stronger, as is obvious, than that of which we have just stated.

Even though it is not meant to be taken literally, still, for Jesus to use the examples of *"Cutting off one's hand, or foot, or plucking out one's eye,"* should, as it is meant to do, portray the seriousness of the situation.

This means to put the things of God first in any and all situations. It means that every other consideration, such as economic welfare, geographical location, education, or likes and dislikes, should be last.

As well, inasmuch as Jesus gave three examples, each almost identical with the other, such is done by design. The Believer is meant to understand the severity of the situation, therefore, it is repeated three times for effect.

The suggested acute measures recommended are given that we may know how

strongly the powers of darkness may come against us. It is with both Believer and unbeliever in mind that Jesus makes these statements. Consequently, the Believer is told, in effect, that if the practicing of sin is allowed to continue, hell fire could be the result. This shoots down the unscriptural doctrine of Unconditional Eternal Security. As well, the unbeliever is told that his punishment is certain and increased, if a *"Little One"* is hindered or hurt.

(48) "WHERE THEIR WORM DIETH NOT, AND THE FIRE IS NOT QUENCHED."

Three times here the Lord affirms the fact of the Lake of Fire and the conscious suffering of those cast into it.

The Gehenna outside Jerusalem, on which these statements are based, was not eternal. Its fire was quenched and its worm died because the corruption on which they fed ceased to exist. But the terrible words, *"Their worm,"* reveals the eternal existence of the moral corruption that is *"to go into hell."*

Regrettably, the Doctrine of *"hell"* is little taught and preached from behind most pulpits. The world and the Church have become so psychologized, that the idea of a future Judgment and an eternal hell are anathema to most. However, the failure to believe this Doctrine in no way negates its reality. The Bible teaches that there is such a place called Gehenna *"hell,"* which Jesus graphically describes in these Passages.

The Rabbis used the word, *"Gehenna,"* to indicate the place of final punishment. Jesus maintained this meaning in the Gospels, but with a difference. Whereas, and as we have stated, the *"Gehenna,"* was a place nearby Jerusalem where refuse and garbage were burned, still, at times, the fires would go out. However, Jesus maintains that the fire will never go out in this place called *"hell."* Consequently, the phrase, *"eternal fire,"* is used of hell, and human beings will be punished there in a fire prepared for *"the devil and his angels"* (Mat. 25:41).

The most striking picture of eternal punishment is found in the Book of Revelation. There, the state of the condemned is described. They are in a *"fiery lake of burning sulfur"* (Rev. 19:20; 20:10), a *"Lake of Fire"* (Rev. 20:14-15), where they will *"be tormented day and night for ever and ever"* (Rev. 20:10).

(The following notes on man, the soul and the spirit, and eternal hell, are derived from the teaching of Dr. Finis Jennings Dake.)

THE MERCY OF GOD EXTENDED TO MAN

That God should remember in mercy such miserable beings, is great condescension; that He should actually visit us by assuming our own nature, by dwelling among us, and by giving His Life a ransom for us, is Mercy and Love indescribable and Divine.

MAN'S DOMINION

Psalm 8:6 places man at the head of all God's Works — the heavens, including the sun, moon, and stars, and the earth, including all living things. It makes him next to God in position and power over all creation. However, in his short time before the Fall, no dominion was exercised over planetary bodies, or even the earth.

Thus Adam was originally made higher than the Angels, but by sin he was brought very low and made subject to death. Now, man in his lessened state (short of God's Glory, Rom. 3:23), is below Angels.

Christ, Himself, was made lower for a time to take man's low place and to raise him again higher than Angels, as he originally was. Christ has been exalted to a place higher than Angels, or any other being except the Father (Eph. 1:21-23; Phil. 2:9-11; I Pet. 3:22).

Redeemed man is to be raised up to that exalted position with Him (Rom. 8:17-18; Eph. 2:6-7; 3:8-11; II Tim. 2:12; Heb. 2:5-11; Rev. 1:6; 5:10; 22:4-6).

THE FALL OF MAN

After man's creation by God, one requirement was made of him:

"And the Lord God commanded the man, saying, Of every tree of the Garden thou mayest freely eat:

"But of the Tree of the Knowledge of Good and Evil, thou shalt not eat of it: for in the day that thou eatest thereof thou shalt surely die" (Gen. 2:16-17).

Regrettably, man, and the woman God gave him disobeyed:

"And when the woman saw that the tree was good for food, and that it was pleasant to the eyes, and a tree to be desired to make one wise, she took of the fruit thereof, and did eat, and

NOTES

gave also unto her husband with her; and he did eat" (Gen. 3:6).

Consequently, Adam and Eve died (spiritually died) at the very moment they disobeyed God.

DEATH DEFINED

The word, "death," as applied to man in Scripture, means separation or a cutting off from realizing God's purpose for which he was created. One can logically substitute the word, "separation" for "death" in every Scripture where it is used. It will clarify many Passages to do so.

PHYSICAL DEATH

Physical death is the separation of the inner man from the outer man; the soul and spirit from the body (James 2:26).

SPIRITUAL DEATH

Spiritual death, which Adam and Even suffered immediately, is separation of man from God because of sin. One spiritually dead can be alive physically (Mat. 8:22; Col. 2:14; I Tim. 5:6), or he can be dead physically and alive in hell, conscious in the soul and spirit or the inner man.

SECOND DEATH: ETERNAL DEATH

The second death means the second and eternal separation from God in the Lake of Fire (Rev. 2:11; 20:6, 14; 21:8).

PENALTY FOR SIN

The penalty for sin and the type of death that God was speaking of when He said to Adam concerning the eating of the Tree of the Knowledge of Good and Evil, "Thou shalt surely die," referred to "separation from God" (Gen. 2:17). It did not mean physical death, even though physical death would ultimately be one of the results. Consequently, at the moment Adam and Eve disobeyed, they suffered spiritual death "separation from God." It was because of disobedience, i.e., sin. Actually, sin is the only thing that will separate man from God.

In effect, as man was separated from God at that time, he was separated unto Satan, and, consequently, all the works of evil. Hence Jesus would say to the Pharisees, "Ye are of your father the devil, and the lust of your father you *will do"* (Jn. 8:44). So, at the Fall, man changed Lords! As well, Satan became the *"god of this world"* (II Cor. 4:4). Hence, all the pain, sickness, suffering, sorrow, heartache, war, greed, and man's inhumanity to man!

SALVATION FROM SPIRITUAL DEATH

The Salvation of man from spiritual death, or separation from God, takes place when one is *"born again."* That is the reason Jesus told Nicodemus, *"Ye must be born again"* (Jn. 3:1-8). At this time, one is made a new creature in Christ Jesus (II Cor. 5:17-18), and is fully reconciled to God through Christ (II Cor. 5:14-21; Eph. 2:12-16; Col. 1:20-22; 2:6-13).

THE IMMORTALITY OF THE SOUL AND SPIRIT

The soul and spirit, called the inner man, are immortal. They continue in full consciousness between death and resurrection of the body, and will continue in the new resurrected body into all eternity.

So, the soul and spirit do not suffer physical death, because they are not physical, and, therefore, cannot die. However, they definitely do suffer spiritual death, which is separation from God, and are made alive only at the New Birth (Isa. 14:9-11; Mat. 10:28; Lk. 12:5; Jn. 5:24; 6:40, 47, 51; 10:28; 11:25-26).

Man's soul is the seat of the emotions, passions, desires, appetites and all feelings (Job 7:11; 14:22; 19:2; 23:13; 30:16, 25).

Consequently, one might say that the soul is the part of man which *"feels."*

Man's spirit is the seat of the intellect, will, and conscience. It is capable of all Divine powers only in a far lesser degree (I Cor. 2:11).

Consequently, one can say that man's spirit is the part of man which *"knows."*

MORTALITY OF THE BODY

The body is now mortal. It will die and go back to dust (Gen. 3:19; Eccl. 3:19-21; Heb. 9:27; James 2:26). This procedure will continue until sin is put down and death is destroyed (I Cor. 15:24-28; Rev. 21:3-7; 22:3).

RESURRECTION OF THE DEAD

This refers only to the bodies of all men who die, not to the souls and spirits which are immortal. All Scriptures on the future resurrection of the dead, without exception, refer only to the bodies which die, and which will be resurrected from dust again (Dan. 12:2; Jn. 5:28-29; I Cor. 15; I Thess. 4:13-17; Rev. 20:4-6, 11-15).

There will be no resurrection — a resurrection of the soul and spirit, at the resurrection of the dead, because, and as stated, the soul and the spirit are not physical and cannot die.

However, there certainly can be, and, in fact, is, a spiritual resurrection carried out respecting the soul and the spirit when one is born again (Jn. 3:1-8; Eph. 2:1-10; Col. 2:11-13).

If one is not resurrected spiritually from death in trespasses and sins in this life, he will remain forever spiritually dead, or separated from God (Heb. 9:27; Rev. 22:11).

NO SOUL-SLEEP TAUGHT IN SCRIPTURE

Many false cults teach that the soul sleeps at death, and will continue to do so until the Resurrection. However, all the Scriptures used by these false cults to prove soul-sleep, really refer to the death of the body, which, as would be obvious, knows nothing in the grave. None of these Scriptures refer to the soul or spirit.

Paul said, and concerning his death, *"I . . . have a desire to depart, and to be with Christ"* (Phil. 1:23).

If his soul was going to sleep at death, as taught by some, then it would not be possible to be with Christ at that time, as he said he would be. So, soul-sleep is not taught in Scripture, and is an erroneous doctrine.

THE IMMORTALITY OF THE BODY

The body, which is now mortal, will become immortal in the Resurrection. All Scriptures mentioning future immortality, refer to the body, not to the soul, which is now immortal.

Some refer to the Scripture, *"The soul that sinneth, it shall die,"* as proof that the soul can die (Ezek. 18:4).

However, this is speaking of spiritual death, separation from God, and not physical death, because the soul is not physical, but spiritual.

THE INTERMEDIATE STATE

By this is meant the state of the dead between death and resurrection of the body. After the body goes back to dust at physical death (Gen. 3:19; Eccl. 3:19-21; James 2:26), it remains dead (separated from the inner man) until the future resurrection day, when the body will be made immortal (I Cor. 15:35-54).

At the death of the body, the soul and spirit continue to live, being immortal either in Heaven or hell, until the Resurrection Day when the body will be made immortal also.

At physical death, the soul and spirit leave the body (James 2:26). If one is *"In Christ,"* his soul and spirit go to Heaven immediately at death to await the resurrection of the body (Lk. 20:38; Jn. 11:25-26; II Cor. 5:8; Eph. 4:8-10; Phil. 1:21-24; Heb. 12:22-23; Rev. 6:9-11).

If he is unsaved, consequently not in Christ, his soul and spirit at death go to hell to await the resurrection of the body (Isa. 14:9; Lk. 16:19-31; II Pet. 2:9; Rev. 20:11-15).

HELL IS MADE UP OF FIVE DEPARTMENTS IN THIS UNDERWORLD OF DEPARTED SPIRITS

There are five distinct prisons in the underworld of departed spirits. Not one of these is the same as the grave, but rather a part of hell.

1. Tartarus (I Pet. 3:19; II Pet. 2:4; Jude 6-7). This prison is a special one for fallen angels who sinned before the flood. No human beings or demons ever go to this prison.

2. Paradise (Lk. 16:19-31; 23:43). This was the abode of the Righteous after physical death, where they were held captive by the Devil against their will until Christ conquered death, hell, and the grave, and was located in the heart of the earth. It is now empty of the Righteous who go to Heaven at death since Christ captured the captives in this place, and took them to Heaven with Him when He ascended on high (Eph. 4:8; Heb. 2:15). As stated, this compartment is now empty.

3. Hell (Mat. 16:18; Lk. 16:19-31). This is the torment compartment of Sheol-Hades where wicked souls have always gone and will always go until the end of the Millennium. Then the wicked will be brought out of there to be reunited with their resurrected and immortal bodies, and to be cast into the Lake of Fire for eternity (Rev. 20:11-15).

4. The abyss or bottomless pit (Lk. 8:26-31; Rom. 10:7; Rev. 9:1-3, 11; 11:7; 17:8; 20:1-10). This is the abode of demons and some fallen angels. No human soul and spirit will ever go to the abyss. The Old Testament equivalent is *"Abaddon,"* and is translated destruction

NOTES

(Job 26:5-6; 28:22; 31:12; Ps. 88:11; Prov. 15:11; 27:20).

5. The Lake of Fire. This is the eternal hell and perdition of all fallen angels, demons, and wicked men (Rev. 20:6, 11-15; 21:8; 22:15).

This is the final hell prepared for the Devil and his angels, and all the unsaved (Mat. 25:41). As well, it is eternal in duration (Isa. 66:22-24; Mat. 25:46; Rev. 14:9-14; 19:20; 20:10-15).

HELL

The English word, *"hell,"* is defined in our dictionaries as *"The abode of evil spirits; infernal region; place of eternal punishment or extreme torment; in ancient times, the place of departed spirits.*

"The word, 'infernal,' means 'belonging to hell.'"

As well, and as stated, the fire of hell that Jesus mentioned is literal.

The word, *"fire,"* is found in Scripture 542 times and is used figuratively only a few times. As well, it is always clear when it is used figuratively.

The same words translated *"eternal,"* *"everlasting,"* and *"forever and ever,"* and used to state the eternity of God, Christ the Holy Spirit, Life, etc., are also used of hell and punishment. Therefore, if these persons and things are eternal, then hell and punishment are eternal.

Some teach that *"forever"* means *"age-long."* This may be true when used in a limited and qualified sense of temporary things, as in Exodus 21:6, but when used literally of God's Plan it always means *"eternal."*

The Hebrew words, *"olam,"* and the Greek word, *"aionios,"* mean time out of mind, past or future; eternity; always; forever; everlasting; perpetual; without end.

In view of these great Truths, which leave no room for misinterpretation, one would do well to graphically heed what Jesus said concerning *"hell,"* and its eternal consequence. To be sure, He meant what He said, and said what He meant!

As someone has said, *"There is a Heaven to gain, and a hell to shun!"* It makes no difference if man does not believe in its existence or that some Preachers refuse to preach this Biblical Doctrine. Still, hell exists, and at this very moment, most of humanity who has ever lived, has gone to this horrible place.

That is at least one of the reasons that the Church is commanded to take the Gospel to the world. The eternal consequences of not being saved, are so awful that they defy description. Hence the Scripture says, *"How shall we escape, if we neglect so great Salvation"* (Heb. 2:3).

(49) "FOR EVERY ONE SHALL BE SALTED WITH FIRE, AND EVERY SACRIFICE SHALL BE SALTED WITH SALT."

The phrase, *"For every one shall be salted with fire,"* has two meanings:

1. Everyone who offends, as Jesus has spoken in the preceding verses, will be eternally lost. Everyone must be salted somehow, either with the unquenchable fire of hell or with the severe fire of self-discipline. Wise is he who chooses the latter alternative.

All followers of Christ will be salted with fire, i.e., tested by trial; but it is the Master Who will test them; they are not to test one another.

The phrase, *"And every Sacrifice shall be salted with salt,"* as well, has two meanings:

1. Every Sacrifice was offered with salt as a symbol of preservation (Lev. 2:13), so here salt is mentioned in a reference to the idea that the everlasting fire is not only inconsumable fire, but will have the property of making whatever is in it inconsumable like itself.

Every unbeliever will be salted with the fire of hell, like every Sacrifice was salted with salt, as an eternal victim and example of Divine justice to future eternal generations who will be born in the New Earth (Isa. 66:24).

Salt was rained down with the fire on Sodom (Deut. 29:23), so the reference here is to the terribleness of hell.

2. Every Believer is to *"present your body a living Sacrifice, holy, acceptable unto God, which is your reasonable service"* (Rom. 12:1).

As the Sacrifices of old were offered with salt as a symbol of preservation, likewise, the salt of the Word of God, of which the salt of the Old Testament was a type, is to be constantly applied to the life of every Believer.

The very word, *"Sacrifice,"* at least in the New Testament, and referring to the Believer, refers to the Sacrifice of self-will, and, hence, the dying to self.

Hence, and as stated, the unquenchable fire of hell or the severe fire of self-discipline.

(50) "SALT IS GOOD: BUT IF THE SALT HAVE LOST HIS SALTNESS, WHEREWITH

NOTES

WILL YE SEASON IT? HAVE SALT IN YOURSELVES, AND HAVE PEACE ONE WITH ANOTHER."

The phrase, *"Salt is good,"* refers to Jesus having once called His Disciples, *"The salt of the earth"* (Mat. 5:13). This, of course, refers to all Believers! As we have stated, salt is a type of the Word of God, and is meant to serve as the judge of one's life. The result will be peace, and not the disputation of verse 34.

All Sacrifice of service (Lev. 2:13) should be seasoned with salt, i.e., judged by the health-giving, purifying, and preservative Word of God. Fire and salt are both symbols of purifying and preservative judgment. For the Christian the fire is chastening in its action and only consumes the flesh (I Cor. 11:31-32).

The fire of I Corinthians 3:15 affects doctrine and not conduct. This fire destroys the theory of purgatory. For the non-Christian, the fire is eternal and destroys both soul and body in hell (Mat. 10:28).

Salt expresses fellowship and affection. It signifies an inward sweetening and preservative energy binding the heart to Christ and to His service — an energy of holiness that judges everything contrary to His Nature and Will.

Hence Christians are the salt of the earth because living in fellowship with Him, and judging evil in themselves, they purify society.

The question, *"But if the salt have lost his saltness, wherewith will ye season it?",* means that if we who are of Christ fail in our testimony, where shall anything be found to restore this loss of the Word of God. The salt will have lost its savor, and what can season it? i.e., preserve society!

It is the Believer, as the salt of the earth, which preserves society from total corruption, and, consequently, from destruction.

Were it not for the family of Abraham before Jesus and all Believers thereafter, this world would have long since been destroyed of its own corruption. God would have had to destroy it, or man would have destroyed himself. Actually, this is what caused the destruction of the world by water during the time of Noah. The Scripture says, *"And God saw that the wickedness of man was great in the earth, and that every imagination of the thoughts of his heart was only evil continually"* (Gen. 6:5).

Actually, until Noah, a period of about 1600 years, the only recorded Believers during that period of time were *"Abel,"* and *"Enoch."* There may have been others, but the Bible does not say. Consequently, there was no *"salt,"* because there were no Believers, and, consequently, the world went to its doom.

To be sure, at this moment, and despite the United Nations, the great universities of the world, Governments, etc., were it not for the Believers on this earth, the world would have long since been destroyed.

That is the reason Judgment is going to come quickly after the Rapture of the Church. Paul said, *"And <u>then</u> shall that Wicked* (Antichrist) *be revealed...*

"Even him whose coming is after the working of Satan with all power and signs and lying wonders,

"And with all deceivableness of unrighteousness in them that perish; because they received not the love of the Truth, that they might be saved" (II Thess. 2:8-10).

At that time, the coming Great Tribulation, the world will *"have lost his saltness,"* and with nothing left to *"season it,"* will be destroyed.

Actually, the conclusion of the question, *"Wherewith will ye season it?"*, tells us in no uncertain terms, that there is no alternative to the Christlike Believer. All of man's vaunted knowledge, education, ability, money, talent, state and position, cannot serve as a preservative, only the *"Believer seasoned with salt,"* i.e., The Word of God.

The phrase, *"Have salt in yourselves,"* refers to the Word of God having free course within one's life, thereby preserving the Believer.

The phrase, *"And have peace one with another,"* means that one will be at peace with his brethren, if the *"salt"* is present. This does not mean that one condones wrongdoing or false doctrine in the lives of others, but does mean that despite those things, that is, if they actually exist, that one still loves the individual, and treats him accordingly, while not approving of the wrong.

This *"peace"* is afforded, at least in part, because the Believer understands the struggle of another, due to the struggle within himself, *"Everyone shall be salted with fire."*

One of the most beautiful movings of the Holy Spirit I have ever experienced occurred relative somewhat to this word, *"salt."*

If I remember correctly, it was November

of 1991. Our Ministry was in crisis, and the only thing I knew to do was pray. I felt that the Lord had told me to call two prayer meetings a day (10 a.m. and 6:30 p.m.), which we have continued unto this present time, with no plans to stop. Actually, I do not believe I could have survived the onslaught of darkness without this constant fellowship with the Lord.

At that time we were having the nightly prayer meetings in our home, which would later be changed to the Church. At any rate, the time in question was a Friday night. Frances and I had gone with friends the earlier part of the evening, to the home of another family in the Church, where we enjoyed fellowship and a good meal. We arrived back home in time for the evening prayer meeting.

There were not many people present that particular Friday night, possibly only seven or eight.

Before we went to prayer, I read the short story of the healing of the water at Jericho from II Kings 2:19-22. I made a few remarks and we went to prayer.

This beautiful illustration speaks of Elisha being in Jericho, with the men of that city coming to him and telling him of the bad water which had made the ground barren. This evidently was a well which bubbled out of a spring, and, in fact, was called the *"spring of the waters"* (II Ki. 2:21).

(Some time ago I was in Jericho, and was shown this spring, which was said to be the same spring of Elisha.)

When the men of the city came to Elisha, telling him of this problem, he told them to bring unto him *"a new cruse, and put salt therein."*

The *"new cruse,"* as Bible teachers know, was a type of the humanity of Christ. The *"salt"* was a type of the Word of God, which filled the life of Christ as no other.

He walked to the *"spring of the waters,"* and *"cast the salt in there."* He then said:

"Thus saith the Lord, I have healed these waters; there shall not be from thence any more death or barren land" (II Ki. 2:21).

Of course, the salt in the natural had nothing to do with the healing of the waters, but simply served as a symbol of the Word of God which emanates from the *"Living Word,"* i.e., *"New Cruse,"* the Lord Jesus, and is the solution to any problem.

As I began to pray that night, after a few moments the Spirit of God came over me in one of the greatest ways ever. Actually, the Presence of God lingered all night long, even into the next day.

The Holy Spirit began to bring to my spirit what the healing of these waters meant, and how that this Ministry would be healed. I remember saying over and over before the Lord, *"I believe that the Telecast is healed!" "I believe that the Church is healed!"* etc. As I would say it, the Spirit of God would wash over me in powerful waves of Glory. As stated, the Spirit of the Lord lingered all night long, even until nearly noon the following day.

From that time until this, to be sure, it has not been easy. At times I have refreshed myself by going back to that moment when the Spirit of God spoke to me that Friday night, and told me *"I have healed these waters."* At times, my Faith has weakened, but then I know and realize that the Word of God will not fail.

From that moment, God has blessed abundantly so. However, I do believe what the Lord is going to do in the near future will far eclipse that which has been done in the past, and will totally fulfill that which I believe the Lord gave me that night in November 1991.

He said it, and despite the obstacles, hindrances, and powers of darkness, it will happen, and exactly as He has said.

From that time I have literally lived in the Word of God. I have applied the *"salt"* to every single problem. I have attempted to fill my life with the Word of God. And even though, at least at the time of this writing (Dec. 1995), I have not seen all of that which I believe the Lord is going to do, still, I know, and beyond the shadow of a doubt, that what He said will be fulfilled in totality.

"Thus saith the Lord, I have healed these waters; there shall not be from thence anymore death or barren land."

CHAPTER 10

(1) "AND HE AROSE FROM THENCE, AND COMETH INTO THE COASTS OF JUDAEA BY THE FARTHER SIDE OF JORDAN: AND THE PEOPLE RESORT UNTO

HIM AGAIN; AND, AS HE WAS WONT, HE TAUGHT THEM AGAIN."

The phrase, *"And He arose from thence,"* refers to Jesus quitting Galilee, and, consequently, going to Jerusalem. The words are far sadder than one may realize, because He is on His way to the Crucifixion, which will take place in a very short time. Consequently, the greatest Move of God the world has ever known, which took place in Galilee, and as the Prophet Isaiah called it, *"Galilee of the Nations"* (Gentiles) (Isa. 9:1-2), would be no more.

In describing this time, Matthew said, *"The people which sat in darkness saw great Light; and to them which sat in the region and shadow of death light is sprung up"* (Mat. 4:16).

The *"Light"* he speaks of here in the Greek Text is *"phos,"* and means *"underived and absolute light — the opposite of all darkness."*

However, the Religious Leaders of Galilee rejected this *"Light,"* and, consequently, Jesus said of them, *"Woe unto thee Chorazin! . . . Bethsaida! . . . .*

"And thou, Capernaum, which art exalted unto Heaven, shalt be brought down to hell" (Mat. 11:21-23).

So, they would not accept Him, despite the fact that blinded eyes were opened, lame legs made to walk, lepers cleansed, and even the dead raised, in effect, and as stated, the greatest Move of God ever known by any people anywhere. No wonder Jesus said of them, *"Woe . . . ."*

The ability of men to resist Light and to rebel against God, even in the face of such a witness as none other than the Son of God, is amazing to say the least!

So His departure, even though spoken in few words, is a happening of eternal consequence. To be sure, as He left Galilee, He has been forced to leave others. They did not want Him, never realizing they were sealing their own doom.

However, I want all to know that I want Him, and with every fiber of my being. I realize I have nothing to offer Him, while, at the same time, He has everything to offer me. On that basis, I can only throw myself at His Feet, as the *"woman of Canaan"* so long ago. Even though she was not a child of the Promise, still, taking the position of a mere *"dog"* she could then appeal to His Mercy and Grace, which He gladly supplied to her, and instead of the crumb which she sought, she was given everything.

I, too, and in whatever capacity, bow at His Feet. I have caught a glimpse of His Grace and Glory, and nothing else will ever satisfy.

The phrase, *"And cometh into the coasts of Judaea by the farther side of Jordan,"* means that He came to Judaea on the east side of the Jordan River, and would consequently cross over at Jericho.

The phrase, *"And the people resort unto Him again,"* means that on this journey from Galilee to Judaea, many other people on their way to the Feast of Passover, would take up step with Him. Many, no doubt, had been healed by Him, with others being kindly disposed toward Him. These journeyed with the Lord and the Disciples along the road.

The phrase, *"And as He was wont, He taught them again,"* means that He taught them and kept on teaching them.

Of all the times these people had made this journey to Jerusalem to keep the Passover, this would be the most momentous occasion. How blessed they were to have had Jesus to teach them along the way. Even though the Scripture does not say, no doubt any sick among them were healed as well. It would be a journey to remember!

And yet, they could little know or understand that He was on His way to His Crucifixion. Little did they realize that the One the Passover represented, and had done so from the time of its institution in Egypt some 1500 years before when Israel was delivered, was actually walking among them. In other words, Jesus was the Passover, and would fulfill its type and symbolism.

While many of them loved Him, there were probably very few who knew exactly Who He was.

(2) "AND THE PHARISEES CAME TO HIM, AND ASKED HIM, IS IT LAWFUL FOR A MAN TO PUT AWAY HIS WIFE? TEMPTING HIM."

The phrase, *"And the Pharisees came to Him, and asked Him,"* refers to this trip from Galilee to Judaea. There were Pharisees in the crowd, and so the wonderful things He was teaching the people would be interrupted by their question.

Regarding the question, *"Is it lawful for a man to put away his wife?"*, Dake says:

"In Christ's day there was a great controversy about divorce and remarriage. It was known as the 'Hillel-Shammai' dispute. Hillel taught that a man could divorce his wife for any cause

whatsoever. Shammai held that a man could not for every cause, but for the one cause of fornication or adultery.

"With the Jews the right to divorce was a right to remarriage, and this was accepted without question by all in Israel.

"However, the question here is not the right to remarry, but only the right to divorce. The Pharisees wanted to know which side of the controversy Jesus was on. It was the prevailing custom to divorce and remarry several times, that is if desired, hence the strategy was to make Jesus unpopular or even come into the disfavor of Herod as had John the Baptist.

"Jesus agreed with Shammai that fornication was the only exception (Mat. 5:32; 19:3-12). He did not change the Jewish universal practice that a right to divorce was a right to remarriage. He let this be as it was in Deuteronomy 24:1-4.

"This is clear from the fact that He referred them to what Moses commanded (vs. 3). He did not say that Moses was out of the Divine Will in making a law of divorce, but merely that it was because of their hardness of heart that such was permitted by God, but that from the beginning this was not the Will of God."

About 75 or so years before Christ, a learned Rabbi named Hillel, a native of Babylon, who, afterwards came to Jerusalem, studied the Law of Moses with great success, and became the head of the chief school in that city.

One of his Disciples named Shammai separated from his master and set up another school; so that in the time of our Lord the Scribes and Doctors of the Law were ranged in two parties, namely the followers of Hillel, the most influential; and the followers of Shammai.

So this question put to the Lord, was meant to bring Him into collision with one or the other of the two opposing parties. For if He had said that it was not lawful for a man to put away his wife, He would have exposed Himself to the hostility of many of the wealthy class, who put away their wives for any cause.

But if He had allowed the lawfulness of divorce at all, they would have found fault with His Doctrine as imperfect and carnal, although He professed to be a spiritual Teacher of a perfect system sent down from Heaven.

Therefore, their question was crafted very perfectly respecting one of the most controversial subjects ever discussed — the subject of divorce.

The phrase, *"Tempting Him,"* means that they were putting Him to the test as a Teacher, hoping to show that He was unorthodox, therefore, putting Him in an unfavorable light with the people.

(3) "AND HE ANSWERED AND SAID UNTO THEM, WHAT DID MOSES COMMAND YOU?"

The phrase, *"And He answered and said unto them,"* would take them to a degree of Bible knowledge that they had never known or heard before. They did not know how to rightly divide the Word. He knew how to rightly divide it, because He was the *"Living Word."*

If they had known the Word, they would have known Who He was!

The question, *"What did Moses command you?",* takes them to the place where they feel comfortable, because they professed much reverence for Moses.

However, the Expositors tell us that Jesus had in view not what Moses allowed in Deuteronomy 24:1, but what He in Genesis enjoined as the ideal state of things (Moses from the Jewish point of view, is the author of the Pentateuch and all its legislation).

When He mentioned Moses, they naturally supposed He had in view Moses' Commandment. As well, by Jesus using the word, *"Command,"* He showed the correctness of Moses' position, but, yet, would taken them to the ideal in Genesis, instead of the permissible.

Man is always attempting to make allowances for his failures, instead of coming up to the ideal as commanded by the Lord.

(4) "AND THEY SAID, MOSES SUFFERED TO WRITE A BILL OF DIVORCEMENT, AND TO PUT HER AWAY."

The phrase, *"And they said,"* presents them giving the statement of Moses, but still improperly interpreting it.

The phrase, *"Moses suffered to write a bill of divorcement, and to put her away,"* is found in Deuteronomy 24:1.

From this statement by Moses, the school of Hillel concluded that it was proper to obtain a divorce for *"every cause"* (Mat. 19:3).

As a result of this liberal interpretation, which was error by the way, divorce was now being permitted on many frivolous grounds, such as careless seasoning of food by the wife, going into the street with loose or uncombed hair, loud talk or constant talking in the home, etc.

So, by the time of Christ, divorce was easily obtained in Israel, with the sanctity of the home being greatly threatened.

As stated, the other school under Shammai contended that divorce must be permitted only in the case of moral defilement, which was correct.

(5) "AND JESUS ANSWERED AND SAID UNTO THEM, FOR THE HARDNESS OF YOUR HEART HE WROTE YOU THIS PRECEPT."

The phrase, *"And Jesus answered and said unto them,"* will constitute an answer they had not expected.

The phrase, *"For the hardness of your heart he wrote you this precept,"* means two things:

1. *"Hardness of the heart"*: This had to do with unbelief on the part of the people, and, above all, being outside the Will of God. In other words, doing that which is not according to the Word of God, which is the Will of God!

Such causes a *"hardness of heart"* in individuals. It even happened in the very hearts of the Disciples when they misunderstood the Mission of Christ, attempting to make Him King, instead of Lord (Mk. 6:52).

Consequently, for the Pharisees to shelter themselves under the temporary recognition of a necessary evil, was to confess that they had not outgrown the moral stature of their fathers (Wuest).

2. *"He wrote you this precept"*: Swete says: *"The Lord does not deny that Moses permitted divorce; command it he did not."* Consequently, the Commandment given by Moses, and allowed by the Holy Spirit, consisted of *"regulations tending to limit it and preclude its abuse."* No such regulations would have been necessary but for the hardness of heart in the Jews.

If this had not been permitted, many women, plus children, would have been placed in an intolerable situation, the occasion for much suffering. The more sinful man became, the more sin changed and corrupted his nature. Consequently, the institution of marriage became corrupted as well!

Even then, Moses put particular legal steps into the act of divorce, which made it somewhat difficult. Thus this legislation was adapted to the imperfect moral condition of the people, who were as yet quite unprepared for a higher moral code.

(It should be obvious that the women at this time did not have much, if any equality. Consequently, this ruling by Moses and, as stated, allowed by the Holy Spirit, was primarily to protect them.)

(6) "BUT FROM THE BEGINNING OF THE CREATION GOD MADE THEM MALE AND FEMALE."

The phrase, *"But from the beginning of the creation,"* does not mean from the beginning of creation of all things, but, rather, from the beginning of the creation of man and woman.

The phrase, *"God made them male and female,"* is the only type of creation made in this fashion respecting living beings. Adam was created first, and then Eve was created second, but with a distinction. She was created from Adam, and, therefore, both were created from one (Gen. 2:21-23).

(7) "FOR THIS CAUSE SHALL A MAN LEAVE HIS FATHER AND MOTHER, AND CLEAVE TO HIS WIFE;"

The phrase, *"For this cause,"* contains a powerful statement within itself. It has reference to the nuclear family, which means *"a family group that consists of father, mother, and children."* It has to do with the way man and woman were created, and, therefore, meant to live.

The phrase, *"Shall a man leave his father and mother,"* constitutes a strong inclination. In other words, the inborn instinct is to ultimately be weaned away from one's parents and be joined to a wife or husband. Even though it does not constitute sin for one not to do this, still, this is the natural order intended by God.

The phrase, *"And cleave to his wife,"* pertains to the initial command of a man joining himself to a wife and then remaining thus joined.

As well, and as should be obvious, this condemns all homosexuality and, by all means, so-called homosexual marriages. Such is an affront to God and His plan of creation, which should be glaringly obvious!

Homosexuality is a sin against society, against nature, against the human body (which should be a temple of the Holy Spirit), and against God.

Paul said this: *"For this cause God gave them up unto vile affections: for even their women did change the natural use into that which is against nature:*

"And likewise also the men, leaving the natural use of the woman, burned in their lust

NOTES

one toward another; men with men working that which is unseemly, and receiving in themselves that recompence of their error which was meet" (Rom. 1:26-27).

IS HOMOSEXUALITY THE WORST SIN?

Whether it is the worst sin, one cannot answer. All sin in the eyes of God is terribly wrong, with some sins, of course, worse than others. Jesus spoke of the Religious Leaders of Israel, and said they had committed *"the greater sin"* (Jn. 19:11).

We do know that the destruction of Sodom and Gomorrah was at least in part because of the sin of Sodomy. *"The Lord said . . . their sin is very grievous"* (Gen. 18:20).

"Then the Lord rained upon Sodom and upon Gomorrah brimstone and fire from the Lord out of Heaven" (Gen. 19:24).

It seems these twin cities had become so evil, at least with a part of this evil being the sin of sodomy, that the Lord Personally took a hand and rained fire and brimstone upon these twin cities and destroyed them from the face of the earth until there is left no record of their former position and place.

The sins of homosexuality and lesbianism are Satan's diabolical thrusts against God's choice creation; namely man. Satan hates man because man was originally created in God's Image. The breath of God is actually in him. His body should be the temple of the Holy Spirit. God has chosen man to rule and reign under Christ Jesus over His creation forever and forever. God deemed man's Salvation so important that He paid a price so staggering it is impossible for our imagination to conceive of its significance.

The sin of homosexuality is Satan's strongest and most conscientious effort to destroy the human family; and since man is favored by God, this would be a great victory for the forces of evil. If this terrible sin became pandemic, Satan's effort would be fastly achieved, for humanity would cease to exist; but Satan has not succeeded, and he never will. This is what he was attempting in Sodom and Gomorrah.

THE CAUSE OF HOMOSEXUALITY

The homosexual claims he is born this way, and, consequently, it was God Who made him so, and, therefore, his lifestyle, he claims, is not wrong.

Consequently, society is encouraged by some sociologists and some psychologists, etc., to accept this lifestyle, even to the point of sanctioning homosexual marriages. Courts in some places are allowing homosexual marriage partners to adopt children and demanding that these *"marriages"* be given the same rights as marriages between men and women.

Powerful political lobbies are working virtually day and night to bring about legislation that would make it a crime to refuse to hire a person because of their sexual orientation, i.e., homosexuality and lesbianism. Actually, there are already laws on the books in America and Canada of this nature, although, at the present time, exempting certain professions.

The nation has watched as President Clinton has attempted to lower the standards of the Armed Forces respecting homosexuality. He has not altogether, thank the Lord, been successful.

At any rate, the homosexual lobby in Washington is so powerful that every effort is being made, and with ground steadily being gained, to not only guarantee homosexuals the rights of everyone else, which they already have, but, rather, to give them rights above everyone else.

Once again, the idea is that inasmuch as these people are born the way they are, their sexual orientation is not their fault, but rather God's, and, therefore, they must be treated as everyone else, with a special place made for their lifestyle.

It is true that due to the Fall, which brought about the sin nature, that every type of evil is ingrained in the human soul and spirit, even homosexuality. From studying the Scriptures, and observing that even children can be demon possessed, the terrible degeneration in the human family is obvious respecting wickedness. Consequently, due to the manner in which man fell, babies are born with original sin. In that original sin, some could very well have, and no doubt do, propensities toward particular wickednesses, which are literally born in them, such as criminal leanings, excessive rebellion, alcoholism, drug addiction, hatred, perversion, and, yes, homosexuality.

This does not mean that one is born a *"criminal,"* or an *"alcoholic,"* or a *"homosexual,"* etc., but that certain tendencies are stronger in some children than others.

NOTES

Science, whether medical or otherwise, continues to look for these *"causes"* in brain cells, with even a suggestion that the problem could be in the *"genes."*

Respecting the *"genes,"* they are closer to the truth than they realize. (Genes are an element of the germ plasm that controls transmission of a hereditary character by specifying the structure of a particular protein or by controlling the function of other genetic material. In plain language, it has to do with our physical and mental make-up, which we have inherited from our forefathers.)

However, the reason for those *"genes"* being the way they are, is not physical or mental, neither is it sociological, etc. It is spiritual! It was caused by the Fall of man and original sin. Man fell from God-consciousness to the far lower level of self-consciousness.

So, these terrible problems, be they homosexuality or whatever, are in a sense hereditary, and, as we have stated, because of original sin. This means that a baby is born a sinner, with all type of propensities toward evil, some with different and more perverse leanings than others.

Due to this, many psychologists, sociologists, and anthropologists, have attempted to claim that man is not to blame for the predicament he is in, etc., which is the main argument of the homosexual.

However, God did not leave man in this perilous condition, but sent His Son, the Lord Jesus Christ, to lift man out of this terrible fallen state, and to give him New Life. Jesus called it *"born again!"* (Jn. 3:3-8).

When one is *"born again"* in Christ, and by the Power of Christ, and due to Faith in Christ, one is literally *"regenerated,"* i.e., *"re-gened."* This is why the *"born-again"* experience changes a person so radically. Actually, it is only by this experience that one can truly change. All the other efforts of man are doomed to failure.

THE DOCTRINE OF REGENERATION

This doctrine must be considered in the context of man in sin (Jn. 3:6; Eph. 2:1-3, 5). The affects of sin on human nature are considered to be so serious that without the new birth, the sinner cannot see, let alone enter into the Kingdom of God (Jn. 3:3, 5; I Cor. 2:6-16).

The initiative in regeneration is ascribed to God (Jn. 1:13); it is from above (Jn. 3:3, 7), and of the Holy Spirit (Jn. 3:5, 8). The same idea occurs in Ephesians 2:4-5; I Jn. 2:29; 4:7. This Divine act is decisive and once for all.

The way the language is structured in these Scriptures indicates that this single, initial act of Regeneration (born again) carries with it far-reaching effects, as in I John 2:29; 3:9; 4:7; 5:1, 4, 18.

The abiding results given in these Passages are doing Righteousness, not committing sin, loving one another, believing that Jesus is the Christ, and overcoming the world. These results indicate that in spiritual matters man is not altogether passive. He is somewhat passive, one might say, in the New Birth; God acts on him. But the result of such an act is far-reaching activity; he actively repents, believes in Christ, and henceforth walks in newness of life.

Actually, the question must be asked as to what does actually happen to the individual in the New Birth?

I think one would be safe to say that there is no great change in the personality itself; the person is still the same. But now he is <u>differently controlled</u>, and that is the secret of the New Birth.

Before the New Birth sin controlled the man and made him a rebel against God; now the Spirit of God controls him and directs him towards God. The regenerate man walks after the Spirit, lives in the Spirit, is led by the Spirit, and is commanded to be filled with the Spirit (Rom. 8:4, 9, 14; Eph. 5:18). However, this does not mean he is perfect, for he is not. He must grow in Grace and progress in the Lord (I Pet. 2:2), but in every department of his personality he is directed towards God.

Consequently, we may define Regeneration as a drastic act on fallen human nature by the Holy Spirit, leading to a change in the person's whole outlook. He can now be described as a new man who seeks, finds, and follows God in Christ, consequently, leaving the old life and actually becoming a new creature in Christ Jesus (II Cor. 5:17).

HOW DOES REGENERATION COME?

First, as stated, it is God Who always takes the initiative respecting Salvation tendered toward man. Man in his natural state, is so fallen he cannot receive the things of the Spirit of God, at least within himself. Consequently,

NOTES

within himself, he makes no overt act toward God. Therefore, all initiative must be from the Lord, and, in fact, is from the Lord.

The Word of God is the vehicle used by the Holy Spirit to awaken man to his need (James 1:18; I Pet. 1:23).

As the Word of God comes to the heart of man, and delivered by whatever means, man is awakened to his fallen condition, and made to realize his need for Redemption. Regrettably, many, if not most, spurn this clarion call, but some accept and receive.

As the Holy Spirit, using the Word of God, makes man aware of his need, a *"measure of Faith"* is given to the individual by the Lord, making it possible for him to believe, that is if he desires to do so (Rom. 12:3).

Even though man's understanding of God at that time is extremely limited, still, because of the action of the Holy Spirit upon the Word of God, the individual knows enough to accept the Lord as his Saviour, which, if done, brings about an immediate, even miraculous change (II Cor. 5:17).

Consequently, medical science attempting to solve man's problem in the physical, is a fruitless exercise. It has already been solved, and by Jesus Christ. However, man, as always, keeps seeking to find a way out of his dilemma without going God's Way. In this effort, he will ever fail, as ever fail he must!

In answer to the question: No, man is not born a homosexual, nor a criminal, etc., but definitely can be born, and no doubt is, with a proclivity or tendency towards certain predispositions. As stated, the only answer to it is Jesus Christ.

So, for man to claim that God made him the way he is due to his birth or any other tendency, is blasphemy against God. Man is in the condition he is because of his own sin and failure, or others, and not because of God. To blame God with our problem, only exacerbates the problem, making it even more difficult to solve. James said, *"Let no man say when he is tempted, I am tempted of God: for God cannot be tempted with evil, neither tempteth He any man:*

"But every man is tempted, when he is drawn away of his own lust, and enticed.

"Then when lust hath conceived, it bringeth forth sin: and sin, when it is finished, bringeth forth death.

"Do not err, My beloved Brethren" (James 1:13-16).

From this Passage we learn that a person is born with *"his own lust,"* and then when Satan sets the stage by tempting the individual, he yields to the temptation, and then becomes snared and bound by the horrible thing.

The word, *"enticed,"* is an interesting word as well. While it is *"his own lust"* which *"entices him,"* still, once recruited, the homosexual tends to recruit others. Consequently, multiple thousands of young boys and girls are enticed into this web of deceit, as the lust continues to work within and upon itself, as a result of this malignity of darkness.

Many of those enticed eventually become homosexuals, because some have a predisposition towards this evil.

THE RECOMPENSE OF THEIR ERROR

The Scripture tells us that those who walk in this deception of darkness will receive in themselves the *"recompence of their error"* (Rom. 1:27). The Greek word for *"error"* means *"wandering, wrong action, wickedness."*

This means that once the person is fully bound by the sin of homosexuality, their mind and body becomes debilitated to receive in themselves the penalty of their wickedness. Consequently, a homosexual is usually known by his mannerisms, actions, personality, and even facial expressions. The sordid lifestyle actually changes the individual's personality.

Some may refer to professional athletes and others who are homosexuals and do not seem to be changed in this manner presently. However, to be sure, if they continue in this dreadful path of darkness, it will change them just as surely as the Scripture says it will. It is impossible for them not to change and for the worse!

THE CURE

Many have asked me, *"Can a homosexual be saved?"* The answer is obvious!

Of course a homosexual can be saved, as well as an alcoholic, drug addict, or good Church member for that matter. When Jesus came and died on Calvary for the sins of lost humanity, the homosexual definitely was included.

However, once the homosexual is brought to Christ, he will cease being a homosexual, as the alcoholic will cease being an alcoholic, etc.

NOTES

Now this is where the controversy begins. As always, men desire to continue in their sin, while, at the same time, having Salvation. Let it ever be known that Jesus does not save in sin, but from sin. Jesus came to destroy the works of Satan, not perpetuate them. John said, *"And ye know that He was manifested to take away our sins; and in Him is no sin"* (I Jn. 3:5).

So when the homosexual comes to Christ, he ceases to be a homosexual; when the alcoholic comes to Christ, he ceases to be an alcoholic, etc. Consequently, the homosexual churches and homosexual preachers, etc., are an abomination in the eyes of God. One might as well have *"alcoholic churches"* or *"drug-addict churches,"* etc.

Please allow us to say it again, Jesus does not save in sin, but from sin!

There is not a power of darkness that the power of Almighty God cannot break. There is not a darkened stain of sin that His Blood cannot cleanse.

The Bible speaks of *"abusers of themselves with mankind"* (I Cor. 6:9). The Greek word for *"abusers"* is *"arsenoloites."* It means *"a person guilty of unnatural offenses: a Sodomite, a homosexual, a sexual pervert."*

Paul, in writing to the Church at Corinth, said, *"Such were some of you: but ye are washed, but ye are sanctified, but ye are justified in the Name of the Lord Jesus, and by the Spirit of our God"* (I Cor. 6:11). In other words, the Lord Jesus Christ can deliver a person from this dreadful sin of homosexuality.

The Devil's tactics are according to the following:

He will first of all try to make a person believe such perversion is normal. If that does not work, he will tell him that he cannot be free, that he cannot be normal; attempting to make him believe there is no hope. Consequently, many homosexuals have committed suicide, as many others caught in a terrible web of Satan's lies.

However, and let it be ever known, there is absolutely no sin that the Blood of Jesus Christ cannot cover and cleanse.

Trying to normalize sin to make it acceptable will not work — it only makes it worse. Turning from sin to the Lord Jesus Christ is the only answer.

"What can wash away my sin?
"Nothing but the Blood of Jesus.

"What can make me whole again?
"Nothing but the Blood of Jesus."

In respect to the phrase, *"God made them male and female,"* in Mark 10:6, let us say that *"God created Adam and Eve, not Adam and Steve!"*

(8) "AND THEY TWAIN SHALL BE ONE FLESH: SO THEN THEY ARE NO MORE TWAIN, BUT ONE FLESH."

The phrase, *"And they twain shall be one flesh,"* means that the *"two"* shall be *"one."*

In other words, the man and his wife, at least in a sense, becomes what God originally created them, *"one flesh."*

This is evident in every capacity of the marriage bond, that is, if it is a marriage as God intended. The union becomes such a union that it becomes *"one flesh."* Ideally, it should be *"one"* spiritually, mentally, and physically. It becomes *"one"* spiritually by a union with God in the Salvation process.

The marriage becomes *"one"* mentally, because both, in Christ, have a renewed mind (Rom. 12:2).

It becomes *"one"* physically by the sexual union. This is what makes adultery so sinful and wicked!

The phrase, *"So then they are no more twain, but one flesh,"* proclaims the action of the union. The first phrase proclaims the Will of God, with the second phrase proclaiming the Will of God carried out to its logical and beautiful conclusion.

(9) "WHAT THEREFORE GOD HATH JOINED TOGETHER, LET NOT MAN PUT ASUNDER."

The phrase, *"What therefore God hath joined together,"* places the seal of God's approval on the marriage union. This means the nuclear family, husband, wife, and children, are His Divine Will.

As well, it means that for every young man in the world, there is a young lady who is God's Will for his wife. This means that marriage is not a random selection, but rather an order of the Will of God. Consequently, every young man and young lady should seek the Lord extensively regarding this all-important life choice — for it is meant to be for life.

Consequently, if a mate is chosen on looks alone, or other considerations other than the Will of God, the stage is already set for disaster. If the young man and young lady earnestly

seek the Lord about this all-important matter, to be sure, the Lord will give Divine guidance and direction. He will give that boy or girl the one He wants them to have, and it will be the perfect choice.

However, this does not mean that marriage is trouble free, for actually it is not. But, if a few simple directions are followed, marriage can be a little bit of Heaven on earth.

1. All the needs of a person cannot be fulfilled in their husband or wife. This is the cause of many, if not most, divorces. The husband demands more of the wife, or the wife of the husband, than is possible to give.

Why?

There are many needs in every individual, be they spiritual, physical, or mental. While it is true that the husband or wife can meet some of these needs, and are, in fact, supposed to do so, still, the ultimate needs of any individual can only be met in Christ.

This is the reason that people get disillusioned with their mates, with their jobs, or country, etc. They try to make these things fulfill the inherent needs within their lives which only God can meet.

The husband demands more and more of the wife, or the wife of the husband, until the person is consumed, with the marriage ultimately falling apart. Therefore, if the husband and wife will have a true relationship with Jesus Christ, the crying needs within their lives which can only be met by Him, will be met. Then the demands are greatly lessened upon the mate.

2. If self is hidden in Christ, self-will, which is the cause of so many marriage problems, will be eradicated. Self-will is really selfishness. It is the opposite of Christlikeness. It wants its way, and irrespective of what it does to others.

If the husband, in Christ, will seek to please the wife and the wife the husband, the servant mentality, of which Jesus demands, will solve most marriage problems (Mk. 9:35).

If the Believer has the servant mentality, he will be kind and gracious toward his wife, and she her husband.

The servant mentality comes about only through true Christ-likeness, and, regrettably, is lacking even in many Believers. If one is to notice, the entirety of the success of any marriage is wrapped up in Christ. A marriage without Christ is no marriage at all. Consequently, about fifty percent of all marriages conclude in the divorce courts. And, many, if not most of the other fifty percent are marriages in name only.

3. Be quick to forgive, which is another command of Christ (Mat. 6:14-15).

Irrespective of our Christlikeness, and even though we attempt to do our very best, still, at times, and due to the fact that we are human, things will be said or done which are wrong. When this happens, the wronged party should be quick to forgive the one who has committed the wrong. As well, the one who has committed the wrong, should be quick to admit that, in fact, he (or she) is in the wrong. The matter is then settled, with God's Way making it right.

4. The two shall be *"one."* And yet there are distinctions! The husband is meant by God to be the head of the family (Eph. 5:23).

Consequently, the husband is to love the wife *"even as Christ also loved the Church, and gave Himself for it"* (Eph. 5:25).

I think it is obvious, if the husband obeys the Lord in loving his wife, even as Christ loves the Church, this would be love unexcelled.

Consequently, it would not then be difficult for the wife to submit to such a husband, as the Lord commands (Eph. 5:22).

Some have argued that wives are to submit to their husbands, even unsaved husbands, irrespective as to what they want them to do. This is an incorrect interpretation of this Passage. The wives are to submit, only as long as it is *"unto the Lord,"* meaning that the Lord would be pleased with the action.

As long as the husband conducts himself as the Lord, then the wife can be subject to her husband *"in everything"* (Eph. 5:24).

If one is to notice, everything is based on the Lord as the example.

Actually, and as is obvious in Ephesians 5, the Godly family is to be a symbol of the Lord and His Church. Consequently, if there are strong, Godly families, likewise, the Church is strong. Conversely, if the families begin to break apart, and because of their lack of relationship with Christ, the Church, as well, becomes fragmented.

Even though it should not have to be mentioned, the subject of money, and because it causes so many problems in marriages, should be addressed.

The *"two becoming one,"* refers to money, as well as all else. Even though the husband is

the head of the family, the wife is the head of the house (I Tim. 5:14). That means she has authority in this domain, which covers much. While every viewpoint should be considered and taken into consideration, still, where the family lives should be more decided by the wife than the husband. The order of the house and its routine should be guided by the wife as well! The last decision concerning style, furnishings, and routine should be hers.

As well, and in this capacity, most husbands would be very wise to let their wives take care of the money. The wife pays more attention to detail, can generally make the money go further, and will generally take care of it better than the husband. That refers to paying bills, savings accounts, checking accounts, and budgets, etc.

While at times some wives are not turned in this direction, still, I think generally most are, and can do a better job than the husband in this department.

If the wife is capable of handling the money (and most are), this solves the problem of the wife having to go to the husband for every dollar she has to have, with him parceling it out to her as he would an allowance to a child. Such is not proper, and does not constitute the *"one"* as designed by the Lord. Even though the husband is the head, and as such should serve as a type of Christ, still, he is not the master. There is only one Master and that is Jesus Christ.

If these simple directions laid out in the Word of God are adhered to, marriage can be a little bit of Heaven on earth. All is tied to Christ. All is in Christ.

If marriage is attempted without Christ, it can quickly become a hell on earth.

The phrase, *"Let not man put asunder,"* means that the marriage should be for life, with no thought of divorce, etc. In fact, God hates divorce (Mal. 2:16).

There are only two Scriptural grounds for divorce, one given by Jesus and the other by Paul. They are as follows:

1. *"Fornication":* (Mat. 5:32). All fornication is adultery, but all adultery is not fornication.

As well, many have erroneously thought that fornication pertains to unmarried people, while adultery pertains to married people. That is incorrect!

The meaning of *"fornication"* is severalfold:

A. Repeated adultery, going from one partner to the next (I Cor. 7:2; 10:8; I Thess. 4:3; Rev. 9:21).

B. Incest (I Cor. 5:1; 10:8).

C. Idolatry: This is adultery in honor of idol gods (II Chron. 21:11; Isa. 23:17; Ezek. 16:15, 26, 29; Acts 15:20, 29; 21:25; Rev. 2:14-21; 14:8).

D. Sodomy and male prostitution: (Rom. 1:24-29; I Cor. 6:9-11; II Cor. 12:21; Gal. 5:19; Eph. 5:3; Col. 3:5; Heb. 12:16; Jude 6-7).

2. Desertion on spiritual grounds: (I Cor. 7:14-15).

If the unbeliever refuses to live with a wife or husband because of Christianity, and if he or she is determined to leave on this account, the Christian is not under further marriage bonds and is not held responsible or punished by requirement to remain single the rest of his or her life because of the rebellion of another. The Christian is to submit to the breaking of the marriage covenant under such circumstances, and because there is no choice (Dake).

(10) "AND IN THE HOUSE HIS DISCIPLES ASKED HIM AGAIN OF THE SAME MATTER."

The phrase, *"And in the house His Disciples,"* refers to them leaving the crowd and the Pharisees, and going into someone's house. Quite possibly, on their way to Jerusalem, they had stopped for the night.

The phrase, *"Asked Him again of the same matter,"* proclaims the Disciples continuing to ply Jesus with questions concerning divorce, etc. In other words, they asked Him over and over!

(11) "AND HE SAITH UNTO THEM, WHOSOEVER SHALL PUT AWAY HIS WIFE, AND MARRY ANOTHER, COMMITTETH ADULTERY AGAINST HER."

The phrase, *"And He saith unto them,"* evidently concerns marriage after divorce. Jesus had spoken plainly about divorce as He dealt with the Pharisees; however, at that time He had said nothing about marriage after divorce. Consequently, the Disciples ply Him with questions concerning this.

The phrase, *"Whosoever shall put away his wife,"* refers to divorce.

The phrase, *"And marry another,"* refers to doing so without Scriptural grounds, which are fornication and desertion, as we have said, and

as Jesus and Paul mentioned (Mat. 5:32; I Cor. 7:14-15).

The phrase, *"Committeth adultery against her,"* means that if they have no Scriptural grounds, at the time of the union of the second marriage, etc., *"adultery"* was committed.

The words, *"against her,"* means *"in reference to her."*

If the man leaves his wife (or the wife the husband), and without Scriptural grounds, he commits sin not only against God, but against his wife (or against her husband, as the case may be). The marriage bond instituted by God, and which the partner was selected, has now been broken, which is in direct contradiction to the original Command, *"What therefore God hath joined together, let not man put asunder"* (vs. 9).

(12) "AND IF A WOMAN SHALL PUT AWAY HER HUSBAND, AND BE MARRIED TO ANOTHER, SHE COMMITTETH ADULTERY."

The phrase, *"And if a woman shall put away her husband,"* places the woman in the same position as the man, and holds her just as responsible.

The phrase, *"And be married to another, she committeth adultery,"* indicates, and according to the Lord, that wives and husbands have equal rights in reference to divorce, and equal responsibility.

Consequently, these simple words of Jesus gave the woman more rights than she had ever had in history. Josephus makes it evident that in his time, which was the time of Christ, the wife by no means had equal rights with the husband. Consequently, the Words of Christ make it clear that the lesser rights given to the woman were not pleasing to God.

(13) "AND THEY BROUGHT YOUNG CHILDREN TO HIM, THAT HE SHOULD TOUCH THEM: AND HIS DISCIPLES REBUKED THOSE THAT BROUGHT THEM."

The phrase, *"And they brought young children to Him, that He should touch them,"* refers to Jesus with His Disciples being in the house, probably having stopped for the night on their way to Jerusalem.

As there were great crowds on the road on their way to keep the Passover in Jerusalem, parents desired that Jesus lay His Hands on their children, who were traveling with them, and pray for them (Mat. 19:13).

This was, no doubt, a beautiful scene, with little children crowding around Jesus, and Him laying His Hands on them, praying for them, and, no doubt, even taking some on His knee.

Swete says: *"The custom of laying on of hands with prayer upon children for the purpose of blessing, finds its symbolism in Genesis 48:14-15. Generally, the rulers of the Synagogues performed this task; however, to have Jesus do this was of the highest magnitude. I wonder how many of them actually knew that the God of all creation was blessing their children?"*

The phrase, *"And His Disciples rebuked those that brought them,"* proclaims this situation quickly developing a paradox. The Disciples were strongly rebuking the people for bringing their children to Jesus, while Jesus was strongly blessing those brought to Him.

No doubt, the motives of the Disciples were right. After walking and teaching, and even healing all day, Jesus was no doubt very tired. Therefore, in looking out for Him, they probably felt that the children were an imposition. They were to quickly find out otherwise!

(14) "BUT WHEN JESUS SAW IT, HE WAS MUCH DISPLEASED, AND SAID UNTO THEM, SUFFER THE LITTLE CHILDREN TO COME UNTO ME, AND FORBID THEM NOT: FOR OF SUCH IS THE KINGDOM OF GOD."

The phrase, *"But when Jesus saw it, He was much displeased,"* concerns His perception respecting this activity, almost as quickly as the Disciples were doing such. Therefore, it seems that none of the children were turned away.

The Word, *"much displeased,"* is strong, and it means *"to be moved with indignation."* In other words, there was some anger in Christ, because of what the Disciples were doing.

Wuest says that *"The very fact that our sinless Lord manifested such feeling, is enough to show that under proper circumstances it is not only right, but its absence would show a serious defect in Christian character."*

The phrase, *"And said unto them, Suffer the little children to come unto Me, and forbid them not,"* means that the Disciples were to stop forthwith!

This simple narrative portrays to us the responsibility of parents in educating their children respecting the Word of God. Basically, this had to do with Solomon's statement, *"Train up*

NOTES

a child in the way he should go: and when he is old, he will not depart from it" (Prov. 22:6).

Consequently, a child should be encouraged in the Ways of the Lord at the tenderest of age. The moment they can grasp or understand, which is very early, should be the time their training begins. Nothing in the world is more important.

In dedicating babies at Family Worship Center in Baton Rouge, Louisiana, I constantly remind the parents that they are actually holding the eternal destiny of their child in their hands. In other words, if they obey Solomon's command, and train that child in the Ways of the Lord, they have the Promise of God that he will not depart from it.

What a promise!

This means, as well, that the parents must live for God as an example to the child.

My parents were saved when I was five years old. Immediately our home changed, and that change was instantly recognizable, even by me!

My Mother and Dad, and even though they loved each other very much, seemed to quarrel constantly before they were saved. I remember the terrible hurt that would come to me when I would hear one or the other speak harshly. However, when Jesus came into their lives, I noticed an instant change. The quarreling stopped! The arguing stopped! The fighting stopped! I think I was the happiest of all!

How homes would be changed if Jesus were allowed entrance! The cause of all juvenile delinquency is found in these very statements. Without Christ, there cannot truly be a home. With Christ, anywhere is home.

Immediately, even at five years old, my parents began to witness to me about Jesus. However, I was eight years old before I accepted the Lord as my Saviour.

Strangely enough, I was *"born again"* standing in front of a theater in Ferriday, Louisiana, on a Saturday afternoon, sometime in the early Spring of 1943. As I said, I was eight years old.

As I was standing in line waiting to purchase a ticket to go into the movie that Saturday afternoon, the Spirit of God spoke to my heart that which I will never forget.

"Do not go into this place, give your heart to Me, as I desire to use you in My service."

I may not be remembering the words exactly, but what I have quoted is very similar, if not exact.

This was the first time I had ever sensed the Presence of God. As well, it was certainly the first time the Lord had ever spoken to me. I realize that many would argue with this statement, claiming that a child could not know or understand the Voice of God!

No, I did not hear an audible voice, but, instead, a voice in my spirit. However, it was just as real as if it had been audible.

To doubt what I say, is to doubt God. It is to say that He is not able to do such! To be sure, it is probably much easier for a child to hear the Lord, and to understand, even than an adult.

I was greatly moved by that which came over me. It was unexpected and sudden! I had been doing nothing that day which would have been termed *"spiritual."* And yet in a moment the Spirit of God spoke to my heart.

I did not respond the first time, and with the line inching forward due to the ticket window having opened, I began to walk forward to purchase a ticket.

I will never forget that moment. I stepped up to the window and laid my quarter on the counter. The lady reached up to tear off a ticket and give it to me, when the spool of tickets jammed. As she began to free the spool, the Spirit of God spoke again. This time the words were the same, but even more powerful.

"Do not go in this place, give your heart to me, for I desire to use you in My service."

I never really said anything audibly, but in my heart I said, *"Yes!"* And then I grabbed my quarter!

The lady who was dispensing the tickets looked at me when I grabbed my quarter, and said, *"Well, Jimmy, do you want a ticket or not?"*

I don't even remember if I answered her. I just took the quarter and walked away. I would never be the same again.

Arriving home much earlier than I was supposed to, my Mother asked me what had happened?

Somewhat matter of factly, I told her, *"I got saved!"* She was somewhat taken aback, wondering how this could have happened.

Then I explained it to her, telling her exactly what the Lord had said to me. I remember her beginning to weep, putting her arms around me, and hugging me to her.

A few weeks later I was Baptized in the Holy Spirit with the evidence of speaking with other

tongues as the Spirit of God gives the utterance (Acts 2:4).

The next year, 1944, when I was nine years old, the Lord called me to preach, a call which in reality, came the moment I was saved. During that time, and especially in the Summer months, I was in a prayer meeting almost every day of my life, whether at the Church or at the house of my Grandmother or Aunt. Some of the most wonderful experiences that words could ever begin to express took place at these particular times. A number of times during these prayer meetings, I would begin to pray, and then literally go into a trance. When I would awaken, or *"come to,"* I would think only a few minutes had passed, when, at times, it had been several hours.

Even at that time, I knew I would be an Evangelist, and that this Ministry would be worldwide. I knew that many people would be saved and many lives would be changed.

So, Jesus words, *"Suffer the little children to come unto Me, and forbid them not,"* are very, very special to me, because of what they meant to me as well as many others.

The phrase, *"For of such is the Kingdom of God,"* has powerful meanings. They are as follows:

1. The innocence of *"little children"* is typical of the *"Kingdom of God."* Inasmuch as children are innocent, they are, at the same time, free of prejudice, bias, unforgiveness, anger or hate.

2. Children, as Christ here exclaims, can be saved at an early age, which not only saves the soul, but the life.

As such, this would bring to a sudden halt all juvenile delinquency, gang warfare, drug addiction, and alcoholism, so prevalent among teenagers. This terrible drain on society would be completely stopped.

3. The tremendous significance of the child in the eyes of God is portrayed here. Consequently, if the spiritual direction of these children are that important to Jesus, it certainly should be that important to us!

(15) "VERILY I SAY UNTO YOU, WHOSOEVER SHALL NOT RECEIVE THE KINGDOM OF GOD AS A LITTLE CHILD, HE SHALL NOT ENTER THEREIN."

The phrase, *"Verily I say unto you,"* is meant to portray an extremely significant statement. Of course, anything Christ says is of extreme importance; however, some statements, as this, are of utmost importance, simply because it ties together all that has gone before.

The phrase, *"Whosoever shall not receive the Kingdom of God as a little child,"* proclaims the manner in which the Kingdom is to be received, which means to give up ambitious aims and earthly contests, and imitate the simple unworldly ways of little children.

Bickersteth says, *"The simplicity of the little child is the model and the rule for everyone who desires, by the Grace of Christ, to obtain the Kingdom of Heaven."*

Of course, Christ is not speaking of doing so literally, but figuratively.

A child is generally trusting, and will believe whatever he is told. Likewise, and regarding the Word of God, the seeker must have the same attitude.

Actually, as this refusal to *"receive the Kingdom of God as a little child,"* keeps millions of unbelievers out, likewise, the refusal to believe and trust *"as a little child,"* keeps many Believers from receiving from God.

The term, *"child-like Faith"* is derived from this 15th verse.

The phrase, *"He shall not enter therein,"* presents a double negative in the Greek, and, consequently, presents an emphatic denial. In other words, there is no way that one will receive the Kingdom of God, unless he does so with the same spirit and attitude of a *"little child."* As we have repeatedly stated, this is the main reason why many never accept Christ. They are not willing to humble themselves, nor trust the Word of the Lord. Therefore, because of this prideful attitude, they die lost!

And yet, when one finally does break before the Lord, he finds what he receives is so much more than what he lost. Actually, what was lost was a prideful deceit, which was merely a facade, which covered his insecurities. Once this is stripped away, with Christ taking its place, the prideful deceit is no longer needed, with Christ absorbing self.

It actually comes down to the person recognizing God as his Creator and, consequently, True Parent. For some reason men are loathe to admit this, rather claiming *"I did it my way,"* which somehow makes them feel self-made. However, that which is self-made is also, ultimately, self-destroyed.

Jesus wants the person to believe Him exactly as the child believes his parent. The only way a child will not believe his parent, is that the parent has lied to him several times. Otherwise, he will believe him without fail.

Of course, the Lord has never lied to anyone, and His Word can be trusted implicitly. He simply desires that we believe Him, exactly as we believed our earthly parents when we were little children.

(16) "AND HE TOOK THEM UP IN HIS ARMS, PUT HIS HANDS UPON THEM, AND BLESSED THEM."

The phrase, *"And He took them up in His Arms,"* refers to the child being embraced by Christ.

The phrase, *"Put His Hands upon them, and blessed them,"* was of far greater magnitude than the parents had at first envisioned.

Wuest says that the very word, *"blessed,"* is intensive in its force, meaning that He *"blessed them fervently."* As well, He *"kept on blessing them."*

Also, this Passage, although intending to express an action by Christ respecting these little children, still, expresses far more!

Spiritually speaking, Christ takes the trusting Believer in His Arms, thereby signaling love, devotion, attention, and protection. This emphasizes the *"security"* craved by the soul since the Fall of man, with every attempt made to secure it elsewhere, but without success. Once the individual comes to Christ, he has come home, i.e., to his rightful Parent. As such, the craving for *"security"* will finally be realized, thereby needing no more the things of the world, such as alcohol, gambling, drugs, immorality, love of money, or worldly ambition, etc. All of these things were a false security, and could never really satisfy. Only Christ can do that.

This is the reason that religion, which is always a work of man, is so damnable; it continues to promise but never delivers, because, in fact, it cannot deliver. Consequently, the Preacher of the Gospel who does not *"preach Christ,"* is, in effect, committing spiritual high treason.

As well, when Christ takes us up in His Arms, spiritually speaking, He also *"puts His Hands on us,"* in order to mold us in His Image. It is a work He commences at conversion, and continues throughout our life.

Regrettably, many Believers really do not allow Him this freedom of action, because they misunderstand what He is doing. His entire purpose is to *"bless us,"* exactly as He blessed these little children. Actually, everything Christ does for the person, even the times of *"chastisement,"* proves to be a *"blessing."* If we obey His Word, He never curses, but, rather, blesses!

A long time ago, Baalim prophesied, saying, *"God is not a man, that he should lie; neither the son of man, that He should repent: Hath He said, and shall He not do it? or hath He spoken, and shall He not make it good?*

"Behold, I have received commandment to bless: and He hath blessed; and I cannot reverse it" (Num. 23:19-20).

One can only shout *"Hallelujah!"*

(17) "AND WHEN HE WAS GONE FORTH INTO THE WAY, THERE CAME ONE RUNNING, AND KNEELED TO HIM, AND ASKED HIM, GOOD MASTER, WHAT SHALL I DO THAT I MAY INHERIT ETERNAL LIFE?"

The phrase, *"And when He was gone forth into the way,"* means as He was leaving the house, on His way to Jerusalem.

The phrase, *"There came one running, and kneeled to Him,"* proclaims one of note. Luke called Him *"a certain ruler,"* which refers to one of preeminence. The term, *"ruler,"* as used by Luke, was understood by Josephus as applying to a member of the Sanhedrin. At any rate, it was a general term for a great man or prince.

Quite possibly, and as the structure of the sentence indicates, he had been waiting for Jesus to come out of the house. At that moment, he ran to Christ *"and kneeled to Him."*

Swete says that the homage paid Jesus by this man is remarkable because he is not asking for material or physical help. He is asking for spiritual help.

The question, *"And asked Him, Good Master, what shall I do that I may inherit Eternal Life?"*, is basically the question of most all humanity, at least in one form or the other! However, several things are wrong with this request. They are as follows:

1. *"Good Master"*: In the Greek Text the words are reversed, and therefore say, *"Teacher, good One."* Consequently, the man regarded Jesus as merely a *"good Teacher,"* and not the Son of God. Consequently, he was looking for advice — what Christ could give, instead of Who Christ was!

He misunderstood, as most of the world misunderstands. Salvation is not a philosophy, but, rather, a Person. That Person is Christ Jesus! Men seek Salvation in Buddhism, Hinduism, Shintoism, Mormonism, Catholicism, and Islam, as well as Humanism. They never find it in these sources, because, basically, all of these religions are a form of *"Humanism,"* because they are devised by humans and not God. God's Salvation is Jesus. He Alone says, *"I am the Way, the Truth, and the Life"* (Jn. 14:6).

2. *"What shall I do that I may inherit Eternal Life?"*: The phrase in the Greek actually says, *"What good thing shall I do that I may inherit Eternal Life?"*

Men ever seek to *"do"* something, and especially something good. This is indicative not only with the religions of the world, which we have just named, but, as well, of much of Christianity.

In effect, no one can *"do"* anything which will give them *"Eternal Life,"* for no matter what they do, it would never be enough! In Truth, one does not have to *"do,"* because all that is needed has already been <u>done</u>. So, to *"inherit Eternal Life,"* all one has to do is to simply *"confess with thy mouth the Lord Jesus, and shalt believe in thine heart that God hath raised him from the dead."*

The Apostle then said, *"Thou shalt be saved"* (Rom. 10:9).

However, inasmuch as it is so simple that which the Lord demands, most will not do it, or simply will not believe it.

The religions of the world are constantly saying *"do,"* when, in Truth, Bible Christianity says *"done."* That simply means that Christ has already done all that needs to be done regarding one's Salvation, when He died on Calvary. There the *"doing"* was *"done!"* Consequently, all one has to *"do"* is simply believe that, thereby accepting Christ as their Saviour (Jn. 3:16).

WHAT IS ETERNAL LIFE?

Christ is *"The True God, and Eternal Life"* (Jn. 1:4; 14:6; I Jn. 5:20). He is, as well, the *"Prince (Author) of Life"* (Acts 3:15), to Whom the Father has granted *"to have life in Himself"* (Jn. 5:26). He is *"The Resurrection and the Life"* (Jn. 11:25), *"The Bread of Life"* (Jn. 6:35), and His Words are *"Spirit and Life"* (Jn. 6:63).

Consequently, one receives this *"Eternal Life"* by receiving Christ, Who, in effect, not only bestows *"Eternal Life"* on all who believe, but, in effect, is, and as stated, *"Eternal Life,"* which was portrayed in His Resurrection.

In the Resurrection of Christ, immortal life has been actualized on the plane of history. His Resurrection becomes the basis of all Resurrection, and all Resurrection is to be understood in terms of His (I Cor. 15; Col. 3:4; I Jn. 3:2).

No longer does the hope of Resurrection rest, as in the Old Testament, merely upon prophetic vision or upon inferences from God's Covenant relationships. Resurrection-Life now finds its meaning in the Image of Jesus Christ (Rom. 8:29).

HOW THE RESURRECTION OF CHRIST RELATES TO MAN

For man, then, True Life is grounded in Jesus Christ, Who *"became a Life-giving Spirit"* (Jn. 6:63; I Cor. 15:45; II Cor. 3:17). The core of the Gospel proclamation is that He Who was dead is *"alive forevermore"* (Acts 2:31; I Cor. 15:3-4; Rev. 1:5, 18), and by the power of an indestructible life gives life to the world (Jn. 6:33; Heb. 7:16).

If Christ has not been raised from death one must write over the Christian dead, *"Finish,"* (I Cor. 15:18, 32). But Christ is risen from the dead, and has the *"keys to hell,"* because hell could not conquer Him, neither can it prevail against His Church (Mat. 16:18; Rev. 1:18).

His Life is given to the Believer through Repentance and Faith. Paul said, *"Repentance toward God, and Faith toward our Lord Jesus Christ"* (Jn. 3:16; 11:25; Acts 20:21), and by such one is *"saved,"* and given *"Eternal Life"* (Rom. 5:10).

In Christ's Death and Resurrection God pierces radically into the world of man to make him see the fatality of sin and the utter Grace of the New Life from God — an unfathomable, unexpected and freely-bestowed act of Salvation.

This New Life is a Resurrection, and New Birth, a sovereign and gracious act of the Creator God (Jn. 1:13; 5:24; Rom. 6:4; Eph. 2:1; Col. 3:1).

A PRESENT POSSESSION OF THE BELIEVER

Resurrection-Life is viewed as a present possession of the Believer. One passes *"from death to life"* at conversion (Jn. 5:24; Eph. 2:1; I Jn. 3:14), and one may even speak in the past tense of having been crucified (in Christ), raised to

NOTES

life, brought into Christ's Kingdom, glorified and made to sit in heavenly places (Rom. 8:30; Gal. 2:20; Eph. 2:5; Col. 1:13). However, this is always viewed as a corporate participation in Christ's Death and Resurrection (Jn. 6:33, 51; Rom. 6:4; 8:2; II Tim. 1:1). All of this is a *"downpayment"* of the New Life we now have in Christ, but which will be realized in its fullness at the Resurrection (II Cor. 4:12; 5:5). Our life is hid with Christ (Col. 3:3) and to have life means simply to have Christ (I Jn. 5:11).

At present, this *"Eternal Life"* is actualized Personally only in Jesus Christ, *"The firstfruits of those who have fallen asleep,"* *"The firstborn among many brethren"* (Rom. 8:29; I Cor. 15:20).

(The thoughts on *"Eternal Life"* were derived from *"The New Bible Dictionary."*)

(18) "AND JESUS SAID UNTO HIM, WHY CALLEST THOU ME GOOD? THERE IS NONE GOOD BUT ONE, THAT IS, GOD."

The phrase, *"And Jesus said unto him,"* concerns the greatest words this rich young ruler will ever hear.

If one scans the Gospels, and without diligence, even though he knows that Jesus is God, still, the simple directives given in the teaching of Jesus will by and large escape the reader.

In the first place, their utter simplicity, which was of course designed by the Holy Spirit, causes many to miss the exceptional height and depth of their wisdom.

As well, the teaching given by Christ, which is the foundation of all knowledge and wisdom, little addresses itself to many things men are searching for, such as scientific achievements, economic power, or a host of other such pursuits. Jesus does not address these things, because those things do not in any way constitute the true problem of mankind.

Man's problem is not in knowing how to build an automobile that will give 100 miles to a gallon of gasoline, but, rather, how to live. Due to the Fall, which brought about the sin nature, man simply does not know how to live. Consequently, the lives of many brilliant scientists are but shambles. The same can be said for billionaires, and educators, etc. Irrespective of one's knowledge in the field of science, or the billions of dollars that one may possess, if he does not know how to live, very little has actually been accomplished. And, as well, those things do not teach people how to live.

Knowing that something is wrong, man searches, but most of the time in all the wrong places. Only Christ can tell one how to live! Peter said, when responding to the question of Christ, *"Will ye also go away?"*:

He was not long in answering, and said, *"Lord, to whom shall we go? Thou hast the Words of Eternal Life"* (Jn. 6:67-68).

Let it be said again that Peter's affirmation is not only true, but, in fact, Jesus is the <u>only</u> One Who has these Words! He is not One of several choices, but, in fact, the <u>only</u> choice!

Therefore, if one takes the time to explore the teaching of Christ, one will find the answer to every perplexing problem of life. Absolutely nothing is left unaddressed, with a simple but yet all-wise answer given to man's quest for life.

And yet, the mere study of the teaching of Christ will reap little harvest if divorced from the Person of Christ. The moralist has attempted to do this, but without success! Christ must be accepted, not merely as a great Teacher, as this rich young ruler thinks, but, rather, as the Son of the Living God. As well, a mere affirmation of that is not enough. Man must accept Christ as His Lord and Saviour, which will then bring about an impartation of the Holy Spirit, Who leads into all Truth (Jn. 16:13). Then and only then, will these all-wise Words of Christ become what they are intended — *"more abundant life"* (Jn. 10:10).

The question, *"Why callest Thou Me good?"*, is not meant to state that Christ is not *"good,"* but, rather, that the word *"good"* be placed in its proper perspective.

Man's label of that which he calls *"good,"* is predicated on many factors. Almost all comes from the *"good"* side of *"The Tree of the Knowledge of Good and Evil"* (Gen. 2:17). Consequently, it is *"good"* that God can never accept, and because of its source.

The concept that links all the uses of the word *"good"* is evaluation. To determine the good, one compares things, qualities, and actions with other things, qualities, and actions. One must contrast the beneficial and the right with other things, qualities, and action that are not beneficial and are wrong.

The account of the Creation introduces Biblically the manner in which God viewed each day's work and pronounced it *"good"* (Gen. 1). Consequently, God evaluates, just as we are to

evaluate. Actually, it is because God has shared His Image and Likeness with mankind that human beings have the capacity to make value judgments.

However, man's value judgments are skewed because sin has distorted humanity's perceptions of what *"good"* really is! Consequently, man is unable to properly evaluate as he should. God can only evaluate perfectly.

In view of this, the Prophets of old proclaimed that God was the Giver and Measure of good, but also that He Alone knows what is truly beneficial for us and what is morally right. Only because God has shared His evaluation of the good in His Word, are we who rely on Him, able to affirm with confidence that a certain thing, quality, or course of action is beneficial, i.e., *"good."*

Whatever is truly good, is free from flaw, in full balance and harmony with the ideal, Who is God.

Sin, as stated, has warped the Divine pattern, to where man's evaluation is no longer trustworthy.

In the ultimate sense, and as Jesus will say here, only God is good. Although human beings may be *"good"* in comparison with one another (Lk. 6:45; 19:17), nothing in any human action can be beneficial to God in the sense that it will merit Salvation.

Man is constantly comparing his standard of *"good"* with other men's standard of *"good."* However, even though such may satisfy man, it can never satisfy God. He can never accept man's standard, and for the obvious reasons. The only standard for proper measurement is God's standard, which is the *"Word of God."* If men do not accept that as the standard, they are left only with their own standard, which can murder millions of unborn babies in their mother's womb, and call it *"good!"*

The rich young ruler, by addressing Jesus as *"Good Master,"* was disavowing the true position of Christ as the Messiah, God manifest in the flesh. Consequently, the efforts of the Lord are not meant to instigate an argument, but, hopefully, to put this man on the right track.

The phrase, *"There is none good but One, that is, God,"* places everything in its proper perspective. If man does not begin with this premise, the entire fabric of his philosophy becomes unworkable. In fact, almost all of mankind falls into this trap. Man thinks he is good within himself, and because he performs a so-called good deed on an occasional basis. Or he thinks he is *"good"* because he doesn't do certain bad things, etc. However, man's standard of goodness simply will not work. This is the reason wars continue to be fought, with jails continuing to be filled, with marriages continuing to be broken.

Fortunately for man there are particular laws of science designed by God that forces man into a certain mode respecting engineering, etc. In other words, these laws must be adhered to, or airplanes will not fly, bridges will not hold up, or machinery will not function. Irrespective of what man likes or doesn't like, these laws must be adhered to.

However, concerning Spiritual Laws which God has laid down, and which we find in God's Word, and God's Word alone, man, due to his fallen nature, will not obey. As a result, and using the vernacular, his spiritual airplanes will not fly, nor will his spiritual bridges hold up, so to speak!

As we have stated, man is loathe to admit that he is not good, and, as well, that most all he does falls into the same category. And yet, man, even unconverted man, is capable of doing some good things, and because he was originally made in the Image of God. Consequently, man equates the *"good things"* he occasionally does, as coming from a *"good man."*

However, the occasional good things done by unconverted man, in no way means that he within himself constitutes that which is *"good."* In fact, he is not *"good,"* and nothing he does can make him *"good!"* And this is where the great problem arises.

Almost all of humanity equate their lives with the so-called good things they have done, or the bad things they have not done. Such is a false premise, and in no way can be accepted by God. Man must come to the conclusion that he is not *"good,"* and, as well, there is absolutely nothing he can do, no matter how seemingly good on the surface, that will make him *"good."* But yet he keeps trying!

Only God can make one *"good,"* and He does so through Faith exhibited in His Son, The Lord Jesus Christ. Consequently, upon Faith in Christ, one can be *"bad"* one minute, even *"notoriously bad,"* and the next minute be *"good."* It is called *"Imputed Righteousness."* Regrettably, it is a

NOTES

"goodness," i.e., *"Righteousness"* the world will not accept, nor much of the Church.

(19) "THOU KNOWEST THE COMMANDMENTS, DO NOT COMMIT ADULTERY, DO NOT KILL, DO NOT STEAL, DO NOT BEAR FALSE WITNESS, DEFRAUD NOT, HONOUR THY FATHER AND MOTHER."

The phrase, *"Thou knowest the Commandments,"* draws the young man to the Word of God, in both a positive and negative sense. Positive, because the Word alone holds the answer; negative, because it will show him as a mirror where he is wrong.

Jesus did not say, *"Commandment,"* singular, but, *"Commandments,"* plural, actually meaning all of them. And yet of the Ten Commandments, Jesus will only deal with Six, which pertain to man's dealings with his fellowman. The remaining Four pertain to man's dealings with God, which actually constitute the first Four. The idea is this:

If man properly loves God, he will, at the same time, love his fellowman.

1. *"Do not commit adultery"*: This is the Seventh Commandment, with all Ten listed in Exodus 20. This speaks of sexual relations between a man and woman before marriage, or unfaithfulness on the part of man or woman after marriage. The man claimed he had not broken this Commandment which was no doubt right concerning the actual physical act of carrying out the deed.

2. *"Do not kill"*: This is the Sixth Commandment. This was kept as well, he says!

3. *"Do not steal"*: This is the Eighth Commandment, and claimed as kept!

4. *"Do not bear false witness"*: He claimed he had not broken this Commandment; however, it is extremely doubtful that he was correct in this claim.

5. *"Defraud not"*: This is the Tenth Commandment, *"Thou shalt not covet."* He claims obedience to this one as well!

6. *"Honour thy father and mother"*: This is the Fifth Commandment to which he claims obedience.

Concerning the man's question as to how he may obtain or inherit Eternal Life, why did Jesus, by quoting a list of Commandments, answer him as He did?

In Truth, there was no Salvation, i.e., *"Eternal Life"* in the Commandments.

Jesus answered him in this manner, because to have done otherwise would have been fruitless. The man, as most, had an entirely erroneous concept of what obtaining *"Eternal Life"* actually meant. So, Jesus set out to show him that his way was wrong, and would do so by dealing with him in the very area which he prized, and thought he had accomplished, the *"keeping of the Commandments."* Most of the world falls into the same category, thinking that by the doing of certain good things, and by not doing certain bad things, *"Eternal Life"* will be theirs.

(20) "AND HE ANSWERED AND SAID UNTO HIM, MASTER, ALL THESE HAVE I OBSERVED FROM MY YOUTH."

The phrase, *"And he answered and said unto Him,"* constitutes the reaction of most of humanity. Because he did not know Who Jesus was (The Son of God), he, consequently, did not know What Jesus was (The Saviour of mankind). He will answer accordingly!

The phrase, *"Master, all these have I observed from my youth,"* states his claim of perfection (Mat. 19:21).

The word, *"observed,"* as used by this man, is a military term meaning *"to guard, watch."* It was used of sentinels keeping guard.

As it is used here, it refers not only to the act, Wuest says, of obeying them, but to that preciousness and honor which belongs to them.

And yet, the very fact of this young man's question concerning the obtaining of *"Eternal Life,"* portrays the emptiness of his heart that precipitates such a question in the first place. Whatever he <u>was</u> doing, was not satisfying the thirst of his heart. Consequently, every single individual who claims Salvation, should take a lesson from him.

If one truly wants Salvation and is trusting in the Church to provide it, one will find an emptiness exactly as this rich young ruler. The Church cannot provide Salvation, only Jesus can do such!

For those who are depending on their good works, they too will find an emptiness in their heart, because such cannot save!

If one is truly saved, one will not thirst again (Jn. 4:13-14).

(21) "THEN JESUS BEHOLDING HIM LOVED HIM, AND SAID UNTO HIM, ONE THING THOU LACKEST: GO THY WAY, SELL WHATSOEVER THOU HAST, AND

NOTES

GIVE TO THE POOR, AND THOU SHALT HAVE TREASURE IN HEAVEN: AND COME, TAKE UP THE CROSS, AND FOLLOW ME."

The phrase, *"Then Jesus beholding him loved him,"* means that Jesus fixed His eyes on the young man, which saw to the very depths of his soul. And seeing, He *"loved him,"* and not because He saw good things, but because He saw a desire for good things, i.e., *"Eternal Life."* In fact, and as his answer showed, this man was not honest, even with himself. He had not truly kept these Commandments! In Truth, no man ever kept them all the time, except Christ. Jesus will now show him, that even in that which he rashly claims, he is, in fact, woefully deficient.

The phrase, *"And said unto him, One thing thou lackest,"* will put its finger on the very heart of this man's problem. This phrase is not used by Christ in the sense that He believes the young man has kept these Commandments, but, instead, to show him that he does not have *"Eternal Life,"* and the reason why!

In Truth, the *"one thing"* he *"lacked,"* was the *"one thing"* which really mattered! The keeping of Commandments is not the cause of one's Salvation, but, rather, the result of one's Salvation. This man had it backwards, as do most!

The phrase, *"Go thy way, sell whatsoever thou hast, and give to the poor,"* in effect, is saying, *"If what you are saying is true, you will do this which I ask of you."*

This man's possessions were his god. As we have stated, all the Commandments listed by Christ pertained to one's conduct toward one's fellowman. So if he really loved his fellowman, as he claims, what Jesus asks of him will be readily done.

No! Jesus was not making the selling of one's goods and giving all to the poor a criteria for Salvation. He was merely putting His finger on what was keeping this young man from having *"Eternal Life."* Without coming out and saying it publicly, He was portraying the hypocrisy and deceit. And yet He *"loved him"* exactly as He loves us.

The phrase, *"And thou shalt have treasure in Heaven,"* concerned the True Treasure.

Even though the subject matter is not *"Treasure in Heaven,"* it is a valid subject which must be addressed.

Jesus had previously said in the Sermon on the Mount, *"Where your treasure is, there will*

NOTES

your heart be also" (Mat. 6:21). So, we learn from this exchange that this man's heart was not with God, and, consequently, was not right with God, but, instead, was with the world. Consequently, this scenario tells us what the Lord expects of all, both rich and poor!

The *"Treasure in Heaven"* consists of our life lived for Jesus, and our resources used for His Work.

The phrase, *"And come,"* actually constitutes an Altar Call. It is the invitation of the ages.

The phrase, *"Take up the Cross, and follow Me,"* constitutes True Salvation.

The *"Taking up of the Cross,"* referred to the dying to self-will, which was actually this young man's problem, with his attitude toward his possessions being but a symptom. A *"Cross"* is made on which to die, which pertains to self, where lies the Believer's greatest struggle.

Millions claim to follow Christ, but refuse the Cross of self-denial, and, consequently, the abrogation of self-will.

In this man's case, as with all, it is not enough to merely sell all he had and give to the poor, but, as well, he had to *"take up his Cross, and follow Jesus."*

Some few have even divested themselves of worldly possessions, but without continuing on to *"take up the Cross and follow Christ."* There is no Salvation in this type of sacrifice. Salvation is only in Christ! The possessions, at least within themselves, constituted neither right or wrong. It was the man's attitude toward them which constituted the wrong. He let them keep him from Jesus, therefore, they constituted the true feelings of his heart.

(22) "AND HE WAS SAD AT THAT SAYING, AND WENT AWAY GRIEVED: FOR HE HAD GREAT POSSESSIONS."

The phrase, *"And he was sad at that saying,"* constitutes the attitude of multiple millions. They, as he, desire Salvation, but on their own terms!

Why was he sad?

The price was too high, or so he thought!

The phrase, *"and went away grieved: for he had great possessions,"* pertained to his treasure, which captured his heart. And yet, he did not have the greatest possession of all, *"Eternal Life."*

Can one have both, *"possessions, and Eternal Life?"*

Actually, the possessions were not his problem, only the occasion of it. The problem was his heart. It was fastened onto these possessions, and would not let go in order to follow Christ.

The answer to the question is twofold:

1. If the *"possessions,"* or anything, capture the heart, then it has to go before Christ can be followed.

2. If the possessions do not capture the heart, they are of no consequence, and Christ can be adequately followed.

The idea is that one cannot follow both! Jesus addressed Himself to this by saying, *"No man can serve two masters: for either he will hate the one, and love the other; or else he will hold to the one, and despise the other. Ye cannot serve God and mammon"* (Mat. 6:24).

As an example, Zacchaeus *"was rich,"* and said to Jesus, *"The half of my goods I give to the poor; and if I have taken any thing from any man by false accusation, I restore him fourfold."*

Jesus did not tell him to give the other half also, but rather said, *"This day is Salvation come to this house"* (Lk. 19:1-9).

So, the criteria is not the giving of all, or half, but rather the *"heart."*

Paul summed it up by saying, *"But what things were gain to me, those I counted loss for Christ."*

He then said, *"Yea doubtless, and I count all things but loss for the excellency of the knowledge of Christ Jesus my Lord: for Whom I have suffered the loss of all things, and do count them but dung, that I may win Christ"* (Phil. 3:7-8).

The only *"possession"* that really matters, is *"Eternal Life,"* and that can only be found in Jesus. If we allow anything to come in between us and Him, whatever it is must be put away.

Let no one think that the Message given to this *"rich young ruler"* was for him alone. Actually, it is for all!

(23) "AND JESUS LOOKED ROUND ABOUT, AND SAITH UNTO HIS DISCIPLES, HOW HARDLY SHALL THEY THAT HAVE RICHES ENTER INTO THE KINGDOM OF GOD!"

The phrase, *"And Jesus looked round about,"* means that as Jesus previously *"beheld"* the young man, He now beholds His Disciples. As He looked searchingly then, He looks searchingly now!

The phrase, *"And saith unto His Disciples, How hardly shall they that have riches enter into the Kingdom of God,"* comes as a bombshell to the Disciples!

It was something they had never heard before, and, in fact, the very opposite of what they believed.

Jesus did not say that it was impossible for one who had riches to be saved, but, rather, that it was more difficult for them.

Why?

Many who have riches, tend to trust those riches. In other words, their dependence and Faith is not in God, but, instead, in the things of this world. As such, they think they can buy whatever they need! However, Salvation cannot be bought, though millions have tried!

As well, many who are rich, and because of the riches, place themselves in a different category than others. They are loathe to think, and not desirous of hearing that they must come to Christ in the same manner, and with the same heart attitude, as the poorest of the poor. Many desire to be treated as a special case, which God will not do. As a result of their riches, they are loathe to humble themselves.

Actually, it is not the *"riches"* which constitute the sin, but the attitude toward them.

(24) "AND THE DISCIPLES WERE ASTONISHED AT HIS WORDS. BUT JESUS ANSWERETH AGAIN, AND SAITH UNTO THEM, CHILDREN, HOW HARD IS IT FOR THEM THAT TRUST IN RICHES TO ENTER INTO THE KINGDOM OF GOD?"

The phrase, *"And the Disciples were astonished at His Words,"* concerns the attitude of the Disciples, and for reason.

Why were they astonished?

Jews equated riches with the favor and blessings of God. In other words, if one had riches, that meant he was right with God, and, consequently, greatly blessed by Him.

Conversely, poverty, at least in the eyes of the Jews, meant God's disfavor, or even His curse.

So, the more riches one had, the closer to God he was. The less riches, the less close to God. Consequently, the poverty-stricken were deemed to be under the curse of God, and, therefore, eternally lost.

Jesus has just turned their theology upside down, or rather right side up, which astonished them.

The phrase, *"But Jesus answereth again, and saith unto them, Children,"* adds another

condition to Salvation, while, at the same time, clarifying what He has just said about riches.

He uses the word, *"Children,"* taking them back to the dissertation He has just given concerning *"receiving the Kingdom of God as a little child."* A child does not grasp after things, nor seeks to own great numbers of things. In effect, *"riches"* mean nothing to a child.

Children who are poor really do not know it, at least if they have enough to eat. Children who are rich pretty well fall into the same category.

So, Jesus is telling His Disciples, as well as all others, that one must have the attitude of a child toward these things.

The phrase, *"How hard is it for them that trust in riches to enter into the Kingdom of God,"* proclaims Him explaining His statement concerning *"riches."* As we have stated, it was not the *"riches"* per se which constituted the wrong, but rather *"trust in riches!"*

In effect, the Lord is saying that it is *"hard"* for anyone to *"enter into the Kingdom of God,"* and especially *"hard"* for those who have added incumberances, such as *"riches!"*

He will explain it further by the following statement:

(25) "IT IS EASIER FOR A CAMEL TO GO THROUGH THE EYE OF A NEEDLE, THAN FOR A RICH MAN TO ENTER INTO THE KINGDOM OF GOD."

The phrase, *"It is easier for a camel to go through the eye of a needle,"* spoke of an ancient Jewish proverb.

Most cities in those days were encircled by walls for protection, with the gates being closed at night. However, for late comers, there was a small opening cut in the gate (an actual smaller gate), which would admit a man, or even a camel if it was stripped of all baggage and got down on its knees.

The idea being that it would be easier to get a camel through this small opening, than it would for a *"rich man"* to be saved. It is not too difficult to get all the baggage off a camel, but it borders on the impossibility for a rich person to purposely strip himself of all the baggage which accompanies riches. That baggage concerned itself with *"trust in riches,"* which Jesus had just mentioned.

However, Wuest says that the *"needle"* spoken of here, was the type of needle used with thread. Consequently, it meant the tiny eye of a sewing needle. Actually, whether the small opening in the large gate, or the actual eye of a needle, the impossibility continues to present itself regarding Salvation, that is if one trusts in riches.

The phrase, *"Than for a rich man to enter into the Kingdom of God,"* is a blatant statement! It leaves absolutely no room for misinterpretation. The absolute impossibility of such a thing, as Jesus will momentarily state, is not the idea of the statement, but, rather, the infrequency of it. In fact, there are rich people who have come to Christ, and who faithfully serve Him. That number, however, is infinitesimally small. Most, as we have stated, trust their riches, consequently refusing to admit that they need a Saviour like all others.

Due to the Fall, the nature of man is such that he tends to puff himself up, if given even the slightest opportunity. Consequently, if he is adept at making large sums of money, he has a tendency to believe that he is a cut above others. The idea that he is a poor lost sinner, with a spiritual need just as desperate as the poorest pauper, is totally foreign to him. Actually, this is the reason for class distinction and racism. Men love to think of themselves as better than others. They reason that their state in life brought on by economic opportunity and educational privilege negates their need for Christ.

As I have mentioned elsewhere in these volumes, I have had the opportunity, and in whatever capacity, to have dialogue with some who consider themselves to be intellectually superior. They are the individuals, or at least they think they are, who mold the thinking of the common people. They are the political pundits of the news media.

Concerning Christ, their attitude, at least for the most part, places them in a position totally different from the mainstream of society. They feel that accepting Christ may be necessary as a crutch for the intellectually inferior. However, they, the intellectually superior, are above this need. In other words, only the ignorant, at least in their thinking, would bother with such foolishness. Consequently, their intellectual cleverness becomes their god.

Most of these, and in whatever category they fall, do not know or believe the Bible. If they did, they would realize how intellectually superior the Word of God is to all philosophies of

man. They would also understand that true riches are found only in loving and serving God.

(26) "AND THEY WERE ASTONISHED OUT OF MEASURE, SAYING AMONG THEMSELVES, WHO THEN CAN BE SAVED?"

The phrase, *"And they were astonished out of measure,"* takes them a step beyond the astonishment of verse 24. If they were astonished then, their astonishment now is beyond measure. They are totally flabbergasted at the Words of Christ!

The question, *"Saying among themselves, Who then can be saved?",* presents, as stated, their theology being completely turned over.

As we have stated, the Jews, including the Disciples, thought that riches were a Blessing of God, and, consequently, the rich person was the most saved of all. Those in poverty were thought to have the curse of God upon them, and, consequently, lost! In other words, they equated riches, i.e., material possessions, as a barometer of one's Salvation. And now Jesus proclaims the very opposite of what they have studiously believed. Hence they begin to converse among themselves in acclaimed surprise, finally blurting out the question, *"Who then can be saved?"*

The belief of Israel at that time concerning Salvation, was pretty much the same as their modern counterparts respecting Faith.

Those who proclaim the Prosperity Message by and large judge a person's Faith by worldly possessions, etc. Such is just as wrongheaded as the belief of the Disciples concerning Salvation. Material possessions were the criteria then, and material possessions are the criteria now! At least in these erroneous doctrines.

(27) "AND JESUS LOOKING UPON THEM SAITH, WITH MEN IT IS IMPOSSIBLE, BUT NOT WITH GOD: FOR WITH GOD ALL THINGS ARE POSSIBLE."

The phrase, *"And Jesus looking upon them saith,"* presents Him gazing steadfastly at them, knowing that His statement would produce this type of reaction.

If the truth be known, most of the theology in modern Christendom is just as skewed as the theology of the Disciples. And yet, despite this wrong thinking, as serious as it was, these men were definitely saved.

This means that one can be wrong in the head, and right in the heart, and, as I must quickly add, we all have been at one time or the other.

The phrase, *"With men it is impossible, but not with God,"* puts everything in a different perspective.

Jesus was not saying that rich men could not be saved, but that, and because of their riches, it was more difficult to bring them to a place of repentance. In effect, Salvation is impossible with all men respecting their own efforts and abilities, etc.

The idea of the Text is, that none of man's machinations, be he rich or poor, will afford him Salvation.

The phrase, *"For with God all things are possible,"* presents God as Omnipotent (all-powerful), Omniscient (all-knowing), Omnipresent (everywhere).

The Miracle of the New Birth, and a Miracle it is, presents all being saved by Grace, without works of the Law and human merit. As such, the rich must humble themselves and meet God's terms exactly as the poor. As we have stated, there is no difference! All have sinned and come short of the Glory of God (Jn. 3:16-18; I Tim. 2:4; II Pet. 3:9; Rev. 22:17).

Being rich does not have to be a barrier in finding the Lord if one will humble himself and renounce all human sins and human merits (Rom. 3:24-31; 5:1-11; 10:9-10; Eph. 2:8-9; I Jn. 1:9).

To be sure, riches, and as here exclaimed by Christ, definitely can prove to be an even greater barrier to Salvation, as it most of the time is. However, and as stated, if the rich will meet God's terms, as all others, they will be saved as all others.

As well, a rich man does not necessarily have to give up all he possesses to be a Disciple, but he must become willing to do so if God would require it of him. In effect, the riches must become the property of the Lord, before such a one can be saved.

The reason the Salvation process is impossible with man, whether rich or poor, is because the spiritual rebirth Believers experience does not come through any natural process. God is the instigator of Salvation, Who effects the New Birth in those who believe and receive the Son (Jn. 1:12-13). The New Birth, consequently, makes us Children of God, and leads us to moral transformation. As stated, only God can do this, and not man.

NOTES

So, the Salvation process in the rich is identical to that in the poor. The process of which Jesus speaks, is not in question, but, rather, the barrier to that process which can be riches.

Therefore, just because a person is rich, or famous, or powerful, etc., doesn't mean that we are not to pray for their Salvation. We should pray for them irrespective of whom they may be, believing that *"with God all things are possible."*

(28) "THEN PETER BEGAN TO SAY UNTO HIM, LO, WE HAVE LEFT ALL, AND HAVE FOLLOWED THEE."

The phrase, *"Then Peter began to say unto Him,"* respects Peter, as usual, the spokesman of the group. The statement Peter will make, means that all the Disciples concerned with what Jesus had said about riches, had been avidly discussing this subject. As stated, their theology has been completely upended.

The phrase, *"Lo, we have left all, and have followed Thee,"* in effect, says, *"We have abandoned all in order to follow You, and what reward will we get for becoming poor for Your sake?"*

Actually, several of the Disciples had left what seemed to be a lucrative fishing business, and Matthew had left his tax-collector's office, all to follow this poor itinerant Preacher. Consequently, Peter, as spokesman for the Disciples, showed by his question that they were still thinking in terms of material rather than spiritual riches (Wuest). In fact, and as the following exchange proclaims, their eyes continued to be on an earthly kingdom, with Jesus as its King, and they as His chosen lieutenants. Of course, at least in their thinking, this would bring great riches and power.

However, one is not to mistake Peter's statement as a proclamation of second thought. The Disciples had made an irrevocable decision to leave all they had, and forever, and to follow with the Lord permanently (Wuest). There was no thought of going back, even if the answer given by Jesus was not according to their thinking.

While it was true that they had things somewhat confused about the Mission of Christ, they were not confused concerning His Person. They knew He was the Messiah! Of that, there was no doubt! So, wherever He led, they were determined to follow, but, still, they also wanted to know where all this was leading. As of yet, they had not learned their lesson respecting the *"servant ministry"* (Mk. 9:35), but continued to exhibit the self-will of *"What's in it for me?"*

If one is to notice, while Jesus did definitely promise great things, as the following verses proclaim, nevertheless, what He said was somewhat vague concerning material possessions. What He actually did say is a lesson we must learn if we are to properly understand His purpose, which must become our purpose.

(29) "AND JESUS ANSWERED AND SAID, VERILY I SAY UNTO YOU, THERE IS NO MAN THAT HATH LEFT HOUSE, OR BRETHREN, OR SISTERS, OR FATHER, OR MOTHER, OR WIFE, OR CHILDREN, OR LANDS, FOR MY SAKE, AND THE GOSPEL'S,"

The phrase, *"And Jesus answered and said, Verily I say unto you,"* concerns itself with the lesson which must be learned by all!

The phrase, *"There is no man that hath left,"* concerns not only what one has, but also what one desires to have. This is a great Truth which must be understood by all followers of the Lord. It is the reason that some continue and some don't.

Many are not willing to leave all, with many attempting to use Christ to get what they want, as was the spirit of the Disciples, at least at this present time. To them, Jesus was a means to an end, just as He is with millions. Thankfully, they would climb out over this, but many, sadly, never do.

Actually, most, if not the entirety, of the *"Prosperity Message"* is made up of this premise. Jesus is the way to earthly riches and material possessions. It is a heady doctrine chased by many devotees, and because of the inherent greed in most hearts.

It must ever be understood that Jesus is not a means to an end. That is blatant self-will, and will never be honored by God.

When men follow Jesus, they are to leave all, with Him Alone charting the course. It is somewhat the same as the military.

When one joins the Service, or is drafted, one does not tell the military what he wants to do, but does what the military wants him to do, whatever that may be. Men have their way, but the Service has its way. To be sure, it is the *"Army way"* which will be done. This is somewhat akin to following Jesus, but with one great difference.

The military forces its way, while Jesus does the opposite, desiring, even demanding, that

those who follow Him do so out of their own free will and volition.

The phrase, *"House, or brethren, or sisters, or father, or mother, or wife, or children, or lands,"* places everything under three headings of *"home, relatives, and property."* In effect, Jesus is saying, that if all of this is not given up, *"He cannot be My Disciple"* (Lk. 14:26).

The phrase, *"For My sake, and the Gospel's,"* speaks as to the reason. Many have done these things, but for other purposes and reasons. Many declare a vow of poverty, but not for the sake of Christ or the Gospel. In effect, many in the world, if not most, give up, or at least put all of these things in a secondary position, in order that they may do certain things. Those things may be the pursuit of money, fame, power, or position. Then, again, it may be alcohol or drugs, etc.

This is the reason for so many broken homes, alienation of affection, anger and hatred!

So, what Christ is demanding is not all that unusual, at least the regarding of leaving all. Most just do it for the wrong reason, and, consequently, reap a bitter harvest.

What does Jesus mean by leaving all, and for His sake, and the Gospel's?

He definitely does not mean that a person should desert his parents, wife, husband, children, nor responsibilities in these areas. Nor does He mean that one should necessarily sell everything he owns, etc. What He does mean is this:

Everything must be subservient to Christ, and, in effect, placed in Christ. Many people boast that Christ is first in their lives, with other things taking second or third place, etc. That too is improper!

Jesus not only must have first place, but, as well, second and third, and so forth. Everything else, and irrespective as to what it is, must have no place at all except in Him.

However, when this is done, and properly so, the true meaning and purpose of all these things become readily obvious, with a greater love or appreciation for them than ever, but in the proper perspective.

In other words, a husband cannot truly love his wife, at least as he ought to, until she is properly placed in Christ. The same would hold for all else! True love, respect, appreciation, and worth, are found only as these things, as dear as they may be, are properly placed in Christ. It is a matter of God's Will in relationship to man's will.

If one is to notice, Jesus said, *"For My sake, and the Gospel's."* Why did He say it in this manner?

If one has truly given up all these things to follow Jesus, the evidence will portray itself regarding the direction it takes. If the course is true, and the direction straight, meaning that Jesus is truly being followed, every effort will be made on the part of the follower to proclaim the Good News of the Gospel to all others. This is the criteria of following Jesus.

If one is to notice, the one great thrust of the followers of Christ, and especially headed up by the Apostle Paul in the Book of Acts, is the taking of the Gospel to those who had never heard it. This alone constituted the true following of Jesus Christ.

Those who claim to be following Jesus and have little or no concern for the lost, are, in effect, following their own self-will. If they truly follow Christ, the Gospel and its proclamation will be first and foremost. Everyone has his part to play. All can pray and all can give, and some can go. Nevertheless, and as stated, all are to have their part. The Great Commission is not the obligation of a few, but all (Mk. 16:15).

(30) "BUT HE SHALL RECEIVE AN HUNDREDFOLD NOW IN THIS TIME, HOUSES, AND BRETHREN, AND SISTERS, AND MOTHERS, AND CHILDREN, AND LANDS, WITH PERSECUTIONS; AND IN THE WORLD TO COME ETERNAL LIFE."

The phrase, *"But he shall receive an hundredfold now in this time,"* refers to this present life.

What did Jesus mean by the hundredfold return?

Some have made a doctrine of this, claiming that if one gives a dollar to the Work of the Lord, or whatever amount, he will receive back a hundred times what he gave.

Is this what Jesus meant?

Concerning our giving to the Lord, whether money or otherwise, the Lord may in turn give back a hundredfold or even greater. At times it may even be a thousandfold! However, if that is our purpose and reason for giving, then our giving has been reduced to the level of a gamble, which God will never honor. This means that almost all given in that which I refer to as the *"Prosperity Gospel,"* is not looked at by the Lord

as *"giving"* at all, but rather some type of investment or gamble. Such will never be honored by God, and will receive no return whatsoever.

If one is to notice, Jesus said, *"Hath left,"* meaning that it is given, and with no thought of getting it back. The person *"has left"* it! This should be the same, and, in fact, must be the same in our giving to God. If it is done with any other motive, it is the wrong motive and will garner no favorable response.

If one gives to *"prove the sincerity of one's love,"* as the Holy Spirit demands, one can then expect the Lord to *"open you the windows of Heaven, and pour you out a Blessing, that there shall not be room enough to receive it"* (Mal. 3:10; II Cor. 8:8).

As well, that of which the Lord speaks regarding family relations and the forsaking of such, pertains to the members of the family of God which He gives us in turn to take their place. Actually, Believers are much closer many times to other Believers, even than to members of their own family, and especially if those members are unsaved. This is what Jesus meant.

While many may understand this, still, others may wonder how this could be fulfilled (the hundredfold return) respecting *"houses and lands?"* Please allow me to give an example from my own experience.

Frances and I have not personally owned an automobile in many years, but yet we are privileged to drive two very nice cars. A dear Brother in the Lord, in his kindness, has afforded us cars. While we do not own them, at the same time, we have the use of them exactly as if we did own them. Isn't this what Jesus was saying?

As another example, when I was eight years old, I asked the Lord to give me the talent to play the piano, etc. He was gracious and kind to do what I asked. In 1961, if I remember correctly, I made my first recording. During those early times of Evangelistic Work, had it not been for the income from the sale of this product, our income would have been meager indeed! Consequently, the recordings were a blessing to the people and to us.

In 1969, and according to the leading of the Lord, I went on radio with our daily program called *"The Campmeeting Hour."* The Lord greatly blessed it, with us quickly developing a very large daily audience. (The program was a fifteen minute daily, aired Monday through Friday.)

In 1970, even before the program became popular, the Lord began to deal with me about our recordings. He asked me to give all the proceeds to Him. As stated, Frances and I had previously kept the profits from these sales for our own use. However, those profits were very small at that particular time.

The Lord, in His dealings with me, did not explain at all, but simply, as is His method, told me that He desired that we place these recordings in the name of the Ministry, and for all proceeds to be used in His Work.

During this time, we were struggling to pay for the radio program, and, as well, the Devil made certain that I remembered the very difficult times we had had financially in getting started. At times the finances were so lean that we would not even have the money to buy bare necessities. Consequently, when we began making the recordings, the extra help this gave was a life saver.

At any rate, I asked the Lord if He would allow me to take half the profits, such as they were, with me giving Him the other half? There was no answer! I came to the place that I asked the Lord to allow me to keep ten percent, with me giving Him ninety percent?

I remember that time of prayer very vividly. I felt somewhat pleased with myself in making this particular offer, that is, until the Lord spoke to me again.

"If you insist, you can have all of it, if that is what you really want!" He said. *"However, if you want My Will, you will do as I have asked!"*

At that moment, I broke before Him, gladly pledging it all. In days, Frances and I called in a lawyer, and drew up the papers, designating all recordings as belonging to the Ministry, with none of the profits accruing to us personally, but all going to the Work of God.

To be sure, at that particular time, the sales were very small. However, the Lord knew what they would ultimately be. In fact, to this day (1995), we have sold approximately 15,000,000 recordings. As well, I am glad I can say that every dollar of the money has gone to the Work of God. Frances and I have not been enriched from the sales of these products, nor any members of our family. Actually, all that we personally own in this world is our home, with that a long ways from being paid for.

However, along with the home I have spoken of, of which we are so thankful to the Lord, He has given us, as stated, beautiful cars to drive, plus good clothes to wear, and good food to eat. On top of that, we have multiple thousands of people around the world who love us dearly, and are a part of our *"family,"* in Christ. What more could anyone ask?

Have I ever regretted consigning all those recording profits over to the Work of the Lord, especially considering the tremendous number sold?

A million times *"no!"* God's Ways are always, and by far, the best ways. Actually, there are no suitable ways but His!

I believe the great Blessings of the Lord given to us respecting the acceptance of our music all around the world, has been because of our obedience to Him. To be sure, He gave me the talent that I possess, and, consequently, He had every right to ask what He did. Of course, He has every right anyway!

A hundredfold return? It is that and more!

The phrase, *"With persecutions,"* is added by the Lord for purpose and reason.

Even though the Lord does bless abundantly, still, the *"persecutions"* will come, because of the animosity of the world and the apostate Church. When one totally sells out to the Lord, such consecration will never be met by approval, but only sarcasm, and even hurt, if possible. Let no one think that such can be avoided or evaded. If the person truly follows the Lord, he will always travel against the current, and, therefore, be greatly opposed. The implication as given by Christ, proclaims that if *"persecutions"* do not come, it is a good sign that one is not truly following the Lord.

So, we have the second sign of such consecration, with the first being the priority of the spread of the Gospel.

The phrase, *"And in the world to come eternal life,"* is the second, and by far greater reward.

What did Jesus mean by *"the world to come?"*

He was speaking of the coming Kingdom Age, when all Believers shall rule and reign with Him for a thousand years on this earth (Rev. 20:1-6). This coming time will present a world as it has never been seen before. Jesus will rule Personally from Jerusalem, with Satan, along with all his minions of darkness, locked away in the bottomless pit. For the first time, the world will know peace and safety, and, as well, worldwide prosperity. War will cease, with even the nature of the animal kingdom to be changed (Isa. 11:6-7; 65:25).

Immediately after the *"thousand years are expired, Satan shall be loosed out of his prison."* For a short period of time he will be allowed the attempt of another overthrow, of which we are given very little information. The Scripture simply says, *"And fire came down from God out of Heaven and devoured them"* (Rev. 20:7-9).

At that time, Satan, along with all his followers, will be *"cast into the lake of fire and brimstone, . . . and shall be tormented day and night forever and ever"* (Rev. 20:10).

This will write *"finish"* for Satan, and his efforts to overthrow the *"Kingdom of God."* To be sure, this effort has resulted in the loss of uncounted millions of souls, along with suffering and heartache unparalleled. But at long last it is over!

At that time there will be *"a new Heaven and a new earth,"* meaning the purging of such, and not their destruction. The Greek word is *"parerchomi,"* and means *"to pass from one condition to another"* (Rev. 21:1).

At that time, the Lord will transfer His Capital City, *"The New Jerusalem,"* from Heaven to earth (Rev. 21:2-3).

At that time, *"There shall be no more curse: but the Throne of God and of the Lamb shall be in it; and His servants shall serve Him . . . .*

"And they shall reign forever and ever" (Rev. 22:3-5).

This is what is meant by *"the world to come."*

"Eternal Life" is something the Saint of God now has, and, in Truth, will have forever. It is the *"Life"* imparted by Christ at conversion, and is consequently *"eternal!"*

I do not know what the thoughts of Peter and the Disciples were upon hearing this. However, what Jesus promised them, so far eclipsed their petty thoughts, that no comparison is possible. Let it ever be understood that the Believer must not plan and then ask God's Blessings on the plan. He should instead let God plan, and the Blessings will automatically come, and of far greater magnitude than anyone could ever think possible.

(31) "BUT MANY THAT ARE FIRST SHALL BE LAST; AND THE LAST FIRST."

What did Jesus mean by this statement?

NOTES

The phrase, *"But many that are first shall be last,"* concerns Israel who was the first to receive the Gospel, but rejected it. However, they will ultimately accept Christ and the Gospel, which will be at the Second Coming. As such, they will be *"last."*

The phrase, *"And the last first,"* refers to those, the Gentiles, who were the last to be offered the Gospel, and the first to receive it. Consequently, the *"last are first."*

In effect, this has a far greater meaning than at first realized.

When Jesus comes the second time, most who will accompany Him will be those who were the *"last"* to be offered the Gospel, and the first to receive, i.e., the Church. However, and as well, all who believed Christ from the very beginning, including the Children of Abraham, will also be in that number. However, that number will be few, with the greater part being made up of the Church.

If one is to notice, Jesus used the word, *"many,"* meaning that most before the Church refused the Gospel, which pertains to the majority of Israel, and from its beginning.

(32) "AND THEY WERE IN THE WAY GOING UP TO JERUSALEM; AND JESUS WENT BEFORE THEM: AND THEY WERE AMAZED; AND AS THEY FOLLOWED, THEY WERE AFRAID. AND HE TOOK AGAIN THE TWELVE, AND BEGAN TO TELL THEM WHAT THINGS SHOULD HAPPEN UNTO HIM,"

The phrase, *"And they were in the way going up to Jerusalem,"* contains in the Greek Text little inference respecting the road, but rather the Lord and His Disciples, but more importantly the Mission that Jesus would carry out, the Redemption of mankind by dying on Calvary. This is the moment of which the Prophets had spoken, and to which everything had led in the great Plan of God. It was awful in more ways than one.

Israel had been raised up from the loins of Abraham for the express purpose of bringing the Messiah into the world. This they did, but with all hatred, and would refuse to recognize Him. As well, and even more horrible, they would kill the Lord of Glory.

Jerusalem was the city chosen by God in which to place His Name (II Chron. 6:6). And yet, this city which He had chosen would be the site of His murder, and by His Own people at that!

(As an aside, the road, and from all points, did lead *"up,"* because Jerusalem stands near the highest point of the backbone of Palestine, namely, the line of hills running north and south between the Mediterranean Sea and the Jordan River. The city cannot be approached from any direction without an ascent.) (Wuest).

The phrase, *"And Jesus went before them,"* speaks of an habitual practice. Jesus often walked alone, ahead of His Disciples. He no doubt did this in order that He may have solitude and privacy with the Father. The evidence points to the fact that Jesus lived a life of constant prayer. Not that He stayed on His knees constantly, but that He was in a constant state and attitude of prayer, as alluded to here.

The phrase, *"And they were amazed,"* speaks of His manner and even of His countenance. In other words, there was something about Him that spoke of impending doom.

Even though the Disciples little understood what He had been telling them respecting His coming Death, still, this Text proclaims the fact that they sensed around Him, and strongly, the spirit of this terrible moment. I think it was not so much in His Spirit the thought of dying, which produced this aura, but, instead, of His Own people doing this to Him, and thereby sealing their doom.

So, the word, *"amazed,"* lends credence to the thought that the Disciples, as well as the crowds going up to the Passover, were so struck by His manner that they did not disturb Him.

The phrase, *"And as they followed, they were afraid,"* speaks of not only the Disciples, but, as well, of all who were near Him.

As stated, the roads were filled with people going to Jerusalem for the Passover, and the occasion which normally would have been joyful, was, at this time, the very opposite! Even the people who did not personally know Him, sensed the awe of this moment.

There is no way that one could properly describe this time. The Heart of the Master was so heavy that it could not be hidden.

The phrase, *"And He took again the Twelve,"* refers to Him slowing His pace until the Disciples caught up with Him. The word, *"again,"* stresses that He will relate to them that which had been previously related.

The phrase, *"And began to tell them what things should happen unto Him,"* is an attempt to prepare them for the horror of these coming events. And yet, even though it would be plainly spoken, they would little understand!

(33) "SAYING, BEHOLD, WE GO UP TO JERUSALEM; AND THE SON OF MAN SHALL BE DELIVERED UNTO THE CHIEF PRIESTS, AND UNTO THE SCRIBES; AND THEY SHALL CONDEMN HIM TO DEATH, AND SHALL DELIVER HIM TO THE GENTILES:"

The phrase, *"Saying, Behold, we go up to Jerusalem,"* is proclaimed in the manner that says, *"Now is the time."* They had been to Jerusalem several times, but this time would be different.

The phrase, *"And the Son of Man shall be delivered unto the Chief Priests, and unto the Scribes,"* speaks of the betrayal by Judas unto these apostates. It is ironical and yet awful that the very ones, *"the Chief Priests and the Scribes,"* who should have been heralding His Name, instead, would kill Him. Such is religion!

The plural, *"Chief Priests,"* describes members of the high- priestly families who served in the Sanhedrin. This was the highest court of the Jews which met in Jerusalem. Traditionally it is said to have originated with the seventy Elders who assisted Moses (Num. 11:16-24). Ezra is supposed to have reorganized this body after the Exile. It appears that the High Priest presided over this ruling body.

The jurisdiction of the Sanhedrin was wide at the time of Christ. It exercised not only civil jurisdiction according to Jewish Law, but also criminal jurisdiction in some degree. It had administrative authority and could order arrests by its own officers of justice (Mat. 26:47; Mk. 14:43). It was empowered to judge cases which did not involve Capital Punishment (Acts 4-5). Capital cases required the confirmation of the Roman procurator (Jn. 18:31), hence, Jesus using the phrase, *"And shall deliver Him to the Gentiles."*

The Scribes were supposed to be scholars in the Mosaic Law. They were the originators of Synagogue service. Some of them even sat as members of the Sanhedrin (Mat. 16:21; 26:3).

Their duty was to preserve the Mosaic Law, and to apply it to daily life. Most of them were Pharisees, and they claimed the oral law was more important even than the written Law

(Mk. 7:5). By their efforts, religion was reduced to heartless formalism.

They were at times referred to as *"lawyers"* or *"teachers of the Law."*

The phrase, *"And they shall condemn Him to death,"* concerns the attitude of the Church of that day, to the Person and Ministry of Christ.

The word, *"condemn,"* means that they could not themselves carry out the act of execution, but would seek to get their sentence carried out by the Roman authorities, which they did! Even though the following statement is strong, still, I believe it to be true.

If the Time and Plan of God had been changed, and Jesus were to come presently, the modern Church, at least for the most part, would take the same attitude toward Him as their counterparts of 2,000 years ago. Religion is Satan's most fertile field. It alone has caused more people to die eternally lost than every vice in the world put together. Up beside religion, alcohol, drugs, immorality, etc., are but beginners.

As these Chief Priest and Scribes had reduced the Law of Moses to mere formalism, likewise, the modern Church has so added to, or taken away, from the Word of God, that its true meaning has long since been lost. Most worship has been reduced to ceremony and formalism. Most Churches have denied the veracity and power of the Holy Spirit, even those who claim to be Pentecostal. Psychology has replaced Him. Consequently, instead of being Preachers of the Word, many, if not most Preachers, are amateur psychologists.

In one of the major Pentecostal Denominations, the crowning achievement of education for their Ministers is a degree in psychology. The Word of God is given lip service, while the Holy Spirit and His Ways have all but been abandoned.

As a result, Pentecostals and Charismatics run hither and yon seeking for some type of demonstration, which is quick to be labeled as spiritual, and too often readily accepted. Prayer and the study of the Word are all but ignored. Much of the Charismatic community claims that prayer is by and large a wasted effort, with confession having taken its place. The convicting Power of the Holy Spirit is ridiculed if believed at all!

Hollywood has invaded the Church, with the *"star"* syndrome paramount, primarily through Television.

Even though what I say, I say with sorrow, I believe it to be true; *"The Church in America and Canada has never been weaker. Its only hope is Revival, and yet it is far from admitting such need!"* My prayer is that God will greatly move on hungry hearts and lives in order that they may intercede that Revival may truly come.

In spirit, and exactly as the Religious Leadership of old, the Church is either killing Christ, or ardently serving Him. There is no middle ground!

The phrase, *"And shall deliver Him to the Gentiles,"* proclaims the action that would follow their condemnation, in order that the Roman Governor, in this case Pilate, would carry out the execution, which he did!

(34) "AND THEY SHALL MOCK HIM, AND SHALL SCOURGE HIM, AND SHALL SPIT UPON HIM, AND SHALL KILL HIM: AND THE THIRD DAY HE SHALL RISE AGAIN."

The phrase, *"And they shall mock Him,"* refers to both Jews and Gentiles (Mat. 26:68; 27:29).

The phrase, *"And shall scourge Him,"* referred to the soldiers of Pilate carrying out this dreadful act (Jn. 19:1).

A scourge was a Roman implement for severe bodily punishment. It consisted of a handle with about a dozen leather cords with jagged pieces of bone or metal at each end to make the blow more painful and effective.

The victim was tied to a post and the blows were applied to the bare back and loins, and sometimes to the face and bowels. The flesh was cut in several places by each blow.

So hideous was the punishment that the victim often fainted, and some died under it.

The Jews permitted flogging up to forty stripes (Deut. 25:3). However, Jesus endured the Roman flogging, which had no limit. In other words, the one wielding the lash would continue to strike the victim until he was ordered to stop (Dake).

The phrase, *"And shall spit upon Him,"* constituted the highest form of insult. This was done by the Temple guards, and possibly even by members of the Sanhedrin (Mk. 14:65).

The phrase, *"And shall kill Him,"* spoke of His Death by Crucifixion, the most horrible form of death one could begin to imagine. Consequently, both the Jews and Gentiles were guilty of this horrid crime.

Why did they do such to Him?

They did so because their hearts were evil and wicked! The Jews did not know God, despite the fact that they spoke of Him constantly! So, instead of serving Him, they would *"kill Him!"*

The phrase, *"And the third day He shall rise again,"* plainly proclaims to the Disciples what will happen. Therefore, there was absolutely no excuse for their not understanding that He would be raised from the dead, and the exact time it would happen. However, and despite what He said, none believed that He would actually come from the dead. Thomas said he would not believe it, *"Except I shall see in His Hands the print of the nails, and put my finger into the print of the nails, and thrust my hand into His side"* (Jn. 20:25).

Why didn't they believe Him?

It goes back to Mark 6:52 and 8:17, where it says, *"For their heart was hardened."*

Their *"heart was hardened"* because self-will had taken the place of God's Will. In their minds, Jesus was going to be King of Israel, consequently overthrowing the Roman yoke, and they would be His Chief Lieutenants, and have great power and riches. This is evidenced even at this late date by the request of James and John, as recorded in verses 35-37.

Any time self-will is promoted, which of necessity abrogates God's Will, the hardened heart is the result! Consequently, the person will not believe anything that contradicts his self-will. Therefore, the Disciples little believed what Jesus said concerning His Death and Resurrection.

(35) "AND JAMES AND JOHN, THE SONS OF ZEBEDEE, COME UNTO HIM, SAYING, MASTER, WE WOULD THAT THOU SHOULDEST DO FOR US WHATSOEVER WE SHALL DESIRE."

The phrase, *"And James and John, the sons of Zebedee, come unto Him, saying, Master,"* proclaims a request that is totally opposite of what Jesus has just said. Matthew proclaims Salome, their mother, who evidently was traveling with them, as making the request (Mat. 20:20). Both accounts are correct, with the sons prompting her to do such!

The phrase, *"We would that Thou shouldest do for us whatsoever we shall desire,"* constitutes a most selfish request! Jesus was going to the Cross, while they had their thoughts centered on self-advancement in the Kingdom.

I think the attitude of the modern Church is little different, in that it is what *"we desire,"* instead of what *"He desires!"* This episode will proclaim the difference in the two.

The request reeks with selfish ambition. Even though Jesus had just made the most solemn announcement that could ever be made, they took little note, rather thinking of themselves. They would use Jesus to get what they wanted.

One can tell from the tenor of their request, that they knew Jesus had the power to do whatever was needed, consequently, they could not see Him being delivered to death.

(36) "AND HE SAID UNTO THEM, WHAT WOULD YE THAT I SHOULD DO FOR YOU?"

Even with a heavy heart, He will speak kindly unto them, even asking what they desired! How patient He is with us!

And yet, in the tenor of His question to them, one can sense that He knew the wrongness of what their request would be.

By the tone of His Voice, which the Text implies, they should have been warned of the wrongness of their desires. It should have been a rebuke, which it was intended to be, even though mild. But yet, self-will very seldom is slowed in its quest for gratification.

(37) "THEY SAID UNTO HIM, GRANT UNTO US THAT WE MAY SIT, ONE ON THY RIGHT HAND, AND THE OTHER ON THY LEFT HAND, IN THY GLORY."

The phrase, *"They said unto Him, Grant unto us that we may sit . . . ,"* refers to a position of honor, as well as power.

They are actually referring back to Peter's statement as to how they had left all to follow Him, and because of that, what would their reward be? (vss. 28-31).

The phrase, *"One on Thy right hand, and the other on Thy left hand,"* concerns the greatest positions of all! They wanted to get in their request first of all, even before the other Disciples. Consequently, the jockeying for position is taking place in His Own ranks.

This spirit, the political spirit of self-will, did not die with the request of James and John. Unfortunately, it plagues the Church even unto the present.

The modern Church is far more political than it is spiritual. That is unfortunate but true! Its members are little content to let the Lord promote them, but, instead, promote themselves, and too often use any and all means to carry out selfish ambition.

I remember years ago when Frances and I first began in Evangelistic Work. We were attending a particular meeting concerning the Denomination we were presently associated with.

I happened to pass a group of Preachers standing in the hall and overheard one say to another, *"I will vote for you and get several others to do so, if you will do thus and so,"* or words to that effect.

In this scenario, even though insignificant, one can readily see the jockeying for power, with little thought as to what the Lord wanted or desired.

In Truth, and with some exceptions, most offices in Religious Denominations are political, and, consequently, carry no spiritual content.

Considering how close to Jesus these men were, how could they be of such mind? This shows us that association, participation, and environment, do not guarantee a close walk with God. In fact, the association, participation, and environment could not have been better! But, still, self-will, even at this late date, prevailed.

As we have said elsewhere in these Volumes, Jesus died on Calvary to save man from sin and self. Many understand the sin problem, but they little understand the self problem. In fact, sin can be easily forgiven in a few moments time upon proper confession and repentance. However, *"self"* is not so easily subdued and placed in its proper position, i.e., in Christ.

One can easily see in the Disciples, that even though their sins had been washed, cleansed, and forgiven, still, they had a long way to go respecting *"self."*

The phrase, *"In Thy Glory,"* shows that they understood the coming Glory and Kingdom of the Messiah (Mat. 16:27-28). However, their timing, as with so many, was wrong.

They still had it in their minds that Jesus was about to set up His earthly Kingdom, and His statements concerning Death and Resurrection did not deter their thinking. If anything, His statement concerning being raised on the *"third day"* only fueled their wrong thoughts.

In fact, this Kingdom Age has not yet come, but will do so at the Second Coming (Rev. 19).

(38) "BUT JESUS SAID UNTO THEM, YE KNOW NOT WHAT YE ASK: CAN YE DRINK OF THE CUP THAT I DRINK OF? AND BE

BAPTIZED WITH THE BAPTISM THAT I AM BAPTIZED WITH?"

The phrase, *"But Jesus said unto them, Ye know not what ye ask,"* characterizes so many petitions made by Believers. Any time one prays after self-will instead of *"after the Spirit,"* one falls into this category (Rom. 8:1, 6).

Knowing how susceptible all of us are to the flesh, it is my practice when engaging in prayer to ask the Lord that the Holy Spirit may guide my petitions along with my worship that I may not pray wrongly.

The question, *"Can ye drink of the cup that I drink of?"*, implies that they will indeed have to do so.

The *"Cup"* in Scripture, signifies a man's portion, which is determined for him by God and sent to him.

The figure is derived from the ancient custom at feasts by which the ruler of the feast tempered the wine according to his own will, and appointed to each guest his own portion, which it was his duty to drink (Bickersteth).

The *"Cup"* spoken of by Jesus, was the Cross and all that it meant.

Even though the Disciples and all others, would not be asked to bear the Cross to this extent, still, it must be borne by all, at least those who follow Christ, as determined by the Lord.

The question, *"And be baptized with the Baptism that I am baptized with?"*, had to do with the Baptism of His sufferings. (The statement had nothing to do with Water Baptism, or the Baptism in the Holy Spirit.)

(39) "AND THEY SAID UNTO HIM, WE CAN. AND JESUS SAID UNTO THEM, YE SHALL INDEED DRINK OF THE CUP THAT I DRINK OF; AND WITH THE BAPTISM THAT I AM BAPTIZED WITHAL SHALL YE BE BAPTIZED:"

The phrase, *"And they said unto Him, We can,"* concerns itself with a brash reply.

Wuest says, *"The 'We can' of the Disciples, is a mere profession of moral courage, not a claim to spiritual power."*

In fact, all of them would desert Him at the Crucifixion. But yet, the later years would prove the veracity of the prediction of Jesus concerning them.

The phrase, *"And Jesus said unto them, Ye shall indeed drink of the Cup that I drink of; and with the Baptism that I am baptized withal shall ye be baptized,"* concerned not only the Disciples, but all who follow Christ, and for all time!

As we have stated, every Believer is appointed a *"Cup"* by the Lord, and of it they must drink. Always, it is a portion of some type of suffering.

In the drinking of this portion, the *"Baptism of suffering"* is brought into being.

These twin appointments for the Child of God are guaranteed, for Jesus said, *"Ye shall indeed drink . . . ."*

In the last few years, a major part of the Charismatic community has attempted to abrogate this statement by Christ, claiming that a proper confession will remove all difficulties and sufferings. Many have even gone so far as to remove any and all songs that speak of such, even songs of the Cross, from their repertoire. They claim that the Cross is *"past miseries,"* and is not applicable to the modern Believer.

Such shows a complete misunderstanding of the Scriptures, and, as well, of the Mission of Christ. As distasteful as they are, these things are necessary for every Believer. The primary objective is the eradication of self-supremacy, in favor of Christ, which can only be brought about by this method. Unfortunately, self-will cannot be confessed away. It is brought to its place only by this *"Baptism"* which is a result of the portion of the *"Cup"* determined by the Father.

While one certainly does not court such a thing, still, if there is proper consecration, the *"Cup"* is automatically appointed, with the *"Baptism"* automatically the result.

(40) "BUT TO SIT ON MY RIGHT HAND AND ON MY LEFT HAND IS NOT MINE TO GIVE: BUT IT SHALL BE GIVEN TO THEM FOR WHOM IT IS PREPARED."

The phrase, *"But to sit on My right and on My left hand is not Mine to give,"* proclaims such being given in accordance with the Father's disposition. In fact, Christ is indeed the appointed Distributor of all eternal rewards (II Tim. 4:8; Rev. 22:12); however, He seeks and determines the Father's Will in all that He does (Jn. 4:34).

Consequently, in making this statement, Jesus proclaims to His Disciples that even He does not seek to carry out His Will, but rather the Will of the Father. Therefore, it should not be *"Whatsoever we shall desire,"* but, instead, *"Whatsoever He shall desire!"*

NOTES

The phrase, *"But it shall be given to them for whom it is prepared,"* says several things:

1. Actually, someone will occupy these positions, and, in fact, the Father is preparing them for it, whomever they may be.

2. Jerome said, *"Our Lord does not say, 'Ye shall not sit,' lest He should put to shame these two. Neither does He say, 'Ye shall sit,' lest the others should be envious. But by holding out the price to all, He animates all to contend for it."*

3. As well, the Lord is careful to point out that he who humbles himself shall be exalted. In other words, this goal is not attained by the ways of the world, self-promotion, but, instead, by the road of humility, which is the very opposite (Mat. 23:12; Lk. 14:11).

(41) "AND WHEN THE TEN HEARD IT, THEY BEGAN TO BE MUCH DISPLEASED WITH JAMES AND JOHN."

The sons of Zebedee wanted to be first, and the Ten were unwilling to be last! Such was the energy of the carnal nature in all Twelve (Williams).

Political quests in the Church always lead to strife. Such is always the result of self-made plans.

The Believer is to let God plan for him, and then walk in the way laid out. Too many Believers make their own plans and then ask God to bless them. Such is not to be! Actually, this is what James and John were doing.

(42) "BUT JESUS CALLED THEM TO HIM, AND SAITH UNTO THEM, YE KNOW THAT THEY WHICH ARE ACCOUNTED TO RULE OVER THE GENTILES EXERCISE LORDSHIP OVER THEM; AND THEIR GREAT ONES EXERCISE AUTHORITY UPON THEM."

The phrase, *"But Jesus called them to Him, and saith unto them,"* expresses itself in a very serious discussion. If this spirit of self-will had continued, it would have destroyed the very fabric of all that Jesus taught. Quite possibly, this problem of self-aggrandizement as evidenced here by the Disciples, which is the opposite of the *"Servant Principle,"* is the greatest danger to the Body of Christ. Consequently, Jesus would call the Disciples close to Him in order to give them this most important teaching concerning the *"Servant Principle."*

The phrase, *"Ye know that they which are accounted to rule over the Gentiles exercise lordship over them,"* points out the way of the world.

So, Christ will show the Disciples the difference between that which is esteemed great in the Gentile world system, and the standard of greatness in the spiritual kingdom which He was inaugurating (Wuest).

The great danger in the Church has always been the tendency to bring the world's system into the Work of God, which can never be accepted by the Lord.

The phrase, *"And their great ones exercise authority upon them,"* speaks of pomp and circumstance, privilege and power, position and authority in the Gentile world, which was esteemed great, and the greatness of the individual came from his place in the system.

Jesus is teaching that Bible Christianity is the very opposite. Were that not the case, Jesus would have never chosen these men to be His Disciples. There was no greatness about them, at least as far as the world was concerned. However, the Lord does not choose on the basis of greatness, but rather on the basis of what He can do through an individual's life. In fact, none of what the world calls *"great"* can be used at all by the Lord. Should such a person come to Christ, all of this *"husk"* has to be stripped from Him before the Way of Christ can become evident in such a life.

This is what John the Baptist was speaking of when he spoke of Jesus Baptizing *"You with the Holy Ghost, and with fire."*

He then said, *"Whose fan is in His Hand, and He will thoroughly purge His floor, and gather His wheat into the garner; but He will burn up the chaff with unquenchable fire"* (Mat. 3:11-12).

The *"chaff"* He speaks of, is that which is of the world!

When He called Paul, who was probably the most educated ever called by the Lord, dependence on these things had to be stripped from him. Of that, Paul was speaking when he said, *"What things were gain to me, those I counted loss for Christ"* (Phil. 3:7).

This is the reason that *"Not many wise men after the flesh, not many mighty, not many noble, are called"* (I Cor. 1:26).

Paul was one of the few who would allow the Lord to strip him of all this *"wisdom after the flesh,"* and, consequently, use him mightily.

This is in no way meant to imply that God uses ignorance, etc. He doesn't! In fact, He can definitely use talent, education, ability, etc.,

exactly as He did in Paul. However, it must be totally dedicated to Him, consequently, led entirely by the Holy Spirit. Again we emphasize, the Holy Spirit will use nothing which pertains to the ways of the world, but only that which is of His origin and design (Zech. 4:6).

Through the years I have had many Christians speak to me of particular entertainers, etc., saying that if they were saved, how God could use them. They were implying that their talent or ability would be greatly used by the Lord, and because of such talent and ability.

However, such is totally unscriptural. In fact, God cannot use such talent and ability, etc., unless it is totally dedicated to Him, as we have stated! Unfortunately, the Church has repeatedly attempted to bring such into its bosom, but always without any spiritual results.

I recently witnessed on one of the major news programs over Television, a *"Christian rock group,"* who was supposedly winning many young people to their banner. After observing this group, as it was portrayed over Television, I might quickly state that while this group may be drawing young people to their banner, they are not drawing them to the Lord.

And how do I know that?

My statement is not based on musical preference, but rather the *"ways of the world."* This group, as all others of similar effort, attempts to copy the rock or rap groups of the world, using their mannerisms, style, etc. To be sure, the Lord will have none of it, with no work of the Spirit being performed in any heart and life. God's Ways are not man's ways, and the attempt to pull man's ways into God's Ways only leads to death (Prov. 16:25).

Consequently, this teaching by Christ concerning the ways of the world versus the *"Ways of God,"* is of supreme importance.

(43) "BUT SO SHALL IT NOT BE AMONG YOU: BUT WHOSOEVER WILL BE GREAT AMONG YOU, SHALL BE YOUR MINISTER:"

The phrase, *"But so shall it not be among you,"* proclaims the necessity of the Church in expelling all that which is not of God, but rather of the world.

The phrase, *"But whosoever will be great among you, shall be your minister,"* proclaims God's standard of greatness. It is, as we have stated, the *"Servant Principle."* The word, *"minister,"* in the Greek is *"diakonos,"* and means, "one who runs errands," or "a waiter on tables or other menial duties."

It does not mean literally that one is to do these things, but that one must be willing to do them, looking at no task for the Lord as menial. If one thinks he is too good to do such things, the Christlike spirit is obviously missing!

(44) "AND WHOSOEVER OF YOU WILL BE THE CHIEFEST, SHALL BE SERVANT OF ALL."

The phrase, "And whosoever of you will be the chiefest," proclaims that the Lord does not condemn the desire for greatness, but only the wrong way of it being achieved.

The phrase, "Shall be servant of all," shows in the Kingdom of God that the greatness of the individual comes from the lowly place he takes as a servant of all.

So, the Believer can desire to be great before other men, or before God. He cannot have both!

To be sure, if he takes the place of the "servant" as the Lord demands, in no way will he be acclaimed great or "chief" from those in the world, and, sadly, from most in the Church. However, with God, Who Alone matters, humility assures greatness.

(45) "FOR EVEN THE SON OF MAN CAME NOT TO BE MINISTERED UNTO, BUT TO MINISTER, AND TO GIVE HIS LIFE A RANSOM FOR MANY."

The phrase, "For even the Son of Man came not to be ministered unto," proclaims Christ as the example.

The phrase, "But to Minister, and to give His life a ransom for many," proclaims that the resplendent beauty of the Son of Man came from the fact that He as Very God of Very God, became incarnate in human flesh and a Servant to mankind (Wuest). What a rebuke this was to the personal ambitions of the Disciples, and what a rebuke it should be to us as well!

As "Minister" referred to the activity of serving, likewise, the word, "Servant," in verse 44, and pertaining to verse 45, is in the Greek "doulos," and means "a slave."

The word, "ransom," in the Greek is "lutron," and means "the price for redeeming, the ransom paid for slaves." It refers to substitution.

The Lord paid the ransom for sinners who could not pay it themselves, namely His Own Precious Blood. Consequently, Christ served

NOTES

as the greatest example of all respecting the "Servant Principle."

The phrase, "A ransom for many," does not teach "limited Atonement," as some claim. The word, "many," is here used in the sense of the whole of mankind, and for all time, which, of course, was "many."

It does not mean that Jesus died for some, but not for others. He died for the entirety of the world, and, as stated, for all time.

Consequently, He once again refers to the death He will die, which will be to set the captive free from sin. However, the Disciples little understood it at the time.

(46) "AND THEY CAME TO JERICHO: AND AS HE WENT OUT OF JERICHO WITH HIS DISCIPLES AND A GREAT NUMBER OF PEOPLE, BLIND BARTIMAEUS, THE SON OF TIMAEUS, SAT BY THE HIGHWAY SIDE BEGGING."

The phrase, "And they came to Jericho," denotes something of great significance which is to happen here. In effect, and as we shall see, it is the healing of Bartimaeus.

The phrase, "And as He went out of Jericho with His Disciples and a great number of people," proclaims this incident exactly as Matthew, "As they departed from Jericho" (Mat. 20:29-34).

Luke said, "As He was come nigh unto Jericho," (Lk. 18:35-43). Is there a discrepancy?

No! There is no discrepancy. Some have claimed that two different incidents entirely are recorded, and this may be correct. However, it is probable that all, Matthew, Mark, and Luke, are speaking of the same incident.

As well, Matthew mentions "two blind men," while Mark and Luke mention only one.

The explanation could be as follows:

1. Only one, Bartimaeus, is mentioned by Mark and Luke, because in some way he stands out. However, this does not mean that the other one as recorded by Matthew, was not present, or healed. In fact he was!

Many times, individuals when giving an account of a particular incident, will highlight certain things, while leaving other things out entirely. This happens constantly, and with purpose. However, it does not mean that the situations not mentioned, did not happen. In fact they did happen, but were not mentioned for some particular reason.

The way it is given by all three is the way the Holy Spirit desired that it be given, and for purpose and reason. Perhaps the reason in Matthew, as it spoke of two blind men, was because Jesus was portrayed in that account as King. As such, the two could have represented the Hebrew nation in its two divisions of Israel and Judah. Their both receiving sight could illustrate the light that will ultimately shine on them when they accept Jesus as their Lord and Saviour at the Second Coming, when He will then be crowned *"KING OF KINGS AND LORD OF LORDS!"* (Rev. 19:16).

2. Luke just simply made mention that they were *"Coming nigh unto Jericho,"* and then gave the account of the healing of the *"blind man."* His account merely states that it was in Jericho this great Miracle took place, and not the location, whether coming in or going out.

If one is to notice, Mark mentions both. He spoke of them coming to Jericho, as Luke, and then he gave the place of the healing, *"As He went out of Jericho,"* which Luke did not give. As stated, there is no discrepancy.

The phrase, *"Blind Bartimaeus, the son of Timaeus,"* suggests, and because of its careful description, that Bartimaeus may have come from a family of some note. Of course, there is no way this can be ascertained, but we do know that Mark's careful description was not without purpose.

More than likely, Peter informed him of this situation, as of most of the experiences in this Book. Consequently, there was a reason he gave to Mark the name of the father of Bartimaeus.

The phrase, *"Sat by the highway side begging,"* denotes the low station in life to which he had fallen.

If, in fact, it was true that Bartimaeus came from a family of note, he would serve as a perfect example of the Fall of mankind. As we have repeatedly stated, every Miracle performed by Christ was meant not only to meet the need of the person or persons involved, but, as well, to serve as a teaching vehicle or example to the whole of humanity.

God was the Father of Adam, and, as obvious, of great note. Nevertheless, man fell from this lofty position, and was reduced to spiritual blindness, and, in effect, the low station of a beggar. Consequently, Bartimaeus epitomizes the whole of humanity.

NOTES

Some would object to such a comparison, claiming that much of mankind is far above the station of *"begging."* However, the richest and most educated of men, can be labeled as none other than *"beggars"* in comparison to what man was before the Fall. Man was intended to be a *"Son of God,"* but due to the Fall, is now a *"son of Adam"* (Gen. 5:3), and, as such, encumbered with all the terrible baggage of that terrible state. Consequently, the term, *"beggar,"* as affixed to *"blind Bartimaeus,"* is an apt description of man in his fallen state, and irrespective of his financial, social, or educational status.

(47) "AND WHEN HE HEARD THAT IT WAS JESUS OF NAZARETH, HE BEGAN TO CRY OUT, AND SAY, JESUS, THOU SON OF DAVID, HAVE MERCY ON ME."

The phrase, *"And when he heard that it was Jesus of Nazareth,"* does not proclaim to us how he heard, but that he did hear. He probably heard the great commotion of the crowd, and asked someone who it was! They would have said, *"Jesus of Nazareth."*

The name, *"Joshua of Nazareth,"* is the name Bartimaeus would have heard because that is the Hebrew derivative of *"Jesus"* which is Greek.

Joshua, the namesake of Christ, came through this very area about 1500 years before. At that time, God would perform a Miracle and open Jordan. Now He will open the eyes of a blind beggar.

Then, Joshua would defeat every enemy on the soil of the Promised Land. Now, Jesus will defeat *"the enemy,"* of men's souls, Satan himself.

Then, Joshua took the land, and it became the habitation of God's people. Now, Jesus will take Salvation, and it too will become the habitation of God's people.

Then, the physical battle was won! Now, the spiritual battle will be won!

(There were many named *"Jesus,"* or *"Joshua,"* at that time, therefore, Jesus was designated by *"Nazareth"* being affixed to His Name, as that was the place of His upbringing.)

How did Bartimaeus know about Jesus? This is the only time it is recorded that Jesus visited Jericho. However, no doubt, as His fame spread throughout all of Israel, the great Power of Christ came to the ears of Bartimaeus. He no doubt asked, and thinking of his own terrible situation, *"Can He open the eyes of the blind?"*

Of course, the answer would have been in the affirmative! From that moment, whenever it was, he no doubt dreamed of the time Jesus would pass this way. As well, he no doubt prayed extensively for this coming moment. To be sure, God would answer this prayer, as He will answer all prayers of such desperation.

The Scripture says that he *"heard!"* What would have happened, had he not heard? The answer is obvious.

What about the hundreds of millions in the world today, who have not had the privilege to *"hear?"* Whereas Jesus could only be in one place at one time during His earthly sojourn, now, He is everywhere, at least where men will tell about Him. Paul said, *"How shall they hear without a Preacher?"* (Rom. 10:14).

Consequently, it is the task of every Believer, with none excluded, to do all within his power, whether through prayer, giving, and witnessing, that others may hear about Jesus. As the blind beggar of so long ago, they too deserve that opportunity!

The phrase, *"He began to cry out,"* means in the Greek that he kept crying over and over to Jesus.

This is a *"cry"* from the soul of this man. In the *"cry"* is desperation, because he senses that this will be the only opportunity he will ever have.

Let it ever be known that anyone who will *"cry"* as Bartimaeus cried, will be heard by the Lord.

The phrase, *"And say, Jesus, Thou Son of David,"* was a title that referred to the Messiah. All Jews thought of David as their father, and of the Messiah as the Son of David in a special sense (Wuest). So, Bartimaeus had already made up his mind that anyone who could perform the Miracles they said Jesus was performing, had to be the *"Messiah."* He was right! He knew it, even though a blind beggar, but the Religious Leaders of Israel did not know.

The phrase, *"Have mercy on me,"* in the Greek indicates that he desired Jesus to heal him at once. The idea is that he felt that Christ may not pass this way again, and if he was to receive his eyesight, it had to be now.

The horror of living in darkness cannot even be remotely understood unless one has experienced such. The knowledge that Jesus could do it, seems to have been implanted in the

beggar's mind. The problem, in his imprisoned world of darkness, was to get to Him.

(48) "AND MANY CHARGED HIM THAT HE SHOULD HOLD HIS PEACE: BUT HE CRIED THE MORE A GREAT DEAL, THOU SON OF DAVID, HAVE MERCY ON ME."

The phrase, *"And many charged him that he should hold his peace,"* proclaims the crowd attempting to stop him from getting to Jesus. The word, *"charged,"* is strong, meaning to *"censure severely."* In other words, they were telling him, and in no uncertain terms, to *"shut up!"*

Why were they doing this?

Perhaps they felt that Jesus, the Great Prophet, should not be troubled by this beggar. However, if these were, in fact, their thoughts, they completely misunderstood Christ and His Mission.

Perhaps at the moment other things were demanding His attention, and they felt the cry of Bartimaeus was an intrusion.

At any rate, they, as us, should learn a lesson from the quest of this blind beggar.

The phrase, *"But he cried the more a great deal,"* proclaims their demand as having the opposite effect on him. The One Who could open his eyes was within shouting distance, and he had absolutely no intention of letting this moment pass.

This should be an example to all, inasmuch as most of the time when one truly seeks the Lord, there will be very little encouragement, if any! The crowd will mostly say, and for any number of reasons, that we cannot have that for which we are seeking. So, if Bartimaeus had listened to the crowd, he would have remained blind. Likewise, if we listen to those who tell us we cannot reach Christ, and for whatever reason, our need will never be met. However, if we take a lesson from this blind beggar, we can, as he, receive what is needed.

The phrase, *"Thou Son of David, have mercy on me,"* proclaims such being cried with even more vigor!

He did not change his petition, because a change was not necessary. The rich young ruler called Him *"Good Master,"* and did not receive what he asked for, and because he felt the price was too high.

The beggar called Him *"Son of David,"* and received everything for which he asked.

The former labeled Jesus only as a Teacher, while the latter labeled Him as *"God"*; and in fact continued to do it, and did not care who heard him.

(49) "AND JESUS STOOD STILL, AND COMMANDED HIM TO BE CALLED. AND THEY CALL THE BLIND MAN, SAYING UNTO HIM, BE OF GOOD COMFORT, RISE; HE CALLETH THEE."

The phrase, *"And Jesus stood still,"* is a beautiful and precious statement. Bartimaeus had Faith, as is evident in his continued petition. Even though Jesus was on His way to Calvary, which was the very reason for which He came, and which was the culmination of the Great Plan of God regarding the Redemption of humanity, still, on this journey which had taken so very long, and was now coming to a climax, He would stop! This shows us the great power of Faith in God. This man, a blind beggar, exhibiting his Faith, would cause Christ to stop, even though He was on His way to redeem the whole of humanity.

Among all the lessons we should learn from this episode, the lesson of Faith in God boldly stands out. No one could be in a worse position than blind Bartimaeus! It seems that very few people cared if he lived or died. He certainly had nothing going for him, except one thing — his Faith in Jesus; and that is enough!

There are very few in worse shape than this man. And yet, because of his Faith, which is expressed in his determination, he received everything for which he asked. Cannot we do the same?

The phrase, *"And commanded him to be called,"* constitutes the greatest moment in the life of this blind beggar. Everything he had dreamed about, no doubt praying himself to sleep many nights, is about to be realized. The One Who spoke the worlds into existence, now sends for him!

The phrase, *"And they call the blind man, saying unto him, Be of good comfort, rise; He calleth thee,"* proclaims the crowd obeying Christ, and giving the good news to Bartimaeus.

Someone has said, *"Defeat is an orphan, while victory has many fathers."* Before Jesus recognized him, the crowd had no interest, but that he *"shut up!"* Now that Jesus has recognized him, the mood of the crowd changes.

In Truth, the Message, *"Be of good comfort, rise; He calleth thee,"* should be the Message of every single Believer to every lost soul. Sadly,

most of the world has a misconception of God. They do not realize that His purpose is to bring *"comfort,"* and, as well, He will *"pick up,"* i.e., *"rise,"* all found in His *"call."*

While it is true that tomorrow He will be the Judge, still, at the present He is the Saviour. Consequently, His *"call"* is for healing, health, happiness, joy, and peace.

(50) "AND HE, CASTING AWAY HIS GARMENT, ROSE, AND CAME TO JESUS."

The two words, *"And he,"* refers to receiving the Message as given by Christ, meaning that of all the people in Israel, the attention of Jesus was solely upon him.

The phrase, *"Casting away his garment,"* has a far greater meaning than just the fact of a garment being left behind.

It is said that many beggars in those days used this outer garment for several purposes. First of all, this type of garment denoted their status as a beggar. As well, it was removed during the day, and used somewhat as a receptacle for gifts, as it was positioned on the ground accordingly. At night it was used for a covering.

When Bartimaeus *"cast away"* this garment, he was, in effect, saying that he would no longer need it. He was this sure of his healing! One can only shout *"Hallelujah!"*

The single word, *"rose,"* actually means that he *"leaped up,"* upon hearing of the call of Christ.

The phrase, *"And came to Jesus,"* was the greatest short distance he had ever traversed. His joy must have known no bounds!

(51) "AND JESUS ANSWERED AND SAID UNTO HIM, WHAT WILT THOU THAT I SHOULD DO UNTO THEE? THE BLIND MAN SAID UNTO HIM, LORD, THAT I MIGHT RECEIVE MY SIGHT."

The phrase, *"And Jesus answered and said unto him,"* refers to the cry of, *"Thou Son of God, have mercy on me."*

The question, *"What wilt thou that I should do unto thee?",* constitutes a question that is open-ended, and could apply to anything. In other words, Jesus is saying to him, *"Whatever you need, that I will do!"*

Quite possibly, and more than likely, Jesus knew exactly what he wanted and needed, but would ask this question in order to bring Faith to its highest pinnacle.

The phrase, *"The blind man said unto Him, Lord, that I might receive my sight,"* constitutes what he was (blind) and what he wanted (sight). He minced no words!

I wonder what his thoughts were when he answered Christ? His heart must have been racing out of his breast. Quite possibly, and because of the anticipation of the moment, his breath may have been coming in short gasps.

The implication in the Greek is, that he had at one time been able to see. He now desires to *"recover his sight."*

The word, *"Lord,"* is *"Rabboni,"* in the Greek Text, and means *"My Master."* It was a term of reverent respect, and in no way meant to lessen his belief in Jesus as the Messiah.

(52) "AND JESUS SAID UNTO HIM, GO THY WAY; THY FAITH HATH MADE THEE WHOLE. AND IMMEDIATELY HE RECEIVED HIS SIGHT, AND FOLLOWED JESUS IN THE WAY."

The phrase, *"And Jesus said unto him,"* should be an example of what Jesus says to all! To those who believe, and despite their past or present circumstances, His Words are always Words of help and healing. What a wonderful Lord we serve.

The phrase, *"Go thy way; thy Faith hath made thee whole,"* was Jesus' answer to the plea of Bartimaeus.

It is said that the word, *"whole,"* in the Greek is in the perfect tense, and, consequently, speaks of a permanent cure. In other words, whatever had caused Bartimaeus to become blind, would never return. He would retain his eyesight until the day he died.

As well, the word, *"whole,"* in the Greek is *"sozo,"* and means *"to save."* It is used either of physical healing or of spiritual Salvation (Wuest). Consequently, the implication is that Bartimaeus was not only healed, but saved as well!

Dake says, *"Personal Faith will always be rewarded, regardless of what the need is or how impossible it seems beyond fulfillment (Mat. 17:20; 21:21-22; Mk. 9:23; 11:22-24).*

"Men receive 'according to' Faith (Mat. 9:29). No instance is given in Scripture where True Faith has been exercised for anything promised by God and the answer has been withheld by God."

As an aside, we should add that *"personal Faith"* must always be according to the Will and Word of God. As well, sometimes it is His *"Will"* but not His *"Wisdom!"*

NOTES

The phrase, *"And immediately he received his sight,"* means exactly what it said, that his sight returned instantly. I wonder what he did upon the opening of those blinded eyes?

How many years he had remained in this condition, we do not know. However, the joy that filled his heart upon his eyesight being immediately restored, must have known no bounds. One can well imagine, but imagine only, such joy!

As well, it is very similar to the moment a person turns to Christ. Instantly the load of sin is lifted, with the terrible guilt instantly removed. Possibly the Miracle of Jesus opening blinded eyes, is the greatest example of the born-again experience.

The phrase, *"And followed Jesus in the way,"* is said by some to mean that he followed Jesus to Jerusalem, and became an ardent Disciple in the Early Church. If this is correct, it might explain Mark and Luke only mentioning him, while not speaking of the second blind man who was healed, which Matthew does mention.

The song says:

VERSE 1:

"Love Divine, all loves excelling,
"Joy of Heaven, to earth come down;
"Fix in us Thy humble dwelling;
"All thy faithful mercies crown.

CHORUS:

"Jesus, Thou art all compassion,
"Pure, unbounded love Thou art;
"Visit us with Thy Salvation;
"Enter every trembling heart."

VERSE 2:

"Come, Almighty to deliver,
"Let us all Thy life receive;
"Suddenly return, and never,
"Never more Thy Temple leave:

CHORUS:

"Thee we would be always blessing,
"Serve Thee as Thy host above,
"Pray, and praise Thee without ceasing,
"Glory in Thy perfect love."

CHAPTER 11

(1) "AND WHEN THEY CAME NIGH TO JERUSALEM, UNTO BETHPHAGE AND BETHANY, AT THE MOUNT OF OLIVES, HE SENDETH FORTH TWO OF HIS DISCIPLES,"

The phrase, *"And when they came nigh to Jerusalem,"* concerns the last time they will visit this city before the Crucifixion. It must have been with heavy heart that Jesus drew near.

Jesus was a King, and not just a King, but, *"The King."* And yet, precious few there recognized Him as such! However, as is the manner of God, the opportunity will be given Israel, as recorded in this Chapter, to recognize her King. It is called the *"Triumphant Entry."* Even though the Person of Christ would be triumphant as always, still, it would be anything but such for Israel. They would deny their King, and, consequently, go to their doom. To accept Christ is to accept life; to refuse Christ is to refuse life, and, therefore, to accept death!

The phrase, *"Unto Bethphage and Bethany,"* concerned two villages close to Jerusalem, east of the city. They would have been on the way from Jericho to Jerusalem, a distance of about seventeen miles. From Jericho to Jerusalem was about a day's journey. The road is winding, through a hilly, rugged, even desolate area. It was often plagued by robbers and bandits. But today, the Son of God would traverse its distance.

"Bethphage" means *"house of figs,"* while *"Bethany"* means *"house of dates."* As stated, they were very close together, approximately a mile separating the two. It appears from John 12:1, that Jesus arrived in this area *"six days before the Passover,"* and, consequently, His Crucifixion.

Bethany was the home of Jesus' beloved friends, Mary, Martha, and Lazarus. Its most central role in the Gospel history is as the place of Jesus' Anointing, as Mark will later relate (Mk. 14:3-9).

The phrase, *"At the Mount of Olives,"* figures a very prominent place in the Gospel narrative. It is a small range of four summits, the highest being about 3,000 feet. This high summit overlooks Jerusalem and the Temple Mount from the East across the Kidron Valley and the Pool of Siloam.

It was thickly wooded in Jesus' day, rich in olives which occasioned its name. It was stripped of trees when Titus, the Roman General, invaded Jerusalem. On a clear day, its summit can be seen from the Jordan River near Jericho, where tradition says Jesus was baptized, a distance of approximately twenty miles.

NOTES

This Mount is the site of Gethsemane, and from its tallest peak the place of the Ascension of Jesus, and where Zechariah said He would touch down at the Second Coming (Zech. 14:4). It is also the area from which Jesus made the Triumphant Entry into Jerusalem.

Approximately a thousand years before, after Solomon completed the Temple, the Mount of Olives was famous for observing this beautiful edifice.

It is said that pilgrims, travelers, and merchants, on their way into the city, would purposely spend the night on Olivet, in order that they may see the rising of the sun the following morning. As the sun rose in the East, it would burst above Olivet, casting its rays on the two Temple columns, which were made of copper, and polished brightly. The sun's rays striking these pillars, it is said, produced an amazing array of light. Now the Greatest Light of all, the Lord Jesus Christ, of which the other was only a symbol, will grace its summit.

The phrase, *"He sendeth forth two of His Disciples,"* does not tell us which Two, but many suppose it was Peter and John, because a little after this Christ sent these Two to prepare for the Passover. Their Mission will pertain to the Triumphant Entry.

From that day until the present, He is still *"Sending forth His Disciples,"* to tell the world of another Triumphant Entry soon to come, the Second Coming of Jesus Christ. It is the Greatest Story ever told!

(2) "AND SAITH UNTO THEM, GO YOUR WAY INTO THE VILLAGE OVER AGAINST YOU: AND AS SOON AS YE BE ENTERED INTO IT, YE SHALL FIND A COLT TIED, WHEREON NEVER MAN SAT; LOOSE HIM, AND BRING HIM."

The phrase, *"And saith unto them, Go your way into the village over against you,"* probably referred to Bethphage, because it was nearer.

The phrase, *"And as soon as ye be entered into it, ye shall find a colt tied,"* refers to a Word of Knowledge given to Jesus by the Holy Spirit, because the Master would not have known this otherwise (I Cor. 12:8).

All nine Gifts of the Spirit were possessed by Christ, and due to the Advent of the Holy Spirit, can be had by the modern Believer as well (Acts 2:1-4; I Cor. 12:8-10). However, I think no one can say that these Gifts of the Spirit work in the lives of Believers, as in Christ, not even remotely so! He walked so after the Spirit, that the Communion was constant. As well, He always did the Father's Will, which even the most consecrated Believer cannot claim.

The phrase, *"Whereon never man sat,"* presents another unique situation in the Life and Ministry of Jesus.

He was born of one who *"did not know a man,"* and was buried where *"no one was ever yet laid."* Now He will ride an animal, *"whereon never man sat"* (Wuest).

The phrase, *"Loose him, and bring him,"* means it is to be done at once!

Matthew not only mentions the colt, but, as well, the mother of the animal. Mark, Luke, and John, only mention the one animal. According to Matthew, the mother of the colt will accompany them. The two animals spoken of by Matthew, could well have represented both Israel and the Gentiles. The mother of the colt, which probably trod alongside, would denote Israel who would not accept Christ.

The unbroken *"colt"* ridden by Christ, could denote the Gentile Church, which would, in effect, accept Christ.

Inasmuch as Matthew presented Jesus as King, the mentioning of both animals would have been appropriate for him, whereas it would not have served any consequence with Mark, Luke, and John, due to the manner in which they presented Christ in their Gospels. (Matthew presented Jesus as King; Mark as Servant; Luke as Man; while John presented Him as God. However, there would have been some of all in each presentation.)

(3) "AND IF ANY MAN SAY UNTO YOU, WHY DO YE THIS? SAY YE THAT THE LORD HATH NEED OF HIM; AND STRAIGHTWAY HE WILL SEND HIM HITHER."

The question, *"And if any man say unto you, Why do ye this?",* represents the possible contingency of such, which did happen. The idea being that if the owners objected, the Lord would not use the animal.

If one is to notice, there is a strong authority presented by Christ throughout the entirety of this scenario. Jesus, at least at this time, is functioning as King, and Kings little ask permission. Consequently, there is no evidence that preparation had been made at all for the borrowing of this animal, but only the

sudden request, with the instant approval by the owners.

The phrase, *"Say ye that the Lord hath need of him,"* represents a remarkable statement.

Is it proper to say that presently, the Lord *"has need"* of certain things in order that His Work be carried out?

As God, the Lord needs nothing! However, inasmuch as He has allowed Believers to be a part of His Work on earth, in that context, He does *"need"* certain things.

For the Holy Spirit to do what must be done, and I speak of the taking of the Gospel to the world, the Lord *"needs"* consecration on the part of Believers. As well, He *"needs"* Believers to exhibit their Faith, trusting Him for the Work to be done.

In the consecration of Believers, He *"needs"* Believers to pray and intercede on behalf of the lost. As well, He *"needs"* Believers to give generously of their income in order that this Work be accomplished.

So, the scenario of this *"colt"* and the manner in which Jesus secured him, is to be a lesson to all Believers everywhere, and for all time.

The phrase, *"And straightway he will send him hither,"* proclaims the Lord knowing in advance that the owners of this animal would immediately acquiesce to the request of the two Disciples.

Do all Believers obey that quickly?

(4) "AND THEY WENT THEIR WAY, AND FOUND THE COLT TIED BY THE DOOR WITHOUT IN A PLACE WHERE TWO WAYS MET; AND THEY LOOSE HIM."

The phrase, *"And they went their way,"* proclaims the obedience of the Disciples, and, as well, *"their way,"* which was *"His Way."* To go *"His Way,"* always brings victory, although greatly opposed by Satan.

The phrase, *"And found the colt tied by the door without in a place where two ways met,"* referred to an intersection where two streets crossed. The *"colt"* was exactly where Jesus said he would be.

The phrase, *"And they loose him,"* concerns them doing exactly what Jesus had said!

They did not at first ask permission, but proceeded to take the animal, when they were then questioned by the owners.

No! Jesus would not have allowed the animal to have been taken without permission.

However, the Disciples were instructed in this manner, because Jesus knew the owners would be nearby and would give permission. The entire scenario speaks of a prearranged plan, which it was — arranged by the Holy Spirit.

This is the reason that Believers should seek the Lord incessantly, in order that they may know His Mind. To follow and obey Him is an exciting journey! To be sure, He continues to do the same presently, as He did 2,000 years ago.

Back in about 1970, if I remember the year correctly, we applied to the FCC (Federal Communications Commission) in Washington, for the right to purchase a bankrupt radio station in Baton Rouge, Louisiana. At that time, Baton Rouge had no Christian Radio whatsoever, and I felt the Lord wanted this Station in the city, which would broadcast Gospel constantly.

The securing of the Station was not easy or simple, due to Satan doing everything possible to hinder all along the way. However, it eventually became ours, which proved to be a blessing to the greater Baton Rouge area. However, one particular episode in the securing of the Station stands out, which is somewhat similar to the Disciples sent to fetch the colt.

The FCC had ruled that all who desired the Station could bid on it, with the highest bidder being awarded the Station. There were to be only two bidders, myself and another man, who desired to air a rock n' roll format. We were to meet at the office of a particular lawyer in the city, who had been appointed as the referee by the FCC. We were to meet at 10 a.m.

That morning in prayer, the Lord spoke to my heart, and told me to go to the bank and get the sum of $250,000, which I did. It was not in cash, but it was in C.D.'s, which were as good as cash.

At that time, the Lord did not tell me why I was to do this, but just to do it. I obeyed, going to the bank and securing the funds, putting the Certificates in my inside coat pocket. No one knew I had these funds, not even my lawyer.

At 10 a.m. sharp, several of us met at the appointed place. A lawyer from Washington was present, representing our side, as well as the lawyer I had secured from Baton Rouge. As well, the other man was there to bid against me, and, of course, the Referee was also present.

For some unknown reason, which I think was orchestrated by the Holy Spirit, the Referee had

NOTES

ruled that the bid could go no higher than $80,000.

As the bidding began, both of us quickly arrived at the $80,000 level, when the bidding stopped, as instructed. (I think that was the amount the Station owed its creditors, etc.)

Now we faced an impasse, with both of us bidding the same amount, with the question quickly asked as to how the deadlock could be broken?

The lawyers began to propose several things, when the Spirit of the Lord spoke to me again, and told me to ask the Referee to make the other bidder prove that he, in fact, had $80,000.

I immediately ventured the question, with the other bidder quickly becoming uncomfortable. He went on to state that he was certain that he could borrow the money, should the bid be awarded to him.

I then remonstrated by saying, *"Your Honor, what happens if he, in fact, cannot borrow the money?"* I then went on to say, *"It seems to me, that whoever is awarded the bid today, in order to purchase this Station, should be able to prove that he has the money to do so!"*

The Judge thought a moment, and then surmised that my statement was correct. The man obviously could not prove at that moment that he could secure these funds, with me now knowing why the Holy Spirit had told me to secure these funds that morning, bringing them with me, while telling no one about it.

All the time, both my lawyers were whispering in my ear, telling me to shut up! As stated, they did not know what I knew, that I had the funds in my inside coat pocket.

My own lawyers were quickly growing exasperated with me, with one of them saying to me, *"If you don't be quiet, we are going to lose this Station."*

I kept wondering when the Referee (the Judge) would turn from the other bidder to me, asking me if I could produce the funds?

Finally it happened! The Referee looked at me and stated, *"You have been questioning this man about his ability to get the funds, should he be awarded the bid; however, can you produce the funds, or proof that you can obtain them?"*

I heard one of my lawyers groan, with the room growing deathly quiet.

I reached in my inside coat pocket, pulled out the C.D.'s totaling $250,000, and laid them on the table. For a moment you could have heard a pin drop. The Referee, plus one of my lawyers, picked up the negotiable instruments, looked carefully at them, and realized they were C.D.'s, and, consequently, were the same as cash.

My lawyer then began to jump up and down, saying, *"Your Honor, we have the money, as is obvious, and you must award us the bid!"*

The Referee turned to the opposing bidder and said, *"Can you match this?"*

Of course, he could not!

I remember him grabbing his briefcase, saying, *"I am in the wrong business,"* and then suddenly leaving the room.

The Referee turned to me and said, *"I award you the Station."*

We operated WLUX for over twenty years, constantly proclaiming the Gospel of Jesus Christ to the city of Baton Rouge and surrounding areas. It was sold in 1995 to another Church in Baton Rouge, after which the Lord had given us a twenty-four hour F.M. Station (WJFM-FM). (The A.M. Station was a day-timer, with the F.M. Station giving around-the-clock coverage.)

If the Lord had not spoken to my heart that morning about securing those funds, there is a possibility I would not have been awarded the Station. However, to follow Him, is to guarantee success. Consequently, the colt was secured, and the Radio Station was secured, all because of leading and direction by the Lord.

(5) "AND CERTAIN OF THEM THAT STOOD THERE SAID UNTO THEM, WHAT DO YE, LOOSING THE COLT?"

The phrase, *"And certain of them that stood there said unto them,"* represents the owners, as Luke identifies them (Lk. 19:33).

The question, *"What do ye, loosing the colt?",* represents, as stated, that no prior arrangements had been made.

I wonder what the thoughts of these men were, when they saw the Disciples taking the colt, who they probably did not know? Little did they realize that this animal which belonged to them, was about to be used by the Creator of all the ages. How blessed and honored they were!

As well, how blessed and honored anyone is, who is privileged to have a part in the Work of God.

Would they have been privileged to have loaned their colt to the Chief Priests, who crucified Christ?

I think the answer to that would be obvious! And yet, millions of Believers support that which is not of God, and which, in effect, opposes the Lord.

We need to know to whom we are loaning our *"colt!"*

(6) AND THEY SAID UNTO THEM EVEN AS JESUS HAD COMMANDED: AND THEY LET THEM GO."

The phrase, *"And they said unto them even as Jesus had commanded,"* were the words, *"The Lord hath need of him."*

The phrase, *"And they let them go,"* respects an instant obedience.

This shows that they knew Jesus, although possibly not being personally acquainted with Him. His Name, Fame, and Reputation, had spread throughout all of Israel, causing all to know Him.

There is no record that the owners questioned the Disciples further, not actually knowing for what purpose the animal was to be used. As stated, how honored they were to be privileged to have a part in the *"Triumphant Entry."* How privileged all of us are to have a part in the Work of God.

(7) "AND THEY BROUGHT THE COLT TO JESUS, AND CAST THEIR GARMENTS ON HIM; AND HE SAT UPON HIM."

The phrase, *"And they brought the colt to Jesus,"* shows that the Disciples did not, at least at this time, know the purpose of the animal. Consequently, if the owners had asked them, they could not have given an answer beyond *"The Lord has need of him!"* What that *"need"* was, they would not at that time have known.

The phrase, *"And cast their garments on him,"* proclaims Jesus finally telling them He is to ride the animal. Even now they probably did not know why He would ride him.

The Disciples probably took extra garments they had brought with them, placing them on the animal's back.

The phrase, *"And He sat upon him,"* proclaims the beginning of the *"Triumphant Entry."*

Several things should be noted:

1. This was in fulfillment of the Prophecy given by Zechariah. *"Rejoice greatly, O daughter of Zion; shout, O daughter of Jerusalem: behold, thy King cometh unto thee: He is just, and having Salvation; lowly, and riding upon an ass, and upon a colt the foal of an ass"* (Zech. 9:9).

Had Israel accepted her King at that time, the Kingdom of God would have come, physically, materially, as well as spiritually.

Inasmuch as Israel rejected her King, the *"Times of the Gentiles"* were lengthened, whereas they would have been brought to an end had Jesus been accepted. As a result, the world, and for some 2,000 years, has been plagued by war, poverty, famine, plagues, and pestilence. As well, Israel has suffered horribly so, which all could have been avoided upon acceptance of Jesus.

When Jesus comes again, which He certainly shall, Israel will then accept Him, with the *"Times of the Gentiles"* coming to an end, with Israel finally taking her place as the conduit of the Blessings of God, which the Lord intended from the beginning (Lk. 21:24).

2. Jesus sitting on the back of this colt, the foal of an ass, portrayed to any and all, that His intentions were peaceful, and, consequently, carried no threat, as He was later accused (Lk. 23:2).

In fact, in times of old, the riding of an *"ass"* denoted leadership and great importance (Jud. 5:10; 10:4). However, all of this changed with the advent of Alexander the Great, about 300 years before Christ.

Then the war-horse replaced the lowly *"ass"* as a symbol of pomp, power, and majesty.

So, if Jesus had intended to do that of which they accused Him, insurrection against Rome, He would not have ridden this lowly *"colt,"* but rather a war-horse.

In Truth, at the Second Coming, when He will come in Power and Glory, He will at that time be riding a war-horse (Rev. 19:11).

3. The presentation by Jesus of Himself, as King of Israel, although rejected, would seal the doom of that nation. Their rejection of Him, caused to be thrown aside the only protection they had, which was God. Without Him, they would be left to the mercy of the world, which would show little mercy, as the last 2,000 years have shown.

During this time, Israel has wandered as a people all over the world, scattered as outcasts, and, regrettably, despised by most all. Only since 1948 have they had a place they could call home, once again the sacred land of Israel. And yet, they are in constant turmoil respecting their claim, with even now (as I dictate these words) portions of it being given to the Palestinians.

NOTES

Regrettably, their times of sorrow have not ended, with the coming Great Tribulation, as proclaimed by Jesus, to be the worst of all (Mat. 24:21).

Nevertheless, they will yet accept Christ, which will be at the Second Coming, with this scenario being played out once again, the Triumphant Entry, but then with a different conclusion.

(8) "AND MANY SPREAD THEIR GARMENTS IN THE WAY: AND OTHERS CUT DOWN BRANCHES OFF THE TREES, AND STRAWED THEM IN THE WAY."

The phrase, *"And many spread their garments in the way,"* represents the crowd understanding what Jesus was doing. Of course, the Disciples also understood it now as well!

Robertson says that the deliberate conduct of Jesus here could have but one meaning, namely, that this was His formal presentation of Himself as the Messiah. The crowds realized this and entered into the spirit of the occasion.

However, the attitude of the people would have been the same as that of the Disciples, expecting the Lord to set up His rule in opposition to that of Rome, and, consequently, to deliver them from the yoke of their oppressors.

While Jesus definitely would deliver them; however, it would be from a far greater oppressor, Satan himself! But this they did not know or understand, although they should have!

Observing Jesus on the animal and riding toward Jerusalem, the people, as the Disciples, began to throw their garments on the road in order to make a grand procession.

The phrase, *"And others cut down branches off the trees, and strawed them in the way,"* probably referred to palm fronds, as well as olive branches, etc. At any rate, it was a sign of their approval, but certainly did not include the Chief Priests and Scribes, etc.

In fact, this very action by Christ would arouse the anger of the Sadducees who occupied the high priestly offices of Israel, which had actually been given to them by Rome. They saw this as a threat to their position, which brought them much power and money. (The office of the High Priest at this time was appointed by Rome, and, consequently, was not occupied by a descendant of Aaron, as it should have been.)

(9) "AND THEY THAT WENT BEFORE, AND THEY THAT FOLLOWED, CRIED,

SAYING, HOSANNA; BLESSED IS HE THAT COMETH IN THE NAME OF THE LORD:"

The phrase, *"And they that went before, and they that followed, cried, saying,"* represented crowds in both the back and front of Jesus.

The crowds could well have numbered into the thousands, with possibly hundreds among them who had been healed by Christ. Consequently, most of them knew Him, with many of them believing He was actually the Messiah.

The phrase, *"Hosanna; Blessed is He that cometh in the Name of the Lord,"* is taken from Psalm 118:25-26.

The word, *"Hosanna,"* means *"O Say."*

The word, *"Blessed,"* means *"to eulogize,"* or *"to praise."*

This acclamation was given at the *"Feast of Tabernacles,"* as the Priests marched once daily for seven days around the Altar, with palm branches in their hands, etc.

On the eighth day they marched seven times, which was the *"Great Hosannah,"* somewhat reminiscent of Jericho.

Even though this was the Passover, still, these people knew from the Prophecies of Zechariah that *"The Feast of Tabernacles"* would be kept in the coming Kingdom Age (Zech. 14:16).

Believing that Jesus was now about to take the Throne, they felt the great Kingdom Age was now beginning, hence the *"Hosannas"* and garments and branches spread on the road.

Some would say that these same people who were now shouting the praises of Christ would, some five days later, clamor for His life. However, that is untrue!

The trial of Jesus took place at night, with these people in bed. The ones who clamored for His life were, by and large, the rabble of the city.

(10) "BLESSED BE THE KINGDOM OF OUR FATHER DAVID, THAT COMETH IN THE NAME OF THE LORD: HOSANNA IN THE HIGHEST."

The phrase, *"Blessed be the Kingdom of our Father David,"* should have been translated, *"Blessed be the Kingdom that cometh, the Kingdom of our Father David."*

As we have stated, Israel looked at David as their Father, and, likewise, the Messiah as his Son, which He actually was (II Sam. 7). The *"Kingdom"* spoken of, is the *"Kingdom Age,"* when Jesus will rule and reign Personally from

Jerusalem. The crowd thought this was the time; however, the Religious Leaders did not!

In Truth, the *"Kingdom Age"* has not yet come, but most assuredly will, upon the Second Advent of Christ.

The phrase, *"That cometh in the Name of the Lord,"* should have been translated, *"Who cometh...."* Jesus was that Person!

The phrase, *"Hosanna in the highest,"* meant that He was the Highest One, and, consequently, the only One Who could save them.

In that they were correct, but did not fully understand His Mission. They thought only of themselves and their nation, actually giving very little consideration to the Gentiles, if any at all!

They really did not fully understand what the *"Kingdom Age"* actually meant. They saw only greatness and glory for themselves, not really realizing that their great need was deliverance from sin, which could only be brought about by Calvary. Regrettably, the Church has by and large followed suit, never quite understanding the real need.

Even at the present time, much of the Church is busily engaged in pursuits that have little true bearing on the True Purpose of God. Jesus is attempting to pull the Church to Himself, while the Church is busily engaged in *"get-rich-quick schemes."* While the Church should be confessing *"The Lord Jesus,"* it is instead busily confessing prosperity and such like! (Rom. 10:9-10).

So, as the *"Kingdom"* was denied Israel at that time, likewise, it is denied many in the modern Church.

(11) "AND JESUS ENTERED INTO JERUSALEM, AND INTO THE TEMPLE: AND WHEN HE HAD LOOKED ROUND ABOUT UPON ALL THINGS, AND NOW THE EVENTIDE WAS COME, HE WENT OUT UNTO BETHANY WITH THE TWELVE."

The phrase, *"And Jesus entered into Jerusalem, and into the Temple,"* represents a visit not recorded by Matthew. At this time, He will not cleanse the Temple, but will do so the next day.

It would not have been the proper time at the moment due to the fact that He has just concluded the Triumphant Entry, with, no doubt, many of these people near Him presently.

The part of the Temple into which Jesus went, was probably the *"Court of the Gentiles."* He would not have gone into the inner structure containing the Holy Place and Holy of Holies, because He was not a Priest after the Order of Aaron, but after the Order of Melchizedek.

The phrase, *"And when He had looked round about upon all things,"* presents a searching, penetrating gaze, which was a comprehensive inspection. He observed all the haggling, bartering, and arguing over prices, etc.

The *"Court of the Gentiles"* was more than likely where this action took place, which would have kept any Gentiles from worshiping God, for which it was originally intended. The entire situation would have grieved Him to no end. However, that which was taking place in the *"Court of the Gentiles,"* was indicative of all of Israel. Judaism had degenerated into religion, which was no more than a business. Regrettably, the religion business is just as rampant presently as then!

The phrase, *"And now the eventide was come, He went out unto Bethany with the Twelve,"* probably referred to the home of Lazarus, which He often visited when in this vicinity; however, it could well have referred to the open air on the Mount of Olives. This momentous day was drawing to a close, and Jesus would retire for the night. It was probably Sunday, and, if so, one week later Jesus would rise from the dead. Consequently, the intervening week would be one of such magnitude of sorrow as to defy description.

(12) "AND ON THE MORROW, WHEN THEY WERE COME FROM BETHANY, HE WAS HUNGRY:"

The phrase, *"And on the morrow,"* suggests it was Monday. Matthew says it was early, probably before 6 a.m.

The phrase, *"When they were come from Bethany, He was hungry,"* suggests one of two things:

1. He and His Disciples spent the night at the home of Lazarus, arose before dawn, slipping out before the host arose, and without breakfast.

2. Or they had spent the night in the open air on Mount Olivet, and, consequently, would have had nothing for breakfast.

Many do not quite understand the Incarnation of Christ. They think of Him as somewhat half God and half Man. This is totally incorrect.

Jesus was Very God and Very Man. In other words, He was one hundred percent God, and one hundred percent Man.

However, He did not at all use His attributes of Deity while in the Incarnate state. As someone has said, *"He lost, or freely laid aside, His expression of Deity, while never losing the possession of Deity."*

Paul said, *"But made Himself of no reputation, and took upon Him the form of a servant, and was made in the likeness of men"* (Phil. 2:7).

The word, *"made,"* in the Greek is *"kenoo,"* and means *"to empty out,"* or to *"make void."* In other words, He *"emptied Himself."*

OF WHAT DID CHRIST EMPTY HIMSELF?

It could not have been His Divine Nature, for He was God not only from all eternity (Mic. 5:1-2; Jn. 1:1-2; Heb. 1:8; Rev. 1:8-11), but as well, God manifest in the flesh during His life on earth (Isa. 7:14; 9:6-7; Mat. 1:18-25; Jn. 1:1-2, 14; I Tim. 3:16).

Dake gives the following of that which He emptied Himself:

1. Equality with the Father (Jn. 14:28; I Cor. 11:3; Phil. 2:6-7).

2. The Spirit Body that He lived in from eternity, in order to take human-form (Zech. 13:6; Mat. 1:18-25; Lk. 1:35; 24:37-40; Jn. 1:14; Rom. 8:3; Gal. 4:4; Phil. 2:6-8; 3:21).

3. The immortality of His Body, at least the impossibility of it dying (Ps. 16:10; I Cor. 15:3; I Pet. 2:24; 3:18). Even though His Body could die, as it obviously did, still, it would not have died had He not laid it down freely (Jn. 10:18). His Body was as Adam's before the Fall. Death came about because of the Fall, and Jesus was not subject to death, because He had not fallen, neither came under its curse.

4. The Glory that He had with the Father before the world was (Mat. 16:27; Jn. 12:23; 17:5; Phil. 2:5-11).

5. His authority in Heaven and in earth, which was given back to Him after the Resurrection (Mat. 28:18; Eph. 1:20-23; Phil. 2:9-11; I Pet. 3:22).

6. His Divine Attributes and outward Powers that He had with the Father from eternity. He had no power to do miracles until He received the Holy Spirit in all fullness (Isa. 11:1-2; 42:1-7; 61:1-2; Mat. 12:28; Lk. 3:21-22; 4:16-21; Jn. 2:11; 3:34; Acts 10:38). He could do nothing of

Himself in all His earthly life. He attributed all His Works, Doctrines, Powers, etc., to the Father through the Anointing of the Holy Spirit.

THIS IS PROVED BY THE FOLLOWING FACTS IN SCRIPTURE

A. He was limited to the status of a man (Phil. 2:6-8; Heb. 2:14-18; 5:8-9).

B. He was God's Agent using God's Power of Attorney (Jn. 8:28; Acts 10:38).

C. He was our example that we should walk in His steps (I Pet. 2:21).

D. The temptations prove that He was limited as a man so that He would overcome as a man and not as God (Heb. 4:14-16; 5:7-9).

E. Isaiah (7:14-16) speaks of the Messiah being born without knowledge enough to know to refuse the evil and choose the good, as all babies.

F. Isaiah (11:2; 53:1-12) speaks of the Messiah being limited as an ordinary baby, showing that God would give Him the Spirit of Wisdom, Understanding, Counsel, Might, Knowledge, and Fear of the Lord. If He had these attributes as God from all eternity and did not lay them aside in becoming Man, when was this Prophecy ever true of Him?

G. Isaiah (50:4-11) predicted that the Messiah would be born without the tongue of the learned, without knowing how to speak a word in season to help any soul, and that He would be wakened day by day to increase in Knowledge and Wisdom.

H. Isaiah (42:1-7; 61:1-2) speaks of the Messiah receiving His Power to manifest Divine acts by the Anointing of the Holy Spirit and not by retaining His Own former attributes and powers. Is it necessary for God to be Anointed with the Holy Spirit to do what He is naturally capable of doing? The answer to that is obviously *"no!"*

If it became necessary to anoint Jesus during His earthly life, then it proves He did not retain His former glory and attributes which He had from all eternity when He emptied Himself to become like men in all things (Phil. 2:6-8; Heb. 2:14-18; 5:8-9).

I. History records that Christ was limited as a baby and grew in body, soul, and spirit, mind, grace, wisdom, stature, and favor with God and man (Lk. 2:40, 52; I Cor. 2:11).

Even after coming to manhood and His full Anointing and Gifts of the Spirit, He was still

NOTES

limited in Knowledge (Mk. 13:32). He even learned obedience by the things He suffered (Heb. 4:14-16; 5:7-9).

J. He did not claim the Attributes of God, but only the Anointing of the Spirit to do His Works (Mat. 12:28; Lk. 4:16-21; Jn. 8:28). Others stated this was the source of His Power (Jn. 3:34; Acts 10:38).

Most Scriptures used in Doctrine Books proving that Christ had Divine Attributes on earth are statements true of Him since His Glory has been restored and do not prove anything during His life on earth. All Scriptures relating to His earthly life can be explained as referring to the exercise of the Gifts of the Spirit and not natural attributes.

K. The fact that Christ promised all Believers power to do the works He did, proves that it was through the Anointing of the Spirit, not by His Deity and natural attributes, that He did His Works (Mat. 10:1-20; 16:18; 18:18; Mk. 16:15-20; Lk. 10; 24:49; Jn. 14:12-15; Acts 1:4-8).

So, when the Text says, *"He was hungry,"* it was the same as any other man being hungry.

(13) "AND SEEING A FIG TREE AFAR OFF HAVING LEAVES, HE CAME, IF HAPLY HE MIGHT FIND ANY THING THEREON: AND WHEN HE CAME TO IT, HE FOUND NOTHING BUT LEAVES; FOR THE TIME OF FIGS WAS NOT YET."

The phrase, *"And seeing a fig tree afar off having leaves,"* constituted the variety which bore early figs (Isa. 28:4; Jer. 24:2).

"Fig trees" were probably plentiful in the area of Bethphage, because its very name means *"the house of figs."* Consequently, seeing such a tree growing at random, and on public property, was nothing unusual. This would answer the question of the critics, of Christ having the right to curse this tree.

The phrase, *"He came, if haply He might find any thing thereon,"* means that according to all appearances, there should have been figs.

The phrase, *"And when He came to it, He found nothing but leaves,"* means it was absolutely fruitless.

The phrase, *"For the time of figs was not yet,"* means that despite its appearance, which suggested fruit, and which there should have been fruit, it was barren.

(14) "AND JESUS ANSWERED AND SAID UNTO IT, NO MAN EAT FRUIT OF THEE

HEREAFTER FOR EVER. AND HIS DIS-
CIPLES HEARD IT."

The phrase, *"And Jesus answered and said
unto it,"* proclaims the Lord forgetting His
natural hunger in the thought of the spiritual
figure which the sight of this tree began to
present to His mind (Bickersteth).

No doubt, as He looked at the tree, He saw
Israel, as well, having indeed the leaves of a
great profession, but yielding no fruit.

The phrase, *"No man eat fruit of thee hereafter for ever,"* speaks of the Jewish nation. And
so the fig tree was cursed, not necessarily for
being barren, but for being false.

The word, *"forever,"* in the Hebrew language
literally means, *"for the age."* Consequently, it
should have been translated, *"No man eat fruit
of thee henceforward, for the age;"* that is, until
the Times of the Gentiles be fulfilled. This will
be at the Second Coming, when Israel, now realizing her spiritually destitute condition, will
finally accept Christ as her Lord and Messiah.
Then she will produce *"much fruit,"* and because of Christ. Without Christ there can be
no fruit!

The phrase, *"And His Disciples heard it,"*
somewhat lends credence to the thought that
Jesus did this thing concerning the fig tree, not
necessarily at that time, for the benefit of the
Disciples. But yet, the Holy Spirit saw to it that
they were witnesses. Bickersteth says, *"This
Miracle would show His Disciples how soon He
could have withered His enemies, who were
about to crucify Him; but He waited with longsuffering for their Salvation, by Repentance and
Faith in Him."* Even though that Repentance
has not yet materialized, one can rest certain
that most assuredly it shall. We speak of the
Restoration of Israel at a Coming Glad Day.

(15) "AND THEY COME TO JERUSALEM:
AND JESUS WENT INTO THE TEMPLE,
AND BEGAN TO CAST OUT THEM THAT
SOLD AND BOUGHT IN THE TEMPLE, AND
OVERTHREW THE TABLES OF THE
MONEYCHANGERS, AND THE SEATS OF
THEM THAT SOLD DOVES;"

The phrase, *"And they come to Jerusalem,"*
should have constituted the city, utterly joyous
because the One Who had chosen Jerusalem,
that His Name might be there, was in their midst
(II Chron. 6:6). Instead, in a matter of hours the
city would find its Religious Leaders scheming

NOTES

as to how they could put to death the very One
Who they claimed to serve, but yet did not know
Him. The Holy Spirit, in giving us this phrase,
does so with the sob of a broken heart. The actions of Jerusalem would seal its own doom!

The phrase, *"And Jesus went into the
Temple,"* refers to the fact that its condition,
spiritually speaking, had been on His mind all
night. He probably went into the part of the
Temple, as stated, called *"The Court of the Gentiles,"* which is where the buying and selling
took place.

The phrase, *"And began to cast out them that
sold and bought in the Temple,"* concerned this
area minutely overseen by the High Priests. The
booths of this market are mentioned in the
Rabbinical Writings as the booths of the son of
Hanan, or Annas. However, this market is never
mentioned in the Old Testament, and seems to
have sprung up after the captivity (Bickersteth).

The phrase, *"And overthrew the tables of the
moneychangers,"* concerned traders who exchanged the half-shekel, which was required of
every Israelite to be paid on the 15th of March.
In every city there were collectors to receive it.
It was called a tribute in Matthew 17:24-27.

Money-changers exchanged Jewish coins for
foreign ones for those who came to the Feast.
Foreign coins with idols on them could not be
used in the worship. Many took advantage of
this to practice fraud and get rich (Dake).

Are their money-changers in the Church
today?

Unfortunately, yes! For instance, the Catholic Doctrine of Purgatory, a place which, in fact,
does not exist, takes in untold amounts of
money, as people pay to get their loved ones ex-
tricated. Money-changers!

As well, some of the schemes promoted in
order to raise money in some Pentecostal and
Charismatic efforts, can only be labeled as
"money-changers!"

A particular brother looks into a Television
camera, telling the people that the Spirit of the
Lord has just come on him, and told him that
everything given in the next fifteen minutes,
etc., will be returned a hundredfold. That is a lie
pure and simple, and, to say the least, unscriptural. Under such gimmickry, the people will
not receive a hundredfold return, and, in fact, will
lose what they give, as well as having the dubi-
ous honor of aiding and abetting Satan! In fact,

the entirety of the *"Prosperity Message Scheme"* falls under the same category. One could say the same for money spent on the promotion of false doctrine. Somebody raised those funds under the pretext of promoting the Gospel. Maybe they were sincere, but being sincerely wrong in no way changes the outcome.

In fact, the modern Temple is filled with money-changers!

The phrase, *"And the seats of them that sold doves,"* concerned those used in Sacrifices, that is if the person could not afford a lamb or a bullock. Not only were the animals sold, but, as well, *"wine, oil, salt, etc., and whatever else was used in the ritual."*

This area was quite large, some say as big as three football fields.

As the Lord began to cast out these traffickers, He made no distinction between sellers and buyers.

This *"Court of the Gentiles"* was supposed to be a place where Gentiles could come pray. However, who could pray in a place which was both a cattle-market and an exchange, where the lowing of oxen mingled with the clinking of silver and the haggling of the dealers and those who came to purchase? (Swete).

(16) "AND WOULD NOT SUFFER THAT ANY MAN SHOULD CARRY ANY VESSEL THROUGH THE TEMPLE."

The idea of this statement regarding Christ, concerned people on their everyday duties, taking a short-cut through the Temple, when going from one side of the city to the other. Such saved distance and time. So the Priests permitted servants and laborers, laden with goods, to take this shorter way through the great court of the Temple.

Jesus, if one could imagine this scenario, would have held up His Hand, and with an authority which could not be denied, compelled these individuals to go back. He would have the whole of His Father's House regarded as sacred (Bickersteth).

Consequently, when Jesus upset the tables of the money-changers, and the *"seats of them that sold doves,"* etc., and especially that it was at the Passover, the height of activity for the year, the anger of the High Priest would have known no bounds. It hit them in the pocketbook, because a large profit was made from these activities, and especially at this time.

NOTES

(17) "AND HE TAUGHT, SAYING UNTO THEM, IS IT NOT WRITTEN, MY HOUSE SHALL BE CALLED OF ALL NATIONS THE HOUSE OF PRAYER? BUT YE HAVE MADE IT A DEN OF THIEVES."

The phrase, *"And He taught, saying unto them,"* no doubt pointed to a large crowd of people which had gathered, watching, as it seems, with open-mouthed astonishment!

The question, *"Is it not written . . . ?"*, proclaims Jesus giving Scripture as a foundation for that which He has just done, the cleansing of the Temple. If one is to notice, everything He did always had Scripture as the foundation. The Bible at that time would have consisted of Genesis through Malachi.

It is my contention that if one does not know and understand the Old Testament, he cannot know and understand the New Testament. Someone has said that the Old Testament is the New Testament concealed, while the New Testament is the Old Testament revealed.

One of the reasons that many Charismatics go into false doctrine, despite being Baptized in the Holy Spirit, is because many of them do not know the Old Testament. Consequently, the foundation is removed from some of what they teach.

The continuing of the question, *"My House shall be called of all nations the house of prayer?"*, is derived from Isaiah 56:7 and Jeremiah 7:11.

Under the Old Economy of God, the Lord dwelt between the Mercy Seat and the Cherubim in the Holy of Holies (Ex. 25:22). In Truth, this was the only place on earth where God dwelt. This was first in the Tabernacle in the wilderness, and then in Solomon's Temple.

Inasmuch as the Ark was lost (or spirited away), at the invasion of Nebuchadnezzar, there is no record that God resided thusly in Zerubbabel's Temple, or Herod's at the time of Christ. In fact, Ezekiel saw the Holy Spirit leave the Temple not long before it was destroyed by Nebuchadnezzar (Ezek. 11:22-23), and it will not return until the Millennial Temple is built in the coming Kingdom Age (Ezek. 43:1-5).

Israel, as a beneficiary of the Word, was obligated to give it to the Gentiles, hence the phrase *"of all nations."* But Israel failed! What they had done to the *"Court of the Gentiles,"* in Herod's Temple, amply illustrated the entirety of the Nation. They had no interest in taking the Great Message of the Lord to others, but, instead, of making money. I wonder if the present Church is any different!

There is presently very little interest in World Evangelism, and I speak primarily of America and Canada. Conversely, there is great interest in the *"Prosperity Gospel,"* which promises great riches to its devotees.

If Jesus cleansed the Temple now, I wonder how many would be left!

The phrase, *"But ye have made it a den of thieves,"* should have been translated, *"robbers."*

The *"robber"* conducted his operations on a large and systematic scale, and with the aid of bands or helpers, is thus to be distinguished from the thieves who purloin or pilfer whatever comes to hand (Vincent).

Swete says: *"No bandit's cave along the Jericho road* (Lk. 10:30), *by which our Lord had lately come, was the scene of such wholesale robbery as the Mountain of His House."*

Under the Old Economy of God, and as stated, the Temple was the *"House of God."* Since the New Covenant, God no longer dwells in a house made with hands, but rather the human heart. Paul said, *"Know ye not that ye are the Temple of God, and that the Spirit of God dwelleth in you?"* (I Cor. 3:16).

So, instead of God being in one place, at least as far as the Sacrifices were concerned, as in days of old, He now resides everywhere, at least where the human heart will have Him. However, the principle outlined in the cleansing of the Temple, is just as apropos presently as then.

1. The occupant of the House is to be Jesus, even as Jesus came into the Temple of old! It is *"His House,"* and, consequently, He is to be free to do whatever He desires.

If Jesus is not Lord <u>of</u> all, He is not Lord <u>at</u> all!

So, for the Temple to be a True Temple of the Lord, Jesus must reside there. He does so in the Power and Person of the Holy Spirit (Eph. 2:22).

This means that every house which does not have Jesus as its Lord, is no House of God. This would exclude Islam, Buddhism, Hinduism, Shintoism, and Mormonism. It would as well exclude Catholicism, and much of what is called *"Christianity."*

2. When He comes in, He will *"cast out"* everything that is undesirable.

It is the business of the Spirit of God to take the Believer from the *"image of the earthy"* to the *"image of the heavenly"* (I Cor. 15:49). Everything not of the Spirit, must be *"cast out!"*

3. It is to be a *"House of Prayer."* In other words, *"prayer"* should be the constant exercise of every Believer. If this is to be taken literally, and it certainly should, intercession and travail should be the major focus of the Child of God. Regrettably, in many religious circles prayer is a lost art!

If one is to notice, Jesus did <u>not</u> say, *"A house of good confession,"* as important as that may be! Regrettably, *"confession"* has taken the place of *"prayer"* in many hearts and lives. Please allow me to say the following:

It is impossible to confess a lost loved one to Jesus Christ, even though *"confession"* certainly does play an important part. The Believer must intercede before God in earnest travail for the unsaved to truly be brought under the convicting power of the Holy Spirit.

No Revival has ever begun by *"confession,"* with every Revival beginning with Intercession and Prayer.

4. *"Of all nations,"* suggests the worldwide scope of the Gospel, intended by the Lord. The Scripture says, *"For God so loved the world,"* and that doesn't mean just a part of it!

It has been suggested that the phrase, *"Of all nations,"* would have been better translated, *"For all nations."*

This translation is double-barrelled, and, consequently, proclaims two directions. *"All nations"* are intended to come, and prayer is to be made *"For all nations."*

(18) "AND THE SCRIBES AND CHIEF PRIESTS HEARD IT, AND SOUGHT HOW THEY MIGHT DESTROY HIM: FOR THEY FEARED HIM, BECAUSE ALL THE PEOPLE WERE ASTONISHED AT HIS DOCTRINE."

The phrase, *"And the Scribes and Chief Priests heard it,"* proclaims for the first time, both groups combined against Jesus.

They *"heard"* about the Temple cleansing, instantly realizing how much money they had lost. Wuest says that the Lord's attack against the Temple-market incensed them.

The phrase, *"And sought how they might destroy Him,"* meant to not only kill Him, but to utterly destroy His influence as a great spiritual energy in the world. To do this, they would accuse Him of many things, including insurrection against Rome, blasphemy respecting the Law of Moses, performing miracles by the power of Satan, etc.

Of course, all these charges were false. However, their biggest ploy was the Crucifixion, at least if they could persuade Pilate to carry out this act.

They knew, and they knew the people knew, that the Law of Moses said, *"For He that is hanged is accursed of God"* (Deut. 21:22-23). That spoke of a sin that was worthy of such death. Consequently, if they could manage to have Him crucified, it would speak to the people that their accusations of Him were correct, and that God had *"cursed Him"* by allowing Him to be crucified (hanged). In their minds, this would destroy His influence among the people.

In Truth, He would be *"cursed of God,"* not for His Own sins, but, instead, for the sins of the world. That is when He would cry, *"My God, My God, Why hast Thou forsaken Me?"* (Mk. 15:34).

At this moment, He would be bearing the sin of the world, suffering as the *"Lamb of God, which took away the sin of the world"* (Jn. 1:29).

The phrase, *"For they feared Him,"* expresses the idea that their authority and interests were attacked. In other words, they were losing control of the people. Religion majors on two specifics: A. Control; and, B. Money. Jesus had hurt them severely in both areas.

The phrase, *"All the people was astonished at His Doctrine,"* referred to the teaching of the Lord being in such contrast to that of the Jewish Leaders, which caused the people to see the difference at once. The difference was that the teaching of the Lord sparkled with life, and because it was Anointed by the Holy Spirit, whereas the type of teaching they had been receiving from the Pharisees, etc., was a dry, formal, stereotyped, powerless garble, which was above their heads and made little sense! (Wuest)

(19) "AND WHEN EVEN WAS COME, HE WENT OUT OF THE CITY."

In this statement, two things are said:

1. It seemed as if the Lord attempted to cram everything into these final hours that was possible. Swete remarks that hunger and fatigue were forgotten in the Work of God, and that only the approach of the hour when the gates were closed, induced Him to retire for rest.

2. There is no indication that Jesus ever spent the night in Jerusalem. There are indications that He did not desire to visit the city at all, day or night. However, on the times when He felt He had to be there, when night fell, He would retreat to the environs of the city, whether to Bethany or the Mount of Olives.

The sadness knows no bounds, concerning the city which should have welcomed Him with open arms, but, instead, crucified Him!

(20) "AND IN THE MORNING, AS THEY PASSED BY, THEY SAW THE FIG TREE DRIED UP FROM THE ROOTS."

The phrase, *"And in the morning,"* probably refers to Tuesday.

The phrase, *"As they passed by,"* proclaimed the morning light as making the fig tree and what had happened to it, plainly visible.

When Jesus and the Disciples had left the city late the previous afternoon, the possibility existed that the twilight hindered the observance of the tree at that time, which may have already withered.

The phrase, *"They saw the fig tree dried up from the roots,"* means that it was completely withered away. Israel would in a short time, dry up from the roots, actually ceasing to be as a nation.

(21) "AND PETER CALLING TO REMEMBRANCE SAITH UNTO HIM, MASTER, BEHOLD, THE FIG TREE WHICH THOU CURSEDST IS WITHERED AWAY."

The phrase, *"And Peter calling to remembrance saith unto Him,"* seems to indicate that Peter was shocked by the condition of the tree, that some twenty-four hours earlier was alive and vibrant.

The phrase, *"Master, behold, the fig tree which Thou cursedst is withered away,"* proclaims a startled Apostle! He has difficulty understanding how the mere words of Jesus, *"No man eat fruit of thee hereafter forever,"* could bring about this obvious and almost instant result! However, it was not the words spoken, but rather Who spoke them.

(22) "AND JESUS ANSWERING SAITH UNTO THEM, HAVE FAITH IN GOD."

The phrase, *"And Jesus answering saith unto them,"* indicates Jesus dealing with <u>what</u> happened, rather than <u>why</u> it happened.

Due to the Disciples thinking so strongly about the prospective supremacy of Israel, and despite what Jesus had constantly taught them, perhaps the Master thought it would be point-less at this time to point out the fruitless tree as a type of Israel, and, consequently, of no value. In a short time, they would understand!

The phrase, *"Have Faith in God,"* literally says, *"Have the Faith of God."*

Dake implies that man was created with God's Faith, but doubt entered in at the Fall (Gen. 3:1-7). Faith is restored in the New Birth, and if normally exercised and maintained, it will grow to fullness and power (Rom. 1:5, 17; 10:17; Gal. 2:20; Col. 1:23; 2:6-7; II Thess. 1:3; II Pet. 1:1-5).

The structure of the Greek shows *"God"* as the object of Faith.

WHAT DOES IT MEAN TO HAVE FAITH IN GOD?

God has chosen to operate His Work from the basis of Faith. It follows in two directions:

1. Paul wrote, *"Through Faith we under-stand that the worlds were framed by the Word of God, so that things which are seen were not made of things which do appear"* (Heb. 11:3).

Actually, this verse or Hebrews 11:1, is not a definition of Faith so much as it is a declara-tion of its action. It makes promises present and real, and unseen things visible.

God's vast creation of *"worlds"* was created, not by existing materials, but rather by Faith. This means that God spoke these things into existence. Consequently, His Word carries not only power, but, as well, creativity.

2. God desires, and actually insists, that man accepts everything done for him on the premise of Faith. The idea is that man at times may little understand what God is doing, but, nev-ertheless, is to accept His Word at face value. His Word is all-important! It is so important, that the simple fact of Abraham believing Him, that is, believing God's Word, caused Righ-teousness to be accounted unto him (Gen. 15:6). God's method of Imputed Righteousness has not differed from that time until the present. Actually, it was the same at the very beginning, although not as clearly defined (Gen. 4:3-5). Consequently, the Jews constantly demanding *"signs"* from Jesus, showed that they had no confidence in the Word of God (Mat. 12:38-39).

Faith in God ensures Salvation, and pro-duces Miracles, as Jesus will portray here. It is

so important that Paul wrote, *"Without Faith it is impossible to please Him: for he that cometh to God must believe* (have Faith) *that He is* (able), *and that He is a rewarder of them that diligently seek Him"* (Heb. 11:6).

So, the ingredient to God and that which will please God, is *"Faith in God,"* i.e., His Word.

(23) "FOR VERILY I SAY UNTO YOU, THAT WHOSOEVER SHALL SAY UNTO THIS MOUNTAIN, BE THOU REMOVED, AND BE THOU CAST INTO THE SEA; AND SHALL NOT DOUBT IN HIS HEART, BUT SHALL BELIEVE THAT THOSE THINGS WHICH HE SAITH SHALL COME TO PASS; HE SHALL HAVE WHATSOEVER HE SAITH."

The phrase, *"For verily I say unto you,"* is used often by Christ, and is meant to announce a Truth of unusual consequence. This Great Truth concerns Faith in God.

In this one Scripture, with even added em-phasis given in the next one, Jesus tells us what Faith in God will do, and, as well, the manner in which it is to be used. As the Holy Spirit generally does, the information given for such a weighty subject, is couched in very simple ter-minology, and very brief in content. But yet, it is the greatest form of teaching in the world, as should be obvious. Hopefully, the Lord will help us in dissecting this great Passage, to rightly divide it in such a way as to make it applicable to the hungry, seeking heart. Let's take it step by step:

1. *"That whosoever"*: First of all, the word, *"whosoever,"* puts mountain-moving Faith in reach of <u>anyone</u>. It is not limited to Bible schol-ars, nationality, or race. It is open to all! That means that whatever problem may be besetting you, the reader, if proper Faith in God is en-joined, the first step to the road of victory can begin instantly. When Jesus said, *"Whosoever,"* the Believer should say in his heart, *"That means me!"* This is not for Preachers only, but includes any and all Believers.

2. *"Shall say"*: These two words proclaim to us the power of proper Scriptural confession. God has given each person a tongue, which is fu-eled by the mind and heart. Consequently, what-ever we *"say"* shows where our Faith actually is, and the direction we are heading. Faith speaks, and does not remain silent. What does it say?

It actually says two things: A. What the Word of God says; and, B. How it applies to one's particular need, which incorporates the Will of God. In other words, even though Faith can move mountains, the Lord will not allow a mountain to be moved in such a way that it will hurt or harm others. So, the Believer is to confess the Word of God and the Will of God. And if we are led by the Spirit, we will never confess anything but that which the Lord desires.

So, one cannot move mountains by speaking doubt. One must speak that which one wants and believes to be the Will of God.

3. *"Unto this mountain"*: Jesus chose about the hardest thing that could be thought of, a mountain, in order to describe the utter unlimited power of Faith in God. Whatever problem that you, the reader, may have, cannot be any larger than a mountain. So, automatically, the Lord places every single problem in the world, and irrespective of its situation, in the context of its possible solution. In other words, *"All things are possible with God."*

If Satan can get the Believer to think that his or her problem is beyond solution, he has won the battle. Please allow me to give a personal illustration.

If I remember correctly, it was 1990. Our situation was such, especially regarding our Ministry, that little by little I had come to believe that it was hopeless. Satan is a genius at maneuvering certain things into place to make one believe such a lie. How in the world could we overcome the prejudice and bias of almost all the Church world? With almost every Preacher in the land turned against us, how would it be possible to have any effective Ministry? These questions of such magnitude filled my mind, with Satan constantly fueling this train of thought.

Under such circumstances, there seemed to be no hope, with Faith little by little giving way to despair.

However, the Lord does not leave His people without a witness. He loves us dearly, and will bring things to pass to increase our Faith if we will only love Him and trust Him.

During this time, a Preacher called me, of whom I had known for years, but not in a direct way. If I remember correctly, this was the first time I had ever spoken with him.

He called the office and asked if he and his wife could have lunch with Frances and me, and that he felt God had given him something for me. The date was set.

NOTES

As the four of us met on that particular day, I enjoyed the fellowship extensively so, and I wondered in my mind exactly what he was going to say.

After the meal was finished, he looked at me and said, *"Brother Swaggart, what I'm about to say sounds foolish. It seems to be so trivial that I'm ashamed to claim that God gave it to me to give to you. And yet,"* he went on to say, *"I can't shake it. Consequently, I must obey the Lord."*

He sat there for a few moments saying nothing, and then finally said, *"The Lord told me to tell you these two words, 'God can!'"*

That was the entirety of the Message, *"God can!"*

Almost immediately upon saying these words, he began to apologize, saying, *"I really don't know what it means, but that's what the Lord said to say to you."*

For a few moments I said nothing. However, when those two words, *"God can!"*, were given to me, I sat there stunned for a few moments, and then the tears began to roll down my cheeks. Actually, it was a few moments before I <u>could</u> say anything.

I then said, *"My Brother, maybe you don't understand what you've said, but I understand it perfectly."* I then added, *"Thank you so much for obeying God."*

It doesn't matter what it is or how large the mountain is, *"God can!"*

As well, Jesus did not put a limit on the size of the *"mountain."* To be frank, it is actually no more difficult to move a large mountain than a small mountain, as should be obvious. Both in the natural are impossible. However, with God, there is no impossibility.

4. *"Be thou removed"*: This proclaims the Word of Faith. It doesn't ask how it can be done, or whether it is possible for it to be done. It just simply says, *"Be done!"*

This is actually the proper confession of the words *"Shall say."*

Conversely, most will say it cannot be removed. However, Jesus tells us otherwise. Consequently, one can believe doubters or one can believe Jesus. I prefer to believe the Lord.

5. *"And be thou cast into the sea"*: Consequently, such Faith in God not only moves the mountain, but puts it in a place to where it can hurt or harm no one else. That is the reason we said that God will not bring something to pass

for the Believer that would harm others. This *"mountain"* is thrown into the sea, where it will do no one any harm. In effect, it is totally removed. This is somewhat the opposite of that which is known as *"Hamilton's Law."*

This Law states that for anything to be constructed, something must be first destroyed. It means that if one builds a house, trees have to be cut down, and other things used, in order to provide the materials from which the house is built. Consequently, things are destroyed in order to construct other things. That is Hamilton's Law.

However, when Jesus builds something, He does not deplete things elsewhere to get it done.

As well, if He removes something for us, as this mountain, He does not make our gain someone else's loss. That is the reason it is thrown into the *"sea."*

6. *"And shall not doubt in his heart"*: The word, *"doubt,"* in the Greek is *"diakrino."* It means *"to judge between two."* In this case, it means to judge whether Faith in God can, or cannot! Everything within the Believer is to understand that God can, and that He not only can, but will.

Many Believers agree that He can, but they are not sure if He will. It is not enough to believe that He can. One must believe as well that *"He will!"*

When the Lord sent Moses to the Children of Israel in Egypt, He did not tell Moses to tell them, *"I can hath sent me unto you,"* but rather, *"I AM hath sent me unto you"* (Ex. 3:14). There is a vast difference in *"I can"* and *"I AM,"* i.e., *"I will."* Actually, *"I AM"* is even stronger than *"I will!"*

"I will" treats it in the sense of being done in the future. However, True Faith, as *"I AM"* represents, calls it done, even though it has not yet happened. In the mind of God, True Faith says that whatever is needed is already done, even though not yet carried out.

7. *"But shall believe"*: Not only does the person not doubt, but, as well, he *"believes"* what Jesus has said here. Jesus said if we have the proper Faith in God, that we can say to a mountain, *"Be thou moved into the sea, and it shall be done."* We are to believe that.

8. *"That those things"*: This speaks of our particular needs, and whatever they may be!

9. *"Which he saith"*: Once again we are told to *"say"* what we want. Actually, this is the

second of three times this phrase will be used. Consequently, the Holy Spirit is showing us the significance of a proper confession.

10. *"Shall come to pass"*: These words are present tense in the Greek Text. Consequently, it more accurately translates, *"Comes to pass."* The idea is, that it may not happen instantly, but happen it shall! We are to keep believing and continue confessing. It is what some refer to as a *"futuristic present,"* and has to do with the word, *"believing."* However, this is the hard part.

It is called the *"trying of your Faith, worketh patience"* (James 1:3).

Many Believers continue to believe for a while, but then grow weary and quit, and lose what they have been seeking for. An excellent example for the opposite, is the Patriarch Isaac.

The Scripture says, *"And Isaac entreated the Lord for his wife, because she was barren"* (Gen. 25:21).

Many people do not realize how <u>long</u> Isaac entreated the Lord. Rebekah, his wife, was barren for nineteen years. Consequently, Isaac continued to entreat the Lord for this period of time. If Jesus were to come into the world, it was imperative that a little boy be born to Rebekah. Consequently, Satan would make it as hard as possible.

However, Isaac did not quit. Regrettably, many, if not most, Christians quit after one or two petitions, much less nineteen years. But Isaac continued to *"entreat the Lord,"* and the Scripture says, *"And Rebekah his wife conceived"* (Gen. 25:21).

The mountain of her *"barrenness"* had to be removed. As so much was at stake, actually the Salvation of the world, Satan would fight horrendously so! Nevertheless, the Patriarch did not discontinue his entreaty of the Lord. He kept believing, and I think He kept confessing. Every indication is that he did! Actually, it would have been impossible for Rebekah to conceive if Isaac had been confessing that it was impossible for her to conceive.

No doubt, Satan taunted him constantly, telling him any lie that seemed plausible at the moment. But Isaac kept believing, asking, and confessing. Ultimately, he received what he wanted!

11. *"He shall have"*: Jesus did not say *"maybe,"* but emphatically states, *"He shall have."* If it is the Will of God, and we keep believing, asking, and confessing, the outcome is certain.

I realize that many object to me using the phrase, *"The Will of God."* They claim that the *"Word of God"* is the *"Will of God"* which is certainly correct. However, many err in claiming that the Promises of the Word of God apply to them on a personal basis, in any and all circumstances. In other words, if God gave Abraham and Sarah a child, when he was 100 years old and she was 90, He will do the same for them, because *"God is no respecter of persons,"* they say!

While it is certainly true that God is no respecter of persons, still, He does have respect according to His Promises. In other words, some of the Promises He gave were personal, and not meant to apply to others. Actually, and despite all the Faith that has been exhibited through the thousands of years since Abraham and Sarah, I do not know of any other couple who has experienced the birth of a child at 100 years old and 90 years old respectively.

God gave a particular Promise to Abraham, which applied to him only, and had to do with the Great Plan of God in the world. To be sure, He has given great Promises to others that he never gave to Abraham, and which Abraham could not have had, because they did not apply to him. So, the Believer must be very careful that he does not try to use the Word of God against God. In other words, to try to force God to do certain things, when it may not be the Will of God, and for the obvious reasons.

Some Promises are indigenous to all. This refers to Salvation, healing, and prosperity. In other words, these things are promised to all. And yet, healing and prosperity must be taken in proper context.

What would be prosperity to one would not necessarily be such to the other. So we must allow God to decide what type of *"prosperity"* He wants us to have.

As well, the Promise of healing for all, as I believe the Scripture proclaims, as well, has limitations. Such will not stop the aging of the human body, and the attendant problems that accompany such. In other words, irrespective of how much Faith in God a person has, a 70-year-old man does not have the reflexes of a 20 year old. So, things must be looked at in their proper context. Please allow me to give another personal example:

When I was about ten years old, the Lord healed me of a very serious malady. What the

sickness was, the doctors were never able to ascertain, although giving me a number of tests, etc. I stayed nauseous almost constantly, and came to the place that I would go unconscious, which happened at school several times. Actually, the teachers had told my parents that if the situation did not improve, they would have to remove me from school.

During this time I was prayed for often by our Pastor and others, but seemingly to no avail!

Immediately after Church on a particular Sunday, my parents had invited the Pastor and his wife out to lunch with them. However, before we all went to lunch, we went by the home of a particular parishioner who was ill, and needed prayer. I remember the scene very vividly.

Prayer was offered for the Brother in question, with all them about to leave. I was the first one to the door, with all standing behind me.

Before I could open the door, my Dad spoke to the Pastor, asking him to anoint me with oil, and pray for me regarding this particular sickness. The Pastor stood there with the bottle of oil in his hand, which he had just used respecting the other Brother. As stated, he had previously prayed for me several times, but to no avail.

The Pastor walked over to me, anointed me with oil, and began to pray. Instantly the Power of God came all over me, and I felt a hot sensation from the top of my head to the soles of my feet. I was instantly healed, and have never been troubled with that malady, or any other disease, from that day until this.

Actually, I have by and large experienced excellent health from that day until this, which, at the time of this writing, has been a little over half a century.

And yet, even though the Lord healed me totally and completely, still, at times, I have experienced colds, and even pneumonia at one particular time. But this did not mean God had not healed me, and that His healing He gave me was not total and complete.

Why didn't the Lord heal me the other times this same Pastor prayed for me?

To these things I have no answer, and I suspect no one else does either.

Every Believer, when asking the Lord for something, must first settle it in his mind that what he is asking is according to the Word of God, and according to the Will of God. God's Will is an extraordinary thing. It is predicated not only on His Word, but, as well, according to His particular dealings with us as individuals. Please allow me to give another example:

I have had many people through the years come up to me and say, *"I am going to believe God to give me the talent to play the piano exactly as He did you!"*

They possibly had heard me relate how I had asked the Lord for this talent when I was eight years old, and He had answered my childlike Faith, and had given me this talent.

And yet, and even though God is no respecter of persons, still, it may not be God's Will to give this particular talent to all who would ask Him. I realize that some would not agree with that statement, claiming that if we have enough Faith in God, we can have anything we desire. Nevertheless, God's Promises are always predicated on His particular Will for our life and ministry, whatever that may be.

If we have concluded that what we are asking for is according to God's Word, and is His Will for our lives, then we should set our mind and heart to it, refusing to take *"no"* for an answer, believing that God will ultimately give us what we are seeking. We should not allow circumstances to hinder us, or obstacles to impede our progress. We must not let doubters turn us aside, or unbelievers deter us from that which the Lord has promised us. We must attack that mountain with Faith in God, believing ultimately that it will be removed, and not stop until it is done.

12. *"Whatsoever he saith"*: This represents the third time this phrase is used. So here is what He tells us to do:

A. Shall say.

B. Shall not doubt.

C. Shall believe.

D. Shall have.

E. He saith.

(24) "THEREFORE I SAY UNTO YOU, WHAT THINGS SOEVER YE DESIRE, WHEN YE PRAY, BELIEVE THAT YE RECEIVE THEM, AND YE SHALL HAVE THEM."

The phrase, *"Therefore I say unto you,"* is meant to serve as an enlargement on this profound Truth regarding Faith. It is the most important Truth, without which the result of Faith can never be realized.

The phrase, *"What things soever ye desire,"* is a profound promise, but yet misunderstood by most people.

NOTES

It means, *"Whatsoever things we desire in the Will of God."* As should be obvious, these Promises are given to mature Believers. And by mature, we do not necessarily mean Believers of longstanding, but, rather, Believers who truly and fully understand that one is to desire the Will of God in all matters, and irrespective as to how long one has been a Believer.

The Believer is to desire only what the Lord wants him to have. Paul said this, *"And be not conformed to this world: but be ye transformed by the renewing of your mind, that ye may prove what is that good, and acceptable, and perfect, Will of God"* (Rom. 12:2). In other words, nothing is *"acceptable"* to God, but the *"Perfect Will of God,"* which negates any idea of that which is referred to as a *"permissive will."* God cannot accept a *"permissive will,"* only a *"perfect Will."*

Many Believers, immature in the Ways of the Lord, have read this Passage of Scripture, automatically making them a shopper's list of things they *"desire,"* and then set about to confess them into existence. Such is foolishness!

Some time back, I heard of a Preacher confessing for himself a Mercedes, and some such like thing for his wife.

As stated, this is foolishness, and has absolutely no relationship to this Promise as given here by Christ. Such requests reeks of selfishness. Regrettably, the so-called *"Faith Ministry,"* which, in reality, is no Faith at all, has pretty much deteriorated to these sub-strata levels. And yet, it continues to have a wide following, because such appeals to greed.

Jesus, in the Garden of Gethsemane, epitomizes the hunger and desire for the Will of God.

He said, and concerning the coming Crucifixion, *"All things are possible unto Thee; take away this Cup from Me"* (Mk. 14:36). In other words, this statement by Christ proclaims that it was possible with God for the Plan of Salvation to be carried out in another fashion. However, Jesus only wanted that other way if it is what the Father wanted. His statement, *"Nevertheless not what I will, but what Thou wilt,"* is the criteria for every Believer.

Is it possible for God to do any and all things for me? Of course it is! However, that is not the point or the desire. The Will of God for my immediate life, is what I desire, and it is what every Believer should want and desire.

So, if the Believer majors only in what God can do, he completely misses the point. We must be careful that we seek only that which we know is His Will for our lives (Mk. 14:36).

The phrase, *"When ye pray,"* has been misunderstood by many as well!

Most have shortened the act of *"praying,"* merely to *"confession."* While *"confession"* certainly will play a part in prayer, still, it is only a part.

The idea is, that such *"prayer"* is not only to receive *"what things soever we desire,"* but, also, that we make certain that we desire the right things.

Prayer is consecration, or it is not really prayer at all. By that we mean, that we seek to consecrate ourselves to the highest, which is the noble Will of God. Nothing else will be satisfactory.

The word, *"pray,"* is *"proseuchomai,"* and means *"to offer prayer addressed to God, to Him as the object of Faith and the One Who will answer one's prayer."*

If God is the object of Faith, and which He must be, then His Will must be paramount. Otherwise, the petition will not, and, in fact, cannot be granted.

So, Faith must be the constant attitude of the mind when one prays, and with the object in view that we want to please God.

Paul wrote, *"But without Faith it is impossible to please Him"* (Heb. 11:6).

It is obvious that we must have Faith in God, to please God. And yet, Faith used for that which is not His Will, could not be pleasing to Him, as should be obvious!

The phrase, *"Believe that ye receive them,"* is the test of Faith, the kind that sees the fulfillment before it happens. This is the Great Truth which we previously spoke of, that this Passage brings out.

Most of the time, what we ask for is not given immediately. A test of Faith results. Actually, sometimes the answer is long in coming. But through it all, we must continue to *"believe,"* with the assurance that if this is properly done, we will ultimately *"receive."*

The word, *"believe,"* in the Greek is *"pisteuo,"* and means, *"to put in trust with."* It means that we are to trust not only for our request to be granted, but, as well, in God's time.

The phrase, *"And ye shall have them,"* refers to a present tense, with a futuristic conclusion.

He doesn't say exactly as to when we *"shall have them,"* but that it will be done, that is if we keep believing, and in due time. The *"timing"* is that which we entrust to Him.

(25-26) "AND WHEN YE STAND PRAYING, FORGIVE, IF YE HAVE OUGHT AGAINST ANY: THAT YOUR FATHER ALSO WHICH IS IN HEAVEN MAY FORGIVE YOU YOUR TRESPASSES.

"BUT IF YOU DO NOT FORGIVE, NEITHER WILL YOUR FATHER WHICH IS IN HEAVEN FORGIVE YOUR TRESPASSES."

Williams said, *"Such a Faith judges profession* (the fig tree, vs. 20); *removes difficulties* (the mountain, vs. 23); *and forgives injuries* (a sinner, vs. 25).*"

The phrase, *"And when ye stand praying, forgive,"* is only meant to point to the standing posture when praying, as it was a practice among the Jews. It in no way means that it is the only posture allowed.

As the previously two verses are some of the most powerful in the Word of God, likewise, verses 25 and 26 fall into the same category.

Irrespective of what someone has done to us, or whether they have asked forgiveness or not, the Scriptural Command is to *"forgive!"* It is to be an automatic thing with every Child of God. Failure to do so, carries an awesome penalty.

WHAT DOES IT MEAN TO FORGIVE?

The New Testament places considerable stress on the importance of forgiving others. In Matthew 18, Jesus tells three stories to illustrate forgiveness. He portrays human beings as sheep, prone to go astray. When this happens, we are to seek the straying. We are to bring the straying home, bearing them in our arms, rejoicing. The image is of a forgiveness that frees us from bitterness or recrimination and provides a joy that is able to heal every hurt (Mat. 18:10-14).

Jesus then spoke of the hurts and sins that mar family relationships. *"If your brother sins against you"* (Mat. 18:15), He began, and then He went on to explain that we are to take the initiative when we are hurt, and we should seek reconciliation.

Peter recognized the difficulty of this teaching, and objected. He asked how often such hurts should be forgiven. Jesus answered, *"Seventy times seven"* (Mat. 18:22) — a phrase indicating unlimited forgiveness.

Following this, Jesus told a Parable about a servant with a debt equivalent to a staggering sum of money (possibly billions of dollars in 1996 rates). When the servant could not pay and begged for time, the ruler to whom he owed the sum simply forgave the entire obligation.

But the same servant later demanded the minor amount a fellow servant owed him (equivalent to a few hundred dollars). He actually went so far as to throw the fellow servant into prison for nonpayment. Jesus' intention is clear: We who are forgiven an unimaginable debt by God (and all of us have been) surely must be so moved by gratitude that we treat our fellows as we have been treated.

This theme — forgive as you are forgiven — is often stressed in the New Testament, and the theme has two applications.

First, God's treatment of us provides an example that we are to follow in our relationships with other persons. We are to be *"kind and compassionate to one another, forgiving one another, just as in Christ God forgave us"* (Eph. 4:32).

The second application seems to introduce a conditional aspect to the promise of forgiveness. In Matthew 6:14-15, we read, *"For if you forgive men when they sin against you, your Heavenly Father will also forgive you.*

"But if you do not forgive men their sins, your Father will not forgive your sins." Mark 11:25 expresses the same thought in the same way. These Passages seem to trouble many. However, there is no reason they should!

FORGIVENESS AFFECTS OUR PERSONALITY

Just as every coin has two sides, never only one, so forgiveness has two aspects that can never be separated. These two sides of forgiveness are accepting and extending.

The person who accepts forgiveness becomes deeply aware of his own weakness and need. Pride is ruled out as we take our place as supplicants before the Lord. This basic attitude releases us from our tendency to become angry with, or judgmental of, others. We begin to see others as creatures who are, like us, flawed by weakness. Rather than react with enflamed pride (he can't do this to me!), we are freed to respond as God does, with loving concern and forgiveness.

NOTES

It isn't that God will not forgive the unforgiving. It is simply that the unforgiving lack the humble attitude that both permits them to accept forgiveness and frees them to extend forgiveness.

THE INNER DYNAMICS OF FORGIVENESS

The foregoing discussion should demonstrate something of the transforming impact of forgiveness. One who accepts forgiveness from God adopts an attitude toward himself that transforms his or her attitude toward others. The person who accepts forgiveness becomes forgiving.

But there are other aspects of forgiveness as well. Jesus once confronted a critical Pharisee who observed with contempt the tearful devotion a woman who seemed to be fallen had for Jesus. The Pharisee thought, *"If this man were a Prophet, he would know who is touching Him and what kind of woman she is"* (Lk. 7:39).

Jesus responded to the Pharisee's unexpressed thought. He told a story of two men in debt to a money-lender. The one owed $200 and the other $2,000. If the money-lender should cancel the debts, Jesus asked, what man would love him more? The Pharisee answered, *"I suppose the one who had the bigger debt canceled"* (Lk. 7:43). Jesus then nodded toward the weeping woman and confirmed the principle. Her sins were many, but when she was forgiven, she knew the wonder of God's gift of love, and she responded with love. As we meditate on God's forgiveness and realize how much we have been forgiven, love for the Lord is nurtured in our hearts.

WHAT TYPE OF FORGIVENESS DOES GOD EXTEND TO THE REPENTANT SINNER?

The Book of Hebrews perhaps develops the type of forgiveness offered to us by Christ, as no other Book in the Bible. The writer compares the Sacrifice of Jesus with the Old Testament Sacrifices that prefigured Him. Had the earlier Sacrifices the power to make the worshipers perfect, they *"would have been cleansed once for all, and would no longer have felt guilty for their sins"* (Heb. 10:2).

But Jesus' Sacrifice does make us perfect! Through Jesus, all our sins are actually taken away! Thus the Believer who realizes that he is truly forgiven is released from a sense of guilt and from bondages to past mistakes. Because God has forgiven our sins (Heb. 10:17), we can forget our past. Forgiven, we can concentrate all our energies on living a Godly life. That is the reason Paul also said, *"Forgetting those things which are behind, and reaching forth unto those things which are before,*

"I press toward the mark for the prize of the high calling of God in Christ Jesus" (Phil. 3:13-14).

He also wrote, *"There is therefore now no condemnation to them which are in Christ Jesus, who walk not after the flesh, but after the Spirit"* (Rom. 8:1).

This means that all the past is washed and cleansed by the precious Blood of Jesus Christ. It is what John was speaking of when he said, *"Behold the Lamb of God, which taketh away the sin of the world"* (Jn. 1:29).

When Jesus *"takes our sin away,"* they can no longer be brought against us. Consequently, we are treated by the Lord as if the sin or sins were never committed. It is called *"Justification by Faith."* Paul wrote, *"Therefore being justified by Faith, we have peace with God through our Lord Jesus Christ"* (Rom. 5:1).

Consequently, the sins which once marred that *"peace,"* have been taken away, and *"peace"* has now been restored.

The Believer should never go back and drag out sins which have been washed and cleansed by the Blood of Jesus, and actually should not even mention these sins anymore. As we have stated, and as Paul wrote, *"Forgetting those things...."*

HOW SHOULD FELLOW BELIEVERS CONDUCT THEMSELVES TOWARD A PENITENT ONE?

I think we have been replete in giving example after example where Jesus demanded that we understand just how much we have been forgiven by God, and that we treat others accordingly. In other words, the same type of forgiveness that God extends to the penitent Believer, must be extended to others by us, or else it is no forgiveness at all! Anything less is not constituted by God as forgiveness.

However, for the Believer to conduct himself accordingly toward a fellow Believer, as we have stated, necessitates the fellow Believer being truly repentant.

If he is not repentant, while in our hearts we should still forgive him, fellowship is necessarily curtailed. However, even then Paul said, *"Yet count him not as an enemy, but admonish him as a brother,"* in other words, continuing to make every effort to bring him to a place of repentance (II Thess. 3:15).

(Some of the thoughts on forgiveness were from the writings of Lawrence Richards.)

The phrase, *"If ye have ought against any,"* places this type of action on a personal basis. In other words, Jesus is speaking of someone who has wronged us, or at least we think they have. We are to forgive that person, as stated, whether they ask or not! Nothing is to be held in our hearts against anyone. Realizing what the Lord has done for us, we must, even at all times, show grace, love, and forgiveness toward all others.

However, and as we have alluded to, if the individual has not asked our forgiveness, and, in fact, is continuing in their wrong or evil way, while forgiveness must be tendered, still, fellowship cannot be enjoined. The Prophet Amos said, *"Can two walk together, except they be agreed?"* (Amos 3:3).

The phrase, *"That your Father also which is in Heaven may forgive you your trespasses,"* constitutes a tremendously important principle, which should be obvious.

The word, *"trespasses,"* in the Greek is *"paraptoma,"* and means *"a fall from the right course,"* or *"a false step."*

It is foolish to think that such will not occur in our own lives, and, therefore, considering our own weaknesses, we must as well consider the weakness of others.

So, the implication is clear, if we want forgiveness for our *"trespasses,"* we must forgive others and be quick to do so.

The phrase, *"But if you do not forgive,"* proclaims an extremely solemn statement to say the least!

This Passage of Scripture is basically the same as verse 25. However, inasmuch as the matter of *"forgiveness"* is so very important, the Holy Spirit had Christ to say it again, even more direct this time, that no one misunderstand.

The phrase, *"Neither will your Father which is in Heaven forgive your trespasses,"* puts the unforgiving one in a terrible state. If one is in the posture in which his sins cannot be forgiven, and because of his lack of forgiveness toward others, if the situation is not somewhere rectified, the individual will die lost. No one can continue in this state until they die and still be saved. To be sure, the Holy Spirit will deal with them, making it abundantly clear that they must obey the Word of God; however, if they refuse to do so, forgive others, there is no alternative but eternal darkness.

Considering the seriousness of what our Lord is saying, every Believer must constantly search his heart in order that no unforgiveness lodges there. And yet, I suspect that many little heed these dire admonitions, and because so little attention is given to the Word of God, many Believers have little or no knowledge of these statements. However, ignorance is no excuse!

(27) "AND THEY COME AGAIN TO JERUSALEM: AND AS HE WAS WALKING IN THE TEMPLE, THERE CAME TO HIM THE CHIEF PRIESTS, AND THE SCRIBES, AND THE ELDERS,"

The phrase, *"And they come again to Jerusalem,"* is thought by some to represent the third day in which He visits this edifice. The Crucifixion is drawing ever closer.

The phrase, *"And as He was walking in the Temple,"* probably spoke of the colonnades. He was probably teaching the people as He walked slowly among them. No doubt, a great crowd had gathered, as it always did when He was present.

The phrase, *"There come to Him the Chief Priests, and the Scribes, and the Elders,"* represents three different groups or orders, and, as well, leaders in these particular orders.

1. Chief Priests: These were members of the vaunted Sanhedrin, and could well have been the High Priests or former members who held that highest office. They were, at times, called *"Chief Priests."*

These could have been representatives of these particular groups; however, inasmuch as the definite article in the Greek is used in each case, quite possibly these were not representatives, but, rather, the High Priests themselves, whether present or former.

This group opposed Christ greatly, and as His claims and mission became more clear, their opposition increased, as here. As well, He strongly denounced them in His Parables, etc.

Considering the cleansing of the Temple, and the great crowds which flocked to Him,

such fueled their opposition. It would reach its bitter climax only in the arrest and trial of the Saviour.

(As well, as the term *"Chief Priests"* describing members of the high-priestly families who served in the Sanhedrin, the title could also have included Temple Officers such as the Treasurer and Captain of Police.)

2. Scribes: These, in effect, were to be the Pastors of the people, and were supposed to be scholars of the Law of Moses.

3. Elders: These were members of the Sanhedrin, and shared with the Chief Priests the power of determining religious affairs and, if necessary, of expulsion from the Synagogue.

These were actually the Religious Leaders of Israel, and bitterly opposed Christ.

They saw in Him a threat to their position, and would not recognize Him as being sent from God. In Truth, they would not have recognized anyone truly sent from God. These individuals were religious but exceedingly evil.

When one reads these Passages, one is reading the greatest thrust of Satan which has caused more people to die eternally lost than possibly anything else. I speak of religion! It has always opposed God, and, consequently, has ever attempted to stop His True Work.

In Truth, and sadly so, most of modern Christendom falls in the same category. This would include virtually all of Catholicism and most of that which calls itself *"Protestant."* Most of the Old-line Churches, such as Baptist, Methodist, Presbyterian, etc., little believe at all in the Holy Spirit. Consequently, precious little, if anything, can be done for the Lord in these circles. They have a *"form of Godliness, but they deny the power thereof"* (II Tim. 3:5).

Regrettably, those who go under the Holiness banner, such as Nazarene, etc., fall into the same category, most having rejected the Holy Spirit, and have consequently sunk into the quagmire of legalism.

Sadder still, the Pentecostal Denominations such as the Assemblies of God, Church of God, Pentecostal Holiness, etc., have pretty much abandoned the Holy Spirit in favor of the knowledge of this world, i.e., psychology, etc. (The old-line Churches have long since embraced these philosophies.)

The Charismatics, which probably number approximately 100,000 Churches in America alone, are, for the most part, mired in false doctrine, such as the *"Prosperity Message,"* or the *"Political Message."*

And yet, there are exceptions to everything stated, with some Godly Preachers and people in any and all of these particular Churches, etc. But for the far greater majority, if the situation presented itself now as then, almost all would fall into step with the Religious Leaders in opposition to Christ. Even though many of these speak favorably of Him presently, still, He is window dressing in most Churches.

(28) "AND SAY UNTO HIM, BY WHAT AUTHORITY DOEST THOU THESE THINGS? AND WHO GAVE THEE THIS AUTHORITY TO DO THESE THINGS?"

The phrase, *"And say unto Him,"* constitutes the very opposite of what they should have said. They should have fallen on their knees before Him, worshiping Him, but, instead, they will do the very opposite!

The question, *"By what authority doest Thou these things?",* was reasonable in their minds.

They were the custodians of the Temple. Our Lord, by forcibly ejecting those who were engaged in business in the Temple, was claiming a superior jurisdiction. Consequently, they asked Him in public now to produce His credentials, first, to state the nature of His authority, and, second, to name the person from whom He had received it (Wuest).

They were highly angered for a number of reasons: First of all, His action concerning cleansing the Temple, had cost them a considerable amount of money, especially since it was Passover, which enjoyed the greatest crowds of the year.

As well, He was teaching the massive crowd particular things in His Parables, which greatly incriminated them. Inasmuch as it was clearly obvious as to whom He was speaking, they are now placed in a very awkward position.

As well, they greatly resent His popularity, especially considering the healings and miracles.

As stated, they in no way considered Him to be the Messiah, but instead to be far beneath them, socially, spiritually, and in every way, especially since He was but a peasant. Were it not for the accolades of the crowds, and His vast popularity, they would have long since taken Him in hand. They had not done so, simply because they felt the could not do so. However,

the situation was now becoming desperate, at least in their eyes.

By the use of the word, *"authority,"* they were speaking of delegated power, the liberty and right to act. Such authority as men have is delegated to them by God, whether directly or indirectly, to Whom they must answer for the way they use it.

God's Authority is an aspect of His unalterable, universal, and eternal dominion over His world (Ex. 15:18; Ps. 29:10; 93:1; 146:10; Dan. 4:34).

Throughout the Bible, the reality of God's Authority is proved by the fact that all who ignore or flout this claim incur Divine Judgment. The Royal Judge has the last word, and so His Authority is vindicated.

In Old Testament times, which were still in force as recorded in the Gospels, God exercised authority over His people through the agency of Prophets, Priests, and Kings, whose respective work it was to proclaim His Messages (Jer. 1:7), teach His Laws (Deut. 31:11; Mal. 2:7), and rule in accordance with those Laws (Deut. 17:18). In so doing, they were to be respected as God's representatives, having authority from Him.

However, the authority held by these Religious Rulers who questioned Jesus, was not derived from God, but rather from Rome. Consequently, it was man-devised authority, which the people were to obey up to a point, providing it did not abrogate the Word of God, which it often did. However, Jesus in no way was subject to the Laws of Rome, or anyone else for that matter, even though He willingly and Personally subjected Himself to such authority, providing it did not abrogate the Word of God.

The Authority of Jesus Christ is an aspect of Kingship, which these Religious Leaders would not recognize. It is both personal and official, for Jesus is both Son of God and Son of Man (The Messiah). As Man and Messiah, His Authority is real because it is delegated to Him by the God at Whose Command He does His Work. (Christ applauded the Centurion for seeing and recognizing this, Mat. 8:9.)

As the Son, His Authority is real because He is Himself God. Authority to judge has been given Him, both that He may be honored as the Son of God (for judgment is God's Work), and also because He is the Son of Man (for judgment is the Messiah's Work) (Jn. 5:22, 27).

In short, His Authority is that of a Divine Messiah; of a God-Man, doing His Father's Will in the double capacity of: A. Human Servant, in Whom meet the saving offices of Prophet, Priest, and King; and, B. Divine Son, co-creator and sharer in all the Father's Works (Jn. 5:19).

The more-than-human Authority of Jesus was manifested during His Ministry in various ways, such as the finality and independence of His Teaching (Mat. 7:28); His Power to cast out devils (Mk. 1:27); His Mastery over storms (Lk. 8:24); His forgiving of sin (a thing which, as the bystanders rightly pointed out, only God can do) and, when challenged, proving His claim (Mat. 9:8; Mk. 2:5-12).

After His Resurrection, He declared that He had been given *"All Power in Heaven and earth"* — a Messianic Dominion, to be exercised in such a way as effectively to bring the elect into His Kingdom of Salvation (Mat. 28:18; Jn. 12:31; 17:2; Acts 1:8-9; 5:31).

The New Testament proclaims the exalted Jesus as *"both Lord and Christ"* (Acts 2:36) — Divine Ruler of all things, and Saviour-King of His people. The Gospel is in the first instance a demand for ascent to this estimate of His Authority.

In short, He did the things He did, by Divine Authority from His Heavenly Father. He said, *"The Son can do nothing of Himself, but what He seeth the Father do: for what things soever He doeth, these also doeth the Son likewise"* (Jn. 5:19).

The question, *"And who gave Thee this authority to do these things?"*, concerned the Source. The first question pertained to His Authority being Divine, and the second question pertained to its Source, God the Father.

It would have done Him no good to have answered them outright, for they would not have accepted His answers. Consequently, He must address their questions from another angle.

(29) "AND JESUS ANSWERED AND SAID UNTO THEM, I WILL ALSO ASK OF YOU ONE QUESTION, AND ANSWER ME, AND I WILL TELL YOU BY WHAT AUTHORITY I DO THESE THINGS."

The phrase, *"And Jesus answered and said unto them,"* pertains to the Holy Spirit telling Him how to answer these questions. However, it must be understood that the Holy Spirit only helped Him respecting information that

was already in His Heart. He knew the Word of God as no one had ever known it, and for several reasons.

First of all, He had never sinned even one time, and, consequently, His mind was not dulled in any manner regarding the debilitating effects of sin. He said, *"I have refrained My feet from every evil way, that I might keep Thy Word"* (Ps. 119:101). Consequently, we learn from this that sin (the evil way) dulls the sense perception and Spirit perception of the Word of God.

As well, Christ had a love for the Word that no one else had ever had. He said, *"O how love I Thy Law! it is My meditation all the day"* (Ps. 119:97). There is no one who has devoted the time and attention to the Word of God as Christ. As I have said elsewhere in these Volumes, I have had the privilege several times to visit Nazareth, the boyhood home of Jesus.

I have stood on some of those hills near the city, where Jesus no doubt had spent much time in His boyhood years, and especially during the years of His twenties. During this time, even while He was working as a carpenter, His mind and spirit were continually on the Word of God.

In writing these Commentaries, I have had the privilege of spending several hours each day in the Word of God. There is no way that words could begin to express the strength I derive from this. As well, and before beginning on the Commentaries several years ago, I was reading the Bible completely through every three to four months. So, I have a faint idea of the devotion He had to this all-important purpose.

Also, He had the help of the Holy Spirit as no other person has ever had, simply because He was *"Anointed with the oil of gladness above Thy fellows"* (Ps. 45:7).

Many people think because He was the Son of God that He knew the Word automatically, and especially considering He was the Word (Jn. 1:1). However, even though He did have some advantages, as we have stated, still, other than that, He had to learn the Word exactly as we do.

The phrase, *"I will also ask of you one question, and answer Me,"* points to only one question which will address their two. It will greatly simplify the issue.

The phrase, *"And I will tell you by what authority I do these things,"* actually means that the correct response to His question will provide the answer.

NOTES

(30) "THE BAPTISM OF JOHN, WAS IT FROM HEAVEN, OR OF MEN? ANSWER ME."

The question which begins with the phrase, *"The Baptism of John,"* concerned the Ministry of John the Baptist, with its Baptism of Repentance demanded of Israel (Mk. 1:4).

As well, he was the one who *"Prepared ye the Way of the Lord,"* i.e., Messiah, the Lord Jesus Christ (Mk. 1:3). He also introduced Jesus as the Messiah, by saying, *"Behold the Lamb of God, Which taketh away the sin of the world"* (Jn. 1:29).

The question, *"Was it from Heaven, or of men?",* puts these Religious Leaders on the spot! In effect, their answer, that is if they would give one, must either proclaim John as being of God, or the Devil!

The words, *"Answer Me,"* are asked before the crowd, which had no doubt assembled. They had tried to put Him on the spot, and now the tables are turned.

(31) "AND THEY REASONED WITH THEMSELVES, SAYING, IF WE SHALL SAY, FROM HEAVEN; HE WILL SAY, WHY THEN DID YE NOT BELIEVE HIM?"

The phrase, *"And they reasoned with themselves,"* in essence, means they went into a huddle. It would have been somewhat embarrassing with the crowd looking on awaiting their answer. They are thrown on the horns of a dilemma.

The phrase, *"Saying, If we shall say, From Heaven,"* proclaims them having no regard for who John really was, only for an answer which would get them out of this dilemma.

The question, *"He will say, Why then did ye not believe him?",* means they would have to believe John, at least if this admittance is made, regarding His introduction of Jesus as the Messiah.

(32) "BUT IF WE SHALL SAY, OF MEN; THEY FEARED THE PEOPLE: FOR ALL MEN COUNTED JOHN, THAT HE WAS A PROPHET INDEED."

The phrase, *"But if we shall say, Of men; they feared the people,"* presents the only thing that stopped them from claiming John the Baptist was *"of men,"* i.e., the Devil.

The phrase, *"For all men counted John, that he was a Prophet indeed,"* means that the respect for John by the people had even deepened since his martyrdom.

These Religious Leaders feared that if they said what they really believed, the people might even stone them, even then and there!

(33) "AND THEY ANSWERED AND SAID UNTO JESUS, WE CANNOT TELL. AND JESUS ANSWERING SAITH UNTO THEM, NEITHER DO I TELL YOU BY WHAT AUTHORITY I DO THESE THINGS."

The phrase, *"And they answered and said unto Jesus, We cannot tell,"* concerns them giving an answer before the crowd that was ridiculous to say the least. They were the very ones who were supposed to know, and yet they say, *"We cannot tell."*

These were supposed to be the scholars of the Mosaic Law. They were the spiritual guides of the people. They were supposed to know if something was of God or men! Their weak, tepid answer shows what they really were! They did not know God, and had no knowledge of spiritual things, and yet they considered themselves *"spiritual leaders."*

To be sure, most fall into the same category even today!

The phrase, *"And Jesus answering saith unto them, Neither do I tell you by what authority I do these things,"* in effect says, *"I will not answer you, because your answer to My question, is the answer to your own."*

Jerome says, *"He thus shows, that they knew, but would not answer; and that He knew, but did not speak, because they were silent as to what they knew."*

Wuest said, *"The Jewish Leaders saved themselves from this dilemma by professing ignorance."*

CHAPTER 12

(1) "AND HE BEGAN TO SPEAK UNTO THEM BY PARABLES. A CERTAIN MAN PLANTED A VINEYARD, AND SET AN HEDGE ABOUT IT, AND DIGGED A PLACE FOR THE WINEFAT, AND BUILT A TOWER, AND LET IT OUT TO HUSBANDMEN, AND WENT INTO A FAR COUNTRY."

The phrase, *"And He began to speak unto them by Parables,"* represents the first time He had used this method in Jerusalem, although it had been used plentifully in Galilee.

Many of the Parables of Jesus are not merely illustrations of general principles; instead they embody messages which cannot be conveyed any other way, at least to present the desired Truth.

Parables are the appropriate form of communication for bringing to men the Message of the Kingdom, since their function is to jolt them into seeing things in a new way. They are means of enlightenment and persuasion, intended to bring the hearers to the point of decision.

Jesus, as it were, stands where His hearers stand, and uses imagery familiar to them to bring new and unfamiliar insights to them. Just as a betrothed finds himself restricted by common expression, and must resort to poetry to express his feelings, so Jesus expresses the Message of the Kingdom in the appropriate forms of language.

Parables, and especially those given by Jesus, have a tendency to enlighten the Believer, while, at the same time, confusing the unbeliever. Actually, Isaiah prophesied that the preaching of the Word of God would do the same thing. The Truth is that Jesus' Parables are unique.

Parables of other teachers can, to some extent, be separated from the teachers themselves, but Jesus and His Parables are inseparable. To fail to understand Him is to fail to understand His Parables.

In this *"Parable of the Householder,"* Jesus is accusing the Religious Leaders of Israel of being the future murderers of the Messiah, and this in the presence of the crowd. His purpose was to expose the true character of the hostility of the Sanhedrin.

The phrase, *"A certain Man planted a Vineyard,"* constitutes no other than God Himself.

The *"Vineyard"* as well, was a recognized symbol of Israel as the Covenant people, and both the members of the Sanhedrin and the better-taught among the crowd could not but understand the symbolism (Wuest).

As the *"Church"* belongs to Jesus, likewise, the *"Vineyard"* belongs to God (Mat. 16:18). This *"Vineyard"* sprang from the loins of Abraham. The members of each of the Twelve Tribes sprang, as well, from the twelve sons of Jacob. In the midst of a sinful, wicked, idol-worshiping world, God formed a people unto Himself, who would do three things:

1. Give the Word of God to the world, which they did. Every writer of the Bible is Jewish.

NOTES

(Some claim that Luke was Gentile; however, there is evidence that points otherwise.)

2. To be the womb of the Messiah, consequently, bringing the Redeemer into the world, The Last Adam.

3. To evangelize the world, hence the *"Temple being a house of prayer for all nations"* (Mk. 11:17).

However, as we shall see, the *"Husbandmen"* i.e., Israel, little attended the Vineyard as the Owner desired.

The phrase, *"And set an hedge about it,"* actually refers to the manner in which Israel is situated in the Middle East. The nation was somewhat guarded on the east by the River Jordan, and on the west by the Mediterranean Sea. On the north lay the mountains of Lebanon, and down south was the desert. So, in a sense, there was *"an hedge about it."*

As well, and of far greater significance, there was a *"hedge"* of the Power of God about the nation. Consequently, when Israel conducted herself according to the Word of God, no nation or group of nations in the world could conquer her.

Only when Israel forsook the Lord, did the *"hedge"* come down. Ultimately, and as this Parable will proclaim, the hedge would be torn down completely.

Regarding the phrase, *"And digged a place for the winefat,"* the word, *"fat,"* is from the old Anglo-Saxon *"foet,"* for *"vessel,"* and the Dutch *"vatten,"* to catch. It was a word used in Northern England for *"vat."* So, the better translation of the word would have been *"winevat."* The *"winevat"* referred to the receptacle into which the wine ran after it had been pressed out of the grapes. As is obvious, this speaks of the product of the Vineyard, and, as well, speaks of the *"fruit"* which came from Israel. At times, there was *"much fruit,"* and because of strong spiritual leadership, such as David, Jehoshaphat, Hezekiah, Josiah, and others!

The manner in which the wine is produced by the crushing of the grapes, spoke of the suffering and opposition that Israel underwent from other nations. It was allowed by God, with no intention of destruction, but rather that Israel would run to Him.

As well as this Parable applying to Israel of old, it can by symbolism apply to the Church, and even to the individual.

Entire Religious Denominations have experienced the results of this Parable, and simply because they ultimately set Jesus aside, and, consequently, their *"Vineyard"* was given to others.

Every Believer should read this Parable not only with Israel in mind, but with the understanding that its lesson applies to all, even to the individual Believer.

The phrase, *"And built a tower,"* referred to the watch-tower, where a watchman was placed to guard the Vineyard from plunderers. It spoke of the Spiritual Leaders of Israel. It speaks as well of the modern Ministry. Every Preacher of the Gospel, along with the type of Ministry that God has given him (Eph. 4:11), likewise, is called to be a *"watchman."*

Jude said, *"That ye should earnestly contend for the faith which was once delivered unto the Saints"* (Jude 3).

As well, Paul said, *"Preach the Word; be instant in season, out of season; reprove, rebuke, exhort with all longsuffering and doctrine.*

"For the time will come when they will not endure sound doctrine; but after their own lusts shall they heap to themselves teachers, having itching ears;"

He then said, *"And they shall turn away their ears from the Truth, and shall be turned unto fables."*

And then, *"But watch thou in all things,"* means to serve as a *"watchman"* (II Tim. 4:2-5).

Sadly and regrettably, the modern *"watch-tower"* is occupied too much by those who little care regarding the encroachment of enemies, exactly as Israel of old!

The phrase, *"And let it out to Husbandmen,"* refers to the teachers of the people, as well as the people. Each member of the Church, then, as now, is required to seek the welfare of the whole Body (Bickersteth). All are responsible, and yet, the leaders are always the far more responsible!

The phrase, *"And went into a far country,"* refers to God's residence as being in Heaven. While He was here with His people in Spirit, still, the responsibility of the *"Vineyard,"* was that of the *"Husbandmen."* It is no different with the Church presently!

The modern Believer, and due to what Jesus did at Calvary and the Resurrection, has a far greater Presence of the Lord than Israel of old.

Then He dwelt in a house made with hands, while now He dwells in every individual Believer (I Cor. 3:16).

However, if that house is defiled, whether the Temple of old, or the individual Temple of the Holy Spirit, it will be destroyed, exactly as the old Temple was destroyed (I Cor. 3:17).

However, even with a greater Presence of the Lord in the modern Church, still, the responsibility still lies with the *"Husbandmen,"* i.e., *"Preachers."*

(2) "AND AT THE SEASON HE SENT TO THE HUSBANDMEN A SERVANT, THAT HE MIGHT RECEIVE FROM THE HUSBANDMEN OF THE FRUIT OF THE VINEYARD."

The phrase, *"And at the season He sent to the Husbandmen a servant,"* refers to the harvest. However, it also refers to the Truth that God has *"seasons"* for the outpouring of His Holy Spirit. In my own lifetime, I have seen two of these *"seasons."*

The first was in the 1950's, with great Divine healing Revivals taking place all over the world. It was the Move of God which brought the Pentecostal Message from obscurity to the limelight. Concerning the Assemblies of God, which we were then with, they were planting on the average one new Church a day, and three on Sunday. In other words, nearly ten a week. Many of the other Pentecostal Movements were doing the same.

I sense the Presence of God even as I dictate these words. Among all the many books written by Gordon Lindsay, who was used mightily in this outpouring, his book, *"Bible Days Are Here Again,"* in my mind, epitomized this outpouring as nothing else. Giant tents seating as many as 10,000 people were being stretched all over America, as well as other parts of the world, housing great Salvation-Healing Revivals. Even though the Lord had continued to heal the sick all the way from the time of Pentecost, still, it was not until this great Move of God, that once again the God of Might and Miracles was introduced to the world.

The second great Move took place in the 1980's. Frances and I had the privilege and opportunity of being a part of this great Outpouring. Our Telecast was aired during that time all over America and Canada, plus Central and South America. We, as well, aired in the Philippines, along with parts of Africa, Europe, and other parts of the world. The Program was translated into the languages of the people, and resulted in hundreds of thousands being brought to a saving knowledge of Jesus Christ.

As well, our Crusades in various countries saw some of the largest crowds ever recorded in these respective countries, with multiple thousands of people answering the Altar Calls. In the Stadium in Santiago, Chile, the Stadium Manager said that 28,000 people answered the Altar Call on the closing Sunday of the meeting. It was a Move of God which touched almost the entirety of the world.

Even in the early 1990's, our Telecast aired in Russia, and translated into Russian, caused untold thousands to be brought to Christ.

Actually, I think one can say without fear of exaggeration, that everywhere the Telecast has aired, tremendous numbers of souls have been saved. We give the Lord Alone the Praise and the Glory!

And yet, I feel that another great *"season"* of moving of the Holy Spirit is coming, a Move so powerful, in fact, that it will eclipse all others. I believe this *"season"* is referred to in the Promise, *"It shall come to pass in the last days, saith God, I will pour out of My Spirit upon all flesh"* (Acts 2:17).

I realize that many conclude the *"Last Days"* to refer to the entirety of the time from the Day of Pentecost until the present; however, verses 19 through 21 let us know that while this may be the case, still, a greater Move will take place at the end, which, I believe, is near!

The *"servant"* He sent, speaks of the Old Testament Prophets sent to Israel.

The phrase, *"That He might receive from the Husbandmen of the fruit of the Vineyard,"* respects that which was rightly His.

The Lord had made a tremendous investment in Israel, as He has in the Church. Consequently, He expects *"Fruit of the Vineyard."*

As stated, it referred to Israel of old, and it also refers to the modern Church, and even to the individual.

(3) "AND THEY CAUGHT HIM, AND BEAT HIM, AND SENT HIM AWAY EMPTY."

The phrase, *"And they caught him,"* refers to them coming to the Prophets, not to heed the Message, but, instead, to stop the Message.

The phrase, *"And beat him,"* means *"to beat severely, to scourge."*

The phrase, *"And sent him away empty,"* according to Wuest means that *"the failure to receive fruit points to the failure of Israel to heed the preaching of the Prophets."*

(4) "AND AGAIN HE SENT UNTO THEM ANOTHER SERVANT; AND AT HIM THEY CAST STONES, AND WOUNDED HIM IN THE HEAD, AND SENT HIM AWAY SHAMEFULLY HANDLED."

The phrase, *"And again He sent unto them another servant,"* does not so much point to the act as to the patience in dealing with these recalcitrant rebels. Once again, these were the Prophets.

The phrase, *"And at him they cast stones,"* refers to the opposition increasingly becoming more severe.

The phrase, *"And wounded him in the head,"* means two things:

1. They were trying to kill him.

2. The projectiles aimed at his *"head,"* were meant to stop the Message.

The phrase, *"And sent him away shamefully handled,"* refers more to their attitude than the condition of the one sent.

In Truth, the True Message of God is seldom met with approval. However, the greatest opposition will always be from the *"Church,"* for Israel was the *"Church"* of that day! So, as one reads these statements, one is reading the present response as well, by the modern Church to the Gospel of Jesus Christ. They try to stop the Message, hence, the striking of the *"head,"* and they *"shamefully handle"* the messenger.

At the present, were it not for the laws of the land, and the separation of Church and State in most countries, this scene would be repeated as well! It is not lack of evil in the heart which stays the hand, but lack of opportunity. There is nothing in the world more evil than Religion. It is far more evil than the vices, such as alcohol, drugs, immorality, etc. Many may blanch at that; however, they must remember that it was not the vices, as sordid as they are, which nailed Jesus to the tree, but, rather, the Church of that day.

(5) "AND AGAIN HE SENT ANOTHER; AND HIM THEY KILLED, AND MANY OTHERS; BEATING SOME, AND KILLING SOME."

The phrase, *"And again He sent another,"* proclaims patience, love, and longsuffering, such as no mortal could ever have. Such is God!

The phrase, *"And him they killed, and many others; beating some, and killing some,"* proclaims an increase in the rebellion and its obvious results. Barring repentance, sin never slows, but, instead, increases.

The word, *"many,"* emphasizes the constant efforts to bring the *"Husbandmen"* to their senses, but to no avail!

(6) "HAVING YET THEREFORE ONE SON, HIS WELLBELOVED, HE SENT HIM ALSO LAST UNTO THEM, SAYING, THEY WILL REVERENCE MY SON."

The phrase, *"Having yet therefore one Son, His wellbeloved,"* refers to the Lord Jesus Christ. Jesus may have had in mind the Words of the Father at His Baptism, *"This is My Son, the Beloved One in Whom I am well pleased"* (Mat. 3:17) (Wuest).

The phrase, *"He sent Him also last unto them,"* refers to Christ coming after all the Prophets had been sent.

The phrase, *"Saying, They will reverence My Son,"* refers to the idea that the Owner, rather *"God,"* expected *"reverence,"* especially considering as to Who the Son actually was!

Of course, one understands that God knows all, past, present, and future. However, the implication is that the depths of depravity to which Israel had fallen, came as a shock, one might say, even to God. Mankind, and even the Church, does not have any conception of the utter and complete depravity of the fallen race, nor to what lengths it will go in order to hold onto its sin.

In the world there is no *"reverence"* for God, nor His Son, the Lord Jesus Christ.

(7) "BUT THOSE HUSBANDMEN SAID AMONG THEMSELVES, THIS IS THE HEIR; COME, LET US KILL HIM, AND THE INHERITANCE SHALL BE OURS."

The phrase, *"But those Husbandmen said among themselves, This is the Heir,"* in this case, refers to the Sanhedrin, the ruling body of Israel.

The phrase, *"This is the Heir,"* means that these Religious Leaders recognized the Lord for What and Who He was, the Son of God, the Messiah of Israel.

How did the Religious Leaders think they could kill the Lord of Glory and not suffer horrifying consequences?

Sin and rebellion against God warps one's mind, until one does not think straight. Sin

and rebellion are extremely selfish acts. Consequently, these individuals saw only their selfish desires. They wanted nothing or no one to interfere with their self-will, even God. Consequently, they were willing to go to any lengths to ensure their desires, even the murdering of the Son of God.

Regarding how they thought they could succeed in such a task, the question might well be asked how Satan thought he could succeed against God? God is Omnipotent (all-powerful), Omniscient (all-knowing), and Omnipresent (everywhere), whereas Satan is only a created being.

The answer lies in deception. Satan is deceived, as well as all his followers, which included the Religious Leaders of Israel.

The phrase, *"Come, let us kill Him,"* addresses itself to the words of Paul, *"But we speak of the wisdom of God in a mystery, even the hidden wisdom, which God ordained before the world unto our glory:*

"Which none of the princes of this world knew: for had they known it, they would not have crucified the Lord of Glory" (I Cor. 2:7-8).

The reason the Religious Leaders of Israel did what they did, even with full knowledge as to Who Jesus was, is the same reason the whole world conducts itself as it does toward Christ. Most people probably know that Jesus is the Son of God, even though they will not admit it; however, being deceived, unbelief concerning His Redemption Plan, causes their opposition.

The phrase, *"And the inheritance shall be ours,"* actually constitutes the plan of Satan from the very beginning. Satan said, *"I will ascend above the heights of the clouds; I will be like the Most High"* (Isa. 14:14).

Satan maneuvered against Israel through these Religious Leaders, in order to steal the *"inheritance,"* i.e., that which belonged to God. In fact, Satan constantly endeavors to take the *"inheritance"* even from the individual.

(8) "AND THEY TOOK HIM, AND KILLED HIM, AND CAST HIM OUT OF THE VINEYARD."

The phrase, *"And they took Him, and killed Him,"* refers to the Sanhedrin, the ruling body of Israel, crucifying the Lord.

The phrase, *"And cast Him out of the Vineyard,"* means they excommunicated the Lord. In other words, and in today's terminology, He was thrown out of the Church. He was condemned as a blasphemer and handed over to the Romans for Crucifixion. Wuest said that His Crucifixion outside the walls of Jerusalem symbolized His expulsion from the community of Israel.

Bickersteth said, *"This was the last effort of Divine Mercy — the sending of the Incarnate God, Whom the Jews put to death without the city."*

Tragically, this horrible spectacle of what Israel did to Christ, their Messiah and our Saviour, set the example for much of that which is called *"Church,"* and down through the ages. In other words, the *"Church"* has by and large *"cast out"* that which is truly of God. By its very nature, organized religion is man-controlled, and, consequently, man-centered. If it is man-controlled, it cannot be God-controlled! Consequently, anything truly of the Lord will ultimately be *"cast out"* of such an arrangement. Let me give an example:

Some years ago I had the opportunity to help a young man through to the Baptism in the Holy Spirit. He was a celebrated baseball player who had recently played (at the time) in a World Series.

At any rate, not long after he came to Christ, the Lord helped me to explain the Baptism in the Holy Spirit to him, which he ultimately received.

In those days, Frances and I were away from Baton Rouge almost constantly in Evangelistic Meetings. However, some time later, being back in town, I happened to see him and asked how his present relationship with his Church was coming since he had been filled with the Spirit?

He smiled and then said, *"Brother Swaggart, I no longer attend that Church."*

He then said, *"The Pastor called me into his office, and told me that I would probably be happier elsewhere.*

"As long as I was getting drunk, gambling, and being unfaithful to my wife," he said, *"I was welcome in the Church. However, once I found Jesus as my Saviour, and was Baptized in the Holy Spirit with the evidence of speaking with other tongues, I was no longer welcome."*

Sadly, the illustration just given is indicative of many, if not most, of the Churches in America and Canada, and elsewhere in the world for that matter!

As well, and even among Churches which claim to believe in the fullness of the Spirit, many of them have become so man-controlled that they cannot at all tolerate anything that is Christ-controlled. The scenario is somewhat strange.

Many, if not most, of present Religious Denominations had their beginning, as they were *"cast out"* of other Religious Denominations. They grew hungry for God, and their hunger was rewarded by *"excommunication."*

However, almost invariably, after two or three generations, the same Religious Denominations, by now large and rich, begin to practice the same thing. In other words, the fires of Revival are lost, with a new generation coming on that little knows or understands the Moving of the Holy Spirit, consequently becoming man-controlled, where they once were Spirit-controlled. It is almost a vicious circle.

However, I believe that in these last days, the situation with organized religion is going to become even more anti-Christ. The Scriptural evidence is plentiful that the apostate Church will aid and abet the Antichrist, at least in His rise for power (II Tim. 3:12-13; 4:3-4; Rev. 13:11-15).

(9) "WHAT SHALL THEREFORE THE LORD OF THE VINEYARD DO? HE WILL COME AND DESTROY THE HUSBANDMEN, AND WILL GIVE THE VINEYARD UNTO OTHERS."

The question, *"What shall therefore the Lord of the Vineyard do?"*, constitutes the question of questions!

Matthew said that the Scribes thus answered Jesus (Mat. 21:41), and probably He repeated their answer. As well, they knew He was speaking of them.

First of all, the *"Lord"* has the power to do whatever He desires, although they have treated Him as if He had no power at all!

The phrase, *"He will come and destroy the Husbandmen,"* constitutes exactly what happened! In 70 A.D. the Roman General Titus, who commanded the Tenth Legion totally destroyed Jerusalem, slaughtering over 1,000,000 Jews, and selling hundreds of thousands as slaves. At that time the nation was effectively *"destroyed!"*

Some may argue that this was done by Rome. However, while that is true, it was the Lord Who allowed it to be done. God uses men, nations, empires, and all things for that matter, to carry out His Will. Rome was the instrument, but God was the Director.

The phrase, *"And will give the Vineyard unto others,"* speaks of the Church, made up mostly of Gentiles, and this being the channel through which God is operating temporarily while Israel is in dispersion, and until Israel will be regathered at the Second Advent, and restored to fellowship and usefulness to God (Wuest).

So, the portend of the question was weighty to say the least!

As we have stated, while this Parable pointed directly to Israel, still, it can in principle refer to certain segments of the Church, as it has through the ages, and even to individuals. While it is not possible for men to presently kill Christ, as Israel of old, nevertheless, at least in a physical sense, it is done spiritually everyday.

When the Early Church finally did apostate itself, eventually sinking to the level of what is now known as the *"Catholic Church,"* the *"Vineyard"* was taken from them, and *"given unto others."* This would have involved the Reformation under Martin Luther, as well as other giants of the Faith.

Out of this came the Baptist and Methodist Churches, among others, which had such great influence on America and the world. Actually, the great Methodist move in the 1800's, without a doubt, steered this nation toward freedom and prosperity. As well, Methodism pulled England out of the Dark Ages, and could have very well saved that nation from the slaughter that engulfed France.

However, as with so many Religious Denominations, the flames of Revival began to wane and die in these respective Churches, with the *"Holiness"* movements springing up to take their place. Again, God gave the *"Vineyard"* to *"others!"*

The flame burned brightly under the *"Holiness"* banner for some time, and then began to dim low. Ultimately, the flame degenerated into legalism, with God raising up another group called *"Pentecostals."* Once again, the *"Vineyard"* was given to *"others."*

The mighty Pentecostal Move shook the world in the 1900's, and especially in the 1950's and 80's. It was a worldwide move, with tens of millions being brought to Christ and Baptized in the Holy Spirit, with the evidence of

speaking with other tongues. Truly, Bible days were here again!

But sadly, in the 1990's that flame, as others before, began to dim low. At the present, only about a third of the people in Pentecostal Churches, even claim to be Baptized in the Holy Spirit with the evidence of speaking with other tongues. Consequently, and by all rights, these once mighty Pentecostal Denominations can no longer rightly call themselves *"Pentecostal."* As Jesus said of Sardis so long ago, *"Thou hast a name that thou livest, and art dead"* (Rev. 3:1).

Will the *"Vineyard"* be taken from them and given to others? Or has it already been taken from them?

Some may argue that it has been given to the Charismatics; however, I do not think that one can legitimately say that a genuine Move of God has come about from this sector. While some Charismatic Churches have been, and are presently being used greatly by the Lord, still, for the most part, that sector is so freighted with false doctrine respecting the *"Prosperity Message"* and *"Political Message,"* that precious little is actually being done for Christ.

So, if the Rapture holds for any time at all, and if there is not a Revival in the Pentecostal ranks, or even others, to whom shall this *"Vineyard"* be given?

(10) "AND HAVE YE NOT READ THIS SCRIPTURE; THE STONE WHICH THE BUILDERS REJECTED IS BECOME THE HEAD OF THE CORNER:"

The phrase, *"And have ye not read this Scripture,"* refers to Psalms 118:22-23, and is quoted again in Acts 4:11, and I Peter 2:4, 7.

The phrase, *"The Stone which the builders rejected is become the Head of the Corner,"* refers to Christ. He is the *"Stone,"* and *"The Head of the Corner."*

The *"builders"* are the Spiritual Leaders of Israel.

The word, *"rejected,"* means that *"something is put to the test for the purpose of approving."*

This tells the story of the Messiah's rejection by Israel. Israel was looking for its Messiah, especially as Daniel had prophesied that He would come at this time (Dan. Chpt. 9)! Jesus of Nazareth claimed to be the Messiah. The leaders of Israel investigated His claims, found them to be true, substantiated by the miracles He performed (Jn. 3:2), yet with all this evidence, rejected Him as the Messiah because He did not meet their specifications. They were looking for a Messiah who would deliver Israel from the despotism of Rome, not from the dominion of sin (Wuest).

However, this same Messiah, the One murdered by Israel, rose from the dead, and will one day become King of kings and Lord of lords over the earth as the Head of the Millennial Empire, the *"Headstone of the Corner."* The Prophet Zechariah said, *"He shall bring forth the Headstone thereof with shoutings, crying, Grace, Grace unto it"* (Zech. 4:7).

As well, the idea of the phrase, *"The Head of the Corner,"* means that as long as Jesus is the *"Head"* and recognized as such, the blessings continue to flow. However, the moment He is replaced, as with Israel of old, and many in the modern Church, He simply gives the *"Vineyard"* to others, who will recognize Him as the *"Head of the Corner."*

It must ever be remembered that Christ is an active Head, and not a passive Head. Religious Denominations have the tendency to abrogate His position, consequently, replacing it with man-devised offices. In the Kingdom of God, this can never be tolerated!

(11) "THIS WAS THE LORD'S DOING, AND IT IS MARVELLOUS IN OUR EYES?"

This, as stated, comes from Psalm 118:23.

The phrase, *"This was the Lord's doing,"* refers to this Great Plan of God, which necessitated God becoming flesh and dwelling among men, in order to bring about the Redemption of man. Consequently, Israel rejected that which was of God, i.e., *"The Lord's doing."*

To fight against God is an untenable situation. Israel would be totally destroyed as a result of her action. Likewise, anyone who does such a thing.

I have seen major Religious Denominations fight against God and bring spiritual death upon themselves.

At the turn of the century, the latter rain outpouring of the Holy Spirit exploded upon the world. Even though many, if not most of the people Baptized in the Holy Spirit were actually out of old-line Churches, still, these Churches as a whole, at least for the most part, rejected the Holy Spirit.

In an even stronger measure, the Holy Spirit began to be poured out on these hungry hearts

in these particular Churches, including Catholics, in the 1960's and 70's.

On January 1, 1969, according to the leading of the Holy Spirit, we went on the air with our Daily Radio Program, *"The Campmeeting Hour."* It was a fifteen minute, daily program, Monday through Friday. To be sure, our beginnings were of small moment. Nevertheless, God began to bless, until we had one of the largest daily Gospel audiences in radio. This is remarkable, considering that our Program was only fifteen minutes in duration.

Almost from the beginning of our Radio Program, the Lord began to deal with me about teaching on the many and varied attributes of the Holy Spirit. His speaking to me about this matter went on for a period of time; however, it came to a head, I believe, early one morning some time before daylight. This would have been, I think, during the latter part of 1969.

I had awakened that early morning hour at approximately 2 or 3 a.m. I slipped out of bed and went outside to my prayer room, which also doubled as my office, etc. As I began to seek the Lord, I sensed a mighty moving of the Holy Spirit, that was at least one of the greatest experiences I have ever had.

The Lord began to deal with me strongly about the teaching format of the Radio Program. I remember remonstrating to the Lord how unqualified I was, reminding Him that I was an Evangelist and not a Teacher. (Oh! The foolish things we sometimes say when the Lord deals with us.) Even though this was many years ago, I still have a vivid memory of those early morning hours, and what transpired at that time.

I knew what the Lord was telling me, but yet fear gripped my heart because I realized that I actually was woefully inadequate as a Bible Teacher. The thought entered my mind concerning entering Bible College, but I realized that would take years, and could not fit into that which the Lord was telling me to do.

Knowing what I was thinking, the Lord spoke to me and said, *"I will give you the gift of teaching, if you will obey Me."* It was just that simple! And yet, I wondered exactly how the Lord would do this. To me it seemed impossible, at least for it to be done in a short period of time. I knew the Lord was moving upon me to begin teaching on the Holy Spirit immediately.

A few days later, it happened! I realize that many would say that such is impossible, and in the natural it is. Nevertheless, in a short time, the Lord showed me what to do in respect to this all-important subject of teaching on the Holy Spirit, plus other subjects as well! When it fell into place, it seemed so simple and easy. Of course, the Holy Spirit always knows exactly what He is doing.

To be sure, I had excellent Bible knowledge, but, as stated, I had served as an Evangelist all of these years and had made little attempt to teach the Word.

Many have questioned me as to what the Lord told me to do in respect to this all-important aspect of our Ministry?

I attempted to explain once or twice, but soon realized that the ones to whom I was attempting to explain this matter, didn't have the slightest idea what I was talking about. Consequently, I have not attempted that since.

At any rate, I immediately began to teach on the Holy Spirit over our Daily Radio Program. I taught on the Gifts of the Spirit, the Fruit of the Spirit, plus other attributes of the Holy Spirit. I taught for weeks on how to receive the Holy Spirit, plus many other things relating to this all-important subject. I suppose I must have taught several months without a break.

Thousands of letters began to pour into our office in Baton Rouge, many of them from Baptists, Methodists, Presbyterians, and even Catholics! Most were hungry for the Holy Spirit, and readily drank in that which the Lord gave to me for them.

I even received letters addressed to *"Mr. Pentecost,"* Baton Rouge, Louisiana, with them promptly delivered.

During this time, as well, the Lord instructed me to set aside at least one service in our City-Wide Crusades, dedicated to Believers being Baptized in the Holy Spirit. For a period of several years this was done, with multiple thousands being Baptized in the Holy Spirit.

As stated, most of these people were former Baptists, Methodists, Lutherans, etc. As well, many Preachers in these Denominations were filled. However, as a whole, these Denominations strongly resisted the Holy Spirit, and even strongly fought against it.

During this time, strong efforts were made by particular individuals, whomever they may

NOTES

have been, to get our Radio Program off the air. To take the time to enumerate all the incidents, would be a fruitless exercise; however, suffice to say that every effort that could be made was made, but, thankfully, to no avail! The Lord preserved the Program, and despite the efforts of these Preachers who seemed to despise anything about the Holy Spirit, and especially speaking with other tongues.

At that time, I believe the Lord strongly dealt with the leadership of these Religious Denominations. But, sadly, they rejected it. However, *"This was the Lord's doing,"* and they found themselves fighting against God. As a result, there is presently very little, if any, moving and operation of the Holy Spirit in these particular Denominations. To be sure, anything done for the Lord will be by and through the Person and Agency of the Holy Spirit. However, if He is not wanted, then nothing is accomplished, at least for God. Church degenerates into *"dead Preachers, preaching dead sermons, to dead congregations."* It is only the Holy Spirit Who makes the difference in our lives. If He does not do it, it is not done!

As well, to reject a part of what He does, is to reject all of what He does. Many claim they want the Holy Spirit, but they don't want the tongues. I do not think it is possible to have one without the other (Acts 2:4).

The question, *"And it is marvellous in our eyes?"*, probably would have been better translated as an exclamation! The idea is this:

It is marvellous in the eyes of God, this great Work of Redemption wrought by the Holy Spirit through Jesus Christ. As well, it is *"marvellous"* in the eyes of all Believers, and it should have been *"marvellous"* in the eyes of Israel. But, tragically, it wasn't, and Israel died.

Anything done by the Lord should be *"marvellous"* in the eyes of all who are privileged to behold its wonders! If it isn't, that which happened to Israel will, as well, happen to others.

These Denominations which I have mentioned, and with possibly some few exceptions among certain Churches, have all but died spiritually. I realize that is a strong statement, but I believe it to be true. If it is the *"Lord's doing,"* it had better be *"our doing,"* and it had better be *"marvellous"* in our eyes.

(12) "AND THEY SOUGHT TO LAY HOLD ON HIM, BUT FEARED THE PEOPLE: FOR

THEY KNEW THAT HE HAD SPOKEN THE PARABLE AGAINST THEM: AND THEY LEFT HIM, AND WENT THEIR WAY."

The phrase, *"And they sought to lay hold on Him,"* refers to the fact that they knew beyond the shadow of a doubt that this Parable was directed at them. However, their response was according to the evil of their own hearts, and not because of the Parable. In effect, it should have brought them to repentance, which the Word of God is always designed to do, at least when it is directed at men, which most of the time it is. (At times it is directed at Satan, with whom there can be no repentance.)

The word, *"sought,"* means that these Religious Leaders immediately began to make plans to stop Christ, and by whatever means!

At this point, Matthew records that Jesus then gave the *"Parable of the Marriage Feast,"* which Mark does not mention, and which pointed at these hypocrites again. So, they are now casting about for any means at their disposal in order to silence the Lord.

The phrase, *"But feared the people,"* shows the true heart of religion. The true man of God fears God, and not people, while religion fears people and not God!

At this Passover time, Jerusalem was filled with people, perhaps as many as a half million or more. Josephus, the Jewish Historian, said that approximately 250,000 lambs were offered at this time, which would have necessitated at least a half million people in the city, or more!

Some of these people had been healed by Christ, and, in effect, their lives actually given back to them. Consequently, they loved Him dearly! So, whatever would be done, must be done under cover, so as not to arouse the ire of the people. In other words, the foul deed would have to be crafted in such a way that the people would think the worst of Him, and, more importantly, done quickly!

The phrase, *"For they knew that He had spoken the Parable against them,"* referred to the fact that if this got out among the people, their situation (these Religious Leaders) might quickly become perilous.

The phrase, *"And they left Him, and went their way,"* refers to them taking a position that Jesus must be stopped, and at whatever price. They were now determined to find a way to

NOTES

bring it about. Regrettably, in a matter of hours Judas will offer them the opportunity.

(13) "AND THEY SEND UNTO HIM CERTAIN OF THE PHARISEES AND OF THE HERODIANS, TO CATCH HIM IN HIS WORDS."

The phrase, *"And they send unto Him certain of the Pharisees,"* referred to their most brilliant minds.

The phrase, *"And of the Herodians,"* concerned a sect of Jews who supported the house of Herod, and were in favor of giving tribute to Rome. This began with Herod the Great, who, some thirty years earlier, had put to death the infants at Bethlehem, that he might thus get rid of Christ, lest any other than himself might be regarded as Christ.

Tertullian, St. Jerome, and others say that these Herodians believed, or claimed to do so, that Herod was the Promised Messiah, because they saw that in him the sceptre had departed from Judah (Gen. 49:10).

They said it was on this account that he rebuilt the Temple with such magnificence.

The Herod who ruled now, was called *"Herod the Tetrarch,"* and was the youngest son of *"Herod the Great."* Jesus is recorded as having once described him as *"That fox"*(Lk. 13:32). He, like his father, was a great builder; the city of Tiberias on the Lake of Galilee was built by him in 22 A.D. and named in honor of the Emperor Tiberius. (*"Herod the Tetrach"* was also called *"Herod Antipas."*)

The Herodians thought of him as the Messiah, as they had of his father, *"Herod the Great."*

The Pharisees, on the other hand, claimed to be defenders of the Law of Moses, to which the Herodians gave no credence. In fact, the Pharisees and Herodians hated each other, but would now join together, temporarily laying aside their hatred in order to stop Christ. Consequently, the Church would join with the world in their attempt to destroy Christ. They did this, even though they hated each other, because they both had the same father, the Devil.

On a personal basis, I am well acquainted with this spirit of the apostate Church joining with the world in their efforts to destroy the Work of God. Consequently, the perfidiousness of this action of the Pharisees and Herodians, would probably have a greater sting for me personally than most! I think one could probably say without fear of contradiction, that in this union of the apostate Church and the world, the depths of evil are reached. I think no vice, or work of the flesh, as sinful as they may be, can remotely compare with the evil here enjoined. It is Satan's master stroke, and is reserved for his greatest efforts. All other evil is subservient to this evil. This is the reason that the greatest enemy to the Work of God is not alcohol, drugs, immorality, as evil as these things may be. The greatest enemy is the Church, i.e., the apostate Church, which includes almost all of organized religion, and almost all that which is not organized.

Yes! There is a *"True Church,"* made up of born-again, Blood-washed Believers, who love Jesus with all of their hearts, and who seek to please Him exclusively of all else. But in comparison to the whole, this number is few. Jesus Himself said, *"Because strait is the gate, and narrow is the way, which leadeth unto life, and few there be that find it"* (Mat. 7:14).

The phrase, *"To catch Him in His Words,"* is somewhat humorous to say the least!

First of all, Jesus was the most intelligent human being who has ever lived. The level of such intelligence the world has never seen, and because He is the only One Who has lived absolutely free from sin. Actually, He was born without the sin nature, and as a result, was not subject to the terrible debilitations of the Fall. His intelligence regarding Life and Godliness was perfect, plus anything else He needed to know (II Pet. 1:3).

As well, He directed that super-intelligence strictly toward the Word of God. It was not used in the realm of economics, or personal aggrandizement or power. It was used in the realm of learning the Word of God, and applying it to His heart and life, and teaching it to others. The Psalmist said of Him, *"I have more understanding than all My teachers: for Thy Testimonies are My meditation.*

"I understand more than the ancients, because I keep Thy precepts" (Ps. 119:99-100).

He also said, *"Through Thy precepts I get understanding: therefore I hate every false way"* (Ps. 119:104).

As stated, these Passages were spoken of Christ. So, for these hypocrites to think they could entangle or snare Christ *"in His Words,"* was facetious indeed!

Knowing that a great crowd would be gathered, they planned to pose a question to Him,

NOTES

that either way He answered it would place Him in a position of incriminating Himself. He would then lose face in front of the people, and be humiliated in their eyes. Consequently, whatever they then desired to do to Him, would be made easier.

(14) "AND WHEN THEY WERE COME, THEY SAY UNTO HIM, MASTER, WE KNOW THAT THOU ART TRUE, AND CAREST FOR NO MAN: FOR THOU REGARDEST NOT THE PERSON OF MEN, BUT TEACHEST THE WAY OF GOD IN TRUTH: IS IT LAWFUL TO GIVE TRIBUTE TO CAESAR, OR NOT?"

The phrase, *"And when they were come,"* concerns them ready to spring their trap. It is so sad, He could have given them Eternal Life, but instead they seek to destroy Him. And yet, doesn't almost the entirety of the world follow in their train?

The phrase, *"They say unto Him, Master,"* means *"Teacher."* The word is not used without design.

As the great crowd looks on, they call Him *"Teacher,"* and, consequently, the crowd thinks of Him in the same way; therefore, He must answer the question which will now be posed.

The phrase, *"We know that Thou art true, and carest for no man: for Thou regardest not the person of men,"* is skillfully arranged with the view of disarming suspicion, and, at the same time, preventing escape.

So independent and fearless a Teacher of Truth could not from fear of consequences, either refuse an answer to honest and perplexed inquiries, or conceal His real opinion. Consequently, there is veiled irony in their words.

Jesus had shown little consideration for men of learning and hierarchial rank; doubtless, at least in their minds, He would be equally indifferent to the views of Rome, and even the Emperor himself; when the Truth was concerned, His independence would assert itself with fearless impartiality (Swete).

The phrase, *"But teacheth the Way of God in Truth,"* presents a paradox. Every evidence is that these Pharisees and Herodians, and especially the Pharisees, knew that what He taught was indeed Truth, i.e., *"The Way of God,"* and, in fact, that He was the *"Son of God."* The word, *"know,"* in *"Master, we know,"* in the Greek is *"oida,"* and refers to positive knowledge. In other words, they were absolutely convinced of the fact.

And yet, they would not publicly admit to the nation that He, indeed, was the Messiah, and that all of Israel should accept Him as such.

Why?

There are a thousand excuses and ways to do wrong, while there is only one reason and way to do right.

One is to do right because it is right, and because it is the Way of the Lord, and according to His Word.

In order to do right, one must make a determination that he is going to obey the Lord irrespective of the price, or what other people say. In other words, there is no self agenda, but only the desire to carry out the Will of the Lord.

The Religious Leaders of Israel, as most, had no desire to obey God. To them, religion was a business in which they did very well financially, socially, and in other ways. Consequently, Jesus was a threat to this, therefore they would oppose Him, even though the evidence was irrefutable as to Who He was.

They, as most, did not know or realize that truly serving God is the most rewarding and fulfilling thing that could ever be, far surpassing anything the world or the Devil has to offer. As someone has said, *"The worst day I have ever had in serving Jesus, by far surpasses the very best Satan has to offer."*

The question, *"Is it lawful to give tribute to Caesar, or not?",* presented an argument that was then raging in Israel.

This *"tribute"* referred to the poll tax which the Jews paid the Emperor. This payment was objectionable to them for two reasons, first, because the coin with which it was to be paid, the denarius, bore the Emperor's effigy stamped upon it. As well, and to make matters worse, Rome demanded that this Emperor be thought of, and worshiped as a god. Consequently, many Jews were incensed at this intrusion into their religion by a foreign religion, and into their daily lives.

The word, *"lawful,"* as used here, means, *"Is it permissible, is it allowed, permitted?"*

Wuest says that the Jews were not necessarily discussing the legality of paying a poll tax to Caesar, but whether a Jew should do so in view of his theocratic relationship to God.

They pressed for an answer from Him regarding this question, feeling they had Him trapped either way it went.

Actually, they hoped He would say *"no"* to their question, because this would involve Him at once with the Roman authorities. He might even be charged with treason (Lk. 23:2).

On the other hand, if He said, *"yes,"* such an answer would incur the displeasure of the Jewish people.

(15) "SHALL WE GIVE, OR SHALL WE NOT GIVE? BUT HE, KNOWING THEIR HYPOCRISY, SAID UNTO THEM, WHY TEMPT YE ME? BRING ME A PENNY, THAT I MAY SEE IT."

The question, *"Shall we give, or shall we not give?",* places the situation in strictly a *"yes"* or *"no"* mode, or so they thought! As they reasoned, this was a trap which would snare Him either way He answered.

Once again allow us to allude to His intelligence — an intelligence, we might add, which was far superior to theirs, or anyone else in the world for that matter! Also, the Holy Spirit was constantly informing Him of what He should say. Isaiah said, concerning Him, *"The Lord God hath given Me the tongue of the learned, that I should know how to speak a word in season to Him that is weary: He wakeneth morning by morning, He wakeneth Mine ear to hear as the learned."*

He then said, *"The Lord God hath opened Mine ear, and I was not rebellious, neither turned away back"* (Isa. 50:4-5).

This means that the Lord spoke into His ear that which He wanted Him to know, and that *"morning by morning,"* or day by day.

So, the instant communication He had with the Father was of such a direct manner, in which no other human being has ever had or known. Consequently, their trying to snare Him, was a task doomed to failure!

The phrase, *"But He, knowing their hypocrisy, said unto them,"* means that He knew they had no desire for the true answer, but only to embarrass Him before the crowd, or to have something in order to accuse Him to Rome. The Holy Spirit spoke into His ear exactly who they were, and what they were, these Religious Leaders!

The question, *"Why tempt ye Me?",* proclaims His relating to them that He knew what their subtle trap was all about.

As someone has said, it is necessary for one who finds himself in the place of Jesus, to know the mind of the questioner, and to adapt His answer accordingly. This Jesus would do!

The phrase, *"Bring Me a penny, that I may see it,"* referred to the Roman denarius, the coin with which the tax was to be paid.

There would not have been a coin of that nature in the Temple, and for the obvious reasons; therefore, it was necessary for them to send for one. During this pause, it is easy to imagine the tension aroused by this breathless wait.

What would Jesus say when the coin was finally brought?

Furthermore, why did He want such a coin?

(16) "AND THEY BROUGHT IT. AND HE SAITH UNTO THEM, WHOSE IS THIS IMAGE AND SUPERSCRIPTION? AND THEY SAID UNTO HIM, CAESAR'S."

The phrase, *"And they brought it,"* refers to a period of time which lapsed as the coin was being obtained.

The question, *"And He saith unto them, Whose is this image and superscription?",* probably was perplexing to these Religious Leaders, even though the answer was obvious.

The phrase, *"And they said unto Him, Caesar's,"* referred to the image of Tiberius Caesar, the then reigning Roman Emperor. Consequently, the coin of the country proved the subjection of the country to him whose image was upon it, in this case, Caesar.

(17) "AND JESUS ANSWERING SAID UNTO THEM, RENDER TO CAESAR THE THINGS THAT ARE CAESAR'S, AND TO GOD THE THINGS THAT ARE GOD'S. AND THEY MARVELLED AT HIM."

The phrase, *"And Jesus answering said unto them,"* would refer to far more than they had asked. Actually, and in a sense, Jesus placed His approval by His answer on the separation of Church and State.

Heretofore, Israel's Government, and by Divine design, had united Church and State, so to speak, into one. In other words, the Mosaic Law was, as well, the Civil Law. In effect, if they had thought through what Jesus was saying, they would have realized that Israel was not about to regain dominion. Actually, Roman power would continue for some time, even destroying the nation in 70 A.D.

As well, when the founding fathers of America drew up the Constitution of the United States, guaranteeing separation of Church and State, and freedom of religion, they were, in effect, following direction already laid down by

Christ, about 1800 years earlier. It has proven to be one of the greatest foundations of freedom ever enjoyed by any nation.

The phrase, *"Render to Caesar the things that are Caesar's, and to God the things that are God's,"* says it all.

The Jewish Leaders had used the word *"give"* respecting tribute or taxes paid to Caesar, while Jesus used the word, *"render,"* which speaks of paying something as a debt. In other words, He was saying that Israel owed Rome certain obligations, such as taxes, etc. This paid or the occupation forces, which provided protection for Israel, etc.

In effect, Jesus was saying, *"The coin is Caesar's; let him have his own. The fact that it circulates in Judaea shows that it is in the ordering of God's providence"* (Swete). Israel should have known that Rome could not have subjected them, without the approval of Jehovah. Consequently, they must recognize these facts and submit.

As well, the *"rendering unto Caesar, that which is his,"* means that Believers are obligated to pay taxes, and, as well, to submit to Civil Government in every respect, providing its demands do not abrogate the Word of God. This means that we obey laws which we do not like, that is, if they do not violate our conscience and the Word of God. Paul said the same thing in Romans 13:1-7.

As well, that which is owed to God, must be paid as well!

On the material side, this would speak of our Tithes and Offerings. As well, it would speak of consecration and dedication, plus obedience to His Word.

The question posed by these Religious Leaders rested on an implied incompatibility of the payment of tribute with the requirements of the Law of God; and the Lord replies that there is no such incompatibility. Debts to man and debts to God are both to be discharged, and the two spheres of duty are at once distinct and reconcilable (Swete).

The phrase, *"And they marvelled at Him,"* referred not only to His answer, but, as well, at His Person, which contained perfect wisdom.

He vaulted over the trap set for Him, leaving them entangled in it. He lifted up the question far above the petty controversy of the hour, and affirmed a great principle of natural and spiritual obligation which belongs alike to all times and persons and places (Bickersteth).

In Truth, they could have been beneficiaries of this great wisdom, had they only accepted Him for Who He actually was, the Messiah. In fact, every Believer is presently a beneficiary of such wisdom. However, so few take advantage of it, simply because so few truly know His Word. His Word, as should be obvious, is His Wisdom!

If this made His enemies *"marvel,"* how much more should it make His followers! That is the reason every Believer should do all within his power to master the Word of God. It alone contains the wisdom of the ages, and because it is the Word of God. But, sadly, many Believers have not even read the Bible completely through even once, much less sought diligently to understand it.

The Word of God alone must be the standard for Life and Godliness. If anything intrudes into this sacred precinct, the results are always disastrous. Actually, this is Satan's greatest effort, whether taking from or adding to the Word of God.

(18) "THEN COME UNTO HIM THE SADDUCEES, WHICH SAY THERE IS NO RESURRECTION; AND THEY ASKED HIM, SAYING,"

The phrase, *"Then come unto Him the Sadducees,"* concerns the third major party in Israel, after the Pharisees and Herodians.

The Sadducees denied the doctrines which connect us more immediately with another world, such as the existence of spirits and of angels, and the resurrection of the body. Even though under Roman authority, the Sadducees controlled the High Priesthood of Israel. Caiaphas, the High Priest of Israel, was a Sadducee, as was his father-in-law, Annas, who had been High Priest preceding him.

The Sadducees had little following among the people, but were more so restricted to the well-to-do. Many, but not all, Priests were Sadducees; nearly all Sadducees, however, appear to have been Priests, especially of the most powerful priestly families.

Under the Herods and Romans, the Sadducees predominated in the Sanhedrin. The party died out with the destruction of the Temple in 70 A.D.

The phrase, *"Which say there is no resurrection,"* means that this denial was their major

platform. It was a denial of the possibility of such a thing as a resurrection from the dead.

Inasmuch as the Pharisees believed strongly in a Resurrection, the contention was sharp between the two parties. However, they would join together, temporarily laying aside their animosity, in order to ensnare Christ, or at least attempt to do so.

The phrase, *"And they asked Him, saying,"* refers to a question they are certain He cannot answer.

For each group quieted by our Lord, another ignorant group takes their place. They seem to not be able to learn that they cannot best Him with their trick questions.

(19) "MASTER, MOSES WROTE UNTO US, IF A MAN'S BROTHER DIE, AND LEAVE HIS WIFE BEHIND HIM, AND LEAVE NO CHILDREN, THAT HIS BROTHER SHOULD TAKE HIS WIFE, AND RAISE UP SEED UNTO HIS BROTHER."

The title, *"Master,"* in no way meant that they considered Jesus to be a great teacher, which this title implied! Their use was purely formal. Their question was not posed in order that they may learn, but that hopefully they may ensnare Him.

The phrase, *"Moses wrote unto us,"* proclaims them quoting the Scripture, but attempting, as many, to subvert it. The Truth was they believed in a historical Moses, but not all that he taught in the Pentateuch.

The phrase, *"If a man's brother die, and leave his wife behind him, and leave no children,"* is quoted from Deuteronomy 25:5-6.

The phrase, *"That his brother should take his wife, and raise up seed unto his brother,"* was given to prevent a family inheritance from being broken up.

In fact, the statement as given by Moses and inspired by the Holy Spirit, had nothing to do with Resurrection, but something else entirely. However, these hypocrites, and as well ignorant of the Word of God, would attempt to use this Passage from Deuteronomy to prove their pet theory regarding no Resurrection.

The phrase, *"And raise up seed unto his brother,"* as stated, pertained to the preventing of the family inheritance from being broken up.

(20-22) "NOW THERE WERE SEVEN BRETHREN: AND THE FIRST TOOK A WIFE, AND DYING LEFT NO SEED.

"AND THE SECOND TOOK HER, AND DIED, NEITHER LEFT HE ANY SEED: AND THE THIRD LIKEWISE.

"AND THE SEVEN HAD HER, AND LEFT NO SEED: LAST OF ALL THE WOMAN DIED ALSO."

None of the above Text is in the Law of Moses. It is all a made-up story in order to prove, they think, their argument against the Resurrection. These skeptics will have a good laugh at Jesus' expense.

This is in the same spirit as the question concerning where Cain got his wife (Gen. 4:17). Ignorant skeptics ask such questions thinking to disprove the Bible.

Incidentally, Cain was over 100 years old when he took his wife and went into the land of Nod, where enough people already existed and lived to build and form a city. There he knew his wife, that is, had relationship with her, and started his family (Gen. 4:16-26).

Inasmuch as Adam and Eve were the first and only people on earth immediately after the six days' work of re-creation, they were commanded to multiply and replenish the earth with their own kind (Gen. 1:26-28). They had sons and daughters (Gen. 4:1; 5:4; 6:1). However, the Bible does not tell us exactly how many sons and daughters Adam and Eve had. One tradition says that Adam had 30 sons and 30 daughters; another says 300 sons and 300 daughters.

At any rate, the first marriages had to be between brothers and sisters in order to get the race started. After that, marrying close relatives was forbidden (Lev. 18).

Consequently, by the time Cain married his wife, it is possible that there were from 250,000 to 500,000 people on the earth.

So, these skeptics will ply Jesus with a question they think He cannot answer, and, as well, prove the fallacy of the Resurrection.

(23) "IN THE RESURRECTION THEREFORE, WHEN THEY SHALL RISE, WHOSE WIFE SHALL SHE BE OF THEM? FOR THE SEVEN HAD HER TO WIFE."

The Sadducees were characterized by their denial of a Resurrection. They had posed their question according to the Mosaic Law; therefore thinking that it repudiated the Doctrine of the Resurrection. Their hypothetical story concerning seven brothers who had been married to one wife, will now prove to be, at least in

their thinking, a great confusion in the afterlife, should there be one.

The phrase, *"In the Resurrection therefore, when they shall rise,"* is presented in sarcasm! As stated, they did not believe there was such a thing as a Resurrection.

The question, *"Whose wife shall she be of them?"*, is the pivot point of their trap.

The Sadducees had absolutely no knowledge, at least properly so, of God or His Plan for the human family. They did not understand that God had originally *"breathed into the nostrils of man the breath of life,"* and as a result, *"man became a living soul"* (Gen. 2:7). By its very definition, the word, *"living,"* refers to *"life without end."* Consequently, man was created by God to live forever. The original intention by God was that man reside with Him forever; however, due to the Fall, even though man's companionship and position were changed, at least for those who will not accept Christ, the eternal consequence was not. Man continues to live forever, whether with the Lord or with Satan (Rev. 20:10-15).

WHAT IS THE DOCTRINE OF THE RESURRECTION?

The Doctrine of the Resurrection is pivotal in the Christian Faith. Paul wrote, *"If in this life only we have hope in Christ, we are of all men most miserable"* (I Cor. 15:19).

What does this *"hope"* really mean?

The New Testament speaks decisively concerning this matter. It is not simply the continuation of existence. It is Resurrection, with all that Resurrection implies!

Even though the Old Testament is not as defined as the New, still, there are salient Passages which delineate the Resurrection. Isaiah said, *"He will swallow up death in victory; and the Lord God will wipe away tears from off all faces"* (Isa. 25:8).

He also said, *"Thy dead men shall live, together with my dead body shall they arise. Awake and sing, ye that dwell in dust: for thy dew is as the dew of herbs, and the earth shall cast out the dead"* (Isa. 26:19).

Daniel said, *"And many of them that sleep in the dust of the earth shall awake, some to everlasting life, and some to shame and everlasting contempt"* (Dan. 12:2).

While the Doctrine of the Resurrection is

not fully developed in the Old Testament, even as Salvation is not fully developed; still, the foundation is adequately laid.

The Pharisees, who held to the Doctrine of Resurrection (and they were right), and the Sadducees, who denied it, might argue about the Old Testament's implications for the Resurrection, but Jesus justly condemned the denial of the Sadducees, as we shall see, saying, *"You are in error because you do not know the Scriptures or the Power of God."*

THE RESURRECTION OF JESUS

Jesus is called the *"Firstfruits of those who have fallen asleep"* (I Cor. 15:20). His Resurrection is the guarantee that the death which grips the human race because of Adam has been conquered and that life is now our destiny. Consequently, the significance of Jesus' Resurrection is beyond imagination. Just a few of the New Testament themes associated with Resurrection show the central place that His Resurrection must play in our Faith.

First, Paul points out that Jesus *"through the Spirit of Holiness was declared with power to be the Son of God by His Resurrection from the dead"* (Rom. 1:4). The Resurrection is proof of all of Christ's claims and a solid foundation for our Faith.

Next, Jesus' Resurrection to endless life guarantees that *"because Jesus lives forever, He has a permanent Priesthood. Therefore He is able to save completely those who come to God through Him, because He always lives to interceded for them"* (Heb. 7:24-25).

Finally, Jesus' Resurrection is the key to fulfillment of all the Old Testament and New Testament Promises about the future. God's purposes will be achieved only when Jesus returns.

Consequently, the Resurrection of Jesus was a keystone in Apostolic proclamation of the Gospel (Acts 2:24-36; 3:15-26; 4:10; 5:30; 10:40; 13:34, 37; 17:18-32).

THE RESURRECTION OF THE BELIEVER

The New Testament makes it clear that the dead must appear before God for Judgment (Heb. 9:27; Rev. 20:11-15). But Resurrection as transformation to a different state of being is for Believers only.

What do we know of Resurrection as transformation?

NOTES

John wrote that God has made us His Own Children (I Jn. 3:1), and then added, *"What we will be has not yet been made known;"* but we do know that when Jesus *"appears, we shall be like Him."*

Paul, in I Thessalonians 4, provides the broad outline. When Jesus returns, *"Those who have fallen asleep,"* will come with Him, and those left alive will meet them in the air. The *"dead in Christ"* (I Thess. 4:16) will be raised before the living Believers are caught up, and together the whole family will meet Jesus in the air. Paul concludes, *"So we will be with the Lord forever"* (I Thess. 4:17).

There are more details in I Corinthians 15. To the questions, *"How are the dead raised?"*, and *"With what kind of body will they come?"* (I Cor. 15:35), Paul simply notes that the Resurrection Body will correspond to our present body, but in contrast it will be imperishable, glorious, infused with power — spiritual rather than natural (I Cor. 15:42-44).

As well, it will be in *"the likeness of the Man from Heaven"* (I Cor. 15:49), through a transformation that will happen *"in the twinkling of an eye, at the last trumpet"* (I Cor. 15:52). Then the *"dead will be raised imperishable, and we"* (those alive at the time) *will be changed."*

In the asking of these questions, some of the Corinthians did not understand what the Resurrection Body of the dead would be like, considering that the body had gone back to dust. Paul answered that by saying, *"But God giveth it a body as it hath pleased Him, and to every seed his own body"* (I Cor. 15:38).

In other words, God would give a new body, which is indestructible, and very similar to our former body, but without its imperfections, which will be joined to the soul and spirit of the individual already with Him. As well, males will continue to be males in the Resurrection, and females will continue to be females, *"every seed his own body."*

WHAT DO WE KNOW ABOUT THE RESURRECTION STATE?

Actually, not very much! As stated, John said that we would be *"like Him"* (I Jn. 3:2).

For instance, the Resurrected Jesus had a body of *"flesh and bones"* (Lk. 24:39). That means that it was not of *"flesh and blood,"* as our present bodies. Presently, *"The life of the flesh is in the blood"* (Lev. 17:11). Then the Resurrected person will be infused with a different kind of life, the Spirit of God.

As well, Jesus could appear and disappear at will, with doors or walls being no barrier to Him in the Resurrected state (Jn. 20:26).

It seems that in the Resurrected state, the limitations of our physical nature will be gone, and whereas we are now perishable, we will then be imperishable. Power will replace weakness; immortality will end mortality.

WHAT IS RESURRECTION POWER?

Resurrection Power now resides within the lives of Believers, as an earnest or down-payment of the Resurrection that is to come. This Resurrection Power which we presently have, is given to us in order that we may live an overcoming life. Paul writes that, *"If the Spirit of Him Who raised Jesus from the dead is living in you, He Who raised Christ from the dead will also give life to your mortal bodies through His Spirit, Who lives in you"* (Rom. 8:11).

The point Paul makes is that the Holy Spirit, the Agent of Jesus' Resurrection, lives within the Believer. This means that Resurrection Power is available to us presently even in our mortal bodies. Through the Holy Spirit we are raised beyond our human limitations and enabled to live a Righteous life.

This Doctrine is sometimes overlooked, and certain Biblical Passages are therefore misinterpreted. For instance, in Philippians 3, Paul is not expressing uncertainty about his own Resurrection when he yearns, *"somehow, to attain to the Resurrection from the dead"* (Phil. 3:11). The entire sentence reads, *"That I may know Him, and the Power of His Resurrection, and the fellowship of His sufferings, being made conformable unto His death"* (Phil. 3:10).

Paul's thought in this statement is focused on the present — living a Resurrected kind of life now, and by the Power of the Resurrected Christ.

However, he did not discount the Resurrection of the coming day, when he said, *"If by any means I might attain unto the Resurrection of the dead"* (Phil. 3:11).

By that statement, he means that even though the Power of the Resurrected Christ presently resides in the Believer, still, we have not yet *"attained unto the Resurrection of the dead,"* which refers to that coming day when

all the Saints will be Resurrected, and given Glorified Bodies (I Thess. 4:16-17).

FINALLY

The New Testament makes clear the Doctrine of the Resurrection, which is only in shadow in the Old Testament. However, Jesus' Own appeals to the Old Testament (Mk. 12:26-27), show evidence sometimes overlooked.

The Bible makes it clear that there is an Eternal Destiny, a life beyond this life. Resurrection lies ahead. As well, it is the Resurrection of Jesus that is the final proof. Jesus' Resurrection not only declared Him to be what He claimed to be, the Son of God, but also provided a guarantee for us who believe. Because Jesus lives, we too shall live. And we will share His Destiny: As John said, *"When He appears, we shall be like Him, for we shall see Him as He is"* (I Jn. 3:2).

(Most of the thoughts on Resurrection were derived from the teaching of Lawrence Richards.)

The question, *"Whose wife shall she be of them? for the seven had her to wife,"* shows a complete misunderstanding, as Jesus will say, of the Scriptures.

(24) "AND JESUS ANSWERING SAID UNTO THEM, DO YE NOT THEREFORE ERR, BECAUSE YE KNOW NOT THE SCRIPTURES, NEITHER THE POWER OF GOD?"

The phrase, *"And Jesus answering said unto them,"* proclaims an answer they had never yet received, even though having argued about this matter with the Pharisees for many years.

The question, *"Do ye not therefore err, because ye know not the Scriptures . . . ?",* points to their ignorance which was inexcusable, seeing that most Sadducees were members of the Priesthood.

All error regarding *"Life and Godliness,"* is because of not knowing the Scriptures (II Pet. 1:3).

This is the reason for the acceptance by the Church of the modern philosophy of psychology. The Christian propagators of this error simply do not know the Word of God. If they did, there would be no question in their minds concerning this matter.

The continuing of the question, *"Neither the Power of God,"* portrays the Sadducees as incapable of conceiving a power which could produce that outlined in the Scriptures concerning the Resurrection. Swete said, *"They assumed either that God could not raise the dead, or that He could raise them only to a life which would be a counterpart of the present, etc."* This gives rise to the wild intentions of reincarnation, etc.

The failure to know the *"Power of God"* stems from unbelief. This was characteristic not only of the Sadducees, but, as well, of their modern counterparts. In Truth, most of the modern Church does not believe in the *"Power of God."* As alluded to, this is the reason for the belief in psychology. Men who call themselves Believers, simply do not believe that God delivers people, hence they doubt His Power.

In Truth, the entirety of life is wrapped up in the *"Scriptures,"* and, consequently, the *"Power of God."* If one truly knows the Scriptures, one truly knows and understands the Power of God. The two are inseparable.

(25) "FOR WHEN THEY SHALL RISE FROM THE DEAD, THEY NEITHER MARRY, NOR ARE GIVEN IN MARRIAGE; BUT ARE AS THE ANGELS WHICH ARE IN HEAVEN."

The phrase, *"For when they shall rise from the dead,"* proclaims the guarantee by Christ of the Resurrection.

The pronoun, *"they,"* speaks not only of the Sainted dead, but, as well, of unbelievers. In other words, all will ultimately *"rise"* whether in the First Resurrection of Life, or the Second Resurrection of Damnation (Jn. 5:29), or sometimes called *"The Second Death"* (Rev. 20:14).

The phrase, *"They neither marry, nor are given in marriage,"* has to do with at least one of the reasons for marriage, the bringing of offspring into the world, hence the propagation of the human race. In the Resurrection, there will be no marriages, simply because none of the Resurrected Saints will ever die, and, consequently, it will not be necessary any longer to bring children into the world, at least by this group.

As well, this sentence by Christ tells us that husband and wife relationships, as on earth, will not be continued as such in the Resurrection, consequently, blowing to pieces the hypotheses of the Sadducees concerning the one woman and seven husbands, etc. It eliminates the Mormon claims as well!

While recognition will no doubt be continued, relationship will be different, in that Christ will be the focal point and not a husband or wife, etc.

The phrase, *"But are as the Angels which are in Heaven,"* is used only in a limited context.

Every evidence is that all Angels were originally created at the same time. Due to them not dying, there are the same number of Angels in existence today as when they were created. They do not propagate their kind. Consequently, human beings in the next life will be like Angels in this respect, they will not propagate their kind. This does not mean that human beings will be Angels, for they will not. Human beings will continue to be human beings, and as Paul said, *"Every seed his own body"* (I Cor. 15:38).

(26) "AND AS TOUCHING THE DEAD, THAT THEY RISE: HAVE YE NOT READ IN THE BOOK OF MOSES, HOW IN THE BUSH GOD SPAKE UNTO HIM, SAYING, I AM THE GOD OF ABRAHAM, AND THE GOD OF ISAAC, AND THE GOD OF JACOB?"

The phrase, *"And as touching the dead, that they rise,"* refers to dead bodies, and not the soul and spirit.

Physical death always refers to the body, never to the death of the soul and spirit. The soul of all unsaved men are dead while they live. Spiritual death means merely separation from God by sin (Isa. 59:2; Eph. 2:1-9; I Tim. 5:6).

Physical death is separation of the inner man from the body (James 2:26). The body only dies at physical death and it goes to the grave; whereas the soul goes to other places until the Resurrection of the body.

The Righteous go to Heaven (II Cor. 5:8; Phil. 1:21-24; Heb. 12:22-23; Rev. 6:9-11), and the wicked go to hell (Isa. 14:9; Lk. 16:19-31; Rev. 20:11-15).

In the Resurrection, the bodies only are made alive and immortal, then the immortal souls and spirits enter them so that the bodies, souls, and spirits of all men can exist in eternal consciousness in punishment or bliss (Isa. 66:22-24; Mat. 10:28; 25:41, 46; Mk. 9:43-49; Rev. 20:11-15) (Dake).

The phrase, *"Have ye not read in the Book of Moses, how in the bush God spake unto him,"* takes the Sadducees to the Scriptures, but, more importantly, to the very part of the Bible they claim to believe, the Pentateuch. The idea that Jesus would prove the Doctrine of the Resurrection from this part of the Word of God, was something they did not count on, to say the least! Jesus is referring to Exodus 3:5-6.

The continuing of the question, *"Saying, I am the God of Abraham, and the God of Isaac, and the God of Jacob?"*, proves the validity of the Doctrine of the Resurrection.

God did not say, *"I was the God of Abraham ...,"* referring to someone who was dead, out of existence, and was no more. He instead said, *"I am the God of Abraham ...,"* meaning that these individuals continued to be alive at the time of Moses, even though their bodies were dead, and, in Truth, were alive even at the present. As well, Jehovah was their God when they were here on this earth, continued to be their God during the time of Moses, hence saying, *"I am,"* and because they were still alive, and, in Truth, were alive even as Jesus spoke, and will be alive forevermore. As Jehovah is the God of these Patriarchs, likewise, He is the God of all!

(27) "HE IS NOT THE GOD OF THE DEAD, BUT THE GOD OF THE LIVING: YE THEREFORE DO GREATLY ERR."

The phrase, *"He is not the God of the dead,"* as Jesus is using it, and referring to the erroneous belief of the Sadducees, means that which no longer exists. The Sadducees were claiming that when a person dies, they are no more, ceasing to exist, and will never be Resurrected. That is what Jesus is referring to by His use of the word, *"dead,"* in this instance.

The phrase, *"But the God of the living,"* means that the Doctrine of the Sadducees is wrong, in that no individual goes out of existence, but actually lives forever, whether Redeemed or in a fallen state.

The Lord is saying that God is not presiding over people who do not exist, for what use would that be? He is rather presiding over those who continue to live, even though their bodies are dead. This speaks of the soul and spirit which live forever, and, in fact, cannot die.

Actually, in Heaven at this very moment, if one could go to that blessed abode for observation, one would see Abraham, Isaac, and Jacob, as well as every other Believer who has ever lived, and would recognize them, even though they were only in the form of their soul and spirit. In the Resurrection, which is soon to come, a Glorified Body will be given to every Believer now in Heaven, and even to those alive on the earth at that time. They (those alive) will be *"changed"* (I Cor. 15:51-57).

NOTES

For there not to be a Resurrection of the Body (for God to give a new body) would leave Believers in an imperfect condition. The living soul must in due time recover its partner (the body), and this will happen at the Resurrection.

The phrase, *"Ye therefore do greatly err,"* proclaims this Doctrine of the Sadducees as not only error, but *"great error."* For men not to believe in the Coming Resurrection, is to undermine the entirety of the Plan of God for the human family. It shows a gross misunderstanding and even ignorance of Who God is, and what God is doing!

Tragically, and despite 2,000 years of access to the Bible, for most of the Church, and concerning many Doctrines, Jesus would probably continue to say, *"Ye therefore do greatly err!"*

(28) "AND ONE OF THE SCRIBES CAME, AND HAVING HEARD THEM REASONING TOGETHER, AND PERCEIVING THAT HE HAD ANSWERED THEM WELL, ASKED HIM, WHICH IS THE FIRST COMMANDMENT OF ALL?"

The phrase, *"And one of the Scribes came, and having heard them reasoning together,"* no doubt spoke of a Pharisee.

The implication is that this exchange took place a short time after the exchange with the Sadducees. Possibly this *"Scribe"* related to the Pharisees what Jesus had said concerning the Resurrection, and greatly impressed by Jesus' answer, will now pose a question himself.

There is no indication that his question was framed with deceit, but rather an earnest, sincere desire for Bible knowledge. He is one of the few who took advantage of the Perfect Knowledge of Christ. What a shame!

The phrase, *"And perceiving that He had answered them well,"* could as well be said concerning every answer given by Jesus.

As we have alluded to, the Religious Leaders of Israel, plus anyone else for that matter, could have asked Jesus the deepest questions concerning Life and Godliness, and it would have been forthrightly answered. The wisdom of the ages was in their presence and they did not know it. Sadly, the Religious Leaders too often sought only to trap Him, instead of seeking answers which they desperately needed.

Their pride would not allow them to admit Who and What He was. The idea that this

"Peasant" had perfect knowledge of the Bible, and furthermore was *"The Messiah,"* was a Truth they could not come to grips with. Consequently, they opposed Him, and, thereby, missed Eternal Life.

Is it any different presently?

Jesus is no less today, and, in Truth, because of Calvary and the Resurrection, even more! And yet, the world as a whole ignores Him, or else bitterly opposes Him.

If anyone will seek Him, He will, and without fail, *"answer them well."*

The question, *"Asked Him, Which is the first Commandment of all?",* was not really referring to the single most important Commandment of the Ten Commandments.

This argument concerning the *"first,"* or *"greatest"* Commandment, then raged in Israel. The idea was the distinction between the ritual and ethical. Which was the most important?

The Pharisees were hung up on the many rituals of the Mosaic Law, which they attempted to fastidiously keep, while others, and rightly so, were more concerned about the ethical, or moral principles of the Law.

(29) "AND JESUS ANSWERED HIM, THE FIRST OF ALL THE COMMANDMENTS IS, HEAR, O ISRAEL; THE LORD OUR GOD IS ONE LORD:"

The phrase, *"And Jesus answered him,"* is typical of the Lord. Every legitimate question, and even many of the previous ones, which were not legitimate, received answers, and, above all, *"the answer."*

The phrase, *"The first of all the Commandments is,"* proclaims an instant response respecting the correct interpretation of the Bible.

The phrase, *"Hear, O Israel; The Lord our God is one Lord,"* is taken from Deuteronomy 6:4-5. It is said that it was recited daily by every Jew, and even written on a miniature roll which every Scribe carried in his phylactery. This was a small case, made of parchment bound to the forehead or arm, in which was placed small pieces of parchment inscribed with Scripture portions (Wuest).

The word, *"one,"* in the Hebrew is *"echad,"* and means *"to be united as one, one in number."*

In Greek it is *"heis,"* and has the same meaning.

Dake says, *"Whether one in number or one in unity is meant must be determined by Scripture and by the subject matter. That these words*

NOTES

are used in the sense of unity is clear from Genesis 2:24; 11:6; John 10:30; 11:52; 17:11, 21-23."

He went on to say, *"There are three separate Persons called 'God' and 'Lord' in Scripture, so one in unity must be the true meaning here.*

"On the other hand, 'one' could refer to the Head Person of the Divine Trinity, Who is the Father and Head of Christ and the Holy Spirit" (Jn. 14:16-17, 26, 28; 15:26; 16:7-15; I Cor. 8:4-6; 11:3; Eph. 4:4-6; I Jn. 5:7).

(30) "AND THOU SHALT LOVE THE LORD THY GOD WITH ALL THY HEART, AND WITH ALL THY SOUL, AND WITH ALL THY MIND, AND WITH ALL THY STRENGTH: THIS IS THE FIRST COMMANDMENT."

The phrase, *"And thou shalt love the Lord thy God with all thy heart,"* refers to *"Agape"* Love, which speaks of Holy Spirit-generated Love in the heart of the yielded Saint. It is a Divine Love, which is due God from His creatures.

So, we are speaking of a type of *"Love"* that the world cannot have, and, in fact, only a Believer can have, and which can only be given by the Lord.

Among the Pharisees there was great profession of love to God, but little practice of love to man. Today there seems to be great evidence of love to man, i.e., philanthropy, social schemes, hospitals, and such like, but little evidence of love to God (Williams).

The *"heart"* as spoken of here, does not refer to the physical organ, but, instead, to the seat of all affections and desires, and must be centered upon God.

The idea is not, as some think, that God is to be first, with other things second and third, etc., but that God is to be all in all, and with every desire and affection brought into this sphere.

In other words, God does not occupy the largest portion of our affections and desires, but, instead, all of our affections and desires. When this is done, other things, such as family, etc., will enjoy the proper type of love, which makes for the happiest relationships and home life that one could ever have! It is all found in God, and not found at all outside of God.

The phrase, *"And with all thy soul,"* has to do with feelings and emotions.

If the Lord is loved with all our *"soul,"* then our emotions will be healthy, instead of a runaway engine, as it is in many people. Feelings and emotions not anchored in Christ, fuel psychological problems, which, in reality, are spiritual problems. Consequently, in this short statement given by Christ, we find the answer to these problems. Feelings and emotions must be centered in Christ, as stated, and must give vent through Praise and Worship.

The phrase, *"And with all thy mind,"* concerns the will and the intellect. In essence, the *"mind"* is the gateway to the spirit. So, if the *"mind"* wills love for God, and worship of God, as it must, the spirit of man will as well be fed and nurtured.

The *"heart"* is mentioned first, because the desire must be generated first of all, and can only come from the heart.

As the desire for God comes from the heart, the emotions are then stirred through the *"soul."* Then the will to love and worship God comes into play through the *"mind."*

The mind is the last to really be brought to bear, and is the reason that many begin correctly, but do not follow through. The desire is there and the emotions are in play, but the *"will"* is lacking.

The phrase, *"And with all thy strength,"* means that whatever strength is shown for the procurement of other things, is to always be secondary to our efforts made respecting love for God.

"Strength" refers to effort, and speaks of determination.

The phrase, *"This is the First Commandment,"* leaves no room for doubt! Succinctly and specifically, even dogmatically, the Lord proclaims the answer to this man's question. Consequently, mere ritual which was followed so minutely by the Pharisees, was given no credence at all by the Lord. He went far beyond the ritual and the ceremony, going to the very seat of man's being, which generates the true state of the individual.

Consequently, this *"First Commandment,"* completely abrogates all religious ceremony, religion, rules, and works. These things (ceremonies, etc.,) can be done without any change of heart, while this of which Jesus speaks, must involve a change of heart, which can only be done by the Lord, and must come from within a person. This is the reason the *"born-again"* experience, which generates these things, is the only Power on earth which can change a person.

This alone is the answer to marriage problems, social problems, economic problems, and even most physical problems.

NOTES

(31) "AND THE SECOND IS LIKE, NAMELY THIS, THOU SHALT LOVE THY NEIGHBOUR AS THYSELF. THERE IS NONE OTHER COMMANDMENT GREATER THAN THESE."

The phrase, *"And the Second is like, namely this,"* gives the man that for which he did not ask. However, it is impossible to separate the two, hence, Jesus including the *"Second."*

The phrase, *"Thou shalt love thy neighbour as thyself,"* in effect, is telling us this:

If we truly love God as we should love Him, we will, as well, *"love our neighbour."* This is the answer to all wars, prejudice, hate, bias, and racism.

If one says he loves God, and accommodating love is not shown to one's neighbor, then his claims of love for God are obviously false. However, and as stated, philanthropic efforts, as engaged in by many, are not exactly what Jesus is speaking of here. It does not refer to action towards one's neighbor, as a result of works, but, instead, of *"Love."* There is a vast difference!

So there would be no mistake as to what Jesus was saying, He added the words, *"As thyself."* The love we have for ourselves is to be the barometer respecting love for others.

The phrase, *"There is none other Commandment greater than these,"* in effect, has just explained the entirety of the Bible. It is so simple that a child could understand it, and, yet, the answer to all the problems which plague humanity, and as one must quickly add, *"the only answer."*

In writing these Commentaries on the four Gospels, the Words of Christ have intrigued me in a manner that I really cannot properly express. The wisdom He gave, so far eclipses anything else known to man, that all else pales by comparison. But yet, it is ignored by most all the world, and even by much of the Church!

He beautifully takes complex questions, reducing them to the lowest possible, and most common denominator, consequently so simple, and yet they remain profound! Anyone can understand the answers He gives, and, yet, the most brilliant intellectuals could never begin to plumb their depths or scale their heights. Truly, He is *"the Way, the Truth, and the Life"* (Jn. 14:6).

(32) "AND THE SCRIBE SAID UNTO HIM, WELL, MASTER, THOU HAST SAID THE TRUTH: FOR THERE IS ONE GOD; AND THERE IS NONE OTHER BUT HE:"

The phrase, *"And the Scribe said unto Him,"* refers to the man who had asked the question to begin with.

The phrase, *"Well, Master, Thou hast said the Truth,"* refers to a Pharisee, who, for a change, spoke kindly to and of Jesus. The word, *"well,"* means *"good,"* and means that the Scribe was greatly blessed and instructed by the answer. And yet, by him calling Jesus, *"Master,"* he merely referred to Him as a Teacher. There is no evidence that he recognized Jesus as the Messiah.

It would seem that the tremendous answers given by Christ, would have made the man realize that while Jesus was definitely a great Teacher, actually the greatest, more than all, He was *"The Messiah."* Jesus not only spoke *"Truth,"* actually He <u>was</u> *"Truth."*

The phrase, *"For there is one God; and there is none other but He,"* was certainly true; however, it is obvious that the man did not fully understand this *"Truth."* In effect, he was standing in front of God, i.e., The Son of God, but did not know it!

(33) "AND TO LOVE HIM WITH ALL THE HEART AND WITH ALL THE UNDERSTANDING, AND WITH ALL THE SOUL, AND WITH ALL THE STRENGTH, AND TO LOVE HIS NEIGHBOUR AS HIMSELF, IS MORE THAN ALL WHOLE BURNT OFFERINGS AND SACRIFICES."

This man reciting the First Commandment, *"And to love Him . . . ,"* and the Second, *"To love his neighbour as himself,"* proclaims him understanding what Christ had said. To it he did not add or take away, and, consequently, portrays the rightful dividing of the Word.

The phrase, *"Is more than all whole Burnt Offerings and Sacrifices,"* proclaims him going beyond most Pharisees, in that he now understands what the Law was all about. While the *"Whole Burnt Offerings"* and *"Sacrifices,"* were important, still, many, if not the majority, engaged in these rituals and ceremonies, but received no spiritual benefit.

It is the same presently as people who belong to Churches, are baptized in water, and frequently take the Lord's Supper, but, in reality, do not know Jesus as their personal Saviour.

And yet, as most of Israel fell into this ceremony trap, likewise, most in modern Christendom follow suit.

Some time ago I received a letter from a dear lady who had been saved as a result of watching our Telecast.

She went on to state how she was a member of a well-known Church, actually teaching a Sunday School Class, having done so for several years. She knew the Doctrine of this Church backwards and forwards, even at times teaching Doctrine Classes.

On the Sunday Morning in question, as she began to watch the Telecast, the Spirit of God began to deal with her soul, convicting her of her lost condition. She was religious but lost! In a few moments time, the Spirit of God let her know that she really did not know Jesus as her personal Saviour, and that she had never really been truly *"born again."* In a few moments time, as the Holy Spirit dealt with her, that was rectified, with her truly accepting Christ as her Saviour.

In the past she had made some type of mental affirmation toward Christ, as millions have, but really did not know Him. As stated, she was religious but lost!

In Truth, her situation, plus multiple millions of others, falls into the same category as Israel at the time of Christ, which was busily engaged in *"Whole Burnt Offerings and Sacrifices,"* but, in reality, did now know God Whom these Sacrifices represented. In other words, they thought they were saved simply because they were Jews, and engaged in these rituals. They were as the lady, religious but lost!

(34) "AND WHEN JESUS SAW THAT HE ANSWERED DISCRETELY, HE SAID UNTO HIM, THOU ART NOT FAR FROM THE KINGDOM OF GOD. AND NO MAN AFTER THAT DURST ASK HIM ANY QUESTION."

The phrase, *"And when Jesus saw that he answered discretely, He said unto him,"* represents Christ not only taking stock of his answer, but, as well, seeing into the very depths of this man's heart.

The word, *"discretely,"* in the Greek Text is *"nounechos,"* and means, *"intelligence, as one who has a mind of his own."* This is far more significant than meets the eye.

Most of the people in Jesus' day, as now, blindly followed Religious Leaders, believing what they were told. Consequently, to meet someone who searched the Word of God himself, and, as well, formed conclusions on what he found, rather than blindly following others, is refreshing, to say the least!

Most people, presently, as always, are either on their way to Heaven or hell, because of what someone else has told them. In other words, most little search the Word of God, forming their own conclusions, but rather blindly take the word of others. As well, this is strongly encouraged in both Catholic and Protestant circles.

In a sense, Catholic Bishops claim infallibility, at least regarding interpretation of Scripture. Consequently, the people are taught to blindly follow and not question. *"If a mistake is made,"* they are told, *"it will be the problem of the Priest and not the person."* The tragedy is that most Priests do not know the Word of God, therefore, the entire scenario points to double jeopardy for Catholic adherents. However, let not the reader think that Catholics alone are in this category. Many if not most Protestants are hard on their heels.

For instance, the Pentecostal Denomination I was formerly associated with, pretty much espouses the same terrible error.

For instance, one of their leading officials called a Pastor acquaintance of mine, of that Denomination, demanding that he do a particular thing, which was obviously unscriptural. The Pastor quickly remonstrated by declaring the lack of Scriptural foundation for such an act. The Official quickly answered, *"That is of no concern of yours. If it's wrong, I will be responsible and not you. It is your duty to obey me irrespective of what I ask!"*

When the conversation ended, the Pastor hung up the phone, stunned, to say the least! He related the incident to his wife, and she answered by saying, *"Surely you misunderstood him!"*

He instantly picked up the telephone, and dialed the man, asking him to state again what had just been said.

"No, you did not misunderstand," he said, *"you heard me exactly right.*

"You are to do exactly what I say, whether it is right or wrong, and the responsibility will be mine."

Of course, anyone who has even a rudimentary knowledge of the Word of God, knows the absolute fallacy of such thinking. Millions have gone to hell, eternally losing their souls because of such error.

NOTES

I do not know if the Pastor obeyed this unscriptural command or not! However, this I do know:

He should have instantly rebuked this man, and then immediately disassociated himself with this Religious Denomination. To continue to associate with such error, and especially after it has become so blatantly obvious, makes one a part and parcel of the error. Blindly closing one's eyes, and then making the lame excuse that all in that Denomination are not of that belief, can only be labeled as compromise of the highest sort! Paul said, *"Be ye not unequally yoked together with unbelievers."*

He also said, *"Wherefore come out from among them, and be ye separate, saith the Lord, and touch not the unclean thing; and I will receive you"* (II Cor. 6:14, 17).

Some may argue that this Religious Official of my illustration was not an unbeliever! And yet, I think one must conclude that the Pharisees of Jesus' day were unbelievers. Consequently, those who follow in their train, as this man, can only be labeled accordingly. One either follows the Word of God, or one doesn't! While it is certainly true that no Believer has all the light on every subject in the Bible, still, to be in error on such a fundamental question, as personal Salvation certainly is, is to basically be in error regarding all.

The phrase, *"Thou art not far from the Kingdom of God,"* constitutes one of, if not the most positive recorded statement offered by Christ to a Pharisee.

The distance from the *"Kingdom of God"* is measured neither by miles, nor by ceremonial standards, but by spiritual conditions. However, being close is not enough. Millions, as well, fall into this category.

Expositors commented that it would be interesting to work out a comparison between this Scribe and the ruler of Mark 10:17. In both cases something was wanting to convert admiration into Discipleship. If wealth was the bar in one case, pride of intellect may have been fatal in the other. The mental acumen which detects and approves spiritual Truth, may, in the tragedy of human life, keep its possessor from entering the Kingdom of God.

As this man, millions attend Churches presently, even making professions of Faith. However, many of these millions have never really had a heartfelt experience with Christ. They are religious and actively in the Church, and, as well, give mental assent to the acceptance of Christ, but, in Truth, do not know the Lord as their own personal Saviour. What a tragedy! They are *"near the Kingdom of God,"* but not *"in the Kingdom of God."*

The phrase, *"And no man after that durst ask Him any question,"* proclaims all three groups of Religious Leaders, Pharisees, Sadducees, and Herodians, as being unable to match wits with Jesus. It is tragic that they approached Christ in this fashion, and not in worship and adoration. However, many, if not most, approach Christ in the same fashion. He is used and abused, but seldom proclaimed as to Who He really is, *"The Son of God."* He was so near, but yet so very far away.

(35) "AND JESUS ANSWERED AND SAID, WHILE HE TAUGHT IN THE TEMPLE, HOW SAY THE SCRIBES THAT CHRIST IS THE SON OF DAVID?"

The phrase, *"And Jesus answered and said,"* is presented by Matthew as Jesus talking with the Pharisees (Mat. 22:41-42).

The phrase, *"While He taught in the Temple,"* presents Him only hours before the Crucifixion.

The question, *"How say the Scribes that Christ is the Son of David?"*, concerned the Incarnation, i.e., God becoming Man, and dwelling among men.

THE INCARNATION

The title, *"Christ,"* in the Greek is *"Christos,"* and means *"The Anointed One."* In the Hebrew, it is translated *"Messiah."* Consequently, this question asked by Christ, carries all types of implications.

The word, *"Son,"* refers to a descendant, which Jesus was of David.

Both the Scribes and the people believed that the Jewish Messiah would come from the Royal Line of David. David was human, so would the Messiah be human. Thus, He would be David's Son.

Actually, the Lord had promised David, *"The Lord telleth thee that He will make thee an house.*

"And when thy days be fulfilled, and thou shalt sleep with thy fathers, I will set up thy Seed after thee, which shall proceed out of thy bowels, and I will establish His Kingdom.

"He shall build an house for My Name, and I will establish the Throne of His Kingdom for ever" (II Sam. 7:11-13).

The word, *"Seed,"* as used, referred to all of David's lineage, which spoke of the Kings of Judah who followed David, but, more specifically, the Lord Jesus Christ, the fulfillment of these Prophecies, Who was in the direct lineage of David, and Who would have been King of Israel at this time, had He been accepted. Actually, the lineage of Jesus went all the way back to Adam. Paul called Him, *"The Last Adam"* (I Cor. 15:45).

WHY WAS THE INCARNATION SO IMPORTANT?

Even though he word, *"Incarnation,"* is not found in the Bible, its meaning is found in some important New Testament Statements about the Person and Work of Jesus Christ. Paul said, *"God* (Jesus) *was manifest in the flesh"* (I Tim. 3:16).

John ascribed to the spirit of Antichrist any denial that Jesus Christ has *"come in the flesh"* (I Jn. 4:2; II Jn. 7). Paul says that Christ did His reconciling work *"in His Body of flesh"* (Eph. 2:15; Col. 1:22), and that by sending His Son *"in the likeness of sinful flesh,"* God *"condemned sin in the flesh"* (Rom. 8:3).

Peter speaks of Christ dying for us *"in the flesh"* (I Pet. 3:18; 4:1).

All these Texts are enforcing the same Truth, but from different angles: that it was precisely by coming and dying *"in the flesh"* that Christ secured our Salvation. Theology calls His Coming the *"Incarnation,"* and His dying the *"Atonement."*

(The word, *"Incarnation,"* in its most simple form, means that Deity, Who has no physical body, takes upon Himself a physical body, and lives among men. Hence the phrase, *"God manifest in the flesh,"* or *"God with us"* (Isa. 7:14). The word, *"Immanuel"* in Isaiah 7:14, means *"God with us."* Thus was Jesus.)

As a result of the Incarnation, Jesus, Who is God and became flesh, at the same time, is *"Very God"* and *"Very Man."* In other words, He is one-hundred percent God and one-hundred percent Man. He is not, as some teach, half God and half man, etc.

The New Testament writers never attempted to dissect the mystery of His Person; it is enough for them to proclaim the Incarnation as a fact, one of the sequence of mighty works whereby God has wrought Salvation for sinners. Basically, the only sense in which the New Testament writers ever attempt to explain the Incarnation is by showing how it fits into God's over-all Plan for redeeming mankind (Jn. 1:18; Rom. 8:3; Phil. 2:6-11; Col. 1:13-22; Heb. 1:2; 4:14-5:10; 7:1-10:18; I Jn. 1:1-2:2).

The basic explanation and understanding of the Incarnation, concerns Jesus as the *"Last Adam."*

THE FIRST ADAM

Adam was created or formed as a *"Son of God"* (Lk. 3:38). God, in His creation, gave Adam and Eve the power or ability of procreation, which means to *"bring offspring into the world."* Had Adam not fallen, their offspring would have been *"sons of God."*

As it was, and due to the Fall, they could not bring *"sons of God"* into the world, but rather *"sons of Adam,"* in other words, *"after his image,"* instead of after the *"Image of God"* (Gen. 1:26; 5:3).

The Fall, and all its resultant action, is the cause of all the pain, suffering, sickness, and death in the world. Consequently, man must be redeemed from this fallen state, or else all is lost.

How could this be done?

The penalty for disobedience by Adam was death, which meant separation from God, and, consequently, the cause of all death (Gen. 2:17).

Consequently, the price of Redemption was *"Life,"* i.e., a perfect life, which could be offered in Sacrifice, which would satisfy the claims of heavenly justice (John 3:16). However, there was a catch to all of this:

Inasmuch as Adam was the federal head, under Christ, of the entirety of the human family, which meant all who were to come, when he acted (sinned) he, in effect, sinned for the entirety of the human family, and for all time. Consequently, when he fell, the entirety of the human race fell. Every baby born would be born *"in sin,"* consequently, lost! (Ps. 51:5; Rom. 3:10-18; 5:17). So, this meant there were no uncontaminated human beings, at least that God would accept, who could redeem fallen humanity.

Angels could not redeem man, because they were of another creation. So, the only way that man could be redeemed, was for God to become

a man, live a perfect, spotless life, free and uncontaminated by sin, and die on Calvary, thereby paying the price for man's Redemption. As stated, he was called the *"Last Adam"* (I Cor. 15:45). What the First Adam failed to do, the Last Adam would have to do.

The only way that God could fulfill this task, thereby redeeming man, was to become man, hence, the Incarnation.

THE VIRGIN BIRTH

However, for God to simply become flesh was not enough. Were He to be born in the manner of all other babies, He, as well, would be born *"in sin,"* and, therefore, unacceptable as a Perfect Sacrifice. And yet, to be the *"Last Adam,"* He had to be man in every respect. As stated, He could not be half God and half man. So, how was it possible to do this?

Inasmuch as Adam under Christ was the federal head of the human family, the seed of procreation (bringing offspring into the world) was contained in man. In effect, the woman has no seed. Therefore, if Jesus was born of a Virgin, which means a woman who had never had sexual relations with a man, He would not be born *"in sin"* as all other babies. Consequently, this is exactly what happened!

The Scripture says, *"Now the birth of Jesus Christ was on this wise: when as His Mother Mary was espoused (engaged) to Joseph, before they came together, she was found with child of the Holy Ghost"* (Mat. 1:18).

Inasmuch as the First Adam was not born of woman, but, instead, formed by God, Jesus, being born of the Virgin Mary, did not violate the type.

So, He was born without sin, and, therefore, a fit subject for the Perfect Sacrifice.

However, He must, as well, as the Last Adam, walk perfect before God, never failing or sinning. If He failed even one time, He, as well, would be fallen, just as the original Adam. He had to live a fully human life, just as all other men. As such, He had to face every temptation that man faces. This He did, and did so perfectly sinless, as several times asserted in the Bible (Mat. 3:14-17; Jn. 8:46; II Cor. 5:21; Heb. 4:15; I Pet. 2:22; I Jn. 2:1). Consequently, when He died on Calvary, He did not die for sins of His Own, but for others. He died vicariously and representatively, the Righteous taking the place of the unrighteous (Rom. 5:16; II Cor. 5:21; Gal. 3:13; I Pet. 3:18).

WHAT EXACTLY WAS THE INCARNATE STATE?

It was a state of *"dependence and obedience."* The Incarnation did not change the relationship between the Son and the Father. They continued in unbroken fellowship, the Son saying and doing what the Father gave Him to say and do, and not going beyond the Father's will at any single moment.

During the time of the Incarnation, He emptied Himself of the qualities of Deity, while never ceasing to be Deity. As the Son, He did not wish or seek to know more than the Father wished Him to know (Phil. 2:5-8).

As well, and as we have already stated, His Life was a state of sinlessness and impeccability. It had to be this way, in order for Him to die as *"a Lamb without blemish and without spot"* (I Pet. 1:19).

He had to keep the Law of Moses in every respect, which He did, and which no other man ever did, even Moses. Consequently, by keeping the Law, He became our Representative Man of victory, and Faith in Him guarantees the Believer the victory won by Jesus. He was our Substitute, and a perfect One at that, and upon identification with Him, all that He gained, which is what Adam lost, is now given to us.

The Incarnation was also a state of temptation and moral conflict. It had to be, in order to be a true entry into the conditions of man's moral life. Being man, as the original Adam, it was necessary for Him to fight temptation, and do it God's Way in order to overcome it. This He did, and never failed in even one point.

The writer to the Hebrews stresses that by virtue of His firsthand experience of temptation and the costliness of obedience, He is able to extend effective sympathy and help to tempted and distraught Christians (Heb. 2:18; 4:14; 5:2, 7).

THE PERFECT SACRIFICE

So, as the Perfect Man, the Last Adam, He did what the First Adam failed to do, and, therefore, redeemed humanity.

To fulfill the requirements of heavenly justice, His perfect Life, which was ensconced in His Perfect Body, was offered as a Perfect Sacrifice

—a Sacrifice, incidentally, which God could, and would accept. Therefore, as the Last Adam, He met Satan on even worse terms than the First Adam, but, nevertheless, overcame him in every respect. He came to the end of His human life, and said, *"The prince of this world* (Satan) *cometh, and hath nothing in Me"* (Jn. 14:30).

So, the Incarnation was an absolute necessity if man was to be redeemed. Thank God that He loved us enough, even when we did not love Him, that He would come down to this world, taking upon Himself the wrappings of human flesh, living in humiliation as a man, and would pay the price for our Redemption. Such is incomprehensible to the human mind, and, as well, simply beyond the ability of man to fully grasp. And yet He did it for you and me.

As the Last Adam, He won back, or rather purchased, with His Own precious Blood, that which we had lost; that and more!

As a Man, He faced Satan in every respect, and in every respect overcame him. As well, He satisfied the claims of heavenly justice, that nothing is left owing on man's ledger, at least for those who will believe (Jn. 3:16).

(36) "FOR DAVID HIMSELF SAID BY THE HOLY GHOST, THE LORD SAID TO MY LORD, SIT THOU ON MY RIGHT HAND, TILL I MAKE THINE ENEMIES THY FOOTSTOOL."

The phrase, *"For David himself said by the Holy Ghost,"* affirms by Christ that David wrote Psalm 110. As well, it proclaims that it was inspired by the Holy Spirit.

The phrase, *"The Lord said to my Lord,"* refers to *"Lord"* as the translation of the Greek word, *"Kurios,"* and is the august title of God in the Hebrew Old Testament, i.e., *"Jehovah."*

The first *"Lord"* in this phrase refers to God, the Father, with the second *"Lord"* referring to God, the Son. Consequently, this phrase proclaims two *"Lords"* in the Deity. Actually, there are three, with the *"Holy Spirit"* mentioned in the first phrase. Therefore, there are three Persons in the Trinity, *"The Father, The Son, and The Holy Spirit"* (Mat. 3:16-17; 28:19; Jn. 14:16, 26; 15:26; 16:7-15; Acts 2:33; 7:55; II Cor. 13:14; Eph. 4:4-6; I Jn. 5:7; Rev. 1:4; 4:2-5; 5:7).

The phrase, *"Sit Thou on My Right Hand,"* refers to the time after His Death, and Resurrection, when the Father exalted Him far above all principality and power, actually placing Him next to Him in Heaven, that He may reign with supreme Power and Glory over all. As should be obvious, Christ is there this moment.

The phrase, *"Till I make Thine enemies Thy footstool,"* does not imply that Christ will then cease to reign, but that He will then formerly deliver up the Kingdom to God, even the Father.

The defeating of these *"enemies,"* which refers to Satan and his kingdom of darkness, began with the Life of Christ, and especially Calvary and the Resurrection. It has continued through the Church Age, and will continue through the Millennial Reign. At the end of the Millennial Reign, Satan, along with all his minions of darkness, will be *"cast into the Lake of Fire and Brimstone"* (Rev. 20:10). At that time, and as well, the *"Last enemy"* which is *"Death"* will be destroyed (I Cor. 15:26).

Paul then said, and as we have referred to, *"Then cometh the end, when He shall have delivered up the Kingdom to God, even the Father; when He shall have put down all rule and all authority and power"* (I Cor. 15:24).

When all enemies are subdued, as they shall be, and the Kingdom is delivered to *"God, the Father,"* then God will transfer His Headquarters from Heaven to earth. John gives us that description in Revelation Chapters 21 and 22.

As a result, the Scripture says, *"And there shall be no more curse: but the Throne of God and of the Lamb shall be in it; and His servants shall serve Him:*

"And they shall see His Face; and His Name shall be in their foreheads."

And then it says, *"And they shall reign for ever and ever"* (Rev. 22:3-5)

(37) "DAVID THEREFORE HIMSELF CALLETH HIM LORD; AND WHENCE IS HE THEN HIS SON? AND THE COMMON PEOPLE HEARD HIM GLADLY."

The phrase, *"David therefore himself calleth Him Lord,"* recognizes Him as Deity, the Jehovah of the Old Testament.

The question, *"And whence is He then his Son?"*, refers to Him, The Messiah, as not only God, but, human as well!

This question is posed to these Religious Leaders, as to how the Messiah as Jehovah, can also be human? At once the Incarnation is brought before them.

Wuest says, *"One of the charges brought against the Lord Jesus was that He called God*

NOTES

His (His private, unique) *Father, making Himself equal with God, thus Deity"* (Jn. 5:18).

Plainly and clearly, Jesus tells these Religious Leaders exactly Who and How the Messiah would be. Consequently, His statement cleared up misunderstanding and outright false interpretation. In view of what the Scripture plainly said, there was no reason for them to be confused. They were in this state because of their self-will, and would reject Jesus because of self-will.

They knew that the Messiah would come from the Royal Line of David. As well, they no doubt checked the genealogy in the Temple, where such of every family in Israel was kept, and knew that Joseph, the foster father of Jesus, was in the direct lineage of David. In fact, had the Davidic dynasty continued, Joseph would now be King.

As well, whereas Joseph's lineage traced back to David through Solomon, they also knew that Mary's lineage, the Mother of Jesus, traced back to David through Nathan, another son of David, and brother to Solomon. Consequently, the lineage of Jesus was perfect, which, of course, would characterize the Messiah.

Therefore, they are faced with a dilemma. Jesus is Who He said He was, and which there was incontrovertible proof, or else He is an imposter, of which there is no evidence whatsoever! Sadly, and despite the proof otherwise, they branded Him as an imposter.

This appeal to them just hours before the Crucifixion, was another effort by Christ to bring them to their senses in order that they may not do this dastardly thing. The killing of Him was bad enough; however, He would rise from the dead in three days. Worst of all, their killing of Him would destroy themselves, for they would not rise from the dead!

The phrase, *"And the common people heard Him gladly,"* means that they, *"The common people,"* heard Him, and believed Him respecting His claim as Messiah, but the Religious Leaders did not! Regrettably, such continues to the present!

The fault of most spiritual declension is not the pew, but, rather, the pulpit.

One Methodist layman told me once, *"Brother Swaggart, it was not the Methodist people who destroyed the Methodist Church, but, rather, the Seminaries which turned out Preachers who no longer believed in God, or the Bible."* He said, *"They destroyed the Methodist Church!"*

(38-40) "AND HE SAID UNTO THEM IN HIS DOCTRINE, BEWARE OF THE SCRIBES, WHICH LOVE TO GO IN LONG CLOTHING, AND LOVE SALUTATIONS IN THE MARKETPLACES,

"AND THE CHIEF SEATS IN THE SYNAGOGUES, AND THE UPPERMOST ROOMS AT FEASTS:

"WHICH DEVOUR WIDOWS' HOUSES, AND FOR A PRETENCE MAKE LONG PRAYERS: THESE SHALL RECEIVE GREATER DAMNATION."

The phrase, *"And He said unto them in His Doctrine,"* refers to these Religious Leaders, who have denied His claims.

The phrase, *"Beware of the Scribes,"* does not demean their official character, but rather their conduct. In effect, these *"Scribes"* were the Pastors of the people. They were supposed to be experts in the Law of Moses, and, consequently, guide the people in the Ways of the Lord. Jesus' condemnation of this group, proclaims them doing any and everything totally opposite of the Ways of God.

As we shall see, He did not condemn them all, but only those who fit His following description, which, sadly, included the vast majority.

Would He say presently, *"Beware of the Preachers?"*

I think it can be said without any fear of contradiction, that without a doubt He would!

The scene is very little different now than then. As there were only a few *"Scribes"* then who truly followed the Lord, likewise, there are only a few Preachers who truly follow. Consequently, of most Preachers standing behind modern pulpits, Jesus would say of them, *"Beware!"*

Why?

Paul said it well, when in prison in Rome, and looking for a Preacher to send to Philippi. *"For I have no man like-minded, who will naturally care for your state.*

"For all seek their own, not the things which are Jesus Christ's" (Phil. 2:20-21).

As Scribes then sought their own *"will and way,"* likewise, modern Preachers too often do the same!

The phrase, *"Which love to go in long clothing,"* spoke of Priestly or Royal robes. What the Lord was condemning was ostentatious display, and not necessarily the type of clothing itself. In other words, they wanted to look important!

The phrase, *"And love salutations in the marketplaces,"* referred to them being fond of being called *"Rabbi,"* or *"Doctor,"* or *"Master."*

Once again, He was not condemning these titles, but only the greedy grasping after them. To be called by these titles in public places, and in the hearing of many people, once again, made these individuals feel important.

The phrase, *"And the chief seats in the Synagogues,"* referred to seats or benches up front, which faced the congregation, and were reserved for officials and persons of distinction. Wuest said, *"The Scribes claimed these places of honor also at social gatherings."*

The phrase, *"And the uppermost rooms at feasts,"* referred to the place reserved for the most honored guest at a feast.

The custom at that time, while at meals, was not to sit in chairs as now, but, rather, to recline on couches around the table. Whoever the host was, the *"Scribes"* desired the *"Uppermost room,"* or place, beside him.

The phrase, *"Which devour widows' houses,"* referred to money.

People often left their whole fortunes to the Temple, and a good part of the money went finally to the Scribes and Pharisees (Wuest).

They would spend much time with wealthy widows, getting them to make out a will, with the money and property seemingly going to the Temple, but which was worded in such a way, that most of the funds came to the Scribe himself.

The phrase, *"And for a pretence make long prayers,"* referred to the Scribes praying long and loud for these widows and in their presence, which helped to ultimately impress upon them the making out of a will in favor of the Scribe, etc.

The phrase, *"These shall receive greater damnation,"* means that God holds them more guilty than He does a dishonest man who makes no pretence to piety. The idea is, that to the sentence of the hypocrite, which these Scribes were, will be added in their case the sentence of the robber.

As well, this phrase teaches degrees of punishment in the coming Judgment.

(41) "AND JESUS SAT OVER AGAINST THE TREASURY, AND BEHELD HOW THE PEOPLE CAST MONEY INTO THE TREASURY: AND MANY THAT WERE RICH CAST IN MUCH."

The phrase, *"And Jesus sat over against the treasury,"* pertains to the woman's court, surrounded by a colonnade. Inside, against the wall, were thirteen receptacles shaped like trumpets and labeled for their special purposes. Nine were for legal dues and four for free-will offerings (Dake).

The phrase, *"and beheld how the people cast money into the treasury,"* of which He would present a great lesson. I think it can be said, and beyond the shadow of a doubt, that He does the same presently!

The phrase, *"And many that were rich cast in much,"* pertains not as much to the amount, but the manner in which it was given. With some of the rich, there was a display of their gift, with it known to the bystanders as to its large amount, and with them receiving accolades and well-wishes for these large gifts.

If one is to notice, Jesus constantly condemns ostentatious display, whether in clothing, gifts, or public appearances. As stated, it was not the clothing or the gifts that were condemned, but rather the showy displays. It was the grasping for recognition, and, therefore, praise.

(42) "AND THERE CAME A CERTAIN POOR WIDOW, AND SHE THREW IN TWO MITES, WHICH MAKE A FARTHING."

The phrase, *"And there came a certain poor widow,"* proclaims her being little noticed, if at all, by others, but greatly noticed by the Lord.

When will we ever learn that this is the only notice that really matters!

The word, *"poor,"* in the Greek Text is *"ptochos,"* and is used to designate a pauper rather than a mere peasant. Consequently, the woman was destitute, and yet she gave from her meager income, actually, *"All that she had, even all her living."*

The phrase, *"And she threw in two mites, which make a farthing,"* referred to the *"lepton,"* which was the smallest Greek copper coin, with both of them being presently worth about five cents in 1996 value.

The *"farthing,"* was the smallest Roman brass coin, and worth, as stated, about a nickel.

(43) "AND HE CALLED UNTO HIM HIS DISCIPLES, AND SAITH UNTO THEM, VERILY I SAY UNTO YOU, THAT THIS POOR WIDOW HATH CAST MORE IN, THAN ALL THEY WHICH HAVE CAST INTO THE TREASURY."

The phrase, *"And He called unto Him His Disciples,"* concerns an important lesson about to be taught to them.

The phrase, *"And saith unto them, Verily I say unto you, That this poor widow hath cast more in, than all they which have cast into the treasury,"* proclaims the manner in which God looks at our giving.

First of all, the motive is pointed out. Many of the rich gave for show, while she gave because she loved God.

How do we know that?

As little as it was, she gave all she had, and, to be sure, such would not have been done unless she loved the Lord deeply.

Second, it is not so much what we give, but how much we have left. Someone who gives a dollar, and only has a little left, is looked at with much higher regard by the Lord, than someone who gives $10,000, and who has hundreds of thousands left.

However, at times, it is easier for some people to give from a meager income, than it is when they come into large sums of money. Somehow, the giving of small amounts does not trouble some, with them remaining faithful in this endeavor. However, some balk at giving large amounts, if such comes into their hands.

And then again, there are many who, unlike this *"poor widow,"* will not give their small amounts, claiming they cannot afford to. I think Christ lays that to rest. Anyone can afford to give to the Lord, and no amount, no matter how small, is looked at by Him with disdain, as this illustration proves. Actually, it is looked at with great favor, and, to be sure, will garner great blessing.

One cannot imagine that Jesus allowed this woman to go unblessed. I believe that He saw to it that her needs were met.

(44) "FOR ALL THEY DID CAST IN OF THEIR ABUNDANCE; BUT SHE OF HER WANT DID CAST IN ALL THAT SHE HAD, EVEN ALL HER LIVING."

The phrase, *"For all they did cast in of their abundance,"* was not necessarily criticized by the Lord, except in the showy display. Neither was it praised at all, because in His eyes, which are the only eyes that count, these rich men had not given very much, simply because of the *"abundance"* they had left. In other words, there was no sacrifice at all on their part.

The phrase, *"But she of her want did cast in all that she had, even all her living,"* means that in the eyes of God, Who sees not as man sees, she gave more than all the others put together. God does not weigh the gift so much as the mind of the giver. This *"poor widow's"* gift was a Sacrifice of tremendous proportions, because she gave all she had.

St. Ambrose says, *"That which God esteems is not that which you proudly present, but what you offer with humility and devotion."*

If I remember correctly, the year was 1970. I was at Brightmoor Tabernacle in Detroit, Michigan, in a Revival Meeting. One particular night after the service, a dear lady came up to me and pressed a roll of bills into my hand. That night, as well as several other nights, I had received an offering for our Radio Program, *"The Campmeeting Hour."*

After she gave the money, I did something that I seldom do. I looked at the worn appearance of her coat, and asked her, *"How much money is this?"*

She dropped her eyes and said, *"Thirty-two dollars."*

I then asked her, *"What do you do for a living?"*

As stated, this was something I seldom ever did, but I asked for a purpose and reason. I did not feel she could afford the giving of the money she had placed in my hands.

In reply to my question, she said, *"I work in an office building, and I scrub floors for a living."*

I then asked her, *"How much money do you make each week?"*

She replied, *"thirty-two dollars."*

I said to her, *"You have given everything you worked for this week!"*

I then attempted to put the money back into her hand, saying to her, *"Sister, the Lord does not need these funds this badly. I want you to take the money back."*

For the first time she looked at me, and her eyes literally flashed with fire. She said, *"I'm not giving this money to you, I'm giving it to the Lord. The Lord told me to do it, and if you don't want to take it, I'll leave it laying on the floor!"*

I thanked her, and in a few moments she turned and walked away. It is very difficult for me to express exactly how I felt at that moment. I sensed somewhat the tremendous love that God has for those who will give so sacrificially.

During this exchange, I was standing on the platform, and she was standing down on the main floor. After she left, I walked over to the corner of the platform, and I could not hold back the tears. The Lord, I believe, spoke to me at that time. This is what He said:

"Much money will come into your hands to be used for My Work. Much of it will come from people just like this woman. Let it be a lesson to you, if you misuse it, you will not only answer to Me in the Judgment, but you will answer to the people who gave it as well!"

I have never forgotten that moment, or that dear lady. True enough, since that time, the Lord has placed large sums of money into my hands respecting His Work. It has been used to pay for Television air time and production, the building of schools for children, Churches, Bible Schools, as well as other efforts for the Cause of Christ. I have tried my best that this lesson given to me that cold January night in 1970 in Detroit, Michigan, be a lesson that I learned well. I have tried my best to remember exactly what the Lord spoke to my heart. Also, I have seen that woman's face, so to speak, in the faces of countless thousands since then, realizing how precious their gifts are in the sight of God. Especially those who give so sacrificially, as some do!

What a wonderful illustration the Lord gave us concerning this *"poor widow."* How little did she know that day, when she went into the Temple, possibly with much concern and anxiety on her mind respecting her poverty-stricken state, that the Lord of Glory was observing her, and that her story would be known for time and eternity.

But the Lord was observing, as He observes all. As well, His observation includes not only that which is done outwardly, but, as well, the very motives of our hearts.

CHAPTER 13

(1) "AND AS HE WENT OUT OF THE TEMPLE, ONE OF HIS DISCIPLES SAITH UNTO HIM, MASTER, SEE WHAT MANNER OF STONES AND WHAT BUILDINGS ARE HERE!"

The phrase, *"And as He went out of the Temple,"* portrays a far greater meaning than the mere act itself. He will not return except at His arrest and trial. Consequently, when He went out, its protection left as well! As He, the Lord of the Temple, was not wanted, there remained no more use for the Temple. In effect, He left the Temple and the city (Mat. 23:39; 24:1).

About 600 years before, He had left the Temple reluctantly and in stages, withdrawing to the Mount of Olives, and the Prophet Ezekiel saw Him as the God of Glory (Ezek. 9:3; 10:4, 19; 11:23).

When men saw Him now leaving the second Temple and withdrawing to the Mount of Olives, they saw in Him neither beauty nor glory, but only a man, the Carpenter of Nazareth!

When Israel finally does accept Him, which they shall at the Second Coming, the Temple will be rebuilt. At that time Ezekiel saw in a vision Him return as the God of Glory, which is even yet future (Ezek. 43:1-7). This will signal the beginning of the coming Kingdom Age.

The phrase, *"One of His Disciples saith unto Him,"* concerns a conversation probably held on the Mount of Olives, as Jesus and the Disciples overlook the Temple and surrounding area.

It seems that Matthew Chapters 24 and 25, along with Mark 13, were spoken after Luke 21, which seems to have been uttered *"in the Temple"* (Lk. 21:1-5, 37-38). As stated, this latter discourse (Mk. 13; Mat. 24) was spoken *"On the Mount of Olives."* Both Prophecies are similar down to Luke 21:12, and should be studied together.

(The Prophecy in Luke 21 gives information concerning the near destruction of Jerusalem and the Temple in 70 A.D., not given in Matthew or Mark.)

The phrase, *"Master, see what manner of stones and what buildings are here!"* spoke of the beauty and grandeur of the Temple.

It is said that this building was one of the wonders of the world. Josephus says that it wanted nothing that the eye and the mind could admire. Built of white marble, it shown with a fiery splendor; so that when the eye gazed upon it, it turned away as from the rays of the sun.

The size of the foundation-stones was enormous. Josephus speaks of some of the stones as nearly seventy feet long, seven and one-half feet in height, and nine feet in breadth. However, all this magnificence had no affect upon our Lord, Who only repeated the sentence of its downfall (Bickersteth).

(2) "AND JESUS ANSWERING SAID UNTO HIM, SEEST THOU THESE GREAT BUILDINGS? THERE SHALL NOT BE LEFT ONE STONE UPON ANOTHER, THAT SHALL NOT BE THROWN DOWN."

The phrase, *"And Jesus answering said unto him,"* proclaims a response concerning the grandeur of the Temple and its coming destruction. It is obvious that the Disciple who pointed out the glory of the Temple to Jesus, did not at all have in mind the destruction of which Jesus would now speak.

Despite Him telling them several times that He would be killed, and rise on the third day, they could not grasp such a statement. On the minds of the Disciples was the grandeur of the Temple and Jerusalem. Jesus would use His Power, they thought, to overthrow Rome, with Israel once again becoming the greatest nation in the world. The glory of the times of David and Solomon would now return. Until the Advent of the Holy Spirit on the Day of Pentecost, they seemingly could not grasp the Truths which He repeatedly told them. Hence, the necessity of the Holy Spirit in the modern Church!

The question, *"Seest thou these great buildings?",* was probably uttered with a sweep of His hand. In fact, the buildings were great!

The word, *"buildings,"* referred to the mass of separate edifices, enclosures, colonnades, halls, sanctuaries, composing the Temple enclosure.

Herod the Great had commenced work on the Temple in 19 B.C., over fifty years before. His building of the Temple was an attempt to reconcile the Jews to him, who was Idumaean, rather than to glorify God. Even though the main structure was finished in approximately ten years, work continued until 64 A.D.

The plan of the shrine somewhat copied Solomon's. The porch was about 150 feet wide and 150 feet high. A doorway some 30 feet wide and 60 feet high gave entry, and one half that size led into the Holy Place. This was about 60 feet long and 30 feet wide. A curtain divided the Holy Place from the inner Sanctuary, called *"the veil"* (Mat. 27:51; Mk. 15:38).

The inner Sanctuary was 30 feet square and like the Holy Place, 60 feet high. An empty room above the Holy Place and the inner Sanctuary rose to the height of the porch, 150 feet, thus making a level roof.

The phrase, *"There shall not be left one stone upon another, that shall not be thrown down,"* was fulfilled in totality, in 70 A.D.

The soldiers of the Roman General Titus, had heard that gold was in the mortar between the stones, which they pulled apart with teams of oxen. There was no gold in the mortar. Nevertheless, they pulled them all down in their search, fulfilling the Prophecy of Christ. Thus this magnificent structure of cream stone was barely finished (A.D. 64) before it was destroyed by the Roman Army.

The Golden Candelabrum, the Table of Shewbread, and other objects, were carried in triumph to Rome, as depicted on the Arch of Titus in that city.

Consequently, the destruction of the Temple signalled the destruction of the nation. Over a million Jews died in that carnage, with hundreds of thousands of others sold as slaves at trifling prices. The burning fires of rebellion against Rome, burned in the hearts of zealots, as they attempted to overthrow the Roman yoke. Of course, they were no match for Roman power. Even though the Roman Army suffered some losses in the several years it took to quell this rebellion, nevertheless, it ultimately succeeded, with the nation being destroyed.

Even though an attempt was made after that to hold the nation together somewhat, the future destruction about sixty-five years later, in 135 A.D., completely destroyed Israel as any semblance of a nation. Consequently, they were then scattered all over the world, where they wandered as outcasts, even as the Prophets had proclaimed, until finally once again becoming a nation, such as it was, in 1948.

Even yet, their most difficult time is ahead, with the nation of Israel and its people coming close to total destruction. Actually, even as Jesus foretells in this Chapter, they will be saved only by the Second Coming.

So, when the Temple was *"thrown down,"* the nation as well was *"thrown down"*— all because of their rejection of Jesus Christ!

(3) "AND AS HE SAT UPON THE MOUNT OF OLIVES OVER AGAINST THE TEMPLE, PETER AND JAMES AND JOHN AND ANDREW ASKED HIM PRIVATELY,"

The phrase, *"And as He sat upon the Mount of Olives over against the Temple,"* proclaims the occasion when the Disciples will

question Him further concerning these momentous events.

The phrase, *"Peter and James and John and Andrew asked Him privately,"* proclaims these four pulling Him aside, not only from the multitude, but, as well, even from the other Disciples.

As Jesus was leaving the Temple, He with the Disciples crossed the Brook Kidron, ascended the steep road over the Mount of Olives which led to Bethany, and was now seated and resting on the top of the Mountain overlooking the Temple and city.

Hearing Jesus mention the destruction of the Temple, even as they walked, they now pull Him aside to a place of privacy, and ply Him with more questions.

It was extremely dangerous to speak of the destruction of the Temple, or anything that resembled such, for fear of the Scribes and Pharisees. It was this accusation that led to the stoning of Stephen. The Temple authorities considered such discussion as high treason against Israel. Consequently, the four would *"ask Him privately."*

It is ironical, and yet planned by the Holy Spirit, that Jesus opened His Ministry with the Sermon on the Mount (Mat. 5), and closed it with a Sermon on the Mount. The first was near the Sea of Galilee, and signaled Grace, while this, as is obvious, was on Mount Olivet, and signaled Judgment.

(4) "TELL US, WHEN SHALL THESE THINGS BE? AND WHAT SHALL BE THE SIGN WHEN ALL THESE THINGS SHALL BE FULFILLED?"

The question, *"Tell us, when shall these things be?"*, proclaims the first of two questions asked by these Disciples.

These things spoken by Christ were startling to say the least! So the Disciples want to know *"when"* it will happen?

The question, *"And what shall be the sign when all these things shall be fulfilled?"*, is the question Christ will actually answer.

"All these things," referred to far more than what the Disciples had in mind. They were thinking, no doubt, of the near future, while Jesus will give them an account of the entirety of the future of Israel. The span of time He covered has now been nearly 2,000 years, and has not concluded yet. Even though He answered what they asked, still, they would have little

understood what He was saying, at least at that time. The future, as the evidence portrays, would greatly improve their understanding of this momentous Message given by Christ.

As well, they would ask for a *"sign"* concerning the near fulfillment of these predictions, which Jesus would adequately give.

There is even a possibility that one or two of the four took down notes while Jesus was speaking. Of course, there is no evidence of that, with the idea being only speculative; however, their accounts are so similar (Matthew, Mark, and Luke), that such certainly may have been the case. As well, inasmuch as their accounts are very similar but not identical, shows that little, if any collaboration was engaged before the writing of the Gospels.

(5) "AND JESUS ANSWERING THEM BEGAN TO SAY, TAKE HEED LEST ANY MAN DECEIVE YOU:"

The phrase, *"And Jesus answering them began to say,"* proclaims the beginning of this momentous answer, which has, and shall, come to pass exactly as predicted.

Due to Israel rejecting Jesus as her Messiah, the *"Kingdom of God,"* which was then ready to be given, and would have brought unprecedented peace and prosperity, instead, was postponed, resulting in the terrible predictions which have come to pass, and shall yet come to pass. Untold sorrow and heartache have been the result.

Man has ever attempted to rebuild the Garden of Eden, but without the Tree of Life. Such is not to be done, and, in fact, cannot be done! Jesus is the *"Tree of Life,"* and unless He is in the Garden, it cannot be rebuilt.

While the intelligence of man has increased greatly since the turn of the century, and as prophesied by Daniel (Dan. 12:4), still, man has not succeeded in learning how to live. Actually, the increase of this vast intelligence has only given man the ability to become more destructive. He has little learned the Words of Christ, that *"A man's life consisteth not in the abundance of things which he possesseth"* (Lk. 12:15).

Consequently, as we study this Chapter, much of that predicted by Christ is even yet to come to pass. However, its fulfillment is even at the door. As such, we should study it minutely, prayerfully, and with dedication. How momentous the occasion, considering we are living on

NOTES

the very eve of the fulfillment of the most cataclysmic happenings the world has ever known; happenings, we might quickly add, which will usher in the Second Coming of Christ.

As well, as we study this Chapter, we must keep in mind that the predictions concern Israel, even though affecting the entirety of the world. They do not pertain to the Church, except in an ancillary way. For instance, the Rapture of the Church is not mentioned in these predictions, because the Church will have been raptured away, when most are brought to fulfillment. Even though spanning the entirety of the last 2,000 years, still, the greatest bulk of these predictions pertain to the final seven years before the Second Coming, the time referred to as *"Daniel's 70th Week"* (Dan. 9:25-27).

The phrase, *"Take heed lest any man deceive you,"* has several implications. They are as follows:

1. Jesus began this discourse with the warning of *"deception,"* simply because Satan is so successful in this effort. Man fell in the Garden of Eden because of deception, and, consequently, deception continues to be man's greatest problem. If it is to be noticed, men would rather believe a lie than the Truth.

2. The greatest deception of all will come to Israel, upon her acceptance of the Antichrist. Thinking he is the Messiah, she will be lulled to sleep by his promises. The awakening, however, will be traumatic, to say the least! She will then face her hardest time, called by Jesus, *"Affliction, such as was not from the beginning of the creation . . ."* (vs. 19).

3. Even though Jesus is speaking of Israel, still, the warning should not go unheeded respecting individual Christians. In effect, deception is just as great in the Church at present, as it was in Israel of old.

The only defense against deception is nearness to Christ, and knowledge of His Word. Regrettably, there is not much of either in the lives of many, if not most, Christians.

(6) "FOR MANY SHALL COME IN MY NAME, SAYING, I AM CHRIST; AND SHALL DECEIVE MANY."

The phrase, *"For many shall come in My Name,"* has to do with false claims. Actually, after the Ascension of Christ, a number of Jews appeared on the scene, claiming to be the Messiah, Who would lead Israel out from under the dominion of the Romans. Those false Messiahs led Israel to her destruction in 70 A.D.

Of these *"many"* who have falsely claimed this role in the past, still, the greatest deception is just ahead. The Antichrist will claim to be the Messiah, and, in fact, will make the greatest claim of all, at least other than Christ Himself. He will deceive not only Israel, but much of the world.

The phrase, *"Saying, I am Christ; and shall deceive many,"* portrays not only the claim of Messiahship, but with even a deeper deception.

The idea presents itself, not only to Israel, but, as well, as a bleed-over to the Church. It holds the idea of individuals claiming to be *"of"* the Lord, or sent *"from"* the Lord. Actually, this is a problem that has raged in the Church from the very beginning.

No doubt, the Judaizers claimed they were sent from the Lord. However, Paul called them, *"False Apostles, deceitful workers, transforming themselves into the Apostles of Christ"* (II Cor. 11:13).

Concerning the Church, most all Preachers claim to be *"of"* the Lord, or sent *"from"* the Lord. The Truth is, some are and some aren't! Tragically, those who aren't are oftentimes successful in leading many astray. As stated, it is only nearness to Christ, and knowledge of His Word which protects against such deception.

The Name, *"Christ,"* means *"The Anointed,"* and refers to the Messiah. However, He is truly the only One of such distinction, of Whom it can be said, *"I, in contradistinction to all others, am He."*

(7) "AND WHEN YE SHALL HEAR OF WARS AND RUMOURS OF WARS, BE YE NOT TROUBLED: FOR SUCH THINGS MUST NEEDS BE; BUT THE END SHALL NOT BE YET."

The phrase, *"And when ye shall hear of wars and rumours of wars,"* has to do with the state of Israel, and the world, which would begin after the Ascension, and actually continues unto this day, and will exacerbate in the near future.

When Christ was born, peace reigned, and for one of the few times in history. As well, there is evidence that it continued through His Life and Ministry. However, with His rejection by Israel, the *"Times of the Gentiles"* continued, and with its baggage of *"wars and rumours of wars."* Because of that rejection, the world has been

bathed in blood from that time until now, and will continue to be so until the Second Coming.

After the Ascension of Christ, three Roman Emperors, Caligula, Claudius, and Nero, almost immediately began to threaten or wage war against the Jews. That continued until Jerusalem was destroyed in 70 A.D., and then the nation totally in 135 A.D. As well, the *"wars and rumours of wars"* were by no means limited to Israel, with almost the entirety of the world bathed in blood, in one way or the other, from then until now.

The phrase, *"Be ye not troubled,"* has to do with the mission at hand of evangelizing the world.

Wuest said, *"Our Lord exhorts the Disciples not to permit political troubles and national upheavals to distract them from their work of Evangelism. There are two kingdoms on this earth moving along side by side, the world's system of evil headed up by Satan and in which the nations are constantly at sword's points, and the Kingdom of God.*

"No matter what happens in the former kingdom, the people of God must carry on toward the God-ordained and predicted conclusion.

"The Disciples were already troubled about the political unrest in Israel. Our Lord says, 'Stop being troubled'."

The total depravity of the human race is the root of all war, and that is the nature of the case that makes war inevitable. However, please allow us to say it again, and because of its vast significance, nothing, as here proclaimed by Christ, must stop World Evangelism. Whatever happens on the world scene, the leading and guidance of the Holy Spirit must be sought, in order that the thrust of Evangelism continue unabated.

Perhaps my own particular burden is much more emphasized in this area than most. World Evangelism is my calling. By and large, the instruments of city-wide Crusades, and Television, are the major thrusts of our activities. Especially through Television, the Lord has helped us to take the Gospel to vast regions of the world. With programs translated into the various languages where it is portrayed, by the Grace of God, we have been able to see hundreds of thousands brought to a saving knowledge of Jesus Christ. To be sure, I am not on Television simply because I saw a need and responded to it. I am there because of an apostolic call in respect to this medium. That is the reason we see so many people brought to Christ, and that is the reason we seek God constantly respecting His Leading and Guidance, and, above all, the Anointing of the Holy Spirit upon our efforts.

The phrase, *"For such things must needs be,"* pertains to the course of evil which fills the world, and of necessity brings about wars, etc. As stated, the Person of Christ was rejected; therefore, this is the alternative.

The phrase, *"But the end shall not be yet,"* in effect, means that the *"end"* will not be brought about until the Second Coming.

Jesus gave, as men say, a sad interpretation of the future. His forecast was very dark. Deception, conflict, suffering, family division, and universal hatred! Such is the experience of the world during His absence.

He predicted that His Coming would be preceded by Religious Movements (vs. 6); Political Movements (vss. 7-8); and Physical Movements (vs. 8).

He warned against religious deception (vss. 5-6), and spiritual failure (vss. 9-13), and against negligence (vs. 23) (Williams).

(8) "FOR NATION SHALL RISE AGAINST NATION, AND KINGDOM AGAINST KINGDOM: AND THERE SHALL BE EARTHQUAKES IN DIVERS PLACES, AND THERE SHALL BE FAMINES AND TROUBLES: THESE ARE THE BEGINNINGS OF SORROWS."

The phrase, *"For nation shall rise against nation, and kingdom against kingdom,"* constitutes the lot of the human family down through the ages. As well, thousands of years of education, culture, and experience, have not ameliorated the problem.

This is what makes the modern *"Kingdom Philosophy"* so ridiculous! This philosophy in the modern Church, which I sometimes refer to as the *"Political Message,"* claims that Christianity is going to invade every culture, coming to terms with the religions of the world, thereby making things better and better, consequently, ushering in the Millennium. Actually, some misguided souls claim that we are already in the Millennium. Such foolishness is proclaimed for two reasons:

1. Ignorance of the Word of God.

2. This erroneous message appeals to the pride of man.

The modern Church, even more and more, and cutting across all Denominational lines, is focusing attention on this world instead of heavenly things. The modern *"Faith Message,"* which, in reality, is no Faith at all, has greatly exacerbated this error. The idea that one can confess into existence almost anything is a heady Doctrine, which appeals to greed and pride in the hearts of all men, even Believers.

When former President Bush mentioned the *"New World Order,"* and especially considering the fall of Communism, this fit in perfectly with many in the modern Church. Much if not most of its message is along political lines, and, therefore, little addressing itself to the true need of the people, Who is Jesus, and the real problem, which is sin. At present, much of the energy of the modern Church is spent on attempting to elect certain individuals to high political office. Precious little energy is spent in trying to get people to Christ.

Sadder still, many, if not most, in the modern Charismatic and Pentecostal Organizations, along with this *"Political Message,"* are running helter-skelter from one emotional fad to the other. This segment of the Church is *"laughing,"* when it ought to be weeping; it is *"reaping"* or at least trying to do so, when it ought to be repenting; it is *"confessing,"* money, etc., when it ought to be crying!

As we have alluded to, these end times, and as Jesus plainly says, are going to see things getting worse and worse instead of better and better. Admittedly, this is not the Gospel that men want to hear. Doom and gloom are not a heady message! However, it does have one thing going for it; it happens to be the Truth!

The phrase, *"And there shall be earthquakes in divers places,"* proclaims disturbance at the very foundations of the earth. The idea is, *"That the whole creation groaneth and travaileth in pain together until now"* (Rom. 8:22). Even though there have been *"earthquakes"* from the very beginning, still, the idea is that the closer to the end, the greater the frequency and intensity of these disturbances.

The phrase, *"And there shall be famines and troubles,"* is the natural product of the course taken by the human family in their rejection of Jesus Christ.

Some may argue that all did not do this, only the Religious Leaders of Israel. While that may be true, still, as the Leaders of the chosen people, chosen for the purpose of bringing the Messiah into the world, they, in effect, acted for the world. Their rejection of Christ, not only brought about their own destruction, but, as well, sentenced the world to a long period of continued war, famine, and pestilence.

As well, this problem cannot be remedied until Israel accepts Christ, regains her place as the leading nation of the world, thereby faithfully serving God, which will be done at the Second Coming. Neither the world, nor even most Believers, fully understands the tremendously important part Israel plays in the entirety of the Plan of God. Even by their rejection of Christ, they have not abrogated their position, except temporarily, although suffering terribly! The great Promises made by the Lord to the Prophets of old, will be realized in totality. Hence, all of these predictions concerning the end time, as asked by the Disciples, and portrayed by Matthew, Mark, and Luke, pertain almost exclusively to Israel. Also, if anyone even half way understands the Word of God, it quickly becomes obvious that these predictions were not fulfilled in 70 A.D., but are even yet future.

The phrase, *"These are the beginnings of sorrows,"* is meant to impress upon all that these *"sorrows"* are not short-lived, but of duration. As stated, they have lasted now for nearly 2,000 years, and, of course, not counting the thousands of years before Christ.

As well, the phrase is meant to point to the greatest *"sorrow"* of all, the coming Great Tribulation, where the possibility exists that over half of the population of the planet could die in a seven year period of time (Rev. Chpts. 6-19).

As I have already stated, these are not pleasant predictions, but they are true predictions.

(9) "BUT TAKE HEED TO YOURSELVES: FOR THEY SHALL DELIVER YOU UP TO COUNCILS; AND IN THE SYNAGOGUES YE SHALL BE BEATEN: AND YE SHALL BE BROUGHT BEFORE RULERS AND KINGS FOR MY SAKE, FOR A TESTIMONY AGAINST THEM."

The phrase, *"But take heed to yourselves,"* takes these predictions from a national scope, and puts them on a personal basis. He is speaking directly to His Disciples, and, as well, to every Believer.

The phrase, *"For they shall deliver you up to councils,"* speaks of the Sanhedrin or Elders of Israel. This happened in the Early Church, and, no doubt, will take place in the coming Great Tribulation.

The phrase, *"And in the Synagogues ye shall be beaten,"* was experienced personally by the Apostle Paul, and because of his strong advocacy of the great Covenant of Grace, which replaced the Covenant of Law. Of course, it was not limited to Paul, with countless others being included.

The phrase, *"And ye shall be brought before rulers and kings for My sake,"* actually pertains to all Believers for all time. Wuest says, *"Paul faced Nero, or at least his representative in the court at Rome, and proclaimed the Gospel to the assembled audience."* Wuest also said, *"But the language goes beyond this, even to the Jewish Remnant in the Great Tribulation."*

The phrase, *"For a testimony against them,"* should have been translated, *"For a testimony to them."*

Wuest says that the setting is Jewish, even though it could include all! However, it basically expresses two particular times: A. The Early Church; and, B. The coming Great Tribulation.

At the beginning, the Early Church was made up entirely of Jews, who experienced tremendous persecution from their own, because of their stand for Christ, as predicted here.

During the coming Great Tribulation, it will include all Believers, Jew and Gentile. Consequently, this tells us that quite a number of Jews will be saved during the coming Great Tribulation. Considering the powerful testimony of the two witnesses, and the conversion of the 144,000, it is obvious that a powerful move by the Holy Spirit will take place in Israel at that time (Rev. 11:3-12; 14:1-5).

(10) "AND THE GOSPEL MUST FIRST BE PUBLISHED AMONG ALL NATIONS."

Several things are said in this short verse:

1. First of all, this speaks of the Church, albeit in shadow. It has been the task of the Church, even from the Day of Pentecost, to take the Gospel to the world.

2. The Jews did not do this; therefore, this tells us that these predictions were not fulfilled in 70 A.D., as great segments of the modern Church insist.

3. To take the Gospel to the world, was the Plan of God for Israel; however, they failed. It

was the Church, therefore, which had to accomplish the task.

4. The *"Gospel"* is Good News. Actually, it is the only truly good news on the face of the earth. All else, which men refer to as *"good news"* is merely an absence of bad news. This *"Good News"* tells us that Jesus died on Calvary and paid the price that man may be saved; therefore, due to what Jesus did at Calvary and the Resurrection, man can now be reconciled to God. It is the *"Greatest Story ever told."*

5. This *"Gospel"* must be the same type as preached by Jesus, Peter, and Paul. It is the whole Gospel for the whole man. Jesus saves, Jesus heals, Jesus baptizes in the Holy Spirit, and Jesus is coming again. Any Gospel which compromises any one of these four points is no Gospel at all! For it to be the *"Gospel,"* it must be that which is given in the Word of God.

6. If it is the True Gospel of Jesus Christ, it will bring forth fruit which will be obvious to all.

7. This verse does not say that the Gospel will have to go to every single person, but it does say that it will have to go to *"all nations."* Quite possibly that has been fulfilled.

However, it is the responsibility and task of every single Believer to do what he or she can, to take the Gospel to every single person. None are to be excluded. Jesus died for all!

8. If one truly studies the Word of God and fully understanding what Jesus did at Calvary and the Resurrection, he cannot help but know that priority with God is the taking of the Gospel to the world. For every single person who does not know what Jesus has done for him, as far as that person is concerned, Jesus died in vain.

The hard part was done by Heaven, with us being given the smaller part of simply telling the story. Regrettably, the proclamation of the Gospel is not priority with many, if not most, Christians.

9. At the Judgment Seat of Christ, I firmly believe that every single Believer is going to have to give account for his or her actions, respecting this all-important task. Did we do what we could? In Truth, did we do anything at all? Many would ask exactly what they can do?

A. There is not a single Believer who cannot pray. Jesus said, *"Pray ye therefore the Lord of the harvest, that He will send forth labourers into His harvest"* (Mat. 9:38). Consequently, our prayer should be twofold:

NOTES

First of all, we should ask the Lord to give us a burden for a certain part of the world, in order that we may intercede for that particular place. It doesn't really matter where it is, or that we have little knowledge of the place. Those things are not important. The important thing is that the Holy Spirit burden our heart for a specific area or people, which He certainly shall, if we will only ask Him.

I believe every single Move of God that has ever taken place has been preceded by travailing intercession.

Second, in our intercession, we should seek the Lord that He would move on individuals to go to these respective places, wherever they may be. These should be persons who are definitely touched by the Holy Spirit, and have a burning Message within their heart.

Prayer alone, however, will not accomplish the task. Somehow, the Word must be gotten to these people, whether by Missionary, Radio, Television, or Literature. So, every Believer should pray that the Lord will bring these things about.

B. Every Believer should give of their finances for this all-important task, even above what they give to their local Church. In other words, the following should be done:

The Believer should seek the Lord earnestly respecting where this tremendously important money should be given. If the Lord is earnestly sought, He will lead and direct.

To be sure, when He directs, the money will be given to someone who preaches the Gospel, and with the Anointing of the Holy Spirit, which is obvious by the <u>fruit</u> it produces.

Tragically, most money given by Believers for this task of World Evangelism, is by and large wasted. This will not only <u>not</u> be rewarded by the Lord, but at the Judgment Seat of Christ, the Believer who supported that which is not of God, is going to have to give an account. Due to its vast significance, please allow me to state it again:

This all-important task of World Evangelism is the responsibility of every single Believer. Consequently, considering what Jesus did at Calvary and the Resurrection, all of us must be diligent, giving time and attention to this task. In essence, it should be the most important thing in our lives.

If one is to notice, of all the things done in the Early Church as recorded in the Book of

Acts, the major thrust outlined by the Holy Spirit was that of taking the Gospel of Jesus Christ to a lost world. If He set this example for us, and He certainly did, then we should follow that example.

It is a wonderful fact that within fifty years after the Death and Resurrection of Christ, Churches had been planted in almost every district of the earth as then known to the Romans.

It is even more wonderful when one considers that this was done without the aid of the printing press or modern methods of communication or transportation. It was done by the Power of the Holy Spirit!

(11) "BUT WHEN THEY SHALL LEAD YOU, AND DELIVER YOU UP, TAKE NO THOUGHT BEFOREHAND WHAT YE SHALL SPEAK, NEITHER DO YE PREMEDITATE: BUT WHATSOEVER SHALL BE GIVEN YOU IN THAT HOUR, THAT SPEAK YE: FOR IT IS NOT YE THAT SPEAK, BUT THE HOLY GHOST."

The phrase, *"But when they shall lead you, and deliver you up,"* refers to persecution. The idea is this:

To those who take the Gospel, and do so by the Power of the Holy Spirit, Satan is going to do everything within his power to hinder this. Such was evident in the life of the Apostle Paul and others in the Early Church.

If the true presentation of the Gospel stops, as it has in many circles, then the persecution will stop.

Satan will oppose; the world will oppose; the apostate Church will oppose!

The phrase, *"Take no thought beforehand what ye shall speak, neither do ye premeditate,"* has nothing to do with the preaching of the Gospel. Many have taken this Passage to mean that Preachers should not study, but rather go into the pulpit without any preparation. Only lazy people believe such a thing!

This is speaking of Believers who are taken before hostile judges, officials, or magistrates.

The Lord does not mean that we are not to premeditate a prudent and wise answer, but that we are not to be anxious about it. He is speaking of fear, and that it is not to beset us.

The phrase, *"But whatsoever shall be given you in that hour, that speak ye,"* infers that if we look to the Lord, He will serve as our defense, giving us what to say.

NOTES

The phrase, *"For it is not ye that speak, but the Holy Ghost,"* concerns His constant leading, guidance, companionship, and counsel. Let me give a minor example:

In 1985, I believe it was, Frances and I, along with others, were in the Soviet Union preaching a series of meetings. Every city we went to, we first had to go to the Commissar of Religion for an interview of sorts. This particular city in Siberia would be no exception.

Almost immediately upon being introduced to the man, who spoke fairly good English, he began to accuse me of preaching against Communism.

"You preach over Television," he said, *"and you say some very strong and negative things about our form of Government!"*

While I did not feel that we were in any type of danger, at the same time, I did not know where this was going to lead.

The man was right! I had preached very strongly against Communism, with these Messages being carried by Television over a great part of the world. Obviously, it had come to his ears, even in the far north of Siberia.

One of my Associates was with me, with several other Communist Officials standing in the room. To say the least, the tension mounted. One could look at the man's face and tell that he was very sincere about what he was saying.

Very quietly I breathed a prayer to the Lord, asking Him to tell me what to say.

I noticed when we walked into the room, that this man, the Commissar of Religion, walked with a slight limp. As well, he had a row of medals pinned to the tunic of his coat, which evidently had been given to him for service rendered in the war.

If I remember correctly, one medal was larger than the others, and stood out.

As he stood there awaiting an answer to his charge respecting my opposition to Communism, I, instead, asked him what this particular medal represented?

Very quickly, he said, *"It was the battle at Kursk!"* I am sure he thought I had never heard of the place; however, it just so happened I had heard of it, and had actually read the account of that battle fought there in World War II.

I said to him, *"Sir, do you mean that you fought in this battle, which was the largest tank battle in the history of the world, up to that time?"* (It was between the Germans and the Russians.)

In a moment, his face softened, and then he asked, *"You mean you have heard of this battle?"*

"Oh yes," I answered, *"but there are a lot of things I would like to ask you, if you don't mind."*

I then said, *"You are the only person I have ever met who actually participated in this battle."*

All thoughts by him of what I had preached against Communism were forgotten. For a goodly period of time, I plied him with questions, which he eagerly answered. He told me how he was wounded, and his eyes lit up as he related this experience to me.

When we got ready to leave, he put his arm around my shoulder, and told me that his office was at my disposal, and, furthermore, he would do anything he could to help us in our visit to his city.

As I have stated, even though this was not a dangerous situation, still, I believe the Holy Spirit brought to my mind the question concerning his medal, and the discussion which followed.

(12) "NOW THE BROTHER SHALL BETRAY THE BROTHER TO DEATH, AND THE FATHER THE SON; AND CHILDREN SHALL RISE UP AGAINST THEIR PARENTS, AND SHALL CAUSE THEM TO BE PUT TO DEATH."

This Passage has been fulfilled countless times in the past 2,000 years. It was true in the Early Church, and especially true during the Catholic Inquisition.

Some time ago, Frances and I, along with friends, were in Toledo, Spain. This was the center of the Spanish Inquisition which saw untold thousands put to death in the most torturous ways by Catholic Authorities.

If there was any hint that anyone had less than total allegiance to the Pope, they were placed on the torture racks. Those instruments of torture are still there today, and visible for all to see.

Countless times, brother betraying brother, and father betraying son, etc., brought about these horrible tortures, and ultimate deaths. Multiple thousands died, tortured to death, because of their allegiance to Jesus Christ, and not to the Pope of Rome.

For the reader's enlightenment, *"Fox's Book of Martyrs,"* should be read! The tremendous price paid for the freedoms we now enjoy, did not come cheaply.

Even in modern times under Communism, multiple thousands, if not millions died for their testimony of Jesus Christ. At times, the betrayals would be brought about by relatives, exactly as Jesus here predicted.

In the coming Great Tribulation, this treachery will be exacerbated manyfold. No doubt, hundreds of thousands will have to die at that time for their testimony of their faithfulness to Christ. It will include both Jews and Gentiles, as the Antichrist declares all-out war on all those who profess the Name of Jesus.

Even though the fact of this prediction is obvious, still, it should be noted that True Bible Christianity alone draws this type of persecution. The religions of the world, such as Islam, Buddhism, Hinduism, etc., draw no such negative response. The reason is simple!

These religions are fostered and nurtured by Satan; consequently, he does not oppose his own efforts.

On the other hand, Bible Christianity is opposed greatly by Satan for all the obvious reasons. It alone lays waste his kingdom of darkness! It alone snatches souls from the edge of the burning pit. It alone offers Jesus!

Someone has said that if a person is not ready to die for Jesus, then he is not ready to live for Him!

(13) "AND YE SHALL BE HATED OF ALL MEN FOR MY NAME'S SAKE: BUT HE THAT SHALL ENDURE UNTO THE END, THE SAME SHALL BE SAVED."

The phrase, *"And ye shall be hated of all men for My Name's sake,"* proclaims the reason for this hatred and resultant persecution. It is *"The Name of Jesus!"*

Why is He hated so much?

The reason should be obvious. Jesus is the One Who died on Calvary, thereby satisfying the claims of heavenly justice, and, as well, defeating Satan and his powers of darkness. He is the One Who overcame death, hell, and the grave.

He is the One Who opens the door to the Heavenly Father (Jn. 10:7). In fact, *"Neither is there Salvation in any other: for there is none other name under Heaven given among men, whereby we must be saved"* (Acts 4:12).

That is the reason Jesus is hated so much!

It is natural that Satan's children would hate Him. It is natural, as well, that an apostate Church would follow suit!

It is ironical, the Jews hate the Name of Jesus, and they in turn are hated because of the Name of Jesus.

The phrase, *"But he that shall endure unto the end, the same shall be saved,"* has to do with this Promise. *"Be thou faithful unto death, and I will give thee a Crown of Life"* (Rev. 2:10).

(14) "BUT WHEN YE SHALL SEE THE ABOMINATION OF DESOLATION, SPOKEN OF BY DANIEL THE PROPHET, STANDING WHERE IT OUGHT NOT, (LET HIM THAT READETH UNDERSTAND,) THEN LET THEM THAT BE IN JUDAEA FLEE TO THE MOUNTAINS:"

The phrase, *"But when ye shall see the abomination of desolation, spoken of by Daniel the Prophet,"* speaks of the coming Great Tribulation. This is found in Daniel 9:27.

It speaks of the seven-year Covenant that the Antichrist will make with Israel, with them thinking he is the Messiah. Either immediately before the seven-year period begins, or at its beginning, he will make it possible for the Jews to rebuild their Temple on its ancient site.

That site is presently occupied by the Moslem *"Dome of the Rock,"* the second most holy place in Islam.

That one may know how near we are to this event, according to *"Newsweek"* and *"Time"* magazines, young men, supposedly of the Tribe of Levi, are now training in Jerusalem for Temple duties. I am told that plans have been drawn, or else are being drawn, for the construction of this edifice. To be sure, it must be rebuilt, because Bible Prophecy says that it shall (Dan. 9:27; Mat. 24:15; II Thess. 2:4; Rev. 13; 14:9-11; 15:2-4; 16:10; 20:4-6).

At the midpoint of the seven-year period, the Antichrist will break his Covenant with Israel, actually invading the country, with Israel suffering her first defeat since becoming a nation in 1948 (Dan. 9:27; Rev. 12:6).

The Antichrist at that time will set up an image of himself in the Temple in Jerusalem, even in the Holy Place where it is to be worshiped. This is the *"abomination of desolation"* spoken of by Christ (Dan. 9:27; II Thess. 2:4).

The phrase, *"Standing where it ought not,"* refers to the Holy Place in the Temple, where nothing of this sort should be.

In the Holy Place in the Temple, the only items were to be the Tables of Shewbread, the

NOTES

Golden Lampstands, and the Altar of Worship. Quite possibly, he will replace the Altar of Worship with his image, demanding that it be worshiped.

The phrase, *"Let him that readeth understand,"* means that there is no reason to misunderstand.

Many claim that this was fulfilled when Antiochus Epiphanies set up the statue of Jupiter on the great Altar of Burnt Sacrifice. However, this is incorrect, because all of this happened about 200 years before Christ made these predictions.

What Antiochus did was truly an *"abomination"*; however, it was not *"the abomination of desolation"* spoken of by Daniel, and referred to by Christ.

The phrase, *"Then let them that be in Judaea flee to the mountains,"* refers to the Antichrist breaking his seven-year Covenant with Israel at the midway point, actually invading this country.

At that time, Israel is to *"Flee to the mountains,"* i.e., Petra (Ps. 60:6-12; Isa. 16:1-5; 26:20-21; 63:1-6; Ezek. 20:43-44; Dan. 11:40-45; Hos. 2:14-23; Mat. 24:15-22; Rev. 12:6).

(15-18) "AND LET HIM THAT IS ON THE HOUSETOP NOT GO DOWN INTO THE HOUSE, NEITHER ENTER THEREIN, TO TAKE ANY THING OUT OF HIS HOUSE:

"AND LET HIM THAT IS IN THE FIELD NOT TURN BACK AGAIN FOR TO TAKE UP HIS GARMENT.

"BUT WOE TO THEM THAT ARE WITH CHILD, AND TO THEM THAT GIVE SUCK IN THOSE DAYS?

"AND PRAY YE THAT YOUR FLIGHT BE NOT IN THE WINTER."

The idea of these Passages is severalfold:

1. The betrayal of Israel by the Antichrist will be sudden. Without warning, he will break his seven-year treaty with Israel, by attacking her with his army. Israel will suffer her first defeat since her formation as a nation in 1948. Inasmuch as the attack is sudden and without warning, Israel will be caught completely by surprise. The Antichrist will then show himself to be, not the reputed friend and protector of Israel, but, in reality, its bitter enemy. In fact, were it not for a series of events, Israel would be totally destroyed at this time. However, these events, as described in Daniel 11:44 and Revelation

12:15-16, will turn the attention of the Antichrist elsewhere, at least for the time being.

2. This attack will be so sudden that Israel will not have time to prepare her retreat. The haste required will be so great that Jesus warns them that if they are on the housetop, they should not take the time to go in the house and retrieve things needed for the retreat. (Houses then and even now in Israel had a flat roof, which was used for various activities. So, the admonishment given concerning not going into the house, lets us know how much haste will be required at that time.)

As well, for those who are working in the fields, they are not to even go a few yards to retrieve a garment, but flee immediately.

As should be obvious, women who are several months pregnant would have a difficult time fleeing as speedily as suggested, and, as well, those with small children.

The *"winter"* has to do with possible adverse weather conditions, which could impede progress.

The entirety of the statements as used by Christ, are merely symbolisms, reflecting the suddenness of the invasion, and the necessary haste required to escape.

3. This will begin the last three and a half years of the Great Tribulation, which will bring Israel close to annihilation. It is called by Jeremiah, *"The Time of Jacob's Trouble"* (Jer. 30:7). It will be worse than any tribulation they have ever experienced, but is necessary in order to bring them to a saving knowledge of Jesus Christ.

(19) "FOR IN THOSE DAYS SHALL BE AFFLICTION, SUCH AS WAS NOT FROM THE BEGINNING OF THE CREATION WHICH GOD CREATED UNTO THIS TIME, NEITHER SHALL BE."

The phrase, *"For in those days,"* refers, as stated, to the last three and a half years of the Great Tribulation.

It is regrettable that the far greater majority of the modern Church has such little knowledge of futuristic events, that it little believes in this of which Jesus spoke. As well, this lack of knowledge is inexcusable, for the simple reason that the Bible clearly outlines that which is coming. Consequently, this lack of knowledge pertains to rabid unbelief.

If people believed the Bible, they would read it and study it more. They neglect and ignore

NOTES

it, because they little believe it, or else simply have no interest in it.

And then again, the foolish teaching of *"Kingdom Now"* fills the hearts of many. This teaching claims, as we have previously stated, that the world, due to the influence of Christianity, is going to get better, ultimately ushering in the Millennium. The Truth is the very opposite is this case! The world situation and on all fronts, is not going to get better, but progressively worse, and regrettably so!

The phrase, *"Shall be affliction,"* proclaims a dogmatic certitude of such action. In other words, Jesus is not saying that it may come, but for a certainty it shall come!

Wuest says the correct translation should be, *"Those days will be a tribulation."* He then said, *"The Judgments of God which will fall upon unbelieving Israel and the Gentile nations will have no precedent in all past history, and no counterpart in all succeeding history."*

Even though it will affect the entirety of the world, still, its greatest concentration will be in the Middle East, and in Israel more specifically. The cause of this tribulation, as brought by God, will be twofold:

1. It is called, *"The great day of His wrath"* (Rev. 6:17). It is a time of God's Judgment poured out on a world which has forgotten Him days without number. Millions have asked the question, *"When will the Lord do something about the sin and the wickedness in this world?"* The Great Tribulation will be His answer to that question. Revelation Chapters 6-19 give this account.

2. The cause of the Great Tribulation is to bring Israel to a state of repentance. As stated, she will come close to annihilation, and actually would be annihilated were it not for the Second Coming of the Lord. Perhaps it would be helpful to comment on Israel's present position.

Due to the peace accords with the Palestinians, Israel is opening up to the world, and, consequently, being accepted as never before. The nation is more prosperous today in an economic sense than ever! Actually, it is predicted that by the year 2020, the present land area of Israel will be completely filled with businesses and housing, with the exception possibly being the very heart of the desert.

At this moment (1996), agreements and joint ventures with the Jordanians are in the works, totaling multiple billions of dollars. As well, conciliatorial agreements with Syria, Israel's ancient enemy, are in the works. This fits right in with Bible Prophecy.

Paul prophesied that Israel at this time would say, *"Peace and safety,"* which they are now beginning to do (I Thess. 5:3).

In the very near future, a strong man is going to make his appearance in the Middle East. He will have economic and diplomatic intelligence, as no one has ever had. He will come in by flattery, seemingly increasing the stability and prosperity of the region. Daniel wrote, *"And through his policy also he shall cause craft* (deceit) *to prosper in his hand; and he shall magnify himself in his heart, and by peace shall destroy many"* (Dan. 8:25).

In this great amalgamation of economic and diplomatic prosperity, this man, who is actually the Antichrist, will endear himself to the world, and more specifically to Israel. They will actually think he is the Messiah. During this time, he may well be instrumental in helping Israel build her Temple. If, in fact, he is involved in this effort, which it seems he shall, he will find a way to satisfy both Israel and the Moslems regarding the Temple site, where the Moslem Dome of the Rock presently sits. Some time during these happenings, he will sign a seven-year agreement with Israel and other nations, guaranteeing prosperity and growth (Dan. 9:27). It is called in Bible terminology, *"Daniel's 70th Week"* (Dan. 9:24-27).

Consequently, the present peace accords with the Palestinians and the present prosperity of Israel, are the beginning, so to speak, of these happenings.

As we have stated, in the midst of this seven-year Covenant, the Antichrist will show his true colors, attacking Israel and breaking the Covenant. Then will begin this time of *"affliction,"* which will be the worst the world has ever known.

Before this time, the Church will have been raptured away, and because this period refers basically to Israel, and not the Church (I Thess. 4:16-18; II Thess. 2:7-8).

The phrase, *"Such as was not from the beginning of the creation which God created unto this time, neither shall be,"* is a startling proclamation! To be sure, the world has seen some bad times in its recorded history of approximately 6,000 years. One thinks of World War

II with some 60,000,000 dead, including 6,000,000 Jews dying in the horror known as the *"holocaust"* as being beyond compare, as it was! However, the coming time of the Great Tribulation will be worse, and because of the Wrath of God. War and its hell is bad enough; however, compared to what the anger of God can bring about, there is no comparison. This is what the world is facing!

In Truth, the Rapture will be the Salvation of the Church, as the Second Coming will be the Salvation of the world.

The Church presently is apostatizing at a frightful pace. However, it is an apostasy that is very subtle.

Much of the modern Church does not deny the Bible or Jesus Christ, as the modernists. It just ignores them, at least as to their rightful place. The Bible is set aside in favor of modern psychology. Jesus Christ is used as a means of *"getting rich,"* etc., i.e., the Prosperity Message. The Holy Spirit is all but ignored, if not outrightly denied, or else made a part of nefarious activities.

So, if the Bible Doctrine of the Rapture is not true, as many claim, it is doubtful that even a True Remnant would survive. Even though Faith is presently much talked about, still, True Faith has never been in shorter supply. Jesus said, *"Nevertheless when the Son of Man cometh, shall He find Faith on the earth?"* (Lk. 18:8).

Because of the coming activities of the Antichrist, and especially the Battle of Armageddon, were it not for the Second Coming, not only would Israel be completely lost, but the world as well!

So, these twin happenings of the *"Rapture,"* and the *"Second Coming,"* are of vast significance, as should be obvious.

(20) "AND EXCEPT THAT THE LORD HAD SHORTENED THOSE DAYS, NO FLESH SHOULD BE SAVED: BUT FOR THE ELECT'S SAKE, WHOM HE HATH CHOSEN, HE HATH SHORTENED THE DAYS."

The phrase, *"And except that the Lord had shortened those days, no flesh should be saved,"* is startling indeed! Even though the world, or even much of the Church pays little attention to this statement, nevertheless, its horror, and without fail, is going to break upon this world.

This statement could well apply to the entirety of the world, and not just to Israel, as many believe! The great plagues and judgments referred to in Revelation Chapters 6-19, while centered in the Middle East, still, because of the moon and planetary bodies being affected, all of the world will suffer as well (Rev. 6:12-17). The possibility actually exists that half or more of the world's population at that time could die. What is being spoken of, is of such consequence that it beggars description.

The phrase, *"But for the elect's sake, whom He hath chosen,"* refers to Israel and not the Church. The Church will by now have been raptured away (II Thess. 2:6-8).

What does the word, *"chosen,"* mean?

Wuest says, *"The verb 'eklego' means 'to choose out from a number,' and refers to the act of God, Who in sovereign grace, chooses certain from among mankind for Himself, and for a specific purpose."*

As we have stated several times, God chose Israel in the beginning for three reasons:

1. To be the womb of the Messiah (Gen. 12:3).

2. To give the world the Word of God. All of the Word of God was written by Jews. (Some think that Luke, who wrote the Gospel that bears his name, and the Book of Acts, was a Gentile. However, the proof seems to be that he was a Jew, as well.)

3. To evangelize the world. In this they miserably failed, but will yet succeed in the coming Kingdom Age (Isa. 66:18-19).

In the context of which Israel was chosen, they were to be a holy people, consequently, having a close relationship with God. Actually, they were the only people on the face of the earth who had such a relationship. As such, they were to convey this message to the Gentiles. Perhaps they came closer to doing this under the administration of David and the first years of Solomon, than any other. However, by and large, they failed in this respect.

As being the people of God, they were to be the premier nation in the world. Consequently, whenever Judah was defeated by Nebuchadnezzar, and Jerusalem destroyed, the scepter of power passed from the hands of the *"chosen"* to the Gentiles, where it has remained ever since. When Jesus came, their great opportunity was lost in them not recognizing Him as the Messiah, and, consequently, rejecting Him. In effect, in rejecting Him, they rejected themselves, which brought about their destruction.

The entirety of their purpose, in one way or the other, was Christ. Without Him they were of no consequence. Therefore, they were destroyed.

However, the Promises to the Prophets included a Restoration, which will be brought about at the Second Coming (Ezek. 37; Hosea 14; Joel 3; Amos 9:14-15; Obad. 19-21; Micah 4; Zeph. 3:18-20; Zech. 12-14; Rev. 19).

The phrase, *"He hath shortened the days,"* means that the Lord will limit the most destructive times of the Great Tribulation, or else the entirety of Israel, in fact, would be destroyed. Even then, Zechariah prophesied that two-thirds of the population of Israel will die during that time (Zech. 13:8).

(21) "AND THEN IF ANY MAN SHALL SAY TO YOU, LO, HERE IS CHRIST; OR, LO, HE IS THERE; BELIEVE HIM NOT:"

The two words, *"And then,"* lets us know the time element of which Jesus is speaking. From verses 24 through 27, we know that these warnings do not pertain to the time preceding the destruction of Jerusalem by Titus, which took place about twenty-seven to thirty years after the Ascension of Christ. Actually, these warnings apply to the coming Great Tribulation. As a result, they have not yet been fulfilled.

The phrase, *"If any man shall say to you, Lo, here is Christ; or, lo, He is there,"* records the fact that false Messiahs will plentifully arise during that time.

However, and even more so, it pertains to the coming Antichrist. Jesus plainly warns concerning the acclamations of such a deceiver, *"Believe him not!"* Consequently, there will be no excuse for Israel accepting this fraud, especially considering the warnings given here by Christ. However, Israel does not believe the New Testament, and, in Truth, precious little of the Old. Consequently, these warnings fall on deaf ears, at least for most!

As we have stated, the word, *"Christ,"* is the English spelling of the Greek, *"Christos,"* which means, *"The Anointed One."*

It refers to the promised and coming King of Israel, who comes in the dynasty of David to rule over Israel in the Messianic Kingdom. Thus, our Lord was speaking of false Messiahs. This false Christ does not deny the Being of a Christ. He builds on the world's expectation of such a person. He appropriates to himself the title and identity, and claims that he is the foretold one (Wuest).

(22) "FOR FALSE CHRISTS AND FALSE PROPHETS SHALL RISE, AND SHALL SHEW SIGNS AND WONDERS, TO SEDUCE, IF IT WERE POSSIBLE, EVEN THE ELECT."

The phrase, "For false Christs and false Prophets shall rise," proclaims the certitude of those coming at that particular time, claiming to be the "Real Thing." Above all, the "Antichrist" and the "False Prophet" will be included in this group, and, in fact, will be accepted by Israel, and much of the world, and despite these warnings given by Christ.

The phrase, "And shall shew signs and wonders," proclaims the working of miracles by these false ones, and especially the Antichrist and False Prophet.

(While others may arise before the Antichrist, claiming to be the Messiah, still, upon the Advent of the Antichrist, all other claimants thereafter will be quickly put down, with the field left exclusively to the Antichrist and the False Prophet.)

The "Signs and wonders" spoken of here, are fulfilled in the Passage, "And deceiveth them that dwell on the earth by the means of those miracles which he had power to do in the sight of the beast" (Rev. 13:14). These miracles will be performed by the False Prophet, described by John as "another beast."

It also says, "And he doeth great wonders, so that he maketh fire come down from Heaven on the earth in the sight of men" (Rev. 13:11-13).

The "signs" in the Greek Text are "semeion," and mean, "a miracle whose purpose is that of attesting the claims of the one performing the miracle to be true."

The word, "wonders," in the Greek Text is "teras," and means, "a miracle whose purpose it is to awaken amazement in the beholder," typified by calling fire down from Heaven, and such like!

Consequently, Israel, as well as all are warned against accepting the claims of one who performs miracles solely upon the basis of the fact that he performs miracles. The person and his message must also be taken into consideration (Wuest).

The phrase, "To seduce, if it were possible, even the elect," proclaims the powerful force of Satanic seduction.

The word, "seduce," means "to stray from Truth." Regrettably, this problem is going to increase as we near the end, even as Jesus is saying.

NOTES

The words, "If it were possible," leave the possibility undetermined (Swete).

Even though the Jews as a whole are referred to by the Lord as "the elect," the word is used here in a slightly different manner. It refers not just to Jews in general, but, instead, to those Jews who have accepted Christ as their Saviour in the coming Great Tribulation. The idea is that the force of this seduction, as a result of the "signs and wonders," will be so powerful that even those who truly know the Lord and His Word, can be swayed in the wrong direction. Even though this does not exactly pertain to the Church, still, the principle is the same. The closer to the end, the more powerful the seduction. Satan is pulling out all stops in order to seduce the Church.

Paul said, in speaking of the very time in which we live, "And they shall turn away their ears from the Truth, and shall be turned unto fables" (II Tim. 4:4).

The word, "fables," has the idea of "a mystery," or in other words, a superior knowledge. Much of the modern "Faith Ministry" falls into this category, teaching that a certain type of knowledge guarantees great success, etc. It is ancient gnosticism under a new label. The modern Church is inundated with this type of teaching, which pulls people from the foundation of the Faith, making them think they have some "new revelation," etc.

(23) "BUT TAKE YE HEED: BEHOLD, I HAVE FORETOLD YOU ALL THINGS."

The phrase, "But take ye heed," is repeated four times in this Chapter (vss. 5, 9, 23, 33).

The pronoun, "ye," or rather "you," is emphatic, specifically meaning that each individual must take heed. This places a far greater emphasis on the warning.

Many take these admonitions as directions to the entirety of Israel and the Church, which they certainly are. However, the Greek Text emphasizes the fact that each individual must be very cautious, realizing that this attack by Satan is not only directed at the Church as a whole, but, as well, toward each individual.

The phrase, "Behold, I have foretold you all things," proclaims Jesus clearly giving this information, which leaves no one with an excuse.

How can the modern Believer keep himself from being seduced by Satan, especially considering the tremendous power of this evil of darkness?

As we have stated, spiritual seduction is rampant at present, and speedily growing worse. In Truth, much if not most of the modern Church has been seduced by Satan. It supports false doctrine; for the most part, it has its priorities wrong; it, as well, has gotten its eyes off Jesus.

This is obvious by the type of *"fruit"* presently being borne.

What is the *"fruit"* of the modern Church?

With exceptions, it is entertainment, fads, and philosophies.

Hundreds of millions of dollars are presently pouring in to certain Television programming which claims to be *"Christian,"* but, in reality, is not. It is, without a doubt, doing greater harm to the Body of Christ, than words could ever begin to express. Much of the money given goes to what could be better labeled *"entertainment."* Regrettably, this is, by and large, financed by Pentecostals and Charismatics who should know better. However, they are *"seduced."*

As well, great segments of the modern Church are running after *"fads,"* whether so-called *"holy laughter,"* or other types of phenomenon, which claim to be of the Spirit, but have little or no Scriptural foundation. To be sure, Satan does not care how *"spiritual"* we become, providing it's not *"on-track."*

Almost all the Church has accepted the humanistic philosophy of psychology, which is as opposed to Scripture as would be humanly possible.

Regrettably, that is the *"fruit"* of much of the modern Church. As stated, there are some exceptions, but those exceptions are few!

The *"fruit"* ought to be souls saved, Believers baptized in the Holy Spirit, sick bodies healed, and bondages broken. Such will result in *"love, joy, peace, longsuffering, gentleness, goodness, Faith, meekness, and temperance"* (Mk. 16:15; Gal. 5:22-23).

Sadly, there isn't much of this type of *"fruit"* being produced.

(24) "BUT IN THOSE DAYS, AFTER THAT TRIBULATION, THE SUN SHALL BE DARKENED, AND THE MOON SHALL NOT GIVE HER LIGHT,"

The phrase, *"But in those days,"* refers to the time *"immediately after the Tribulation,"* when Christ comes (Zech. 14; Mat. 24:29-31; Rev. 19:11-21).

The phrase, *"After that Tribulation,"* refers to the seven-year Tribulation which is to take

NOTES

place in the very near future. It will affect the entirety of the world, but have its greater impact in the Middle East. At the very end of that Great Tribulation, certain phenomenon will take place in the heavens, as outlined here by Christ. It pertains to the Second Coming.

The phrase, *"The sun shall be darkened, and the moon shall not give her light,"* pertains to the fifth time the planets will be affected in part, or in whole, during Daniel's 70th Week, i.e., the seven-year Tribulation period.

(25) "AND THE STARS OF HEAVEN SHALL FALL, AND THE POWERS THAT ARE IN HEAVEN SHALL BE SHAKEN."

The phrase, *"And the stars of Heaven shall fall,"* proclaims the second of two times the stars or meteors are spoken of as falling:

1. In the sixth seal (Rev. 6:12-17).

2. At Christ's coming (here and Matthew 24:29) (Dake).

The phrase, *"And the powers that are in Heaven shall be shaken,"* refers to the Satanic hosts that now rule the air (Eph. 2:1-3; 6:12).

They are now above us, but will not be at the Coming of Christ, for they will be cast down to earth three and a half years before then (Rev. 12:7-12). Isaiah spoke of them being defeated at the end of this age (Isa. 24:21-22; 34:4). Both Isaiah and Jesus made predictions of them while they were powers in the heavenlies.

At Christ's Coming, they will not only be shaken and completely defeated, but will be cast into prison for 1,000 years (Isa. 24:21-22; Rev. 20:1-10).

The planets and the hosts of Heaven are distinguished in II Kings 23:4-5. The hosts of Heaven are intelligent beings and have been worshiped and served by men in past ages (II Ki. 17:16; 21:3, 5; II Chron. 33:3-5; Jer. 8:2; 19:13; Zeph. 1:5; Acts 7:42).

That such could not refer to the material heavens is clear from Hebrews 12:26, where God says He will shake Heaven only once more, and this will be when the heavens and earth are renovated by fire at the end of the Millennium, or 1,000 years after *"the host"* and *"powers of Heaven"* are shaken, as in the above Prophecies (II Pet. 3:5-13).

The word, *"host,"* means a mass of persons, an army, great company, and is so used over 400 times of men and Angels (Dake).

(26) "AND THEN SHALL THEY SEE THE SON OF MAN COMING IN THE CLOUDS WITH GREAT POWER AND GLORY."

The two words, *"And then,"* refers to the time of the stars or meteorites falling from Heaven, as well as the Satanic powers of Heaven being shaken.

The phrase, *"Shall they see the Son of Man coming,"* refers to the Second Coming.

At the beginning of this Chapter, as well as Matthew 24, Jesus warned against believing reports of the Messiah being in *"the desert,"* or *"secret chambers,"* etc. (Mat. 24:26). As we have stated, this refers to the beginning of the Great Tribulation. However, His Coming will be at the end of the Great Tribulation, actually during the Battle of Armageddon.

In essence, the Lord is saying that the time of His coming will be so glorious and even cataclysmic, that there will be absolutely no doubt as to Who He actually is. The very heavens will announce His coming by a display of meteorite activity, along with other heavenly phenomenon, which added to the Glory of Christ, will present a display of power such as the world has never known before. So, no one will have to wonder if this is the Messiah! It will be very obvious to the entirety of the world that it is the Messiah, and He is the Lord Jesus Christ.

The phrase, *"In the clouds,"* does not speak of clouds as we think of such, but, rather, a great multitude of people who will be with Him, namely all the Saints who have ever lived (Rev. 19:14). Not only will all the Saints of God accompany the Lord at the Second Coming, but, as well, an innumerable company of Angels.

The phrase, *"With great Power and Glory,"* proclaims that of which we have been speaking.

It will be a display such as the world has never seen. Quite possibly, at least if the atmospheric conditions do not knock out satellite transmission, Television will record this event, portraying it over most of the world.

This will happen at the Battle of Armageddon, and, no doubt, every major Television Network in the world will be there to record this event. With the Antichrist pressing Jerusalem, actually with half of it falling, and with total annihilation of Israel seeming certain, Television transmission will be going into most of the homes of the world. It will be news as it happens!

NOTES

However, the world eagerly observing this battle of all battles taking place, will little expect what is about to transpire. It is the Second Coming!

The very creation which has groaned for deliverance (Rom. 8:22), now realizes that deliverance is at hand. Jesus Christ is coming back, and the powers of darkness which have caused so much heartache, death, and trouble, are about to be totally defeated. It is the times of which the Prophets spoke, and, therefore, the fulfillment of all the Prophecies.

As meteorites crisscross the heavens in a display of glory, and one might quickly add, of ecstatic joy, Jesus, with all the Glorified Saints and Angels will present a display of glory, which will be a scene totally eclipsing anything that man could ever begin to imagine. Hollywood has faked these scenes for years; however, this one is for real!

At that time, the Antichrist will be totally defeated, and defeated to such an extent that Satan's power will be completely broken.

Ezekiel said, and concerning the defeat of the Antichrist by the Lord, *"And I will plead against him with pestilence and with blood; I will rain upon him, and upon his bands, and upon the many people that are with him, an overflowing rain, and great hailstones, fire, and brimstone."*

He then said, *"Thus will I magnify Myself, and sanctify Myself; and I will be known in the eyes of many nations, and they shall know that I am the Lord"* (Ezek. 38:22-23).

(27) AND THEN SHALL HE SEND HIS ANGELS, AND SHALL GATHER TOGETHER HIS ELECT FROM THE FOUR WINDS, FROM THE UTTERMOST PART OF THE EARTH TO THE UTTERMOST PART OF HEAVEN."

This verse of Scripture proclaims the fulfillment of all the Prophecies concerning the Restoration of Israel. Israel's Salvation is omitted here, with Jesus portraying the Second Coming, and then the regathering of Israel, which will be after their acceptance of Christ. However, the Prophet Zechariah proclaims this moment of Israel's Salvation graphically so:

He said, *"In that day there shall be a fountain opened to the House of David, and to the inhabitants of Jerusalem for sin and for uncleanness"* (Zech. 13:1).

At that time, Zechariah also prophesied, *"One shall say unto Him, What are these wounds in*

Thine hands? Then He shall answer, those with which I was wounded in the house of My friends" (Zech. 13:6).

They will then know that the Jesus they crucified was indeed the Messiah, the Son of God, the Saviour of the world.

When this information is known, Zechariah also said, *"And they shall look upon Me Whom they have pierced, and they shall mourn for Him, as one mourneth for his only son"* (Zech. 12:10).

The phrase, *"And then shall He send His Angels, and gather together His elect from the four winds,"* refers to the regathering of Jews from all over the world (Isa. 11:11-12; 60:8-9; 65:9, 22; 66:19-21; Jer. 31:36-40; 33:17-26; Ezek. 36:8-24; 37:21-28; 39:25-29; Amos 9:11-15; Acts 15:13-18).

The phrase, *"From the uttermost part of the earth to the uttermost part of Heaven,"* has a double meaning.

1. Knowing that Jesus is now reigning in Jerusalem, with Israel once again the premier nation in the world, and especially that Israel now has a different spirit since her acceptance of Christ, most every Jew in the world will now want to relocate to Israel. They will be aided and abetted in this endeavor by Angels. More than likely the Angels will be visible.

Irrespective as to who these Jews are, whether rich or poor, the evidence from Scripture is that even the various Governments of particular nations will help in this endeavor, in order that the expense be minimal if any.

It is difficult to imagine the feelings which will fill the hearts of Jews all over the world, when they come to the realization that Jesus is the Messiah, and actually reigns in Jerusalem. No doubt, everything that Jesus does and says will be heralded all over the world by Television, plus every other type of media. Consequently, the new order of things will be known by the entirety of the world. It will be unparalleled in all history. Now the great Promises of God for blessing will fill the entirety of the earth, as this planet begins its Kingdom Age.

As we have repeatedly stated, many in the modern Church have little understanding as to the tremendous part played by Israel in the great Plan of God. While it is true that she has suffered terribly due to her rejection of Christ, still, the Prophecies given by the Prophets of old still hold true!

NOTES

When Nebuchadnezzar, the Babylonian Monarch, defeated Judah approximately 600 years before Christ, at that time the scepter of world power passed from the faltering hands of the Kings of Judah, the sons of David, to the Gentiles. There it has remained ever since. However, at this particular time, that scepter will be returned to the House of David. Israel will once again be the greatest nation in the world. However, its greatness will be totally different than the greatness of the Gentile nations of the past. The Glory of God will be its strength, and the Power of God its Salvation. As such, it will rule the world in Righteousness.

As well, it will be a rulership of fairness and equity, resulting in such prosperity as the world has never known. Poverty will be eliminated; man's inhumanity to man will be over; racism will end; in Christ all will be equal.

As well, sickness, disease, death, and sorrow, will be a thing of the past. It will be what the Righteous human heart has longed for! Then, spiritually speaking, the Garden of Eden will be brought back, an effort, incidently, that man has made constantly, but without success. However, at this time, the *"Tree of Life"* will be in its midst, i.e., the Lord Jesus Christ.

All is in Christ, as all must be in Christ!

2. Not only will every Jew be gathered from the entirety of the earth, but, as well, every son of Jacob who went to be with the Lord in all the intervening centuries, will return to this earth, even with all the Saints of the Church, and with Glorified Bodies, will help administer the affairs not only of Israel, but the entirety of the world.

Consequently, there will be two types of Jews and Gentiles, in the world at that time.

There will be Jews with Glorified Bodies, as well as Gentiles, which incorporates every single Believer who has ever lived, and had part in the First Resurrection. This will be all those who accepted Christ as their personal Saviour, even from Adam's day unto the Second Coming of the Lord.

As well, there will be all the Jews, plus Gentiles, who will be alive after the Second Coming, and will accept Jesus as their personal Saviour. These will not have Glorified Bodies. They will have normal human bodies, but will be kept alive indefinitely by virtue of eating the *"fruit"* which grows on the Trees beside the River, which will flow from the Temple in Jerusalem (Ezek. 47:1-12).

These from the *"Uttermost part of Heaven,"* will include all the Bible Greats, such as Abraham, Moses, David, etc. As stated, it will include every believing Jew, and for all time, who died in Christ, or was taken in the Rapture.

(28) "NOW LEARN A PARABLE OF THE FIG TREE; WHEN HER BRANCH IS YET TENDER, AND PUTTETH FORTH LEAVES, YE KNOW THAT SUMMER IS NEAR:"

The phrase, *"Now learn a Parable of the Fig Tree,"* is used in the same sense as the vine and the olive, with which it is associated in God's Promises of prosperity and in prophetic warnings (Jer. 5:17; Hos. 2:12; Joel 1:7, 12; Hab. 3:17).

Actually, the fig is often planted with the vine (Lk. 13:6), so that its branches and the vine's foliage led to the well-known expression, *"To sit down under one's own vine and fig tree,"* as a symbol of long-continued well-being and prosperity (I Ki. 4:25; II Ki. 18:31; Isa. 36:16; Micah 4:4; Zech. 3:10).

So, the *"fig tree"* is here as a symbol of Israel, and, more particularly, the Second Coming of Christ.

The phrase, *"When her branch is yet tender, and putteth forth leaves,"* has a double meaning:

1. It refers to the rebirth of Israel, as it began in 1948. For about 1900 years this *"fig tree"* produced nothing. Now, this tree, taking life from the roots, is beginning to *"put forth leaves."*

Since the Palestinian peace accords, many nations have opened up to Israel respecting trade, etc. From an economic viewpoint, Israel is prospering greatly, with her G.N.P. increasing at the rate of approximately five percent a year. Factories are being speedily built in Israel, employing the latest technological advancements, and turning out high-tech goods in abundance. As we have previously stated, this will continue until the Advent of the Antichrist, who they will accept as their Messiah.

2. The second meaning merely concerns the fig tree, that is used here by Jesus as a symbol of the Second Coming. When it puts forth leaves, it is about ready to bear fruit, i.e., Jesus is soon to come!

The phrase, *"Ye know that summer is near,"* refers to the fig tree about to bring forth fruit, and, consequently, the advent of *"summer."*

(29) "SO YE IN LIKE MANNER, WHEN YE SHALL SEE THESE THINGS COME TO PASS, KNOW THAT IT IS NIGH, EVEN AT THE DOORS."

The phrase, *"So ye in like manner, when ye shall see these things come to pass,"* is referring to all the predictions of the preceding verses, i.e., *"false Messiahs," "signs and wonders,"* etc.

The phrase, *"Know that it is nigh, even at the doors,"* should have been translated, *"He is nigh,"* because it refers to Christ.

This Parable of the Fig Tree pertains to Israel and the Second Coming, and is meant to explain the time of that world-shaking event.

No doubt many Jews during the coming Great Tribulation, who have accepted Christ as their Saviour, will read these very words with encouragement.

As well, there is no reason for the world to be in ignorance concerning this all-important event. However, ignorance prevails, because most people simply do not believe the Bible, hence, they do not believe these words.

(30) "VERILY I SAY UNTO YOU, THAT THIS GENERATION SHALL NOT PASS, TILL ALL THESE THINGS BE DONE."

"This generation," spoken of by Jesus, concerns the generation in existence at the time of these happenings. Actually, this will be the last generation living on earth at the time all these things will be fulfilled — the last generation before the beginning of the Kingdom Age.

This proves that all these things will be fulfilled in one generation only, and, actually, in less than one generation. The Great Tribulation, called *"Daniel's 70th Week,"* will last for seven years (Dan. 9:27). All of the predictions in Revelation Chapters 6-19, will take place during this seven years. Consequently, as is obvious, that is much shorter than a generation, but, yet, many things will no doubt take place, leading up to the Great Tribulation. (It is possible that the *"generation"* of which Jesus spoke, is this generation alive now. That should be a sobering thought.)

Once again, there is no excuse for Israel's rebellion, and their acceptance of the Antichrist, especially considering that Jesus plainly tells them what will take place. However, and sadly, the nation of Israel gives no credence at all to the New Testament, and especially Christ and

His Words. To be sure, this unbelief will cost them dearly!

Sadder still, even much of the Church has little knowledge of futuristic events as they are predicted in the Bible. The reason, as with Israel, is unbelief!

(31) "HEAVEN AND EARTH SHALL PASS AWAY: BUT MY WORDS SHALL NOT PASS AWAY."

The phrase, *"Heaven and earth shall pass away,"* would have probably been better translated, *"Heaven and earth shall pass from one condition to another."*

The Greek word for *"pass away,"* is *"parerchomai,"* and means, *"to change from one condition or state to another."* It never means annihilation, but change only.

Actually, the heavens and earth are eternal (Ps. 72:5-17; 89:3-37; 104:5; Eccl. 1:4), and cannot pass out of existence. They will be *"changed"* (Rom. 8:21-23; Heb. 1:10-12; 12:25-28), be renovated by fire (II Pet. 3:5-13), and be renewed (Rev. 21:1), but never pass out of existence (Dake).

The phrase, *"But My Words shall not pass away,"* means that Heaven and earth may change, and, in fact, will change, but *"My Words shall never change."*

In other words, what He is saying is going to come to pass, and without fail! It will not, and, in fact, cannot be changed by world events, unbelief in God's Word, or the machinations of evil men.

In fact, God's Word is always unchangeable, and, in Truth, is the only thing that is unchangeable. God said, *"For I am the Lord, I change not"* (Mal. 3:6).

Perfection cannot change, because perfection does not need to change!

(32) "BUT OF THAT DAY AND THAT HOUR KNOWETH NO MAN, NO, NOT THE ANGELS WHICH ARE IN HEAVEN, NEITHER THE SON, BUT THE FATHER."

The phrase, *"But of that day and that hour knoweth no man,"* refers to the exact time it will happen. In fact, since the utterance of these Words by Christ, it has been nearly 2,000 years.

However, if, in fact, the *"fig tree"* typifies Israel, we know these events are not far off, and simply because Israel, so to speak, is *"putting forth leaves."*

NOTES

The phrase, *"No, not the Angels which are in Heaven,"* means they did not know then; however, they probably do know now!

The phrase, *"Neither the Son,"* means that the Lord Jesus, speaking in the capacity of the Son of Man under the self-imposed limitations of the Incarnation, says that even He Himself did not at that time know the hour of the Second Advent, and of the time of the fulfillment of these other things grouped around that event (Wuest).

Without a doubt, He now knows!

The phrase, *"But the Father,"* means that at that time, the time when Christ was speaking these Words, only the Father knew the exact time of the fulfillment of these coming events.

As well, this tells us that the Lord sought to know only the things the Father desired that He know. This spoke of total submission to the Father, leaving all in His Hands.

Now that He is seated by the Right Hand of the Father, the Incarnation with its limitations is now past. As such, He is now *"Omnipotent"* (all-powerful), *"Omniscient"* (all-knowing), and *"Omnipresent"* (everywhere), and has been since the Ascension (Acts 1:9; Eph. 1:20-23).

(33) "TAKE YE HEED, WATCH AND PRAY: FOR YE KNOW NOT WHEN THE TIME IS."

The phrase, *"Take ye heed, watch and pray,"* is an admonition given not only to Israel, but to the Church as well! The idea is a state of watchfulness, which is seasoned by prayer.

If the Believer does not have a strong prayer life, these predictions will grow more and more dim, such as is happening in the modern Church!

The phrase, *"For ye know not when the time is,"* means that the *"time"* itself is not that important, but that *"watchfulness"* is!

Even though the Rapture is not mentioned here, still, the same principle applies. When that important event will take place, no one knows; however, we are admonished to be ready at all times, and live as if it will happen at any time (I Thess. 1:10; 5:6).

John said, and concerning the Rapture, *"And every man that hath this hope in him purifieth himself, even as he is pure"* (I Jn. 3:3).

The idea is, and as is obvious, that the *"hope"* of the Rapture, and realizing it could happen at any time, causes one to draw closer to Jesus Christ.

NOTES

(34) "FOR THE SON OF MAN IS AS A MAN TAKING A FAR JOURNEY, WHO LEFT HIS HOUSE, AND GAVE AUTHORITY TO HIS SERVANTS, AND TO EVERY MAN HIS WORK, AND COMMANDED THE PORTER TO WATCH."

The phrase, *"For the Son of Man is as a man taking a far journey,"* refers to the Lord speaking of Himself. He left this earth and went back to Heaven, where He resides even at this present time, seated by the Right Hand of the Father, making intercession for the Saints (Eph. 1:20-23; Heb. 7:25).

The phrase, *"Who left His house,"* refers to the Work He established on earth, constituted as the *"Church"* (Mat. 16:18).

The phrase, *"And gave authority to His servants,"* concerns those to whom belongs the responsibility of guarding the house and of being ready to open the door to the Master at His return (Wuest). In a sense, this stands for every Believer, but, more particularly, for every full-time Christian worker, such as a Pastor, Evangelist, Bible Teacher, Missionary, etc.

The phrase, *"And commanded the porter to watch,"* is a little different than the word, *"watch,"* in verse 33. That *"watch"* speaks of a sleeping man arousing himself, while this *"watch"* conveys the idea of wakefulness (Wuest).

(35) "WATCH YE THEREFORE: FOR YE KNOW NOT WHEN THE MASTER OF THE HOUSE COMETH, AT EVEN, OR AT MIDNIGHT, OR AT THE COCKCROWING, OR IN THE MORNING:"

The phrase, *"Watch ye therefore,"* is used again to portray the seriousness of the matter, referring to the Coming of the Lord.

The phrase, *"For ye know not when the Master of the house cometh, at even, or at midnight, or at the cockcrowing, or in the morning,"* according to Vincent, pertains to Preachers, and in a sense every Believer, who are thus compared with the doorkeepers of verse 34. The night season as here represented is an apt description. In the Temple, during the night, the Captain of the Temple made his rounds, and the guards had to rise at his approach and salute him in a particular manner. Any guard found asleep on duty was beaten, or his garments set on fire. One can compare Revelation 16:15, *"Blessed is he that watcheth, and keepeth his garments,"* with this illustration.

The preparations for the morning service required all to be early astir. The superintending Priest might knock at the door at any moment.

(36) "LEST COMING SUDDENLY HE FIND YOU SLEEPING."

After the establishment of Roman power in Judaea, the Jews copied the Roman method of dividing the night into four watches. Jesus continues with that custom in verse 35.

The first watch would have begun at 6 p.m. and continued until 9 p.m.

The second watch would have begun at 9 p.m. and ended at midnight.

The third watch would have begun at midnight and concluded at 3 a.m., or at *"cockcrowing,"* which would have been the first crowing of the rooster.

The fourth watch began at 3 a.m., and concluded at 6 a.m., or the last *"cockcrowing"* (the roosters crowed twice at about 3 a.m. and approximately 6 a.m.)

"Sleeping" on *"watch,"* of course, was a serious offense. With the Romans it was punishable by death, and with the Temple guards, as stated, it could result in a severe beating, etc.

Once again, the constant vigilance respecting the Coming of the Lord is here intoned.

(37) "AND WHAT I SAY UNTO YOU I SAY UNTO ALL, WATCH."

This was said to the Apostles, but was meant for all Israel, and, as well, it pertains to the Church.

For Jesus to be as elaborate as He was in this explanation, and to even repeat Himself several times, one should realize the seriousness of His Words.

What does He mean by the word, *"Watch?"*

1. The certitude of His Coming is portrayed here. Nothing can stop this, it is a foregone conclusion.

2. The time of that Coming is not given, with even Him, at least at that time, not knowing the date (vs. 32).

3. As stated, the idea of this short Message concerning the Second Coming, is *"watchfulness."*

The Believer is importuned to stay ready at all times. Even though Jesus is not speaking here of the Rapture, still, as stated, it definitely could apply in principle to that event.

The manner in which Jesus spoke of this event, in essence referring to the guards and each watch of the night, is an excellent example. No guard would want to be found sleeping at his post, or even conducting himself in a way that spoke of lack of diligence. Consequently, during the time of his watch, he was to remain alert, realizing that the Priest could show up at any time.

The principle of these statements as they pertain to modern Believers, concerns the attitude and consecration of our everyday life before the Lord. We are to live as if Jesus may come at any moment. This is the thrust of what Christ is saying.

If the Believer felt the Trump of God would sound tomorrow morning at daybreak, I greatly suspect that many Christians would hurriedly attempt to right wrongs, pay back tithe, ask forgiveness, as well as calling out to God in prayer and worship. The idea is that we live in this manner of consecration at all times.

How different the Church would be were this truly the case!

CHAPTER 14

(1) "AFTER TWO DAYS WAS THE FEAST OF THE PASSOVER, AND OF UNLEAVENED BREAD: AND THE CHIEF PRIESTS AND THE SCRIBES SOUGHT HOW THEY MIGHT TAKE HIM BY CRAFT, AND PUT HIM TO DEATH."

The phrase, *"After two days was the Feast of the Passover,"* pertained to the Paschal Lamb which was offered for Sacrifice by the ancient Israelites in Egypt, with the Blood being sprinkled on the doorposts of their dwellings in Egypt so that the destroying Angel might pass over their homes without entering and taking the life of the firstborn.

Moses wrote, *"And the Blood shall be to you for a token upon the houses where ye are: and when I see the Blood, I will pass over you, and the plague shall not be upon you to destroy you, when I smite the land of Egypt"* (Ex. 12:13).

After that, they were instructed to *"Keep this ordinance in his season from year to year"* (Ex. 13:10). Consequently, for nearly 1600 years it had been kept, with the exception of the time spent in dispersion in Babylon, and times of Spiritual declension.

NOTES

The Passover is very significant to Christians as well as to Jews. To God's Old Testament, the Passover recalled a redemption linked with death and the shedding of blood.

To the Christian, the Passover speaks of Jesus, for He actually was the Passover Lamb, fulfilling the symbolism which the slain lambs represented.

Consequently, as the symbolic Passover was about to be celebrated at this time in Israel, the actual Passover Lamb was entering Jerusalem to fulfill the type by dying on the Cross.

As Israel's redemption was linked to their trust in what the Passover Lamb represented, namely Jesus, likewise, our Redemption is linked in totality to what Jesus did at Calvary, which not only saves us, but protects us as well from the ultimate destroyer.

The phrase, *"And of Unleavened Bread,"* pertained to the same Feast which lasted for seven days, during which time only Unleavened Bread was used. The killing of the Paschal Lamb and the celebration of that Feast took place on the first of these seven days.

As the Passover Lamb typified Jesus Who would shed His Blood, likewise, the *"Unleavened Bread"* typified His perfect Body and unspotted Life.

Leaven in Bible times was sourdough, which with added juices served as a fermenting agent to leaven (make to rise) new dough. It is used in a figurative and symbolic sense in the New Testament.

So, inasmuch as leaven was used as a symbol for sin, it being removed from all bread during this seven-day period symbolized, as stated, the pure and spotless Life and Body of the Lord Jesus Christ.

(Both Feasts, that of the Passover and Unleavened Bread, were celebrated in the same week.)

The phrase, *"And the Chief Priests and the Scribes sought how they might take Him by craft, and put Him to death,"* spoke of representatives of each order of the Sanhedrin who were gathered together in counsel to discuss ways and means of putting Jesus to death.

Actually, they were assembled in the house of Caiaphas, the High Priest, who had for some time been advocating the policy of sacrificing Jesus to the Roman power (Jn. 11:49).

They were not divided as to whether to do such a thing, but only as to how it should be done. The point under consideration was the strategic, opportune, safe time to give Jesus over to the Roman authorities (Wuest).

As sordid as it sounds, in effect, we have before us what was the *"Church"* of that day plotting the Death of Christ. In Truth, the Church has always been the biggest enemy of the Lord. Of course, I speak of the Apostate Church, which makes up the far greater majority. Consequently, the most dangerous place in town is oftentimes the Church. Therefore, it is extremely important as to where a person attends Church.

Inasmuch as the leaders of most Churches do not follow the Lord, do not preach the Bible, and, consequently, do not have the power of the Holy Spirit, for one to associate with one of these Churches, whatever their names may be, is tantamount to spiritual death.

There are some good Churches led by Spirit-filled Preachers, but not many! The person who has the privilege to attend such a Church is privileged indeed!

(2) "BUT THEY SAID, NOT ON THE FEAST DAY, LEST THERE BE AN UPROAR OF THE PEOPLE."

The phrase, *"But they said, Not on the Feast Day,"* spoke of the Day of the Passover.

The phrase, *"Lest there be an uproar of the people,"* concerned the vast population of Jerusalem which swelled during the Passover Feast, and could have numbered as many as 500,000 people, or even more.

Scores of these people had experienced Healings and even Miracles at the Hand of Christ, and, as well, many at least considered Jesus a great Prophet, if not the Messiah. Consequently, these Church leaders felt that if this matter was not handled delicately, it could cause severe problems, even a riot, should the people rise in His defense. Their first intention, therefore, was not to destroy Him until after the close of the Passover Feast.

However, they were overruled by events, all ordered by God's never-failing providence. The sudden betrayal by Judas led them to change their minds. Consequently, Jesus would be handed over to the Roman authorities, and would, therefore, die on the Passover Day, even at 3 p.m. which was the exact time the Paschal Lamb was offered.

And thus the Divine purpose was fulfilled that Christ should suffer at that particular time, and so the type be satisfied (Bickersteth).

NOTES

(3) "AND BEING IN BETHANY IN THE HOUSE OF SIMON THE LEPER, AS HE SAT AT MEAT, THERE CAME A WOMAN HAVING AN ALABASTER BOX OF OINTMENT OF SPIKENARD VERY PRECIOUS; AND SHE BRAKE THE BOX, AND POURED IT ON HIS HEAD."

The phrase, *"And being in Bethany,"* spoke of the small village where Jesus and His Disciples spent much time when in the vicinity of Jerusalem. Actually, there is no evidence that Jesus ever spent the night in Jerusalem, with the exception of the night He was arrested. He had close friends in Bethany, including Lazarus, and his sisters, Mary and Martha. It seems that *"Simon the Leper"* also was in this favored group.

The phrase, *"In the house of Simon the leper,"* probably referred to a man who Jesus had healed. Oftentimes, something was linked, as here, to the name of a person, and done so for recognition.

The phrase, *"As He sat at meat,"* referred, more than likely, to the evening meal.

The meals in those days were not taken as presently, with people sitting in chairs, but, instead, reclining on cushions or couches on the floor.

The phrase, *"There came a woman,"* probably refers to Mary, the sister of Lazarus, and spoken of in John 11:1-2.

Some have claimed it was another woman, and thereby another anointing. However, there is little evidence of such!

The phrase, *"Having an alabaster box of ointment of spikenard very precious,"* referred to a perfume which came from India, and was well-known to the Greeks and Romans, and procured from the hills on the banks of the Ganges River.

The Greek word, *"pistikos,"* is used, meaning that it was genuine, not imitation or adulterated.

As well, the Greek word *"poluteles"* (precious), tells us that it was very costly.

The phrase, *"And she brake the box,"* means that she broke the seal that kept the fragrance preserved. It did not mean that the bottle was smashed or broken.

The phrase, *"And poured it on His Head,"* spoke of her anointing Him for His burial.

Williams said of this anointing, *"Her action denoted affection and intelligence. Having heard that He was to die, she purchased a costly spikenard to assist in the embalming of His Body; but instructed by the Resurrection of her brother, Lazarus, hearing that Jesus was Himself the Resurrection and the Life, learning that He was to rise on the third day, and recognizing that embalmment would be needless, she poured it upon His Living Body and so testified her belief in the Resurrection."*

Consequently, it seems that she was the only person who believed and understood the Lord's teaching as to His Death and Resurrection. None of the Disciples seemed to have understood what He said to them on that matter until after Pentecost.

As recorded in John, she anointed both the Lord's Feet and His Head.

(Some believe that Martha was the wife of Simon the leper, Lazarus and Mary being, consequently, brother-in-law and sister-in-law to Simon.)

(4) "AND THERE WERE SOME THAT HAD INDIGNATION WITHIN THEMSELVES, AND SAID, WHY WAS THIS WASTE OF THE OINTMENT MADE?"

The phrase, *"And there were some that had indignation within themselves,"* pertained to some of the Disciples, but with Judas Iscariot taking the lead.

This shows how fault-finding can quickly spread! It is the same in a local Church. One individual finds fault, and then attempts to pedal it to others. They usually succeed!

Continuing in the vein of the local Church, no one should be a party to such action. If false doctrine is being presented, it should be examined according to Scripture, and then confronted. If it seems the situation or direction will not change, the individual should leave that particular Church Body and go elsewhere. He should not remain, at least in those circumstances, and become a part of a Church fight.

It is obvious why Judas did as he did. His affections had already found root other than Christ. Consequently, he would grow *"indignant"* at what he considered a *"waste."*

Regrettably, the minds and hearts of some of the other Disciples were more carnal than spiritual. Consequently, it was very easy for these to join him.

Other than Judas, how badly they must have felt afterward, when thinking back upon this situation.

Jesus was about to die! The anointing He received would be the only such anointing.

Mary anointed His *"Head,"* signifying His Death, and His Feet (Jn. 12:3), signifying that He would walk out of that tomb, whether she understood that at the time or not!

The question, *"And said, Why was this waste of the ointment made?"*, concerned, according to some, a worth of approximately $10,000 in 1996 money. Consequently, it was, and as stated, *"very precious."*

First of all, to refer to this as *"waste,"* shows a woeful lack of spiritual knowledge! Such must have been grievous to the Heart of Jesus.

In Truth, the entirety of the spirit of the world follows in this train. Anything done for God, plus anything spent for the Work of the Lord is termed *"waste."*

Through the years, I have dealt often with the media, and along these very lines. They greatly complained about our appealing to people for funds to help us take the Gospel to the world. They professed to be extremely agitated at elderly people on fixed incomes giving for this cause and purpose. However, I have not noticed the media saying anything in a negative sense concerning the scores of elderly and destitute poor buying lottery tickets, which they can ill afford.

To give to God, is the most noble thing that one could ever do, and irrespective of his status or position in life. To throw away one's money on lottery tickets is truly the biggest *"waste"* in which one could ever engage.

Why is it that the media says nothing about that sort of *"waste,"* i.e., gambling?

The answer is simple! Their spirit and the gambling spirit are one and the same. In other words, it all comes from the same parent, Satan!

In Truth, the only thing in this world that is not a *"waste"* is that which is done for God! Of course, that would include the care of one's family, etc.

(5) "FOR IT MIGHT HAVE BEEN SOLD FOR MORE THAN THREE HUNDRED PENCE, AND HAVE BEEN GIVEN TO THE POOR. AND THEY MURMURED AGAINST HER."

The phrase, *"For it might have been sold for more than three hundred pence,"* represented, as stated, approximately $10,000.

The phrase, *"And have been given to the poor,"* originated with Judas (Jn. 12:4-6).

He did not care for the poor, but only that this money could be brought within his reach. The

Scripture said, *"This he said, not that he cared for the poor; but because he was a thief, and had the bag, and bare what was put therein"* (Jn. 12:6).

The phrase, *"And they murmured against her,"* concerned whichever Disciples had joined in with Judas in complaining about this *"Anointing!"*

Dake says, *"No case of murmuring has ever been justified or sanctioned by God in Scripture regardless of how right the cause. It is always condemned and cursed, and for the obvious reasons"* (Ex. 15:24; 16:2-12; 17:3-5; Num. 14:2-36; 17:5-10; Deut. 1:27; Josh. 9:18; Ps. 106:25; Mat. 20:11; Lk. 5:30; 15:2; 19:7; Jn. 6:41, 61; 7:12, 32; Acts 6:1; I Cor. 10:10; Phil. 2:14; Jude 16).

(6) "AND JESUS SAID, LET HER ALONE; WHY TROUBLE YE HER? SHE HATH WROUGHT A GOOD WORK ON ME."

The phrase, *"And Jesus said, Let her alone,"* proclaims the same Word He says to all who would attempt to hinder that done for Him.

It appears from John 12:7 that Jesus here addressed Himself pointedly to Judas in these words.

The question, *"Why trouble ye her,"* concerns itself with the *"murmuring."*

What she did was not the business of Judas, or anyone else. So, what right did any of them have in saying anything?

Judas was accusing her of *"waste,"* which, in reality, was no waste at all, while he was guilty of the largest *"waste"* ever perpetrated by a human being. He would *"waste"* himself, all of Israel, and, most of all, the Lord Jesus Christ.

Actually, almost all the world falls into this category. They waste themselves, their families, and all of humanity in which they come in contact with, and, above all, the Plan of God for their lives.

No! The Anointing of Jesus with this costly *"box of ointment"* was no waste. What Judas did was!

People waste their time, talent, and money on that which is of no use or consequence.

Conversely, anything done for the Lord, and in whatever capacity, that is, if our motives are right, is not only <u>not</u> a *"waste,"* but, in reality, a profit of incalculable proportions.

The phrase, *"She hath wrought a good work on Me,"* is epitomized in the following statement:

"One life will soon be past, only what's done for Christ will last."

NOTES

(7) "FOR YE HAVE THE POOR WITH YOU ALWAYS, AND WHENSOEVER YE WILL YE MAY DO THEM GOOD: BUT ME YE HAVE NOT ALWAYS."

The phrase, *"For ye have the poor with you always,"* regrettably, portrays a condition resulting from the Fall in the Garden of Eden.

While it is certainly no sin to be poor, still, poverty is a crushing, debilitating weight on humanity.

The word, *"always,"* speaks of the time up to the Second Coming. At that time, the beginning of the Kingdom Age, poverty will be completely eliminated.

To be poor, often means the lacking of adequate basic necessities. The poor are always in need of the resources that provide for an improved quality of life. However, more than material need is implied by poverty.

Poverty assumes a low social status and a terrible vulnerability to the abuses of those with power. Because the poor lack resources, they are defenseless against those in society who are above them. They are likely to be treated unfairly in the courts (Deut. 15:1-4).

When defrauded by the well-to-do, they have no recourse but to appeal to the Lord. Because of their powerlessness, the poor are the most easily robbed in any society (Ps. 35:10). Poverty strips the individual of rights, respect as a human being, and a place in society.

THE CAUSE OF POVERTY

In the Old Testament, and especially in Proverbs, there is sometimes strong emphasis on individual responsibility. Solomon said, *"Lazy hands make a man poor, but diligent hands bring wealth"* (Prov. 10:4).

He also said, *"Drunkards and gluttons become poor, and drowsiness clothes them in rags"* (Prov. 23:21; 24:34).

However, the Book of Proverbs also recognizes causes of poverty that an individual has no control over. Solomon said, *"A poor man's field may produce abundant food, but injustice sweeps it away"* (Prov. 13:23).

Clearly, it is the injustice of those who oppress the poor and the helpless that the Old Testament portrays as the most common cause of poverty.

Although certain Laws in the Law of Moses were intended to guard the poor, Israel's failure in this regard is reflected both in history and in the Old Testament Prophets' pronouncements.

Calling for a return to God, Isaiah communicated God's Message that His people are to stop their practice of empty ritual and begin to live a life acceptable to the Lord: *"Is not this the kind of fasting that I have chosen: to loose the chains of injustice and untie the cords of the yoke, to set the oppressed free and break every yoke?*

"Is it not to share your food with the hungry and to provide the poor wanderer with shelter — when you see the naked, to clothe him, and not to turn away from your own flesh and blood?" (Isa. 58:6-7).

As well, the Lord through the Prophet Zechariah said, *"Administer true justice; show Mercy and Compassion to one another.*

"Do not oppress the widow or the fatherless, the alien or the poor" (Zech. 7:9-10).

Solomon also said, *"He who oppresses the poor shows contempt for their Maker, but whoever is kind to the needy honors God"* (Prov. 14:31).

ISRAEL AND THE POOR

Even though the Laws of God were strong respecting the poor, none of the mechanisms worked on a society-wide scale in Israel's entire history! God's people remained hardened; and although individuals may have approached the ideal, no generation of Israelites ever achieved it.

This may be the one reason why commitment to God is closely associated with concern for the poor and oppressed in Scripture. Only by putting God and His Way first would someone exhibit compassion, surrendering material possessions to meet the needs of others.

However, in the Old Testament, there is a strong linkage between sin entrenched in society and practiced by individuals and the crushing poverty that many suffered. God Himself sometimes brought the nation to a state of poverty. This came as a Judgment to those generations that would not serve the Lord in times of prosperity. Such Judgment brought hunger and thirst, nakedness and dire poverty (Deut. 28:48).

THE POOR WITHIN THE CHURCH

Regarding the teaching on poverty, the Epistles differ in several striking ways from the Old Testament.

First, the Old Testament links poverty in society with oppression and establishes social mechanisms that people of good will can use to reduce poverty.

The New Testament does not explore the relationship between social oppression and the state of the lower classes. Nor does it suggest social mechanisms by which a society can deal with poverty. This is primarily because Israel was a nation as well as a community of Faith. Old Testament Law was civil as well as ethical in nature.

The New Testament Church, by contrast, exists as a community of Faith within a variety of societies and cultures. The Christian may influence his or her society, but the Church is never envisioned as a State. Thus, no New Testament writer felt that it was his mission to set up the constitution of an ideal society.

Second, social class differences are assumed in the New Testament. But these differences are not to be considered within the fellowship of those who follow Jesus. James warns against showing favoritism to the rich (James 2:1-7). He reminds us that early Christianity was a movement of the lower classes and that the rich were exploiting the Believers.

Paul makes a similar point in writing to the Corinthians (I Cor. 1:20-30): *"Not many of you were wise by human standards; not many were influential; not many were of noble birth."* They were instead *"the lowly things of this world"* (I Cor. 1:26-28). Paul insisted that those now clothed with Christ *"are all one in Christ Jesus"* and not to be categorized as slave or free, male or female (Gal. 3:28).

It follows, then, that class distinctions are to be rejected in the Body of Christ. As Paul says to the Romans, do not be proud, but be willing to associate with people of low position. Do not be conceited (Rom. 12:12-13).

THE RESPONSE OF THE CHURCH
TO THE POOR

The New Testament definitely focuses on the plight of the poor and on the way in which the Church and the individual Believer are to respond.

The New Testament records that when one part of the ancient world suffered famine or persecution, Believers in more prosperous areas responded by sending funds to meet the survival needs of their brothers and sisters. However, due to the influence of Christianity for the last 2,000 years, Governments are now very much involved respecting needs as a result of famine or catastrophe. Thankfully, this relieves this burden on the Church, in order that it may use its funds for World Evangelism.

Individual Believers are also to respond to the immediate needs of others whom he or she knows (James 2:14-16; I Jn. 3:16-18). However, this is done only if the individual truly cannot help himself. Paul also said, *"That if any would not work, neither should he eat"* (II Thess. 3:10).

This statement was given no doubt, because of lazy busybodies and shiftless individuals in the Church who had become professional moochers.

As well, the New Testament does not command the distribution of wealth to bring about a level society, but the rich are to see their wealth as a gift God has given them to help alleviate the needs of brothers and sisters.

Generosity is to be the basic principle as a sharing modeled after Christ, Who sacrificed Himself to meet our needs (II Cor. 8:8-9).

Because God ultimately is the One Who supplies our needs, we can give generously, knowing that He will care for us when we have need. Then, having all that you need, you will abound in every good work (II Cor. 9:8-11).

Although Believers are exhorted to *"Do good to all people,"* they are to do so *"especially to those who belong to the family of Believers"* (Gal. 6:10).

Someone has well said, and regarding the poor, that if every person in the world was given $1,000,000, at the end of twelve months or less, one percent would have all the money, with the other ninety-nine percent having little or none. Regrettably, that is true! Consequently, we *"have the poor with us always,"* at least until the coming Kingdom Age.

The phrase, *"And whensoever ye will ye may do them good,"* was in no way an intention on the Lord's part to contrast services rendered to Himself in person with services rendered to the poor for His Sake — the two are equivalent in His sight (Mat. 25:40-45).

The phrase, *"But Me ye have not always,"* is meant to point out that this privilege would very soon be impossible, while opportunity for the poor would abound to the end of this age.

(8) "SHE HATH DONE WHAT SHE COULD: SHE IS COME AFOREHAND TO ANOINT MY BODY TO THE BURYING."

The phrase, *"She hath done what she could,"* pertained to Mary. She had been moved upon by the Holy Spirit to do this, and because of its great significance.

She did *"what she could"*; are we doing what we can? As a result, her unselfish act has been spoken of for 2,000 years. As well, of the millions of Believers who have praised her, not one has taken the position that Judas took.

The phrase, *"She is come aforehand to anoint My Body to the burying,"* represented something so very important that it defies all description. Sadly, Judas and some of the Disciples did not see or understand this extremely important event.

The *"Body"* of Jesus was to be the Sacrifice that would redeem humanity from the terrible grip of sin. As well, His Sacrifice would satisfy the claims of heavenly justice, in that the debt owed by mankind would be paid in full.

For this very cause, Jesus came into the world. The Prophet had said, *"A Body hast Thou prepared Me"* (Heb. 10:5).

So, Mary was anointing this Body of Christ which had been prepared by God for this very purpose. Inasmuch as the embalming process was never really carried out, the Resurrection preventing the fulfillment of this purpose, the only anointing which the Lord received was the anticipatory one by Mary.

What an honor that God chose a woman to do this! As well, a woman, Mary Magdalene, was the first to announce the Resurrection (Mk. 16:9-10).

(9) "VERILY I SAY UNTO YOU, WHERESOEVER THIS GOSPEL SHALL BE PREACHED THROUGHOUT THE WHOLE WORLD, THIS ALSO THAT SHE HATH DONE SHALL BE SPOKEN OF FOR A MEMORIAL OF HER."

The phrase, *"Verily I say unto you, Wheresoever this Gospel shall be preached throughout the whole world,"* tells us several things:

1. This tells us that the Gospel will be preached *"Throughout the whole world."*

2. As well, it will be *"This Gospel,"* the Gospel of Jesus Christ.

Even though False Prophets abound, propagating their false message, still, there are probably more Preachers proclaiming the Truth today than ever before in the history of the Gospel. To be sure, that number is not nearly as large as those who preach a false message; however, it is larger today than ever!

3. This which Mary did, which was so very important, will ever be heralded, and because anything and everything done for Christ bears eternal consequences.

The phrase, *"This also that she hath done shall be spoken of for a memorial of her,"* has been fulfilled in totality, and will continue to be fulfilled.

If one is to notice, it says, *"A memorial of her,"* signifying this act is connected with her and will never be forgotten.

I believe one could say without fear of contradiction, that every single thing done for Christ, and by anyone, is written down in a *"Memorial Book"* in Heaven. The *"Books"* are mentioned in Revelation 20:12, and proclaim that everything is noted, whether good or bad. However, upon Trust in the shed Blood of Jesus Christ, and because of Justification by Faith, all of that which is negative or bad is erased. Only the good remains!

(10) "AND JUDAS ISCARIOT, ONE OF THE TWELVE, WENT UNTO THE CHIEF PRIESTS, TO BETRAY HIM UNTO THEM."

The phrase, *"And Judas Iscariot, one of the Twelve,"* is noted by design by the Holy Spirit. He desires all to know that Judas was chosen by the Lord as one of the *"Twelve,"* and, consequently, one of the Twelve most important offices ever given to a human being in the history of mankind.

The phrase, *"Went unto the Chief Priests,"* means that he had lost one opportunity of gain; he would seek another.

Judas had entered such a state of rebellion, that the rebuke tendered by Christ caused the other Disciples to be brought to their senses, but not Judas. Whereas it softened them, it only served to harden him.

Such is the Gospel! It is like the sun; it hardens clay, while softening wax. The fault is not in the sun, as it is not in the Gospel, but the material.

The phrase, *"To betray Him unto them,"* proclaims the most perfidious act ever carried out by any human being.

Any wrong thing done to anyone is always censored by the Lord, and stringently so!

However, nothing can compare with that which was done to Christ, for He was absolutely sinless, and, therefore, perfect. He had never done anything to anyone, but be kind and gracious to them. He had never made a leg to be lame, but made many to walk. He had never caused an eye to be blind, but had opened many. So, why would anyone want to betray Him?

That question could be asked concerning the rejection of Christ by almost the entirety of the world.

Why?

Unbelief! (Jn. 16:9).

Judas would fall into the same category. He simply did not believe in the Mission of Christ regarding the Salvation of humanity, but, instead, placed his own self-will in the forefront. When it looked as if Christ was not going to use His Power to bring about the selfish desires of Judas, he consented to betray Him.

The word, *"betray,"* is *"paradidomai,"* in the Greek, and means *"to hand over or alongside,"* or *"sell him down the river."*

The pronoun, *"Them,"* and referring to the *"Chief Priests,"* is said with some sarcasm by the Holy Spirit.

They were supposed to be *"Priests"* of God; however, they were *"Priests"* of man, actually, lackeys of Rome.

To this level the Church had fallen!

(11) "AND WHEN THEY HEARD IT, THEY WERE GLAD, AND PROMISED TO GIVE HIM MONEY. AND HE SOUGHT HOW HE MIGHT CONVENIENTLY BETRAY HIM."

The phrase, *"And when they heard it, they were glad,"* proclaims them more delighted than they cared to show. Swete remarks that the burden of finding a way to do away with Jesus so that the Passover crowds would not see, now was definitely on the shoulders of Judas. His position in the inner circle of Disciples gave him an advantage which the Chief Priests did not have.

The phrase, *"And promised to give him money,"* proclaims the amount given by Matthew as *"thirty pieces of silver"* (Mat. 26:15). Some five hundred years earlier, the Prophet Zechariah had prophesied the exact amount (Zech. 11:12).

Some Commentators think that this was only an installment of what they promised him if he completed his treasonable design (Bickersteth).

The phrase, *"And he sought how he might conveniently betray Him,"* proclaims the devilish deed about to be carried out. He betrayed Him at night, when He was alone with His Disciples in the Garden of Gethsemane.

The word, *"conveniently,"* is interesting! Judas would betray Him, but he would attempt to carry it out in a manner in which his part and activity would be concealed. However, it was not to be!

It would be observed by all the Disciples, plus all the Temple Guards, and would be written in all four Gospels. Consequently, his perfidious act would be known to all, and for all time!

(12) "AND THE FIRST DAY OF UNLEAVENED BREAD, WHEN THEY KILLED THE PASSOVER, HIS DISCIPLES SAID UNTO HIM, WHERE WILT THOU THAT WE GO AND PREPARE THAT THOU MAYEST EAT THE PASSOVER?"

The phrase, *"And the first day of Unleavened Bread, when they killed the Passover,"* according to Dake, was the 14th of Nisan (April), our Tuesday sunset to Wednesday sunset. This was the day of preparation, as stated, when the Passover Lamb must be killed.

The next day would be the *"high day,"* the great special Sabbath, not the ordinary weekly Sabbath (Lev. 23:6-7; Jn. 19:30-31).

The regular Feast of Unleavened Bread did not officially begin until a day after the Passover, but Jews began to eat this Bread on the day of the preparation, and that is what is referred to here.

The question, *"His Disciples said unto Him, Where wilt Thou that we go and prepare that Thou mayest eat the Passover?"*, in effect, concerns the greatest Passover of all!

The Sacrifice had to be eaten in Jerusalem; therefore, the question was in what *"house"* it was to be prepared.

(Some claim that the first day of Unleavened Bread was the evening of Thursday, actually the beginning of the Jewish Friday. However, the evidence points to that being incorrect, due to the fact that Christ must remain in the tomb three days and three nights (Mat. 12:40).

(13) "AND HE SENDETH FORTH TWO OF HIS DISCIPLES, AND SAITH UNTO THEM, GO YE INTO THE CITY, AND THERE SHALL MEET YOU A MAN BEARING A PITCHER OF WATER: FOLLOW HIM."

The phrase, *"And He sendeth forth two of His Disciples,"* referred to Peter and John (Lk. 22:8).

NOTES

The phrase, *"And saith unto them, Go ye into the city,"* proclaims the identical way in which the Lord continues to deal with His people. Although He is not here physically, still, through the Agency and Person of the Holy Spirit, He is here now even in a greater way than when here physically.

The Holy Spirit does *"not speak of Himself,"* but instead, Christ. Jesus said of Him, *"He shall glorify Me: for He shall receive of Mine, and shall shew it unto you"* (Jn. 16:13-14).

Some time ago, while speaking with a noted Preacher of one of the major Religious Denominations in America, he made mention to me that this organization, which claims to be fundamental in their beliefs (believe all the Bible), does not believe that God speaks to people in this day and time. This man, who is Spirit-filled, although retaining his ordination in this organization, was not a party to this concept.

When he told me this, to be sure, I was shocked!

I asked him how they carried on their work?

His answer was revealing, and yet typical of most of that which today refers to itself as *"Christian."*

"Men direct it," he said, *"making decisions as they think best."*

In other words, there is no leading of the Holy Spirit whatsoever! Consequently, what is done, and in every capacity, is man-originated, man-led, and man-directed. While there may be much religious machinery, under these circumstances there is absolutely nothing done for the Lord.

Anything that is truly done for the Lord on this earth is done by the unction, guidance, power, and leading of the Holy Spirit (Zech. 4:6). As stated, He shows to the Believer what Jesus wants, Who always carries out the Will of the Heavenly Father.

Any Believer who attempts any type of work for the Lord without being led by the Holy Spirit, is *"in the flesh,"* and, consequently, *"cannot please God"* (Rom. 8:8).

As well, the leading of the Holy Spirit is not an automatic process. To be led by the Spirit, one must be filled with the Spirit and seek actively to walk close to God. Regrettably, most in modern Christendom little do this, and are little led by the Spirit.

In Truth, most of the modern Religious Denominations do not even believe in the Holy Spirit. They may claim to do so, but, in reality, He is totally ignored, just as the Brother related concerning the major Denomination.

The last two or three years I was associated with a major Pentecostal Denomination, I began to notice things which sounded strange to my ears. I would mention the Anointing of the Holy Spirit, and some of the Preachers in that particular Denomination would ridicule my statement, in effect, asking, *"What is that?"*

Their questions and sarcasm confused me at first, because I could not imagine someone calling himself *"Pentecostal"* and not knowing that of which I spoke! However, they did not know! Actually, those particular Preachers, they were no more led by the Spirit of God than their counterparts in the Denomination I spoke of.

The problem of ignoring the Holy Spirit is not indicative to any Religious Denomination, but seemingly problematic in all. In reality, this is a personal position, and has very little to do with particular Denominations.

By and large, there are some few Believers in all Denominations who are Spirit-led. However that number is small.

RESIDENCE OF THE HOLY SPIRIT

There is a verse in James that may help explain this all-important subject a little better.

James said, *"Do ye think that the Scripture saith in vain, The Spirit that dwelleth in us lusteth to envy?"* (James 4:5).

The Greek Scholars say that the verb, *"dwell,"* is not from the Greek word which means *"to take up one's residence,"* but from a closely allied verb meaning *"to cause to take up residence, to send or bring to an abode."*

In other words, the Holy Spirit does not of Himself take up His residence in the heart of the Believer. He is caused to do so, and by God the Father. In the outworking of the Plan of Salvation, there is a subordination among the members of the Godhead. Here the Holy Spirit, Very God Himself, the Third Person of the Triune God, is sent by God the Father, caused to take up His residence in our hearts.

But that is not all. The simple verb means, as we have stated, *"To cause to take up residence."* The idea is one of permanency. Thus the Holy

Spirit has been caused to take up His permanent residence in our hearts.

This agrees with I John 2:27, where the word translated *"abide"* means *"to abide"* in the sense of *"to remain."* Thus, the Holy Spirit never leaves the Believer, that is, on His Own! He will only leave if the Believer no longer desires Him.

Concerning this statement by James, the words, *"Lusteth to envy,"* have been confusing to many.

The word, *"lusteth,"* is the translation of a Greek word that means *"to earnestly or passionately desire."* Consequently, the meaning is that the indwelling Holy Spirit within our lives, possessing all the potential power and help a Saint needs, has a passionate desire to the point of envy. Of what is He envious, and what does He passionately desire? The context makes this clear.

James is speaking of Christians who are not separated unto God, but, in reality, are playing false with their Lord and fellowshipping with the world. They are allowing their evil natures to control them, those evil natures from which they had been delivered when God saved them. The Holy Spirit is envious of any control which that fallen nature might have over the Believer, and passionately desirous of Himself controlling the thoughts, words, and deeds of the Believer. He is desirous of having the Believer depend upon Him for His Ministry to him, in order that He might discharge His responsibility to the One Who sent Him, namely the Heavenly Father, which is to cause the Believer to grow in his Christian life.

GIVING THE HOLY SPIRIT LIBERTY

The Anointing with the Spirit forms the basis of all His Ministry to and in behalf of the Believer. Let us remember that it is potential in its nature. In other words, the mere indwelling of the Spirit, as important as that may be, does not guarantee the full efficacy of His Work in us, since that indwelling is not automatic in its nature. God's ideal for the indwelling of the Spirit is found in the word translated, *"Cause to take up His residence."* Its root is in the word, *"home."*

The Spirit was sent to the Believer's heart to make His home there. That means that the Christian must make Him feel at home. He can do that by giving the Holy Spirit absolute liberty of action in his heart, the home in which He lives. This means that the Believer is to yield himself, all of himself, to the Spirit's control, depending upon the Spirit for guidance, teaching, and strength. Then will the potential power resident in the presence of the Spirit in the heart of the Believer be operative in his life.

FELLOWSHIP OF THE SPIRIT

Some think that *"fellowship of the Spirit,"* means *"companionship with the Spirit."* To think such, leaves the path of sound doctrine and practice. Such individuals seek the Holy Spirit and His fullness for His sake alone. They seek intercourse with Him as an end in itself. Thus they lay themselves open to the snares of Satan and even to be controlled by evil spirits, etc. There is no such thing in Scripture as the Believer's fellowship or companionship with the Spirit comparable to the Believer's fellowship or companionship with the Lord Jesus. The Ministry of the Holy Spirit is to glorify the Son, and in doing that He always calls the Believer's attention to the Lord Jesus, never to Himself. He keeps Himself always in the background. The Lord Jesus must always be central in the life of the Saint. He is the One with Whom we have fellowship in the commonly accepted usage of the word today. The Holy Spirit makes this possible (Jn. 16:13-14).

As Sir Robert Anderson said, *"In proportion therefore as mind and heart are fixed on Christ, we may count on the Spirit's Presence and Power, but if we make the Holy Spirit Himself the object of our aspirations and worship, some false spirit may counterfeit the true and take us for a prey."*

The association which the correctly instructed Saint has with the Holy Spirit is in the form of a moment-by-moment conscious dependence upon Him, and trust in Him for His guidance and strength, and a yielding to Him for His Ministry of putting sin out of the life and keeping it out, and of radiating the beauty of the Lord Jesus through his every thought, word, and deed. This, together with a cooperation with Him, if carried out in this manner, takes the form of a mutual interest and active participation in the things of God.

G. D. Watson said this: *"The Holy Spirit will put a strict watch over you with a jealous love, and will rebuke you for little words and feelings,*

or for wasting your time, which other Christians never seem distressed over. So make up your mind that God is an infinite Sovereign, and has a right to do as He pleases with His Own.

"He may not explain to you a thousand things which puzzle your reason in His dealings with you, but if you absolutely sell yourself to be His love slave, He will wrap you up in a jealous love, and bestow upon you many blessings which come only to those who are in the inner circle."

He went on to say, *"Settle it forever, then, that you are to deal directly with the Holy Spirit, and that He is to have the privilege of tying your tongue or chaining your hand or closing your eyes, in ways that He does not seem to use with others. Now when you are so possessed with the Living God that you are, in your secret heart, pleased and delighted over this peculiar, personal, private, jealous guardianship and management of the Holy Spirit over your life, you will have found the vestibule of Heaven."*

CONTROLLED BY THE SPIRIT

The Believer is exhorted, *"Be filled with the Spirit"* (Eph. 5:18), or, as we have translated it, *"Be controlled by the Spirit."*

Thus, the expression, *"Filled with the Holy Spirit,"* speaks of the Spirit possessing the mind and heart of the Believer. This possession implies His control over that mind and heart. Thus the words, *"full"* and *"filled"* refer to the control which the Spirit exerts over the Believer who is said to be filled with Him. Thus the *"Spirit"* exerts the control.

We must not think of the Holy Spirit filling our hearts as water fills a bottle, or air a vacuum, or a bushel of oats an empty basket, etc. The heart of a Christian is not a receptacle to be emptied in order that the Holy Spirit may fill it. The Holy Spirit is not a substance to fill an empty receptacle. He is a Person to control another person, the Believer. He does not fill a Christian's life with Himself. He controls that person, or, rather, desires to do so!

The heart is a symbol used to refer to the passions. Thus, the Holy Spirit possesses or controls the volitional, rational, and emotional activities of the Believer who is said to be filled with Him. He brings all these into the place of obedience and conformity to the Word of God. Therefore, when we speak of a Christian filled with the Spirit, we are referring to the control which a Divine Person, the Holy Spirit, has over a human being, the Believer.

It is the business of the Holy Spirit, among other things, to maintain the actual experience of the Christian, which God did for him the moment He saved him. The Holy Spirit suppresses the activities of the evil nature whose power was broken, and produces His fruit in the life. The very fact that an individual is exhorted by the Spirit to do something, demands as a logical accompaniment, that person's exercise of his will in the doing of that thing. That is, the Believer here is not automatically controlled by the Spirit just because the Spirit indwells him. The control which the Spirit exerts over the Believer is dependent upon the Believer's active and correct adjustment to the Spirit. In other words, the Holy Spirit will never take control, He must be given control, and freely and willingly so.

As an example, the Lord Jesus did not save us until we recognized Him as the Saviour and put our trust in Him for Salvation. Just so, the Holy Spirit does not control us in the sense of permeating our will, reason, and emotions, until we recognize Him as the One Who has been sent by the Father to sanctify our lives, and trust Him to perform His Ministry in and through us.

There must be an ever-present conscious dependence upon and definite subjection to the Holy Spirit, a constant yielding to His Ministry and leaning upon Him for guidance and power, if He is to control the Believer in the most efficient manner and with the largest and best results. The Lord Jesus waited for you and me to recognize Him as Saviour before He saved us. The Holy Spirit indwelling a Believer, as well, is waiting to be recognized as the One to come to that Believer's aid.

Salvation is by Faith from start to finish. It is a Work of God for man. But God waits for man, unsaved or saved as the case might be, to avail himself of the Salvation he needs, by means of Faith. One of the reasons why the Holy Spirit has so little control over many Christians is because they think He works automatically in their hearts.

TWO REQUIREMENTS

Our Lord in John 7:37-38 lays down two simple requirements for the fullness of the

Spirit, a thirst for His control, and a trust in the Lord Jesus for the Spirit's control.

"If any man thirst," refers to a desire on the part of the Believer that the Holy Spirit be the One to control his every thought, word, and deed. We do not take a drink of water unless we are thirsty. We do not appropriate the control of the Spirit unless we desire Him to control us. A desire for His control will include, among other things, a desire that He call us to judge sin in our lives, a desire that He put sin out of our lives and keep it out, a desire that He separate us from all the ties we might have with the system of evil called the world, a desire that He dethrone our self-life and enthrone the Lord Jesus as absolute Lord and Master, a desire that He produce in us His Own fruit, a desire that He make us Christlike, a desire that He lead us and teach us.

Such a desire is a serious thing. It involves crucifixion of self, and self dies hard. The Spirit-controlled life is a crucified life.

The other requirement is trust. Our Lord said, *"He that believeth on Me, out from his inmost being shall flow rivers of Living Water."* The trust here in this context is not only trust in Him as Saviour, but trust in Him as the One Who fills with the Spirit. The Spirit-controlled life is a matter of trust. Salvation is by Faith. We receive our Justification by Faith. We are, as well, to receive our Sanctification by Faith. It is this constant desire for the Spirit's control and a trust in the Lord Jesus for the Spirit's control that result in the Spirit-controlled life. When one faces a new day, it is well to include in our prayers thanksgiving for the presence of the Holy Spirit in our hearts, the expression of our desire for His control, and a definite assertion of our trust in the Lord Jesus for the Spirit's control during that day.

It is well when we are faced with temptation, have a definite Christian service to perform, are in need of instruction from the Word, need strength for some duty to quietly recognize at intervals during the day the Ministry of the Spirit and depend upon Him for all needed guidance, wisdom, and strength. He is waiting for us to recognize Him and trust Him for His aid. He is there, the indwelling Spirit, always at the service of the Believer.

But the point is that He comes to our aid when we avail ourselves of His help. Therefore, there are just two things which the Believer must do in order to be controlled by the Spirit, desire that control and trust the Lord Jesus for that control.

The greatest need of the Church is the Holy Spirit, and that refers to Him working in the hearts and lives of Believers. He desires to control, lead, and guide, but cannot do so without our submission of self-will to His Will, and an ardent seeking of His leading, guidance, and direction. He can anoint us, lead us, guide us, direct us, help us, strengthen us, and instruct us, only as we allow Him control in our lives.

(Many of the thoughts on the Holy Spirit and His guidance were derived from material prepared by Dr. Kenneth Wuest.)

The phrase, *"And there shall meet you a man bearing a pitcher of water,"* was not as difficult as it might at first seem.

Inasmuch as Jerusalem was thronged with people, during the Passover time, it would seem that such a task might be impossible. However, the carrying of water was usually a woman's work, and was seldom done by men. Hence, a man carrying out this activity would be very noticeable.

As well, the words, *"Shall meet you,"* express a design by the Holy Spirit. In other words, the Holy Spirit told Jesus exactly what to do, and what to tell the Disciples to look for. As well, there seemed to be no further directions than, *"Go ye into the city."* Consequently, the Holy Spirit would bring about the meeting, which He did.

This example beautifully portrays the manner in which the Holy Spirit works. He very seldom gives total information, only part. We are expected to trust and believe that He will provide the balance as we proceed.

As an example, He told Samuel to go to the house of Jesse in order to anoint one of his sons as King. However, He did not tell him which son, inasmuch as Jesse had seven. Samuel was to trust the Lord for that information after he arrived, which he did, and which was ultimately given (I Sam. 16:1, 6-13).

Such teaches trust and dependence.

The words, *"Follow him,"* present another beautiful symbolism.

The entirety of this episode can serve as a beautiful example of that which Jesus does for the Believer. It is as follows:

NOTES

1. The Passover speaks of Salvation, and the sinner's acceptance of Christ as his Saviour.

2. Immediately upon finding Christ, the Lord *"sends"* the Believer to *"meet the Man bearing a pitcher of water,"* Who is a symbol of the Holy Spirit.

The last Words Jesus gave to His Disciples before His Ascension were, *"Wait for the Promise of the Father,"* . . . .

"Ye shall be Baptized with the Holy Ghost" (Acts 1:4-5).

In other words, these followers were not to go build Churches, witness, or do anything for the Lord until they were first Baptized in the Holy Spirit. That Command continues to be apropos unto this moment.

3. *"Follow Him"*: Once the Believer is Baptized in the Holy Spirit (Acts 2:4), the Spirit will then *"guide you into all Truth"* (Jn. 16:13). His business will be to *"glorify Me,"* i.e., Jesus.

4. *"He will show you a large upper room furnished"*: This *"upper room,"* spiritually speaking, to which the Holy Spirit will lead the trusting Believer, is thoroughly furnished with all the Believer needs pertaining to *"Life and Godliness"* (II Pet. 1:3-4).

5. *"And prepared"*: This means it is prepared by the Spirit, and not by man. This one word, *"prepared,"* is the bane of the modern Church. Instead of allowing the Holy Spirit to prepare, religious man attempts to prepare of his own abilities, which God cannot accept. Let Him *"prepare"* for us, and the preparation will be perfect.

6. *"And as they sat and did eat"*: This speaks of fellowship, not only with other Disciples, but, above all, with Jesus. While service for Him is definitely important, still, fellowship with Him is the most important. Without that fellowship, there can be no proper service.

(14) "AND WHERESOEVER HE SHALL GO IN, SAY YE TO THE GOODMAN OF THE HOUSE, THE MASTER SAITH, WHERE IS THE GUESTCHAMBER, WHERE I SHALL EAT THE PASSOVER WITH MY DISCIPLES?"

The phrase, *"And wheresoever he shall go in,"* is thought by some to have been the house of John whose surname was Mark, and the writer of the Gospel according to Mark.

Considering how large this room had to have been to accommodate Jesus and all the Disciples, John Mark must have been a man of some substance, if, in fact, it was his house.

The phrase, *"Say ye to the goodman of the house,"* referred to the owner, and, as stated, could have been John Mark.

The question, *"The Master saith, Where is the guestchamber, where I shall eat the Passover with My Disciples?"*, actually says, *"My guestchamber."* The indication is that there seems to have been some type of previous understanding between the Lord and the owner of this house, who undoubtedly was a follower of His.

What an honor to have had Jesus and His Disciples partake of the Last Supper in this house!

(15) "AND HE WILL SHEW YOU A LARGE UPPER ROOM FURNISHED AND PREPARED: THERE MAKE READY FOR US."

The phrase, *"And He will shew you a large upper room furnished and prepared,"* means that he himself (maybe Mark) personally conducted Peter and John to the room.

The room being *"furnished,"* means that it was in a state of readiness. It was furnished with carpets and hall couches around the table properly spread. The room was prepared for the eating of the Passover, speaking of the removal of all leaven, also possibly of the Master of the house sharing His Passover Lamb with our Lord and His Disciples, as the custom was in Israel in the case of small families.

The phrase, *"There make ready for us,"* has to do with the preparation of the Passover ingredients, as the room was already prepared.

(16) "AND HIS DISCIPLES WENT FORTH, AND CAME INTO THE CITY, AND FOUND AS HE HAD SAID UNTO THEM: AND THEY MADE READY THE PASSOVER."

The phrase, *"And His Disciples went forth, and came into the city,"* refers to Peter and John obeying the Lord implicitly.

The phrase, *"And found as He had said unto them,"* is a beautiful expression! Of all the countless things He has said to His many followers, everything has always been exactly as He said it would be.

Not one jot or tittle of inspired Prophecy has yet failed of literally thousands of details uttered even up to thousands of years before fulfillment (Dake). What a wonderful Lord we serve!

The phrase, *"And they made ready the Passover,"* meant that Peter and John took the Paschal Lamb to the Temple, where it was there killed, with the Priests officiating, with the

blood poured out at the base of the giant Brazen Altar.

The carcass of the Lamb would have then been brought back to this house, where it would have been roasted and prepared by the Disciples.

Actually, it was not supposed to be eaten until the next day. However, Christ had to partake of it a day early because He was to be on trial all night and was to be our Passover Sacrifice for us at the regular time the next afternoon (I Cor. 5:7).

Making ready and eating the Passover in this case had to be before the regular time. John 13:1 tells us that it was *"before the Feast of the Passover"* that Christ and His Disciples observed it.

They would have brought the Lamb to the house, and prepared the Unleavened Bread, the bitter herbs, the wine, and water for purification.

Exactly what Peter and John personally did in this case is not stated. However, they either prepared the Passover themselves or saw to it that it was done.

(17) "AND IN THE EVENING HE COMETH WITH THE TWELVE."

The *"evening"* mentioned here, as we have stated, referred to the same day. Because of His being arrested that night, and being unable to eat the Passover the next day when it was supposed to be observed, they would eat it a day early.

The phrase, *"He cometh with the Twelve,"* means that Peter and John went back to Bethany in order to inform Christ that all was ready. Then Jesus and the entirety of the Twelve, which included Judas, would come for the purpose of eating the Passover, i.e., *"The Last Supper."*

(18) "AND AS THEY SAT AND DID EAT, JESUS SAID, VERILY I SAY UNTO YOU, ONE OF YOU WHICH EATETH WITH ME SHALL BETRAY ME."

The phrase, *"And as they sat and did eat,"* refers, as is obvious, to the partaking of the Passover.

Of all the approximate 1600 years in which the Passover had been observed, this was the most important of all. As stated, Jesus would literally become the Passover, Who this solemn and beautiful Feast was meant to portray.

The phrase, *"Jesus said, Verily I say unto you, One of you which eateth with me shall betray Me,"* narrows down the prediction to the point where the traitor is said to be one of the Disciples.

The words, *"Eateth with Me,"* are not meant merely to point to the individual who would betray Christ, but to the enormity of the offense (Swete).

Partaking of food together, at least in those times, was of far greater consequence than presently. Then, and especially in the type of setting as the Last Supper, such fellowship denoted deep friendship. Actually, this very moment had been prophesied by David approximately one thousand years earlier: *"Yea, Mine Own familiar friend, in whom I trusted, which did eat of My bread, hath lifted up his heel against Me"* (Ps. 41:9). Actually, Jesus would quote this very verse in John 13:18.

It was at this time that Satan entered into Judas, and impelled him onwards to this terrible sin.

It was considered an act of utmost severity among Eastern nations of those days for one to do an evil deed against those who had given of such hospitality and friendship as Jesus.

(19) "AND THEY BEGAN TO BE SORROWFUL, AND TO SAY UNTO HIM ONE BY ONE, IS IT I? AND ANOTHER SAID, IS IT I?"

The phrase, *"And they began to be sorrowful,"* speaks of the opposite of that which this occasion, the Passover, should have enjoyed. It was normally a festive time, especially considering that it was to commemorate the great deliverance of the Children of Israel from Egyptian bondage. However, the Words of Christ cast a pall over the entire proceedings.

The phrase, *"And to say unto Him one by one,"* speaks of each understanding the significance of the accusation. It was a moment of heart searching for each.

The question one asked, *"Is it I? and another said, Is it I?"*, would have probably been better translated, *"It is not me, is it?"*, from each of them!

(20) "AND HE ANSWERED AND SAID UNTO THEM, IT IS ONE OF THE TWELVE, THAT DIPPETH WITH ME IN THE DISH."

The phrase, *"And He answered and said unto them,"* now presents a scenario of tremendous proportions. As we shall see, the Lord made every effort to appeal to Judas that he not do this thing, but to no avail!

The phrase, *"It is one of the Twelve, that dippeth with Me in the dish,"* little answered the question, because all of the Disciples were dipping with Him in the dish.

NOTES

The *"dish"* referred to a sauce made of dates, raisins, and vinegar, into which each dipped pieces of the unleavened bread with bitter herbs. As we have alluded to, this further statement is meant to point to the seriousness of the act of which Judas was even then contemplating.

Even though Mark does not take the situation further, John records that Peter hinted to John, who was *"reclining on Jesus' bosom,"* that he should ask Him to say definitely and by name who it was that should betray Him. Our Lord then said to John, *"He it is, to whom I shall give a sop, when I have dipped it"* (Jn. 13:23-26). The Lord then dipped the sop, and gave it to Judas Iscariot. That is when Jesus said unto him, *"That thou doest, do quickly"* (Jn. 13:27).

It was at that time that Satan entered into Judas, even though Satan had put it into his heart long before this. It was now that Judas repelled all efforts by Christ for him not to do this dastardly thing, which pushed him over the edge. Judas hardened his heart at the last appeal of Jesus, so now he was open for Satanic control.

Jesus, now knowing that Judas had submitted to Satan and that further appeal was useless, dismissed him for the work he was to do (Dake).

(21) "THE SON OF MAN INDEED GOETH, AS IT IS WRITTEN OF HIM: BUT WOE TO THAT MAN BY WHOM THE SON OF MAN IS BETRAYED! GOOD WERE IT FOR THAT MAN IF HE HAD NEVER BEEN BORN."

The phrase, *"The Son of Man indeed goeth, as it is written of Him,"* refers to Psalm 22 and Isaiah 51, as well as Genesis 3:15. Actually, the tenor of the entirety of the Old Testament points to Christ giving His Life as a ransom for many, even to which all the Sacrifices pointed. However, this predestined purpose of God did not make the guilt any the less of those who brought the Saviour to His Cross (Bickersteth).

The phrase, *"But woe to that man by whom the Son of Man is betrayed,"* does not present a *"woe"* of vindictiveness, or of the nature of a curse, but as Swete said, *"Reveals a misery which love itself could not prevent."*

The phrase, *"Good were it for that man if he had never been born,"* is one of the saddest pronouncements of doom in Scripture.

As we have alluded to, and Williams further says, *"Obedient to the Divine purpose,*

Christ must die as a Sacrifice for sin, but that necessity did not excuse the free agent who brought it about."

Bickersteth says, *"Existence is no blessing, but a curse, to him who consciously and willfully defeats the purpose of his existence."*

As the statement, *"Good were it for that man if he had never been born,"* was said of Judas, tragically, the same can be said for all of the human family who does not accept Christ as their Saviour.

The scenario of pointing out Judas as the one guilty of the betrayal, seems to have been done with only Judas fully hearing and understanding, at least at that moment, that it was him. Had the conversation and act been fully heard and understood by others, such as Peter and John, they might have risen at once to inflict vengeance upon the apostate traitor.

Many who hold to an erroneous concept of the Doctrine of Predestination, mistakenly think that Judas was predestined to do what he did, and, consequently, had no choice. However, this is incorrect. Judas did what he did of his own free will.

While it is true that Satan moved upon him regarding this evil, and, as well, the Holy Spirit through the Person of Christ moved upon him for the opposite effect, still, the choice alone belonged to Judas.

Many Believers misunderstand the foreknowledge of God for predestination. God foreknowing that Judas would do this thing, in no way meant that God forced this action. In other words, Judas was not elected by God to do this thing, as many suggest!

ELECTION

In Scripture, there is not the slightest reference to an election of God whereby one person is chosen to be saved and another is not. There is no teaching that a man is saved because of God's choice alone; there must also be the choice of the individual to meet God's terms of Salvation.

IT IS THE PLAN OF GOD THAT IS ELECTED

The Plan of God is elected, chosen, foreknown, and predestined — not the individual or national choice of man to conform to that Plan. In other words, it was the Plan of God that Jesus would die on Calvary; however, the individual

actors in this drama were not the Plan of God, but was of their own choice and making.

The Plan is the same for all alike; and everyone is invited, chosen, elected, foreknown, and predestined to Salvation, without exception, on the sole basis of the individual's choice and total conformity to the Gospel, to the end of life; otherwise, one will be lost, and there is no exception, nor can there be an exception to this, the Divine Plan.

GOD'S PART

God's part in Salvation for all men has been completed, and whosoever meets His terms will be saved. This means everyone, with no one previously elected to be saved or lost.

The whole program of Salvation is simply that of becoming born again — becoming a new creature in Christ (Mat. 18:3; Jn. 3:1-8, 14:18; II Cor. 5:17-18), and of living soberly, Righteously, and Godly in this present world (Gal. 5:18-21, 24; Tit. 2:11-14; I Jn. 1:7; 2:29; 3:5-10; 5:1-4, 18).

God has played His part respecting the Salvation Plan. It is *"Whosoever will"* (Rev. 22:17). The choice is left up to the individual.

ISRAEL AS AN ELECTED OR CHOSEN NATION

The word, *"election,"* as used in connection with Israel as a chosen nation (Isa. 45:4), simply means that God elected or predestined what this nation or people would be, respecting their purpose. It did not mean that all who were in this nation would be elected or predestined to Salvation. Actually, most Israelites died lost, even though their nation as a people was elected by God, and because they refused God's simple Plan of Salvation.

In turn, the Lord elected the Gentiles to take their place (Mat. 21:43; 23:37-39; Rom. 11:11-29).

In neither case was the election absolute. All was conditional as far as final Salvation was concerned. Nothing was by personal merit. All were called to blessings, which, if properly used, would lead them to personal and eternal Salvation.

That these blessings and even the calling and election of either class (Jews and Gentiles) could be abused, become finally useless and forfeited by them, is clear from the state of the Jews, who, after being the elect for approximately

2,300 years, were now rejected and reprobate (Rom. 11).

JACOB OVER ESAU

In Romans 9, Paul deals with the choice of God in Jacob over Esau. However, it is clear that all such individual choices of God are based upon the disposition and attitude of the individual in conforming to Him and His Will. Not even Jacob would have been chosen if he had behaved as Esau toward God.

One becomes a special subject of God's dealings when he chooses to be and as long as he chooses to be. But if one rebels against the choice all must make to be saved, no benefits of the election of God can be made manifest to him.

These simple facts should answer all questions on election, predestination, foreknowledge, and like subjects. Truly God is just and the justifier of him that believeth, and the Judge of him that believeth not, as stated in Scripture (Mat. 16:15-16; Lk. 13:1-5; Jn. 3:16-18; I Tim. 2:4-5; II Pet. 3:9; Rev. 22:17) (Dake).

(22) "AND AS THEY DID EAT, JESUS TOOK BREAD, AND BLESSED, AND BRAKE IT, AND GAVE TO THEM, AND SAID, TAKE, EAT: THIS IS MY BODY."

The phrase, *"And as they did eat,"* pertained to the Passover, but out of this was instituted that which we know as the *"Lord's Supper."*

Up to this point in the Paschal meal, only unleavened cakes and bitter herbs, along with the sauce, as mentioned, were consumed. The Lamb would be reserved for the end. However, at this Passover, and as we have stated, the Lord would use the ingredients of the *"Bread,"* and the *"Cup,"* to institute the *"Lord's Supper,"* which is sacred to the Church. The meaning of both, the Passover and the Supper, is similar, but yet totally different.

The *"Passover"* represented something which was to come, and the *"Supper"* represents something which has already come, namely Christ. The *"Passover"* represented a work not yet finished, while the *"Supper"* represents a work completely finished.

The phrase, *"Jesus took bread, and blessed, and brake it, and gave to them,"* represents the first step in the *"Lord's Supper,"* and pertains to His Body.

Once again, the order is maintained even as Jesus multiplied the loaves and the fishes,

which, in a sense, was a type of Christ being given to the world (Mk. 6:41; 8:6). The order is as follows:

1. *"Jesus took bread"*: As He stated, this represents His Body, which was offered at Calvary's Cross for the Redemption of humanity.

As well, it represents the Believer who comes to Christ.

2. *"And blessed"*: Jesus' offering of Himself for the Salvation of humanity was *"blessed"* by God.

As well, once the sinner comes to Christ, he, likewise, is *"blessed"* by the Lord in many and varied ways.

3. *"And brake it"*: However, for Jesus to be a blessing, His Body must be broken, as it was at Calvary.

Likewise, for the Believer to be a blessing, the self life must be *"broken"* in order that it become Christlike. This is what Jesus was speaking of when He gave the Command to *"Take up his Cross and follow Me"* (Mk. 8:34-35). Many Believers want only the *"blessing"* and not the *"breaking"*; however, if we are to be a blessing to others, as Christ, we must be *"broken."* It is not something that is done easily or quickly.

4. *"And gave to them"*: Jesus, before Calvary could not save anyone except by Faith in that which was to come, namely His Death and Resurrection. Even though the Incarnation was necessary, still, it did not within itself save anyone. Likewise, the miracles, etc.

Unfortunately, much of the modern Church is attempting to give to the world the Miracles of Christ, etc. It is only the Crucified Christ Who will save. That is the reason Paul said, *"I determined not to know anything among you, save Jesus Christ, and Him crucified"* (I Cor. 2:2).

Even though all the other things are very important, still, we must never forget, it is only the Crucified Christ Who saves!

Likewise, far too many Believers are attempting to give themselves to the world instead of Christ. It is only Christ within us which can accomplish the desired task.

The phrase, *"And said, Take, eat: this is My Body,"* is said in the same sense that Jesus said, *"I am the door of the sheep"* (Jn. 10:7). He did not mean that He was the literal, actual door or gate of the sheepfold, but that He, as Saviour, constituted the way whereby a sinner could enter into Salvation. Just as the actual sheep gate pictured, illustrated, and symbolized our Lord in His position and work as Saviour, so the bread symbolized Him as the spiritual nourishment upon which a sinner may feed and have eternal life (Wuest).

Salvation is a gift. Hence the word *"take."*

As well, the word, *"is,"* means *"represents."*

(For a full Commentary on the erroneous conclusion of the Catholic Church regarding the Mass, or what we refer to as the *"Lord's Supper,"* please see the Jimmy Swaggart Bible Commentary, Vol. VII - Matthew, Chpt. 26.)

(23) "AND HE TOOK THE CUP, AND WHEN HE HAD GIVEN THANKS, HE GAVE IT TO THEM: AND THEY ALL DRANK OF IT."

The phrase, *"And He took the cup,"* probably represents the third cup, of which the Talmud says four cups were consumed during the Paschal Feast. The third was known as the *"cup of blessing,"* which adequately described that which the Lord would do for the human family at Calvary.

The phrase, *"And when He had given thanks, He gave it to them,"* proclaims two extremely important attributes of Christ. They are as follows:

1. He lived a life of perpetual thanksgiving to the Lord, as is epitomized in the last five Psalms. Even though He was facing Calvary with all its darkness, still, He was thanking the Lord that He had the privilege to do this for humanity, even though humanity loved Him not at all. However, His thanksgiving and praise had nothing to do with the attitude of those for whom He was dying, but, instead, was centered in the Will of God. What a lesson for us!

If one is in the Will of God, such is the highest attainment of life. It gives occasion for all Praise and Thanksgiving. Everything else is of small consequence.

2. His life which was poured out for humanity, and typified by the *"Cup,"* was done for others, hence, *"Gave it to them."* Inasmuch as it is freely given, it is to be freely received.

The phrase, *"And they all drank of it,"* signifies the shedding of the Saviour's Blood at Calvary, and that which it afforded, Eternal Life being granted to the one who takes Christ as his Saviour.

The *"eating"* of the *"Bread"* signifying His Body offered in Sacrifice, and the *"drinking"* of His *"Blood,"* which signified His Life being

NOTES

poured out in that Sacrifice, is a perfect portrayal of accepting Christ, and a fulfillment of John 6:54.

Salvation is not a ceremony, creed, dogma, theory, Church or philosophy. It is rather a Person, and more particularly a Man, *"The Man, Jesus Christ."*

Millions desire to accept Him as a good Man, but not as the Son of God, and, consequently, the Saviour. However, unless He is accepted as the Saviour, He cannot be accepted as anything. The born-again experience is totally unlike anything else in which man engages. It is a Work of the Spirit, with man furnishing only the small amount of Faith given to him by God, with the Lord doing everything else (Jn. 3:16). This is what Jesus was speaking of when He said, *"At that day ye shall know that I am in My Father, and ye in Me, and I in you"* (Jn. 14:20). Someone has rightly called it, *"The Divine Entanglement."*

As well, *"They all drank of it,"* and not just the Priests as maintained by the Catholic Church.

(24) "AND HE SAID UNTO THEM, THIS IS MY BLOOD OF THE NEW TESTAMENT, WHICH IS SHED FOR MANY."

The phrase, *"And He said unto them, This is My Blood of the New Testament,"* speaks of the New Covenant and the Sacrifice of our Lord on the Cross, and the New Covenant.

The First Testament was spoken of as the Old Testament, and referred to the system of symbolic Sacrifices known as the Levitical economy (Heb. 8:7).

As well, as the Bread, it was not literally His Blood, but symbolic of His Blood. As the Lamb, symbolic of Christ, did not turn into the literal Body of Christ under the Old Covenant, likewise, the Bread and Grape Juice do not turn into the literal Body and Blood of Christ, as claimed by the Catholic Church.

The phrase, *"Which is shed for many,"* refers to the whole world, and for all time, which is *"many."*

In effect, the *"Lord's Supper"* is symbolic of the Covenant cut at Calvary. This New Covenant (Testament), was cut between God and man, exactly as the Covenants of old, but with one major difference. Jesus Christ was both <u>God</u> and <u>Man</u>, and, therefore, produced a Covenant unlike the First Covenant, which (the New Covenant) cannot fail. He, as God, spilled His Blood, for *"God was in Christ, reconciling the world unto Himself, not imputing their trespasses unto them; and hath committed unto us the Word of Reconciliation"* (II Cor. 5:19).

As well, Jesus was the Substitute Man, Who did all the things that God demanded that man do, but was never able to do. In Christ it was all done. He is our Substitute, and, consequently, when we identify with Him, we become everything He is. Paul called it *"Joint-heirs with Christ"* (Rom. 8:17).

(25) "VERILY I SAY UNTO YOU, I WILL DRINK NO MORE OF THE FRUIT OF THE VINE, UNTIL THAT DAY THAT I DRINK IT NEW IN THE KINGDOM OF GOD."

The phrase, *"Verily I say unto you,"* is meant to portray several things:

1. *"I will drink no more of the fruit of the vine"*: After saying *"This is My Blood,"* He now says it is *"the fruit of the vine,"* proclaiming that it was not literal Blood, and neither does it turn into literal Blood, as claimed by the Catholics in the Doctrine of Transubstantiation.

As well, the words, *"No more,"* speak of the one Sacrifice of Christ at Calvary, performing and accomplishing all that was needed for the Salvation of mankind. No repeat performance is needed or necessary.

2. *"Until that day"*: This refers to His Second Coming.

3. *"That I drink it new"*: The word, *"new,"* does not refer to time, but *"new"* as to quality. His drinking it at that time, simply refers to His Personal Presence, and not that Calvary is needed all over again.

4. *"In the Kingdom of God"*: This refers to the coming Millennial Kingdom which will begin at the Second Coming, when the Messiah and His cleansed and restored Israel will drink in a new and glorious way, the fruit of the mystical Vine (Jn. 15:1) in the worldwide Kingdom where He will reign as a King upon the Throne of His Father David.

In respect to this coming time, the Holy Spirit through the Apostle Paul said, *"For as often as ye eat this bread, and drink this cup, ye do shew the Lord's Death till He come"* (I Cor. 11:26).

(26) "AND WHEN THEY HAD SUNG AN HYMN, THEY WENT OUT INTO THE MOUNT OF OLIVES."

The phrase, *"And when they had sung an hymn,"* refers, no doubt, to Psalm 118.

When we read this Psalm, it gives it an added preciousness to the heart to know that the Lord and His Disciples sang this immediately before setting out for Gethsemane. As the True Israel He could perfectly sing it, and as the High Priest of His people thus express His Faith in her Faith, and make real and bring near the joys of the morning, which are predicted to follow the sorrows of that dark night and the afflictions of Jacob's long exile.

As well, this Song will be sung by Israel on the happy morning of her renewed espousal, as Jesus alluded to in the previous verse.

In Psalm 117, Israel will invite the nations of the world to trust Jehovah and to praise Him. She will testify that the Messiah is her One and Efficient Saviour. In Psalm 118 that Praise is offered.

The phrase, *"They went out into the Mount of Olives,"* refers to the moment of His betrayal being carried out. His hour had come, so He voluntarily put Himself in the way of the traitor (Jn. 18:2). There is no evidence at all that the Disciples had any idea what awaited them that night. The things Jesus will say, as outlined in the following verses, and Peter's answer (vs. 29), portray their spiritual insensitivity.

(27) "AND JESUS SAITH UNTO THEM, ALL YE SHALL BE OFFENDED BECAUSE OF ME THIS NIGHT: FOR IT IS WRITTEN, I WILL SMITE THE SHEPHERD, AND THE SHEEP SHALL BE SCATTERED."

The phrase, *"And Jesus saith unto them,"* is to be an announcement the Disciples do not desire to hear, and actually do not believe.

The phrase, *"All ye shall be offended because of Me this night,"* referred to His betrayal, and subsequent arrest by the Romans.

The word, *"offended,"* in the Greek is *"skandalizo,"* and means *"to find occasion of stumbling,"* or *"to see in another what is disapproving and what hinders one from acknowledging authority."*

The Disciples deserted their Lord and fled. This was their act of stumbling. The occasion for their stumbling was in the fact that our Lord's arrest and treatment by Rome might involve them in the same kind of treatment. In other words, they were out to save themselves (Wuest).

However, the tone of the announcement of the desertion by the Disciples was not made by Christ as a reproach, nor intended as such, but is intended to point to a better moment when their Faith would return.

The phrase, *"For it is written, I will smite the shepherd, and the sheep shall be scattered,"* is quoted from Zechariah 13:7. Even though Israel and the Romans were the instruments, still, the Hand was God's. At the same time, this does not mean, as we have already stated, that they were destined to do this, but that God will use their wicked desires to carry out His Plan.

The *"sheep"* being scattered, proclaims a weakening of their Faith. They felt doubtful for the moment whether He was indeed the Son of God. *"They trusted that it was He Who should redeem Israel,"* but now saw that such would not be, at least in the manner in which they had thought, with their hopes giving way to fear and doubt.

The word, *"scattered,"* describes it perfectly, with Peter and John coming to the empty tomb on the testimony of Mary Magdalene, with the other Disciples elsewhere. As well, He appeared unto the Ten without Thomas (Jn. 20:19-24). However, they were not to remain *"scattered"* very long.

(28) "BUT AFTER THAT I AM RISEN, I WILL GO BEFORE YOU INTO GALILEE."

The phrase, *"But after that I am risen,"* although a startling and glorious announcement, still, fell on deaf ears. His Death was so horrible that not one single Disciple remembered these words, or else failed to believe them.

The phrase, *"I will go before you into Galilee,"* was fulfilled as recorded in John 21:1. However, there were first two other appearances in Jerusalem, the first being to the Ten, which was without Thomas, and the second appearance being to the Eleven (Jn. 20:19-24, 26).

(29) "BUT PETER SAID UNTO HIM, ALTHOUGH ALL SHALL BE OFFENDED, YET WILL NOT I."

The phrase, *"But Peter said unto Him,"* portrays, as we shall see, a disavowal of what Christ has just said respecting *"All being offended."* After three and a half years of walking by the side of Christ, Peter should have known that whatever Jesus said was going to happen would, and exactly as He had said it. But he, as we, was slow to learn!

The phrase, *"Although all shall be offended, yet will not I,"* constitutes presumption on his part, and an insult toward the others.

Peter's statement contains the idea that he felt the other Disciples most probably would stumble, but he considered himself to be far above them, and, therefore, above such weakness.

His answer, if anything at all, should have been, *"I know that through my own infirmity this may easily happen. Nevertheless, I trust to Thy mercy and goodness to save me"* (Bickersteth).

Bickersteth further said, *"The true remedy against temptation is the consciousness of our own weakness, and supplication for Divine strength."*

As well, all who would read these words as uttered by Peter, and, consequently, think lightly of him in your heart, such attitude proclaims a moral weakness even greater than that shown by the fisherman.

We often think that we are strong in Faith, strong in purity, strong in patience. But when temptation arises, we often falter and fall.

Many who criticize Peter have never faced the onslaught of Satan as faced by Peter. In Truth, most who criticize, at least in this capacity, have never faced the same type of oppression. The few who have faced such, and come out victorious, have no criticism whatsoever. Many years ago the following statement was made in a particular sermon:

1. Upon hearing that a Brother or Sister in the Lord has failed, one should realize they are hearing gossip, and treat it accordingly. An accusation should not be received against an Elder, but before two or three witnesses (I Tim. 5:19).

2. If, in fact, one feels that they do have inside information respecting a failure by a fellow Christian, still, they have little or no knowledge of the spiritual warfare involved.

3. If placed in the same circumstances, as the one who failed, would we do any better, or even as well?

(30) "AND JESUS SAITH UNTO HIM, VERILY I SAY UNTO THEE, THAT THIS DAY, EVEN IN THIS NIGHT, BEFORE THE COCK CROW TWICE, THOU SHALT DENY ME THRICE."

The phrase, *"And Jesus saith unto him, Verily I say unto thee,"* is meant to proclaim a very solemn announcement.

The phrase, *"That this day, even in this night,"* means that Peter would not even have the strength to last out the night. Consequently, and despite what he thought, his strength was small.

The phrase, *"Thou shalt deny Me thrice,"* speaks of three times. In other words, Peter would deny Christ, not once, but again, and again, and again.

At the very time he thought he was so very strong, in fact, he was so very weak.

It is regrettable, but the far greater majority of the modern Church think of themselves as Peter first thought of himself. And how do I know that?

The modern Church would not be so critical, as Peter was at first, if it did not think of itself so very highly. As stated, Peter not only boasted of his own strength, but, as well, criticized the small strength, at least as he saw it in the remaining Ten. However, most boasting is done in this manner. The putting down of someone else, somehow makes us feel superior.

(31) "BUT HE SPAKE THE MORE VEHEMENTLY, IF I SHOULD DIE WITH THEE, I WILL NOT DENY THEE IN ANY WISE. LIKEWISE ALSO SAID THEY ALL."

The phrase, *"But he spake the more vehemently,"* has a double meaning: A. He kept on speaking, disavowing that he would ever fail Christ; and, B. He said it strongly, and loudly, as well as repeatedly!

The phrase, *"If I should die with Thee, I will not deny Thee in any wise,"* was uttered before all the other Disciples, as well as Christ.

Hilary says respecting this statement of Peter, *"Peter was so carried away by the fervor of his zeal and love for Christ, that he regarded neither the weakness of his own flesh nor the truth of his Master's word."* An emphatic denial will turn into an emphatic failure.

The words, *"any wise,"* mean that whatever happens, even to the forfeiting of his life, he will not deny Christ. However, his strength was so small that he began to deny long before his life was even thought of being threatened. He never made it past the little servant girl, much less the Sanhedrin or Romans (vs. 66).

The phrase, *"Likewise also said they all,"* proclaims the other Disciples being carried forth by Peter's bold declaration, with them joining their voices.

All of them minutes before had heard Jesus state that *"All would be offended because of Me this night."* He even quoted the Prophecy as given by the Holy Spirit through the Prophet Zechariah, proclaiming what they would do,

NOTES

but still they denied it. How so typical of most of us.

When we should be on our knees crying to God for strength, instead, we are boldly proclaiming what we will or won't do.

The modern Faith Message, which, in reality, is no Faith at all, perhaps fosters this presumptuous spirit more so than anything else. To admit that one is weak and must have the help and strength of the Lord, is considered a bad confession. However, the so-called *"good confession"* too often proclaims not the Strength of Christ, but, more so the spiritual ignorance of the individual.

While a *"good confession"* is certainly important, still, we must be very careful that we see ourselves as we really are, thereby extolling the Power and Strength of Christ.

(32) "AND THEY CAME TO A PLACE WHICH WAS NAMED GETHSEMANE: AND HE SAITH TO HIS DISCIPLES, SIT YE HERE, WHILE I SHALL PRAY."

The phrase, *"And they came to a place which was named Gethsemane,"* spoke of a Garden at the foot of the Mount of Olives. John called it a Garden, or Orchard (Jn. 18:1).

The word, *"Gethsemane,"* means literally *"The place of the olive-press."* This was the place where the olives were brought, in order that the oil contained in them might be pressed out. As well, Gethsemane would *"press out"* the self-will of the Disciples, or at least would begin the process. Sooner or later every Believer comes to Gethsemane. The conclusion of its effect is that we might say as Christ, *"Not my will, but Thine, be done"* (Lk. 22:42).

The phrase, *"And He saith to His Disciples, Sit ye here, while I shall pray,"* proclaims the prescription for every other Believer as well!

It is sad, that much of the modern Church for such a time recommends the services of the psychologist. Much of the remaining Church claims that if a proper confession is maintained, there will never be a Gethsemane.

Precious few recommend prayer, as the Holy Spirit did to Jesus. James said, *"Is any among you afflicted? Let him pray"* (James 5:13).

(33) "AND HE TAKETH WITH HIM PETER AND JAMES AND JOHN, AND BEGAN TO BE SORE AMAZED, AND TO BE VERY HEAVY;"

The phrase, *"And He taketh with Him Peter and James and John,"* proclaims the third time such a thing was done, in reference to the other Disciples.

1. First of all, these Three witnessed the Power of Christ when He raised the daughter of Jairus from the dead (Mk. 5:37-43).

2. These Three were chosen to witness the Transfiguration of Christ, thereby, witnessing His Glory (Mk. 9:1-10).

3. Last of all, these Three witnessed His passion, and therefore His sufferings (Mk. 14:32-42).

Some have claimed that the Three Disciples here chosen, had been fortified to endure the sight of the passion of Christ by the glories of the Transfiguration. It is suggested that it would have been too much for the Faith of the others. But these Three witnessed it that they might learn themselves and be able to teach others that the way to Glory is by Suffering (Bickersteth).

Regarding the phrase, *"And began to be sore amazed,"* the Greek word for *"sore amazed"* is *"ekthambeo,"* and means, *"to throw into terror, alarm, and distress."*

Swete says: *"The Lord was overwhelmed with sorrow, but His first feeling was one of terrified surprise. His forseeing the passion was one thing, but when it came clearly into view, its terrors exceeded His anticipations. This is when Hebrews 5:7 and 8 were fulfilled."*

This means He learned upon the basis of the things He suffered, and the last lesson of obedience began with a sensation of inconceivable awe.

The phrase, *"And to be very heavy,"* in the Greek is *"ademoneo,"* and means, *"an experience of which one is not familiar, and which one does not feel at home, that is, at rest, and which distresses him."*

Dake asks the question what it was that affected Christ so dramatically?

"Was it," he asked, *"the concentration of the Satanic forces to kill Him before He could get to the Cross, thus to avert their own defeat in the Cross?"* (Col. 2:14-17; I Pet. 2:24).

Or, *"Is not this the cup into which He looked, and saw a greater degree of vileness than He had anticipated?"* (Mat. 20:22-23).

(34) "AND SAITH UNTO THEM, MY SOUL IS EXCEEDING SORROWFUL UNTO DEATH: TARRY YE HERE, AND WATCH."

The phrase, *"And saith unto them,"* has to do with Peter, James, and John. They were

called upon to witness His sufferings, even though at the time, they little understood it, if at all!

The phrase, *"My soul is exceeding sorrowful unto death,"* means that grief so overwhelmed Him, that He was close to dying. In fact, Satan definitely tried to kill Him at this time!

That which caused this had to be *"this Cup,"* which He spoke of in verse 36. What *"this Cup"* contained was horrible beyond belief.

First of all, He Who knew no sin, would be forced to take upon Himself the penalty for every sin that had ever been committed, and would be committed. This was the judgment and anger of God which would smite Him, instead of us (Isa. 53:4).

As well, and even worse, during this time He would be separated from the Father. This agony is described in Psalm 22.

Consequently, there is no way that mere human mortals could ever begin to realize the extent of the price that was paid for our Redemption. Into this *"price"* it is possible for man to go so far, and no further! The full brunt of what He suffered will never be known or understood by the human heart and mind. We can only surmise, and even then, the greatest stretch of our imagination cannot begin to encompass what He did, and, in effect, had to do to bring about our Redemption.

The phrase, *"Tarry ye here, and watch,"* was addressed, as stated at the beginning, to Peter, James, and John.

Of this third expression, which was suffering, it is my personal belief that these Three learned more at this time than the other two times combined. The lessons of all the experiences would never be lost upon them, but, even more so, what they witnessed in Gethsemane, no other human mortals have ever witnessed.

They saw a side of Christ that they did not know existed. As well, they were taken to a depth of human suffering, at least as far as observation was concerned, that no one else has ever experienced.

What were their thoughts at this particular time? Or were they even able to half way comprehend what they were seeing?

I think not, and neither could we! They saw it, but they did not understand it. In fact, they could not understand it, at least at this time!

Quite possibly, at a later time, the Holy Spirit

helped them to more fully grasp what they had seen and experienced.

Why these Three, and not the others?

The only answer that could be given, is that He undoubtedly saw a degree of hunger in their hearts for God that the others did not quite possess, and that despite their present weaknesses. The Lord never looks at us as we are, but, instead, as to what He can make of us, at least if the desire is present in the soul.

Peter would ultimately be the spokesman for the Early Church, at least in its beginning stages, and would be mightily used of God. He would write two of the Epistles in the New Testament.

John would outlive any of the Apostles, and would write five Books in the New Testament, with the depth of his writing reaching a level that is truly beyond comprehension. In the Book of Revelation, which would close out the Canon of Scripture, He would be given the greatest Revelation of all.

Not much is known about James, even though he was one of the chosen Three. He was martyred about ten or eleven years after the Day of Pentecost (Acts 12:1-2). He was the brother of John.

(35) "AND HE WENT FORWARD A LITTLE, AND FELL ON THE GROUND, AND PRAYED THAT, IF IT WERE POSSIBLE, THE HOUR MIGHT PASS FROM HIM."

The phrase, *"And He went forward a little, and fell on the ground,"* actually means in the Greek Text that He fell on the ground repeatedly. In other words, He would fall, arise, and then fall again. More than anything else, this portrays the desperation of the struggle in which our Lord was engaged at the time. Quite possibly it was at this time that, as Luke reported it, *"His sweat was as it were great drops of blood falling down to the ground"*(Lk. 22:44).

It is medically known, that under extreme mental pressure the pores may become so dilated that blood may issue from them, producing a bloody sweat.

As well, even though the Disciples a little later are shown sleeping, the indication is that they were eyewitnesses of these happenings.

The phrase, *"And prayed that, if it were possible, the hour might pass from Him,"* as well, means that He continued to pray and put forth this same petition, saying it over and over.

NOTES

The *"hour"* spoken of here pertains to the Cross and His terrible death in this fashion, which pertained to the bearing of the sin of the world. Even though He had looked ahead to this hour (Jn. 2:4; 7:30; 8:20; 12:23, 27; 13:1), still, as it now drew near, the horror of it, along with the terrible opposition by Satanic powers produced an oppression, or spectacle, if you will, such as no human being has ever had to face.

Him going *"forward,"* means that this action probably took place about a hundred feet from the three Disciples.

(36) "AND HE SAID, ABBA, FATHER, ALL THINGS ARE POSSIBLE UNTO THEE; TAKE AWAY THIS CUP FROM ME: NEVERTHELESS NOT WHAT I WILL, BUT WHAT THOU WILT."

The phrase, *"And He said, Abba Father,"* is actually the expression of two languages. Some feel that Mark only added the word *"Father"* which was in the Greek, with Jesus using the Aramaic word, *"Abba,"* which actually means *"Father."* However, it is far more natural to conclude that Mark is taking his narrative from an eye and ear witness, Peter, and that both the words were uttered by him; so that He thus in His agony cried to God in the name of the whole human family, the Jew first, and also the Gentile (Bickersteth).

As well, the address to the Heavenly Father, as used by Christ, portrays a relationship which no one else has, or, in fact, could have! Actually, it seems this relationship between the Father and the Son even deepens at this terrible time of suffering, if, in fact, it was possible to deepen more than it already was!

Consequently, this tells us that our relationship with the Heavenly Father cannot be deepened except through suffering. No doubt this was the major lesson, among others, that was taught to Peter, James, and John.

While it is certainly true that no one desires suffering for the sake of suffering, but still, if one truly takes up the Cross, and, thereby, truly follows Christ, the suffering definitely will come. Unfortunately, great segments of the modern Church have attempted to eliminate this part of the Christian experience, claiming that inasmuch as Christ suffered, we do not have to suffer. However, while it is certainly true that none of us will ever have to suffer as Christ suffered, still, this part of the Christian walk is not deleted, and, in fact, should not be deleted. It, and it alone, deepens the relationship. Paul said, *"If so be that we suffer with Him, that we may be also glorified together"* (Rom. 8:17; I Cor. 4:12; Gal. 5:11; 6:12; Phil. 1:29; I Tim. 4:10; II Tim. 2:12; 3:12; Heb. 11:25).

The phrase, *"All things are possible unto Thee,"* tells us that God being Omnipotent and Omniscient could have affected the Salvation and Redemption of humanity in another way. Such was possible! But such was not His Will!

The phrase, *"Take away this cup from Me,"* refers to the lot or portion, whether good or evil, which is appointed for us by God. In the case of Christ, it was a bitter cup, from which He naturally and sinlessly shrank. Wuest says, *"If He had not offered this petition, He would not have been Who and What He was."*

One of them was to be made sin, to be charged by the High Court of Heaven with the guilt of all human sin. From that, the Holy Son of God drew back with all the infinite hatred of sin that was His. Knowing that sin was the cause of all the hurt and harm in the creation of God, the horror of it overwhelmed Him, as it should have.

The other was the agony of being deprived of the fellowship of the Father from 9 o'clock in the morning to 3 in the afternoon (Ps. 22:1-2). The fellowship between Father and Son had had no beginning. Wuest further said, *"For a sinner who has never known the bliss of the Father's fellowship, to be deprived of it all through eternity, is bad enough. But for the Holy Son of God Who knew nothing else up to that moment, the loss of that fellowship meant infinite suffering."*

To most, even Believers, the loss of six hours of fellowship may not seem like a large thing. However, only spiritual ignorance would think such a thing.

Even though the relationship with the Heavenly Father by the Believer is of necessity far less than between Jesus and His Father, still, for the Believer to have to do without the Presence of God even for a minute, is an appalling thought. The Lord is everything to us, and in every capacity. Even the weakest Believer enjoys a relationship that is supernatural to say the least. The longer one lives for the Lord, the deeper that relationship becomes. Consequently, to view it in that light, lets us know

the horror that overwhelmed Christ by that relationship being broken. Even though it was only approximately six hours, still, the horror of that filled Christ with revulsion, which is understandable once we comprehend the seriousness of the matter.

The phrase, *"Nevertheless not what I will, but what Thou wilt,"* proclaims far more than the acquiescence of Christ to the Will of God, but, instead, proclaims the principle of Faith for all Believers. His Will was subject to the Will of the Father, as our wills must be subject.

In this one Passage is found the cause of all spiritual declension, disobedience, suffering, problems, etc., experienced by the Believer. It is God's Will versus our will.

Even though it was possible for the Heavenly Father to have carried out Redemption in another fashion, still, it was not His Will to do so. This way was the best way, and it was the business of Christ, as He wondrously did, to acquiesce His Will to the Father's Will.

Most, if not all, Believers would automatically agree with the statements I have just made. However, the great error is in erroneously interpreting the Will of God. The modern Faith teaching, which, in reality, is precious little Faith at all, claims for the most part a life free of disturbances, hindrances, and difficulties, at least if one has the proper Faith and Confession. Such teaching is attractive, and draws many adherents. There aren't many who desire a Gethsemane, and, in Truth, no one would desire such. However, one must understand the certitude of a personal Gethsemane, at least in a limited way, that is, if we are to be what we should be in Christ.

Some time back, I was listening to the News, and heard the announcer say that Tommy Dorsey had died the day before. He also mentioned that Thurgood Marshall had passed away on the same day. Mr. Marshall was the first Black to grace the august Supreme Court of the United States.

The man went on to say that Mr. Marshall had influenced America. But then he said, *"Tommy Dorsey influenced the world."*

What did he mean?

Tommy Dorsey wrote many songs for the Cause of Christ. However, one stands out, and it was that song of which the announcer spoke. The song was, *"Take my hand precious Lord, and lead me on.*" That one song has blessed the world.

Tommy Dorsey lost his wife and six children in a fire. He was away preaching a meeting in a distant city when he received the news.

Is it possible to imagine how one would feel in being given this type of message?

Out of that trial and heartache came the song, *"Take my hand precious Lord, and lead me on."*

Most, if not all, that truly blesses the world in Christ, comes out of a Gethsemane. I think this is evident in the Word of God from Genesis to Revelation.

It is not that the suffering itself, and of whatever direction it may take, has any special cleansing or redemptive power, for it doesn't! What it does do is to drive a person to their knees, and, thereby, closer to God. Then the work that Christ desires can be accomplished in our hearts and lives, out of which comes the Blessing.

Perhaps David said it best when he said, *"Neither will I offer Burnt Offerings unto the Lord my God of that which doth cost me nothing"* (II Sam. 24:24).

(37) "AND HE COMETH, AND FINDETH THEM SLEEPING, AND SAITH UNTO PETER, SIMON, SLEEPEST THOU? COULDEST NOT THOU WATCH ONE HOUR?"

The phrase, *"And He cometh, and findeth them sleeping,"* presents, as Luke explained it, a sleep resulting from the exhaustion produced by their deepening realization of what was really happening all around them — that Jesus was really going to die (Lk. 22:45).

The question, *"And saith unto Peter, Simon, sleepest thou?"*, presents Jesus addressing Peter by his old name. Wuest says, *"For the time he is 'Peter' no more; the new character which he owes to association with Jesus is in abeyance. He who was ready to die with the Master has been proved not to possess the strength of will requisite for resisting sleep during the third part of a single watch"* (Wuest).

The question, *"Couldest not thou watch one hour?"*, pertains to the struggle between the flesh and the spirit.

Swete explains the flesh here as follows: *"The flesh is man as belonging to the sphere of the material life, under the limitations of a corporeal nature, frail, mortal, and, in fact, impure"* (Gen. 6:12). The spirit he explains as the *"vital force* (Gen. 6:17), *which in man is directly*

dependent on the Spirit of God (Gen. 2:7), *and the organ of communication with God and the spiritual world."*

THE FLESH AS EXPLAINED BY THE APOSTLE PAUL

In Paul's Epistles, a number of Passages expand implications of the Old Testament view of human nature expressed regarding the *"flesh."* According to Paul, human nature is not just frail and weak; human nature is also twisted and tangled. Human perspectives, human understanding, and human efforts are actually hostile to the perspective, understanding, and Plan of God. In other words, we are morally inadequate, and we are driven toward rebellion.

The contrasts are drawn between human powers, perspectives, and abilities and the powers, perspectives, and abilities of God, most importantly His ability to enable people to do His Will.

The whole of human nature, not merely a *"part"* of human beings, is in view when Scripture uses *"flesh"* in a moral or theological sense to make statements about human nature.

ISOLATION FROM GOD

The Scripture presents human beings in isolation from God. Human beings are cut off from the Lord, because they are morally inadequate (Rom. 6:19; 7:7-11, 15-20; 8:3). To live according to the *"flesh"* is completely different from living according to God's Spirit (Rom. 8:4-13; Gal. 5:16-26).

Apart from God, humanity is characterized by a complex web of thoughts, desires, values, and actions that are in opposition to God's intended pattern for us. This is what is meant by the *"flesh."*

Several intended Passages in Paul's Letters explore the nature and meaning of the flesh.

THE STRUGGLE WITH SIN

Exploring his own struggle with sin, Paul faced his moral inadequacy. The Law of God is spiritual, but Paul was attempting to overcome by the flesh, failing, and, therefore, trapped in sin. Paul then realized that *"nothing good"* lived in him, that is, in his *"flesh,"* i.e., *"in my sinful nature."* Trapped by his moral frailty, which characterizes all of us, Paul, at least in the flesh, could not live the Righteous life that is revealed in God's Law, even though he acknowledged its beauty (Rom. 7:4-25). Paul would find the secret to victory in the Holy Spirit, which he gave us in Romans 8.

THE SINFUL NATURE

In Galatians 5:16-26, the *"flesh"* could be translated *"sinful nature."* Paul here describes the flesh as energized and motivated by desires that find expression in a number of actions, ranging from sexual immorality to jealousy and fits of rage.

In contrast, as Believers are called on to *"live by the Spirit,"* God Himself becomes the Source of transformed desires that can motivate a new life. What's more, He is also the Source of Power for such a life. When we keep in step with the Spirit rather than the flesh, God will fill us and our actions with love, joy, peace, and the other aspects of the Fruit of the Spirit.

THE BEHAVIOR OF CHRISTIANS

In I Corinthians 3:1-4, Paul alludes to the behavior of the Christians at Corinth. Their bickering and factions show that despite their relationship with Jesus, the Corinthians were acting like *"mere men."* Their outlook was human, rather than being shaped by God's perspective on the issues they found so important.

We Christians do have the potential to live beyond the possibilities of our *"sinful human nature."* But such an enabled life is not guaranteed. We make daily choices beyond our initial choice of trusting and loving Jesus that affect our experience of the Christian Life.

To break out of this pattern of the flesh, these Corinthians had to return to God's Word and search out His perspective.

GOD'S REMEDY

Release from the limits of our human nature is possible. Romans 8:3-14 explains God's remedy for the limitations and sin of the flesh. That remedy is not found in the Law. Law was unable to lift us to Righteousness, because it was *"weakened by our sinful nature,"* in other words, dependent upon the strength of mere man, which is not sufficient.

So God through Christ provided the Holy Spirit to Believers. Now we have the possibility of being controlled by the Spirit, not by the flesh. It is the Spirit Whose life-giving power

NOTES

raised Jesus from the dead. It is the Spirit Who can bring us life and power despite our mortality. Consequently, we are now raised to a new level entirely.

If we choose to rely on the Spirit and if we commit ourselves to His control, we will experience a Resurrection kind of life now. The limits imposed by our fleshly human nature will no longer contain us, and we will be freed from the mastery of the flesh.

The Old Testament emphasized the frailty of human beings. Because of our weakness, we must look to God for everything good. He Alone is the Source of our help. To recognize His Power brings us release from fear of other persons, who are ultimately as powerless as we are.

The New Testament took the explanation of the flesh further, by emphasizing humanity's moral inadequacy, even of Believers. When humans are isolated from God, they become energized by evil desires and guided by perceptions that distort God's Will and His Nature. The word, *"flesh,"* reminds us that we are caught in the grip of sin. Even a desire for Righteousness cannot enable us to actually become Righteous, as Paul's experience teaches us (Rom. 7).

God deals with our *"flesh"* in a surprising way. He does not free us now from the fleshly nature (sin nature). Instead, He provides a source of power that will release us from the domination of that sin nature. Jesus has paid for sins generated by our flesh, whether sins of our past or those yet in our future. But, as well, Christ has also provided us with His Holy Spirit.

The Spirit lives within us, and He is the Source of new desires and a new perspective. Even more, the spiritual power unleashed in the Resurrection is made available to us in the Spirit.

Consequently, the bonds of our mortality and all that mortality implies can be shattered if we live according to the Spirit, with our desires and motives shaped by Him, with His Power enabling us to do what is truly good.

Consequently, we are made to see through Romans 8, just how important the Holy Spirit is within the life of the Believer. Without Him, the victorious life is impossible, and that despite all our good intentions. With Him, the unlawful passions of the sin nature can be defeated.

(Most of the thoughts on the *"flesh"* were provided by the comments of Rev. Lawrence O. Richards.)

A FURTHER DEFINITION

The *"flesh,"* as by now is clear, is the earthly part of man. It has its *"lust"* and its *"desires"* (Eph. 2:3). If men concentrate on these, they may be said to *"set their minds on the things of the flesh"* (Rom. 8:5). And to set the mind on the *"flesh"* is *"death"* (Rom. 8:6). This is explained as *"enmity against God"* (Rom. 8:7).

The man whose horizon is limited by the *"flesh,"* is by that very fact opposed to God. He lives *"according to the flesh"* (Rom. 8:13), that flesh that *"lusteth against the Spirit"* (Gal. 5:17). Actually, the *"desires of the flesh are against the Spirit"* (Gal. 5:19-21). The flesh in this sense denotes the whole personality of man as organized in the wrong direction, as directed to earthly pursuits rather than the service of God (Bible Dictionary).

(38) "WATCH YE AND PRAY, LEST YE ENTER INTO TEMPTATION. THE SPIRIT TRULY IS READY, BUT THE FLESH IS WEAK."

The phrase, *"Watch ye and pray, lest ye enter into temptation,"* provides us with the true remedy against temptation of every kind.

"Prayer" teaches us reliance on the Holy Spirit, and, as well, creates within us a *"watchfulness"* able to recognize the craft and subtlety of the devil or man.

Incidentally, this was not a suggestion by Christ, but, actually, a Command! The Believer who does not *"watch and pray,"* will not only be subject to temptation, but, as well, will have no means to overcome its pull.

As well, this is a problem that is constant, and, therefore, requires continuous *"watchfulness and prayer."*

Many have asked me why I am so persistent respecting our two prayer meetings a day? It is this very reason mentioned here by Christ. To be sure, it has provided a strength and solace obtainable from no other source.

Someone else asked how long I plan to continue these prayer meetings?

We plan to continue them until the Lord comes. The reason is simple:

Satan never ceases with his persistent efforts to steal, kill, and destroy. Consequently, I

NOTES

must never cease in my efforts respecting the Command of Christ to *"watch and pray."*

I am certain that Peter, along with the other Disciples, learned this valuable lesson, and even from this very experience in Gethsemane. When the Early Church began to grow, *"The Twelve,"* and no doubt headed up by Peter, advised the large number of Believers to *"Look ye out among you seven men of honest report, full of the Holy Ghost and wisdom, whom we may appoint over this business."*

They then said, *"But we will give ourselves continually to prayer, and to the Ministry of the Word"* (Acts 6:3-4).

Peter and the Disciples were doing their best to obey Christ, as modern Believers must do as well!

The *"Entering into temptation,"* has the meaning of being pulled into a trap laid by Satan. The *"watching and praying"* circumvents those traps.

The phrase, *"The spirit truly is ready, but the flesh is weak,"* could be translated, *"The spirit (of man) truly is ready, but the 'flesh' (of man) is weak."*

The *"spirit"* here refers to the spirit of man. In the Believer, the regenerated spirit is willing, or rather has the desire to fully obey God, but has no power within itself to do so, and certainly cannot override the evil passions and desires of the *"flesh,"* i.e., *"sin nature."* However, as we have stated, the Lord has given us the Holy Spirit with all His Great Power, Who can easily override the sin nature (flesh). This is the reason the Holy Spirit is so absolutely important. Paul said, *"For the Law of the Spirit of Life in Christ Jesus hath made me free from the law of sin and death"* (Rom. 8:2).

Does the Spirit of God come into the life of the Believer at conversion with the power needed to overcome the *"flesh?"*

While the Spirit of God definitely does come into the heart and life of the Believer at conversion, He does not come in with the power needed to effect this work within the life of the Believer. This awaits the Baptism in the Holy Spirit, which initial physical evidence is the speaking with other tongues as the Spirit gives utterance (Acts 2:4). This is the reason that Jesus *"Commanded them that they should not depart from Jerusalem, but wait for the Promise of the Father"* (Acts 1:4).

The *"Promise of the Father"* is the *"Baptism in the Holy Spirit"* (Acts 1:5).

It should be obvious that these people to whom Jesus was speaking, which included the Disciples, were definitely saved; however, they had not yet been Baptized in the Holy Spirit. Consequently, in effect, Jesus told them not to evangelize, build Churches, preach the Gospel, etc., until they <u>first</u> were *"Baptized in the Holy Spirit."*

Incidentally, it was not a suggestion, but a Command!

The reason is found in Acts 1:8, *"But ye shall receive power, after that the Holy Spirit is come upon you."*

However, just because an individual has been Baptized in the Holy Spirit, in no way means that the knowledge of using this *"Power"* is automatic. Actually, it isn't, with many Spirit-filled Believers falling short of what the Holy Spirit desires to do within our lives. This was evident in the life of the Apostle Paul, as we have previously mentioned, even after He was Spirit-filled (Acts 9:17). He said, *"For that which I do I allow not: for what I would, that do I not; but what I hate, that do I"* (Rom. 7:15).

Even though he was saved and Spirit-filled, he further said, *"O wretched man that I am! Who shall deliver me from the body of this death?"* (Rom. 7:24).

This proclaims him, though Spirit-filled, still not allowing the Holy Spirit to perform the work. However, there came a time that *"in Christ,"* he learned to *"walk not after the flesh,"* but *"after the Spirit"* (Rom. 8:1).

Actually, Romans 8:1 tells us that it is possible to be *"in Christ Jesus,"* in other words, *"born again,"* but still continue to *"walk after the flesh."* In fact, millions of Christians experience this defeat on a daily basis, and, in Truth, every single Believer, even as Paul, has at times walked *"after the flesh."*

At the time, Jesus did not explain what He meant by the statement, *"The spirit truly is ready, but the flesh is weak."* There was really little point in explaining it then, because the Holy Spirit was not yet given, at least as it would be on the Day of Pentecost (Jn. 7:39).

Jerome said, and rightly so, *"In whatever degree we trust to the Power of the Spirit, in the same degree ought we to fear because of the infirmity of the flesh."*

In other words, it is a constant struggle, with the *"flesh"* ready to take the upper hand the moment we relax our vigil. The Lord has designed this Christian walk in order that we may constantly need to depend on the Spirit. Yesterday's blessings, as wonderful as they were, will not suffice for today. Consecration and yielding to the Spirit must be fresh, even on a daily and constant basis (Eph. 5:18).

(39) "AND AGAIN HE WENT AWAY, AND PRAYED, AND SPAKE THE SAME WORDS."

The phrase, *"And again He went away, and prayed,"* is meant to portray to us a valuable lesson.

First of all, He felt the necessity of more prayer. He set the example for us by continuing to seek the Face of the Heavenly Father, in order that the Will of God may be carried out. This, and this alone, was His concern.

If these words are studied closely, we learn that they abrogate the teaching of many who claim that we should not pray or ask about something more than once. These false teachers claim that such shows a lack of Faith. I think this Passage tells us that such thinking is error.

The phrase, *"And spake the same words,"* does not show lack of Faith, but rather Great Faith. Of His statement, *"Nevertheless not what I will, but what Thou wilt,"* there must not be any doubt. Consequently, He will repeat this all-important Doctrine. In effect, He was saying it not just for Himself, but for all Believers.

(40) "AND WHEN HE RETURNED, HE FOUND THEM ASLEEP AGAIN, (FOR THEIR EYES WERE HEAVY,) NEITHER WIST THEY WHAT TO ANSWER HIM."

The phrase, *"And when He returned, He found them asleep again, (for their eyes were heavy,)"* in the Greek Text means literally they were *"weighed down."* Their sleep was not deliberate, but the result of an oppressive sorrow.

At the time of the Transfiguration, these three had experienced the same over-powering drowsiness, and the same inability to give expression to their thoughts. Then their situation was the result of fear, and here the result of grief (Wuest).

The phrase, *"Neither wist they what to answer Him,"* concerns the question He had previously asked, and probably asks again, *"Couldest not thou watch one hour?"*

They did not know what to answer, so they said nothing!

Peter has claimed that he would even die for Christ, and, *"Likewise also said they all,"* but they cannot even *"Watch one hour."* The lesson should be well taken for all.

Within the spiritual arena, without the Power of God we have no strength against the evil one. How foolish for man to say what he will or will not do!

(41) "AND HE COMETH THE THIRD TIME, AND SAITH UNTO THEM, SLEEP ON NOW, AND TAKE YOUR REST: IT IS ENOUGH, THE HOUR IS COME; BEHOLD, THE SON OF MAN IS BETRAYED INTO THE HANDS OF SINNERS."

The phrase, *"And He cometh the third time, and saith unto them, Sleep on now, and take your rest,"* is actually said in irony. In fact, there would be no more *"rest!"*

The implication is that all of these terrible scenes of the agony of Christ were repeated three times. If we are to take the 37th verse literally, this entire scenario lasted approximately three hours. However, we have no way of knowing if the last two times of the Passion of Christ were as long as the first.

As an aside, and observing the effect all of this had on Peter, James, and John, who were, no doubt, in excellent physical shape, we are made to realize how prime actually was the manhood of Christ. Such oppression would have killed a normal human being. His manhood which had never been touched by sin, and, consequently, by sickness or disease, was, no doubt, of such excellence that it defied description. I think this is evident considering the torture He would undergo up to and during the Crucifixion.

The phrase, *"It is enough, the hour is come,"* is a statement so important that it beggars description. This is the *"hour"* which had been planned even before the foundation of the world (Rev. 13:8).

Even though this *"hour"* would be one of absolute horror for Him, on the other hand it would be an *"hour"* of triumph for the entirety of the world. The price would be paid for man's Redemption. The door would be opened for all to enter in, with Jesus Himself being the *"Door"* (Jn. 10:7).

The phrase, *"Behold, the Son of Man is betrayed into the hands of sinners,"* reflects the perfidiousness of Judas. As well, the word, *"sinners,"* not only expresses Judas, but the Pharisees as well!

In fact, the reputations of the Pharisees in Israel at that time, were literally impeccable, at least as far as man was concerned. However, Jesus calls them *"sinners!"*

In Truth, the world does not recognizes at all, and the Church but little, the reputation which Christ Alone can give. That which He cleanses by His Blood, is cleansed indeed! However, precious few recognize and honor His finished work in the lives of those who truly trust Him. Nevertheless, it is not what man thinks that counts, but what God knows.

It is ironical, these Pharisees were so deceived they would kill the Lord in the Name of the Lord.

(42) "RISE UP, LET US GO; LO, HE THAT BETRAYETH ME IS AT HAND."

The two words, *"Rise up,"* mean that the Disciples were still lying on the ground. Jesus was standing.

The phrase, *"Let us go,"* refers to the approach of Judas and those with him, and that Jesus and the Disciples would meet them. There is no idea here of Jesus contemplating flight. Wuest says, *"This was His hour and He was there to meet it."*

The phrase, *"Lo, he that betrayeth Me is at hand,"* means that the Holy Spirit had informed Christ of their immediate arrival.

So, it is obvious that even at this tremendously trying time with Satan trying to kill Him, the Holy Spirit was watching over Him constantly. Luke said, *"And there appeared an Angel unto Him from Heaven, strengthening Him"* (Lk. 22:43). His Father would not forsake Him until He actually hung on the Cross, which, as stated, was from approximately 9 a.m. to 3 p.m.

(43) "AND IMMEDIATELY, WHILE HE YET SPAKE, COMETH JUDAS, ONE OF THE TWELVE, AND WITH HIM A GREAT MULTITUDE WITH SWORDS AND STAVES, FROM THE CHIEF PRIESTS AND THE SCRIBES AND THE ELDERS."

The phrase, *"And immediately, while He yet spake, cometh Judas, one of the Twelve,"* speaks of their arrival, even while Jesus was speaking.

The Holy Spirit is careful to delineate the fact that it was *"Judas, one of the Twelve,"* who betrayed Christ. The implication is dark indeed!

NOTES

No man had any greater opportunity than Judas. He was shoulder to shoulder with Christ, the Son of God, for a period of approximately three and a half years. However, association does not bring Salvation, and neither does environment or participation. There must be a heart changing work of Repentance that takes place in the life, and, as well, there must be an ongoing relationship.

I think the evidence is clear that Judas once had an experience with the Lord. Luke wrote of him, *"Which Judas by transgression fell, that he might go to his own place"* (Acts 1:25). It is impossible to *"fall"* from something that one has not previously had. Consequently, this refutes the erroneous Doctrine of Unconditional Eternal Security.

Judas, as many, allowed his relationship with Christ to wane and weaken until he became grist for Satan's mill. Judas did what he did of his own free will. Consequently, he would reap the bitter results!

Luke says that Judas *"Went before them,"* in other words, eager to accomplish this hateful task (Lk. 22:47).

The phrase, *"And with him a great multitude with swords and staves,"* consisted of some of the members of the vaunted Sanhedrin, members of the Temple Police, and some of the regular Roman soldiers, along with some of the personal servants of the High Priest. Thus Gentiles and Jews were united in the daring act of arresting the Son of God. John 18:3 says they had *"lanterns and torches."*

The phrase, *"From the Chief Priests and the Scribes and the Elders,"* constituted the entirety of the Religious Order of Israel. Truly, *"He came unto His Own, and His Own received Him not"* (Jn. 1:11).

As we have previously stated, it was not the thieves, drunks, or gamblers who killed Christ, but actually the *"Church"* of that day. It is my firm belief that if time and the Plan of God were changed, and Jesus came now as He did then, the modern Church would do the same to Him as the Church of old! There is no evil like religious evil!

If my memory is correct, the year was 1982. It was a Saturday morning, and I had left the house to go to a particular place close to the Mississippi River, where I often went, and which I would spend much of the day in prayer and study of the Word. That morning was to present a momentous occasion.

I suppose I had been there an hour or so when the Spirit of God began to come upon me very heavily. It was so heavy in fact that I doubled over as a deep spirit of intercession gripped me. I remember looking around to see if anyone was watching me, inasmuch as I was walking back and forth in the open air. (It was on the levee beside the Mississippi River.)

That morning the Lord spoke some things to my heart which would come to pass in amazing clarity. He said to me, *"I have a Message I want you to deliver to the Catholics, the Denominational Churches, and to your own,"* which referred to the Pentecostals. At that time, we had the largest Television audience in the world, at least regarding Christian programming.

Concerning the Catholics, the Message was simple. The Lord simply told me to tell them, *"The just shall live by Faith."* However, I was to find that that Message, even though seeing multiple thousands of Catholics brought to Christ, would not meet with approval from most of the Church world, and especially from the Pentecostals.

To the Denominational world, the Lord told me to proclaim to them the necessity of the Holy Spirit. As well, we would see multiple thousands of these people Baptized in the Holy Spirit, but, at the same time, tremendous opposition.

To the Pentecostals, the Lord told me to tell them, *"Your Own,"* as He had put it, *"they must return to the Holy Spirit."*

If the opposition from Catholicism and the Denominational world had been strong, it was nothing in comparison to the opposition from *"my own."* They reacted to My Message with great anger.

Actually, the Lord told me that if I obeyed Him and preached what He told me to preach, we would suffer great loss. He said, *"Your own will turn against you."* And then He asked, *"Will you do what I ask you to do?"*

I did not answer immediately. As I have stated, the Spirit of God was on me to such an extent that I could barely stand.

The words spoken to me by the Lord weighed extremely heavy upon my heart. The implications were clear. He had told me that we might lose everything.

At that time, and as I have stated, our Telecast had the largest audience in Christendom in the world. We were even at that moment constructing Family Worship Center, which would grow to some 7,000 in attendance. As well, the Bible College was under construction, and would begin its first semester very shortly.

Our Missions works of building Churches, Bible Schools, and schools for children, were in high gear all over the world, and would grow to large proportions. All of this flashed before my eyes, with the words of the Lord, *"You could lose it all,"* constantly flashing before me.

After a period of time, I said to the Lord, *"I will do my best, and irrespective of the cost."* Actually, and even though the Lord had spelled it out to me, I little knew or understood just what that *"cost"* would be.

As stated, the opposition was fierce, even to the place at times that I was concerned for my life. And when the time came that my enemies, which seemed to be many, had something they could use against me, they lost no time or spared no expense in doing so. Exactly as the Lord said, *"My own turned against Me,"* and in a way that I could not even begin to have imagined. The hatred was so intense that in some small measure I know and understand what the Lord experienced. As well, that hatred and opposition was worldwide.

I realize that many think that the action taken by the religious world was because of what happened, however, that was only an excuse. They hated me for two reasons: because of the Message I preached, and because of the Anointing of the Holy Spirit upon that Message, which garnered tremendous results.

In the last year of Jesus' public Ministry, He was banned from most all Synagogues. I, as well, have suffered that same opposition.

As we will soon see, when Christ was rendered helpless, or so they thought, as well as condemned, with men able to do anything to Him they so desired, then the wickedness of these *"Chief Priests, Scribes, and Elders,"* becomes obvious.

As well, I know the feeling of total helplessness, with anyone permitted to do any negative thing desired, which would not be censored, but rather applauded. Then one sees how many True Believers there really are! Regrettably, now, as then, there aren't many.

NOTES

However, as the songwriter said, *"Through it all, I have learned to depend upon the Lord."*

What a person suffers is designed by Satan and allowed by the Lord. Satan means for it to destroy us, while the Lord means for it to draw us closer to Him. Thankfully, this that Frances and I have faced, along with our entire family, has, instead, drawn us closer to the Lord, much closer!

No! The Lord never gets glory out of sin, but He does get glory out of victory over sin.

(44) "AND HE THAT BETRAYED HIM HAD GIVEN THEM A TOKEN, SAYING, WHOMSOEVER I SHALL KISS, THAT SAME IS HE; TAKE HIM, AND LEAD HIM AWAY SAFELY."

The phrase, *"And he that betrayed Him had given them a token,"* proclaims the scheme that had been perpetrated by Judas and the Religious Leaders.

The phrase, *"Saying Whomsoever I shall kiss, that same is He,"* portrays the most perfidious act in human history. The *"kiss"* was the customary mode of saluting a Rabbi. So, Judas had told his co-conspirators that the one he kissed would be Jesus. Now, the strong words spoken of Judas in Psalm 109 take on completely new meaning. Before the terrible curse was rendered through the lips of David concerning Judas by the Holy Spirit (Ps. 109:6-20), the reason was given; *"And they have rewarded Me evil for good, and hatred for My love"* (Ps. 109:5).

The phrase, *"Take Him, and lead Him away safely,"* is a somewhat ridiculous statement!

First of all, Judas had seen Jesus walk through hate-filled mobs several times, when they were bent on killing Him. He had seen Him raise the dead and perform miracles of unprecedented proportions. How did he think they could *"Take Him,"* unless He would simply allow them to do so?

Actually, John recorded at this time, that when Judas and these brigands approached, Jesus *"Said unto them, Whom seek ye?"*

The Scripture says, *"They answered Him, Jesus of Nazareth."*

Then, *"Jesus saith unto them, I am He."*

Then John said, *"As soon then as He had said unto them, I am He, they went backward, and fell to the ground"* (Jn. 18:4-6).

At this time, the Power of God was on Him so strong that His mere words caused all of them to fall backward to the ground. Consequently, there is no way they could have taken Him unless He allowed them to do so, which He did!

This portrays how insensitive and dull these Religious Leaders were to the moving and operation of the Holy Spirit. In Truth, they did not know God, despite all their religious claims! They were not children of God, but, instead, children of Satan. And to be sure, the worst child of Satan in the world is the religious child of Satan. This evil is unequalled!

(45) "AND AS SOON AS HE WAS COME, HE GOETH STRAIGHTWAY TO HIM, AND SAITH, MASTER, MASTER; AND KISSED HIM."

The phrase, *"And as soon as he was come, he goeth straightway to Him,"* proclaims Judas carrying out this perfidious action. The words, *"As soon as he was come,"* seem to imply that he was in a hurry to carry out this ungodly act.

The phrase, *"And saith, Master, Master; and kissed Him,"* means that it was an affectionate, fervent kiss the traitor gave the Lord, but, as obvious, hypocritical. The words, *"Master, Master,"* mean, *"Rabbi, Rabbi,"* or *"Teacher, Teacher!"*

Chrysostom said, *"Judas felt assured by the gentleness of Christ that He would not repel him, or that if He did, the treacherous action would have answered its purpose."*

(46) "AND THEY LAID THEIR HANDS ON HIM, AND TOOK HIM."

The phrase, *"And they laid their hands on Him,"* portrays in glaring detail the difference in the action of Christ and these hypocrites.

The Hands of Jesus were used to heal the sick and cast out devils. Not one time did those Hands ever minister sickness, suffering, heartache, disappointment, or failure. Every single time, when His Hands touched anyone, it was for blessing.

Conversely, the only time it is recorded that the Church used their hands to touch Him, it was for the purpose of hurt and harm. The contrast should be obvious!

Jesus had said, *"Ye shall know them by their fruits"* (Mat. 7:16).

The *"fruits"* of His Life and Ministry were saved souls, changed lives, broken bondages, with the sick brought to health. In other words, the *"fruits"* were obvious!

What were the *"fruits"* of the Lives and Ministries of these Religious Leaders, etc.?

No lives were changed, no souls were saved, no bondages broken, and no sick were healed. All they could do was kill.

The reader should take a lesson from this. That which is not of God has no good *"fruits."* And yet, most of the money goes to support that which produces nothing, at least nothing good.

The phrase, *"And took Him,"* was after, and as John recorded, they had all fallen backward to the ground. Their hypocrisy was overshadowed only by their ignorance! There was no way they could have *"taken Him,"* unless He had allowed them to do so!

(47) "AND ONE OF THEM THAT STOOD BY DREW A SWORD, AND SMOTE A SERVANT OF THE HIGH PRIEST, AND CUT OFF HIS EAR."

The phrase, *"And one of them that stood by drew a sword,"* refers to Peter (Jn. 18:10).

The phrase, *"And smote a servant of the High Priest,"* proclaims as well, according to John, that the servant's name was *"Malchus."*

The phrase, *"And cut off his ear,"* no doubt pictures Peter as attempting to cleave his skull.

Luke is the only one who mentions the healing of the wound by our Lord (Lk. 22:51).

Of all the thousands of healings performed by Christ in His public Ministry, the last healing He performed before His Death, at least that is recorded, was performed on an enemy. How so much He lived and proclaimed His Own Message, *"Bless them that curse you"* (Mat. 5:44).

Incidently, if the authorities had desired to press charges against Peter, they would have had difficulty, since no evidence remained. The man's ear was whole.

In a way this is a picture of *"Justification by Faith."* No evidence is left of the sin. Jesus not only forgives, but cleanses and heals, until no trace remains. Satan attempting to press charges, finds no evidence.

(48) "AND JESUS ANSWERED AND SAID UNTO THEM, ARE YE COME OUT, AS AGAINST A THIEF, WITH SWORDS AND WITH STAVES TO TAKE ME?"

The phrase, *"And Jesus answered and said unto them,"* is spoken after the Lord had rebuked His Disciples for their resistance; after which He proceeded to rebuke those who were bent upon apprehending Him (Mat. 26:52) (Bickersteth).

The question, *"Are ye come out, as against a thief, with swords and with staves to take Me?",* proclaims the Lord protesting the manner in which this act is carried out. He was not a thief, so why were they treating Him as one?

As well, why were they armed, inasmuch as He led no rebellion?

(49) "I WAS DAILY WITH YOU IN THE TEMPLE TEACHING, AND YE TOOK ME NOT: BUT THE SCRIPTURES MUST BE FULFILLED."

The phrase, *"I was daily with you in the Temple teaching, and ye took Me not,"* proclaims the wickedness of their act. Jesus had appeared in the Temple some three times in the last few days. He had taught and healed, so why didn't they take Him then?

They did not take Him then, because they did not have any legitimate charge to bring against Him. As well, they feared the people. Consequently, they would have to carry out their perfidious act by night. Never was anything done in such an underhanded, ungodly, wicked, demeaning way.

The phrase, *"But the Scriptures must be fulfilled,"* spoke of Prophecies given to the Prophets of old, as the Lord through foreknowledge saw what would happen (Isa. 53; Zech. 11:13; 13:7).

As we have previously stated, this does not mean that these individuals were foreordained to do these dastardly deeds, but, instead, simply that God saw what they would do of their own free choice, and then foretold it through the Prophets. It is not predestination, but, instead, foreknowledge.

(50) "AND THEY ALL FORSOOK HIM, AND FLED."

As someone has said, not being allowed to fight, they fled. The flesh will fight or flee, but it will not *"trust."*

"They all," refer to the Eleven Disciples. This fulfilled 14:27.

However, Peter and John took courage, and followed Him to the house of the High Priest, where Peter was to deny Him.

As well, this is the beginning of the fulfillment of the Prophecy of David, *"I looked on My Right Hand, and behold, but there was no man that would know Me: refuge failed Me; no man cared for My soul"* (Ps. 142:4).

It is too awful to contemplate, but at this time not a single individual, not even His Disciples, stood up for Him. He had healed thousands, but none were there to speak up for Him.

NOTES

He had taught tens of thousands, even with Words of Life which they had never heard before, and yet, there is no one to speak a word of kindness to Him at this terrible time!

Even those He had purposely chosen, now refuse to choose Him.

(51) "AND THERE FOLLOWED HIM A CERTAIN YOUNG MAN, HAVING A LINEN CLOTH CAST ABOUT HIS NAKED BODY; AND THE YOUNG MEN LAID HOLD ON HIM:"

The phrase, *"And there followed Him a certain young man,"* is given only here.

Who was this young man?

Inasmuch as the Scripture is silent regarding identity, no one knows for sure. However, Hahn said, *"In this curious incident we have the monogram of the painter* (Mark) *in a dark corner of the picture."*

The phrase, *"Having a linen cloth cast about his naked body,"* tells us several things:

1. Whoever this young man was, he must have been in bed when news was given to him of the arrest of Christ.

2. The *"linen cloth"* spoken of here was that which people of poor circumstances could not have owned. Therefore, he belonged to a family of means.

3. As well, this was a kind of light cloak frequently worn in hot weather.

The phrase, *"And the young men laid hold on him,"* means the soldiers were setting about to arrest him.

(52) "AND HE LEFT THE LINEN CLOTH, AND FLED FROM THEM NAKED."

This incident portrays to us the great hatred of the Jews against Jesus, inasmuch as they endeavored to seize a young man who was merely following at a distance.

The idea of the verse is, that the soldiers grabbed him, with him struggling to get away. In the struggle, his garment was pulled from him.

The word, *"naked,"* probably means that he only had undergarments. There is no evidence they pursued him.

In the idea that this may have been John Mark, some suggest that it may have been his house in which the Lord celebrated the Passover, and from whence He went out to the Mount of Olives. If this is correct, there is even a possibility that Mark was present at the Last Supper, and if, in fact, that was the case, sensed that something was about to happen to Christ.

There is even a possibility that after the arrest of Christ, the group passed by the house of Mark awakening him, which occasioned this scenario.

(53) "AND THEY LED JESUS AWAY TO THE HIGH PRIEST: AND WITH HIM WERE ASSEMBLED ALL THE CHIEF PRIESTS AND THE ELDERS AND THE SCRIBES."

The phrase, *"And they led Jesus away to the High Priest,"* refers to Caiaphas. However, we learn from John 18:13, that Jesus was first brought before Annas, the father-in-law of Caiaphas.

Annas and his five sons held the High Priesthood in succession. Caiaphas, his son-in-law, stepping in between the first and the second son, and holding the office for twelve years.

It is supposed that it was at the house of Annas where the price of the betrayal was paid to Judas. Annas, though not then High Priest, must have had considerable influence in the counsels of the Sanhedrin; and this will probably explain the fact of our Lord having been taken first to him (Bickersteth).

The phrase, *"And with Him were assembled all the Chief Priests and the Elders and the Scribes,"* proclaims the Religious Hierarchy of Israel.

It is very difficult, if not impossible, for all organized religion not to fall into this category of wickedness. Most of the laity do not realize it, but organized religion is just as political, if not more so, than its worldly counterpart. As such, the Will of God is totally abrogated, with the will of man becoming paramount. As such, it becomes Satanic!

This does not mean that every one associated with organized religion is Satanic, for there were even two members of the Jewish Sanhedrin who were Godly, Nicodemus and Joseph of Arimathaea.

However, as particular Church groups begin to apostatize, the idea is almost always ventured forth that association with that particular Denomination or group plays a part in one's Salvation. An elitist attitude develops, which is indicative of self-righteousness. As the spiritual deterioration becomes more and more acute, however, less and less people in this particular Denomination truly know Christ. This happens to almost all Religious Denominations.

Many Denominations begin with true Holy Ghost Revival; however, if the following

NOTES

generation does not experience the same moving of the Spirit, the spiritual deterioration begins. Most do not spiritually survive three generations. They become more and more man-led, and, consequently, less and less God-led. Unless there is a Move of God, the end result is identical to that which crucified Christ.

(54) "AND PETER FOLLOWED HIM AFAR OFF, EVEN INTO THE PALACE OF THE HIGH PRIEST: AND HE SAT WITH THE SERVANTS, AND WARMED HIMSELF AT THE FIRE."

The phrase, *"And Peter followed Him afar off,"* now begins the saga of the fisherman.

At this time, a great turmoil no doubt is going on the heart of Peter. The Holy Spirit delineates the *"afar off."* The idea is meant to call our attention to the boasts of Peter, which this following at a distance occasioned.

What would have happened had Peter followed in the very Presence of Christ, instead of far off?

To be sure, nothing would have happened to him because Christ would have seen to it that he would have been spared. However, it is a moot point!

The phrase, *"Even into the palace of the High Priest,"* actually refers to the court of the palace where the guards and servants of the High Priest were assembled.

Jesus had been taken inside the palace to be arraigned before the Council. John tells us that inasmuch as he was known to the High Priest, he had been the means of bringing in Peter, who had been standing outside at the door leading into the court (Jn. 18:15).

The phrase, *"And he sat with the servants, and warmed himself at the fire,"* proclaims the coolness of the early spring, and especially considering that it was now after midnight. The glow of the fire would have clearly outlined his features, as he crouched to warm himself.

The idea of having a trial at this ridiculous time of the night, is indicative of the perverseness of this action. Such action was clearly opposed to Mosaic Law, which they so loudly claimed to keep. To be honest, the worst criminal would not have been tried at this time of night. However, among other things, they were fearful that if Jesus had been tried during the day, the vast crowds filling Jerusalem for the Passover would have come to His aid.

Even above that, Jesus must die at the same time the Passover Lambs were killed, which would be 3 o'clock p.m. the following afternoon.

Once again, we emphasize that these evil men did this of their own free will, not at all coerced by God. While it is true that they would fulfill Bible Prophecy, still, it is not true that they were predestined to do so. The predestination only pertained to Christ and how and when He would die, and not who would bring about this evil process.

(55) "AND THE CHIEF PRIESTS AND ALL THE COUNCIL SOUGHT FOR WITNESS AGAINST JESUS TO PUT HIM TO DEATH; AND FOUND NONE."

The phrase, *"And the Chief Priests and all the Council,"* refers to the vaunted Sanhedrin, the great Council of the Jews at Jerusalem consisting of 71 members, made up of Scribes, Elders, and prominent members of the High-Priestly families. The High Priest Caiaphas was the President of this body.

The most important cases in the land were brought before this tribunal, inasmuch as Rome had left it in the power of this group to try such cases, and also of pronouncing the sentence of death. However, a capital sentence of death was not valid unless it was confirmed by the Roman Procurator, in this case, Pilate.

The word, *"all,"* indicates that it was a full meeting of this body of men. However, it is not known whether Nicodemus or Joseph of Arimathaea or members of this body were present. The word, *"all,"* could have very well referred to those opposed to Christ, which pertained to all except the two mentioned.

The phrase, *"Sought for witness against Jesus to put Him to death,"* proclaims this group attempting to legalize their vile action. They were attempting to find a way to kill the Lord in the Name of the Lord! Deception is a cruel thing!

How could these Religious Leaders have sunk so low until they, who were supposed to know God more so than anyone in the world, didn't even recognize Him even though He stood before them?

Even though my statement is strong, I feel it must be said. If the Truth were known, many, if not most, of present Religious Leaders of modern Christendom fall into the same category. Jesus said as much concerning the Church in the last days.

He said, *"The Kingdom of Heaven is like unto leaven, which a woman took, and hid in three measures of meal, till the whole was leavened"* (Mat. 13:33).

This means that in these last days, which are now upon us, the *"whole"* of the modern Church would become so corrupted by false doctrines and unscriptural programs, that its entirety would be *"leavened,"* i.e., corrupted.

The phrase, *"And found none,"* refers to the emptiness of their accusations. There was nothing they could legally or morally put their hands on in which to condemn Him. Consequently, He was arraigned before this Court, not because He had done something wrong, but simply because they hated Him. The Psalmist had prophesied some one thousand years before, saying, *"For the mouth of the wicked and the mouth of the deceitful are opened against Me: they have spoken against Me with a lying tongue.*

"They compassed Me about also with words of hatred; and fought against Me without a cause" (Ps. 109:2-3).

(56) "FOR MANY BARE FALSE WITNESS AGAINST HIM, BUT THEIR WITNESS AGREED NOT TOGETHER."

The phrase, *"For many bare false witness against Him,"* proclaims such being contrary to the Law of Moses, which required them to begin a trial with those things which would acquit the accused, instead of condemning Him.

In this case, not one thing was sought that could acquit Christ. They were determined to kill Him, so they looked for every excuse possible, not realizing they were fulfilling Prophecy.

The phrase, *"But their witness agreed not together,"* proclaims them not even being able to find one honest witness against Him, much less two, which were required before charges could be legally brought.

Whatever things these witnesses brought forward were either false, or self-contradictory. In other words, the trial was a farce!

(57-58) "AND THERE AROSE CERTAIN, AND BARE FALSE WITNESS AGAINST HIM, SAYING,

"WE HEARD HIM SAY, I WILL DESTROY THIS TEMPLE THAT IS MADE WITH HANDS, AND WITHIN THREE DAYS I WILL BUILD ANOTHER MADE WITHOUT HANDS."

The phrase, *"And there arose certain,"* speaks of two men, as given in Matthew 26:60.

The phrase, *"And bare false witness against Him, saying,"* proclaims the Sanhedrin as thinking they finally had a proper accusation against Him. However, they were to see that this was false as well!

The phrase, *"We heard Him say,"* constitutes a lie, because He did not say what they accused Him of saying.

The phrase, *"I will destroy this Temple,"* was not what He said.

What He really said, and as is recorded in John 2:19, is *"Destroy this Temple, and in three days I will raise it up."*

First of all, He was not speaking of Herod's Temple, as they were accusing Him, but His Own Body.

As well, He was not speaking of destroying His Body Himself, but that they, the Jews, even this very Sanhedrin, would destroy it, i.e., kill Him. It was a Prophecy concerning the way He would die, and that He would raise it up, hence, the Resurrection.

The phrase, *"That is made with hands, and within three days I will build another made without hands,"* is not, as we have stated, what He said!

They had added the words, *"That is made with hands,"* and *"I will build another made without hands,"* to make it seem as if Jesus was talking about the Jerusalem Temple.

This is a favorite method of Satan, especially when he is successful in getting religious people to do his work, which he often is. Words are twisted to make it seem as if something else is said altogether.

The idea is, that those who do such things have no regard or concern for the Truth, but just the lying accusation. As is obvious, this court was not seeking Truth, as Satan never seeks Truth. Likewise, those in the religious world who follow in Satan's train do not seek Truth either!

(59) "BUT NEITHER SO DID THEIR WITNESS AGREE TOGETHER."

As they begin to venture forth this accusation, they found themselves opposing each other. One was saying that He said thus and so, while another was saying *"No, He said this...."* Consequently, their testimony falls down.

As we have alluded to, according to the Law in Deuteronomy 19:15, the testimony of two witnesses was required for a conviction. No two witnesses could be found who agreed on essential points. The idea in the Greek Text is that they made repeated attempts to bring testimony that would warrant conviction, but without success (Wuest).

(60) "AND THE HIGH PRIEST STOOD UP IN THE MIDST, AND ASKED JESUS, SAYING, ANSWEREST THOU NOTHING? WHAT IS IT WHICH THESE WITNESS AGAINST THEE?"

The phrase, *"And the High Priest stood up in the midst,"* suggests that this man had become exasperated by their inability to bring forth a credible witness, and sought to make up by bluster the lack of evidence (Robertson). As stated, they had no regard for Truth, but only their determination to kill, and, therefore, silence Him, which they were determined to do at whatever cost. To be sure, the price would be high, the destruction of their nation and their banishment among the nations of the world, to wander as outcasts for nearly 2,000 years.

The question, *"And asked Jesus, saying, Answerest Thou nothing?",* now presents a change of tactics.

Unable to get credible witnesses, Caiaphas will now attempt to trap Jesus by getting Him to say something which will give them grounds for some type of condemnation. They are, by now, desperate! With this tactic they will succeed. However, it will not be what Jesus says is wrong, but that they claim it is.

Jesus did not answer these accusations made by these false witnesses because such was pointless. Silence was the greatest answer of all!

Had they been seeking Truth, that would have been a different story. However, they had no interest in what was truly said!

The question, *"What is it which these witness against Thee?",* proclaims Caiaphas demanding an answer from Christ concerning the accusations, but Jesus says nothing, at least to that charge.

(61) "BUT HE HELD HIS PEACE, AND ANSWERED NOTHING. AGAIN THE HIGH PRIEST ASKED HIM, AND SAID UNTO HIM, ART THOU THE CHRIST, THE SON OF THE BLESSED?"

The phrase, *"But He held His peace, and answered nothing,"* means in the Greek Text that He kept on maintaining His silence.

To answer these foolish questions, would have been admitting the authority of this assembly which had been brought together by an unjust arrest and by the employment of perjured witnesses. Consequently, Christ would lend no credence to this unlawful assembly. The efforts of Caiaphas to force Jesus to incriminate Himself was, within itself, unlawful in jurisprudence. However, this wicked assembly had long since ceased to abide by any degree of honesty and integrity.

The phrase, *"Again the High Priest asked Him,"* will now present another tactic. The question that Caiaphas will now ask, he already knows the answer, because Jesus had made it clear several times Who He actually was.

The question, *"And said unto Him, Art Thou the Christ, the Son of the Blessed?",* actually would have been said, *"Art Thou the Messiah?",* namely, *"The Anointed of God."*

The word, *"Blessed,"* in the Greek Text is *"Eulogetos,"* and is used as a Name for God.

Dake says, *"This was the central controversy about Jesus. He claimed to be the Christ and the Son of God but Satan and the Jews were determined to disprove these claims (Mat. 4:3, 6; 27:40; Jn. 5:18; 10:36; 19:7).*

"God acknowledged His claims (Mat. 3:17; 17:5); demons were forced to acknowledge them (Mat. 8:29; Mk. 3:11; 5:7); Disciples confessed them (Mat. 14:33; 16:16); but His enemies rebelled against facts and refused to believe even after His Resurrection (Mat. 27:40; 28:11-15; Acts 4:16-22; 5:17-28, 40-42).

"However, some Jews repented and confessed His claims after Miraculous and Resurrection facts were known (Jn. 3:2; Acts 6:7). A few years after the Resurrection of Christ, Josephus, a noted Jewish Historian, gave one of the most valuable confessions of honest Faith in Christ.

"He said, 'Now there was about this time Jesus, a wise man, if it be lawful to call Him a man; for He was a doer of wonderful works, a Teacher of such men as received the Truth with pleasure. He drew over to Him both many of the Jews and many of the Gentiles. He was the Christ. And when Pilate, at the suggestion of the principle men amongst us, had condemned Him to the Cross, those that loved Him at the first did not forsake Him; for He appeared to them alive again the third day; as the Divine Prophets had foretold these and ten thousand other wonderful things concerning Him. And the Tribe of Christians so named from Him, are

not extinct at this day' (Josephus, Ant. of the Jews, page 535, 3)."

(62) "AND JESUS SAID, I AM: AND YE SHALL SEE THE SON OF MAN SITTING ON THE RIGHT HAND OF POWER, AND COMING IN THE CLOUDS OF HEAVEN."

The phrase, *"And Jesus said, I am,"* constitutes a bold declaration of Who He was. Christ either deceived men by a conscious fraud, or He deceived Himself, or He was God. It is impossible to get out of this dilemma.

Wuest says, *"The pronoun 'I' is used for emphasis. It is, 'As for Myself, in contradistinction to all others, I am.'"*

In other words, the answer given by Jesus left absolutely no doubt as to Who He claimed to be, and, in Truth, was!

Whereas Jesus had refused to answer the false accusations, to this question concerning His Divinity, He must answer, because to refuse to do so would have been a denial of Who He was.

As well, and as Chrysostom said, *"Our Lord answered thus that He might leave without excuse all those who listen to Him, who would not hereafter be able to plead in the Day of Judgment that, when our Lord was solemnly asked in the Council whether He was the Son of God, He had refused to answer, or had answered evasively. The answer of our Lord is full of majesty and sublimity."*

Not only must He answer Who He was, but, as well, these men must know, and without doubt, that they are condemning the Messiah, the Holy One of God, even the *"I am"* of the Old Testament.

When Jesus gave this solemn witness as to His Divinity, it must have hit like a bombshell. There is no way it could have been otherwise. Grown men must have trembled, and yet, they refused to heed this, the last appeal to their hearts and consciences, which would have saved them and their nation. Instead, they pressed on, even to their own doom.

Considering the three and a half years of miracles, even to the raising of the dead, and in a manner the world had never seen before, and even with the fulfilling of all Prophecy, still, they would not believe! Truly, as the Prophet Jeremiah said, *"The heart is deceitful above all things, and desperately wicked: who can know it?"* (Jer. 17:9).

The phrase, *"And ye shall see,"* proclaims that Caiaphas, as well as the entirety of the Jewish Sanhedrin, would ultimately *"see"* that what Jesus had just said was absolutely true.

It is as if Jesus said, and stated by Bickersteth, *"You, O Caiaphas, and you the Chief Priests and Elders of the Jews, are now unjustly condemning Me as a false Prophet and a false Christ; but the day is at hand when I, Who am now a prisoner at your judgment seat, shall sit on the Throne of Glory as the Judge of you and of all mankind. You are now about to condemn Me to the death of the Cross; but I shall then sit in judgment upon you, and condemn you for this terrible guilt of slaying Me, Who am the True God and the Judge of the world."*

The phrase, *"The Son of Man sitting on the right hand of power, and coming in the clouds of Heaven,"* is a reference to Psalm 110:1 and Daniel 7:13.

These two statements were considered as a claim to Messiahship by the Jews, as these Old Testament Passages to which reference was made were looked upon as Messianic.

Consequently, these words as uttered by Christ at this trial before the Sanhedrin, as we have alluded to, were a final but ineffective summons to Repentance and Faith, in that the Jewish Leaders, instead of repenting of their rejection of Jesus as Messiah, and accepting Him as such, caused Him to be crucified (Swete).

Jesus is saying, *"You are judging Me now, but one day I will judge you, and even though you will now kill Me, still, I will rise again, and one day come back to this earth in Power and Glory.*

"That which you now deny Me, I will have at the Second Coming."

The answer of Jesus was so ringing, so declarative, that there was absolutely no way of misunderstanding what He had said. To be sure, that which He said will one day come to pass, and exactly as He said it.

Actually, the latter part concerning the Second Coming will be fulfilled first. At the conclusion of the Kingdom Age, which the Second Coming will precipitate, the Great White Throne Judgment will commence, with Jesus judging all, as He sits *"On the Right Hand of Power,"* i.e., God (Rev. 20:11-15).

It is as well a solemn announcement to the world that Jesus is now the Saviour, but, at a point in time, He will become the Judge. As well, as wonderful as He was, and is, as Saviour, likewise, He will be as Judge.

(63) "THEN THE HIGH PRIEST RENT HIS CLOTHES, AND SAITH, WHAT NEED WE ANY FURTHER WITNESSES?"

The phrase, *"Then the High Priest rent his clothes,"* signified the garment immediately under the outward robe. The Jewish tunic was open under the chin, in which the wearer could seize the garment at this opening with both hands, and violently tear it asunder down to the waist.

The tearing of garments was an old sign of mourning or sorrow first mentioned in Genesis 37:29. The Mosaic Law forbad the High Priest from rending His garments in the case of private troubles (Lev. 10:6, 21:10), but when acting as a judge, he was required by custom to express in this way his horror of that which he considered to be blasphemy, at least that uttered in his presence (Wuest).

Some of the Early Church Fathers think that by this action, Caiaphas involuntarily typified the rending of the Priesthood from himself and from the Jewish nation.

As the abrogation of the Throne of David was carried out by Nebuchadnezzar some 600 years before, as well, the Priesthood was now destroyed, or soon would be, placing Israel in a position of no more reason to exist. And that is exactly what happened!

For nearly 2,000 years the Jewish people have wandered from nation to nation as outcasts, and because by their rejection of Jesus Christ, they, during this time, have had no Divine purpose.

As all know, in 1948 Israel once again became a nation. This is brought about by the Lord, in order that they may fulfill the Divine Prophecies, and ultimately accept Jesus Christ as Messiah and Redeemer. They will then resume their role and place as originally intended by God (Zech. 14).

The question, *"And saith, What need we any further witnesses?",* proclaims the statement of Christ concerning His Deity as being the sought-for evidence. The prisoner had incriminated Himself (Swete).

The liars they had produced as *"witnesses"* could not agree among themselves; therefore, Caiaphas felt that this was the only opportunity of condemnation he would have. Therefore, he seized upon it.

(64) "YE HAVE HEARD THE BLASPHEMY: WHAT THINK YE? AND THEY ALL CONDEMNED HIM TO BE GUILTY OF DEATH."

The exclamation, *"Ye have heard the blasphemy,"* proclaims the High Priest rendering his conclusion even before testing the claims of Jesus. Consequently, it becomes more and more obvious that this farce of a trial was not convened to seek for the Truth, but, instead, to find a way, any way, to condemn Christ.

No! What they heard was not *"blasphemy,"* but rather a proclamation of the Son of God respecting His Deity. There was *"blasphemy"* all right, but it was on their part instead!

The question, *"What think ye?"*, would be the singular most important question ever asked of these men. Their answer would seal their eternal doom.

As well, the question, *"What think ye?"*, as asked by Caiaphas so long ago, is a question that not only the Jewish Sanhedrin had to answer, but also every single human being who has ever lived. Actually, this is the question of the ages.

The controversy is not so much with God, as it is with His Son, the Lord Jesus Christ. Much of the world steeped in heathenistic religions do not believe Jesus Christ is the Son of God, and, therefore, the Redeemer of the world. So, as Caiaphas and the Sanhedrin, they have given their answer.

Even in the ranks of that which proposes to be *"Christian,"* this is the question of the hour. The world of Roman Catholicism claims to believe that Jesus is the Son of God, but almost altogether ignore Him, in favor of His Mother, Mary. She is lionized and even deified, whether they claim such or not! Consequently, by their actions centered up in Mary worship, Jesus Christ is denied, whether they realize it or not.

Even in Christian Protestant circles, a very great percentage do not believe that Jesus Christ is the Son of God.

On this question hangs the Salvation of the entirety of mankind, and for all time. While no Salvation is afforded for the mere acclamation that Jesus is the Son of God, still, it is certain that one cannot be saved without embracing this cardinal doctrine. Believing that He is the Son of God is the first step in the Salvation process, with accepting Him as one's Lord and Saviour being the concluding step (Jn. 3:16).

So, *"What think ye?"*

The phrase, *"And they all condemned Him to be guilty of death,"* thus fulfilling the Prophecy of 8:31.

According to Luke 23:51, Joseph of Arimathaea was not present since he did not consent to the death of Jesus. It seems that Nicodemus was not present as well, probably not having been invited because of his sympathy with Christ. So, the *"all"* pertained to those present, and not those absent.

Even though these two men were members of the highest ruling religious body in Israel, which spoke of unparalleled success, still, the emptiness in their hearts was not satisfied until they met Jesus. Then they found what the soul of man craved.

Salvation is not a philosophy, nor a set of rules and regulations. Neither is it a Church, but rather a Person, and, more particularly, a Man, The Man, Jesus Christ.

Considering there were only two of the seventy-one members of the vaunted Sanhedrin who knew and served the Lord, and, therefore, accepted Christ, this ratio would probably be very close to modern Christendom respecting those in religious hierarchy who are truly saved.

I am not saying that the Holy Spirit intended for this to serve as an example, but I suspect, especially when one considers all of Christendom, that most modern Christian Leaders would fall into the category of those who condemned Christ to death. I realize this statement is strong, but I believe it to be true. And how do I come to this conclusion?

Jesus said, *"Ye shall know them by their fruits"* (Mat. 7:16). Most in religious hierarchy oppose anything that is of God, exactly as their counterparts of 2,000 years ago. While it is true that they are religious, even very religious, even as the Pharisees of old, still, it is religion and not Christlikeness. Actually, religion is the biggest business in the world, whether Apostate Christendom or the other major religions, far eclipsing General Motors, Honda, Microsoft, etc. It actually enslaves much of the world.

When Lenin, the father of Communism, said, *"Religion is the opiate of the masses,"* he was actually correct. However, that in no way includes a true relationship with Jesus Christ.

I have been in Russia, even in the services of the Russian Orthodox Church. I have watched the people kissing the feet of the Priests, and kissing the religious icons on the walls or places of prominence in all of these Churches. I know how the Apostle Paul felt as *"His spirit was stirred in him, when he saw the city* (Athens) *wholly given to idolatry"* (Acts 17:16). The Russian Orthodox Church, as well as Catholicism, the Church of England, along with much of Protestant Christendom, can be labeled only as *"idolatry."*

And yet, there is a True Remnant called the *"Body of Christ,"* who truly know the Lord as their Saviour and Redeemer. To be sure, that group is small, at least when compared with the whole. But, nevertheless, 'tis *"A glorious Church, not having spot, or wrinkle, or any such thing; but that it should be holy and without blemish"* (Eph. 5:27).

(65) "AND SOME BEGAN TO SPIT ON HIM, AND TO COVER HIS FACE, AND TO BUFFET HIM, AND TO SAY UNTO HIM, PROPHECY: AND THE SERVANTS DID STRIKE HIM WITH THE PALMS OF THEIR HANDS."

The phrase, *"And some began to spit on Him,"* fulfilled Isaiah 50:6, *"I hid not My Face from shame and spitting."*

The evidence is that the *"some"* included members of the Sanhedrin, as well as the Temple guards and soldiers. Actually, the evidence is that the latter did not join in these indignities until they observed the members of the Sanhedrin engaging in these vile acts.

There is no way the mind of man can adequately comprehend the depths to which the religious heart can sink. These verses will show that it is the most vile of all. Even hardened Roman soldiers, who were pagans, were not this cruel. Such action is reserved for professors of religion.

The phrase, *"And to cover His Face,"* means they wrapped a covering around the Lord's Head so as to blindfold Him. This was for the purpose of asking Him to identify the one who struck Him, and with great sarcasm.

The phrase, *"And to buffet Him,"* in the Greek Text is *"kolaphizo,"* and means *"to strike with the fist,"* thus, *"to pummel."*

Isaiah, some 800 years before, had prophesied, *"His visage was so marred more than any man"* (Isa. 52:14).

The effect of the brutalities described here, caused His Face to be so marred that His appearance was not that of a man, but rather like something not human.

As well, it must be noted that modern Religious Leaders who do not know Christ would do the same to the true followers of Christ, if the law of the land did not prevent them. Actually, more blood has been spilled in this fashion than words could ever begin to describe.

As an aside, this one Scripture pretty well destroys the myth of the Shroud of Turin, which is alleged by some in Catholicism to be the cloth which covered the Face of Jesus after His death. To be sure, whatever type of cloth was placed over His Face at that particular time, would have had no discernable imprint because of the disfigurement of His Features.

The phrase, *"And to say unto Him, Prophesy,"* now adds the spiritual abuse to the physical abuse.

The phrase, *"And the servants did strike Him with the palms of their hands,"* proclaims them, as stated, joining in after they see the Religious Leaders of Israel conducting themselves accordingly.

How could these people do such a thing?

Despite their religious activity, these men were wicked, vile reprobates. They claimed to know God, but were actually children of Satan. Had they known God, they would have known that which belonged to God, namely His Son, the Lord Jesus Christ.

As well, people who truly know the Lord, will know that which is of the Lord. If they oppose that which is truly of God, it is a sign they do not know God, or at least have very little relationship with Him, if any!

(66) "AND AS PETER WAS BENEATH IN THE PALACE, THERE COMETH ONE OF THE MAIDS OF THE HIGH PRIEST."

The phrase, *"And as Peter was beneath in the palace,"* speaks of the porch of the palace. The trial of Jesus was held in an upper story.

The phrase, *"There cometh one of the maids of the High Priest,"* concerns one of the domestics who had the very early morning shift which evidently began some time before daylight.

(67) "AND WHEN SHE SAW PETER WARMING HIMSELF, SHE LOOKED UPON HIM, AND SAID, AND THOU ALSO WAST WITH JESUS OF NAZARETH."

The phrase, *"And when she saw Peter warming himself,"* now begins the saga which will prove the boastings of Peter as being hollow.

The very fact that Peter was there, shows that he did not want to desert Jesus. However, his actions will show that he will not desire to stand up for Him either! He is in the same position as multiple millions who want Christ, but not enough to stand up and be counted. They are in a spiritual twilight zone, which is neither here nor there. However, almost all in such a position, when tested, which will come about sooner or later, will fail in the same manner as Peter. There is no middle ground in serving Jesus Christ. One either serves Him with his whole heart, or serves Him not at all!

The phrase, *"She looked upon Him, and said,"* in the Greek Text means that she *"Gazed intently at."*

The phrase, *"And thou also wast with Jesus of Nazareth,"* means that even though she possibly did not know his name, yet she knew he was a follower of Christ. Quite possibly she had seen him with Jesus at an earlier time.

As well, her statement suggests much more than this knowledge, but, rather, that she was well aware of the proceedings which were taking place even then concerning Jesus.

(68) "BUT HE DENIED, SAYING, I KNOW NOT, NEITHER UNDERSTAND I WHAT THOU SAYEST. AND HE WENT OUT INTO THE PORCH; AND THE COCK CREW."

The phrase, *"But he denied, saying, I know not, neither understand I what Thou sayest,"* proclaims him doing exactly what Jesus had said he would do!

Swete suggests: *"Had Peter been called to go with the Master to judgment and death, possibly he would have done so. However, his test came in an unexpected form, and discovered a weak point — his lack of moral courage."*

In simple terminology, he was attempting to act as if he was a stranger to Christ, consequently, not knowing or understanding what the girl was speaking of.

The phrase, *"And he went out into the porch; and the cock crew,"* proclaims his consternation after he answered the girl. No doubt, filled with guilt, he leaves the fire, walking away from the small crowd which had possibly gathered, probably to get away from the girl more so than anything else.

Then he heard the rooster crow!

I wonder what was in his mind when this happened, no doubt recalling the Words of Jesus, *"That this day, even in this night, before the cock crow twice, thou shalt deny me thrice"* (vs. 30).

NOTES

Did he resolve not to deny again? Or was he so caught up in the act of the moment that he momentarily forgot that Jesus said he would do this thing three times?

(69) "AND A MAID SAW HIM AGAIN, AND BEGAN TO SAY TO THEM THAT STOOD BY, THIS IS ONE OF THEM."

The phrase, *"And a maid saw him again,"* implies that this is a different *"maid"* than the previous.

The phrase, *"And began to say to them that stood by, This is one of them,"* probably means that Peter had by now returned to the fire, with him being pointed out once more.

(70) "AND HE DENIED IT AGAIN. AND A LITTLE AFTER, THEY THAT STOOD BY SAID AGAIN TO PETER, SURELY THOU ART ONE OF THEM: FOR THOU ART A GALILAEAN, AND THY SPEECH AGREETH THERETO."

The phrase, *"And he denied it again,"* proclaims the second denial. He possibly said basically the same words that he had said previously.

Quite possibly, when the second maid pointed him out, a man joined in with her because Luke records Peter as saying at this time, and concerning his association with Jesus, *"Man, I am not"* (Lk. 22:58).

The phrase, *"And a little after, they that stood by said again to Peter, Surely thou art one of them,"* proclaims the occasion for the third denial. The people standing around the fire, both men and women, began to pick up on what the *"maid"* had said.

The phrase, *"For thou art a Galilaean, and thy speech agreeth thereto,"* is actually used in contempt. Many people in Jerusalem looked down on the Galileans for various reasons, with their accent being one of those reasons. In other words, they were looked at somewhat like country bumpkins. As well, it was commonly known that most of the Twelve who were the chosen Disciples of Jesus were from Galilee.

(71) "BUT HE BEGAN TO CURSE AND TO SWEAR, SAYING, I KNOW NOT THIS MAN OF WHOM YE SPEAK."

The phrase, *"But he began to curse and to swear,"* does not refer to profanity. The Greek word for *"curse"* is *"anathematizo,"* which means *"to declare anathema or cursed."* Peter thus declares himself subject to the Divine curse if he is not telling the truth when he disclaims all acquaintance with Jesus (Wuest).

The word, *"swear,"* is the same word found in Hebrews 3:11, where God is said to swear, that is, to put Himself under oath.

Peter's sin was about as bad as could be imagined, inasmuch as he brought God into his lie. In effect, he was calling on God to curse him to eternal damnation, if he was not telling the truth concerning his disavowal of any association with Christ — and this at the very moment that the Sanhedrin and others were spitting on the Face of Jesus, and striking Him repeatedly.

The phrase, *"Saying, I know not this Man of Whom ye speak,"* proclaims the third denial, and, therefore, completely fulfilling the prediction of Christ.

(72) "AND THE SECOND TIME THE COCK CREW. AND PETER CALLED TO MIND THE WORD THAT JESUS SAID UNTO HIM, BEFORE THE COCK CROW TWICE, THOU SHALT DENY ME THRICE. AND WHEN HE THOUGHT THEREON, HE WEPT."

The phrase, *"And the second time the cock crew,"* was probably pretty close to daylight. Some have suggested that the first time could have been as early as 1 a.m.

At any rate, these several intervening hours were momentous to say the least!

All the Disciples would forsake Jesus, with Peter denying Him. As well, by their perfidious action, the Religious Leaders of Israel would seal the doom of themselves and their nation. They would condemn and crucify the Lord of Glory.

The phrase, *"And Peter called to mind the Word that Jesus said unto him,"* may have been the time that Jesus walked by and looked at him (Lk. 22:61).

As it was not daylight, the Sanhedrin would meet again to formerly condemn Jesus, because it was not legal for them to do so during the night. Consequently, before taking Jesus to Pilate, they would *"legalize"* their insidious activities. When Jesus looked at Peter, was probably when he was being led to the formal meeting place of the Sanhedrin. There is no record that Jesus said anything to Peter. However, that one look was enough to stamp on Peter's mind the things Christ had said.

The phrase, *"Before the cock crow twice, thou shalt deny Me thrice,"* proclaims exactly what Jesus had said.

The phrase, *"And when he thought thereon, he wept,"* is proclaimed by Matthew, *"And wept*

bitterly" (Mat. 26:75). This refers to wracking sobs, which came from the depths of his being. This was the time of Peter's Repentance, which is portrayed by *"A broken and a contrite heart"* (Ps. 51:17).

It is said that ever after, when Peter would hear the crowing of a rooster, he would fall to his knees, consequently, never forgetting this moment.

And yet, the Lord would wondrously and graciously recommission him (Jn. 21:15-17), and use him mightily. He was one of the greatest men of God who ever lived.

Did Peter fall?

Almost all would say he did. However, the Scripture is replete with the wonderful Truth that despite failures, one is never fallen who continues to trust Christ (I Jn. 1:9). While it is true that Peter did sin, and grievously so, still, he did not turn away from the Lord, but rather to Him. Sin in any form is a horrible and wicked thing. However, if sin is properly taken to Christ, and with proper confession made to Him, the act is cleansed and canceled by the Precious Blood of Jesus (I Jn. 2:1-2).

Some may claim that such is too easy, thereby providing a license for people to sin. Such thinking is foolishness, simply because no True Believer desires to sin. Sin is repugnant to Him, and if it does happen, he is quick to take it to Christ. Only unbelievers practice sin (I Jn. 5:18).

Anyone who would suggest that Peter wanted and desired to do what he did, evidently knows little of the situation. No True Believer desires to sin. Even the very thoughts of failing God are abhorrent to the soul. And yet, there is not a Believer who has ever lived, that has not had to go to the Lord quite a number of times, pleading Mercy and Grace. Thank God, such Mercy and Grace is available.

Furthermore, on such occasions we are invited to *"Come boldly unto the Throne of Grace, that we may obtain Mercy, and find Grace to help in time of need"* (Heb. 4:16).

No! Even though Peter failed, he did not fall!

CHAPTER 15

(1) "AND STRAIGHTWAY IN THE MORNING THE CHIEF PRIESTS HELD A CONSULTATION WITH THE ELDERS AND SCRIBES

AND THE WHOLE COUNCIL, AND BOUND JESUS, AND CARRIED HIM AWAY, AND DELIVERED HIM TO PILATE."

The phrase, *"And straightway in the morning,"* refers to the approximate time of daylight.

The phrase, *"The Chief Priests held a consultation with the Elders and Scribes and the whole Council,"* referred to the entire Sanhedrin, with the possible exception, as stated, of Nicodemus and Joseph of Arimathaea. (It is not known for certain if they were present.)

The proceedings recorded in the last Chapter probably terminated a little before daylight. And, as stated, they were illegal. Now comes the more formal trial. However, they will continue to break their own Law.

In capital cases, sentences of condemnation might not be legally pronounced on the day of trial. Yet our Lord was tried, condemned, and crucified on the same day (Bickersteth).

The phrase, *"And bound Jesus,"* refers to the time they finished the second trial. By now, He must have been a grotesque sight! His Face would have been unrecognizable, but the torture had not ended, actually, only begun.

The phrase, *"And carried Him away,"* means that even while they were taking Him to Pilate, they were doing so with violence and force. In other words, they continue to strike and beat Him, even while He is attempting to walk from one building to another.

He is by now *"fair game,"* a term used to denote that *"anything goes."*

Due to Roman control, they were unable to carry out the death sentence on Him; however, they would torture Him to near death. In these actions, their true hearts begin to show. When one is helpless, and, consequently, anything can be done to that person without any fear of reprisal, but rather commendation, one quickly sees what people really are.

Jesus was now helpless, and by His Own choice. Consequently, they would be allowed to do whatever they desired. What they desired, was exactly what Satan desired, to *"steal, kill, and destroy"* (Jn. 10:10).

The phrase, *"And delivered Him to Pilate,"* meant that knowing such action, within itself, and even their own charges against Him, would not guarantee His death. Therefore, they would put a political construction on the confession of Jesus regarding His claim of Deity. They

NOTES

would claim that He was a pretender to the Throne of Israel. This will force Pilate to deal with Jesus from a political stance instead of a religious stance, because failure to do so could involve him in a dereliction of duty towards the Throne of the Caesars. The accusation would boil down to the Jews accusing Jesus of setting Himself up as a King in opposition to Caesar, which, of course, was a serious charge.

Judaea had now been added to the Province of Syria, and governed by Procurators, of whom Pontius Pilate was the fifth.

It was necessary for the Jews to deliver Christ to Roman power, because, as stated, the power of life and death had been taken from them since they became subject to the Romans. John recorded them saying, *"It is not lawful for us to put any man to death"* (Jn. 18:31).

Pontius Pilate was a Roman of the upper middle-class order. Little is known of his career before 26 A.D. But in that year, the Emperor Tiberius appointed him, as stated, to be the fifth Procurator.

Before A.D. 21, such Governors could not be accompanied by their wives. However, in 21 A.D. the Roman Senate reversed its policy on that issue. Consequently, Pilate had his wife with him in Judaea (Mat. 27:19).

As Procurator (Governor), he had full control in the Province, being in charge of an army of approximately 5,000 men. They were stationed at Caesarea, with a detachment on garrison duty at Jerusalem in the fortress of Antonia.

Pilate had full powers of life and death, and could reverse capital sentences passed by the Sanhedrin, which had to be submitted to him for ratification. He also appointed the High Priests and controlled the Temple and its funds. The very vestments of the High Priest were in his custody and were released only for festivals, when the Governor took up residence in Jerusalem, consequently, bringing in additional troops to patrol the city, as he did at this Passover time.

It is somewhat ironical that even pagan historians mention Pilate only in connection with his authorization of the death of Jesus.

Philo finds nothing good to say about Pilate. He describes him as *"by nature rigid and stubbornly harsh and of spiteful disposition and an exceeding wrathful man."*

The verdict of the New Testament is that he was a weak man, ready to serve expediency rather than principle, whose authorization of the judicial murder of the Saviour was due less to a desire to please the Jewish authorities than the fear of imperial displeasure if Tiberius heard of further unrest in Judaea. This is made abundantly evident by his mockery of the Jews in the wording of the superscription on the Cross of Christ (Jn. 19:19-22).

Due to extensive trouble at Mt. Gerizim, to which Pilate responded by executing the ringleaders, he was ultimately called to Rome where he was to appear before the Emperor to answer the charges brought against him. However, on his way to Rome Tiberius died. This was in 37 A.D. Nothing is known of the outcome of this trial, as he appeared before Emperor Gaius who succeeded Tiberius. However, Eusebius says that Pilate committed suicide shortly thereafter.

(2) "AND PILATE ASKED HIM, ART THOU THE KING OF THE JEWS? AND HE ANSWERING SAID UNTO HIM, THOU SAYEST IT."

The question, *"And Pilate asked Him, Art Thou the King of the Jews?"*, proclaims the Governor going to the very heart of the matter, which to him was a political question. He had no regard or concern for the religious controversy.

It seems the Jews had brought three charges against Jesus, at least as far as Pilate was concerned. They are as follows:

1. He perverted the nation.
2. That He forbade to give tribute to Caesar.
3. That He said He was Christ, a King.

It would have been virtually impossible for Pilate to have not heard of Jesus. He was no doubt familiar with His blameless life, His pure Doctrine, and the many Miracles that were performed.

As we have alluded, his disposition before Jesus portrayed him as a weak man. He seemed to have enemies in Rome, as well as elsewhere. Consequently, as facts would later prove, his hold on his governorship was weak to say the least! As a result, he saw in Jesus the possibility of another threat to his position, so he would yield to expediency, allowing these reprobates to have their way.

The phrase, *"And He answering said unto him, Thou sayest it,"* refers to Jesus answering in the affirmative. In effect, Jesus said, *"Thou sayest that which is true."*

(3) "AND THE CHIEF PRIESTS ACCUSED HIM OF MANY THINGS: BUT HE ANSWERED NOTHING."

Even though he answered Pilate, he would not answer the accusations of the *"Chief Priests."* Why?

Even though they *"accused Him of many things,"* He said nothing, simply because their accusations were false.

Pilate's question was legitimate and thereby received a legitimate answer. Their accusations were not legitimate, so *"He answered nothing."*

(4) "AND PILATE ASKED HIM AGAIN, SAYING, ANSWEREST THOU NOTHING? BEHOLD HOW MANY THINGS THEY WITNESS AGAINST THEE."

The phrase, *"And Pilate asked Him again,"* proclaims the astonishment of the Governor at Jesus saying nothing, especially considering how serious these allegations were! To Pilate this self-restraint was incomprehensible. Actually, he had never met anyone like Christ, and, in Truth, no one else had ever met anyone like Christ.

The question, *"Answerest Thou nothing?",* is perplexing to the Governor. The Lord does not defend Himself, and the Governor does not understand the reason why.

It is obvious that he does not believe Jesus to be a political pretender, but does not quite know what to make of Him!

The phrase, *"How many things they witness against Thee,"* proclaims the startlement of the Governor more so than anything else. He had never seen a man who would not defend himself.

(5) "BUT JESUS YET ANSWERED NOTHING; SO THAT PILATE MARVELLED."

The phrase, *"But Jesus yet answered nothing,"* proclaims the answer of Christ to the constant exclamation of Pilate. The answer was silence.

Someone has said, *"The silence of a blameless life pleads more powerfully than any defense, however elaborate."*

Such was Christ!

The phrase, *"So that Pilate marvelled,"* proclaims the Governor startled and marvelling about several things: the silence of Christ in the face of these vehement accusations by the leading men of the Jews, His contempt of death, and His calmness. As stated, He had never met anyone even remotely so like Jesus.

(6) "NOW AT THAT FEAST HE RELEASED UNTO THEM ONE PRISONER, WHOMSO-EVER THEY DESIRED."

Immediately before the situation concerning Barabbas, Pilate sent Jesus to Herod, which is omitted by Mark (Lk. 23:6-12).

By this act, Pilate hoped to rid himself of the responsibility of Jesus. However, Herod mockingly sent Him back to Pilate. So, this strategy failed!

The phrase, *"Now at that feast he released unto them one prisoner,"* constitutes his second effort to rid himself of the responsibility of Christ. However, it will succeed no better than the former.

In John 18:39, we read that Pilate said, *"Ye have a custom, that I should release unto you one at the Passover."*

There is no record in the Law of Moses where such a custom originated. However, some maintain that the custom began with the Jews at some point in time, to commemorate the deliverance of the Children of Israel from Egyptian bondage. Others claim that it was a practice engaged in by the Romans all over the world of that day, and that they instituted it in Israel as well! It was deemed to be a political ploy which would find favor with the people. Consequently, this custom and its origin is anyone's guess.

The phrase, *"Whomsoever they desired,"* it seems, means exactly what it said.

(7) "AND THERE WAS ONE NAMED BARABBAS, WHICH LAY BOUND WITH THEM THAT HAD MADE INSURRECTION WITH HIM, WHO HAD COMMITTED MURDER IN THE INSURRECTION."

The phrase, *"And there was one named Barabbas,"* speaks of a leader of insurrection and a murderer. He was arrested for homicidal political terrorism. From the way Mark describes it, the incident in which he was engaged seemed to be well known. His crime was an insurrection against Rome, which had the sympathy of many people. Actually, there were many insurrectionists at this particular time, with this problem continuing to increase in one form or the other until Rome finally destroyed Jerusalem in 70 A.D.

There is some evidence that he was referred to as *"Jesus Barabbas."* If so, the Jews had the choice of *"Jesus Barabbas"* or *"Jesus Christ."*

The phrase, *"Which lay bound with them that had made insurrection with him,"* concerned the

entire group, however large it was, which had been apprehended by Pilate. Rome was quick to put down any hint of insurrection, so Pilate is going to be thrown into another quandary.

He is going to be forced to make the choice between a murderous leader of insurrection, or a pretender to the Throne of Israel. At first glance, it would seem that the choice should be easily made. Barabbas is a known enemy of Rome, while Jesus has expressed no tendency in this direction whatsoever. However, the weakness of Pilate will see him succumbing to the expediency of the moment.

The phrase, *"Who had committed murder in the insurrection,"* probably pertained to the murder of a Roman soldier, or at least someone favorable to Rome.

(8) "AND THE MULTITUDE CRYING ALOUD BEGAN TO DESIRE HIM TO DO AS HE HAD EVER DONE UNTO THEM."

The phrase, *"And the multitude crying aloud,"* concerns this custom of releasing a prisoner at this time of the year, and the loud clamor for this to be done. This activity would have had little or nothing to do with Jesus, with the interruption coming at a particular time of which Pilate attempted to take advantage. He was to be disappointed!

The phrase, *"Began to desire him to do as he had ever done unto them,"* concerned the releasing of a particular prisoner.

At this stage, it does not seem as if the clamoring crowd had anyone in particular in mind respecting release. At this stage, they seemed to be more concerned regarding the custom than the person.

(9) "BUT PILATE ANSWERED THEM, SAYING, WILL YE THAT I RELEASE UNTO YOU THE KING OF THE JEWS?"

The phrase, *"But Pilate answered them, saying,"* proclaims the Governor attempting to take advantage of this which he sees as another opportunity to rid himself of the responsibility of Jesus. His efforts will be fruitless.

The question, *"Will ye that I release unto you the King of the Jews?",* referred to Jesus, and that which He hoped this crowd would do.

However, the manner in which he referred to Jesus, using the title *"King of the Jews,"* was done in sarcasm.

He would have reasoned that inasmuch as Jesus had claimed such, he (Pilate) was entitled to use it as well, which, at least in his mind, was ludicrous considering the present appearance of Christ. Whatever he thought of Jesus, he, in no way thought of Him as being a King. Consequently, he was to make the greatest mistake of his life. Jesus was not only *"King of the Jews,"* but, as well, The Son of the Living God.

(10) "FOR HE KNEW THAT THE CHIEF PRIESTS HAD DELIVERED HIM FOR ENVY."

Inasmuch as the *"envy"* was so obvious that even this pagan could see it, tells us exactly to what level these Religious Leaders had sunk.

The *"Chief Priests"* saw that Jesus was gaining popularity and increasing influence over the people, as a result of His Person, His Miracles, and the Power of His Words. As they saw His influence gaining, they saw theirs lessening. Consequently, He must be destroyed.

This evil passion, *"envy,"* is the ruling factor of most, if not all, religion. Inasmuch as religion is man-directed, and, consequently, man-led, it is extremely political in nature. As such, it cannot be God-directed; therefore, it must protect its interest at whatever cost.

That which is God-directed is protected by the Lord, with His followers giving no consideration to place or position.

However, place and position is everything to those who are man-led, and they will do anything to protect it. Such makes up the world of religion, even to this present hour.

When men fight to hold on to whatever they think they presently have, at least in the realm of religion, one can be certain that it was not given by God. The Apostle Paul would greatly defend the Gospel, but he did little to defend himself, at least where the Gospel was not at stake.

Pilate now knows that the real offense of Jesus was His great influence with the people. Swete says: *"The pretense of loyalty to the Emperor, was too flimsy to deceive a man of the world, and he detected under their disguise, the vulgar vice of envy."*

(11) "BUT THE CHIEF PRIESTS MOVED THE PEOPLE, THAT HE SHOULD RATHER RELEASE BARABBAS UNTO THEM."

The phrase, *"But the Chief Priests moved the people,"* proclaims at least some interval of time after Pilate had asked, at least in a roundabout way that they should request the release of Jesus.

NOTES

What these *"Chief Priests"* told the people is not known, at least respecting the choice of Barabbas. Whatever it was, it swayed the people.

The phrase, *"That he should rather release Barabbas unto them,"* presents them with the choice, as stated, *"Jesus Barabbas,"* or *"Jesus Christ!"*

The crowd who had gathered at this very early morning hour, was probably the rabble of the city, which could be easily influenced, and especially for evil. So they demanded the release of *"Barabbas,"* even though he was a murderer.

As a result of this demand, Israel has had murderers ruling over them for nearly 2,000 years. Only since 1948, have they gained some type of autonomy and safety. Up until then they were at the mercy of the world, which showed no mercy. They wanted a murderer, so they received a murderer, and Adolph Hitler is but one example of the many.

Some would claim that whatever was done then should not apply to succeeding generations. However, the succeeding generations of Jewish people, at least as a whole, have held Jesus Christ with the same contempt as their forefathers, consequently, with even worse days immediately ahead (Jer. 30:7).

(12) "AND PILATE ANSWERED AND SAID AGAIN UNTO THEM, WHAT WILL YE THEN THAT I SHALL DO UNTO HIM WHOM YE CALL THE KING OF THE JEWS?"

The phrase, *"And Pilate answered and said again unto them,"* probably proclaims him not knowing at the moment who the crowd will demand for release. It seems he still has hope that they will request Jesus Christ. But yet he will continue with his sarcasm!

The question, *"What will ye then that I shall do unto Him Whom ye call the King of the Jews?"*, presents a slight twist from the first time he asked the question.

Now he says, *"Whom ye call...,"* which curtailed his chances, even though in reality he had none at all.

Some claim he was appealing to their national pride by adding the words, *"Whom ye call."* However, even though that may have been possible, it is doubtful!

He seems to be more and more disgusted with the entire scenario, and even though he certainly does not give Jesus any credence as a King, he knows that the accusations of these Religious

Leaders have no credence. Jesus is harmless, at least as far as a threat to Rome is concerned.

So, whatever was in his mind did not work at all, with the situation now being taken completely out of his hands, at least considering that he only desired to please the people.

(13) "AND THEY CRIED OUT AGAIN, CRUCIFY HIM."

The phrase, *"And they cried out again,"* constituted a response that seemed to shock even Pilate.

The phrase, *"Crucify Him,"* is not only what he did not expect, but he also knew there were no grounds for such action.

Stoning was the Jewish method of punishment for blasphemy. Crucifixion was the Roman punishment for treason, which means the *"Chief Priests"* had been working the crowd. As stated, what they told them, which caused them to bring forth such a response, is not known. This rabble could probably be easily persuaded to believe anything, at least if it could provide them with some sort of entertainment, as disgusting as that may be. These were more than likely the drunks and thieves who prowled the city at night. Little did they realize that they were being used as a pawn in the most horrifying spectacle the world had ever known. Their cry for crucifixion would come back to haunt them.

About thirty-seven years later, when Titus laid siege to Jerusalem, so many Jews were crucified that there were literally no more places to put crosses. Tens of thousands, if not hundreds of thousands died in this agonizing manner — quite possibly some who screamed these very words that very day.

(14) "THEN PILATE SAID UNTO THEM, WHY, WHAT EVIL HATH HE DONE? AND THEY CRIED OUT THE MORE EXCEEDINGLY, CRUCIFY HIM."

The question, *"Then Pilate said unto them, Why, what evil hath He done?"*, rings out through the ages! The Truth is, He has done no evil. He had never harmed anyone, but rather had helped everyone; He had never caused sickness, but rather healing; He had never brought disappointment or sorrow, but rather joy and more abundant life; He had not added to the terrible weight of sin, but rather had delivered men from sin. In Truth, He is the only truly good Man Who has ever lived. He is the only

NOTES

One Who has ever walked perfect in character, whether by word, thought, or deed.

It was not for *"evil"* that they wanted to crucify Him, but because of His *"good."* His perfection and goodness was a constant rebuke to their evil.

To be sure, all who attempt to follow Him will face the same type of opposition. As well, it will come from the same source; the world, the Devil, and the apostate Church.

The phrase, *"And they cried out the more exceedingly, Crucify Him,"* represents their intensified answer. Luke says they repeated the cry again and again (Lk. 23:23).

Pilate was attempting to reason with them; however, a mob cannot be reasoned with, and this was a mob! Consequently, Pilate's last half-hearted effort to free Christ has been thwarted.

(15) "AND SO PILATE, WILLING TO CONTENT THE PEOPLE, RELEASED BARABBAS UNTO THEM, AND DELIVERED JESUS, WHEN HE HAD SCOURGED HIM, TO BE CRUCIFIED."

The phrase, *"And so Pilate, willing to content the people,"* shows what type of leader he actually was — weak and vacillating.

A strong leader would have done what he felt was right, irrespective of the demands of the people. He had approximately 5,000 soldiers to ensure his decision; however, instead of acting like a statesman, he conducted himself like a politician. Consequently, he would destroy himself.

Who were these people he was willing to content?

Some have claimed that these were the same people, who, some hours before during the triumphant entry, had cried *"Hosanna to the highest!"* However, that is incorrect. Those people who lined the roads during the momentous occasion were now in bed.

These *"people"* were, no doubt, as we have previously stated, the rabble of the city. They were, for the most part, the night prowlers, i.e., a baser sort. As is obvious, they were for sale to the highest bidder. The Chief Priests were the bidders, and these *"people"* would sell cheap!

What all of them did not know or realize, was that this was the Lord of Glory, the Creator of the ages, they were dealing with. Consequently, every action toward Him would ultimately be answered in kind.

As well, let it ever be known that the treatment of His, is, as well, the treatment of Him.

Even though He had the Power to call down any number of Angels, who would have come to His rescue at the slightest signal, He, instead, allowed evil to take its course. However, His allowing such, in no way abrogated the penalty all these participants would ultimately pay. In the Sermon on the Mount, He had plainly stated, *"For with what judgment ye judge, ye shall be judged: and with what measure ye mete, it shall be measured to you again"* (Mat. 7:2).

That day the Religious Leaders of Israel, along with the mob and Pilate, *"measured"* Jesus, and, in turn, they were measured!

Caiaphas committed suicide not long thereafter, and so did Pilate. About thirty-seven years later, when Titus, the Roman General, laid siege to Jerusalem, at this very site blood ran in the streets, even the blood of those who had cried, *"Crucify Him!"*

Pilate was *"willing to content the people,"* but he was not willing to content God. Tragically, tens of thousands of Preachers do the same every Sunday.

The phrase, *"Released Barabbas unto them,"* is a study in irony! They accused Christ of being an insurrectionist, which He was not, and yet demanded Barabbas be released, who had actually made insurrection! Such is evil!

In evil, as here, everything is upside down. Truth becomes a lie, and a lie becomes the Truth; right becomes wrong, and wrong becomes right; darkness becomes light, and light becomes darkness. Tragically, almost the entirety of the world operates on this basis, hence the wars, insurrection, starvation, hate, etc.

The phrase, *"And delivered Jesus,"* is said by the Holy Spirit with a broken heart.

Even though it was God's Will that His Son would die on a Cross, in order that the terrible price of sin would be paid and that men would be saved; still, it was not God's Will at all that these people do what they did. This terrible act, the condemnation of Christ, the most vile act in human history, was carried out by people who desired to do such a thing because their hearts were evil.

In the entirety of this scenario, Pilate, representing the world, is placed on one side, with the Religious Leaders of Israel placed on the other. Pilate, although a pagan and knowing nothing

NOTES

about God, still, had a far greater sense of fairness and integrity than the Religious Leaders of Israel. They had none at all! Their evil was the evil of refusing light and purposely accepting darkness. Pilate's evil, at least in part, was an evil of ignorance. Theirs was an evil of rebellion.

Consequently, in this scenario, a picture is drawn by the Holy Spirit of the true opposition against God and His Work. While the world definitely opposes that which is of God, still, the greater opposition by far comes from organized religion.

In almost every foreign country to which we travel in order to conduct Evangelistic Crusades, there has never been much opposition from the world. Most of the Governments remain neutral, with little hindrance from that sector. However, organized religion, and from whatever source, opposes these meetings in every conceivable way possible.

Why?

The reason then, and I speak of the Crucifixion of Christ, is the reason now! It doesn't matter to these people that many souls are saved in our Crusades, which means that lives are changed, with the Glory of the New Birth taking place, which is the greatest Miracle that one could ever know. To these people, it doesn't matter that Love replaces hate, and Light replaces darkness, with all of its glorious results. They bitterly oppose it, even while all of the time claiming to be of God. As well, the Religious Leaders of Israel claimed to be of God, while all the time crucifying the Son of God.

Of course it should be obvious that they were not of God, but rather Satan! That which is truly of God will not oppose God. So, the Believer at present is placed in the same position as the people during the time of Christ. Who was right, Jesus or the Religious Leaders? The people had to make a choice, as the people today have to make a choice.

Actually, that choice was not hard to make then, just as it is not hard to make now. The Fruit of Jesus' Ministry was obvious. The Religious Leaders had no Fruit in their Ministry. So why didn't the people readily choose Christ?

In Truth, many did; however, many, even though they knew Jesus was actually Who He said He was, would not follow Him, because they feared excommunication. Millions fear the same presently!

Religion controls people. Actually, its power is in its *"control."* It controls their money and their minds. In doing so, it desires to think for them, and decide for them. This is the earmark of religion.

The Religious Leaders of Israel saw their control of the people slipping away, so they felt they must destroy the One, and at any cost, Who was undermining this control.

The same spirit that killed Christ is alive and well presently, attempting to do the same identical thing to all those who truly follow Him, instead of religion.

As we have repeatedly stated, religion is that which is instituted by man, even though it speaks of God constantly. True Bible Christianity is not a religion, because it is instituted by God. Bible Christianity is rather a relationship with a Person, actually the Man, Christ Jesus. It is all of God and none of man.

Whenever man begins to add to, or take from, that which God has given, it then becomes *"religion."*

The phrase, *"When he had scourged Him,"* spoke of something so terrible that many men did not survive it.

Scourging was usually inflicted on slaves, but was also inflicted upon those who were condemned to death, even though free men. This scourging, which was a part of the punishment of Crucifixion, was of frightful severity. However, it seems from John 19:1 that the scourging of Jesus took place before His formal condemnation to be crucified.

It seems that Pilate may have used this tactic, hoping that the mob, upon seeing the brutally beaten Body of Jesus, would have their blood lust satisfied, and would relent in their demand for Crucifixion. However, if that was his thought, he was again to be disappointed (Jn. 19:1-16).

Wuest says, *"The Roman scourge was a lash usually made of leather thongs loaded at intervals with bone or metal. Peter, using the phrase, 'By Whose stripes ye were healed,' gives us a vivid picture of his recollection of how our Lord's Back looked after the scourging (I Pet. 2:24). The word 'stripes' in the Greek Text is in the singular number. The word refers to a bloody wale trickling with blood that arises under a blow. Our Lord's Back was so lacerated by the scourge, that it was one mass of open, raw, quivering flesh, trickling*

with blood, not a series of stripes or cuts, but one mass of torn flesh."

The phrase, *"To be crucified,"* proclaims Mark omitting the details given by John of how Pilate once again tried to reason with the Religious Leaders of Israel concerning the release of Jesus, but to no avail. They would be satisfied with nothing except His death, and that by Crucifixion. Then they could claim to the people that Rome demanded His execution, because of Him pretending to be a King. So, their demands upon this weak, vacillating Governor will bring about the desired results, *"Crucifixion!"*

(16) "AND THE SOLDIERS LED HIM AWAY INTO THE HALL, CALLED PRAETORIUM; AND THEY CALL TOGETHER THE WHOLE BAND."

The phrase, *"And the soldiers led Him away into the hall, called Praetorium,"* was actually the barracks of the soldiers, which could have numbered as many as 600.

The phrase, *"And they called together the whole band,"* referred to all the soldiers, which actually constituted Pilate's body guard.

Jesus had been condemned by the Religious Leaders of Israel, now He is condemned as well by the State. As He was *"fair game"* then, He is *"fair game"* now! Anything these soldiers desire to do to Him, short of death, they can do without any fear of censure.

(17) "AND THEY CLOTHED HIM WITH PURPLE, AND PLATTED A CROWN OF THORNS, AND PUT IT ABOUT HIS HEAD,"

The phrase, *"And they clothed Him with purple,"* probably spoke of the cloak of one of the soldiers, possibly a cast-off and faded rag.

The phrase, *"And platted a crown of thorns, and put it about His Head,"* spoke, some say, of *"victor's thorns,"* which were about six inches long. When puncturing the skin, they often created a festering wound.

The soldiers made a crude crown of sorts, which was meant to serve as a mockery of His claim at being King of the Jews.

However, it was also meant to denote, and again in mockery, His claim of Deity.

The Religious Leaders had no doubt spread this bit of information to the mob, as well as others, that Jesus claimed Divinity. Consequently, this poor pathetic figure standing before the soldiers, was mocked as God as well as King. To them, it was one big joke!

However, despite His appearance, and refusal to defend Himself, He was God, the Creator of all things. Little did they know what they were doing!

It is known that the scalp swells quickly when struck or lacerated. Consequently, as the thorns were pressed onto the brow of Christ, no doubt piercing the skin, for the soldiers would have had no mercy, His Head must have looked grotesque, enlarged as it was!

(18) "AND BEGAN TO SALUTE HIM, HAIL, KING OF THE JEWS!"

All was done in mockery, because they in no way knew Who and What He was!

Cyril said that the purple cloak symbolized the Kingdom of the whole world, which Christ was about to receive, and which He was to obtain by the shedding of His Most Precious Blood.

He would not receive the world at the hand of Satan, but He would receive it by the terrible price He paid. However, the possession of it is yet to be obtained, but, to be certain, it shall be obtained. The world awaits His Coming! As certain as He paid the price, as certain He shall come!

(19) "AND THEY SMOTE HIM ON THE HEAD WITH A REED, AND DID SPIT UPON HIM, AND BOWING THEIR KNEES WORSHIPPED HIM."

The phrase, "And they smote Him on the Head with a reed," spoke of a stiff object approximately two feet long, which would have driven the thorns deep within His Scalp, possibly even creasing the Skull. The pain must have been unbearable! And, as stated, the swelling and shedding of blood would have made Him not only unrecognizable, but inhuman respecting appearance as well!

The phrase, "And did spit upon Him," in effect, says they "kept spitting." This was a part of their contempt they showed Him.

I suspect it would be impossible for one to imagine exactly what He looked like, with His Head swollen as it was, and spittle mixed with blood covering His Face.

The phrase, "And bowing their knees worshipped Him," spoke to His claim of being God and King. In their "worship," which was mockery, even as the next verse proclaims, they were no doubt telling Him to perform a miracle, etc.

When the full impact of this horror is even partly comprehended, the Love of God takes on a completely different complexion. How could

He love people who would do such a thing? And yet we know He does. Paul wrote, "But God commendeth His Love toward us, in that, while we were yet sinners, Christ died for us" (Rom. 5:8). This is Love that is beyond the comprehension of man, but yet the Love that God gives to all who truly accept and follow Him.

(20) "AND WHEN THEY HAD MOCKED HIM, THEY TOOK OFF THE PURPLE FROM HIM, AND PUT HIS OWN CLOTHES ON HIM, AND LED HIM OUT TO CRUCIFY HIM."

The phrase, "And when they had mocked Him," sadly, did not conclude the "mocking." Men have been mocking Him ever since!

However, let it be known that the One Who is now the Saviour, is, at the same time, the Judge. Assuming these soldiers did not make this horrible thing right with God, (which some of them may well have done in the near future), they will one day stand at the Great White Throne Judgment to give account for these actions. Their deeds, as vile as they were, were written down in Heaven and will be recalled in glaring detail (Rev. 20:11-15).

As we have repeatedly stated, the contention of the world and the Church is with Jesus Christ. He Alone is the Way to the Father (Jn. 10:7). He said, "No man cometh unto the Father, but by Me" (Jn. 14:6).

Hundreds of millions of people in the world claim to know God, but without Jesus Christ. Such claims are spurious; no man knows God, nor can he know God, without accepting Jesus Christ as His Saviour. Christ Alone is the Way to the Father.

A newsman once exclaimed to me that such was not fair, because "The Jews do not believe in Christ," he said! If my memory is correct, I said to him, "You don't believe in Him either!"

He looked somewhat startled, I would hope, realizing that this subject has nothing to do with a class of people, but actually with Faith or the lack thereof.

The phrase, "They took off the purple from Him, and put His Own clothes on Him," referred to the seamless Robe.

The phrase, "And led Him out to crucify Him," constitutes the injustice of all injustices. Pilate, as recorded by Luke, had said that Jesus had done nothing worthy of death (Lk. 23:15). And yet he will "crucify Him" for political expediency, or so he thinks!

(21) "AND THEY COMPEL ONE SIMON A CYRENIAN, WHO PASSED BY, COMING OUT OF THE COUNTRY, THE FATHER OF ALEXANDER AND RUFUS, TO BEAR HIS CROSS."

The phrase, *"And they compel one Simon a Cyrenian,"* means they pressed him into service.

It seems that Jesus carried the Cross toward Golgotha as long as He could, but exhausted from the beatings and torture, there is evidence that He could not carry it further.

That which was being carried was probably only the cross-bar, which was probably about eight feet long and two or three inches thick. it could have weighed anywhere from fifty to a hundred pounds.

The long part of the Cross on which the body of the victim was placed was normally left suspended in the ground. When arriving at the scene of the Crucifixion, the victim would have been laid on the ground. The cross-bar would have been laid under his back, with his arms extended on the cross-beam on either side. The arms were either tied or nailed to the cross-bar, and in this case nailed.

Once the hands were nailed to the cross-bar, the victim was picked up, cross-bar and all, and suspended on the upright portion of the cross. The cross-bar was laid on top of the suspended portion, held in place by either being tied or nailed. The feet would have then been placed one on top of the other, and nailed through the instep to the suspended portion of the cross. It was the most cruel form of death that one could ever begin to imagine.

It is supposed to have been invented by Semiramis, Queen of Nimrod, who founded the Babylonian system of mysteries. As stated, it was reserved for slaves and the worst criminals.

The weight of the body hung on nails through the hands and feet. The victim was left on the cross until he died of pain and untold sufferings.

(At times, victims carried the entire cross, while at other times the cross-bar only. It is not known for certain which Jesus carried; however, most of the times it seems the victims carried only the cross-bar.)

It is thought by some that Simon may have been a black man, inasmuch as he lived on the north coast of Africa. However, there is no proof of that. Actually, the name *"Simon"* lends credence to the fact that he was a Jew who lived in Cyrene. Actually, the Cyrenians had a

NOTES

Synagogue in Jerusalem (Acts 6:9). He may well have come to Jerusalem at this time, making the long journey in order to keep the Passover, as many did!

However, whether black or white, he had the distinct honor of helping Jesus at this crucial time. To be sure, precious few did help Him.

The phrase, *"Who passed by, coming out of the country,"* means that he was not a party in any way to these insidious proceedings, but just happened to be standing there when Jesus came by. Quite possibly he saw the commotion and stopped to see what was happening. The Lord in bearing the Cross, evidently became so exhausted that He could not proceed under its terrible weight, especially considering the torture already endured. His legs must have buckled in that He could no longer carry the wooden beam. It all happened very close to where Simon was standing, along with many others.

There was probably a Roman soldier riding a horse who was leading the procession. If, in fact, that was the case, he would have wheeled around on seeing Jesus stumble and fall, spotted Simon, and then demanded that he carry the Cross.

It may have been by chance, or so he thought, that he was standing there at that time, but it was not by chance as far as God was concerned. The Heavenly Father no doubt orchestrated this very moment. Even though it was an extremely saddened occasion, still, it was to be the greatest day of Simon's life. He would meet Jesus.

The phrase, *"The Father of Alexander and Rufus, to bear His Cross,"* speaks of two who would give their hearts to the Lord, becoming well-known Disciples, and all because of what happened here this day.

By the time Mark wrote his Gospel, these two were well known.

Paul, writing to the Romans, sends a special salutation to Rufus, *"Chosen in the Lord, and his mother, and mine"*; which, no doubt, spoke of some special care bestowed upon him by the mother of Rufus (Rom. 16:13). By the time Paul wrote this Epistle, it is probable that Simon had passed on, and maybe even Alexander had died as well.

Rufus is honorably mentioned by Polycarp, a Disciple of John the Beloved, in one of his letters.

There is a tradition, as well, that Rufus became a Bishop (Pastor) in Spain, and that his brother, Alexander, suffered martyrdom.

What an honor it was for Simon to bear the Cross of Jesus Christ. It was to change the entirety of his life, and the lives of his children.

Even as I write these words, I sense the Presence of the Lord. Any contact with Jesus leaves one immeasurably bettered, and gloriously changed. As the song says:

"What the world needs is Jesus,

"Just a glimpse of Him."

Simon had that glimpse, and it was to change his life forever.

(22) "AND THEY BRING HIM UNTO THE PLACE GOLGOTHA, WHICH IS, BEING INTERPRETED, THE PLACE OF A SKULL."

The phrase, *"And they bring Him unto the place Golgotha,"* has been interpreted two ways. The word, *"bring,"* in the Greek Text is *"phero,"* and means *"to carry a burden,"* or *"to lead."* Consequently, and as stated, it can be interpreted two ways.

1. Some think that Jesus was being *"led"* as a prisoner to execution, or as a victim to the Sacrifice.

2. It could also mean that Jesus was so weak through the strain of the last few days, especially considering the scourging and torture, that, at a point in time, perhaps when He could no longer carry the Cross, He, as well, became unable to walk. As a consequence, He had to be helped or half carried.

Even though there is no definitive answer either way, I think my opinion would rest with this latter version.

If Jesus had become so weak that He could not bear the Cross, more than likely He was so weak that He needed help to even continue to walk.

As well, there has been disagreement as to the actual site of *"Golgotha."* From Scripture all that's known is that it was outside Jerusalem, fairly conspicuous, and probably not far from a city gate and a highway, and that a garden containing a tomb lay nearby.

Two sites are pointed out presently as the location of the Cross and Tomb. The one is the Church of the Holy Sepulchre, claimed by the Catholics to be the correct site; and the other is Gordon's Calvary, with the Garden Tomb being nearby.

The Catholic site seems to indicate a tomb of slightly too late a date to be authentic.

Calvary (Golgotha) and the Garden Tomb were first pointed out in 1849 by General Gordon of

NOTES

the British Army. The rock formation of Golgotha indeed resembles a skull; as well, the site accords with the Biblical data.

The phrase, *"Which is, being interpreted, The place of a skull,"* has two or three meanings as well!

An ancient tradition says that *"Golgotha"* was the place where Adam was buried, and his skull later found. However, there is no evidence whatsoever of this tradition.

Others think the interpretation simply means that the rock face of the hill resembles a skull, which is probably the correct interpretation.

It was here where Jesus redeemed lost humanity. It was here that the justice of God was satisfied, in that the Perfect Sacrifice was offered in the Person of the Lord Jesus Christ. As such, even though an extremely saddened spectacle, still, it is the most glorious moment in human history. The entirety of the world turns on this pivot — the Crucifixion of Christ at Calvary. There He bore the sin of the world (Jn. 1:29).

(23) "AND THEY GAVE HIM TO DRINK WINE MINGLED WITH MYRRH: BUT HE RECEIVED IT NOT."

The phrase, *"And they gave Him to drink wine mingled with myrrh,"* referred to a strong narcotic made of the sour wine of the country and mingled with bitter herbs. It was supposed to dull the sense of pain.

Some think that Christ was offered drink twice, but there is some indication that it was offered three times:

1. On arrival at Calvary (Mat. 27:33-34; Mk. 15:22-23). There is evidence that this was offered to Him just before He was nailed to the Cross. This is the time of which Mark now speaks. Jesus refused it.

2. When He was on the Cross before the thief cried for mercy (Lk. 23:36). The Scripture does not say if He accepted it or not. It seems to have been a drink which was not drugged.

3. Just before He died (Mat. 27:48; Jn. 19:29). It seems He accepted this drink. However, there is no evidence that it was a narcotic.

The phrase, *"But He received it not,"* as stated, refers to the first drink offered to Him upon arriving at the place of Crucifixion.

Bickersteth said, *"He would not seek alleviation of the agonies of the Crucifixion by any drugged potion which might render Him insensible. He would bear the full burden consciously."*

(24) "AND WHEN THEY HAD CRUCIFIED HIM, THEY PARTED HIS GARMENTS, CASTING LOTS UPON THEM, WHAT EVERY MAN SHOULD TAKE."

The phrase, *"And when they had crucified Him,"* referred to them nailing Him to the Cross, which Mark omits. The Religious Leaders of Israel had their desires granted. Even though God had no part in their wickedness and evil, still, He would use it to further His Own Will, for it was His Will that Jesus die on Calvary.

In Truth, God uses everything, be it people or happenings, to ultimately carry out His Plan. He even uses Satan!

However, in no way does He involve Himself in the evil or wickedness, only using what transpires in whatever way He chooses. That is how Paul could say, *"And we know that all things work together for good to them that love God, to them who are the called according to His purpose"* (Rom. 8:28).

However, it should be noted that *"All things working together for good,"* applies only to those who: A. *"Love God";* and, B. *"Are the called according to His purpose."*

The phrase, *"They parted His garments,"* means they divided them among the four soldiers employed for the Crucifixion. It was an unwritten rule that the clothing of the condemned belonged to the executioners.

Unless Jesus had other clothing elsewhere, what is spoken of here was all He possessed in the world. He owned no real estate, places of business, nor anything else for that matter! That does not mean that it is wrong to own these things, it just simply means that He came for one purpose, and that was to die for lost humanity, and rise again the third day.

These *"garments,"* however many they were, included the Robe without seam (Jn. 19:23).

Some have claimed this seamless Robe was an undergarment, with others claiming it was the outer Robe.

The phrase, *"Casting lots upon them, what every man should take,"* basically refers to the seamless Robe.

The other garments were divided among them, with the seamless Robe of such workmanship that they felt they should not rend it. Consequently, they gambled (cast lots) with the winner taking ownership of the garment. This was the fulfillment of Psalms 22:18.

(25) "AND IT WAS THE THIRD HOUR, AND THEY CRUCIFIED HIM."

The *"third hour"* was 9 a.m. in Jewish time, which was the time of the morning Sacrifice. He died at 3 p.m., the time of the evening Sacrifice.

As well, it was not only the time of the evening Sacrifice, but the time the Passover Lambs at this Passover season were killed (Mat. 27:45-50; Lk. 23:44-46).

(26) "AND THE SUPERSCRIPTION OF HIS ACCUSATION WAS WRITTEN OVER, **THE KING OF THE JEWS.**"

The phrase, *"And the superscription,"* pertained to that which was written concerning Who and What Jesus was.

John says that this *"superscription"* was written in three languages, Hebrew, Latin, and Greek.

It is spoken of in all four Gospels, but no two carry precisely the same words. It appears by the comparison of them that the whole title was, *"This is Jesus of Nazareth, the King of the Jews"* (Bickersteth).

The difference in the wording in each account could probably be explained in the three languages in which it was originally written by Pilate.

The phrase, *"Of his accusation was written over,"* normally pertained to the type of crime committed which occasioned the Crucifixion. In the case of remarkable prisoners, the accusation was written on a white tablet, and carried before them as they went to the place of execution. It was then placed over their heads, fastened to the top of the cross.

In the case of Jesus, no accusation concerning any crime was attributed to Him, and because He committed no crime.

Out of anger, no doubt toward the Jews, Pilate wrote the title himself (Jn. 19:19). The *"Chief Priests"* were visibly angry over this, and strongly requested that Pilate change the statement to read instead, *"He said, I am King of the Jews."*

Pilate would have none of it, answering, *"What I have written I have written"* (Jn. 19:21-22).

So, Who and What Jesus really was, was fitly placed over His Head on the Cross.

Bede says, *"He was crucified in weakness for us, yet He shone with the majesty of a King above His Cross. The Title proclaimed that He was after all a King; and that from henceforth He began to reign from His Cross over the Jews"* — and I might quickly add, over the entirety of the world. Consequently, Pilate was Divinely restrained from making any alteration in the title, so that it should mean anything less than Who and What He actually was.

The phrase, *"The King Of The Jews,"* is a title the Jews did not then recognize, but one day shall! Zechariah prophesied that moment:

"And one shall say unto Him, What are these wounds in Thine Hands? Then He shall answer, Those with which I was wounded in the house of My friends" (Zech. 13:6).

He then said, *"And the Lord shall be King over all the earth: in that day shall there be one Lord, and His Name One"* (Zech. 14:9).

That awaits the Second Coming, and the Kingdom Age.

(27) "AND WITH HIM THEY CRUCIFY TWO THIEVES; THE ONE ON HIS RIGHT HAND, AND THE OTHER ON HIS LEFT."

The phrase, *"And with Him they crucify two thieves,"* would have probably been better translated, *"robbers."*

As well, these two robbers formed a part of the procession to Calvary. However, the evidence is that they were crucified after Him.

The phrase, *"The one on His right Hand, and the other on His left,"* proclaims Him crucified in the middle.

Luke tells us that one of these robbers was saved; while it would appear that the other died in his sins (Lk. 23:40).

Ambrose stated, *"Christ upon His Cross, between these two men, and with the title of King over His Head, presented a striking and awful picture of the final Judgment."*

Augustine said, *"This Cross, if you mark it well, was a Judgment Seat. For the Judge being placed in the midst, the one who believed was set free; the other who reviled Him was condemned; and thus He signified what He will do with the quick and the dead."*

(28) "AND THE SCRIPTURE WAS FULFILLED, WHICH SAITH, AND HE WAS NUMBERED WITH THE TRANSGRESSORS."

The phrase, *"And the Scripture was fulfilled,"* proclaims the Holy Spirit as always, going back to the Scripture. It was always fulfilled, and because it was and is the Word of God. How much should the Believer take advantage of the Word of God to master its contents. How so few do!

As the *"Scripture"* was fulfilled concerning His First Coming, likewise, all will be fulfilled

NOTES

concerning His Second Coming. And yet the world pays precious little attention to these august Prophecies given concerning the days just ahead. Regrettably, most of the Church falls into the same category.

The phrase, *"Which saith, And He was numbered with the transgressors,"* is taken from Isaiah 53:12.

He was *"numbered with the transgressors,"* because He took the place of the transgressors. So, His Death, its manner, and with whom He died, was fitting!

(29) "AND THEY THAT PASSED BY RAILED ON HIM, WAGGING THEIR HEADS, AND SAYING, AH, THOU THAT DESTROYEST THE TEMPLE, AND BUILDEST IT IN THREE DAYS,"

The phrase, *"And they that passed by railed on Him, wagging their heads,"* is also a fulfillment of Prophecy. The Psalmist said, *"All they that see Me laugh Me to scorn: they shoot out the lip, they shake the head, saying,*

"He trusted on the Lord that He would deliver Him: let Him deliver Him, seeing He delighteth in Him" (Ps. 22:7-8).

The pronoun, *"they,"* referred to *"the Chief Priests, Scribes and Elders,"* among others (Mat. 27:41).

The *"railing"* would have included mockery, reproach, and insults. It is difficult to imagine human beings doing that to another.

Even if Jesus had been guilty of all they said, still, their actions and attitude were ungodly to say the least! Considering that He was guilty of nothing, and, in fact, was the Son of God, the very personification of Goodness and Righteousness, their crime is beyond belief. Even the pagan Romans did not do such a thing. Such cruelty is reserved for professors of religion.

The phrase, *"And saying, Ah, Thou that destroyest the Temple, and buildest it in three days,"* constitutes an error on their part. Jesus had never said such a thing.

They were referring to the statement He did make in John 2:19-21, which referred to His Body as the Temple, its death, and resurrection in three days.

But, of course, they were not interested in what He really said or meant, only in their own devious designs.

(30) "SAVE THYSELF, AND COME DOWN FROM THE CROSS."

The phrase, *"Save Thyself,"* constituted that which He would not do! Had He saved himself, which He certainly could have done, He could not have saved others. The entire purpose of His Coming, was to give Himself. This He did, in a manner in which no other ever has, or ever shall!

The phrase, *"And come down from the Cross,"* constituted the very opposite of the real purpose for which He came. His entire purpose was to die on a Cross, as the perfect Sacrifice, which would save the souls of men, at least those who would believe (Jn. 3:16).

However, Swete remarks: *"The jest was the harder to endure since it appealed to a consciousness of power held back only by the self-restraint of a sacrificed will."*

Calvary was probably near one of the thoroughfares leading to the city so that there would be a continual stream of persons passing to and fro, more especially at this time, when Jerusalem was thronged with visitors (Bickersteth).

(31) "LIKEWISE ALSO THE CHIEF PRIESTS MOCKING SAID AMONG THEMSELVES WITH THE SCRIBES, HE SAVED OTHERS; HIMSELF HE CANNOT SAVE."

The phrase, *"Likewise also the Chief Priests mocking said among themselves with the Scribes,"* presents these two groups conversing among themselves. They watch Him die even suffering an agony that is indescribable, and register no pity or sympathy whatsoever!

Religion hardens the hearts of men, until there is no sympathy for others. It is the product of acute self-righteousness.

The Lord helped us to build 176 schools for under-privileged children in third world countries during the 1980's.

To be sure, these were not elaborate buildings, with each school costing approximately $50,000. Basically, they were walls and roof. However, from 200 to 1000 children attended each school. As well, we did our best to give each child a hot meal each day at noon. For many of these children, it was the only meal they received all day, for there was nothing at home.

For the most part, the schools only went through the elementary grades: however, without this the children would have received no education at all.

One of the men who was a part of the Religious Denomination we were formerly associated with, and actually placed in charge of a

particular area of the world, was greatly opposed to us building these schools, or anything else for that matter. I did not know him to well, but was shocked at his ideas.

He said, I am told, *"These people should not be educated, and as well, better that they starve to death, because there are to many of them anyway,"* or words to that effect.

Despite being a leader in that particular Denomination, I do not believe that man knew God. He died shortly thereafter, I do pray that he made his peace with God.

Even though there were certainly some godly Preachers and Missionaries in that particular Denomination, still, there were far to many of the stripe just mentioned. They had no heart, no pity, no sympathy, and in Truth had the same spirit as these *"Chief Priests and Scribes."*

I realize that is a serious indictment, but I believe it to be true.

The phrase, *"He saved others; Himself He cannot save,"* in effect is the old charge that His miracles of healing and deliverance had been wrought by Beelzebub, because, if they had been wrought by God, God would have interposed in this, His sore extremity and have set Him free (Bickersteth).

They cannot deny the fact that He saved others, but they attempt to turn that fact against Him, by alleging that He performed these miracles by the power of Satan, rather than by the Power of God.

They would take advantage of this opportunity to publicly expose Him as an imposter. They must do everything within their power, to destroy any influence He may have had.

How could they come to this terrible state of unbelief?

This was the Church of Israel, and actually the very Leaders who were supposed to lead the people to Righteousness. They were the ones who were to point people toward God. And yet they did not even know God when He was in their very midst. They were not Children of God, but rather of Satan!

Jesus had said as much of them and to them, *"Ye are of your father the devil, and the lusts of your father ye will do. He was a murderer from the beginning, and abode not in the truth, because there is no truth in him. When he speaketh a lie, he speaketh of his own: for he is liar and the father of it"* (Jn. 8:44).

Exactly as Jesus said they were, that they did.

Their father Satan was a *"murderer"*; consequently, they would murder Christ as well!

Satan was also a *"liar"*; consequently, his children are liars and would lie about Christ.

How could they be so blind that they did not recognize Jesus for Who He was?

Deception is a powerful thing, and they were deceived.

The human family fell in the Garden of Eden through deception; consequently, deception plagues the human race. The very word *"deception"* means *"to lead astray by words or behavior."*

If a person knows the Lord, deception can come from without, that is if that individual does not know the Word of God as they should. However, for those who do not know the Lord, deception comes from within, as the desires impel in that direction. To be sure, these religious leaders of Israel were not saved, and, in fact, had never been saved.

From the very beginning men have made the truth relative. In other words, those who are deceived speak of something as being *"true for you,"* (subjective) but not necessarily being *"true for me."* In other words, they deny absolute truth which is objective.

The Bible clearly affirms objective truth, and it grounds that belief in the Biblical concept of God. God is Truth. All that He says is in strict accord with reality. His Words are firm and trustworthy.

By contrast, human beings, at least those who do not truly know God, are trapped in illusion. They struggle to understand the meaning of the world around them and of their experiences. But, unaided, they cannot distinguish between the real and the counterfeit, the truth and the lie. As stated, it is because they do not know the Lord, Who is Truth.

Only reliance on God's Word, which is Truth, enables us to build our lives on a firm foundation.

These religious leaders did not know Truth, because they did not know God. Consequently, they were very easily deceived, because in Truth, the entirety of their lives was a deception. Everything they taught and believed was skewed until its true meaning was lost. Consequently when Jesus came, they saw Him only in the light of their wicked ungodly hearts. In the state they

were in, it was impossible for them to see Him as He truly was. Willful unrighteousness cannot see righteousness! Willful ungodliness cannot see Godliness! So, these religious leaders, and despite all the proof in the world, actually believed that Jesus was an imposter.

In their deception they reasoned, that if He really was the Son of God, He would not be on a Cross, because it was known that only those who committed terrible sins were hanged, and thereby cursed of God (Deut. 21:22-23). Consequently, they deemed Jesus cursed by God.

Had they truly known and understood Isaiah 53, they would have known exactly who He was and His mission. However, they did not know Isaiah 53, nor did they properly interpret any other part of the Bible.

They reasoned in their minds, that if He were truly of God, God surely would not allow Him to remain in this position. They understood not at all. They were truly congratulating themselves, on having rid the world of this imposter.

Such is deception!

In a sense, they were right concerning their statement, *"He saved others; Himself He cannot save,"* in that had he saved Himself, He could not have saved others.

(32) "LET CHRIST THE KING OF ISRAEL DESCEND NOW FROM THE CROSS, THAT WE MAY SEE AND BELIEVE. AND THEY THAT WERE CRUCIFIED WITH HIM REVILED HIM."

Their phrase, *"Let Christ the King of Israel,"* is said in mockery. They did not believe He was the *"King of Israel."*

They believe now, but it is too late!

The phrase, *"Descend now from the Cross, that we may see and believe,"* constituted a lie!

He rose from the dead, which was far greater then coming down from the cross while He was still alive, and they still would not *"believe."*

While they were mocking Him, He in His terrible torment, never said a word against these tormentors. On the contrary, He proclaimed mercy: for as He hung there, He said, *"Father, forgive them: for they know not what they do."*

They had seen him open blinded eyes, but they would not believe. They had seen Him, instantly cleanse lepers, but they would not believe. They had even seen Him raise the dead, but they still would not believe. In effect, there was nothing that God could have done which would have brought them to a place of Faith. As stated, they were woefully deceived.

The phrase, *"And they that were crucified with Him reviled Him,"* constitutes something unusual, for most of the time those in such circumstances, will not mock others in the same plight.

And yet, one of these very robbers who was reviling Him, would observe something about Jesus that he had never witnessed before. Consequently, before this horrible day was over, he would except Christ as his Saviour (Lk. 23:40).

(33) "AND WHEN THE SIXTH HOUR WAS COME, THERE WAS DARKNESS OVER THE WHOLE LAND UNTIL THE NINTH HOUR."

The phrase, *"And when the sixth hour was come,"* denoted 12 noon. Jesus had now been on the cross for three hours.

The phrase, *"There was darkness over the whole land until the ninth hour,"* records this beginning at noon, which meant it lasted for three hours. Consequently, this supernatural darkness, for that's what it was, came when the day was at its brightest.

As it was the Passover, the moon was now at the full, so that it could not have been caused by an eclipse. For when the moon is full it cannot intervene between the earth and the sun.

An account of it is given by Phlegon of Tralles, a man who was personally set free by the Emperor Andrian. Eusebius, in his records of the year A.D. 33 quoted at length from Phlegon, who says, *"That in the fourth year of the 202nd Olympiad, there was a great and remarkable eclipse of the sun, above any that had happened before."* (He said it was an eclipse, because that's actually what he thought it was, even though it wasn't.)

He went on to say that at the sixth hour the day was turned into the darkness of night, so that the stars were seen in the heavens; and there was a great earthquake in Bithynia, which overthrew many houses in the city of Nicaea.

His mention of an earthquake also brings into account the Sacred narrative (Mat. 27:51-54).

Exactly how far this darkness extended, is not known. However, Dionysius says that he saw this phenomenon at Heliopolis, in Egypt. He is reported to have exclaimed, *"Either the God of nature, the Creator, is suffering, or the universe is dissolving."*

Cyprian said, and looking back at that time some years later, *"The sun was constrained to*

withdraw its rays, and close its eyes, that it might not be compelled to look upon this crime of the Jews."

Someone else said that God pulled the blinds on earth at this time, that He, nor anyone else, might have to look at His Son bearing the sin of the world. During this final three hours that Jesus hung on the cross, there is no way the mind of man could even begin to comprehend that which He suffered. The physical pain was nothing in comparison to the spiritual agony. *"For He Hath made Him to be sin for us, Who knew no sin; that we might be made the Righteousness of God in Him"* (II Cor. 5:21).

It was at this hour that He became the Burnt-Offering and the Sin-Offering of Leviticus 1 and 4.

Even then, with nature convulsing, darkness covering the land, an earthquake causing it to tremble, and even though the Roman Centurion said, *"Truly this Man was the Son of God,"* the religious leaders of Israel still would not believe!

(34) "AND AT THE NINTH HOUR JESUS CRIED WITH A LOUD VOICE, SAYING, ELOI, ELOI, LAMA SA-BACH-THA-NI? WHICH IS, BEING INTERPRETED, MY GOD, MY GOD, WHY HAST THOU FORSAKEN ME?"

The phrase, *"And at the ninth hour,"* referred to three o'clock in the afternoon, which was the time, as stated, of the evening Sacrifice. As well, it was the time that the Passover lamb was to be killed.

The phrase, *"Jesus cried with a loud voice,"* proclaims the fact, that the torture and wounds did not kill Him, but, rather He laid down His own life.

The question, *"Saying, Eloi, Eloi, Lama Sabach-tha-ni?"*, seems not to explain exactly what language Jesus spoke. Even though, we have the interpretation given to us, the controversy still rages as to whether He spoke Hebrew, Syriac, or Aramaic? One thing is certain, no one near the cross seemed to understand what He said and there were people there who could understand all these languages (Dake).

Some say that Jesus was speaking Aramaic, which Mark uses, with Matthew referring to the original Hebrew.

The question, *"Which is, being interpreted, My God, My God, why hast Thou forsaken Me?"*, is taken from Psalm 22:1.

Some believe that He quoted the entirety of Psalm 22. At any rate, whether part or whole,

His reciting this Psalm showed Himself to be the very Being to Whom the words refer; so that the Jewish Scribes and people might examine and see the cause why He would not descend from the cross; mainly, because this very Psalm showed that it was appointed that He should suffer these things (Bickersteth).

The question, *"Why hast Thou forsaken Me?"*, actually proclaimed Him bearing the sin of the world, on which the Heavenly Father could not look. The Prophet Habakkuk said, *"Thou art of purer eyes than to behold evil, and canst not look on iniquity"* (Hab. 1:13).

Of course, God being God, see's everything, even *"evil"* however, He cannot countenance such, even though borne by His Only Son.

Some religious teachers denied that Jesus was forsaken by God. They say He was permitted to think so. They also teach that He was not personally judged, for God only judged man's sin which was upon Him. Were these doctrines true, then man is forever lost; for the sentence of death rested on man personally because of his sinful nature and because of his sinful actions. If Christ, therefore, would redeem him from this doom He must suffer it Himself, must load Himself with the sinners' sins and, Himself sinless, be constituted sin itself (II Cor. 5:21; Gal. 3:13).

Because of sin and sins (Rom. 1-8) God justly doomed to perpetual banishment from His Presence, i.e., to death, guilty man (Rom. 5:12).

To deliver man Christ became the Sin-Offering. As such He bore their sins in His Own Body on the tree (I Pet. 2:24). He abolished sin by the sacrifice of Himself (Heb. 9:26). He suffered the wrath of God due to disobedience but not His disobedience (Eph. 5:6); and the sword of that wrath awoke not only against the sins that were laid upon Him, but against Himself as being the Sinner, and yet the Fellow of Jehovah (Zech. 8:7); and, therefore, He was accursed of God personally (Gal. 3:10), i.e. condemned to death, the mysterious death of separation from God and seclusion in hell (the paradise part). But He could not be holden of the abyss for He was sinless and He was God, so He carried away its gates, as Samson the gates of Gaza.

Herein lies the mystery of Christ as the Burnt-Offering and the Sin-Offering of Leviticus 1 and 4. Never was He more perfect and more precious to the Heart of God, more truly a Sweet

Savour, than when hanging on the Tree; and yet, at that same moment, He was accursed as being the impersonation of sin itself. Hence He Himself declared (Jn. 3:14) that the serpent on the pole, the similitude of the deadly stinging serpent, pre-figured Himself.

(The statements on Jesus bearing the sin of the world while on the cross, and suffering its punishment, was derived from Dr. George Williams.)

(35) "AND SOME OF THEM THAT STOOD BY, WHEN THEY HEARD IT, SAID, BEHOLD, HE CALLETH ELIAS."

The phrase, *"And some of them that stood by,"* refers to the Roman soldiers, and even possibly some of the religious leaders of Israel.

The Phrase, *"When they heard it,"* refers to the cry of Jesus. Actually there were seven sayings of Christ on the Cross. The following is probably the order in which they were uttered:

1. *"Woman, behold thy son . . . Behold thy mother"* (Jn. 19:26-27).

2. *"Father, forgive them; for they know not what they do"* (Lk. 23:34).

3. *"Verily, I say unto thee, To day shalt thou be with Me in paradise"* (Lk. 23:43).

4. *"I thirst"* (Jn. 19:28).

5. *"My God, My God, why hast Thou forsaken Me"* (Ps. 22:1; Mat. 27:46; Mk. 15:34).

6. *"Father, into Thy Hands I commend My spirit"* (Lk. 23:46).

7. *"It is finished"* (Jn. 19:30).

The phrase, *"Said, Behold, He calleth Elias (Elijah),"* proclaims them not understanding what He said, or else not understanding the language.

However, the statement concerning Elijah could have been made in sarcasm, only pretending to misunderstand, which was probably the case.

(36) "AND ONE RAN AND FILLED A SPONGE FULL OF VINEGAR, AND PUT IT ON A REED, AND GAVE HIM TO DRINK, SAYING, LET ALONE; LET US SEE WHETHER ELIAS WILL COME TO TAKE HIM DOWN."

The phrase, *"And one ran and filled a sponge full of vinegar,"* was probably in response to the words of Jesus, *"I thirst"* (Jn. 19:28). Expositors differ as to whether this was a drugged potion, or the ordinary drink of the soldiers, which contained no narcotics, called *"posca."* It doesn't actually say whether Jesus drank the *"vinegar"* or not, but according to John that He *"received the vinegar"* (Jn. 19:30). At any rate, it touched His lips, whether He was able to consume any or not.

The phrase, *"And put it on a reed,"* according to John was *"hyssop"* (Jn. 19:29).

This would have been a fitting symbol, as hyssop was used to apply the blood to the door post in Egypt when the Children of Israel were delivered from Egyptian bondage (Ex. 12:22).

When the *"hyssop"* touched His lips, no doubt it came back stained with His Blood. As such, it fulfilled the type in every way of what happened in Egypt so long ago.

As the blood was then applied to the door post by Faith, likewise, it is applied to our hearts presently by Faith.

The glorious promise that was then rich with life, continues to hold true unto today, *"when I see the Blood, I will pass over you"* (Ex. 12:13).

The phrase, *"And gave Him to drink,"* may or may not have represented an act of kindness. If it was truly kindness, it was the only such kindness shown to Him at this horrible time.

It is not known if the phrase, *"Let alone,"* was uttered in kindness or not?

The phrase, *"Let us see whether Elias will come to take Him down,"* once again, was said either in jest or true kindness.

If in jest, of course it was in sarcasm, meant only to mock.

If in compassion, his motive was to offer our Lord the liquid in an effort to prolong His life, so that Elijah would have an opportunity to work an effectual deliverance by taking Him down from the cross.

Elijah was regarded by Jews as a deliverer in time of trouble. But of course, the Word of God promised no such thing regarding Elijah, but only that his ministry would touch Israel in the coming Great Tribulation Period (Mal. 4:5-6).

(37) "AND JESUS CRIED WITH A LOUD VOICE, AND GAVE UP THE GHOST."

The phrase, *"And Jesus cried with a loud voice,"* portrays something very unusual when dying, and is recorded by Matthew, Mark, and Luke.

Usually the voice fails the dying, more especially when the natural forces have been weakened by long agony, as in the case of our Lord.

This tells us that He did not die of necessity, but voluntarily, in accordance with what He had Himself said, *"No man taketh My life*

from Me . . . I have power to lay it down, and I have power to take it again" (Jn. 10:18).

Antiochanus said, *"By this action the Lord Jesus proved that He had His whole life, and His death, in His Own free power."*

In Truth, had He not purposely laid it down, due to the fact that the Lord was not born of the seed of Adam, and, consequently, did not have the *"sin nature,"* His human body would have lived forever, not seeing death, as God originally intended with Adam. In effect, if Adam and Eve had not fallen, all children born to them would have been born, *"sons and daughters of God"* (Lk. 3:38). As such they would not have died, nor were they intended to die. However, Adam and Eve, as is known, fell before a child was born to them.

After the Fall, all children born to Adam and his seed, were not born in the likeness of God, but rather in the likeness of Adam (Gen. 5:3), and, therefore, subject to death, which passed upon all men (Rom. 5:12).

Thank God that Jesus came, serving as the *"Last Adam,"* purchasing back by His Own Precious Blood, what the first Adam lost! Paul said, *"For as in Adam all die, even so in Christ shall all be made alive"* (I Cor. 15:22).

So, when Jesus died, He purposely laid down His Own life, for no man took it from Him. This is shown by the strength He exhibited, even at the last moment.

The phrase, *"And gave up the ghost,"* would have probably been better translated, *"Breathed out His life,"* because the words *"gave up"* are literally, *"breathed out."*

At this moment, Jesus purposely gave up His life, and thus ended that which had been planned *"before the foundation of the world"* (I Pet. 1:20).

The penalty for disobedience to God in the Garden of Eden had been death, spiritual death, i.e., separation from God. The price for Redemption had been death as well, but the death of a Perfect Sacrifice. That Perfect Sacrifice was the Lord Jesus Christ (Jn. 3:16).

The Word of God makes it clear that Jesus' Life is the price of Redemption (Mat. 20:28; Mk. 10:45). The Redemption price, as stated, the *"Precious Blood of Christ, a Lamb without blemish or defect,"* was paid to release people from *"the empty way of life"* received from the forefathers (I Pet. 1:18-19). Redemption is a release *"from all wickedness"* (Tit. 2:14). The Redemption that Jesus accomplished by His Blood is an eternal Redemption (Heb. 9:12), intended to so cleanse us that *"we may serve the Living God."* Thus, Redemption in the New Testament focuses on the condition of the Believer, who had been locked in a wicked and empty way of life, and on the price of Redemption, the Blood of Christ. It also focuses on the results of Redemption, a commitment by the Believer to serve God.

This last aspect of Redemption has a parallel in Roman law. A person who had been captured in war and released through the payment of a ransom by another Roman citizen was obligated to his ransomer until the price had been repaid. You and I, ransomed at incalculable cost, are forever in the debt of God and must rightfully surrender ourselves to Him (Rom. 6:12-14). But it is in bondage to Him that our true freedom lies.

The idea is, that each person in the world is in the grip of sin. Sin's bondage can be broken only through Christ's Blood. Redeemed, the Believer is given a place in the family of God and is called to live a life that reflects his new standing.

Only the Bible, the Word of God, among all the world's great religious writings, so portray the relation between human beings and God in terms of Redemption. Redemption reveals a helpless humanity; and Redemption affirms a God Whose love drives Him to take the part of the near kinsman. At His Own expense, He paid the price needed to win our release. That price was the life of His Only Son, poured out at Calvary in the shedding of His Own Blood (Richards).

(38) "AND THE VEIL OF THE TEMPLE WAS RENT IN TWAIN FROM THE TOP TO THE BOTTOM."

The Phrase, *"And the Veil of the Temple,"* referred to the curtain which separated the Holy Place and the Holy of Holies.

The Holy Place contained the Table(s) of Shewbread, the Golden Lampstand(s), as well as the Altar of Worship.

The Holy of Holies contained the Ark of the Covenant, on which was placed the Mercy Seat, over which were the Cherubim. God dwelt between the Mercy Seat and the Cherubim, or rather was supposed to. Actually, this room, the Holy of Holies in Herod's Temple, was empty due to the fact that the Ark of the Covenant had been lost when Nebuchadnezzar desecrated

NOTES

and destroyed Solomon's Temple, some six hundred years earlier. Consequently, from that time the Blood of the sacrificial Lamb could not be applied once a year to the Mercy Seat on the Great Day of Atonement. This was fitting. Because of sinful rebellion, Israel had forfeited her right to be led by God, and since that time was led by Gentile powers.

The phrase, *"Was rent in twain from the top to the bottom,"* signified the finish of the Old Mosaic Law, meaning that the Sufferer Who had just died on the Cross, had fulfilled all the Levitical Sacrifices and had abrogated them.

As well, the rending of the *"Veil"* specified that with Jesus' death, the way into the Holiest — where God Himself dwells — was opened for all. Because of Jesus, and what He did at Calvary, we can *"approach the Throne of Grace with confidence"* (Heb. 4:16).

Whereas under the Old Levitical Law, the Holy of Holies, as stated, could only be approached by the Great High Priest, and once a year, can now be approached by anyone at anytime who has Faith in the Lord Jesus Christ and what He did at Calvary. The Scripture is emphatically clear in this, saying, *"And the Spirit and the bride say, Come. And let him that heareth say, Come. And let him that is athirst come. And whosoever will, let him take the water of life freely"* (Rev. 22:17).

Even as I dictate these words, I since the Presence of God. It is as if the Holy Spirit is saying to any and all which He is, that this great Way of Salvation has been opened to any and all, and for all time!

Paul said it beautifully, *"But now in Christ Jesus ye who sometimes were far off* (Gentiles, who were unable to approach God) *are made nigh* (now able to come) *by the Blood of Christ"* (Eph. 2:13).

The rending of this *"Veil"* at the time of the death of Jesus, is of far greater significance, than even the brightest spiritual mind could ever begin to comprehend. Because of the Blood of Jesus the most sinful of men can approach with confidence, that God will not strike them dead, but in Truth, will wash and cleanse them from all sin. The *"Veil"* signified that heaven was closed to all, until Christ by His death rent this Veil in twain, and laid open the way. The justice of God had been satisfied. The price had been paid. Now, unholy men could approach a thrice holy God. The song says:

"Hallelujah what a thought,
"Jesus full Salvation brought,
"Victory, yes victory!
"Let the powers of sin assail,
"Heavens Grace can never fail,
"Victory, yes victory!"

According to Josephus this *"Veil"* was sixty feet high and fifteen feet wide. It is said that it was four inches thick, and so strong, that four yolk of oxen could not pull it apart. However, the very moment Jesus died, the Hand of God immediately ripped this giant veil from top to bottom, signifying that the way was now open to all. From this action, we can see the Great Heart of God.

He so desired the Way to be opened, that not a second was lost after the price had been paid. Immediately, He ripped this barrier asunder, and with a violent action, signifying that all may come. Hallelujah!

As well, He ripped it from the top, which would have been impossible for man to do, at least at that time. As well, the rending it from the top, portrayed that this action came from heaven, and was ordained by God.

It was the duty of the officiating Priest on the evening of the day of preparation which would have been at 3 p.m. to enter into the holy place where he would open the outer veil, thus exposing the Holy Place to the people in the Outer Court. This time (3 p.m.) was the actual time of the evening Sacrifice and, in this case, the offering of the Passover Lamb and the moment Jesus died.

Without a doubt, as he opened the Outer Veil, exposing the Inner Veil, hiding the Holy of Holies, he, as well as many others, saw something that was so startling it must have defied description.

To his shocked amazement, as well as all who were observing, he saw this giant Veil begin to rend from the top, slowly making its way to the bottom, until it was completely rent asunder.

There had been many strange happenings this day, the darkness which had lasted from noon until now, the earthquake, and now the strangest of all, the *"rending of the Veil."*

Did he understand the significance of this momentous occasion?

More than likely not! However, his lack of understanding, if so, in no way would have weakened the effectiveness of this which was wondrously done.

"Saved by the blood of the Crucified One!
"Now Ransomed from sin and a new work begun,
"Sing praise to the Father and praise to the Son,
"Saved by the blood of the Crucified One!"

(39) "AND WHEN THE CENTURION, WHICH STOOD OVER AGAINST HIM, SAW THAT HE SO CRIED OUT, AND GAVE UP THE GHOST, HE SAID, TRULY THIS MAN WAS THE SON OF GOD."

The phrase, *"And when the Centurion which stood over against Him,"* presents something somewhat unusual! A *"Centurion"* who was in charge of one hundred men, normally would not have officiated at a crucifixion. More than likely there were not a hundred soldiers present. However, the possibility definitely exists that Pilate assigned this man this duty because of the unusual circumstances which surrounded the Crucifixion of Christ. At any rate, a duty which no doubt repulsed him, in which he probably had no desire to serve, turned out to be the greatest day of his life. For there he met Jesus, and would make a ringing declaration which would carry forth through the ages.

The evidence is, that this man closely observed all the things that happened, such as the darkness and earthquake. But more importantly, the evidence seems to be, that he stood very near Jesus, closely observing Him, at least as much as one could in the darkness. What he would see, would change his life.

The phrase, *"Saw that He so cried out, and gave up the ghost,"* concerned the manner in which Jesus died. No doubt, this *"Centurion"* had seen many men die. However, he had never seen one die in the manner that Jesus did. He no doubt heard Jesus when he uttered the word, *"Father, forgive them, for they know not what they do!"* This was something he had never heard in all his life, someone forgiving their tormentors, especially the kind of tormentors that Jesus had!

And then he heard Him cry, *"My God, My God, why has Thou forsaken Me?"* It seems the way that Jesus uttered these words, proclaimed, at least to the Centurion's ears, a relationship unexplainable in the natural. How much knowledge he had of Jehovah is anyone's guess. However, he knew that this One hanging on the cross, was different than anyone he had ever known, and, as well, that the God to Whom He spoke, was more, far more, than these superstitious pagan gods of Rome.

The phrase, *"He said, Truly this Man was the Son of God,"* presents a controversy in some circles.

Some say that he actually said *"a"* Son of God instead of *"the"* Son of God.

However, tradition affirms that the Centurion's name was Longinus, that he became a devoted follower of Christ, preached the Faith, and died a martyr's death.

If, in fact, this is true, the evidence seems to conclude that he said *"the"* Son of God and referring to Christ. As well, if he used the word "the," he was distinguishing Jesus from the many called by the Romans a *"son of god"*. Even Caesar claimed to be God! So, in effect he was saying, *"Many have claimed to be, but this is 'The One.'"*

As well, the testimony of the Centurion is conclusive proof that Jesus really died, for his testimony was impartial, as should be obvious. (Some claim he only swooned, and regained consciousness in the tomb. The lengths that men go to attempting to boast of their unbelief, are amazing!)

(40) "THERE WERE ALSO WOMEN LOOKING ON AFAR OFF: AMONG WHOM WAS MARY MAGDALENE, AND MARY THE MOTHER OF JAMES THE LESS AND JOSES, AND SALOME;"

The phrase, *"There were also women looking on afar off,"* spoke of women from Galilee as the text proclaims, and not women from Jerusalem.

John 19:25 says these women stood near the cross, which is no contradiction. Jesus was on the Cross for some six hours, and the account as given by John seems to point to those first hours. To be sure, they could have come closer, and then stood further away several times, dependent on the immediate happenings. However, when He died, Mark says they were *"looking on afar off."*

The phrase, *"Among whom was Mary Magdalene, and Mary the mother of James the less and of Joses, and Salome,"* proclaims some of the most ardent followers of Christ.

"Mary Magdalene" came from Magdala, a little village near Capernaum. Jesus cast seven devils out of her (Mk. 16:9; Lk. 8:2). The horror

of that defies description, and the devotion this woman gave to Christ, proclaims to all the great deliverance effected by Christ. He literally gave her life back to her. The agony she underwent before her deliverance, can only be measured by her love shown to Christ after her deliverance. She had the honor of being the first person to herald the Resurrection.

The other *"Mary"* mentioned here, is said to be the wife of Cleophas and sister of Mary the mother of Jesus (Jn. 19:25).

"James the Less" is distinguished from the Apostle James the brother of John, and James the half-brother of Jesus (Mat. 13:55).

"Salome" was the mother of James and John (Mat. 27:56), and wife of Zebedee (Mat. 4:21; 20:20; 27:56).

While the Scripture is clear that Mary the Mother of Jesus was there, at least at the beginning of the Crucifixion, it is not clear if she was there at the last or not! The evidence seems to indicate that she wasn't. Undoubtedly, the horror of this was more than she could bear, so possibly John the Beloved took her away (Jn. 19:25-27).

(41) "(WHO ALSO, WHEN HE WAS IN GALILEE, FOLLOWED HIM, AND MINISTERED UNTO HIM;) AND MANY OTHER WOMEN WHICH CAME UP WITH HIM UNTO JERUSALEM."

The phrase, *"Who also, when he was in Galilee, followed Him,"* concerned the many meetings He conducted in this area.

Other than the terrible opposition by the Pharisees, these were the most glorious days that the earth had ever known. The crowds were tremendous in size, but above all the display of the Power of God was unlike anything anyone had ever seen before. Before the very eyes of onlookers, the lame walked, the dumb spake, and the blind saw.

As well, when He spoke, His Words were totally unlike anything anyone had ever heard previously. Above all, everything He did, was accompanied by the Power of God, and in a fashion never before experienced. Jesus Himself said, *"The Spirit of the Lord is upon Me…"* (Lk. 4:18).

No wonder they *"followed Him,"* and even though I was not privileged to be there at that time, nevertheless it is my glorious privilege to follow Him now! Once you have *"followed Him"* everything else is mundane.

As Peter responded, *"Lord, to whom shall we go? Thou hast the Words of Eternal Life."*

And then he said, *"And we believe and are sure that Thou art that Christ, the Son of the Living God"* (Jn. 6:67-69).

The phrase, *"And ministered unto Him,"* means they did the best they could to help with the various needs of His humanity. This would speak no doubt, of the washing of clothes, helping to arrange meals, or anything else they were able to do. What a privilege it was to have the opportunity to do anything for Christ, even menial.

From this one phrase, and which the Holy Spirit wanted us to know and remember, we learn that nothing is overlooked in our efforts for the Cause of Christ. No one must ever think or believe that their task, no matter how seemingly small, is insignificant. All is dear and precious to the Heart of God, as this proclaims.

As stated, Mary Magdalene had been delivered from seven devils, so in her own mind, she no doubt thought that what little she could do, although not serving as payment, still, would proclaim her love. It would be wonderful, if every Believer felt the same way. To be sure, every Believer has been delivered in one way or the other, exactly as Mary Magdalene.

The phrase, *"And many other women which came up with him unto Jerusalem,"* gives us no indication who they were, but no doubt, had experienced great things from His Ministry, and desired to be near His Presence.

(42) "AND NOW WHEN THE EVEN WAS COME, BECAUSE IT WAS THE PREPARATION, THAT IS, THE DAY BEFORE THE SABBATH,"

The phrase, *"And now when the even was come,"* referred to approximately 6 p.m. when the High Sabbath of the Feast would begin. It was now just after 3 p.m. in the afternoon, with much work to be done before the Passover Sabbath began, when all work had to stop. During this three hour period of time, Joseph of Arimathaea had to go to Pilate, and ask for the Body of Jesus. As well, Jesus had to be taken down from the cross, with some care given, and placed in the Tomb before sundown.

The phrase, *"Because it was the preparation,"* spoke of all the work being done in preparation for the Passover. This was the day the lambs were killed for the Passover, with all activity having to cease, as stated, at sundown.

The phrase, *"That is, the day before the Sabbath,"* spoke of the High Sabbath of the Passover Feast, which was Thursday, and not the ordinary weekly Sabbath, which was Saturday (Lev. 23:6-7).

The misinterpretation of this one passage, with most thinking it referred to the normal weekly Sabbath of Saturday, confuses many, causing them to think that Jesus died on a Friday. Actually, He was crucified on a Wednesday, and spent three full days and nights in the Tomb, rising on Sunday Morning, as He had said He would do (Mat. 12:40).

(43) "JOSEPH OF ARIMATHAEA, AN HONOURABLE COUNSELLOR, WHICH ALSO WAITED FOR THE KINGDOM OF GOD, CAME, AND WENT IN BOLDLY UNTO PILATE, AND CRAVED THE BODY OF JESUS."

The name *"Joseph of Arimathaea,"* stands out boldly in that which he did for Christ at this time. The Scripture says of him, *"he was a good man, and a just: ..."*

"Who also himself waited for the Kingdom of God" (Lk. 23:50-51). He was also *"a Disciple of Jesus, but secretly, for fear of the Jews"* (Jn. 19:38). He was also a member of the Sanhedrin who had not voted for Jesus' death. Whether that meant he was present at the illegal trial of Jesus, is not exactly known.

From what description is given of this man, it seems he struggled inwardly concerning his devotion to Christ before the Crucifixion. He was rich, respected, occupied one of the highest offices in the land, and it seems, had trouble openly declaring his devotion to Christ.

Sadly, there are many, even presently, who are secret disciples of Christ. However, as with Joseph, sooner or later, the *"secret"* will have to be divulged, or else Jesus denied.

The record is clear that all this man had, concerning riches, office, place, and position, in no way satisfied the longing and craving in his heart. That was only stirred and satisfied, when he first heard Jesus. What this occasion was is not known. However, he would never be the same again.

Now, he will fulfill Bible prophesy, by giving Jesus his tomb (Isa. 53:9). Had he not done this Christ would have been buried with criminals.

The phrase, *"An honourable Counsellor,"* referred to his being a member of the Grand Council of Jerusalem, the Sanhedrin. Even though he was a native of Arimathaea, every evidence is, that he now lived in Jerusalem.

Jerome says that this city, Arimathaea, was called Ramathaim-Zophim and was where Samuel was born.

The Holy Spirit uses the word *"honourable"* and for specific reasons. This man, although not as bold as he should have been, had a heart for God.

The phrase, *"Which also waited for the Kingdom of God,"* spoke of this hunger. It was to be fulfilled in Jesus.

The phrase, *"Came, and went in boldly unto Pilate,"* means that what he did, was not commonly done. Pilate, no doubt, consented to see him, because of who he was, rich, and a member of the Sanhedrin.

The phrase, *"And craved the Body of Jesus,"* means that he strongly requested that he be given the remains.

He *"craved"* the *"Body"* simply because, if such was not granted, Jesus, as stated, would have been buried in a common grave with criminals.

As well, and as stated, time was running out. What was done, must be done quickly!

(44) "AND PILATE MARVELLED IF HE WERE ALREADY DEAD: AND CALLING UNTO HIM THE CENTURION, HE ASKED HIM WHETHER HE HAD BEEN ANY WHILE DEAD."

The phrase, *"And Pilate marvelled if He were already dead,"* is understandable, because it normally took from two to three days for one to die on the cross. Inasmuch as Jesus had only been on the cross for six hours, Pilate was skeptical. The time was probably about 4 p.m.

The phrase, *"And calling unto him the Centurion, he asked him whether He had been any while dead,"* pertained to the man who had said, *"Truly this man was the Son of God."* Pilate was not satisfied that Jesus was dead, and, if in fact, He truly was dead, how long had it been since He expired?

There is a possibility that the Centurion had come with Joseph, but had not actually gone in before Pilate, remaining in a side room, until called.

(45) "AND WHEN HE KNEW IT OF THE CENTURION, HE GAVE THE BODY TO JOSEPH."

The phrase, *"And when he knew it of the Centurion,"* proclaims the fact that he satisfied

himself that Jesus truly was dead. Consequently, and as previously stated, the unprejudiced testimony of an unbiased witness, in this case a Roman Centurion, placed the official stamp of Rome on the death of Jesus.

Although some skeptics have attempted to claim otherwise, if it is to be noticed, the Jews, even though they hated Christ, never claimed that He did not die, only that He did not rise from the dead. They knew He died, because they watched Him die. And, as stated, the uncontestable testimony of the Centurion verified it.

The phrase, *"He gave the Body to Joseph,"* proclaims such being done, not so much out of a feeling of generosity, but that he would rid himself of this most inconvenient and troublesome affair.

The word *"Body"* as it is used here, in the Greek Text is *"ptoma,"* which means *"a corpse."*

(46) "AND HE BOUGHT FINE LINEN, AND TOOK HIM DOWN, AND WRAPPED HIM IN THE LINEN, AND LAID HIM IN A SEPULCHRE WHICH WAS HEWN OUT OF A ROCK, AND ROLLED A STONE UNTO THE DOOR OF THE SEPULCHRE."

The phrase, *"And he bought fine linen,"* proclaims such being purchased on the way back from Pilate to Golgotha. The *"linen"* was not a garment, but rather a piece of cloth fresh and unused. It would be used to wrap around the body of Jesus.

The phrase, *"And took him down,"* constituted one of the most touching and heart rending moments in human history.

From John's account, it seems that Nicodemus was at the Crucifixion sight waiting on Joseph. As well, there may have been others present, with even the possibility of the Roman Centurion helping.

The taking him down from the cross would not have been a simple or easy task. Somehow they would have to remove the large nails from His hands as well as His feet.

Using some type of instrument to pull the nails out, they would have tried to be as gentle as possible, so as not to enlarge the wound any worse than it already was, whether in His hands or feet. They would have been the first to look upon those wounds, which He will bear forever (Zech. 13:6).

When they finally were able to remove the nails, two or three of the men would have gently laid Him on the ground at the foot of the Cross. Even though the Scripture is silent, they undoubtedly at this time, attempted to cleanse the Blood from the wounds in his hands and feet, as well as His side. As they held His Hands, attempting to wipe away the blood, their minds no doubt would have gone to the countless scores whom He had touched, instantly bringing healing.

They would have had little success in attempting to cleanse His back, and because the wounds were too many, with hardly any skin left intact. As well, His face would have been unrecognizable. So, regarding His face, there would have been almost nothing they could have done except close His eyes.

The song says:
*"Were you there when they crucified
   my Lord.*
*"Were you there when they crucified
   my Lord.*
*"Sometimes it makes me, to tremble,
   tremble, tremble,*
*"Were you there when they crucified
   my Lord."*

The phrase, *"And wrapped Him in the linen,"* speaks of the cloth purchased by Joseph.

The phrase, *"And laid Him in a sepulchre which was hewn out of a rock,"* pertained to Joseph's own tomb. The tomb was in the garden adjacent to the place of Crucifixion, most certainly the property of Joseph. Golgotha being as close as it was to the Garden Tomb, more than likely Joseph and Nicodemus, plus others who may have been near, no doubt carried the Body that short distance.

The phrase, *"And rolled a stone unto the door of the Sepulchre,"* refers to the tomb being a new one. If the tomb had been previously used, the opening would have been closed with a stone. Inasmuch as they rolled the stone over the opening, after the Body was carefully placed inside, lets us know that it had never been used.

Consequently, thus, while our Lord died with the wicked (the thieves on the cross), He was with the rich in His death (Isa. 53:9).

Tradition says that Joseph of Arimathaea was sent by Philip from Gaul to Britain in A.D. 63 and founded the first Christian settlement in this country, afterwards the site of Glastonbury.

NOTES

(47) "AND MARY MAGDALENE AND MARY THE MOTHER OF JOSES BEHELD WHERE HE WAS LAID,"

Evidently, these two women remained behind after the other women had left. They no doubt watched as Joseph and Nicodemus prepared the body, probably at both the Crucifixion site and at the Tomb.

It is obvious that Mary Magdalene did not want to leave, even though there was nothing left but a corpse. The horror of this moment must have been indescribable. Little did she realize that approximately seventy two hours later, she would see Him standing near this tomb in all His Resurrection Power. However, at this time, no one believed He would rise from the dead, and despite what He had said!

The song says:
*"Were you there when they laid Him in
   the tomb.*
*"Were you there when they laid Him in
   the tomb.*
*"Sometimes it makes me to tremble,
   tremble, tremble,*
*"Were you there when the laid Him in
   the tomb."*

At this time, demon powers must have exulted in hellish glee. Jesus Christ was dead! Evil, it seemed, had triumphed! The sun would never rise again. There would never be the bloom of another flower, nor the chuckle of a baby. Darkness had prevailed, or so it seemed!

Sometime ago I stood on the field of Waterloo, where Napoleon, the French Emperor, was defeated by the British General, Wellington. On that memorable day the world awaited the outcome of this battle. But especially in England they did wait. If the Corsician tyrant, as they referred to Napoleon, defeated Wellington, he would easily occupy England.

On the day in question, multiple tens of thousands gathered in London, awaiting news from the battle front. Before modern communications, the method was to post the news on the top of tallest building for all to see.

At last, the news came, and the tens of thousands of people in the streets below held there breath as they watched the workmen on top of the building putting up the big block letters which would give the news.

The letters to the first word were placed on the giant back drop. They spelled W-E-L-L-I-

N-G-T-O-N. They eagerly awaited the second word. What would it be?

Quickly the workmen spelled it out D-E-F-E-A-T-E-D.

A groan went up from the crowd. They said that women fainted, and men wept! England was vanquished! And then all of a sudden, the crowd grew quiet, for the workmen were putting up another word.

It read N-A-P-O-L-E-O-N.

They now had the total message, *"WELLINGTON DEFEATED NAPOLEON!"*

One can well imagine the joy that filled London, as the news spread all over the British Empire. *"Wellington Defeated Napoleon!"*

When they laid Jesus in that tomb, the spirit world of darkness must have shouted *"J-E-S-U-S D-E-F-E-A-T-E-D."*

However, hell will celebrate too soon! Sunday morning is coming, and then the message will read, *"J-E-S-U-S D-E-F-E-A-T-E-D S-A-T-A-N!"*

CHAPTER 16

(1) "AND WHEN THE SABBATH WAS PAST, MARY MAGDALENE, AND MARY THE MOTHER OF JAMES, AND SALOME, HAD BOUGHT SWEET SPICES, THAT THEY MIGHT COME AND ANOINT HIM."

The phrase, *"And when the Sabbath was past,"* spoke of the regular weekly Sabbath on Saturday. Three full days and four full nights had already passed since the burial of Jesus (Mat. 12:40). Days were reckoned then from sunset to sunset (Lev. 23:32). This destroys the myth that Jesus was crucified on Friday. Were that the case, it would not have fulfilled His Own statement, *"For as Jonah was three days and three nights in the whale's belly; so shall the Son of Man be three days and three nights in the heart of the earth"*(Mat. 12:40). As stated, there is no way the Friday concept can fulfill this.

Jesus was put in the tomb Wednesday just before sunset and was Resurrected at the end of Saturday (or their beginning of Sunday) at sunset. Consequently, Good Friday should be changed to Good Wednesday. No statement in the Bible says that He was buried Friday at sunset. This would make Him in the tomb only

one day and two nights, proving His Own Words untrue.

That which confuses many, and as we have stated, is the Sabbath of John 19:31. This was not the regular weekly Sabbath of Saturday, but the special Sabbath of the Passover Feast, which fell on Thursday. John 19:31 plainly says, *"For that Sabbath Day was an high day,"* speaking of the special Sabbath of the Passover, and not the weekly Sabbath of Saturday.

The Jews understood Christ to mean *"After three days"* or three full days and three full nights (Mat. 27:63), hence the soldiers had orders to guard the tomb at least that long (Dake).

The phrase, *"Mary Magdalene, and Mary the mother of James, and Salome,"* once again speaks of these three ladies, who, in this case, had thought to finish the embalming process.

The phrase, *"Had bought sweet spices, that they might come and anoint Him."* proves that none of them thought He would rise from the dead. If so, it would have been pointless to have wasted money on the purchase of these expensive items.

One is not to condemn Mary, the Mother of Jesus for not being there, due to what she had undergone the last three days and nights. The Prophecy of Simeon had come to pass exactly as predicted, *"Yea, a sword shall pierce through thy own soul also"* (Lk. 2:35).

Joseph and Nicodemus had begun the embalming process late Wednesday afternoon. They had *"brought a mixture of myrrh and aloes, about an hundred pound weight"*(Jn. 19:39).

This was a compound of the gum of the myrrh tree, and a powder of the fragrant aloe wood mixed together, with which they would completely cover the body, which was then swathed with linen. According to John, it seems that they finished this first part of the embalming process, with the ladies now to complete the task.

(2) "AND VERY EARLY IN THE MORNING THE FIRST DAY OF THE WEEK, THEY CAME UNTO THE SEPULCHRE AT THE RISING OF THE SUN."

The phrase, *"And very early in the morning the first day of the week,"* spoke of daybreak on Sunday morning. What had happened, was probably according to the following:

Jesus was placed in the tomb just before sunset on Wednesday evening. According to Jewish reckoning, Thursday would have begun at sunset. For all of that night, and the next day, which was the High Sabbath of the Passover Feast, all businesses were closed, and all work was condemned. This was the day that the Passover Feast was supposed to be eaten, having been prepared the day before. (Jesus and His Disciples had eaten it a day early.)

The next day being Friday, all the businesses were to be open once again, with normal activity. On this day, the ladies had probably purchased the *"sweet spices,"* etc.

Beginning at sunset Friday, the weekly Jewish Sabbath of Saturday began, with all activity ceasing once again. Consequently, the embalming process could not be completed on this day, hence them coming *"very early in the morning,"* which would have been Sunday, the *"first day of the week,"* and the first time they would have the opportunity to apply these spices, due to the two Sabbath's which had fallen during the past three days.

The phrase, *"They came unto the sepulchre at the rising of the sun,"* proclaimed their first opportunity, as stated, to finish this process. However, the *"rising of the sun"* on this day, also meant the *"rising of the 'SON!'"* in effect, it would be the greatest day in history.

Of course, as is obvious, without the Resurrection Calvary would have been in vain. The Resurrection, consequently, was the ratification of what Jesus had done on the Cross.

So, this day would not be one of sorrow as these ladies had envisioned, but rather the happiest, the most joyful, the most wonderful day they would ever know. Jesus is alive again!

(3) "AND THEY SAID AMONG THEMSELVES, WHO SHALL ROLL US AWAY THE STONE FROM THE DOOR OF THE SEPULCHRE?"

The phrase, *"And they said among themselves,"* means in the Greek Text that *"they kept on saying among themselves."*

The question, *"Who shall roll us away the stone from the door of the sepulchre?",* means that this was their chief concern. They had no anticipation of a Resurrection. As well, the stone was so heavy, they knew they did not have the strength to dislodge it.

From their conversation, and not having been there the past three days and nights, they had no knowledge of the Roman soldiers who had stood watch all of this time, nor of the sealing

of the stone which would have been unlawful to break (Mat. 27:62-66).

As well, they would have had no knowledge of the Angel which descended from Heaven, *"rolled back the stone from the door,"* which frightened the Roman soldiers so much, that they quickly fled the scene (Mat. 28:2-4).

Actually, this had happened several hours earlier, or quite possibly immediately before they came.

However, the evidence is that the Angel descending and rolling away the stone, took place hours earlier, because the Scripture says, *"And, behold, there was a great earthquake"* (Mat. 28:2). If this earthquake, which the Scripture says was severe, had taken place while the ladies were on the way to the Tomb, it seems that some mention would have been made of it. However, if it had taken place hours earlier, when they possibly were in bed, it would not have been noticed as much as otherwise. The indication is, that God did not make His Son stay in that prison house of death, one hour or even one minute more than necessary. Consequently, Jesus probably rose from the dead shortly after dark on Saturday evening, which would have been the Jewish Sunday, the first day of the week.

So, when the women arrived at the tomb that early morning hour, *"at the rising of the sun,"* they find the tomb deserted, the soldiers already having fled in terror. (Mat.28:11-15).

(4) "AND WHEN THEY LOOKED, THEY SAW THAT THE STONE WAS ROLLED AWAY: FOR IT WAS VERY GREAT."

The phrase, *"And when they looked,"* probably means they approached the tomb with downcast eyes. In no manner did they expect to see what awaited them.

The phrase, *"They saw that the stone was rolled away,"* proclaims them staring intently at the scene that greeted them, which was totally unexpected!

The phrase, *"For it was very great,"* means it was not something, which could be done easily or quickly.

If one carefully reads all four accounts of the Resurrection, one will see a diversity of testimony. Swete says, *"The very diversity of the accounts strengthens the certitude that the story rests upon the basis of Truth; the impressions of the witnesses differed, but they agree upon the main facts."*

Had it been a *"made up"* story, as many suggest, the stories of all of them would have been identical.

This account is identical to the accounts given by any of several people who witness a traumatic happening. Each account differs a little bit, with one seeing something another did not see, etc.

The evidence seems to be at this stage, that upon seeing the stone rolled away from the door, Mary Magdalene immediately left to go tell Peter and John (Jn. 20:2). If that is the case, she would not have seen the Angel in the Tomb, as *"Mary and Salome,"* who entered the tomb.

In John's account, she never mentioned the Angel. It stands to reason, had she seen him she surely would have mentioned it. As it was, she only said, *"They have taken away the Lord out of the Sepulchre, and we know not where they have laid Him"* (Jn. 20:1-2).

(5) "AND ENTERING INTO THE SEPULCHRE, THEY SAW A YOUNG MAN SITTING ON THE RIGHT SIDE, CLOTHED IN A LONG WHITE GARMENT; AND THEY WERE AFFRIGHTED."

The phrase, *"And entering into the Sepulchre,"* spoke only, as stated, of Mary the mother of James, and Salome.

The phrase, *"They saw a young man sitting on the right side,"* speaks of one of the several Angels who were present (Jn. 20:12). He was *"sitting"* on the raised projection which had contained the Body of Jesus. Him *"sitting"* portrayed far more than posture. It meant that the work of the Resurrection was completed, and death had been defeated.

The phrase, *"Clothed in a long white garment,"* in the Greek Text, refers to a long stately robe, reaching to the feet, even sweeping the ground. The word was used of any garment of special solemnity, richness, or beauty. Expositors remark that *"no such robe was warn by young men on earth."* The implication is that the individual described was not a human being, but an Angel.

No doubt, this *"white garment,"* and of such beauty, was especially worn to celebrate the Resurrection in particular.

If that is the case, what must have been taking place in heaven at this time? It would have had to have been a time of unprecedented celebration and rejoicing. Jesus Christ had

redeemed man, and, as well, had defeated death, hell and the grave. Hallelujah!

The phrase, *"And they were affrighted,"* is no wonder! Matthew said, *"His countenance was like lightening"* (Mat. 28:3).

They had come expecting to find a corpse, but instead found an Empty Tomb, and, as well, an Angel sitting where the Body of Jesus had been, and with the Glory of God displayed on his countenance in such a fashion, that they were terrified.

By now they should have learned that anything pertaining to Jesus always resulted in the miraculous. Wherever He was, the sick were healed, lives were changed, Miracles performed, and Angles appeared! This is the Jesus Who is the Head of the Church. And that is the reason True Bible Christianity is a Miracle experience. Nothing in the world can even remotely compare with it! Tragically and sadly, the Headship of Christ in the Church has been too often replaced by pitiful men. Consequently, there are few Miracles, few Healings, few True Salvations, etc. When and where Jesus reigns, that which He does is obvious. When men reign, nothing happens!

(6) "AND HE SAITH UNTO THEM, BE NOT AFFRIGHTED: YE SEEK JESUS OF NAZARETH, WHICH WAS CRUCIFIED: HE IS RISEN; HE IS NOT HERE: BEHOLD THE PLACE WHERE THEY LAID HIM."

The phrase, *"And he saith unto them, be not affrighted,"* proclaims the very first words uttered by the Angel to the new Church, in effect, *"fear not!"*

In other words, this thing is not ending as you had thought, but, in reality, just beginning.

The phrase, *"Ye seek Jesus of Nazareth, which was crucified,"* specifies exactly Who they were looking for, and, as well, an identification rendered, which left absolutely no doubt as to Who it was! It was *"Jesus of Nazareth!"*

For quite some time *"Nazareth"* had been looked at with disdain. A Roman garrison was located nearby, which gave rise to Gentile contamination. So, up to now, to have *"Nazareth"* attached to one's name, was not exactly complimentary.

But now all of this will change. The greatest happening the world has ever known, the Resurrection, has just taken place. It was *"Jesus of Nazareth"* Who was Resurrected; consequently, proclaiming to the world that He was exactly Who He said He was, the Son of God, and What He said He was, the Redeemer of mankind.

So, as He changed the complexion of *"Nazareth,"* likewise, He can, and will, if given the opportunity, change the complexion of any and all who come to Him.

The words, *"He is risen,"* is, without doubt, the greatest statement ever made in the annals of human history. Even though Calvary effected man's Redemption, still, had Jesus not risen from the dead, all would have been in vain! The song says:

"He's alive again, the stone's been
  rolled away.
"He's alive again, He's no longer in
  the grave.
"He's alive again, I can hear the Angel say,
"Let all the world rejoice, He's alive."

The phrase, *"He is not here"* speaks of victory over death, hell and the grave.

I have visited the tomb of Lenin in Moscow. I have looked upon his waxen cold face. The founder of Communism is dead! Likewise, every other pretender. However, no one ever found the Body of Jesus, because there was no Body, due to the Resurrection. To be sure, inasmuch as the Roman officials were greatly embarrassed, with the members of the Jewish Sanhedrin doing everything they could to secure the Tomb, if the Disciples had stolen Him away, as was suggested, no stone would have been unturned until that Body was found. It was not found, because it did not exist. As the Angel said, and speaking of the Tomb, or anywhere else for that matter referring to a corpse, *"He is not here!"*

The phrase, *"Behold the place where they laid Him,"* signifies the empty Tomb. In other words, He definitely was dead, but is now definitely alive!

It is sad! Multiple millions have visited that empty Tomb in Jerusalem, but Israel still will not believe. Their Greatest Son was denied, and because of that, their suffering has lasted for nearly two thousand years.

Nevertheless, in the coming near future, this will all change. The sons of Jacob will finally come home. And I speak of the acceptance of their Lord and Saviour, the Lord Jesus Christ.

(7) "BUT GO YOUR WAY, TELL HIS DISCIPLES AND PETER THAT HE GOETH

BEFORE YOU INTO GALILEE: THERE SHALL YE SEE HIM, AS HE SAID UNTO YOU."

The phrase, *"But go your way, tell His Disciples and Peter,"* presents a special comfort.

There is no censure or reprimand concerning the unbelief of the Disciples. Only a proclamation that they should be told the Good News.

As well, *"Peter"* is added to let him know that he is included, because after his denial of Christ, he probably felt he was no longer a part of the Disciples. He was to find out different. Actually, the Lord personally appeared to Peter a very short time after this (Lk. 24:34).

The grief of failure, and especially failure concerning one's commitment to the Lord, has no counterpart. It would kill one, at least one who is totally dedicated as Peter, were not Grace and Mercy extended, as it certainly was.

The modern Church would have in no way said *"and Peter,"* but the Angel did!

The modern Church, by and large, says that the words *"and Peter,"* can be included after two years of probation, etc. In other words, the Protestant Church pretty much demands penance, exactly as the Catholics. As such, the Grace, Mercy, and Finished Work of Christ, are denied. In the Bible, there is no such thing as probation, at least pertaining to the Mercy and Grace of the Lord.

Why does the Church insist on such?

It does so because of self-righteousness. Self-righteousness cannot abide failure of any nature, even though, within itself, it is the greatest failure of all.

Jesus says that Ministry begins with Repentance (Rev. 2:5). Strangely enough, the modern Church Ministry ends with Repentance!

The tragedy is, most of the time the ones doing the judging in the modern Church are in worse condition spiritually than the one they are judging! That is sad, but true. Such is done, because men have departed from the Word of God, instituting their own rules instead.

Every Believer in the world should be hilariously thrilled and overjoyed, that the Angel said *"and Peter,"* because, in effect, and in one way or the other, he said it to all!

The phrase, *"That He goeth before you into Galilee: there shall ye see Him, as He said unto you,"* is exactly what Jesus had told them in Mark 14:28.

Why Galilee?

Even though immediately after the Resurrection, He appeared to them several times in Jerusalem, still, He did not recommission them until He appeared to them in Galilee. John records this incident in his closing Chapter.

Galilee is where He first commissioned them, and Galilee is where He will recommission them.

There is every evidence that Jesus, during the entirety of His Ministry, did not visit Jerusalem unless it was on the Feast Days, when He had to come. There is no record that He ever spent the night in Jerusalem, except the night of His arrest and trial. Religious opposition in this city was so bitterly against Him, that the rejection was felt almost immediately upon commencement of His Public Ministry. In effect, they hated Him!

Even though the major cities of Galilee did not repent, and, in fact, would not repent, though the recipient of the greatest visitation from God ever known, still, their opposition was not nearly as pronounced as that in Jerusalem. The arrest, trial and Crucifixion, attest to that.

Knowing that there would be no acceptance of Him in Jerusalem, the Holy Spirit proclaimed hundreds of years before, that Galilee would be the place primarily of His Ministry (Isa. 9:1-2). There He called them, and there, after the Resurrection, He let them know that call was still in force.

(8) "AND THEY WENT OUT QUICKLY, AND FLED FROM THE SEPULCHRE; FOR THEY TREMBLED AND WERE AMAZED: NEITHER SAID THEY ANY THING TO ANY MAN; FOR THEY WERE AFRAID."

The phrase, *"And they went out quickly, and fled from the Sepulchre; for they trembled and were amazed,"* proclaims them seeing more than they could comprehend, digest, or even except for the moment!

They had come to finish the embalming of the Body of Christ, with the shock of the Crucifixion still very much evident within and upon their persons. If they even thought of His Words where He spoke of rising again, they dismissed them from their minds, or else felt that even though He did say such a thing, it must have a meaning to it that they did not understand. In no way did they expect Him to rise from the dead.

They had seen His Back cut to pieces by the whip, and His face so disfigured that He was

NOTES

unrecognizable. They had watched the nails driven into His Hands and Feet, and had seen Him die. As well, His death was horrible, to say the least! It was so final, so total, and so complete, that as far as they were concerned, He was dead, and would remain so!

As well, and perhaps of even greater magnitude, they knew that anyone, at least One such as Christ, who hung on a Cross, was cursed by God (Deut. 21:22-23). So, not only were their minds shattered by what they had seen, but their Faith was shattered as well! How could Jesus be the Messiah, which they at first thought, and be cursed by God? They really had very little understanding as to Who He actually was, and especially His Mission.

While He was truly cursed by God, it was not for any sin He had committed, but for the sin of the world. This they did not understand, at least at that time!

And now, these further developments are beyond comprehension! Jesus is not in the Tomb, but, instead, a Being of such startling appearance that they could scarcely look upon Him. Furthermore, with their own ears they heard him say, *"Ye seek Jesus of Nazareth, which was crucified: He is risen; He is not here: behold the place where they laid Him."*

No doubt they are wondering in their minds if what they have seen is actually real? They do not want to mislead the Disciples, and make their hurt and pain even worse; therefore, they will say nothing!

The phrase, *"Neither said they any thing to any man; for they were afraid,"* means that what they had witnessed was too much for them to comprehend, at least at this time. They would say nothing! However, Mary Magdalene had not seen the Angel, nor heard his announcement concerning the Resurrection of Christ; therefore, she will tell Peter and John at least that the Tomb is empty. They will come to investigate, according to John, and will find, as she has said, the Tomb empty, but no Angel is there.

Matthew records the account of the women leaving the Tomb with *"fear,"* but also with *"great joy."* They, in fact, were going to *"bring the Disciples Word,"* but never were able to do so, because in fact, *"Jesus met them,"* and they, *"held Him by the Feet, and worshipped Him"* (Mat. 28:8-10). This was very shortly after Jesus had first appeared to Mary Magdalene. Later, these two women related this incident, but, at the time, and as Mark said, and due to events, *"neither said they any thing to any man."*

(9) "NOW WHEN JESUS WAS RISEN EARLY THE FIRST DAY OF THE WEEK, HE APPEARED FIRST TO MARY MAGDALENE, OUT OF WHOM HE HAD CAST SEVEN DEVILS."

The phrase, *"Now when Jesus was risen early the first day of the week,"* probably referred to sometime after sundown Saturday, which would have been the beginning of the Jewish Sunday, the first day of the week.

The phrase, *"He appeared first to Mary Magdalene,"* constitutes an honor of unparalleled proportions. He appeared to her *"first,"* no doubt, because of her Love, Devotion, and Faith.

After she had told Peter and John about the Tomb being empty, they had immediately come to see for themselves. Finding it as she said, they had left. However, she had lingered behind, which occasioned the appearance of Christ (Jn. 20:1-18). This was even before Jesus appeared to the other women, which must have been almost immediately after He appeared to Mary (Mat. 28:8-10).

The phrase, *"Out of whom He had cast seven devils,"* gives us at least a hint as to the cause of her Love and Devotion. As we have previously stated, the horror of this woman's life before Jesus delivered her, due to being possessed by these devils, would be beyond imagination. How and when Jesus delivered her, the Scriptures are silent. However, it seems that from the moment of her Salvation, she immediately began to follow Christ, and never stopped, even after the Crucifixion.

The terrible bondages binding humanity, are of spiritual origin. As such, all the psychology, or psychologists, in the world cannot alleviate this terrible problem. Jesus is not only the Answer, but, in Truth, the only Answer! It is sad when much of the Church world opts for other than Jesus.

(10) "AND SHE WENT AND TOLD THEM THAT HAD BEEN WITH HIM, AS THEY MOURNED AND WEPT."

The phrase, *"And she went and told them that had been with Him,"* referred to His Disciples, and, as well, was the second time she had left the Sepulchre, the first time going to Peter and John. However, at that time, she only

NOTES

reported and empty Tomb, with this time reporting that she had seen Jesus.

The phrase, *"As they mourned and wept,"* expresses their grief, which was natural, but also expressed, as the next verse shows, that they did not believe her.

Mary Magdalene had the distinct privilege of being the first person to preach the Gospel. Actually, the first Preachers of a risen Saviour were women. No other speakers are mentioned as addressing the Church on that first Sunday morning. Many, misunderstanding the language of I Corinthians 14:34, and I Timothy 2:11-12 believe that the Scriptures forbid a woman to preach the Gospel. However, such is incorrect, as proven here.

(11) "AND THEY, WHEN THEY HAD HEARD THAT HE WAS ALIVE, AND HAD BEEN SEEN OF HER, BELIEVED NOT."

The words, *"And they,"* are said by the Holy Spirit in this fashion, to denote their unbelief, which was inexcusable. They knew that Mary Magdalene was trustworthy, having seen her life in the last months. Possibly they thought she was overwrought with grief, and had imagined that she had seen Him.

The phrase, *"When they had heard that He was alive, and had been seen of her,"* should have been enough to have awakened His Words in them, which He had foretold concerning His Resurrection.

The words, *"Believed not,"* means they flatly rejected her testimony.

They did not believe her story, for it seemed *"as idle tales"* (Lk. 24:11). They did not seem to remember, even though they should have, what Christ had said on numerous occasions — that He would rise after the third day and would see them in Galilee (Mat. 16:21).

The repeated unbelief of the Apostles in the Resurrection, destroys the theory that they invented the Resurrection.

(12) "AFTER THAT HE APPEARED IN ANOTHER FORM UNTO TWO OF THEM, AS THEY WALKED, AND WENT INTO THE COUNTRY."

This *"appearance"* pertains to that which is given in detail in Luke 24:13-35.

The words, *"Another form,"* in the Greek Text literally say, *"In a different outward expression or appearance."* However, there is nothing in the Greek Text which meant that the Lord's

NOTES

appearance distinguished Him from any other wayfaring man.

With Mary Magdalene, He had seemed to her to be a gardener (Jn. 20:15). And now these *"two"* who were Cleophas, and maybe Luke thought He was just another traveler on the road. As Mary did not instantly recognize Him, neither did they!

Why?

There is really no way that any natural explanation will suffice. About the only thing that can be said is, after the Resurrection He was known as He pleased and not necessarily at once. It seems that a particular spiritual harmony with the Lord had to be entered into before He could be recognized. Mary Magdalene, along with the other two were preoccupied with their sorrow.

When the Disciples on the Lake failed to recognize Him (Jn. 21:4), they were, as well, preoccupied with their grief and consternation. There is undoubtedly an excellent lesson to be learned from this.

I personally believe the lack of recognition, at least concerning the examples we are given, was meant to portray *"recognition"* or the *"lack"* of it for all time. It is sad but true, that most Believers presently, even though truly saved as the Disciples of old, most of the time do not recognize the Lord, i.e., that which is truly of Him. The lack of recognition presently is, as then, the lack of spiritual harmony.

If a Believer, as the Disciples, is clouded by unbelief, and especially unbelief, I personally think that *"recognition"* is impossible. This could well account for many in the modern Church falling for whatever looks spiritual, even though it has precious little, if any, Scriptural foundation.

Sometime back while in the country of Brazil, some of the leading Believers (Preachers) in that country were questioning me concerning particular religious phenomenon being accepted so readily in the U.S. and Canada. That which had been so readily accepted in America and Canada, was accepted there little, if at all! If one has had the opportunity to preach in both America and Brazil, one will readily see the spiritual harmony with the Word of God, which is far more pronounced in Brazil than in America or Canada. I take no delight in saying that, but I believe it to be true.

So, I think that this lesson respecting *"recognition"* of Jesus after the Resurrection was not merely a spiritual quirk, but, instead, designed by the Holy Spirit concerning spiritual harmony with Christ, according to the Word of God.

(13) "AND THEY WENT AND TOLD IT UNTO THE RESIDUE: NEITHER BELIEVED THEY THEM."

The phrase, *"And they went and told it unto the residue,"* speaks of Cleophus and the other Disciple giving the Grand Message of the Resurrection of Christ to the other Disciples. However, they met with no greater success than had Mary Magdalene.

The phrase, *"Neither believed they them,"* places them in the position of disbelieving two different and distinct sources.

To not believe Mary Magdalene was bad enough, but to refuse the second witness, which came from two men, and in detail, is inexcusable. There was no spiritual harmony of Faith, which actually means they disbelieved the Words of Christ, when He told them, He would rise from the dead. To not believe these individuals is one thing. To disbelieve Christ, is to disbelieve the Word of God. All unbelief is wrapped up in this premise, a failure to know the Word, or else to disbelieve the Word that is known. *"Faith cometh by hearing, and hearing by the Word of God"* (Rom. 10:17).

Millions *"hear"* the Word of God, exactly as the Disciples heard Jesus speak of His coming Death and Resurrection. However, they really don't *"hear"* it! They *"hear"* it with their ears, but do not "hear" with their hearts.

The Disciples heard what Jesus said, but their hearing was superficial, and, therefore, not really understood.

To truly *"hear"* the Word of God, is to truly believe the Word of God and to act upon what has been heard.

The Disciples did not *"hear"* Jesus properly, therefore, they do not *"hear"* these testimonies properly!

Why didn't they *"hear"* Him as they should, concerning this all important issue of His Death and Resurrection?

As it is unbelief now concerning the fact of His Resurrection, it was unbelief then, concerning the Truth of His Resurrection.

Their unbelief was a misinterpretation of the Word of God, concerning the Mission and

Work of Christ. In their minds, He was going to overthrow the Roman yoke, and set Israel up as the premier nation as in the days of David and Solomon. They did not understand that His true mission, was to liberate the entirety of the world from the terrible grip of sin. Their thinking, as such thinking usually does, had some Scriptural validity, but was completely misplaced according to time and fulfillment.

So, when He spoke to them of Who He really was, the Messiah of Israel, they misinterpreted that. In their minds, He was the victorious Messiah, instead of the suffering Messiah. Isaiah 53 spelled it out to them perfectly, but they either did not know these Passages, or else dismissed them. In their minds Jesus was going to be King, and they were going to be powerful men by His side. Consequently, they only heard what they wanted to *"hear,"* instead of what they should have heard. This was the cause of their unbelief, and is the cause of unbelief presently.

(14) "AFTERWARD HE APPEARED UNTO THE ELEVEN AS THEY SAT AT MEAT, AND UPBRAIDED THEM WITH THEIR UNBELIEF AND HARDNESS OF HEART, BECAUSE THEY BELIEVED NOT THEM WHICH HAD SEEN HIM AFTER HE WAS RISEN."

The phrase, *"Afterward He appeared unto the Eleven as they sat at meat,"* could have well referred to His appearance to them by the Sea of Galilee (Jn. 21:4-23).

The phrase, *"Upbraided them with their unbelief and hardness of heart,"* proclaims that which I have just said. Unbelief causes *"hardness of heart,"* and means hardness toward God. In this state, people do not know what is of God, and what is not of God.

The words, *"Upbraided them,"* is strong, meaning *"He rebuked them."*

The phrase, *"Because they believed not them which had seen Him after He was risen,"* means there was no reason they should not have received the testimony of competent witnesses. They were in this state because of unbelief.

In the true sense, *"hardness of heart"* comes about because of being out of the Will of God. However, this is caused, as well, by unbelief.

Even as I dictate these words, in the last few months the Lord has given us some particularly good services in our Camp Meetings, or in the

regular worship services at Family Worship Center, which have registered a powerful moving and operation of the Holy Spirit. When these types of programs are aired over Television, it would seem surely that they would have a positive effect on Believers. However, and despite the powerful moving and operation of the Holy Spirit, the effect would be little.

To be sure, we would receive letters from people who had been saved as a result of these programs, and with a ringing testimony of such deliverances that defied description; however, almost nothing from Believers. The reason then, is the reason now.

As we have stated, unbelief among Believers stems from failing to adhere to the Word of God. As a consequence, many of these Believers, whomever they may have been, simply do not recognize the moving and operation of the Holy Spirit when they see it.

In one of our prayer meetings in 1994 (I believe it was), I had addressed our small group for a few minutes on Luke 24, where the account is given of the Two Disciples who did not recognize Christ, even though He walked with them. I dealt with the subject very briefly, and then we went to prayer.

As I began to seek the Lord that evening, the Holy Spirit brought back to my mind this account which I had just dealt with. The Lord began to speak to me basically saying the following:

"These two men could not have been convinced of My Resurrection, and irrespective of the proof, other than My appearance unto them. Likewise, you cannot convince people of what I have called you to do, nor can you make them see what I presently am doing, and irrespective of any argument you may use."

Then He said this to me: *"However, I can make them see!"*

From that day until this, I have lived on that Promise. Little by little I am beginning to see it come to pass. While I realize, at least at this present time, that we have a long way to go; still, I believe with all my heart that He has promised me that He will open their eyes.

(15) "AND HE SAID UNTO THEM, GO YE INTO ALL THE WORLD, AND PREACH THE GOSPEL TO EVERY CREATURE."

The phrase, *"And He said unto them,"* constitutes the introduction of the Great Commission. Some think He spoke these words to the

Disciples in Galilee, while some think the statement was given at Bethany, immediately before the Ascension. I tend to think it was given at this particular time.

The phrase, *"Go ye into all the world,"* tells us several things:

1. As this Commission begins with the word *"Go,"* someone has pointed out that two-thirds of the Name of God is *"Go!"* This means that the thrust of the Gospel is that it be taken to everyone. For the person who does no know of the Saving Grace of Christ, the Lord's Death on Calvary was in vain. Considering that, I think one should well understand the significance the Lord places on the taking of the Gospel to the world.

If one knows and properly understands the Bible, it will be quickly recognized that the Lord places great stock in everyone having an opportunity to hear, whether they accept or not (Ezek. 3:17-21; Rom. 10:14-17).

Every Believer should understand that the Lord requires that every person in each particular generation must be reached with the Gospel, and if they are not reached, as He told Ezekiel, *"His blood will I require at thine hand"* (Ezek. 3:18). Consequently, the seriousness of taking lightly these words of the Lord is serious indeed!

2. As well, this Commission is intended to be the responsibility of every single Believer, and not just a select few. While it is true that some have a greater calling of leadership in this capacity, still, all must do their part. However, the sad truth is that only about one percent of those who call themselves *"born again,"* truly take this burden to heart. Most Christians do absolutely nothing toward this all- important task.

What does the Lord expect of each Believer in this capacity?

First of all, and whatever it is, He expects our best. He gave His best, and He requires the same of us. The following is something everyone can do:

A. Pray: Jesus said, *"The harvest truly is great, but the labourers are few: pray ye therefore the Lord of the harvest, that He would send forth labourers into His harvest"* (Lk. 10:2). So, every Believer can pray.

Each should pray that God would lay particular parts of the world upon his or her heart, in order that intercession be made for that particular part of the world. It doesn't really matter if

the person has been there, or even knows anything about the area. That has little to do with it. The Holy Spirit knows all about it, and if sought, will give us the place and the manner in which we are to pray for that particular place.

Many would ask the question, why it is necessary to do such, considering that the Lord already knows what is needed, and where it is needed!

While that is certainly true, He has given us the Glorious privilege of entering into the carrying out of His Plan, and, consequently, the harvest. However, with that privilege comes a great responsibility.

Many Believers have the erroneous idea that the Lord being the Lord, and able to do all things, will get His Work done, whether they do it or not. That is totally incorrect!

The Lord has a part for everyone to play. That part, whatever it may be, was decided in the High Councils of Heaven. Consequently, if certain Believers do not carry out that which God has called them to do, that part of the great Plan of God is left undone. Actually, that is what the Lord was speaking of when He gave the Parable of the Talents (Mat. 25:14-30). The tragedy is, most Believers not only do not do their part, but actually have no idea as to what their part is. In other words, they are not even close enough to God to discern His Will for their lives.

This I know, if the Believer, any Believer, will begin to seek the Lord on a daily basis concerning this all-important task, soon, the Holy Spirit will begin to deal with them concerning their part in the Great Plan of God.

What an honor to have a part, and what an honor by the help of the Lord, to carry out that part.

To be sure, when all of us one day stand before God, the only thing that is going to be remembered, is that which we were supposed to do for the Lord, and whether we did it or not! At that time, it will not matter who won the World Series, or what other things we did, only what was done for Christ.

B. Give: There is not a single individual who cannot give of their resources to God, as little as it may be. Many have the erroneous idea that their small amount will make no difference, and, consequently, they might as well keep it.

That shows a total lack of understanding regarding God and how He looks at our gifts.

When Jesus was ready to use as an example the giving of a particular individual, He chose a woman who gave only two mites. In today's money, that was about 5 cents. He judged her motives, not the amount. As well, He judged the Sacrifice, because her giving was a Sacrifice, and, consequently, used as an example for all time (Mk. 12:42). So, let not anyone think that their gift is too small.

As well, those whom God has blessed respecting financial prosperity, should be extremely generous with the Work of God. They should stop and think, that this is the real reason the Lord has blessed them.

As well, every Believer ought to know exactly what his or her money is going for. I have had many years of experience in taking the Gospel of Jesus Christ to the world. In these years, I have learned a few things regarding what should or should not be done in this respect. Tragically, I have observed that the far greater amount of money given for that which is purported to be for the Work of God, much of the time is not.

Regrettably, most Believers little seek the Lord for this all-important work and ministry. They blindly support particular Religious Denominations, with most of the time their money being wasted. So, not only is the giving important, but how and where it is given is just as important.

Many Believers are going to stand before the Judgement Seat of Christ and find out that their financial support for what they thought was the Work of God, many times was not only not of God, but actually supported the work of the Devil. While such Believers will not lose their soul in such a situation, they will lose their reward (I Cor. 3:11-15).

Each Believer should be concerned enough about the Work of God, realizing how important it actually is, to check the fruit of that which they support (Mat. 7:15-20).

The fruit should be souls saved, lives changed, sick bodies healed, bondages broken, Believers filled with the Holy Spirit, and the Fruit of the Spirit made evident in people's lives.

One should pray earnestly over what they give, and especially where it is given. If prayer is earnestly engaged, with the Lord sincerely sought, direction will be given by the Holy Spirit (Jn. 16:13-15).

NOTES

To give the reader an example of a waste of God's money, please allow me to relate one incident.

Some time ago, I was in a particular large American city, and happened to be visiting a Church pastored by a dear friend. Very close to his Church was a large building, costing approximately $15,000,000. It was brand new. Money had been raised by a particular Ministry, so-called, to build this structure. It was claimed that the Gospel was going to be translated into many languages in this building, and sent all over the world. Consequently, Believers sent at least $15,000,000, if not much more.

The building sits there unused for anything, and above all, no Gospel is being translated from English into other languages, as claimed.

Why?

First of all, Preachers have to be called of God and given a special Ministry for this task. It is not something that anyone can do. With some, if not many of the Preachers associated with that organization, even if their messages were translated, the results would be small, if any at all. Due to the lack of the Anointing of the Holy Spirit, very little can be done.

As well, it costs a great deal of money to translate languages, and it is a continuous cost, occurring every week. Consequently, most do not truly have the burden to continue to shoulder that expense.

This building was constructed for this particular task, because it was an easy way to raise money. In other words, there was never any real intention to use this structure to take the Gospel to the world, and simply because there is no real burden.

Having said that, what happens to the multiple thousands of Christians who give to such a project?

First of all, they are not truly supporting the Work of God as they think; consequently, their money is wasted. They give because they do not have enough spiritual discernment to know right from wrong. In other words, and as we have previously stated, there is not enough spiritual harmony with the Lord to know what is of God or not of God. Consequently, they are led by what their eyes see and their ears hear, instead of the Holy Spirit.

It is sad, but most of the giving of Christendom falls into the same category! Very little truly goes to help take the True Gospel of Jesus Christ to a lost world. Satan is very successful in his efforts to deceive, in order that things be grandly supported which have no Scriptural foundation whatsoever. As a result, most of the money in Christendom is siphoned off into worthless projects, which accomplish little or nothing for the Lord. One day every Believer will answer, and with that in mind, we should be more responsible with that which is so very important.

C. Witness: Not only should every Believer pray, and give, but every Believer should be a witness in whatever capacity the Lord helps him to be. This means that we are responsible to tell the Grand Story of Jesus Christ and His Power to Save, to our next-door neighbor, also to the man or woman we work with in the marketplace, and those we have the privilege of associating with in any capacity.

As well, we should seek the Lord earnestly concerning this all-important task. Regrettably, *"witnessing"* has been reduced in many Church circles to little more than a formula, etc. While there certainly should be some order to our efforts, still, if we are not truly Spirit led, precious little, if anything, will be accomplished for the Lord.

There are hearts and lives which are more fertile for the reception of the Gospel than others. Consequently, we must ask the Lord to lead us to these people. If we earnestly seek Him in this capacity, He will answer, and we will be led.

3. Not only should we *"Go,"* and with the responsibility resting upon everyone, as well, the *"world,"* in its entirety must be our field. Christians who use as an excuse that there are plenty of people in their indigenous locality not yet saved, in order to abrogate their responsibility to the rest of the world, are simply shirking their Spiritual and Scriptural responsibility. Such thinking is a cop-out!

While all of us certainly must be concerned about our immediate locality, still, He who does not have a burden for the entirety of the world, does not have a burden at all!

As well, this is not a *"western Gospel,"* or a *"eastern Gospel,"* but, rather, a *"World Gospel."* When Jesus died, He died for all, and that includes the entirety of the world (Jn. 3:16).

While it is true that some parts of the world are more open to the Gospel than others, still, that does not mean that any part of the world

should be ignored. As I dictate these words, technology is advancing at a rapid pace respecting Satellite Television, and which could prove to be the greatest opportunity for World Evangelism ever known.

As all know and realize, some nations of the world are literally fenced in regarding keeping out the Gospel. I speak of Moslem countries, etc. However, even though they can build a fence, they cannot build a roof.

As I dictate these words, in a matter of days we should begin airing on Television in India. That nation, one of the largest in the world, with a billion population, is mostly steeped in heathenistic Hinduism. There are some Moslems there, as well as Buddhists, but only about one hundredth of one percent of the total population, according to the information I have received, are truly *"born again."* Consequently, it is one of the greatest fields of Evangelism in the world.

The Satellite over which we will air our program, will, at this particular time, cover approximately one-tenth of this great country, and also goes into surrounding countries, many of them Moslem. To bring in this Satellite, a small dish is purchased, which enables not only the owner of the dish to receive the signal, but, as well, any number of surrounding homes, etc. In other words, quite a number of dwellings, paying a small fee, can feed off this dish, and receive the programming. To be sure, most of the programming from this satellite is like any other Television programming in the world, with one exception. Our program will be on this Satellite, consequently, reaching many millions of people — many who have never heard the Gospel before!

God has called me to do this, and that is the reason we see so many people brought to Christ as a result of our Telecast. As should be obvious, it is not my ability or talent, but rather God's call, and the Anointing of the Holy Spirit. That is the reason we seek the Face of the Lord incessantly, that we may be a usable vessel, serving as a channel for the moving and operation of the Holy Spirit. To be sure, at this particular time, we are receiving some of the greatest testimonies of conversions and deliverances that we have ever received. They are coming from all over the world. Of course, as all know and realize, for everyone who writes, several hundred never write and let us know. Actually, most of these in foreign countries have little way to converse with us. However, that is not important. The important thing is them hearing the Gospel, with some of them most assuredly accepting Christ.

That is the reason our Telecast is aired in many countries of the world, translated into several languages. I have a mandate from the Lord to do this. In other words, I do not have a choice. Irrespective of the difficulties, obstacles and hindrances, I must do everything within my power, seeking the Lord constantly, in order to carry out this Commission.

I personally believe that Satan will fight and oppose the taking of the Gospel to the world, more so than anything else. This is where his greatest concentration is. Sadly and regrettably, to carry out this evil task, he uses the apostate Church more than anything else. It was that way with Paul, and it is that way presently. Rome little opposed Christ, but the apostate Church opposed Him greatly, even crucifying Him.

Likewise, Paul had a little problem with Rome, but his biggest opposition came from the Church. This is sad but true. In other words, the very thing (World Evangelism) the Church ought to be engaged in, they opposed the most.

While it is true that the modern Church carries out extensive Missions Works, with some of it definitely being of the Lord, still, for the most part, it is not of the Lord. Religious Denominations desire to exert total control, under the guise of proper management and administration, but, in reality, is Satanic. In the doing of this, the Headship of Christ is abrogated, and, consequently, the Organization or Denomination becomes man-led instead of God-led. This is Satan's greatest trump card, so to speak!

These Religious Leaders, with some exceptions, are not satisfied to preach their powerless Gospel, they, as well, feel they must use every method at their disposal to stop anything and anyone who does not have their seal of approval. To be sure, if one has the approval of the Lord, he will not have their approval, whomever they may be.

I realize the reader may peruse these words with some astonishment. However, that which is hindering the Church, and the carrying out of the Great Commission, is not so much the sins of the flesh, as damnable as they may be, but

NOTES

instead, this of which we speak. I remind the reader, it was not the gamblers, harlots or thieves, who nailed Christ to the Cross, but, rather, the Church of that day. No! The Lord in no way condones the vile sins which I have alluded to, but again I emphasize, that has never been the true hinderance of the Gospel. The great hinderance has always been *"religious control!"*

The phrase, *"And preach the Gospel to every creature,"* likewise, is powerful indeed!

1. Preach: Preaching is God's method of proclaiming His Word, of heralding the Good News, and calling attention to Truth. The method cannot be improved upon, and because it was given by the Holy Spirit.

As the Church weakens and wanes spiritually, preaching does as well! One might well say, that with the weakening of *"preaching,"* everything else in the Church begins to weaken. Spiritually illiterate men attempt to take its place with singspirations, talk shows, symposiums, seminars, etc. However, to accomplish that which the Lord demands, there must be Spirit filled, and, therefore, Spirit-led Preachers of the Gospel, who strongly, and without fear or favor, portray the Truth. True Spirit-anointed preaching, angers, upsets, threatens, and at times blisters, while at the same time, comforts, soothes, and inspires, but never bores. Paul wrote, *"It pleased God by the foolishness of preaching to save them that believe"* (I Cor. 1:21). However, the Holy Spirit through Paul, turned around and said, *"Because the foolishness of God is wiser than men"* (I Cor. 1:25).

It is regrettable that True Bible Preaching is weaker in America and Canada presently, maybe more than ever before. The energy of the Church has instead turned to the secular political process in an attempt to steer America correctly. While Believers should be diligent in backing political candidates who seem to be more in line with the Bible, still, the final effect will fall out to very little True Bible direction. The answer to the ills of this nation, or any nation for that matter, is not a President, or Senator, etc., who holds to certain issues which Christians think are proper, but rather a Holy Ghost Revival, which can only be brought about by the preaching of the Gospel, which brings True Bible Repentance. However, this is seldom espoused by religious man, because it is always God-inspired, and, consequently, God-centered, whereas the other is man-centered. Now as ever, in the Church the biggest problem is following God or men. To follow the Lord takes consecration, dedication, and relationship. Consequently, He is followed but little! To follow man requires nothing. Consequently, most follow men.

2. The Gospel: The Gospel is Good News, and, in fact, the only truly Good News that man could ever hear. As well, it is only the Gospel which is truly the Word of God, and truly Anointed by The Holy Spirit, Which will set the captive free. A compromised, watered-down Gospel is of no positive consequence to anyone. Regrettably, most fall into that category.

Most Preachers do not even believe in the Holy Spirit, or if they claim to do so, only pay Him lip service. In fact, entire Religious Denominations, even those who call themselves *"fundamentalists"* which mean by its definition, that they claim to believe all of the Bible, in fact, do not believe that the Holy Spirit leads, directs, or anoints. So, by their unbelief they little seek His help, if at all! As a result, what they say, even if the Truth, carries little weight, and because of no unction by the Holy Spirit. Tragically, most modern Christians, are Christians little at all, at least by Bible standards, and because they have accepted, at least for the most part, a philosophy instead of a Person. The Person I speak of is Christ Jesus.

Through the years, I have seen thousands of *"Christians"* give their hearts to the Lord, saying, after they were truly convicted by the Holy Spirit, *"I thought I was saved, but I really was not!"* For the first time, they truly came under the Word of God, as it was preached under the anointing of the Holy Spirit. As a result, the Holy Spirit convicted them, and, truly, brought them to a saving knowledge of Jesus Christ. Previously they had been indoctrinated, but not truly *"born again."* Regrettably, most of that which calls itself *"Christian"* falls into the category, of mere indoctrination, instead of true conversion. Two things must always be done, before people can be truly brought to Christ. They are as follows:

A. The True Gospel must be preached, and not a compromised version (Mat. 24:14).

B. It must be preached under the Anointing of the Holy Spirit (Acts 1:8).

3. To every creature: it can be translated, *"Preach the Gospel to the whole creation."* It

actually refers to man, and to all nations. However, the Gospel of Jesus Christ has an effect not only upon man, and in a very positive way, but as well, the whole of God's creation, including the animal kingdom, etc. Regarding that part of the creation, I speak only in the physical and material sense. Paul said, *"For we know that the whole creation groaneth and travaileth in pain together until now"* (Rom. 8:22).

Isaiah said, *"For ye shall go out with joy, and be led forth with peace: The mountains and the hills shall break forth before you into singing, and all the trees of the fields shall clap their hands"* (Isa. 55:12).

Of course, this is speaking of the time that the curse will be removed from plants and trees, and the very earth itself, which pertains to the coming Kingdom Age. However, the Gospel even now, if accepted, has an extremely positive effect in every capacity.

If one is to notice, in the nations of the world which offer at least a semblance of the acceptance of Jesus Christ, the product of its farms and ranches, as well as every other capacity, is of far greater magnitude than the countries of the world which reject Him. The former Soviet Union is a prime example. Even though it has one of the largest areas of fertile soil in the world, and some of the greatest natural resources, still, it cannot feed its own population. If the Truth were known, it is because of that of which we speak — a lack of the Gospel of Jesus Christ.

By and large, America and Canada have served as the granaries of the world, and because the Gospel has had a positive effect on the very nature of the earth to produce, along with enhanced ability.

So, it is the spiritual tide which decides the destiny of nations, and not its economical production, or educational institutions. Of course, those things are very important; still, it is the spiritual tide that drives them, and not vice versa.

(16) "HE THAT BELIEVETH AND IS BAPTIZED SHALL BE SAVED; BUT HE THAT BELIEVETH NOT SHALL BE DAMNED."

The phrase, *"He that believeth and is baptized shall be saved,"* tells us how to be saved, and what Salvation actually means. However, it is probably one of the most misinterpreted Passages in the Word of God.

First of all, the word *"believeth"* pertains to believing in a Person, and in this instance, the

Lord Jesus Christ, and not a philosophy, etc. The simple meaning of the word from the Greek Text is, *"to put in trust with."*

Jesus Himself said, *"For God so loved the world, that He gave His Only Begotten Son, that whosoever believeth in Him should not perish, but have everlasting life"* (Jn. 3:16).

Regrettably, the Faith of millions is not solely in Christ, but rather a Church, Doctrine, or Sacrament. Such affords no Salvation, because it constitutes *"Christ plus."*

To believe in Christ, simply means to believe that He is the Son of God, and He died on Calvary in order to pay for the sin of man. In other words, the penalty we rightly deserved, He took upon Himself. He literally died for us. On the third day He rose from the dead, which, in effect, ratified what He did at Calvary.

To be saved, one must believe this Truth, even though he may have very little understanding of all that it means.

This is brought about by the preaching of the Word, as we have already mentioned, which the Holy Spirit moves upon to convict the heart. Man is not brought to Christ by a mental affirmation, or in other words, intellectualism, but, rather, by heart felt conviction. It is impossible for him to come to a place of Faith, or the act of believing, otherwise!

As well, and as we have alluded to, to truly believe, means more than mental affirmation. Hundreds of millions believe in one way or the other, but still are not saved. In other words, they mentally agree that Jesus is the Son of God, but that is as far as they go. Such does not bring Salvation. *"The devils also believe, and tremble,"* but they are not saved (James 2:19).

What does it mean to truly believe in Jesus?

To truly believe in something or someone, means to take upon oneself the thrust, action, and even nature and character of what is believed. It is not mere acquiescence to something, or affirmation of something, but, rather, a conviction.

To believe in Jesus, means not only to accept Him as one's Saviour, but, as well, strive to be like Him in any and all respects. This is what Jesus meant when He said, *"At that day* (the day one truly believes in Christ, thereby effecting the entrance of the Holy Spirit) *ye shall know that I am in my Father, and ye in Me, and I in you"* (Jn. 14:20).

NOTES

Churches are filled with people who claim to *"believe,"* but, in reality, have only mentally affirmed, instead of truly accepting.

The word *"baptize"* as used here by Christ, has nothing to do with water baptism, as is commonly believed.

Paul said, *"Know ye not, that so many of us as were baptized into Jesus Christ were baptized into His death?"*

He then said, *"Therefore we are buried with Him by baptism into death: that like as Christ was raised up from the dead by the Glory of the Father, even so we also should walk in newness of life"* (Rom. 6:3-4).

As stated, this is a Baptism into Christ which takes place at conversion, and has nothing to do with Baptism by water (I Cor. 12:13; Gal. 3:28-29; Eph. 4:5; Col. 2:11-13).

To be sure, Water Baptism is meant to serve as a symbol of Baptism into Christ, but a symbol only. It is not that of which Jesus speaks in Mark 16:16.

If Baptism in water is meant in this verse, then that means that Salvation is impossible without it. Consequently, the penitent thief is not now in Heaven; and the many tens of thousands who, through the ages, have truly believed and not been baptized, and because of particular reasons such as a death bed Repentance, etc., are perished.

But if Water Baptism were fundamental to Salvation or essential to obedience, the Apostle Paul could not possibly have rejoiced that he saved so few or made so few obedient (I Cor. 1:14-17).

And, further, if Water Baptism were a necessity for Salvation, God would have so ordered the climate of the earth that it would have been possible of performance in all countries, and at all seasons of the year. But in the Arctic and Antarctic regions, and in the vast deserts of Arabia and Central Asia and Africa, emersion in water is, at times, impossible.

If Water Baptism saves then all persons so baptized will be saved, which is absurd. What proves too much, proves nothing.

If the ellipses in the Greek Text be fully supplied, the verse will become clearer to the reader: *"He that believeth on Me, and is Baptized by Me* (I Cor. 12:13) *shall be saved."*

Even though the following on Water Baptism and Infant Baptism has been given elsewhere in these Volumes, due to the manner in which Commentaries are generally studied, I think it would be profitable to again relate this information.

WATER BAPTISM

As we have stated, Water Baptism is a symbol, although a very important symbol, but cannot save anyone. It is the answer of a clean conscience toward God and a symbol of the Birth, Death, and Resurrection of our Lord. In essence, it is a type of our birth (our born-again experience), death (our death to the world), and resurrection (risen in His likeness and His image).

Some people misunderstand when they read, *"The like figure whereunto even Baptism doth also now save us (not the putting away of the filth of the flesh, but the answer of a good conscience toward God,) by the Resurrection of Jesus Christ"* (I Pet. 3:21). Many people focus on the Passage *"Baptism doth also now save us,"* consequently, missing the point of what is being said when it says, the *"like figure whereunto even Baptism"* saves us. Is it the water that saves or the *"like figure"* that saves? Water Baptism has never saved any soul. It is a person's Faith in the Death, Burial, and Resurrection of Jesus Christ that saves the soul. In other words, it is the *"like figure,"* i.e., Baptism into Christ, that saves the soul.

Water Baptism is a type or figure of what has already happened in the heart and the life of an individual. A mere figure has no power to save but the reality of the figure can, and that real figure is Jesus. Lest anyone should trust in Water Baptism to save his soul, Peter made it clear that Water Baptism does not save a person from the filth or moral depravity of the flesh. Water Baptism is the answer of a good conscience toward God — a conscience that has been made clean by Faith in the Precious Blood of Jesus Christ.

It is not possible for a person who trusts in the Lord Jesus Christ to be only partially saved until he is baptized in water, and then be completely saved. The moment an individual trusts Jesus Christ as his Saviour, that person is saved — instantly, totally, and completely. He can never be more saved no matter what else he may or may not do.

Now we come back to the *"works syndrome."* I heard a Preacher say once, *"The water saves."* I wondered what kind of water he was talking

about — river water, flowing water, deep water, shallow water, water from the River Jordan? What kind of water?

Not meaning to be facetious, but still, if, in fact, Water Baptism does save as many claim, what type of water is the best?

Water Baptism, in Truth, is a sacred, holy, and precious symbol that a person should by all means follow after, but he should partake of it for the reasons given, and not for Salvation. Water Baptism does not save; it is a public confession of Faith in the Lord Jesus Christ, of that which has already been brought about in the heart by the acceptance of Christ as one's Saviour.

Regrettably, many people attempt to tack some kind of works onto Salvation. Many claim that one has to join a particular Church, or be baptized in the manner of their Church, or take the Lord's Supper in their particular fashion, etc. However, such is nothing short of adding to the Great Price that Jesus Christ paid. Of course that is not possible, much less needful! As wonderful as these symbols and sacraments are, they only represent the reality; they are not the reality. The reality is Jesus. The Scripture still says, *"Looking unto Jesus the Author and Finisher of our Faith"* (Heb. 12:2), not Water Baptism, not the Lord's Supper, not Church membership, not religious traditions, but Jesus!

INFANT BAPTISM

Infant baptism is not a Scriptural doctrine; and more probable, Infant Baptism is responsible for causing more people to be eternally lost than perhaps any other doctrine or religious error.

It is a terrible thing when a person has been erroneously led to believe that his being baptized as a baby constitutes his Salvation, and consequently he is on his way to Heaven.

JESUS AND THE CHILDREN

The fact that Jesus loves children very much was made evident when He stated, *"Suffer little children, and forbid them not, to come unto Me"* (Mat. 19:14). As we have said many times, we believe all babies and children below the age of accountability are protected by the Lord respecting their eternal souls. In other words, I do not believe any child below the age of accountability, who has died, has ever died lost.

As well, the age of accountability varies with children, and according to their environment. It could range anywhere from six years old to eight or nine. Accountability is when a child is able to understand and comprehend enough about the Salvation Message to accept Christ. Surprisingly enough, children are able to grasp these truths very early and very readily when presented unto them.

HISTORY OF INFANT BAPTISM

Infant Baptism appeared in Church history about the year 370 A.D. It came about as a result of the Doctrine of Baptismal Regeneration — the teaching that Baptism is essential to Salvation; or if one desires to turn it around, that Water Baptism saves the soul (or at least constitutes a part of one's Salvation). So, consequently, as the teaching of Baptismal Regeneration began being propagated, it was natural for those holding to this Doctrine to believe that everyone should be baptized as soon as possible. Thus, Baptism of Infants still in the innocent state (and as yet unaccountable for their actions), came into vogue among many of the Churches. Once again I state: these two grievous errors (Baptismal Regeneration and Infant Baptism) have probably caused more people to die lost than any other Doctrine.

EMPEROR CONSTANTINE

The professed conversion of Emperor Constantine in 313 A.D. was looked upon by many persons as a great triumph for Christianity. However, it more than likely was the greatest tragedy in Church history because it resulted in the union of Church and State and the establishment of a hierarchy that ultimately developed into the Roman Catholic system.

There is a great question as to whether or not Constantine was ever truly converted. At the time of his supposed vision of the sign of the Cross, he promised to become a Christian. But he was not baptized in water until near death, having postponed the act in the belief that baptism washed away all past sins, and he wanted all his sins to be in the past tense before he was baptized. Such thinking is indicative of a lack of knowledge of the Word of God, and, more specifically, what true Bible Salvation really means.

In 416 A.D. Infant Baptism was made compulsory throughout the Roman Empire. Naturally

NOTES

this filled the Churches with unconverted members who had only been *"baptized into favor."* So whatever power the Church had in the past relative to actual conversions was now null and void. The world consequently was plunged into the gloom of the Dark Ages, which endured for more than twelve centuries, until the Reformation.

During this time God had a Remnant who remained faithful to Him; they never consented to the union of Church and State, Baptismal Regeneration, or Infant Baptism. These people were called by various names, but probably could better be summed up by their generic name, *"Anabaptist"* meaning rebaptizers. These people ignored Infant Baptism and rebaptized those who had been saved through personal Faith. They also had a generic name for themselves, *"Antipedobaptists"* meaning *"against Infant Baptism."*

THE STRANGE THING

The strange thing about these two diabolical doctrines of Baptismal Regeneration and Infant Baptism is that the great reformers (Martin Luther, for one) brought with them out of Rome these two dreaded errors: the union of Church and State and Infant Baptism. Strangely enough, in those days not only did the Roman Catholic Church persecute those who would not conform to its ways, but after the Lutheran Church became the established Church of Germany, it persecuted the nonconformist as well — of course, not as stringently so and not in such numbers as those before them.

John Calvin, as well as Cromwell in England and John Knox in Scotland, all stuck to the union of Church and State and Infant Baptism and used their power, when they had power, to seek to force others to conform to their own views.

Unaware to a lot of people, this thing came to the Americas well in the early days of this Republic. Before the Massachusetts Bay Colony was twenty years old, it was decreed by statute that *"If any person or persons within this jurisdiction shall either openly condemn or oppose the baptizing of infants, or go about secretly to seduce others from the approbation or use thereof, or shall purposely depart from the congregation at the administration of the ordinance — after due time and means of conviction — every such person or persons shall be subject to banishment."*

So, Religious persecution existed even in the early days of the United States of America. Roger Williams and others were banished (when banishment meant to go and live with the Indians), because they would not submit to the Doctrine of Baptismal Regeneration or the Baptizing of Infants.

However, it was the Constitution of the Rhode Island Colony (founded by Roger Williams, John Clark, and others) that established religious liberty by law for the first time in 1,300 years (over the world). Thus it was that Rhode Island, founded by a small group of Believers, was the first spot on earth where religious liberty became the Law of the Land. The settlement was made in 1638, and the colony was legally established in 1663. Virginia followed, to be the second, in 1786.

As you can see, the Doctrine of Infant Baptism has a long and bloody history, and it has been one of Satan's chief weapons to condemn untold millions of people to hell.

FURTHER EXPLANATION

What does the above have to do with us today? A great deal!

The union of Church and State continues today in many countries of the world, or else a particular Church recognized more readily by the State.

In these State Churches, or Churches recognized somewhat by the State, Pastors and Leaders christen babies, which means they make them *"Christians"* by baptizing them; thus the person having been christened as a baby believes he is on his way to Heaven simply because he was christened (or baptized) in infancy. Having been taught all his life that this saved him, he naturally considers himself saved by the act of Infant Baptism. The Roman Catholic Church teaches Baptismal Regeneration and practices Infant Baptism. Its Statement of Doctrine says, *"The Sacrament of Baptism is administered on adults by the pouring of water and the pronouncement of the proper words, and cleanses from original sin."*

The Reformed Church says, *"Children are baptized as heirs of the Kingdom of God and of His Covenant."*

The Lutheran Church teaches that Baptism, whether of infants or adults, is a means of Regeneration.

Because of the following declaration, I believe the Episcopal Church teaches that Salvation comes from Infant Baptism. In his confirmation the catechist answers a question about his Baptism in infancy by saying: *"In my Baptism . . . I was made a member of Christ, a Child of God, and an Inheritor of the Kingdom of God."* (This is printed in the prayer book and can be read by anyone interested enough to look for it.)

Most people who practice Infant Baptism believe the ceremony has something to do with the Salvation of the child. These are traditions of men, and we can follow the Commandments of God or follow after the traditions of men; we cannot follow both!

CLEAR BIBLE TEACHING

The Word of God is clear regarding the matter of Salvation. Jesus said, *"He that believeth on the Son hath everlasting life: and he that believeth not the Son shall not see life; but the wrath of God abideth on him"* (Jn. 3:36).

"He that believeth on Him is not condemned: but he that believeth not is condemned already, because he hath not believed in the Name of the Only Begotten Son of God" (Jn. 3:18).

Basically there are two groups of people in the world today: those who do believe on the Son and those who do not. Those who believe are not condemned; they have everlasting life (whatever Church they may belong to). Those who believe not on the Son are condemned already, and they shall not see life, but the wrath of God abides on them.

This is the clear, unmistakable teaching and language of the Bible.

If you will notice, the Word of God never says simply believe and be saved, but rather believe on the Lord Jesus Christ and be saved. The Word of God always identifies the object of Faith, which is the Lord Jesus Himself. *"For God so loved the world, that He gave His Only Begotten Son, that whosoever believeth in Him should not perish, but have everlasting life"* (Jn. 3:16). It is not enough just to believe; a person must believe in Him.

When the Philippian jailer asked, *"Sirs, what must I do to be saved?"* Paul answered, *"Believe on the Lord Jesus Christ, and thou shalt be saved"* (Acts 16:30-31). It was not enough simply to believe; that belief, that trust, that dependance had to be *"in Him."*

If a person is trusting in Baptism for Salvation, he cannot be trusting *"in Him."* Christ is not one way of Salvation; He is the only way of Salvation (Jn. 10:1, 7, 9; 14:6). There is no promise in the Word of God to those who believe partially in Christ. In other words, a person cannot trust the Lord Jesus 90% and baptism 10%, or Jesus 50% and baptism 50%, or Jesus 95% and some Church 5%, etc. As a matter of fact, there is no such thing as partially trusting Christ. The man who is partially trusting is not trusting at all. Yet the sad fact is that the majority of people in Churches in the United States and the world today are not trusting Christ at all — they believe they are trusting Him, while only partially doing so.

It is even sadder to realize that more people are going to hell through religious organizations than any other way. That is a shocking, startling statement, but it is true. Jesus said, *"Many will say to Me in that day, Lord, Lord, have we not prophesied in Thy Name? and in Thy Name have cast out devils? and in Thy Name done many wonderful Works?*

"And then will I profess unto them, I never knew you: depart from Me, ye that work iniquity" (Mat. 7:22-23).

This Scripture makes it clear that any works offered to Christ for Salvation are called by Jesus Himself, *"Works of iniquity."*

There is an old song that expresses true Faith. It says:

"My hope is built on nothing less
"Than Jesus' Blood and Righteousness;
"I dare not trust the sweetest frame,
"But wholly lean on Jesus' Name.
"On Christ, the Solid Rock, I stand;
"All other ground is sinking sand,
"All other ground is sinking sand."

(Note: Portions of source material for the article on Infant Baptism were derived from a Message by the late Dr. William Pettingill, entitled *"Infant Baptism.")*

The phrase, *"But he that believeth not shall be damned,"* refers to final damnation.

One is not damned until the end of a life of sowing to the flesh and until the end of the broad road (Mat. 7:13-14; Rom. 6:23; 8:12-13; Gal. 6:7-8).

One can make things right with God at any time between now and final damnation (Jn. 3:16; Rom. 10:9-10; I Jn. 1:7).

Our reaping life eternal is also at the end of a life of sowing to the Spirit (Gal. 6:7-8), at the end of the narrow road (Mat. 7:13-14), and at the end of our Faith (Jn. 6:27) (Dake).

In other words, we have been saved; we are being saved; and we shall be saved.

As we have stated, *"Believing in Christ,"* is the manner in which one is *"Baptized into Christ,"* and, thereby, saved. If one is to notice, Jesus did not say, *"But he that believeth not, and is not baptized, shall be damned."*

If, in fact, He was speaking of *"Water Baptism,"* when He used the word *"Baptize,"* He would, in fact, have said that. However, He did not do so, because He was not speaking of Water Baptism, but that which Believing in Christ affords, *"Baptism into Christ,"* i.e., Salvation.

If a person truly *"Believes in Christ,"* that person is instantly and completely at that moment *"Baptized into Christ."* It is a work of the Spirit, and not of the flesh.

(17) "AND THESE SIGNS SHALL FOLLOW THEM THAT BELIEVE; IN MY NAME SHALL THEY CAST OUT DEVILS; THEY SHALL SPEAK WITH NEW TONGUES;"

The phrase, *"And these signs shall follow them that believe,"* specifically tells us how it can be known if one is merely professing Salvation, rather than truly possessing Salvation. The criteria is laid out in verses 17 and 18.

One of the reasons many claim that verses 17-20 are not in the original Manuscripts, of which we will address ourselves to in commentary on verse 19, is because these *"signs"* are not evident in their lives and ministries. However, the real reason is that most have strayed considerably from the Book of Acts criteria.

If one studies the Book of Acts, which is given by the Holy Spirit, and intended to be the criteria for the Church, one finds that these *"signs"* were common in that account.

Knowing that to be true, many make up the excuses that such was to be in the Early Church, but not intended to continue thereafter, or that such *"signs"* ceased with the Apostles, etc. However, Jesus did not say, *"And these signs shall follow the Apostles, or the Early Church,"* but *"shall follow them that believe,"* including any and all, and for all time!

One thing is certain, it is only through the Power of the Holy Spirit that these things can be carried out, and if the Holy Spirit is denied, ignored, or misinterpreted, there will not be *"signs."* Consequently, as we see, at least for the most part, the modern Church bereft of these *"signs,"* tells us it is also bereft of the Holy Spirit.

The criteria is *"believing,"* and, sadly, most Christians simply do not *"believe."* The greatest oxymoron of all is *"Believers who do not believe."*

As well, one does not have to be an Apostle, an Evangelist, a Prophet, etc., to have these *"signs,"* only *"believe!"*

The phrase, *"In My Name shall they cast out devils,"* presents such Believers as the only authority against evil spirits. This is done in many and varied ways; at times by the laying on of hands, and at times by the Word being preached to individuals, which upon the acceptance of Christ, causes devils to depart.

It is regrettable that presently, the modern Church has turned into a giant referral system. It refers the alcoholics to Alcoholics Anonymous; the drug addicts to psychological therapy, etc.

The Truth is, the Bible holds the answer to all of the these problems, and the Bible alone we might add; however, most Preachers no longer believe the Bible. Even many who profess to do so, really do not! Only Jesus Christ by the Power of the Holy Spirit can set the captive free from domination of evil spirits (Lk. 4:18).

The phrase, *"They shall speak with new tongues,"* refers to the Baptism in the Holy Spirit, in which the physical evidence is *"speaking with other tongues, as the Spirit of God gave them utterance"* (Acts 2:4; 10:46; 19:6).

In a catalog outlining the Course Offerings of a particular *"Christian College,"* in its policy section, the statement was made that anyone who speaks with tongues is either mentally unbalanced, or demon possessed. Consequently, those who believe in the Baptism in the Holy Spirit, with the evidence of speaking with other tongues, were not welcome at that school. As well, anyone at the school caught *"speaking in tongues,"* would be summarily dismissed.

Considering the statements made, one can easily see why there are few Biblical *"signs"* of Salvation registered in such an atmosphere, with even acute spiritual danger being engaged by referring to the Holy Spirit in the realm of *"demon possession."* This is the same thing the Pharisees did concerning Christ, linking the Holy Spirit with demon powers (Mat. 12:24-32).

NOTES

While there is much religious machinery manifested at this particular school and ministry, there are few *"signs"* of true Salvation. Where that leaves these people, is left up to the Lord. However, sadly and regrettably, most fall into the same category!

Considering the significance of the Baptism in the Holy Spirit, perhaps more detailed information on this all-important subject would be helpful at this point.

THE BAPTISM IN THE HOLY SPIRIT

Salvation is God's greatest gift to the world. The Holy Spirit is God's greatest gift to His Children, the Church. The Baptism in the Holy Spirit might properly be called the Baptism of Power. As such, it is an invaluable asset to the Christian committed to seeking the furtherance of God's plan for the world.

As well, we believe that every Christian who receives the Baptism in the Holy Spirit speaks in other tongues as the Spirit gives the utterance. We believe speaking in other tongues is the initial evidence that one has received the Holy Spirit (Acts 2:4). (It is certainly not the only evidence, but we believe it is the initial physical evidence.)

We believe (and teach) that any Preacher, Teacher, or Church which does not acknowledge and proclaim the Mighty Baptism in the Holy Spirit (with the evidence of speaking in other tongues) is remiss in their teaching and will spiritually weaken those who depend on them for guidance.

Sending a Christian into the world without the Holy Spirit, and His full operation in our lives, is tantamount to sending a soldier into battle without a weapon. Admittedly, at the moment a person is saved, he becomes a Christian just as a person becomes a soldier the moment he is sworn into the Army. But the inductee is not ready for battle until he has basic training and has been issued his weapons.

And the Christian is in the same condition at the time of Salvation. If he isn't encouraged to receive the Baptism in the Holy Spirit, preparing him for the ever-continuing battle against Satan, he is being sent out onto a battlefield woefully unprepared.

Our Lord Jesus Christ said (Acts 1:8), *"But ye shall receive power, after that the Holy Spirit is come upon you."* We need power if we are to work effectively against the perverting, destructive conspiracy promoted by the enemy. Anyone hindering the Christian in any way as he enters this battle, is tacitly working for Satan, even though he may be appalled at the thought of doing so.

It is God's Wish (and Command) that every Christian should be filled with the Holy Spirit. Therefore, anyone working against that infilling, whether consciously or through erroneous doctrine, is, in effect, working at cross purposes to the Will of God.

WHO IS THE HOLY SPIRIT?

The Holy Spirit is a distinct and separate Member of the Divine Trinity. He works in association and in complete harmony with the Father and the Son.

The Holy Spirit should not be confused with either the Father or the Son. I John 5:7 tells us, *"There are Three that bear record in Heaven, the Father, the Word, and the Holy Spirit."* The Lord Himself said (Mat. 28:19), to *"teach all nations, baptizing them in the Name of the Father, and of the Son, and of the Holy Spirit."*

The Holy Spirit is God, just as the Father is God, and the Son is God. There are, however, differences between the Father, and the Son, and the Holy Spirit. The Three are not carbon copies. They have individual characteristics which set their roles apart, even though their purposes and their aims are inseparable.

THE LAST MESSAGE JESUS PREACHED

The last Message Jesus preached (Acts 1:4-9) was confined to the subject of the Holy Spirit Baptism. This was an historic occasion. The Lord was leaving the earth, His lifetime of work completed. He was about to depart for Heaven. This would be the last time He would be physically present to advise His Disciples and other followers. This unique situation stamps His Words with unusual importance. He might have spoken of Prophesy, Salvation, Worship, or any number of other important subjects. But He mentioned none of these things, at least directly!

Being God, Who knew (and knows) everything, He told them, in effect, that they should attempt nothing concerning the Salvation of the world, until they would first receive the Promise of the Father (Acts 1:4). In view of the dramatic circumstances surrounding this

NOTES

pronouncement, we can assume that every Word contained within these verses (Acts 1:4-9) was among the most important ever uttered by our Lord and Master.

RECEIVING THE HOLY SPIRIT AT SALVATION

There is controversy today as to whether one receives the Holy Spirit at the moment of conversion. Actually, the only proper answer to this question is, *"Yes and no!"*

The responsibilities of the Holy Spirit are many and varied. One of the most important of these responsibilities is that of regeneration. Paul states (I Cor. 12:3), *"No man can say that Jesus Christ is Lord, but by the Holy Spirit."* This demonstrates without question that the Holy Spirit plays a unique role in bringing a sinner to Conviction, Repentance, and Salvation. The activities of the Holy Spirit, as well, are many. He is a Comforter. He is a Leader. He is a Teacher. He is a Communicator. He is a Guide. He is the Director of all God's activities on earth today. So when the sinner comes to the moment of Salvation certainly he has received the Holy Spirit within the context of Regeneration. However, that is not in the context of Acts 1:8 and 2:4.

While it is true that every Believer definitely has the Holy Spirit, it is not true that every Believer is Baptized in the Holy Spirit, according to Acts 2:4. The Work of the Holy Spirit in the capacity of Regeneration is one thing altogether, with His work in the capacity of Power, in referring to the Baptism, being something else entirely. There is a difference in being Born of the Spirit and being Baptized in the Spirit. They are two separate things altogether.

However, while all Believers, although truly saved by the Blood of Jesus, are not Baptized in the Holy Spirit, they certainly can be if they so desire, and will *"ask, seek, and knock"* (Lk. 11:9-13).

At Salvation, life is imparted to someone who is heretofore spiritually dead. At the Baptism in the Holy Spirit, power is imparted to the Christian who was previously weak and ineffectual. He is henceforth fitted for service to God, whether he utilizes it or not! It is clearly the mandate of God that every Christian should be Baptized in the Holy Spirit (Acts 1:4).

Salvation and the Baptism in the Holy Spirit are two separate and distinct experiences. They are different as to source, time, and nature. A person may experience Salvation without experiencing the Baptism in the Holy Spirit (Acts 2:4). They cannot, however, experience the Baptism without first experiencing Salvation. The Baptism in the Holy Spirit must, therefore, be preceded by Regeneration (Salvation), and only then can the Holy Spirit function within us as He so desires. It is this indwelling of the Holy Spirit, which, incidentally, is not automatic, that endows us with power and enables us to be of greater service to God.

FROM THE WORD OF GOD

Are there Scriptures to support the contention that the Baptism in the Holy Spirit and Salvation are not simultaneous? Let's look at the Word of God.

In Luke 10:20, Jesus said to the Disciples upon their return from spreading the Gospel, *"Rejoice, because your names are written in Heaven."* What can we assume from this? We can assume that these men were saved. If their names were written in Heaven (in the Lamb's Book of Life), they were unquestionably saved. But they did not receive the Baptism in the Holy Spirit until the Day of Pentecost, some time later!

And then there was Paul (Saul of Tarsus). Chapter 9 in the Book of Acts tells of the dramatic, glorious, and sudden conversion of Paul as he traveled toward Damascus. It also tells that it was three days later before the Lord sent Ananias to Paul for the laying on of hands for healing, and for the Baptism in the Holy Spirit! Obviously, Paul was not Baptized in the Holy Spirit at the time of his Salvation on the road to Damascus.

In Acts 19:1-6, we are told of Paul's experience in Ephesus. Arriving there he found a party of twelve. They were saved, water baptized Believers.

He said unto them, *"Have ye received the Holy Spirit since ye believed?"*

And they answered him, *"We have not so much as heard whether there be any Holy Spirit."*

So Paul laid his hands upon them, the Holy Spirit came upon them; and they spake with tongues and prophesied.

The Bible states, without room for doubt, these men were saved. They were Believers.

Scripture refers to them as Disciples. But when Paul met them, he asked them, *"Have you received the Holy Spirit, since ye believed?"* Anyone reading this sentence cannot help but feel that *"since ye believed"* stands out in bold type. It is almost as if Paul, anticipating the future debate over whether the Holy Spirit comes simultaneously with Salvation, would include this phrase to prove that these men were Believers (saved), who had not received the Holy Spirit at the time of Salvation. This should have laid the question to rest before it ever started. Some, though, see what they want in Scripture, despite all the evidence to the contrary. Was the Lord foreseeing this when He said in Mark 8:18, *"Having eyes, see ye not?"*

To those who like additional proof that the Holy Spirit Baptism comes subsequent to Salvation, I would refer them to Acts 8:5-16. In this Chapter it tells how Philip went to Samaria where he held a Revival meeting. During the course of the meeting many were delivered and many were healed. Upon seeing all these Miracles, the people were convicted and accepted Jesus as their Saviour and were Baptized in the Name of Jesus Christ.

Read verses 15 and 16 carefully: They say, *"When* (Peter and John) *came down* (to Samaria from Jerusalem at a later date), *they prayed that they might receive the Holy Spirit; for as yet He was not fallen upon them, they were only Baptized in the Name of the Lord Jesus."* This is another definite Scriptural proof that the Baptism in the Holy Spirit is not simultaneous with Salvation.

Another aspect of this question of whether we are automatically Baptized in the Holy Spirit at the time of Salvation is revealed in the Words of our Lord as quoted in Luke 11:11-13. He says, *"How much more shall your Heavenly Father give the Holy Spirit to them that ask Him?"*.

The simple fact of the matter is that we must seek the Baptism in the Holy Spirit. It is not something imposed unknowingly (or unwillingly) upon anyone at the moment they become Christians. The Baptism in the Holy Spirit imparts power and fire to those who receive it. Anyone desirous of being a retiring, ineffectual Christian has the right to accept Salvation without accepting the next step, the Baptism in the Holy Spirit. However, they will be a powerless, and, by and large, ineffective Christian (Acts 1:8).

DOES EVERY RECIPIENT SPEAK IN OTHER TONGUES?

We teach and preach that every recipient of the Holy Spirit does speak in other tongues. And before we pursue this, let us clarify something in the beginning.

One does not have to speak in tongues to be saved. In fact, speaking in tongues has nothing to do with one being saved. Such comes about by simple Faith in the Lord Jesus Christ.

A person is not saved by seeing visions, delivering prophetic utterances, working miracles, or speaking in tongues. A person is saved by confessing the Lord Jesus with his mouth and believing in his heart (Rom. 10:9-10).

A person can be saved in a Church, in his home, on a street corner, or anywhere. It is not the place, it is the action. The person who believes in his heart and confesses with his mouth is saved! And once he is saved, he cannot be more saved by speaking in tongues, or seeing visions, etc.

Some, therefore, ask the question, *"If I already have a complete Gift of Grace in Salvation, why do I need the additional endowment of the Baptism?"*

First of all, if we did not need it, the Lord would not have commanded His followers to receive it (Acts 1:4).

As well, to be what one ought to be in Christ, the Baptism in the Holy Spirit is imperative. Also, for Power to do the work of the Lord, the Baptism in the Holy Spirit is an absolute necessity.

During our Lord's Ministry here on earth the Disciples had Him as a personal Advisor, Comforter, Leader and Manager. Today we do not have Him on hand personally to fill these essential roles. And this is why He said, before he left *"He would send the Comforter"* (Jn. 15:26). He knew His personal time on earth would be short; that He would personally oversee only the beginning of the great Salvation story; and that those committed to sharing the responsibility for bringing the Gospel to unsaved millions, would need direction beyond their human capabilities. Basically this is the inestimable value of the Baptism in the Holy Spirit.

As well, every Believer, active or passive, is going to be forced to confront the powers of darkness described by the Apostle Paul in Ephesians

NOTES

6:12. Satan has his army of demons committed to interfering with and even destroying Christian lives. The mighty Power of the indwelling Holy Spirit is the only thing that can augment our feeble powers to the point where we can live the lives we should live and become the type of Christians we should become.

Salvation equips us to enter into the Presence of God after mortal life is over. The Baptism in the Holy Spirit equips us to live fruitfully during those years before we go to be with the Lord. To willingly eschew this God-given assistance is to handicap ourselves throughout our Christian lifetime.

SCRIPTURAL EVIDENCE FOR TONGUES

Acts 2:4 says, *"And they were all filled with the Holy Spirit, and began to speak with other tongues, as the Spirit gave them utterance."* This is very clear and uncomplicated. It says *"They began to speak with other tongues."*

Acts 9:17 describes the incident where Paul was Baptized in the Holy Spirit. It does not say specifically that he spoke with tongues at that moment, and because it gives no description as to exactly what happened when he was filled. But turning to his Epistle to the Corinthians (I Cor. 14:18) he said, *"I thank my God, I speak with tongues more than ye all."*

Obviously, he spoke in tongues as a result of his Baptism in the Spirit, or he would not have mentioned it here. As well, this has nothing to do with Paul being linguistic, as some have taught!

Acts 10 tells the story of the house of Cornelius (the first of the Gentiles to come to the Lord) receiving Salvation. Verses 45 and 46 bear retelling. *"And they of the circumcision which believed were astonished, as many as came with Peter, because that on the Gentiles also was poured out the Gift of the Holy Spirit.*

"For they heard them speak with tongues, and magnify God."

We mentioned the incident of Paul laying hands on the twelve at Ephesus, and their being Baptized in the Holy Spirit some time after Salvation. This incident also enters into the question of the moment whether tongues is valid evidence of the Baptism in the Holy Spirit. Acts 19:6 says, *"And when Paul had laid his hands upon them, the Holy Spirit came on them; and they spake with tongues, and prophesied."*

In the 8th Chapter of Acts, Simon the Sorcerer offered money to the Apostles if they would teach him how to bring about the Baptism in the Holy Spirit by laying on of hands. This indicates there was some observable manifestation to prove something definitive had happened.

If there were no tangible demonstration (such as speaking in tongues by the recipients), why would Simon have gone to the extreme of offering money to learn the secret? He could very easily have set up shop on his own, pretending to bring about the results.

Only a supernatural proof, like speaking in tongues, could have forced Simon to: A. Believe there was some dramatic change taking place; and, B. Make him greedy enough to offer money so he could share in the unique ability to produce this result.

Without doubt, speaking in tongues was evidence of the Baptism in the Spirit throughout the accounts in Acts, even where not specified.

GREAT CONTROVERSY

Today, great controversy swirls about the Baptism in the Holy Spirit with the evidence of speaking with other tongues. It is not surprising, perhaps, that this should be so. Satan hates with all his being, seeing individuals and Churches transformed and set on fire as a result of the Baptism in the Holy Spirit. It is not surprising he would promote doctrines suggesting this *"is not for today,"* etc. Certainly, if the Devil had his say, it would not have been for any day.

But Scripture does not agree with what Satan is trying to promote with false doctrine. Misguided Christians, who admit tongues were an evidence of the Baptism in the Holy Spirit during apostolic days, say, *"It ended when the last Apostle died. It is not for today."* But what does Scripture say?

In Joel 2:28 and Acts 2:17-18, Almighty God makes a statement concerning this. He says, *"In the last days . . .*

"On My servants and on My handmaidens I will pour out in those days of My Spirit . . . ." And then in Acts 2:38 and 39, our Father further confirms this with these words, *". . . Ye shall receive the Gift of the Holy Spirit.*

"For the Promise is unto you, and to your children, and to all that are afar off, even as many as the Lord our God shall call." This does

NOTES

not sound like an offer with an expiration date stamped on it.

Why does Satan fight so hard to discredit this Biblical experience? Because he knows far better than we ever can, the frustration he faces when the mighty Holy Spirit Power falls on an individual or group. Ineffectual, Christ-denying *"Churches"* are suddenly turned around to become bastions of power for the Lord. Weak and frightened Christians become raging lions in the Cause of Christ. People who could not be persuaded to tell others about their Saviour are suddenly turned into adept and dedicated witnesses. Backsliding Christians suddenly straighten out their lives and become examples of Righteous Christian living.

The Holy Spirit is the single most important factor in the world today, as far as the Church is concerned. Without Him, Christ is not glorified, and the Church is ineffectual. With Him, the Church becomes effective, dedicated, and productive.

I thank God the Holy Spirit is being poured out today all over the world. People from every denominational background are being Baptized in the Holy Spirit. This shouldn't surprise us. The Lord said He was going to do it (Joel 2:28; Acts 2:17-18).

UNKNOWN TONGUES?

Too many people are confused about *"speaking in tongues."* They think speaking in tongues is an end in itself, or that speaking in tongues is the main manifestation of the Baptism in the Holy Spirit. They are unfortunately looking at things incorrectly

The mere act of speaking in tongues is not, in itself, life-changing or all-important. What is important, is the yielding of our unruly member (James 3:1-8), the tongue, to the control of God's Spirit.

It is very similar to Salvation. The act of publicly confessing our acceptance of the Lord accomplishes nothing within itself. However, it is crucially important within the context of our acknowledging the Lordship of Christ. Jesus said, *"Whosoever therefore shall confess Me before men, him will I confess also before My Father which is in Heaven"* (Mat. 10:32).

I believe a willingness to yield our unruly member, the tongue, to the Holy Spirit is exactly parallel to publicly confessing Christ.

Giving our tongues and voices to the use of God's Spirit, is, I believe, the same principle. *"Speaking in tongues"* sets one apart, not only from the unsaved, but from formal religion as well. Relinquishing our will to God, to allow this radical departure, serves as a *"sign."* A sign not only to ourselves, but to God as well, that we are ready to yield our will to His.

Even though this is, I believe, the basic significance of speaking in tongues, there are other tremendous benefits as well.

A REFRESHING AND REST

Isaiah prophesied long ago, *"For with stammering lips and another tongue will He speak to this people.*

"To whom He said, This is the rest wherewith ye may cause the weary to rest; and this is the refreshing; yet they would not hear" (Isa. 28:11-12).

1. *"The rest"*: In the Hebrew, this word speaks of comfort, ease, quiet, and a *"resting place."* It is the attribute of the Holy Spirit, through speaking in other tongues, which humanistic psychology attempts to fulfill, but cannot. Regrettably, most of the modern Church, including Pentecostals, have opted for psychology instead of the Holy Spirit.

While many would argue that they have not forsaken the Holy Spirit by embracing psychology, still, it is impossible for one to trust in both God and man at the same time, for the same help, especially considering that one originates with God and the other with Satan.

Speaking in tongues, and as the Scripture plainly says, provides this *"rest,"* which the soul desperately needs. It does so because it *"speaks not unto men, but unto God"* (I Cor. 14:2). This is expressed by the words of Paul as well, *"In the Spirit he speaketh mysteries."* If the words could be understood, they, within themselves, would not be a mystery. However, it would certainly be a mystery to Satan, as the Lord uses them according to His Word to minister to the individual doing the speaking. That is the reason Paul also said, *"He that speaketh in an unknown tongue edifieth himself"* (I Cor. 14:4).

Even though *"edifying oneself"* is not the purpose of the Holy Spirit in a public service, still, it is definitely the purpose of the Holy Spirit respecting the individual in his own private devotions.

The human mind and spirit is so constructed that it needs rest and comfort. Such can only be truly received from the Lord. Although *"speaking in other tongues"* is not the only way, still, it is certainly one way outlined by the Lord, and probably one of the greatest ways. Drugs, therapy, psychological counseling, etc., as well intentioned as these may be, cannot in any way take the place of the Holy Spirit. I am persuaded if Believers who are Spirit Baptized, would speak in tongues more as they go about their daily duties, they would find stress levels falling, and nervous disorders lessened, which in turn would create a far more healthy physical and emotional atmosphere — all generated by the Power and Operation of the Holy Spirit.

Incidentally, the Spirit-filled Believer can utilize this Gift of *"speaking in tongues"* as often and as much as he or she desires. One can even speak in tongues subconsciously and, in fact, should do so as much as possible, which will help provide a needed *"rest."*

2. *"The refreshing"*: This word in the Hebrew has the idea of a violent, stormy sea, with an oasis of repose in the very midst of the storm. In essence, this tells us that *"speaking with other tongues,"* gives the speaker a refreshing, while storms are raging all about him. This is beautiful beyond description! Life is turbulent, and seemingly more so by the day. Without this wonderful Gift, our ability to come into this beautiful *"refreshing"* which is so desperately needed for body, soul, and spirit, is desperately impaired.

So, for one to ridicule *"tongues"* by asking *"What good is it?"*, only portrays one's Scriptural and Spiritual ignorance.

3. *"Praying in the Holy Spirit"*: This is spoken of in Jude 20. While one can certainly pray in the *"Holy Spirit"* without praying in *"tongues,"* still, *"praying in tongues"* is certainly a part of this tremendous privilege. To do so, Jude said, *"Builds up ourselves in our most Holy Faith."*

The word, *"Build,"* in the Greek has to do with *"architecture and design."* In other words, the spiritual structure is built in the manner the Holy Spirit desires it. Faith is then not misplaced. Such comes about, at least in part, by *"praying in the Spirit."*

SOME ERRONEOUS CONTENTIONS

We have discussed some of the major arguments raised against the Baptism in the Holy

Spirit (with the evidence of speaking in other tongues). I hope we have clarified the fact that God does not change His methods every few years, and the methods employed during the Apostolic years are still operative today. As well, we would like to deal with some of the other arguments, Scriptural and otherwise.

1. Do all speak with tongues?

Disputants love I Corinthians 12:29-30. Paul says here, *"Have all the gifts of healing? do all speak with tongues?"*

Those who resist the testimony of millions, use this line of Scripture to convince themselves they are on God's side when they refuse to be drawn into this business of *"glossolalia."* They say Paul was indicating that while some may receive the Gift of tongues, it is certainly not mandatory that the Gift of tongues be present to prove the Baptism in the Holy Spirit. They will be shocked to hear me say this, but they are right!

What they do not realize, however, is that Paul is speaking throughout this Chapter (I Corinthians 12) about *"Spiritual gifts."* Careful reading of this Chapter, beginning with verse 8, will reveal that the *"Gifts of the Spirit"* include such things as the *"Word of Wisdom,"* the *"Word of Knowledge,"* the *"Working of Miracles,"* and so forth. Among these Gifts is the Gift of *"Diverse Tongues"*; that is, the ability, in the Spirit, to give an utterance in a tongue or tongues not known by the speaker, and as would be obvious, without ever having studied or learned them, and is meant to be interpreted (I Cor. 14:27-28).

In verses 28 through 30, Paul is explaining to the Church at Corinth, and all others as well, that they must all pull together, using their individual gifts in concert, in order to be a complete body, effective in the Lord's Work. Obviously, all do not have the Gift of Diversity of Tongues as mentioned in verse 30. Most have just one unknown tongue, given to them at the moment of Baptism in the Spirit, which is a prayer and worship tongue between that person and God. Careful reading of the Epistle to the Corinthians makes this clear.

In Chapter 12 the Apostle is speaking of the *"Gift of Tongues,"* which is used to give an utterance in a group, which, as stated, should be interpreted. He is not discussing speaking in tongues which accompanies every Spirit-filled Believer. As stated, all obviously do not have

"Gifts of Healing" or *"Gifts of Tongues,"* etc. While speaking with other tongues is certainly a Gift, as one is Baptized in the Holy Spirit, and continues to use thereafter, still, it is not one of the nine *"Gifts"* that Paul is speaking of. Our unbelieving friends confuse this issue.

2. The tongues of men and of Angels:

Paul is referring to I Corinthians 13:1 and 14:2. Some claim from this Passage that most have *"tongues of men,"* a language understood by all, while a few might have *"tongues of Angels."*

No! Paul is not saying this. He is saying that if we are able to speak in every type of *"tongues of men"* and even possibly of *"Angels,"* that if we have not *"love,"* we become as *"sounding brass, or a tinkling cymbal"* (I Cor. 13:1). He is not denigrating *"tongues,"* and in any capacity, but only a lack of love.

As well, he is not saying that one must have love and not tongues. That is not the idea at all!

He is merely reminding the Corinthians, and all others, that nothing can take the place of *"love."*

3. Whether there be tongues, they shall cease:

Once again this is an example of taking a few words out of context and building a doctrine on them. In order to put this statement in proper perspective, one must read all of I Corinthians 13:8-10 to get the full meaning of what Paul is saying. He was not saying, as some claim, tongues would cease when the last Apostle died.

"Charity never faileth," he said. *"But whether there be Prophecies, they shall fail, whether there be tongues, they shall cease; whether there be knowledge, it shall vanish away."*

Some, looking for a time frame in which to assign this day when tongues will cease, have claimed that *"When that which is perfect is come,"* refers to the day in which the Bible was collected into a single work.

Actually, this error is so ridiculous, as not to warrant serious discussion.

The One spoken of here as *"Perfect"* is the Lord Jesus Christ, and pertains to His Second Coming.

When He comes, many things will be changed, or no longer necessary. However, until He, the Perfect One, comes, we need everything the Holy Spirit gives us.

4. I had rather speak five words with my understanding, than ten thousand words in an unknown tongue:

This is a favorite Scripture for those who are antagonistic to the concept of speaking in tongues.

This is I Corinthians 14:19. However, the careful reading of the whole of the 14th Chapter, tells us what Paul was actually saying.

The Church at Corinth had become somewhat unbalanced in their worship services, concentrating unduly on the matter of speaking in tongues during their service. Paul spends the whole 14th Chapter teaching the proper place of tongues in a public service.

Obviously, if someone were opposed to speaking in tongues, he would hardly devote the amount of teaching encompassed in the 14th Chapter to its proper utilization. He could have simply said, *"Do not speak in tongues."*

But does he say this? Hardly! He says, *"I would that ye all speak in tongues."* He says, *"I thank my God, I speak with tongues more than you all."*

Why would those who stress the 19th verse completely ignore the 39th?

The 39th verse says, *"Forbid not to speak in tongues."*

Paul was simply saying, when it came time for the Preacher to deliver the Word, that it would do no one any good for him to stand behind the pulpit (or wherever) and address the people in tongues. They would not know what he was talking about, so would not be edified or helped. Consequently, when it came time to teach the people, five words in a tongue they could understand was of greater value than ten thousand words in an unknown tongue which they could not understand. The idea is *"teaching and instruction,"* and not worship.

5. The least of all the gifts:

Some say, since Paul placed tongues last in his index of gifts in I Corinthians 12:28, that it might well be eliminated.

What a hornet's nest of Satanic confusion would be opened if we were to accept this proposal. Do we begin with the Ten Commandments and eliminate the Tenth because it is listed last? Then with the Tenth removed, do we strike out the Ninth? I think one can see the foolishness of such thinking.

Obviously, any list has to contain something first and something last. It should not imply, however, that items on the list become optional to a greater or lesser degree depending on their position. Nothing from God is insignificant. No

statement from God is to be considered *"optional"* by man.

The Lord set up the roster of Spiritual Gifts. Evidently, He intended all the gifts to be operational in the Church. Without all the gifts, a body becomes less effective than it would be with all the gifts.

Any man who takes over God's authority and begins picking and choosing from among those God-given Gifts is assuming an authority I would not want to assume. The mere fact that placement on a list might be above or below something else is small authority to remove anything instituted by God. I think the argument that *"tongues"* is the least of all gifts is a dangerous argument, and one belittling God's ability to decide whether or not something is of value to man and his Church.

IS THE BAPTISM IN THE HOLY SPIRIT FOR US TODAY?

The question, ultimately, is this. Is the mighty Baptism in the Holy Spirit, with the evidence of speaking with other tongues, for every Believer today? I believe it is. And more than that, I believe it is a *"must"* for every Christian. It isn't something to be placed on the *"optional"* shelf where the Christian shopper can browse and debate whether or not it will be *"desirable."*

Without the Baptism in the Holy Spirit, the Christian will never be what he could be within God's Plan for his life. John the Baptist said (Lk. 3:16), *"He shall Baptize you with the Holy Spirit and with fire!"* Anyone who has seen a lukewarm Christian transformed by the Holy Spirit, knows what John was talking about.

All the arguments against the Baptism in the Holy Spirit stem from unbelief. There is not a hint in the Word of God that such passed away, or was only for a certain period of time. Such thinking is ludicrous to say the least!

To fall short of God's intentions, is to fall short indeed. To be sure, He did not suggest that Believers be Baptized in the Holy Spirit, but rather commanded it (Acts 1:4).

His Commands are not to be taken lightly!

The Church today, and in any age for that matter, without the Holy Spirit, is lackluster, man-led, and therefore ineffective as far as the Work of God is concerned. To be sure, I have no interest whatsoever in what man wants or desires. I want what the Lord wants. As well, He has said I can have this mighty Holy Spirit Baptism. In obedience to His Word, I have received it, and so have multiple millions of others.

We must ever remember, it is *"Not by might, nor by power, but by My Spirit, saith the Lord of Hosts"* (Zech. 4:6).

(18) "THEY SHALL TAKE UP SERPENTS; AND IF THEY DRINK ANY DEADLY THING, IT SHALL NOT HURT THEM; THEY SHALL LAY HANDS ON THE SICK, AND THEY SHALL RECOVER."

The phrase, *"They shall take up serpents,"* has absolutely nothing to do with the handling of poisonous snakes, etc. Actually, to do such is a sin. This is the same sin that Satan attempted to get Jesus to commit by throwing Himself off the pinnacle of the Temple (Mat. 4:6-7). Jesus answered by saying, *"Thou shalt not tempt the Lord thy God."* It is the sin of presumption.

The words, *"Take up,"* in the Greek Text is *"airo,"* and means to *"remove, take away, put away, do away with, or kill."* So, the correct translation would have been, *"They shall remove serpents."*

As well, the word, *"serpents,"* has nothing to do with vipers, etc. It speaks of demon spirits. In other words, the proclamation of the Gospel removes demon spirits from their control of people and areas. Satan is called *"That old serpent, which is the Devil, and Satan"* (Rev. 20:2). As well, Jesus also said, *"Behold, I give unto you power to tread on serpents and scorpions, and over all the power of the enemy: and nothing shall by any means hurt you"* (Lk. 10:19).

The seventy had been on a preaching mission, and came back rejoicing that *"The devils were subject unto them through the Name of Jesus"* (Lk. 10:17).

The answer as given by Jesus had nothing to do with vipers, etc., but rather with demon spirits.

The phrase, *"And if they drink any deadly thing, it shall not hurt them,"* simply speaks of protection. In no way does it speak of purposely drinking poison, etc., in order to prove one's Faith. The word, *"if,"* speaks of accidental ingestion.

The idea of this statement comes from the previous phrase concerning the removal of serpents (demon spirits), and mastery over the world of darkness.

Spirit-filled Believers alone have power over Satan. Education, money, or culture, have no authority whatsoever in this arena.

Actually, the authority possessed by the Believer is that which is derived from the *"Name of Jesus."* The phrase, *"In My Name...,"* as used in verse 17, as well, is implied in the other phrases. For instance, *"In My Name, they shall speak with new tongues,"* etc.

So, it is the *"Name of Jesus,"* which gives the Believer the authority and power to do the Works of Christ. The idea is, that the Ministry of Christ continue on in the lives and ministries of Believers. An example is given in the sending out of the *"seventy"* as recorded in Luke 10:17, and just mentioned. Regrettably, the modern Church, and especially in America and Canada, is a far cry from True Christlike Ministry. The modern Church is little more than a glorified social club. For the most part, it impacts the world of darkness not at all.

Consequently, a powerless Church, bereft of the Holy Spirit, attempts to disavow these verses. It does so, because it in no way resembles this which Christ proclaimed.

So, if we take Jesus' Words at face value, which we certainly should, and we look at the lack of *"signs,"* which will follow True Believers, then we have to assume that most claiming Salvation, in fact aren't even saved.

The phrase, *"They shall lay hands on the sick, and they shall recover,"* once again means to do so *"In the Name of Jesus."*

Laying hands on the sick to heal and to bless men is a practice of both Testaments (Gen. 48:14; Num. 8:10; 27:23; Deut. 34:9; Mat. 19:15; Mk. 5:23; 6:2, 5; Lk. 4:40; 13:13; Acts 5:12; 13:3; 14:3; 19:11; 28:8; I Tim. 4:14; II Tim. 1:6; Heb. 6:2) (Dake).

The *"Laying on of hands in the Name of Jesus,"* is meant to portray Blessing. Actually, such is the only Blessing afforded in this world. Consequently, Believers ought to be quick to lay hands on others for this purpose.

(19) "SO THEN AFTER THE LORD HAD SPOKEN UNTO THEM, HE WAS RECEIVED UP INTO HEAVEN, AND SAT ON THE RIGHT HAND OF GOD."

The phrase, *"So then after the Lord had spoken unto them,"* refers to verses 15-18.

Skeptics claim that verses 17 through 20 are not in the original Greek Text. I think the following will prove otherwise:

1. GREEK MANUSCRIPTS: There are over 4,200 Gr. MSS. of the New Testament. At least

618 contain the Gospels, and only two do not have these verses.

2. SYRIAC VERSIONS: Syriac is the first language into which the New Testament was translated. The *"Peshito"* MSS., 150 A.D., and *"Curetonian,"* 3rd Century, contained these verses.

3. LATIN VERSIONS: Eight thousand of them now exist, copied from Jerome's Vulgate, 382 A.D. (He had access to the Gr. Testaments of his day.) It contains these verses. His version was a revision of the Vetus Itala (2nd Century), which also contained these verses.

4. THE GOTHIC VERSION: (350 A.D.) contains these verses.

5. THE EGYPTIAN VERSIONS: The Memphitic (Coptic), 4th Century, and the Thebaic (Sahidic), 3rd Century, contained these verses.

6. THE ARMENIAN: (5th Century), the Ethiopic (4th Century), and the Georgian (6th Century), all have these verses.

7. THE FATHERS: Whether they were correct in doctrine or not, the fact remains that their testimony as to whether a verse or verses existed or not in their day, is even more valuable than MSS. and versions. There are about 100 writers older than the oldest Gr. MSS., and about 200 more of them between 300 to 600 A.D., and they all refer to these verses as being written by Mark as part of his Gospel. For instance, the *"Ante-Nicene Fathers"* referred to these verses some 16 times in their writings, confirming Mark as their author.

8. It is admitted by all that the overwhelming mass of witnesses — MSS., versions and Fathers are in favor of them, and that the two oldest Gr. MSS. — the Sinaitic and the Vatican are the only two that do not have them. It is also admitted that in one of these — the Vatican, a blank space is left for these verses, indicating that the Chapter is incomplete. It was not until the 4th Century that they were questioned.

9. The Doctrines taught in these verses can be proved by many other Scriptures (Mat. 10:1-8; 17:20; Mk. 9:23; 11:22-24; Lk. 10:19; Jn. 14:12).

10. If we leave these verses out just because they are not in a few MSS., then to be consistent we must leave out great portions of the Bible. For example, the Codex Vaticanus that leaves out Mark 16:9-20 also leaves out Genesis 1-46; Psalms 105-137; Hebrews 9:14-13:25; and all of I and II Timothy; Titus; Philemon; and Revelation.

NOTES

Actually, every early MSS. leaves out some portion, so if we are going to leave out all these parts, we shall have a much smaller Bible.

Since these verses are in perfect harmony with the other Gospels and a necessary part of Mark, why question them further? (Dake).

The Truth is, the Great Commission of Jesus Christ given at the conclusion of Mark, Matthew, and Luke, is supposed to be carried out exactly as He said. If the True Gospel is preached, and not some watered-down, compromised version, *"These signs shall follow them that believe."* If they don't follow, it is because the Gospel is not truly being preached.

Sadly, most modern Missionaries are little more than glorified social workers. Many are amateur psychologists or sociologists, which means they are not Preachers of the Gospel at all! Most of these do not even believe in the Power of the Holy Spirit, which is obvious in their lack of *"signs."*

If the True Gospel of Jesus Christ is preached, it will be done so by the Power of the Holy Spirit, which will automatically dispel demon spirits, resulting in bondages being broken, and darkness dispelled. This will result in people being saved, Baptized in the Holy Spirit, and healed by the Power of God. It is impossible for it to be otherwise! Consequently, these things *"Spoken unto them,"* are extremely important, as should be obvious, and were meant to be spoken to all. Anyone denying verses 17 and 18 is, in effect, denying the Lord Jesus Christ.

The Church has a choice to make. It can accept the doubt and skepticism of unbelievers, or it can accept the Words of Christ, as recorded in the Bible. I will say as Joshua of old, *"As for me and my house, we will serve the Lord"* (Josh. 24:15).

The phrase, *"He was received up into Heaven,"* pertains to the Ascension. It speaks of the Mission of Christ to redeem humanity, as finished and complete, victorious in every capacity.

The phrase, *"And sat on the Right Hand of God,"* speaks of His rightful place. There He serves as our *"High Priest," "making intercession for the Saints"* (Heb. 7:25; 8:1). As such, *"He is the Mediator of a Better Covenant, which was established upon Better Promises"* (Heb. 8:6).

Even though Jesus resides literally on the *"Right Hand of God,"* even more so, this speaks of the Power of God, which is resident in Christ.

In other words, He has the Power to back up the use of *"His Name."* Actually, He said, *"All Power is given unto Me in Heaven and in earth"* (Mat. 28:18). Through the Agency and the Person of the Holy Spirit this *"Power"* is freely given to the Spirit-filled Believer (Acts 1:8). It is given, as stated, to carry on the Work and Ministry of Christ.

(20) "AND THEY WENT FORTH, AND PREACHED EVERY WHERE, THE LORD WORKING WITH THEM, AND CONFIRMING THE WORD WITH SIGNS FOLLOWING. AMEN."

The phrase, *"And they went forth,"* refers to the entirety of the Early Church, and not just the Twelve Apostles. They did exactly what Jesus told them to do, *"Go"* (Mk. 16:15).

If one is to carefully study the Book of Acts as given by the Holy Spirit, which is meant to be a blueprint for the Church for all time, one will quickly ascertain the thrust that is intended. The Church, as was ultimately spearheaded by the Apostle Paul, was meant to take the Gospel to the entirety of the world, in obedience to Christ. This was priority. Consequently, without the aid of modern transportation or modern communications, they were able to touch much of the world of that day. They did so by the Power, Leading, and Operation of the Holy Spirit. Over fifty times in the Book of Acts it alludes to the Holy Spirit in one form or the other. He empowered, He led, He spoke. Consequently, it is impossible to miss His leadership in the Book of Acts, and the following of it by the Apostles and others! So, *"They went forth in the Power of the Holy Spirit."*

When the modern Church does the same, we will have the same results.

The phrase, *"And preached every where,"* once again proclaims them doing exactly what Jesus said do, *"And preach the Gospel to every creature"* (Mk. 16:15).

What did they preach?

They *"Preached Christ unto them"* (Acts 8:5, 35).

The phrase, *"The Lord working with them,"* proclaims such being done if His Commands are followed. Otherwise, He will not *"work!"* As stated, He does so through the Power and Agency of the Holy Spirit. As well, it hasn't changed from then until now.

The phrase, *"And confirming the Word with signs following,"* is another clear reference to

NOTES

the New Testament program for the Church. If the *"signs"* are not *"following,"* the Gospel is not being preached.

In January of 1969, I felt led of the Lord to go on radio with a daily program, which we called *"The Campmeeting Hour."* It was fifteen minutes in length, airing Monday through Friday. The Lord began to bless, and soon we were on approximately 600 stations.

In 1975, the Lord began to deal with me respecting Television. Consequently, we began airing our Telecast that year. To be sure, it was a very simple beginning. However, the Lord began to bless that as well.

In 1980, if I remember correctly, the Lord began to deal with me concerning the placement of our Telecast in foreign countries. This we did, translating from English to whatever language was necessary. We ultimately translated into Spanish, Portuguese, Japanese, Chinese, French, Arabic, and Russian. If I remember correctly, we even translated into Zulu. This is a very difficult process, but yet very effective, that is if you have the proper Interpreter.

At any rate, the Lord began to bless immeasurably so, with our offices receiving literally millions of letters over a period of time. Many of these letters contained some of the greatest testimonies of Salvation and Deliverance that one could ever begin to imagine. To be sure, it was similar to the Book of Acts, and continues unto this very day. Perhaps the following will serve as an example.

One particular area of the country of Peru was noted for its lawlessness. It is said that even the Army was afraid to go into these locations. Drunkenness, dope, and crime were pretty much the agenda.

In one particular area, there was one Television set, which the villagers would hook up to an automobile battery in order to bring in sporting events, or whatever they wanted to see.

The ringleader of the area on a particular Sunday, was attempting to bring in a soccer match from Lima. As it so happened, he was unable to bring in the Channel on which this sporting event was portrayed, but, instead, was able to only receive the Channel over which our program was being aired. Being in Peru, it was translated into Spanish.

To be sure, he was not too happy about this arrangement, but inasmuch as they could not pull in any other Channel, he, along with others, sat back to watch the Program.

The Spirit of God moved that day, and in a great way. When I gave the Altar Call, I really do not know how many accepted Christ in this little group, but this ringleader was among those who did. He was said to be one of the meanest men in the area, and guilty of just about anything one could think of. But that day, he was gloriously and wondrously saved by the Precious Blood of Jesus Christ.

Some time later, a Missionary came through Baton Rouge, and told of going into that part of Peru. When he came, this dear brother who had been gloriously saved, thought he had been sent by me in order to build a Church. Even though I had not sent him, still, he preached the Gospel to these people, and a little later a Church was built.

This entire community changed. Men who had formerly been drunkards, now were sober. Thieves were now no longer thieves, and because of accepting Jesus Christ. As mean as this ringleader had previously been, now he was totally opposite, and because of the Gospel of Jesus Christ.

Soon, many in this area were Baptized in the Holy Spirit, and, of course, the power of demon spirits was broken in these hearts and lives that had come to Christ. Actually, this power of darkness was greatly weakened in the entirety of this area, as it always is when a moving of the Holy Spirit takes place as a result of the Gospel being preached.

This is just one of multiple thousands of examples of what has and is transpiring as a result of the Gospel we preach over the Telecast. These *"signs"* have followed, simply because we believe. As well, they will follow all who believe.

The word, *"Amen,"* is meant to portray what Jesus has said and done is to be continued. It is not to be changed.

"Down from the Glories of Heaven,
"Down to a world of woe,
"When there was no eye to pity,
"Jesus said, 'I will go'."

"Go, go, go, go, leave what He asks you
*   to leave;*
"Pray for your part in the harvest,
"Give what he asks you to give."

"Out in the dark they are dying,
"For them His life He gave;

"Go, tell the lost of salvation,
"Give them a chance to live."

"Uttermost part is His order,
"Dare any answer no?
"What will you do when you meet Him,
"If you refuse to go?"

NOTES

For all orders of the
Jimmy Swaggart Bible Commentary,
please refer to the prices below:

One copy .... $ 55   Three copies.............. $ 135
Two copies .... $ 100   Four copies .... $ 170

When ordering in lots of more than four, please add $30 for each additional copy. These prices apply to multiple copies in one order only and cannot be broken into separate orders. You may mix the volumes as desired in any single order. We pay all shipping & handling.

Please order using product numbers.

Volume 1: Genesis-II Chronicles (11-067)
Volume 2: Ezra-Psalms (11-068)
Volume 3: Proverbs-Isaiah (11-069)
Volume 4: Jeremiah-Lamentations (11-070)
Volume 5: Ezekiel-Daniel (11-071)
Volume 6: Hosea-Malachi (11-072)
Volume 7: Matthew (11-073)
Volume 8: Mark (11-074)

For telephone orders you may call (504) 768-7000 with bankcard information. For mail orders send to:

Jimmy Swaggart Ministries
P.O. Box 262550
Baton Rouge, LA 70826-2550